America's
Top-Rated Cities:
A Statistical Handbook

Volume 3

2023
Thirtieth Edition

America's
Top-Rated Cities:
A Statistical Handbook

Volume 3: Central Region

Grey House
Publishing

Cover image: Green Bay, Wisconsin

PUBLISHER: Leslie Mackenzie
EDITORIAL DIRECTOR: Stuart Paterson
SENIOR EDITOR: David Garoogian

RESEARCHER & WRITER: Jael Bridgemahon; Laura Mars
MARKETING DIRECTOR: Jessica Moody

Grey House Publishing, Inc.
4919 Route 22
Amenia, NY 12501
518.789.8700 • Fax 845.373.6390
www.greyhouse.com
books@greyhouse.com

While every effort has been made to ensure the reliability of the information presented in this publication, Grey House Publishing neither guarantees the accuracy of the data contained herein nor assumes any responsibility for errors, omissions or discrepancies. Grey House accepts no payment for listing; inclusion in the publication of any organization, agency, institution, publication, service or individual does not imply endorsement of the editors or publisher.

Errors brought to the attention of the publisher and verified to the satisfaction of the publisher will be corrected in future editions.

Except by express prior written permission of the Copyright Proprietor no part of this work may be copied by any means of publication or communication now known or developed hereafter including, but not limited to, use in any directory or compilation or other print publication, in any information storage and retrieval system, in any other electronic device, or in any visual or audio-visual device or product.

This publication is an original and creative work, copyrighted by Grey House Publishing, Inc. and is fully protected by all applicable copyright laws, as well as by laws covering misappropriation, trade secrets and unfair competition.

Grey House has added value to the underlying factual material through one or more of the following efforts: unique and original selection; expression; arrangement; coordination; and classification.

Grey House Publishing, Inc. will defend its rights in this publication.

Copyright © 2023 Grey House Publishing, Inc.
All rights reserved

Thirtieth Edition
Printed in the U.S.A.

Publisher's Cataloging-in-Publication Data
(Prepared by The Donohue Group, Inc.)

America's top-rated cities. Vol. 3, Central region : a statistical handbook. — 1992-

v. : ill. ; cm.
Annual, 1995-
Irregular, 1992-1993
ISSN: 1082-7102

1. Cities and towns—Ratings—Central States—Statistics—Periodicals. 2. Cities and towns—Central States—Statistics—Periodicals. 3. Social indicators—Central States—Periodicals. 4. Quality of life—Central States—Statistics—Periodicals. 5. Central States—Social conditions—Statistics—Periodicals. I. Title: America's top rated cities. II. Title: Central region

HT123.5.S6 A44
307.76/0973/05   95644648

4-Volume Set   ISBN: 978-1-63700-534-7
Volume 1   ISBN: 978-1-63700-536-1
Volume 2   ISBN: 978-1-63700-537-8
Volume 3   ISBN: 978-1-63700-538-5
Volume 4   ISBN: 978-1-63700-539-2

Ann Arbor, Michigan

Cedar Rapids, Iowa

Chicago, Illinois

Columbia, Missouri

Grand Rapids, Michigan

Green Bay, Wisconsin

Indianapolis, Indiana

Kansas City, Missouri

Lincoln, Nebraska

Little Rock, Arkansas

Madison, Wisconsin

Milwaukee, Wisconsin

Minneapolis, Minnesota

Oklahoma City, Oklahoma

Omaha, Nebraska

Rochester, Minnesota

Saint Louis, Missouri

Springfield, Illinois

Sioux Falls, South Dakota

Tulsa, Oklahoma

Wichita, Kansas

Appendixes

Introduction

This thirtieth edition of *America's Top-Rated Cities* is a concise, statistical, 4-volume work identifying America's top-rated cities with estimated populations of approximately 100,000 or more. It profiles 100 cities that have received high marks for business and living from prominent sources such as *Forbes, Fortune, U.S. News & World Report, The Brookings Institution, U.S. Conference of Mayors, The Wall Street Journal,* and *CNNMoney.*

Each volume covers a different region of the country—Southern, Western, Central, Eastern—and includes a detailed Table of Contents, City Chapters, Appendices, and Maps. Each city chapter incorporates information from hundreds of resources to create the following major sections:
- **Background**—lively narrative of significant, up-to-date news for both businesses and residents. These combine historical facts with current developments, "known-for" annual events, and climate data.
- **Rankings**—fun-to-read, bulleted survey results from over 221 books, magazines, and online articles, ranging from general (Great Places to Live), to specific (Friendliest Cities), and everything in between.
- **Statistical Tables**—88 tables and detailed topics that offer an unparalleled view of each city's Business and Living Environments. They are carefully organized with data that is easy to read and understand.
- **Appendices**—five in all, appearing at the end of each volume. These range from listings of Metropolitan Statistical Areas to Comparative Statistics for all 100 cities.

This new edition of *America's Top-Rated Cities* includes cities that not only surveyed well, but ranked highest using our unique weighting system. We looked at violent crime, property crime, population growth, median household income, housing affordability, poverty, educational attainment, and unemployment. You'll find that we have included several American cities despite less-than-stellar numbers. New York, Los Angeles, and Miami remain world-class cities despite challenges faced by many large urban centers. Part of the criteria, in most cases, is that it be the "primary" city in a given metropolitan area. For example, if the metro area is Raleigh-Cary, NC, we would consider Raleigh, not Cary. This allows for a more equitable core city comparison. In general, the core city of a metro area is defined as having substantial influence on neighboring cities. A final consideration is location—we strive to include as many states in the country as possible.

New to this edition are:
Volume 1 - Brownsville, TX
Volume 2 - Greeley, CO; Salem, OR
Volume 4 - Greensboro, NC; Worcester, MA

Praise for previous editions:

> *"...[ATRC] has...proven its worth to a wide audience...from businesspeople and corporations planning to launch, relocate, or expand their operations to market researchers, real estate professionals, urban planners, job-seekers, students...interested in...reliable, attractively presented statistical information about larger U.S. cities."*
> —ARBA

> *"...For individuals or businesses looking to relocate, this resource conveniently reports rankings from more than 300 sources for the top 100 US cities. Recommended..."*
> —Choice

> *"...While patrons are becoming increasingly comfortable locating statistical data online, there is still something to be said for the ease associated with such a compendium of otherwise scattered data. A well-organized and appropriate update...*
> —Library Journal

BACKGROUND
Each city begins with an informative Background that combines history with current events. These narratives often reflect changes that have occurred during the past year, and touch on the city's environment, politics, employment, cultural offerings, and climate, and include interesting trivia. For example: Peregrine Falcons were rehabilitated and released into the wild from Boise City's World Center for Birds of Prey; Grand Rapids was the first city to introduce fluoride into its drinking water in 1945; and Thomas Alva Edison discovered the phonograph and the light bulb in the city whose name was changed in 1954 from Raritan Township to Edison in his honor.

RANKINGS

This section has rankings from a possible 221 books, articles, and reports. For easy reference, these Rankings are categorized into 16 topics including Business/Finance, Dating/Romance, and Health/Fitness.

The Rankings are presented in an easy-to-read, bulleted format and include results from both annual surveys and one-shot studies. **Fastest-Growing Economies . . . Best Drivers . . . Most Well-Read . . . Most Wired . . . Healthiest for Women . . . Best for Minority Entrepreneurs . . . Safest . . . Best to Retire . . . Most Polite . . . Best for Moviemakers . . . Most Frugal . . . Best for Bikes . . . Most Cultured . . . Least Stressful . . . Best for Families . . . Most Romantic . . . Most Charitable . . . Best for Telecommuters . . . Best for Singles . . . Nerdiest . . . Fittest . . . Best for Dogs . . . Most Tattooed . . . Best for Wheelchair Users**, and more.

Sources for these Rankings include both well-known magazines and other media, including *Forbes, Fortune, USA Today, Condé Nast Traveler, Gallup, Kiplinger's Personal Finance, Men's Journal,* and *Travel + Leisure,* as well as *Asthma & Allergy Foundation of America, American Lung Association, League of American Bicyclists, The Advocate, National Civic League, National Alliance to End Homelessness, MovieMaker Magazine, National Insurance Crime Bureau, Center for Digital Government, National Association of Home Builders,* and *Milken Institute.*

Rankings cover a variety of geographic areas; see Appendix B for full geographic definitions.

STATISTICAL TABLES

Each city chapter includes 88 tables and detailed topics—45 in Business and 43 in Living. Over 90% of statistical data has been updated. This edition also includes newly released data from the 2020 Census. A new table on household relationships has also be added, which includes information on same-sex spouses and unmarried partners.

Business Environment includes hard facts and figures on 8 major categories, including Demographics, Income, Economy, Employment, and Taxes. *Living Environment* includes 11 major categories, such as Cost of Living, Housing, Health, Education, Safety, and Climate.

To compile the Statistical Tables, editors have again turned to a wide range of sources, some well known, such as the *U.S. Census Bureau, U.S. Environmental Protection Agency, Bureau of Labor Statistics, Centers for Disease Control and Prevention,* and the *Federal Bureau of Investigation,* plus others like *The Council for Community and Economic Research, Texas A&M Transportation Institute,* and *Federation of Tax Administrators.*

APPENDIXES: Data for all cities appear in all volumes.
- **Appendix A**—*Comparative Statistics*
- **Appendix B**—*Metropolitan Area Definitions*
- **Appendix C**—*Government Type and County*
- **Appendix D**—*Chambers of Commerce and Economic Development Organizations*
- **Appendix E**—*State Departments of Labor and Employment*

Material provided by public and private agencies and organizations was supplemented by original research, numerous library sources and Internet sites. *America's Top-Rated Cities, 2023,* is designed for a wide range of readers: private individuals considering relocating a residence or business; professionals considering expanding their businesses or changing careers; corporations considering relocating, opening up additional offices or creating new divisions; government agencies; general and market researchers; real estate consultants; human resource personnel; urban planners; investors; and urban government students.

Customers who purchase the four-volume set receive free online access to *America's Top-Rated Cities* allowing them to download city reports and sort and rank by 50-plus data points.

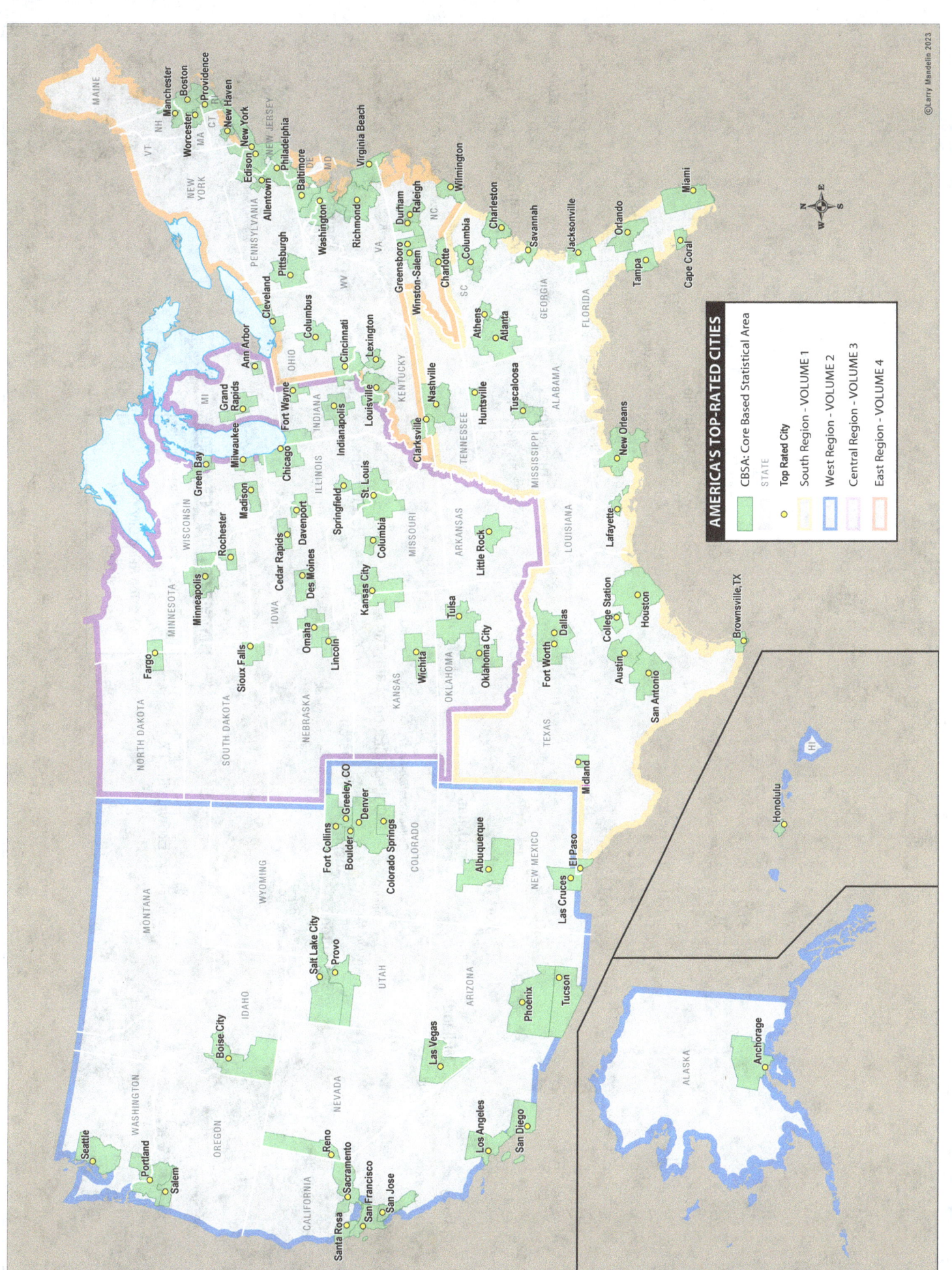

AMERICA'S TOP-RATED CITIES

- **CBSA: Core Based Statistical Area**
- STATE
- Top Rated City
- South Region - VOLUME 1
- West Region - VOLUME 2
- Central Region - VOLUME 3
- East Region - VOLUME 4

©Larry Mandelin 2023

AMERICA'S TOP-RATED CITIES

CBSA: Core Based Statistical Area

STATE

Top Rated City

South Region – VOLUME 1

©Larry Mandelin 2023

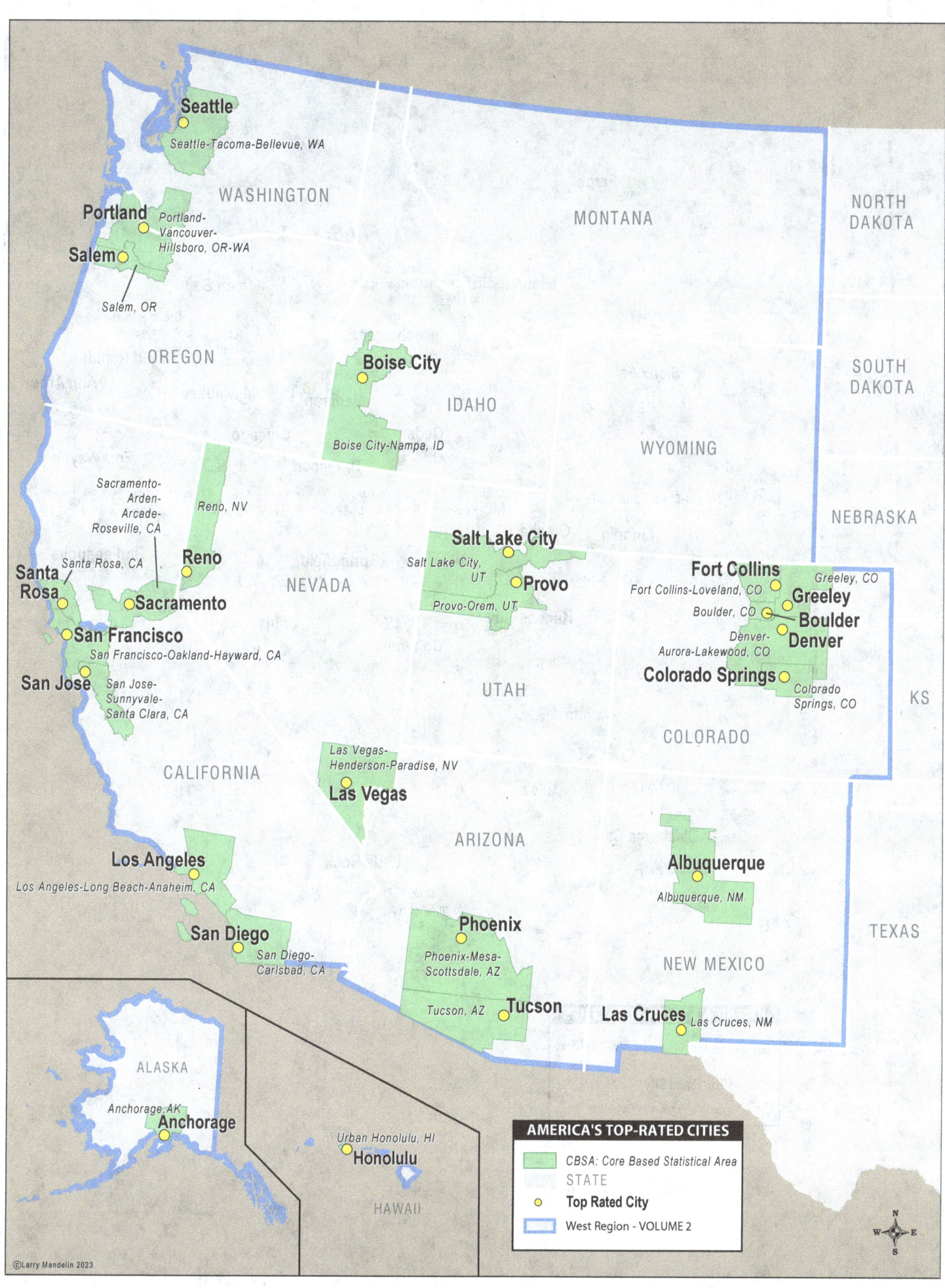

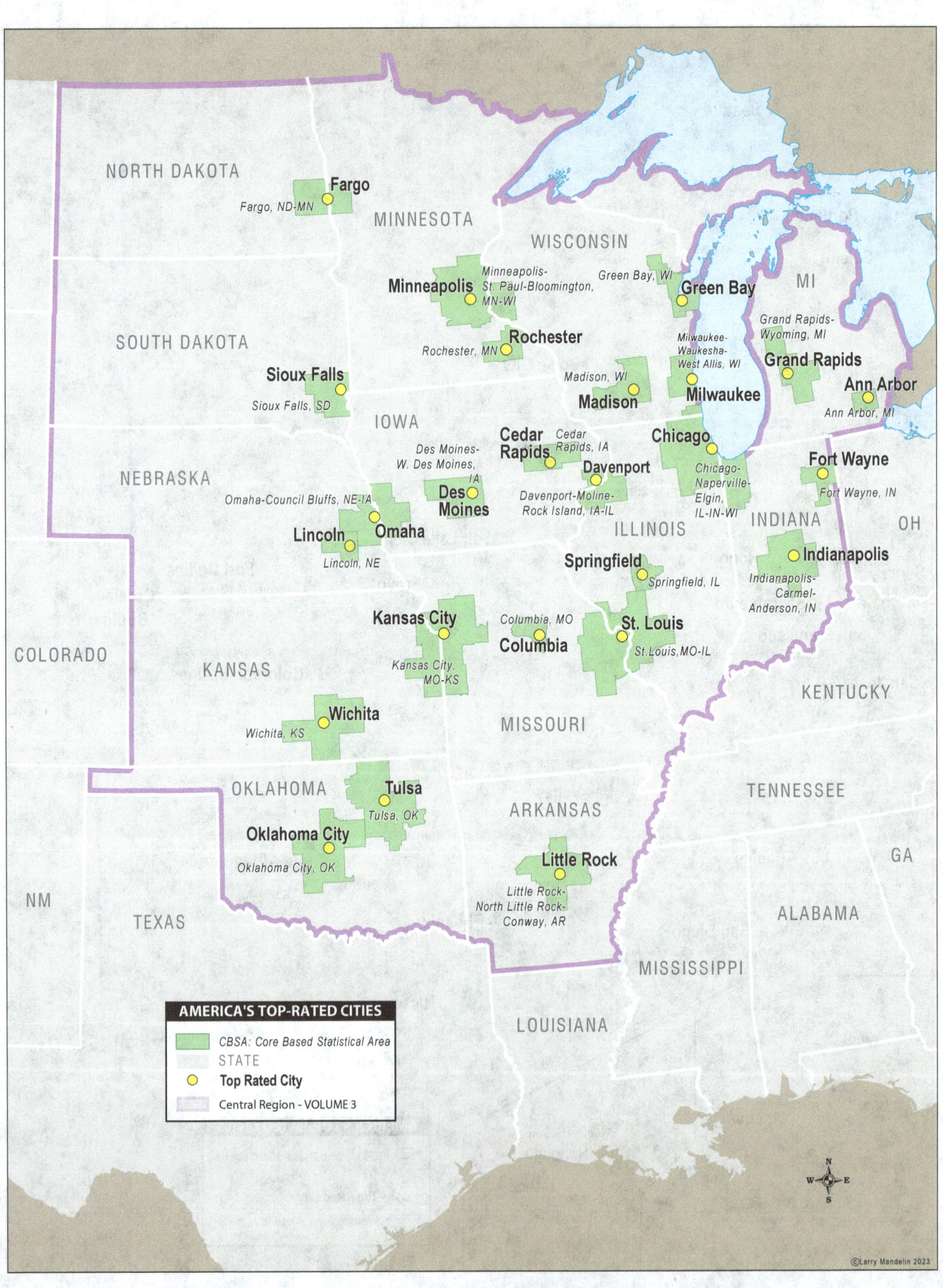

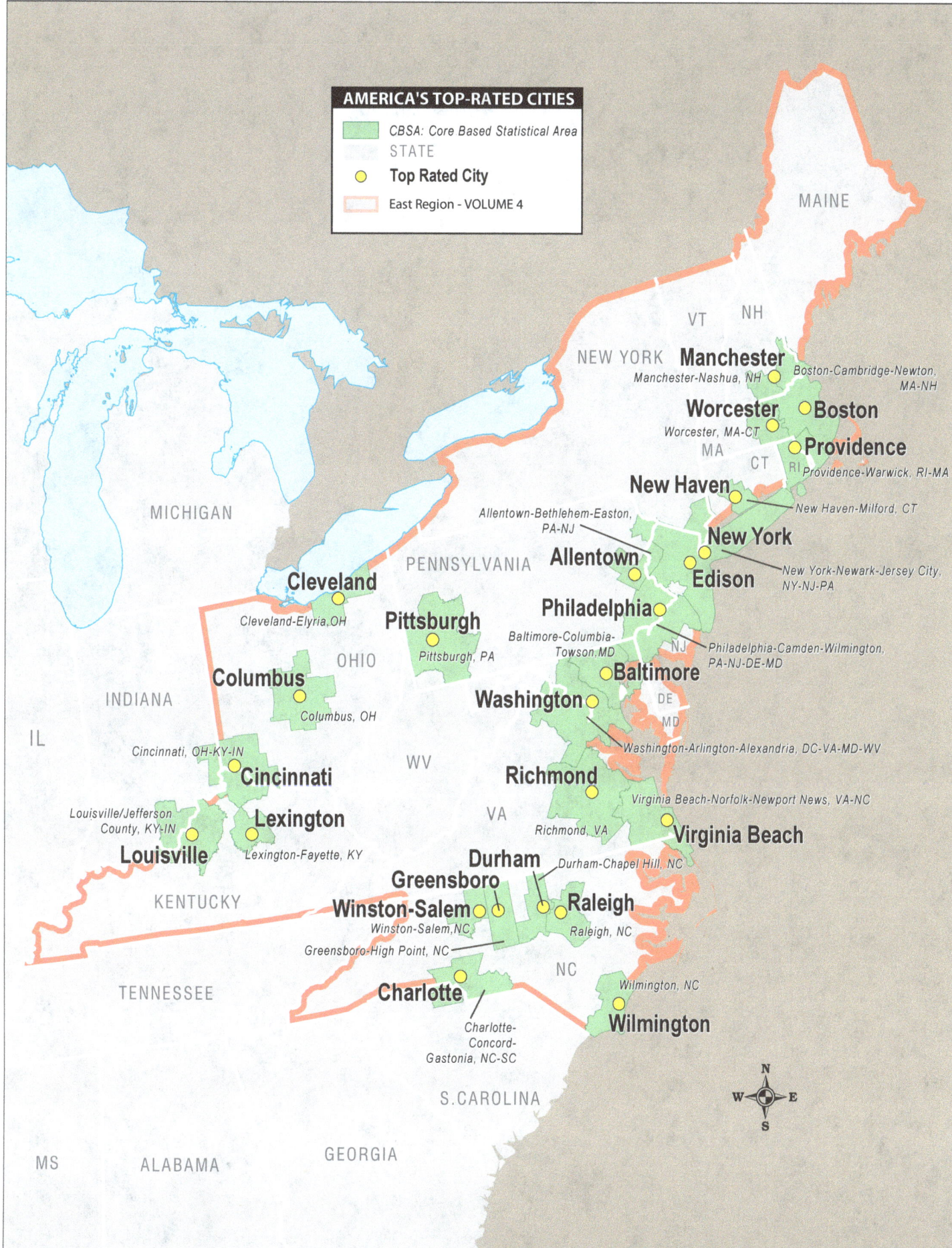

AMERICA'S TOP-RATED CITIES

CBSA: Core Based Statistical Area
STATE
Top Rated City
East Region - VOLUME 4

MAINE

VT   NH

NEW YORK   **Manchester**
Manchester-Nashua, NH   Boston-Cambridge-Newton, MA-NH

Worcester   **Boston**
Worcester, MA-CT   MA   CT   **Providence**
RI   Providence-Warwick, RI-MA

New Haven
Allentown-Bethlehem-Easton, PA-NJ   New Haven-Milford, CT

Allentown   **New York**
Edison   New York-Newark-Jersey City, NY-NJ-PA

PENNSYLVANIA   **Philadelphia**

Cleveland   NJ
Cleveland-Elyria, OH   Baltimore-Columbia-Towson, MD   Philadelphia-Camden-Wilmington, PA-NJ-DE-MD

Pittsburgh   DE
Pittsburgh, PA   **Baltimore**   MD

OHIO   **Washington**
Columbus   Washington-Arlington-Alexandria, DC-VA-MD-WV
Columbus, OH

INDIANA   WV
IL   **Richmond**   Virginia Beach-Norfolk-Newport News, VA-NC
Cincinnati, OH-KY-IN   VA

Cincinnati   Richmond, VA   **Virginia Beach**
Louisville/Jefferson County, KY-IN   **Lexington**
Louisville   Lexington-Fayette, KY   **Durham**   Durham-Chapel Hill, NC

Greensboro   **Raleigh**
KENTUCKY   **Winston-Salem**   Raleigh, NC
Winston-Salem, NC
Greensboro-High Point, NC

TENNESSEE   NC   Wilmington, NC

Charlotte   **Wilmington**
Charlotte-Concord-Gastonia, NC-SC

S.CAROLINA   N
W   E
S

MS   ALABAMA   GEORGIA

©Larry Mandelin 2023

Ann Arbor, Michigan

Background

Ann Arbor is located on the Huron River, 36 miles west of Detroit. It was founded in 1824 by John Allen and Elisha W. Rumsey, two East Coast entrepreneurs who named the settlement for their wives—both Ann—and for the community's location within natural groves. In 1851, Ann Arbor was chartered as a city.

After the arrival of the Michigan Central Railroad in 1839, the settlement developed as an agricultural center, and it continues to be such for the rich agricultural area surrounding it.

Before the arrival of settlers, the Ojibwa tribe roamed the area, which they called Washtenaw—the land beyond—which now serves as the county for which Ann Arbor is the seat.

The city manufactures machinery, tools, steel ball bearings, scientific instruments, doors and blinds, cameras, and coil springs. Lasers, computers, hospital and laboratory equipment, automotive parts, and high-tech/software products are also vibrant industries. The University of Michigan Medical Centers and St. Joseph Mercy Hospital employ over 12,000, and the region is also strong in book printing and manufacturing.

Ann Arbor's population is about one-third college or university students. The University of Michigan, the town's largest employer, played a prominent role in Ann Arbor's development as a major Midwest center for aeronautical, space, nuclear, chemical, and metallurgical research. The university's Museum of Natural History is known for an outstanding collection of dinosaur and mastodon skeletons and fossils, detailed dioramas of prehistoric life and Native American cultures, exhibits on Michigan wildlife, anthropology, and geology, and its planetarium. Also located at the university is a 250-acre botanical garden with a conservatory featuring tropical, temperate, and arid houses, over six miles of nature trails, and a variety of outdoor display gardens. The University of Michigan Museum of Art (UMMA), with more than 18,000 works of art from all over the world, and the university's Detroit Observatory, a historic scientific laboratory built in 1854, make this a truly unique, world-class institution. UMMA expanded in 2009, more than doubling its space.

The university is also home to the Gerald R. Ford School of Policy, named in honor of the former President, who graduated from the university in 1935. The 85,000 square-foot Joan and Sanford Weill Hall, designed by the noted firm of Robert A. M. Stern Architects, opened in 2006. The University of Michigan is also the site of the Ford Presidential Library.

Other cultural attractions in the city include: the African American Cultural and Historical Museum; the Ann Arbor Art Center, including two contemporary art galleries and art classes for all ages; the Ann Arbor Hands-On Museum, offering interactive exhibits in physics, mathematics, biology, physiology, botany and geology; and Gallery Von Glahn, specializing in serigraphs, lithographs, and original bronze and porcelain art. The Detroit Institute of Arts displays Diego Rivera's spectacular "Detroit Industry" frescoes. In addition, Ann Arbor offers dozens of artists' guilds, museums, top-rated art fairs, music and film festivals, and its share of fine restaurants with cuisine ranging from Italian to Ethiopian.

In nearby Dearborn are the Henry Ford Estate and Museum and the Automotive Hall of Fame. Historic Ypsilanti hosts the annual Orphan Car Show, which pays homage to elegant vehicles of a bygone era such as the Kaiser, Triumph, and Packard.

With its high-tech industries and great university, Ann Arbor is an exceptionally livable city and full of cultural events, including an annual arts fair, and jazz, film, and summer festivals. The city boasts 161 city parks, 12 golf courses, and more than 40 hiking trails.

Located in the humid continental climate zone, Ann Arbor's summers are hot, winters are cold, and there is an above-average occurrence of snow and rain. Proximity to the Great Lakes causes extreme temperatures, but also results in high humidity and cloud cover two-thirds of the year.

Rankings

General Rankings

- *US News & World Report* conducted a survey of more than 3,600 people and analyzed the 150 largest metropolitan areas to determine what matters most when selecting where to settle down. Ann Arbor ranked #11 out of the top 25 as having the best combination of desirable factors. Criteria: cost of living; quality of life and education; net migration; job market; desirability; and other factors. *money.usnews.com, "The 25 Best Places to Live in the U.S. in 2022-2023," May 17, 2022*

- Ann Arbor was selected as one of the best places to live in the United States by *Money* magazine. The city ranked #8 out of 50. This year's list focused on cities that would be welcoming to a broader group of people and with populations of at least 20,000. Beginning with a pool of 1,370 candidates, editors looked at 350 data points, organized into the these nine categories: income and personal finance, cost of living, economic opportunity, housing market, fun and amenities, health and safety, education, diversity, and quality of life. *Money, "The 50 Best Places to Live in the U.S. in 2022-2023" September 29, 2022*

- In their ninth annual survey, Livability.com looked at data for more than 2,300 mid-sized U.S. cities to determine the rankings for Livability's "Top 100 Best Places to Live" in 2022. Ann Arbor ranked #2. Criteria: housing and economy; social and civic engagement; education; demographics; health care options; transportation & infrastructure; and community amenities. *Livability.com, "Top 100 Best Places to Live 2022" July 19, 2022*

Business/Finance Rankings

- *24/7 Wall St.* used metro data from the Bureau of Labor Statistics' Occupational Employment database to identify the cities with the highest percentage of those employed in jobs requiring knowledge in the science, technology, engineering, and math (STEM) fields as well as average wages for STEM jobs. The Ann Arbor metro area was #13. *247wallst.com, "15 Cities with the Most High-Tech Jobs," January 11, 2020*

- The Ann Arbor metro area appeared on the Milken Institute "2022 Best Performing Cities" list. Rank: #97 out of 200 large metro areas (population over 250,000). Criteria: job growth; wage and salary growth; high-tech output growth; housing affordability; household broadband access. *Milken Institute, "Best-Performing Cities 2022," March 28, 2022*

- *Forbes* ranked the 200 most populous metro areas to determine the nation's "Best Places for Business and Careers." The Ann Arbor metro area was ranked #71. Criteria: costs (business and living); job growth (past and projected); income growth; quality of life; educational attainment (college and high school); projected economic growth; cultural and leisure opportunities; workplace tolerance laws; net migration patterns. *Forbes, "The Best Places for Business and Careers 2019: Seattle Still On Top," October 30, 2019*

Dating/Romance Rankings

- Ann Arbor was selected as one of America's best cities for singles by the readers of *Travel + Leisure* in their annual "America's Favorite Cities" survey. Criteria included good-looking locals, cool shopping, an active bar scene and hipster-magnet coffee bars. *Travel + Leisure, "Best Cities in America for Singles," July 21, 2017*

- Ann Arbor was selected as one of the nation's most romantic cities with 100,000 or more residents by Amazon.com. The city ranked #10 of 20. Criteria: per capita sales of romance novels, relationship books, romantic comedy movies, romantic music, and sexual wellness products. *Amazon.com, "Top 20 Most Romantic Cities in the U.S.," February 1, 2017*

Education Rankings

- Personal finance website *WalletHub* analyzed the 150 largest U.S. metropolitan statistical areas to determine where the most educated Americans are putting their degrees to work. Criteria: education levels; percentage of workers with degrees; education quality and attainment gap; public school quality rankings; quality and enrollment of each metro area's universities. Ann Arbor was ranked #1 (#1 = most educated city). *www.WalletHub.com, "Most & Least Educated Cities in America," July 18, 2022*

Environmental Rankings

- Niche compiled a list of the nation's snowiest cities, based on the National Oceanic and Atmospheric Administration's 30-year average snowfall data. Among cities with a population of at least 50,000, Ann Arbor ranked #19. *Niche.com, Top 25 Snowiest Cities in America, December 10, 2018*

Food/Drink Rankings

- Ann Arbor was selected as one of America's 10 most vegan-friendly areas. The city was ranked #8. Criteria now includes smaller urban areas, following the migration to smaller cities due to the pandemic. *People for the Ethical Treatment of Animals, "Top 10 Vegan-Friendly Towns and Small Cities of 2020," December 14, 2020*

Health/Fitness Rankings

- The Sharecare Community Well-Being Index evaluates 10 individual and social health factors in order to measure what matters to Americans in the communities in which they live. The Ann Arbor metro area ranked #8 in the top 10 across all 10 domains. Criteria: access to healthcare, food, and community resources; housng and transportation; economic security; feeling of purpose; physical, financial, social, and community well-being. *www.sharecare.com, "Community Well-Being Index: 2020 Metro Area & County Rankings Report," August 30, 2021*

Real Estate Rankings

- Ann Arbor was ranked #83 out of 235 metro areas in terms of housing affordability in 2022 by the National Association of Home Builders (#1 = most affordable). Criteria: the share of homes sold in that area affordable to a family earning the local median income, based on standard mortgage underwriting criteria. *National Association of Home Builders®, NAHB-Wells Fargo Housing Opportunity Index, 4th Quarter 2022*

Safety Rankings

- The National Insurance Crime Bureau ranked 390 metro areas in the U.S. in terms of per capita rates of vehicle theft. The Ann Arbor metro area ranked #306 (#1 = highest rate). Criteria: number of vehicle theft offenses per 100,000 inhabitants in 2021. *National Insurance Crime Bureau, "Hot Spots 2021," September 1, 2022*

Seniors/Retirement Rankings

- From its Best Cities for Successful Aging indexes, the Milken Institute generated rankings for metropolitan areas, weighing data in nine categories—health care, wellness, living arrangements, transportation and convenience, financial characteristics, education, employment, community engagement, and overall livability. The Ann Arbor metro area was ranked #6 overall in the small metro area category. *Milken Institute, "Best Cities for Successful Aging, 2017" March 14, 2017*

Women/Minorities Rankings

- *24/7 Wall St.* compared median annual earnings for men and women who worked full-time, year-round, female employment in management roles, bachelor's degree attainment among women, female life expectancy, uninsured rates, and preschool enrollment to identify the best cities for women. The U.S. metropolitan area, Ann Arbor was ranked #7 in pay disparity and other gender gaps. *24/7 Wall St., "The Easiest (and Toughest) Cities to Be a Woman," January 11, 2020*

Business Environment

DEMOGRAPHICS

Population Growth

Area	1990 Census	2000 Census	2010 Census	2020 Census	Population Growth (%) 1990-2020	Population Growth (%) 2010-2020
City	111,018	114,024	113,934	123,851	11.6	8.7
MSA[1]	282,937	322,895	344,791	372,258	31.6	8.0
U.S.	248,709,873	281,421,906	308,745,538	331,449,281	33.3	7.4

Note: (1) Figures cover the Ann Arbor, MI Metropolitan Statistical Area
Source: U.S. Census Bureau, 1990 Census, 2000 Census, 2010 Census, 2020 Census

Race

Area	White Alone[2] (%)	Black Alone[2] (%)	Asian Alone[2] (%)	AIAN[3] Alone[2] (%)	NHOPI[4] Alone[2] (%)	Other Race Alone[2] (%)	Two or More Races (%)
City	67.6	6.8	15.7	0.2	0.1	1.8	7.9
MSA[1]	69.2	11.5	9.0	0.3	0.1	2.0	7.9
U.S.	61.6	12.4	6.0	1.1	0.2	8.4	10.2

Note: (1) Figures cover the Ann Arbor, MI Metropolitan Statistical Area; (2) Alone is defined as not being in combination with one or more other races; (3) American Indian and Alaska Native; (4) Native Hawaiian and Other Pacific Islander
Source: U.S. Census Bureau, 2020 Census

Hispanic or Latino Origin

Area	Total (%)	Mexican (%)	Puerto Rican (%)	Cuban (%)	Other (%)
City	4.6	2.4	0.3	0.3	1.7
MSA[1]	5.0	2.8	0.5	0.2	1.5
U.S.	18.4	11.2	1.8	0.7	4.7

Note: Persons of Hispanic or Latino origin can be of any race; (1) Figures cover the Ann Arbor, MI Metropolitan Statistical Area
Source: U.S. Census Bureau, 2017-2021 American Community Survey 5-Year Estimates

Age

Area	Under Age 5	Age 5–19	Age 20–34	Age 35–44	Age 45–54	Age 55–64	Age 65–74	Age 75–84	Age 85+	Median Age
City	3.9	15.5	42.4	9.6	7.8	8.1	7.3	3.6	1.7	27.9
MSA[1]	4.7	17.5	28.4	11.6	11.3	11.6	9.1	4.1	1.6	34.5
U.S.	5.6	19.2	20.2	12.7	12.4	13.1	10.0	4.9	1.9	38.8

Note: (1) Figures cover the Ann Arbor, MI Metropolitan Statistical Area
Source: U.S. Census Bureau, 2020 Census

Disability by Age

Area	All Ages	Under 18 Years Old	18 to 64 Years Old	65 Years and Over
City	7.1	4.2	4.9	24.0
MSA[1]	9.7	3.8	7.7	27.2
U.S.	12.6	4.4	10.3	33.4

Note: Figures show percent of the civilian noninstitutionalized population that reported having a disability. Disability status is determined from six types of difficulty: vision, hearing, cognitive, ambulatory, self-care, and independent living. For children under 5 years old, hearing and vision difficulty are used to determine disability status. For children between the ages of 5 and 14, disability status is determined from hearing, vision, cognitive, ambulatory, and self-care difficulties. For people aged 15 years and older, they are considered to have a disability if they have difficulty with any one of the six difficulty types; Note: (1) Figures cover the Ann Arbor, MI Metropolitan Statistical Area
Source: U.S. Census Bureau, 2017-2021 American Community Survey 5-Year Estimates

Ancestry

Area	German	Irish	English	American	Italian	Polish	French[2]	Scottish	Dutch
City	17.0	10.4	10.1	2.7	4.9	6.0	2.7	2.6	2.4
MSA[1]	18.3	10.6	10.8	5.9	4.6	6.3	2.9	2.7	2.0
U.S.	12.8	9.6	8.1	5.7	5.0	2.7	2.2	1.6	1.1

Note: Figures are the percentage of the total population reporting a particular ancestry. The nine most commonly reported ancestries in the U.S. are shown. Figures include multiple ancestries (e.g. if a person reported being Irish and Italian, they were included in both columns); (1) Figures cover the Ann Arbor, MI Metropolitan Statistical Area; (2) Excludes Basque
Source: U.S. Census Bureau, 2017-2021 American Community Survey 5-Year Estimates

Foreign-born Population

Area	Any Foreign Country	Asia	Mexico	Europe	Caribbean	Central America[2]	South America	Africa	Canada
				Percent of Population Born in					
City	18.6	12.3	0.5	2.9	0.1	0.1	0.7	1.2	0.8
MSA[1]	12.5	7.3	0.6	2.3	0.1	0.2	0.5	0.9	0.6
U.S.	13.6	4.2	3.3	1.5	1.4	1.1	1.1	0.8	0.2

Note: (1) Figures cover the Ann Arbor, MI Metropolitan Statistical Area; (2) Excludes Mexico.
Source: U.S. Census Bureau, 2017-2021 American Community Survey 5-Year Estimates

Household Size

Area	One	Two	Three	Four	Five	Six	Seven or More	Average Household Size
			Persons in Household (%)					
City	33.7	37.5	13.0	10.7	2.9	1.7	0.6	2.20
MSA[1]	30.0	36.6	14.7	11.7	4.2	1.9	0.8	2.40
U.S.	28.1	33.8	15.5	12.9	6.0	2.3	1.4	2.60

Note: (1) Figures cover the Ann Arbor, MI Metropolitan Statistical Area
Source: U.S. Census Bureau, 2017-2021 American Community Survey 5-Year Estimates

Household Relationships

Area	House-holder	Opposite-sex Spouse	Same-sex Spouse	Opposite-sex Unmarried Partner	Same-sex Unmarried Partner	Child[2]	Grand-child	Other Relatives	Non-relatives
City	40.3	13.3	0.3	2.4	0.2	17.1	0.5	1.6	11.5
MSA[1]	39.7	17.0	0.3	2.4	0.2	24.3	1.3	2.5	5.8
U.S.	38.3	17.5	0.2	2.5	0.2	28.3	2.4	4.8	3.4

Note: Figures are percent of the total population; (1) Figures cover the Ann Arbor, MI Metropolitan Statistical Area; (2) Includes biological, adopted, and stepchildren of the householder
Source: U.S. Census Bureau, 2020 Census

Gender

Area	Males	Females	Males per 100 Females
City	61,263	62,588	97.9
MSA[1]	182,825	189,433	96.5
U.S.	162,685,811	168,763,470	96.4

Note: (1) Figures cover the Ann Arbor, MI Metropolitan Statistical Area
Source: U.S. Census Bureau, 2020 Census

Marital Status

Area	Never Married	Now Married[2]	Separated	Widowed	Divorced
City	56.5	34.4	0.4	2.4	6.3
MSA[1]	43.1	44.4	0.7	3.6	8.1
U.S.	33.8	48.0	1.8	5.6	10.8

Note: Figures are percentages and cover the population 15 years of age and older; (1) Figures cover the Ann Arbor, MI Metropolitan Statistical Area; (2) Excludes separated
Source: U.S. Census Bureau, 2017-2021 American Community Survey 5-Year Estimates

Religious Groups by Family

Area	Catholic	Baptist	Methodist	LDS[2]	Pentecostal	Lutheran	Islam	Adventist	Other
MSA[1]	9.7	2.0	2.4	0.8	1.5	2.3	2.2	0.9	10.0
U.S.	18.7	7.3	3.0	2.0	1.8	1.7	1.3	1.3	11.6

Note: Figures are the number of adherents as a percentage of the total population and cover the eight largest religious groups in the U.S; (1) Figures cover the Ann Arbor, MI Metropolitan Statistical Area; (2) Church of Jesus Christ of Latter-day Saints
Sources: 2020 U.S. Religion Census, Association of Statisticians of American Religious Bodies; The Association of Religion Data Archives (ARDA)

Religious Groups by Tradition

Area	Catholic	Evangelical Protestant	Mainline Protestant	Black Protestant	Islam	Judaism	Hinduism	Orthodox	Buddhism
MSA[1]	9.7	8.1	5.6	2.5	2.2	0.8	0.5	0.4	0.3
U.S.	18.7	16.5	5.2	2.3	1.3	0.6	0.4	0.4	0.3

Note: Figures are the number of adherents as a percentage of the total population; (1) Figures cover the Ann Arbor, MI Metropolitan Statistical Area
Sources: 2020 U.S. Religion Census, Association of Statisticians of American Religious Bodies; The Association of Religion Data Archives (ARDA)

ECONOMY

Gross Metropolitan Product

Area	2020	2021	2022	2023	Rank[2]
MSA[1]	25.8	28.1	30.4	32.1	113

Note: Figures are in billions of dollars; (1) Figures cover the Ann Arbor, MI Metropolitan Statistical Area; (2) Rank is based on 2021 data and ranges from 1 to 381
Source: U.S. Conference of Mayors, U.S. Metro Economies: U.S. Metros Compared to Global and State Economies, June 2022

Economic Growth

Area	2018-20 (%)	2021 (%)	2022 (%)	2023 (%)	Rank[2]
MSA[1]	-0.4	5.0	2.9	2.6	164
U.S.	-0.6	5.7	3.1	2.9	–

Note: Figures are real gross metropolitan product (GMP) growth rates and represent average annual percent change; (1) Figures cover the Ann Arbor, MI Metropolitan Statistical Area; (2) Rank is based on 2020 2-year average annual percent change and ranges from 1 to 381
Source: U.S. Conference of Mayors, U.S. Metro Economies: U.S. Metros Compared to Global and State Economies, June 2022

Metropolitan Area Exports

Area	2016	2017	2018	2019	2020	2021	Rank[2]
MSA[1]	1,207.9	1,447.4	1,538.7	1,432.7	1,183.1	1,230.7	141

Note: Figures are in millions of dollars; (1) Figures cover the Ann Arbor, MI Metropolitan Statistical Area; (2) Rank is based on 2021 data and ranges from 1 to 388
Source: U.S. Department of Commerce, International Trade Administration, Office of Trade and Economic Analysis, Industry and Analysis, Exports by Metropolitan Area, data extracted March 16, 2023

Building Permits

Area	Single-Family			Multi-Family			Total		
	2021	2022	Pct. Chg.	2021	2022	Pct. Chg.	2021	2022	Pct. Chg.
City	175	135	-22.9	52	4	-92.3	227	139	-38.8
MSA[1]	795	580	-27.0	121	49	-59.5	916	629	-31.3
U.S.	1,115,400	975,600	-12.5	621,600	689,500	10.9	1,737,000	1,665,100	-4.1

Note: (1) Figures cover the Ann Arbor, MI Metropolitan Statistical Area; Figures represent new, privately-owned housing units authorized (unadjusted data); All permit data are based on estimates with imputation
Source: U.S. Census Bureau, Manufacturing, Mining, and Construction Statistics, Building Permits, 2021, 2022

Bankruptcy Filings

Area	Business Filings			Nonbusiness Filings		
	2021	2022	% Chg.	2021	2022	% Chg.
Washtenaw County	8	24	200.0	352	350	-0.6
U.S.	14,347	13,481	-6.0	399,269	374,240	-6.3

Note: Business filings include Chapter 7, Chapter 9, Chapter 11, Chapter 12, Chapter 13, Chapter 15, and Section 304; Nonbusiness filings include Chapter 7, Chapter 11, and Chapter 13
Source: Administrative Office of the U.S. Courts, Business and Nonbusiness Bankruptcy, County Cases Commenced by Chapter of the Bankruptcy Code, During the 12-Month Period Ending December 31, 2021 and Business and Nonbusiness Bankruptcy, County Cases Commenced by Chapter of the Bankruptcy Code, During the 12-Month Period Ending December 31, 2022

Housing Vacancy Rates

Area	Gross Vacancy Rate[2] (%)			Year-Round Vacancy Rate[3] (%)			Rental Vacancy Rate[4] (%)			Homeowner Vacancy Rate[5] (%)		
	2020	2021	2022	2020	2021	2022	2020	2021	2022	2020	2021	2022
MSA[1]	n/a	n/a	n/a	n/a	n/a	n/a	n/a	n/a	n/a	n/a	n/a	n/a
U.S.	10.6	10.8	10.5	8.2	8.4	8.2	6.3	6.1	5.8	1.0	0.9	0.8

Note: (1) Figures cover the Ann Arbor, MI Metropolitan Statistical Area; (2) The percentage of the total housing inventory that is vacant; (3) The percentage of the housing inventory (excluding seasonal units) that is year-round vacant; (4) The percentage of rental inventory that is vacant for rent; (5) The percentage of homeowner inventory that is vacant for sale; n/a not available
Source: U.S. Census Bureau, Housing Vacancies and Homeownership Annual Statistics: 2020, 2021, 2022

INCOME

Income

Area	Per Capita ($)	Median Household ($)	Average Household ($)
City	47,883	73,276	107,368
MSA[1]	45,500	79,198	110,102
U.S.	37,638	69,021	97,196

Note: (1) Figures cover the Ann Arbor, MI Metropolitan Statistical Area
Source: U.S. Census Bureau, 2017-2021 American Community Survey 5-Year Estimates

Household Income Distribution

Area	Percent of Households Earning							
	Under $15,000	$15,000 -$24,999	$25,000 -$34,999	$35,000 -$49,999	$50,000 -$74,999	$75,000 -$99,999	$100,000 -$149,999	$150,000 and up
City	14.5	6.2	6.2	8.9	15.2	11.2	15.7	22.2
MSA[1]	9.7	6.0	6.9	9.7	15.5	12.5	17.4	22.3
U.S.	9.4	7.8	8.2	11.4	16.8	12.8	16.3	17.3

Note: (1) Figures cover the Ann Arbor, MI Metropolitan Statistical Area
Source: U.S. Census Bureau, 2017-2021 American Community Survey 5-Year Estimates

Poverty Rate

Area	All Ages	Under 18 Years Old	18 to 64 Years Old	65 Years and Over
City	22.5	10.8	27.7	6.3
MSA[1]	13.4	11.1	15.8	5.8
U.S.	12.6	17.0	11.8	9.6

Note: Figures are percentage of people whose income during the past 12 months was below the poverty level;
(1) Figures cover the Ann Arbor, MI Metropolitan Statistical Area
Source: U.S. Census Bureau, 2017-2021 American Community Survey 5-Year Estimates

EMPLOYMENT

Labor Force and Employment

Area	Civilian Labor Force			Workers Employed		
	Dec. 2021	Dec. 2022	% Chg.	Dec. 2021	Dec. 2022	% Chg.
City	63,522	64,736	1.9	62,006	63,139	1.8
MSA[1]	192,598	196,315	1.9	187,000	190,417	1.8
U.S.	161,696,000	164,224,000	1.6	155,732,000	158,872,000	2.0

Note: Data is not seasonally adjusted and covers workers 16 years of age and older; (1) Figures cover the Ann Arbor, MI Metropolitan Statistical Area
Source: Bureau of Labor Statistics, Local Area Unemployment Statistics

Unemployment Rate

Area	2022											
	Jan.	Feb.	Mar.	Apr.	May	Jun.	Jul.	Aug.	Sep.	Oct.	Nov.	Dec.
City	2.7	3.1	2.5	2.5	3.0	3.4	3.3	2.9	2.7	2.7	2.5	2.5
MSA[1]	3.3	3.7	3.1	3.0	3.6	4.1	4.0	3.5	3.3	3.3	3.1	3.0
U.S.	4.4	4.1	3.8	3.3	3.4	3.8	3.8	3.8	3.3	3.4	3.4	3.3

Note: Data is not seasonally adjusted and covers workers 16 years of age and older; (1) Figures cover the Ann Arbor, MI Metropolitan Statistical Area
Source: Bureau of Labor Statistics, Local Area Unemployment Statistics

Average Wages

Occupation	$/Hr.	Occupation	$/Hr.
Accountants and Auditors	41.17	Maintenance and Repair Workers	22.11
Automotive Mechanics	24.91	Marketing Managers	66.72
Bookkeepers	22.53	Network and Computer Systems Admin.	43.40
Carpenters	27.04	Nurses, Licensed Practical	28.93
Cashiers	13.30	Nurses, Registered	41.54
Computer Programmers	46.31	Nursing Assistants	18.36
Computer Systems Analysts	50.46	Office Clerks, General	19.11
Computer User Support Specialists	26.14	Physical Therapists	46.21
Construction Laborers	23.76	Physicians	120.10
Cooks, Restaurant	16.10	Plumbers, Pipefitters and Steamfitters	33.25
Customer Service Representatives	19.39	Police and Sheriff's Patrol Officers	34.05
Dentists	76.15	Postal Service Mail Carriers	27.10
Electricians	34.45	Real Estate Sales Agents	33.57
Engineers, Electrical	48.28	Retail Salespersons	16.77
Fast Food and Counter Workers	13.66	Sales Representatives, Technical/Scientific	128.93
Financial Managers	71.39	Secretaries, Exc. Legal/Medical/Executive	22.52
First-Line Supervisors of Office Workers	31.10	Security Guards	18.34
General and Operations Managers	62.22	Surgeons	n/a
Hairdressers/Cosmetologists	19.87	Teacher Assistants, Exc. Postsecondary*	15.21
Home Health and Personal Care Aides	14.08	Teachers, Secondary School, Exc. Sp. Ed.*	35.99
Janitors and Cleaners	17.50	Telemarketers	n/a
Landscaping/Groundskeeping Workers	17.82	Truck Drivers, Heavy/Tractor-Trailer	24.45
Lawyers	60.75	Truck Drivers, Light/Delivery Services	23.48
Maids and Housekeeping Cleaners	15.15	Waiters and Waitresses	17.37

Note: Wage data covers the Ann Arbor, MI Metropolitan Statistical Area; (*) Hourly wages were calculated from annual wage data based on a 40 hour work week; n/a not available.
Source: Bureau of Labor Statistics, Metro Area Occupational Employment & Wage Estimates, May 2022

Employment by Industry

Sector	MSA[1]		U.S.
	Number of Employees	Percent of Total	Percent of Total
Construction, Mining, and Logging	4,700	2.0	5.4
Private Education and Health Services	30,100	13.1	16.1
Financial Activities	7,100	3.1	5.9
Government	88,000	38.2	14.5
Information	5,900	2.6	2.0
Leisure and Hospitality	16,100	7.0	10.3
Manufacturing	12,700	5.5	8.4
Other Services	6,000	2.6	3.7
Professional and Business Services	31,400	13.6	14.7
Retail Trade	16,600	7.2	10.2
Transportation, Warehousing, and Utilities	5,000	2.2	4.9
Wholesale Trade	6,800	3.0	3.9

Note: Figures are non-farm employment as of December 2022. Figures are not seasonally adjusted and include workers 16 years of age and older; (1) Figures cover the Ann Arbor, MI Metropolitan Statistical Area
Source: Bureau of Labor Statistics, Current Employment Statistics, Employment, Hours, and Earnings

Employment by Occupation

Occupation Classification	City (%)	MSA[1] (%)	U.S. (%)
Management, Business, Science, and Arts	66.9	55.7	40.3
Natural Resources, Construction, and Maintenance	1.9	4.1	8.7
Production, Transportation, and Material Moving	5.2	9.1	13.1
Sales and Office	14.3	16.4	20.9
Service	11.8	14.7	17.0

Note: Figures cover employed civilians 16 years of age and older; (1) Figures cover the Ann Arbor, MI Metropolitan Statistical Area
Source: U.S. Census Bureau, 2017-2021 American Community Survey 5-Year Estimates

Occupations with Greatest Projected Employment Growth: 2021 – 2023

Occupation[1]	2021 Employment	2023 Projected Employment	Numeric Employment Change	Percent Employment Change
Fast Food and Counter Workers	116,260	126,010	9,750	8.4
Laborers and Freight, Stock, and Material Movers, Hand	84,660	94,000	9,340	11.0
Waiters and Waitresses	61,590	67,760	6,170	10.0
Stockers and Order Fillers	69,390	75,390	6,000	8.6
Cooks, Restaurant	29,850	34,490	4,640	15.5
Retail Salespersons	123,250	126,400	3,150	2.6
Heavy and Tractor-Trailer Truck Drivers	61,520	64,670	3,150	5.1
Janitors and Cleaners, Except Maids and Housekeeping Cleaners	64,490	67,530	3,040	4.7
General and Operations Managers	69,180	72,210	3,030	4.4
First-Line Supervisors of Food Preparation and Serving Workers	27,070	29,760	2,690	9.9

Note: Projections cover Michigan; Projections for 2022-2024 were not available at time of publication; (1) Sorted by numeric employment change
Source: www.projectionscentral.com, State Occupational Projections, 2021–2023 Short-Term Projections

Fastest-Growing Occupations: 2021 – 2023

Occupation[1]	2021 Employment	2023 Projected Employment	Numeric Employment Change	Percent Employment Change
Ushers, Lobby Attendants, and Ticket Takers	1,930	2,290	360	18.7
Cooks, Restaurant	29,850	34,490	4,640	15.5
Flight Attendants	3,150	3,580	430	13.7
Conveyor Operators and Tenders	650	730	80	12.3
Industrial Truck and Tractor Operators	22,030	24,680	2,650	12.0
Bartenders	15,110	16,830	1,720	11.4
Hosts and Hostesses, Restaurant, Lounge, and Coffee Shop	9,630	10,720	1,090	11.3
Laborers and Freight, Stock, and Material Movers, Hand	84,660	94,000	9,340	11.0
Dining Room and Cafeteria Attendants and Bartender Helpers	10,100	11,150	1,050	10.4
Waiters and Waitresses	61,590	67,760	6,170	10.0

Note: Projections cover Michigan; Projections for 2022-2024 were not available at time of publication; (1) Sorted by percent employment change and excludes occupations with numeric employment change less than 50
Source: www.projectionscentral.com, State Occupational Projections, 2021–2023 Short-Term Projections

CITY FINANCES

City Government Finances

Component	2020 ($000)	2020 ($ per capita)
Total Revenues	286,726	2,390
Total Expenditures	269,762	2,248
Debt Outstanding	290,215	2,419
Cash and Securities[1]	329,640	2,747

Note: (1) Cash and security holdings of a government at the close of its fiscal year, including those of its dependent agencies, utilities, and liquor stores.
Source: U.S. Census Bureau, State & Local Government Finances 2020

City Government Revenue by Source

Source	2020 ($000)	2020 ($ per capita)	2020 (%)
General Revenue			
From Federal Government	35,297	294	12.3
From State Government	27,807	232	9.7
From Local Governments	1,615	13	0.6
Taxes			
Property	109,187	910	38.1
Sales and Gross Receipts	0	0	0.0
Personal Income	0	0	0.0
Corporate Income	0	0	0.0
Motor Vehicle License	0	0	0.0
Other Taxes	7,617	63	2.7
Current Charges	53,321	444	18.6
Liquor Store	0	0	0.0
Utility	25,277	211	8.8

Source: U.S. Census Bureau, State & Local Government Finances 2020

City Government Expenditures by Function

Function	2020 ($000)	2020 ($ per capita)	2020 (%)
General Direct Expenditures			
Air Transportation	768	6	0.3
Corrections	0	0	0.0
Education	0	0	0.0
Employment Security Administration	0	0	0.0
Financial Administration	3,845	32	1.4
Fire Protection	16,647	138	6.2
General Public Buildings	0	0	0.0
Governmental Administration, Other	3,589	29	1.3
Health	0	0	0.0
Highways	40,218	335	14.9
Hospitals	0	0	0.0
Housing and Community Development	20,025	166	7.4
Interest on General Debt	6,939	57	2.6
Judicial and Legal	6,929	57	2.6
Libraries	0	0	0.0
Parking	1,688	14	0.6
Parks and Recreation	17,237	143	6.4
Police Protection	29,728	247	11.0
Public Welfare	0	0	0.0
Sewerage	16,449	137	6.1
Solid Waste Management	17,103	142	6.3
Veterans' Services	0	0	0.0
Liquor Store	0	0	0.0
Utility	31,927	266	11.8

Source: U.S. Census Bureau, State & Local Government Finances 2020

TAXES

State Corporate Income Tax Rates

State	Tax Rate (%)	Income Brackets ($)	Num. of Brackets	Financial Institution Tax Rate (%)[a]	Federal Income Tax Ded.
Michigan	6.0	Flat rate	1	(a)	No

Note: Tax rates as of January 1, 2023; (a) Rates listed are the corporate income tax rate applied to financial institutions or excise taxes based on income. Some states have other taxes based upon the value of deposits or shares.
Source: Federation of Tax Administrators, State Corporate Income Tax Rates, January 1, 2023

State Individual Income Tax Rates

State	Tax Rate (%)	Income Brackets ($)	Personal Exemptions ($) Single	Personal Exemptions ($) Married	Personal Exemptions ($) Depend.	Standard Ded. ($) Single	Standard Ded. ($) Married
Michigan	4.25	Flat rate	5,000	10,000	5,000	–	–

Note: Tax rates as of January 1, 2023; Local- and county-level taxes are not included; Federal income tax is not deductible on state income tax returns
Source: Federation of Tax Administrators, State Individual Income Tax Rates, January 1, 2023

Various State Sales and Excise Tax Rates

State	State Sales Tax (%)	Gasoline[1] ($/gal.)	Cigarette[2] ($/pack)	Spirits[3] ($/gal.)	Wine[4] ($/gal.)	Beer[5] ($/gal.)	Recreational Marijuana (%)
Michigan	6	0.466	2.00	13.57	0.51	0.20	(i)

Note: All tax rates as of January 1, 2023; (1) The American Petroleum Institute has developed a methodology for determining the average tax rate on a gallon of fuel. Rates may include any of the following: excise taxes, environmental fees, storage tank fees, other fees or taxes, general sales tax, and local taxes; (2) The federal excise tax of $1.0066 per pack and local taxes are not included; (3) Rates are those applicable to off-premise sales of 40% alcohol by volume (a.b.v.) distilled spirits in 750ml containers. Local excise taxes are excluded; (4) Rates are those applicable to off-premise sales of 11% a.b.v. non-carbonated wine in 750ml containers; (5) Rates are those applicable to off-premise sales of 4.7% a.b.v. beer in 12 ounce containers; (i) 10% excise tax (retail price)
Source: Tax Foundation, 2023 Facts & Figures: How Does Your State Compare?

State Business Tax Climate Index Rankings

State	Overall Rank	Corporate Tax Rank	Individual Income Tax Rank	Sales Tax Rank	Property Tax Rank	Unemployment Insurance Tax Rank
Michigan	12	20	12	11	25	8

Note: The index is a measure of how each state's tax laws affect economic performance. The lower the rank, the more favorable a state's tax system is for business. States without a given tax are given a ranking of 1. The scores/rankings for the District of Columbia do not affect other states. The 2023 index represents the tax climate as of July 1, 2022.
Source: Tax Foundation, State Business Tax Climate Index 2023

TRANSPORTATION

Means of Transportation to Work

Area	Car/Truck/Van		Public Transportation			Bicycle	Walked	Other Means	Worked at Home
	Drove Alone	Car-pooled	Bus	Subway	Railroad				
City	48.5	4.9	7.9	0.2	0.0	3.1	15.5	0.6	19.1
MSA[1]	66.1	6.5	4.1	0.1	0.0	1.3	6.9	0.8	14.2
U.S.	73.2	8.6	2.0	1.6	0.5	0.5	2.5	1.5	9.7

Note: Figures are percentages and cover workers 16 years of age and older; (1) Figures cover the Ann Arbor, MI Metropolitan Statistical Area
Source: U.S. Census Bureau, 2017-2021 American Community Survey 5-Year Estimates

Travel Time to Work

Area	Less Than 10 Minutes	10 to 19 Minutes	20 to 29 Minutes	30 to 44 Minutes	45 to 59 Minutes	60 to 89 Minutes	90 Minutes or More
City	13.9	45.7	18.6	14.0	5.0	2.4	0.5
MSA[1]	11.5	32.6	24.5	19.1	7.3	3.8	1.1
U.S.	12.4	28.5	21.0	20.9	8.2	6.2	2.9

Note: Note: Figures are percentages and include workers 16 years old and over; (1) Figures cover the Ann Arbor, MI Metropolitan Statistical Area
Source: U.S. Census Bureau, 2017-2021 American Community Survey 5-Year Estimates

Key Congestion Measures

Measure	1990	2000	2010	2015	2020
Annual Hours of Delay, Total (000)	n/a	n/a	n/a	6,900	3,239
Annual Hours of Delay, Per Auto Commuter	n/a	n/a	n/a	22	10
Annual Congestion Cost, Per Auto Commuter ($)	n/a	n/a	n/a	461	228

Note: n/a not available
Source: Texas A&M Transportation Institute, 2021 Urban Mobility Report

Freeway Travel Time Index

Measure	1985	1990	1995	2000	2005	2010	2015	2020
Urban Area Index[1]	n/a	n/a	n/a	n/a	n/a	n/a	1.11	1.07
Urban Area Rank[1,2]	n/a	n/a	n/a	n/a	n/a	n/a	n/a	n/a

Note: Freeway Travel Time Index—the ratio of travel time in the peak period to the travel time at free-flow conditions. For example, a value of 1.30 indicates a 20-minute free-flow trip takes 26 minutes in the peak (20 minutes x 1.30 = 26 minutes); (1) Covers the Ann Arbor MI urban area; (2) Rank is based on 101 larger urban areas (#1 = highest travel time index); n/a not available
Source: Texas A&M Transportation Institute, 2021 Urban Mobility Report

Public Transportation

Agency Name / Mode of Transportation	Vehicles Operated in Maximum Service[1]	Annual Unlinked Passenger Trips[2] (in thous.)	Annual Passenger Miles[3] (in thous.)
Ann Arbor Transportation Authority (AATA)			
Bus (directly operated)	75	1,729.4	6,172.5
Demand Response (directly operated)	24	53.9	288.6
Demand Response (purchased transportation)	36	33.6	136.1
Demand Response - Taxi	5	12.4	62.2
Vanpool (purchased transportation)	87	139.7	5,282.7

Note: (1) Number of revenue vehicles operated by the given mode and type of service to meet the annual maximum service requirement. This is the revenue vehicle count during the peak season of the year; on the week and day that maximum service is provided. Vehicles operated in maximum service (VOMS) exclude atypical days and one-time special events; (2) Number of passengers who boarded public transportation vehicles. Passengers are counted each time they board a vehicle no matter how many vehicles they use to travel from their origin to their destination. (3) Sum of the distances ridden by all passengers during the entire fiscal year.
Source: Federal Transit Administration, National Transit Database, 2021

Air Transportation

Airport Name and Code / Type of Service	Passenger Airlines[1]	Passenger Enplanements	Freight Carriers[2]	Freight (lbs)
Detroit Metro Wayne County (25 miles) (DTW)				
Domestic service (U.S. carriers - 2022)	31	12,672,501	15	123,138,882
International service (U.S. carriers - 2021)	7	396,588	3	18,581,730

Note: (1) Includes all U.S.-based major, minor and commuter airlines that carried at least one passenger during the year; (2) Includes all U.S.-based airlines and freight carriers that transported at least one pound of freight during the year.
Source: Bureau of Transportation Statistics, The Intermodal Transportation Database, Air Carriers: T-100 Domestic Market (U.S. Carriers), 2022; Bureau of Transportation Statistics, The Intermodal Transportation Database, Air Carriers: T-100 International Market (U.S. Carriers), 2021

BUSINESSES

Major Business Headquarters

Company Name	Industry	Rankings	
		Fortune[1]	Forbes[2]
No companies listed	-	-	-

Note: (1) Companies that produce a 10-K are ranked 1 to 500 based on 2021 revenue; (2) All private companies with at least $2 billion in annual revenue through the end of their most current fiscal year are ranked 1 to 246; companies listed are headquartered in the city; dashes indicate no ranking
Source: Fortune, "Fortune 500," 2022; Forbes, "America's Largest Private Companies," 2022

Fastest-Growing Businesses

According to Deloitte, Ann Arbor is home to one of North America's 500 fastest-growing high-technology companies: **AdAdapted** (#374). Companies are ranked by percentage growth in revenue over a four-year period. Criteria for inclusion: company must be headquartered within North America; must own proprietary intellectual property or technology that is sold to customers in products that contributes to a significant portion of the company's operating revenue; must have been in business for a minumum of four years with 2018 operating revenues of at least $50,000 USD/CD and 2021 operating revenues of at least $5 million USD/CD. *Deloitte, 2022 Technology Fast 500*[TM]

Living Environment

COST OF LIVING

Cost of Living Index

Composite Index	Groceries	Housing	Utilities	Trans- portation	Health Care	Misc. Goods/ Services
n/a	n/a	n/a	n/a	n/a	n/a	n/a

Note: The Cost of Living Index measures regional differences in the cost of consumer goods and services, excluding taxes and non-consumer expenditures, for professional and managerial households in the top income quintile. It is based on more than 50,000 prices covering almost 60 different items for which prices are collected three times a year by chambers of commerce, economic development organizations or university applied economic centers in each participating urban area. The numbers shown should be read as a percentage above or below the national average of 100. For example, a value of 115.4 in the groceries column indicates that grocery prices are 15.4% higher than the national average. Small differences in the index numbers should not be interpreted as significant; n/a not available.
Source: The Council for Community and Economic Research, Cost of Living Index, 2022

Grocery Prices

Area[1]	T-Bone Steak ($/pound)	Frying Chicken ($/pound)	Whole Milk ($/half gal.)	Eggs ($/dozen)	Orange Juice ($/64 oz.)	Coffee ($/11.5 oz.)
City[2]	n/a	n/a	n/a	n/a	n/a	n/a
Avg.	13.81	1.59	2.43	2.25	3.85	4.95
Min.	10.17	0.90	1.51	1.30	2.90	3.46
Max.	19.35	3.30	4.32	4.32	5.31	8.59

Note: (1) Values for the local area are compared with the average, minimum and maximum values for all 286 areas in the Cost of Living Index; (2) Figures cover the Ann Arbor MI urban area; n/a not available; **T-Bone Steak** (price per pound); **Frying Chicken** (price per pound, whole fryer); **Whole Milk** (half gallon carton); **Eggs** (price per dozen, Grade A, large); **Orange Juice** (64 oz. Tropicana or Florida Natural); **Coffee** (11.5 oz. can, vacuum-packed, Maxwell House, Hills Bros, or Folgers).
Source: The Council for Community and Economic Research, Cost of Living Index, 2022

Housing and Utility Costs

Area[1]	New Home Price ($)	Apartment Rent ($/month)	All Electric ($/month)	Part Electric ($/month)	Other Energy ($/month)	Telephone ($/month)
City[2]	n/a	n/a	n/a	n/a	n/a	n/a
Avg.	450,913	1,371	176.41	99.93	76.96	190.22
Min.	229,283	546	100.84	31.56	27.15	174.27
Max.	2,434,977	4,569	356.86	249.59	272.24	208.31

Note: (1) Values for the local area are compared with the average, minimum and maximum values for all 286 areas in the Cost of Living Index; (2) Figures cover the Ann Arbor MI urban area; n/a not available; **New Home Price** (2,400 sf living area, 8,000 sf lot, in urban area with full utilities); **Apartment Rent** (950 sf 2 bedroom/1.5 or 2 bath, unfurnished, excluding all utilities except water); **All Electric** (average monthly cost for an all-electric home); **Part Electric** (average monthly cost for a part-electric home); **Other Energy** (average monthly cost for natural gas, fuel oil, coal, wood, and any other forms of energy except electricity); **Telephone** (price includes the base monthly rate plus taxes and fees for three lines of mobile phone service).
Source: The Council for Community and Economic Research, Cost of Living Index, 2022

Health Care, Transportation, and Other Costs

Area[1]	Doctor ($/visit)	Dentist ($/visit)	Optometrist ($/visit)	Gasoline ($/gallon)	Beauty Salon ($/visit)	Men's Shirt ($)
City[2]	n/a	n/a	n/a	n/a	n/a	n/a
Avg.	124.91	107.77	117.66	3.86	43.31	34.21
Min.	36.61	58.25	51.79	2.90	22.18	13.05
Max.	250.21	162.58	371.96	5.54	85.61	63.54

Note: (1) Values for the local area are compared with the average, minimum and maximum values for all 286 areas in the Cost of Living Index; (2) Figures cover the Ann Arbor MI urban area; n/a not available; **Doctor** (general practitioners routine exam of an established patient); **Dentist** (adult teeth cleaning and periodic oral examination); **Optometrist** (full vision eye exam for established adult patient); **Gasoline** (one gallon regular unleaded, national brand, including all taxes, cash price at self-service pump if available); **Beauty Salon** (woman's shampoo, trim, and blow-dry); **Men's Shirt** (cotton/polyester dress shirt, pinpoint weave, long sleeves).
Source: The Council for Community and Economic Research, Cost of Living Index, 2022

HOUSING

Homeownership Rate

Area	2015 (%)	2016 (%)	2017 (%)	2018 (%)	2019 (%)	2020 (%)	2021 (%)	2022 (%)
MSA[1]	n/a	n/a	n/a	n/a	n/a	n/a	n/a	n/a
U.S.	63.7	63.4	63.9	64.4	64.6	66.6	65.5	65.8

Note: (1) Figures cover the Ann Arbor, MI Metropolitan Statistical Area; n/a not available
Source: U.S. Census Bureau, Housing Vacancies and Homeownership Annual Statistics: 2015-2022

House Price Index (HPI)

Area	National Ranking[2]	Quarterly Change (%)	One-Year Change (%)	Five-Year Change (%)	Since 1991Q1 (%)
MSA[1]	210	-4.46	8.26	40.08	220.18
U.S.[3]	–	0.34	8.41	58.44	289.08

Note: The HPI is a weighted repeat sales index. It measures average price changes in repeat sales or refinancings on the same properties. This information is obtained by reviewing repeat mortgage transactions on single-family properties whose mortgages have been purchased or securitized by Fannie Mae or Freddie Mac since January 1975; (1) Figures cover the Ann Arbor, MI Metropolitan Statistical Area; (2) Rankings are based on annual percentage change for all metro areas containing at least 15,000 transactions over the last 10 years and ranges from 1 to 257; (3) figures based on a weighted average of Census Division estimates using a seasonally adjusted, purchase-only index; all figures are for the period ending December 31, 2022
Source: Federal Housing Finance Agency, Change in FHFA Metropolitan Area House Price Indexes, 2022Q4

Median Single-Family Home Prices

Area	2020	2021	2022p	Percent Change 2021 to 2022
MSA[1]	312.4	348.8	373.8	7.2
U.S. Average	300.2	357.1	392.6	9.9

Note: Figures are median sales prices of existing single-family homes in thousands of dollars; (p) preliminary; (1) Figures cover the Ann Arbor, MI Metropolitan Statistical Area
Source: National Association of Realtors, Median Sales Price of Existing Single-Family Homes for Metropolitan Areas, 4th Quarter 2022

Qualifying Income Based on Median Sales Price of Existing Single-Family Homes

Area	With 5% Down ($)	With 10% Down ($)	With 20% Down ($)
MSA[1]	106,091	100,507	89,339
U.S. Average	112,234	106,237	94,513

Note: Figures are preliminary; Qualifying income is based on a mortgage rate of 6.77%. Monthly principal and interest payment is limited to 25% of income; (1) Figures cover the Ann Arbor, MI Metropolitan Statistical Area
Source: National Association of Realtors, Qualifying Income Based on Median Sales Price of Existing Single-Family Homes for Metropolitan Areas, 4th Quarter 2022

Home Value

Area	Under $100,000	$100,000 -$199,999	$200,000 -$299,999	$300,000 -$399,999	$400,000 -$499,999	$500,000 -$999,999	$1,000,000 or more	Median ($)
City	2.4	10.8	20.5	24.6	18.8	19.9	3.0	366,600
MSA[1]	9.2	18.2	24.0	19.4	12.7	14.5	1.9	293,800
U.S.	16.2	24.2	20.1	13.6	8.3	13.6	4.1	244,900

Note: Figures are percentages except for median and cover owner-occupied housing units; (1) Figures cover the Ann Arbor, MI Metropolitan Statistical Area
Source: U.S. Census Bureau, 2017-2021 American Community Survey 5-Year Estimates

Year Housing Structure Built

Area	2020 or Later	2010 -2019	2000 -2009	1990 -1999	1980 -1989	1970 -1979	1960 -1969	1950 -1959	1940 -1949	Before 1940	Median Year
City	0.2	5.0	5.8	11.7	11.3	16.9	18.0	11.1	5.0	15.0	1971
MSA[1]	0.2	4.8	12.8	17.0	11.2	16.0	12.4	9.7	4.5	11.5	1977
U.S.	0.2	7.3	13.6	13.6	13.2	14.8	10.3	10.0	4.7	12.2	1979

Note: Figures are percentages except for Median Year; Note: (1) Figures cover the Ann Arbor, MI Metropolitan Statistical Area
Source: U.S. Census Bureau, 2017-2021 American Community Survey 5-Year Estimates

Gross Monthly Rent

Area	Under $500	$500 -$999	$1,000 -$1,499	$1,500 -$1,999	$2,000 -$2,499	$2,500 -$2,999	$3,000 and up	Median ($)
City	3.9	17.0	37.0	24.4	9.7	3.5	4.4	1,382
MSA[1]	5.1	24.0	40.6	18.9	6.1	2.2	3.1	1,218
U.S.	8.1	30.5	30.8	16.8	7.3	3.1	3.5	1,163

Note: Figures are percentages except for median; Gross rent is the contract rent plus the estimated average monthly cost of utilities (electricity, gas, and water and sewer) and fuels (oil, coal, kerosene, wood, etc.) if these are paid by the renter (or paid for the renter by someone else); (1) Figures cover the Ann Arbor, MI Metropolitan Statistical Area
Source: U.S. Census Bureau, 2017-2021 American Community Survey 5-Year Estimates

HEALTH

Health Risk Factors

Category	MSA[1] (%)	U.S. (%)
Adults aged 18–64 who have any kind of health care coverage	n/a	90.9
Adults who reported being in good or better health	n/a	85.2
Adults who have been told they have high blood cholesterol	n/a	35.7
Adults who have been told they have high blood pressure	n/a	32.4
Adults who are current smokers	n/a	14.4
Adults who currently use e-cigarettes	n/a	6.7
Adults who currently use chewing tobacco, snuff, or snus	n/a	3.5
Adults who are heavy drinkers[2]	n/a	6.3
Adults who are binge drinkers[3]	n/a	15.4
Adults who are overweight (BMI 25.0 - 29.9)	n/a	34.4
Adults who are obese (BMI 30.0 - 99.8)	n/a	33.9
Adults who participated in any physical activities in the past month	n/a	76.3

Note: (1) Figures for the Ann Arbor, MI Metropolitan Statistical Area were not available.
(2) Heavy drinkers are classified as adult men having more than 14 drinks per week and adult women having more than 7 drinks per week; (3) Binge drinkers are classified as males having five or more drinks on one occasion or females having four or more drinks on one occasion
Source: Centers for Disease Control and Prevention, Behaviorial Risk Factor Surveillance System, SMART: Selected Metropolitan Area Risk Trends, 2021

Acute and Chronic Health Conditions

Category	MSA[1] (%)	U.S. (%)
Adults who have ever been told they had a heart attack	n/a	4.0
Adults who have ever been told they have angina or coronary heart disease	n/a	3.8
Adults who have ever been told they had a stroke	n/a	3.0
Adults who have ever been told they have asthma	n/a	14.9
Adults who have ever been told they have arthritis	n/a	25.8
Adults who have ever been told they have diabetes[2]	n/a	10.9
Adults who have ever been told they had skin cancer	n/a	6.6
Adults who have ever been told they had any other types of cancer	n/a	7.5
Adults who have ever been told they have COPD	n/a	6.1
Adults who have ever been told they have kidney disease	n/a	3.0
Adults who have ever been told they have a form of depression	n/a	20.5

Note: (1) Figures for the Ann Arbor, MI Metropolitan Statistical Area were not available.
(2) Figures do not include pregnancy-related, borderline, or pre-diabetes
Source: Centers for Disease Control and Prevention, Behaviorial Risk Factor Surveillance System, SMART: Selected Metropolitan Area Risk Trends, 2021

Health Screening and Vaccination Rates

Category	MSA[1] (%)	U.S. (%)
Adults who have ever been tested for HIV	n/a	34.9
Adults who have had their blood cholesterol checked within the last five years	n/a	85.2
Adults aged 65+ who have had flu shot within the past year	n/a	68.6
Adults aged 65+ who have ever had a pneumonia vaccination	n/a	71.0

Note: (1) Figures for the Ann Arbor, MI Metropolitan Statistical Area were not available.
Source: Centers for Disease Control and Prevention, Behaviorial Risk Factor Surveillance System, SMART: Selected Metropolitan Area Risk Trends, 2021

Disability Status

Category	MSA[1] (%)	U.S. (%)
Adults who reported being deaf	n/a	7.2
Are you blind or have serious difficulty seeing, even when wearing glasses?	n/a	4.8
Are you limited in any way in any of your usual activities due to arthritis?	n/a	11.1
Do you have difficulty doing errands alone?	n/a	7.0
Do you have difficulty dressing or bathing?	n/a	3.6
Do you have serious difficulty concentrating/remembering/making decisions?	n/a	12.1
Do you have serious difficulty walking or climbing stairs?	n/a	12.8

Note: (1) Figures for the Ann Arbor, MI Metropolitan Statistical Area were not available.
Source: Centers for Disease Control and Prevention, Behaviorial Risk Factor Surveillance System, SMART: Selected Metropolitan Area Risk Trends, 2021

Mortality Rates for the Top 10 Causes of Death in the U.S.

ICD-10[a] Sub-Chapter	ICD-10[a] Code	Crude Mortality Rate[1] per 100,000 population	
		County[2]	U.S.
Malignant neoplasms	C00-C97	148.1	182.6
Ischaemic heart diseases	I20-I25	85.3	113.1
Other forms of heart disease	I30-I51	43.6	64.4
Other degenerative diseases of the nervous system	G30-G31	48.5	51.0
Cerebrovascular diseases	I60-I69	42.7	47.8
Other external causes of accidental injury	W00-X59	38.9	46.4
Chronic lower respiratory diseases	J40-J47	27.0	45.7
Organic, including symptomatic, mental disorders	F01-F09	22.8	35.9
Hypertensive diseases	I10-I15	39.0	35.0
Diabetes mellitus	E10-E14	12.1	29.6

Note: (a) ICD-10 = International Classification of Diseases 10th Revision; (1) Crude mortality rates are a three-year average covering 2019-2021; (2) Figures cover Washtenaw County.
Source: Centers for Disease Control and Prevention, National Center for Health Statistics. National Vital Statistics System, Mortality 2018-2021 on CDC WONDER Online Database

Mortality Rates for Selected Causes of Death

ICD-10[a] Sub-Chapter	ICD-10[a] Code	Crude Mortality Rate[1] per 100,000 population	
		County[2]	U.S.
Assault	X85-Y09	3.7	7.0
Diseases of the liver	K70-K76	11.1	19.8
Human immunodeficiency virus (HIV) disease	B20-B24	Suppressed	1.5
Influenza and pneumonia	J09-J18	7.2	14.7
Intentional self-harm	X60-X84	13.0	14.3
Malnutrition	E40-E46	4.4	4.3
Obesity and other hyperalimentation	E65-E68	Unreliable	3.0
Renal failure	N17-N19	9.2	15.7
Transport accidents	V01-V99	7.6	13.6
Viral hepatitis	B15-B19	Suppressed	1.2

Note: (a) ICD-10 = International Classification of Diseases 10th Revision; (1) Crude mortality rates are a three-year average covering 2019-2021; (2) Figures cover Washtenaw County; Data are suppressed when the data meet the criteria for confidentiality constraints; Crude mortality rates are flagged as unreliable when the rate would be calculated with a numerator of 20 or less.
Source: Centers for Disease Control and Prevention, National Center for Health Statistics. National Vital Statistics System, Mortality 2018-2021 on CDC WONDER Online Database

Health Insurance Coverage

Area	With Health Insurance	With Private Health Insurance	With Public Health Insurance	Without Health Insurance	Population Under Age 19 Without Health Insurance
City	97.4	87.5	20.3	2.6	1.3
MSA[1]	96.6	82.5	27.2	3.4	1.8
U.S.	91.2	67.8	35.4	8.8	5.3

Note: Figures are percentages that cover the civilian noninstitutionalized population; (1) Figures cover the Ann Arbor, MI Metropolitan Statistical Area
Source: U.S. Census Bureau, 2017-2021 American Community Survey 5-Year Estimates

Number of Medical Professionals

Area	MDs[3]	DOs[3,4]	Dentists	Podiatrists	Chiropractors	Optometrists
County[1] (number)	4,905	157	733	29	99	68
County[1] (rate[2])	1,319.8	42.2	198.4	7.9	26.8	18.4
U.S. (rate[2])	289.3	23.5	72.5	6.2	28.7	17.4

Note: Data as of 2021 unless noted; (1) Data covers Washtenaw County; (2) Rate per 100,000 population; (3) Data as of 2020 and includes all active, non-federal physicians; (4) Doctor of Osteopathic Medicine
Source: U.S. Department of Health and Human Services, Health Resources and Services Administration, Bureau of Health Professions, Area Resource File (ARF) 2021-2022

Best Hospitals

According to *U.S. News,* the Ann Arbor, MI metro area is home to five of the best hospitals in the U.S.: **University of Michigan Health Frankel Cardiovascular Center** (Honor Roll/13 adult specialties and 9 pediatric specialties); **University of Michigan Health Kellogg Eye Center** (Honor Roll/13 adult specialties and 9 pediatric specialties); **University of Michigan Health Rogel Cancer Center** (Honor Roll/13 adult specialties and 9 pediatric specialties); **University of Michigan Health Von Voigtlander Women's Hospital** (Honor Roll/13 adult specialties and 9 pediatric specialties); **University of Michigan Health-Ann Arbor** (Honor Roll/13 adult specialties and 9 pediatric specialties). The hospitals listed were nationally ranked in at least one of 15 adult or 10 pediatric specialties. The number of specialties shown cover the parent hospital. Only 164 U.S. hospitals performed well enough to be nationally ranked in one or more specialties. Twenty hospitals in the U.S. made the Honor Roll. The Best Hospitals Honor Roll takes both the national rankings and the procedure and condition ratings into account. Hospitals received points if they were nationally ranked in one of the 15 adult specialties—the higher they ranked, the more points they got—and how many ratings of "high performing" they earned in the 17 procedures and conditions. *U.S. News Online, "America's Best Hospitals 2022-23"*

According to *U.S. News,* the Ann Arbor, MI metro area is home to one of the best children's hospitals in the U.S.: **University of Michigan Health C.S. Mott Children's Hospital** (9 pediatric specialties). The hospital listed was highly ranked in at least one of 10 pediatric specialties. Eighty-six children's hospitals in the U.S. were nationally ranked in at least one specialty. Hospitals received points for being ranked in a specialty, and the 10 hospitals with the most points across the 10 specialties make up the Honor Roll. *U.S. News Online, "America's Best Children's Hospitals 2022-23"*

EDUCATION

Public School District Statistics

District Name	Schls	Pupils	Pupil/ Teacher Ratio	Minority Pupils[1] (%)	LEP/ELL[2] (%)	IEP[3] (%)
Ann Arbor Public Schools	32	17,070	13.6	49.5	9.1	12.4

Note: Table includes school districts with 2,000 or more students; (1) Percentage of students that are not non-Hispanic white; (2) Percentage of students that are Limited English Proficient or English Language Learners (2018-19); (3) Percentage of students that have an Individualized Education Program (2019-20).
Source: U.S. Department of Education, National Center for Education Statistics, Common Core of Data, Local Education Agency (School District) Universe Survey: School Year 2021-2022

Best High Schools

According to *U.S. News,* Ann Arbor is home to one of the top 500 high schools in the U.S.: **Skyline High School** (#493). Nearly 18,000 public, magnet and charter schools were ranked based on their performance on state assessments and how well they prepare students for college. *U.S. News & World Report, "Best High Schools 2022"*

Highest Level of Education

Area	Less than H.S.	H.S. Diploma	Some College, No Deg.	Associate Degree	Bachelor's Degree	Master's Degree	Prof. School Degree	Doctorate Degree
City	2.2	7.6	8.9	4.0	30.5	26.8	8.3	11.6
MSA[1]	4.3	14.6	17.0	6.9	26.9	19.0	5.0	6.2
U.S.	11.1	26.5	20.0	8.7	20.6	9.3	2.2	1.5

Note: Figures cover persons age 25 and over; (1) Figures cover the Ann Arbor, MI Metropolitan Statistical Area
Source: U.S. Census Bureau, 2017-2021 American Community Survey 5-Year Estimates

Educational Attainment by Race

Area	High School Graduate or Higher (%)					Bachelor's Degree or Higher (%)				
	Total	White	Black	Asian	Hisp.[2]	Total	White	Black	Asian	Hisp.[2]
City	97.8	98.5	93.2	98.0	92.7	77.2	79.5	36.4	85.6	69.9
MSA[1]	95.7	96.8	90.8	95.7	87.2	57.2	58.9	29.1	82.1	46.1
U.S.	88.9	91.4	87.2	87.6	71.2	33.7	35.5	23.3	55.6	18.4

Note: Figures shown cover persons 25 years old and over; (1) Figures cover the Ann Arbor, MI Metropolitan Statistical Area; (2) People of Hispanic origin can be of any race
Source: U.S. Census Bureau, 2017-2021 American Community Survey 5-Year Estimates

School Enrollment by Grade and Control

Area	Preschool (%)		Kindergarten (%)		Grades 1 - 4 (%)		Grades 5 - 8 (%)		Grades 9 - 12 (%)	
	Public	Private	Public	Private	Public	Private	Public	Private	Public	Private
City	34.0	66.0	86.6	13.4	88.7	11.3	87.6	12.4	94.0	6.0
MSA[1]	49.9	50.1	89.4	10.6	87.1	12.9	88.1	11.9	93.0	7.0
U.S.	58.8	41.2	86.3	13.7	88.3	11.7	88.6	11.4	89.4	10.6

Note: Figures shown cover persons 3 years old and over; (1) Figures cover the Ann Arbor, MI Metropolitan Statistical Area
Source: U.S. Census Bureau, 2017-2021 American Community Survey 5-Year Estimates

Higher Education

Four-Year Colleges			Two-Year Colleges			Medical Schools[1]	Law Schools[2]	Voc/ Tech[3]
Public	Private Non-profit	Private For-profit	Public	Private Non-profit	Private For-profit			
2	1	0	1	0	0	1	1	1

Note: Figures cover institutions located within the Ann Arbor, MI Metropolitan Statistical Area and include main campuses only; (1) includes schools accredited by the Liaison Committee on Medical Education and the American Osteopathic Association's Commission on Osteopathic College Accreditation; (2) includes ABA-accredited schools, schools with provisional ABA accreditation, and state accredited schools; (3) includes all schools with programs that are less than 2 years.
Source: National Center for Education Statistics, Integrated Postsecondary Education System (IPEDS), 2021-22; Wikipedia, List of Medical Schools in the United States, accessed April 10, 2023; Wikipedia, List of Law Schools in the United States, accessed April 10, 2023

According to *U.S. News & World Report,* the Ann Arbor, MI metro area is home to one of the top 200 national universities in the U.S.: **University of Michigan—Ann Arbor** (#25 tie). The indicators used to capture academic quality fall into a number of categories: assessment by administrators at peer institutions; retention of students; faculty resources; student selectivity; financial resources; alumni giving; high school counselor ratings of colleges; and graduation rate. *U.S. News & World Report, "America's Best Colleges 2023"*

According to *U.S. News & World Report,* the Ann Arbor, MI metro area is home to one of the top 100 law schools in the U.S.: **University of Michigan—Ann Arbor** (#10). The rankings are based on a weighted average of 12 measures of quality: peer assessment score; assessment score by lawyers/judges; median LSAT scores; median undergrad GPA; acceptance rate; employment rates for graduates; placement success; bar passage rate; faculty resources; expenditures per student; student/faculty ratio; and library resources. *U.S. News & World Report, "America's Best Graduate Schools, Law, 2023"*

According to *U.S. News & World Report,* the Ann Arbor, MI metro area is home to one of the top 75 medical schools for research in the U.S.: **University of Michigan—Ann Arbor** (#17 tie). The rankings are based on a weighted average of 11 measures of quality: quality assessment; peer assessment score; assessment score by residency directors; research activity; total research activity; average research activity per faculty member; student selectivity; median MCAT total score; median undergraduate GPA; acceptance rate; and faculty resources. *U.S. News & World Report, "America's Best Graduate Schools, Medical, 2023"*

According to *U.S. News & World Report,* the Ann Arbor, MI metro area is home to one of the top 75 business schools in the U.S.: **University of Michigan—Ann Arbor (Ross)** (#10). The rankings are based on a weighted average of the following nine measures: quality assessment; peer assessment; recruiter assessment; placement success; mean starting salary and bonus; student selectivity; mean GMAT and GRE scores; mean undergraduate GPA; and acceptance rate. *U.S. News & World Report, "America's Best Graduate Schools, Business, 2023"*

EMPLOYERS

Major Employers

Company Name	Industry
Ann Arbor Public Schools	Education
Citizens Insurance Company of America	FInance & insurance
City of Ann Arbor	Municipal government
Domino's Pizza	Food services
Eastern Michigan University	Education
Faurecia Interior Systems	Automotive component mfg.
Ford Motor Company	Automotive component mfg.
General Motors Milford Proving Grounds	OEM research
Grupo Antolin	Automotive component mfg.
Integrated Health Associates (IHA)	Medical center
JAC Products	Auto component mfg.
ProQuest	Data & information
Terumo Carviocascular Systems	Medical device manufacturer
Thai Summit America	Automotive component mfg.
Thomson Reuters	Software/IT
Toyota Technical Center	Automotive research & development
Trinity Health	Medical center
Truven Health Analytics	Data & information
University of Michigan	Education
University of Michigan Medical Center	Medical center
VA Ann Arbor Healthcare System	Medical center
Washtenaw Community College	Education
Washtenaw County Government	Government
Ypsilanti Public Schools	Education
Zingerman's	Food processing

Note: Companies shown are located within the Ann Arbor, MI Metropolitan Statistical Area.
Source: Hoovers.com; Wikipedia

PUBLIC SAFETY

Crime Rate

Area	Total Crime	Violent Crime Rate				Property Crime Rate		
		Murder	Rape[3]	Robbery	Aggrav. Assault	Burglary	Larceny -Theft	Motor Vehicle Theft
City	1,563.2	0.8	40.6	31.5	170.7	126.8	1,125.6	67.1
Suburbs[1]	1,734.3	3.2	74.1	38.7	378.3	167.6	942.7	129.7
Metro[2]	1,678.4	2.4	63.2	36.3	310.4	154.3	1,002.5	109.3
U.S.	2,356.7	6.5	38.4	73.9	279.7	314.2	1,398.0	246.0

Note: Figures are crimes per 100,000 population; (1) All areas within the metro area that are located outside the city limits; (2) Figures cover the Ann Arbor, MI Metropolitan Statistical Area; (3) All figures shown were reported using the revised Uniform Crime Reporting (UCR) definition of rape; Due to the transition to the National Incident-Based Reporting System (NIBRS), limited city and metro area data was released for 2021.
Source: FBI Uniform Crime Reports, 2020

Hate Crimes

Area	Number of Quarters Reported	Number of Incidents per Bias Motivation					
		Race/Ethnicity/ Ancestry	Religion	Sexual Orientation	Disability	Gender	Gender Identity
City	4	3	0	0	0	0	1
U.S.	4	5,227	1,244	1,110	130	75	266

Note: Due to the transition to the National Incident-Based Reporting System (NIBRS), limited crime data was released for 2021.
Source: Federal Bureau of Investigation, Hate Crime Statistics 2020

Identity Theft Consumer Reports

Area	Reports	Reports per 100,000 Population	Rank[2]
MSA[1]	915	248	107
U.S.	1,108,609	339	-

Note: (1) Figures cover the Ann Arbor, MI Metropolitan Statistical Area; (2) Rank ranges from 1 to 391 where 1 indicates greatest number of identity theft reports per 100,000 population
Source: Federal Trade Commission, Consumer Sentinel Network Data Book 2022

Fraud and Other Consumer Reports

Area	Reports	Reports per 100,000 Population	Rank[2]
MSA[1]	3,778	1,026	87
U.S.	4,064,520	1,245	-

Note: (1) Figures cover the Ann Arbor, MI Metropolitan Statistical Area; (2) Rank ranges from 1 to 391 where 1 indicates greatest number of fraud and other consumer reports per 100,000 population
Source: Federal Trade Commission, Consumer Sentinel Network Data Book 2022

POLITICS

2020 Presidential Election Results

Area	Biden	Trump	Jorgensen	Hawkins	Other
Washtenaw County	72.4	25.9	0.9	0.3	0.4
U.S.	51.3	46.8	1.2	0.3	0.5

Note: Results are percentages and may not add to 100% due to rounding
Source: Dave Leip's Atlas of U.S. Presidential Elections

SPORTS

Professional Sports Teams

Team Name	League	Year Established
No teams are located in the metro area		

Source: Wikipedia, Major Professional Sports Teams of the United States and Canada, April 12, 2023

CLIMATE

Average and Extreme Temperatures

Temperature	Jan	Feb	Mar	Apr	May	Jun	Jul	Aug	Sep	Oct	Nov	Dec	Yr.
Extreme High (°F)	62	65	81	89	93	104	102	100	98	91	77	68	104
Average High (°F)	30	33	44	58	70	79	83	81	74	61	48	35	58
Average Temp. (°F)	23	26	36	48	59	68	72	71	64	52	40	29	49
Average Low (°F)	16	18	27	37	47	56	61	60	53	41	32	21	39
Extreme Low (°F)	-21	-15	-4	10	25	36	41	38	29	17	9	-10	-21

Note: Figures cover the years 1958-1990
Source: National Climatic Data Center, International Station Meteorological Climate Summary, 9/96

Average Precipitation/Snowfall/Humidity

Precip./Humidity	Jan	Feb	Mar	Apr	May	Jun	Jul	Aug	Sep	Oct	Nov	Dec	Yr.
Avg. Precip. (in.)	1.8	1.8	2.5	3.0	2.9	3.6	3.1	3.4	2.8	2.2	2.6	2.7	32.4
Avg. Snowfall (in.)	10	9	7	2	Tr	0	0	0	0	Tr	3	11	41
Avg. Rel. Hum. 7am (%)	80	79	79	78	78	79	82	86	87	84	82	81	81
Avg. Rel. Hum. 4pm (%)	67	63	59	53	51	52	52	54	55	55	64	70	58

Note: Figures cover the years 1958-1990; Tr = Trace amounts (<0.05 in. of rain; <0.5 in. of snow)
Source: National Climatic Data Center, International Station Meteorological Climate Summary, 9/96

Weather Conditions

Temperature			Daytime Sky			Precipitation		
5°F & below	32°F & below	90°F & above	Clear	Partly cloudy	Cloudy	0.01 inch or more precip.	0.1 inch or more snow/ice	Thunder-storms
15	136	12	74	134	157	135	38	32

Note: Figures are average number of days per year and cover the years 1958-1990
Source: National Climatic Data Center, International Station Meteorological Climate Summary, 9/96

HAZARDOUS WASTE

Superfund Sites

The Ann Arbor, MI metro area has no sites on the EPA's Superfund Final National Priorities List. There are a total of 1,165 Superfund sites with a status of proposed or final on the list in the U.S. *U.S. Environmental Protection Agency, National Priorities List, April 12, 2023*

AIR QUALITY

Air Quality Trends: Ozone

	1990	1995	2000	2005	2010	2015	2018	2019	2020	2021
MSA[1]	0.025	0.034	0.035	0.023	0.034	0.064	0.072	0.058	0.067	0.063
U.S.	0.087	0.089	0.081	0.072	0.067	0.067	0.069	0.065	0.065	0.067

Note: (1) Data covers the Ann Arbor, MI Metropolitan Statistical Area. The values shown are the composite ozone concentration averages among trend sites based on the highest fourth daily maximum 8-hour concentration in parts per million. These trends are based on sites having an adequate record of monitoring data during the trend period. Data from exceptional events are included.
Source: U.S. Environmental Protection Agency, Air Quality Monitoring Information, "Air Quality Trends by City, 1990-2021"

Air Quality Index

Area	Percent of Days when Air Quality was...[2]					AQI Statistics[2]	
	Good	Moderate	Unhealthy for Sensitive Groups	Unhealthy	Very Unhealthy	Maximum	Median
MSA[1]	76.2	23.8	0.0	0.0	0.0	100	40

Note: (1) Data covers the Ann Arbor, MI Metropolitan Statistical Area; (2) Based on 365 days with AQI data in 2021. Air Quality Index (AQI) is an index for reporting daily air quality. EPA calculates the AQI for five major air pollutants regulated by the Clean Air Act: ground-level ozone, particle pollution (aka particulate matter), carbon monoxide, sulfur dioxide, and nitrogen dioxide. The AQI runs from 0 to 500. The higher the AQI value, the greater the level of air pollution and the greater the health concern. There are six AQI categories: "Good" AQI is between 0 and 50. Air quality is considered satisfactory; "Moderate" AQI is between 51 and 100. Air quality is acceptable; "Unhealthy for Sensitive Groups" When AQI values are between 101 and 150, members of sensitive groups may experience health effects; "Unhealthy" When AQI values are between 151 and 200 everyone may begin to experience health effects; "Very Unhealthy" AQI values between 201 and 300 trigger a health alert; "Hazardous" AQI values over 300 trigger warnings of emergency conditions (not shown).
Source: U.S. Environmental Protection Agency, Air Quality Index Report, 2021

Air Quality Index Pollutants

Area	Percent of Days when AQI Pollutant was...[2]					
	Carbon Monoxide	Nitrogen Dioxide	Ozone	Sulfur Dioxide	Particulate Matter 2.5	Particulate Matter 10
MSA[1]	0.0	0.0	62.5	(3)	37.5	0.0

Note: (1) Data covers the Ann Arbor, MI Metropolitan Statistical Area; (2) Based on 365 days with AQI data in 2021. The Air Quality Index (AQI) is an index for reporting daily air quality. EPA calculates the AQI for five major air pollutants regulated by the Clean Air Act: ground-level ozone, particle pollution (also known as particulate matter), carbon monoxide, sulfur dioxide, and nitrogen dioxide. The AQI runs from 0 to 500. The higher the AQI value, the greater the level of air pollution and the greater the health concern; (3) Sulfur dioxide is no longer included in this table (as of December 8, 2021) because SO_2 concentrations tend to be very localized and not necessarily representative of broad geographical areas like counties and CBSAs.
Source: U.S. Environmental Protection Agency, Air Quality Index Report, 2021

Maximum Air Pollutant Concentrations: Particulate Matter, Ozone, CO and Lead

	Particulate Matter 10 (ug/m³)	Particulate Matter 2.5 Wtd AM (ug/m³)	Particulate Matter 2.5 24-Hr (ug/m³)	Ozone (ppm)	Carbon Monoxide (ppm)	Lead (ug/m³)
MSA[1] Level	n/a	8.8	18	0.066	n/a	n/a
NAAQS[2]	150	15	35	0.075	9	0.15
Met NAAQS[2]	n/a	Yes	Yes	Yes	n/a	n/a

Note: (1) Data covers the Ann Arbor, MI Metropolitan Statistical Area; Data from exceptional events are included; (2) National Ambient Air Quality Standards; ppm = parts per million; ug/m³ = micrograms per cubic meter; n/a not available.
Concentrations: Particulate Matter 10 (coarse particulate)—highest second maximum 24-hour concentration; Particulate Matter 2.5 Wtd AM (fine particulate)—highest weighted annual mean concentration; Particulate Matter 2.5 24-Hour (fine particulate)—highest 98th percentile 24-hour concentration; Ozone—highest fourth daily maximum 8-hour concentration; Carbon Monoxide—highest second maximum non-overlapping 8-hour concentration; Lead—maximum running 3-month average
Source: U.S. Environmental Protection Agency, Air Quality Monitoring Information, "Air Quality Statistics by City, 2021"

Maximum Air Pollutant Concentrations: Nitrogen Dioxide and Sulfur Dioxide

	Nitrogen Dioxide AM (ppb)	Nitrogen Dioxide 1-Hr (ppb)	Sulfur Dioxide AM (ppb)	Sulfur Dioxide 1-Hr (ppb)	Sulfur Dioxide 24-Hr (ppb)
MSA[1] Level	n/a	n/a	n/a	n/a	n/a
NAAQS[2]	53	100	30	75	140
Met NAAQS[2]	n/a	n/a	n/a	n/a	n/a

Note: (1) Data covers the Ann Arbor, MI Metropolitan Statistical Area; Data from exceptional events are included; (2) National Ambient Air Quality Standards; ppm = parts per million; ug/m³ = micrograms per cubic meter; n/a not available.
Concentrations: Nitrogen Dioxide AM—highest arithmetic mean concentration; Nitrogen Dioxide 1-Hr—highest 98th percentile 1-hour daily maximum concentration; Sulfur Dioxide AM—highest annual mean concentration; Sulfur Dioxide 1-Hr—highest 99th percentile 1-hour daily maximum concentration; Sulfur Dioxide 24-Hr—highest second maximum 24-hour concentration
Source: U.S. Environmental Protection Agency, Air Quality Monitoring Information, "Air Quality Statistics by City, 2021"

Cedar Rapids, Iowa

Background

Cedar Rapids, on the Cedar River that gave it its name, is the principal city in eastern Iowa, located some 100 miles northeast of Des Moines. The Cedar Rapids of today is one of the Midwest's most diversified and modern cities.

Prior to European expansion, the site was intermittently home to nomadic bands of Fox, Meskwaki, and Winnebago Indians. Its first western settler was Osgood Shephard, a hunter, trapper, and horse trader who lived in a cabin on the river at the current corner of First Avenue and First Street SE. A stainless-steel sculpture, The Tree of Five Seasons, commemorates Shephard's first settlement, and is a common point of reference for the city's citizens.

Cedar Rapids, first called Rapids City, was incorporated as a town in 1849 and as a city in 1856. By 1858 the city boasted a population of 1,400. The city itself and its immediate environs is steeped in rich ethnic traditions and a pride in the preservation of local performing and visual arts.

Cedar Rapids was the original home of the North Star Oatmeal Mill, which eventually became Quaker Oats, long a giant in the cereal industry. The Cedar Rapids-based company still operates, under one roof, the largest cereal mill in the world.

The city has extensively diversified, however, from its original agricultural focus. Many industries, both locally and internationally owned, provide stability and dynamism to the local economy, which is increasingly tied into a larger global framework. Cedar Rapids today depends on an economy strengthened by food processing, construction machinery, pharmaceuticals, financial services, and biotechnology, and is one of the largest exporters per capita in the United States, with the nearby Eastern Iowa Airport designated as a foreign trade zone. The city is also a major telecommunications hub.

Cedar Rapids is home to Coe College, founded in 1851, and Mount Mercy College, founded in 1928. The National Capital Language Resource Center (NCLRC) in Washington DC maintains 93 schools that teach Arabic, one of which is in Cedar Rapids. The town also benefits from the presence of the Cedar Rapids Museum of Art, the Cedar Rapids Symphony Orchestra, the Science Station, which boasts the first IMAX Theater in Iowa, the History Center, and the National Czech and Slovak Museum and Library. Other area attractions include Duffy's Collectible Cars, Brucemore Mansion, the Iowa Children's Museum, the Indian Creek Nature Center, and the Czech Village. Government buildings are located on Municipal Island in the main channel of the Cedar River. Within a half-hour's drive are 75 public parks and seven public golf courses.

Nearby points of historical interest include the Herbert Hoover Birthplace and Library, and the Amana Colonies, founded in the 1850s as a utopian society by members of a German religious sect. At the Amana villages, visitors can view the operations of working farms, wool mills, and bakeries. Cedar Rapids is also the home to a large number of American Muslims, and the city boasts the oldest exclusively Muslim cemetery in the United States and the historic Mother Mosque of America.

Grant Wood—the famous painter of *American Gothic* and other icons of the Great Plains—was a resident of the city and taught there for many years. The Cedar Rapids Museum houses 7,200 works of art, including the world's largest collections of works by Wood, Marvin D. Cone, and Mauricio Lasansky. The Museum also operates the Grant Wood Studio and Visitor Center.

In June 2008, the Cedar River flooded its banks, leaving 1,300 city blocks under water and causing much of the city to be evacuated. Rebuilding efforts for the hundreds of homes destroyed have been strong and a restored City Hall and Paramount Theater opened in 2012, with other facilities opening in 2013, including fire stations, the library, and the ground transportation center. In 2016, a $37 million office tower opened on the river's east bank.

In September 2016, when Hurricane Paine threatened to flood Cedar Rapids again, the residents were prepared as hundreds of thousands of volunteers, as well as over 400 National Guard troops, filled more than 250,000 sandbags that prevented major flooding of the city. In 2020 an intense derecho (windstorm) caused major damage to the city.

There are four distinct seasons in Cedar Rapids. Winters are cold and dry, with winds out of the northwest. Some summer days bring rain from the Gulf of Mexico, and hot dry air from the southwest can cause unusually high temperatures. Fall and spring are usually mild, tempered by air from the Pacific. Precipitation throughout the year is moderate.

Rankings

Business/Finance Rankings

- *Forbes* ranked the 200 most populous metro areas to determine the nation's "Best Places for Business and Careers." The Cedar Rapids metro area was ranked #154. Criteria: costs (business and living); job growth (past and projected); income growth; quality of life; educational attainment (college and high school); projected economic growth; cultural and leisure opportunities; workplace tolerance laws; net migration patterns. *Forbes, "The Best Places for Business and Careers 2019: Seattle Still On Top," October 30, 2019*

Environmental Rankings

- Cedar Rapids was highlighted as one of the top 59 cleanest metro areas for short-term particle pollution (24-hour PM 2.5) in the U.S. during 2019 through 2021. Monitors in these cities reported no days with unhealthful PM 2.5 levels. *American Lung Association, "State of the Air 2023," April 19, 2023*

Health/Fitness Rankings

- The Cedar Rapids metro area was identified as one of the worst cities for bed bugs in America by pest control company Orkin. The area ranked #31 out of 50 based on the number of bed bug treatments Orkin performed from December 2021 to November 2022. *Orkin, "The Windy City Can't Blow Bed Bugs Away: Chicago Ranks #1 For Third Consecutive Year On Orkin's Bed Bug Cities List," January 9, 2023*

Real Estate Rankings

- *WalletHub* compared the most populated U.S. cities to determine which had the best markets for real estate agents. Cedar Rapids ranked #150 where demand was high and pay was the best. Criteria: sales per agent; annual median wage for real-estate agents; monthly average starting salary for real estate agents; real estate job density and competition; unemployment rate; home turnover rate; housing-market health index; and other relevant metrics. *www.WalletHub.com, "2021 Best Places to Be a Real Estate Agent," May 12, 2021*

Safety Rankings

- The National Insurance Crime Bureau ranked 390 metro areas in the U.S. in terms of per capita rates of vehicle theft. The Cedar Rapids metro area ranked #213 (#1 = highest rate). Criteria: number of vehicle theft offenses per 100,000 inhabitants in 2021. *National Insurance Crime Bureau, "Hot Spots 2021," September 1, 2022*

Seniors/Retirement Rankings

- From its Best Cities for Successful Aging indexes, the Milken Institute generated rankings for metropolitan areas, weighing data in nine categories—health care, wellness, living arrangements, transportation and convenience, financial characteristics, education, employment, community engagement, and overall livability. The Cedar Rapids metro area was ranked #82 overall in the small metro area category. *Milken Institute, "Best Cities for Successful Aging, 2017" March 14, 2017*

Women/Minorities Rankings

- Personal finance website *WalletHub* compared more than 180 U.S. cities across two key dimensions, "Hispanic Business-Friendliness" and "Hispanic Purchasing Power," to arrive at the most favorable conditions for Hispanic entrepreneurs. Cedar Rapids was ranked #89 out of 182. Criteria includes: share of Hispanic-Owned Businesses; Hispanic entrepreneurship rate to median annual income of Hispanics; Small Business-Friendliness score; cost of living; and number of Hispanics with at least a bachelor's degree. *WalletHub.com, "2019's Best Cities for Hispanic Entrepreneurs," May 1, 2019*

Miscellaneous Rankings

- *WalletHub* compared the 150 most populated U.S. cities to determine their operating efficiency. A "Quality of Services" score was constructed for each city and then divided by the total budget per capita to reveal which were managed the best. Cedar Rapids ranked #28. Criteria: financial stability; economy; education; safety; health; infrastructure and pollution. *www.WalletHub.com, "2022's Best- & Worst-Run Cities in America," June 21, 2022*

Business Environment

DEMOGRAPHICS

Population Growth

Area	1990 Census	2000 Census	2010 Census	2020 Census	Population Growth (%) 1990-2020	Population Growth (%) 2010-2020
City	110,829	120,758	126,326	137,710	24.3	9.0
MSA[1]	210,640	237,230	257,940	276,520	31.3	7.2
U.S.	248,709,873	281,421,906	308,745,538	331,449,281	33.3	7.4

Note: (1) Figures cover the Cedar Rapids, IA Metropolitan Statistical Area
Source: U.S. Census Bureau, 1990 Census, 2000 Census, 2010 Census, 2020 Census

Race

Area	White Alone[2] (%)	Black Alone[2] (%)	Asian Alone[2] (%)	AIAN[3] Alone[2] (%)	NHOPI[4] Alone[2] (%)	Other Race Alone[2] (%)	Two or More Races (%)
City	77.8	10.4	2.7	0.3	0.4	1.7	6.8
MSA[1]	84.7	6.1	2.0	0.2	0.2	1.2	5.6
U.S.	61.6	12.4	6.0	1.1	0.2	8.4	10.2

Note: (1) Figures cover the Cedar Rapids, IA Metropolitan Statistical Area; (2) Alone is defined as not being in combination with one or more other races; (3) American Indian and Alaska Native; (4) Native Hawaiian and Other Pacific Islander
Source: U.S. Census Bureau, 2020 Census

Hispanic or Latino Origin

Area	Total (%)	Mexican (%)	Puerto Rican (%)	Cuban (%)	Other (%)
City	4.4	3.2	0.2	0.1	1.0
MSA[1]	3.2	2.4	0.1	0.0	0.7
U.S.	18.4	11.2	1.8	0.7	4.7

Note: Persons of Hispanic or Latino origin can be of any race; (1) Figures cover the Cedar Rapids, IA Metropolitan Statistical Area
Source: U.S. Census Bureau, 2017-2021 American Community Survey 5-Year Estimates

Age

Area	Under Age 5	Age 5–19	Age 20–34	Age 35–44	Age 45–54	Age 55–64	Age 65–74	Age 75–84	Age 85+	Median Age
City	6.3	19.1	22.5	13.0	11.2	12.0	8.9	4.6	2.4	36.4
MSA[1]	5.9	19.9	19.1	12.8	11.9	13.2	9.7	5.1	2.2	38.8
U.S.	5.6	19.2	20.2	12.7	12.4	13.1	10.0	4.9	1.9	38.8

Note: (1) Figures cover the Cedar Rapids, IA Metropolitan Statistical Area
Source: U.S. Census Bureau, 2020 Census

Disability by Age

Area	All Ages	Under 18 Years Old	18 to 64 Years Old	65 Years and Over
City	10.0	3.1	8.1	27.2
MSA[1]	10.3	4.1	8.1	27.2
U.S.	12.6	4.4	10.3	33.4

Note: Figures show percent of the civilian noninstitutionalized population that reported having a disability. Disability status is determined from six types of difficulty: vision, hearing, cognitive, ambulatory, self-care, and independent living. For children under 5 years old, hearing and vision difficulty are used to determine disability status. For children between the ages of 5 and 14, disability status is determined from hearing, vision, cognitive, ambulatory, and self-care difficulties. For people aged 15 years and older, they are considered to have a disability if they have difficulty with any one of the six difficulty types; Note: (1) Figures cover the Cedar Rapids, IA Metropolitan Statistical Area
Source: U.S. Census Bureau, 2017-2021 American Community Survey 5-Year Estimates

Ancestry

Area	German	Irish	English	American	Italian	Polish	French[2]	Scottish	Dutch
City	29.0	13.5	9.0	3.6	1.7	1.3	1.9	1.7	1.6
MSA[1]	32.6	14.2	9.1	4.1	1.7	1.1	2.2	1.9	2.0
U.S.	12.8	9.6	8.1	5.7	5.0	2.7	2.2	1.6	1.1

Note: Figures are the percentage of the total population reporting a particular ancestry. The nine most commonly reported ancestries in the U.S. are shown. Figures include multiple ancestries (e.g. if a person reported being Irish and Italian, they were included in both columns); (1) Figures cover the Cedar Rapids, IA Metropolitan Statistical Area; (2) Excludes Basque
Source: U.S. Census Bureau, 2017-2021 American Community Survey 5-Year Estimates

Foreign-born Population

Area	Any Foreign Country	Asia	Mexico	Europe	Caribbean	Central America[2]	South America	Africa	Canada
City	6.8	2.6	0.7	0.5	0.1	0.2	0.2	2.3	0.1
MSA[1]	4.3	1.8	0.4	0.3	0.1	0.1	0.1	1.2	0.1
U.S.	13.6	4.2	3.3	1.5	1.4	1.1	1.1	0.8	0.2

Note: (1) Figures cover the Cedar Rapids, IA Metropolitan Statistical Area; (2) Excludes Mexico.
Source: U.S. Census Bureau, 2017-2021 American Community Survey 5-Year Estimates

Household Size

Area	Persons in Household (%)							Average Household Size
	One	Two	Three	Four	Five	Six	Seven or More	
City	33.8	34.3	14.7	10.3	4.5	1.4	1.0	2.30
MSA[1]	29.5	36.7	14.2	11.9	5.1	1.6	0.9	2.40
U.S.	28.1	33.8	15.5	12.9	6.0	2.3	1.4	2.60

Note: (1) Figures cover the Cedar Rapids, IA Metropolitan Statistical Area
Source: U.S. Census Bureau, 2017-2021 American Community Survey 5-Year Estimates

Household Relationships

Area	House-holder	Opposite-sex Spouse	Same-sex Spouse	Opposite-sex Unmarried Partner	Same-sex Unmarried Partner	Child[2]	Grand-child	Other Relatives	Non-relatives
City	42.2	16.7	0.2	3.5	0.2	26.8	1.3	2.9	3.4
MSA[1]	40.9	19.3	0.1	3.0	0.1	27.9	1.2	2.3	2.5
U.S.	38.3	17.5	0.2	2.5	0.2	28.3	2.4	4.8	3.4

Note: Figures are percent of the total population; (1) Figures cover the Cedar Rapids, IA Metropolitan Statistical Area; (2) Includes biological, adopted, and stepchildren of the householder
Source: U.S. Census Bureau, 2020 Census

Gender

Area	Males	Females	Males per 100 Females
City	67,218	70,492	95.4
MSA[1]	136,845	139,675	98.0
U.S.	162,685,811	168,763,470	96.4

Note: (1) Figures cover the Cedar Rapids, IA Metropolitan Statistical Area
Source: U.S. Census Bureau, 2020 Census

Marital Status

Area	Never Married	Now Married[2]	Separated	Widowed	Divorced
City	35.5	45.7	1.0	5.6	12.2
MSA[1]	30.6	51.3	1.1	5.5	11.5
U.S.	33.8	48.0	1.8	5.6	10.8

Note: Figures are percentages and cover the population 15 years of age and older; (1) Figures cover the Cedar Rapids, IA Metropolitan Statistical Area; (2) Excludes separated
Source: U.S. Census Bureau, 2017-2021 American Community Survey 5-Year Estimates

Religious Groups by Family

Area	Catholic	Baptist	Methodist	LDS[2]	Pentecostal	Lutheran	Islam	Adventist	Other
MSA[1]	16.8	1.0	5.3	1.0	1.3	8.1	1.3	0.6	9.6
U.S.	18.7	7.3	3.0	2.0	1.8	1.7	1.3	1.3	11.6

Note: Figures are the number of adherents as a percentage of the total population and cover the eight largest religious groups in the U.S; (1) Figures cover the Cedar Rapids, IA Metropolitan Statistical Area; (2) Church of Jesus Christ of Latter-day Saints
Sources: 2020 U.S. Religion Census, Association of Statisticians of American Religious Bodies; The Association of Religion Data Archives (ARDA)

Religious Groups by Tradition

Area	Catholic	Evangelical Protestant	Mainline Protestant	Black Protestant	Islam	Judaism	Hinduism	Orthodox	Buddhism
MSA[1]	16.8	11.9	12.2	0.4	1.3	0.1	0.7	0.1	<0.1
U.S.	18.7	16.5	5.2	2.3	1.3	0.6	0.4	0.4	0.3

Note: Figures are the number of adherents as a percentage of the total population; (1) Figures cover the Cedar Rapids, IA Metropolitan Statistical Area
Sources: 2020 U.S. Religion Census, Association of Statisticians of American Religious Bodies; The Association of Religion Data Archives (ARDA)

ECONOMY

Gross Metropolitan Product

Area	2020	2021	2022	2023	Rank[2]
MSA[1]	18.5	20.7	21.9	23.3	147

*Note: Figures are in billions of dollars; (1) Figures cover the Cedar Rapids, IA Metropolitan Statistical Area;
(2) Rank is based on 2021 data and ranges from 1 to 381*
*Source: U.S. Conference of Mayors, U.S. Metro Economies: U.S. Metros Compared to Global and State
Economies, June 2022*

Economic Growth

Area	2018-20 (%)	2021 (%)	2022 (%)	2023 (%)	Rank[2]
MSA[1]	-2.3	4.9	-0.2	3.5	310
U.S.	-0.6	5.7	3.1	2.9	–

*Note: Figures are real gross metropolitan product (GMP) growth rates and represent average annual percent
change; (1) Figures cover the Cedar Rapids, IA Metropolitan Statistical Area; (2) Rank is based on 2020
2-year average annual percent change and ranges from 1 to 381*
*Source: U.S. Conference of Mayors, U.S. Metro Economies: U.S. Metros Compared to Global and State
Economies, June 2022*

Metropolitan Area Exports

Area	2016	2017	2018	2019	2020	2021	Rank[2]
MSA[1]	945.0	1,071.6	1,025.0	1,028.4	832.0	980.0	160

*Note: Figures are in millions of dollars; (1) Figures cover the Cedar Rapids, IA Metropolitan Statistical Area;
(2) Rank is based on 2021 data and ranges from 1 to 388*
*Source: U.S. Department of Commerce, International Trade Administration, Office of Trade and Economic
Analysis, Industry and Analysis, Exports by Metropolitan Area, data extracted March 16, 2023*

Building Permits

Area	Single-Family			Multi-Family			Total		
	2021	2022	Pct. Chg.	2021	2022	Pct. Chg.	2021	2022	Pct. Chg.
City	158	129	-18.4	280	225	-19.6	438	354	-19.2
MSA[1]	546	453	-17.0	352	494	40.3	898	947	5.5
U.S.	1,115,400	975,600	-12.5	621,600	689,500	10.9	1,737,000	1,665,100	-4.1

*Note: (1) Figures cover the Cedar Rapids, IA Metropolitan Statistical Area; Figures represent new,
privately-owned housing units authorized (unadjusted data); All permit data are based on estimates with
imputation*
*Source: U.S. Census Bureau, Manufacturing, Mining, and Construction Statistics, Building Permits, 2021,
2022*

Bankruptcy Filings

Area	Business Filings			Nonbusiness Filings		
	2021	2022	% Chg.	2021	2022	% Chg.
Linn County	6	10	66.7	193	166	-14.0
U.S.	14,347	13,481	-6.0	399,269	374,240	-6.3

*Note: Business filings include Chapter 7, Chapter 9, Chapter 11, Chapter 12, Chapter 13, Chapter 15, and
Section 304; Nonbusiness filings include Chapter 7, Chapter 11, and Chapter 13*
*Source: Administrative Office of the U.S. Courts, Business and Nonbusiness Bankruptcy, County Cases
Commenced by Chapter of the Bankruptcy Code, During the 12-Month Period Ending December 31, 2021 and
Business and Nonbusiness Bankruptcy, County Cases Commenced by Chapter of the Bankruptcy Code, During
the 12-Month Period Ending December 31, 2022*

Housing Vacancy Rates

Area	Gross Vacancy Rate[2] (%)			Year-Round Vacancy Rate[3] (%)			Rental Vacancy Rate[4] (%)			Homeowner Vacancy Rate[5] (%)		
	2020	2021	2022	2020	2021	2022	2020	2021	2022	2020	2021	2022
MSA[1]	n/a	n/a	n/a	n/a	n/a	n/a	n/a	n/a	n/a	n/a	n/a	n/a
U.S.	10.6	10.8	10.5	8.2	8.4	8.2	6.3	6.1	5.8	1.0	0.9	0.8

*Note: (1) Figures cover the Cedar Rapids, IA Metropolitan Statistical Area; (2) The percentage of the total
housing inventory that is vacant; (3) The percentage of the housing inventory (excluding seasonal units) that is
year-round vacant; (4) The percentage of rental inventory that is vacant for rent; (5) The percentage of
homeowner inventory that is vacant for sale; n/a not available*
Source: U.S. Census Bureau, Housing Vacancies and Homeownership Annual Statistics: 2020, 2021, 2022

INCOME

Income

Area	Per Capita ($)	Median Household ($)	Average Household ($)
City	35,566	63,170	82,815
MSA[1]	37,291	70,210	90,560
U.S.	37,638	69,021	97,196

Note: (1) Figures cover the Cedar Rapids, IA Metropolitan Statistical Area
Source: U.S. Census Bureau, 2017-2021 American Community Survey 5-Year Estimates

Household Income Distribution

Area	Percent of Households Earning							
	Under $15,000	$15,000 -$24,999	$25,000 -$34,999	$35,000 -$49,999	$50,000 -$74,999	$75,000 -$99,999	$100,000 -$149,999	$150,000 and up
City	7.1	8.5	9.5	13.6	19.9	14.8	14.9	11.7
MSA[1]	6.6	7.4	8.5	12.1	19.2	14.9	17.0	14.4
U.S.	9.4	7.8	8.2	11.4	16.8	12.8	16.3	17.3

Note: (1) Figures cover the Cedar Rapids, IA Metropolitan Statistical Area
Source: U.S. Census Bureau, 2017-2021 American Community Survey 5-Year Estimates

Poverty Rate

Area	All Ages	Under 18 Years Old	18 to 64 Years Old	65 Years and Over
City	11.2	15.5	10.9	6.4
MSA[1]	9.5	12.0	9.4	6.5
U.S.	12.6	17.0	11.8	9.6

Note: Figures are percentage of people whose income during the past 12 months was below the poverty level;
(1) Figures cover the Cedar Rapids, IA Metropolitan Statistical Area
Source: U.S. Census Bureau, 2017-2021 American Community Survey 5-Year Estimates

EMPLOYMENT

Labor Force and Employment

Area	Civilian Labor Force			Workers Employed		
	Dec. 2021	Dec. 2022	% Chg.	Dec. 2021	Dec. 2022	% Chg.
City	69,935	70,822	1.3	66,849	68,200	2.0
MSA[1]	140,768	142,727	1.4	135,170	137,743	1.9
U.S.	161,696,000	164,224,000	1.6	155,732,000	158,872,000	2.0

Note: Data is not seasonally adjusted and covers workers 16 years of age and older; (1) Figures cover the
Cedar Rapids, IA Metropolitan Statistical Area
Source: Bureau of Labor Statistics, Local Area Unemployment Statistics

Unemployment Rate

Area	2022											
	Jan.	Feb.	Mar.	Apr.	May	Jun.	Jul.	Aug.	Sep.	Oct.	Nov.	Dec.
City	4.9	3.9	3.6	2.7	2.9	3.4	3.7	3.8	3.3	3.4	3.7	3.7
MSA[1]	4.9	4.0	3.7	2.6	2.6	3.0	3.2	3.4	2.9	3.0	3.3	3.5
U.S.	4.4	4.1	3.8	3.3	3.4	3.8	3.8	3.8	3.3	3.4	3.4	3.3

Note: Data is not seasonally adjusted and covers workers 16 years of age and older; (1) Figures cover the
Cedar Rapids, IA Metropolitan Statistical Area
Source: Bureau of Labor Statistics, Local Area Unemployment Statistics

Average Wages

Occupation	$/Hr.	Occupation	$/Hr.
Accountants and Auditors	36.04	Maintenance and Repair Workers	22.16
Automotive Mechanics	23.48	Marketing Managers	61.42
Bookkeepers	22.67	Network and Computer Systems Admin.	41.95
Carpenters	24.39	Nurses, Licensed Practical	25.54
Cashiers	13.19	Nurses, Registered	33.68
Computer Programmers	42.82	Nursing Assistants	17.02
Computer Systems Analysts	43.29	Office Clerks, General	19.34
Computer User Support Specialists	27.05	Physical Therapists	40.86
Construction Laborers	22.70	Physicians	125.70
Cooks, Restaurant	14.19	Plumbers, Pipefitters and Steamfitters	32.41
Customer Service Representatives	20.25	Police and Sheriff's Patrol Officers	31.90
Dentists	95.40	Postal Service Mail Carriers	27.18
Electricians	28.53	Real Estate Sales Agents	30.06
Engineers, Electrical	47.69	Retail Salespersons	15.63
Fast Food and Counter Workers	12.59	Sales Representatives, Technical/Scientific	51.91
Financial Managers	60.69	Secretaries, Exc. Legal/Medical/Executive	20.40
First-Line Supervisors of Office Workers	29.72	Security Guards	17.15
General and Operations Managers	45.54	Surgeons	n/a
Hairdressers/Cosmetologists	15.24	Teacher Assistants, Exc. Postsecondary*	14.26
Home Health and Personal Care Aides	16.20	Teachers, Secondary School, Exc. Sp. Ed.*	28.59
Janitors and Cleaners	15.98	Telemarketers	n/a
Landscaping/Groundskeeping Workers	16.78	Truck Drivers, Heavy/Tractor-Trailer	25.17
Lawyers	57.59	Truck Drivers, Light/Delivery Services	19.97
Maids and Housekeeping Cleaners	13.71	Waiters and Waitresses	13.27

Note: Wage data covers the Cedar Rapids, IA Metropolitan Statistical Area; (*) Hourly wages were calculated
from annual wage data based on a 40 hour work week; n/a not available.
Source: Bureau of Labor Statistics, Metro Area Occupational Employment & Wage Estimates, May 2022

Employment by Industry

Sector	MSA[1]		U.S.
	Number of Employees	Percent of Total	Percent of Total
Construction, Mining, and Logging	8,700	6.0	5.4
Private Education and Health Services	22,000	15.3	16.1
Financial Activities	10,600	7.4	5.9
Government	16,600	11.5	14.5
Information	3,000	2.1	2.0
Leisure and Hospitality	11,800	8.2	10.3
Manufacturing	20,000	13.9	8.4
Other Services	5,000	3.5	3.7
Professional and Business Services	15,600	10.8	14.7
Retail Trade	14,800	10.3	10.2
Transportation, Warehousing, and Utilities	10,000	6.9	4.9
Wholesale Trade	5,900	4.1	3.9

Note: Figures are non-farm employment as of December 2022. Figures are not seasonally adjusted and include workers 16 years of age and older; (1) Figures cover the Cedar Rapids, IA Metropolitan Statistical Area
Source: Bureau of Labor Statistics, Current Employment Statistics, Employment, Hours, and Earnings

Employment by Occupation

Occupation Classification	City (%)	MSA[1] (%)	U.S. (%)
Management, Business, Science, and Arts	38.5	39.0	40.3
Natural Resources, Construction, and Maintenance	8.0	8.7	8.7
Production, Transportation, and Material Moving	16.7	15.9	13.1
Sales and Office	21.8	22.2	20.9
Service	15.0	14.2	17.0

Note: Figures cover employed civilians 16 years of age and older; (1) Figures cover the Cedar Rapids, IA Metropolitan Statistical Area
Source: U.S. Census Bureau, 2017-2021 American Community Survey 5-Year Estimates

Occupations with Greatest Projected Employment Growth: 2022 – 2024

Occupation[1]	2022 Employment	2024 Projected Employment	Numeric Employment Change	Percent Employment Change
Fast Food and Counter Workers	39,300	41,100	1,800	4.6
Cooks, Restaurant	12,190	13,530	1,340	11.0
Waiters and Waitresses	19,970	21,220	1,250	6.3
Farmers, Ranchers, and Other Agricultural Managers	85,770	86,980	1,210	1.4
Home Health and Personal Care Aides	24,530	25,690	1,160	4.7
Maids and Housekeeping Cleaners	11,530	12,500	970	8.4
Registered Nurses	34,440	35,270	830	2.4
Bartenders	8,970	9,770	800	8.9
Laborers and Freight, Stock, and Material Movers, Hand	31,300	32,000	700	2.2
Heavy and Tractor-Trailer Truck Drivers	46,230	46,880	650	1.4

Note: Projections cover Iowa; (1) Sorted by numeric employment change
Source: www.projectionscentral.com, State Occupational Projections, 2022–2024 Short-Term Projections

Fastest-Growing Occupations: 2022 – 2024

Occupation[1]	2022 Employment	2024 Projected Employment	Numeric Employment Change	Percent Employment Change
Entertainers and Performers, Sports and Related Workers, All Other	210	260	50	23.8
Hotel, Motel, and Resort Desk Clerks	3,170	3,780	610	19.2
Ushers, Lobby Attendants, and Ticket Takers	800	950	150	18.8
Audio and Video Equipment Technicians	340	400	60	17.6
Gaming Change Persons and Booth Cashiers	340	400	60	17.6
Wind Turbine Service Technicians	460	540	80	17.4
Gaming Dealers	1,180	1,370	190	16.1
Musicians and Singers	420	480	60	14.3
Gaming Service Workers, All Other	370	420	50	13.5
Passenger Vehicle Drivers, Except Bus Drivers, Transit and Intercity	1,950	2,200	250	12.8

Note: Projections cover Iowa; (1) Sorted by percent employment change and excludes occupations with numeric employment change less than 50
Source: www.projectionscentral.com, State Occupational Projections, 2022–2024 Short-Term Projections

CITY FINANCES

City Government Finances

Component	2020 ($000)	2020 ($ per capita)
Total Revenues	438,575	3,284
Total Expenditures	420,770	3,150
Debt Outstanding	507,596	3,800
Cash and Securities[1]	552,415	4,136

Note: (1) Cash and security holdings of a government at the close of its fiscal year, including those of its dependent agencies, utilities, and liquor stores.
Source: U.S. Census Bureau, State & Local Government Finances 2020

City Government Revenue by Source

Source	2020 ($000)	2020 ($ per capita)	2020 (%)
General Revenue			
From Federal Government	32,667	245	7.4
From State Government	40,369	302	9.2
From Local Governments	616	5	0.1
Taxes			
Property	112,326	841	25.6
Sales and Gross Receipts	40,632	304	9.3
Personal Income	0	0	0.0
Corporate Income	0	0	0.0
Motor Vehicle License	0	0	0.0
Other Taxes	3,367	25	0.8
Current Charges	136,512	1,022	31.1
Liquor Store	0	0	0.0
Utility	37,564	281	8.6

Source: U.S. Census Bureau, State & Local Government Finances 2020

City Government Expenditures by Function

Function	2020 ($000)	2020 ($ per capita)	2020 (%)
General Direct Expenditures			
Air Transportation	32,282	241	7.7
Corrections	0	0	0.0
Education	0	0	0.0
Employment Security Administration	0	0	0.0
Financial Administration	6,026	45	1.4
Fire Protection	21,446	160	5.1
General Public Buildings	1,009	7	0.2
Governmental Administration, Other	3,463	25	0.8
Health	1,367	10	0.3
Highways	23,585	176	5.6
Hospitals	0	0	0.0
Housing and Community Development	6,824	51	1.6
Interest on General Debt	14,202	106	3.4
Judicial and Legal	943	7	0.2
Libraries	6,680	50	1.6
Parking	646	4	0.2
Parks and Recreation	10,924	81	2.6
Police Protection	46,957	351	11.2
Public Welfare	0	0	0.0
Sewerage	49,338	369	11.7
Solid Waste Management	10,847	81	2.6
Veterans' Services	0	0	0.0
Liquor Store	0	0	0.0
Utility	48,393	362	11.5

Source: U.S. Census Bureau, State & Local Government Finances 2020

TAXES

State Corporate Income Tax Rates

State	Tax Rate (%)	Income Brackets ($)	Num. of Brackets	Financial Institution Tax Rate (%)[a]	Federal Income Tax Ded.
Iowa	5.5 - 8.4	100,000 - 250,001	3	4.7	Yes (h)

Note: Tax rates as of January 1, 2023; (a) Rates listed are the corporate income tax rate applied to financial institutions or excise taxes based on income. Some states have other taxes based upon the value of deposits or shares; (h) 50% of the federal income tax is deductible.
Source: Federation of Tax Administrators, State Corporate Income Tax Rates, January 1, 2023

State Individual Income Tax Rates

State	Tax Rate (%)	Income Brackets ($)	Personal Exemptions ($) Single	Married	Depend.	Standard Ded. ($) Single	Married
Iowa (a)	4.4 - 6.0 (bb)	6,000 - 75,000	40	80	40 (c)	–	–

Note: Tax rates as of January 1, 2023; Local- and county-level taxes are not included; Federal income tax is deductible on state income tax returns; (a) 16 states have statutory provision for automatically adjusting to the rate of inflation the dollar values of the income tax brackets, standard deductions, and/or personal exemptions. Oregon does not index the income brackets for $125,000 and over; (c) The personal exemption takes the form of a tax credit instead of a deduction; (bb) Louisiana tax rates may be adjusted down if revenue trigger is met on April 1st. Iowa is phasing-in a flat rate by 2027, while Nebraska and South Carolina is phasing-in a reduced top rate by 2027.
Source: Federation of Tax Administrators, State Individual Income Tax Rates, January 1, 2023

Various State Sales and Excise Tax Rates

State	State Sales Tax (%)	Gasoline[1] ($/gal.)	Cigarette[2] ($/pack)	Spirits[3] ($/gal.)	Wine[4] ($/gal.)	Beer[5] ($/gal.)	Recreational Marijuana (%)
Iowa	6	0.30	1.36	14.10	1.75	0.19	Not legal

Note: All tax rates as of January 1, 2023; (1) The American Petroleum Institute has developed a methodology for determining the average tax rate on a gallon of fuel. Rates may include any of the following: excise taxes, environmental fees, storage tank fees, other fees or taxes, general sales tax, and local taxes; (2) The federal excise tax of $1.0066 per pack and local taxes are not included; (3) Rates are those applicable to off-premise sales of 40% alcohol by volume (a.b.v.) distilled spirits in 750ml containers. Local excise taxes are excluded; (4) Rates are those applicable to off-premise sales of 11% a.b.v. non-carbonated wine in 750ml containers; (5) Rates are those applicable to off-premise sales of 4.7% a.b.v. beer in 12 ounce containers.
Source: Tax Foundation, 2023 Facts & Figures: How Does Your State Compare?

State Business Tax Climate Index Rankings

State	Overall Rank	Corporate Tax Rank	Individual Income Tax Rank	Sales Tax Rank	Property Tax Rank	Unemployment Insurance Tax Rank
Iowa	38	34	40	15	40	33

Note: The index is a measure of how each state's tax laws affect economic performance. The lower the rank, the more favorable a state's tax system is for business. States without a given tax are given a ranking of 1. The scores/rankings for the District of Columbia do not affect other states. The 2023 index represents the tax climate as of July 1, 2022.
Source: Tax Foundation, State Business Tax Climate Index 2023

TRANSPORTATION

Means of Transportation to Work

Area	Car/Truck/Van Drove Alone	Car-pooled	Public Transportation Bus	Subway	Railroad	Bicycle	Walked	Other Means	Worked at Home
City	80.2	7.6	0.4	0.0	0.0	0.5	2.0	1.0	8.5
MSA[1]	80.3	7.0	0.3	0.0	0.0	0.3	1.8	0.8	9.4
U.S.	73.2	8.6	2.0	1.6	0.5	0.5	2.5	1.5	9.7

Note: Figures are percentages and cover workers 16 years of age and older; (1) Figures cover the Cedar Rapids, IA Metropolitan Statistical Area
Source: U.S. Census Bureau, 2017-2021 American Community Survey 5-Year Estimates

Travel Time to Work

Area	Less Than 10 Minutes	10 to 19 Minutes	20 to 29 Minutes	30 to 44 Minutes	45 to 59 Minutes	60 to 89 Minutes	90 Minutes or More
City	20.0	48.9	17.0	9.2	1.9	1.5	1.5
MSA[1]	18.8	40.1	20.6	12.8	4.3	2.0	1.5
U.S.	12.4	28.5	21.0	20.9	8.2	6.2	2.9

Note: Note: Figures are percentages and include workers 16 years old and over; (1) Figures cover the Cedar Rapids, IA Metropolitan Statistical Area
Source: U.S. Census Bureau, 2017-2021 American Community Survey 5-Year Estimates

Key Congestion Measures

Measure	1990	2000	2010	2015	2020
Annual Hours of Delay, Total (000)	n/a	n/a	n/a	2,974	2,287
Annual Hours of Delay, Per Auto Commuter	n/a	n/a	n/a	15	11
Annual Congestion Cost, Per Auto Commuter ($)	n/a	n/a	n/a	307	259

Note: n/a not available
Source: Texas A&M Transportation Institute, 2021 Urban Mobility Report

Freeway Travel Time Index

Measure	1985	1990	1995	2000	2005	2010	2015	2020
Urban Area Index[1]	n/a	n/a	n/a	n/a	n/a	n/a	1.07	1.07
Urban Area Rank[1,2]	n/a	n/a	n/a	n/a	n/a	n/a	n/a	n/a

Note: Freeway Travel Time Index—the ratio of travel time in the peak period to the travel time at free-flow conditions. For example, a value of 1.30 indicates a 20-minute free-flow trip takes 26 minutes in the peak (20 minutes x 1.30 = 26 minutes); (1) Covers the Cedar Rapids IA urban area; (2) Rank is based on 101 larger urban areas (#1 = highest travel time index); n/a not available
Source: Texas A&M Transportation Institute, 2021 Urban Mobility Report

Public Transportation

Agency Name / Mode of Transportation	Vehicles Operated in Maximum Service[1]	Annual Unlinked Passenger Trips[2] (in thous.)	Annual Passenger Miles[3] (in thous.)
Five Seasons Transportation and Parking (FSTP)			
Bus (directly operated)	22	556.7	2,671.9
Demand Response (purchased transportation)	5	14.1	107.2

Note: (1) Number of revenue vehicles operated by the given mode and type of service to meet the annual maximum service requirement. This is the revenue vehicle count during the peak season of the year; on the week and day that maximum service is provided. Vehicles operated in maximum service (VOMS) exclude atypical days and one-time special events; (2) Number of passengers who boarded public transportation vehicles. Passengers are counted each time they board a vehicle no matter how many vehicles they use to travel from their origin to their destination. (3) Sum of the distances ridden by all passengers during the entire fiscal year.
Source: Federal Transit Administration, National Transit Database, 2021

Air Transportation

Airport Name and Code / Type of Service	Passenger Airlines[1]	Passenger Enplanements	Freight Carriers[2]	Freight (lbs)
The Eastern Iowa (CID)				
Domestic service (U.S. carriers - 2022)	22	610,543	9	42,933,213
International service (U.S. carriers - 2021)	0	0	0	0

Note: (1) Includes all U.S.-based major, minor and commuter airlines that carried at least one passenger during the year; (2) Includes all U.S.-based airlines and freight carriers that transported at least one pound of freight during the year.
Source: Bureau of Transportation Statistics, The Intermodal Transportation Database, Air Carriers: T-100 Domestic Market (U.S. Carriers), 2022; Bureau of Transportation Statistics, The Intermodal Transportation Database, Air Carriers: T-100 International Market (U.S. Carriers), 2021

BUSINESSES

Major Business Headquarters

Company Name	Industry	Rankings	
		Fortune[1]	Forbes[2]
No companies listed	-	-	-

Note: (1) Companies that produce a 10-K are ranked 1 to 500 based on 2021 revenue; (2) All private companies with at least $2 billion in annual revenue through the end of their most current fiscal year are ranked 1 to 246; companies listed are headquartered in the city; dashes indicate no ranking
Source: Fortune, "Fortune 500," 2022; Forbes, "America's Largest Private Companies," 2022

Fastest-Growing Businesses

According to *Inc.*, Cedar Rapids is home to one of America's 500 fastest-growing private companies: **Ready IoT/Ready Wireless** (#282). Criteria: must be an independent, privately-held, for-profit, U.S. corporation, proprietorship or partnership as of December 31, 2021; revenues must be at least $100,000 in 2018 and $2 million in 2021; must have four-year operating/sales history. *Inc., "America's 500 Fastest-Growing Private Companies," 2022*

Living Environment

COST OF LIVING

Cost of Living Index

Composite Index	Groceries	Housing	Utilities	Trans-portation	Health Care	Misc. Goods/ Services
89.0	96.8	71.2	91.7	100.2	101.6	94.9

Note: The Cost of Living Index measures regional differences in the cost of consumer goods and services, excluding taxes and non-consumer expenditures, for professional and managerial households in the top income quintile. It is based on more than 50,000 prices covering almost 60 different items for which prices are collected three times a year by chambers of commerce, economic development organizations or university applied economic centers in each participating urban area. The numbers shown should be read as a percentage above or below the national average of 100. For example, a value of 115.4 in the groceries column indicates that grocery prices are 15.4% higher than the national average. Small differences in the index numbers should not be interpreted as significant; Figures cover the Cedar Rapids IA urban area.
Source: The Council for Community and Economic Research, Cost of Living Index, 2022

Grocery Prices

Area[1]	T-Bone Steak ($/pound)	Frying Chicken ($/pound)	Whole Milk ($/half gal.)	Eggs ($/dozen)	Orange Juice ($/64 oz.)	Coffee ($/11.5 oz.)
City[2]	14.03	1.66	2.19	2.32	3.68	5.08
Avg.	13.81	1.59	2.43	2.25	3.85	4.95
Min.	10.17	0.90	1.51	1.30	2.90	3.46
Max.	19.35	3.30	4.32	4.32	5.31	8.59

*Note: (1) Values for the local area are compared with the average, minimum and maximum values for all 286 areas in the Cost of Living Index; (2) Figures cover the Cedar Rapids IA urban area; **T-Bone Steak** (price per pound); **Frying Chicken** (price per pound, whole fryer); **Whole Milk** (half gallon carton); **Eggs** (price per dozen, Grade A, large); **Orange Juice** (64 oz. Tropicana or Florida Natural); **Coffee** (11.5 oz. can, vacuum-packed, Maxwell House, Hills Bros, or Folgers).*
Source: The Council for Community and Economic Research, Cost of Living Index, 2022

Housing and Utility Costs

Area[1]	New Home Price ($)	Apartment Rent ($/month)	All Electric ($/month)	Part Electric ($/month)	Other Energy ($/month)	Telephone ($/month)
City[2]	339,825	846	-	106.96	45.22	189.46
Avg.	450,913	1,371	176.41	99.93	76.96	190.22
Min.	229,283	546	100.84	31.56	27.15	174.27
Max.	2,434,977	4,569	356.86	249.59	272.24	208.31

*Note: (1) Values for the local area are compared with the average, minimum and maximum values for all 286 areas in the Cost of Living Index; (2) Figures cover the Cedar Rapids IA urban area; **New Home Price** (2,400 sf living area, 8,000 sf lot, in urban area with full utilities); **Apartment Rent** (950 sf 2 bedroom/1.5 or 2 bath, unfurnished, excluding all utilities except water); **All Electric** (average monthly cost for an all-electric home); **Part Electric** (average monthly cost for a part-electric home); **Other Energy** (average monthly cost for natural gas, fuel oil, coal, wood, and any other forms of energy except electricity); **Telephone** (price includes the base monthly rate plus taxes and fees for three lines of mobile phone service).*
Source: The Council for Community and Economic Research, Cost of Living Index, 2022

Health Care, Transportation, and Other Costs

Area[1]	Doctor ($/visit)	Dentist ($/visit)	Optometrist ($/visit)	Gasoline ($/gallon)	Beauty Salon ($/visit)	Men's Shirt ($)
City[2]	139.68	101.88	94.68	3.84	34.39	26.11
Avg.	124.91	107.77	117.66	3.86	43.31	34.21
Min.	36.61	58.25	51.79	2.90	22.18	13.05
Max.	250.21	162.58	371.96	5.54	85.61	63.54

*Note: (1) Values for the local area are compared with the average, minimum and maximum values for all 286 areas in the Cost of Living Index; (2) Figures cover the Cedar Rapids IA urban area; **Doctor** (general practitioners routine exam of an established patient); **Dentist** (adult teeth cleaning and periodic oral examination); **Optometrist** (full vision eye exam for established adult patient); **Gasoline** (one gallon regular unleaded, national brand, including all taxes, cash price at self-service pump if available); **Beauty Salon** (woman's shampoo, trim, and blow-dry); **Men's Shirt** (cotton/polyester dress shirt, pinpoint weave, long sleeves).*
Source: The Council for Community and Economic Research, Cost of Living Index, 2022

HOUSING

Homeownership Rate

Area	2015 (%)	2016 (%)	2017 (%)	2018 (%)	2019 (%)	2020 (%)	2021 (%)	2022 (%)
MSA[1]	n/a	n/a	n/a	n/a	n/a	n/a	n/a	n/a
U.S.	63.7	63.4	63.9	64.4	64.6	66.6	65.5	65.8

Note: (1) Figures cover the Cedar Rapids, IA Metropolitan Statistical Area; n/a not available
Source: U.S. Census Bureau, Housing Vacancies and Homeownership Annual Statistics: 2015-2022

House Price Index (HPI)

Area	National Ranking[2]	Quarterly Change (%)	One-Year Change (%)	Five-Year Change (%)	Since 1991Q1 (%)
MSA[1]	243	-4.60	5.29	30.92	170.24
U.S.[3]	–	0.34	8.41	58.44	289.08

Note: The HPI is a weighted repeat sales index. It measures average price changes in repeat sales or refinancings on the same properties. This information is obtained by reviewing repeat mortgage transactions on single-family properties whose mortgages have been purchased or securitized by Fannie Mae or Freddie Mac since January 1975; (1) Figures cover the Cedar Rapids, IA Metropolitan Statistical Area; (2) Rankings are based on annual percentage change for all metro areas containing at least 15,000 transactions over the last 10 years and ranges from 1 to 257; (3) figures based on a weighted average of Census Division estimates using a seasonally adjusted, purchase-only index; all figures are for the period ending December 31, 2022
Source: Federal Housing Finance Agency, Change in FHFA Metropolitan Area House Price Indexes, 2022Q4

Median Single-Family Home Prices

Area	2020	2021	2022[p]	Percent Change 2021 to 2022
MSA[1]	173.1	182.8	196.4	7.4
U.S. Average	300.2	357.1	392.6	9.9

Note: Figures are median sales prices of existing single-family homes in thousands of dollars; (p) preliminary; (1) Figures cover the Cedar Rapids, IA Metropolitan Statistical Area
Source: National Association of Realtors, Median Sales Price of Existing Single-Family Homes for Metropolitan Areas, 4th Quarter 2022

Qualifying Income Based on Median Sales Price of Existing Single-Family Homes

Area	With 5% Down ($)	With 10% Down ($)	With 20% Down ($)
MSA[1]	58,131	55,072	48,953
U.S. Average	112,234	106,237	94,513

Note: Figures are preliminary; Qualifying income is based on a mortgage rate of 6.77%. Monthly principal and interest payment is limited to 25% of income; (1) Figures cover the Cedar Rapids, IA Metropolitan Statistical Area
Source: National Association of Realtors, Qualifying Income Based on Median Sales Price of Existing Single-Family Homes for Metropolitan Areas, 4th Quarter 2022

Home Value

Area	Under $100,000	$100,000 -$199,999	$200,000 -$299,999	$300,000 -$399,999	$400,000 -$499,999	$500,000 -$999,999	$1,000,000 or more	Median ($)
City	18.6	53.5	19.0	5.4	1.7	1.5	0.3	149,000
MSA[1]	17.2	44.7	22.6	8.4	3.7	3.0	0.5	165,500
U.S.	16.2	24.2	20.1	13.6	8.3	13.6	4.1	244,900

Note: Figures are percentages except for median and cover owner-occupied housing units; (1) Figures cover the Cedar Rapids, IA Metropolitan Statistical Area
Source: U.S. Census Bureau, 2017-2021 American Community Survey 5-Year Estimates

Year Housing Structure Built

Area	2020 or Later	2010 -2019	2000 -2009	1990 -1999	1980 -1989	1970 -1979	1960 -1969	1950 -1959	1940 -1949	Before 1940	Median Year
City	0.1	7.7	11.5	10.5	7.1	14.6	14.8	12.8	4.1	16.8	1971
MSA[1]	0.1	8.3	13.7	12.7	7.2	13.8	12.3	10.4	3.5	18.0	1974
U.S.	0.2	7.3	13.6	13.6	13.2	14.8	10.3	10.0	4.7	12.2	1979

Note: Figures are percentages except for Median Year; Note: (1) Figures cover the Cedar Rapids, IA Metropolitan Statistical Area
Source: U.S. Census Bureau, 2017-2021 American Community Survey 5-Year Estimates

Gross Monthly Rent

Area	Under $500	$500 -$999	$1,000 -$1,499	$1,500 -$1,999	$2,000 -$2,499	$2,500 -$2,999	$3,000 and up	Median ($)
City	12.8	56.9	24.8	3.1	0.6	0.2	1.7	836
MSA[1]	13.4	57.1	23.0	4.2	0.8	0.1	1.4	806
U.S.	8.1	30.5	30.8	16.8	7.3	3.1	3.5	1,163

Note: Figures are percentages except for median; Gross rent is the contract rent plus the estimated average monthly cost of utilities (electricity, gas, and water and sewer) and fuels (oil, coal, kerosene, wood, etc.) if these are paid by the renter (or paid for the renter by someone else); (1) Figures cover the Cedar Rapids, IA Metropolitan Statistical Area
Source: U.S. Census Bureau, 2017-2021 American Community Survey 5-Year Estimates

HEALTH

Health Risk Factors

Category	MSA[1] (%)	U.S. (%)
Adults aged 18–64 who have any kind of health care coverage	95.0	90.9
Adults who reported being in good or better health	86.5	85.2
Adults who have been told they have high blood cholesterol	35.8	35.7
Adults who have been told they have high blood pressure	36.5	32.4
Adults who are current smokers	14.2	14.4
Adults who currently use e-cigarettes	6.4	6.7
Adults who currently use chewing tobacco, snuff, or snus	3.9	3.5
Adults who are heavy drinkers[2]	6.7	6.3
Adults who are binge drinkers[3]	22.8	15.4
Adults who are overweight (BMI 25.0 - 29.9)	33.5	34.4
Adults who are obese (BMI 30.0 - 99.8)	40.2	33.9
Adults who participated in any physical activities in the past month	76.7	76.3

Note: (1) Figures cover the Cedar Rapids, IA Metropolitan Statistical Area; (2) Heavy drinkers are classified as adult men having more than 14 drinks per week and adult women having more than 7 drinks per week; (3) Binge drinkers are classified as males having five or more drinks on one occasion or females having four or more drinks on one occasion
Source: Centers for Disease Control and Prevention, Behaviorial Risk Factor Surveillance System, SMART: Selected Metropolitan Area Risk Trends, 2021

Acute and Chronic Health Conditions

Category	MSA[1] (%)	U.S. (%)
Adults who have ever been told they had a heart attack	4.0	4.0
Adults who have ever been told they have angina or coronary heart disease	3.4	3.8
Adults who have ever been told they had a stroke	3.0	3.0
Adults who have ever been told they have asthma	13.5	14.9
Adults who have ever been told they have arthritis	24.3	25.8
Adults who have ever been told they have diabetes[2]	9.8	10.9
Adults who have ever been told they had skin cancer	5.0	6.6
Adults who have ever been told they had any other types of cancer	7.9	7.5
Adults who have ever been told they have COPD	7.1	6.1
Adults who have ever been told they have kidney disease	3.2	3.0
Adults who have ever been told they have a form of depression	21.1	20.5

Note: (1) Figures cover the Cedar Rapids, IA Metropolitan Statistical Area; (2) Figures do not include pregnancy-related, borderline, or pre-diabetes
Source: Centers for Disease Control and Prevention, Behaviorial Risk Factor Surveillance System, SMART: Selected Metropolitan Area Risk Trends, 2021

Health Screening and Vaccination Rates

Category	MSA[1] (%)	U.S. (%)
Adults who have ever been tested for HIV	27.1	34.9
Adults who have had their blood cholesterol checked within the last five years	84.7	85.2
Adults aged 65+ who have had flu shot within the past year	77.7	68.6
Adults aged 65+ who have ever had a pneumonia vaccination	84.8	71.0

Note: (1) Figures cover the Cedar Rapids, IA Metropolitan Statistical Area.
Source: Centers for Disease Control and Prevention, Behaviorial Risk Factor Surveillance System, SMART: Selected Metropolitan Area Risk Trends, 2021

Disability Status

Category	MSA[1] (%)	U.S. (%)
Adults who reported being deaf	6.2	7.2
Are you blind or have serious difficulty seeing, even when wearing glasses?	n/a	4.8
Are you limited in any way in any of your usual activities due to arthritis?	9.6	11.1
Do you have difficulty doing errands alone?	4.5	7.0
Do you have difficulty dressing or bathing?	n/a	3.6
Do you have serious difficulty concentrating/remembering/making decisions?	9.9	12.1
Do you have serious difficulty walking or climbing stairs?	9.4	12.8

Note: (1) Figures cover the Cedar Rapids, IA Metropolitan Statistical Area.
Source: Centers for Disease Control and Prevention, Behaviorial Risk Factor Surveillance System, SMART: Selected Metropolitan Area Risk Trends, 2021

Mortality Rates for the Top 10 Causes of Death in the U.S.

ICD-10[a] Sub-Chapter	ICD-10[a] Code	Crude Mortality Rate[1] per 100,000 population	
		County[2]	U.S.
Malignant neoplasms	C00-C97	176.9	182.6
Ischaemic heart diseases	I20-I25	120.6	113.1
Other forms of heart disease	I30-I51	53.0	64.4
Other degenerative diseases of the nervous system	G30-G31	59.5	51.0
Cerebrovascular diseases	I60-I69	35.4	47.8
Other external causes of accidental injury	W00-X59	46.5	46.4
Chronic lower respiratory diseases	J40-J47	46.2	45.7
Organic, including symptomatic, mental disorders	F01-F09	35.6	35.9
Hypertensive diseases	I10-I15	21.9	35.0
Diabetes mellitus	E10-E14	14.5	29.6

Note: (a) ICD-10 = International Classification of Diseases 10th Revision; (1) Crude mortality rates are a three-year average covering 2019-2021; (2) Figures cover Linn County.
Source: Centers for Disease Control and Prevention, National Center for Health Statistics. National Vital Statistics System, Mortality 2018-2021 on CDC WONDER Online Database

Mortality Rates for Selected Causes of Death

ICD-10[a] Sub-Chapter	ICD-10[a] Code	Crude Mortality Rate[1] per 100,000 population	
		County[2]	U.S.
Assault	X85-Y09	5.6	7.0
Diseases of the liver	K70-K76	20.2	19.8
Human immunodeficiency virus (HIV) disease	B20-B24	Suppressed	1.5
Influenza and pneumonia	J09-J18	11.1	14.7
Intentional self-harm	X60-X84	19.3	14.3
Malnutrition	E40-E46	8.5	4.3
Obesity and other hyperalimentation	E65-E68	Suppressed	3.0
Renal failure	N17-N19	13.5	15.7
Transport accidents	V01-V99	8.2	13.6
Viral hepatitis	B15-B19	Suppressed	1.2

Note: (a) ICD-10 = International Classification of Diseases 10th Revision; (1) Crude mortality rates are a three-year average covering 2019-2021; (2) Figures cover Linn County; Data are suppressed when the data meet the criteria for confidentiality constraints; Crude mortality rates are flagged as unreliable when the rate would be calculated with a numerator of 20 or less.
Source: Centers for Disease Control and Prevention, National Center for Health Statistics. National Vital Statistics System, Mortality 2018-2021 on CDC WONDER Online Database

Health Insurance Coverage

Area	With Health Insurance	With Private Health Insurance	With Public Health Insurance	Without Health Insurance	Population Under Age 19 Without Health Insurance
City	95.2	73.2	34.4	4.8	2.2
MSA[1]	96.2	75.9	33.5	3.8	1.8
U.S.	91.2	67.8	35.4	8.8	5.3

Note: Figures are percentages that cover the civilian noninstitutionalized population; (1) Figures cover the Cedar Rapids, IA Metropolitan Statistical Area
Source: U.S. Census Bureau, 2017-2021 American Community Survey 5-Year Estimates

Number of Medical Professionals

Area	MDs[3]	DOs[3,4]	Dentists	Podiatrists	Chiropractors	Optometrists
County[1] (number)	419	54	170	18	134	40
County[1] (rate[2])	182.0	23.5	74.3	7.9	58.5	17.5
U.S. (rate[2])	289.3	23.5	72.5	6.2	28.7	17.4

Note: Data as of 2021 unless noted; (1) Data covers Linn County; (2) Rate per 100,000 population; (3) Data as of 2020 and includes all active, non-federal physicians; (4) Doctor of Osteopathic Medicine
Source: U.S. Department of Health and Human Services, Health Resources and Services Administration, Bureau of Health Professions, Area Resource File (ARF) 2021-2022

EDUCATION

Public School District Statistics

District Name	Schls	Pupils	Pupil/ Teacher Ratio	Minority Pupils[1] (%)	LEP/ELL[2] (%)	IEP[3] (%)
Cedar Rapids CSD	33	15,728	14.8	41.2	6.4	16.0
College Comm School District	10	5,719	15.5	26.3	2.9	11.0

Note: Table includes school districts with 2,000 or more students; (1) Percentage of students that are not non-Hispanic white; (2) Percentage of students that are Limited English Proficient or English Language Learners (2018-19); (3) Percentage of students that have an Individualized Education Program (2019-20).
Source: U.S. Department of Education, National Center for Education Statistics, Common Core of Data, Local Education Agency (School District) Universe Survey: School Year 2021-2022

Highest Level of Education

Area	Less than H.S.	H.S. Diploma	Some College, No Deg.	Associate Degree	Bachelor's Degree	Master's Degree	Prof. School Degree	Doctorate Degree
City	6.2	25.7	22.8	12.5	22.7	7.2	2.0	0.8
MSA[1]	5.2	28.0	21.3	13.4	22.1	7.4	1.7	0.9
U.S.	11.1	26.5	20.0	8.7	20.6	9.3	2.2	1.5

Note: Figures cover persons age 25 and over; (1) Figures cover the Cedar Rapids, IA Metropolitan Statistical Area
Source: U.S. Census Bureau, 2017-2021 American Community Survey 5-Year Estimates

Educational Attainment by Race

Area	High School Graduate or Higher (%)					Bachelor's Degree or Higher (%)				
	Total	White	Black	Asian	Hisp.[2]	Total	White	Black	Asian	Hisp.[2]
City	93.8	95.3	83.0	86.2	82.8	32.8	33.6	17.8	51.5	22.4
MSA[1]	94.8	95.7	83.9	87.6	79.9	32.1	32.5	18.5	49.3	23.6
U.S.	88.9	91.4	87.2	87.6	71.2	33.7	35.5	23.3	55.6	18.4

Note: Figures shown cover persons 25 years old and over; (1) Figures cover the Cedar Rapids, IA Metropolitan Statistical Area; (2) People of Hispanic origin can be of any race
Source: U.S. Census Bureau, 2017-2021 American Community Survey 5-Year Estimates

School Enrollment by Grade and Control

Area	Preschool (%)		Kindergarten (%)		Grades 1 - 4 (%)		Grades 5 - 8 (%)		Grades 9 - 12 (%)	
	Public	Private	Public	Private	Public	Private	Public	Private	Public	Private
City	69.1	30.9	85.6	14.4	88.0	12.0	91.4	8.6	87.2	12.8
MSA[1]	69.0	31.0	86.7	13.3	89.3	10.7	90.5	9.5	91.0	9.0
U.S.	58.8	41.2	86.3	13.7	88.3	11.7	88.6	11.4	89.4	10.6

Note: Figures shown cover persons 3 years old and over; (1) Figures cover the Cedar Rapids, IA Metropolitan Statistical Area
Source: U.S. Census Bureau, 2017-2021 American Community Survey 5-Year Estimates

Higher Education

Four-Year Colleges			Two-Year Colleges			Medical Schools[1]	Law Schools[2]	Voc/ Tech[3]
Public	Private Non-profit	Private For-profit	Public	Private Non-profit	Private For-profit			
0	3	0	1	1	1	0	0	1

Note: Figures cover institutions located within the Cedar Rapids, IA Metropolitan Statistical Area and include main campuses only; (1) includes schools accredited by the Liaison Committee on Medical Education and the American Osteopathic Association's Commission on Osteopathic College Accreditation; (2) includes ABA-accredited schools, schools with provisional ABA accreditation, and state accredited schools; (3) includes all schools with programs that are less than 2 years.
Source: National Center for Education Statistics, Integrated Postsecondary Education System (IPEDS), 2021-22; Wikipedia, List of Medical Schools in the United States, accessed April 10, 2023; Wikipedia, List of Law Schools in the United States, accessed April 10, 2023

According to *U.S. News & World Report,* the Cedar Rapids, IA metro area is home to one of the top 100 liberal arts colleges in the U.S.: **Cornell College** (#100 tie). The indicators used to capture academic quality fall into a number of categories: assessment by administrators at peer institutions; retention of students; faculty resources; student selectivity; financial resources; alumni giving; high school counselor ratings of colleges; and graduation rate. *U.S. News & World Report, "America's Best Colleges 2023"*

EMPLOYERS

Major Employers

Company Name	Industry
AEGON USA	Insurance
Alliant Energy	Energy
Amana Refrigeration Products	Appliances
Cedar Rapids Community School District	Education
City of Cedar Rapids	Municipal government
Gazette Communications	Publishing
General Mills	Food products
Hy-Vee Food Stores	Grocery stores
Kirkwood Community College	Education
Linn County Offices	Government
Linn-Mar Community Schools	Education
Maytag Appliances	Appliances
MCI	Communications
McLeodUSA Incorporated	Communications
Mercy Medical Center	Healthcare
Nash Finch Company	Retail
Rockwell Collins	Aerospace/defense
St. Luke's Hospital	Education
Wal-Mart Stores	Retail
Yellowbook USA	Publisher

Note: Companies shown are located within the Cedar Rapids, IA Metropolitan Statistical Area.
Source: Hoovers.com; Wikipedia

Best Companies to Work For

RSM US, headquartered in Cedar Rapids, is among the "100 Best Places to Work in IT." To qualify, companies had to have a minimum of 100 total employees and five IT employees. The best places to work were selected based on DEI (diversity, equity, and inclusion) practices; IT turnover, promotions, and growth; IT retention and engagement programs; remote/hybrid working; benefits and perks (such as elder care and child care, flextime, and reimbursement for college tuition); and training and career development opportunities. *Computerworld, "Best Places to Work in IT," 2023*

PUBLIC SAFETY

Crime Rate

Area	Total Crime	Violent Crime Rate				Property Crime Rate		
		Murder	Rape[3]	Robbery	Aggrav. Assault	Burglary	Larceny -Theft	Motor Vehicle Theft
City	3,488.4	8.2	11.9	75.9	225.6	619.4	2,132.8	414.7
Suburbs[1]	1,291.6	0.7	39.3	10.0	135.0	318.6	660.1	127.9
Metro[2]	2,367.4	4.4	25.9	42.3	179.4	465.9	1,381.3	268.3
U.S.	2,356.7	6.5	38.4	73.9	279.7	314.2	1,398.0	246.0

Note: Figures are crimes per 100,000 population; (1) All areas within the metro area that are located outside the city limits; (2) Figures cover the Cedar Rapids, IA Metropolitan Statistical Area; (3) All figures shown were reported using the revised Uniform Crime Reporting (UCR) definition of rape; Due to the transition to the National Incident-Based Reporting System (NIBRS), limited city and metro area data was released for 2021.
Source: FBI Uniform Crime Reports, 2020

Hate Crimes

Area	Number of Quarters Reported	Number of Incidents per Bias Motivation					
		Race/Ethnicity/ Ancestry	Religion	Sexual Orientation	Disability	Gender	Gender Identity
City	4	0	0	0	0	0	0
U.S.	4	5,227	1,244	1,110	130	75	266

Note: Due to the transition to the National Incident-Based Reporting System (NIBRS), limited crime data was released for 2021.
Source: Federal Bureau of Investigation, Hate Crime Statistics 2020

Identity Theft Consumer Reports

Area	Reports	Reports per 100,000 Population	Rank[2]
MSA[1]	299	110	345
U.S.	1,108,609	339	-

Note: (1) Figures cover the Cedar Rapids, IA Metropolitan Statistical Area; (2) Rank ranges from 1 to 391 where 1 indicates greatest number of identity theft reports per 100,000 population
Source: Federal Trade Commission, Consumer Sentinel Network Data Book 2022

Fraud and Other Consumer Reports

Area	Reports	Reports per 100,000 Population	Rank[2]
MSA[1]	1,809	666	313
U.S.	4,064,520	1,245	-

Note: (1) Figures cover the Cedar Rapids, IA Metropolitan Statistical Area; (2) Rank ranges from 1 to 391 where 1 indicates greatest number of fraud and other consumer reports per 100,000 population
Source: Federal Trade Commission, Consumer Sentinel Network Data Book 2022

POLITICS

2020 Presidential Election Results

Area	Biden	Trump	Jorgensen	Hawkins	Other
Linn County	55.6	41.9	1.6	0.3	0.7
U.S.	51.3	46.8	1.2	0.3	0.5

Note: Results are percentages and may not add to 100% due to rounding
Source: Dave Leip's Atlas of U.S. Presidential Elections

SPORTS

Professional Sports Teams

Team Name	League	Year Established

No teams are located in the metro area
Source: Wikipedia, Major Professional Sports Teams of the United States and Canada, April 12, 2023

CLIMATE

Average and Extreme Temperatures

Temperature	Jan	Feb	Mar	Apr	May	Jun	Jul	Aug	Sep	Oct	Nov	Dec	Yr.
Extreme High (°F)	58	66	87	100	94	103	105	105	97	95	76	65	105
Average High (°F)	24	30	43	59	71	81	84	82	73	62	45	29	57
Average Temp. (°F)	15	21	34	48	60	69	73	71	62	50	36	21	47
Average Low (°F)	6	11	24	36	48	58	62	59	50	39	26	12	36
Extreme Low (°F)	-33	-29	-34	-4	25	38	42	38	22	11	-17	-27	-34

Note: Figures cover the years 1960-1995
Source: National Climatic Data Center, International Station Meteorological Climate Summary, 9/96

Average Precipitation/Snowfall/Humidity

Precip./Humidity	Jan	Feb	Mar	Apr	May	Jun	Jul	Aug	Sep	Oct	Nov	Dec	Yr.
Avg. Precip. (in.)	0.8	1.0	2.3	3.6	4.1	4.5	4.8	4.0	3.5	2.5	1.9	1.3	34.4
Avg. Snowfall (in.)	7	7	6	2	Tr	0	0	0	0	Tr	4	8	33
Avg. Rel. Hum. 6am (%)	77	80	82	81	81	83	87	90	89	84	83	82	83
Avg. Rel. Hum. 3pm (%)	68	66	62	52	51	51	55	55	55	52	62	70	58

Note: Figures cover the years 1960-1995; Tr = Trace amounts (<0.05 in. of rain; <0.5 in. of snow)
Source: National Climatic Data Center, International Station Meteorological Climate Summary, 9/96

Weather Conditions

Temperature			Daytime Sky			Precipitation		
5°F & below	32°F & below	90°F & above	Clear	Partly cloudy	Cloudy	0.01 inch or more precip.	0.1 inch or more snow/ice	Thunder-storms
38	156	16	89	132	144	109	28	42

Note: Figures are average number of days per year and cover the years 1960-1995
Source: National Climatic Data Center, International Station Meteorological Climate Summary, 9/96

HAZARDOUS WASTE

Superfund Sites

The Cedar Rapids, IA metro area has no sites on the EPA's Superfund Final National Priorities List. There are a total of 1,165 Superfund sites with a status of proposed or final on the list in the U.S. *U.S. Environmental Protection Agency, National Priorities List, April 12, 2023*

AIR QUALITY

Air Quality Trends: Ozone

	1990	1995	2000	2005	2010	2015	2018	2019	2020	2021
MSA[1]	n/a	n/a	n/a	n/a	n/a	n/a	n/a	n/a	n/a	n/a
U.S.	0.087	0.089	0.081	0.080	0.072	0.067	0.069	0.065	0.065	0.067

Note: (1) Data covers the Cedar Rapids, IA Metropolitan Statistical Area; n/a not available. The values shown are the composite ozone concentration averages among trend sites based on the highest fourth daily maximum 8-hour concentration in parts per million. These trends are based on sites having an adequate record of monitoring data during the trend period. Data from exceptional events are included.
Source: U.S. Environmental Protection Agency, Air Quality Monitoring Information, "Air Quality Trends by City, 1990-2021"

Air Quality Index

Area	Percent of Days when Air Quality was...[2]					AQI Statistics[2]	
	Good	Moderate	Unhealthy for Sensitive Groups	Unhealthy	Very Unhealthy	Maximum	Median
MSA[1]	64.4	34.5	1.1	0.0	0.0	123	44

Note: (1) Data covers the Cedar Rapids, IA Metropolitan Statistical Area; (2) Based on 365 days with AQI data in 2021. Air Quality Index (AQI) is an index for reporting daily air quality. EPA calculates the AQI for five major air pollutants regulated by the Clean Air Act: ground-level ozone, particle pollution (aka particulate matter), carbon monoxide, sulfur dioxide, and nitrogen dioxide. The AQI runs from 0 to 500. The higher the AQI value, the greater the level of air pollution and the greater the health concern. There are six AQI categories: "Good" AQI is between 0 and 50. Air quality is considered satisfactory; "Moderate" AQI is between 51 and 100. Air quality is acceptable; "Unhealthy for Sensitive Groups" When AQI values are between 101 and 150, members of sensitive groups may experience health effects; "Unhealthy" When AQI values are between 151 and 200 everyone may begin to experience health effects; "Very Unhealthy" AQI values between 201 and 300 trigger a health alert; "Hazardous" AQI values over 300 trigger warnings of emergency conditions (not shown).
Source: U.S. Environmental Protection Agency, Air Quality Index Report, 2021

Air Quality Index Pollutants

Area	Percent of Days when AQI Pollutant was...[2]					
	Carbon Monoxide	Nitrogen Dioxide	Ozone	Sulfur Dioxide	Particulate Matter 2.5	Particulate Matter 10
MSA[1]	0.0	0.0	35.1	(3)	64.7	0.3

Note: (1) Data covers the Cedar Rapids, IA Metropolitan Statistical Area; (2) Based on 365 days with AQI data in 2021. The Air Quality Index (AQI) is an index for reporting daily air quality. EPA calculates the AQI for five major air pollutants regulated by the Clean Air Act: ground-level ozone, particle pollution (also known as particulate matter), carbon monoxide, sulfur dioxide, and nitrogen dioxide. The AQI runs from 0 to 500. The higher the AQI value, the greater the level of air pollution and the greater the health concern; (3) Sulfur dioxide is no longer included in this table (as of December 8, 2021) because SO_2 concentrations tend to be very localized and not necessarily representative of broad geographical areas like counties and CBSAs.
Source: U.S. Environmental Protection Agency, Air Quality Index Report, 2021

Maximum Air Pollutant Concentrations: Particulate Matter, Ozone, CO and Lead

	Particulate Matter 10 (ug/m^3)	Particulate Matter 2.5 Wtd AM (ug/m^3)	Particulate Matter 2.5 24-Hr (ug/m^3)	Ozone (ppm)	Carbon Monoxide (ppm)	Lead (ug/m^3)
MSA[1] Level	57	8.8	24	0.064	n/a	n/a
NAAQS[2]	150	15	35	0.075	9	0.15
Met NAAQS[2]	Yes	Yes	Yes	Yes	n/a	n/a

Note: (1) Data covers the Cedar Rapids, IA Metropolitan Statistical Area; Data from exceptional events are included; (2) National Ambient Air Quality Standards; ppm = parts per million; ug/m^3 = micrograms per cubic meter; n/a not available.
Concentrations: Particulate Matter 10 (coarse particulate)—highest second maximum 24-hour concentration; Particulate Matter 2.5 Wtd AM (fine particulate)—highest weighted annual mean concentration; Particulate Matter 2.5 24-Hour (fine particulate)—highest 98th percentile 24-hour concentration; Ozone—highest fourth daily maximum 8-hour concentration; Carbon Monoxide—highest second maximum non-overlapping 8-hour concentration; Lead—maximum running 3-month average
Source: U.S. Environmental Protection Agency, Air Quality Monitoring Information, "Air Quality Statistics by City, 2021"

Maximum Air Pollutant Concentrations: Nitrogen Dioxide and Sulfur Dioxide

	Nitrogen Dioxide AM (ppb)	Nitrogen Dioxide 1-Hr (ppb)	Sulfur Dioxide AM (ppb)	Sulfur Dioxide 1-Hr (ppb)	Sulfur Dioxide 24-Hr (ppb)
MSA[1] Level	n/a	n/a	n/a	40	n/a
NAAQS[2]	53	100	30	75	140
Met NAAQS[2]	n/a	n/a	n/a	Yes	n/a

Note: (1) Data covers the Cedar Rapids, IA Metropolitan Statistical Area; Data from exceptional events are included; (2) National Ambient Air Quality Standards; ppm = parts per million; ug/m^3 = micrograms per cubic meter; n/a not available.
Concentrations: Nitrogen Dioxide AM—highest arithmetic mean concentration; Nitrogen Dioxide 1-Hr—highest 98th percentile 1-hour daily maximum concentration; Sulfur Dioxide AM—highest annual mean concentration; Sulfur Dioxide 1-Hr—highest 99th percentile 1-hour daily maximum concentration; Sulfur Dioxide 24-Hr—highest second maximum 24-hour concentration
Source: U.S. Environmental Protection Agency, Air Quality Monitoring Information, "Air Quality Statistics by City, 2021"

Chicago, Illinois

Background

City of Big Shoulders, The Windy City, That Toddling Town, and The Second City, are all Chicago's nicknames. Whatever one calls Chicago, it has always exemplified a great American city, from a bustling downtown with towering skyscrapers to a quaint collection of tightly packed urban neighborhoods stretching into the suburban landscape, then into the fields of the Illinois prairie.

Innovation has been part of Chicago's history from the very start. Cyrus McCormick invented his McCormick Reaper in 1831 and put Chicago on the map, revolutionizing harvesting across the world. The first mail-order business, Montgomery Ward, was established in Chicago in 1872. The world's first skyscraper was built in Chicago in 1885 for the Home Insurance Company. In 1907, University of Chicago's Albert Michelson, received the first American Nobel Prize for science. In 1931, Enrico Fermi split the atom underneath the University of Chicago football field. In 1983, Motorola set up the first modern portable cellular phone system in Chicago. The city also boasts 78 Nobel Prize Winners, more than any other city in the world.

Present-day Chicago is "greener" than ever before. It has 300 square miles of protected lands and is home to 131 plant species of global importance. The city is the nation's largest municipal marina with over 5,000 boat slips. Bicycling, walking trails, beaches and golf are all abundant and top notch. The Oceanarium is the world's largest indoor marine mammal pavilion.

Chicago, with the third largest gross metropolitan product in the nation, has been rated the most balanced economy in the United States, due to its elevated level of diversification. The Boeing Company relocated its corporate headquarters from Seattle to Chicago in 2001. The city, a major convention destination, is first in the country and third worldwide, in number of annual conventions. Chicago and its metro area are home to 10 Fortune 500 companies.

Chicago was the home of former President Barack Obama and his family; the Barack Obama Presidential Center opened in 2020 at the University of Chicago.

When the Willis (formerly Sears) Tower was completed in 1973, it was the tallest building in North America. Today, Chicago is home to the tenth and twenty-second tallest buildings in the world, and the work of homegrown architects Frank Lloyd Wright, Louis Sullivan, and Helmut Jahn. In addition, Mies van der Rohe immigrated here and became one of the most influential architects of the post-World War II era. In 2019, the city elected the first African American women and openly LBGTQ+ mayor.

Chicago boasts the Art Institute of Chicago, the Adler Planetarium, the Chicago Architecture Foundation, and the Hellenic Museum and Cultural Center. Classical musical offerings include the Chicago Symphony Orchestra, its Chamber Music Series, the Chicago Opera Theater, and the Lyric Opera of Chicago. The city is famous for its eclectic nightlife. You can hear music at dozens of clubs, and comedy at Second City, where such comics as John Belushi, John Candy, Chris Farley, and Stephen Colbert had their start.

Chicago professional sports have long been in the national spotlight. Chicago is home to two major league baseball teams, the Chicago Cubs who play at Wrigley Field in the city's North Side and the Chicago White Sox who play in the city's South Side at U.S. Cellular Field and who won the 2016 World Series, ending a 108-year record World Series drought. The Chicago Bears, the city's NFL team, won thirteen NFL championships, and Chicago's professional basketball team, the Chicago Bulls, is one of the world's most recognized teams. In 2021, Chicago Sky, the city's Women's National Basketball Association team, became WNBA champions.

The Chicago Marathon, one of five world marathon events, has been held every October since 1977. Chicago is also the starting point for the Chicago Yacht Club Race to Mackinac—the longest annual freshwater sailboat race in the world. Chicago was a candidate to host the 2016 games, but lost the bid to Rio de Janeiro.

Outstanding educational institutions in Chicago include the University of Chicago (1891); Northwestern University (1851); DePaul University; Loyola University; and the School of the Art Institute of Chicago.

Located along the southwest shore of Lake Michigan, Chicago has four true seasons, with a white Christmas, spring flowers, a steamy summer, and the beautiful colors of fall. Summers can be very hot, and winters are often quite cold.

Rankings

General Rankings

- *Insider* listed 23 places in the U.S. that travel industry trends reveal would be popular destinations in 2023. This year the list trends towards cultural and historical happenings, sports events, wellness experiences and invigorating outdoor escapes. According to the website insider.com Chicago is a place to visit in 2023. *Insider, "23 of the Best Places You Should Travel to in the U.S. in 2023," December 17, 2022*

- Chicago was selected as one of the best places to live in America by *Outside Magazine*. Criteria centered on diversity; sustainability; outdoor equity; and affordability. Local experts shared highlights from hands-on experience in each location. *Outside Magazine, "The 20 Most Livable Towns and Cities in America," October 15, 2021*

- Chicago was selected as one of the best places to live in the United States by *Money* magazine. The city ranked #5 out of 50. This year's list focused on cities that would be welcoming to a broader group of people and with populations of at least 20,000. Beginning with a pool of 1,370 candidates, editors looked at 350 data points, organized into the these nine categories: income and personal finance, cost of living, economic opportunity, housing market, fun and amenities, health and safety, education, diversity, and quality of life. *Money, "The 50 Best Places to Live in the U.S. in 2022-2023" September 29, 2022*

- The human resources consulting firm Mercer ranked 231 major cities worldwide in terms of overall quality of life. Chicago ranked #49. Criteria: political, social, economic, and socio-cultural factors; medical and health considerations; schools and education; public services and transportation; recreation; consumer goods; housing; and natural environment. *Mercer, "Mercer 2019 Quality of Living Survey," March 13, 2019*

- Chicago appeared on *Travel + Leisure's* list of "The 15 Best Cities in the United States." The city was ranked #7. Criteria: sights/landmarks; culture; food; friendliness; shopping; and overall value. *Travel + Leisure, "The World's Best Awards 2022" July 12, 2022*

- For its 35th annual "Readers' Choice Awards" survey, *Condé Nast Traveler* ranked its readers' favorite cities in the U.S. Whether it be a longed-for visit or a first on the list, these are the places that inspired a return to travel. The list was broken into large cities and cities under 250,000. Chicago ranked #1 in the big city category. *Condé Nast Traveler, Readers' Choice Awards 2022, "Best Big Cities in the U.S." October 4, 2022*

Business/Finance Rankings

- According to *Business Insider*, the Chicago metro area is a prime place to run a startup or move an existing business to. The area ranked #14. More than 300 metro areas were analyzed for factors that were of top concern to new business owners. Data was based on the 2019 U.S. Census Bureau American Community Survey, statistics from the CDC, Bureau of Labor Statistics employment report, and University of Chicago analysis. Criteria: business formations; percentage of vaccinated population; percentage of households with internet subscriptions; median household income; and share of work that can be done from home. *www.businessinsider.com, "The 20 Best Cities for Starting a Business in 2022 Include Baltimore, Boulder, and Boston," January 5, 2022*

- Based on metro area social media reviews, the employment opinion group Glassdoor surveyed 50 of the most populous U.S. metro areas and equally weighed cost of living, hiring opportunity, and job satisfaction to compose a list of "25 Best Cities for Jobs." Median pay and home value, and number of active job openings were also factored in. The Chicago metro area was ranked #15 in overall job satisfaction. *www.glassdoor.com, "Best Cities for Jobs," February 25, 2020*

- The Brookings Institution ranked the nation's largest cities based on income inequality. Chicago was ranked #22 (#1 = greatest inequality). Criteria: the "95/20 ratio," a figure representing the income at which a household earns more than 95 percent of all other households, divided by the income at which a household earns more than only 20 percent of all other households. *Brookings Institution, "Household Income Inequality, Largest Cities of 97 Large U.S. Metro Areas, 2014-2016," February 5, 2018*

- The Brookings Institution ranked the 100 largest metro areas in the U.S. based on income inequality. Chicago was ranked #15 (#1 = greatest inequality). Criteria: the "95/20 ratio," a figure representing the income at which a household earns more than 95 percent of all other households, divided by the income at which a household earns more than only 20 percent of all other households. *Brookings Institution, "Household Income Inequality, 100 Largest U.S. Metro Areas, 2014-2016," February 5, 2018*

- Payscale.com ranked the 32 largest metro areas in terms of wage growth. The Chicago metro area ranked #18. Criteria: quarterly changes in private industry employee and education professional wage growth from the previous year. *PayScale, "Wage Trends by Metro Area-1st Quarter," April 20, 2023*

- The Chicago metro area was identified as one of the most debt-ridden places in America by the finance site Credit.com. The metro area was ranked #12. Criteria: residents' average credit card debt as well as median income. *Credit.com, "25 Cities With the Most Credit Card Debt," February 28, 2018*

- Chicago was cited as one of America's top metros for total corporate facility investment in 2022. The area ranked #1 in the large metro area category (population over 1 million). *Site Selection, "Top Metros of 2022," March 2023*

- Chicago was identified as one of the happiest cities to work in by CareerBliss.com, an online community for career advancement. The city ranked #2 out of 10. Criteria: an employee's relationship with his or her boss and co-workers; daily tasks; general work environment; compensation; opportunities for advancement; company culture and job reputation; and resources. *Businesswire.com, "CareerBliss Happiest Cities to Work 2019," February 12, 2019*

- The Chicago metro area appeared on the Milken Institute "2022 Best Performing Cities" list. Rank: #121 out of 200 large metro areas (population over 250,000). Criteria: job growth; wage and salary growth; high-tech output growth; housing affordability; household broadband access. *Milken Institute, "Best-Performing Cities 2022," March 28, 2022*

- *Forbes* ranked the 200 most populous metro areas to determine the nation's "Best Places for Business and Careers." The Chicago metro area was ranked #75. Criteria: costs (business and living); job growth (past and projected); income growth; quality of life; educational attainment (college and high school); projected economic growth; cultural and leisure opportunities; workplace tolerance laws; net migration patterns. *Forbes, "The Best Places for Business and Careers 2019: Seattle Still On Top," October 30, 2019*

- Mercer Human Resources Consulting ranked 227 cities worldwide in terms of cost-of-living. Chicago ranked #36 (the lower the ranking, the higher the cost-of-living). The survey measured the comparative cost of over 200 items (such as housing, food, clothing, domestic supplies, transportation, and recreation/entertainment) in each location. *Mercer, "2022 Cost of Living City Ranking," June 29, 2022*

Children/Family Rankings

- Chicago was selected as one of the most playful cities in the U.S. by KaBOOM! The organization's Playful City USA initiative honors cities and towns across the nation that have made their communities more playable. Criteria: pledging to integrate play as a solution to challenges in their communities; making it easy for children to get active and balanced play; creating more family-friendly and innovative communities as a result. *KaBOOM! National Campaign for Play, "2017 Playful City USA Communities"*

Culture/Performing Arts Rankings

- Chicago was selected as one of the 25 best cities for moviemakers in North America. Great film cities are places where filmmaking dreams can come true, that offer more creative space, lower costs, and great outdoor locations. NYC & LA were intentionally excluded. Criteria: longstanding reputations as film-friendly communities; film community and culture; affordability; and quality of life. The city was ranked #7. *MovieMaker Magazine, "Best Places to Live and Work as a Moviemaker, 2023," January 18, 2023*

- Chicago was selected as one of "America's Favorite Cities." The city ranked #3 in the "Architecture" category. Respondents to an online survey were asked to rate their favorite place (population over 100,000) in over 65 categories. *Travelandleisure.com, "America's Favorite Cities for Architecture 2016," March 2, 2017*

Education Rankings

- Personal finance website *WalletHub* analyzed the 150 largest U.S. metropolitan statistical areas to determine where the most educated Americans are putting their degrees to work. Criteria: education levels; percentage of workers with degrees; education quality and attainment gap; public school quality rankings; quality and enrollment of each metro area's universities. Chicago was ranked #31 (#1 = most educated city). *www.WalletHub.com, "Most & Least Educated Cities in America," July 18, 2022*

- Chicago was selected as one of America's most literate cities. The city ranked #19 out of the 84 largest U.S. cities. Criteria: number of booksellers; library resources; Internet resources; educational attainment; periodical publishing resources; newspaper circulation. *Central Connecticut State University, "America's Most Literate Cities, 2018," February 2019*

Environmental Rankings

- The U.S. Environmental Protection Agency (EPA) released its list of U.S. metropolitan areas with the most ENERGY STAR certified buildings in 2022. The Chicago metro area was ranked #8 out of 25. *U.S. Environmental Protection Agency, "2023 Energy Star Top Cities," April 26, 2023*

- Chicago was highlighted as one of the 25 most ozone-polluted metro areas in the U.S. during 2019 through 2021. The area ranked #17. *American Lung Association, "State of the Air 2023," April 19, 2023*

- Chicago was highlighted as one of the 25 metro areas most polluted by year-round particle pollution (Annual PM 2.5) in the U.S. during 2019 through 2021. The area ranked #23. *American Lung Association, "State of the Air 2023," April 19, 2023*

Food/Drink Rankings

- The U.S. Chamber of Commerce Foundation conducted an in-depth study on local food truck regulations, surveyed 288 food truck owners, and ranked 20 major American cities based on how friendly they are for operating a food truck. The compiled index assessed the following: procedures for obtaining permits and licenses; complying with restrictions; and financial obligations associated with operating a food truck. Chicago ranked #13 overall (1 being the best). *www.foodtrucknation.us, "Food Truck Nation," March 20, 2018*

Health/Fitness Rankings

- For each of the 100 largest cities in the United States, the American Fitness Index®, compiled in partnership between the American College of Sports Medicine and the Elevance Health Foundation, evaluated community infrastructure and 34 health behaviors including preventive health, levels of chronic disease conditions, food insecurity, sleep quality, pedestrian safety, air quality, and community/environment resources that support physical activity. Chicago ranked #10 for "community fitness." *americanfitnessindex.org, "2022 ACSM American Fitness Index Summary Report," July 12, 2022*

- Chicago was identified as one of the 10 most walkable cities in the U.S. by Walk Score. The city ranked #6. Walk Score measures walkability by analyzing hundreds of walking routes to nearby amenities, and also measures pedestrian friendliness by analyzing population density and road metrics such as block length and intersection density. *WalkScore.com, April 13, 2021*

- The Chicago metro area was identified as one of the worst cities for bed bugs in America by pest control company Orkin. The area ranked #1 out of 50 based on the number of bed bug treatments Orkin performed from December 2021 to November 2022. *Orkin, "The Windy City Can't Blow Bed Bugs Away: Chicago Ranks #1 For Third Consecutive Year On Orkin's Bed Bug Cities List," January 9, 2023*

- Chicago was identified as a "2022 Spring Allergy Capital." The area ranked #71 out of 100. Three groups of factors were used to identify the most challenging cities for people with allergies during the spring season: annual spring pollen scores; over the counter allergy medicine use; number of board-certified allergy specialists. *Asthma and Allergy Foundation of America, "Spring Allergy Capitals 2022," March 2, 2022*

- Chicago was identified as a "2022 Fall Allergy Capital." The area ranked #65 out of 100. Three groups of factors were used to identify the most challenging cities for people with allergies during the fall season: annual fall pollen scores; over the counter allergy medicine use; number of board-certified allergy specialists. *Asthma and Allergy Foundation of America, "Fall Allergy Capitals 2022," March 2, 2022*

- Chicago was identified as a "2022 Asthma Capital." The area ranked #28 out of the nation's 100 largest metropolitan areas. Criteria: estimated asthma prevalence; asthma-related mortality; and ER visits due to asthma. Risk factors analyzed but not factored in the rankings: annual pollen score; annual air quality; public smoking laws; access to board-certified asthma specialists; rescue and controller medication use; uninsured rate; poverty rate. *Asthma and Allergy Foundation of America, "Asthma Capitals 2022: The Most Challenging Places to Live With Asthma," September 14, 2022*

Real Estate Rankings

- *WalletHub* compared the most populated U.S. cities to determine which had the best markets for real estate agents. Chicago ranked #134 where demand was high and pay was the best. Criteria: sales per agent; annual median wage for real-estate agents; monthly average starting salary for real estate agents; real estate job density and competition; unemployment rate; home turnover rate; housing-market health index; and other relevant metrics. *www.WalletHub.com, "2021 Best Places to Be a Real Estate Agent," May 12, 2021*

- Chicago was ranked #82 out of 235 metro areas in terms of housing affordability in 2022 by the National Association of Home Builders (#1 = most affordable). Criteria: the share of homes sold in that area affordable to a family earning the local median income, based on standard mortgage underwriting criteria. *National Association of Home Builders®, NAHB-Wells Fargo Housing Opportunity Index, 4th Quarter 2022*

- The nation's largest metro areas were analyzed in terms of the percentage of households entering some stage of foreclosure in 2022. The Chicago metro area ranked #5 out of 8 (#1 = highest foreclosure rate). *ATTOM Data Solutions, "2022 Year-End U.S. Foreclosure Market Report™," January 12, 2023*

Safety Rankings

- Allstate ranked the 200 largest cities in America in terms of driver safety. Chicago ranked #133. Criteria: internal property damage claims over a two-year period from January 2016 to December 2017. The report helps increase the importance of safety and awareness behind the wheel. *Allstate, "Allstate America's Best Drivers Report, 2019" June 24, 2019*

Seniors/Retirement Rankings

- From its Best Cities for Successful Aging indexes, the Milken Institute generated rankings for metropolitan areas, weighing data in nine categories—health care, wellness, living arrangements, transportation and convenience, financial characteristics, education, employment, community engagement, and overall livability. The Chicago metro area was ranked #52 overall in the large metro area category. *Milken Institute, "Best Cities for Successful Aging, 2017" March 14, 2017*

Sports/Recreation Rankings

- Chicago was chosen as one of America's best cities for bicycling. The city ranked #6 out of 50. Criteria: cycling infrastructure that is safe and friendly for all ages; energy and bike culture. The editors evaluated cities with populations of 100,000 or more. *Bicycling, "The 50 Best Bike Cities in America," October 10, 2018*

Transportation Rankings

- Business Insider presented an AllTransit Performance Score ranking of public transportation in major U.S. cities and towns, with populations over 250,000, in which Chicago earned the #6-ranked "Transit Score," awarded for frequency of service, access to jobs, quality and number of stops, and affordability. *www.businessinsider.com, "The 17 Major U.S. Cities with the Best Public Transportation," April 17, 2018*

- According to the INRIX "2022 Global Traffic Scorecard," Chicago was identified as one of the most congested metro areas in the U.S. The area ranked #1 out of 25. Criteria: average annual time spent in traffic and average cost of congestion per motorist. *Inrix.com, "Return to Work, Higher Gas Prices & Inflation Drove Americans to Spend Hundreds More in Time and Money Commuting," January 10, 2023*

Women/Minorities Rankings

- *Travel + Leisure* listed the best cities in and around the U.S. for a memorable and fun girls' trip, even on a budget. Whether it is for a special occasion, to make new memories or just to get away, Chicago is sure to have something for all the ladies in your tribe. *Travel + Leisure, "25 Affordable Girls Weekend Getaways That Won't Break the Bank," November 25, 2022*

- The *Houston Chronicle* listed the Chicago metro area as #8 in top places for young Latinos to live in the U.S. Research was largely based on housing and occupational data from the largest metropolitan areas performed by *Forbes* and NBC Universo. Criteria: percentage of 18-34 year-olds; Latino college grad rates; and diversity. *blog.chron.com, "The 15 Best Big Cities for Latino Millenials," January 26, 2016*

- Personal finance website *WalletHub* compared more than 180 U.S. cities across two key dimensions, "Hispanic Business-Friendliness" and "Hispanic Purchasing Power," to arrive at the most favorable conditions for Hispanic entrepreneurs. Chicago was ranked #122 out of 182. Criteria includes: share of Hispanic-Owned Businesses; Hispanic entrepreneurship rate to median annual income of Hispanics; Small Business-Friendliness score; cost of living; and number of Hispanics with at least a bachelor's degree. *WalletHub.com, "2019's Best Cities for Hispanic Entrepreneurs," May 1, 2019*

Miscellaneous Rankings

- In its roundup of St. Patrick's Day parades "Gayot" listed the best festivals and parades of all things Irish. The festivities in Chicago as among the best in North America. *www.gayot.com, "Best St. Patrick's Day Parades," March 2023*

- The watchdog site, Charity Navigator, conducted a study of charities in major markets both to analyze statistical differences in their financial, accountability, and transparency practices and to track year-to-year variations in individual philanthropic communities. The Chicago metro area was ranked #11 among the 30 metro markets in the rating category of Overall Score. *www.charitynavigator.org, "2017 Metro Market Study," May 1, 2017*

- In *Condé Nast Traveler* magazine's 2022 Readers' Choice Survey, Chicago made the top ten list of friendliest American cities. Chicago ranked #9. *www.cntraveler.com, "The 10 Friendliest Cities in the U.S.," December 20, 2022*

- *WalletHub* compared the 150 most populated U.S. cities to determine their operating efficiency. A "Quality of Services" score was constructed for each city and then divided by the total budget per capita to reveal which were managed the best. Chicago ranked #140. Criteria: financial stability; economy; education; safety; health; infrastructure and pollution. *www.WalletHub.com, "2022's Best- & Worst-Run Cities in America," June 21, 2022*

- The National Alliance to End Homelessness listed the 25 most populous metro areas with the highest rate of homelessness. The Chicago metro area had a high rate of homelessness. Criteria: number of homeless people per 10,000 population in 2016. *National Alliance to End Homelessness, "Homelessness in the 25 Most Populous U.S. Metro Areas," September 1, 2017*

Business Environment

DEMOGRAPHICS

Population Growth

Area	1990 Census	2000 Census	2010 Census	2020 Census	Population Growth (%) 1990-2020	Population Growth (%) 2010-2020
City	2,783,726	2,896,016	2,695,598	2,746,388	-1.3	1.9
MSA[1]	8,182,076	9,098,316	9,461,105	9,618,502	17.6	1.7
U.S.	248,709,873	281,421,906	308,745,538	331,449,281	33.3	7.4

Note: (1) Figures cover the Chicago-Naperville-Elgin, IL-IN-WI Metropolitan Statistical Area
Source: U.S. Census Bureau, 1990 Census, 2000 Census, 2010 Census, 2020 Census

Race

Area	White Alone[2] (%)	Black Alone[2] (%)	Asian Alone[2] (%)	AIAN[3] Alone[2] (%)	NHOPI[4] Alone[2] (%)	Other Race Alone[2] (%)	Two or More Races (%)
City	35.9	29.2	7.0	1.3	0.0	15.8	10.8
MSA[1]	54.0	16.4	7.1	0.9	0.0	11.3	10.2
U.S.	61.6	12.4	6.0	1.1	0.2	8.4	10.2

Note: (1) Figures cover the Chicago-Naperville-Elgin, IL-IN-WI Metropolitan Statistical Area; (2) Alone is defined as not being in combination with one or more other races; (3) American Indian and Alaska Native; (4) Native Hawaiian and Other Pacific Islander
Source: U.S. Census Bureau, 2020 Census

Hispanic or Latino Origin

Area	Total (%)	Mexican (%)	Puerto Rican (%)	Cuban (%)	Other (%)
City	28.7	21.2	3.5	0.3	3.8
MSA[1]	22.5	17.5	2.2	0.3	2.6
U.S.	18.4	11.2	1.8	0.7	4.7

Note: Persons of Hispanic or Latino origin can be of any race; (1) Figures cover the Chicago-Naperville-Elgin, IL-IN-WI Metropolitan Statistical Area
Source: U.S. Census Bureau, 2017-2021 American Community Survey 5-Year Estimates

Age

Area	Under Age 5	Age 5–19	Age 20–34	Age 35–44	Age 45–54	Age 55–64	Age 65–74	Age 75–84	Age 85+	Median Age
City	5.5	16.9	27.5	14.4	11.9	11.1	7.7	3.7	1.4	35.1
MSA[1]	5.5	19.3	20.8	13.4	12.9	12.9	9.0	4.3	1.8	38.2
U.S.	5.6	19.2	20.2	12.7	12.4	13.1	10.0	4.9	1.9	38.8

Note: (1) Figures cover the Chicago-Naperville-Elgin, IL-IN-WI Metropolitan Statistical Area
Source: U.S. Census Bureau, 2020 Census

Disability by Age

Area	All Ages	Under 18 Years Old	18 to 64 Years Old	65 Years and Over
City	10.9	3.3	8.8	34.8
MSA[1]	10.1	3.3	7.9	30.3
U.S.	12.6	4.4	10.3	33.4

Note: Figures show percent of the civilian noninstitutionalized population that reported having a disability. Disability status is determined from six types of difficulty: vision, hearing, cognitive, ambulatory, self-care, and independent living. For children under 5 years old, hearing and vision difficulty are used to determine disability status. For children between the ages of 5 and 14, disability status is determined from hearing, vision, cognitive, ambulatory, and self-care difficulties. For people aged 15 years and older, they are considered to have a disability if they have difficulty with any one of the six difficulty types; Note: (1) Figures cover the Chicago-Naperville-Elgin, IL-IN-WI Metropolitan Statistical Area
Source: U.S. Census Bureau, 2017-2021 American Community Survey 5-Year Estimates

Ancestry

Area	German	Irish	English	American	Italian	Polish	French[2]	Scottish	Dutch
City	7.3	7.3	2.8	2.1	3.9	5.2	0.9	0.7	0.5
MSA[1]	13.7	10.5	4.5	2.5	6.4	8.3	1.3	0.9	1.1
U.S.	12.8	9.6	8.1	5.7	5.0	2.7	2.2	1.6	1.1

Note: Figures are the percentage of the total population reporting a particular ancestry. The nine most commonly reported ancestries in the U.S. are shown. Figures include multiple ancestries (e.g. if a person reported being Irish and Italian, they were included in both columns); (1) Figures cover the Chicago-Naperville-Elgin, IL-IN-WI Metropolitan Statistical Area; (2) Excludes Basque
Source: U.S. Census Bureau, 2017-2021 American Community Survey 5-Year Estimates

Foreign-born Population

Area	Any Foreign Country	Percent of Population Born in							
		Asia	Mexico	Europe	Caribbean	Central America[2]	South America	Africa	Canada
City	20.2	5.1	8.1	3.4	0.3	0.9	1.1	1.0	0.2
MSA[1]	17.7	5.3	6.3	3.7	0.2	0.5	0.7	0.7	0.2
U.S.	13.6	4.2	3.3	1.5	1.4	1.1	1.1	0.8	0.2

Note: (1) Figures cover the Chicago-Naperville-Elgin, IL-IN-WI Metropolitan Statistical Area; (2) Excludes Mexico.
Source: U.S. Census Bureau, 2017-2021 American Community Survey 5-Year Estimates

Household Size

Area	Persons in Household (%)							Average Household Size
	One	Two	Three	Four	Five	Six	Seven or More	
City	38.2	29.5	13.6	10.0	5.0	2.2	1.5	2.40
MSA[1]	29.3	31.2	15.6	13.6	6.5	2.4	1.4	2.60
U.S.	28.1	33.8	15.5	12.9	6.0	2.3	1.4	2.60

Note: (1) Figures cover the Chicago-Naperville-Elgin, IL-IN-WI Metropolitan Statistical Area
Source: U.S. Census Bureau, 2017-2021 American Community Survey 5-Year Estimates

Household Relationships

Area	House-holder	Opposite-sex Spouse	Same-sex Spouse	Opposite-sex Unmarried Partner	Same-sex Unmarried Partner	Child[2]	Grand-child	Other Relatives	Non-relatives
City	41.6	12.2	0.3	3.0	0.3	26.6	3.0	6.4	4.8
MSA[1]	38.2	17.1	0.2	2.3	0.1	30.3	2.4	5.1	2.8
U.S.	38.3	17.5	0.2	2.5	0.2	28.3	2.4	4.8	3.4

Note: Figures are percent of the total population; (1) Figures cover the Chicago-Naperville-Elgin, IL-IN-WI Metropolitan Statistical Area; (2) Includes biological, adopted, and stepchildren of the householder
Source: U.S. Census Bureau, 2020 Census

Gender

Area	Males	Females	Males per 100 Females
City	1,332,725	1,413,663	94.3
MSA[1]	4,694,560	4,923,942	95.3
U.S.	162,685,811	168,763,470	96.4

Note: (1) Figures cover the Chicago-Naperville-Elgin, IL-IN-WI Metropolitan Statistical Area
Source: U.S. Census Bureau, 2020 Census

Marital Status

Area	Never Married	Now Married[2]	Separated	Widowed	Divorced
City	48.9	35.5	2.3	5.0	8.3
MSA[1]	37.2	47.0	1.6	5.2	8.9
U.S.	33.8	48.0	1.8	5.6	10.8

Note: Figures are percentages and cover the population 15 years of age and older; (1) Figures cover the Chicago-Naperville-Elgin, IL-IN-WI Metropolitan Statistical Area; (2) Excludes separated
Source: U.S. Census Bureau, 2017-2021 American Community Survey 5-Year Estimates

Religious Groups by Family

Area	Catholic	Baptist	Methodist	LDS[2]	Pentecostal	Lutheran	Islam	Adventist	Other
MSA[1]	28.6	3.4	1.4	0.3	1.5	2.1	4.7	1.1	9.2
U.S.	18.7	7.3	3.0	2.0	1.8	1.7	1.3	1.3	11.6

Note: Figures are the number of adherents as a percentage of the total population and cover the eight largest religious groups in the U.S; (1) Figures cover the Chicago-Naperville-Elgin, IL-IN-WI Metropolitan Statistical Area; (2) Church of Jesus Christ of Latter-day Saints
Sources: 2020 U.S. Religion Census, Association of Statisticians of American Religious Bodies; The Association of Religion Data Archives (ARDA)

Religious Groups by Tradition

Area	Catholic	Evangelical Protestant	Mainline Protestant	Black Protestant	Islam	Judaism	Hinduism	Orthodox	Buddhism
MSA[1]	28.6	8.2	3.7	3.6	4.7	0.7	0.4	0.7	0.4
U.S.	18.7	16.5	5.2	2.3	1.3	0.6	0.4	0.4	0.3

Note: Figures are the number of adherents as a percentage of the total population; (1) Figures cover the Chicago-Naperville-Elgin, IL-IN-WI Metropolitan Statistical Area
Sources: 2020 U.S. Religion Census, Association of Statisticians of American Religious Bodies; The Association of Religion Data Archives (ARDA)

ECONOMY

Gross Metropolitan Product

Area	2020	2021	2022	2023	Rank[2]
MSA[1]	693.0	757.2	819.9	861.2	3

Note: Figures are in billions of dollars; (1) Figures cover the Chicago-Naperville-Elgin, IL-IN-WI Metropolitan Statistical Area; (2) Rank is based on 2021 data and ranges from 1 to 381
Source: U.S. Conference of Mayors, U.S. Metro Economies: U.S. Metros Compared to Global and State Economies, June 2022

Economic Growth

Area	2018-20 (%)	2021 (%)	2022 (%)	2023 (%)	Rank[2]
MSA[1]	-2.4	5.5	2.6	1.8	324
U.S.	-0.6	5.7	3.1	2.9	—

Note: Figures are real gross metropolitan product (GMP) growth rates and represent average annual percent change; (1) Figures cover the Chicago-Naperville-Elgin, IL-IN-WI Metropolitan Statistical Area; (2) Rank is based on 2020 2-year average annual percent change and ranges from 1 to 381
Source: U.S. Conference of Mayors, U.S. Metro Economies: U.S. Metros Compared to Global and State Economies, June 2022

Metropolitan Area Exports

Area	2016	2017	2018	2019	2020	2021	Rank[2]
MSA[1]	43,932.7	46,140.2	47,287.8	42,438.8	41,279.4	54,498.1	4

Note: Figures are in millions of dollars; (1) Figures cover the Chicago-Naperville-Elgin, IL-IN-WI Metropolitan Statistical Area; (2) Rank is based on 2021 data and ranges from 1 to 388
Source: U.S. Department of Commerce, International Trade Administration, Office of Trade and Economic Analysis, Industry and Analysis, Exports by Metropolitan Area, data extracted March 16, 2023

Building Permits

Area	Single-Family			Multi-Family			Total		
	2021	2022	Pct. Chg.	2021	2022	Pct. Chg.	2021	2022	Pct. Chg.
City	414	412	-0.5	4,927	6,712	36.2	5,341	7,124	33.4
MSA[1]	10,071	8,563	-15.0	8,440	9,073	7.5	18,511	17,636	-4.7
U.S.	1,115,400	975,600	-12.5	621,600	689,500	10.9	1,737,000	1,665,100	-4.1

Note: (1) Figures cover the Chicago-Naperville-Elgin, IL-IN-WI Metropolitan Statistical Area; Figures represent new, privately-owned housing units authorized (unadjusted data); All permit data are based on estimates with imputation
Source: U.S. Census Bureau, Manufacturing, Mining, and Construction Statistics, Building Permits, 2021, 2022

Bankruptcy Filings

Area	Business Filings			Nonbusiness Filings		
	2021	2022	% Chg.	2021	2022	% Chg.
Cook County	270	237	-12.2	10,430	10,849	4.0
U.S.	14,347	13,481	-6.0	399,269	374,240	-6.3

Note: Business filings include Chapter 7, Chapter 9, Chapter 11, Chapter 12, Chapter 13, Chapter 15, and Section 304; Nonbusiness filings include Chapter 7, Chapter 11, and Chapter 13
Source: Administrative Office of the U.S. Courts, Business and Nonbusiness Bankruptcy, County Cases Commenced by Chapter of the Bankruptcy Code, During the 12-Month Period Ending December 31, 2021 and Business and Nonbusiness Bankruptcy, County Cases Commenced by Chapter of the Bankruptcy Code, During the 12-Month Period Ending December 31, 2022

Housing Vacancy Rates

Area	Gross Vacancy Rate[2] (%)			Year-Round Vacancy Rate[3] (%)			Rental Vacancy Rate[4] (%)			Homeowner Vacancy Rate[5] (%)		
	2020	2021	2022	2020	2021	2022	2020	2021	2022	2020	2021	2022
MSA[1]	7.4	8.7	7.3	7.2	8.6	7.1	7.4	8.0	6.1	1.2	1.3	1.1
U.S.	10.6	10.8	10.5	8.2	8.4	8.2	6.3	6.1	5.8	1.0	0.9	0.8

Note: (1) Figures cover the Chicago-Naperville-Elgin, IL-IN-WI Metropolitan Statistical Area; (2) The percentage of the total housing inventory that is vacant; (3) The percentage of the housing inventory (excluding seasonal units) that is year-round vacant; (4) The percentage of rental inventory that is vacant for rent; (5) The percentage of homeowner inventory that is vacant for sale
Source: U.S. Census Bureau, Housing Vacancies and Homeownership Annual Statistics: 2020, 2021, 2022

INCOME

Income

Area	Per Capita ($)	Median Household ($)	Average Household ($)
City	41,821	65,781	100,347
MSA[1]	42,097	78,790	109,339
U.S.	37,638	69,021	97,196

Note: (1) Figures cover the Chicago-Naperville-Elgin, IL-IN-WI Metropolitan Statistical Area
Source: U.S. Census Bureau, 2017-2021 American Community Survey 5-Year Estimates

Household Income Distribution

Area	Percent of Households Earning							
	Under $15,000	$15,000 -$24,999	$25,000 -$34,999	$35,000 -$49,999	$50,000 -$74,999	$75,000 -$99,999	$100,000 -$149,999	$150,000 and up
City	13.1	8.7	8.2	10.2	14.9	11.7	14.7	18.6
MSA[1]	8.7	6.6	7.1	9.9	15.6	12.8	17.9	21.5
U.S.	9.4	7.8	8.2	11.4	16.8	12.8	16.3	17.3

Note: (1) Figures cover the Chicago-Naperville-Elgin, IL-IN-WI Metropolitan Statistical Area
Source: U.S. Census Bureau, 2017-2021 American Community Survey 5-Year Estimates

Poverty Rate

Area	All Ages	Under 18 Years Old	18 to 64 Years Old	65 Years and Over
City	17.1	24.2	15.1	15.9
MSA[1]	11.1	15.1	10.1	9.4
U.S.	12.6	17.0	11.8	9.6

Note: Figures are percentage of people whose income during the past 12 months was below the poverty level;
(1) Figures cover the Chicago-Naperville-Elgin, IL-IN-WI Metropolitan Statistical Area
Source: U.S. Census Bureau, 2017-2021 American Community Survey 5-Year Estimates

EMPLOYMENT

Labor Force and Employment

Area	Civilian Labor Force			Workers Employed		
	Dec. 2021	Dec. 2022	% Chg.	Dec. 2021	Dec. 2022	% Chg.
City	1,370,152	1,365,082	-0.4	1,301,665	1,299,230	-0.2
MD[1]	3,826,621	3,838,545	0.3	3,671,983	3,676,358	0.1
U.S.	161,696,000	164,224,000	1.6	155,732,000	158,872,000	2.0

Note: Data is not seasonally adjusted and covers workers 16 years of age and older; (1) Figures cover the Chicago-Naperville-Evanston, IL Metropolitan Division
Source: Bureau of Labor Statistics, Local Area Unemployment Statistics

Unemployment Rate

Area	2022											
	Jan.	Feb.	Mar.	Apr.	May	Jun.	Jul.	Aug.	Sep.	Oct.	Nov.	Dec.
City	5.8	5.5	5.0	4.7	4.9	5.7	5.8	5.9	5.6	5.2	5.3	4.8
MD[1]	5.2	5.0	4.4	4.3	4.5	5.3	5.1	5.2	4.6	4.5	4.4	4.2
U.S.	4.4	4.1	3.8	3.3	3.4	3.8	3.8	3.8	3.3	3.4	3.4	3.3

Note: Data is not seasonally adjusted and covers workers 16 years of age and older; (1) Figures cover the Chicago-Naperville-Evanston, IL Metropolitan Division
Source: Bureau of Labor Statistics, Local Area Unemployment Statistics

Average Wages

Occupation	$/Hr.	Occupation	$/Hr.
Accountants and Auditors	42.15	Maintenance and Repair Workers	26.11
Automotive Mechanics	25.15	Marketing Managers	70.74
Bookkeepers	25.13	Network and Computer Systems Admin.	44.98
Carpenters	35.45	Nurses, Licensed Practical	30.01
Cashiers	14.91	Nurses, Registered	40.99
Computer Programmers	43.54	Nursing Assistants	18.37
Computer Systems Analysts	49.11	Office Clerks, General	21.22
Computer User Support Specialists	29.52	Physical Therapists	48.81
Construction Laborers	32.85	Physicians	100.40
Cooks, Restaurant	17.06	Plumbers, Pipefitters and Steamfitters	43.17
Customer Service Representatives	21.26	Police and Sheriff's Patrol Officers	41.59
Dentists	67.54	Postal Service Mail Carriers	27.84
Electricians	42.79	Real Estate Sales Agents	21.56
Engineers, Electrical	50.03	Retail Salespersons	17.49
Fast Food and Counter Workers	14.28	Sales Representatives, Technical/Scientific	56.01
Financial Managers	78.05	Secretaries, Exc. Legal/Medical/Executive	23.34
First-Line Supervisors of Office Workers	33.78	Security Guards	17.98
General and Operations Managers	63.64	Surgeons	136.81
Hairdressers/Cosmetologists	21.49	Teacher Assistants, Exc. Postsecondary*	16.89
Home Health and Personal Care Aides	15.66	Teachers, Secondary School, Exc. Sp. Ed.*	37.13
Janitors and Cleaners	17.40	Telemarketers	15.52
Landscaping/Groundskeeping Workers	18.93	Truck Drivers, Heavy/Tractor-Trailer	27.99
Lawyers	78.47	Truck Drivers, Light/Delivery Services	24.27
Maids and Housekeeping Cleaners	17.07	Waiters and Waitresses	15.53

Note: Wage data covers the Chicago-Naperville-Elgin, IL-IN-WI Metropolitan Statistical Area; (*) Hourly wages were calculated from annual wage data based on a 40 hour work week; n/a not available.
Source: Bureau of Labor Statistics, Metro Area Occupational Employment & Wage Estimates, May 2022

Employment by Industry

Sector	MD[1]		U.S.
	Number of Employees	Percent of Total	Percent of Total
Construction	130,600	3.4	5.0
Private Education and Health Services	617,600	16.2	16.1
Financial Activities	273,800	7.2	5.9
Government	401,000	10.5	14.5
Information	73,600	1.9	2.0
Leisure and Hospitality	362,200	9.5	10.3
Manufacturing	276,300	7.3	8.4
Mining and Logging	1,200	<0.1	0.4
Other Services	156,400	4.1	3.7
Professional and Business Services	728,600	19.2	14.7
Retail Trade	338,300	8.9	10.2
Transportation, Warehousing, and Utilities	252,700	6.6	4.9
Wholesale Trade	192,000	5.0	3.9

Note: Figures are non-farm employment as of December 2022. Figures are not seasonally adjusted and include workers 16 years of age and older; (1) Figures cover the Chicago-Naperville-Evanston, IL Metropolitan Division
Source: Bureau of Labor Statistics, Current Employment Statistics, Employment, Hours, and Earnings

Employment by Occupation

Occupation Classification	City (%)	MSA[1] (%)	U.S. (%)
Management, Business, Science, and Arts	45.5	42.3	40.3
Natural Resources, Construction, and Maintenance	5.0	6.7	8.7
Production, Transportation, and Material Moving	12.1	13.9	13.1
Sales and Office	19.3	21.1	20.9
Service	18.1	16.0	17.0

Note: Figures cover employed civilians 16 years of age and older; (1) Figures cover the Chicago-Naperville-Elgin, IL-IN-WI Metropolitan Statistical Area
Source: U.S. Census Bureau, 2017-2021 American Community Survey 5-Year Estimates

Occupations with Greatest Projected Employment Growth: 2022 – 2024

Occupation[1]	2022 Employment	2024 Projected Employment	Numeric Employment Change	Percent Employment Change
Laborers and Freight, Stock, and Material Movers, Hand	197,270	205,510	8,240	4.2
Fast Food and Counter Workers	144,440	149,210	4,770	3.3
Cooks, Restaurant	42,630	46,710	4,080	9.6
Home Health and Personal Care Aides	100,160	104,050	3,890	3.9
Waiters and Waitresses	73,770	77,220	3,450	4.7
Heavy and Tractor-Trailer Truck Drivers	76,720	79,980	3,260	4.2
General and Operations Managers	126,240	129,310	3,070	2.4
Software Developers and Software Quality Assurance Analysts and Testers	67,670	70,440	2,770	4.1
Light Truck or Delivery Services Drivers	64,670	67,340	2,670	4.1
Stockers and Order Fillers	80,950	83,070	2,120	2.6

Note: Projections cover Illinois; (1) Sorted by numeric employment change
Source: www.projectionscentral.com, State Occupational Projections, 2022–2024 Short-Term Projections

Fastest-Growing Occupations: 2022 – 2024

Occupation[1]	2022 Employment	2024 Projected Employment	Numeric Employment Change	Percent Employment Change
Gaming Service Workers, All Other	150	220	70	46.7
Gaming Dealers	1,200	1,740	540	45.0
First-Line Supervisors of Gambling Services Workers	380	540	160	42.1
Gaming Change Persons and Booth Cashiers	340	480	140	41.2
Gaming Cage Workers	220	300	80	36.4
Hotel, Motel, and Resort Desk Clerks	6,430	7,520	1,090	17.0
Ushers, Lobby Attendants, and Ticket Takers	3,830	4,350	520	13.6
Lodging Managers	820	910	90	11.0
Baggage Porters and Bellhops	1,200	1,330	130	10.8
Cooks, Restaurant	42,630	46,710	4,080	9.6

Note: Projections cover Illinois; (1) Sorted by percent employment change and excludes occupations with numeric employment change less than 50
Source: www.projectionscentral.com, State Occupational Projections, 2022–2024 Short-Term Projections

CITY FINANCES

City Government Finances

Component	2020 ($000)	2020 ($ per capita)
Total Revenues	9,672,991	3,591
Total Expenditures	9,283,901	3,446
Debt Outstanding	27,453,234	10,191
Cash and Securities[1]	10,546,309	3,915

Note: (1) Cash and security holdings of a government at the close of its fiscal year, including those of its dependent agencies, utilities, and liquor stores.
Source: U.S. Census Bureau, State & Local Government Finances 2020

City Government Revenue by Source

Source	2020 ($000)	2020 ($ per capita)	2020 (%)
General Revenue			
From Federal Government	148,073	55	1.5
From State Government	1,146,225	425	11.8
From Local Governments	5,284	2	0.1
Taxes			
Property	1,278,091	474	13.2
Sales and Gross Receipts	2,192,812	814	22.7
Personal Income	0	0	0.0
Corporate Income	0	0	0.0
Motor Vehicle License	23,348	9	0.2
Other Taxes	373,268	139	3.9
Current Charges	2,281,673	847	23.6
Liquor Store	0	0	0.0
Utility	744,378	276	7.7

Source: U.S. Census Bureau, State & Local Government Finances 2020

City Government Expenditures by Function

Function	2020 ($000)	2020 ($ per capita)	2020 (%)
General Direct Expenditures			
Air Transportation	1,783,382	662	19.2
Corrections	0	0	0.0
Education	0	0	0.0
Employment Security Administration	0	0	0.0
Financial Administration	160,835	59	1.7
Fire Protection	611,180	226	6.6
General Public Buildings	241,318	89	2.6
Governmental Administration, Other	54,469	20	0.6
Health	137,684	51	1.5
Highways	579,618	215	6.2
Hospitals	0	0	0.0
Housing and Community Development	295,511	109	3.2
Interest on General Debt	981,096	364	10.6
Judicial and Legal	32,019	11	0.3
Libraries	107,996	40	1.2
Parking	7,724	2	0.1
Parks and Recreation	33,485	12	0.4
Police Protection	1,619,079	601	17.4
Public Welfare	363,451	134	3.9
Sewerage	227,947	84	2.5
Solid Waste Management	165,635	61	1.8
Veterans' Services	0	0	0.0
Liquor Store	0	0	0.0
Utility	612,305	227	6.6

Source: U.S. Census Bureau, State & Local Government Finances 2020

TAXES

State Corporate Income Tax Rates

State	Tax Rate (%)	Income Brackets ($)	Num. of Brackets	Financial Institution Tax Rate (%)[a]	Federal Income Tax Ded.
Illinois	9.5 (g)	Flat rate	1	9.5 (g)	No

Note: Tax rates as of January 1, 2023; (a) Rates listed are the corporate income tax rate applied to financial institutions or excise taxes based on income. Some states have other taxes based upon the value of deposits or shares; (g) The Illinois rate of 9.5% is the sum of a corporate income tax rate of 7.0% plus a replacement tax of 2.5%.
Source: Federation of Tax Administrators, State Corporate Income Tax Rates, January 1, 2023

State Individual Income Tax Rates

State	Tax Rate (%)	Income Brackets ($)	Personal Exemptions ($)			Standard Ded. ($)	
			Single	Married	Depend.	Single	Married
Illinois (a)	4.95	Flat rate	2,425	4,850	2,425	–	–

Note: Tax rates as of January 1, 2023; Local- and county-level taxes are not included; Federal income tax is not deductible on state income tax returns; (a) 16 states have statutory provision for automatically adjusting to the rate of inflation the dollar values of the income tax brackets, standard deductions, and/or personal exemptions. Oregon does not index the income brackets for $125,000 and over.
Source: Federation of Tax Administrators, State Individual Income Tax Rates, January 1, 2023

Various State Sales and Excise Tax Rates

State	State Sales Tax (%)	Gasoline[1] ($/gal.)	Cigarette[2] ($/pack)	Spirits[3] ($/gal.)	Wine[4] ($/gal.)	Beer[5] ($/gal.)	Recreational Marijuana (%)
Illinois	6.25	0.654	2.98	8.55	1.39	0.23	(f)

Note: All tax rates as of January 1, 2023; (1) The American Petroleum Institute has developed a methodology for determining the average tax rate on a gallon of fuel. Rates may include any of the following: excise taxes, environmental fees, storage tank fees, other fees or taxes, general sales tax, and local taxes; (2) The federal excise tax of $1.0066 per pack and local taxes are not included; (3) Rates are those applicable to off-premise sales of 40% alcohol by volume (a.b.v.) distilled spirits in 750ml containers. Local excise taxes are excluded; (4) Rates are those applicable to off-premise sales of 11% a.b.v. non-carbonated wine in 750ml containers; (5) Rates are those applicable to off-premise sales of 4.7% a.b.v. beer in 12 ounce containers; (f) 7% excise tax of value at wholesale level; 10% tax on cannabis flower or products with less than 35% THC; 20% tax on products infused with cannabis, such as edible products; 25% tax on any product with a THC concentration higher than 35%
Source: Tax Foundation, 2023 Facts & Figures: How Does Your State Compare?

State Business Tax Climate Index Rankings

State	Overall Rank	Corporate Tax Rank	Individual Income Tax Rank	Sales Tax Rank	Property Tax Rank	Unemployment Insurance Tax Rank
Illinois	36	38	13	38	44	43

Note: The index is a measure of how each state's tax laws affect economic performance. The lower the rank, the more favorable a state's tax system is for business. States without a given tax are given a ranking of 1. The scores/rankings for the District of Columbia do not affect other states. The 2023 index represents the tax climate as of July 1, 2022.
Source: Tax Foundation, State Business Tax Climate Index 2023

TRANSPORTATION

Means of Transportation to Work

Area	Car/Truck/Van		Public Transportation			Bicycle	Walked	Other Means	Worked at Home
	Drove Alone	Car-pooled	Bus	Subway	Railroad				
City	47.4	7.5	11.1	10.7	1.4	1.5	5.8	2.2	12.3
MSA[1]	66.7	7.6	3.7	3.6	2.6	0.6	2.8	1.5	10.9
U.S.	73.2	8.6	2.0	1.6	0.5	0.5	2.5	1.5	9.7

Note: Figures are percentages and cover workers 16 years of age and older; (1) Figures cover the Chicago-Naperville-Elgin, IL-IN-WI Metropolitan Statistical Area
Source: U.S. Census Bureau, 2017-2021 American Community Survey 5-Year Estimates

Travel Time to Work

Area	Less Than 10 Minutes	10 to 19 Minutes	20 to 29 Minutes	30 to 44 Minutes	45 to 59 Minutes	60 to 89 Minutes	90 Minutes or More
City	4.7	16.4	18.4	30.5	15.1	11.9	3.1
MSA[1]	8.5	21.9	19.0	25.3	12.2	10.0	3.1
U.S.	12.4	28.5	21.0	20.9	8.2	6.2	2.9

Note: Note: Figures are percentages and include workers 16 years old and over; (1) Figures cover the Chicago-Naperville-Elgin, IL-IN-WI Metropolitan Statistical Area
Source: U.S. Census Bureau, 2017-2021 American Community Survey 5-Year Estimates

Key Congestion Measures

Measure	1990	2000	2010	2015	2020
Annual Hours of Delay, Total (000)	134,309	221,112	280,745	315,669	172,876
Annual Hours of Delay, Per Auto Commuter	40	52	59	70	39
Annual Congestion Cost, Per Auto Commuter ($)	1,122	1,387	1,401	1,455	852

Note: Covers the Chicago IL-IN urban area
Source: Texas A&M Transportation Institute, 2021 Urban Mobility Report

Freeway Travel Time Index

Measure	1985	1990	1995	2000	2005	2010	2015	2020
Urban Area Index[1]	1.16	1.19	1.23	1.25	1.27	1.26	1.29	1.10
Urban Area Rank[1,2]	10	12	8	16	18	19	18	29

Note: Freeway Travel Time Index—the ratio of travel time in the peak period to the travel time at free-flow conditions. For example, a value of 1.30 indicates a 20-minute free-flow trip takes 26 minutes in the peak (20 minutes x 1.30 = 26 minutes); (1) Covers the Chicago IL-IN urban area; (2) Rank is based on 101 larger urban areas (#1 = highest travel time index)
Source: Texas A&M Transportation Institute, 2021 Urban Mobility Report

Public Transportation

Agency Name / Mode of Transportation	Vehicles Operated in Maximum Service[1]	Annual Unlinked Passenger Trips[2] (in thous.)	Annual Passenger Miles[3] (in thous.)
Chicago Transit Authority (CTA)			
Bus (directly operated)	1,525	117,357.5	296,815.6
Heavy Rail (directly operated)	1,160	78,623.0	501,767.8
Northeast Illinois Regional Commuter Railroad (Metra)			
Commuter Rail (directly operated)	422	6,194.1	133,021.3
Commuter Rail (purchased transportation)	396	7,886.7	171,968.1

Note: (1) Number of revenue vehicles operated by the given mode and type of service to meet the annual maximum service requirement. This is the revenue vehicle count during the peak season of the year; on the week and day that maximum service is provided. Vehicles operated in maximum service (VOMS) exclude atypical days and one-time special events; (2) Number of passengers who boarded public transportation vehicles. Passengers are counted each time they board a vehicle no matter how many vehicles they use to travel from their origin to their destination. (3) Sum of the distances ridden by all passengers during the entire fiscal year.
Source: Federal Transit Administration, National Transit Database, 2021

Air Transportation

Airport Name and Code / Type of Service	Passenger Airlines[1]	Passenger Enplanements	Freight Carriers[2]	Freight (lbs)
O'Hare International (ORD)				
Domestic service (U.S. carriers - 2022)	37	27,555,665	20	433,912,871
International service (U.S. carriers - 2021)	16	1,174,135	16	166,978,304
Midway International (MDW)				
Domestic service (U.S. carriers - 2022)	18	9,302,140	2	21,488,974
International service (U.S. carriers - 2021)	7	87,721	2	10,175

Note: (1) Includes all U.S.-based major, minor and commuter airlines that carried at least one passenger during the year; (2) Includes all U.S.-based airlines and freight carriers that transported at least one pound of freight during the year.
Source: Bureau of Transportation Statistics, The Intermodal Transportation Database, Air Carriers: T-100 Domestic Market (U.S. Carriers), 2022; Bureau of Transportation Statistics, The Intermodal Transportation Database, Air Carriers: T-100 International Market (U.S. Carriers), 2021

BUSINESSES

Major Business Headquarters

Company Name	Industry	Rankings Fortune[1]	Rankings Forbes[2]
Amsted Industries	Capital goods	-	157
Archer Daniels Midland	Food production	38	-
Berlin Packaging	Materials	-	214
Boeing	Aerospace and defense	60	-
Conagra Brands	Food consumer products	331	-
Echo Global Logistics	Transportation	-	147
Exelon	Utilities, gas and electric	99	-
Heico Cos	Capital goods	-	219
Jones Lang LaSalle	Real estate	185	-
Kirkland & Ellis	Services	-	84
LKQ	Wholesalers, diversified	283	-
Newly Weds Foods	Food, drink & tobacco	-	239
Northern Trust	Commercial banks	493	-
Old Republic International	Insurance, property and casualty (stock)	376	-
Sidley Austin	Services	-	197
United Airlines Holdings	Airlines	146	-
Walsh Group	Construction	-	97

Note: (1) Companies that produce a 10-K are ranked 1 to 500 based on 2021 revenue; (2) All private companies with at least $2 billion in annual revenue through the end of their most current fiscal year are ranked 1 to 246; companies listed are headquartered in the city; dashes indicate no ranking
Source: Fortune, "Fortune 500," 2022; Forbes, "America's Largest Private Companies," 2022

Fastest-Growing Businesses

According to *Inc.*, Chicago is home to 18 of America's 500 fastest-growing private companies: **CDL 1000** (#3); **TransLoop** (#12); **TheMathCompany** (#77); **Threekit** (#80); **CoinFlip** (#92); **QualSights** (#94); **Eve International Logistics** (#102); **Foxbox Digital** (#121); **M1** (#150); **Clearcover** (#151); **Songfinch** (#166); **Turn Technologies** (#169); **Petalura** (#233); **Lextegrity** (#295); **Amplify HR Management** (#313); **Kin Insurance** (#349); **Givenly** (#378); **Packed with Purpose** (#422). Criteria: must be an independent, privately-held, for-profit, U.S. corporation, proprietorship or partnership as of December 31, 2021; revenues must be at least $100,000 in 2018 and $2 million in 2021; must have four-year operating/sales history. *Inc., "America's 500 Fastest-Growing Private Companies," 2022*

According to *Initiative for a Competitive Inner City (ICIC)*, Chicago is home to six of America's 100 fastest-growing "inner city" companies: **Rudd Resources** (#7); **Transportation One** (#17); **Nova Driving School** (#43); **Paket Corporation** (#51); **Lasalle Network** (#59); **Laystrom Manufacturing** (#64). Criteria for inclusion: company must be headquartered in or have 51 percent or more of its physical operations in an economically distressed urban area; must be an independent, for-profit corporation, partnership or proprietorship; must have 10 or more employees and have a five-year sales history that includes sales of at least $200,000 in the base year and at least $1 million in the current year with no decrease in sales over the two most recent years. Companies were ranked overall by revenue growth over the five-year period between 2017 and 2021. *Initiative for a Competitive Inner City (ICIC), "Inner City 100 Companies," 2022*

According to Deloitte, Chicago is home to 10 of North America's 500 fastest-growing high-technology companies: **CoinFlip** (#36); **QualSights** (#37); **Clearcover** (#50); **Rush Street Interactive** (#68); **Copado** (#152); **LogicGate** (#171); **Loadsmart** (#214); **ShipBob** (#282); **XSELL Technologies** (#314); **G2** (#393). Companies are ranked by percentage growth in revenue over a four-year period. Criteria for inclusion: company must be headquartered within North America; must own proprietary intellectual property or technology that is sold to customers in products that contributes to a significant portion of the company's operating revenue; must have been in business for a minumum of four years with 2018 operating revenues of at least $50,000 USD/CD and 2021 operating revenues of at least $5 million USD/CD. *Deloitte, 2022 Technology Fast 500*™

Living Environment

COST OF LIVING

Cost of Living Index

Composite Index	Groceries	Housing	Utilities	Trans-portation	Health Care	Misc. Goods/ Services
n/a	n/a	n/a	n/a	n/a	n/a	n/a

Note: The Cost of Living Index measures regional differences in the cost of consumer goods and services, excluding taxes and non-consumer expenditures, for professional and managerial households in the top income quintile. It is based on more than 50,000 prices covering almost 60 different items for which prices are collected three times a year by chambers of commerce, economic development organizations or university applied economic centers in each participating urban area. The numbers shown should be read as a percentage above or below the national average of 100. For example, a value of 115.4 in the groceries column indicates that grocery prices are 15.4% higher than the national average. Small differences in the index numbers should not be interpreted as significant; n/a not available.
Source: The Council for Community and Economic Research, Cost of Living Index, 2022

Grocery Prices

Area[1]	T-Bone Steak ($/pound)	Frying Chicken ($/pound)	Whole Milk ($/half gal.)	Eggs ($/dozen)	Orange Juice ($/64 oz.)	Coffee ($/11.5 oz.)
City[2]	n/a	n/a	n/a	n/a	n/a	n/a
Avg.	13.81	1.59	2.43	2.25	3.85	4.95
Min.	10.17	0.90	1.51	1.30	2.90	3.46
Max.	19.35	3.30	4.32	4.32	5.31	8.59

*Note: (1) Values for the local area are compared with the average, minimum and maximum values for all 286 areas in the Cost of Living Index; (2) Figures cover the Chicago IL urban area; n/a not available; **T-Bone Steak** (price per pound); **Frying Chicken** (price per pound, whole fryer); **Whole Milk** (half gallon carton); **Eggs** (price per dozen, Grade A, large); **Orange Juice** (64 oz. Tropicana or Florida Natural); **Coffee** (11.5 oz. can, vacuum-packed, Maxwell House, Hills Bros, or Folgers).*
Source: The Council for Community and Economic Research, Cost of Living Index, 2022

Housing and Utility Costs

Area[1]	New Home Price ($)	Apartment Rent ($/month)	All Electric ($/month)	Part Electric ($/month)	Other Energy ($/month)	Telephone ($/month)
City[2]	n/a	n/a	n/a	n/a	n/a	n/a
Avg.	450,913	1,371	176.41	99.93	76.96	190.22
Min.	229,283	546	100.84	31.56	27.15	174.27
Max.	2,434,977	4,569	356.86	249.59	272.24	208.31

*Note: (1) Values for the local area are compared with the average, minimum and maximum values for all 286 areas in the Cost of Living Index; (2) Figures cover the Chicago IL urban area; n/a not available; **New Home Price** (2,400 sf living area, 8,000 sf lot, in urban area with full utilities); **Apartment Rent** (950 sf 2 bedroom/1.5 or 2 bath, unfurnished, excluding all utilities except water); **All Electric** (average monthly cost for an all-electric home); **Part Electric** (average monthly cost for a part-electric home); **Other Energy** (average monthly cost for natural gas, fuel oil, coal, wood, and any other forms of energy except electricity); **Telephone** (price includes the base monthly rate plus taxes and fees for three lines of mobile phone service).*
Source: The Council for Community and Economic Research, Cost of Living Index, 2022

Health Care, Transportation, and Other Costs

Area[1]	Doctor ($/visit)	Dentist ($/visit)	Optometrist ($/visit)	Gasoline ($/gallon)	Beauty Salon ($/visit)	Men's Shirt ($)
City[2]	n/a	n/a	n/a	n/a	n/a	n/a
Avg.	124.91	107.77	117.66	3.86	43.31	34.21
Min.	36.61	58.25	51.79	2.90	22.18	13.05
Max.	250.21	162.58	371.96	5.54	85.61	63.54

*Note: (1) Values for the local area are compared with the average, minimum and maximum values for all 286 areas in the Cost of Living Index; (2) Figures cover the Chicago IL urban area; n/a not available; **Doctor** (general practitioners routine exam of an established patient); **Dentist** (adult teeth cleaning and periodic oral examination); **Optometrist** (full vision eye exam for established adult patient); **Gasoline** (one gallon regular unleaded, national brand, including all taxes, cash price at self-service pump if available); **Beauty Salon** (woman's shampoo, trim, and blow-dry); **Men's Shirt** (cotton/polyester dress shirt, pinpoint weave, long sleeves).*
Source: The Council for Community and Economic Research, Cost of Living Index, 2022

HOUSING

Homeownership Rate

Area	2015 (%)	2016 (%)	2017 (%)	2018 (%)	2019 (%)	2020 (%)	2021 (%)	2022 (%)
MSA[1]	64.3	64.5	64.1	64.6	63.4	66.0	67.5	66.8
U.S.	63.7	63.4	63.9	64.4	64.6	66.6	65.5	65.8

Note: (1) Figures cover the Chicago-Naperville-Elgin, IL-IN-WI Metropolitan Statistical Area
Source: U.S. Census Bureau, Housing Vacancies and Homeownership Annual Statistics: 2015-2022

House Price Index (HPI)

Area	National Ranking[2]	Quarterly Change (%)	One-Year Change (%)	Five-Year Change (%)	Since 1991Q1 (%)
MD[1]	205	-1.86	8.51	31.58	168.46
U.S.[3]	–	0.34	8.41	58.44	289.08

Note: The HPI is a weighted repeat sales index. It measures average price changes in repeat sales or refinancings on the same properties. This information is obtained by reviewing repeat mortgage transactions on single-family properties whose mortgages have been purchased or securitized by Fannie Mae or Freddie Mac since January 1975; (1) Figures cover the Chicago-Naperville-Arlington Heights, IL Metropolitan Division; (2) Rankings are based on annual percentage change for all metro areas containing at least 15,000 transactions over the last 10 years and ranges from 1 to 257; (3) figures based on a weighted average of Census Division estimates using a seasonally adjusted, purchase-only index; all figures are for the period ending December 31, 2022
Source: Federal Housing Finance Agency, Change in FHFA Metropolitan Area House Price Indexes, 2022Q4

Median Single-Family Home Prices

Area	2020	2021	2022p	Percent Change 2021 to 2022
MSA[1]	287.6	330.4	345.6	4.6
U.S. Average	300.2	357.1	392.6	9.9

Note: Figures are median sales prices of existing single-family homes in thousands of dollars; (p) preliminary; (1) Figures cover the Chicago-Naperville-Elgin, IL-IN-WI Metropolitan Statistical Area
Source: National Association of Realtors, Median Sales Price of Existing Single-Family Homes for Metropolitan Areas, 4th Quarter 2022

Qualifying Income Based on Median Sales Price of Existing Single-Family Homes

Area	With 5% Down ($)	With 10% Down ($)	With 20% Down ($)
MSA[1]	96,696	91,607	81,428
U.S. Average	112,234	106,237	94,513

Note: Figures are preliminary; Qualifying income is based on a mortgage rate of 6.77%. Monthly principal and interest payment is limited to 25% of income; (1) Figures cover the Chicago-Naperville-Elgin, IL-IN-WI Metropolitan Statistical Area
Source: National Association of Realtors, Qualifying Income Based on Median Sales Price of Existing Single-Family Homes for Metropolitan Areas, 4th Quarter 2022

Home Value

Area	Under $100,000	$100,000 -$199,999	$200,000 -$299,999	$300,000 -$399,999	$400,000 -$499,999	$500,000 -$999,999	$1,000,000 or more	Median ($)
City	8.5	22.4	24.5	16.5	9.6	14.2	4.3	277,600
MSA[1]	8.6	25.3	26.7	17.5	8.5	10.9	2.5	258,500
U.S.	16.2	24.2	20.1	13.6	8.3	13.6	4.1	244,900

Note: Figures are percentages except for median and cover owner-occupied housing units; (1) Figures cover the Chicago-Naperville-Elgin, IL-IN-WI Metropolitan Statistical Area
Source: U.S. Census Bureau, 2017-2021 American Community Survey 5-Year Estimates

Year Housing Structure Built

Area	2020 or Later	2010 -2019	2000 -2009	1990 -1999	1980 -1989	1970 -1979	1960 -1969	1950 -1959	1940 -1949	Before 1940	Median Year
City	<0.1	3.8	8.0	5.1	4.8	7.7	9.6	11.8	8.8	40.3	1951
MSA[1]	0.1	3.6	11.4	11.2	9.1	14.1	11.5	12.7	5.9	20.5	1969
U.S.	0.2	7.3	13.6	13.6	13.2	14.8	10.3	10.0	4.7	12.2	1979

Note: Figures are percentages except for Median Year; Note: (1) Figures cover the Chicago-Naperville-Elgin, IL-IN-WI Metropolitan Statistical Area
Source: U.S. Census Bureau, 2017-2021 American Community Survey 5-Year Estimates

Gross Monthly Rent

Area	Under $500	$500 -$999	$1,000 -$1,499	$1,500 -$1,999	$2,000 -$2,499	$2,500 -$2,999	$3,000 and up	Median ($)
City	8.6	25.4	32.7	17.7	8.6	3.9	3.2	1,209
MSA[1]	6.9	25.3	36.0	18.6	7.6	2.9	2.5	1,209
U.S.	8.1	30.5	30.8	16.8	7.3	3.1	3.5	1,163

Note: Figures are percentages except for median; Gross rent is the contract rent plus the estimated average monthly cost of utilities (electricity, gas, and water and sewer) and fuels (oil, coal, kerosene, wood, etc.) if these are paid by the renter (or paid for the renter by someone else); (1) Figures cover the Chicago-Naperville-Elgin, IL-IN-WI Metropolitan Statistical Area
Source: U.S. Census Bureau, 2017-2021 American Community Survey 5-Year Estimates

HEALTH

Health Risk Factors

Category	MSA[1] (%)	U.S. (%)
Adults aged 18–64 who have any kind of health care coverage	91.9	90.9
Adults who reported being in good or better health	85.7	85.2
Adults who have been told they have high blood cholesterol	32.2	35.7
Adults who have been told they have high blood pressure	28.5	32.4
Adults who are current smokers	10.0	14.4
Adults who currently use e-cigarettes	5.4	6.7
Adults who currently use chewing tobacco, snuff, or snus	2.3	3.5
Adults who are heavy drinkers[2]	5.5	6.3
Adults who are binge drinkers[3]	15.7	15.4
Adults who are overweight (BMI 25.0 - 29.9)	34.6	34.4
Adults who are obese (BMI 30.0 - 99.8)	33.2	33.9
Adults who participated in any physical activities in the past month	74.7	76.3

Note: (1) Figures cover the Chicago-Naperville-Elgin, IL-IN-WI Metropolitan Statistical Area; (2) Heavy drinkers are classified as adult men having more than 14 drinks per week and adult women having more than 7 drinks per week; (3) Binge drinkers are classified as males having five or more drinks on one occasion or females having four or more drinks on one occasion
Source: Centers for Disease Control and Prevention, Behaviorial Risk Factor Surveillance System, SMART: Selected Metropolitan Area Risk Trends, 2021

Acute and Chronic Health Conditions

Category	MSA[1] (%)	U.S. (%)
Adults who have ever been told they had a heart attack	3.5	4.0
Adults who have ever been told they have angina or coronary heart disease	2.6	3.8
Adults who have ever been told they had a stroke	3.5	3.0
Adults who have ever been told they have asthma	12.9	14.9
Adults who have ever been told they have arthritis	20.3	25.8
Adults who have ever been told they have diabetes[2]	9.4	10.9
Adults who have ever been told they had skin cancer	4.7	6.6
Adults who have ever been told they had any other types of cancer	7.2	7.5
Adults who have ever been told they have COPD	4.8	6.1
Adults who have ever been told they have kidney disease	2.2	3.0
Adults who have ever been told they have a form of depression	15.8	20.5

Note: (1) Figures cover the Chicago-Naperville-Elgin, IL-IN-WI Metropolitan Statistical Area; (2) Figures do not include pregnancy-related, borderline, or pre-diabetes
Source: Centers for Disease Control and Prevention, Behaviorial Risk Factor Surveillance System, SMART: Selected Metropolitan Area Risk Trends, 2021

Health Screening and Vaccination Rates

Category	MSA[1] (%)	U.S. (%)
Adults who have ever been tested for HIV	31.2	34.9
Adults who have had their blood cholesterol checked within the last five years	86.7	85.2
Adults aged 65+ who have had flu shot within the past year	73.1	68.6
Adults aged 65+ who have ever had a pneumonia vaccination	68.7	71.0

Note: (1) Figures cover the Chicago-Naperville-Elgin, IL-IN-WI Metropolitan Statistical Area.
Source: Centers for Disease Control and Prevention, Behaviorial Risk Factor Surveillance System, SMART: Selected Metropolitan Area Risk Trends, 2021

Disability Status

Category	MSA[1] (%)	U.S. (%)
Adults who reported being deaf	7.2	7.2
Are you blind or have serious difficulty seeing, even when wearing glasses?	4.1	4.8
Are you limited in any way in any of your usual activities due to arthritis?	8.1	11.1
Do you have difficulty doing errands alone?	6.9	7.0
Do you have difficulty dressing or bathing?	4.1	3.6
Do you have serious difficulty concentrating/remembering/making decisions?	11.9	12.1
Do you have serious difficulty walking or climbing stairs?	14.7	12.8

Note: (1) Figures cover the Chicago-Naperville-Elgin, IL-IN-WI Metropolitan Statistical Area.
Source: Centers for Disease Control and Prevention, Behaviorial Risk Factor Surveillance System, SMART: Selected Metropolitan Area Risk Trends, 2021

Mortality Rates for the Top 10 Causes of Death in the U.S.

ICD-10[a] Sub-Chapter	ICD-10[a] Code	Crude Mortality Rate[1] per 100,000 population	
		County[2]	U.S.
Malignant neoplasms	C00-C97	172.3	182.6
Ischaemic heart diseases	I20-I25	92.0	113.1
Other forms of heart disease	I30-I51	77.0	64.4
Other degenerative diseases of the nervous system	G30-G31	37.0	51.0
Cerebrovascular diseases	I60-I69	50.9	47.8
Other external causes of accidental injury	W00-X59	47.3	46.4
Chronic lower respiratory diseases	J40-J47	28.5	45.7
Organic, including symptomatic, mental disorders	F01-F09	35.6	35.9
Hypertensive diseases	I10-I15	38.6	35.0
Diabetes mellitus	E10-E14	25.3	29.6

Note: (a) ICD-10 = International Classification of Diseases 10th Revision; (1) Crude mortality rates are a three-year average covering 2019-2021; (2) Figures cover Cook County.
Source: Centers for Disease Control and Prevention, National Center for Health Statistics. National Vital Statistics System, Mortality 2018-2021 on CDC WONDER Online Database

Mortality Rates for Selected Causes of Death

ICD-10[a] Sub-Chapter	ICD-10[a] Code	Crude Mortality Rate[1] per 100,000 population	
		County[2]	U.S.
Assault	X85-Y09	17.2	7.0
Diseases of the liver	K70-K76	14.3	19.8
Human immunodeficiency virus (HIV) disease	B20-B24	1.6	1.5
Influenza and pneumonia	J09-J18	16.3	14.7
Intentional self-harm	X60-X84	9.2	14.3
Malnutrition	E40-E46	3.9	4.3
Obesity and other hyperalimentation	E65-E68	2.4	3.0
Renal failure	N17-N19	19.4	15.7
Transport accidents	V01-V99	9.4	13.6
Viral hepatitis	B15-B19	0.7	1.2

Note: (a) ICD-10 = International Classification of Diseases 10th Revision; (1) Crude mortality rates are a three-year average covering 2019-2021; (2) Figures cover Cook County; Data are suppressed when the data meet the criteria for confidentiality constraints; Crude mortality rates are flagged as unreliable when the rate would be calculated with a numerator of 20 or less.
Source: Centers for Disease Control and Prevention, National Center for Health Statistics. National Vital Statistics System, Mortality 2018-2021 on CDC WONDER Online Database

Health Insurance Coverage

Area	With Health Insurance	With Private Health Insurance	With Public Health Insurance	Without Health Insurance	Population Under Age 19 Without Health Insurance
City	90.2	61.6	35.5	9.8	3.6
MSA[1]	92.4	70.5	31.6	7.6	3.3
U.S.	91.2	67.8	35.4	8.8	5.3

Note: Figures are percentages that cover the civilian noninstitutionalized population; (1) Figures cover the Chicago-Naperville-Elgin, IL-IN-WI Metropolitan Statistical Area
Source: U.S. Census Bureau, 2017-2021 American Community Survey 5-Year Estimates

Number of Medical Professionals

Area	MDs[3]	DOs[3,4]	Dentists	Podiatrists	Chiropractors	Optometrists
County[1] (number)	22,846	1,186	4,936	651	1,508	1,093
County[1] (rate[2])	434.1	22.5	95.4	12.6	29.2	21.1
U.S. (rate[2])	289.3	23.5	72.5	6.2	28.7	17.4

Note: Data as of 2021 unless noted; (1) Data covers Cook County; (2) Rate per 100,000 population; (3) Data as of 2020 and includes all active, non-federal physicians; (4) Doctor of Osteopathic Medicine
Source: U.S. Department of Health and Human Services, Health Resources and Services Administration, Bureau of Health Professions, Area Resource File (ARF) 2021-2022

Best Hospitals

According to *U.S. News,* the Chicago-Naperville-Evanston, IL metro area is home to 12 of the best hospitals in the U.S.: **Advocate Christ Medical Center** (2 adult specialties and 1 pediatric specialty); **Advocate Good Samaritan Hospital** (1 adult specialty); **Advocate Illinois Masonic Medical Center** (1 adult specialty); **Advocate Lutheran General Hospital** (1 adult specialty); **Loyola University Medical Center** (2 adult specialties); **Midwest Orthopaedics at Rush University Medical Center** (Honor Roll/10 adult specialties); **NorthShore University Health System-Metro Chicago** (2 adult specialties); **Northwest Community Hospital** (1 adult specialty); **Northwestern Medicine-Northwestern Memorial Hospital** (Honor Roll/10 adult specialties); **Rush University Medical Center** (Honor Roll/10 adult specialties); **Shirley Ryan AbilityLab (formerly Rehabilitation Institute of**

Chicago) (1 adult specialty); **University of Chicago Medical Center** (10 adult specialties and 4 pediatric specialties). The hospitals listed were nationally ranked in at least one of 15 adult or 10 pediatric specialties. The number of specialties shown cover the parent hospital. Only 164 U.S. hospitals performed well enough to be nationally ranked in one or more specialties. Twenty hospitals in the U.S. made the Honor Roll. The Best Hospitals Honor Roll takes both the national rankings and the procedure and condition ratings into account. Hospitals received points if they were nationally ranked in one of the 15 adult specialties—the higher they ranked, the more points they got—and how many ratings of "high performing" they earned in the 17 procedures and conditions. *U.S. News Online, "America's Best Hospitals 2022-23"*

According to *U.S. News,* the Chicago-Naperville-Evanston, IL metro area is home to three of the best children's hospitals in the U.S.: **Ann and Robert H. Lurie Children's Hospital-Prentice Women's Hospital** (9 pediatric specialties); **University of Chicago Comer Children's Hospital** (4 pediatric specialties); **Advocate Children's Hospital** (1 pediatric specialty). The hospitals listed were highly ranked in at least one of 10 pediatric specialties. Eighty-six children's hospitals in the U.S. were nationally ranked in at least one specialty. Hospitals received points for being ranked in a specialty, and the 10 hospitals with the most points across the 10 specialties make up the Honor Roll. *U.S. News Online, "America's Best Children's Hospitals 2022-23"*

EDUCATION

Public School District Statistics

District Name	Schls	Pupils	Pupil/ Teacher Ratio	Minority Pupils[1] (%)	LEP/ELL[2] (%)	IEP[3] (%)
City of Chicago SD 299	646	329,836	14.5	89.1	18.2	14.6

Note: Table includes school districts with 2,000 or more students; (1) Percentage of students that are not non-Hispanic white; (2) Percentage of students that are Limited English Proficient or English Language Learners (2018-19); (3) Percentage of students that have an Individualized Education Program (2019-20).
Source: U.S. Department of Education, National Center for Education Statistics, Common Core of Data, Local Education Agency (School District) Universe Survey: School Year 2021-2022

Best High Schools

According to *U.S. News,* Chicago is home to eight of the top 500 high schools in the U.S.: **Payton College Preparatory High School** (#5); **Northside College Preparatory High School** (#31); **Jones College Prep High School** (#51); **Young Magnet High School** (#67); **Lane Technical High School** (#84); **Brooks College Prep Academy High School** (#322); **Hancock College Preparatory High School** (#453); **Lindblom Math and Science Academy** (#489). Nearly 18,000 public, magnet and charter schools were ranked based on their performance on state assessments and how well they prepare students for college. *U.S. News & World Report, "Best High Schools 2022"*

Highest Level of Education

Area	Less than H.S.	H.S. Diploma	Some College, No Deg.	Associate Degree	Bachelor's Degree	Master's Degree	Prof. School Degree	Doctorate Degree
City	13.7	21.9	17.0	5.7	24.1	12.2	3.6	1.8
MSA[1]	10.5	23.4	19.0	7.3	23.8	11.6	2.8	1.5
U.S.	11.1	26.5	20.0	8.7	20.6	9.3	2.2	1.5

Note: Figures cover persons age 25 and over; (1) Figures cover the Chicago-Naperville-Elgin, IL-IN-WI Metropolitan Statistical Area
Source: U.S. Census Bureau, 2017-2021 American Community Survey 5-Year Estimates

Educational Attainment by Race

Area	High School Graduate or Higher (%)					Bachelor's Degree or Higher (%)				
	Total	White	Black	Asian	Hisp.[2]	Total	White	Black	Asian	Hisp.[2]
City	86.3	90.8	86.4	87.6	70.9	41.7	55.5	23.5	64.1	18.5
MSA[1]	89.5	92.9	88.7	91.1	70.5	39.7	44.4	24.5	66.5	16.8
U.S.	88.9	91.4	87.2	87.6	71.2	33.7	35.5	23.3	55.6	18.4

Note: Figures shown cover persons 25 years old and over; (1) Figures cover the Chicago-Naperville-Elgin, IL-IN-WI Metropolitan Statistical Area; (2) People of Hispanic origin can be of any race
Source: U.S. Census Bureau, 2017-2021 American Community Survey 5-Year Estimates

School Enrollment by Grade and Control

Area	Preschool (%)		Kindergarten (%)		Grades 1 - 4 (%)		Grades 5 - 8 (%)		Grades 9 - 12 (%)	
	Public	Private	Public	Private	Public	Private	Public	Private	Public	Private
City	54.2	45.8	80.2	19.8	82.7	17.3	84.1	15.9	86.0	14.0
MSA[1]	56.6	43.4	84.4	15.6	88.3	11.7	88.6	11.4	90.3	9.7
U.S.	58.8	41.2	86.3	13.7	88.3	11.7	88.6	11.4	89.4	10.6

Note: Figures shown cover persons 3 years old and over; (1) Figures cover the Chicago-Naperville-Elgin, IL-IN-WI Metropolitan Statistical Area
Source: U.S. Census Bureau, 2017-2021 American Community Survey 5-Year Estimates

Higher Education

Four-Year Colleges			Two-Year Colleges			Medical Schools[1]	Law Schools[2]	Voc/ Tech[3]
Public	Private Non-profit	Private For-profit	Public	Private Non-profit	Private For-profit			
9	58	8	22	1	9	7	7	65

Note: Figures cover institutions located within the Chicago-Naperville-Elgin, IL-IN-WI Metropolitan Statistical Area and include main campuses only; (1) includes schools accredited by the Liaison Committee on Medical Education and the American Osteopathic Association's Commission on Osteopathic College Accreditation; (2) includes ABA-accredited schools, schools with provisional ABA accreditation, and state accredited schools; (3) includes all schools with programs that are less than 2 years.
Source: National Center for Education Statistics, Integrated Postsecondary Education System (IPEDS), 2021-22; Wikipedia, List of Medical Schools in the United States, accessed April 10, 2023; Wikipedia, List of Law Schools in the United States, accessed April 10, 2023

According to *U.S. News & World Report,* the Chicago-Naperville-Evanston, IL metro division is home to one of the top 100 liberal arts colleges in the U.S.: **Wheaton College (IL)** (#63 tie). The indicators used to capture academic quality fall into a number of categories: assessment by administrators at peer institutions; retention of students; faculty resources; student selectivity; financial resources; alumni giving; high school counselor ratings of colleges; and graduation rate. *U.S. News & World Report, "America's Best Colleges 2023"*

EMPLOYERS

Major Employers

Company Name	Industry
Abbott Laboratories	Pharmaceutical preparations
Addus HomeCare Corporation	Home health care services
Advocate Lutheran General Hospital	General medical & surgical hospitals
BMO Bankcorp	National commercial banks
City of Chicago	Municipal government
Cook County Bureau of Health Services	Administration of public health programs
Graphic Packaging International	Folding boxboard
Loyola University Health System	General medical & surgical hospitals
Northshore University Healthsystem	General medical & surgical hospitals
Northwestern Memorial Hospital	General medical & surgical hospitals
SCC Holding Co.	Cups, plastics, except foam
Schneider Electric Holdings	Air transportation, scheduled
SOLO Cup Company	Cups, plastics, except foam
The Allstate Corporation	Fire, marine, & casualty insurance
The University of Chicago Medical Center	General medical & surgical hospitals
United Parcel Service	Package delivery services
United States Steel Corporation	Steel foundries
WM Recycle America	Material recovery

Note: Companies shown are located within the Chicago-Naperville-Elgin, IL-IN-WI Metropolitan Statistical Area.
Source: Hoovers.com; Wikipedia

Best Companies to Work For

Crowe; Hyatt Hotels Corporation; RSM US, headquartered in Chicago, are among "The 100 Best Companies to Work For." To pick the best companies, *Fortune* partnered with the Great Place to Work Institute. Two-thirds of a company's score is based on the results of the Institute's Trust Index survey, which is sent to a random sample of employees from each company. The questions related to attitudes about management's credibility, job satisfaction, and camaraderie. The other third of the scoring is based on the company's responses to the Institute's Culture Audit, which includes detailed questions about pay and benefit programs, and a series of open-ended questions about hiring practices, internal communication, training, recognition programs, and diversity efforts. Any company that is at least five years old with more than 1,000 U.S. employees is eligible. *Fortune, "The 100 Best Companies to Work For," 2023*

Baker Tilly US; Basis Technologies; Hyatt Hotels Corporation; RSM US; West Monroe Partners, headquartered in Chicago, are among "Fortune's Best Workplaces for Women." To pick the best companies, *Fortune* partnered with the Great Place to Work Institute. To be considered for the list, companies must be Great Place To Work-Certified. Companies must also employ at least 50 women, at least 20% of their non-executive managers must be female, and at least one executive must be female. To determine the Best Workplaces for Women, Great Place To Work measured the differences in women's survey responses to those of their peers and assesses the impact of demographics and roles on the quality and consistency of women's experiences. Great Place To Work also analyzed the gender balance of each workplace, how it compared to each company's industry, and patterns in representation as women rise from front-line positions to the board of directors. *Fortune, "Best Workplaces for Women," 2022*

Q-Centrix, headquartered in Chicago, is among "Best Workplaces in Health Care." To determine the Best Workplaces in Health Care list, Great Place To Work analyzed the survey responses of over

161,000 employees from Great Place To Work-Certified companies in the health care industry. Survey data analysis and company-provided datapoints are then factored into a combined score to compare and rank the companies that create the most consistently positive experience for all employees in this industry. *Fortune, "Best Workplaces in Health Care," 2022*

Baker Tilly US; RSM US; Sprout Social; West Monroe Partners, headquartered in Chicago, are among "Fortune's Best Workplaces for Parents." To pick the best companies, *Fortune* partnered with the Great Place to Work Institute. To be considered for the list, companies must be Great Place To Work-Certified and have at least 50 responses from parents in the US. The survey enables employees to share confidential quantitative and qualitative feedback about their organization's culture by responding to 60 statements on a 5-point scale and answering two open-ended questions. Collectively, these statements describe a great employee experience, defined by high levels of trust, respect, credibility, fairness, pride, and camaraderie. In addition, companies provide organizational data like size, location, industry, demographics, roles, and levels; and provide information about parental leave, adoption, flexible schedule, childcare and dependent health care benefits. *Fortune, "Best Workplaces for Parents," 2022*

ADM; CME Group; Enova; Health Care Service Corporation (HCSC); Nitel, headquartered in Chicago, are among the "100 Best Places to Work in IT." To qualify, companies had to have a minimum of 100 total employees and five IT employees. The best places to work were selected based on DEI (diversity, equity, and inclusion) practices; IT turnover, promotions, and growth; IT retention and engagement programs; remote/hybrid working; benefits and perks (such as elder care and child care, flextime, and reimbursement for college tuition); and training and career development opportunities. *Computerworld, "Best Places to Work in IT," 2023*

PUBLIC SAFETY

Crime Rate

Area	Total Crime	Violent Crime Rate				Property Crime Rate		
		Murder	Rape[3]	Robbery	Aggrav. Assault	Burglary	Larceny -Theft	Motor Vehicle Theft
City	n/a	28.6	50.0	292.1	616.2	320.9	n/a	373.2
Suburbs[1]	n/a	n/a	n/a	n/a	n/a	n/a	n/a	n/a
Metro[2]	n/a	n/a	n/a	n/a	n/a	n/a	n/a	n/a
U.S.	2,356.7	6.5	38.4	73.9	279.7	314.2	1,398.0	246.0

Note: Figures are crimes per 100,000 population; (1) All areas within the metro area that are located outside the city limits; (2) Figures cover the Chicago-Naperville-Arlington Heights, IL Metropolitan Division; n/a not available; (3) All figures shown were reported using the revised Uniform Crime Reporting (UCR) definition of rape; Due to the transition to the National Incident-Based Reporting System (NIBRS), limited city and metro area data was released for 2021.
Source: FBI Uniform Crime Reports, 2020

Hate Crimes

Area	Number of Quarters Reported	Number of Incidents per Bias Motivation					
		Race/Ethnicity/ Ancestry	Religion	Sexual Orientation	Disability	Gender	Gender Identity
City	4	9	3	7	0	0	2
U.S.	4	5,227	1,244	1,110	130	75	266

Note: Due to the transition to the National Incident-Based Reporting System (NIBRS), limited crime data was released for 2021.
Source: Federal Bureau of Investigation, Hate Crime Statistics 2020

Identity Theft Consumer Reports

Area	Reports	Reports per 100,000 Population	Rank[2]
MSA[1]	37,048	391	34
U.S.	1,108,609	339	-

Note: (1) Figures cover the Chicago-Naperville-Elgin, IL-IN-WI Metropolitan Statistical Area; (2) Rank ranges from 1 to 391 where 1 indicates greatest number of identity theft reports per 100,000 population
Source: Federal Trade Commission, Consumer Sentinel Network Data Book 2022

Fraud and Other Consumer Reports

Area	Reports	Reports per 100,000 Population	Rank[2]
MSA[1]	106,139	1,120	60
U.S.	4,064,520	1,245	-

Note: (1) Figures cover the Chicago-Naperville-Elgin, IL-IN-WI Metropolitan Statistical Area; (2) Rank ranges from 1 to 391 where 1 indicates greatest number of fraud and other consumer reports per 100,000 population
Source: Federal Trade Commission, Consumer Sentinel Network Data Book 2022

POLITICS

2020 Presidential Election Results

Area	Biden	Trump	Jorgensen	Hawkins	Other
Cook County	74.2	24.0	0.8	0.5	0.5
U.S.	51.3	46.8	1.2	0.3	0.5

Note: Results are percentages and may not add to 100% due to rounding
Source: Dave Leip's Atlas of U.S. Presidential Elections

SPORTS

Professional Sports Teams

Team Name	League	Year Established
Chicago Bears	National Football League (NFL)	1921
Chicago Blackhawks	National Hockey League (NHL)	1926
Chicago Bulls	National Basketball Association (NBA)	1966
Chicago Cubs	Major League Baseball (MLB)	1874
Chicago Fire	Major League Soccer (MLS)	1997
Chicago White Sox	Major League Baseball (MLB)	1900

Note: Includes teams located in the Chicago-Naperville-Elgin, IL-IN-WI Metropolitan Statistical Area.
Source: Wikipedia, Major Professional Sports Teams of the United States and Canada, April 12, 2023

CLIMATE

Average and Extreme Temperatures

Temperature	Jan	Feb	Mar	Apr	May	Jun	Jul	Aug	Sep	Oct	Nov	Dec	Yr.
Extreme High (°F)	65	71	88	91	93	104	102	100	99	91	78	71	104
Average High (°F)	29	33	45	59	70	79	84	82	75	63	48	34	59
Average Temp. (°F)	21	26	37	49	59	69	73	72	65	53	40	27	49
Average Low (°F)	13	17	28	39	48	57	63	62	54	42	32	19	40
Extreme Low (°F)	-27	-17	-8	7	24	36	40	41	28	17	1	-25	-27

Note: Figures cover the years 1958-1990
Source: National Climatic Data Center, International Station Meteorological Climate Summary, 9/96

Average Precipitation/Snowfall/Humidity

Precip./Humidity	Jan	Feb	Mar	Apr	May	Jun	Jul	Aug	Sep	Oct	Nov	Dec	Yr.
Avg. Precip. (in.)	1.6	1.4	2.7	3.6	3.3	3.7	3.7	4.1	3.7	2.4	2.8	2.3	35.4
Avg. Snowfall (in.)	11	8	7	2	Tr	0	0	0	0	1	2	9	39
Avg. Rel. Hum. 6am (%)	76	77	79	77	77	78	82	85	85	82	80	80	80
Avg. Rel. Hum. 3pm (%)	65	63	59	53	51	52	54	55	55	53	61	68	57

Note: Figures cover the years 1958-1990; Tr = Trace amounts (<0.05 in. of rain; <0.5 in. of snow)
Source: National Climatic Data Center, International Station Meteorological Climate Summary, 9/96

Weather Conditions

Temperature			Daytime Sky			Precipitation		
5°F & below	32°F & below	90°F & above	Clear	Partly cloudy	Cloudy	0.01 inch or more precip.	0.1 inch or more snow/ice	Thunder-storms
21	132	17	84	135	146	125	31	38

Note: Figures are average number of days per year and cover the years 1958-1990
Source: National Climatic Data Center, International Station Meteorological Climate Summary, 9/96

HAZARDOUS WASTE

Superfund Sites

The Chicago-Naperville-Evanston, IL metro division has no sites on the EPA's Superfund Final National Priorities List. There are a total of 1,165 Superfund sites with a status of proposed or final on the list in the U.S. *U.S. Environmental Protection Agency, National Priorities List, April 12, 2023*

AIR QUALITY

Air Quality Trends: Ozone

	1990	1995	2000	2005	2010	2015	2018	2019	2020	2021
MSA[1]	0.074	0.094	0.073	0.084	0.070	0.066	0.073	0.069	0.076	0.071
U.S.	0.087	0.089	0.081	0.080	0.072	0.067	0.069	0.065	0.065	0.067

Note: (1) Data covers the Chicago-Naperville-Elgin, IL-IN-WI Metropolitan Statistical Area. The values shown are the composite ozone concentration averages among trend sites based on the highest fourth daily maximum 8-hour concentration in parts per million. These trends are based on sites having an adequate record of monitoring data during the trend period. Data from exceptional events are included.
Source: U.S. Environmental Protection Agency, Air Quality Monitoring Information, "Air Quality Trends by City, 1990-2021"

Air Quality Index

Area	Percent of Days when Air Quality was...[2]					AQI Statistics[2]	
	Good	Moderate	Unhealthy for Sensitive Groups	Unhealthy	Very Unhealthy	Maximum	Median
MSA[1]	34.2	58.1	7.1	0.5	0.0	169	58

Note: (1) Data covers the Chicago-Naperville-Elgin, IL-IN-WI Metropolitan Statistical Area; (2) Based on 365 days with AQI data in 2021. Air Quality Index (AQI) is an index for reporting daily air quality. EPA calculates the AQI for five major air pollutants regulated by the Clean Air Act: ground-level ozone, particle pollution (aka particulate matter), carbon monoxide, sulfur dioxide, and nitrogen dioxide. The AQI runs from 0 to 500. The higher the AQI value, the greater the level of air pollution and the greater the health concern. There are six AQI categories: "Good" AQI is between 0 and 50. Air quality is considered satisfactory; "Moderate" AQI is between 51 and 100. Air quality is acceptable; "Unhealthy for Sensitive Groups" When AQI values are between 101 and 150, members of sensitive groups may experience health effects; "Unhealthy" When AQI values are between 151 and 200 everyone may begin to experience health effects; "Very Unhealthy" AQI values between 201 and 300 trigger a health alert; "Hazardous" AQI values over 300 trigger warnings of emergency conditions (not shown).
Source: U.S. Environmental Protection Agency, Air Quality Index Report, 2021

Air Quality Index Pollutants

Area	Percent of Days when AQI Pollutant was...[2]					
	Carbon Monoxide	Nitrogen Dioxide	Ozone	Sulfur Dioxide	Particulate Matter 2.5	Particulate Matter 10
MSA[1]	0.0	4.9	34.2	(3)	51.0	9.9

Note: (1) Data covers the Chicago-Naperville-Elgin, IL-IN-WI Metropolitan Statistical Area; (2) Based on 365 days with AQI data in 2021. The Air Quality Index (AQI) is an index for reporting daily air quality. EPA calculates the AQI for five major air pollutants regulated by the Clean Air Act: ground-level ozone, particle pollution (also known as particulate matter), carbon monoxide, sulfur dioxide, and nitrogen dioxide. The AQI runs from 0 to 500. The higher the AQI value, the greater the level of air pollution and the greater the health concern; (3) Sulfur dioxide is no longer included in this table (as of December 8, 2021) because SO_2 concentrations tend to be very localized and not necessarily representative of broad geographical areas like counties and CBSAs.
Source: U.S. Environmental Protection Agency, Air Quality Index Report, 2021

Maximum Air Pollutant Concentrations: Particulate Matter, Ozone, CO and Lead

	Particulate Matter 10 (ug/m³)	Particulate Matter 2.5 Wtd AM (ug/m³)	Particulate Matter 2.5 24-Hr (ug/m³)	Ozone (ppm)	Carbon Monoxide (ppm)	Lead (ug/m³)
MSA[1] Level	166	10.8	27	0.079	1	0.03
NAAQS[2]	150	15	35	0.075	9	0.15
Met NAAQS[2]	No	Yes	Yes	No	Yes	Yes

Note: (1) Data covers the Chicago-Naperville-Elgin, IL-IN-WI Metropolitan Statistical Area; Data from exceptional events are included; (2) National Ambient Air Quality Standards; ppm = parts per million; ug/m³ = micrograms per cubic meter; n/a not available.
Concentrations: Particulate Matter 10 (coarse particulate)—highest second maximum 24-hour concentration; Particulate Matter 2.5 Wtd AM (fine particulate)—highest weighted annual mean concentration; Particulate Matter 2.5 24-Hour (fine particulate)—highest 98th percentile 24-hour concentration; Ozone—highest fourth daily maximum 8-hour concentration; Carbon Monoxide—highest second maximum non-overlapping 8-hour concentration; Lead—maximum running 3-month average
Source: U.S. Environmental Protection Agency, Air Quality Monitoring Information, "Air Quality Statistics by City, 2021"

Maximum Air Pollutant Concentrations: Nitrogen Dioxide and Sulfur Dioxide

	Nitrogen Dioxide AM (ppb)	Nitrogen Dioxide 1-Hr (ppb)	Sulfur Dioxide AM (ppb)	Sulfur Dioxide 1-Hr (ppb)	Sulfur Dioxide 24-Hr (ppb)
MSA[1] Level	17	54	n/a	73	n/a
NAAQS[2]	53	100	30	75	140
Met NAAQS[2]	Yes	Yes	n/a	Yes	n/a

Note: (1) Data covers the Chicago-Naperville-Elgin, IL-IN-WI Metropolitan Statistical Area; Data from exceptional events are included; (2) National Ambient Air Quality Standards; ppm = parts per million; ug/m³ = micrograms per cubic meter; n/a not available.
Concentrations: Nitrogen Dioxide AM—highest arithmetic mean concentration; Nitrogen Dioxide 1-Hr—highest 98th percentile 1-hour daily maximum concentration; Sulfur Dioxide AM—highest annual mean concentration; Sulfur Dioxide 1-Hr—highest 99th percentile 1-hour daily maximum concentration; Sulfur Dioxide 24-Hr—highest second maximum 24-hour concentration
Source: U.S. Environmental Protection Agency, Air Quality Monitoring Information, "Air Quality Statistics by City, 2021"

Columbia, Missouri

Background

In the middle of the state, along its namesake river, Columbia is a college town teeming with bright young minds and technological breakthroughs.

The city, located in Boone County, has ridden out the economic downturn with less trauma than the rest of Missouri. Recent surveys give the city high marks in general and for retirees.

The founding of its colleges and university dovetails with the growth and founding of the city itself. A settlement called Smithton grew from the Smithton Land Company's 2,000-acre land purchase on the other side of Flat Branch, not far from where Lewis and Clark travelled during their 1803 explorations. In 1821 the settlement moved across the river and Columbia was established. Daniel Boone and sons ran a salt lick about forty miles away.

Six counties competed for the right to host Missouri's university when it was founded in 1838, the first public university west of the Mississippi River. Boone County responded by raising more than $118,000 in land, cash, and buildings. It was forced to repeat its largess decades later, when the academic hall burned down and talk turned to moving the university. The city responded by raising $50,000 to build Jesse Hall, now a local landmark.

Two other institutions of higher learning contributed to Columbia's focus on education. Stephens College, a private women's college, was founded in 1833, and Columbia College was founded as the Christian Female College in 1851, now with 30,000 students. This school was the first women's college west of the Mississippi chartered by a state legislature; it became co-ed in 1970.

Although these three institutions help to define the historic downtown area, it is the state's massive flagship university—with a rare combination of law school, medical school, and veterinary school all on the same campus—that is Boone County's largest employer. As a major research institution, "Mizzou" conducts nearly $400 million in research and houses a nuclear research reactor on campus. It is the nation's largest supplier of radioisotopes for diagnosing and treating cancer and hosts interdisciplinary research in a range of scientific enterprises: biofuels, energy logistics, energy policy, wind, biomass, and solar. The licensing of products invented by MU products by various companies is a huge market.

The MU Life Science Business Incubator, which opened in 2008, encourages and supports business based on these technologies. The Indian pharma company Shasun collaborated to create a cancer treatment, Shasun-NBI. Also in the city is Discovery Ridge, with other research centers under development.

The campus also houses a well-regarded journalism school and IRE, Investigative Reporters and Editors, Inc. The 1,250-acre campus is also home to a botanic garden and several cultural opportunities enjoyed by the community at large including the Missouri Theatre Center for the Arts, Jesse Auditorium, and the university's Museum of Art and Architecture. The State Historical Society of Missouri also operates a research center at the university.

The county's other large employers include University Hospital and Clinics, Columbia Public Schools, Boone Hospital Center, the City of Columbia, and the U.S. Dept. of Veterans Affairs.

The city operates a regional airport, a short line railroad, and utilities for both water and electricity. Its Office of Cultural Affairs distributes art guides and a cultural newsletter, funds local arts organizations, and supports local arts opportunities. Columbia's "percent for art" program allows one percent of the cost of new city construction or renovation to be used for site-specific public art. The town is also full of galleries and various arts organizations.

Columbia has four distinct seasons, with highs in the upper 80s in July and August, lows below 20 degrees in January, and rainfall peaking in May.

Rankings

General Rankings

- In their ninth annual survey, Livability.com looked at data for more than 2,300 mid-sized U.S. cities to determine the rankings for Livability's "Top 100 Best Places to Live" in 2022. Columbia ranked #97. Criteria: housing and economy; social and civic engagement; education; demographics; health care options; transportation & infrastructure; and community amenities. *Livability.com, "Top 100 Best Places to Live 2022" July 19, 2022*

Business/Finance Rankings

- The Columbia metro area appeared on the Milken Institute "2022 Best Performing Cities" list. Rank: #30 out of 201 small metro areas (population over 60,000). Criteria: job growth; wage and salary growth; high-tech output growth; housing affordability; household broadband access. *Milken Institute, "Best-Performing Cities 2022," March 28, 2022*

- *Forbes* ranked 203 smaller metro areas (population under 268,000) to determine the nation's "Best Small Places for Business and Careers." The Columbia metro area was ranked #43. Criteria: costs (business and living); job growth (past and projected); income growth; quality of life; educational attainment (college and high school); projected economic growth; cultural and leisure opportunities; workplace tolerance laws; net migration patterns. *Forbes, "The Best Small Places for Business and Careers 2019," October 30, 2019*

Dating/Romance Rankings

- Columbia was selected as one of the most romantic cities in the U.S. by video-rental kiosk company Redbox. The city ranked #6 out of 20. Criteria: number of romance-related rentals in 2016. *Redbox, "20 Most Romantic Cities," February 6, 2017*

Environmental Rankings

- Columbia was highlighted as one of the cleanest metro areas for ozone air pollution in the U.S. during 2019 through 2021. The list represents cities with no monitored ozone air pollution in unhealthful ranges. *American Lung Association, "State of the Air 2023," April 19, 2023*

Safety Rankings

- The National Insurance Crime Bureau ranked 390 metro areas in the U.S. in terms of per capita rates of vehicle theft. The Columbia metro area ranked #140 (#1 = highest rate). Criteria: number of vehicle theft offenses per 100,000 inhabitants in 2021. *National Insurance Crime Bureau, "Hot Spots 2021," September 1, 2022*

Seniors/Retirement Rankings

- From its Best Cities for Successful Aging indexes, the Milken Institute generated rankings for metropolitan areas, weighing data in nine categories—health care, wellness, living arrangements, transportation and convenience, financial characteristics, education, employment, community engagement, and overall livability. The Columbia metro area was ranked #4 overall in the small metro area category. *Milken Institute, "Best Cities for Successful Aging, 2017" March 14, 2017*

- Columbia made the 2022 *Forbes* list of "25 Best Places to Retire." Criteria, focused on overall affordability as well as quality of life indicators, include: housing/living costs compared to the national average and state taxes; air quality; crime rates; home price appreciation; risk associated with climate-change/natural hazards; availability of medical care; bikeability; walkability; healthy living. *Forbes.com, "The Best Places to Retire in 2022," May 13, 2022*

Sports/Recreation Rankings

- Columbia was chosen as one of America's best cities for bicycling. The city ranked #46 out of 50. Criteria: cycling infrastructure that is safe and friendly for all ages; energy and bike culture. The editors evaluated cities with populations of 100,000 or more. *Bicycling, "The 50 Best Bike Cities in America," October 10, 2018*

Miscellaneous Rankings

- Columbia was selected as a 2022 Digital Cities Survey winner. The city ranked #6 in the small city (75,000 to 124,999 population) category. The survey examined and assessed how city governments are utilizing technology to continue innovation, engage with residents, and persevere through the challenges of the pandemic. Survey questions focused on ten initiatives: cybersecurity; citizen experience; disaster recovery; business intelligence; IT personnel; data governance; business automation; IT governance; infrastructure modernization; and broadband connectivity. *Center for Digital Government, "2022 Digital Cities Survey," November 10, 2022*

Business Environment

DEMOGRAPHICS

Population Growth

Area	1990 Census	2000 Census	2010 Census	2020 Census	Population Growth (%)	
					1990-2020	2010-2020
City	71,069	84,531	108,500	126,254	77.6	16.4
MSA[1]	122,010	145,666	172,786	210,864	72.8	22.0
U.S.	248,709,873	281,421,906	308,745,538	331,449,281	33.3	7.4

Note: (1) Figures cover the Columbia, MO Metropolitan Statistical Area
Source: U.S. Census Bureau, 1990 Census, 2000 Census, 2010 Census, 2020 Census

Race

Area	White Alone[2] (%)	Black Alone[2] (%)	Asian Alone[2] (%)	AIAN[3] Alone[2] (%)	NHOPI[4] Alone[2] (%)	Other Race Alone[2] (%)	Two or More Races (%)
City	72.5	11.9	5.6	0.3	0.1	2.2	7.4
MSA[1]	77.7	9.3	3.8	0.3	0.1	1.8	7.1
U.S.	61.6	12.4	6.0	1.1	0.2	8.4	10.2

Note: (1) Figures cover the Columbia, MO Metropolitan Statistical Area; (2) Alone is defined as not being in combination with one or more other races; (3) American Indian and Alaska Native; (4) Native Hawaiian and Other Pacific Islander
Source: U.S. Census Bureau, 2020 Census

Hispanic or Latino Origin

Area	Total (%)	Mexican (%)	Puerto Rican (%)	Cuban (%)	Other (%)
City	3.7	2.1	0.3	0.0	1.2
MSA[1]	3.4	2.1	0.2	0.1	1.0
U.S.	18.4	11.2	1.8	0.7	4.7

Note: Persons of Hispanic or Latino origin can be of any race; (1) Figures cover the Columbia, MO Metropolitan Statistical Area
Source: U.S. Census Bureau, 2017-2021 American Community Survey 5-Year Estimates

Age

Area	Percent of Population									Median Age
	Under Age 5	Age 5–19	Age 20–34	Age 35–44	Age 45–54	Age 55–64	Age 65–74	Age 75–84	Age 85+	
City	5.5	20.5	32.8	11.4	9.1	8.9	7.0	3.3	1.5	29.2
MSA[1]	5.7	20.6	26.7	12.0	10.2	10.9	8.4	3.9	1.5	32.8
U.S.	5.6	19.2	20.2	12.7	12.4	13.1	10.0	4.9	1.9	38.8

Note: (1) Figures cover the Columbia, MO Metropolitan Statistical Area
Source: U.S. Census Bureau, 2020 Census

Disability by Age

Area	All Ages	Under 18 Years Old	18 to 64 Years Old	65 Years and Over
City	11.4	4.6	9.8	33.9
MSA[1]	12.8	4.9	11.1	33.8
U.S.	12.6	4.4	10.3	33.4

Note: Figures show percent of the civilian noninstitutionalized population that reported having a disability. Disability status is determined from six types of difficulty: vision, hearing, cognitive, ambulatory, self-care, and independent living. For children under 5 years old, hearing and vision difficulty are used to determine disability status. For children between the ages of 5 and 14, disability status is determined from hearing, vision, cognitive, ambulatory, and self-care difficulties. For people aged 15 years and older, they are considered to have a disability if they have difficulty with any one of the six difficulty types; Note: (1) Figures cover the Columbia, MO Metropolitan Statistical Area
Source: U.S. Census Bureau, 2017-2021 American Community Survey 5-Year Estimates

Ancestry

Area	German	Irish	English	American	Italian	Polish	French[2]	Scottish	Dutch
City	24.6	12.0	11.0	4.4	3.6	2.2	1.9	2.3	1.2
MSA[1]	25.0	11.7	11.6	6.2	2.9	1.7	2.1	2.1	1.3
U.S.	12.8	9.6	8.1	5.7	5.0	2.7	2.2	1.6	1.1

Note: Figures are the percentage of the total population reporting a particular ancestry. The nine most commonly reported ancestries in the U.S. are shown. Figures include multiple ancestries (e.g. if a person reported being Irish and Italian, they were included in both columns); (1) Figures cover the Columbia, MO Metropolitan Statistical Area; (2) Excludes Basque
Source: U.S. Census Bureau, 2017-2021 American Community Survey 5-Year Estimates

Foreign-born Population

Area	Percent of Population Born in								
	Any Foreign Country	Asia	Mexico	Europe	Caribbean	Central America[2]	South America	Africa	Canada
City	8.4	5.1	0.6	0.9	0.1	0.2	0.3	1.0	0.1
MSA[1]	5.7	3.3	0.5	0.7	0.1	0.2	0.2	0.7	0.1
U.S.	13.6	4.2	3.3	1.5	1.4	1.1	1.1	0.8	0.2

Note: (1) Figures cover the Columbia, MO Metropolitan Statistical Area; (2) Excludes Mexico.
Source: U.S. Census Bureau, 2017-2021 American Community Survey 5-Year Estimates

Household Size

Area	Persons in Household (%)							Average Household Size
	One	Two	Three	Four	Five	Six	Seven or More	
City	35.7	31.8	13.7	11.1	5.7	1.2	0.8	2.30
MSA[1]	31.5	35.2	13.8	11.9	5.3	1.4	0.9	2.40
U.S.	28.1	33.8	15.5	12.9	6.0	2.3	1.4	2.60

Note: (1) Figures cover the Columbia, MO Metropolitan Statistical Area
Source: U.S. Census Bureau, 2017-2021 American Community Survey 5-Year Estimates

Household Relationships

Area	House-holder	Opposite-sex Spouse	Same-sex Spouse	Opposite-sex Unmarried Partner	Same-sex Unmarried Partner	Child[2]	Grand-child	Other Relatives	Non-relatives
City	40.5	14.1	0.2	2.8	0.2	22.4	1.0	2.5	7.8
MSA[1]	39.8	16.5	0.2	2.8	0.2	24.9	1.4	2.5	5.7
U.S.	38.3	17.5	0.2	2.5	0.2	28.3	2.4	4.8	3.4

Note: Figures are percent of the total population; (1) Figures cover the Columbia, MO Metropolitan Statistical Area; (2) Includes biological, adopted, and stepchildren of the householder
Source: U.S. Census Bureau, 2020 Census

Gender

Area	Males	Females	Males per 100 Females
City	60,766	65,488	92.8
MSA[1]	102,929	107,935	95.4
U.S.	162,685,811	168,763,470	96.4

Note: (1) Figures cover the Columbia, MO Metropolitan Statistical Area
Source: U.S. Census Bureau, 2020 Census

Marital Status

Area	Never Married	Now Married[2]	Separated	Widowed	Divorced
City	47.8	39.2	1.3	3.1	8.7
MSA[1]	40.0	44.8	1.3	4.0	9.8
U.S.	33.8	48.0	1.8	5.6	10.8

Note: Figures are percentages and cover the population 15 years of age and older; (1) Figures cover the Columbia, MO Metropolitan Statistical Area; (2) Excludes separated
Source: U.S. Census Bureau, 2017-2021 American Community Survey 5-Year Estimates

Religious Groups by Family

Area	Catholic	Baptist	Methodist	LDS[2]	Pentecostal	Lutheran	Islam	Adventist	Other
MSA[1]	7.1	9.0	3.5	1.7	1.1	1.6	1.4	1.2	12.4
U.S.	18.7	7.3	3.0	2.0	1.8	1.7	1.3	1.3	11.6

Note: Figures are the number of adherents as a percentage of the total population and cover the eight largest religious groups in the U.S; (1) Figures cover the Columbia, MO Metropolitan Statistical Area; (2) Church of Jesus Christ of Latter-day Saints
Sources: 2020 U.S. Religion Census, Association of Statisticians of American Religious Bodies; The Association of Religion Data Archives (ARDA)

Religious Groups by Tradition

Area	Catholic	Evangelical Protestant	Mainline Protestant	Black Protestant	Islam	Judaism	Hinduism	Orthodox	Buddhism
MSA[1]	7.1	19.4	6.3	1.9	1.4	0.2	0.1	0.1	<0.1
U.S.	18.7	16.5	5.2	2.3	1.3	0.6	0.4	0.4	0.3

Note: Figures are the number of adherents as a percentage of the total population; (1) Figures cover the Columbia, MO Metropolitan Statistical Area
Sources: 2020 U.S. Religion Census, Association of Statisticians of American Religious Bodies; The Association of Religion Data Archives (ARDA)

ECONOMY

Gross Metropolitan Product

Area	2020	2021	2022	2023	Rank[2]
MSA[1]	10.4	11.6	12.5	13.3	211

Note: Figures are in billions of dollars; (1) Figures cover the Columbia, MO Metropolitan Statistical Area; (2) Rank is based on 2021 data and ranges from 1 to 381
Source: U.S. Conference of Mayors, U.S. Metro Economies: U.S. Metros Compared to Global and State Economies, June 2022

Economic Growth

Area	2018-20 (%)	2021 (%)	2022 (%)	2023 (%)	Rank[2]
MSA[1]	2.1	5.6	2.9	3.3	29
U.S.	-0.6	5.7	3.1	2.9	—

Note: Figures are real gross metropolitan product (GMP) growth rates and represent average annual percent change; (1) Figures cover the Columbia, MO Metropolitan Statistical Area; (2) Rank is based on 2020 2-year average annual percent change and ranges from 1 to 381
Source: U.S. Conference of Mayors, U.S. Metro Economies: U.S. Metros Compared to Global and State Economies, June 2022

Metropolitan Area Exports

Area	2016	2017	2018	2019	2020	2021	Rank[2]
MSA[1]	213.7	224.0	238.6	291.4	256.2	335.4	255

Note: Figures are in millions of dollars; (1) Figures cover the Columbia, MO Metropolitan Statistical Area; (2) Rank is based on 2021 data and ranges from 1 to 388
Source: U.S. Department of Commerce, International Trade Administration, Office of Trade and Economic Analysis, Industry and Analysis, Exports by Metropolitan Area, data extracted March 16, 2023

Building Permits

Area	Single-Family			Multi-Family			Total		
	2021	2022	Pct. Chg.	2021	2022	Pct. Chg.	2021	2022	Pct. Chg.
City	487	303	-37.8	189	135	-28.6	676	438	-35.2
MSA[1]	838	628	-25.1	191	151	-20.9	1,029	779	-24.3
U.S.	1,115,400	975,600	-12.5	621,600	689,500	10.9	1,737,000	1,665,100	-4.1

Note: (1) Figures cover the Columbia, MO Metropolitan Statistical Area; Figures represent new, privately-owned housing units authorized (unadjusted data); All permit data are based on estimates with imputation
Source: U.S. Census Bureau, Manufacturing, Mining, and Construction Statistics, Building Permits, 2021, 2022

Bankruptcy Filings

Area	Business Filings			Nonbusiness Filings		
	2021	2022	% Chg.	2021	2022	% Chg.
Boone County	1	5	400.0	193	171	-11.4
U.S.	14,347	13,481	-6.0	399,269	374,240	-6.3

Note: Business filings include Chapter 7, Chapter 9, Chapter 11, Chapter 12, Chapter 13, Chapter 15, and Section 304; Nonbusiness filings include Chapter 7, Chapter 11, and Chapter 13
Source: Administrative Office of the U.S. Courts, Business and Nonbusiness Bankruptcy, County Cases Commenced by Chapter of the Bankruptcy Code, During the 12-Month Period Ending December 31, 2021 and Business and Nonbusiness Bankruptcy, County Cases Commenced by Chapter of the Bankruptcy Code, During the 12-Month Period Ending December 31, 2022

Housing Vacancy Rates

Area	Gross Vacancy Rate[2] (%)			Year-Round Vacancy Rate[3] (%)			Rental Vacancy Rate[4] (%)			Homeowner Vacancy Rate[5] (%)		
	2020	2021	2022	2020	2021	2022	2020	2021	2022	2020	2021	2022
MSA[1]	n/a	n/a	n/a	n/a	n/a	n/a	n/a	n/a	n/a	n/a	n/a	n/a
U.S.	10.6	10.8	10.5	8.2	8.4	8.2	6.3	6.1	5.8	1.0	0.9	0.8

Note: (1) Figures cover the Columbia, MO Metropolitan Statistical Area; (2) The percentage of the total housing inventory that is vacant; (3) The percentage of the housing inventory (excluding seasonal units) that is year-round vacant; (4) The percentage of rental inventory that is vacant for rent; (5) The percentage of homeowner inventory that is vacant for sale; n/a not available
Source: U.S. Census Bureau, Housing Vacancies and Homeownership Annual Statistics: 2020, 2021, 2022

INCOME

Income

Area	Per Capita ($)	Median Household ($)	Average Household ($)
City	32,784	57,463	80,898
MSA[1]	33,131	61,901	82,741
U.S.	37,638	69,021	97,196

Note: (1) Figures cover the Columbia, MO Metropolitan Statistical Area
Source: U.S. Census Bureau, 2017-2021 American Community Survey 5-Year Estimates

Household Income Distribution

Area	Percent of Households Earning							
	Under $15,000	$15,000 -$24,999	$25,000 -$34,999	$35,000 -$49,999	$50,000 -$74,999	$75,000 -$99,999	$100,000 -$149,999	$150,000 and up
City	12.8	9.6	9.8	12.6	17.3	11.5	13.2	13.2
MSA[1]	10.8	8.5	9.5	12.3	18.3	13.3	14.8	12.5
U.S.	9.4	7.8	8.2	11.4	16.8	12.8	16.3	17.3

Note: (1) Figures cover the Columbia, MO Metropolitan Statistical Area
Source: U.S. Census Bureau, 2017-2021 American Community Survey 5-Year Estimates

Poverty Rate

Area	All Ages	Under 18 Years Old	18 to 64 Years Old	65 Years and Over
City	19.9	14.9	23.7	6.1
MSA[1]	16.2	14.6	18.7	6.8
U.S.	12.6	17.0	11.8	9.6

Note: Figures are percentage of people whose income during the past 12 months was below the poverty level;
(1) Figures cover the Columbia, MO Metropolitan Statistical Area
Source: U.S. Census Bureau, 2017-2021 American Community Survey 5-Year Estimates

EMPLOYMENT

Labor Force and Employment

Area	Civilian Labor Force			Workers Employed		
	Dec. 2021	Dec. 2022	% Chg.	Dec. 2021	Dec. 2022	% Chg.
City	68,593	68,729	0.2	67,043	67,523	0.7
MSA[1]	100,630	100,708	0.1	98,278	98,981	0.7
U.S.	161,696,000	164,224,000	1.6	155,732,000	158,872,000	2.0

Note: Data is not seasonally adjusted and covers workers 16 years of age and older; (1) Figures cover the Columbia, MO Metropolitan Statistical Area
Source: Bureau of Labor Statistics, Local Area Unemployment Statistics

Unemployment Rate

Area	2022											
	Jan.	Feb.	Mar.	Apr.	May	Jun.	Jul.	Aug.	Sep.	Oct.	Nov.	Dec.
City	3.0	2.2	2.4	1.7	2.4	1.9	2.4	2.5	1.5	1.9	1.9	1.8
MSA[1]	3.0	2.3	2.6	1.7	2.3	1.8	2.3	2.4	1.4	1.9	1.8	1.7
U.S.	4.4	4.1	3.8	3.3	3.4	3.8	3.8	3.8	3.3	3.4	3.4	3.3

Note: Data is not seasonally adjusted and covers workers 16 years of age and older; (1) Figures cover the Columbia, MO Metropolitan Statistical Area
Source: Bureau of Labor Statistics, Local Area Unemployment Statistics

Average Wages

Occupation	$/Hr.	Occupation	$/Hr.
Accountants and Auditors	32.30	Maintenance and Repair Workers	20.64
Automotive Mechanics	21.77	Marketing Managers	52.19
Bookkeepers	20.39	Network and Computer Systems Admin.	38.68
Carpenters	25.95	Nurses, Licensed Practical	23.50
Cashiers	12.91	Nurses, Registered	34.00
Computer Programmers	37.12	Nursing Assistants	15.71
Computer Systems Analysts	38.74	Office Clerks, General	18.99
Computer User Support Specialists	26.05	Physical Therapists	41.76
Construction Laborers	25.63	Physicians	132.62
Cooks, Restaurant	14.43	Plumbers, Pipefitters and Steamfitters	28.50
Customer Service Representatives	17.49	Police and Sheriff's Patrol Officers	24.89
Dentists	80.29	Postal Service Mail Carriers	26.18
Electricians	27.19	Real Estate Sales Agents	20.94
Engineers, Electrical	40.87	Retail Salespersons	14.99
Fast Food and Counter Workers	12.77	Sales Representatives, Technical/Scientific	n/a
Financial Managers	n/a	Secretaries, Exc. Legal/Medical/Executive	18.33
First-Line Supervisors of Office Workers	27.71	Security Guards	16.33
General and Operations Managers	47.42	Surgeons	n/a
Hairdressers/Cosmetologists	18.61	Teacher Assistants, Exc. Postsecondary*	14.65
Home Health and Personal Care Aides	13.29	Teachers, Secondary School, Exc. Sp. Ed.*	n/a
Janitors and Cleaners	15.66	Telemarketers	n/a
Landscaping/Groundskeeping Workers	15.24	Truck Drivers, Heavy/Tractor-Trailer	24.11
Lawyers	58.60	Truck Drivers, Light/Delivery Services	22.20
Maids and Housekeeping Cleaners	13.42	Waiters and Waitresses	15.51

Note: Wage data covers the Columbia, MO Metropolitan Statistical Area; (*) Hourly wages were calculated from annual wage data based on a 40 hour work week; n/a not available.
Source: Bureau of Labor Statistics, Metro Area Occupational Employment & Wage Estimates, May 2022

Employment by Industry

Sector	MSA[1]		U.S.
	Number of Employees	Percent of Total	Percent of Total
Construction, Mining, and Logging	n/a	n/a	5.4
Private Education and Health Services	n/a	n/a	16.1
Financial Activities	n/a	n/a	5.9
Government	29,600	28.2	14.5
Information	n/a	n/a	2.0
Leisure and Hospitality	n/a	n/a	10.3
Manufacturing	n/a	n/a	8.4
Other Services	n/a	n/a	3.7
Professional and Business Services	n/a	n/a	14.7
Retail Trade	11,000	10.5	10.2
Transportation, Warehousing, and Utilities	n/a	n/a	4.9
Wholesale Trade	n/a	n/a	3.9

Note: Figures are non-farm employment as of December 2022. Figures are not seasonally adjusted and include workers 16 years of age and older; (1) Figures cover the Columbia, MO Metropolitan Statistical Area; n/a not available
Source: Bureau of Labor Statistics, Current Employment Statistics, Employment, Hours, and Earnings

Employment by Occupation

Occupation Classification	City (%)	MSA[1] (%)	U.S. (%)
Management, Business, Science, and Arts	49.3	46.3	40.3
Natural Resources, Construction, and Maintenance	4.4	7.1	8.7
Production, Transportation, and Material Moving	7.5	9.4	13.1
Sales and Office	19.4	19.4	20.9
Service	19.3	17.8	17.0

Note: Figures cover employed civilians 16 years of age and older; (1) Figures cover the Columbia, MO Metropolitan Statistical Area
Source: U.S. Census Bureau, 2017-2021 American Community Survey 5-Year Estimates

Occupations with Greatest Projected Employment Growth: 2022 – 2024

Occupation[1]	2022 Employment	2024 Projected Employment	Numeric Employment Change	Percent Employment Change
Home Health and Personal Care Aides	80,580	84,180	3,600	4.5
Stockers and Order Fillers	58,060	60,440	2,380	4.1
General and Operations Managers	86,320	88,430	2,110	2.4
Cooks, Restaurant	30,940	33,020	2,080	6.7
Registered Nurses	73,620	74,860	1,240	1.7
Laborers and Freight, Stock, and Material Movers, Hand	42,770	43,710	940	2.2
Maintenance and Repair Workers, General	38,300	39,130	830	2.2
Janitors and Cleaners, Except Maids and Housekeeping Cleaners	45,160	45,960	800	1.8
Industrial Truck and Tractor Operators	13,420	14,180	760	5.7
Waiters and Waitresses	41,390	42,140	750	1.8

Note: Projections cover Missouri; (1) Sorted by numeric employment change
Source: www.projectionscentral.com, State Occupational Projections, 2022–2024 Short-Term Projections

Fastest-Growing Occupations: 2022 – 2024

Occupation[1]	2022 Employment	2024 Projected Employment	Numeric Employment Change	Percent Employment Change
Nurse Practitioners	7,420	8,030	610	8.2
Logisticians	2,520	2,710	190	7.5
Ushers, Lobby Attendants, and Ticket Takers	2,670	2,860	190	7.1
Computer Numerically Controlled Tool Programmers	740	790	50	6.8
Cooks, Restaurant	30,940	33,020	2,080	6.7
Information Security Analysts (SOC 2018)	2,110	2,250	140	6.6
Operations Research Analysts	980	1,040	60	6.1
Fitness Trainers and Aerobics Instructors	7,500	7,940	440	5.9
Weighers, Measurers, Checkers, and Samplers, Recordkeeping	850	900	50	5.9
Physical Therapist Assistants	2,230	2,360	130	5.8

Note: Projections cover Missouri; (1) Sorted by percent employment change and excludes occupations with numeric employment change less than 50
Source: www.projectionscentral.com, State Occupational Projections, 2022–2024 Short-Term Projections

CITY FINANCES

City Government Finances

Component	2020 ($000)	2020 ($ per capita)
Total Revenues	347,755	2,823
Total Expenditures	345,450	2,804
Debt Outstanding	295,578	2,399
Cash and Securities[1]	586,848	4,764

Note: (1) Cash and security holdings of a government at the close of its fiscal year, including those of its dependent agencies, utilities, and liquor stores.
Source: U.S. Census Bureau, State & Local Government Finances 2020

City Government Revenue by Source

Source	2020 ($000)	2020 ($ per capita)	2020 (%)
General Revenue			
From Federal Government	13,705	111	3.9
From State Government	5,696	46	1.6
From Local Governments	20,784	169	6.0
Taxes			
Property	8,546	69	2.5
Sales and Gross Receipts	57,397	466	16.5
Personal Income	0	0	0.0
Corporate Income	0	0	0.0
Motor Vehicle License	1,461	12	0.4
Other Taxes	1,840	15	0.5
Current Charges	60,117	488	17.3
Liquor Store	0	0	0.0
Utility	156,043	1,267	44.9

Source: U.S. Census Bureau, State & Local Government Finances 2020

City Government Expenditures by Function

Function	2020 ($000)	2020 ($ per capita)	2020 (%)
General Direct Expenditures			
Air Transportation	9,897	80	2.9
Corrections	0	0	0.0
Education	0	0	0.0
Employment Security Administration	0	0	0.0
Financial Administration	4,488	36	1.3
Fire Protection	13,411	108	3.9
General Public Buildings	204	1	0.1
Governmental Administration, Other	7,392	60	2.1
Health	5,715	46	1.7
Highways	15,396	125	4.5
Hospitals	0	0	0.0
Housing and Community Development	1,487	12	0.4
Interest on General Debt	4,485	36	1.3
Judicial and Legal	2,743	22	0.8
Libraries	0	0	0.0
Parking	3,772	30	1.1
Parks and Recreation	21,736	176	6.3
Police Protection	19,172	155	5.5
Public Welfare	965	7	0.3
Sewerage	11,069	89	3.2
Solid Waste Management	18,110	147	5.2
Veterans' Services	0	0	0.0
Liquor Store	0	0	0.0
Utility	156,913	1,273	45.4

Source: U.S. Census Bureau, State & Local Government Finances 2020

TAXES

State Corporate Income Tax Rates

State	Tax Rate (%)	Income Brackets ($)	Num. of Brackets	Financial Institution Tax Rate (%)[a]	Federal Income Tax Ded.
Missouri	4.0	Flat rate	1	4.48	Yes (h)

Note: Tax rates as of January 1, 2023; (a) Rates listed are the corporate income tax rate applied to financial institutions or excise taxes based on income. Some states have other taxes based upon the value of deposits or shares; (h) 50% of the federal income tax is deductible.
Source: Federation of Tax Administrators, State Corporate Income Tax Rates, January 1, 2023

State Individual Income Tax Rates

State	Tax Rate (%)	Income Brackets ($)	Personal Exemptions ($) Single	Married	Depend.	Standard Ded. ($) Single	Married
Missouri (a)	0.0 - 4.95	1,207 - 8,449	(d)	(d)	(d)	13,850	27,700 (d)

Note: Tax rates as of January 1, 2023; Local- and county-level taxes are not included; (a) 16 states have statutory provision for automatically adjusting to the rate of inflation the dollar values of the income tax brackets, standard deductions, and/or personal exemptions. Oregon does not index the income brackets for $125,000 and over; (d) These states use the personal exemption/standard deduction amounts provided in the federal Internal Revenue Code.
Source: Federation of Tax Administrators, State Individual Income Tax Rates, January 1, 2023

Various State Sales and Excise Tax Rates

State	State Sales Tax (%)	Gasoline[1] ($/gal.)	Cigarette[2] ($/pack)	Spirits[3] ($/gal.)	Wine[4] ($/gal.)	Beer[5] ($/gal.)	Recreational Marijuana (%)
Missouri	4.225	0.2242	0.17	2.00	0.42	0.06	(j)

Note: All tax rates as of January 1, 2023; (1) The American Petroleum Institute has developed a methodology for determining the average tax rate on a gallon of fuel. Rates may include any of the following: excise taxes, environmental fees, storage tank fees, other fees or taxes, general sales tax, and local taxes; (2) The federal excise tax of $1.0066 per pack and local taxes are not included; (3) Rates are those applicable to off-premise sales of 40% alcohol by volume (a.b.v.) distilled spirits in 750ml containers. Local excise taxes are excluded; (4) Rates are those applicable to off-premise sales of 11% a.b.v. non-carbonated wine in 750ml containers; (5) Rates are those applicable to off-premise sales of 4.7% a.b.v. beer in 12 ounce containers; (j) 6% excise tax (retail price)
Source: Tax Foundation, 2023 Facts & Figures: How Does Your State Compare?

State Business Tax Climate Index Rankings

State	Overall Rank	Corporate Tax Rank	Individual Income Tax Rank	Sales Tax Rank	Property Tax Rank	Unemployment Insurance Tax Rank
Missouri	11	3	21	26	7	4

Note: The index is a measure of how each state's tax laws affect economic performance. The lower the rank, the more favorable a state's tax system is for business. States without a given tax are given a ranking of 1. The scores/rankings for the District of Columbia do not affect other states. The 2023 index represents the tax climate as of July 1, 2022.
Source: Tax Foundation, State Business Tax Climate Index 2023

TRANSPORTATION

Means of Transportation to Work

Area	Car/Truck/Van Drove Alone	Car-pooled	Public Transportation Bus	Subway	Railroad	Bicycle	Walked	Other Means	Worked at Home
City	75.0	9.0	0.9	0.0	0.0	1.2	6.4	0.7	6.8
MSA[1]	77.1	9.6	0.6	0.0	0.0	0.8	4.4	0.8	6.7
U.S.	73.2	8.6	2.0	1.6	0.5	0.5	2.5	1.5	9.7

Note: Figures are percentages and cover workers 16 years of age and older; (1) Figures cover the Columbia, MO Metropolitan Statistical Area
Source: U.S. Census Bureau, 2017-2021 American Community Survey 5-Year Estimates

Travel Time to Work

Area	Less Than 10 Minutes	10 to 19 Minutes	20 to 29 Minutes	30 to 44 Minutes	45 to 59 Minutes	60 to 89 Minutes	90 Minutes or More
City	20.0	54.4	13.7	7.3	2.5	1.0	1.1
MSA[1]	17.3	44.2	19.4	11.9	3.8	1.7	1.7
U.S.	12.4	28.5	21.0	20.9	8.2	6.2	2.9

Note: Note: Figures are percentages and include workers 16 years old and over; (1) Figures cover the Columbia, MO Metropolitan Statistical Area
Source: U.S. Census Bureau, 2017-2021 American Community Survey 5-Year Estimates

Key Congestion Measures

Measure	1990	2000	2010	2015	2020
Annual Hours of Delay, Total (000)	n/a	n/a	n/a	2,665	2,006
Annual Hours of Delay, Per Auto Commuter	n/a	n/a	n/a	19	14
Annual Congestion Cost, Per Auto Commuter ($)	n/a	n/a	n/a	400	335

Note: n/a not available
Source: Texas A&M Transportation Institute, 2021 Urban Mobility Report

Freeway Travel Time Index

Measure	1985	1990	1995	2000	2005	2010	2015	2020
Urban Area Index[1]	n/a	n/a	n/a	n/a	n/a	n/a	1.10	1.07
Urban Area Rank[1,2]	n/a	n/a	n/a	n/a	n/a	n/a	n/a	n/a

Note: Freeway Travel Time Index—the ratio of travel time in the peak period to the travel time at free-flow conditions. For example, a value of 1.30 indicates a 20-minute free-flow trip takes 26 minutes in the peak (20 minutes x 1.30 = 26 minutes); (1) Covers the Columbia MO urban area; (2) Rank is based on 101 larger urban areas (#1 = highest travel time index); n/a not available
Source: Texas A&M Transportation Institute, 2021 Urban Mobility Report

Public Transportation

Agency Name / Mode of Transportation	Vehicles Operated in Maximum Service[1]	Annual Unlinked Passenger Trips[2] (in thous.)	Annual Passenger Miles[3] (in thous.)
Columbia Transit (CT)			
Bus (directly operated)	14	500.3	1,380.7
Demand Response (directly operated)	6	34.6	125.8

Note: (1) Number of revenue vehicles operated by the given mode and type of service to meet the annual maximum service requirement. This is the revenue vehicle count during the peak season of the year; on the week and day that maximum service is provided. Vehicles operated in maximum service (VOMS) exclude atypical days and one-time special events; (2) Number of passengers who boarded public transportation vehicles. Passengers are counted each time they board a vehicle no matter how many vehicles they use to travel from their origin to their destination. (3) Sum of the distances ridden by all passengers during the entire fiscal year.
Source: Federal Transit Administration, National Transit Database, 2021

Air Transportation

Airport Name and Code / Type of Service	Passenger Airlines[1]	Passenger Enplanements	Freight Carriers[2]	Freight (lbs)
Columbia Regional (COU)				
Domestic service (U.S. carriers - 2022)	13	81,605	2	4,101
International service (U.S. carriers - 2021)	0	0	0	0

Note: (1) Includes all U.S.-based major, minor and commuter airlines that carried at least one passenger during the year; (2) Includes all U.S.-based airlines and freight carriers that transported at least one pound of freight during the year.
Source: Bureau of Transportation Statistics, The Intermodal Transportation Database, Air Carriers: T-100 Domestic Market (U.S. Carriers), 2022; Bureau of Transportation Statistics, The Intermodal Transportation Database, Air Carriers: T-100 International Market (U.S. Carriers), 2021

BUSINESSES

Major Business Headquarters

Company Name	Industry	Rankings	
		Fortune[1]	Forbes[2]
No companies listed	-	-	-

Note: (1) Companies that produce a 10-K are ranked 1 to 500 based on 2021 revenue; (2) All private companies with at least $2 billion in annual revenue through the end of their most current fiscal year are ranked 1 to 246; companies listed are headquartered in the city; dashes indicate no ranking
Source: Fortune, "Fortune 500," 2022; Forbes, "America's Largest Private Companies," 2022

Living Environment

COST OF LIVING

Cost of Living Index

Composite Index	Groceries	Housing	Utilities	Trans-portation	Health Care	Misc. Goods/ Services
95.0	99.8	86.4	96.0	98.8	91.5	99.3

Note: The Cost of Living Index measures regional differences in the cost of consumer goods and services, excluding taxes and non-consumer expenditures, for professional and managerial households in the top income quintile. It is based on more than 50,000 prices covering almost 60 different items for which prices are collected three times a year by chambers of commerce, economic development organizations or university applied economic centers in each participating urban area. The numbers shown should be read as a percentage above or below the national average of 100. For example, a value of 115.4 in the groceries column indicates that grocery prices are 15.4% higher than the national average. Small differences in the index numbers should not be interpreted as significant; Figures cover the Columbia MO urban area.
Source: The Council for Community and Economic Research, Cost of Living Index, 2022

Grocery Prices

Area[1]	T-Bone Steak ($/pound)	Frying Chicken ($/pound)	Whole Milk ($/half gal.)	Eggs ($/dozen)	Orange Juice ($/64 oz.)	Coffee ($/11.5 oz.)
City[2]	12.00	1.39	3.08	2.51	3.99	5.68
Avg.	13.81	1.59	2.43	2.25	3.85	4.95
Min.	10.17	0.90	1.51	1.30	2.90	3.46
Max.	19.35	3.30	4.32	4.32	5.31	8.59

Note: (1) Values for the local area are compared with the average, minimum and maximum values for all 286 areas in the Cost of Living Index; (2) Figures cover the Columbia MO urban area; **T-Bone Steak** *(price per pound);* **Frying Chicken** *(price per pound, whole fryer);* **Whole Milk** *(half gallon carton);* **Eggs** *(price per dozen, Grade A, large);* **Orange Juice** *(64 oz. Tropicana or Florida Natural);* **Coffee** *(11.5 oz. can, vacuum-packed, Maxwell House, Hills Bros, or Folgers).*
Source: The Council for Community and Economic Research, Cost of Living Index, 2022

Housing and Utility Costs

Area[1]	New Home Price ($)	Apartment Rent ($/month)	All Electric ($/month)	Part Electric ($/month)	Other Energy ($/month)	Telephone ($/month)
City[2]	442,644	861	-	96.49	65.29	194.74
Avg.	450,913	1,371	176.41	99.93	76.96	190.22
Min.	229,283	546	100.84	31.56	27.15	174.27
Max.	2,434,977	4,569	356.86	249.59	272.24	208.31

Note: (1) Values for the local area are compared with the average, minimum and maximum values for all 286 areas in the Cost of Living Index; (2) Figures cover the Columbia MO urban area; **New Home Price** *(2,400 sf living area, 8,000 sf lot, in urban area with full utilities);* **Apartment Rent** *(950 sf 2 bedroom/1.5 or 2 bath, unfurnished, excluding all utilities except water);* **All Electric** *(average monthly cost for an all-electric home);* **Part Electric** *(average monthly cost for a part-electric home);* **Other Energy** *(average monthly cost for natural gas, fuel oil, coal, wood, and any other forms of energy except electricity);* **Telephone** *(price includes the base monthly rate plus taxes and fees for three lines of mobile phone service).*
Source: The Council for Community and Economic Research, Cost of Living Index, 2022

Health Care, Transportation, and Other Costs

Area[1]	Doctor ($/visit)	Dentist ($/visit)	Optometrist ($/visit)	Gasoline ($/gallon)	Beauty Salon ($/visit)	Men's Shirt ($)
City[2]	125.84	92.11	110.19	3.84	43.33	29.87
Avg.	124.91	107.77	117.66	3.86	43.31	34.21
Min.	36.61	58.25	51.79	2.90	22.18	13.05
Max.	250.21	162.58	371.96	5.54	85.61	63.54

Note: (1) Values for the local area are compared with the average, minimum and maximum values for all 286 areas in the Cost of Living Index; (2) Figures cover the Columbia MO urban area; **Doctor** *(general practitioners routine exam of an established patient);* **Dentist** *(adult teeth cleaning and periodic oral examination);* **Optometrist** *(full vision eye exam for established adult patient);* **Gasoline** *(one gallon regular unleaded, national brand, including all taxes, cash price at self-service pump if available);* **Beauty Salon** *(woman's shampoo, trim, and blow-dry);* **Men's Shirt** *(cotton/polyester dress shirt, pinpoint weave, long sleeves).*
Source: The Council for Community and Economic Research, Cost of Living Index, 2022

HOUSING

Homeownership Rate

Area	2015 (%)	2016 (%)	2017 (%)	2018 (%)	2019 (%)	2020 (%)	2021 (%)	2022 (%)
MSA[1]	n/a	n/a	n/a	n/a	n/a	n/a	n/a	n/a
U.S.	63.7	63.4	63.9	64.4	64.6	66.6	65.5	65.8

Note: (1) Figures cover the Columbia, MO Metropolitan Statistical Area; n/a not available
Source: U.S. Census Bureau, Housing Vacancies and Homeownership Annual Statistics: 2015-2022

House Price Index (HPI)

Area	National Ranking[2]	Quarterly Change (%)	One-Year Change (%)	Five-Year Change (%)	Since 1991Q1 (%)
MSA[1]	148	1.10	10.69	48.19	225.68
U.S.[3]	–	0.34	8.41	58.44	289.08

Note: The HPI is a weighted repeat sales index. It measures average price changes in repeat sales or refinancings on the same properties. This information is obtained by reviewing repeat mortgage transactions on single-family properties whose mortgages have been purchased or securitized by Fannie Mae or Freddie Mac since January 1975; (1) Figures cover the Columbia, MO Metropolitan Statistical Area; (2) Rankings are based on annual percentage change for all metro areas containing at least 15,000 transactions over the last 10 years and ranges from 1 to 257; (3) figures based on a weighted average of Census Division estimates using a seasonally adjusted, purchase-only index; all figures are for the period ending December 31, 2022
Source: Federal Housing Finance Agency, Change in FHFA Metropolitan Area House Price Indexes, 2022Q4

Median Single-Family Home Prices

Area	2020	2021	2022p	Percent Change 2021 to 2022
MSA[1]	225.4	255.0	288.9	13.3
U.S. Average	300.2	357.1	392.6	9.9

Note: Figures are median sales prices of existing single-family homes in thousands of dollars; (p) preliminary; (1) Figures cover the Columbia, MO Metropolitan Statistical Area
Source: National Association of Realtors, Median Sales Price of Existing Single-Family Homes for Metropolitan Areas, 4th Quarter 2022

Qualifying Income Based on Median Sales Price of Existing Single-Family Homes

Area	With 5% Down ($)	With 10% Down ($)	With 20% Down ($)
MSA[1]	84,549	80,099	71,199
U.S. Average	112,234	106,237	94,513

Note: Figures are preliminary; Qualifying income is based on a mortgage rate of 6.77%. Monthly principal and interest payment is limited to 25% of income; (1) Figures cover the Columbia, MO Metropolitan Statistical Area
Source: National Association of Realtors, Qualifying Income Based on Median Sales Price of Existing Single-Family Homes for Metropolitan Areas, 4th Quarter 2022

Home Value

Area	Under $100,000	$100,000 -$199,999	$200,000 -$299,999	$300,000 -$399,999	$400,000 -$499,999	$500,000 -$999,999	$1,000,000 or more	Median ($)
City	8.9	35.8	29.2	14.1	6.5	5.1	0.5	215,300
MSA[1]	14.6	36.8	24.4	12.8	5.2	5.2	1.0	195,600
U.S.	16.2	24.2	20.1	13.6	8.3	13.6	4.1	244,900

Note: Figures are percentages except for median and cover owner-occupied housing units; (1) Figures cover the Columbia, MO Metropolitan Statistical Area
Source: U.S. Census Bureau, 2017-2021 American Community Survey 5-Year Estimates

Year Housing Structure Built

Area	2020 or Later	2010 -2019	2000 -2009	1990 -1999	1980 -1989	1970 -1979	1960 -1969	1950 -1959	1940 -1949	Before 1940	Median Year
City	0.1	15.5	20.0	18.1	11.8	12.1	10.5	4.4	2.3	5.3	1992
MSA[1]	<0.1	12.1	18.1	17.6	13.2	14.8	9.6	4.7	2.6	7.2	1988
U.S.	0.2	7.3	13.6	13.6	13.2	14.8	10.3	10.0	4.7	12.2	1979

Note: Figures are percentages except for Median Year; Note: (1) Figures cover the Columbia, MO Metropolitan Statistical Area
Source: U.S. Census Bureau, 2017-2021 American Community Survey 5-Year Estimates

Gross Monthly Rent

Area	Under $500	$500 -$999	$1,000 -$1,499	$1,500 -$1,999	$2,000 -$2,499	$2,500 -$2,999	$3,000 and up	Median ($)
City	5.7	52.3	30.3	6.6	4.2	0.8	0.1	935
MSA[1]	7.4	52.9	29.9	5.6	3.5	0.6	0.2	917
U.S.	8.1	30.5	30.8	16.8	7.3	3.1	3.5	1,163

Note: Figures are percentages except for median; Gross rent is the contract rent plus the estimated average monthly cost of utilities (electricity, gas, and water and sewer) and fuels (oil, coal, kerosene, wood, etc.) if these are paid by the renter (or paid for the renter by someone else); (1) Figures cover the Columbia, MO Metropolitan Statistical Area
Source: U.S. Census Bureau, 2017-2021 American Community Survey 5-Year Estimates

HEALTH

Health Risk Factors

Category	MSA[1] (%)	U.S. (%)
Adults aged 18–64 who have any kind of health care coverage	n/a	90.9
Adults who reported being in good or better health	n/a	85.2
Adults who have been told they have high blood cholesterol	n/a	35.7
Adults who have been told they have high blood pressure	n/a	32.4
Adults who are current smokers	n/a	14.4
Adults who currently use e-cigarettes	n/a	6.7
Adults who currently use chewing tobacco, snuff, or snus	n/a	3.5
Adults who are heavy drinkers[2]	n/a	6.3
Adults who are binge drinkers[3]	n/a	15.4
Adults who are overweight (BMI 25.0 - 29.9)	n/a	34.4
Adults who are obese (BMI 30.0 - 99.8)	n/a	33.9
Adults who participated in any physical activities in the past month	n/a	76.3

Note: (1) Figures for the Columbia, MO Metropolitan Statistical Area were not available.
(2) Heavy drinkers are classified as adult men having more than 14 drinks per week and adult women having more than 7 drinks per week; (3) Binge drinkers are classified as males having five or more drinks on one occasion or females having four or more drinks on one occasion
Source: Centers for Disease Control and Prevention, Behaviorial Risk Factor Surveillance System, SMART: Selected Metropolitan Area Risk Trends, 2021

Acute and Chronic Health Conditions

Category	MSA[1] (%)	U.S. (%)
Adults who have ever been told they had a heart attack	n/a	4.0
Adults who have ever been told they have angina or coronary heart disease	n/a	3.8
Adults who have ever been told they had a stroke	n/a	3.0
Adults who have ever been told they have asthma	n/a	14.9
Adults who have ever been told they have arthritis	n/a	25.8
Adults who have ever been told they have diabetes[2]	n/a	10.9
Adults who have ever been told they had skin cancer	n/a	6.6
Adults who have ever been told they had any other types of cancer	n/a	7.5
Adults who have ever been told they have COPD	n/a	6.1
Adults who have ever been told they have kidney disease	n/a	3.0
Adults who have ever been told they have a form of depression	n/a	20.5

Note: (1) Figures for the Columbia, MO Metropolitan Statistical Area were not available.
(2) Figures do not include pregnancy-related, borderline, or pre-diabetes
Source: Centers for Disease Control and Prevention, Behaviorial Risk Factor Surveillance System, SMART: Selected Metropolitan Area Risk Trends, 2021

Health Screening and Vaccination Rates

Category	MSA[1] (%)	U.S. (%)
Adults who have ever been tested for HIV	n/a	34.9
Adults who have had their blood cholesterol checked within the last five years	n/a	85.2
Adults aged 65+ who have had flu shot within the past year	n/a	68.6
Adults aged 65+ who have ever had a pneumonia vaccination	n/a	71.0

Note: (1) Figures for the Columbia, MO Metropolitan Statistical Area were not available.
Source: Centers for Disease Control and Prevention, Behaviorial Risk Factor Surveillance System, SMART: Selected Metropolitan Area Risk Trends, 2021

Disability Status

Category	MSA[1] (%)	U.S. (%)
Adults who reported being deaf	n/a	7.2
Are you blind or have serious difficulty seeing, even when wearing glasses?	n/a	4.8
Are you limited in any way in any of your usual activities due to arthritis?	n/a	11.1
Do you have difficulty doing errands alone?	n/a	7.0
Do you have difficulty dressing or bathing?	n/a	3.6
Do you have serious difficulty concentrating/remembering/making decisions?	n/a	12.1
Do you have serious difficulty walking or climbing stairs?	n/a	12.8

Note: (1) Figures for the Columbia, MO Metropolitan Statistical Area were not available.
Source: Centers for Disease Control and Prevention, Behaviorial Risk Factor Surveillance System, SMART: Selected Metropolitan Area Risk Trends, 2021

Mortality Rates for the Top 10 Causes of Death in the U.S.

ICD-10[a] Sub-Chapter	ICD-10[a] Code	Crude Mortality Rate[1] per 100,000 population	
		County[2]	U.S.
Malignant neoplasms	C00-C97	144.0	182.6
Ischaemic heart diseases	I20-I25	59.9	113.1
Other forms of heart disease	I30-I51	61.9	64.4
Other degenerative diseases of the nervous system	G30-G31	40.2	51.0
Cerebrovascular diseases	I60-I69	34.0	47.8
Other external causes of accidental injury	W00-X59	34.0	46.4
Chronic lower respiratory diseases	J40-J47	36.8	45.7
Organic, including symptomatic, mental disorders	F01-F09	30.0	35.9
Hypertensive diseases	I10-I15	22.2	35.0
Diabetes mellitus	E10-E14	23.3	29.6

Note: (a) ICD-10 = International Classification of Diseases 10th Revision; (1) Crude mortality rates are a three-year average covering 2019-2021; (2) Figures cover Boone County.
Source: Centers for Disease Control and Prevention, National Center for Health Statistics. National Vital Statistics System, Mortality 2018-2021 on CDC WONDER Online Database

Mortality Rates for Selected Causes of Death

ICD-10[a] Sub-Chapter	ICD-10[a] Code	Crude Mortality Rate[1] per 100,000 population	
		County[2]	U.S.
Assault	X85-Y09	8.6	7.0
Diseases of the liver	K70-K76	12.7	19.8
Human immunodeficiency virus (HIV) disease	B20-B24	Suppressed	1.5
Influenza and pneumonia	J09-J18	7.5	14.7
Intentional self-harm	X60-X84	16.7	14.3
Malnutrition	E40-E46	Unreliable	4.3
Obesity and other hyperalimentation	E65-E68	Unreliable	3.0
Renal failure	N17-N19	13.8	15.7
Transport accidents	V01-V99	10.0	13.6
Viral hepatitis	B15-B19	Suppressed	1.2

Note: (a) ICD-10 = International Classification of Diseases 10th Revision; (1) Crude mortality rates are a three-year average covering 2019-2021; (2) Figures cover Boone County; Data are suppressed when the data meet the criteria for confidentiality constraints; Crude mortality rates are flagged as unreliable when the rate would be calculated with a numerator of 20 or less.
Source: Centers for Disease Control and Prevention, National Center for Health Statistics. National Vital Statistics System, Mortality 2018-2021 on CDC WONDER Online Database

Health Insurance Coverage

Area	With Health Insurance	With Private Health Insurance	With Public Health Insurance	Without Health Insurance	Population Under Age 19 Without Health Insurance
City	92.5	80.0	22.1	7.5	3.8
MSA[1]	92.4	78.6	25.0	7.6	4.7
U.S.	91.2	67.8	35.4	8.8	5.3

Note: Figures are percentages that cover the civilian noninstitutionalized population; (1) Figures cover the Columbia, MO Metropolitan Statistical Area
Source: U.S. Census Bureau, 2017-2021 American Community Survey 5-Year Estimates

Number of Medical Professionals

Area	MDs[3]	DOs[3,4]	Dentists	Podiatrists	Chiropractors	Optometrists
County[1] (number)	1,487	106	133	10	71	53
County[1] (rate[2])	808.6	57.6	71.6	5.4	38.2	28.5
U.S. (rate[2])	289.3	23.5	72.5	6.2	28.7	17.4

Note: Data as of 2021 unless noted; (1) Data covers Boone County; (2) Rate per 100,000 population; (3) Data as of 2020 and includes all active, non-federal physicians; (4) Doctor of Osteopathic Medicine
Source: U.S. Department of Health and Human Services, Health Resources and Services Administration, Bureau of Health Professions, Area Resource File (ARF) 2021-2022

EDUCATION

Public School District Statistics

District Name	Schls	Pupils	Pupil/ Teacher Ratio	Minority Pupils[1] (%)	LEP/ELL[2] (%)	IEP[3] (%)
Columbia 93	36	18,470	12.6	43.8	6.8	11.1

Note: Table includes school districts with 2,000 or more students; (1) Percentage of students that are not non-Hispanic white; (2) Percentage of students that are Limited English Proficient or English Language Learners (2018-19); (3) Percentage of students that have an Individualized Education Program (2019-20).
Source: U.S. Department of Education, National Center for Education Statistics, Common Core of Data, Local Education Agency (School District) Universe Survey: School Year 2021-2022

Highest Level of Education

Area	Less than H.S.	H.S. Diploma	Some College, No Deg.	Associate Degree	Bachelor's Degree	Master's Degree	Prof. School Degree	Doctorate Degree
City	4.5	17.5	17.6	6.6	28.4	15.5	4.6	5.3
MSA[1]	5.9	23.1	18.3	7.5	25.4	12.6	3.3	3.8
U.S.	11.1	26.5	20.0	8.7	20.6	9.3	2.2	1.5

Note: Figures cover persons age 25 and over; (1) Figures cover the Columbia, MO Metropolitan Statistical Area
Source: U.S. Census Bureau, 2017-2021 American Community Survey 5-Year Estimates

Educational Attainment by Race

Area	High School Graduate or Higher (%)					Bachelor's Degree or Higher (%)				
	Total	White	Black	Asian	Hisp.[2]	Total	White	Black	Asian	Hisp.[2]
City	95.5	96.6	92.6	94.7	89.1	53.8	56.5	29.4	68.9	47.1
MSA[1]	94.1	94.7	91.6	94.2	88.0	45.1	46.2	25.5	67.1	38.5
U.S.	88.9	91.4	87.2	87.6	71.2	33.7	35.5	23.3	55.6	18.4

Note: Figures shown cover persons 25 years old and over; (1) Figures cover the Columbia, MO Metropolitan Statistical Area; (2) People of Hispanic origin can be of any race
Source: U.S. Census Bureau, 2017-2021 American Community Survey 5-Year Estimates

School Enrollment by Grade and Control

Area	Preschool (%)		Kindergarten (%)		Grades 1 - 4 (%)		Grades 5 - 8 (%)		Grades 9 - 12 (%)	
	Public	Private	Public	Private	Public	Private	Public	Private	Public	Private
City	42.1	57.9	84.4	15.6	86.5	13.5	85.4	14.6	91.4	8.6
MSA[1]	52.3	47.7	87.6	12.4	85.9	14.1	87.6	12.4	91.3	8.7
U.S.	58.8	41.2	86.3	13.7	88.3	11.7	88.6	11.4	89.4	10.6

Note: Figures shown cover persons 3 years old and over; (1) Figures cover the Columbia, MO Metropolitan Statistical Area
Source: U.S. Census Bureau, 2017-2021 American Community Survey 5-Year Estimates

Higher Education

Four-Year Colleges			Two-Year Colleges			Medical Schools[1]	Law Schools[2]	Voc/ Tech[3]
Public	Private Non-profit	Private For-profit	Public	Private Non-profit	Private For-profit			
1	4	0	0	0	0	1	1	1

Note: Figures cover institutions located within the Columbia, MO Metropolitan Statistical Area and include main campuses only; (1) includes schools accredited by the Liaison Committee on Medical Education and the American Osteopathic Association's Commission on Osteopathic College Accreditation; (2) includes ABA-accredited schools, schools with provisional ABA accreditation, and state accredited schools; (3) includes all schools with programs that are less than 2 years.
Source: National Center for Education Statistics, Integrated Postsecondary Education System (IPEDS), 2021-22; Wikipedia, List of Medical Schools in the United States, accessed April 10, 2023; Wikipedia, List of Law Schools in the United States, accessed April 10, 2023

According to *U.S. News & World Report*, the Columbia, MO metro area is home to one of the top 200 national universities in the U.S.: **University of Missouri** (#121 tie). The indicators used to capture academic quality fall into a number of categories: assessment by administrators at peer institutions; retention of students; faculty resources; student selectivity; financial resources; alumni giving; high school counselor ratings of colleges; and graduation rate. *U.S. News & World Report, "America's Best Colleges 2023"*

According to *U.S. News & World Report*, the Columbia, MO metro area is home to one of the top 100 law schools in the U.S.: **University of Missouri** (#67 tie). The rankings are based on a weighted average of 12 measures of quality: peer assessment score; assessment score by lawyers/judges; median LSAT scores; median undergrad GPA; acceptance rate; employment rates for graduates; placement success; bar passage rate; faculty resources; expenditures per student; student/faculty ratio; and library resources. *U.S. News & World Report, "America's Best Graduate Schools, Law, 2023"*

EMPLOYERS

Major Employers

Company Name	Industry
BJC Health System	Hospital management
City of Columbia	Courts
Columbia College	Colleges & universities
Kraft Foods Global	Frankfurters, from purchased meat
MBS Textbook Exchange	Books, periodicals, & newspapers
MCI Worldcom Communications	Telephone communication, except radio
Regional Medical Pharmacy	Home health care services
Schneider Electric USA	Switchgear & switchboard apparatus
Shelter Insurance Companies	Fire, marine, & casualty insurance
State Farm Mutual Automobile Insurance	Insurance agents & brokers
University of Missouri Hospital	General medical & surgical hospitals
University of Missouri System	Colleges & universities
University Physicians Hospital	Gynecologist
Veterans Health Administration	Administration of veterans' affairs

Note: Companies shown are located within the Columbia, MO Metropolitan Statistical Area.
Source: Hoovers.com; Wikipedia

Best Companies to Work For

Veterans United Home Loans, headquartered in Columbia, is among "The 100 Best Companies to Work For." To pick the best companies, *Fortune* partnered with the Great Place to Work Institute. Two-thirds of a company's score is based on the results of the Institute's Trust Index survey, which is sent to a random sample of employees from each company. The questions related to attitudes about management's credibility, job satisfaction, and camaraderie. The other third of the scoring is based on the company's responses to the Institute's Culture Audit, which includes detailed questions about pay and benefit programs, and a series of open-ended questions about hiring practices, internal communication, training, recognition programs, and diversity efforts. Any company that is at least five years old with more than 1,000 U.S. employees is eligible. *Fortune, "The 100 Best Companies to Work For," 2023*

Veterans United Home Loans, headquartered in Columbia, is among "Fortune's Best Workplaces for Women." To pick the best companies, *Fortune* partnered with the Great Place to Work Institute. To be considered for the list, companies must be Great Place To Work-Certified. Companies must also employ at least 50 women, at least 20% of their non-executive managers must be female, and at least one executive must be female. To determine the Best Workplaces for Women, Great Place To Work measured the differences in women's survey responses to those of their peers and assesses the impact of demographics and roles on the quality and consistency of women's experiences. Great Place To Work also analyzed the gender balance of each workplace, how it compared to each company's industry, and patterns in representation as women rise from front-line positions to the board of directors. *Fortune, "Best Workplaces for Women," 2022*

PUBLIC SAFETY

Crime Rate

Area	Total Crime	Violent Crime Rate				Property Crime Rate		
		Murder	Rape[3]	Robbery	Aggrav. Assault	Burglary	Larceny -Theft	Motor Vehicle Theft
City	3,106.6	10.4	71.3	46.5	314.0	323.6	1,985.1	355.7
Suburbs[1]	1,789.7	2.3	52.8	19.9	179.4	218.1	1,128.2	188.8
Metro[2]	2,572.2	7.1	63.8	35.7	259.4	280.8	1,637.3	288.0
U.S.	2,356.7	6.5	38.4	73.9	279.7	314.2	1,398.0	246.0

Note: Figures are crimes per 100,000 population; (1) All areas within the metro area that are located outside the city limits; (2) Figures cover the Columbia, MO Metropolitan Statistical Area; (3) All figures shown were reported using the revised Uniform Crime Reporting (UCR) definition of rape; Due to the transition to the National Incident-Based Reporting System (NIBRS), limited city and metro area data was released for 2021.
Source: FBI Uniform Crime Reports, 2020

Hate Crimes

Area	Number of Quarters Reported	Number of Incidents per Bias Motivation					
		Race/Ethnicity/ Ancestry	Religion	Sexual Orientation	Disability	Gender	Gender Identity
City	4	1	0	0	0	0	0
U.S.	4	5,227	1,244	1,110	130	75	266

Note: Due to the transition to the National Incident-Based Reporting System (NIBRS), limited crime data was released for 2021.
Source: Federal Bureau of Investigation, Hate Crime Statistics 2020

Identity Theft Consumer Reports

Area	Reports	Reports per 100,000 Population	Rank[2]
MSA[1]	499	241	117
U.S.	1,108,609	339	-

Note: (1) Figures cover the Columbia, MO Metropolitan Statistical Area; (2) Rank ranges from 1 to 391 where 1 indicates greatest number of identity theft reports per 100,000 population
Source: Federal Trade Commission, Consumer Sentinel Network Data Book 2022

Fraud and Other Consumer Reports

Area	Reports	Reports per 100,000 Population	Rank[2]
MSA[1]	1,610	777	235
U.S.	4,064,520	1,245	-

Note: (1) Figures cover the Columbia, MO Metropolitan Statistical Area; (2) Rank ranges from 1 to 391 where 1 indicates greatest number of fraud and other consumer reports per 100,000 population
Source: Federal Trade Commission, Consumer Sentinel Network Data Book 2022

POLITICS

2020 Presidential Election Results

Area	Biden	Trump	Jorgensen	Hawkins	Other
Boone County	54.8	42.3	2.2	0.3	0.4
U.S.	51.3	46.8	1.2	0.3	0.5

Note: Results are percentages and may not add to 100% due to rounding
Source: Dave Leip's Atlas of U.S. Presidential Elections

SPORTS

Professional Sports Teams

Team Name	League	Year Established

No teams are located in the metro area
Source: Wikipedia, Major Professional Sports Teams of the United States and Canada, April 12, 2023

CLIMATE

Average and Extreme Temperatures

Temperature	Jan	Feb	Mar	Apr	May	Jun	Jul	Aug	Sep	Oct	Nov	Dec	Yr.
Extreme High (°F)	74	76	85	90	90	103	111	110	101	93	83	76	111
Average High (°F)	36	42	54	66	74	83	89	87	79	67	53	41	64
Average Temp. (°F)	28	33	44	55	64	73	78	76	68	56	44	33	54
Average Low (°F)	19	23	34	44	53	62	67	65	57	45	34	24	44
Extreme Low (°F)	-19	-15	-5	19	29	40	48	42	32	22	0	-20	-20

Note: Figures cover the years 1969-1995
Source: National Climatic Data Center, International Station Meteorological Climate Summary, 9/96

Average Precipitation/Snowfall/Humidity

Precip./Humidity	Jan	Feb	Mar	Apr	May	Jun	Jul	Aug	Sep	Oct	Nov	Dec	Yr.
Avg. Precip. (in.)	1.6	2.0	3.2	4.3	5.1	3.9	3.9	3.8	3.7	3.1	3.5	2.6	40.6
Avg. Snowfall (in.)	7	7	4	1	0	0	0	0	0	Tr	2	5	25
Avg. Rel. Hum. 6am (%)	80	80	79	79	85	86	87	89	88	84	82	81	83
Avg. Rel. Hum. 3pm (%)	62	59	53	52	57	56	53	52	54	53	59	64	56

Note: Figures cover the years 1969-1995; Tr = Trace amounts (<0.05 in. of rain; <0.5 in. of snow)
Source: National Climatic Data Center, International Station Meteorological Climate Summary, 9/96

Weather Conditions

Temperature			Daytime Sky			Precipitation		
10°F & below	32°F & below	90°F & above	Clear	Partly cloudy	Cloudy	0.01 inch or more precip.	0.1 inch or more snow/ice	Thunder-storms
17	108	36	99	127	139	110	17	52

Note: Figures are average number of days per year and cover the years 1969-1995
Source: National Climatic Data Center, International Station Meteorological Climate Summary, 9/96

HAZARDOUS WASTE

Superfund Sites

The Columbia, MO metro area has no sites on the EPA's Superfund Final National Priorities List. There are a total of 1,165 Superfund sites with a status of proposed or final on the list in the U.S. *U.S. Environmental Protection Agency, National Priorities List, April 12, 2023*

AIR QUALITY

Air Quality Trends: Ozone

	1990	1995	2000	2005	2010	2015	2018	2019	2020	2021
MSA[1]	n/a	n/a	n/a	n/a	n/a	n/a	n/a	n/a	n/a	n/a
U.S.	0.087	0.089	0.081	0.080	0.072	0.067	0.069	0.065	0.065	0.067

Note: (1) Data covers the Columbia, MO Metropolitan Statistical Area; n/a not available. The values shown are the composite ozone concentration averages among trend sites based on the highest fourth daily maximum 8-hour concentration in parts per million. These trends are based on sites having an adequate record of monitoring data during the trend period. Data from exceptional events are included.
Source: U.S. Environmental Protection Agency, Air Quality Monitoring Information, "Air Quality Trends by City, 1990-2021"

Air Quality Index

Area	Percent of Days when Air Quality was...[2]					AQI Statistics[2]	
	Good	Moderate	Unhealthy for Sensitive Groups	Unhealthy	Very Unhealthy	Maximum	Median
MSA[1]	95.1	4.9	0.0	0.0	0.0	77	37

Note: (1) Data covers the Columbia, MO Metropolitan Statistical Area; (2) Based on 245 days with AQI data in 2021. Air Quality Index (AQI) is an index for reporting daily air quality. EPA calculates the AQI for five major air pollutants regulated by the Clean Air Act: ground-level ozone, particle pollution (aka particulate matter), carbon monoxide, sulfur dioxide, and nitrogen dioxide. The AQI runs from 0 to 500. The higher the AQI value, the greater the level of air pollution and the greater the health concern. There are six AQI categories: "Good" AQI is between 0 and 50. Air quality is considered satisfactory; "Moderate" AQI is between 51 and 100. Air quality is acceptable; "Unhealthy for Sensitive Groups" When AQI values are between 101 and 150, members of sensitive groups may experience health effects; "Unhealthy" When AQI values are between 151 and 200 everyone may begin to experience health effects; "Very Unhealthy" AQI values between 201 and 300 trigger a health alert; "Hazardous" AQI values over 300 trigger warnings of emergency conditions (not shown).
Source: U.S. Environmental Protection Agency, Air Quality Index Report, 2021

Air Quality Index Pollutants

Area	Percent of Days when AQI Pollutant was...[2]					
	Carbon Monoxide	Nitrogen Dioxide	Ozone	Sulfur Dioxide	Particulate Matter 2.5	Particulate Matter 10
MSA[1]	0.0	0.0	100.0	(3)	0.0	0.0

Note: (1) Data covers the Columbia, MO Metropolitan Statistical Area; (2) Based on 245 days with AQI data in 2021. The Air Quality Index (AQI) is an index for reporting daily air quality. EPA calculates the AQI for five major air pollutants regulated by the Clean Air Act: ground-level ozone, particle pollution (also known as particulate matter), carbon monoxide, sulfur dioxide, and nitrogen dioxide. The AQI runs from 0 to 500. The higher the AQI value, the greater the level of air pollution and the greater the health concern; (3) Sulfur dioxide is no longer included in this table (as of December 8, 2021) because SO_2 concentrations tend to be very localized and not necessarily representative of broad geographical areas like counties and CBSAs.
Source: U.S. Environmental Protection Agency, Air Quality Index Report, 2021

Maximum Air Pollutant Concentrations: Particulate Matter, Ozone, CO and Lead

	Particulate Matter 10 (ug/m³)	Particulate Matter 2.5 Wtd AM (ug/m³)	Particulate Matter 2.5 24-Hr (ug/m³)	Ozone (ppm)	Carbon Monoxide (ppm)	Lead (ug/m³)
MSA[1] Level	n/a	n/a	n/a	0.058	n/a	n/a
NAAQS[2]	150	15	35	0.075	9	0.15
Met NAAQS[2]	n/a	n/a	n/a	Yes	n/a	n/a

Note: (1) Data covers the Columbia, MO Metropolitan Statistical Area; Data from exceptional events are included; (2) National Ambient Air Quality Standards; ppm = parts per million; ug/m³ = micrograms per cubic meter; n/a not available.
Concentrations: Particulate Matter 10 (coarse particulate)—highest second maximum 24-hour concentration; Particulate Matter 2.5 Wtd AM (fine particulate)—highest weighted annual mean concentration; Particulate Matter 2.5 24-Hour (fine particulate)—highest 98th percentile 24-hour concentration; Ozone—highest fourth daily maximum 8-hour concentration; Carbon Monoxide—highest second maximum non-overlapping 8-hour concentration; Lead—maximum running 3-month average
Source: U.S. Environmental Protection Agency, Air Quality Monitoring Information, "Air Quality Statistics by City, 2021"

Maximum Air Pollutant Concentrations: Nitrogen Dioxide and Sulfur Dioxide

	Nitrogen Dioxide AM (ppb)	Nitrogen Dioxide 1-Hr (ppb)	Sulfur Dioxide AM (ppb)	Sulfur Dioxide 1-Hr (ppb)	Sulfur Dioxide 24-Hr (ppb)
MSA[1] Level	n/a	n/a	n/a	n/a	n/a
NAAQS[2]	53	100	30	75	140
Met NAAQS[2]	n/a	n/a	n/a	n/a	n/a

Note: (1) Data covers the Columbia, MO Metropolitan Statistical Area; Data from exceptional events are included; (2) National Ambient Air Quality Standards; ppm = parts per million; ug/m^3 = micrograms per cubic meter; n/a not available.
Concentrations: Nitrogen Dioxide AM—highest arithmetic mean concentration; Nitrogen Dioxide 1-Hr—highest 98th percentile 1-hour daily maximum concentration; Sulfur Dioxide AM—highest annual mean concentration; Sulfur Dioxide 1-Hr—highest 99th percentile 1-hour daily maximum concentration; Sulfur Dioxide 24-Hr—highest second maximum 24-hour concentration
Source: U.S. Environmental Protection Agency, Air Quality Monitoring Information, "Air Quality Statistics by City, 2021"

Davenport, Iowa

Background

The city of Davenport was first incorporated in 1836 on the site of the bloody "Black Hawk War" between the Native American Sac tribe and eastern settlers who were intent on westward expansion. In 1828, John Quincy Adams had declared that all land east of the Mississippi would be sold to settlers. When Chief Black Hawk and his warriors refused to leave their land, the Black Hawk War ensued, resulting in a treaty now known as the Black Hawk Purchase. Credit Island, which had originally been a fur trading post, hosted the treaty signing between the Sac chief and Colonel George Davenport, from whom Davenport derives its name.

In 1856, a new bridge was constructed between Davenport and Rock Island, Illinois—the first railroad bridge to span the Mississippi. Months later, the riverboat *Effie Afton*, struck and damaged the bridge. The ensuing court case, *Hurd v. Rock Island Railroad Company*, remained the most notable case in the law career of Abraham Lincoln.

The decade preceding the Civil War saw a major influx of German immigrants to Davenport, increasing the population fivefold; it is estimated that about 50 percent of today's Davenport citizenry are of German descent. Many of these immigrants were fleeing political persecution and were instrumental in the creation of the Republican Party, which, within a decade, would provide the country with one of its most influential presidents. The culture and work ethic of these immigrants remains a key factor in the Davenport ethos of hard work and industry. At the turn of the 19th century, Davenport earned the rather amusing moniker of "Washing Machine Capital of the World."

In 1861, Rock Island opened a munitions arsenal to help the Union war efforts. It is now home to the largest, government-owned weapons manufacturing facility in the United States, and a designated national historic landmark. Today, Davenport supports a diverse base of manufacturing industries that include everything from farm and military machinery to publishing products and food processing. Its central, mid-continent location makes Davenport an important, inland U.S. Customs Port of Entry for freight distribution. It is also designated a Foreign Trade Zone.

The largest employers in the area comprise a veritable who's who of American manufacturing, including John Deere & Co., Aluminum Co. of America (ALCOA), Oscar Meyer Food Corp. and Eagle Food Center. Davenport is also home to the regional headquarters of the United Parcel Service and serves as the headquarters of the Von Maur department stores.

Davenport is home to four institutes of higher learning, including the Catholic liberal arts St. Ambrose University, the city's oldest college. The Palmer College of Chiropractic, the first college of its kind, was established by the inventor of chiropractic practice and Davenport resident David Palmer. Within commuting distance of Davenport are Augustana College (Rock Island), the University of Iowa (Iowa City), and Knox College (Galesburg).

Iowa's first municipal art museum, the Figge Museum, is home to the *Grant Wood Archive*. The collection features Wood's wire-rimmed glasses, his easel and painting tools, and the iconic cameo broach in both the portrait of his mother, *Woman with Plants*, 1929, and his most famous painting, *American Gothic*, 1930.

Given Davenport's central location in the heart of America's Midwest, the climate is relatively temperate. Temperatures can fluctuate considerably; summers are hot and winters severe, with an average snowfall just over 30 inches.

Rankings

Business/Finance Rankings

- The Davenport metro area appeared on the Milken Institute "2022 Best Performing Cities" list. Rank: #165 out of 200 large metro areas (population over 250,000). Criteria: job growth; wage and salary growth; high-tech output growth; housing affordability; household broadband access. *Milken Institute, "Best-Performing Cities 2022," March 28, 2022*

- *Forbes* ranked the 200 most populous metro areas to determine the nation's "Best Places for Business and Careers." The Davenport metro area was ranked #175. Criteria: costs (business and living); job growth (past and projected); income growth; quality of life; educational attainment (college and high school); projected economic growth; cultural and leisure opportunities; workplace tolerance laws; net migration patterns. *Forbes, "The Best Places for Business and Careers 2019: Seattle Still On Top," October 30, 2019*

Children/Family Rankings

- Davenport was selected as one of the most playful cities in the U.S. by KaBOOM! The organization's Playful City USA initiative honors cities and towns across the nation that have made their communities more playable. Criteria: pledging to integrate play as a solution to challenges in their communities; making it easy for children to get active and balanced play; creating more family-friendly and innovative communities as a result. *KaBOOM! National Campaign for Play, "2017 Playful City USA Communities"*

Education Rankings

- Personal finance website *WalletHub* analyzed the 150 largest U.S. metropolitan statistical areas to determine where the most educated Americans are putting their degrees to work. Criteria: education levels; percentage of workers with degrees; education quality and attainment gap; public school quality rankings; quality and enrollment of each metro area's universities. Davenport was ranked #108 (#1 = most educated city). *www.WalletHub.com, "Most & Least Educated Cities in America," July 18, 2022*

Real Estate Rankings

- The Davenport metro area was identified as one of the 20 most affordable housing markets in the U.S. in 2022. The area ranked #13 out of 186 markets. Criteria: qualification for a mortgage loan with a 10 percent down payment on a typical home. *National Association of Realtors®, Qualifying Income Based on Sales Price of Existing Single-Family Homes for Metropolitan Areas, 2022*

- Davenport was ranked #4 out of 235 metro areas in terms of housing affordability in 2022 by the National Association of Home Builders (#1 = most affordable). Criteria: the share of homes sold in that area affordable to a family earning the local median income, based on standard mortgage underwriting criteria. *National Association of Home Builders®, NAHB-Wells Fargo Housing Opportunity Index, 4th Quarter 2022*

Seniors/Retirement Rankings

- From its Best Cities for Successful Aging indexes, the Milken Institute generated rankings for metropolitan areas, weighing data in nine categories—health care, wellness, living arrangements, transportation and convenience, financial characteristics, education, employment, community engagement, and overall livability. The Davenport metro area was ranked #153 overall in the small metro area category. *Milken Institute, "Best Cities for Successful Aging, 2017" March 14, 2017*

Business Environment

DEMOGRAPHICS

Population Growth

Area	1990 Census	2000 Census	2010 Census	2020 Census	Population Growth (%) 1990-2020	Population Growth (%) 2010-2020
City	95,705	98,359	99,685	101,724	6.3	2.0
MSA[1]	368,151	376,019	379,690	384,324	4.4	1.2
U.S.	248,709,873	281,421,906	308,745,538	331,449,281	33.3	7.4

Note: (1) Figures cover the Davenport-Moline-Rock Island, IA-IL Metropolitan Statistical Area
Source: U.S. Census Bureau, 1990 Census, 2000 Census, 2010 Census, 2020 Census

Race

Area	White Alone[2] (%)	Black Alone[2] (%)	Asian Alone[2] (%)	AIAN[3] Alone[2] (%)	NHOPI[4] Alone[2] (%)	Other Race Alone[2] (%)	Two or More Races (%)
City	74.1	12.0	2.2	0.4	0.0	2.6	8.7
MSA[1]	78.2	8.3	2.4	0.4	0.0	3.2	7.5
U.S.	61.6	12.4	6.0	1.1	0.2	8.4	10.2

Note: (1) Figures cover the Davenport-Moline-Rock Island, IA-IL Metropolitan Statistical Area; (2) Alone is defined as not being in combination with one or more other races; (3) American Indian and Alaska Native; (4) Native Hawaiian and Other Pacific Islander
Source: U.S. Census Bureau, 2020 Census

Hispanic or Latino Origin

Area	Total (%)	Mexican (%)	Puerto Rican (%)	Cuban (%)	Other (%)
City	8.9	8.2	0.3	0.1	0.3
MSA[1]	9.1	8.0	0.3	0.1	0.7
U.S.	18.4	11.2	1.8	0.7	4.7

Note: Persons of Hispanic or Latino origin can be of any race; (1) Figures cover the Davenport-Moline-Rock Island, IA-IL Metropolitan Statistical Area
Source: U.S. Census Bureau, 2017-2021 American Community Survey 5-Year Estimates

Age

Area	Under Age 5	Age 5–19	Age 20–34	Age 35–44	Age 45–54	Age 55–64	Age 65–74	Age 75–84	Age 85+	Median Age
City	6.1	18.8	21.8	12.5	11.5	12.8	9.7	4.6	2.1	37.5
MSA[1]	5.7	19.5	17.9	12.4	11.8	13.6	11.0	5.6	2.3	40.3
U.S.	5.6	19.2	20.2	12.7	12.4	13.1	10.0	4.9	1.9	38.8

Note: (1) Figures cover the Davenport-Moline-Rock Island, IA-IL Metropolitan Statistical Area
Source: U.S. Census Bureau, 2020 Census

Disability by Age

Area	All Ages	Under 18 Years Old	18 to 64 Years Old	65 Years and Over
City	13.1	5.2	11.3	31.6
MSA[1]	12.7	5.2	10.4	30.1
U.S.	12.6	4.4	10.3	33.4

Note: Figures show percent of the civilian noninstitutionalized population that reported having a disability. Disability status is determined from six types of difficulty: vision, hearing, cognitive, ambulatory, self-care, and independent living. For children under 5 years old, hearing and vision difficulty are used to determine disability status. For children between the ages of 5 and 14, disability status is determined from hearing, vision, cognitive, ambulatory, and self-care difficulties. For people aged 15 years and older, they are considered to have a disability if they have difficulty with any one of the six difficulty types; Note: (1) Figures cover the Davenport-Moline-Rock Island, IA-IL Metropolitan Statistical Area
Source: U.S. Census Bureau, 2017-2021 American Community Survey 5-Year Estimates

Ancestry

Area	German	Irish	English	American	Italian	Polish	French[2]	Scottish	Dutch
City	27.7	15.3	7.5	3.4	2.2	2.0	1.5	1.6	1.6
MSA[1]	25.9	13.5	8.2	4.0	2.3	2.1	1.7	1.4	1.8
U.S.	12.8	9.6	8.1	5.7	5.0	2.7	2.2	1.6	1.1

Note: Figures are the percentage of the total population reporting a particular ancestry. The nine most commonly reported ancestries in the U.S. are shown. Figures include multiple ancestries (e.g. if a person reported being Irish and Italian, they were included in both columns); (1) Figures cover the Davenport-Moline-Rock Island, IA-IL Metropolitan Statistical Area; (2) Excludes Basque
Source: U.S. Census Bureau, 2017-2021 American Community Survey 5-Year Estimates

Foreign-born Population

Area	Any Foreign Country	Asia	Mexico	Europe	Caribbean	Central America[2]	South America	Africa	Canada
City	4.5	1.6	1.8	0.4	0.2	0.1	0.0	0.2	0.1
MSA[1]	5.3	1.7	1.7	0.5	0.1	0.1	0.1	0.9	0.1
U.S.	13.6	4.2	3.3	1.5	1.4	1.1	1.1	0.8	0.2

Note: (1) Figures cover the Davenport-Moline-Rock Island, IA-IL Metropolitan Statistical Area; (2) Excludes Mexico.
Source: U.S. Census Bureau, 2017-2021 American Community Survey 5-Year Estimates

Household Size

Area	Persons in Household (%)							Average Household Size
	One	Two	Three	Four	Five	Six	Seven or More	
City	34.3	35.7	13.1	9.1	5.1	1.7	0.9	2.40
MSA[1]	31.2	36.3	13.3	11.4	5.1	1.8	0.9	2.40
U.S.	28.1	33.8	15.5	12.9	6.0	2.3	1.4	2.60

Note: (1) Figures cover the Davenport-Moline-Rock Island, IA-IL Metropolitan Statistical Area
Source: U.S. Census Bureau, 2017-2021 American Community Survey 5-Year Estimates

Household Relationships

Area	House-holder	Opposite-sex Spouse	Same-sex Spouse	Opposite-sex Unmarried Partner	Same-sex Unmarried Partner	Child[2]	Grand-child	Other Relatives	Non-relatives
City	41.9	15.9	0.2	3.7	0.2	27.0	2.0	3.0	3.2
MSA[1]	41.4	18.8	0.2	2.9	0.1	27.9	1.8	2.5	2.2
U.S.	38.3	17.5	0.2	2.5	0.2	28.3	2.4	4.8	3.4

Note: Figures are percent of the total population; (1) Figures cover the Davenport-Moline-Rock Island, IA-IL Metropolitan Statistical Area; (2) Includes biological, adopted, and stepchildren of the householder
Source: U.S. Census Bureau, 2020 Census

Gender

Area	Males	Females	Males per 100 Females
City	49,751	51,973	95.7
MSA[1]	189,247	195,077	97.0
U.S.	162,685,811	168,763,470	96.4

Note: (1) Figures cover the Davenport-Moline-Rock Island, IA-IL Metropolitan Statistical Area
Source: U.S. Census Bureau, 2020 Census

Marital Status

Area	Never Married	Now Married[2]	Separated	Widowed	Divorced
City	36.9	43.5	1.3	5.6	12.7
MSA[1]	30.5	49.9	1.4	6.2	12.0
U.S.	33.8	48.0	1.8	5.6	10.8

Note: Figures are percentages and cover the population 15 years of age and older; (1) Figures cover the Davenport-Moline-Rock Island, IA-IL Metropolitan Statistical Area; (2) Excludes separated
Source: U.S. Census Bureau, 2017-2021 American Community Survey 5-Year Estimates

Religious Groups by Family

Area	Catholic	Baptist	Methodist	LDS[2]	Pentecostal	Lutheran	Islam	Adventist	Other
MSA[1]	13.2	3.2	3.6	0.8	1.5	6.6	0.7	0.8	6.7
U.S.	18.7	7.3	3.0	2.0	1.8	1.7	1.3	1.3	11.6

Note: Figures are the number of adherents as a percentage of the total population and cover the eight largest religious groups in the U.S; (1) Figures cover the Davenport-Moline-Rock Island, IA-IL Metropolitan Statistical Area; (2) Church of Jesus Christ of Latter-day Saints
Sources: 2020 U.S. Religion Census, Association of Statisticians of American Religious Bodies; The Association of Religion Data Archives (ARDA)

Religious Groups by Tradition

Area	Catholic	Evangelical Protestant	Mainline Protestant	Black Protestant	Islam	Judaism	Hinduism	Orthodox	Buddhism
MSA[1]	13.2	8.5	10.6	1.9	0.7	0.1	0.2	0.1	n/a
U.S.	18.7	16.5	5.2	2.3	1.3	0.6	0.4	0.4	0.3

Note: Figures are the number of adherents as a percentage of the total population; (1) Figures cover the Davenport-Moline-Rock Island, IA-IL Metropolitan Statistical Area
Sources: 2020 U.S. Religion Census, Association of Statisticians of American Religious Bodies; The Association of Religion Data Archives (ARDA)

ECONOMY

Gross Metropolitan Product

Area	2020	2021	2022	2023	Rank[2]
MSA[1]	22.1	24.6	26.3	27.6	126

Note: Figures are in billions of dollars; (1) Figures cover the Davenport-Moline-Rock Island, IA-IL Metropolitan Statistical Area; (2) Rank is based on 2021 data and ranges from 1 to 381
Source: U.S. Conference of Mayors, U.S. Metro Economies: U.S. Metros Compared to Global and State Economies, June 2022

Economic Growth

Area	2018-20 (%)	2021 (%)	2022 (%)	2023 (%)	Rank[2]
MSA[1]	-0.6	5.6	1.2	1.8	184
U.S.	-0.6	5.7	3.1	2.9	—

Note: Figures are real gross metropolitan product (GMP) growth rates and represent average annual percent change; (1) Figures cover the Davenport-Moline-Rock Island, IA-IL Metropolitan Statistical Area; (2) Rank is based on 2020 2-year average annual percent change and ranges from 1 to 381
Source: U.S. Conference of Mayors, U.S. Metro Economies: U.S. Metros Compared to Global and State Economies, June 2022

Metropolitan Area Exports

Area	2016	2017	2018	2019	2020	2021	Rank[2]
MSA[1]	4,497.6	5,442.7	6,761.9	6,066.3	5,097.5	6,341.0	52

Note: Figures are in millions of dollars; (1) Figures cover the Davenport-Moline-Rock Island, IA-IL Metropolitan Statistical Area; (2) Rank is based on 2021 data and ranges from 1 to 388
Source: U.S. Department of Commerce, International Trade Administration, Office of Trade and Economic Analysis, Industry and Analysis, Exports by Metropolitan Area, data extracted March 16, 2023

Building Permits

Area	Single-Family			Multi-Family			Total		
	2021	2022	Pct. Chg.	2021	2022	Pct. Chg.	2021	2022	Pct. Chg.
City	84	160	90.5	0	0	0.0	84	160	90.5
MSA[1]	436	416	-4.6	193	181	-6.2	629	597	-5.1
U.S.	1,115,400	975,600	-12.5	621,600	689,500	10.9	1,737,000	1,665,100	-4.1

Note: (1) Figures cover the Davenport-Moline-Rock Island, IA-IL Metropolitan Statistical Area; Figures represent new, privately-owned housing units authorized (unadjusted data); All permit data are based on estimates with imputation
Source: U.S. Census Bureau, Manufacturing, Mining, and Construction Statistics, Building Permits, 2021, 2022

Bankruptcy Filings

Area	Business Filings			Nonbusiness Filings		
	2021	2022	% Chg.	2021	2022	% Chg.
Scott County	5	9	80.0	163	140	-14.1
U.S.	14,347	13,481	-6.0	399,269	374,240	-6.3

Note: Business filings include Chapter 7, Chapter 9, Chapter 11, Chapter 12, Chapter 13, Chapter 15, and Section 304; Nonbusiness filings include Chapter 7, Chapter 11, and Chapter 13
Source: Administrative Office of the U.S. Courts, Business and Nonbusiness Bankruptcy, County Cases Commenced by Chapter of the Bankruptcy Code, During the 12-Month Period Ending December 31, 2021 and Business and Nonbusiness Bankruptcy, County Cases Commenced by Chapter of the Bankruptcy Code, During the 12-Month Period Ending December 31, 2022

Housing Vacancy Rates

Area	Gross Vacancy Rate[2] (%)			Year-Round Vacancy Rate[3] (%)			Rental Vacancy Rate[4] (%)			Homeowner Vacancy Rate[5] (%)		
	2020	2021	2022	2020	2021	2022	2020	2021	2022	2020	2021	2022
MSA[1]	n/a	n/a	n/a	n/a	n/a	n/a	n/a	n/a	n/a	n/a	n/a	n/a
U.S.	10.6	10.8	10.5	8.2	8.4	8.2	6.3	6.1	5.8	1.0	0.9	0.8

Note: (1) Figures cover the Davenport-Moline-Rock Island, IA-IL Metropolitan Statistical Area; (2) The percentage of the total housing inventory that is vacant; (3) The percentage of the housing inventory (excluding seasonal units) that is year-round vacant; (4) The percentage of rental inventory that is vacant for rent; (5) The percentage of homeowner inventory that is vacant for sale; n/a not available
Source: U.S. Census Bureau, Housing Vacancies and Homeownership Annual Statistics: 2020, 2021, 2022

INCOME

Income

Area	Per Capita ($)	Median Household ($)	Average Household ($)
City	32,431	56,315	76,281
MSA[1]	34,859	63,282	83,352
U.S.	37,638	69,021	97,196

Note: (1) Figures cover the Davenport-Moline-Rock Island, IA-IL Metropolitan Statistical Area
Source: U.S. Census Bureau, 2017-2021 American Community Survey 5-Year Estimates

Household Income Distribution

Area	Percent of Households Earning							
	Under $15,000	$15,000 -$24,999	$25,000 -$34,999	$35,000 -$49,999	$50,000 -$74,999	$75,000 -$99,999	$100,000 -$149,999	$150,000 and up
City	10.9	9.1	9.0	13.6	20.8	12.8	14.6	9.2
MSA[1]	9.6	8.2	8.7	12.4	18.8	13.7	16.5	12.0
U.S.	9.4	7.8	8.2	11.4	16.8	12.8	16.3	17.3

Note: (1) Figures cover the Davenport-Moline-Rock Island, IA-IL Metropolitan Statistical Area
Source: U.S. Census Bureau, 2017-2021 American Community Survey 5-Year Estimates

Poverty Rate

Area	All Ages	Under 18 Years Old	18 to 64 Years Old	65 Years and Over
City	15.8	24.7	14.1	9.8
MSA[1]	12.6	18.5	11.8	7.6
U.S.	12.6	17.0	11.8	9.6

Note: Figures are percentage of people whose income during the past 12 months was below the poverty level;
(1) Figures cover the Davenport-Moline-Rock Island, IA-IL Metropolitan Statistical Area
Source: U.S. Census Bureau, 2017-2021 American Community Survey 5-Year Estimates

EMPLOYMENT

Labor Force and Employment

Area	Civilian Labor Force			Workers Employed		
	Dec. 2021	Dec. 2022	% Chg.	Dec. 2021	Dec. 2022	% Chg.
City	50,142	51,938	3.6	47,788	49,912	4.4
MSA[1]	185,485	190,708	2.8	177,815	183,615	3.3
U.S.	161,696,000	164,224,000	1.6	155,732,000	158,872,000	2.0

Note: Data is not seasonally adjusted and covers workers 16 years of age and older; (1) Figures cover the
Davenport-Moline-Rock Island, IA-IL Metropolitan Statistical Area
Source: Bureau of Labor Statistics, Local Area Unemployment Statistics

Unemployment Rate

Area	2022											
	Jan.	Feb.	Mar.	Apr.	May	Jun.	Jul.	Aug.	Sep.	Oct.	Nov.	Dec.
City	5.5	4.4	4.1	3.1	3.2	4.0	4.0	3.9	3.3	3.4	3.8	3.9
MSA[1]	5.3	4.6	4.4	3.7	3.8	3.7	3.8	3.8	3.4	3.5	3.7	3.7
U.S.	4.4	4.1	3.8	3.3	3.4	3.8	3.8	3.8	3.3	3.4	3.4	3.3

Note: Data is not seasonally adjusted and covers workers 16 years of age and older; (1) Figures cover the
Davenport-Moline-Rock Island, IA-IL Metropolitan Statistical Area
Source: Bureau of Labor Statistics, Local Area Unemployment Statistics

Average Wages

Occupation	$/Hr.	Occupation	$/Hr.
Accountants and Auditors	34.44	Maintenance and Repair Workers	22.09
Automotive Mechanics	23.03	Marketing Managers	60.27
Bookkeepers	21.58	Network and Computer Systems Admin.	40.41
Carpenters	25.54	Nurses, Licensed Practical	25.09
Cashiers	13.39	Nurses, Registered	32.77
Computer Programmers	41.58	Nursing Assistants	16.26
Computer Systems Analysts	42.03	Office Clerks, General	18.58
Computer User Support Specialists	27.11	Physical Therapists	41.53
Construction Laborers	23.89	Physicians	n/a
Cooks, Restaurant	14.54	Plumbers, Pipefitters and Steamfitters	32.66
Customer Service Representatives	19.17	Police and Sheriff's Patrol Officers	32.09
Dentists	75.24	Postal Service Mail Carriers	26.31
Electricians	30.25	Real Estate Sales Agents	33.24
Engineers, Electrical	46.40	Retail Salespersons	15.72
Fast Food and Counter Workers	12.80	Sales Representatives, Technical/Scientific	50.09
Financial Managers	60.84	Secretaries, Exc. Legal/Medical/Executive	19.78
First-Line Supervisors of Office Workers	29.38	Security Guards	18.10
General and Operations Managers	47.04	Surgeons	n/a
Hairdressers/Cosmetologists	16.42	Teacher Assistants, Exc. Postsecondary*	15.10
Home Health and Personal Care Aides	14.44	Teachers, Secondary School, Exc. Sp. Ed.*	31.35
Janitors and Cleaners	16.52	Telemarketers	14.97
Landscaping/Groundskeeping Workers	16.43	Truck Drivers, Heavy/Tractor-Trailer	26.12
Lawyers	56.57	Truck Drivers, Light/Delivery Services	20.97
Maids and Housekeeping Cleaners	13.68	Waiters and Waitresses	13.22

Note: Wage data covers the Davenport-Moline-Rock Island, IA-IL Metropolitan Statistical Area; (*) Hourly
wages were calculated from annual wage data based on a 40 hour work week; n/a not available.
Source: Bureau of Labor Statistics, Metro Area Occupational Employment & Wage Estimates, May 2022

Employment by Industry

Sector	MSA[1]		U.S.
	Number of Employees	Percent of Total	Percent of Total
Construction, Mining, and Logging	n/a	n/a	5.4
Private Education and Health Services	n/a	n/a	16.1
Financial Activities	n/a	n/a	5.9
Government	n/a	n/a	14.5
Information	n/a	n/a	2.0
Leisure and Hospitality	n/a	n/a	10.3
Manufacturing	n/a	n/a	8.4
Other Services	n/a	n/a	3.7
Professional and Business Services	n/a	n/a	14.7
Retail Trade	n/a	n/a	10.2
Transportation, Warehousing, and Utilities	n/a	n/a	4.9
Wholesale Trade	n/a	n/a	3.9

Note: Figures are non-farm employment as of December 2022. Figures are not seasonally adjusted and include workers 16 years of age and older; (1) Figures cover the Davenport-Moline-Rock Island, IA-IL Metropolitan Statistical Area; n/a not available
Source: Bureau of Labor Statistics, Current Employment Statistics, Employment, Hours, and Earnings

Employment by Occupation

Occupation Classification	City (%)	MSA[1] (%)	U.S. (%)
Management, Business, Science, and Arts	34.5	36.2	40.3
Natural Resources, Construction, and Maintenance	9.0	9.0	8.7
Production, Transportation, and Material Moving	17.3	17.8	13.1
Sales and Office	21.3	20.5	20.9
Service	17.9	16.5	17.0

Note: Figures cover employed civilians 16 years of age and older; (1) Figures cover the Davenport-Moline-Rock Island, IA-IL Metropolitan Statistical Area
Source: U.S. Census Bureau, 2017-2021 American Community Survey 5-Year Estimates

Occupations with Greatest Projected Employment Growth: 2022 – 2024

Occupation[1]	2022 Employment	2024 Projected Employment	Numeric Employment Change	Percent Employment Change
Fast Food and Counter Workers	39,300	41,100	1,800	4.6
Cooks, Restaurant	12,190	13,530	1,340	11.0
Waiters and Waitresses	19,970	21,220	1,250	6.3
Farmers, Ranchers, and Other Agricultural Managers	85,770	86,980	1,210	1.4
Home Health and Personal Care Aides	24,530	25,690	1,160	4.7
Maids and Housekeeping Cleaners	11,530	12,500	970	8.4
Registered Nurses	34,440	35,270	830	2.4
Bartenders	8,970	9,770	800	8.9
Laborers and Freight, Stock, and Material Movers, Hand	31,300	32,000	700	2.2
Heavy and Tractor-Trailer Truck Drivers	46,230	46,880	650	1.4

Note: Projections cover Iowa; (1) Sorted by numeric employment change
Source: www.projectionscentral.com, State Occupational Projections, 2022–2024 Short-Term Projections

Fastest-Growing Occupations: 2022 – 2024

Occupation[1]	2022 Employment	2024 Projected Employment	Numeric Employment Change	Percent Employment Change
Entertainers and Performers, Sports and Related Workers, All Other	210	260	50	23.8
Hotel, Motel, and Resort Desk Clerks	3,170	3,780	610	19.2
Ushers, Lobby Attendants, and Ticket Takers	800	950	150	18.8
Audio and Video Equipment Technicians	340	400	60	17.6
Gaming Change Persons and Booth Cashiers	340	400	60	17.6
Wind Turbine Service Technicians	460	540	80	17.4
Gaming Dealers	1,180	1,370	190	16.1
Musicians and Singers	420	480	60	14.3
Gaming Service Workers, All Other	370	420	50	13.5
Passenger Vehicle Drivers, Except Bus Drivers, Transit and Intercity	1,950	2,200	250	12.8

Note: Projections cover Iowa; (1) Sorted by percent employment change and excludes occupations with numeric employment change less than 50
Source: www.projectionscentral.com, State Occupational Projections, 2022–2024 Short-Term Projections

CITY FINANCES

City Government Finances

Component	2020 ($000)	2020 ($ per capita)
Total Revenues	195,756	1,927
Total Expenditures	194,737	1,917
Debt Outstanding	296,018	2,914
Cash and Securities[1]	192,306	1,893

Note: (1) Cash and security holdings of a government at the close of its fiscal year, including those of its dependent agencies, utilities, and liquor stores.
Source: U.S. Census Bureau, State & Local Government Finances 2020

City Government Revenue by Source

Source	2020 ($000)	2020 ($ per capita)	2020 (%)
General Revenue			
From Federal Government	14,318	141	7.3
From State Government	21,731	214	11.1
From Local Governments	776	8	0.4
Taxes			
Property	77,893	767	39.8
Sales and Gross Receipts	25,348	250	12.9
Personal Income	0	0	0.0
Corporate Income	0	0	0.0
Motor Vehicle License	0	0	0.0
Other Taxes	2,239	22	1.1
Current Charges	44,945	442	23.0
Liquor Store	0	0	0.0
Utility	321	3	0.2

Source: U.S. Census Bureau, State & Local Government Finances 2020

City Government Expenditures by Function

Function	2020 ($000)	2020 ($ per capita)	2020 (%)
General Direct Expenditures			
Air Transportation	324	3	0.2
Corrections	0	0	0.0
Education	0	0	0.0
Employment Security Administration	0	0	0.0
Financial Administration	1,928	19	1.0
Fire Protection	20,059	197	10.3
General Public Buildings	948	9	0.5
Governmental Administration, Other	2,436	24	1.3
Health	0	0	0.0
Highways	18,298	180	9.4
Hospitals	0	0	0.0
Housing and Community Development	8,646	85	4.4
Interest on General Debt	6,008	59	3.1
Judicial and Legal	0	0	0.0
Libraries	5,241	51	2.7
Parking	866	8	0.4
Parks and Recreation	7,303	71	3.8
Police Protection	28,694	282	14.7
Public Welfare	0	0	0.0
Sewerage	16,210	159	8.3
Solid Waste Management	5,589	55	2.9
Veterans' Services	0	0	0.0
Liquor Store	0	0	0.0
Utility	9,471	93	4.9

Source: U.S. Census Bureau, State & Local Government Finances 2020

TAXES

State Corporate Income Tax Rates

State	Tax Rate (%)	Income Brackets ($)	Num. of Brackets	Financial Institution Tax Rate (%)[a]	Federal Income Tax Ded.
Iowa	5.5 - 8.4	100,000 - 250,001	3	4.7	Yes (h)

Note: Tax rates as of January 1, 2023; (a) Rates listed are the corporate income tax rate applied to financial institutions or excise taxes based on income. Some states have other taxes based upon the value of deposits or shares; (h) 50% of the federal income tax is deductible.
Source: Federation of Tax Administrators, State Corporate Income Tax Rates, January 1, 2023

State Individual Income Tax Rates

State	Tax Rate (%)	Income Brackets ($)	Personal Exemptions ($)			Standard Ded. ($)	
			Single	Married	Depend.	Single	Married
Iowa (a)	4.4 - 6.0 (bb)	6,000 - 75,000	40	80	40 (c)	–	–

Note: Tax rates as of January 1, 2023; Local- and county-level taxes are not included; Federal income tax is deductible on state income tax returns; (a) 16 states have statutory provision for automatically adjusting to the rate of inflation the dollar values of the income tax brackets, standard deductions, and/or personal exemptions. Oregon does not index the income brackets for $125,000 and over; (c) The personal exemption takes the form of a tax credit instead of a deduction; (bb) Louisiana tax rates may be adjusted down if revenue trigger is met on April 1st. Iowa is phasing-in a flat rate by 2027, while Nebraska and South Carolina is phasing-in a reduced top rate by 2027.
Source: Federation of Tax Administrators, State Individual Income Tax Rates, January 1, 2023

Various State Sales and Excise Tax Rates

State	State Sales Tax (%)	Gasoline[1] ($/gal.)	Cigarette[2] ($/pack)	Spirits[3] ($/gal.)	Wine[4] ($/gal.)	Beer[5] ($/gal.)	Recreational Marijuana (%)
Iowa	6	0.30	1.36	14.10	1.75	0.19	Not legal

Note: All tax rates as of January 1, 2023; (1) The American Petroleum Institute has developed a methodology for determining the average tax rate on a gallon of fuel. Rates may include any of the following: excise taxes, environmental fees, storage tank fees, other fees or taxes, general sales tax, and local taxes; (2) The federal excise tax of $1.0066 per pack and local taxes are not included; (3) Rates are those applicable to off-premise sales of 40% alcohol by volume (a.b.v.) distilled spirits in 750ml containers. Local excise taxes are excluded; (4) Rates are those applicable to off-premise sales of 11% a.b.v. non-carbonated wine in 750ml containers; (5) Rates are those applicable to off-premise sales of 4.7% a.b.v. beer in 12 ounce containers.
Source: Tax Foundation, 2023 Facts & Figures: How Does Your State Compare?

State Business Tax Climate Index Rankings

State	Overall Rank	Corporate Tax Rank	Individual Income Tax Rank	Sales Tax Rank	Property Tax Rank	Unemployment Insurance Tax Rank
Iowa	38	34	40	15	40	33

Note: The index is a measure of how each state's tax laws affect economic performance. The lower the rank, the more favorable a state's tax system is for business. States without a given tax are given a ranking of 1. The scores/rankings for the District of Columbia do not affect other states. The 2023 index represents the tax climate as of July 1, 2022.
Source: Tax Foundation, State Business Tax Climate Index 2023

TRANSPORTATION

Means of Transportation to Work

Area	Car/Truck/Van		Public Transportation			Bicycle	Walked	Other Means	Worked at Home
	Drove Alone	Car-pooled	Bus	Subway	Railroad				
City	83.4	6.5	0.6	0.0	0.0	0.2	2.3	0.7	6.3
MSA[1]	83.9	6.8	0.7	0.0	0.0	0.2	2.2	0.7	5.6
U.S.	73.2	8.6	2.0	1.6	0.5	0.5	2.5	1.5	9.7

Note: Figures are percentages and cover workers 16 years of age and older; (1) Figures cover the Davenport-Moline-Rock Island, IA-IL Metropolitan Statistical Area
Source: U.S. Census Bureau, 2017-2021 American Community Survey 5-Year Estimates

Travel Time to Work

Area	Less Than 10 Minutes	10 to 19 Minutes	20 to 29 Minutes	30 to 44 Minutes	45 to 59 Minutes	60 to 89 Minutes	90 Minutes or More
City	16.5	47.5	22.0	8.2	3.1	1.8	1.0
MSA[1]	18.3	36.1	24.9	13.1	3.9	2.4	1.3
U.S.	12.4	28.5	21.0	20.9	8.2	6.2	2.9

Note: Note: Figures are percentages and include workers 16 years old and over; (1) Figures cover the Davenport-Moline-Rock Island, IA-IL Metropolitan Statistical Area
Source: U.S. Census Bureau, 2017-2021 American Community Survey 5-Year Estimates

Key Congestion Measures

Measure	1990	2000	2010	2015	2020
Annual Hours of Delay, Total (000)	n/a	n/a	n/a	4,084	2,579
Annual Hours of Delay, Per Auto Commuter	n/a	n/a	n/a	14	9
Annual Congestion Cost, Per Auto Commuter ($)	n/a	n/a	n/a	286	193

Note: n/a not available
Source: Texas A&M Transportation Institute, 2021 Urban Mobility Report

Freeway Travel Time Index

Measure	1985	1990	1995	2000	2005	2010	2015	2020
Urban Area Index[1]	n/a	n/a	n/a	n/a	n/a	n/a	1.05	1.04
Urban Area Rank[1,2]	n/a	n/a	n/a	n/a	n/a	n/a	n/a	n/a

Note: Freeway Travel Time Index—the ratio of travel time in the peak period to the travel time at free-flow conditions. For example, a value of 1.30 indicates a 20-minute free-flow trip takes 26 minutes in the peak (20 minutes x 1.30 = 26 minutes); (1) Covers the Davenport IA-IL urban area; (2) Rank is based on 101 larger urban areas (#1 = highest travel time index); n/a not available
Source: Texas A&M Transportation Institute, 2021 Urban Mobility Report

Public Transportation

Agency Name / Mode of Transportation	Vehicles Operated in Maximum Service[1]	Annual Unlinked Passenger Trips[2] (in thous.)	Annual Passenger Miles[3] (in thous.)
Davenport Public Transit			
Bus (directly operated)	15	396.8	n/a

Note: (1) Number of revenue vehicles operated by the given mode and type of service to meet the annual maximum service requirement. This is the revenue vehicle count during the peak season of the year; on the week and day that maximum service is provided. Vehicles operated in maximum service (VOMS) exclude atypical days and one-time special events; (2) Number of passengers who boarded public transportation vehicles. Passengers are counted each time they board a vehicle no matter how many vehicles they use to travel from their origin to their destination. (3) Sum of the distances ridden by all passengers during the entire fiscal year.
Source: Federal Transit Administration, National Transit Database, 2021

Air Transportation

Airport Name and Code / Type of Service	Passenger Airlines[1]	Passenger Enplanements	Freight Carriers[2]	Freight (lbs)
Quad City International Airport (MLI)				
Domestic service (U.S. carriers - 2022)	13	269,730	4	12,531
International service (U.S. carriers - 2021)	0	0	0	0

Note: (1) Includes all U.S.-based major, minor and commuter airlines that carried at least one passenger during the year; (2) Includes all U.S.-based airlines and freight carriers that transported at least one pound of freight during the year.
Source: Bureau of Transportation Statistics, The Intermodal Transportation Database, Air Carriers: T-100 Domestic Market (U.S. Carriers), 2022; Bureau of Transportation Statistics, The Intermodal Transportation Database, Air Carriers: T-100 International Market (U.S. Carriers), 2021

BUSINESSES

Major Business Headquarters

Company Name	Industry	Rankings	
		Fortune[1]	Forbes[2]
No companies listed	-	-	-

Note: (1) Companies that produce a 10-K are ranked 1 to 500 based on 2021 revenue; (2) All private companies with at least $2 billion in annual revenue through the end of their most current fiscal year are ranked 1 to 246; companies listed are headquartered in the city; dashes indicate no ranking
Source: Fortune, "Fortune 500," 2022; Forbes, "America's Largest Private Companies," 2022

Living Environment

COST OF LIVING

Cost of Living Index

Composite Index	Groceries	Housing	Utilities	Trans-portation	Health Care	Misc. Goods/ Services
90.2	113.3	66.9	91.4	94.3	95.9	96.7

Note: The Cost of Living Index measures regional differences in the cost of consumer goods and services, excluding taxes and non-consumer expenditures, for professional and managerial households in the top income quintile. It is based on more than 50,000 prices covering almost 60 different items for which prices are collected three times a year by chambers of commerce, economic development organizations or university applied economic centers in each participating urban area. The numbers shown should be read as a percentage above or below the national average of 100. For example, a value of 115.4 in the groceries column indicates that grocery prices are 15.4% higher than the national average. Small differences in the index numbers should not be interpreted as significant; Figures cover the Davenport-Moline-Rock Is IA-IL urban area.
Source: The Council for Community and Economic Research, Cost of Living Index, 2022

Grocery Prices

Area[1]	T-Bone Steak ($/pound)	Frying Chicken ($/pound)	Whole Milk ($/half gal.)	Eggs ($/dozen)	Orange Juice ($/64 oz.)	Coffee ($/11.5 oz.)
City[2]	13.66	2.17	2.57	2.18	3.81	5.91
Avg.	13.81	1.59	2.43	2.25	3.85	4.95
Min.	10.17	0.90	1.51	1.30	2.90	3.46
Max.	19.35	3.30	4.32	4.32	5.31	8.59

*Note: (1) Values for the local area are compared with the average, minimum and maximum values for all 286 areas in the Cost of Living Index; (2) Figures cover the Davenport-Moline-Rock Is IA-IL urban area; **T-Bone Steak** (price per pound); **Frying Chicken** (price per pound, whole fryer); **Whole Milk** (half gallon carton); **Eggs** (price per dozen, Grade A, large); **Orange Juice** (64 oz. Tropicana or Florida Natural); **Coffee** (11.5 oz. can, vacuum-packed, Maxwell House, Hills Bros, or Folgers).*
Source: The Council for Community and Economic Research, Cost of Living Index, 2022

Housing and Utility Costs

Area[1]	New Home Price ($)	Apartment Rent ($/month)	All Electric ($/month)	Part Electric ($/month)	Other Energy ($/month)	Telephone ($/month)
City[2]	285,682	1,014	-	88.01	57.06	198.79
Avg.	450,913	1,371	176.41	99.93	76.96	190.22
Min.	229,283	546	100.84	31.56	27.15	174.27
Max.	2,434,977	4,569	356.86	249.59	272.24	208.31

*Note: (1) Values for the local area are compared with the average, minimum and maximum values for all 286 areas in the Cost of Living Index; (2) Figures cover the Davenport-Moline-Rock Is IA-IL urban area; **New Home Price** (2,400 sf living area, 8,000 sf lot, in urban area with full utilities); **Apartment Rent** (950 sf 2 bedroom/1.5 or 2 bath, unfurnished, excluding all utilities except water); **All Electric** (average monthly cost for an all-electric home); **Part Electric** (average monthly cost for a part-electric home); **Other Energy** (average monthly cost for natural gas, fuel oil, coal, wood, and any other forms of energy except electricity); **Telephone** (price includes the base monthly rate plus taxes and fees for three lines of mobile phone service).*
Source: The Council for Community and Economic Research, Cost of Living Index, 2022

Health Care, Transportation, and Other Costs

Area[1]	Doctor ($/visit)	Dentist ($/visit)	Optometrist ($/visit)	Gasoline ($/gallon)	Beauty Salon ($/visit)	Men's Shirt ($)
City[2]	136.67	84.83	102.07	3.46	34.89	37.75
Avg.	124.91	107.77	117.66	3.86	43.31	34.21
Min.	36.61	58.25	51.79	2.90	22.18	13.05
Max.	250.21	162.58	371.96	5.54	85.61	63.54

*Note: (1) Values for the local area are compared with the average, minimum and maximum values for all 286 areas in the Cost of Living Index; (2) Figures cover the Davenport-Moline-Rock Is IA-IL urban area; **Doctor** (general practitioners routine exam of an established patient); **Dentist** (adult teeth cleaning and periodic oral examination); **Optometrist** (full vision eye exam for established adult patient); **Gasoline** (one gallon regular unleaded, national brand, including all taxes, cash price at self-service pump if available); **Beauty Salon** (woman's shampoo, trim, and blow-dry); **Men's Shirt** (cotton/polyester dress shirt, pinpoint weave, long sleeves).*
Source: The Council for Community and Economic Research, Cost of Living Index, 2022

HOUSING

Homeownership Rate

Area	2015 (%)	2016 (%)	2017 (%)	2018 (%)	2019 (%)	2020 (%)	2021 (%)	2022 (%)
MSA[1]	n/a	n/a	n/a	n/a	n/a	n/a	n/a	n/a
U.S.	63.7	63.4	63.9	64.4	64.6	66.6	65.5	65.8

Note: (1) Figures cover the Davenport-Moline-Rock Island, IA-IL Metropolitan Statistical Area; n/a not available
Source: U.S. Census Bureau, Housing Vacancies and Homeownership Annual Statistics: 2015-2022

House Price Index (HPI)

Area	National Ranking[2]	Quarterly Change (%)	One-Year Change (%)	Five-Year Change (%)	Since 1991Q1 (%)
MSA[1]	220	0.26	7.72	30.21	202.26
U.S.[3]	–	0.34	8.41	58.44	289.08

Note: The HPI is a weighted repeat sales index. It measures average price changes in repeat sales or refinancings on the same properties. This information is obtained by reviewing repeat mortgage transactions on single-family properties whose mortgages have been purchased or securitized by Fannie Mae or Freddie Mac since January 1975; (1) Figures cover the Davenport-Moline-Rock Island, IA-IL Metropolitan Statistical Area; (2) Rankings are based on annual percentage change for all metro areas containing at least 15,000 transactions over the last 10 years and ranges from 1 to 257; (3) figures based on a weighted average of Census Division estimates using a seasonally adjusted, purchase-only index; all figures are for the period ending December 31, 2022
Source: Federal Housing Finance Agency, Change in FHFA Metropolitan Area House Price Indexes, 2022Q4

Median Single-Family Home Prices

Area	2020	2021	2022[p]	Percent Change 2021 to 2022
MSA[1]	142.8	152.3	160.4	5.3
U.S. Average	300.2	357.1	392.6	9.9

Note: Figures are median sales prices of existing single-family homes in thousands of dollars; (p) preliminary; (1) Figures cover the Davenport-Moline-Rock Island, IA-IL Metropolitan Statistical Area
Source: National Association of Realtors, Median Sales Price of Existing Single-Family Homes for Metropolitan Areas, 4th Quarter 2022

Qualifying Income Based on Median Sales Price of Existing Single-Family Homes

Area	With 5% Down ($)	With 10% Down ($)	With 20% Down ($)
MSA[1]	48,647	46,087	40,966
U.S. Average	112,234	106,237	94,513

Note: Figures are preliminary; Qualifying income is based on a mortgage rate of 6.77%. Monthly principal and interest payment is limited to 25% of income; (1) Figures cover the Davenport-Moline-Rock Island, IA-IL Metropolitan Statistical Area
Source: National Association of Realtors, Qualifying Income Based on Median Sales Price of Existing Single-Family Homes for Metropolitan Areas, 4th Quarter 2022

Home Value

Area	Under $100,000	$100,000 -$199,999	$200,000 -$299,999	$300,000 -$399,999	$400,000 -$499,999	$500,000 -$999,999	$1,000,000 or more	Median ($)
City	28.0	44.6	17.1	7.5	1.1	1.4	0.3	138,000
MSA[1]	27.9	41.0	17.1	8.3	2.8	2.6	0.4	145,200
U.S.	16.2	24.2	20.1	13.6	8.3	13.6	4.1	244,900

Note: Figures are percentages except for median and cover owner-occupied housing units; (1) Figures cover the Davenport-Moline-Rock Island, IA-IL Metropolitan Statistical Area
Source: U.S. Census Bureau, 2017-2021 American Community Survey 5-Year Estimates

Year Housing Structure Built

Area	2020 or Later	2010 -2019	2000 -2009	1990 -1999	1980 -1989	1970 -1979	1960 -1969	1950 -1959	1940 -1949	Before 1940	Median Year
City	<0.1	3.9	8.5	8.7	6.8	15.2	12.5	10.9	5.6	27.8	1965
MSA[1]	0.1	4.6	7.9	8.5	6.8	15.9	12.8	12.1	7.2	24.2	1965
U.S.	0.2	7.3	13.6	13.6	13.2	14.8	10.3	10.0	4.7	12.2	1979

Note: Figures are percentages except for Median Year; Note: (1) Figures cover the Davenport-Moline-Rock Island, IA-IL Metropolitan Statistical Area
Source: U.S. Census Bureau, 2017-2021 American Community Survey 5-Year Estimates

Gross Monthly Rent

Area	Under $500	$500 -$999	$1,000 -$1,499	$1,500 -$1,999	$2,000 -$2,499	$2,500 -$2,999	$3,000 and up	Median ($)
City	9.4	61.7	21.9	4.3	0.7	0.5	1.5	815
MSA[1]	12.9	58.7	21.1	4.7	1.2	0.4	1.1	808
U.S.	8.1	30.5	30.8	16.8	7.3	3.1	3.5	1,163

Note: Figures are percentages except for median; Gross rent is the contract rent plus the estimated average monthly cost of utilities (electricity, gas, and water and sewer) and fuels (oil, coal, kerosene, wood, etc.) if these are paid by the renter (or paid for the renter by someone else); (1) Figures cover the Davenport-Moline-Rock Island, IA-IL Metropolitan Statistical Area
Source: U.S. Census Bureau, 2017-2021 American Community Survey 5-Year Estimates

HEALTH

Health Risk Factors

Category	MSA[1] (%)	U.S. (%)
Adults aged 18–64 who have any kind of health care coverage	n/a	90.9
Adults who reported being in good or better health	n/a	85.2
Adults who have been told they have high blood cholesterol	n/a	35.7
Adults who have been told they have high blood pressure	n/a	32.4
Adults who are current smokers	n/a	14.4
Adults who currently use e-cigarettes	n/a	6.7
Adults who currently use chewing tobacco, snuff, or snus	n/a	3.5
Adults who are heavy drinkers[2]	n/a	6.3
Adults who are binge drinkers[3]	n/a	15.4
Adults who are overweight (BMI 25.0 - 29.9)	n/a	34.4
Adults who are obese (BMI 30.0 - 99.8)	n/a	33.9
Adults who participated in any physical activities in the past month	n/a	76.3

Note: (1) Figures for the Davenport-Moline-Rock Island, IA-IL Metropolitan Statistical Area were not available.
(2) Heavy drinkers are classified as adult men having more than 14 drinks per week and adult women having more than 7 drinks per week; (3) Binge drinkers are classified as males having five or more drinks on one occasion or females having four or more drinks on one occasion
Source: Centers for Disease Control and Prevention, Behaviorial Risk Factor Surveillance System, SMART: Selected Metropolitan Area Risk Trends, 2021

Acute and Chronic Health Conditions

Category	MSA[1] (%)	U.S. (%)
Adults who have ever been told they had a heart attack	n/a	4.0
Adults who have ever been told they have angina or coronary heart disease	n/a	3.8
Adults who have ever been told they had a stroke	n/a	3.0
Adults who have ever been told they have asthma	n/a	14.9
Adults who have ever been told they have arthritis	n/a	25.8
Adults who have ever been told they have diabetes[2]	n/a	10.9
Adults who have ever been told they had skin cancer	n/a	6.6
Adults who have ever been told they had any other types of cancer	n/a	7.5
Adults who have ever been told they have COPD	n/a	6.1
Adults who have ever been told they have kidney disease	n/a	3.0
Adults who have ever been told they have a form of depression	n/a	20.5

Note: (1) Figures for the Davenport-Moline-Rock Island, IA-IL Metropolitan Statistical Area were not available.
(2) Figures do not include pregnancy-related, borderline, or pre-diabetes
Source: Centers for Disease Control and Prevention, Behaviorial Risk Factor Surveillance System, SMART: Selected Metropolitan Area Risk Trends, 2021

Health Screening and Vaccination Rates

Category	MSA[1] (%)	U.S. (%)
Adults who have ever been tested for HIV	n/a	34.9
Adults who have had their blood cholesterol checked within the last five years	n/a	85.2
Adults aged 65+ who have had flu shot within the past year	n/a	68.6
Adults aged 65+ who have ever had a pneumonia vaccination	n/a	71.0

Note: (1) Figures for the Davenport-Moline-Rock Island, IA-IL Metropolitan Statistical Area were not available.
Source: Centers for Disease Control and Prevention, Behaviorial Risk Factor Surveillance System, SMART: Selected Metropolitan Area Risk Trends, 2021

Disability Status

Category	MSA[1] (%)	U.S. (%)
Adults who reported being deaf	n/a	7.2
Are you blind or have serious difficulty seeing, even when wearing glasses?	n/a	4.8
Are you limited in any way in any of your usual activities due to arthritis?	n/a	11.1
Do you have difficulty doing errands alone?	n/a	7.0
Do you have difficulty dressing or bathing?	n/a	3.6
Do you have serious difficulty concentrating/remembering/making decisions?	n/a	12.1
Do you have serious difficulty walking or climbing stairs?	n/a	12.8

Note: (1) Figures for the Davenport-Moline-Rock Island, IA-IL Metropolitan Statistical Area were not available.
Source: Centers for Disease Control and Prevention, Behaviorial Risk Factor Surveillance System, SMART: Selected Metropolitan Area Risk Trends, 2021

Mortality Rates for the Top 10 Causes of Death in the U.S.

ICD-10[a] Sub-Chapter	ICD-10[a] Code	Crude Mortality Rate[1] per 100,000 population	
		County[2]	U.S.
Malignant neoplasms	C00-C97	198.9	182.6
Ischaemic heart diseases	I20-I25	137.8	113.1
Other forms of heart disease	I30-I51	60.2	64.4
Other degenerative diseases of the nervous system	G30-G31	43.6	51.0
Cerebrovascular diseases	I60-I69	48.0	47.8
Other external causes of accidental injury	W00-X59	39.8	46.4
Chronic lower respiratory diseases	J40-J47	63.4	45.7
Organic, including symptomatic, mental disorders	F01-F09	45.9	35.9
Hypertensive diseases	I10-I15	36.3	35.0
Diabetes mellitus	E10-E14	17.5	29.6

Note: (a) ICD-10 = International Classification of Diseases 10th Revision; (1) Crude mortality rates are a three-year average covering 2019-2021; (2) Figures cover Scott County.
Source: Centers for Disease Control and Prevention, National Center for Health Statistics. National Vital Statistics System, Mortality 2018-2021 on CDC WONDER Online Database

Mortality Rates for Selected Causes of Death

ICD-10[a] Sub-Chapter	ICD-10[a] Code	Crude Mortality Rate[1] per 100,000 population	
		County[2]	U.S.
Assault	X85-Y09	5.8	7.0
Diseases of the liver	K70-K76	18.6	19.8
Human immunodeficiency virus (HIV) disease	B20-B24	Suppressed	1.5
Influenza and pneumonia	J09-J18	12.1	14.7
Intentional self-harm	X60-X84	16.9	14.3
Malnutrition	E40-E46	6.3	4.3
Obesity and other hyperalimentation	E65-E68	5.0	3.0
Renal failure	N17-N19	11.1	15.7
Transport accidents	V01-V99	7.9	13.6
Viral hepatitis	B15-B19	Suppressed	1.2

Note: (a) ICD-10 = International Classification of Diseases 10th Revision; (1) Crude mortality rates are a three-year average covering 2019-2021; (2) Figures cover Scott County; Data are suppressed when the data meet the criteria for confidentiality constraints; Crude mortality rates are flagged as unreliable when the rate would be calculated with a numerator of 20 or less.
Source: Centers for Disease Control and Prevention, National Center for Health Statistics. National Vital Statistics System, Mortality 2018-2021 on CDC WONDER Online Database

Health Insurance Coverage

Area	With Health Insurance	With Private Health Insurance	With Public Health Insurance	Without Health Insurance	Population Under Age 19 Without Health Insurance
City	93.3	66.2	39.9	6.7	4.9
MSA[1]	94.5	71.5	37.8	5.5	3.5
U.S.	91.2	67.8	35.4	8.8	5.3

Note: Figures are percentages that cover the civilian noninstitutionalized population; (1) Figures cover the Davenport-Moline-Rock Island, IA-IL Metropolitan Statistical Area
Source: U.S. Census Bureau, 2017-2021 American Community Survey 5-Year Estimates

Number of Medical Professionals

Area	MDs[3]	DOs[3,4]	Dentists	Podiatrists	Chiropractors	Optometrists
County[1] (number)	420	93	141	8	321	30
County[1] (rate[2])	240.7	53.3	81.0	4.6	184.3	17.2
U.S. (rate[2])	289.3	23.5	72.5	6.2	28.7	17.4

Note: Data as of 2021 unless noted; (1) Data covers Scott County; (2) Rate per 100,000 population; (3) Data as of 2020 and includes all active, non-federal physicians; (4) Doctor of Osteopathic Medicine
Source: U.S. Department of Health and Human Services, Health Resources and Services Administration, Bureau of Health Professions, Area Resource File (ARF) 2021-2022

EDUCATION

Public School District Statistics

District Name	Schls	Pupils	Pupil/ Teacher Ratio	Minority Pupils[1] (%)	LEP/ELL[2] (%)	IEP[3] (%)
Davenport Comm School District	30	14,417	14.2	47.9	2.8	18.0

Note: Table includes school districts with 2,000 or more students; (1) Percentage of students that are not non-Hispanic white; (2) Percentage of students that are Limited English Proficient or English Language Learners (2018-19); (3) Percentage of students that have an Individualized Education Program (2019-20).
Source: U.S. Department of Education, National Center for Education Statistics, Common Core of Data, Local Education Agency (School District) Universe Survey: School Year 2021-2022

Highest Level of Education

Area	Less than H.S.	H.S. Diploma	Some College, No Deg.	Associate Degree	Bachelor's Degree	Master's Degree	Prof. School Degree	Doctorate Degree
City	7.9	31.4	22.0	11.7	17.9	6.6	1.6	0.9
MSA[1]	8.2	29.9	22.9	11.1	17.8	7.7	1.5	0.9
U.S.	11.1	26.5	20.0	8.7	20.6	9.3	2.2	1.5

Note: Figures cover persons age 25 and over; (1) Figures cover the Davenport-Moline-Rock Island, IA-IL Metropolitan Statistical Area
Source: U.S. Census Bureau, 2017-2021 American Community Survey 5-Year Estimates

Educational Attainment by Race

Area	High School Graduate or Higher (%)					Bachelor's Degree or Higher (%)				
	Total	White	Black	Asian	Hisp.[2]	Total	White	Black	Asian	Hisp.[2]
City	92.1	93.9	87.7	71.8	78.3	27.1	29.1	13.6	35.3	15.4
MSA[1]	91.8	93.9	80.3	78.7	75.3	27.9	29.0	11.8	51.7	16.9
U.S.	88.9	91.4	87.2	87.6	71.2	33.7	35.5	23.3	55.6	18.4

Note: Figures shown cover persons 25 years old and over; (1) Figures cover the Davenport-Moline-Rock Island, IA-IL Metropolitan Statistical Area; (2) People of Hispanic origin can be of any race
Source: U.S. Census Bureau, 2017-2021 American Community Survey 5-Year Estimates

School Enrollment by Grade and Control

Area	Preschool (%)		Kindergarten (%)		Grades 1 - 4 (%)		Grades 5 - 8 (%)		Grades 9 - 12 (%)	
	Public	Private	Public	Private	Public	Private	Public	Private	Public	Private
City	59.7	40.3	83.7	16.3	85.5	14.5	86.6	13.4	94.0	6.0
MSA[1]	68.6	31.4	88.3	11.7	91.0	9.0	92.0	8.0	92.1	7.9
U.S.	58.8	41.2	86.3	13.7	88.3	11.7	88.6	11.4	89.4	10.6

Note: Figures shown cover persons 3 years old and over; (1) Figures cover the Davenport-Moline-Rock Island, IA-IL Metropolitan Statistical Area
Source: U.S. Census Bureau, 2017-2021 American Community Survey 5-Year Estimates

Higher Education

Four-Year Colleges			Two-Year Colleges			Medical Schools[1]	Law Schools[2]	Voc/ Tech[3]
Public	Private Non-profit	Private For-profit	Public	Private Non-profit	Private For-profit			
0	4	1	2	0	3	0	0	0

Note: Figures cover institutions located within the Davenport-Moline-Rock Island, IA-IL Metropolitan Statistical Area and include main campuses only; (1) includes schools accredited by the Liaison Committee on Medical Education and the American Osteopathic Association's Commission on Osteopathic College Accreditation; (2) includes ABA-accredited schools, schools with provisional ABA accreditation, and state accredited schools; (3) includes all schools with programs that are less than 2 years.
Source: National Center for Education Statistics, Integrated Postsecondary Education System (IPEDS), 2021-22; Wikipedia, List of Medical Schools in the United States, accessed April 10, 2023; Wikipedia, List of Law Schools in the United States, accessed April 10, 2023

According to *U.S. News & World Report*, the Davenport-Moline-Rock Island, IA-IL metro area is home to one of the top 100 liberal arts colleges in the U.S.: **Augustana College** (#94 tie). The indicators used to capture academic quality fall into a number of categories: assessment by administrators at peer institutions; retention of students; faculty resources; student selectivity; financial resources;

alumni giving; high school counselor ratings of colleges; and graduation rate. *U.S. News & World Report, "America's Best Colleges 2023"*

EMPLOYERS

Major Employers

Company Name	Industry
Alcoa	Manufacturer
Deere and Company	Manufacturer
Genesis Health System	Healthcare
HNI Corporation/The Hon Company/Allsteel	Manufacturer
Hy-Vee Food Stores	Grocery stores
Kraft Foods/Oscar Mayer	Food processing
Rock Island Arsenal	U.S. military
Trinity Regional Health System	Healthcare
Tyson Fresh Meats	Food processing
XPAC	Service, parts, packaging

Note: Companies shown are located within the Davenport-Moline-Rock Island, IA-IL Metropolitan Statistical Area.
Source: Hoovers.com; Wikipedia

PUBLIC SAFETY

Crime Rate

Area	Total Crime	Violent Crime Rate				Property Crime Rate		
		Murder	Rape[3]	Robbery	Aggrav. Assault	Burglary	Larceny -Theft	Motor Vehicle Theft
City	4,661.8	9.8	65.8	133.6	527.5	895.8	2,568.6	460.7
Suburbs[1]	n/a	5.8	57.2	48.2	268.5	345.6	n/a	174.3
Metro[2]	n/a	6.9	59.6	71.2	338.3	493.9	n/a	251.4
U.S.	2,356.7	6.5	38.4	73.9	279.7	314.2	1,398.0	246.0

Note: Figures are crimes per 100,000 population; (1) All areas within the metro area that are located outside the city limits; (2) Figures cover the Davenport-Moline-Rock Island, IA-IL Metropolitan Statistical Area; (3) All figures shown were reported using the revised Uniform Crime Reporting (UCR) definition of rape; Due to the transition to the National Incident-Based Reporting System (NIBRS), limited city and metro area data was released for 2021.
Source: FBI Uniform Crime Reports, 2020

Hate Crimes

Area	Number of Quarters Reported	Number of Incidents per Bias Motivation					
		Race/Ethnicity/ Ancestry	Religion	Sexual Orientation	Disability	Gender	Gender Identity
City	4	1	0	0	0	0	0
U.S.	4	5,227	1,244	1,110	130	75	266

Note: Due to the transition to the National Incident-Based Reporting System (NIBRS), limited crime data was released for 2021.
Source: Federal Bureau of Investigation, Hate Crime Statistics 2020

Identity Theft Consumer Reports

Area	Reports	Reports per 100,000 Population	Rank[2]
MSA[1]	515	135	285
U.S.	1,108,609	339	-

Note: (1) Figures cover the Davenport-Moline-Rock Island, IA-IL Metropolitan Statistical Area; (2) Rank ranges from 1 to 391 where 1 indicates greatest number of identity theft reports per 100,000 population
Source: Federal Trade Commission, Consumer Sentinel Network Data Book 2022

Fraud and Other Consumer Reports

Area	Reports	Reports per 100,000 Population	Rank[2]
MSA[1]	2,556	672	308
U.S.	4,064,520	1,245	-

Note: (1) Figures cover the Davenport-Moline-Rock Island, IA-IL Metropolitan Statistical Area; (2) Rank ranges from 1 to 391 where 1 indicates greatest number of fraud and other consumer reports per 100,000 population
Source: Federal Trade Commission, Consumer Sentinel Network Data Book 2022

POLITICS

2020 Presidential Election Results

Area	Biden	Trump	Jorgensen	Hawkins	Other
Scott County	50.7	47.2	1.2	0.2	0.7
U.S.	51.3	46.8	1.2	0.3	0.5

Note: Results are percentages and may not add to 100% due to rounding
Source: Dave Leip's Atlas of U.S. Presidential Elections

SPORTS

Professional Sports Teams

Team Name	League	Year Established
No teams are located in the metro area		

Source: Wikipedia, Major Professional Sports Teams of the United States and Canada, April 12, 2023

CLIMATE

Average and Extreme Temperatures

Temperature	Jan	Feb	Mar	Apr	May	Jun	Jul	Aug	Sep	Oct	Nov	Dec	Yr.
Extreme High (°F)	65	70	91	93	98	103	105	108	99	95	76	69	108
Average High (°F)	29	34	45	61	72	82	86	84	76	65	48	33	60
Average Temp. (°F)	20	25	36	51	62	72	76	74	65	54	39	25	50
Average Low (°F)	11	16	27	40	51	61	66	64	54	43	29	17	40
Extreme Low (°F)	-24	-20	-22	9	28	42	47	40	28	14	-3	-22	-24

Note: Figures cover the years 1945-1990
Source: National Climatic Data Center, International Station Meteorological Climate Summary, 9/96

Average Precipitation/Snowfall/Humidity

Precip./Humidity	Jan	Feb	Mar	Apr	May	Jun	Jul	Aug	Sep	Oct	Nov	Dec	Yr.
Avg. Precip. (in.)	1.1	1.1	2.3	3.1	3.8	4.4	3.5	3.9	3.1	2.4	1.7	1.2	31.8
Avg. Snowfall (in.)	8	7	7	2	Tr	0	0	0	Tr	Tr	3	7	33
Avg. Rel. Hum. 6am (%)	77	79	79	78	78	81	83	86	85	80	79	80	80
Avg. Rel. Hum. 3pm (%)	65	63	57	50	51	52	52	54	52	50	58	66	56

Note: Figures cover the years 1945-1990; Tr = Trace amounts (<0.05 in. of rain; <0.5 in. of snow)
Source: National Climatic Data Center, International Station Meteorological Climate Summary, 9/96

Weather Conditions

Temperature			Daytime Sky			Precipitation		
5°F & below	32°F & below	90°F & above	Clear	Partly cloudy	Cloudy	0.01 inch or more precip.	0.1 inch or more snow/ice	Thunderstorms
25	137	26	99	128	138	106	25	46

Note: Figures are average number of days per year and cover the years 1945-1990
Source: National Climatic Data Center, International Station Meteorological Climate Summary, 9/96

HAZARDOUS WASTE

Superfund Sites

The Davenport-Moline-Rock Island, IA-IL metro area has no sites on the EPA's Superfund Final National Priorities List. There are a total of 1,165 Superfund sites with a status of proposed or final on the list in the U.S. *U.S. Environmental Protection Agency, National Priorities List, April 12, 2023*

AIR QUALITY

Air Quality Trends: Ozone

	1990	1995	2000	2005	2010	2015	2018	2019	2020	2021
MSA[1]	0.065	0.072	0.064	0.065	0.057	0.060	0.067	0.066	0.063	0.066
U.S.	0.087	0.089	0.081	0.080	0.072	0.067	0.069	0.065	0.065	0.067

Note: (1) Data covers the Davenport-Moline-Rock Island, IA-IL Metropolitan Statistical Area. The values shown are the composite ozone concentration averages among trend sites based on the highest fourth daily maximum 8-hour concentration in parts per million. These trends are based on sites having an adequate record of monitoring data during the trend period. Data from exceptional events are included.
Source: U.S. Environmental Protection Agency, Air Quality Monitoring Information, "Air Quality Trends by City, 1990-2021"

Air Quality Index

Area	Percent of Days when Air Quality was...[2]					AQI Statistics[2]	
	Good	Moderate	Unhealthy for Sensitive Groups	Unhealthy	Very Unhealthy	Maximum	Median
MSA[1]	56.2	43.0	0.8	0.0	0.0	112	49

Note: (1) Data covers the Davenport-Moline-Rock Island, IA-IL Metropolitan Statistical Area; (2) Based on 365 days with AQI data in 2021. Air Quality Index (AQI) is an index for reporting daily air quality. EPA calculates the AQI for five major air pollutants regulated by the Clean Air Act: ground-level ozone, particle pollution (aka particulate matter), carbon monoxide, sulfur dioxide, and nitrogen dioxide. The AQI runs from 0 to 500. The higher the AQI value, the greater the level of air pollution and the greater the health concern. There are six AQI categories: "Good" AQI is between 0 and 50. Air quality is considered satisfactory; "Moderate" AQI is between 51 and 100. Air quality is acceptable; "Unhealthy for Sensitive Groups" When AQI values are between 101 and 150, members of sensitive groups may experience health effects; "Unhealthy" When AQI values are between 151 and 200 everyone may begin to experience health effects; "Very Unhealthy" AQI values between 201 and 300 trigger a health alert; "Hazardous" AQI values over 300 trigger warnings of emergency conditions (not shown).
Source: U.S. Environmental Protection Agency, Air Quality Index Report, 2021

Air Quality Index Pollutants

Area	Percent of Days when AQI Pollutant was...[2]					
	Carbon Monoxide	Nitrogen Dioxide	Ozone	Sulfur Dioxide	Particulate Matter 2.5	Particulate Matter 10
MSA[1]	0.0	0.0	33.4	(3)	46.8	19.7

Note: (1) Data covers the Davenport-Moline-Rock Island, IA-IL Metropolitan Statistical Area; (2) Based on 365 days with AQI data in 2021. The Air Quality Index (AQI) is an index for reporting daily air quality. EPA calculates the AQI for five major air pollutants regulated by the Clean Air Act: ground-level ozone, particle pollution (also known as particulate matter), carbon monoxide, sulfur dioxide, and nitrogen dioxide. The AQI runs from 0 to 500. The higher the AQI value, the greater the level of air pollution and the greater the health concern; (3) Sulfur dioxide is no longer included in this table (as of December 8, 2021) because SO_2 concentrations tend to be very localized and not necessarily representative of broad geographical areas like counties and CBSAs.
Source: U.S. Environmental Protection Agency, Air Quality Index Report, 2021

Maximum Air Pollutant Concentrations: Particulate Matter, Ozone, CO and Lead

	Particulate Matter 10 (ug/m^3)	Particulate Matter 2.5 Wtd AM (ug/m^3)	Particulate Matter 2.5 24-Hr (ug/m^3)	Ozone (ppm)	Carbon Monoxide (ppm)	Lead (ug/m^3)
MSA[1] Level	137	9.4	26	0.066	1	n/a
NAAQS[2]	150	15	35	0.075	9	0.15
Met NAAQS[2]	Yes	Yes	Yes	Yes	Yes	n/a

Note: (1) Data covers the Davenport-Moline-Rock Island, IA-IL Metropolitan Statistical Area; Data from exceptional events are included; (2) National Ambient Air Quality Standards; ppm = parts per million; ug/m^3 = micrograms per cubic meter; n/a not available.
Concentrations: Particulate Matter 10 (coarse particulate)—highest second maximum 24-hour concentration; Particulate Matter 2.5 Wtd AM (fine particulate)—highest weighted annual mean concentration; Particulate Matter 2.5 24-Hour (fine particulate)—highest 98th percentile 24-hour concentration; Ozone—highest fourth daily maximum 8-hour concentration; Carbon Monoxide—highest second maximum non-overlapping 8-hour concentration; Lead—maximum running 3-month average
Source: U.S. Environmental Protection Agency, Air Quality Monitoring Information, "Air Quality Statistics by City, 2021"

Maximum Air Pollutant Concentrations: Nitrogen Dioxide and Sulfur Dioxide

	Nitrogen Dioxide AM (ppb)	Nitrogen Dioxide 1-Hr (ppb)	Sulfur Dioxide AM (ppb)	Sulfur Dioxide 1-Hr (ppb)	Sulfur Dioxide 24-Hr (ppb)
MSA[1] Level	n/a	n/a	n/a	4	n/a
NAAQS[2]	53	100	30	75	140
Met NAAQS[2]	n/a	n/a	n/a	Yes	n/a

Note: (1) Data covers the Davenport-Moline-Rock Island, IA-IL Metropolitan Statistical Area; Data from exceptional events are included; (2) National Ambient Air Quality Standards; ppm = parts per million; ug/m^3 = micrograms per cubic meter; n/a not available.
Concentrations: Nitrogen Dioxide AM—highest arithmetic mean concentration; Nitrogen Dioxide 1-Hr—highest 98th percentile 1-hour daily maximum concentration; Sulfur Dioxide AM—highest annual mean concentration; Sulfur Dioxide 1-Hr—highest 99th percentile 1-hour daily maximum concentration; Sulfur Dioxide 24-Hr—highest second maximum 24-hour concentration
Source: U.S. Environmental Protection Agency, Air Quality Monitoring Information, "Air Quality Statistics by City, 2021"

Des Moines, Iowa

In 1843, Fort Des Moines was founded at the confluence of the Des Moines and Raccoon rivers. Though the fort was initially established to protect local Native American populations, within two years the area was opened to white settlers. By 1857, the state capital was moved from Iowa City to Des Moines. Today, Des Moines remains the capital of Iowa and is its largest city.

The city frequently finds itself near the top of best-of lists extolling its reasonable cost of living, quality of life, or job opportunities. It has taken an active role in acquiring properties in its downtown for redevelopment, and takes a progressive approach to planning, having joined with other counties and regional partners to plan for transportation and other future needs. The Capital Corridor encourages the development of creative high-value growth and development for industry, including animal science.

Des Moines's significant industries include the financial services industry, and Greater Des Moines has the nation's highest concentration of employment in financial services. Logistics, bioscience, and data centers are also significant economic sectors in the city.

Greater Des Moines is home to the first statewide fiber optics network in the country. The city proper boasts world-class architecture including the Des Moines Art Center, designed in 1944 by Eliel Saarinen, a Finnish architect and then-president of the renowned Cranbrook Academy of Art in Detroit. In 1968, I.M. Pei, architect of the Pyramid du Louvre and the East Wing of the National Gallery of Art in Washington, D.C., designed a gallery addition to the main Art Center structure. In 1985, Richard Meier, who designed the Museum of Modern Art in Florence, Italy, designed an addition to the Art Center's north wing and went on to design the famed Getty Center in Los Angeles. The city's Home Federal Savings and Loan Building was designed by Mies van der Rohe, of the famous German Bauhaus School of Design, and a sculpture, The Crusoe Umbrella, designed by pop artist Claes Oldenberg, stands in the middle of Nollen Plaza, a wooded park and popular gathering place.

The Greater Des Moines Botanical Center has been renovated to include Iowa's first "living wall," a new office suite and lobby, and improvements to the center's gardens.

Des Moines Civic Center offers ballet, symphony, and other performances. The Science Center of Iowa features hands-on science and technology exhibits, an IMAX theater, and a planetarium with an interactive program and laser light show.

Every four years, Des Moines becomes the center of national attention as correspondents from all over the U.S. and abroad arrive to cover the Iowa political caucuses, which has become a financial boon for the state.

Located in the heart of North America, Des Moines has a continental climate, resulting in a seasonal contrast in both temperature and precipitation. Exceptionally high summer rains have caused the nearby Des Moines River and Raccoon River to breach the city's levees in 1993 and again in 2008. The winter is a season of cold, dry air, interrupted by occasional storms of short duration. The autumn is characteristically sunny with diminishing precipitation.

Rankings

General Rankings

- *US News & World Report* conducted a survey of more than 3,600 people and analyzed the 150 largest metropolitan areas to determine what matters most when selecting where to settle down. Des Moines ranked #14 out of the top 25 as having the best combination of desirable factors. Criteria: cost of living; quality of life and education; net migration; job market; desirability; and other factors. *money.usnews.com, "The 25 Best Places to Live in the U.S. in 2022-2023," May 17, 2022*

- The Des Moines metro area was identified as one of America's fastest-growing areas in terms of population and business growth by *MagnifyMoney*. The area ranked #15 out of 35. The 100 most populous metro areas in the U.S. were evaluated on their change from 2011 to 2016 in the following categories: people and housing; workforce and employment opportunities; growing industry. *www.businessinsider.com, "The 35 Cities in the US with the Biggest Influx of People, the Most Work Opportunities, and the Hottest Business Growth," August 12, 2018*

- In their ninth annual survey, Livability.com looked at data for more than 2,300 mid-sized U.S. cities to determine the rankings for Livability's "Top 100 Best Places to Live" in 2022. Des Moines ranked #90. Criteria: housing and economy; social and civic engagement; education; demographics; health care options; transportation & infrastructure; and community amenities. *Livability.com, "Top 100 Best Places to Live 2022" July 19, 2022*

Business/Finance Rankings

- Des Moines was the #10-ranked city for savers, according to a study by the finance site GOBankingRates, which considered the prospects for people trying to save money. Criteria: average monthly cost of grocery items; median home listing price; median rent; median income; transportation costs; gas prices; and the cost of eating out for an inexpensive and mid-range meal in 100 U.S. cities. *www.gobankingrates.com, "The 20 Best (and Worst) Places to Live If You're Trying to Save Money," August 27, 2019*

- Des Moines was ranked #10 among 100 U.S. cities for most difficult conditions for savers, according to a study by the finance site GOBankingRates. Criteria: average monthly cost of grocery items; median home listing price; median rent; median income; transportation costs; gas prices; and the cost of eating out for an inexpensive and mid-range meal. *www.gobankingrates.com, "The 20 Best (and Worst) Places to Live If You're Trying to Save Money," August 27, 2019*

- The Brookings Institution ranked the nation's largest cities based on income inequality. Des Moines was ranked #88 (#1 = greatest inequality). Criteria: the "95/20 ratio," a figure representing the income at which a household earns more than 95 percent of all other households, divided by the income at which a household earns more than only 20 percent of all other households. *Brookings Institution, "Household Income Inequality, Largest Cities of 97 Large U.S. Metro Areas, 2014-2016," February 5, 2018*

- The Brookings Institution ranked the 100 largest metro areas in the U.S. based on income inequality. Des Moines was ranked #93 (#1 = greatest inequality). Criteria: the "95/20 ratio," a figure representing the income at which a household earns more than 95 percent of all other households, divided by the income at which a household earns more than only 20 percent of all other households. *Brookings Institution, "Household Income Inequality, 100 Largest U.S. Metro Areas, 2014-2016," February 5, 2018*

- For its annual survey of the "Cheapest U.S. Cities to Live In," Kiplinger applied Cost of Living Index statistics developed by the Council for Community and Economic Research to U.S. Census Bureau population and median household income data for 265 urban areas. Only areas with at least 50,000 residents were considered. In the resulting ranking, Des Moines ranked #20. *Kiplinger.com, "The 25 Cheapest Places to Live: U.S. Cities Edition," April 3, 2023*

- Des Moines was cited as one of America's top metros for total major capital investment facility projects in 2022. The area ranked #9 in the mid-sized metro area category (population 200,000 to 1 million). *Site Selection, "Top Metros of 2022," March 2023*

- *Forbes* ranked the 200 most populous metro areas to determine the nation's "Best Places for Business and Careers." The Des Moines metro area was ranked #10. Criteria: costs (business and living); job growth (past and projected); income growth; quality of life; educational attainment (college and high school); projected economic growth; cultural and leisure opportunities; workplace tolerance laws; net migration patterns. *Forbes, "The Best Places for Business and Careers 2019: Seattle Still On Top," October 30, 2019*

Dating/Romance Rankings

- Des Moines was ranked #6 out of 25 cities that stood out for inspiring romance and attracting diners on the website OpenTable.com. Criteria: percentage of people who dined out on Valentine's Day in 2018; percentage of romantic restaurants as rated by OpenTable diner reviews; and percentage of tables seated for two. *OpenTable, "25 Most Romantic Cities in America for 2019," February 7, 2019*

Education Rankings

- Personal finance website *WalletHub* analyzed the 150 largest U.S. metropolitan statistical areas to determine where the most educated Americans are putting their degrees to work. Criteria: education levels; percentage of workers with degrees; education quality and attainment gap; public school quality rankings; quality and enrollment of each metro area's universities. Des Moines was ranked #55 (#1 = most educated city). *www.WalletHub.com, "Most & Least Educated Cities in America," July 18, 2022*

Environmental Rankings

- The U.S. Environmental Protection Agency (EPA) released its list of mid-size U.S. metropolitan areas with the most ENERGY STAR certified buildings in 2022. The Des Moines metro area was ranked #2 out of 10. *U.S. Environmental Protection Agency, "2023 Energy Star Top Cities," April 26, 2023*

- Des Moines was highlighted as one of the cleanest metro areas for ozone air pollution in the U.S. during 2019 through 2021. The list represents cities with no monitored ozone air pollution in unhealthful ranges. *American Lung Association, "State of the Air 2023," April 19, 2023*

Health/Fitness Rankings

- Des Moines was identified as a "2022 Spring Allergy Capital." The area ranked #16 out of 100. Three groups of factors were used to identify the most challenging cities for people with allergies during the spring season: annual spring pollen scores; over the counter allergy medicine use; number of board-certified allergy specialists. *Asthma and Allergy Foundation of America, "Spring Allergy Capitals 2022," March 2, 2022*

- Des Moines was identified as a "2022 Fall Allergy Capital." The area ranked #17 out of 100. Three groups of factors were used to identify the most challenging cities for people with allergies during the fall season: annual fall pollen scores; over the counter allergy medicine use; number of board-certified allergy specialists. *Asthma and Allergy Foundation of America, "Fall Allergy Capitals 2022," March 2, 2022*

- Des Moines was identified as a "2022 Asthma Capital." The area ranked #75 out of the nation's 100 largest metropolitan areas. Criteria: estimated asthma prevalence; asthma-related mortality; and ER visits due to asthma. Risk factors analyzed but not factored in the rankings: annual pollen score; annual air quality; public smoking laws; access to board-certified asthma specialists; rescue and controller medication use; uninsured rate; poverty rate. *Asthma and Allergy Foundation of America, "Asthma Capitals 2022: The Most Challenging Places to Live With Asthma," September 14, 2022*

Real Estate Rankings

- *WalletHub* compared the most populated U.S. cities to determine which had the best markets for real estate agents. Des Moines ranked #61 where demand was high and pay was the best. Criteria: sales per agent; annual median wage for real-estate agents; monthly average starting salary for real estate agents; real estate job density and competition; unemployment rate; home turnover rate; housing-market health index; and other relevant metrics. *www.WalletHub.com, "2021 Best Places to Be a Real Estate Agent," May 12, 2021*

Safety Rankings

- Allstate ranked the 200 largest cities in America in terms of driver safety. Des Moines ranked #38. Criteria: internal property damage claims over a two-year period from January 2016 to December 2017. The report helps increase the importance of safety and awareness behind the wheel. *Allstate, "Allstate America's Best Drivers Report, 2019" June 24, 2019*

- The National Insurance Crime Bureau ranked 390 metro areas in the U.S. in terms of per capita rates of vehicle theft. The Des Moines metro area ranked #128 (#1 = highest rate). Criteria: number of vehicle theft offenses per 100,000 inhabitants in 2021. *National Insurance Crime Bureau, "Hot Spots 2021," September 1, 2022*

Seniors/Retirement Rankings

- From its Best Cities for Successful Aging indexes, the Milken Institute generated rankings for metropolitan areas, weighing data in nine categories—health care, wellness, living arrangements, transportation and convenience, financial characteristics, education, employment, community engagement, and overall livability. The Des Moines metro area was ranked #5 overall in the large metro area category. *Milken Institute, "Best Cities for Successful Aging, 2017" March 14, 2017*

Sports/Recreation Rankings

- Des Moines was chosen as one of America's best cities for bicycling. The city ranked #38 out of 50. Criteria: cycling infrastructure that is safe and friendly for all ages; energy and bike culture. The editors evaluated cities with populations of 100,000 or more. *Bicycling, "The 50 Best Bike Cities in America," October 10, 2018*

Women/Minorities Rankings

- Personal finance website *WalletHub* compared more than 180 U.S. cities across two key dimensions, "Hispanic Business-Friendliness" and "Hispanic Purchasing Power," to arrive at the most favorable conditions for Hispanic entrepreneurs. Des Moines was ranked #158 out of 182. Criteria includes: share of Hispanic-Owned Businesses; Hispanic entrepreneurship rate to median annual income of Hispanics; Small Business-Friendliness score; cost of living; and number of Hispanics with at least a bachelor's degree. *WalletHub.com, "2019's Best Cities for Hispanic Entrepreneurs," May 1, 2019*

Miscellaneous Rankings

- *WalletHub* compared the 150 most populated U.S. cities to determine their operating efficiency. A "Quality of Services" score was constructed for each city and then divided by the total budget per capita to reveal which were managed the best. Des Moines ranked #55. Criteria: financial stability; economy; education; safety; health; infrastructure and pollution. *www.WalletHub.com, "2022's Best-& Worst-Run Cities in America," June 21, 2022*

Business Environment

DEMOGRAPHICS

Population Growth

Area	1990 Census	2000 Census	2010 Census	2020 Census	Population Growth (%) 1990-2020	Population Growth (%) 2010-2020
City	193,569	198,682	203,433	214,133	10.6	5.3
MSA[1]	416,346	481,394	569,633	709,466	70.4	24.5
U.S.	248,709,873	281,421,906	308,745,538	331,449,281	33.3	7.4

Note: (1) Figures cover the Des Moines-West Des Moines, IA Metropolitan Statistical Area
Source: U.S. Census Bureau, 1990 Census, 2000 Census, 2010 Census, 2020 Census

Race

Area	White Alone[2] (%)	Black Alone[2] (%)	Asian Alone[2] (%)	AIAN[3] Alone[2] (%)	NHOPI[4] Alone[2] (%)	Other Race Alone[2] (%)	Two or More Races (%)
City	64.5	11.7	6.8	0.7	0.1	6.6	9.6
MSA[1]	79.8	5.6	4.3	0.4	0.1	3.2	6.7
U.S.	61.6	12.4	6.0	1.1	0.2	8.4	10.2

Note: (1) Figures cover the Des Moines-West Des Moines, IA Metropolitan Statistical Area; (2) Alone is defined as not being in combination with one or more other races; (3) American Indian and Alaska Native; (4) Native Hawaiian and Other Pacific Islander
Source: U.S. Census Bureau, 2020 Census

Hispanic or Latino Origin

Area	Total (%)	Mexican (%)	Puerto Rican (%)	Cuban (%)	Other (%)
City	14.6	11.6	0.3	0.2	2.4
MSA[1]	7.4	5.5	0.3	0.1	1.5
U.S.	18.4	11.2	1.8	0.7	4.7

Note: Persons of Hispanic or Latino origin can be of any race; (1) Figures cover the Des Moines-West Des Moines, IA Metropolitan Statistical Area
Source: U.S. Census Bureau, 2017-2021 American Community Survey 5-Year Estimates

Age

Area	Under Age 5	Age 5–19	Age 20–34	Age 35–44	Age 45–54	Age 55–64	Age 65–74	Age 75–84	Age 85+	Median Age
City	6.6	19.7	24.0	13.1	11.3	11.8	8.2	3.6	1.7	34.8
MSA[1]	6.5	20.8	20.2	13.8	12.0	11.9	8.7	4.1	1.7	36.6
U.S.	5.6	19.2	20.2	12.7	12.4	13.1	10.0	4.9	1.9	38.8

Note: (1) Figures cover the Des Moines-West Des Moines, IA Metropolitan Statistical Area
Source: U.S. Census Bureau, 2020 Census

Disability by Age

Area	All Ages	Under 18 Years Old	18 to 64 Years Old	65 Years and Over
City	13.7	5.3	12.8	35.6
MSA[1]	10.5	3.7	9.0	30.4
U.S.	12.6	4.4	10.3	33.4

Note: Figures show percent of the civilian noninstitutionalized population that reported having a disability. Disability status is determined from six types of difficulty: vision, hearing, cognitive, ambulatory, self-care, and independent living. For children under 5 years old, hearing and vision difficulty are used to determine disability status. For children between the ages of 5 and 14, disability status is determined from hearing, vision, cognitive, ambulatory, and self-care difficulties. For people aged 15 years and older, they are considered to have a disability if they have difficulty with any one of the six difficulty types; Note: (1) Figures cover the Des Moines-West Des Moines, IA Metropolitan Statistical Area
Source: U.S. Census Bureau, 2017-2021 American Community Survey 5-Year Estimates

Ancestry

Area	German	Irish	English	American	Italian	Polish	French[2]	Scottish	Dutch
City	19.1	11.9	8.2	3.1	3.6	1.2	1.5	1.2	2.3
MSA[1]	26.2	13.0	10.1	4.0	3.1	1.4	1.7	1.5	3.6
U.S.	12.8	9.6	8.1	5.7	5.0	2.7	2.2	1.6	1.1

Note: Figures are the percentage of the total population reporting a particular ancestry. The nine most commonly reported ancestries in the U.S. are shown. Figures include multiple ancestries (e.g. if a person reported being Irish and Italian, they were included in both columns); (1) Figures cover the Des Moines-West Des Moines, IA Metropolitan Statistical Area; (2) Excludes Basque
Source: U.S. Census Bureau, 2017-2021 American Community Survey 5-Year Estimates

Foreign-born Population

Area	Any Foreign Country	Asia	Mexico	Europe	Caribbean	Central America[2]	South America	Africa	Canada
City	13.8	5.2	3.6	0.8	0.1	1.1	0.1	2.8	0.1
MSA[1]	8.1	3.2	1.5	1.0	0.1	0.5	0.2	1.5	0.1
U.S.	13.6	4.2	3.3	1.5	1.4	1.1	1.1	0.8	0.2

Note: (1) Figures cover the Des Moines-West Des Moines, IA Metropolitan Statistical Area; (2) Excludes Mexico.
Source: U.S. Census Bureau, 2017-2021 American Community Survey 5-Year Estimates

Household Size

Area	Persons in Household (%)							Average Household Size
	One	Two	Three	Four	Five	Six	Seven or More	
City	34.9	30.6	14.3	10.9	5.1	2.5	1.7	2.40
MSA[1]	28.6	34.2	14.2	13.7	6.2	2.0	1.1	2.50
U.S.	28.1	33.8	15.5	12.9	6.0	2.3	1.4	2.60

Note: (1) Figures cover the Des Moines-West Des Moines, IA Metropolitan Statistical Area
Source: U.S. Census Bureau, 2017-2021 American Community Survey 5-Year Estimates

Household Relationships

Area	House-holder	Opposite-sex Spouse	Same-sex Spouse	Opposite-sex Unmarried Partner	Same-sex Unmarried Partner	Child[2]	Grand-child	Other Relatives	Non-relatives
City	41.1	14.2	0.3	3.5	0.2	27.9	2.0	4.4	3.9
MSA[1]	39.6	19.2	0.2	2.7	0.1	29.6	1.3	2.8	2.6
U.S.	38.3	17.5	0.2	2.5	0.2	28.3	2.4	4.8	3.4

Note: Figures are percent of the total population; (1) Figures cover the Des Moines-West Des Moines, IA Metropolitan Statistical Area; (2) Includes biological, adopted, and stepchildren of the householder
Source: U.S. Census Bureau, 2020 Census

Gender

Area	Males	Females	Males per 100 Females
City	105,618	108,515	97.3
MSA[1]	349,805	359,661	97.3
U.S.	162,685,811	168,763,470	96.4

Note: (1) Figures cover the Des Moines-West Des Moines, IA Metropolitan Statistical Area
Source: U.S. Census Bureau, 2020 Census

Marital Status

Area	Never Married	Now Married[2]	Separated	Widowed	Divorced
City	39.5	39.8	2.1	5.5	13.0
MSA[1]	30.9	51.7	1.2	4.9	11.2
U.S.	33.8	48.0	1.8	5.6	10.8

Note: Figures are percentages and cover the population 15 years of age and older; (1) Figures cover the Des Moines-West Des Moines, IA Metropolitan Statistical Area; (2) Excludes separated
Source: U.S. Census Bureau, 2017-2021 American Community Survey 5-Year Estimates

Religious Groups by Family

Area	Catholic	Baptist	Methodist	LDS[2]	Pentecostal	Lutheran	Islam	Adventist	Other
MSA[1]	12.1	1.8	4.0	0.9	2.5	6.6	1.6	0.8	8.7
U.S.	18.7	7.3	3.0	2.0	1.8	1.7	1.3	1.3	11.6

Note: Figures are the number of adherents as a percentage of the total population and cover the eight largest religious groups in the U.S; (1) Figures cover the Des Moines-West Des Moines, IA Metropolitan Statistical Area; (2) Church of Jesus Christ of Latter-day Saints
Sources: 2020 U.S. Religion Census, Association of Statisticians of American Religious Bodies; The Association of Religion Data Archives (ARDA)

Religious Groups by Tradition

Area	Catholic	Evangelical Protestant	Mainline Protestant	Black Protestant	Islam	Judaism	Hinduism	Orthodox	Buddhism
MSA[1]	12.1	10.3	12.2	1.0	1.6	<0.1	0.2	0.1	0.1
U.S.	18.7	16.5	5.2	2.3	1.3	0.6	0.4	0.4	0.3

Note: Figures are the number of adherents as a percentage of the total population; (1) Figures cover the Des Moines-West Des Moines, IA Metropolitan Statistical Area
Sources: 2020 U.S. Religion Census, Association of Statisticians of American Religious Bodies; The Association of Religion Data Archives (ARDA)

ECONOMY

Gross Metropolitan Product

Area	2020	2021	2022	2023	Rank[2]
MSA[1]	55.0	63.3	67.6	71.4	57

Note: Figures are in billions of dollars; (1) Figures cover the Des Moines-West Des Moines, IA Metropolitan Statistical Area; (2) Rank is based on 2021 data and ranges from 1 to 381
Source: U.S. Conference of Mayors, U.S. Metro Economies: U.S. Metros Compared to Global and State Economies, June 2022

Economic Growth

Area	2018-20 (%)	2021 (%)	2022 (%)	2023 (%)	Rank[2]
MSA[1]	1.7	8.2	0.9	2.7	46
U.S.	-0.6	5.7	3.1	2.9	–

Note: Figures are real gross metropolitan product (GMP) growth rates and represent average annual percent change; (1) Figures cover the Des Moines-West Des Moines, IA Metropolitan Statistical Area; (2) Rank is based on 2020 2-year average annual percent change and ranges from 1 to 381
Source: U.S. Conference of Mayors, U.S. Metro Economies: U.S. Metros Compared to Global and State Economies, June 2022

Metropolitan Area Exports

Area	2016	2017	2018	2019	2020	2021	Rank[2]
MSA[1]	1,052.2	1,141.2	1,293.7	1,437.8	1,414.0	1,706.6	118

Note: Figures are in millions of dollars; (1) Figures cover the Des Moines-West Des Moines, IA Metropolitan Statistical Area; (2) Rank is based on 2021 data and ranges from 1 to 388
Source: U.S. Department of Commerce, International Trade Administration, Office of Trade and Economic Analysis, Industry and Analysis, Exports by Metropolitan Area, data extracted March 16, 2023

Building Permits

Area	Single-Family			Multi-Family			Total		
	2021	2022	Pct. Chg.	2021	2022	Pct. Chg.	2021	2022	Pct. Chg.
City	248	256	3.2	380	284	-25.3	628	540	-14.0
MSA[1]	4,888	3,646	-25.4	2,081	2,476	19.0	6,969	6,122	-12.2
U.S.	1,115,400	975,600	-12.5	621,600	689,500	10.9	1,737,000	1,665,100	-4.1

Note: (1) Figures cover the Des Moines-West Des Moines, IA Metropolitan Statistical Area; Figures represent new, privately-owned housing units authorized (unadjusted data); All permit data are based on estimates with imputation
Source: U.S. Census Bureau, Manufacturing, Mining, and Construction Statistics, Building Permits, 2021, 2022

Bankruptcy Filings

Area	Business Filings			Nonbusiness Filings		
	2021	2022	% Chg.	2021	2022	% Chg.
Polk County	22	17	-22.7	550	474	-13.8
U.S.	14,347	13,481	-6.0	399,269	374,240	-6.3

Note: Business filings include Chapter 7, Chapter 9, Chapter 11, Chapter 12, Chapter 13, Chapter 15, and Section 304; Nonbusiness filings include Chapter 7, Chapter 11, and Chapter 13
Source: Administrative Office of the U.S. Courts, Business and Nonbusiness Bankruptcy, County Cases Commenced by Chapter of the Bankruptcy Code, During the 12-Month Period Ending December 31, 2021 and Business and Nonbusiness Bankruptcy, County Cases Commenced by Chapter of the Bankruptcy Code, During the 12-Month Period Ending December 31, 2022

Housing Vacancy Rates

Area	Gross Vacancy Rate[2] (%)			Year-Round Vacancy Rate[3] (%)			Rental Vacancy Rate[4] (%)			Homeowner Vacancy Rate[5] (%)		
	2020	2021	2022	2020	2021	2022	2020	2021	2022	2020	2021	2022
MSA[1]	n/a	n/a	n/a	n/a	n/a	n/a	n/a	n/a	n/a	n/a	n/a	n/a
U.S.	10.6	10.8	10.5	8.2	8.4	8.2	6.3	6.1	5.8	1.0	0.9	0.8

Note: (1) Figures cover the Des Moines-West Des Moines, IA Metropolitan Statistical Area; (2) The percentage of the total housing inventory that is vacant; (3) The percentage of the housing inventory (excluding seasonal units) that is year-round vacant; (4) The percentage of rental inventory that is vacant for rent; (5) The percentage of homeowner inventory that is vacant for sale; n/a not available
Source: U.S. Census Bureau, Housing Vacancies and Homeownership Annual Statistics: 2020, 2021, 2022

INCOME

Income

Area	Per Capita ($)	Median Household ($)	Average Household ($)
City	31,276	58,444	74,131
MSA[1]	39,333	75,134	97,364
U.S.	37,638	69,021	97,196

Note: (1) Figures cover the Des Moines-West Des Moines, IA Metropolitan Statistical Area
Source: U.S. Census Bureau, 2017-2021 American Community Survey 5-Year Estimates

Household Income Distribution

Area	Percent of Households Earning							
	Under $15,000	$15,000 -$24,999	$25,000 -$34,999	$35,000 -$49,999	$50,000 -$74,999	$75,000 -$99,999	$100,000 -$149,999	$150,000 and up
City	10.0	8.9	9.4	14.7	20.2	14.3	13.6	8.9
MSA[1]	6.4	6.3	7.4	11.8	18.1	14.1	19.0	16.9
U.S.	9.4	7.8	8.2	11.4	16.8	12.8	16.3	17.3

Note: (1) Figures cover the Des Moines-West Des Moines, IA Metropolitan Statistical Area
Source: U.S. Census Bureau, 2017-2021 American Community Survey 5-Year Estimates

Poverty Rate

Area	All Ages	Under 18 Years Old	18 to 64 Years Old	65 Years and Over
City	15.3	22.6	13.6	9.8
MSA[1]	9.0	11.5	8.6	6.6
U.S.	12.6	17.0	11.8	9.6

Note: Figures are percentage of people whose income during the past 12 months was below the poverty level;
(1) Figures cover the Des Moines-West Des Moines, IA Metropolitan Statistical Area
Source: U.S. Census Bureau, 2017-2021 American Community Survey 5-Year Estimates

EMPLOYMENT

Labor Force and Employment

Area	Civilian Labor Force			Workers Employed		
	Dec. 2021	Dec. 2022	% Chg.	Dec. 2021	Dec. 2022	% Chg.
City	109,744	111,230	1.4	104,975	107,148	2.1
MSA[1]	362,322	367,598	1.5	350,192	357,259	2.0
U.S.	161,696,000	164,224,000	1.6	155,732,000	158,872,000	2.0

Note: Data is not seasonally adjusted and covers workers 16 years of age and older; (1) Figures cover the Des Moines-West Des Moines, IA Metropolitan Statistical Area
Source: Bureau of Labor Statistics, Local Area Unemployment Statistics

Unemployment Rate

Area	2022											
	Jan.	Feb.	Mar.	Apr.	May	Jun.	Jul.	Aug.	Sep.	Oct.	Nov.	Dec.
City	5.7	4.7	4.3	3.0	2.8	3.0	3.2	3.3	2.8	2.9	3.2	3.7
MSA[1]	4.2	3.4	3.2	2.1	2.2	2.5	2.6	2.7	2.3	2.5	2.8	2.8
U.S.	4.4	4.1	3.8	3.3	3.4	3.8	3.8	3.8	3.3	3.4	3.4	3.3

Note: Data is not seasonally adjusted and covers workers 16 years of age and older; (1) Figures cover the Des Moines-West Des Moines, IA Metropolitan Statistical Area
Source: Bureau of Labor Statistics, Local Area Unemployment Statistics

Average Wages

Occupation	$/Hr.	Occupation	$/Hr.
Accountants and Auditors	36.71	Maintenance and Repair Workers	22.01
Automotive Mechanics	23.68	Marketing Managers	64.50
Bookkeepers	23.50	Network and Computer Systems Admin.	44.01
Carpenters	25.01	Nurses, Licensed Practical	25.09
Cashiers	13.40	Nurses, Registered	34.16
Computer Programmers	44.45	Nursing Assistants	17.50
Computer Systems Analysts	45.98	Office Clerks, General	19.96
Computer User Support Specialists	27.24	Physical Therapists	41.72
Construction Laborers	22.43	Physicians	105.11
Cooks, Restaurant	14.73	Plumbers, Pipefitters and Steamfitters	31.79
Customer Service Representatives	21.45	Police and Sheriff's Patrol Officers	34.32
Dentists	80.98	Postal Service Mail Carriers	27.78
Electricians	30.12	Real Estate Sales Agents	34.49
Engineers, Electrical	48.91	Retail Salespersons	15.88
Fast Food and Counter Workers	13.07	Sales Representatives, Technical/Scientific	54.80
Financial Managers	72.01	Secretaries, Exc. Legal/Medical/Executive	21.22
First-Line Supervisors of Office Workers	31.64	Security Guards	17.63
General and Operations Managers	49.19	Surgeons	n/a
Hairdressers/Cosmetologists	16.70	Teacher Assistants, Exc. Postsecondary*	14.28
Home Health and Personal Care Aides	15.41	Teachers, Secondary School, Exc. Sp. Ed.*	32.05
Janitors and Cleaners	15.75	Telemarketers	15.86
Landscaping/Groundskeeping Workers	17.60	Truck Drivers, Heavy/Tractor-Trailer	26.85
Lawyers	59.08	Truck Drivers, Light/Delivery Services	21.17
Maids and Housekeeping Cleaners	14.22	Waiters and Waitresses	13.46

Note: Wage data covers the Des Moines-West Des Moines, IA Metropolitan Statistical Area; (*) Hourly wages were calculated from annual wage data based on a 40 hour work week; n/a not available.
Source: Bureau of Labor Statistics, Metro Area Occupational Employment & Wage Estimates, May 2022

Employment by Industry

Sector	MSA[1]		U.S.
	Number of Employees	Percent of Total	Percent of Total
Construction, Mining, and Logging	23,100	5.9	5.4
Private Education and Health Services	55,900	14.3	16.1
Financial Activities	56,100	14.3	5.9
Government	48,200	12.3	14.5
Information	6,200	1.6	2.0
Leisure and Hospitality	34,200	8.7	10.3
Manufacturing	23,200	5.9	8.4
Other Services	13,100	3.3	3.7
Professional and Business Services	53,000	13.5	14.7
Retail Trade	41,400	10.6	10.2
Transportation, Warehousing, and Utilities	17,500	4.5	4.9
Wholesale Trade	19,500	5.0	3.9

Note: Figures are non-farm employment as of December 2022. Figures are not seasonally adjusted and include workers 16 years of age and older; (1) Figures cover the Des Moines-West Des Moines, IA Metropolitan Statistical Area
Source: Bureau of Labor Statistics, Current Employment Statistics, Employment, Hours, and Earnings

Employment by Occupation

Occupation Classification	City (%)	MSA[1] (%)	U.S. (%)
Management, Business, Science, and Arts	34.4	43.5	40.3
Natural Resources, Construction, and Maintenance	8.3	8.0	8.7
Production, Transportation, and Material Moving	16.1	12.4	13.1
Sales and Office	21.7	21.4	20.9
Service	19.4	14.7	17.0

Note: Figures cover employed civilians 16 years of age and older; (1) Figures cover the Des Moines-West Des Moines, IA Metropolitan Statistical Area
Source: U.S. Census Bureau, 2017-2021 American Community Survey 5-Year Estimates

Occupations with Greatest Projected Employment Growth: 2022 – 2024

Occupation[1]	2022 Employment	2024 Projected Employment	Numeric Employment Change	Percent Employment Change
Fast Food and Counter Workers	39,300	41,100	1,800	4.6
Cooks, Restaurant	12,190	13,530	1,340	11.0
Waiters and Waitresses	19,970	21,220	1,250	6.3
Farmers, Ranchers, and Other Agricultural Managers	85,770	86,980	1,210	1.4
Home Health and Personal Care Aides	24,530	25,690	1,160	4.7
Maids and Housekeeping Cleaners	11,530	12,500	970	8.4
Registered Nurses	34,440	35,270	830	2.4
Bartenders	8,970	9,770	800	8.9
Laborers and Freight, Stock, and Material Movers, Hand	31,300	32,000	700	2.2
Heavy and Tractor-Trailer Truck Drivers	46,230	46,880	650	1.4

Note: Projections cover Iowa; (1) Sorted by numeric employment change
Source: www.projectionscentral.com, State Occupational Projections, 2022–2024 Short-Term Projections

Fastest-Growing Occupations: 2022 – 2024

Occupation[1]	2022 Employment	2024 Projected Employment	Numeric Employment Change	Percent Employment Change
Entertainers and Performers, Sports and Related Workers, All Other	210	260	50	23.8
Hotel, Motel, and Resort Desk Clerks	3,170	3,780	610	19.2
Ushers, Lobby Attendants, and Ticket Takers	800	950	150	18.8
Audio and Video Equipment Technicians	340	400	60	17.6
Gaming Change Persons and Booth Cashiers	340	400	60	17.6
Wind Turbine Service Technicians	460	540	80	17.4
Gaming Dealers	1,180	1,370	190	16.1
Musicians and Singers	420	480	60	14.3
Gaming Service Workers, All Other	370	420	50	13.5
Passenger Vehicle Drivers, Except Bus Drivers, Transit and Intercity	1,950	2,200	250	12.8

Note: Projections cover Iowa; (1) Sorted by percent employment change and excludes occupations with numeric employment change less than 50
Source: www.projectionscentral.com, State Occupational Projections, 2022–2024 Short-Term Projections

CITY FINANCES

City Government Finances

Component	2020 ($000)	2020 ($ per capita)
Total Revenues	624,798	2,916
Total Expenditures	613,454	2,863
Debt Outstanding	584,597	2,729
Cash and Securities[1]	354,565	1,655

Note: (1) Cash and security holdings of a government at the close of its fiscal year, including those of its dependent agencies, utilities, and liquor stores.
Source: U.S. Census Bureau, State & Local Government Finances 2020

City Government Revenue by Source

Source	2020 ($000)	2020 ($ per capita)	2020 (%)
General Revenue			
From Federal Government	44,108	206	7.1
From State Government	56,043	262	9.0
From Local Governments	8,034	38	1.3
Taxes			
Property	164,248	767	26.3
Sales and Gross Receipts	69,025	322	11.0
Personal Income	0	0	0.0
Corporate Income	0	0	0.0
Motor Vehicle License	0	0	0.0
Other Taxes	4,428	21	0.7
Current Charges	173,710	811	27.8
Liquor Store	0	0	0.0
Utility	71,022	332	11.4

Source: U.S. Census Bureau, State & Local Government Finances 2020

City Government Expenditures by Function

Function	2020 ($000)	2020 ($ per capita)	2020 (%)
General Direct Expenditures			
Air Transportation	57,543	268	9.4
Corrections	0	0	0.0
Education	0	0	0.0
Employment Security Administration	0	0	0.0
Financial Administration	3,960	18	0.6
Fire Protection	43,231	201	7.0
General Public Buildings	4,499	21	0.7
Governmental Administration, Other	9,973	46	1.6
Health	2,302	10	0.4
Highways	85,562	399	13.9
Hospitals	0	0	0.0
Housing and Community Development	22,817	106	3.7
Interest on General Debt	24,847	116	4.1
Judicial and Legal	2,031	9	0.3
Libraries	10,747	50	1.8
Parking	9,511	44	1.6
Parks and Recreation	20,120	93	3.3
Police Protection	70,839	330	11.5
Public Welfare	9,378	43	1.5
Sewerage	106,754	498	17.4
Solid Waste Management	12,210	57	2.0
Veterans' Services	0	0	0.0
Liquor Store	0	0	0.0
Utility	66,566	310	10.9

Source: U.S. Census Bureau, State & Local Government Finances 2020

TAXES

State Corporate Income Tax Rates

State	Tax Rate (%)	Income Brackets ($)	Num. of Brackets	Financial Institution Tax Rate (%)[a]	Federal Income Tax Ded.
Iowa	5.5 - 8.4	100,000 - 250,001	3	4.7	Yes (h)

Note: Tax rates as of January 1, 2023; (a) Rates listed are the corporate income tax rate applied to financial institutions or excise taxes based on income. Some states have other taxes based upon the value of deposits or shares; (h) 50% of the federal income tax is deductible.
Source: Federation of Tax Administrators, State Corporate Income Tax Rates, January 1, 2023

State Individual Income Tax Rates

State	Tax Rate (%)	Income Brackets ($)	Personal Exemptions ($)			Standard Ded. ($)	
			Single	Married	Depend.	Single	Married
Iowa (a)	4.4 - 6.0 (bb)	6,000 - 75,000	40	80	40 (c)	–	–

Note: Tax rates as of January 1, 2023; Local- and county-level taxes are not included; Federal income tax is deductible on state income tax returns; (a) 16 states have statutory provision for automatically adjusting to the rate of inflation the dollar values of the income tax brackets, standard deductions, and/or personal exemptions. Oregon does not index the income brackets for $125,000 and over; (c) The personal exemption takes the form of a tax credit instead of a deduction; (bb) Louisiana tax rates may be adjusted down if revenue trigger is met on April 1st. Iowa is phasing-in a flat rate by 2027, while Nebraska and South Carolina is phasing-in a reduced top rate by 2027.
Source: Federation of Tax Administrators, State Individual Income Tax Rates, January 1, 2023

Various State Sales and Excise Tax Rates

State	State Sales Tax (%)	Gasoline[1] ($/gal.)	Cigarette[2] ($/pack)	Spirits[3] ($/gal.)	Wine[4] ($/gal.)	Beer[5] ($/gal.)	Recreational Marijuana (%)
Iowa	6	0.30	1.36	14.10	1.75	0.19	Not legal

Note: All tax rates as of January 1, 2023; (1) The American Petroleum Institute has developed a methodology for determining the average tax rate on a gallon of fuel. Rates may include any of the following: excise taxes, environmental fees, storage tank fees, other fees or taxes, general sales tax, and local taxes; (2) The federal excise tax of $1.0066 per pack and local taxes are not included; (3) Rates are those applicable to off-premise sales of 40% alcohol by volume (a.b.v.) distilled spirits in 750ml containers. Local excise taxes are excluded; (4) Rates are those applicable to off-premise sales of 11% a.b.v. non-carbonated wine in 750ml containers; (5) Rates are those applicable to off-premise sales of 4.7% a.b.v. beer in 12 ounce containers.
Source: Tax Foundation, 2023 Facts & Figures: How Does Your State Compare?

State Business Tax Climate Index Rankings

State	Overall Rank	Corporate Tax Rank	Individual Income Tax Rank	Sales Tax Rank	Property Tax Rank	Unemployment Insurance Tax Rank
Iowa	38	34	40	15	40	33

Note: The index is a measure of how each state's tax laws affect economic performance. The lower the rank, the more favorable a state's tax system is for business. States without a given tax are given a ranking of 1. The scores/rankings for the District of Columbia do not affect other states. The 2023 index represents the tax climate as of July 1, 2022.
Source: Tax Foundation, State Business Tax Climate Index 2023

TRANSPORTATION

Means of Transportation to Work

Area	Car/Truck/Van		Public Transportation			Bicycle	Walked	Other Means	Worked at Home
	Drove Alone	Car-pooled	Bus	Subway	Railroad				
City	75.4	10.6	1.4	0.1	0.0	0.5	2.4	1.4	8.2
MSA[1]	78.3	7.6	0.6	0.0	0.0	0.2	1.7	1.1	10.5
U.S.	73.2	8.6	2.0	1.6	0.5	0.5	2.5	1.5	9.7

Note: Figures are percentages and cover workers 16 years of age and older; (1) Figures cover the Des Moines-West Des Moines, IA Metropolitan Statistical Area
Source: U.S. Census Bureau, 2017-2021 American Community Survey 5-Year Estimates

Travel Time to Work

Area	Less Than 10 Minutes	10 to 19 Minutes	20 to 29 Minutes	30 to 44 Minutes	45 to 59 Minutes	60 to 89 Minutes	90 Minutes or More
City	13.5	43.1	26.6	12.3	2.2	1.3	1.1
MSA[1]	15.0	35.0	27.5	16.1	3.7	1.5	1.1
U.S.	12.4	28.5	21.0	20.9	8.2	6.2	2.9

Note: Note: Figures are percentages and include workers 16 years old and over; (1) Figures cover the Des Moines-West Des Moines, IA Metropolitan Statistical Area
Source: U.S. Census Bureau, 2017-2021 American Community Survey 5-Year Estimates

Key Congestion Measures

Measure	1990	2000	2010	2015	2020
Annual Hours of Delay, Total (000)	n/a	n/a	n/a	8,528	3,468
Annual Hours of Delay, Per Auto Commuter	n/a	n/a	n/a	17	7
Annual Congestion Cost, Per Auto Commuter ($)	n/a	n/a	n/a	355	153

Note: n/a not available
Source: Texas A&M Transportation Institute, 2021 Urban Mobility Report

Freeway Travel Time Index

Measure	1985	1990	1995	2000	2005	2010	2015	2020
Urban Area Index[1]	n/a	n/a	n/a	n/a	n/a	n/a	1.07	1.04
Urban Area Rank[1,2]	n/a	n/a	n/a	n/a	n/a	n/a	n/a	n/a

Note: Freeway Travel Time Index—the ratio of travel time in the peak period to the travel time at free-flow conditions. For example, a value of 1.30 indicates a 20-minute free-flow trip takes 26 minutes in the peak (20 minutes x 1.30 = 26 minutes); (1) Covers the Des Moines IA urban area; (2) Rank is based on 101 larger urban areas (#1 = highest travel time index); n/a not available
Source: Texas A&M Transportation Institute, 2021 Urban Mobility Report

Public Transportation

Agency Name / Mode of Transportation	Vehicles Operated in Maximum Service[1]	Annual Unlinked Passenger Trips[2] (in thous.)	Annual Passenger Miles[3] (in thous.)
Des Moines Metropolitan Transit Authority (MTA)			
Bus (directly operated)	85	1,773.1	6,934.0
Demand Response (directly operated)	16	49.1	413.4
Demand Response - Taxi	2	2.9	21.2
Vanpool (directly operated)	49	81.3	3,074.5

Note: (1) Number of revenue vehicles operated by the given mode and type of service to meet the annual maximum service requirement. This is the revenue vehicle count during the peak season of the year; on the week and day that maximum service is provided. Vehicles operated in maximum service (VOMS) exclude atypical days and one-time special events; (2) Number of passengers who boarded public transportation vehicles. Passengers are counted each time they board a vehicle no matter how many vehicles they use to travel from their origin to their destination. (3) Sum of the distances ridden by all passengers during the entire fiscal year.
Source: Federal Transit Administration, National Transit Database, 2021

Air Transportation

Airport Name and Code / Type of Service	Passenger Airlines[1]	Passenger Enplanements	Freight Carriers[2]	Freight (lbs)
Des Moines International (DSM)				
Domestic service (U.S. carriers - 2022)	23	1,367,087	10	35,894,834
International service (U.S. carriers - 2021)	0	0	0	0

Note: (1) Includes all U.S.-based major, minor and commuter airlines that carried at least one passenger during the year; (2) Includes all U.S.-based airlines and freight carriers that transported at least one pound of freight during the year.
Source: Bureau of Transportation Statistics, The Intermodal Transportation Database, Air Carriers: T-100 Domestic Market (U.S. Carriers), 2022; Bureau of Transportation Statistics, The Intermodal Transportation Database, Air Carriers: T-100 International Market (U.S. Carriers), 2021

BUSINESSES

Major Business Headquarters

Company Name	Industry	Rankings	
		Fortune[1]	Forbes[2]
Principal Financial	Insurance, life and health (stock)	256	-

Note: (1) Companies that produce a 10-K are ranked 1 to 500 based on 2021 revenue; (2) All private companies with at least $2 billion in annual revenue through the end of their most current fiscal year are ranked 1 to 246; companies listed are headquartered in the city; dashes indicate no ranking
Source: Fortune, "Fortune 500," 2022; Forbes, "America's Largest Private Companies," 2022

Living Environment

COST OF LIVING

Cost of Living Index

Composite Index	Groceries	Housing	Utilities	Trans-portation	Health Care	Misc. Goods/Services
86.0	98.3	67.8	85.1	88.2	96.3	93.6

Note: The Cost of Living Index measures regional differences in the cost of consumer goods and services, excluding taxes and non-consumer expenditures, for professional and managerial households in the top income quintile. It is based on more than 50,000 prices covering almost 60 different items for which prices are collected three times a year by chambers of commerce, economic development organizations or university applied economic centers in each participating urban area. The numbers shown should be read as a percentage above or below the national average of 100. For example, a value of 115.4 in the groceries column indicates that grocery prices are 15.4% higher than the national average. Small differences in the index numbers should not be interpreted as significant; Figures cover the Des Moines IA urban area.
Source: The Council for Community and Economic Research, Cost of Living Index, 2022

Grocery Prices

Area[1]	T-Bone Steak ($/pound)	Frying Chicken ($/pound)	Whole Milk ($/half gal.)	Eggs ($/dozen)	Orange Juice ($/64 oz.)	Coffee ($/11.5 oz.)
City[2]	11.66	2.33	2.79	2.40	3.41	5.05
Avg.	13.81	1.59	2.43	2.25	3.85	4.95
Min.	10.17	0.90	1.51	1.30	2.90	3.46
Max.	19.35	3.30	4.32	4.32	5.31	8.59

Note: (1) Values for the local area are compared with the average, minimum and maximum values for all 286 areas in the Cost of Living Index; (2) Figures cover the Des Moines IA urban area; *T-Bone Steak* (price per pound); *Frying Chicken* (price per pound, whole fryer); *Whole Milk* (half gallon carton); *Eggs* (price per dozen, Grade A, large); *Orange Juice* (64 oz. Tropicana or Florida Natural); *Coffee* (11.5 oz. can, vacuum-packed, Maxwell House, Hills Bros, or Folgers).
Source: The Council for Community and Economic Research, Cost of Living Index, 2022

Housing and Utility Costs

Area[1]	New Home Price ($)	Apartment Rent ($/month)	All Electric ($/month)	Part Electric ($/month)	Other Energy ($/month)	Telephone ($/month)
City[2]	337,128	741	-	79.63	53.25	188.32
Avg.	450,913	1,371	176.41	99.93	76.96	190.22
Min.	229,283	546	100.84	31.56	27.15	174.27
Max.	2,434,977	4,569	356.86	249.59	272.24	208.31

Note: (1) Values for the local area are compared with the average, minimum and maximum values for all 286 areas in the Cost of Living Index; (2) Figures cover the Des Moines IA urban area; *New Home Price* (2,400 sf living area, 8,000 sf lot, in urban area with full utilities); *Apartment Rent* (950 sf 2 bedroom/1.5 or 2 bath, unfurnished, excluding all utilities except water); *All Electric* (average monthly cost for an all-electric home); *Part Electric* (average monthly cost for a part-electric home); *Other Energy* (average monthly cost for natural gas, fuel oil, coal, wood, and any other forms of energy except electricity); *Telephone* (price includes the base monthly rate plus taxes and fees for three lines of mobile phone service).
Source: The Council for Community and Economic Research, Cost of Living Index, 2022

Health Care, Transportation, and Other Costs

Area[1]	Doctor ($/visit)	Dentist ($/visit)	Optometrist ($/visit)	Gasoline ($/gallon)	Beauty Salon ($/visit)	Men's Shirt ($)
City[2]	131.59	90.21	119.28	3.34	39.44	39.61
Avg.	124.91	107.77	117.66	3.86	43.31	34.21
Min.	36.61	58.25	51.79	2.90	22.18	13.05
Max.	250.21	162.58	371.96	5.54	85.61	63.54

Note: (1) Values for the local area are compared with the average, minimum and maximum values for all 286 areas in the Cost of Living Index; (2) Figures cover the Des Moines IA urban area; *Doctor* (general practitioners routine exam of an established patient); *Dentist* (adult teeth cleaning and periodic oral examination); *Optometrist* (full vision eye exam for established adult patient); *Gasoline* (one gallon regular unleaded, national brand, including all taxes, cash price at self-service pump if available); *Beauty Salon* (woman's shampoo, trim, and blow-dry); *Men's Shirt* (cotton/polyester dress shirt, pinpoint weave, long sleeves).
Source: The Council for Community and Economic Research, Cost of Living Index, 2022

HOUSING

Homeownership Rate

Area	2015 (%)	2016 (%)	2017 (%)	2018 (%)	2019 (%)	2020 (%)	2021 (%)	2022 (%)
MSA[1]	n/a	n/a	n/a	n/a	n/a	n/a	n/a	n/a
U.S.	63.7	63.4	63.9	64.4	64.6	66.6	65.5	65.8

Note: (1) Figures cover the Des Moines-West Des Moines, IA Metropolitan Statistical Area; n/a not available
Source: U.S. Census Bureau, Housing Vacancies and Homeownership Annual Statistics: 2015-2022

House Price Index (HPI)

Area	National Ranking[2]	Quarterly Change (%)	One-Year Change (%)	Five-Year Change (%)	Since 1991Q1 (%)
MSA[1]	108	0.29	12.00	40.34	223.17
U.S.[3]	–	0.34	8.41	58.44	289.08

Note: The HPI is a weighted repeat sales index. It measures average price changes in repeat sales or refinancings on the same properties. This information is obtained by reviewing repeat mortgage transactions on single-family properties whose mortgages have been purchased or securitized by Fannie Mae or Freddie Mac since January 1975; (1) Figures cover the Des Moines-West Des Moines, IA Metropolitan Statistical Area; (2) Rankings are based on annual percentage change for all metro areas containing at least 15,000 transactions over the last 10 years and ranges from 1 to 257; (3) figures based on a weighted average of Census Division estimates using a seasonally adjusted, purchase-only index; all figures are for the period ending December 31, 2022
Source: Federal Housing Finance Agency, Change in FHFA Metropolitan Area House Price Indexes, 2022Q4

Median Single-Family Home Prices

Area	2020	2021	2022p	Percent Change 2021 to 2022
MSA[1]	229.6	258.2	274.9	6.5
U.S. Average	300.2	357.1	392.6	9.9

Note: Figures are median sales prices of existing single-family homes in thousands of dollars; (p) preliminary; (1) Figures cover the Des Moines-West Des Moines, IA Metropolitan Statistical Area
Source: National Association of Realtors, Median Sales Price of Existing Single-Family Homes for Metropolitan Areas, 4th Quarter 2022

Qualifying Income Based on Median Sales Price of Existing Single-Family Homes

Area	With 5% Down ($)	With 10% Down ($)	With 20% Down ($)
MSA[1]	78,087	73,977	65,757
U.S. Average	112,234	106,237	94,513

Note: Figures are preliminary; Qualifying income is based on a mortgage rate of 6.77%. Monthly principal and interest payment is limited to 25% of income; (1) Figures cover the Des Moines-West Des Moines, IA Metropolitan Statistical Area
Source: National Association of Realtors, Qualifying Income Based on Median Sales Price of Existing Single-Family Homes for Metropolitan Areas, 4th Quarter 2022

Home Value

Area	Under $100,000	$100,000 -$199,999	$200,000 -$299,999	$300,000 -$399,999	$400,000 -$499,999	$500,000 -$999,999	$1,000,000 or more	Median ($)
City	20.9	53.8	17.0	4.6	1.5	1.9	0.3	149,700
MSA[1]	12.8	35.7	26.8	13.6	5.6	5.0	0.6	205,200
U.S.	16.2	24.2	20.1	13.6	8.3	13.6	4.1	244,900

Note: Figures are percentages except for median and cover owner-occupied housing units; (1) Figures cover the Des Moines-West Des Moines, IA Metropolitan Statistical Area
Source: U.S. Census Bureau, 2017-2021 American Community Survey 5-Year Estimates

Year Housing Structure Built

Area	2020 or Later	2010 -2019	2000 -2009	1990 -1999	1980 -1989	1970 -1979	1960 -1969	1950 -1959	1940 -1949	Before 1940	Median Year
City	0.1	5.5	6.7	7.0	6.4	13.6	10.0	14.9	7.8	28.0	1960
MSA[1]	0.3	14.1	15.7	12.5	8.0	13.3	7.9	8.8	3.9	15.4	1981
U.S.	0.2	7.3	13.6	13.6	13.2	14.8	10.3	10.0	4.7	12.2	1979

Note: Figures are percentages except for Median Year; Note: (1) Figures cover the Des Moines-West Des Moines, IA Metropolitan Statistical Area
Source: U.S. Census Bureau, 2017-2021 American Community Survey 5-Year Estimates

Gross Monthly Rent

Area	Under $500	$500 -$999	$1,000 -$1,499	$1,500 -$1,999	$2,000 -$2,499	$2,500 -$2,999	$3,000 and up	Median ($)
City	7.8	52.1	31.7	6.4	1.7	0.2	0.2	916
MSA[1]	6.8	46.8	34.7	8.9	2.0	0.3	0.6	972
U.S.	8.1	30.5	30.8	16.8	7.3	3.1	3.5	1,163

Note: Figures are percentages except for median; Gross rent is the contract rent plus the estimated average monthly cost of utilities (electricity, gas, and water and sewer) and fuels (oil, coal, kerosene, wood, etc.) if these are paid by the renter (or paid for the renter by someone else); (1) Figures cover the Des Moines-West Des Moines, IA Metropolitan Statistical Area
Source: U.S. Census Bureau, 2017-2021 American Community Survey 5-Year Estimates

HEALTH

Health Risk Factors

Category	MSA[1] (%)	U.S. (%)
Adults aged 18–64 who have any kind of health care coverage	92.0	90.9
Adults who reported being in good or better health	88.4	85.2
Adults who have been told they have high blood cholesterol	34.0	35.7
Adults who have been told they have high blood pressure	28.6	32.4
Adults who are current smokers	13.2	14.4
Adults who currently use e-cigarettes	7.5	6.7
Adults who currently use chewing tobacco, snuff, or snus	3.5	3.5
Adults who are heavy drinkers[2]	5.9	6.3
Adults who are binge drinkers[3]	21.1	15.4
Adults who are overweight (BMI 25.0 - 29.9)	33.3	34.4
Adults who are obese (BMI 30.0 - 99.8)	35.8	33.9
Adults who participated in any physical activities in the past month	77.8	76.3

Note: (1) Figures cover the Des Moines-West Des Moines, IA Metropolitan Statistical Area; (2) Heavy drinkers are classified as adult men having more than 14 drinks per week and adult women having more than 7 drinks per week; (3) Binge drinkers are classified as males having five or more drinks on one occasion or females having four or more drinks on one occasion
Source: Centers for Disease Control and Prevention, Behaviorial Risk Factor Surveillance System, SMART: Selected Metropolitan Area Risk Trends, 2021

Acute and Chronic Health Conditions

Category	MSA[1] (%)	U.S. (%)
Adults who have ever been told they had a heart attack	3.8	4.0
Adults who have ever been told they have angina or coronary heart disease	3.6	3.8
Adults who have ever been told they had a stroke	1.6	3.0
Adults who have ever been told they have asthma	12.8	14.9
Adults who have ever been told they have arthritis	25.4	25.8
Adults who have ever been told they have diabetes[2]	8.1	10.9
Adults who have ever been told they had skin cancer	6.8	6.6
Adults who have ever been told they had any other types of cancer	6.5	7.5
Adults who have ever been told they have COPD	5.2	6.1
Adults who have ever been told they have kidney disease	1.9	3.0
Adults who have ever been told they have a form of depression	18.5	20.5

Note: (1) Figures cover the Des Moines-West Des Moines, IA Metropolitan Statistical Area; (2) Figures do not include pregnancy-related, borderline, or pre-diabetes
Source: Centers for Disease Control and Prevention, Behaviorial Risk Factor Surveillance System, SMART: Selected Metropolitan Area Risk Trends, 2021

Health Screening and Vaccination Rates

Category	MSA[1] (%)	U.S. (%)
Adults who have ever been tested for HIV	29.2	34.9
Adults who have had their blood cholesterol checked within the last five years	83.4	85.2
Adults aged 65+ who have had flu shot within the past year	77.3	68.6
Adults aged 65+ who have ever had a pneumonia vaccination	77.0	71.0

Note: (1) Figures cover the Des Moines-West Des Moines, IA Metropolitan Statistical Area.
Source: Centers for Disease Control and Prevention, Behaviorial Risk Factor Surveillance System, SMART: Selected Metropolitan Area Risk Trends, 2021

Disability Status

Category	MSA[1] (%)	U.S. (%)
Adults who reported being deaf	6.1	7.2
Are you blind or have serious difficulty seeing, even when wearing glasses?	2.4	4.8
Are you limited in any way in any of your usual activities due to arthritis?	9.0	11.1
Do you have difficulty doing errands alone?	4.9	7.0
Do you have difficulty dressing or bathing?	2.1	3.6
Do you have serious difficulty concentrating/remembering/making decisions?	9.9	12.1
Do you have serious difficulty walking or climbing stairs?	9.7	12.8

Note: (1) Figures cover the Des Moines-West Des Moines, IA Metropolitan Statistical Area.
Source: Centers for Disease Control and Prevention, Behaviorial Risk Factor Surveillance System, SMART: Selected Metropolitan Area Risk Trends, 2021

Mortality Rates for the Top 10 Causes of Death in the U.S.

ICD-10[a] Sub-Chapter	ICD-10[a] Code	Crude Mortality Rate[1] per 100,000 population	
		County[2]	U.S.
Malignant neoplasms	C00-C97	165.8	182.6
Ischaemic heart diseases	I20-I25	106.7	113.1
Other forms of heart disease	I30-I51	53.1	64.4
Other degenerative diseases of the nervous system	G30-G31	41.2	51.0
Cerebrovascular diseases	I60-I69	35.5	47.8
Other external causes of accidental injury	W00-X59	46.1	46.4
Chronic lower respiratory diseases	J40-J47	40.8	45.7
Organic, including symptomatic, mental disorders	F01-F09	37.5	35.9
Hypertensive diseases	I10-I15	21.8	35.0
Diabetes mellitus	E10-E14	21.1	29.6

Note: (a) ICD-10 = International Classification of Diseases 10th Revision; (1) Crude mortality rates are a three-year average covering 2019-2021; (2) Figures cover Polk County.
Source: Centers for Disease Control and Prevention, National Center for Health Statistics. National Vital Statistics System, Mortality 2018-2021 on CDC WONDER Online Database

Mortality Rates for Selected Causes of Death

ICD-10[a] Sub-Chapter	ICD-10[a] Code	Crude Mortality Rate[1] per 100,000 population	
		County[2]	U.S.
Assault	X85-Y09	3.5	7.0
Diseases of the liver	K70-K76	16.3	19.8
Human immunodeficiency virus (HIV) disease	B20-B24	Suppressed	1.5
Influenza and pneumonia	J09-J18	9.4	14.7
Intentional self-harm	X60-X84	17.1	14.3
Malnutrition	E40-E46	6.0	4.3
Obesity and other hyperalimentation	E65-E68	2.6	3.0
Renal failure	N17-N19	7.3	15.7
Transport accidents	V01-V99	9.1	13.6
Viral hepatitis	B15-B19	1.4	1.2

Note: (a) ICD-10 = International Classification of Diseases 10th Revision; (1) Crude mortality rates are a three-year average covering 2019-2021; (2) Figures cover Polk County; Data are suppressed when the data meet the criteria for confidentiality constraints; Crude mortality rates are flagged as unreliable when the rate would be calculated with a numerator of 20 or less.
Source: Centers for Disease Control and Prevention, National Center for Health Statistics. National Vital Statistics System, Mortality 2018-2021 on CDC WONDER Online Database

Health Insurance Coverage

Area	With Health Insurance	With Private Health Insurance	With Public Health Insurance	Without Health Insurance	Population Under Age 19 Without Health Insurance
City	93.7	63.7	42.0	6.3	2.2
MSA[1]	95.7	76.3	31.8	4.3	2.2
U.S.	91.2	67.8	35.4	8.8	5.3

Note: Figures are percentages that cover the civilian noninstitutionalized population; (1) Figures cover the Des Moines-West Des Moines, IA Metropolitan Statistical Area
Source: U.S. Census Bureau, 2017-2021 American Community Survey 5-Year Estimates

Number of Medical Professionals

Area	MDs[3]	DOs[3,4]	Dentists	Podiatrists	Chiropractors	Optometrists
County[1] (number)	1,064	489	384	56	295	108
County[1] (rate[2])	215.9	99.2	77.3	11.3	59.4	21.7
U.S. (rate[2])	289.3	23.5	72.5	6.2	28.7	17.4

Note: Data as of 2021 unless noted; (1) Data covers Polk County; (2) Rate per 100,000 population; (3) Data as of 2020 and includes all active, non-federal physicians; (4) Doctor of Osteopathic Medicine
Source: U.S. Department of Health and Human Services, Health Resources and Services Administration, Bureau of Health Professions, Area Resource File (ARF) 2021-2022

EDUCATION

Public School District Statistics

District Name	Schls	Pupils	Pupil/ Teacher Ratio	Minority Pupils[1] (%)	LEP/ELL[2] (%)	IEP[3] (%)
Des Moines Independent CSD	59	31,323	14.7	65.7	21.7	16.8

Note: Table includes school districts with 2,000 or more students; (1) Percentage of students that are not non-Hispanic white; (2) Percentage of students that are Limited English Proficient or English Language Learners (2018-19); (3) Percentage of students that have an Individualized Education Program (2019-20).
Source: U.S. Department of Education, National Center for Education Statistics, Common Core of Data, Local Education Agency (School District) Universe Survey: School Year 2021-2022

Highest Level of Education

Area	Less than H.S.	H.S. Diploma	Some College, No Deg.	Associate Degree	Bachelor's Degree	Master's Degree	Prof. School Degree	Doctorate Degree
City	12.9	29.6	20.2	9.2	19.3	6.2	1.8	0.8
MSA[1]	6.6	25.6	19.5	10.7	25.8	8.4	2.1	1.3
U.S.	11.1	26.5	20.0	8.7	20.6	9.3	2.2	1.5

Note: Figures cover persons age 25 and over; (1) Figures cover the Des Moines-West Des Moines, IA Metropolitan Statistical Area
Source: U.S. Census Bureau, 2017-2021 American Community Survey 5-Year Estimates

Educational Attainment by Race

Area	High School Graduate or Higher (%)					Bachelor's Degree or Higher (%)				
	Total	White	Black	Asian	Hisp.[2]	Total	White	Black	Asian	Hisp.[2]
City	87.1	91.9	82.1	58.6	60.2	28.1	31.1	16.4	21.8	10.1
MSA[1]	93.4	95.6	84.8	71.0	68.2	37.6	39.0	20.7	37.1	15.8
U.S.	88.9	91.4	87.2	87.6	71.2	33.7	35.5	23.3	55.6	18.4

Note: Figures shown cover persons 25 years old and over; (1) Figures cover the Des Moines-West Des Moines, IA Metropolitan Statistical Area; (2) People of Hispanic origin can be of any race
Source: U.S. Census Bureau, 2017-2021 American Community Survey 5-Year Estimates

School Enrollment by Grade and Control

Area	Preschool (%)		Kindergarten (%)		Grades 1 - 4 (%)		Grades 5 - 8 (%)		Grades 9 - 12 (%)	
	Public	Private	Public	Private	Public	Private	Public	Private	Public	Private
City	73.4	26.6	90.8	9.2	89.8	10.2	89.4	10.6	92.0	8.0
MSA[1]	67.2	32.8	90.4	9.6	91.9	8.1	90.5	9.5	92.2	7.8
U.S.	58.8	41.2	86.3	13.7	88.3	11.7	88.6	11.4	89.4	10.6

Note: Figures shown cover persons 3 years old and over; (1) Figures cover the Des Moines-West Des Moines, IA Metropolitan Statistical Area
Source: U.S. Census Bureau, 2017-2021 American Community Survey 5-Year Estimates

Higher Education

Four-Year Colleges			Two-Year Colleges			Medical Schools[1]	Law Schools[2]	Voc/ Tech[3]
Public	Private Non-profit	Private For-profit	Public	Private Non-profit	Private For-profit			
0	6	0	1	1	3	1	1	1

Note: Figures cover institutions located within the Des Moines-West Des Moines, IA Metropolitan Statistical Area and include main campuses only; (1) includes schools accredited by the Liaison Committee on Medical Education and the American Osteopathic Association's Commission on Osteopathic College Accreditation; (2) includes ABA-accredited schools, schools with provisional ABA accreditation, and state accredited schools; (3) includes all schools with programs that are less than 2 years.
Source: National Center for Education Statistics, Integrated Postsecondary Education System (IPEDS), 2021-22; Wikipedia, List of Medical Schools in the United States, accessed April 10, 2023; Wikipedia, List of Law Schools in the United States, accessed April 10, 2023

According to *U.S. News & World Report,* the Des Moines-West Des Moines, IA metro area is home to one of the top 200 national universities in the U.S.: **Drake University** (#137 tie). The indicators used to capture academic quality fall into a number of categories: assessment by administrators at peer institutions; retention of students; faculty resources; student selectivity; financial resources; alumni giving; high school counselor ratings of colleges; and graduation rate. *U.S. News & World Report, "America's Best Colleges 2023"*

EMPLOYERS

Major Employers

Company Name	Industry
Bridgestone Americas Tire Operations	Global distribution center for tires
DuPont Pioneer	Crop inputs for worldwide agribusiness
Emerson Process Management Fisher Div	Control valves & systems, divisional headquarters
Grinnell Mutual Reinsurance Company	Reinsurance
Hy-Vee Food Stores	Retail grocery & drugstore chain
JBS USA	Pork processing & packaging
John Deere companies	Agricultural machinery, consumer financial services
Lennox Manufacturing	Heating & air conditioners
Mercer	Insurance
Mercy Medical Center	Healthcare
Meredith Corporation	Magazine, book publishing, tv, integrated marketing
Nationwide	Insurance
Principal Financial Group	Financial services
United Parcel Service	Package delivery services
UnityPoint Health	Healthcare
Vermeer Manufacturing Company	Manufacturing
Wellmark	Health insurance
Wells Fargo	Financial services & home mortgage

Note: Companies shown are located within the Des Moines-West Des Moines, IA Metropolitan Statistical Area.
Source: Hoovers.com; Wikipedia

Best Companies to Work For

BH Management Services, headquartered in Des Moines, is among "Fortune's Best Workplaces for Women." To pick the best companies, *Fortune* partnered with the Great Place to Work Institute. To be considered for the list, companies must be Great Place To Work-Certified. Companies must also employ at least 50 women, at least 20% of their non-executive managers must be female, and at least one executive must be female. To determine the Best Workplaces for Women, Great Place To Work measured the differences in women's survey responses to those of their peers and assesses the impact of demographics and roles on the quality and consistency of women's experiences. Great Place To Work also analyzed the gender balance of each workplace, how it compared to each company's industry, and patterns in representation as women rise from front-line positions to the board of directors. *Fortune, "Best Workplaces for Women," 2022*

Principal, headquartered in Des Moines, is among the "100 Best Places to Work in IT." To qualify, companies had to have a minimum of 100 total employees and five IT employees. The best places to work were selected based on DEI (diversity, equity, and inclusion) practices; IT turnover, promotions, and growth; IT retention and engagement programs; remote/hybrid working; benefits and perks (such as elder care and child care, flextime, and reimbursement for college tuition); and training and career development opportunities. *Computerworld, "Best Places to Work in IT," 2023*

PUBLIC SAFETY

Crime Rate

Area	Total Crime	Violent Crime Rate				Property Crime Rate		
		Murder	Rape[3]	Robbery	Aggrav. Assault	Burglary	Larceny -Theft	Motor Vehicle Theft
City	4,606.3	15.3	55.3	114.3	519.8	894.1	2,347.1	660.5
Suburbs[1]	1,384.2	2.2	25.9	9.9	141.1	218.8	859.4	126.9
Metro[2]	2,362.1	6.2	34.8	41.6	256.0	423.8	1,310.9	288.8
U.S.	2,356.7	6.5	38.4	73.9	279.7	314.2	1,398.0	246.0

Note: Figures are crimes per 100,000 population; (1) All areas within the metro area that are located outside the city limits; (2) Figures cover the Des Moines-West Des Moines, IA Metropolitan Statistical Area; (3) All figures shown were reported using the revised Uniform Crime Reporting (UCR) definition of rape; Due to the transition to the National Incident-Based Reporting System (NIBRS), limited city and metro area data was released for 2021.
Source: FBI Uniform Crime Reports, 2020

Hate Crimes

Area	Number of Quarters Reported	Number of Incidents per Bias Motivation					
		Race/Ethnicity/ Ancestry	Religion	Sexual Orientation	Disability	Gender	Gender Identity
City	4	0	0	0	0	0	0
U.S.	4	5,227	1,244	1,110	130	75	266

Note: Due to the transition to the National Incident-Based Reporting System (NIBRS), limited crime data was released for 2021.
Source: Federal Bureau of Investigation, Hate Crime Statistics 2020

Identity Theft Consumer Reports

Area	Reports	Reports per 100,000 Population	Rank[2]
MSA[1]	907	131	292
U.S.	1,108,609	339	-

Note: (1) Figures cover the Des Moines-West Des Moines, IA Metropolitan Statistical Area; (2) Rank ranges from 1 to 391 where 1 indicates greatest number of identity theft reports per 100,000 population
Source: Federal Trade Commission, Consumer Sentinel Network Data Book 2022

Fraud and Other Consumer Reports

Area	Reports	Reports per 100,000 Population	Rank[2]
MSA[1]	4,781	692	298
U.S.	4,064,520	1,245	-

Note: (1) Figures cover the Des Moines-West Des Moines, IA Metropolitan Statistical Area; (2) Rank ranges from 1 to 391 where 1 indicates greatest number of fraud and other consumer reports per 100,000 population
Source: Federal Trade Commission, Consumer Sentinel Network Data Book 2022

POLITICS

2020 Presidential Election Results

Area	Biden	Trump	Jorgensen	Hawkins	Other
Polk County	56.5	41.3	1.3	0.2	0.7
U.S.	51.3	46.8	1.2	0.3	0.5

Note: Results are percentages and may not add to 100% due to rounding
Source: Dave Leip's Atlas of U.S. Presidential Elections

SPORTS

Professional Sports Teams

Team Name	League	Year Established

No teams are located in the metro area
Source: Wikipedia, Major Professional Sports Teams of the United States and Canada, April 12, 2023

CLIMATE

Average and Extreme Temperatures

Temperature	Jan	Feb	Mar	Apr	May	Jun	Jul	Aug	Sep	Oct	Nov	Dec	Yr.
Extreme High (°F)	65	70	91	93	98	103	105	108	99	95	76	69	108
Average High (°F)	29	34	45	61	72	82	86	84	76	65	48	33	60
Average Temp. (°F)	20	25	36	51	62	72	76	74	65	54	39	25	50
Average Low (°F)	11	16	27	40	51	61	66	64	54	43	29	17	40
Extreme Low (°F)	-24	-20	-22	9	28	42	47	40	28	14	-3	-22	-24

Note: Figures cover the years 1945-1990
Source: National Climatic Data Center, International Station Meteorological Climate Summary, 9/96

Average Precipitation/Snowfall/Humidity

Precip./Humidity	Jan	Feb	Mar	Apr	May	Jun	Jul	Aug	Sep	Oct	Nov	Dec	Yr.
Avg. Precip. (in.)	1.1	1.1	2.3	3.1	3.8	4.4	3.5	3.9	3.1	2.4	1.7	1.2	31.8
Avg. Snowfall (in.)	8	7	7	2	Tr	0	0	0	Tr	Tr	3	7	33
Avg. Rel. Hum. 6am (%)	77	79	79	78	78	81	83	86	85	80	79	80	80
Avg. Rel. Hum. 3pm (%)	65	63	57	50	51	52	52	54	52	50	58	66	56

Note: Figures cover the years 1945-1990; Tr = Trace amounts (<0.05 in. of rain; <0.5 in. of snow)
Source: National Climatic Data Center, International Station Meteorological Climate Summary, 9/96

Weather Conditions

Temperature			Daytime Sky			Precipitation		
5°F & below	32°F & below	90°F & above	Clear	Partly cloudy	Cloudy	0.01 inch or more precip.	0.1 inch or more snow/ice	Thunderstorms
25	137	26	99	128	138	106	25	46

Note: Figures are average number of days per year and cover the years 1945-1990
Source: National Climatic Data Center, International Station Meteorological Climate Summary, 9/96

HAZARDOUS WASTE

Superfund Sites

The Des Moines-West Des Moines, IA metro area is home to two sites on the EPA's Superfund National Priorities List: **Des Moines TCE** (final); **Railroad Avenue Groundwater Contamination** (final). There are a total of 1,165 Superfund sites with a status of proposed or final on the list in the U.S.
U.S. Environmental Protection Agency, National Priorities List, April 12, 2023

AIR QUALITY

Air Quality Trends: Ozone

	1990	1995	2000	2005	2010	2015	2018	2019	2020	2021
MSA[1]	n/a	n/a	n/a	n/a	n/a	n/a	n/a	n/a	n/a	n/a
U.S.	0.087	0.089	0.081	0.080	0.072	0.067	0.069	0.065	0.065	0.067

Note: (1) Data covers the Des Moines-West Des Moines, IA Metropolitan Statistical Area; n/a not available. The values shown are the composite ozone concentration averages among trend sites based on the highest fourth daily maximum 8-hour concentration in parts per million. These trends are based on sites having an adequate record of monitoring data during the trend period. Data from exceptional events are included.
Source: U.S. Environmental Protection Agency, Air Quality Monitoring Information, "Air Quality Trends by City, 1990-2021"

Air Quality Index

Area	Percent of Days when Air Quality was...[2]					AQI Statistics[2]	
	Good	Moderate	Unhealthy for Sensitive Groups	Unhealthy	Very Unhealthy	Maximum	Median
MSA[1]	77.8	21.9	0.3	0.0	0.0	110	40

Note: (1) Data covers the Des Moines-West Des Moines, IA Metropolitan Statistical Area; (2) Based on 365 days with AQI data in 2021. Air Quality Index (AQI) is an index for reporting daily air quality. EPA calculates the AQI for five major air pollutants regulated by the Clean Air Act: ground-level ozone, particle pollution (aka particulate matter), carbon monoxide, sulfur dioxide, and nitrogen dioxide. The AQI runs from 0 to 500. The higher the AQI value, the greater the level of air pollution and the greater the health concern. There are six AQI categories: "Good" AQI is between 0 and 50. Air quality is considered satisfactory; "Moderate" AQI is between 51 and 100. Air quality is acceptable; "Unhealthy for Sensitive Groups" When AQI values are between 101 and 150, members of sensitive groups may experience health effects; "Unhealthy" When AQI values are between 151 and 200 everyone may begin to experience health effects; "Very Unhealthy" AQI values between 201 and 300 trigger a health alert; "Hazardous" AQI values over 300 trigger warnings of emergency conditions (not shown).
Source: U.S. Environmental Protection Agency, Air Quality Index Report, 2021

Air Quality Index Pollutants

Area	Percent of Days when AQI Pollutant was...[2]					
	Carbon Monoxide	Nitrogen Dioxide	Ozone	Sulfur Dioxide	Particulate Matter 2.5	Particulate Matter 10
MSA[1]	0.0	3.6	43.3	(3)	51.8	1.4

Note: (1) Data covers the Des Moines-West Des Moines, IA Metropolitan Statistical Area; (2) Based on 365 days with AQI data in 2021. The Air Quality Index (AQI) is an index for reporting daily air quality. EPA calculates the AQI for five major air pollutants regulated by the Clean Air Act: ground-level ozone, particle pollution (also known as particulate matter), carbon monoxide, sulfur dioxide, and nitrogen dioxide. The AQI runs from 0 to 500. The higher the AQI value, the greater the level of air pollution and the greater the health concern; (3) Sulfur dioxide is no longer included in this table (as of December 8, 2021) because SO_2 concentrations tend to be very localized and not necessarily representative of broad geographical areas like counties and CBSAs.
Source: U.S. Environmental Protection Agency, Air Quality Index Report, 2021

Maximum Air Pollutant Concentrations: Particulate Matter, Ozone, CO and Lead

	Particulate Matter 10 (ug/m³)	Particulate Matter 2.5 Wtd AM (ug/m³)	Particulate Matter 2.5 24-Hr (ug/m³)	Ozone (ppm)	Carbon Monoxide (ppm)	Lead (ug/m³)
MSA[1] Level	54	8.3	23	0.061	n/a	n/a
NAAQS[2]	150	15	35	0.075	9	0.15
Met NAAQS[2]	Yes	Yes	Yes	Yes	n/a	n/a

Note: (1) Data covers the Des Moines-West Des Moines, IA Metropolitan Statistical Area; Data from exceptional events are included; (2) National Ambient Air Quality Standards; ppm = parts per million; ug/m³ = micrograms per cubic meter; n/a not available.
Concentrations: Particulate Matter 10 (coarse particulate)—highest second maximum 24-hour concentration; Particulate Matter 2.5 Wtd AM (fine particulate)—highest weighted annual mean concentration; Particulate Matter 2.5 24-Hour (fine particulate)—highest 98th percentile 24-hour concentration; Ozone—highest fourth daily maximum 8-hour concentration; Carbon Monoxide—highest second maximum non-overlapping 8-hour concentration; Lead—maximum running 3-month average
Source: U.S. Environmental Protection Agency, Air Quality Monitoring Information, "Air Quality Statistics by City, 2021"

Maximum Air Pollutant Concentrations: Nitrogen Dioxide and Sulfur Dioxide

	Nitrogen Dioxide AM (ppb)	Nitrogen Dioxide 1-Hr (ppb)	Sulfur Dioxide AM (ppb)	Sulfur Dioxide 1-Hr (ppb)	Sulfur Dioxide 24-Hr (ppb)
MSA[1] Level	6	34	n/a	n/a	n/a
NAAQS[2]	53	100	30	75	140
Met NAAQS[2]	Yes	Yes	n/a	n/a	n/a

Note: (1) Data covers the Des Moines-West Des Moines, IA Metropolitan Statistical Area; Data from exceptional events are included; (2) National Ambient Air Quality Standards; ppm = parts per million; ug/m^3 = micrograms per cubic meter; n/a not available.
Concentrations: Nitrogen Dioxide AM—highest arithmetic mean concentration; Nitrogen Dioxide 1-Hr—highest 98th percentile 1-hour daily maximum concentration; Sulfur Dioxide AM—highest annual mean concentration; Sulfur Dioxide 1-Hr—highest 99th percentile 1-hour daily maximum concentration; Sulfur Dioxide 24-Hr—highest second maximum 24-hour concentration
Source: U.S. Environmental Protection Agency, Air Quality Monitoring Information, "Air Quality Statistics by City, 2021"

Fargo, North Dakota

Background

Fargo sits on the western bank of the Red River in the Red River Valley in the southeastern part of the state. The city is in Cass County and about 300 miles northwest of Minneapolis.

Fargo was originally a stopping point for steamboats on the Red River in the later part of the 19th century. Founded in 1871, the city was first named Centralia, but renamed Fargo in honor of the Northern Pacific Railway Director Wells Fargo. It began to flourish after the arrival of the railroad and became known as the Gateway to the West. During the 1880s, Fargo was also known for its lenient divorce laws.

A major fire in 1893 destroyed hundreds of homes and businesses but the city was quickly rebuilt with new brick buildings, new streets, and a water system. The North Dakota State Agricultural College was founded in 1890 as the state's land-grant university and was accredited by the North Central Association in 1915. The school eventually became known as North Dakota State University during the 1960s.

Fargo grew rapidly after World War II as the connection of two interstates, I-29 and I-94, revolutionized travel in the region and allowed for further expansion in the southern and western parts of the city. In 1972, the West Acres Shopping Center was constructed near the intersection of the two interstates and served as a catalyst for retail growth in the area.

Fargo is the crossroads and economic center of eastern North Dakota and western Minnesota. Though the economy of the region was historically dependent on agriculture, other sectors have become increasingly prevalent in recent years, including food processing, manufacturing, technology, retail trade, higher education, and healthcare. The University is the city's largest public sector employer.

A significant landmark in Fargo is the main campus of North Dakota State University, which has a full-time enrollment of nearly 9,000. The city also features many public parks including Percy Godwin Park, Lindenwood Park, Mickelson Field, Island Park, Roosevelt Playground, and Oak Grove Park.

As the city continues to energize the downtown area, the Renaissance Zone and Storefront Rehab programs encourage new business, renovate deteriorating buildings, and increase the availability of housing in the downtown area. The renovated Fargo Public Library's main downtown branch is popular with the city's residents.

Fargo, an Academy Award-winning 1996 film named after the city, shows the city briefly at the film's opening scene set in a bar, and is mentioned twice in the film. *Fargo*, the TV series based on the film, debuted on FX in 2014. The city was featured in its seventh episode of season 1, "Who Shaves the Barber?" and more prominently in season 2. The series was filmed in Calgary, Alberta, Canada.

Fargo has a moderate northern climate. Summer temperatures average 65 degrees, while winter averages fall to 10 degrees during of December and January. The city averages 2.5 inches of rainfall per month from April to October and 8 inches of snowfall per month from December to March. Natural disaster struck in 2009, when heavy snowfall caused the Red River to flood the area, followed by extended periods of freezing temperatures.

Rankings

General Rankings

- In their ninth annual survey, Livability.com looked at data for more than 2,300 mid-sized U.S. cities to determine the rankings for Livability's "Top 100 Best Places to Live" in 2022. Fargo ranked #48. Criteria: housing and economy; social and civic engagement; education; demographics; health care options; transportation & infrastructure; and community amenities. *Livability.com, "Top 100 Best Places to Live 2022" July 19, 2022*

Business/Finance Rankings

- The Fargo metro area appeared on the Milken Institute "2022 Best Performing Cities" list. Rank: #15 out of 201 small metro areas (population over 60,000). Criteria: job growth; wage and salary growth; high-tech output growth; housing affordability; household broadband access. *Milken Institute, "Best-Performing Cities 2022," March 28, 2022*

- *Forbes* ranked 203 smaller metro areas (population under 268,000) to determine the nation's "Best Small Places for Business and Careers." The Fargo metro area was ranked #23. Criteria: costs (business and living); job growth (past and projected); income growth; quality of life; educational attainment (college and high school); projected economic growth; cultural and leisure opportunities; workplace tolerance laws; net migration patterns. *Forbes, "The Best Small Places for Business and Careers 2019," October 30, 2019*

Dating/Romance Rankings

- Fargo was selected as one of the most romantic cities in the U.S. by video-rental kiosk company Redbox. The city ranked #10 out of 20. Criteria: number of romance-related rentals in 2016. *Redbox, "20 Most Romantic Cities," February 6, 2017*

Environmental Rankings

- Niche compiled a list of the nation's snowiest cities, based on the National Oceanic and Atmospheric Administration's 30-year average snowfall data. Among cities with a population of at least 50,000, Fargo ranked #18. *Niche.com, Top 25 Snowiest Cities in America, December 10, 2018*

- Fargo was highlighted as one of the 25 metro areas most polluted by short-term particle pollution (24-hour PM 2.5) in the U.S. during 2019 through 2021. The area ranked #22. *American Lung Association, "State of the Air 2023," April 19, 2023*

Real Estate Rankings

- *WalletHub* compared the most populated U.S. cities to determine which had the best markets for real estate agents. Fargo ranked #35 where demand was high and pay was the best. Criteria: sales per agent; annual median wage for real-estate agents; monthly average starting salary for real estate agents; real estate job density and competition; unemployment rate; home turnover rate; housing-market health index; and other relevant metrics. *www.WalletHub.com, "2021 Best Places to Be a Real Estate Agent," May 12, 2021*

- The Fargo metro area was identified as one of the 20 best housing markets in the U.S. in 2022. The area ranked #14 out of 187 markets. Criteria: year-over-year change of median sales price of existing single-family homes between the 4th quarter of 2021 and the 4th quarter of 2022. *National Association of Realtors®, Median Sales Price of Existing Single-Family Homes for Metropolitan Areas, 4th Quarter 2022*

Seniors/Retirement Rankings

- From its Best Cities for Successful Aging indexes, the Milken Institute generated rankings for metropolitan areas, weighing data in nine categories—health care, wellness, living arrangements, transportation and convenience, financial characteristics, education, employment, community engagement, and overall livability. The Fargo metro area was ranked #14 overall in the small metro area category. *Milken Institute, "Best Cities for Successful Aging, 2017" March 14, 2017*

- Fargo made the 2022 *Forbes* list of "25 Best Places to Retire." Criteria, focused on overall affordability as well as quality of life indicators, include: housing/living costs compared to the national average and state taxes; air quality; crime rates; home price appreciation; risk associated with climate-change/natural hazards; availability of medical care; bikeability; walkability; healthy living. *Forbes.com, "The Best Places to Retire in 2022," May 13, 2022*

Women/Minorities Rankings

- Personal finance website *WalletHub* compared more than 180 U.S. cities across two key dimensions, "Hispanic Business-Friendliness" and "Hispanic Purchasing Power," to arrive at the most favorable conditions for Hispanic entrepreneurs. Fargo was ranked #111 out of 182. Criteria includes: share of Hispanic-Owned Businesses; Hispanic entrepreneurship rate to median annual income of Hispanics; Small Business-Friendliness score; cost of living; and number of Hispanics with at least a bachelor's degree. *WalletHub.com, "2019's Best Cities for Hispanic Entrepreneurs," May 1, 2019*

Miscellaneous Rankings

- *WalletHub* compared the 150 most populated U.S. cities to determine their operating efficiency. A "Quality of Services" score was constructed for each city and then divided by the total budget per capita to reveal which were managed the best. Fargo ranked #61. Criteria: financial stability; economy; education; safety; health; infrastructure and pollution. *www.WalletHub.com, "2022's Best-& Worst-Run Cities in America," June 21, 2022*

Business Environment

DEMOGRAPHICS

Population Growth

Area	1990 Census	2000 Census	2010 Census	2020 Census	Population Growth (%) 1990-2020	Population Growth (%) 2010-2020
City	74,372	90,599	105,549	125,990	69.4	19.4
MSA[1]	153,296	174,367	208,777	249,843	63.0	19.7
U.S.	248,709,873	281,421,906	308,745,538	331,449,281	33.3	7.4

Note: (1) Figures cover the Fargo, ND-MN Metropolitan Statistical Area
Source: U.S. Census Bureau, 1990 Census, 2000 Census, 2010 Census, 2020 Census

Race

Area	White Alone[2] (%)	Black Alone[2] (%)	Asian Alone[2] (%)	AIAN[3] Alone[2] (%)	NHOPI[4] Alone[2] (%)	Other Race Alone[2] (%)	Two or More Races (%)
City	78.9	8.8	4.1	1.6	0.1	1.2	5.3
MSA[1]	82.8	6.5	2.7	1.5	0.0	1.1	5.3
U.S.	61.6	12.4	6.0	1.1	0.2	8.4	10.2

Note: (1) Figures cover the Fargo, ND-MN Metropolitan Statistical Area; (2) Alone is defined as not being in combination with one or more other races; (3) American Indian and Alaska Native; (4) Native Hawaiian and Other Pacific Islander
Source: U.S. Census Bureau, 2020 Census

Hispanic or Latino Origin

Area	Total (%)	Mexican (%)	Puerto Rican (%)	Cuban (%)	Other (%)
City	3.2	2.0	0.3	0.0	0.9
MSA[1]	3.4	2.4	0.3	0.0	0.7
U.S.	18.4	11.2	1.8	0.7	4.7

Note: Persons of Hispanic or Latino origin can be of any race; (1) Figures cover the Fargo, ND-MN Metropolitan Statistical Area
Source: U.S. Census Bureau, 2017-2021 American Community Survey 5-Year Estimates

Age

Area	Percent of Population Under Age 5	Age 5–19	Age 20–34	Age 35–44	Age 45–54	Age 55–64	Age 65–74	Age 75–84	Age 85+	Median Age
City	6.2	17.8	30.1	13.0	9.7	10.3	7.7	3.5	1.8	32.5
MSA[1]	6.7	19.9	25.7	13.7	10.4	10.7	7.7	3.5	1.7	33.5
U.S.	5.6	19.2	20.2	12.7	12.4	13.1	10.0	4.9	1.9	38.8

Note: (1) Figures cover the Fargo, ND-MN Metropolitan Statistical Area
Source: U.S. Census Bureau, 2020 Census

Disability by Age

Area	All Ages	Under 18 Years Old	18 to 64 Years Old	65 Years and Over
City	10.2	5.1	7.7	32.0
MSA[1]	9.8	4.0	7.8	31.7
U.S.	12.6	4.4	10.3	33.4

Note: Figures show percent of the civilian noninstitutionalized population that reported having a disability. Disability status is determined from six types of difficulty: vision, hearing, cognitive, ambulatory, self-care, and independent living. For children under 5 years old, hearing and vision difficulty are used to determine disability status. For children between the ages of 5 and 14, disability status is determined from hearing, vision, cognitive, ambulatory, and self-care difficulties. For people aged 15 years and older, they are considered to have a disability if they have difficulty with any one of the six difficulty types; Note: (1) Figures cover the Fargo, ND-MN Metropolitan Statistical Area
Source: U.S. Census Bureau, 2017-2021 American Community Survey 5-Year Estimates

Ancestry

Area	German	Irish	English	American	Italian	Polish	French[2]	Scottish	Dutch
City	35.0	8.2	5.0	2.5	1.0	2.1	3.5	1.2	1.0
MSA[1]	35.4	7.8	4.8	2.5	1.1	2.2	3.1	1.1	1.1
U.S.	12.8	9.6	8.1	5.7	5.0	2.7	2.2	1.6	1.1

Note: Figures are the percentage of the total population reporting a particular ancestry. The nine most commonly reported ancestries in the U.S. are shown. Figures include multiple ancestries (e.g. if a person reported being Irish and Italian, they were included in both columns); (1) Figures cover the Fargo, ND-MN Metropolitan Statistical Area; (2) Excludes Basque
Source: U.S. Census Bureau, 2017-2021 American Community Survey 5-Year Estimates

Foreign-born Population

Area	Percent of Population Born in								
	Any Foreign Country	Asia	Mexico	Europe	Caribbean	Central America[2]	South America	Africa	Canada
City	9.9	3.7	0.1	0.5	0.1	0.1	0.2	4.8	0.5
MSA[1]	7.0	2.8	0.1	0.5	0.1	0.0	0.1	3.0	0.4
U.S.	13.6	4.2	3.3	1.5	1.4	1.1	1.1	0.8	0.2

Note: (1) Figures cover the Fargo, ND-MN Metropolitan Statistical Area; (2) Excludes Mexico.
Source: U.S. Census Bureau, 2017-2021 American Community Survey 5-Year Estimates

Household Size

Area	Persons in Household (%)							Average Household Size
	One	Two	Three	Four	Five	Six	Seven or More	
City	38.0	34.0	13.3	9.0	4.1	1.2	0.4	2.20
MSA[1]	33.3	33.8	14.0	11.2	5.4	1.5	0.8	2.30
U.S.	28.1	33.8	15.5	12.9	6.0	2.3	1.4	2.60

Note: (1) Figures cover the Fargo, ND-MN Metropolitan Statistical Area
Source: U.S. Census Bureau, 2017-2021 American Community Survey 5-Year Estimates

Household Relationships

Area	House-holder	Opposite-sex Spouse	Same-sex Spouse	Opposite-sex Unmarried Partner	Same-sex Unmarried Partner	Child[2]	Grand-child	Other Relatives	Non-relatives
City	44.5	15.5	0.1	3.6	0.2	23.5	0.7	2.5	5.0
MSA[1]	41.5	17.7	0.1	3.2	0.1	27.0	0.7	2.2	3.9
U.S.	38.3	17.5	0.2	2.5	0.2	28.3	2.4	4.8	3.4

Note: Figures are percent of the total population; (1) Figures cover the Fargo, ND-MN Metropolitan Statistical Area; (2) Includes biological, adopted, and stepchildren of the householder
Source: U.S. Census Bureau, 2020 Census

Gender

Area	Males	Females	Males per 100 Females
City	63,707	62,283	102.3
MSA[1]	125,674	124,169	101.2
U.S.	162,685,811	168,763,470	96.4

Note: (1) Figures cover the Fargo, ND-MN Metropolitan Statistical Area
Source: U.S. Census Bureau, 2020 Census

Marital Status

Area	Never Married	Now Married[2]	Separated	Widowed	Divorced
City	43.0	43.4	1.0	3.9	8.6
MSA[1]	37.5	49.1	0.9	4.0	8.5
U.S.	33.8	48.0	1.8	5.6	10.8

Note: Figures are percentages and cover the population 15 years of age and older; (1) Figures cover the Fargo, ND-MN Metropolitan Statistical Area; (2) Excludes separated
Source: U.S. Census Bureau, 2017-2021 American Community Survey 5-Year Estimates

Religious Groups by Family

Area	Catholic	Baptist	Methodist	LDS[2]	Pentecostal	Lutheran	Islam	Adventist	Other
MSA[1]	14.2	0.2	1.0	0.6	1.3	24.0	<0.1	0.6	8.1
U.S.	18.7	7.3	3.0	2.0	1.8	1.7	1.3	1.3	11.6

Note: Figures are the number of adherents as a percentage of the total population and cover the eight largest religious groups in the U.S; (1) Figures cover the Fargo, ND-MN Metropolitan Statistical Area; (2) Church of Jesus Christ of Latter-day Saints
Sources: 2020 U.S. Religion Census, Association of Statisticians of American Religious Bodies; The Association of Religion Data Archives (ARDA)

Religious Groups by Tradition

Area	Catholic	Evangelical Protestant	Mainline Protestant	Black Protestant	Islam	Judaism	Hinduism	Orthodox	Buddhism
MSA[1]	14.2	11.1	23.4	n/a	<0.1	<0.1	n/a	0.1	n/a
U.S.	18.7	16.5	5.2	2.3	1.3	0.6	0.4	0.4	0.3

Note: Figures are the number of adherents as a percentage of the total population; (1) Figures cover the Fargo, ND-MN Metropolitan Statistical Area
Sources: 2020 U.S. Religion Census, Association of Statisticians of American Religious Bodies; The Association of Religion Data Archives (ARDA)

ECONOMY

Gross Metropolitan Product

Area	2020	2021	2022	2023	Rank[2]
MSA[1]	15.7	18.0	19.9	20.6	160

Note: Figures are in billions of dollars; (1) Figures cover the Fargo, ND-MN Metropolitan Statistical Area; (2) Rank is based on 2021 data and ranges from 1 to 381
Source: U.S. Conference of Mayors, U.S. Metro Economies: U.S. Metros Compared to Global and State Economies, June 2022

Economic Growth

Area	2018-20 (%)	2021 (%)	2022 (%)	2023 (%)	Rank[2]
MSA[1]	-0.4	6.0	-0.2	1.2	170
U.S.	-0.6	5.7	3.1	2.9	—

Note: Figures are real gross metropolitan product (GMP) growth rates and represent average annual percent change; (1) Figures cover the Fargo, ND-MN Metropolitan Statistical Area; (2) Rank is based on 2020 2-year average annual percent change and ranges from 1 to 381
Source: U.S. Conference of Mayors, U.S. Metro Economies: U.S. Metros Compared to Global and State Economies, June 2022

Metropolitan Area Exports

Area	2016	2017	2018	2019	2020	2021	Rank[2]
MSA[1]	474.5	519.5	553.5	515.0	438.3	539.4	210

Note: Figures are in millions of dollars; (1) Figures cover the Fargo, ND-MN Metropolitan Statistical Area; (2) Rank is based on 2021 data and ranges from 1 to 388
Source: U.S. Department of Commerce, International Trade Administration, Office of Trade and Economic Analysis, Industry and Analysis, Exports by Metropolitan Area, data extracted March 16, 2023

Building Permits

Area	Single-Family			Multi-Family			Total		
	2021	2022	Pct. Chg.	2021	2022	Pct. Chg.	2021	2022	Pct. Chg.
City	410	413	0.7	736	820	11.4	1,146	1,233	7.6
MSA[1]	1,229	1,123	-8.6	1,060	1,191	12.4	2,289	2,314	1.1
U.S.	1,115,400	975,600	-12.5	621,600	689,500	10.9	1,737,000	1,665,100	-4.1

Note: (1) Figures cover the Fargo, ND-MN Metropolitan Statistical Area; Figures represent new, privately-owned housing units authorized (unadjusted data); All permit data are based on estimates with imputation
Source: U.S. Census Bureau, Manufacturing, Mining, and Construction Statistics, Building Permits, 2021, 2022

Bankruptcy Filings

Area	Business Filings			Nonbusiness Filings		
	2021	2022	% Chg.	2021	2022	% Chg.
Cass County	4	2	-50.0	131	100	-23.7
U.S.	14,347	13,481	-6.0	399,269	374,240	-6.3

Note: Business filings include Chapter 7, Chapter 9, Chapter 11, Chapter 12, Chapter 13, Chapter 15, and Section 304; Nonbusiness filings include Chapter 7, Chapter 11, and Chapter 13
Source: Administrative Office of the U.S. Courts, Business and Nonbusiness Bankruptcy, County Cases Commenced by Chapter of the Bankruptcy Code, During the 12-Month Period Ending December 31, 2021 and Business and Nonbusiness Bankruptcy, County Cases Commenced by Chapter of the Bankruptcy Code, During the 12-Month Period Ending December 31, 2022

Housing Vacancy Rates

Area	Gross Vacancy Rate[2] (%)			Year-Round Vacancy Rate[3] (%)			Rental Vacancy Rate[4] (%)			Homeowner Vacancy Rate[5] (%)		
	2020	2021	2022	2020	2021	2022	2020	2021	2022	2020	2021	2022
MSA[1]	n/a	n/a	n/a	n/a	n/a	n/a	n/a	n/a	n/a	n/a	n/a	n/a
U.S.	10.6	10.8	10.5	8.2	8.4	8.2	6.3	6.1	5.8	1.0	0.9	0.8

Note: (1) Figures cover the Fargo, ND-MN Metropolitan Statistical Area; (2) The percentage of the total housing inventory that is vacant; (3) The percentage of the housing inventory (excluding seasonal units) that is year-round vacant; (4) The percentage of rental inventory that is vacant for rent; (5) The percentage of homeowner inventory that is vacant for sale; n/a not available
Source: U.S. Census Bureau, Housing Vacancies and Homeownership Annual Statistics: 2020, 2021, 2022

INCOME

Income

Area	Per Capita ($)	Median Household ($)	Average Household ($)
City	37,522	60,243	82,974
MSA[1]	38,367	68,560	91,642
U.S.	37,638	69,021	97,196

Note: (1) Figures cover the Fargo, ND-MN Metropolitan Statistical Area
Source: U.S. Census Bureau, 2017-2021 American Community Survey 5-Year Estimates

Household Income Distribution

Area	Percent of Households Earning							
	Under $15,000	$15,000 -$24,999	$25,000 -$34,999	$35,000 -$49,999	$50,000 -$74,999	$75,000 -$99,999	$100,000 -$149,999	$150,000 and up
City	9.8	9.1	9.7	12.9	18.4	13.0	15.5	11.7
MSA[1]	8.7	7.9	7.9	11.8	17.3	13.8	17.9	14.7
U.S.	9.4	7.8	8.2	11.4	16.8	12.8	16.3	17.3

Note: (1) Figures cover the Fargo, ND-MN Metropolitan Statistical Area
Source: U.S. Census Bureau, 2017-2021 American Community Survey 5-Year Estimates

Poverty Rate

Area	All Ages	Under 18 Years Old	18 to 64 Years Old	65 Years and Over
City	12.9	14.1	14.1	4.8
MSA[1]	11.3	12.1	12.2	5.5
U.S.	12.6	17.0	11.8	9.6

Note: Figures are percentage of people whose income during the past 12 months was below the poverty level;
(1) Figures cover the Fargo, ND-MN Metropolitan Statistical Area
Source: U.S. Census Bureau, 2017-2021 American Community Survey 5-Year Estimates

EMPLOYMENT

Labor Force and Employment

Area	Civilian Labor Force			Workers Employed		
	Dec. 2021	Dec. 2022	% Chg.	Dec. 2021	Dec. 2022	% Chg.
City	72,514	72,188	-0.4	70,902	70,818	-0.1
MSA[1]	143,613	142,810	-0.6	140,498	140,046	-0.3
U.S.	161,696,000	164,224,000	1.6	155,732,000	158,872,000	2.0

Note: Data is not seasonally adjusted and covers workers 16 years of age and older; (1) Figures cover the Fargo, ND-MN Metropolitan Statistical Area
Source: Bureau of Labor Statistics, Local Area Unemployment Statistics

Unemployment Rate

Area	2022											
	Jan.	Feb.	Mar.	Apr.	May	Jun.	Jul.	Aug.	Sep.	Oct.	Nov.	Dec.
City	2.7	2.5	2.7	2.1	1.8	2.2	1.7	1.8	1.4	1.5	1.6	1.9
MSA[1]	2.8	2.4	2.7	1.9	1.6	2.1	1.7	1.7	1.4	1.4	1.5	1.9
U.S.	4.4	4.1	3.8	3.3	3.4	3.8	3.8	3.8	3.3	3.4	3.4	3.3

Note: Data is not seasonally adjusted and covers workers 16 years of age and older; (1) Figures cover the Fargo, ND-MN Metropolitan Statistical Area
Source: Bureau of Labor Statistics, Local Area Unemployment Statistics

Average Wages

Occupation	$/Hr.	Occupation	$/Hr.
Accountants and Auditors	33.62	Maintenance and Repair Workers	22.10
Automotive Mechanics	23.74	Marketing Managers	61.40
Bookkeepers	21.80	Network and Computer Systems Admin.	39.32
Carpenters	24.78	Nurses, Licensed Practical	25.14
Cashiers	14.30	Nurses, Registered	36.60
Computer Programmers	43.53	Nursing Assistants	17.94
Computer Systems Analysts	46.07	Office Clerks, General	22.07
Computer User Support Specialists	27.94	Physical Therapists	40.35
Construction Laborers	22.00	Physicians	105.75
Cooks, Restaurant	15.80	Plumbers, Pipefitters and Steamfitters	29.18
Customer Service Representatives	19.82	Police and Sheriff's Patrol Officers	34.03
Dentists	80.70	Postal Service Mail Carriers	27.52
Electricians	29.07	Real Estate Sales Agents	29.08
Engineers, Electrical	47.71	Retail Salespersons	17.14
Fast Food and Counter Workers	13.47	Sales Representatives, Technical/Scientific	54.63
Financial Managers	68.39	Secretaries, Exc. Legal/Medical/Executive	20.53
First-Line Supervisors of Office Workers	30.87	Security Guards	16.86
General and Operations Managers	48.98	Surgeons	n/a
Hairdressers/Cosmetologists	16.61	Teacher Assistants, Exc. Postsecondary*	16.83
Home Health and Personal Care Aides	16.62	Teachers, Secondary School, Exc. Sp. Ed.*	28.97
Janitors and Cleaners	16.77	Telemarketers	n/a
Landscaping/Groundskeeping Workers	19.28	Truck Drivers, Heavy/Tractor-Trailer	27.94
Lawyers	61.05	Truck Drivers, Light/Delivery Services	23.00
Maids and Housekeeping Cleaners	14.33	Waiters and Waitresses	14.71

Note: Wage data covers the Fargo, ND-MN Metropolitan Statistical Area; (*) Hourly wages were calculated from annual wage data based on a 40 hour work week; n/a not available.
Source: Bureau of Labor Statistics, Metro Area Occupational Employment & Wage Estimates, May 2022

Employment by Industry

Sector	MSA[1]		U.S.
	Number of Employees	Percent of Total	Percent of Total
Construction, Mining, and Logging	9,000	6.0	5.4
Private Education and Health Services	28,800	19.2	16.1
Financial Activities	11,300	7.5	5.9
Government	20,200	13.5	14.5
Information	2,700	1.8	2.0
Leisure and Hospitality	14,300	9.6	10.3
Manufacturing	11,800	7.9	8.4
Other Services	5,000	3.3	3.7
Professional and Business Services	15,000	10.0	14.7
Retail Trade	15,000	10.0	10.2
Transportation, Warehousing, and Utilities	7,500	5.0	4.9
Wholesale Trade	9,100	6.1	3.9

Note: Figures are non-farm employment as of December 2022. Figures are not seasonally adjusted and include workers 16 years of age and older; (1) Figures cover the Fargo, ND-MN Metropolitan Statistical Area
Source: Bureau of Labor Statistics, Current Employment Statistics, Employment, Hours, and Earnings

Employment by Occupation

Occupation Classification	City (%)	MSA[1] (%)	U.S. (%)
Management, Business, Science, and Arts	41.2	42.9	40.3
Natural Resources, Construction, and Maintenance	7.7	8.4	8.7
Production, Transportation, and Material Moving	11.6	11.6	13.1
Sales and Office	20.3	20.2	20.9
Service	19.2	16.8	17.0

Note: Figures cover employed civilians 16 years of age and older; (1) Figures cover the Fargo, ND-MN Metropolitan Statistical Area
Source: U.S. Census Bureau, 2017-2021 American Community Survey 5-Year Estimates

Occupations with Greatest Projected Employment Growth: 2022 – 2024

Occupation[1]	2022 Employment	2024 Projected Employment	Numeric Employment Change	Percent Employment Change
Heavy and Tractor-Trailer Truck Drivers	10,330	11,070	740	7.2
Service Unit Operators, Oil, Gas, and Mining	2,840	3,530	690	24.3
Roustabouts, Oil and Gas	2,110	2,630	520	24.6
First-Line Supervisors of Construction Trades and Extraction Workers	3,540	4,040	500	14.1
General and Operations Managers	10,120	10,570	450	4.4
Construction Laborers	4,470	4,890	420	9.4
Laborers and Freight, Stock, and Material Movers, Hand	7,640	7,990	350	4.6
Operating Engineers and Other Construction Equipment Operators	3,490	3,780	290	8.3
Fast Food and Counter Workers	11,860	12,130	270	2.3
Registered Nurses	12,070	12,320	250	2.1

Note: Projections cover North Dakota; (1) Sorted by numeric employment change
Source: www.projectionscentral.com, State Occupational Projections, 2022–2024 Short-Term Projections

Fastest-Growing Occupations: 2022 – 2024

Occupation[1]	2022 Employment	2024 Projected Employment	Numeric Employment Change	Percent Employment Change
Rotary Drill Operators, Oil and Gas	340	430	90	26.5
Derrick Operators, Oil and Gas	360	450	90	25.0
Roustabouts, Oil and Gas	2,110	2,630	520	24.6
Service Unit Operators, Oil, Gas, and Mining	2,840	3,530	690	24.3
First-Line Supervisors of Construction Trades and Extraction Workers	3,540	4,040	500	14.1
Wellhead Pumpers	1,260	1,430	170	13.5
Ushers, Lobby Attendants, and Ticket Takers	440	490	50	11.4
Occupational Health and Safety Specialists (SOC 2018)	590	650	60	10.2
Construction Laborers	4,470	4,890	420	9.4
Nurse Practitioners	650	710	60	9.2

Note: Projections cover North Dakota; (1) Sorted by percent employment change and excludes occupations with numeric employment change less than 50
Source: www.projectionscentral.com, State Occupational Projections, 2022–2024 Short-Term Projections

CITY FINANCES

City Government Finances

Component	2020 ($000)	2020 ($ per capita)
Total Revenues	316,855	2,542
Total Expenditures	366,448	2,940
Debt Outstanding	955,338	7,663
Cash and Securities[1]	332,391	2,666

Note: (1) Cash and security holdings of a government at the close of its fiscal year, including those of its dependent agencies, utilities, and liquor stores.
Source: U.S. Census Bureau, State & Local Government Finances 2020

City Government Revenue by Source

Source	2020 ($000)	2020 ($ per capita)	2020 (%)
General Revenue			
From Federal Government	4,826	39	1.5
From State Government	46,137	370	14.6
From Local Governments	181	1	0.1
Taxes			
Property	33,011	265	10.4
Sales and Gross Receipts	61,514	493	19.4
Personal Income	0	0	0.0
Corporate Income	0	0	0.0
Motor Vehicle License	0	0	0.0
Other Taxes	6,265	50	2.0
Current Charges	67,836	544	21.4
Liquor Store	0	0	0.0
Utility	25,617	205	8.1

Source: U.S. Census Bureau, State & Local Government Finances 2020

City Government Expenditures by Function

Function	2020 ($000)	2020 ($ per capita)	2020 (%)
General Direct Expenditures			
Air Transportation	12,575	100	3.4
Corrections	0	0	0.0
Education	0	0	0.0
Employment Security Administration	0	0	0.0
Financial Administration	1,276	10	0.3
Fire Protection	13,507	108	3.7
General Public Buildings	2,027	16	0.6
Governmental Administration, Other	4,022	32	1.1
Health	11,886	95	3.2
Highways	72,904	584	19.9
Hospitals	0	0	0.0
Housing and Community Development	1,294	10	0.4
Interest on General Debt	30,737	246	8.4
Judicial and Legal	3,499	28	1.0
Libraries	4,656	37	1.3
Parking	8,368	67	2.3
Parks and Recreation	11,499	92	3.1
Police Protection	21,924	175	6.0
Public Welfare	1,113	8	0.3
Sewerage	36,303	291	9.9
Solid Waste Management	12,526	100	3.4
Veterans' Services	0	0	0.0
Liquor Store	0	0	0.0
Utility	29,869	239	8.2

Source: U.S. Census Bureau, State & Local Government Finances 2020

TAXES

State Corporate Income Tax Rates

State	Tax Rate (%)	Income Brackets ($)	Num. of Brackets	Financial Institution Tax Rate (%)[a]	Federal Income Tax Ded.
North Dakota	1.41 - 4.31 (q)	25,000 - 50,001	3	1.41 - 4.31 (q)	No

Note: Tax rates as of January 1, 2023; (a) Rates listed are the corporate income tax rate applied to financial institutions or excise taxes based on income. Some states have other taxes based upon the value of deposits or shares; (q) North Dakota imposes a 3.5% surtax for filers electing to use the water's edge method to apportion income.
Source: Federation of Tax Administrators, State Corporate Income Tax Rates, January 1, 2023

State Individual Income Tax Rates

State	Tax Rate (%)	Income Brackets ($)	Personal Exemptions ($) Single	Married	Depend.	Standard Ded. ($) Single	Married
North Dakota (a)	1.1 - 2.9	44,725 - 491,350 (t)	(d)	(d)	(d)	13,850	27,700 (d)

Note: Tax rates as of January 1, 2023; Local- and county-level taxes are not included; Federal income tax is not deductible on state income tax returns; (a) 16 states have statutory provision for automatically adjusting to the rate of inflation the dollar values of the income tax brackets, standard deductions, and/or personal exemptions. Oregon does not index the income brackets for $125,000 and over; (d) These states use the personal exemption/standard deduction amounts provided in the federal Internal Revenue Code; (t) The income brackets reported for North Dakota are for single individuals. For married couples filing jointly, the same tax rates apply to income brackets ranging from $74,750 to $491,350.
Source: Federation of Tax Administrators, State Individual Income Tax Rates, January 1, 2023

Various State Sales and Excise Tax Rates

State	State Sales Tax (%)	Gasoline[1] ($/gal.)	Cigarette[2] ($/pack)	Spirits[3] ($/gal.)	Wine[4] ($/gal.)	Beer[5] ($/gal.)	Recreational Marijuana (%)
North Dakota	5	0.23	0.44	4.68	1.10	0.40	Not legal

Note: All tax rates as of January 1, 2023; (1) The American Petroleum Institute has developed a methodology for determining the average tax rate on a gallon of fuel. Rates may include any of the following: excise taxes, environmental fees, storage tank fees, other fees or taxes, general sales tax, and local taxes; (2) The federal excise tax of $1.0066 per pack and local taxes are not included; (3) Rates are those applicable to off-premise sales of 40% alcohol by volume (a.b.v.) distilled spirits in 750ml containers. Local excise taxes are excluded; (4) Rates are those applicable to off-premise sales of 11% a.b.v. non-carbonated wine in 750ml containers; (5) Rates are those applicable to off-premise sales of 4.7% a.b.v. beer in 12 ounce containers.
Source: Tax Foundation, 2023 Facts & Figures: How Does Your State Compare?

State Business Tax Climate Index Rankings

State	Overall Rank	Corporate Tax Rank	Individual Income Tax Rank	Sales Tax Rank	Property Tax Rank	Unemployment Insurance Tax Rank
North Dakota	17	9	27	28	9	7

Note: The index is a measure of how each state's tax laws affect economic performance. The lower the rank, the more favorable a state's tax system is for business. States without a given tax are given a ranking of 1. The scores/rankings for the District of Columbia do not affect other states. The 2023 index represents the tax climate as of July 1, 2022.
Source: Tax Foundation, State Business Tax Climate Index 2023

TRANSPORTATION

Means of Transportation to Work

Area	Car/Truck/Van Drove Alone	Car-pooled	Public Transportation Bus	Subway	Railroad	Bicycle	Walked	Other Means	Worked at Home
City	79.5	7.8	1.2	0.0	0.0	0.5	3.5	1.9	5.5
MSA[1]	79.8	8.0	0.9	0.0	0.0	0.4	2.6	1.4	6.9
U.S.	73.2	8.6	2.0	1.6	0.5	0.5	2.5	1.5	9.7

Note: Figures are percentages and cover workers 16 years of age and older; (1) Figures cover the Fargo, ND-MN Metropolitan Statistical Area
Source: U.S. Census Bureau, 2017-2021 American Community Survey 5-Year Estimates

Travel Time to Work

Area	Less Than 10 Minutes	10 to 19 Minutes	20 to 29 Minutes	30 to 44 Minutes	45 to 59 Minutes	60 to 89 Minutes	90 Minutes or More
City	20.6	56.3	15.2	3.6	1.4	1.9	0.9
MSA[1]	17.8	52.1	18.3	6.0	2.4	1.9	1.4
U.S.	12.4	28.5	21.0	20.9	8.2	6.2	2.9

Note: Note: Figures are percentages and include workers 16 years old and over; (1) Figures cover the Fargo, ND-MN Metropolitan Statistical Area
Source: U.S. Census Bureau, 2017-2021 American Community Survey 5-Year Estimates

Key Congestion Measures

Measure	1990	2000	2010	2015	2020
Annual Hours of Delay, Total (000)	n/a	n/a	n/a	2,648	1,506
Annual Hours of Delay, Per Auto Commuter	n/a	n/a	n/a	15	8
Annual Congestion Cost, Per Auto Commuter ($)	n/a	n/a	n/a	299	166

Note: n/a not available
Source: Texas A&M Transportation Institute, 2021 Urban Mobility Report

Freeway Travel Time Index

Measure	1985	1990	1995	2000	2005	2010	2015	2020
Urban Area Index[1]	n/a	n/a	n/a	n/a	n/a	n/a	1.15	1.04
Urban Area Rank[1,2]	n/a	n/a	n/a	n/a	n/a	n/a	n/a	n/a

Note: Freeway Travel Time Index—the ratio of travel time in the peak period to the travel time at free-flow conditions. For example, a value of 1.30 indicates a 20-minute free-flow trip takes 26 minutes in the peak (20 minutes x 1.30 = 26 minutes); (1) Covers the Fargo ND-MN urban area; (2) Rank is based on 101 larger urban areas (#1 = highest travel time index); n/a not available
Source: Texas A&M Transportation Institute, 2021 Urban Mobility Report

Public Transportation

Agency Name / Mode of Transportation	Vehicles Operated in Maximum Service[1]	Annual Unlinked Passenger Trips[2] (in thous.)	Annual Passenger Miles[3] (in thous.)
Fargo Metropolitan Area Transit (MAT)			
Bus (purchased transportation)	26	782.2	3,308.9
Demand Response (purchased transportation)	13	52.8	285.1

Note: (1) Number of revenue vehicles operated by the given mode and type of service to meet the annual maximum service requirement. This is the revenue vehicle count during the peak season of the year; on the week and day that maximum service is provided. Vehicles operated in maximum service (VOMS) exclude atypical days and one-time special events; (2) Number of passengers who boarded public transportation vehicles. Passengers are counted each time they board a vehicle no matter how many vehicles they use to travel from their origin to their destination. (3) Sum of the distances ridden by all passengers during the entire fiscal year.
Source: Federal Transit Administration, National Transit Database, 2021

Air Transportation

Airport Name and Code / Type of Service	Passenger Airlines[1]	Passenger Enplanements	Freight Carriers[2]	Freight (lbs)
Hector International (FAR)				
Domestic service (U.S. carriers - 2022)	18	461,765	6	40,797,615
International service (U.S. carriers - 2021)	1	1	2	1,597,013

Note: (1) Includes all U.S.-based major, minor and commuter airlines that carried at least one passenger during the year; (2) Includes all U.S.-based airlines and freight carriers that transported at least one pound of freight during the year.
Source: Bureau of Transportation Statistics, The Intermodal Transportation Database, Air Carriers: T-100 Domestic Market (U.S. Carriers), 2022; Bureau of Transportation Statistics, The Intermodal Transportation Database, Air Carriers: T-100 International Market (U.S. Carriers), 2021

BUSINESSES

Major Business Headquarters

Company Name	Industry	Rankings	
		Fortune[1]	Forbes[2]
No companies listed	-	-	-

Note: (1) Companies that produce a 10-K are ranked 1 to 500 based on 2021 revenue; (2) All private companies with at least $2 billion in annual revenue through the end of their most current fiscal year are ranked 1 to 246; companies listed are headquartered in the city; dashes indicate no ranking
Source: Fortune, "Fortune 500," 2022; Forbes, "America's Largest Private Companies," 2022

Living Environment

COST OF LIVING

Cost of Living Index

Composite Index	Groceries	Housing	Utilities	Trans- portation	Health Care	Misc. Goods/ Services
n/a	n/a	n/a	n/a	n/a	n/a	n/a

Note: The Cost of Living Index measures regional differences in the cost of consumer goods and services, excluding taxes and non-consumer expenditures, for professional and managerial households in the top income quintile. It is based on more than 50,000 prices covering almost 60 different items for which prices are collected three times a year by chambers of commerce, economic development organizations or university applied economic centers in each participating urban area. The numbers shown should be read as a percentage above or below the national average of 100. For example, a value of 115.4 in the groceries column indicates that grocery prices are 15.4% higher than the national average. Small differences in the index numbers should not be interpreted as significant; n/a not available.
Source: The Council for Community and Economic Research, Cost of Living Index, 2022

Grocery Prices

Area[1]	T-Bone Steak ($/pound)	Frying Chicken ($/pound)	Whole Milk ($/half gal.)	Eggs ($/dozen)	Orange Juice ($/64 oz.)	Coffee ($/11.5 oz.)
City[2]	n/a	n/a	n/a	n/a	n/a	n/a
Avg.	13.81	1.59	2.43	2.25	3.85	4.95
Min.	10.17	0.90	1.51	1.30	2.90	3.46
Max.	19.35	3.30	4.32	4.32	5.31	8.59

*Note: (1) Values for the local area are compared with the average, minimum and maximum values for all 286 areas in the Cost of Living Index; (2) Figures cover the Fargo ND urban area; n/a not available; **T-Bone Steak** (price per pound); **Frying Chicken** (price per pound, whole fryer); **Whole Milk** (half gallon carton); **Eggs** (price per dozen, Grade A, large); **Orange Juice** (64 oz. Tropicana or Florida Natural); **Coffee** (11.5 oz. can, vacuum-packed, Maxwell House, Hills Bros, or Folgers).*
Source: The Council for Community and Economic Research, Cost of Living Index, 2022

Housing and Utility Costs

Area[1]	New Home Price ($)	Apartment Rent ($/month)	All Electric ($/month)	Part Electric ($/month)	Other Energy ($/month)	Telephone ($/month)
City[2]	n/a	n/a	n/a	n/a	n/a	n/a
Avg.	450,913	1,371	176.41	99.93	76.96	190.22
Min.	229,283	546	100.84	31.56	27.15	174.27
Max.	2,434,977	4,569	356.86	249.59	272.24	208.31

*Note: (1) Values for the local area are compared with the average, minimum and maximum values for all 286 areas in the Cost of Living Index; (2) Figures cover the Fargo ND urban area; n/a not available; **New Home Price** (2,400 sf living area, 8,000 sf lot, in urban area with full utilities); **Apartment Rent** (950 sf 2 bedroom/1.5 or 2 bath, unfurnished, excluding all utilities except water); **All Electric** (average monthly cost for an all-electric home); **Part Electric** (average monthly cost for a part-electric home); **Other Energy** (average monthly cost for natural gas, fuel oil, coal, wood, and any other forms of energy except electricity); **Telephone** (price includes the base monthly rate plus taxes and fees for three lines of mobile phone service).*
Source: The Council for Community and Economic Research, Cost of Living Index, 2022

Health Care, Transportation, and Other Costs

Area[1]	Doctor ($/visit)	Dentist ($/visit)	Optometrist ($/visit)	Gasoline ($/gallon)	Beauty Salon ($/visit)	Men's Shirt ($)
City[2]	n/a	n/a	n/a	n/a	n/a	n/a
Avg.	124.91	107.77	117.66	3.86	43.31	34.21
Min.	36.61	58.25	51.79	2.90	22.18	13.05
Max.	250.21	162.58	371.96	5.54	85.61	63.54

*Note: (1) Values for the local area are compared with the average, minimum and maximum values for all 286 areas in the Cost of Living Index; (2) Figures cover the Fargo ND urban area; n/a not available; **Doctor** (general practitioners routine exam of an established patient); **Dentist** (adult teeth cleaning and periodic oral examination); **Optometrist** (full vision eye exam for established adult patient); **Gasoline** (one gallon regular unleaded, national brand, including all taxes, cash price at self-service pump if available); **Beauty Salon** (woman's shampoo, trim, and blow-dry); **Men's Shirt** (cotton/polyester dress shirt, pinpoint weave, long sleeves).*
Source: The Council for Community and Economic Research, Cost of Living Index, 2022

HOUSING

Homeownership Rate

Area	2015 (%)	2016 (%)	2017 (%)	2018 (%)	2019 (%)	2020 (%)	2021 (%)	2022 (%)
MSA[1]	n/a	n/a	n/a	n/a	n/a	n/a	n/a	n/a
U.S.	63.7	63.4	63.9	64.4	64.6	66.6	65.5	65.8

Note: (1) Figures cover the Fargo, ND-MN Metropolitan Statistical Area; n/a not available
Source: U.S. Census Bureau, Housing Vacancies and Homeownership Annual Statistics: 2015-2022

House Price Index (HPI)

Area	National Ranking[2]	Quarterly Change (%)	One-Year Change (%)	Five-Year Change (%)	Since 1991Q1 (%)
MSA[1]	133	0.78	11.14	32.39	270.20
U.S.[3]	–	0.34	8.41	58.44	289.08

Note: The HPI is a weighted repeat sales index. It measures average price changes in repeat sales or refinancings on the same properties. This information is obtained by reviewing repeat mortgage transactions on single-family properties whose mortgages have been purchased or securitized by Fannie Mae or Freddie Mac since January 1975; (1) Figures cover the Fargo, ND-MN Metropolitan Statistical Area; (2) Rankings are based on annual percentage change for all metro areas containing at least 15,000 transactions over the last 10 years and ranges from 1 to 257; (3) figures based on a weighted average of Census Division estimates using a seasonally adjusted, purchase-only index; all figures are for the period ending December 31, 2022
Source: Federal Housing Finance Agency, Change in FHFA Metropolitan Area House Price Indexes, 2022Q4

Median Single-Family Home Prices

Area	2020	2021	2022p	Percent Change 2021 to 2022
MSA[1]	233.5	255.9	283.8	10.9
U.S. Average	300.2	357.1	392.6	9.9

Note: Figures are median sales prices of existing single-family homes in thousands of dollars; (p) preliminary; (1) Figures cover the Fargo, ND-MN Metropolitan Statistical Area
Source: National Association of Realtors, Median Sales Price of Existing Single-Family Homes for Metropolitan Areas, 4th Quarter 2022

Qualifying Income Based on Median Sales Price of Existing Single-Family Homes

Area	With 5% Down ($)	With 10% Down ($)	With 20% Down ($)
MSA[1]	85,537	81,035	72,031
U.S. Average	112,234	106,237	94,513

Note: Figures are preliminary; Qualifying income is based on a mortgage rate of 6.77%. Monthly principal and interest payment is limited to 25% of income; (1) Figures cover the Fargo, ND-MN Metropolitan Statistical Area
Source: National Association of Realtors, Qualifying Income Based on Median Sales Price of Existing Single-Family Homes for Metropolitan Areas, 4th Quarter 2022

Home Value

Area	Under $100,000	$100,000 -$199,999	$200,000 -$299,999	$300,000 -$399,999	$400,000 -$499,999	$500,000 -$999,999	$1,000,000 or more	Median ($)
City	7.4	30.1	36.2	16.5	4.6	4.4	0.7	232,900
MSA[1]	8.0	29.3	32.7	16.9	6.0	6.3	0.8	235,600
U.S.	16.2	24.2	20.1	13.6	8.3	13.6	4.1	244,900

Note: Figures are percentages except for median and cover owner-occupied housing units; (1) Figures cover the Fargo, ND-MN Metropolitan Statistical Area
Source: U.S. Census Bureau, 2017-2021 American Community Survey 5-Year Estimates

Year Housing Structure Built

Area	2020 or Later	2010 -2019	2000 -2009	1990 -1999	1980 -1989	1970 -1979	1960 -1969	1950 -1959	1940 -1949	Before 1940	Median Year
City	0.3	18.3	14.2	15.1	13.1	14.2	6.1	8.0	2.3	8.3	1988
MSA[1]	0.4	17.5	17.3	13.6	10.2	15.0	6.8	7.8	2.5	8.9	1989
U.S.	0.2	7.3	13.6	13.6	13.2	14.8	10.3	10.0	4.7	12.2	1979

Note: Figures are percentages except for Median Year; Note: (1) Figures cover the Fargo, ND-MN Metropolitan Statistical Area
Source: U.S. Census Bureau, 2017-2021 American Community Survey 5-Year Estimates

Gross Monthly Rent

Area	Under $500	$500 -$999	$1,000 -$1,499	$1,500 -$1,999	$2,000 -$2,499	$2,500 -$2,999	$3,000 and up	Median ($)
City	5.7	65.4	21.2	5.3	1.9	0.3	0.2	841
MSA[1]	6.6	60.9	22.5	7.6	1.6	0.4	0.3	855
U.S.	8.1	30.5	30.8	16.8	7.3	3.1	3.5	1,163

Note: Figures are percentages except for median; Gross rent is the contract rent plus the estimated average monthly cost of utilities (electricity, gas, and water and sewer) and fuels (oil, coal, kerosene, wood, etc.) if these are paid by the renter (or paid for the renter by someone else); (1) Figures cover the Fargo, ND-MN Metropolitan Statistical Area
Source: U.S. Census Bureau, 2017-2021 American Community Survey 5-Year Estimates

HEALTH

Health Risk Factors

Category	MSA[1] (%)	U.S. (%)
Adults aged 18–64 who have any kind of health care coverage	91.5	90.9
Adults who reported being in good or better health	89.0	85.2
Adults who have been told they have high blood cholesterol	31.6	35.7
Adults who have been told they have high blood pressure	26.9	32.4
Adults who are current smokers	11.7	14.4
Adults who currently use e-cigarettes	6.7	6.7
Adults who currently use chewing tobacco, snuff, or snus	3.9	3.5
Adults who are heavy drinkers[2]	6.1	6.3
Adults who are binge drinkers[3]	21.3	15.4
Adults who are overweight (BMI 25.0 - 29.9)	36.9	34.4
Adults who are obese (BMI 30.0 - 99.8)	32.9	33.9
Adults who participated in any physical activities in the past month	79.5	76.3

Note: (1) Figures cover the Fargo, ND-MN Metropolitan Statistical Area; (2) Heavy drinkers are classified as adult men having more than 14 drinks per week and adult women having more than 7 drinks per week; (3) Binge drinkers are classified as males having five or more drinks on one occasion or females having four or more drinks on one occasion
Source: Centers for Disease Control and Prevention, Behaviorial Risk Factor Surveillance System, SMART: Selected Metropolitan Area Risk Trends, 2021

Acute and Chronic Health Conditions

Category	MSA[1] (%)	U.S. (%)
Adults who have ever been told they had a heart attack	2.5	4.0
Adults who have ever been told they have angina or coronary heart disease	2.6	3.8
Adults who have ever been told they had a stroke	1.6	3.0
Adults who have ever been told they have asthma	11.4	14.9
Adults who have ever been told they have arthritis	20.2	25.8
Adults who have ever been told they have diabetes[2]	7.1	10.9
Adults who have ever been told they had skin cancer	5.9	6.6
Adults who have ever been told they had any other types of cancer	6.1	7.5
Adults who have ever been told they have COPD	3.1	6.1
Adults who have ever been told they have kidney disease	2.7	3.0
Adults who have ever been told they have a form of depression	22.3	20.5

Note: (1) Figures cover the Fargo, ND-MN Metropolitan Statistical Area; (2) Figures do not include pregnancy-related, borderline, or pre-diabetes
Source: Centers for Disease Control and Prevention, Behaviorial Risk Factor Surveillance System, SMART: Selected Metropolitan Area Risk Trends, 2021

Health Screening and Vaccination Rates

Category	MSA[1] (%)	U.S. (%)
Adults who have ever been tested for HIV	29.2	34.9
Adults who have had their blood cholesterol checked within the last five years	79.6	85.2
Adults aged 65+ who have had flu shot within the past year	74.1	68.6
Adults aged 65+ who have ever had a pneumonia vaccination	74.3	71.0

Note: (1) Figures cover the Fargo, ND-MN Metropolitan Statistical Area.
Source: Centers for Disease Control and Prevention, Behaviorial Risk Factor Surveillance System, SMART: Selected Metropolitan Area Risk Trends, 2021

Disability Status

Category	MSA[1] (%)	U.S. (%)
Adults who reported being deaf	5.5	7.2
Are you blind or have serious difficulty seeing, even when wearing glasses?	2.6	4.8
Are you limited in any way in any of your usual activities due to arthritis?	7.6	11.1
Do you have difficulty doing errands alone?	5.6	7.0
Do you have difficulty dressing or bathing?	2.1	3.6
Do you have serious difficulty concentrating/remembering/making decisions?	10.4	12.1
Do you have serious difficulty walking or climbing stairs?	7.6	12.8

Note: (1) Figures cover the Fargo, ND-MN Metropolitan Statistical Area.
Source: Centers for Disease Control and Prevention, Behaviorial Risk Factor Surveillance System, SMART: Selected Metropolitan Area Risk Trends, 2021

Mortality Rates for the Top 10 Causes of Death in the U.S.

ICD-10[a] Sub-Chapter	ICD-10[a] Code	Crude Mortality Rate[1] per 100,000 population	
		County[2]	U.S.
Malignant neoplasms	C00-C97	132.3	182.6
Ischaemic heart diseases	I20-I25	59.7	113.1
Other forms of heart disease	I30-I51	50.0	64.4
Other degenerative diseases of the nervous system	G30-G31	47.4	51.0
Cerebrovascular diseases	I60-I69	29.0	47.8
Other external causes of accidental injury	W00-X59	32.8	46.4
Chronic lower respiratory diseases	J40-J47	26.8	45.7
Organic, including symptomatic, mental disorders	F01-F09	33.9	35.9
Hypertensive diseases	I10-I15	21.0	35.0
Diabetes mellitus	E10-E14	12.9	29.6

Note: (a) ICD-10 = International Classification of Diseases 10th Revision; (1) Crude mortality rates are a three-year average covering 2019-2021; (2) Figures cover Cass County.
Source: Centers for Disease Control and Prevention, National Center for Health Statistics. National Vital Statistics System, Mortality 2018-2021 on CDC WONDER Online Database

Mortality Rates for Selected Causes of Death

ICD-10[a] Sub-Chapter	ICD-10[a] Code	Crude Mortality Rate[1] per 100,000 population	
		County[2]	U.S.
Assault	X85-Y09	Unreliable	7.0
Diseases of the liver	K70-K76	16.3	19.8
Human immunodeficiency virus (HIV) disease	B20-B24	Suppressed	1.5
Influenza and pneumonia	J09-J18	10.5	14.7
Intentional self-harm	X60-X84	15.9	14.3
Malnutrition	E40-E46	Suppressed	4.3
Obesity and other hyperalimentation	E65-E68	9.2	3.0
Renal failure	N17-N19	7.6	15.7
Transport accidents	V01-V99	6.9	13.6
Viral hepatitis	B15-B19	Suppressed	1.2

Note: (a) ICD-10 = International Classification of Diseases 10th Revision; (1) Crude mortality rates are a three-year average covering 2019-2021; (2) Figures cover Cass County; Data are suppressed when the data meet the criteria for confidentiality constraints; Crude mortality rates are flagged as unreliable when the rate would be calculated with a numerator of 20 or less.
Source: Centers for Disease Control and Prevention, National Center for Health Statistics. National Vital Statistics System, Mortality 2018-2021 on CDC WONDER Online Database

Health Insurance Coverage

Area	With Health Insurance	With Private Health Insurance	With Public Health Insurance	Without Health Insurance	Population Under Age 19 Without Health Insurance
City	93.8	79.9	25.1	6.2	3.8
MSA[1]	94.5	80.8	25.2	5.5	4.4
U.S.	91.2	67.8	35.4	8.8	5.3

Note: Figures are percentages that cover the civilian noninstitutionalized population; (1) Figures cover the Fargo, ND-MN Metropolitan Statistical Area
Source: U.S. Census Bureau, 2017-2021 American Community Survey 5-Year Estimates

Number of Medical Professionals

Area	MDs[3]	DOs[3,4]	Dentists	Podiatrists	Chiropractors	Optometrists
County[1] (number)	747	39	154	8	141	61
County[1] (rate[2])	404.1	21.1	82.5	4.3	75.6	32.7
U.S. (rate[2])	289.3	23.5	72.5	6.2	28.7	17.4

Note: Data as of 2021 unless noted; (1) Data covers Cass County; (2) Rate per 100,000 population; (3) Data as of 2020 and includes all active, non-federal physicians; (4) Doctor of Osteopathic Medicine
Source: U.S. Department of Health and Human Services, Health Resources and Services Administration, Bureau of Health Professions, Area Resource File (ARF) 2021-2022

EDUCATION

Public School District Statistics

District Name	Schls	Pupils	Pupil/ Teacher Ratio	Minority Pupils[1] (%)	LEP/ELL[2] (%)	IEP[3] (%)
Fargo 1	25	11,331	12.1	31.1	8.2	15.1

Note: Table includes school districts with 2,000 or more students; (1) Percentage of students that are not non-Hispanic white; (2) Percentage of students that are Limited English Proficient or English Language Learners (2018-19); (3) Percentage of students that have an Individualized Education Program (2019-20).
Source: U.S. Department of Education, National Center for Education Statistics, Common Core of Data, Local Education Agency (School District) Universe Survey: School Year 2021-2022

Highest Level of Education

Area	Less than H.S.	H.S. Diploma	Some College, No Deg.	Associate Degree	Bachelor's Degree	Master's Degree	Prof. School Degree	Doctorate Degree
City	5.2	19.3	20.3	13.6	28.1	9.9	1.8	2.0
MSA[1]	4.8	19.7	21.1	14.1	27.8	8.9	1.8	1.7
U.S.	11.1	26.5	20.0	8.7	20.6	9.3	2.2	1.5

Note: Figures cover persons age 25 and over; (1) Figures cover the Fargo, ND-MN Metropolitan Statistical Area
Source: U.S. Census Bureau, 2017-2021 American Community Survey 5-Year Estimates

Educational Attainment by Race

Area	High School Graduate or Higher (%)					Bachelor's Degree or Higher (%)				
	Total	White	Black	Asian	Hisp.[2]	Total	White	Black	Asian	Hisp.[2]
City	94.8	96.7	79.3	82.7	91.6	41.8	43.5	19.0	57.2	16.4
MSA[1]	95.2	96.5	78.9	85.9	86.7	40.3	41.5	20.4	55.6	21.7
U.S.	88.9	91.4	87.2	87.6	71.2	33.7	35.5	23.3	55.6	18.4

Note: Figures shown cover persons 25 years and over; (1) Figures cover the Fargo, ND-MN Metropolitan Statistical Area; (2) People of Hispanic origin can be of any race
Source: U.S. Census Bureau, 2017-2021 American Community Survey 5-Year Estimates

School Enrollment by Grade and Control

Area	Preschool (%)		Kindergarten (%)		Grades 1 - 4 (%)		Grades 5 - 8 (%)		Grades 9 - 12 (%)	
	Public	Private	Public	Private	Public	Private	Public	Private	Public	Private
City	43.0	57.0	92.4	7.6	92.6	7.4	90.6	9.4	94.5	5.5
MSA[1]	59.7	40.3	91.9	8.1	91.0	9.0	91.1	8.9	91.6	8.4
U.S.	58.8	41.2	86.3	13.7	88.3	11.7	88.6	11.4	89.4	10.6

Note: Figures shown cover persons 3 years old and over; (1) Figures cover the Fargo, ND-MN Metropolitan Statistical Area
Source: U.S. Census Bureau, 2017-2021 American Community Survey 5-Year Estimates

Higher Education

Four-Year Colleges			Two-Year Colleges			Medical Schools[1]	Law Schools[2]	Voc/ Tech[3]
Public	Private Non-profit	Private For-profit	Public	Private Non-profit	Private For-profit			
2	1	1	0	0	2	0	0	1

Note: Figures cover institutions located within the Fargo, ND-MN Metropolitan Statistical Area and include main campuses only; (1) includes schools accredited by the Liaison Committee on Medical Education and the American Osteopathic Association's Commission on Osteopathic College Accreditation; (2) includes ABA-accredited schools, schools with provisional ABA accreditation, and state accredited schools; (3) includes all schools with programs that are less than 2 years.
Source: National Center for Education Statistics, Integrated Postsecondary Education System (IPEDS), 2021-22; Wikipedia, List of Medical Schools in the United States, accessed April 10, 2023; Wikipedia, List of Law Schools in the United States, accessed April 10, 2023

EMPLOYERS

Major Employers

Company Name	Industry
BlueCross BlueShield of North Dakota	Insurance
City of Fargo	Municipal government
CNH Industrial America	Agriculture equipment
Concordia College	Education
Essentia Health	General medical & surgical hospitals
Fargo Public School District	Education
John Deere Electronic Solutions	Manufacturers
Microsoft	Computer software
Minnesota State University Moorhead	Education
Moorhead Area Public Schools	Education
Noridian Heathcare Solutions	Insurance
North Dakota State University	Education
Sanford Fargo Medical Center	Healthcare services
U.S. Bank	Financial services
Veterans Affairs	General medical & surgical hospitals
West Fargo Public School	Education

Note: Companies shown are located within the Fargo, ND-MN Metropolitan Statistical Area.
Source: Hoovers.com; Wikipedia

Best Companies to Work For

Bell Bank, headquartered in Fargo, is among "Fortune's Best Workplaces for Women." To pick the best companies, *Fortune* partnered with the Great Place to Work Institute. To be considered for the list, companies must be Great Place To Work-Certified. Companies must also employ at least 50 women, at least 20% of their non-executive managers must be female, and at least one executive must be female. To determine the Best Workplaces for Women, Great Place To Work measured the differences in women's survey responses to those of their peers and assesses the impact of demographics and roles on the quality and consistency of women's experiences. Great Place To Work also analyzed the gender balance of each workplace, how it compared to each company's industry, and patterns in representation as women rise from front-line positions to the board of directors. *Fortune, "Best Workplaces for Women," 2022*

Blue Cross Blue Shield of North Dakota, headquartered in Fargo, is among the "100 Best Places to Work in IT." To qualify, companies had to have a minimum of 100 total employees and five IT employees. The best places to work were selected based on DEI (diversity, equity, and inclusion) practices; IT turnover, promotions, and growth; IT retention and engagement programs; remote/hybrid working; benefits and perks (such as elder care and child care, flextime, and reimbursement for college tuition); and training and career development opportunities. *Computerworld, "Best Places to Work in IT," 2023*

PUBLIC SAFETY

Crime Rate

Area	Total Crime	Violent Crime Rate				Property Crime Rate		
		Murder	Rape[3]	Robbery	Aggrav. Assault	Burglary	Larceny-Theft	Motor Vehicle Theft
City	3,929.0	5.5	84.3	48.1	322.2	800.5	2,302.1	366.4
Suburbs[1]	2,397.0	5.8	53.5	17.3	159.7	489.9	1,455.9	214.9
Metro[2]	3,180.0	5.6	69.3	33.0	242.8	648.6	1,888.3	292.3
U.S.	2,356.7	6.5	38.4	73.9	279.7	314.2	1,398.0	246.0

Note: Figures are crimes per 100,000 population; (1) All areas within the metro area that are located outside the city limits; (2) Figures cover the Fargo, ND-MN Metropolitan Statistical Area; (3) All figures shown were reported using the revised Uniform Crime Reporting (UCR) definition of rape; Due to the transition to the National Incident-Based Reporting System (NIBRS), limited city and metro area data was released for 2021.
Source: FBI Uniform Crime Reports, 2020

Hate Crimes

Area	Number of Quarters Reported	Number of Incidents per Bias Motivation					
		Race/Ethnicity/ Ancestry	Religion	Sexual Orientation	Disability	Gender	Gender Identity
City	4	3	0	1	0	0	1
U.S.	4	5,227	1,244	1,110	130	75	266

Note: Due to the transition to the National Incident-Based Reporting System (NIBRS), limited crime data was released for 2021.
Source: Federal Bureau of Investigation, Hate Crime Statistics 2020

Identity Theft Consumer Reports

Area	Reports	Reports per 100,000 Population	Rank[2]
MSA[1]	323	132	289
U.S.	1,108,609	339	-

Note: (1) Figures cover the Fargo, ND-MN Metropolitan Statistical Area; (2) Rank ranges from 1 to 391 where 1 indicates greatest number of identity theft reports per 100,000 population
Source: Federal Trade Commission, Consumer Sentinel Network Data Book 2022

Fraud and Other Consumer Reports

Area	Reports	Reports per 100,000 Population	Rank[2]
MSA[1]	1,573	645	325
U.S.	4,064,520	1,245	-

Note: (1) Figures cover the Fargo, ND-MN Metropolitan Statistical Area; (2) Rank ranges from 1 to 391 where 1 indicates greatest number of fraud and other consumer reports per 100,000 population
Source: Federal Trade Commission, Consumer Sentinel Network Data Book 2022

POLITICS

2020 Presidential Election Results

Area	Biden	Trump	Jorgensen	Hawkins	Other
Cass County	46.8	49.5	2.9	0.0	0.7
U.S.	51.3	46.8	1.2	0.3	0.5

Note: Results are percentages and may not add to 100% due to rounding
Source: Dave Leip's Atlas of U.S. Presidential Elections

SPORTS

Professional Sports Teams

Team Name	League	Year Established

No teams are located in the metro area
Source: Wikipedia, Major Professional Sports Teams of the United States and Canada, April 12, 2023

CLIMATE

Average and Extreme Temperatures

Temperature	Jan	Feb	Mar	Apr	May	Jun	Jul	Aug	Sep	Oct	Nov	Dec	Yr.
Extreme High (°F)	52	66	78	100	98	100	106	106	102	93	74	57	106
Average High (°F)	15	21	34	54	69	77	83	81	70	57	36	21	52
Average Temp. (°F)	6	12	26	43	56	66	71	69	58	46	28	13	41
Average Low (°F)	-3	3	17	32	44	54	59	57	46	35	19	4	31
Extreme Low (°F)	-36	-34	-34	-7	20	30	36	33	19	5	-24	-32	-36

Note: Figures cover the years 1948-1995
Source: National Climatic Data Center, International Station Meteorological Climate Summary, 9/96

Average Precipitation/Snowfall/Humidity

Precip./Humidity	Jan	Feb	Mar	Apr	May	Jun	Jul	Aug	Sep	Oct	Nov	Dec	Yr.
Avg. Precip. (in.)	0.6	0.5	1.0	1.7	2.3	3.1	3.2	2.4	1.8	1.5	0.8	0.6	19.6
Avg. Snowfall (in.)	9	6	7	3	Tr	0	0	0	Tr	1	6	7	40
Avg. Rel. Hum. 6am (%)	75	77	82	79	77	82	86	86	85	80	81	78	81
Avg. Rel. Hum. 3pm (%)	70	71	67	51	45	50	50	47	49	51	65	73	57

Note: Figures cover the years 1948-1995; Tr = Trace amounts (<0.05 in. of rain; <0.5 in. of snow)
Source: National Climatic Data Center, International Station Meteorological Climate Summary, 9/96

Weather Conditions

Temperature			Daytime Sky			Precipitation		
5°F & below	32°F & below	90°F & above	Clear	Partly cloudy	Cloudy	0.01 inch or more precip.	0.1 inch or more snow/ice	Thunder-storms
65	180	15	81	145	139	100	38	31

Note: Figures are average number of days per year and cover the years 1948-1995
Source: National Climatic Data Center, International Station Meteorological Climate Summary, 9/96

HAZARDOUS WASTE

Superfund Sites

The Fargo, ND-MN metro area has no sites on the EPA's Superfund Final National Priorities List. There are a total of 1,165 Superfund sites with a status of proposed or final on the list in the U.S. *U.S. Environmental Protection Agency, National Priorities List, April 12, 2023*

AIR QUALITY

Air Quality Trends: Ozone

	1990	1995	2000	2005	2010	2015	2018	2019	2020	2021
MSA[1]	n/a	n/a	n/a	n/a	n/a	n/a	n/a	n/a	n/a	n/a
U.S.	0.087	0.089	0.081	0.080	0.072	0.067	0.069	0.065	0.065	0.067

Note: (1) Data covers the Fargo, ND-MN Metropolitan Statistical Area; n/a not available. The values shown are the composite ozone concentration averages among trend sites based on the highest fourth daily maximum 8-hour concentration in parts per million. These trends are based on sites having an adequate record of monitoring data during the trend period. Data from exceptional events are included.
Source: U.S. Environmental Protection Agency, Air Quality Monitoring Information, "Air Quality Trends by City, 1990-2021"

Air Quality Index

Area	Percent of Days when Air Quality was...[2]					AQI Statistics[2]	
	Good	Moderate	Unhealthy for Sensitive Groups	Unhealthy	Very Unhealthy	Maximum	Median
MSA[1]	76.6	18.7	2.2	2.5	0.0	192	37

Note: (1) Data covers the Fargo, ND-MN Metropolitan Statistical Area; (2) Based on 363 days with AQI data in 2021. Air Quality Index (AQI) is an index for reporting daily air quality. EPA calculates the AQI for five major air pollutants regulated by the Clean Air Act: ground-level ozone, particle pollution (aka particulate matter), carbon monoxide, sulfur dioxide, and nitrogen dioxide. The AQI runs from 0 to 500. The higher the AQI value, the greater the level of air pollution and the greater the health concern. There are six AQI categories: "Good" AQI is between 0 and 50. Air quality is considered satisfactory; "Moderate" AQI is between 51 and 100. Air quality is acceptable; "Unhealthy for Sensitive Groups" When AQI values are between 101 and 150, members of sensitive groups may experience health effects; "Unhealthy" When AQI values are between 151 and 200 everyone may begin to experience health effects; "Very Unhealthy" AQI values between 201 and 300 trigger a health alert; "Hazardous" AQI values over 300 trigger warnings of emergency conditions (not shown).
Source: U.S. Environmental Protection Agency, Air Quality Index Report, 2021

Air Quality Index Pollutants

| Area | Percent of Days when AQI Pollutant was...[2] | | | | | |
	Carbon Monoxide	Nitrogen Dioxide	Ozone	Sulfur Dioxide	Particulate Matter 2.5	Particulate Matter 10
MSA[1]	0.0	1.4	54.5	(3)	44.1	0.0

Note: (1) Data covers the Fargo, ND-MN Metropolitan Statistical Area; (2) Based on 363 days with AQI data in 2021. The Air Quality Index (AQI) is an index for reporting daily air quality. EPA calculates the AQI for five major air pollutants regulated by the Clean Air Act: ground-level ozone, particle pollution (also known as particulate matter), carbon monoxide, sulfur dioxide, and nitrogen dioxide. The AQI runs from 0 to 500. The higher the AQI value, the greater the level of air pollution and the greater the health concern; (3) Sulfur dioxide is no longer included in this table (as of December 8, 2021) because SO_2 concentrations tend to be very localized and not necessarily representative of broad geographical areas like counties and CBSAs.
Source: U.S. Environmental Protection Agency, Air Quality Index Report, 2021

Maximum Air Pollutant Concentrations: Particulate Matter, Ozone, CO and Lead

	Particulate Matter 10 (ug/m^3)	Particulate Matter 2.5 Wtd AM (ug/m^3)	Particulate Matter 2.5 24-Hr (ug/m^3)	Ozone (ppm)	Carbon Monoxide (ppm)	Lead (ug/m^3)
MSA[1] Level	n/a	11	60	0.063	n/a	n/a
NAAQS[2]	150	15	35	0.075	9	0.15
Met NAAQS[2]	n/a	Yes	No	Yes	n/a	n/a

Note: (1) Data covers the Fargo, ND-MN Metropolitan Statistical Area; Data from exceptional events are included; (2) National Ambient Air Quality Standards; ppm = parts per million; ug/m^3 = micrograms per cubic meter; n/a not available.
Concentrations: Particulate Matter 10 (coarse particulate)—highest second maximum 24-hour concentration; Particulate Matter 2.5 Wtd AM (fine particulate)—highest weighted annual mean concentration; Particulate Matter 2.5 24-Hour (fine particulate)—highest 98th percentile 24-hour concentration; Ozone—highest fourth daily maximum 8-hour concentration; Carbon Monoxide—highest second maximum non-overlapping 8-hour concentration; Lead—maximum running 3-month average
Source: U.S. Environmental Protection Agency, Air Quality Monitoring Information, "Air Quality Statistics by City, 2021"

Maximum Air Pollutant Concentrations: Nitrogen Dioxide and Sulfur Dioxide

	Nitrogen Dioxide AM (ppb)	Nitrogen Dioxide 1-Hr (ppb)	Sulfur Dioxide AM (ppb)	Sulfur Dioxide 1-Hr (ppb)	Sulfur Dioxide 24-Hr (ppb)
MSA[1] Level	4	31	n/a	n/a	n/a
NAAQS[2]	53	100	30	75	140
Met NAAQS[2]	Yes	Yes	n/a	n/a	n/a

Note: (1) Data covers the Fargo, ND-MN Metropolitan Statistical Area; Data from exceptional events are included; (2) National Ambient Air Quality Standards; ppm = parts per million; ug/m^3 = micrograms per cubic meter; n/a not available.
Concentrations: Nitrogen Dioxide AM—highest arithmetic mean concentration; Nitrogen Dioxide 1-Hr—highest 98th percentile 1-hour daily maximum concentration; Sulfur Dioxide AM—highest annual mean concentration; Sulfur Dioxide 1-Hr—highest 99th percentile 1-hour daily maximum concentration; Sulfur Dioxide 24-Hr—highest second maximum 24-hour concentration
Source: U.S. Environmental Protection Agency, Air Quality Monitoring Information, "Air Quality Statistics by City, 2021"

Fort Wayne, Indiana

Background

Fort Wayne lies 100 miles northeast of Indianapolis, at the confluence of the St. Mary and St. Joseph rivers, which form the Maumee River. The waters, spanned by 21 bridges, divide the town into three parts.

Once the stronghold of the Miami Native American tribe, the area was prominent in frontier history. The Miami ruled the lower peninsula region, fighting against the Iroquois who were armed by the English colonists. Later, the Miami tribe established itself in the Wabash Valley and built a village at the Lakeside district in Fort Wayne. They continued to side with the British during the American Revolution, after which President Washington ordered armies into the center of the Miami Territory to stop the Miami war parties, which had been encouraged by the British to attack the new nation. After Chief Little Turtle, one of the most feared and respected tribal leaders, defeated the army of General Arthur St. Clair, Washington sought the help of General "Mad" Anthony Wayne, who succeeded in defeating the rebellious tribes. Wayne marched on Miamitown and built the first American fort there. When the fort was turned over to Colonel John Hamtramck on October 21, 1794, the colonel immediately changed the name to Fort Wayne.

Fort Wayne's industrial growth began with the building of the Wabash and Erie Canal in the 1830s and was further stimulated in the 1850s when the railroad reached the region.

Nearly equidistant from Chicago, Cincinnati, and Detroit, the city is a regional transportation and communications center. Although rich in dairy, livestock, and vegetable farming, it is primarily a diversified industrial center, with several strong clusters of industry including advanced manufacturing, defense engineering, automotive-related development and production (home to the world's first full-size hybrid pickup truck), life science, higher education, aerospace/avionics-related, logistics and finance. Fort Wayne also enjoys additional prosperity due to its proximity to Warsaw, Indiana, termed the Orthopedic Capitol of the World due to its many orthopedic-implant manufacturers.

Institutions of higher education in the city include Indiana's Institute of Technology, Indiana University-Purdue University at Fort Wayne, and University of St. Francis. The city is also home to the Northeast Indiana Innovation Center, designed to attract high-tech businesses and provide community outreach to local entrepreneurs and schools. Ongoing projects include the Core Incubation System, which specializes in biomedical, information systems, and advanced manufacturing plans, and the Digital Kids Initiative, which promotes early mastery of digital skills. The city has developed a blueprint for preservation and restoration of various downtown districts, including the Landing District, the Old Canal District, and the Barr Street District, which features an "International Marketplace," a diverse group of businesses representing a variety of ethnicities and cultural centers serving them.

Fort Wayne is sometimes referred to as the "City of Churches," an unofficial moniker dating to the late-19th century when the city was the regional hub of Catholic, Lutheran, and Episcopal faiths. Today, there are nearly 400 churches in the city.

Parkview Field is home to the TinCaps, baseball's minor league team affiliated with the San Diego Padres. Not far from Parkview Field are condominiums, shops and a centrally located Courtyard Marriott hotel. Fort Wayne's renovated Grand Wayne Convention Center encompasses 225,000 square feet.

Fort Wayne's varied cultural and educational attractions combined with a low cost of living continue to earn Fort Wayne many "best of" awards. Arts events are held at the Allen County War Memorial Coliseum, Foellinger Outdoor Theater, and IPFW Performing Arts Center. Additional attractions include the Foellinger-Freimann Botanical Conservatory with a Tropical House and cascading waterfall; Sonoran Desert House; Woody the talking tree and exhibit; Fort Wayne Museum of Art; the nationally acclaimed Fort Wayne Children's Zoo; and Lincoln Museum with its award-winning exhibit honoring the life and legacy of our 16th president.

The land surrounding the city is generally level to the south and east, rolling to the west and southwest, and quite hilly to the north and northwest. The climate is influenced by the Great Lakes, with rain constant throughout the warmer months. Damaging hailstorms occur approximately twice a year, and severe flooding is possible. While snow generally covers the ground for about a month during the winter, heavy snowstorms are infrequent. Except for considerable cloudiness during the winter, Fort Wayne enjoys a good Midwestern average for sunshine.

Rankings

General Rankings

- *Insider* listed 23 places in the U.S. that travel industry trends reveal would be popular destinations in 2023. This year the list trends towards cultural and historical happenings, sports events, wellness experiences and invigorating outdoor escapes. According to the website insider.com Fort Wayne is a place to visit in 2023. *Insider, "23 of the Best Places You Should Travel to in the U.S. in 2023," December 17, 2022*

Business/Finance Rankings

- Fort Wayne was the #18-ranked city for savers, according to a study by the finance site GOBankingRates, which considered the prospects for people trying to save money. Criteria: average monthly cost of grocery items; median home listing price; median rent; median income; transportation costs; gas prices; and the cost of eating out for an inexpensive and mid-range meal in 100 U.S. cities. *www.gobankingrates.com, "The 20 Best (and Worst) Places to Live If You're Trying to Save Money," August 27, 2019*

- Fort Wayne was ranked #18 among 100 U.S. cities for most difficult conditions for savers, according to a study by the finance site GOBankingRates. Criteria: average monthly cost of grocery items; median home listing price; median rent; median income; transportation costs; gas prices; and the cost of eating out for an inexpensive and mid-range meal. *www.gobankingrates.com, "The 20 Best (and Worst) Places to Live If You're Trying to Save Money," August 27, 2019*

- The Fort Wayne metro area appeared on the Milken Institute "2022 Best Performing Cities" list. Rank: #134 out of 200 large metro areas (population over 250,000). Criteria: job growth; wage and salary growth; high-tech output growth; housing affordability; household broadband access. *Milken Institute, "Best-Performing Cities 2022," March 28, 2022*

- *Forbes* ranked the 200 most populous metro areas to determine the nation's "Best Places for Business and Careers." The Fort Wayne metro area was ranked #122. Criteria: costs (business and living); job growth (past and projected); income growth; quality of life; educational attainment (college and high school); projected economic growth; cultural and leisure opportunities; workplace tolerance laws; net migration patterns. *Forbes, "The Best Places for Business and Careers 2019: Seattle Still On Top," October 30, 2019*

Children/Family Rankings

- Fort Wayne was selected as one of the most playful cities in the U.S. by KaBOOM! The organization's Playful City USA initiative honors cities and towns across the nation that have made their communities more playable. Criteria: pledging to integrate play as a solution to challenges in their communities; making it easy for children to get active and balanced play; creating more family-friendly and innovative communities as a result. *KaBOOM! National Campaign for Play, "2017 Playful City USA Communities"*

Education Rankings

- Personal finance website *WalletHub* analyzed the 150 largest U.S. metropolitan statistical areas to determine where the most educated Americans are putting their degrees to work. Criteria: education levels; percentage of workers with degrees; education quality and attainment gap; public school quality rankings; quality and enrollment of each metro area's universities. Fort Wayne was ranked #109 (#1 = most educated city). *www.WalletHub.com, "Most & Least Educated Cities in America," July 18, 2022*

- Fort Wayne was selected as one of America's most literate cities. The city ranked #53 out of the 84 largest U.S. cities. Criteria: number of booksellers; library resources; Internet resources; educational attainment; periodical publishing resources; newspaper circulation. *Central Connecticut State University, "America's Most Literate Cities, 2018," February 2019*

Health/Fitness Rankings

- For each of the 100 largest cities in the United States, the American Fitness Index®, compiled in partnership between the American College of Sports Medicine and the Elevance Health Foundation, evaluated community infrastructure and 34 health behaviors including preventive health, levels of chronic disease conditions, food insecurity, sleep quality, pedestrian safety, air quality, and community/environment resources that support physical activity. Fort Wayne ranked #75 for "community fitness." *americanfitnessindex.org, "2022 ACSM American Fitness Index Summary Report," July 12, 2022*

- The Fort Wayne metro area was identified as one of the worst cities for bed bugs in America by pest control company Orkin. The area ranked #35 out of 50 based on the number of bed bug treatments Orkin performed from December 2021 to November 2022. *Orkin, "The Windy City Can't Blow Bed Bugs Away: Chicago Ranks #1 For Third Consecutive Year On Orkin's Bed Bug Cities List," January 9, 2023*

Real Estate Rankings

- *WalletHub* compared the most populated U.S. cities to determine which had the best markets for real estate agents. Fort Wayne ranked #86 where demand was high and pay was the best. Criteria: sales per agent; annual median wage for real-estate agents; monthly average starting salary for real estate agents; real estate job density and competition; unemployment rate; home turnover rate; housing-market health index; and other relevant metrics. *www.WalletHub.com, "2021 Best Places to Be a Real Estate Agent," May 12, 2021*

Safety Rankings

- Allstate ranked the 200 largest cities in America in terms of driver safety. Fort Wayne ranked #36. Criteria: internal property damage claims over a two-year period from January 2016 to December 2017. The report helps increase the importance of safety and awareness behind the wheel. *Allstate, "Allstate America's Best Drivers Report, 2019" June 24, 2019*

- The National Insurance Crime Bureau ranked 390 metro areas in the U.S. in terms of per capita rates of vehicle theft. The Fort Wayne metro area ranked #242 (#1 = highest rate). Criteria: number of vehicle theft offenses per 100,000 inhabitants in 2021. *National Insurance Crime Bureau, "Hot Spots 2021," September 1, 2022*

Seniors/Retirement Rankings

- From its Best Cities for Successful Aging indexes, the Milken Institute generated rankings for metropolitan areas, weighing data in nine categories—health care, wellness, living arrangements, transportation and convenience, financial characteristics, education, employment, community engagement, and overall livability. The Fort Wayne metro area was ranked #115 overall in the small metro area category. *Milken Institute, "Best Cities for Successful Aging, 2017" March 14, 2017*

Women/Minorities Rankings

- Personal finance website *WalletHub* compared more than 180 U.S. cities across two key dimensions, "Hispanic Business-Friendliness" and "Hispanic Purchasing Power," to arrive at the most favorable conditions for Hispanic entrepreneurs. Fort Wayne was ranked #118 out of 182. Criteria includes: share of Hispanic-Owned Businesses; Hispanic entrepreneurship rate to median annual income of Hispanics; Small Business-Friendliness score; cost of living; and number of Hispanics with at least a bachelor's degree. *WalletHub.com, "2019's Best Cities for Hispanic Entrepreneurs," May 1, 2019*

Miscellaneous Rankings

- *WalletHub* compared the 150 most populated U.S. cities to determine their operating efficiency. A "Quality of Services" score was constructed for each city and then divided by the total budget per capita to reveal which were managed the best. Fort Wayne ranked #3. Criteria: financial stability; economy; education; safety; health; infrastructure and pollution. *www.WalletHub.com, "2022's Best- & Worst-Run Cities in America," June 21, 2022*

Business Environment

DEMOGRAPHICS

Population Growth

Area	1990 Census	2000 Census	2010 Census	2020 Census	Population Growth (%) 1990-2020	Population Growth (%) 2010-2020
City	205,671	205,727	253,691	263,886	28.3	4.0
MSA[1]	354,435	390,156	416,257	419,601	18.4	0.8
U.S.	248,709,873	281,421,906	308,745,538	331,449,281	33.3	7.4

Note: (1) Figures cover the Fort Wayne, IN Metropolitan Statistical Area
Source: U.S. Census Bureau, 1990 Census, 2000 Census, 2010 Census, 2020 Census

Race

Area	White Alone[2] (%)	Black Alone[2] (%)	Asian Alone[2] (%)	AIAN[3] Alone[2] (%)	NHOPI[4] Alone[2] (%)	Other Race Alone[2] (%)	Two or More Races (%)
City	65.0	15.3	5.8	0.5	0.0	5.6	7.8
MSA[1]	73.7	10.6	4.4	0.4	0.0	4.0	6.8
U.S.	61.6	12.4	6.0	1.1	0.2	8.4	10.2

Note: (1) Figures cover the Fort Wayne, IN Metropolitan Statistical Area; (2) Alone is defined as not being in combination with one or more other races; (3) American Indian and Alaska Native; (4) Native Hawaiian and Other Pacific Islander
Source: U.S. Census Bureau, 2020 Census

Hispanic or Latino Origin

Area	Total (%)	Mexican (%)	Puerto Rican (%)	Cuban (%)	Other (%)
City	9.5	7.2	0.6	0.1	1.6
MSA[1]	7.4	5.6	0.4	0.1	1.3
U.S.	18.4	11.2	1.8	0.7	4.7

Note: Persons of Hispanic or Latino origin can be of any race; (1) Figures cover the Fort Wayne, IN Metropolitan Statistical Area
Source: U.S. Census Bureau, 2017-2021 American Community Survey 5-Year Estimates

Age

Area	Percent of Population Under Age 5	Age 5–19	Age 20–34	Age 35–44	Age 45–54	Age 55–64	Age 65–74	Age 75–84	Age 85+	Median Age
City	6.9	20.8	21.9	12.4	11.2	11.9	9.1	4.1	1.9	35.3
MSA[1]	6.7	21.3	19.9	12.4	11.7	12.4	9.4	4.4	1.8	36.6
U.S.	5.6	19.2	20.2	12.7	12.4	13.1	10.0	4.9	1.9	38.8

Note: (1) Figures cover the Fort Wayne, IN Metropolitan Statistical Area
Source: U.S. Census Bureau, 2020 Census

Disability by Age

Area	All Ages	Under 18 Years Old	18 to 64 Years Old	65 Years and Over
City	13.9	5.5	12.8	34.2
MSA[1]	12.4	4.7	11.0	32.0
U.S.	12.6	4.4	10.3	33.4

Note: Figures show percent of the civilian noninstitutionalized population that reported having a disability. Disability status is determined from six types of difficulty: vision, hearing, cognitive, ambulatory, self-care, and independent living. For children under 5 years old, hearing and vision difficulty are used to determine disability status. For children between the ages of 5 and 14, disability status is determined from hearing, vision, cognitive, ambulatory, and self-care difficulties. For people aged 15 years and older, they are considered to have a disability if they have difficulty with any one of the six difficulty types; Note: (1) Figures cover the Fort Wayne, IN Metropolitan Statistical Area
Source: U.S. Census Bureau, 2017-2021 American Community Survey 5-Year Estimates

Ancestry

Area	German	Irish	English	American	Italian	Polish	French[2]	Scottish	Dutch
City	23.1	9.4	7.8	5.5	2.3	2.2	2.7	1.6	1.1
MSA[1]	26.4	9.5	8.3	6.4	2.5	2.1	3.1	1.6	1.1
U.S.	12.8	9.6	8.1	5.7	5.0	2.7	2.2	1.6	1.1

Note: Figures are the percentage of the total population reporting a particular ancestry. The nine most commonly reported ancestries in the U.S. are shown. Figures include multiple ancestries (e.g. if a person reported being Irish and Italian, they were included in both columns); (1) Figures cover the Fort Wayne, IN Metropolitan Statistical Area; (2) Excludes Basque
Source: U.S. Census Bureau, 2017-2021 American Community Survey 5-Year Estimates

Foreign-born Population

Area	\multicolumn{9}{c}{Percent of Population Born in}
	Any Foreign Country	Asia	Mexico	Europe	Caribbean	Central America[2]	South America	Africa	Canada
City	8.6	4.3	2.0	0.6	0.1	0.6	0.2	0.6	0.1
MSA[1]	6.7	3.3	1.5	0.6	0.1	0.4	0.2	0.4	0.1
U.S.	13.6	4.2	3.3	1.5	1.4	1.1	1.1	0.8	0.2

Note: (1) Figures cover the Fort Wayne, IN Metropolitan Statistical Area; (2) Excludes Mexico.
Source: U.S. Census Bureau, 2017-2021 American Community Survey 5-Year Estimates

Household Size

Area	\multicolumn{7}{c}{Persons in Household (%)}	Average Household Size
	One	Two	Three	Four	Five	Six	Seven or More	
City	32.8	32.8	14.1	10.8	5.7	2.7	1.2	2.40
MSA[1]	29.1	34.3	14.2	12.1	6.2	2.7	1.5	2.50
U.S.	28.1	33.8	15.5	12.9	6.0	2.3	1.4	2.60

Note: (1) Figures cover the Fort Wayne, IN Metropolitan Statistical Area
Source: U.S. Census Bureau, 2017-2021 American Community Survey 5-Year Estimates

Household Relationships

Area	House-holder	Opposite-sex Spouse	Same-sex Spouse	Opposite-sex Unmarried Partner	Same-sex Unmarried Partner	Child[2]	Grand-child	Other Relatives	Non-relatives
City	40.7	15.6	0.2	3.1	0.2	29.7	2.0	3.4	3.0
MSA[1]	39.5	18.0	0.2	2.7	0.1	30.5	1.9	2.9	2.5
U.S.	38.3	17.5	0.2	2.5	0.2	28.3	2.4	4.8	3.4

Note: Figures are percent of the total population; (1) Figures cover the Fort Wayne, IN Metropolitan Statistical Area; (2) Includes biological, adopted, and stepchildren of the householder
Source: U.S. Census Bureau, 2020 Census

Gender

Area	Males	Females	Males per 100 Females
City	128,678	135,208	95.2
MSA[1]	205,785	213,816	96.2
U.S.	162,685,811	168,763,470	96.4

Note: (1) Figures cover the Fort Wayne, IN Metropolitan Statistical Area
Source: U.S. Census Bureau, 2020 Census

Marital Status

Area	Never Married	Now Married[2]	Separated	Widowed	Divorced
City	36.1	44.2	1.5	5.9	12.3
MSA[1]	31.5	50.0	1.3	5.6	11.6
U.S.	33.8	48.0	1.8	5.6	10.8

Note: Figures are percentages and cover the population 15 years of age and older; (1) Figures cover the Fort Wayne, IN Metropolitan Statistical Area; (2) Excludes separated
Source: U.S. Census Bureau, 2017-2021 American Community Survey 5-Year Estimates

Religious Groups by Family

Area	Catholic	Baptist	Methodist	LDS[2]	Pentecostal	Lutheran	Islam	Adventist	Other
MSA[1]	13.1	8.1	3.9	0.4	1.1	7.1	1.0	0.9	17.6
U.S.	18.7	7.3	3.0	2.0	1.8	1.7	1.3	1.3	11.6

Note: Figures are the number of adherents as a percentage of the total population and cover the eight largest religious groups in the U.S; (1) Figures cover the Fort Wayne, IN Metropolitan Statistical Area; (2) Church of Jesus Christ of Latter-day Saints
Sources: 2020 U.S. Religion Census, Association of Statisticians of American Religious Bodies; The Association of Religion Data Archives (ARDA)

Religious Groups by Tradition

Area	Catholic	Evangelical Protestant	Mainline Protestant	Black Protestant	Islam	Judaism	Hinduism	Orthodox	Buddhism
MSA[1]	13.1	24.7	6.1	6.5	1.0	0.1	0.1	0.2	0.4
U.S.	18.7	16.5	5.2	2.3	1.3	0.6	0.4	0.4	0.3

Note: Figures are the number of adherents as a percentage of the total population; (1) Figures cover the Fort Wayne, IN Metropolitan Statistical Area
Sources: 2020 U.S. Religion Census, Association of Statisticians of American Religious Bodies; The Association of Religion Data Archives (ARDA)

ECONOMY

Gross Metropolitan Product

Area	2020	2021	2022	2023	Rank[2]
MSA[1]	24.3	27.3	29.8	31.6	114

Note: Figures are in billions of dollars; (1) Figures cover the Fort Wayne, IN Metropolitan Statistical Area; (2) Rank is based on 2021 data and ranges from 1 to 381
Source: U.S. Conference of Mayors, U.S. Metro Economies: U.S. Metros Compared to Global and State Economies, June 2022

Economic Growth

Area	2018-20 (%)	2021 (%)	2022 (%)	2023 (%)	Rank[2]
MSA[1]	-2.0	8.3	3.1	2.7	285
U.S.	-0.6	5.7	3.1	2.9	—

Note: Figures are real gross metropolitan product (GMP) growth rates and represent average annual percent change; (1) Figures cover the Fort Wayne, IN Metropolitan Statistical Area; (2) Rank is based on 2020 2-year average annual percent change and ranges from 1 to 381
Source: U.S. Conference of Mayors, U.S. Metro Economies: U.S. Metros Compared to Global and State Economies, June 2022

Metropolitan Area Exports

Area	2016	2017	2018	2019	2020	2021	Rank[2]
MSA[1]	1,322.2	1,422.8	1,593.3	1,438.5	1,144.6	1,592.7	123

Note: Figures are in millions of dollars; (1) Figures cover the Fort Wayne, IN Metropolitan Statistical Area; (2) Rank is based on 2021 data and ranges from 1 to 388
Source: U.S. Department of Commerce, International Trade Administration, Office of Trade and Economic Analysis, Industry and Analysis, Exports by Metropolitan Area, data extracted March 16, 2023

Building Permits

Area	Single-Family			Multi-Family			Total		
	2021	2022	Pct. Chg.	2021	2022	Pct. Chg.	2021	2022	Pct. Chg.
City	n/a	n/a	n/a	n/a	n/a	n/a	n/a	n/a	n/a
MSA[1]	1,799	1,453	-19.2	179	882	392.7	1,978	2,335	18.0
U.S.	1,115,400	975,600	-12.5	621,600	689,500	10.9	1,737,000	1,665,100	-4.1

Note: (1) Figures cover the Fort Wayne, IN Metropolitan Statistical Area; Figures represent new, privately-owned housing units authorized (unadjusted data); All permit data are based on estimates with imputation
Source: U.S. Census Bureau, Manufacturing, Mining, and Construction Statistics, Building Permits, 2021, 2022

Bankruptcy Filings

Area	Business Filings			Nonbusiness Filings		
	2021	2022	% Chg.	2021	2022	% Chg.
Allen County	6	13	116.7	872	767	-12.0
U.S.	14,347	13,481	-6.0	399,269	374,240	-6.3

Note: Business filings include Chapter 7, Chapter 9, Chapter 11, Chapter 12, Chapter 13, Chapter 15, and Section 304; Nonbusiness filings include Chapter 7, Chapter 11, and Chapter 13
Source: Administrative Office of the U.S. Courts, Business and Nonbusiness Bankruptcy, County Cases Commenced by Chapter of the Bankruptcy Code, During the 12-Month Period Ending December 31, 2021 and Business and Nonbusiness Bankruptcy, County Cases Commenced by Chapter of the Bankruptcy Code, During the 12-Month Period Ending December 31, 2022

Housing Vacancy Rates

Area	Gross Vacancy Rate[2] (%)			Year-Round Vacancy Rate[3] (%)			Rental Vacancy Rate[4] (%)			Homeowner Vacancy Rate[5] (%)		
	2020	2021	2022	2020	2021	2022	2020	2021	2022	2020	2021	2022
MSA[1]	n/a	n/a	n/a	n/a	n/a	n/a	n/a	n/a	n/a	n/a	n/a	n/a
U.S.	10.6	10.8	10.5	8.2	8.4	8.2	6.3	6.1	5.8	1.0	0.9	0.8

Note: (1) Figures cover the Fort Wayne, IN Metropolitan Statistical Area; (2) The percentage of the total housing inventory that is vacant; (3) The percentage of the housing inventory (excluding seasonal units) that is year-round vacant; (4) The percentage of rental inventory that is vacant for rent; (5) The percentage of homeowner inventory that is vacant for sale; n/a not available
Source: U.S. Census Bureau, Housing Vacancies and Homeownership Annual Statistics: 2020, 2021, 2022

INCOME

Income

Area	Per Capita ($)	Median Household ($)	Average Household ($)
City	29,268	53,978	70,654
MSA[1]	32,207	62,031	80,675
U.S.	37,638	69,021	97,196

Note: (1) Figures cover the Fort Wayne, IN Metropolitan Statistical Area
Source: U.S. Census Bureau, 2017-2021 American Community Survey 5-Year Estimates

Household Income Distribution

Area	Percent of Households Earning							
	Under $15,000	$15,000 -$24,999	$25,000 -$34,999	$35,000 -$49,999	$50,000 -$74,999	$75,000 -$99,999	$100,000 -$149,999	$150,000 and up
City	10.4	10.4	10.8	14.8	19.8	13.2	13.1	7.5
MSA[1]	8.2	8.9	9.5	13.5	19.5	14.9	15.3	10.3
U.S.	9.4	7.8	8.2	11.4	16.8	12.8	16.3	17.3

Note: (1) Figures cover the Fort Wayne, IN Metropolitan Statistical Area
Source: U.S. Census Bureau, 2017-2021 American Community Survey 5-Year Estimates

Poverty Rate

Area	All Ages	Under 18 Years Old	18 to 64 Years Old	65 Years and Over
City	15.5	23.9	13.7	8.3
MSA[1]	12.1	17.9	10.9	6.9
U.S.	12.6	17.0	11.8	9.6

Note: Figures are percentage of people whose income during the past 12 months was below the poverty level;
(1) Figures cover the Fort Wayne, IN Metropolitan Statistical Area
Source: U.S. Census Bureau, 2017-2021 American Community Survey 5-Year Estimates

EMPLOYMENT

Labor Force and Employment

Area	Civilian Labor Force			Workers Employed		
	Dec. 2021	Dec. 2022	% Chg.	Dec. 2021	Dec. 2022	% Chg.
City	126,450	130,964	3.6	124,397	127,828	2.8
MSA[1]	213,153	220,727	3.6	210,157	215,921	2.7
U.S.	161,696,000	164,224,000	1.6	155,732,000	158,872,000	2.0

Note: Data is not seasonally adjusted and covers workers 16 years of age and older; (1) Figures cover the Fort Wayne, IN Metropolitan Statistical Area
Source: Bureau of Labor Statistics, Local Area Unemployment Statistics

Unemployment Rate

Area	2022											
	Jan.	Feb.	Mar.	Apr.	May	Jun.	Jul.	Aug.	Sep.	Oct.	Nov.	Dec.
City	2.5	2.7	2.8	2.5	2.6	3.3	3.6	3.1	2.3	2.9	2.9	2.4
MSA[1]	2.2	2.4	2.6	2.2	2.3	3.0	3.2	2.8	2.0	2.7	2.6	2.2
U.S.	4.4	4.1	3.8	3.3	3.4	3.8	3.8	3.8	3.3	3.4	3.4	3.3

Note: Data is not seasonally adjusted and covers workers 16 years of age and older; (1) Figures cover the Fort Wayne, IN Metropolitan Statistical Area
Source: Bureau of Labor Statistics, Local Area Unemployment Statistics

Average Wages

Occupation	$/Hr.	Occupation	$/Hr.
Accountants and Auditors	35.91	Maintenance and Repair Workers	23.13
Automotive Mechanics	21.07	Marketing Managers	56.84
Bookkeepers	20.51	Network and Computer Systems Admin.	37.68
Carpenters	24.46	Nurses, Licensed Practical	25.80
Cashiers	12.43	Nurses, Registered	35.21
Computer Programmers	41.88	Nursing Assistants	15.77
Computer Systems Analysts	40.51	Office Clerks, General	18.98
Computer User Support Specialists	25.05	Physical Therapists	44.25
Construction Laborers	22.43	Physicians	n/a
Cooks, Restaurant	14.31	Plumbers, Pipefitters and Steamfitters	33.18
Customer Service Representatives	19.63	Police and Sheriff's Patrol Officers	31.73
Dentists	81.34	Postal Service Mail Carriers	26.91
Electricians	29.66	Real Estate Sales Agents	27.25
Engineers, Electrical	48.26	Retail Salespersons	14.91
Fast Food and Counter Workers	11.84	Sales Representatives, Technical/Scientific	51.06
Financial Managers	56.74	Secretaries, Exc. Legal/Medical/Executive	18.31
First-Line Supervisors of Office Workers	29.78	Security Guards	17.67
General and Operations Managers	57.29	Surgeons	n/a
Hairdressers/Cosmetologists	15.67	Teacher Assistants, Exc. Postsecondary*	13.32
Home Health and Personal Care Aides	13.51	Teachers, Secondary School, Exc. Sp. Ed.*	27.57
Janitors and Cleaners	15.11	Telemarketers	15.78
Landscaping/Groundskeeping Workers	16.18	Truck Drivers, Heavy/Tractor-Trailer	25.45
Lawyers	62.54	Truck Drivers, Light/Delivery Services	20.20
Maids and Housekeeping Cleaners	13.34	Waiters and Waitresses	13.17

Note: Wage data covers the Fort Wayne, IN Metropolitan Statistical Area; (*) Hourly wages were calculated from annual wage data based on a 40 hour work week; n/a not available.
Source: Bureau of Labor Statistics, Metro Area Occupational Employment & Wage Estimates, May 2022

Employment by Industry

Sector	MSA[1]		U.S.
	Number of Employees	Percent of Total	Percent of Total
Construction, Mining, and Logging	12,300	5.2	5.4
Private Education and Health Services	43,100	18.4	16.1
Financial Activities	12,900	5.5	5.9
Government	22,000	9.4	14.5
Information	1,900	0.8	2.0
Leisure and Hospitality	21,100	9.0	10.3
Manufacturing	38,400	16.4	8.4
Other Services	11,700	5.0	3.7
Professional and Business Services	22,700	9.7	14.7
Retail Trade	25,100	10.7	10.2
Transportation, Warehousing, and Utilities	11,900	5.1	4.9
Wholesale Trade	11,300	4.8	3.9

Note: Figures are non-farm employment as of December 2022. Figures are not seasonally adjusted and include workers 16 years of age and older; (1) Figures cover the Fort Wayne, IN Metropolitan Statistical Area
Source: Bureau of Labor Statistics, Current Employment Statistics, Employment, Hours, and Earnings

Employment by Occupation

Occupation Classification	City (%)	MSA[1] (%)	U.S. (%)
Management, Business, Science, and Arts	33.9	36.1	40.3
Natural Resources, Construction, and Maintenance	6.6	7.6	8.7
Production, Transportation, and Material Moving	21.3	19.9	13.1
Sales and Office	21.6	21.2	20.9
Service	16.6	15.2	17.0

Note: Figures cover employed civilians 16 years of age and older; (1) Figures cover the Fort Wayne, IN Metropolitan Statistical Area
Source: U.S. Census Bureau, 2017-2021 American Community Survey 5-Year Estimates

Occupations with Greatest Projected Employment Growth: 2022 – 2024

Occupation[1]	2022 Employment	2024 Projected Employment	Numeric Employment Change	Percent Employment Change
Laborers and Freight, Stock, and Material Movers, Hand	98,000	103,790	5,790	5.9
Retail Salespersons	87,130	89,970	2,840	3.3
Stockers and Order Fillers	53,700	56,260	2,560	4.8
Heavy and Tractor-Trailer Truck Drivers	57,980	59,970	1,990	3.4
General and Operations Managers	57,130	59,100	1,970	3.4
Cooks, Restaurant	27,050	28,980	1,930	7.1
Industrial Truck and Tractor Operators	26,810	28,690	1,880	7.0
Fast Food and Counter Workers	90,910	92,670	1,760	1.9
Janitors and Cleaners, Except Maids and Housekeeping Cleaners	49,870	51,520	1,650	3.3
Light Truck or Delivery Services Drivers	25,930	27,450	1,520	5.9

Note: Projections cover Indiana; (1) Sorted by numeric employment change
Source: www.projectionscentral.com, State Occupational Projections, 2022–2024 Short-Term Projections

Fastest-Growing Occupations: 2022 – 2024

Occupation[1]	2022 Employment	2024 Projected Employment	Numeric Employment Change	Percent Employment Change
Travel Agents	910	1,000	90	9.9
Nurse Practitioners	6,630	7,280	650	9.8
Information Security Analysts (SOC 2018)	1,710	1,870	160	9.4
Data Scientists	2,170	2,370	200	9.2
Web Developers	1,560	1,690	130	8.3
Logisticians	2,580	2,790	210	8.1
Software Developers	13,210	14,280	1,070	8.1
Veterinarians	1,980	2,130	150	7.6
Veterinary Assistants and Laboratory Animal Caretakers	2,630	2,830	200	7.6
Veterinary Technologists and Technicians	2,700	2,900	200	7.4

Note: Projections cover Indiana; (1) Sorted by percent employment change and excludes occupations with numeric employment change less than 50
Source: www.projectionscentral.com, State Occupational Projections, 2022–2024 Short-Term Projections

CITY FINANCES

City Government Finances

Component	2020 ($000)	2020 ($ per capita)
Total Revenues	478,331	1,769
Total Expenditures	443,073	1,639
Debt Outstanding	552,545	2,043
Cash and Securities[1]	174,221	644

Note: (1) Cash and security holdings of a government at the close of its fiscal year, including those of its dependent agencies, utilities, and liquor stores.
Source: U.S. Census Bureau, State & Local Government Finances 2020

City Government Revenue by Source

Source	2020 ($000)	2020 ($ per capita)	2020 (%)
General Revenue			
From Federal Government	7,846	29	1.6
From State Government	53,035	196	11.1
From Local Governments	702	3	0.1
Taxes			
Property	137,591	509	28.8
Sales and Gross Receipts	4,673	17	1.0
Personal Income	68,575	254	14.3
Corporate Income	0	0	0.0
Motor Vehicle License	9,931	37	2.1
Other Taxes	1,936	7	0.4
Current Charges	120,956	447	25.3
Liquor Store	0	0	0.0
Utility	49,287	182	10.3

Source: U.S. Census Bureau, State & Local Government Finances 2020

City Government Expenditures by Function

Function	2020 ($000)	2020 ($ per capita)	2020 (%)
General Direct Expenditures			
Air Transportation	0	0	0.0
Corrections	0	0	0.0
Education	0	0	0.0
Employment Security Administration	0	0	0.0
Financial Administration	9,235	34	2.1
Fire Protection	40,157	148	9.1
General Public Buildings	1,747	6	0.4
Governmental Administration, Other	3,357	12	0.8
Health	3,567	13	0.8
Highways	63,801	235	14.4
Hospitals	0	0	0.0
Housing and Community Development	42,649	157	9.6
Interest on General Debt	6,568	24	1.5
Judicial and Legal	589	2	0.1
Libraries	0	0	0.0
Parking	1,632	6	0.4
Parks and Recreation	31,883	117	7.2
Police Protection	61,997	229	14.0
Public Welfare	0	0	0.0
Sewerage	106,610	394	24.1
Solid Waste Management	12,189	45	2.8
Veterans' Services	0	0	0.0
Liquor Store	0	0	0.0
Utility	39,383	145	8.9

Source: U.S. Census Bureau, State & Local Government Finances 2020

TAXES

State Corporate Income Tax Rates

State	Tax Rate (%)	Income Brackets ($)	Num. of Brackets	Financial Institution Tax Rate (%)[a]	Federal Income Tax Ded.
Indiana	4.9	Flat rate	1	4.9	No

Note: Tax rates as of January 1, 2023; (a) Rates listed are the corporate income tax rate applied to financial institutions or excise taxes based on income. Some states have other taxes based upon the value of deposits or shares.
Source: Federation of Tax Administrators, State Corporate Income Tax Rates, January 1, 2023

State Individual Income Tax Rates

State	Tax Rate (%)	Income Brackets ($)	Personal Exemptions ($)			Standard Ded. ($)	
			Single	Married	Depend.	Single	Married
Indiana	3.15	Flat rate	1,000	2,000	2,500 (j)	–	–

Note: Tax rates as of January 1, 2023; Local- and county-level taxes are not included; Federal income tax is not deductible on state income tax returns; (j) In Indiana, includes an additional exemption of $1,500 for each dependent child.
Source: Federation of Tax Administrators, State Individual Income Tax Rates, January 1, 2023

Various State Sales and Excise Tax Rates

State	State Sales Tax (%)	Gasoline[1] ($/gal.)	Cigarette[2] ($/pack)	Spirits[3] ($/gal.)	Wine[4] ($/gal.)	Beer[5] ($/gal.)	Recreational Marijuana (%)
Indiana	7	0.516	0.995	2.68	0.47	0.12	Not legal

Note: All tax rates as of January 1, 2023; (1) The American Petroleum Institute has developed a methodology for determining the average tax rate on a gallon of fuel. Rates may include any of the following: excise taxes, environmental fees, storage tank fees, other fees or taxes, general sales tax, and local taxes; (2) The federal excise tax of $1.0066 per pack and local taxes are not included; (3) Rates are those applicable to off-premise sales of 40% alcohol by volume (a.b.v.) distilled spirits in 750ml containers. Local excise taxes are excluded; (4) Rates are those applicable to off-premise sales of 11% a.b.v. non-carbonated wine in 750ml containers; (5) Rates are those applicable to off-premise sales of 4.7% a.b.v. beer in 12 ounce containers.
Source: Tax Foundation, 2023 Facts & Figures: How Does Your State Compare?

State Business Tax Climate Index Rankings

State	Overall Rank	Corporate Tax Rank	Individual Income Tax Rank	Sales Tax Rank	Property Tax Rank	Unemployment Insurance Tax Rank
Indiana	9	11	15	19	2	27

Note: The index is a measure of how each state's tax laws affect economic performance. The lower the rank, the more favorable a state's tax system is for business. States without a given tax are given a ranking of 1. The scores/rankings for the District of Columbia do not affect other states. The 2023 index represents the tax climate as of July 1, 2022.
Source: Tax Foundation, State Business Tax Climate Index 2023

TRANSPORTATION

Means of Transportation to Work

Area	Car/Truck/Van		Public Transportation			Bicycle	Walked	Other Means	Worked at Home
	Drove Alone	Car-pooled	Bus	Subway	Railroad				
City	80.9	9.6	1.0	0.0	0.0	0.5	1.5	0.8	5.8
MSA[1]	82.1	8.7	0.7	0.0	0.0	0.4	1.3	0.7	6.2
U.S.	73.2	8.6	2.0	1.6	0.5	0.5	2.5	1.5	9.7

Note: Figures are percentages and cover workers 16 years of age and older; (1) Figures cover the Fort Wayne, IN Metropolitan Statistical Area
Source: U.S. Census Bureau, 2017-2021 American Community Survey 5-Year Estimates

Travel Time to Work

Area	Less Than 10 Minutes	10 to 19 Minutes	20 to 29 Minutes	30 to 44 Minutes	45 to 59 Minutes	60 to 89 Minutes	90 Minutes or More
City	12.8	38.2	28.0	13.5	3.0	2.6	1.8
MSA[1]	13.0	35.3	28.4	15.7	3.4	2.4	1.8
U.S.	12.4	28.5	21.0	20.9	8.2	6.2	2.9

Note: Note: Figures are percentages and include workers 16 years old and over; (1) Figures cover the Fort Wayne, IN Metropolitan Statistical Area
Source: U.S. Census Bureau, 2017-2021 American Community Survey 5-Year Estimates

Key Congestion Measures

Measure	1990	2000	2010	2015	2020
Annual Hours of Delay, Total (000)	n/a	n/a	n/a	5,835	2,768
Annual Hours of Delay, Per Auto Commuter	n/a	n/a	n/a	18	8
Annual Congestion Cost, Per Auto Commuter ($)	n/a	n/a	n/a	373	186

Note: n/a not available
Source: Texas A&M Transportation Institute, 2021 Urban Mobility Report

Freeway Travel Time Index

Measure	1985	1990	1995	2000	2005	2010	2015	2020
Urban Area Index[1]	n/a	n/a	n/a	n/a	n/a	n/a	1.09	1.04
Urban Area Rank[1,2]	n/a	n/a	n/a	n/a	n/a	n/a	n/a	n/a

Note: Freeway Travel Time Index—the ratio of travel time in the peak period to the travel time at free-flow conditions. For example, a value of 1.30 indicates a 20-minute free-flow trip takes 26 minutes in the peak (20 minutes x 1.30 = 26 minutes); (1) Covers the Fort Wayne IN urban area; (2) Rank is based on 101 larger urban areas (#1 = highest travel time index); n/a not available
Source: Texas A&M Transportation Institute, 2021 Urban Mobility Report

Public Transportation

Agency Name / Mode of Transportation	Vehicles Operated in Maximum Service[1]	Annual Unlinked Passenger Trips[2] (in thous.)	Annual Passenger Miles[3] (in thous.)
Fort Wayne Public Transportation Corp. (Citilink)			
Bus (directly operated)	25	1,229.7	3,725.9
Demand Response (directly operated)	15	57.0	487.5

Note: (1) Number of revenue vehicles operated by the given mode and type of service to meet the annual maximum service requirement. This is the revenue vehicle count during the peak season of the year; on the week and day that maximum service is provided. Vehicles operated in maximum service (VOMS) exclude atypical days and one-time special events; (2) Number of passengers who boarded public transportation vehicles. Passengers are counted each time they board a vehicle no matter how many vehicles they use to travel from their origin to their destination. (3) Sum of the distances ridden by all passengers during the entire fiscal year.
Source: Federal Transit Administration, National Transit Database, 2021

Air Transportation

Airport Name and Code / Type of Service	Passenger Airlines[1]	Passenger Enplanements	Freight Carriers[2]	Freight (lbs)
Fort Wayne International (FWA)				
Domestic service (U.S. carriers - 2022)	11	359,786	9	25,146,721
International service (U.S. carriers - 2021)	0	0	2	18,831

Note: (1) Includes all U.S.-based major, minor and commuter airlines that carried at least one passenger during the year; (2) Includes all U.S.-based airlines and freight carriers that transported at least one pound of freight during the year.
Source: Bureau of Transportation Statistics, The Intermodal Transportation Database, Air Carriers: T-100 Domestic Market (U.S. Carriers), 2022; Bureau of Transportation Statistics, The Intermodal Transportation Database, Air Carriers: T-100 International Market (U.S. Carriers), 2021

BUSINESSES

Major Business Headquarters

Company Name	Industry	Rankings Fortune[1]	Forbes[2]
Steel Dynamics	Metals	196	-

Note: (1) Companies that produce a 10-K are ranked 1 to 500 based on 2021 revenue; (2) All private companies with at least $2 billion in annual revenue through the end of their most current fiscal year are ranked 1 to 246; companies listed are headquartered in the city; dashes indicate no ranking
Source: Fortune, "Fortune 500," 2022; Forbes, "America's Largest Private Companies," 2022

Living Environment

COST OF LIVING

Cost of Living Index

Composite Index	Groceries	Housing	Utilities	Trans-portation	Health Care	Misc. Goods/ Services
89.3	95.2	70.8	98.2	100.7	103.3	94.7

Note: The Cost of Living Index measures regional differences in the cost of consumer goods and services, excluding taxes and non-consumer expenditures, for professional and managerial households in the top income quintile. It is based on more than 50,000 prices covering almost 60 different items for which prices are collected three times a year by chambers of commerce, economic development organizations or university applied economic centers in each participating urban area. The numbers shown should be read as a percentage above or below the national average of 100. For example, a value of 115.4 in the groceries column indicates that grocery prices are 15.4% higher than the national average. Small differences in the index numbers should not be interpreted as significant; Figures cover the Fort Wayne-Allen County IN urban area.
Source: The Council for Community and Economic Research, Cost of Living Index, 2022

Grocery Prices

Area[1]	T-Bone Steak ($/pound)	Frying Chicken ($/pound)	Whole Milk ($/half gal.)	Eggs ($/dozen)	Orange Juice ($/64 oz.)	Coffee ($/11.5 oz.)
City[2]	12.91	1.22	2.46	1.84	3.53	4.98
Avg.	13.81	1.59	2.43	2.25	3.85	4.95
Min.	10.17	0.90	1.51	1.30	2.90	3.46
Max.	19.35	3.30	4.32	4.32	5.31	8.59

*Note: (1) Values for the local area are compared with the average, minimum and maximum values for all 286 areas in the Cost of Living Index; (2) Figures cover the Fort Wayne-Allen County IN urban area; **T-Bone Steak** (price per pound); **Frying Chicken** (price per pound, whole fryer); **Whole Milk** (half gallon carton); **Eggs** (price per dozen, Grade A, large); **Orange Juice** (64 oz. Tropicana or Florida Natural); **Coffee** (11.5 oz. can, vacuum-packed, Maxwell House, Hills Bros, or Folgers).*
Source: The Council for Community and Economic Research, Cost of Living Index, 2022

Housing and Utility Costs

Area[1]	New Home Price ($)	Apartment Rent ($/month)	All Electric ($/month)	Part Electric ($/month)	Other Energy ($/month)	Telephone ($/month)
City[2]	296,241	1,083	-	105.04	65.35	191.60
Avg.	450,913	1,371	176.41	99.93	76.96	190.22
Min.	229,283	546	100.84	31.56	27.15	174.27
Max.	2,434,977	4,569	356.86	249.59	272.24	208.31

*Note: (1) Values for the local area are compared with the average, minimum and maximum values for all 286 areas in the Cost of Living Index; (2) Figures cover the Fort Wayne-Allen County IN urban area; **New Home Price** (2,400 sf living area, 8,000 sf lot, in urban area with full utilities); **Apartment Rent** (950 sf 2 bedroom/1.5 or 2 bath, unfurnished, excluding all utilities except water); **All Electric** (average monthly cost for an all-electric home); **Part Electric** (average monthly cost for a part-electric home); **Other Energy** (average monthly cost for natural gas, fuel oil, coal, wood, and any other forms of energy except electricity); **Telephone** (price includes the base monthly rate plus taxes and fees for three lines of mobile phone service).*
Source: The Council for Community and Economic Research, Cost of Living Index, 2022

Health Care, Transportation, and Other Costs

Area[1]	Doctor ($/visit)	Dentist ($/visit)	Optometrist ($/visit)	Gasoline ($/gallon)	Beauty Salon ($/visit)	Men's Shirt ($)
City[2]	140.00	105.42	88.55	3.70	34.67	39.66
Avg.	124.91	107.77	117.66	3.86	43.31	34.21
Min.	36.61	58.25	51.79	2.90	22.18	13.05
Max.	250.21	162.58	371.96	5.54	85.61	63.54

*Note: (1) Values for the local area are compared with the average, minimum and maximum values for all 286 areas in the Cost of Living Index; (2) Figures cover the Fort Wayne-Allen County IN urban area; **Doctor** (general practitioners routine exam of an established patient); **Dentist** (adult teeth cleaning and periodic oral examination); **Optometrist** (full vision eye exam for established adult patient); **Gasoline** (one gallon regular unleaded, national brand, including all taxes, cash price at self-service pump if available); **Beauty Salon** (woman's shampoo, trim, and blow-dry); **Men's Shirt** (cotton/polyester dress shirt, pinpoint weave, long sleeves).*
Source: The Council for Community and Economic Research, Cost of Living Index, 2022

HOUSING

Homeownership Rate

Area	2015 (%)	2016 (%)	2017 (%)	2018 (%)	2019 (%)	2020 (%)	2021 (%)	2022 (%)
MSA[1]	n/a	n/a	n/a	n/a	n/a	n/a	n/a	n/a
U.S.	63.7	63.4	63.9	64.4	64.6	66.6	65.5	65.8

Note: (1) Figures cover the Fort Wayne, IN Metropolitan Statistical Area; n/a not available
Source: U.S. Census Bureau, Housing Vacancies and Homeownership Annual Statistics: 2015-2022

House Price Index (HPI)

Area	National Ranking[2]	Quarterly Change (%)	One-Year Change (%)	Five-Year Change (%)	Since 1991Q1 (%)
MSA[1]	68	1.56	14.01	67.52	186.04
U.S.[3]	—	0.34	8.41	58.44	289.08

Note: The HPI is a weighted repeat sales index. It measures average price changes in repeat sales or refinancings on the same properties. This information is obtained by reviewing repeat mortgage transactions on single-family properties whose mortgages have been purchased or securitized by Fannie Mae or Freddie Mac since January 1975; (1) Figures cover the Fort Wayne, IN Metropolitan Statistical Area; (2) Rankings are based on annual percentage change for all metro areas containing at least 15,000 transactions over the last 10 years and ranges from 1 to 257; (3) figures based on a weighted average of Census Division estimates using a seasonally adjusted, purchase-only index; all figures are for the period ending December 31, 2022
Source: Federal Housing Finance Agency, Change in FHFA Metropolitan Area House Price Indexes, 2022Q4

Median Single-Family Home Prices

Area	2020	2021	2022[p]	Percent Change 2021 to 2022
MSA[1]	169.3	189.9	214.1	12.7
U.S. Average	300.2	357.1	392.6	9.9

Note: Figures are median sales prices of existing single-family homes in thousands of dollars; (p) preliminary; (1) Figures cover the Fort Wayne, IN Metropolitan Statistical Area
Source: National Association of Realtors, Median Sales Price of Existing Single-Family Homes for Metropolitan Areas, 4th Quarter 2022

Qualifying Income Based on Median Sales Price of Existing Single-Family Homes

Area	With 5% Down ($)	With 10% Down ($)	With 20% Down ($)
MSA[1]	64,474	61,081	54,294
U.S. Average	112,234	106,237	94,513

Note: Figures are preliminary; Qualifying income is based on a mortgage rate of 6.77%. Monthly principal and interest payment is limited to 25% of income; (1) Figures cover the Fort Wayne, IN Metropolitan Statistical Area
Source: National Association of Realtors, Qualifying Income Based on Median Sales Price of Existing Single-Family Homes for Metropolitan Areas, 4th Quarter 2022

Home Value

Area	Under $100,000	$100,000 -$199,999	$200,000 -$299,999	$300,000 -$399,999	$400,000 -$499,999	$500,000 -$999,999	$1,000,000 or more	Median ($)
City	32.7	46.5	14.2	4.0	1.2	1.1	0.2	130,700
MSA[1]	26.2	42.9	18.0	6.8	2.7	2.8	0.5	150,600
U.S.	16.2	24.2	20.1	13.6	8.3	13.6	4.1	244,900

Note: Figures are percentages except for median and cover owner-occupied housing units; (1) Figures cover the Fort Wayne, IN Metropolitan Statistical Area
Source: U.S. Census Bureau, 2017-2021 American Community Survey 5-Year Estimates

Year Housing Structure Built

Area	2020 or Later	2010 -2019	2000 -2009	1990 -1999	1980 -1989	1970 -1979	1960 -1969	1950 -1959	1940 -1949	Before 1940	Median Year
City	0.1	2.2	6.7	13.6	11.5	17.5	14.9	12.8	6.5	14.2	1971
MSA[1]	0.2	5.9	11.5	14.3	10.4	15.3	12.4	11.0	5.4	13.7	1975
U.S.	0.2	7.3	13.6	13.6	13.2	14.8	10.3	10.0	4.7	12.2	1979

Note: Figures are percentages except for Median Year; Note: (1) Figures cover the Fort Wayne, IN Metropolitan Statistical Area
Source: U.S. Census Bureau, 2017-2021 American Community Survey 5-Year Estimates

Gross Monthly Rent

Area	Under $500	$500 -$999	$1,000 -$1,499	$1,500 -$1,999	$2,000 -$2,499	$2,500 -$2,999	$3,000 and up	Median ($)
City	9.5	63.9	22.8	3.0	0.4	0.2	0.2	823
MSA[1]	8.9	62.4	23.7	4.1	0.6	0.2	0.2	839
U.S.	8.1	30.5	30.8	16.8	7.3	3.1	3.5	1,163

Note: Figures are percentages except for median; Gross rent is the contract rent plus the estimated average monthly cost of utilities (electricity, gas, and water and sewer) and fuels (oil, coal, kerosene, wood, etc.) if these are paid by the renter (or paid for the renter by someone else); (1) Figures cover the Fort Wayne, IN Metropolitan Statistical Area
Source: U.S. Census Bureau, 2017-2021 American Community Survey 5-Year Estimates

HEALTH

Health Risk Factors

Category	MSA[1] (%)	U.S. (%)
Adults aged 18–64 who have any kind of health care coverage	93.2	90.9
Adults who reported being in good or better health	83.5	85.2
Adults who have been told they have high blood cholesterol	35.0	35.7
Adults who have been told they have high blood pressure	34.1	32.4
Adults who are current smokers	16.2	14.4
Adults who currently use e-cigarettes	7.2	6.7
Adults who currently use chewing tobacco, snuff, or snus	3.0	3.5
Adults who are heavy drinkers[2]	6.9	6.3
Adults who are binge drinkers[3]	14.2	15.4
Adults who are overweight (BMI 25.0 - 29.9)	33.3	34.4
Adults who are obese (BMI 30.0 - 99.8)	37.0	33.9
Adults who participated in any physical activities in the past month	75.8	76.3

Note: (1) Figures cover the Fort Wayne, IN Metropolitan Statistical Area; (2) Heavy drinkers are classified as adult men having more than 14 drinks per week and adult women having more than 7 drinks per week; (3) Binge drinkers are classified as males having five or more drinks on one occasion or females having four or more drinks on one occasion
Source: Centers for Disease Control and Prevention, Behaviorial Risk Factor Surveillance System, SMART: Selected Metropolitan Area Risk Trends, 2021

Acute and Chronic Health Conditions

Category	MSA[1] (%)	U.S. (%)
Adults who have ever been told they had a heart attack	5.1	4.0
Adults who have ever been told they have angina or coronary heart disease	5.0	3.8
Adults who have ever been told they had a stroke	3.5	3.0
Adults who have ever been told they have asthma	21.2	14.9
Adults who have ever been told they have arthritis	26.9	25.8
Adults who have ever been told they have diabetes[2]	13.9	10.9
Adults who have ever been told they had skin cancer	6.8	6.6
Adults who have ever been told they had any other types of cancer	6.8	7.5
Adults who have ever been told they have COPD	7.6	6.1
Adults who have ever been told they have kidney disease	3.1	3.0
Adults who have ever been told they have a form of depression	20.6	20.5

Note: (1) Figures cover the Fort Wayne, IN Metropolitan Statistical Area; (2) Figures do not include pregnancy-related, borderline, or pre-diabetes
Source: Centers for Disease Control and Prevention, Behaviorial Risk Factor Surveillance System, SMART: Selected Metropolitan Area Risk Trends, 2021

Health Screening and Vaccination Rates

Category	MSA[1] (%)	U.S. (%)
Adults who have ever been tested for HIV	32.7	34.9
Adults who have had their blood cholesterol checked within the last five years	79.3	85.2
Adults aged 65+ who have had flu shot within the past year	57.8	68.6
Adults aged 65+ who have ever had a pneumonia vaccination	73.0	71.0

Note: (1) Figures cover the Fort Wayne, IN Metropolitan Statistical Area.
Source: Centers for Disease Control and Prevention, Behaviorial Risk Factor Surveillance System, SMART: Selected Metropolitan Area Risk Trends, 2021

Disability Status

Category	MSA[1] (%)	U.S. (%)
Adults who reported being deaf	7.0	7.2
Are you blind or have serious difficulty seeing, even when wearing glasses?	3.2	4.8
Are you limited in any way in any of your usual activities due to arthritis?	11.4	11.1
Do you have difficulty doing errands alone?	9.7	7.0
Do you have difficulty dressing or bathing?	2.7	3.6
Do you have serious difficulty concentrating/remembering/making decisions?	11.3	12.1
Do you have serious difficulty walking or climbing stairs?	13.5	12.8

Note: (1) Figures cover the Fort Wayne, IN Metropolitan Statistical Area.
Source: Centers for Disease Control and Prevention, Behaviorial Risk Factor Surveillance System, SMART: Selected Metropolitan Area Risk Trends, 2021

Mortality Rates for the Top 10 Causes of Death in the U.S.

ICD-10[a] Sub-Chapter	ICD-10[a] Code	Crude Mortality Rate[1] per 100,000 population	
		County[2]	U.S.
Malignant neoplasms	C00-C97	182.9	182.6
Ischaemic heart diseases	I20-I25	95.7	113.1
Other forms of heart disease	I30-I51	54.1	64.4
Other degenerative diseases of the nervous system	G30-G31	41.3	51.0
Cerebrovascular diseases	I60-I69	48.5	47.8
Other external causes of accidental injury	W00-X59	54.2	46.4
Chronic lower respiratory diseases	J40-J47	56.4	45.7
Organic, including symptomatic, mental disorders	F01-F09	49.3	35.9
Hypertensive diseases	I10-I15	47.4	35.0
Diabetes mellitus	E10-E14	41.3	29.6

Note: (a) ICD-10 = International Classification of Diseases 10th Revision; (1) Crude mortality rates are a three-year average covering 2019-2021; (2) Figures cover Allen County.
Source: Centers for Disease Control and Prevention, National Center for Health Statistics. National Vital Statistics System, Mortality 2018-2021 on CDC WONDER Online Database

Mortality Rates for Selected Causes of Death

ICD-10[a] Sub-Chapter	ICD-10[a] Code	Crude Mortality Rate[1] per 100,000 population	
		County[2]	U.S.
Assault	X85-Y09	10.3	7.0
Diseases of the liver	K70-K76	19.3	19.8
Human immunodeficiency virus (HIV) disease	B20-B24	Unreliable	1.5
Influenza and pneumonia	J09-J18	10.3	14.7
Intentional self-harm	X60-X84	13.8	14.3
Malnutrition	E40-E46	3.8	4.3
Obesity and other hyperalimentation	E65-E68	1.8	3.0
Renal failure	N17-N19	16.7	15.7
Transport accidents	V01-V99	11.1	13.6
Viral hepatitis	B15-B19	Unreliable	1.2

Note: (a) ICD-10 = International Classification of Diseases 10th Revision; (1) Crude mortality rates are a three-year average covering 2019-2021; (2) Figures cover Allen County; Data are suppressed when the data meet the criteria for confidentiality constraints; Crude mortality rates are flagged as unreliable when the rate would be calculated with a numerator of 20 or less.
Source: Centers for Disease Control and Prevention, National Center for Health Statistics. National Vital Statistics System, Mortality 2018-2021 on CDC WONDER Online Database

Health Insurance Coverage

Area	With Health Insurance	With Private Health Insurance	With Public Health Insurance	Without Health Insurance	Population Under Age 19 Without Health Insurance
City	90.8	64.6	37.0	9.2	6.2
MSA[1]	91.9	69.8	33.3	8.1	6.1
U.S.	91.2	67.8	35.4	8.8	5.3

Note: Figures are percentages that cover the civilian noninstitutionalized population; (1) Figures cover the Fort Wayne, IN Metropolitan Statistical Area
Source: U.S. Census Bureau, 2017-2021 American Community Survey 5-Year Estimates

Number of Medical Professionals

Area	MDs[3]	DOs[3,4]	Dentists	Podiatrists	Chiropractors	Optometrists
County[1] (number)	1,015	113	260	23	91	101
County[1] (rate[2])	263.0	29.3	66.9	5.9	23.4	26.0
U.S. (rate[2])	289.3	23.5	72.5	6.2	28.7	17.4

Note: Data as of 2021 unless noted; (1) Data covers Allen County; (2) Rate per 100,000 population; (3) Data as of 2020 and includes all active, non-federal physicians; (4) Doctor of Osteopathic Medicine
Source: U.S. Department of Health and Human Services, Health Resources and Services Administration, Bureau of Health Professions, Area Resource File (ARF) 2021-2022

EDUCATION

Public School District Statistics

District Name	Schls	Pupils	Pupil/ Teacher Ratio	Minority Pupils[1] (%)	LEP/ELL[2] (%)	IEP[3] (%)
Fort Wayne Community Schools	50	28,778	14.9	61.9	10.1	19.5
M S D Southwest Allen Co. Schls	10	7,800	16.3	24.3	1.0	9.9
Northwest Allen County Schools	12	7,955	16.8	19.1	2.0	15.4

Note: Table includes school districts with 2,000 or more students; (1) Percentage of students that are not non-Hispanic white; (2) Percentage of students that are Limited English Proficient or English Language Learners (2018-19); (3) Percentage of students that have an Individualized Education Program (2019-20).
Source: U.S. Department of Education, National Center for Education Statistics, Common Core of Data, Local Education Agency (School District) Universe Survey: School Year 2021-2022

Highest Level of Education

Area	Less than H.S.	H.S. Diploma	Some College, No Deg.	Associate Degree	Bachelor's Degree	Master's Degree	Prof. School Degree	Doctorate Degree
City	11.1	28.9	21.9	10.1	19.0	7.1	1.1	0.8
MSA[1]	9.8	29.0	21.0	11.0	19.8	7.1	1.5	1.0
U.S.	11.1	26.5	20.0	8.7	20.6	9.3	2.2	1.5

Note: Figures cover persons age 25 and over; (1) Figures cover the Fort Wayne, IN Metropolitan Statistical Area
Source: U.S. Census Bureau, 2017-2021 American Community Survey 5-Year Estimates

Educational Attainment by Race

Area	High School Graduate or Higher (%)					Bachelor's Degree or Higher (%)				
	Total	White	Black	Asian	Hisp.[2]	Total	White	Black	Asian	Hisp.[2]
City	88.9	93.5	85.4	47.6	63.7	28.0	31.6	15.3	21.6	11.6
MSA[1]	90.2	93.3	86.0	55.8	66.3	29.3	31.4	16.4	30.4	12.5
U.S.	88.9	91.4	87.2	87.6	71.2	33.7	35.5	23.3	55.6	18.4

Note: Figures shown cover persons 25 years old and over; (1) Figures cover the Fort Wayne, IN Metropolitan Statistical Area; (2) People of Hispanic origin can be of any race
Source: U.S. Census Bureau, 2017-2021 American Community Survey 5-Year Estimates

School Enrollment by Grade and Control

Area	Preschool (%)		Kindergarten (%)		Grades 1 - 4 (%)		Grades 5 - 8 (%)		Grades 9 - 12 (%)	
	Public	Private	Public	Private	Public	Private	Public	Private	Public	Private
City	50.8	49.2	76.9	23.1	79.4	20.6	82.2	17.8	79.9	20.1
MSA[1]	46.6	53.4	75.5	24.5	76.6	23.4	77.4	22.6	80.7	19.3
U.S.	58.8	41.2	86.3	13.7	88.3	11.7	88.6	11.4	89.4	10.6

Note: Figures shown cover persons 3 years old and over; (1) Figures cover the Fort Wayne, IN Metropolitan Statistical Area
Source: U.S. Census Bureau, 2017-2021 American Community Survey 5-Year Estimates

Higher Education

Four-Year Colleges			Two-Year Colleges			Medical Schools[1]	Law Schools[2]	Voc/ Tech[3]
Public	Private Non-profit	Private For-profit	Public	Private Non-profit	Private For-profit			
1	5	0	0	0	1	0	0	2

Note: Figures cover institutions located within the Fort Wayne, IN Metropolitan Statistical Area and include main campuses only; (1) includes schools accredited by the Liaison Committee on Medical Education and the American Osteopathic Association's Commission on Osteopathic College Accreditation; (2) includes ABA-accredited schools, schools with provisional ABA accreditation, and state accredited schools; (3) includes all schools with programs that are less than 2 years.
Source: National Center for Education Statistics, Integrated Postsecondary Education System (IPEDS), 2021-22; Wikipedia, List of Medical Schools in the United States, accessed April 10, 2023; Wikipedia, List of Law Schools in the United States, accessed April 10, 2023

EMPLOYERS

Major Employers

Company Name	Industry
Allen County Government	Government
BAE Systems Platform Solutions	Aircraft electronics
Benchmark Human Services	Services for people with disabilities
BFGoodrich	Rubber tire manufacturing
City of Fort Wayne	Municipal government
Dana Corp.	Motor vehicle parts manufacturing
Edy's Grand Ice Cream	Ice cream & other frozen treats
Fort Wayne Community Schools	Elementary & secondary schools
Fort Wayne Metals Research Products Corp.	Wire for medical devices
Frontier Communications Corp.	Wired telecommunications carriers
General Motors	Motor vehicle manufacturing
Harris Corporation	Wireless networking systems & satellite imaging systems
IPFW	University
Ivy Tech Community College- Northeast	Community college
Lincoln Financial Group	Insurance carriers
Lutheran Health Network	General medical & surgical hospitals
Norfolk Southern Corp2	Rail transportation
Northwest Allen County Schools	Elementary & secondary schools
Parker Hannifin Corporation	Metal product manufacturing for a/c systems
Parkview Health Systems	General medical & surgical hospitals
Raytheon Systems Co.	Mission solutions for aerospace industry
Shambaugh & Son	Commercial building construction
Steel Dynamics1	Corporate headquarters & scrap metal processing
Sweetwater Sound	Sound recording studio & equipment distribution
Vera Bradley	Handbags, luggage, & accessories

Note: Companies shown are located within the Fort Wayne, IN Metropolitan Statistical Area.
Source: Hoovers.com; Wikipedia

PUBLIC SAFETY

Crime Rate

Area	Total Crime	Violent Crime Rate				Property Crime Rate		
		Murder	Rape[3]	Robbery	Aggrav. Assault	Burglary	Larceny -Theft	Motor Vehicle Theft
City	2,659.5	14.3	35.6	90.0	272.9	240.6	1,818.8	187.3
Suburbs[1]	988.4	1.4	22.3	16.7	146.5	136.7	579.0	85.8
Metro[2]	2,083.1	9.9	31.0	64.7	229.3	204.7	1,391.1	152.3
U.S.	2,356.7	6.5	38.4	73.9	279.7	314.2	1,398.0	246.0

Note: Figures are crimes per 100,000 population; (1) All areas within the metro area that are located outside the city limits; (2) Figures cover the Fort Wayne, IN Metropolitan Statistical Area; (3) All figures shown were reported using the revised Uniform Crime Reporting (UCR) definition of rape; Due to the transition to the National Incident-Based Reporting System (NIBRS), limited city and metro area data was released for 2021.
Source: FBI Uniform Crime Reports, 2020

Hate Crimes

Area	Number of Quarters Reported	Number of Incidents per Bias Motivation					
		Race/Ethnicity/ Ancestry	Religion	Sexual Orientation	Disability	Gender	Gender Identity
City	3	5	1	2	0	0	0
U.S.	4	5,227	1,244	1,110	130	75	266

Note: Due to the transition to the National Incident-Based Reporting System (NIBRS), limited crime data was released for 2021.
Source: Federal Bureau of Investigation, Hate Crime Statistics 2020

Identity Theft Consumer Reports

Area	Reports	Reports per 100,000 Population	Rank[2]
MSA[1]	872	213	149
U.S.	1,108,609	339	-

Note: (1) Figures cover the Fort Wayne, IN Metropolitan Statistical Area; (2) Rank ranges from 1 to 391 where 1 indicates greatest number of identity theft reports per 100,000 population
Source: Federal Trade Commission, Consumer Sentinel Network Data Book 2022

Fraud and Other Consumer Reports

Area	Reports	Reports per 100,000 Population	Rank[2]
MSA[1]	3,737	913	139
U.S.	4,064,520	1,245	-

Note: (1) Figures cover the Fort Wayne, IN Metropolitan Statistical Area; (2) Rank ranges from 1 to 391 where 1 indicates greatest number of fraud and other consumer reports per 100,000 population
Source: Federal Trade Commission, Consumer Sentinel Network Data Book 2022

POLITICS

2020 Presidential Election Results

Area	Biden	Trump	Jorgensen	Hawkins	Other
Allen County	43.2	54.3	2.2	0.0	0.3
U.S.	51.3	46.8	1.2	0.3	0.5

Note: Results are percentages and may not add to 100% due to rounding
Source: Dave Leip's Atlas of U.S. Presidential Elections

SPORTS

Professional Sports Teams

Team Name	League	Year Established

No teams are located in the metro area
Source: Wikipedia, Major Professional Sports Teams of the United States and Canada, April 12, 2023

CLIMATE

Average and Extreme Temperatures

Temperature	Jan	Feb	Mar	Apr	May	Jun	Jul	Aug	Sep	Oct	Nov	Dec	Yr.
Extreme High (°F)	69	69	82	88	94	106	103	101	100	90	79	71	106
Average High (°F)	31	35	46	60	71	81	84	82	76	64	49	36	60
Average Temp. (°F)	24	27	37	49	60	70	74	72	65	53	41	29	50
Average Low (°F)	16	19	28	39	49	59	63	61	53	42	32	22	40
Extreme Low (°F)	-22	-18	-10	7	27	38	44	38	29	19	-1	-18	-22

Note: Figures cover the years 1948-1990
Source: National Climatic Data Center, International Station Meteorological Climate Summary, 9/96

Average Precipitation/Snowfall/Humidity

Precip./Humidity	Jan	Feb	Mar	Apr	May	Jun	Jul	Aug	Sep	Oct	Nov	Dec	Yr.
Avg. Precip. (in.)	2.3	2.1	2.9	3.4	3.6	3.8	3.6	3.4	2.6	2.7	2.8	2.7	35.9
Avg. Snowfall (in.)	8	8	5	2	Tr	0	0	0	0	Tr	3	7	33
Avg. Rel. Hum. 7am (%)	81	81	80	77	76	78	81	86	86	84	83	83	81
Avg. Rel. Hum. 4pm (%)	71	68	62	54	52	52	53	55	53	55	67	74	59

Note: Figures cover the years 1948-1990; Tr = Trace amounts (<0.05 in. of rain; <0.5 in. of snow)
Source: National Climatic Data Center, International Station Meteorological Climate Summary, 9/96

Weather Conditions

Temperature			Daytime Sky			Precipitation		
5°F & below	32°F & below	90°F & above	Clear	Partly cloudy	Cloudy	0.01 inch or more precip.	0.1 inch or more snow/ice	Thunder-storms
16	131	16	75	140	150	131	31	39

Note: Figures are average number of days per year and cover the years 1948-1990
Source: National Climatic Data Center, International Station Meteorological Climate Summary, 9/96

HAZARDOUS WASTE

Superfund Sites

The Fort Wayne, IN metro area is home to one site on the EPA's Superfund National Priorities List: **Fort Wayne Reduction Dump** (final). There are a total of 1,165 Superfund sites with a status of proposed or final on the list in the U.S. *U.S. Environmental Protection Agency, National Priorities List, April 12, 2023*

AIR QUALITY

Air Quality Trends: Ozone

	1990	1995	2000	2005	2010	2015	2018	2019	2020	2021
MSA[1]	0.086	0.094	0.086	0.081	0.067	0.061	0.071	0.063	0.064	0.062
U.S.	0.087	0.089	0.081	0.080	0.072	0.067	0.069	0.065	0.065	0.067

Note: (1) Data covers the Fort Wayne, IN Metropolitan Statistical Area. The values shown are the composite ozone concentration averages among trend sites based on the highest fourth daily maximum 8-hour concentration in parts per million. These trends are based on sites having an adequate record of monitoring data during the trend period. Data from exceptional events are included.
Source: U.S. Environmental Protection Agency, Air Quality Monitoring Information, "Air Quality Trends by City, 1990-2021"

Air Quality Index

Area	Percent of Days when Air Quality was...[2]					AQI Statistics[2]	
	Good	Moderate	Unhealthy for Sensitive Groups	Unhealthy	Very Unhealthy	Maximum	Median
MSA[1]	70.7	29.3	0.0	0.0	0.0	100	41

Note: (1) Data covers the Fort Wayne, IN Metropolitan Statistical Area; (2) Based on 365 days with AQI data in 2021. Air Quality Index (AQI) is an index for reporting daily air quality. EPA calculates the AQI for five major air pollutants regulated by the Clean Air Act: ground-level ozone, particle pollution (aka particulate matter), carbon monoxide, sulfur dioxide, and nitrogen dioxide. The AQI runs from 0 to 500. The higher the AQI value, the greater the level of air pollution and the greater the health concern. There are six AQI categories: "Good" AQI is between 0 and 50. Air quality is considered satisfactory; "Moderate" AQI is between 51 and 100. Air quality is acceptable; "Unhealthy for Sensitive Groups" When AQI values are between 101 and 150, members of sensitive groups may experience health effects; "Unhealthy" When AQI values are between 151 and 200 everyone may begin to experience health effects; "Very Unhealthy" AQI values between 201 and 300 trigger a health alert; "Hazardous" AQI values over 300 trigger warnings of emergency conditions (not shown).
Source: U.S. Environmental Protection Agency, Air Quality Index Report, 2021

Air Quality Index Pollutants

Area	Percent of Days when AQI Pollutant was...[2]					
	Carbon Monoxide	Nitrogen Dioxide	Ozone	Sulfur Dioxide	Particulate Matter 2.5	Particulate Matter 10
MSA[1]	0.0	0.0	51.0	(3)	49.0	0.0

Note: (1) Data covers the Fort Wayne, IN Metropolitan Statistical Area; (2) Based on 365 days with AQI data in 2021. The Air Quality Index (AQI) is an index for reporting daily air quality. EPA calculates the AQI for five major air pollutants regulated by the Clean Air Act: ground-level ozone, particle pollution (also known as particulate matter), carbon monoxide, sulfur dioxide, and nitrogen dioxide. The AQI runs from 0 to 500. The higher the AQI value, the greater the level of air pollution and the greater the health concern; (3) Sulfur dioxide is no longer included in this table (as of December 8, 2021) because SO_2 concentrations tend to be very localized and not necessarily representative of broad geographical areas like counties and CBSAs.
Source: U.S. Environmental Protection Agency, Air Quality Index Report, 2021

Maximum Air Pollutant Concentrations: Particulate Matter, Ozone, CO and Lead

	Particulate Matter 10 (ug/m^3)	Particulate Matter 2.5 Wtd AM (ug/m^3)	Particulate Matter 2.5 24-Hr (ug/m^3)	Ozone (ppm)	Carbon Monoxide (ppm)	Lead (ug/m^3)
MSA[1] Level	n/a	9	21	0.065	n/a	n/a
NAAQS[2]	150	15	35	0.075	9	0.15
Met NAAQS[2]	n/a	Yes	Yes	Yes	n/a	n/a

Note: (1) Data covers the Fort Wayne, IN Metropolitan Statistical Area; Data from exceptional events are included; (2) National Ambient Air Quality Standards; ppm = parts per million; ug/m^3 = micrograms per cubic meter; n/a not available.
Concentrations: Particulate Matter 10 (coarse particulate)—highest second maximum 24-hour concentration; Particulate Matter 2.5 Wtd AM (fine particulate)—highest weighted annual mean concentration; Particulate Matter 2.5 24-Hour (fine particulate)—highest 98th percentile 24-hour concentration; Ozone—highest fourth daily maximum 8-hour concentration; Carbon Monoxide—highest second maximum non-overlapping 8-hour concentration; Lead—maximum running 3-month average
Source: U.S. Environmental Protection Agency, Air Quality Monitoring Information, "Air Quality Statistics by City, 2021"

Maximum Air Pollutant Concentrations: Nitrogen Dioxide and Sulfur Dioxide

	Nitrogen Dioxide AM (ppb)	Nitrogen Dioxide 1-Hr (ppb)	Sulfur Dioxide AM (ppb)	Sulfur Dioxide 1-Hr (ppb)	Sulfur Dioxide 24-Hr (ppb)
MSA[1] Level	n/a	n/a	n/a	n/a	n/a
NAAQS[2]	53	100	30	75	140
Met NAAQS[2]	n/a	n/a	n/a	n/a	n/a

Note: (1) Data covers the Fort Wayne, IN Metropolitan Statistical Area; Data from exceptional events are included; (2) National Ambient Air Quality Standards; ppm = parts per million; ug/m^3 = micrograms per cubic meter; n/a not available.
Concentrations: Nitrogen Dioxide AM—highest arithmetic mean concentration; Nitrogen Dioxide 1-Hr—highest 98th percentile 1-hour daily maximum concentration; Sulfur Dioxide AM—highest annual mean concentration; Sulfur Dioxide 1-Hr—highest 99th percentile 1-hour daily maximum concentration; Sulfur Dioxide 24-Hr—highest second maximum 24-hour concentration
Source: U.S. Environmental Protection Agency, Air Quality Monitoring Information, "Air Quality Statistics by City, 2021"

Grand Rapids, Michigan

Background

The city of Grand Rapids is in the west-central part of Kent County in the picturesque Grand River Valley, about 30 miles east of Lake Michigan. It is known for its fine furniture making.

The presence of an abundant forest, as well as the hydropower and trade afforded by a powerful river, contributed to the reputation of a manufacturing industry that is known worldwide, producing not only furniture, but industrial machinery, metal, paper, plastics, and printing products. Food and information technology industries are also important to the economy of the city. There are 14 universities and colleges in Grand Rapids. In 1945, Grand Rapids became the first city in the United States to add fluoride to its drinking water.

Before Grand Rapids became involved in making seating for churches, buses, and schools, among other furniture, the site was a Native American settlement of the Ottawa, Chippewa, and Potawatomi tribes. The earliest white settlers in the area were fur traders who bought pelts from the Native American tribes in the early nineteenth century. One by one, more white settlers found their way into the area on the rapids of the Grand River. A Baptist mission was established in 1825, and a year after that, Louis Campau erected a trading post. In 1833, the area's first permanent white settlement appeared, led by Samuel Dexter of Herkimer County, New York.

Revitalization efforts have resulted in a thriving downtown district that includes restaurants, hotels, clubs, museums, and the 12,000-square foot Van Andel Arena. The DeVos Place Convention Center boasts a 162,000-square foot, column-free exhibit hall, 40,000-square foot ballroom, 26 individual meeting rooms, and 2,404-seat performing arts theater that is home to the Grand Rapids Symphony, the Grand Rapids Ballet Company, Opera Grand Rapids, and Broadway Grand Rapids.

The city's other attractions include a yearly Festival of the Arts held in June and featuring visual, performing, and culinary arts, and an annual jazz festival. Celebration on the Grand salutes summer with free concerts, West Michigan's largest fireworks display and food booths. The annual Fulton Street Farmers Market has been held since 1922 and offers locally grown produce and handmade items.

The Frederik Meijer Gardens and Sculpture Park blends art and nature, maintaining outdoor (125 acres) and indoor exhibits. Each spring, visitors marvel at the thousands of butterflies, brought from all over the world and released into the Park's tropical conservatory.

Children enjoy the John Ball Zoo as well as the Grand Rapids Children's Museum, which offers a wide range of entertainment and educational programs.

Fall is a very colorful time of year in western Michigan, perhaps compensating for the late spring. During the winter, excessive cloudiness and numerous snow flurries occur with strong westerly winds. Lake Michigan has a tempering effect on winter cold waves coming in from the west. Prolonged, severe cold waves are infrequent. The snowfall season extends from mid-November to mid-March and some winters have had continuous snow cover throughout this period.

Rankings

General Rankings

- *US News & World Report* conducted a survey of more than 3,600 people and analyzed the 150 largest metropolitan areas to determine what matters most when selecting where to settle down. Grand Rapids ranked #16 out of the top 25 as having the best combination of desirable factors. Criteria: cost of living; quality of life and education; net migration; job market; desirability; and other factors. *money.usnews.com, "The 25 Best Places to Live in the U.S. in 2022-2023," May 17, 2022*

- The Grand Rapids metro area was identified as one of America's fastest-growing areas in terms of population and business growth by *MagnifyMoney*. The area ranked #27 out of 35. The 100 most populous metro areas in the U.S. were evaluated on their change from 2011 to 2016 in the following categories: people and housing; workforce and employment opportunities; growing industry. *www.businessinsider.com, "The 35 Cities in the US with the Biggest Influx of People, the Most Work Opportunities, and the Hottest Business Growth," August 12, 2018*

- The Grand Rapids metro area was identified as one of America's fastest-growing areas in terms of population and economy by *Forbes*. The area ranked #25 out of 25. The 100 most populous metro areas in the U.S. were evaluated on the following criteria: estimated population growth; employment; economic output; wages; home values. *Forbes, "America's Fastest-Growing Cities 2018," February 28, 2018*

- In their ninth annual survey, Livability.com looked at data for more than 2,300 mid-sized U.S. cities to determine the rankings for Livability's "Top 100 Best Places to Live" in 2022. Grand Rapids ranked #47. Criteria: housing and economy; social and civic engagement; education; demographics; health care options; transportation & infrastructure; and community amenities. *Livability.com, "Top 100 Best Places to Live 2022" July 19, 2022*

Business/Finance Rankings

- The Brookings Institution ranked the nation's largest cities based on income inequality. Grand Rapids was ranked #85 (#1 = greatest inequality). Criteria: the "95/20 ratio," a figure representing the income at which a household earns more than 95 percent of all other households, divided by the income at which a household earns more than only 20 percent of all other households. *Brookings Institution, "Household Income Inequality, Largest Cities of 97 Large U.S. Metro Areas, 2014-2016," February 5, 2018*

- The Brookings Institution ranked the 100 largest metro areas in the U.S. based on income inequality. Grand Rapids was ranked #97 (#1 = greatest inequality). Criteria: the "95/20 ratio," a figure representing the income at which a household earns more than 95 percent of all other households, divided by the income at which a household earns more than only 20 percent of all other households. *Brookings Institution, "Household Income Inequality, 100 Largest U.S. Metro Areas, 2014-2016," February 5, 2018*

- The Grand Rapids metro area appeared on the Milken Institute "2022 Best Performing Cities" list. Rank: #110 out of 200 large metro areas (population over 250,000). Criteria: job growth; wage and salary growth; high-tech output growth; housing affordability; household broadband access. *Milken Institute, "Best-Performing Cities 2022," March 28, 2022*

- *Forbes* ranked the 200 most populous metro areas to determine the nation's "Best Places for Business and Careers." The Grand Rapids metro area was ranked #68. Criteria: costs (business and living); job growth (past and projected); income growth; quality of life; educational attainment (college and high school); projected economic growth; cultural and leisure opportunities; workplace tolerance laws; net migration patterns. *Forbes, "The Best Places for Business and Careers 2019: Seattle Still On Top," October 30, 2019*

Dating/Romance Rankings

- Grand Rapids was ranked #7 out of 25 cities that stood out for inspiring romance and attracting diners on the website OpenTable.com. Criteria: percentage of people who dined out on Valentine's Day in 2018; percentage of romantic restaurants as rated by OpenTable diner reviews; and percentage of tables seated for two. *OpenTable, "25 Most Romantic Cities in America for 2019," February 7, 2019*

Education Rankings

- Personal finance website *WalletHub* analyzed the 150 largest U.S. metropolitan statistical areas to determine where the most educated Americans are putting their degrees to work. Criteria: education levels; percentage of workers with degrees; education quality and attainment gap; public school quality rankings; quality and enrollment of each metro area's universities. Grand Rapids was ranked #64 (#1 = most educated city). *www.WalletHub.com, "Most & Least Educated Cities in America," July 18, 2022*

Environmental Rankings

- Niche compiled a list of the nation's snowiest cities, based on the National Oceanic and Atmospheric Administration's 30-year average snowfall data. Among cities with a population of at least 50,000, Grand Rapids ranked #8. *Niche.com, Top 25 Snowiest Cities in America, December 10, 2018*

- The U.S. Environmental Protection Agency (EPA) released its list of mid-size U.S. metropolitan areas with the most ENERGY STAR certified buildings in 2022. The Grand Rapids metro area was ranked #4 out of 10. *U.S. Environmental Protection Agency, "2023 Energy Star Top Cities," April 26, 2023*

Health/Fitness Rankings

- The Grand Rapids metro area was identified as one of the worst cities for bed bugs in America by pest control company Orkin. The area ranked #12 out of 50 based on the number of bed bug treatments Orkin performed from December 2021 to November 2022. *Orkin, "The Windy City Can't Blow Bed Bugs Away: Chicago Ranks #1 For Third Consecutive Year On Orkin's Bed Bug Cities List," January 9, 2023*

- Grand Rapids was identified as a "2022 Spring Allergy Capital." The area ranked #23 out of 100. Three groups of factors were used to identify the most challenging cities for people with allergies during the spring season: annual spring pollen scores; over the counter allergy medicine use; number of board-certified allergy specialists. *Asthma and Allergy Foundation of America, "Spring Allergy Capitals 2022," March 2, 2022*

- Grand Rapids was identified as a "2022 Fall Allergy Capital." The area ranked #25 out of 100. Three groups of factors were used to identify the most challenging cities for people with allergies during the fall season: annual fall pollen scores; over the counter allergy medicine use; number of board-certified allergy specialists. *Asthma and Allergy Foundation of America, "Fall Allergy Capitals 2022," March 2, 2022*

- Grand Rapids was identified as a "2022 Asthma Capital." The area ranked #72 out of the nation's 100 largest metropolitan areas. Criteria: estimated asthma prevalence; asthma-related mortality; and ER visits due to asthma. Risk factors analyzed but not factored in the rankings: annual pollen score; annual air quality; public smoking laws; access to board-certified asthma specialists; rescue and controller medication use; uninsured rate; poverty rate. *Asthma and Allergy Foundation of America, "Asthma Capitals 2022: The Most Challenging Places to Live With Asthma," September 14, 2022*

Real Estate Rankings

- *WalletHub* compared the most populated U.S. cities to determine which had the best markets for real estate agents. Grand Rapids ranked #105 where demand was high and pay was the best. Criteria: sales per agent; annual median wage for real-estate agents; monthly average starting salary for real estate agents; real estate job density and competition; unemployment rate; home turnover rate; housing-market health index; and other relevant metrics. *www.WalletHub.com, "2021 Best Places to Be a Real Estate Agent," May 12, 2021*

- The Grand Rapids metro area appeared on Realtor.com's list of hot housing markets to watch in 2023. The area ranked #7. Criteria: forecasted home price and sales growth; overall economy; population trends. *Realtor.com®, "Top 10 Housing Markets Positioned for Growth in 2023," December 7, 2022*

- Grand Rapids was ranked #74 out of 235 metro areas in terms of housing affordability in 2022 by the National Association of Home Builders (#1 = most affordable). Criteria: the share of homes sold in that area affordable to a family earning the local median income, based on standard mortgage underwriting criteria. *National Association of Home Builders®, NAHB-Wells Fargo Housing Opportunity Index, 4th Quarter 2022*

Safety Rankings

- Allstate ranked the 200 largest cities in America in terms of driver safety. Grand Rapids ranked #131. Criteria: internal property damage claims over a two-year period from January 2016 to December 2017. The report helps increase the importance of safety and awareness behind the wheel. *Allstate, "Allstate America's Best Drivers Report, 2019" June 24, 2019*

- Grand Rapids was identified as one of the most dangerous cities in America by NeighborhoodScout. The city ranked #81 out of 100 (#1 = most dangerous). Criteria: number of violent crimes per 1,000 residents. The editors evaluated cities with 25,000 or more residents. *NeighborhoodScout.com, "2023 Top 100 Most Dangerous Cities in the U.S.," January 12, 2023*

- The National Insurance Crime Bureau ranked 390 metro areas in the U.S. in terms of per capita rates of vehicle theft. The Grand Rapids metro area ranked #223 (#1 = highest rate). Criteria: number of vehicle theft offenses per 100,000 inhabitants in 2021. *National Insurance Crime Bureau, "Hot Spots 2021," September 1, 2022*

Women/Minorities Rankings

- Personal finance website *WalletHub* compared more than 180 U.S. cities across two key dimensions, "Hispanic Business-Friendliness" and "Hispanic Purchasing Power," to arrive at the most favorable conditions for Hispanic entrepreneurs. Grand Rapids was ranked #101 out of 182. Criteria includes: share of Hispanic-Owned Businesses; Hispanic entrepreneurship rate to median annual income of Hispanics; Small Business-Friendliness score; cost of living; and number of Hispanics with at least a bachelor's degree. *WalletHub.com, "2019's Best Cities for Hispanic Entrepreneurs," May 1, 2019*

Miscellaneous Rankings

- *MoveHub* ranked 446 hipster cities across 20 countries, using its new and improved *alternative* Hipster Index and Grand Rapids came out as #28 among the top 50. Criteria: population over 150,000; number of vintage boutiques; density of tattoo parlors; vegan places to eat; coffee shops; and density of vinyl record stores. *www.movehub.com, "The Hipster Index: Brighton Pips Portland to Global Top Spot," July 28, 2021*

- *WalletHub* compared the 150 most populated U.S. cities to determine their operating efficiency. A "Quality of Services" score was constructed for each city and then divided by the total budget per capita to reveal which were managed the best. Grand Rapids ranked #40. Criteria: financial stability; economy; education; safety; health; infrastructure and pollution. *www.WalletHub.com, "2022's Best- & Worst-Run Cities in America," June 21, 2022*

- Grand Rapids was selected as one of "America's Friendliest Cities." The city ranked #13 in the "Friendliest" category. Respondents to an online survey were asked to rate 38 top urban destinations in the United States as to general friendliness, as well as manners, politeness and warm disposition. *Travel + Leisure, "America's Friendliest Cities," October 20, 2017*

Business Environment

DEMOGRAPHICS

Population Growth

Area	1990 Census	2000 Census	2010 Census	2020 Census	Population Growth (%) 1990-2020	Population Growth (%) 2010-2020
City	189,145	197,800	188,040	198,917	5.2	5.8
MSA[1]	645,914	740,482	774,160	1,087,592	68.4	40.5
U.S.	248,709,873	281,421,906	308,745,538	331,449,281	33.3	7.4

Note: (1) Figures cover the Grand Rapids-Kentwood, MI Metropolitan Statistical Area
Source: U.S. Census Bureau, 1990 Census, 2000 Census, 2010 Census, 2020 Census

Race

Area	White Alone[2] (%)	Black Alone[2] (%)	Asian Alone[2] (%)	AIAN[3] Alone[2] (%)	NHOPI[4] Alone[2] (%)	Other Race Alone[2] (%)	Two or More Races (%)
City	60.3	18.9	2.3	0.9	0.0	9.0	8.7
MSA[1]	78.0	6.9	2.8	0.6	0.0	4.7	7.0
U.S.	61.6	12.4	6.0	1.1	0.2	8.4	10.2

Note: (1) Figures cover the Grand Rapids-Kentwood, MI Metropolitan Statistical Area; (2) Alone is defined as not being in combination with one or more other races; (3) American Indian and Alaska Native; (4) Native Hawaiian and Other Pacific Islander
Source: U.S. Census Bureau, 2020 Census

Hispanic or Latino Origin

Area	Total (%)	Mexican (%)	Puerto Rican (%)	Cuban (%)	Other (%)
City	15.7	9.6	1.6	0.3	4.1
MSA[1]	9.9	6.8	0.9	0.3	1.9
U.S.	18.4	11.2	1.8	0.7	4.7

Note: Persons of Hispanic or Latino origin can be of any race; (1) Figures cover the Grand Rapids-Kentwood, MI Metropolitan Statistical Area
Source: U.S. Census Bureau, 2017-2021 American Community Survey 5-Year Estimates

Age

Area	Under Age 5	Age 5–19	Age 20–34	Age 35–44	Age 45–54	Age 55–64	Age 65–74	Age 75–84	Age 85+	Median Age
City	6.4	18.1	31.1	12.2	9.3	10.1	7.3	3.4	2.1	31.7
MSA[1]	6.1	20.6	21.8	12.5	11.5	12.5	8.9	4.3	1.8	36.2
U.S.	5.6	19.2	20.2	12.7	12.4	13.1	10.0	4.9	1.9	38.8

Note: (1) Figures cover the Grand Rapids-Kentwood, MI Metropolitan Statistical Area
Source: U.S. Census Bureau, 2020 Census

Disability by Age

Area	All Ages	Under 18 Years Old	18 to 64 Years Old	65 Years and Over
City	11.7	3.9	11.0	30.4
MSA[1]	10.9	3.8	9.4	29.8
U.S.	12.6	4.4	10.3	33.4

Note: Figures show percent of the civilian noninstitutionalized population that reported having a disability. Disability status is determined from six types of difficulty: vision, hearing, cognitive, ambulatory, self-care, and independent living. For children under 5 years old, hearing and vision difficulty are used to determine disability status. For children between the ages of 5 and 14, disability status is determined from hearing, vision, cognitive, ambulatory, and self-care difficulties. For people aged 15 years and older, they are considered to have a disability if they have difficulty with any one of the six difficulty types; Note: (1) Figures cover the Grand Rapids-Kentwood, MI Metropolitan Statistical Area
Source: U.S. Census Bureau, 2017-2021 American Community Survey 5-Year Estimates

Ancestry

Area	German	Irish	English	American	Italian	Polish	French[2]	Scottish	Dutch
City	14.1	8.0	6.4	2.5	3.0	6.3	1.9	1.6	13.0
MSA[1]	18.8	9.5	8.9	3.4	3.0	6.3	2.5	1.7	18.0
U.S.	12.8	9.6	8.1	5.7	5.0	2.7	2.2	1.6	1.1

Note: Figures are the percentage of the total population reporting a particular ancestry. The nine most commonly reported ancestries in the U.S. are shown. Figures include multiple ancestries (e.g. if a person reported being Irish and Italian, they were included in both columns); (1) Figures cover the Grand Rapids-Kentwood, MI Metropolitan Statistical Area; (2) Excludes Basque
Source: U.S. Census Bureau, 2017-2021 American Community Survey 5-Year Estimates

Foreign-born Population

| Area | \multicolumn{9}{c}{Percent of Population Born in} |
	Any Foreign Country	Asia	Mexico	Europe	Caribbean	Central America[2]	South America	Africa	Canada
City	10.8	2.4	3.2	1.0	0.7	1.4	0.2	1.7	0.2
MSA[1]	6.6	2.1	1.6	0.9	0.4	0.5	0.2	0.7	0.2
U.S.	13.6	4.2	3.3	1.5	1.4	1.1	1.1	0.8	0.2

Note: (1) Figures cover the Grand Rapids-Kentwood, MI Metropolitan Statistical Area; (2) Excludes Mexico.
Source: U.S. Census Bureau, 2017-2021 American Community Survey 5-Year Estimates

Household Size

| Area | \multicolumn{7}{c}{Persons in Household (%)} | Average Household Size |
	One	Two	Three	Four	Five	Six	Seven or More	
City	33.2	30.9	15.2	10.2	6.0	2.3	2.2	2.50
MSA[1]	25.0	34.3	15.2	14.3	7.3	2.4	1.5	2.60
U.S.	28.1	33.8	15.5	12.9	6.0	2.3	1.4	2.60

Note: (1) Figures cover the Grand Rapids-Kentwood, MI Metropolitan Statistical Area
Source: U.S. Census Bureau, 2017-2021 American Community Survey 5-Year Estimates

Household Relationships

Area	House-holder	Opposite-sex Spouse	Same-sex Spouse	Opposite-sex Unmarried Partner	Same-sex Unmarried Partner	Child[2]	Grand-child	Other Relatives	Non-relatives
City	40.2	13.1	0.3	3.6	0.3	26.1	2.1	4.0	6.6
MSA[1]	37.3	19.0	0.1	2.5	0.1	29.6	1.7	2.9	3.5
U.S.	38.3	17.5	0.2	2.5	0.2	28.3	2.4	4.8	3.4

Note: Figures are percent of the total population; (1) Figures cover the Grand Rapids-Kentwood, MI Metropolitan Statistical Area; (2) Includes biological, adopted, and stepchildren of the householder
Source: U.S. Census Bureau, 2020 Census

Gender

Area	Males	Females	Males per 100 Females
City	97,037	101,880	95.2
MSA[1]	540,561	547,031	98.8
U.S.	162,685,811	168,763,470	96.4

Note: (1) Figures cover the Grand Rapids-Kentwood, MI Metropolitan Statistical Area
Source: U.S. Census Bureau, 2020 Census

Marital Status

Area	Never Married	Now Married[2]	Separated	Widowed	Divorced
City	45.3	38.1	1.2	4.9	10.5
MSA[1]	32.2	52.1	0.9	4.5	10.3
U.S.	33.8	48.0	1.8	5.6	10.8

Note: Figures are percentages and cover the population 15 years of age and older; (1) Figures cover the Grand Rapids-Kentwood, MI Metropolitan Statistical Area; (2) Excludes separated
Source: U.S. Census Bureau, 2017-2021 American Community Survey 5-Year Estimates

Religious Groups by Family

Area	Catholic	Baptist	Methodist	LDS[2]	Pentecostal	Lutheran	Islam	Adventist	Other
MSA[1]	13.1	1.3	1.8	0.4	1.3	1.8	0.8	1.2	19.9
U.S.	18.7	7.3	3.0	2.0	1.8	1.7	1.3	1.3	11.6

Note: Figures are the number of adherents as a percentage of the total population and cover the eight largest religious groups in the U.S; (1) Figures cover the Grand Rapids-Kentwood, MI Metropolitan Statistical Area; (2) Church of Jesus Christ of Latter-day Saints
Sources: 2020 U.S. Religion Census, Association of Statisticians of American Religious Bodies; The Association of Religion Data Archives (ARDA)

Religious Groups by Tradition

Area	Catholic	Evangelical Protestant	Mainline Protestant	Black Protestant	Islam	Judaism	Hinduism	Orthodox	Buddhism
MSA[1]	13.1	17.6	7.4	1.0	0.8	0.1	0.2	0.2	<0.1
U.S.	18.7	16.5	5.2	2.3	1.3	0.6	0.4	0.4	0.3

Note: Figures are the number of adherents as a percentage of the total population; (1) Figures cover the Grand Rapids-Kentwood, MI Metropolitan Statistical Area
Sources: 2020 U.S. Religion Census, Association of Statisticians of American Religious Bodies; The Association of Religion Data Archives (ARDA)

ECONOMY

Gross Metropolitan Product

Area	2020	2021	2022	2023	Rank[2]
MSA[1]	61.4	67.8	73.0	78.0	55

Note: Figures are in billions of dollars; (1) Figures cover the Grand Rapids-Kentwood, MI Metropolitan Statistical Area; (2) Rank is based on 2021 data and ranges from 1 to 381
Source: U.S. Conference of Mayors, U.S. Metro Economies: U.S. Metros Compared to Global and State Economies, June 2022

Economic Growth

Area	2018-20 (%)	2021 (%)	2022 (%)	2023 (%)	Rank[2]
MSA[1]	-2.1	6.3	1.8	3.7	294
U.S.	-0.6	5.7	3.1	2.9	–

Note: Figures are real gross metropolitan product (GMP) growth rates and represent average annual percent change; (1) Figures cover the Grand Rapids-Kentwood, MI Metropolitan Statistical Area; (2) Rank is based on 2020 2-year average annual percent change and ranges from 1 to 381
Source: U.S. Conference of Mayors, U.S. Metro Economies: U.S. Metros Compared to Global and State Economies, June 2022

Metropolitan Area Exports

Area	2016	2017	2018	2019	2020	2021	Rank[2]
MSA[1]	5,168.5	5,385.8	5,420.9	5,214.1	4,488.3	5,171.7	57

Note: Figures are in millions of dollars; (1) Figures cover the Grand Rapids-Kentwood, MI Metropolitan Statistical Area; (2) Rank is based on 2021 data and ranges from 1 to 388
Source: U.S. Department of Commerce, International Trade Administration, Office of Trade and Economic Analysis, Industry and Analysis, Exports by Metropolitan Area, data extracted March 16, 2023

Building Permits

Area	Single-Family			Multi-Family			Total		
	2021	2022	Pct. Chg.	2021	2022	Pct. Chg.	2021	2022	Pct. Chg.
City	43	23	-46.5	243	211	-13.2	286	234	-18.2
MSA[1]	2,811	2,488	-11.5	894	1,710	91.3	3,705	4,198	13.3
U.S.	1,115,400	975,600	-12.5	621,600	689,500	10.9	1,737,000	1,665,100	-4.1

Note: (1) Figures cover the Grand Rapids-Kentwood, MI Metropolitan Statistical Area; Figures represent new, privately-owned housing units authorized (unadjusted data); All permit data are based on estimates with imputation
Source: U.S. Census Bureau, Manufacturing, Mining, and Construction Statistics, Building Permits, 2021, 2022

Bankruptcy Filings

Area	Business Filings			Nonbusiness Filings		
	2021	2022	% Chg.	2021	2022	% Chg.
Kent County	8	10	25.0	469	439	-6.4
U.S.	14,347	13,481	-6.0	399,269	374,240	-6.3

Note: Business filings include Chapter 7, Chapter 9, Chapter 11, Chapter 12, Chapter 13, Chapter 15, and Section 304; Nonbusiness filings include Chapter 7, Chapter 11, and Chapter 13
Source: Administrative Office of the U.S. Courts, Business and Nonbusiness Bankruptcy, County Cases Commenced by Chapter of the Bankruptcy Code, During the 12-Month Period Ending December 31, 2021 and Business and Nonbusiness Bankruptcy, County Cases Commenced by Chapter of the Bankruptcy Code, During the 12-Month Period Ending December 31, 2022

Housing Vacancy Rates

Area	Gross Vacancy Rate[2] (%)			Year-Round Vacancy Rate[3] (%)			Rental Vacancy Rate[4] (%)			Homeowner Vacancy Rate[5] (%)		
	2020	2021	2022	2020	2021	2022	2020	2021	2022	2020	2021	2022
MSA[1]	7.1	7.0	4.9	4.7	4.2	3.0	4.6	3.4	2.4	1.1	0.7	0.1
U.S.	10.6	10.8	10.5	8.2	8.4	8.2	6.3	6.1	5.8	1.0	0.9	0.8

Note: (1) Figures cover the Grand Rapids-Kentwood, MI Metropolitan Statistical Area; (2) The percentage of the total housing inventory that is vacant; (3) The percentage of the housing inventory (excluding seasonal units) that is year-round vacant; (4) The percentage of rental inventory that is vacant for rent; (5) The percentage of homeowner inventory that is vacant for sale
Source: U.S. Census Bureau, Housing Vacancies and Homeownership Annual Statistics: 2020, 2021, 2022

INCOME

Income

Area	Per Capita ($)	Median Household ($)	Average Household ($)
City	29,060	55,385	72,017
MSA[1]	34,581	70,347	91,126
U.S.	37,638	69,021	97,196

Note: (1) Figures cover the Grand Rapids-Kentwood, MI Metropolitan Statistical Area
Source: U.S. Census Bureau, 2017-2021 American Community Survey 5-Year Estimates

Household Income Distribution

Area	Percent of Households Earning							
	Under $15,000	$15,000 -$24,999	$25,000 -$34,999	$35,000 -$49,999	$50,000 -$74,999	$75,000 -$99,999	$100,000 -$149,999	$150,000 and up
City	12.5	9.8	8.1	14.1	19.0	14.1	14.3	8.0
MSA[1]	7.1	7.4	7.5	12.3	19.2	14.8	17.9	13.9
U.S.	9.4	7.8	8.2	11.4	16.8	12.8	16.3	17.3

Note: (1) Figures cover the Grand Rapids-Kentwood, MI Metropolitan Statistical Area
Source: U.S. Census Bureau, 2017-2021 American Community Survey 5-Year Estimates

Poverty Rate

Area	All Ages	Under 18 Years Old	18 to 64 Years Old	65 Years and Over
City	18.6	25.6	17.1	13.9
MSA[1]	9.8	11.7	9.5	7.8
U.S.	12.6	17.0	11.8	9.6

Note: Figures are percentage of people whose income during the past 12 months was below the poverty level;
(1) Figures cover the Grand Rapids-Kentwood, MI Metropolitan Statistical Area
Source: U.S. Census Bureau, 2017-2021 American Community Survey 5-Year Estimates

EMPLOYMENT

Labor Force and Employment

Area	Civilian Labor Force			Workers Employed		
	Dec. 2021	Dec. 2022	% Chg.	Dec. 2021	Dec. 2022	% Chg.
City	101,134	105,118	3.9	96,771	100,836	4.2
MSA[1]	563,869	586,790	4.1	545,813	568,603	4.2
U.S.	161,696,000	164,224,000	1.6	155,732,000	158,872,000	2.0

Note: Data is not seasonally adjusted and covers workers 16 years of age and older; (1) Figures cover the
Grand Rapids-Kentwood, MI Metropolitan Statistical Area
Source: Bureau of Labor Statistics, Local Area Unemployment Statistics

Unemployment Rate

Area	2022											
	Jan.	Feb.	Mar.	Apr.	May	Jun.	Jul.	Aug.	Sep.	Oct.	Nov.	Dec.
City	5.0	5.0	4.3	4.2	4.6	5.2	5.0	4.6	4.3	4.2	4.0	4.1
MSA[1]	3.7	3.8	3.3	3.1	3.4	3.9	3.8	3.4	3.2	3.1	3.0	3.1
U.S.	4.4	4.1	3.8	3.3	3.4	3.8	3.8	3.8	3.3	3.4	3.4	3.3

Note: Data is not seasonally adjusted and covers workers 16 years of age and older; (1) Figures cover the
Grand Rapids-Kentwood, MI Metropolitan Statistical Area
Source: Bureau of Labor Statistics, Local Area Unemployment Statistics

Average Wages

Occupation	$/Hr.	Occupation	$/Hr.
Accountants and Auditors	36.05	Maintenance and Repair Workers	21.10
Automotive Mechanics	23.88	Marketing Managers	64.10
Bookkeepers	21.43	Network and Computer Systems Admin.	41.89
Carpenters	25.03	Nurses, Licensed Practical	27.34
Cashiers	13.24	Nurses, Registered	36.98
Computer Programmers	43.23	Nursing Assistants	17.03
Computer Systems Analysts	45.05	Office Clerks, General	20.33
Computer User Support Specialists	27.43	Physical Therapists	42.66
Construction Laborers	21.17	Physicians	126.06
Cooks, Restaurant	15.94	Plumbers, Pipefitters and Steamfitters	30.06
Customer Service Representatives	19.17	Police and Sheriff's Patrol Officers	31.96
Dentists	88.95	Postal Service Mail Carriers	27.01
Electricians	27.51	Real Estate Sales Agents	27.56
Engineers, Electrical	43.36	Retail Salespersons	16.20
Fast Food and Counter Workers	13.09	Sales Representatives, Technical/Scientific	52.99
Financial Managers	65.10	Secretaries, Exc. Legal/Medical/Executive	20.23
First-Line Supervisors of Office Workers	29.78	Security Guards	14.75
General and Operations Managers	55.04	Surgeons	121.07
Hairdressers/Cosmetologists	18.45	Teacher Assistants, Exc. Postsecondary*	15.09
Home Health and Personal Care Aides	14.38	Teachers, Secondary School, Exc. Sp. Ed.*	31.35
Janitors and Cleaners	15.34	Telemarketers	15.93
Landscaping/Groundskeeping Workers	17.18	Truck Drivers, Heavy/Tractor-Trailer	24.69
Lawyers	64.19	Truck Drivers, Light/Delivery Services	20.89
Maids and Housekeeping Cleaners	14.27	Waiters and Waitresses	17.53

Note: Wage data covers the Grand Rapids-Kentwood, MI Metropolitan Statistical Area; (*) Hourly wages were
calculated from annual wage data based on a 40 hour work week; n/a not available.
Source: Bureau of Labor Statistics, Metro Area Occupational Employment & Wage Estimates, May 2022

Employment by Industry

Sector	MSA[1]		U.S.
	Number of Employees	Percent of Total	Percent of Total
Construction, Mining, and Logging	27,100	4.7	5.4
Private Education and Health Services	95,800	16.5	16.1
Financial Activities	28,000	4.8	5.9
Government	50,100	8.6	14.5
Information	7,100	1.2	2.0
Leisure and Hospitality	47,400	8.2	10.3
Manufacturing	115,700	20.0	8.4
Other Services	22,600	3.9	3.7
Professional and Business Services	79,900	13.8	14.7
Retail Trade	50,500	8.7	10.2
Transportation, Warehousing, and Utilities	20,100	3.5	4.9
Wholesale Trade	34,900	6.0	3.9

Note: Figures are non-farm employment as of December 2022. Figures are not seasonally adjusted and include workers 16 years of age and older; (1) Figures cover the Grand Rapids-Kentwood, MI Metropolitan Statistical Area
Source: Bureau of Labor Statistics, Current Employment Statistics, Employment, Hours, and Earnings

Employment by Occupation

Occupation Classification	City (%)	MSA[1] (%)	U.S. (%)
Management, Business, Science, and Arts	38.1	37.9	40.3
Natural Resources, Construction, and Maintenance	6.1	7.9	8.7
Production, Transportation, and Material Moving	17.3	18.2	13.1
Sales and Office	19.9	20.7	20.9
Service	18.6	15.3	17.0

Note: Figures cover employed civilians 16 years of age and older; (1) Figures cover the Grand Rapids-Kentwood, MI Metropolitan Statistical Area
Source: U.S. Census Bureau, 2017-2021 American Community Survey 5-Year Estimates

Occupations with Greatest Projected Employment Growth: 2021 – 2023

Occupation[1]	2021 Employment	2023 Projected Employment	Numeric Employment Change	Percent Employment Change
Fast Food and Counter Workers	116,260	126,010	9,750	8.4
Laborers and Freight, Stock, and Material Movers, Hand	84,660	94,000	9,340	11.0
Waiters and Waitresses	61,590	67,760	6,170	10.0
Stockers and Order Fillers	69,390	75,390	6,000	8.6
Cooks, Restaurant	29,850	34,490	4,640	15.5
Retail Salespersons	123,250	126,400	3,150	2.6
Heavy and Tractor-Trailer Truck Drivers	61,520	64,670	3,150	5.1
Janitors and Cleaners, Except Maids and Housekeeping Cleaners	64,490	67,530	3,040	4.7
General and Operations Managers	69,180	72,210	3,030	4.4
First-Line Supervisors of Food Preparation and Serving Workers	27,070	29,760	2,690	9.9

Note: Projections cover Michigan; Projections for 2022-2024 were not available at time of publication; (1) Sorted by numeric employment change
Source: www.projectionscentral.com, State Occupational Projections, 2021–2023 Short-Term Projections

Fastest-Growing Occupations: 2021 – 2023

Occupation[1]	2021 Employment	2023 Projected Employment	Numeric Employment Change	Percent Employment Change
Ushers, Lobby Attendants, and Ticket Takers	1,930	2,290	360	18.7
Cooks, Restaurant	29,850	34,490	4,640	15.5
Flight Attendants	3,150	3,580	430	13.7
Conveyor Operators and Tenders	650	730	80	12.3
Industrial Truck and Tractor Operators	22,030	24,680	2,650	12.0
Bartenders	15,110	16,830	1,720	11.4
Hosts and Hostesses, Restaurant, Lounge, and Coffee Shop	9,630	10,720	1,090	11.3
Laborers and Freight, Stock, and Material Movers, Hand	84,660	94,000	9,340	11.0
Dining Room and Cafeteria Attendants and Bartender Helpers	10,100	11,150	1,050	10.4
Waiters and Waitresses	61,590	67,760	6,170	10.0

Note: Projections cover Michigan; Projections for 2022-2024 were not available at time of publication;
(1) Sorted by percent employment change and excludes occupations with numeric employment change less than 50
Source: www.projectionscentral.com, State Occupational Projections, 2021–2023 Short-Term Projections

CITY FINANCES

City Government Finances

Component	2020 ($000)	2020 ($ per capita)
Total Revenues	466,780	2,322
Total Expenditures	550,516	2,739
Debt Outstanding	697,321	3,469
Cash and Securities[1]	613,637	3,053

Note: (1) Cash and security holdings of a government at the close of its fiscal year,
including those of its dependent agencies, utilities, and liquor stores.
Source: U.S. Census Bureau, State & Local Government Finances 2020

City Government Revenue by Source

Source	2020 ($000)	2020 ($ per capita)	2020 (%)
General Revenue			
From Federal Government	39,162	195	8.4
From State Government	47,867	238	10.3
From Local Governments	2,801	14	0.6
Taxes			
Property	68,492	341	14.7
Sales and Gross Receipts	0	0	0.0
Personal Income	104,591	520	22.4
Corporate Income	0	0	0.0
Motor Vehicle License	0	0	0.0
Other Taxes	6,618	33	1.4
Current Charges	117,981	587	25.3
Liquor Store	0	0	0.0
Utility	48,756	243	10.4

Source: U.S. Census Bureau, State & Local Government Finances 2020

City Government Expenditures by Function

Function	2020 ($000)	2020 ($ per capita)	2020 (%)
General Direct Expenditures			
Air Transportation	0	0	0.0
Corrections	0	0	0.0
Education	0	0	0.0
Employment Security Administration	0	0	0.0
Financial Administration	12,097	60	2.2
Fire Protection	32,413	161	5.9
General Public Buildings	0	0	0.0
Governmental Administration, Other	16,461	81	3.0
Health	657	3	0.1
Highways	23,803	118	4.3
Hospitals	0	0	0.0
Housing and Community Development	37,625	187	6.8
Interest on General Debt	18,184	90	3.3
Judicial and Legal	16,908	84	3.1
Libraries	10,704	53	1.9
Parking	17,869	88	3.2
Parks and Recreation	14,453	71	2.6
Police Protection	55,881	278	10.2
Public Welfare	0	0	0.0
Sewerage	86,787	431	15.8
Solid Waste Management	15,329	76	2.8
Veterans' Services	0	0	0.0
Liquor Store	0	0	0.0
Utility	59,112	294	10.7

Source: U.S. Census Bureau, State & Local Government Finances 2020

TAXES

State Corporate Income Tax Rates

State	Tax Rate (%)	Income Brackets ($)	Num. of Brackets	Financial Institution Tax Rate (%)[a]	Federal Income Tax Ded.
Michigan	6.0	Flat rate	1	(a)	No

Note: Tax rates as of January 1, 2023; (a) Rates listed are the corporate income tax rate applied to financial institutions or excise taxes based on income. Some states have other taxes based upon the value of deposits or shares.
Source: Federation of Tax Administrators, State Corporate Income Tax Rates, January 1, 2023

State Individual Income Tax Rates

State	Tax Rate (%)	Income Brackets ($)	Personal Exemptions ($) Single	Married	Depend.	Standard Ded. ($) Single	Married
Michigan	4.25	Flat rate	5,000	10,000	5,000	–	–

Note: Tax rates as of January 1, 2023; Local- and county-level taxes are not included; Federal income tax is not deductible on state income tax returns
Source: Federation of Tax Administrators, State Individual Income Tax Rates, January 1, 2023

Various State Sales and Excise Tax Rates

State	State Sales Tax (%)	Gasoline[1] ($/gal.)	Cigarette[2] ($/pack)	Spirits[3] ($/gal.)	Wine[4] ($/gal.)	Beer[5] ($/gal.)	Recreational Marijuana (%)
Michigan	6	0.466	2.00	13.57	0.51	0.20	(i)

Note: All tax rates as of January 1, 2023; (1) The American Petroleum Institute has developed a methodology for determining the average tax rate on a gallon of fuel. Rates may include any of the following: excise taxes, environmental fees, storage tank fees, other fees or taxes, general sales tax, and local taxes; (2) The federal excise tax of $1.0066 per pack and local taxes are not included; (3) Rates are those applicable to off-premise sales of 40% alcohol by volume (a.b.v.) distilled spirits in 750ml containers. Local excise taxes are excluded; (4) Rates are those applicable to off-premise sales of 11% a.b.v. non-carbonated wine in 750ml containers; (5) Rates are those applicable to off-premise sales of 4.7% a.b.v. beer in 12 ounce containers; (i) 10% excise tax (retail price)
Source: Tax Foundation, 2023 Facts & Figures: How Does Your State Compare?

State Business Tax Climate Index Rankings

State	Overall Rank	Corporate Tax Rank	Individual Income Tax Rank	Sales Tax Rank	Property Tax Rank	Unemployment Insurance Tax Rank
Michigan	12	20	12	11	25	8

Note: The index is a measure of how each state's tax laws affect economic performance. The lower the rank, the more favorable a state's tax system is for business. States without a given tax are given a ranking of 1. The scores/rankings for the District of Columbia do not affect other states. The 2023 index represents the tax climate as of July 1, 2022.
Source: Tax Foundation, State Business Tax Climate Index 2023

TRANSPORTATION

Means of Transportation to Work

Area	Car/Truck/Van		Public Transportation			Bicycle	Walked	Other Means	Worked at Home
	Drove Alone	Car-pooled	Bus	Subway	Railroad				
City	71.5	10.0	3.3	0.0	0.0	0.9	4.4	1.0	8.8
MSA[1]	79.0	8.5	1.2	0.0	0.0	0.4	2.2	0.7	7.9
U.S.	73.2	8.6	2.0	1.6	0.5	0.5	2.5	1.5	9.7

Note: Figures are percentages and cover workers 16 years of age and older; (1) Figures cover the Grand Rapids-Kentwood, MI Metropolitan Statistical Area
Source: U.S. Census Bureau, 2017-2021 American Community Survey 5-Year Estimates

Travel Time to Work

Area	Less Than 10 Minutes	10 to 19 Minutes	20 to 29 Minutes	30 to 44 Minutes	45 to 59 Minutes	60 to 89 Minutes	90 Minutes or More
City	14.5	44.0	23.5	11.6	3.7	2.0	0.8
MSA[1]	14.8	35.3	24.7	16.1	5.0	2.6	1.5
U.S.	12.4	28.5	21.0	20.9	8.2	6.2	2.9

Note: Note: Figures are percentages and include workers 16 years old and over; (1) Figures cover the Grand Rapids-Kentwood, MI Metropolitan Statistical Area
Source: U.S. Census Bureau, 2017-2021 American Community Survey 5-Year Estimates

Key Congestion Measures

Measure	1990	2000	2010	2015	2020
Annual Hours of Delay, Total (000)	4,010	10,180	13,453	16,394	9,472
Annual Hours of Delay, Per Auto Commuter	19	35	37	40	22
Annual Congestion Cost, Per Auto Commuter ($)	318	601	632	711	435

Note: Covers the Grand Rapids MI urban area
Source: Texas A&M Transportation Institute, 2021 Urban Mobility Report

Freeway Travel Time Index

Measure	1985	1990	1995	2000	2005	2010	2015	2020
Urban Area Index[1]	1.05	1.08	1.12	1.15	1.15	1.14	1.13	1.07
Urban Area Rank[1,2]	64	62	57	53	68	71	83	57

Note: Freeway Travel Time Index—the ratio of travel time in the peak period to the travel time at free-flow conditions. For example, a value of 1.30 indicates a 20-minute free-flow trip takes 26 minutes in the peak (20 minutes x 1.30 = 26 minutes); (1) Covers the Grand Rapids MI urban area; (2) Rank is based on 101 larger urban areas (#1 = highest travel time index)
Source: Texas A&M Transportation Institute, 2021 Urban Mobility Report

Public Transportation

Agency Name / Mode of Transportation	Vehicles Operated in Maximum Service[1]	Annual Unlinked Passenger Trips[2] (in thous.)	Annual Passenger Miles[3] (in thous.)
Interurban Transit Partnership (The Rapid)			
Bus (directly operated)	105	3,553.1	14,818.2
Bus Rapid Transit (directly operated)	6	367.5	1,270.8
Demand Response (purchased transportation)	62	200.5	2,796.8
Vanpool (directly operated)	6	7.7	306.9

Note: (1) Number of revenue vehicles operated by the given mode and type of service to meet the annual maximum service requirement. This is the revenue vehicle count during the peak season of the year; on the week and day that maximum service is provided. Vehicles operated in maximum service (VOMS) exclude atypical days and one-time special events; (2) Number of passengers who boarded public transportation vehicles. Passengers are counted each time they board a vehicle no matter how many vehicles they use to travel from their origin to their destination. (3) Sum of the distances ridden by all passengers during the entire fiscal year.
Source: Federal Transit Administration, National Transit Database, 2021

Air Transportation

Airport Name and Code / Type of Service	Passenger Airlines[1]	Passenger Enplanements	Freight Carriers[2]	Freight (lbs)
Gerald R. Ford International (GRR)				
Domestic service (U.S. carriers - 2022)	22	1,716,240	12	40,070,991
International service (U.S. carriers - 2021)	0	0	0	0

Note: (1) Includes all U.S.-based major, minor and commuter airlines that carried at least one passenger during the year; (2) Includes all U.S.-based airlines and freight carriers that transported at least one pound of freight during the year.
Source: Bureau of Transportation Statistics, The Intermodal Transportation Database, Air Carriers: T-100 Domestic Market (U.S. Carriers), 2022; Bureau of Transportation Statistics, The Intermodal Transportation Database, Air Carriers: T-100 International Market (U.S. Carriers), 2021

BUSINESSES

Major Business Headquarters

Company Name	Industry	Rankings	
		Fortune[1]	Forbes[2]
Gordon Food Service	Food, drink & tobacco	-	16
Meijer	Food markets	-	14
SpartanNash	Wholesalers, food and grocery	392	-
UFP Industries	Wood and wood-alternative products	401	-

Note: (1) Companies that produce a 10-K are ranked 1 to 500 based on 2021 revenue; (2) All private companies with at least $2 billion in annual revenue through the end of their most current fiscal year are ranked 1 to 246; companies listed are headquartered in the city; dashes indicate no ranking
Source: Fortune, "Fortune 500," 2022; Forbes, "America's Largest Private Companies," 2022

Fastest-Growing Businesses

According to *Inc.*, Grand Rapids is home to one of America's 500 fastest-growing private companies: **Campspot** (#487). Criteria: must be an independent, privately-held, for-profit, U.S. corporation, proprietorship or partnership as of December 31, 2021; revenues must be at least $100,000 in 2018 and $2 million in 2021; must have four-year operating/sales history. *Inc., "America's 500 Fastest-Growing Private Companies," 2022*

Living Environment

COST OF LIVING

Cost of Living Index

Composite Index	Groceries	Housing	Utilities	Trans-portation	Health Care	Misc. Goods/ Services
94.7	92.3	84.8	102.8	101.3	95.3	100.1

Note: The Cost of Living Index measures regional differences in the cost of consumer goods and services, excluding taxes and non-consumer expenditures, for professional and managerial households in the top income quintile. It is based on more than 50,000 prices covering almost 60 different items for which prices are collected three times a year by chambers of commerce, economic development organizations or university applied economic centers in each participating urban area. The numbers shown should be read as a percentage above or below the national average of 100. For example, a value of 115.4 in the groceries column indicates that grocery prices are 15.4% higher than the national average. Small differences in the index numbers should not be interpreted as significant; Figures cover the Grand Rapids MI urban area.
Source: The Council for Community and Economic Research, Cost of Living Index, 2022

Grocery Prices

Area[1]	T-Bone Steak ($/pound)	Frying Chicken ($/pound)	Whole Milk ($/half gal.)	Eggs ($/dozen)	Orange Juice ($/64 oz.)	Coffee ($/11.5 oz.)
City[2]	15.24	1.48	1.92	2.07	3.33	3.68
Avg.	13.81	1.59	2.43	2.25	3.85	4.95
Min.	10.17	0.90	1.51	1.30	2.90	3.46
Max.	19.35	3.30	4.32	4.32	5.31	8.59

*Note: (1) Values for the local area are compared with the average, minimum and maximum values for all 286 areas in the Cost of Living Index; (2) Figures cover the Grand Rapids MI urban area; **T-Bone Steak** (price per pound); **Frying Chicken** (price per pound, whole fryer); **Whole Milk** (half gallon carton); **Eggs** (price per dozen, Grade A, large); **Orange Juice** (64 oz. Tropicana or Florida Natural); **Coffee** (11.5 oz. can, vacuum-packed, Maxwell House, Hills Bros, or Folgers).*
Source: The Council for Community and Economic Research, Cost of Living Index, 2022

Housing and Utility Costs

Area[1]	New Home Price ($)	Apartment Rent ($/month)	All Electric ($/month)	Part Electric ($/month)	Other Energy ($/month)	Telephone ($/month)
City[2]	384,672	1,273	-	105.38	79.74	190.37
Avg.	450,913	1,371	176.41	99.93	76.96	190.22
Min.	229,283	546	100.84	31.56	27.15	174.27
Max.	2,434,977	4,569	356.86	249.59	272.24	208.31

*Note: (1) Values for the local area are compared with the average, minimum and maximum values for all 286 areas in the Cost of Living Index; (2) Figures cover the Grand Rapids MI urban area; **New Home Price** (2,400 sf living area, 8,000 sf lot, in urban area with full utilities); **Apartment Rent** (950 sf 2 bedroom/1.5 or 2 bath, unfurnished, excluding all utilities except water); **All Electric** (average monthly cost for an all-electric home); **Part Electric** (average monthly cost for a part-electric home); **Other Energy** (average monthly cost for natural gas, fuel oil, coal, wood, and any other forms of energy except electricity); **Telephone** (price includes the base monthly rate plus taxes and fees for three lines of mobile phone service).*
Source: The Council for Community and Economic Research, Cost of Living Index, 2022

Health Care, Transportation, and Other Costs

Area[1]	Doctor ($/visit)	Dentist ($/visit)	Optometrist ($/visit)	Gasoline ($/gallon)	Beauty Salon ($/visit)	Men's Shirt ($)
City[2]	104.35	109.29	109.72	4.13	36.00	26.03
Avg.	124.91	107.77	117.66	3.86	43.31	34.21
Min.	36.61	58.25	51.79	2.90	22.18	13.05
Max.	250.21	162.58	371.96	5.54	85.61	63.54

*Note: (1) Values for the local area are compared with the average, minimum and maximum values for all 286 areas in the Cost of Living Index; (2) Figures cover the Grand Rapids MI urban area; **Doctor** (general practitioners routine exam of an established patient); **Dentist** (adult teeth cleaning and periodic oral examination); **Optometrist** (full vision eye exam for established adult patient); **Gasoline** (one gallon regular unleaded, national brand, including all taxes, cash price at self-service pump if available); **Beauty Salon** (woman's shampoo, trim, and blow-dry); **Men's Shirt** (cotton/polyester dress shirt, pinpoint weave, long sleeves).*
Source: The Council for Community and Economic Research, Cost of Living Index, 2022

HOUSING

Homeownership Rate

Area	2015 (%)	2016 (%)	2017 (%)	2018 (%)	2019 (%)	2020 (%)	2021 (%)	2022 (%)
MSA[1]	75.8	76.2	71.7	73.0	75.2	71.8	65.0	68.1
U.S.	63.7	63.4	63.9	64.4	64.6	66.6	65.5	65.8

Note: (1) Figures cover the Grand Rapids-Kentwood, MI Metropolitan Statistical Area
Source: U.S. Census Bureau, Housing Vacancies and Homeownership Annual Statistics: 2015-2022

House Price Index (HPI)

Area	National Ranking[2]	Quarterly Change (%)	One-Year Change (%)	Five-Year Change (%)	Since 1991Q1 (%)
MSA[1]	116	n/a	11.72	62.74	262.62
U.S.[3]	–	0.34	8.41	58.44	289.08

Note: The HPI is a weighted repeat sales index. It measures average price changes in repeat sales or refinancings on the same properties. This information is obtained by reviewing repeat mortgage transactions on single-family properties whose mortgages have been purchased or securitized by Fannie Mae or Freddie Mac since January 1975; (1) Figures cover the Grand Rapids-Wyoming, MI Metropolitan Statistical Area; (2) Rankings are based on annual percentage change for all metro areas containing at least 15,000 transactions over the last 10 years and ranges from 1 to 257; (3) figures based on a weighted average of Census Division estimates using a seasonally adjusted, purchase-only index; all figures are for the period ending December 31, 2022
Source: Federal Housing Finance Agency, Change in FHFA Metropolitan Area House Price Indexes, 2022Q4

Median Single-Family Home Prices

Area	2020	2021	2022[p]	Percent Change 2021 to 2022
MSA[1]	230.1	267.7	297.7	11.2
U.S. Average	300.2	357.1	392.6	9.9

Note: Figures are median sales prices of existing single-family homes in thousands of dollars; (p) preliminary; (1) Figures cover the Grand Rapids-Kentwood, MI Metropolitan Statistical Area
Source: National Association of Realtors, Median Sales Price of Existing Single-Family Homes for Metropolitan Areas, 4th Quarter 2022

Qualifying Income Based on Median Sales Price of Existing Single-Family Homes

Area	With 5% Down ($)	With 10% Down ($)	With 20% Down ($)
MSA[1]	85,118	80,638	71,678
U.S. Average	112,234	106,237	94,513

Note: Figures are preliminary; Qualifying income is based on a mortgage rate of 6.77%. Monthly principal and interest payment is limited to 25% of income; (1) Figures cover the Grand Rapids-Kentwood, MI Metropolitan Statistical Area
Source: National Association of Realtors, Qualifying Income Based on Median Sales Price of Existing Single-Family Homes for Metropolitan Areas, 4th Quarter 2022

Home Value

Area	Under $100,000	$100,000 -$199,999	$200,000 -$299,999	$300,000 -$399,999	$400,000 -$499,999	$500,000 -$999,999	$1,000,000 or more	Median ($)
City	16.4	49.8	24.0	6.0	2.0	1.4	0.3	168,700
MSA[1]	14.0	34.9	27.4	12.2	5.7	4.7	1.1	203,500
U.S.	16.2	24.2	20.1	13.6	8.3	13.6	4.1	244,900

Note: Figures are percentages except for median and cover owner-occupied housing units; (1) Figures cover the Grand Rapids-Kentwood, MI Metropolitan Statistical Area
Source: U.S. Census Bureau, 2017-2021 American Community Survey 5-Year Estimates

Year Housing Structure Built

Area	2020 or Later	2010 -2019	2000 -2009	1990 -1999	1980 -1989	1970 -1979	1960 -1969	1950 -1959	1940 -1949	Before 1940	Median Year
City	<0.1	3.8	4.9	6.3	6.6	8.5	9.0	14.9	8.9	37.1	1953
MSA[1]	0.2	6.9	12.6	15.8	11.3	13.6	9.3	10.0	5.1	15.2	1978
U.S.	0.2	7.3	13.6	13.6	13.2	14.8	10.3	10.0	4.7	12.2	1979

Note: Figures are percentages except for Median Year; Note: (1) Figures cover the Grand Rapids-Kentwood, MI Metropolitan Statistical Area
Source: U.S. Census Bureau, 2017-2021 American Community Survey 5-Year Estimates

Gross Monthly Rent

Area	Under $500	$500 -$999	$1,000 -$1,499	$1,500 -$1,999	$2,000 -$2,499	$2,500 -$2,999	$3,000 and up	Median ($)
City	10.7	38.1	37.4	9.2	3.4	0.8	0.4	1,013
MSA[1]	8.4	45.1	34.9	7.7	2.5	0.9	0.6	973
U.S.	8.1	30.5	30.8	16.8	7.3	3.1	3.5	1,163

Note: Figures are percentages except for median; Gross rent is the contract rent plus the estimated average monthly cost of utilities (electricity, gas, and water and sewer) and fuels (oil, coal, kerosene, wood, etc.) if these are paid by the renter (or paid for the renter by someone else); (1) Figures cover the Grand Rapids-Kentwood, MI Metropolitan Statistical Area
Source: U.S. Census Bureau, 2017-2021 American Community Survey 5-Year Estimates

HEALTH

Health Risk Factors

Category	MSA[1] (%)	U.S. (%)
Adults aged 18–64 who have any kind of health care coverage	92.7	90.9
Adults who reported being in good or better health	85.2	85.2
Adults who have been told they have high blood cholesterol	37.4	35.7
Adults who have been told they have high blood pressure	31.1	32.4
Adults who are current smokers	11.9	14.4
Adults who currently use e-cigarettes	5.6	6.7
Adults who currently use chewing tobacco, snuff, or snus	3.2	3.5
Adults who are heavy drinkers[2]	7.8	6.3
Adults who are binge drinkers[3]	19.0	15.4
Adults who are overweight (BMI 25.0 - 29.9)	37.1	34.4
Adults who are obese (BMI 30.0 - 99.8)	33.1	33.9
Adults who participated in any physical activities in the past month	77.5	76.3

Note: (1) Figures cover the Grand Rapids-Wyoming, MI Metropolitan Statistical Area; (2) Heavy drinkers are classified as adult men having more than 14 drinks per week and adult women having more than 7 drinks per week; (3) Binge drinkers are classified as males having five or more drinks on one occasion or females having four or more drinks on one occasion
Source: Centers for Disease Control and Prevention, Behaviorial Risk Factor Surveillance System, SMART: Selected Metropolitan Area Risk Trends, 2021

Acute and Chronic Health Conditions

Category	MSA[1] (%)	U.S. (%)
Adults who have ever been told they had a heart attack	3.6	4.0
Adults who have ever been told they have angina or coronary heart disease	4.4	3.8
Adults who have ever been told they had a stroke	4.3	3.0
Adults who have ever been told they have asthma	15.8	14.9
Adults who have ever been told they have arthritis	25.0	25.8
Adults who have ever been told they have diabetes[2]	9.8	10.9
Adults who have ever been told they had skin cancer	6.2	6.6
Adults who have ever been told they had any other types of cancer	8.1	7.5
Adults who have ever been told they have COPD	5.5	6.1
Adults who have ever been told they have kidney disease	3.9	3.0
Adults who have ever been told they have a form of depression	24.2	20.5

Note: (1) Figures cover the Grand Rapids-Wyoming, MI Metropolitan Statistical Area; (2) Figures do not include pregnancy-related, borderline, or pre-diabetes
Source: Centers for Disease Control and Prevention, Behaviorial Risk Factor Surveillance System, SMART: Selected Metropolitan Area Risk Trends, 2021

Health Screening and Vaccination Rates

Category	MSA[1] (%)	U.S. (%)
Adults who have ever been tested for HIV	34.5	34.9
Adults who have had their blood cholesterol checked within the last five years	87.1	85.2
Adults aged 65+ who have had flu shot within the past year	71.0	68.6
Adults aged 65+ who have ever had a pneumonia vaccination	74.6	71.0

Note: (1) Figures cover the Grand Rapids-Wyoming, MI Metropolitan Statistical Area.
Source: Centers for Disease Control and Prevention, Behaviorial Risk Factor Surveillance System, SMART: Selected Metropolitan Area Risk Trends, 2021

Disability Status

Category	MSA[1] (%)	U.S. (%)
Adults who reported being deaf	8.0	7.2
Are you blind or have serious difficulty seeing, even when wearing glasses?	5.6	4.8
Are you limited in any way in any of your usual activities due to arthritis?	11.6	11.1
Do you have difficulty doing errands alone?	7.9	7.0
Do you have difficulty dressing or bathing?	3.7	3.6
Do you have serious difficulty concentrating/remembering/making decisions?	12.1	12.1
Do you have serious difficulty walking or climbing stairs?	12.5	12.8

Note: (1) Figures cover the Grand Rapids-Wyoming, MI Metropolitan Statistical Area.
Source: Centers for Disease Control and Prevention, Behaviorial Risk Factor Surveillance System, SMART: Selected Metropolitan Area Risk Trends, 2021

Mortality Rates for the Top 10 Causes of Death in the U.S.

ICD-10[a] Sub-Chapter	ICD-10[a] Code	Crude Mortality Rate[1] per 100,000 population	
		County[2]	U.S.
Malignant neoplasms	C00-C97	168.1	182.6
Ischaemic heart diseases	I20-I25	112.8	113.1
Other forms of heart disease	I30-I51	46.9	64.4
Other degenerative diseases of the nervous system	G30-G31	60.8	51.0
Cerebrovascular diseases	I60-I69	38.6	47.8
Other external causes of accidental injury	W00-X59	40.7	46.4
Chronic lower respiratory diseases	J40-J47	33.8	45.7
Organic, including symptomatic, mental disorders	F01-F09	32.2	35.9
Hypertensive diseases	I10-I15	38.0	35.0
Diabetes mellitus	E10-E14	13.9	29.6

Note: (a) ICD-10 = International Classification of Diseases 10th Revision; (1) Crude mortality rates are a three-year average covering 2019-2021; (2) Figures cover Kent County.
Source: Centers for Disease Control and Prevention, National Center for Health Statistics. National Vital Statistics System, Mortality 2018-2021 on CDC WONDER Online Database

Mortality Rates for Selected Causes of Death

ICD-10[a] Sub-Chapter	ICD-10[a] Code	Crude Mortality Rate[1] per 100,000 population	
		County[2]	U.S.
Assault	X85-Y09	5.5	7.0
Diseases of the liver	K70-K76	15.6	19.8
Human immunodeficiency virus (HIV) disease	B20-B24	Unreliable	1.5
Influenza and pneumonia	J09-J18	9.2	14.7
Intentional self-harm	X60-X84	10.2	14.3
Malnutrition	E40-E46	1.9	4.3
Obesity and other hyperalimentation	E65-E68	4.1	3.0
Renal failure	N17-N19	6.4	15.7
Transport accidents	V01-V99	9.9	13.6
Viral hepatitis	B15-B19	Unreliable	1.2

Note: (a) ICD-10 = International Classification of Diseases 10th Revision; (1) Crude mortality rates are a three-year average covering 2019-2021; (2) Figures cover Kent County; Data are suppressed when the data meet the criteria for confidentiality constraints; Crude mortality rates are flagged as unreliable when the rate would be calculated with a numerator of 20 or less.
Source: Centers for Disease Control and Prevention, National Center for Health Statistics. National Vital Statistics System, Mortality 2018-2021 on CDC WONDER Online Database

Health Insurance Coverage

Area	With Health Insurance	With Private Health Insurance	With Public Health Insurance	Without Health Insurance	Population Under Age 19 Without Health Insurance
City	91.6	63.6	37.7	8.4	4.9
MSA[1]	95.0	76.1	31.3	5.0	3.0
U.S.	91.2	67.8	35.4	8.8	5.3

Note: Figures are percentages that cover the civilian noninstitutionalized population; (1) Figures cover the Grand Rapids-Kentwood, MI Metropolitan Statistical Area
Source: U.S. Census Bureau, 2017-2021 American Community Survey 5-Year Estimates

Number of Medical Professionals

Area	MDs[3]	DOs[3,4]	Dentists	Podiatrists	Chiropractors	Optometrists
County[1] (number)	2,358	459	506	33	258	167
County[1] (rate[2])	358.3	69.8	76.9	5.0	39.2	25.4
U.S. (rate[2])	289.3	23.5	72.5	6.2	28.7	17.4

Note: Data as of 2021 unless noted; (1) Data covers Kent County; (2) Rate per 100,000 population; (3) Data as of 2020 and includes all active, non-federal physicians; (4) Doctor of Osteopathic Medicine
Source: U.S. Department of Health and Human Services, Health Resources and Services Administration, Bureau of Health Professions, Area Resource File (ARF) 2021-2022

Best Hospitals

According to *U.S. News,* the Grand Rapids-Kentwood, MI metro area is home to one of the best hospitals in the U.S.: **Mary Free Bed Rehabilitation Hospital** (1 adult specialty). The hospital listed was nationally ranked in at least one of 15 adult or 10 pediatric specialties. The number of specialties shown cover the parent hospital. Only 164 U.S. hospitals performed well enough to be nationally ranked in one or more specialties. Twenty hospitals in the U.S. made the Honor Roll. The Best Hospitals Honor Roll takes both the national rankings and the procedure and condition ratings into account. Hospitals received points if they were nationally ranked in one of the 15 adult specialties—the higher they ranked, the more points they got—and how many ratings of "high performing" they earned in the 17 procedures and conditions. *U.S. News Online, "America's Best Hospitals 2022-23"*

According to *U.S. News,* the Grand Rapids-Kentwood, MI metro area is home to one of the best children's hospitals in the U.S.: **Spectrum Health Helen DeVos Children's Hospital** (4 pediatric specialties). The hospital listed was highly ranked in at least one of 10 pediatric specialties. Eighty-six children's hospitals in the U.S. were nationally ranked in at least one specialty. Hospitals received points for being ranked in a specialty, and the 10 hospitals with the most points across the 10 specialties make up the Honor Roll. *U.S. News Online, "America's Best Children's Hospitals 2022-23"*

EDUCATION

Public School District Statistics

District Name	Schls	Pupils	Pupil/ Teacher Ratio	Minority Pupils[1] (%)	LEP/ELL[2] (%)	IEP[3] (%)
East Grand Rapids Public Schools	5	2,895	17.0	16.7	0.6	5.7
Forest Hills Public Schools	18	9,339	18.0	21.2	4.4	9.1
Godwin Heights Public Schools	5	2,033	17.6	88.2	32.5	13.3
Grand Rapids Public Schools	51	13,900	15.9	79.0	25.6	17.3
Kelloggsville Public Schools	7	2,238	16.6	81.6	27.3	11.8
Kenowa Hills Public Schools	6	3,110	16.4	30.4	5.5	14.6
Kentwood Public Schools	16	9,325	16.9	73.1	22.1	13.5
Michigan Virtual Charter Academy	1	2,860	18.9	45.9	2.3	16.4
Northview Public Schools	8	3,138	18.1	28.5	1.3	13.0

Note: Table includes school districts with 2,000 or more students; (1) Percentage of students that are not non-Hispanic white; (2) Percentage of students that are Limited English Proficient or English Language Learners (2018-19); (3) Percentage of students that have an Individualized Education Program (2019-20).
Source: U.S. Department of Education, National Center for Education Statistics, Common Core of Data, Local Education Agency (School District) Universe Survey: School Year 2021-2022

Best High Schools

According to *U.S. News,* Grand Rapids is home to one of the top 500 high schools in the U.S.: **City High Middle School** (#18). Nearly 18,000 public, magnet and charter schools were ranked based on their performance on state assessments and how well they prepare students for college. *U.S. News & World Report, "Best High Schools 2022"*

Highest Level of Education

Area	Less than H.S.	H.S. Diploma	Some College, No Deg.	Associate Degree	Bachelor's Degree	Master's Degree	Prof. School Degree	Doctorate Degree
City	11.3	22.2	20.1	7.6	25.6	9.7	2.2	1.4
MSA[1]	7.7	26.7	21.6	9.5	22.5	9.1	1.8	1.2
U.S.	11.1	26.5	20.0	8.7	20.6	9.3	2.2	1.5

Note: Figures cover persons age 25 and over; (1) Figures cover the Grand Rapids-Kentwood, MI Metropolitan Statistical Area
Source: U.S. Census Bureau, 2017-2021 American Community Survey 5-Year Estimates

Educational Attainment by Race

Area	High School Graduate or Higher (%)					Bachelor's Degree or Higher (%)				
	Total	White	Black	Asian	Hisp.[2]	Total	White	Black	Asian	Hisp.[2]
City	88.7	92.6	86.4	80.6	57.7	38.8	46.0	20.4	44.7	13.3
MSA[1]	92.3	94.3	87.7	75.5	69.4	34.5	36.4	20.6	40.5	16.2
U.S.	88.9	91.4	87.2	87.6	71.2	33.7	35.5	23.3	55.6	18.4

Note: Figures shown cover persons 25 years old and over; (1) Figures cover the Grand Rapids-Kentwood, MI Metropolitan Statistical Area; (2) People of Hispanic origin can be of any race
Source: U.S. Census Bureau, 2017-2021 American Community Survey 5-Year Estimates

School Enrollment by Grade and Control

Area	Preschool (%)		Kindergarten (%)		Grades 1 - 4 (%)		Grades 5 - 8 (%)		Grades 9 - 12 (%)	
	Public	Private	Public	Private	Public	Private	Public	Private	Public	Private
City	66.8	33.2	74.2	25.8	78.3	21.7	82.3	17.7	82.3	17.7
MSA[1]	61.5	38.5	81.4	18.6	82.3	17.7	85.8	14.2	85.3	14.7
U.S.	58.8	41.2	86.3	13.7	88.3	11.7	88.6	11.4	89.4	10.6

Note: Figures shown cover persons 3 years old and over; (1) Figures cover the Grand Rapids-Kentwood, MI Metropolitan Statistical Area
Source: U.S. Census Bureau, 2017-2021 American Community Survey 5-Year Estimates

Higher Education

Four-Year Colleges			Two-Year Colleges			Medical Schools[1]	Law Schools[2]	Voc/ Tech[3]
Public	Private Non-profit	Private For-profit	Public	Private Non-profit	Private For-profit			
1	10	0	2	1	1	0	0	5

Note: Figures cover institutions located within the Grand Rapids-Kentwood, MI Metropolitan Statistical Area and include main campuses only; (1) includes schools accredited by the Liaison Committee on Medical Education and the American Osteopathic Association's Commission on Osteopathic College Accreditation; (2) includes ABA-accredited schools, schools with provisional ABA accreditation, and state accredited schools; (3) includes all schools with programs that are less than 2 years.
Source: National Center for Education Statistics, Integrated Postsecondary Education System (IPEDS), 2021-22; Wikipedia, List of Medical Schools in the United States, accessed April 10, 2023; Wikipedia, List of Law Schools in the United States, accessed April 10, 2023

EMPLOYERS

Major Employers

Company Name	Industry
Alticor	Consumer products, multi-level marketing
Farmers Insurance Group	Insurance
Grand Rapids Public Schools	Public elementary & secondary schools
Herman Miller	Manufacturing & industrial supply
Johnson Controls	Automotive interiors, HVAC equipment
Meijer	Retail, grocery & discount
Spectrum Health	Healthcare
Steelcase	Furniture

Note: Companies shown are located within the Grand Rapids-Kentwood, MI Metropolitan Statistical Area.
Source: Hoovers.com; Wikipedia

Best Companies to Work For

Corewell Health, headquartered in Grand Rapids, is among the "100 Best Places to Work in IT." To qualify, companies had to have a minimum of 100 total employees and five IT employees. The best places to work were selected based on DEI (diversity, equity, and inclusion) practices; IT turnover, promotions, and growth; IT retention and engagement programs; remote/hybrid working; benefits and perks (such as elder care and child care, flextime, and reimbursement for college tuition); and training and career development opportunities. *Computerworld, "Best Places to Work in IT," 2023*

PUBLIC SAFETY

Crime Rate

Area	Total Crime	Violent Crime Rate				Property Crime Rate		
		Murder	Rape[3]	Robbery	Aggrav. Assault	Burglary	Larceny -Theft	Motor Vehicle Theft
City	2,666.0	13.8	59.7	94.8	544.2	228.6	1,437.9	286.9
Suburbs[1]	1,390.3	2.5	70.8	21.3	172.1	149.8	837.9	135.8
Metro[2]	1,628.8	4.6	68.8	35.1	241.6	164.6	950.1	164.0
U.S.	2,356.7	6.5	38.4	73.9	279.7	314.2	1,398.0	246.0

Note: Figures are crimes per 100,000 population; (1) All areas within the metro area that are located outside the city limits; (2) Figures cover the Grand Rapids-Wyoming, MI Metropolitan Statistical Area; (3) All figures shown were reported using the revised Uniform Crime Reporting (UCR) definition of rape; Due to the transition to the National Incident-Based Reporting System (NIBRS), limited city and metro area data was released for 2021.
Source: FBI Uniform Crime Reports, 2020

Hate Crimes

Area	Number of Quarters Reported	Number of Incidents per Bias Motivation					
		Race/Ethnicity/ Ancestry	Religion	Sexual Orientation	Disability	Gender	Gender Identity
City	4	1	0	0	0	0	0
U.S.	4	5,227	1,244	1,110	130	75	266

Note: Due to the transition to the National Incident-Based Reporting System (NIBRS), limited crime data was released for 2021.
Source: Federal Bureau of Investigation, Hate Crime Statistics 2020

Identity Theft Consumer Reports

Area	Reports	Reports per 100,000 Population	Rank[2]
MSA[1]	1,707	160	231
U.S.	1,108,609	339	-

Note: (1) Figures cover the Grand Rapids-Kentwood, MI Metropolitan Statistical Area; (2) Rank ranges from 1 to 391 where 1 indicates greatest number of identity theft reports per 100,000 population
Source: Federal Trade Commission, Consumer Sentinel Network Data Book 2022

Fraud and Other Consumer Reports

Area	Reports	Reports per 100,000 Population	Rank[2]
MSA[1]	7,590	710	288
U.S.	4,064,520	1,245	-

Note: (1) Figures cover the Grand Rapids-Kentwood, MI Metropolitan Statistical Area; (2) Rank ranges from 1 to 391 where 1 indicates greatest number of fraud and other consumer reports per 100,000 population
Source: Federal Trade Commission, Consumer Sentinel Network Data Book 2022

POLITICS

2020 Presidential Election Results

Area	Biden	Trump	Jorgensen	Hawkins	Other
Kent County	51.9	45.8	1.5	0.3	0.5
U.S.	51.3	46.8	1.2	0.3	0.5

Note: Results are percentages and may not add to 100% due to rounding
Source: Dave Leip's Atlas of U.S. Presidential Elections

SPORTS

Professional Sports Teams

Team Name	League	Year Established

No teams are located in the metro area
Source: Wikipedia, Major Professional Sports Teams of the United States and Canada, April 12, 2023

CLIMATE

Average and Extreme Temperatures

Temperature	Jan	Feb	Mar	Apr	May	Jun	Jul	Aug	Sep	Oct	Nov	Dec	Yr.
Extreme High (°F)	66	67	80	88	92	102	100	100	97	87	81	67	102
Average High (°F)	30	32	42	57	69	79	83	81	73	61	46	34	57
Average Temp. (°F)	23	25	34	47	58	67	72	70	62	51	39	28	48
Average Low (°F)	15	16	25	36	46	56	60	59	51	41	31	21	38
Extreme Low (°F)	-22	-19	-8	3	22	33	41	39	28	18	-10	-18	-22

Note: Figures cover the years 1948-1990
Source: National Climatic Data Center, International Station Meteorological Climate Summary, 9/96

Average Precipitation/Snowfall/Humidity

Precip./Humidity	Jan	Feb	Mar	Apr	May	Jun	Jul	Aug	Sep	Oct	Nov	Dec	Yr.
Avg. Precip. (in.)	1.9	1.6	2.6	3.5	3.0	3.5	3.2	3.2	3.7	2.7	3.1	2.7	34.7
Avg. Snowfall (in.)	21	12	11	3	Tr	0	0	0	Tr	1	8	18	73
Avg. Rel. Hum. 7am (%)	81	80	80	79	79	81	84	88	89	85	83	83	83
Avg. Rel. Hum. 4pm (%)	71	66	61	54	50	52	52	55	58	60	68	74	60

Note: Figures cover the years 1948-1990; Tr = Trace amounts (<0.05 in. of rain; <0.5 in. of snow)
Source: National Climatic Data Center, International Station Meteorological Climate Summary, 9/96

Weather Conditions

Temperature			Daytime Sky			Precipitation		
5°F & below	32°F & below	90°F & above	Clear	Partly cloudy	Cloudy	0.01 inch or more precip.	0.1 inch or more snow/ice	Thunder-storms
15	146	11	67	119	179	142	57	34

Note: Figures are average number of days per year and cover the years 1948-1990
Source: National Climatic Data Center, International Station Meteorological Climate Summary, 9/96

HAZARDOUS WASTE

Superfund Sites

The Grand Rapids-Kentwood, MI metro area is home to five sites on the EPA's Superfund National Priorities List: **Butterworth #2 Landfill** (final); **Chem Central** (final); **H. Brown Co., Inc.** (final); **Kentwood Landfill** (final); **Organic Chemicals, Inc.** (final). There are a total of 1,165 Superfund sites with a status of proposed or final on the list in the U.S. *U.S. Environmental Protection Agency, National Priorities List, April 12, 2023*

AIR QUALITY

Air Quality Trends: Ozone

	1990	1995	2000	2005	2010	2015	2018	2019	2020	2021
MSA[1]	0.098	0.092	0.073	0.084	0.069	0.066	0.070	0.063	0.074	0.067
U.S.	0.087	0.089	0.081	0.080	0.072	0.067	0.069	0.065	0.065	0.067

Note: (1) Data covers the Grand Rapids-Kentwood, MI Metropolitan Statistical Area. The values shown are the composite ozone concentration averages among trend sites based on the highest fourth daily maximum 8-hour concentration in parts per million. These trends are based on sites having an adequate record of monitoring data during the trend period. Data from exceptional events are included.
Source: U.S. Environmental Protection Agency, Air Quality Monitoring Information, "Air Quality Trends by City, 1990-2021"

Air Quality Index

Area	Percent of Days when Air Quality was...[2]					AQI Statistics[2]	
	Good	Moderate	Unhealthy for Sensitive Groups	Unhealthy	Very Unhealthy	Maximum	Median
MSA[1]	62.2	36.4	1.4	0.0	0.0	143	44

Note: (1) Data covers the Grand Rapids-Kentwood, MI Metropolitan Statistical Area; (2) Based on 365 days with AQI data in 2021. Air Quality Index (AQI) is an index for reporting daily air quality. EPA calculates the AQI for five major air pollutants regulated by the Clean Air Act: ground-level ozone, particle pollution (aka particulate matter), carbon monoxide, sulfur dioxide, and nitrogen dioxide. The AQI runs from 0 to 500. The higher the AQI value, the greater the level of air pollution and the greater the health concern. There are six AQI categories: "Good" AQI is between 0 and 50. Air quality is considered satisfactory; "Moderate" AQI is between 51 and 100. Air quality is acceptable; "Unhealthy for Sensitive Groups" When AQI values are between 101 and 150, members of sensitive groups may experience health effects; "Unhealthy" When AQI values are between 151 and 200 everyone may begin to experience health effects; "Very Unhealthy" AQI values between 201 and 300 trigger a health alert; "Hazardous" AQI values over 300 trigger warnings of emergency conditions (not shown).
Source: U.S. Environmental Protection Agency, Air Quality Index Report, 2021

Air Quality Index Pollutants

Area	Percent of Days when AQI Pollutant was...[2]					
	Carbon Monoxide	Nitrogen Dioxide	Ozone	Sulfur Dioxide	Particulate Matter 2.5	Particulate Matter 10
MSA[1]	0.0	1.9	50.1	(3)	47.9	0.0

Note: (1) Data covers the Grand Rapids-Kentwood, MI Metropolitan Statistical Area; (2) Based on 365 days with AQI data in 2021. The Air Quality Index (AQI) is an index for reporting daily air quality. EPA calculates the AQI for five major air pollutants regulated by the Clean Air Act: ground-level ozone, particle pollution (also known as particulate matter), carbon monoxide, sulfur dioxide, and nitrogen dioxide. The AQI runs from 0 to 500. The higher the AQI value, the greater the level of air pollution and the greater the health concern; (3) Sulfur dioxide is no longer included in this table (as of December 8, 2021) because SO_2 concentrations tend to be very localized and not necessarily representative of broad geographical areas like counties and CBSAs.
Source: U.S. Environmental Protection Agency, Air Quality Index Report, 2021

Maximum Air Pollutant Concentrations: Particulate Matter, Ozone, CO and Lead

	Particulate Matter 10 (ug/m^3)	Particulate Matter 2.5 Wtd AM (ug/m^3)	Particulate Matter 2.5 24-Hr (ug/m^3)	Ozone (ppm)	Carbon Monoxide (ppm)	Lead (ug/m^3)
MSA[1] Level	42	10.1	26	0.069	1	n/a
NAAQS[2]	150	15	35	0.075	9	0.15
Met NAAQS[2]	Yes	Yes	Yes	Yes	Yes	n/a

Note: (1) Data covers the Grand Rapids-Kentwood, MI Metropolitan Statistical Area; Data from exceptional events are included; (2) National Ambient Air Quality Standards; ppm = parts per million; ug/m^3 = micrograms per cubic meter; n/a not available.
Concentrations: Particulate Matter 10 (coarse particulate)—highest second maximum 24-hour concentration; Particulate Matter 2.5 Wtd AM (fine particulate)—highest weighted annual mean concentration; Particulate Matter 2.5 24-Hour (fine particulate)—highest 98th percentile 24-hour concentration; Ozone—highest fourth daily maximum 8-hour concentration; Carbon Monoxide—highest second maximum non-overlapping 8-hour concentration; Lead—maximum running 3-month average
Source: U.S. Environmental Protection Agency, Air Quality Monitoring Information, "Air Quality Statistics by City, 2021"

Maximum Air Pollutant Concentrations: Nitrogen Dioxide and Sulfur Dioxide

	Nitrogen Dioxide AM (ppb)	Nitrogen Dioxide 1-Hr (ppb)	Sulfur Dioxide AM (ppb)	Sulfur Dioxide 1-Hr (ppb)	Sulfur Dioxide 24-Hr (ppb)
MSA[1] Level	8	39	n/a	4	n/a
NAAQS[2]	53	100	30	75	140
Met NAAQS[2]	Yes	Yes	n/a	Yes	n/a

Note: (1) Data covers the Grand Rapids-Kentwood, MI Metropolitan Statistical Area; Data from exceptional events are included; (2) National Ambient Air Quality Standards; ppm = parts per million; ug/m^3 = micrograms per cubic meter; n/a not available.
Concentrations: Nitrogen Dioxide AM—highest arithmetic mean concentration; Nitrogen Dioxide 1-Hr—highest 98th percentile 1-hour daily maximum concentration; Sulfur Dioxide AM—highest annual mean concentration; Sulfur Dioxide 1-Hr—highest 99th percentile 1-hour daily maximum concentration; Sulfur Dioxide 24-Hr—highest second maximum 24-hour concentration
Source: U.S. Environmental Protection Agency, Air Quality Monitoring Information, "Air Quality Statistics by City, 2021"

Green Bay, Wisconsin

Background

The city of Green Bay takes its name from an inlet at the mouth of the Fox River, off Lake Michigan. Green Bay is the oldest city in Wisconsin, and the seat of Brown County. The city, laid out on high ground on either side of the river, has always been an important port and is known to Americans as the home of the nation's oldest professional football team, the Green Bay Packers, who play in Lambeau Field, the longest continuously occupied stadium in the NFL.

Prior to European settlement, the area was home to Winnebago and other settled, horticultural tribes. The French explorer Jean Nicolet, who was seeking a route to the Pacific and thence to Asia, was the first recorded European visitor. He landed his canoe in 1634 about 10 miles south of the present city, finding there a community of friendly Winnebago or Oneida, who he thought at first to be Chinese.

Later explorers and traders, mostly French, established a trading post at the site, and in 1720, Fort St. Francis was completed at the mouth of the river. In 1745, the first permanent settlement was begun at "Le Baye" in what are the boundaries of the present city. The so-called "Tank House," built by the voyageur Joseph Roy in 1766, is thought to be the oldest house in the state. Green Bay is also home to the oldest Roman Catholic bishopric in the area. Although the French influence was paramount, many of the fur traders who came into the area were associated with the American fur baron John Jacob Astor, who constructed warehouses and other buildings on the site.

Settlers regarded themselves as French citizens until the fort was occupied by the British in 1763. From 1763 until the War of 1812, they were under British control. When the Americans garrisoned Fort Howard, the city was brought firmly under rule of the new republic. The first newspaper in the state, the *Green Bay Intelligencer*, was established in 1833. In 1854, the city of Green Bay was chartered, and in 1893, the adjoining Fort Howard was incorporated into it. In the late nineteenth century, Green Bay was a major port for the thriving lumber trade.

Forest products, particularly paper, are still a mainstay of the local economy, as are health care, finance, insurance, and logistics. The Oneida Tribe of Indians of Wisconsin is headquartered in the region. Tourism is increasingly important, with visitors drawn to the city both for Green Bay Packers football, and for some of the most attractive vacation spots in the state.

The city's downtown renaissance includes office space and dwelling units along the Fox River, and a walking/biking trail along the river's east side. The CityDeck faces the water for four blocks. Similarly, the Broadway corridor has been revived. The KI Convention Center was expanded by 35,000 square feet and the 15,000-square foot Children's Museum of Green Bay is a popular attraction in the city's downtown.

Other attractions include the National Railroad Museum, which includes the world's largest steam locomotive, and the NEW Zoo, with more than 200 animals of nearly 90 species.

Green Bay is home to a local campus (1965) of the University of Wisconsin and Bellin College (1909), which specializes in nursing and radiologic sciences.

The weather in Green Bay is a mild version of the general northern plains climate, with four seasons, warm summers, and considerable winter snowfall. High and low temperatures are modified by the city's location on Green Bay, as well as its proximity to Lake Superior and Lake Michigan.

Rankings

General Rankings

- *US News & World Report* conducted a survey of more than 3,600 people and analyzed the 150 largest metropolitan areas to determine what matters most when selecting where to settle down. Green Bay ranked #3 out of the top 25 as having the best combination of desirable factors. Criteria: cost of living; quality of life and education; net migration; job market; desirability; and other factors. *money.usnews.com, "The 25 Best Places to Live in the U.S. in 2022-2023," May 17, 2022*

- In their ninth annual survey, Livability.com looked at data for more than 2,300 mid-sized U.S. cities to determine the rankings for Livability's "Top 100 Best Places to Live" in 2022. Green Bay ranked #74. Criteria: housing and economy; social and civic engagement; education; demographics; health care options; transportation & infrastructure; and community amenities. *Livability.com, "Top 100 Best Places to Live 2022" July 19, 2022*

Business/Finance Rankings

- The Green Bay metro area appeared on the Milken Institute "2022 Best Performing Cities" list. Rank: #92 out of 200 large metro areas (population over 250,000). Criteria: job growth; wage and salary growth; high-tech output growth; housing affordability; household broadband access. *Milken Institute, "Best-Performing Cities 2022," March 28, 2022*

- *Forbes* ranked the 200 most populous metro areas to determine the nation's "Best Places for Business and Careers." The Green Bay metro area was ranked #100. Criteria: costs (business and living); job growth (past and projected); income growth; quality of life; educational attainment (college and high school); projected economic growth; cultural and leisure opportunities; workplace tolerance laws; net migration patterns. *Forbes, "The Best Places for Business and Careers 2019: Seattle Still On Top," October 30, 2019*

Safety Rankings

- The National Insurance Crime Bureau ranked 390 metro areas in the U.S. in terms of per capita rates of vehicle theft. The Green Bay metro area ranked #326 (#1 = highest rate). Criteria: number of vehicle theft offenses per 100,000 inhabitants in 2021. *National Insurance Crime Bureau, "Hot Spots 2021," September 1, 2022*

Seniors/Retirement Rankings

- From its Best Cities for Successful Aging indexes, the Milken Institute generated rankings for metropolitan areas, weighing data in nine categories—health care, wellness, living arrangements, transportation and convenience, financial characteristics, education, employment, community engagement, and overall livability. The Green Bay metro area was ranked #162 overall in the small metro area category. *Milken Institute, "Best Cities for Successful Aging, 2017" March 14, 2017*

Business Environment

DEMOGRAPHICS

Population Growth

Area	1990 Census	2000 Census	2010 Census	2020 Census	Population Growth (%)	
					1990-2020	2010-2020
City	96,466	102,313	104,057	107,395	11.3	3.2
MSA[1]	243,698	282,599	306,241	328,268	34.7	7.2
U.S.	248,709,873	281,421,906	308,745,538	331,449,281	33.3	7.4

Note: (1) Figures cover the Green Bay, WI Metropolitan Statistical Area
Source: U.S. Census Bureau, 1990 Census, 2000 Census, 2010 Census, 2020 Census

Race

Area	White Alone[2] (%)	Black Alone[2] (%)	Asian Alone[2] (%)	AIAN[3] Alone[2] (%)	NHOPI[4] Alone[2] (%)	Other Race Alone[2] (%)	Two or More Races (%)
City	66.6	5.5	4.4	4.4	0.1	8.4	10.6
MSA[1]	81.8	2.6	2.7	2.5	0.0	3.8	6.6
U.S.	61.6	12.4	6.0	1.1	0.2	8.4	10.2

Note: (1) Figures cover the Green Bay, WI Metropolitan Statistical Area; (2) Alone is defined as not being in combination with one or more other races; (3) American Indian and Alaska Native; (4) Native Hawaiian and Other Pacific Islander
Source: U.S. Census Bureau, 2020 Census

Hispanic or Latino Origin

Area	Total (%)	Mexican (%)	Puerto Rican (%)	Cuban (%)	Other (%)
City	16.6	13.0	1.9	0.0	1.8
MSA[1]	8.1	6.1	0.9	0.1	1.0
U.S.	18.4	11.2	1.8	0.7	4.7

Note: Persons of Hispanic or Latino origin can be of any race; (1) Figures cover the Green Bay, WI Metropolitan Statistical Area
Source: U.S. Census Bureau, 2017-2021 American Community Survey 5-Year Estimates

Age

Area	Percent of Population									Median Age
	Under Age 5	Age 5–19	Age 20–34	Age 35–44	Age 45–54	Age 55–64	Age 65–74	Age 75–84	Age 85+	
City	6.5	20.6	22.5	12.9	11.1	12.4	8.6	3.7	1.5	35.2
MSA[1]	5.8	19.8	18.8	12.6	12.2	14.0	10.1	4.8	1.8	39.3
U.S.	5.6	19.2	20.2	12.7	12.4	13.1	10.0	4.9	1.9	38.8

Note: (1) Figures cover the Green Bay, WI Metropolitan Statistical Area
Source: U.S. Census Bureau, 2020 Census

Disability by Age

Area	All Ages	Under 18 Years Old	18 to 64 Years Old	65 Years and Over
City	13.8	6.7	12.2	34.9
MSA[1]	11.3	4.5	9.7	27.7
U.S.	12.6	4.4	10.3	33.4

Note: Figures show percent of the civilian noninstitutionalized population that reported having a disability. Disability status is determined from six types of difficulty: vision, hearing, cognitive, ambulatory, self-care, and independent living. For children under 5 years old, hearing and vision difficulty are used to determine disability status. For children between the ages of 5 and 14, disability status is determined from hearing, vision, cognitive, ambulatory, and self-care difficulties. For people aged 15 years and older, they are considered to have a disability if they have difficulty with any one of the six difficulty types; Note: (1) Figures cover the Green Bay, WI Metropolitan Statistical Area
Source: U.S. Census Bureau, 2017-2021 American Community Survey 5-Year Estimates

Ancestry

Area	German	Irish	English	American	Italian	Polish	French[2]	Scottish	Dutch
City	28.7	8.5	4.3	4.1	2.1	8.0	3.6	1.0	2.6
MSA[1]	35.4	9.6	4.8	3.8	2.1	9.5	3.9	0.8	4.1
U.S.	12.8	9.6	8.1	5.7	5.0	2.7	2.2	1.6	1.1

Note: Figures are the percentage of the total population reporting a particular ancestry. The nine most commonly reported ancestries in the U.S. are shown. Figures include multiple ancestries (e.g. if a person reported being Irish and Italian, they were included in both columns); (1) Figures cover the Green Bay, WI Metropolitan Statistical Area; (2) Excludes Basque
Source: U.S. Census Bureau, 2017-2021 American Community Survey 5-Year Estimates

Foreign-born Population

Area	Any Foreign Country	Asia	Mexico	Europe	Caribbean	Central America[2]	South America	Africa	Canada
City	9.2	2.0	5.2	0.4	0.2	0.4	0.3	0.6	0.1
MSA[1]	4.9	1.6	2.1	0.4	0.1	0.3	0.1	0.2	0.1
U.S.	13.6	4.2	3.3	1.5	1.1	1.1	1.1	0.8	0.2

Note: (1) Figures cover the Green Bay, WI Metropolitan Statistical Area; (2) Excludes Mexico.
Source: U.S. Census Bureau, 2017-2021 American Community Survey 5-Year Estimates

Household Size

Area	One	Two	Three	Four	Five	Six	Seven or More	Average Household Size
City	35.0	32.2	13.6	10.7	5.6	1.6	1.4	2.40
MSA[1]	28.4	37.5	14.0	11.8	5.6	1.7	1.0	2.40
U.S.	28.1	33.8	15.5	12.9	6.0	2.3	1.4	2.60

Note: (1) Figures cover the Green Bay, WI Metropolitan Statistical Area
Source: U.S. Census Bureau, 2017-2021 American Community Survey 5-Year Estimates

Household Relationships

Area	House-holder	Opposite-sex Spouse	Same-sex Spouse	Opposite-sex Unmarried Partner	Same-sex Unmarried Partner	Child[2]	Grand-child	Other Relatives	Non-relatives
City	40.7	15.2	0.2	4.0	0.2	28.6	1.6	3.4	3.0
MSA[1]	40.5	19.8	0.1	3.3	0.1	28.1	1.2	2.2	2.2
U.S.	38.3	17.5	0.2	2.5	0.2	28.3	2.4	4.8	3.4

Note: Figures are percent of the total population; (1) Figures cover the Green Bay, WI Metropolitan Statistical Area; (2) Includes biological, adopted, and stepchildren of the householder
Source: U.S. Census Bureau, 2020 Census

Gender

Area	Males	Females	Males per 100 Females
City	53,407	53,988	98.9
MSA[1]	163,689	164,579	99.5
U.S.	162,685,811	168,763,470	96.4

Note: (1) Figures cover the Green Bay, WI Metropolitan Statistical Area
Source: U.S. Census Bureau, 2020 Census

Marital Status

Area	Never Married	Now Married[2]	Separated	Widowed	Divorced
City	37.4	42.2	1.2	5.2	14.0
MSA[1]	30.6	52.2	0.7	5.1	11.4
U.S.	33.8	48.0	1.8	5.6	10.8

Note: Figures are percentages and cover the population 15 years of age and older; (1) Figures cover the Green Bay, WI Metropolitan Statistical Area; (2) Excludes separated
Source: U.S. Census Bureau, 2017-2021 American Community Survey 5-Year Estimates

Religious Groups by Family

Area	Catholic	Baptist	Methodist	LDS[2]	Pentecostal	Lutheran	Islam	Adventist	Other
MSA[1]	31.8	0.3	1.4	0.5	1.1	10.8	0.4	0.9	7.0
U.S.	18.7	7.3	3.0	2.0	1.8	1.7	1.3	1.3	11.6

Note: Figures are the number of adherents as a percentage of the total population and cover the eight largest religious groups in the U.S; (1) Figures cover the Green Bay, WI Metropolitan Statistical Area; (2) Church of Jesus Christ of Latter-day Saints
Sources: 2020 U.S. Religion Census, Association of Statisticians of American Religious Bodies; The Association of Religion Data Archives (ARDA)

Religious Groups by Tradition

Area	Catholic	Evangelical Protestant	Mainline Protestant	Black Protestant	Islam	Judaism	Hinduism	Orthodox	Buddhism
MSA[1]	31.8	14.6	6.2	<0.1	0.4	n/a	n/a	<0.1	<0.1
U.S.	18.7	16.5	5.2	2.3	1.3	0.6	0.4	0.4	0.3

Note: Figures are the number of adherents as a percentage of the total population; (1) Figures cover the Green Bay, WI Metropolitan Statistical Area
Sources: 2020 U.S. Religion Census, Association of Statisticians of American Religious Bodies; The Association of Religion Data Archives (ARDA)

ECONOMY

Gross Metropolitan Product

Area	2020	2021	2022	2023	Rank[2]
MSA[1]	20.5	22.2	24.3	26.0	139

Note: Figures are in billions of dollars; (1) Figures cover the Green Bay, WI Metropolitan Statistical Area; (2) Rank is based on 2021 data and ranges from 1 to 381
Source: U.S. Conference of Mayors, U.S. Metro Economies: U.S. Metros Compared to Global and State Economies, June 2022

Economic Growth

Area	2018-20 (%)	2021 (%)	2022 (%)	2023 (%)	Rank[2]
MSA[1]	-2.5	3.7	3.7	3.9	326
U.S.	-0.6	5.7	3.1	2.9	—

Note: Figures are real gross metropolitan product (GMP) growth rates and represent average annual percent change; (1) Figures cover the Green Bay, WI Metropolitan Statistical Area; (2) Rank is based on 2020 2-year average annual percent change and ranges from 1 to 381
Source: U.S. Conference of Mayors, U.S. Metro Economies: U.S. Metros Compared to Global and State Economies, June 2022

Metropolitan Area Exports

Area	2016	2017	2018	2019	2020	2021	Rank[2]
MSA[1]	1,044.0	1,054.8	1,044.3	928.2	736.4	765.6	185

Note: Figures are in millions of dollars; (1) Figures cover the Green Bay, WI Metropolitan Statistical Area; (2) Rank is based on 2021 data and ranges from 1 to 388
Source: U.S. Department of Commerce, International Trade Administration, Office of Trade and Economic Analysis, Industry and Analysis, Exports by Metropolitan Area, data extracted March 16, 2023

Building Permits

Area	Single-Family			Multi-Family			Total		
	2021	2022	Pct. Chg.	2021	2022	Pct. Chg.	2021	2022	Pct. Chg.
City	58	37	-36.2	2	0	-100.0	60	37	-38.3
MSA[1]	830	627	-24.5	578	622	7.6	1,408	1,249	-11.3
U.S.	1,115,400	975,600	-12.5	621,600	689,500	10.9	1,737,000	1,665,100	-4.1

Note: (1) Figures cover the Green Bay, WI Metropolitan Statistical Area; Figures represent new, privately-owned housing units authorized (unadjusted data); All permit data are based on estimates with imputation
Source: U.S. Census Bureau, Manufacturing, Mining, and Construction Statistics, Building Permits, 2021, 2022

Bankruptcy Filings

Area	Business Filings			Nonbusiness Filings		
	2021	2022	% Chg.	2021	2022	% Chg.
Brown County	2	7	250.0	388	290	-25.3
U.S.	14,347	13,481	-6.0	399,269	374,240	-6.3

Note: Business filings include Chapter 7, Chapter 9, Chapter 11, Chapter 12, Chapter 13, Chapter 15, and Section 304; Nonbusiness filings include Chapter 7, Chapter 11, and Chapter 13
Source: Administrative Office of the U.S. Courts, Business and Nonbusiness Bankruptcy, County Cases Commenced by Chapter of the Bankruptcy Code, During the 12-Month Period Ending December 31, 2021 and Business and Nonbusiness Bankruptcy, County Cases Commenced by Chapter of the Bankruptcy Code, During the 12-Month Period Ending December 31, 2022

Housing Vacancy Rates

Area	Gross Vacancy Rate[2] (%)			Year-Round Vacancy Rate[3] (%)			Rental Vacancy Rate[4] (%)			Homeowner Vacancy Rate[5] (%)		
	2020	2021	2022	2020	2021	2022	2020	2021	2022	2020	2021	2022
MSA[1]	n/a	n/a	n/a	n/a	n/a	n/a	n/a	n/a	n/a	n/a	n/a	n/a
U.S.	10.6	10.8	10.5	8.2	8.4	8.2	6.3	6.1	5.8	1.0	0.9	0.8

Note: (1) Figures cover the Green Bay, WI Metropolitan Statistical Area; (2) The percentage of the total housing inventory that is vacant; (3) The percentage of the housing inventory (excluding seasonal units) that is year-round vacant; (4) The percentage of rental inventory that is vacant for rent; (5) The percentage of homeowner inventory that is vacant for sale; n/a not available
Source: U.S. Census Bureau, Housing Vacancies and Homeownership Annual Statistics: 2020, 2021, 2022

INCOME

Income

Area	Per Capita ($)	Median Household ($)	Average Household ($)
City	29,822	55,221	70,879
MSA[1]	35,678	68,952	87,144
U.S.	37,638	69,021	97,196

Note: (1) Figures cover the Green Bay, WI Metropolitan Statistical Area
Source: U.S. Census Bureau, 2017-2021 American Community Survey 5-Year Estimates

Household Income Distribution

Area	Percent of Households Earning							
	Under $15,000	$15,000 -$24,999	$25,000 -$34,999	$35,000 -$49,999	$50,000 -$74,999	$75,000 -$99,999	$100,000 -$149,999	$150,000 and up
City	10.1	9.4	10.0	15.0	21.7	13.0	13.6	7.3
MSA[1]	7.0	7.1	8.7	12.3	19.2	15.2	18.3	12.1
U.S.	9.4	7.8	8.2	11.4	16.8	12.8	16.3	17.3

Note: (1) Figures cover the Green Bay, WI Metropolitan Statistical Area
Source: U.S. Census Bureau, 2017-2021 American Community Survey 5-Year Estimates

Poverty Rate

Area	All Ages	Under 18 Years Old	18 to 64 Years Old	65 Years and Over
City	15.4	21.5	14.2	10.3
MSA[1]	9.4	12.0	9.0	7.1
U.S.	12.6	17.0	11.8	9.6

Note: Figures are percentage of people whose income during the past 12 months was below the poverty level;
(1) Figures cover the Green Bay, WI Metropolitan Statistical Area
Source: U.S. Census Bureau, 2017-2021 American Community Survey 5-Year Estimates

EMPLOYMENT

Labor Force and Employment

Area	Civilian Labor Force			Workers Employed		
	Dec. 2021	Dec. 2022	% Chg.	Dec. 2021	Dec. 2022	% Chg.
City	53,463	52,666	-1.5	52,235	51,500	-1.4
MSA[1]	173,797	170,959	-1.6	170,171	167,408	-1.6
U.S.	161,696,000	164,224,000	1.6	155,732,000	158,872,000	2.0

Note: Data is not seasonally adjusted and covers workers 16 years of age and older; (1) Figures cover the
Green Bay, WI Metropolitan Statistical Area
Source: Bureau of Labor Statistics, Local Area Unemployment Statistics

Unemployment Rate

Area	2022											
	Jan.	Feb.	Mar.	Apr.	May	Jun.	Jul.	Aug.	Sep.	Oct.	Nov.	Dec.
City	3.1	3.1	3.1	2.9	2.8	3.4	3.2	3.4	3.3	2.9	2.5	2.2
MSA[1]	2.8	3.0	3.0	2.7	2.6	3.2	3.0	3.0	2.9	2.6	2.4	2.1
U.S.	4.4	4.1	3.8	3.3	3.4	3.8	3.8	3.8	3.3	3.4	3.4	3.3

Note: Data is not seasonally adjusted and covers workers 16 years of age and older; (1) Figures cover the
Green Bay, WI Metropolitan Statistical Area
Source: Bureau of Labor Statistics, Local Area Unemployment Statistics

Average Wages

Occupation	$/Hr.	Occupation	$/Hr.
Accountants and Auditors	35.84	Maintenance and Repair Workers	22.47
Automotive Mechanics	24.15	Marketing Managers	75.00
Bookkeepers	21.27	Network and Computer Systems Admin.	42.60
Carpenters	27.33	Nurses, Licensed Practical	23.59
Cashiers	13.29	Nurses, Registered	37.41
Computer Programmers	48.63	Nursing Assistants	17.41
Computer Systems Analysts	44.13	Office Clerks, General	19.40
Computer User Support Specialists	29.31	Physical Therapists	44.40
Construction Laborers	22.68	Physicians	177.48
Cooks, Restaurant	15.04	Plumbers, Pipefitters and Steamfitters	33.56
Customer Service Representatives	20.32	Police and Sheriff's Patrol Officers	34.37
Dentists	81.73	Postal Service Mail Carriers	27.20
Electricians	30.20	Real Estate Sales Agents	29.62
Engineers, Electrical	43.80	Retail Salespersons	16.28
Fast Food and Counter Workers	11.72	Sales Representatives, Technical/Scientific	34.34
Financial Managers	67.97	Secretaries, Exc. Legal/Medical/Executive	20.34
First-Line Supervisors of Office Workers	32.04	Security Guards	16.22
General and Operations Managers	64.87	Surgeons	n/a
Hairdressers/Cosmetologists	16.41	Teacher Assistants, Exc. Postsecondary*	15.77
Home Health and Personal Care Aides	14.33	Teachers, Secondary School, Exc. Sp. Ed.*	29.64
Janitors and Cleaners	15.45	Telemarketers	n/a
Landscaping/Groundskeeping Workers	17.41	Truck Drivers, Heavy/Tractor-Trailer	25.81
Lawyers	72.57	Truck Drivers, Light/Delivery Services	21.30
Maids and Housekeeping Cleaners	14.43	Waiters and Waitresses	15.02

Note: Wage data covers the Green Bay, WI Metropolitan Statistical Area; (*) Hourly wages were calculated
from annual wage data based on a 40 hour work week; n/a not available.
Source: Bureau of Labor Statistics, Metro Area Occupational Employment & Wage Estimates, May 2022

Employment by Industry

Sector	MSA[1]		U.S.
	Number of Employees	Percent of Total	Percent of Total
Construction, Mining, and Logging	8,400	4.7	5.4
Private Education and Health Services	27,600	15.3	16.1
Financial Activities	11,200	6.2	5.9
Government	20,800	11.5	14.5
Information	1,400	0.8	2.0
Leisure and Hospitality	16,000	8.9	10.3
Manufacturing	31,900	17.7	8.4
Other Services	8,100	4.5	3.7
Professional and Business Services	19,100	10.6	14.7
Retail Trade	17,800	9.9	10.2
Transportation, Warehousing, and Utilities	9,300	5.1	4.9
Wholesale Trade	9,000	5.0	3.9

Note: Figures are non-farm employment as of December 2022. Figures are not seasonally adjusted and include workers 16 years of age and older; (1) Figures cover the Green Bay, WI Metropolitan Statistical Area
Source: Bureau of Labor Statistics, Current Employment Statistics, Employment, Hours, and Earnings

Employment by Occupation

Occupation Classification	City (%)	MSA[1] (%)	U.S. (%)
Management, Business, Science, and Arts	31.2	36.1	40.3
Natural Resources, Construction, and Maintenance	8.1	9.1	8.7
Production, Transportation, and Material Moving	20.6	18.4	13.1
Sales and Office	21.3	20.6	20.9
Service	18.9	15.8	17.0

Note: Figures cover employed civilians 16 years of age and older; (1) Figures cover the Green Bay, WI Metropolitan Statistical Area
Source: U.S. Census Bureau, 2017-2021 American Community Survey 5-Year Estimates

Occupations with Greatest Projected Employment Growth: 2022 – 2024

Occupation[1]	2022 Employment	2024 Projected Employment	Numeric Employment Change	Percent Employment Change
Laborers and Freight, Stock, and Material Movers, Hand	64,310	67,940	3,630	5.6
Maids and Housekeeping Cleaners	22,820	26,320	3,500	15.3
Fast Food and Counter Workers	58,230	61,720	3,490	6.0
Farmworkers and Laborers, Crop, Nursery, and Greenhouse	48,090	51,190	3,100	6.4
Cooks, Restaurant	23,140	25,660	2,520	10.9
Childcare Workers	14,930	17,390	2,460	16.5
Industrial Truck and Tractor Operators	17,330	19,540	2,210	12.8
Home Health and Personal Care Aides	75,480	77,560	2,080	2.8
Waiters and Waitresses	34,590	36,650	2,060	6.0
Stockers and Order Fillers	47,340	48,990	1,650	3.5

Note: Projections cover Wisconsin; (1) Sorted by numeric employment change
Source: www.projectionscentral.com, State Occupational Projections, 2022–2024 Short-Term Projections

Fastest-Growing Occupations: 2022 – 2024

Occupation[1]	2022 Employment	2024 Projected Employment	Numeric Employment Change	Percent Employment Change
Personal Care and Service Workers, All Other	140	240	100	71.4
Ushers, Lobby Attendants, and Ticket Takers	1,350	1,630	280	20.7
Childcare Workers	14,930	17,390	2,460	16.5
Maids and Housekeeping Cleaners	22,820	26,320	3,500	15.3
Industrial Truck and Tractor Operators	17,330	19,540	2,210	12.8
Reservation and Transportation Ticket Agents and Travel Clerks	1,000	1,120	120	12.0
Travel Agents	820	910	90	11.0
Cooks, Restaurant	23,140	25,660	2,520	10.9
Medical Scientists, Except Epidemiologists	1,360	1,500	140	10.3
Athletes and Sports Competitors	580	640	60	10.3

Note: Projections cover Wisconsin; (1) Sorted by percent employment change and excludes occupations with numeric employment change less than 50
Source: www.projectionscentral.com, State Occupational Projections, 2022–2024 Short-Term Projections

CITY FINANCES

City Government Finances

Component	2020 ($000)	2020 ($ per capita)
Total Revenues	213,921	2,046
Total Expenditures	216,361	2,069
Debt Outstanding	256,548	2,453
Cash and Securities[1]	172,628	1,651

Note: (1) Cash and security holdings of a government at the close of its fiscal year, including those of its dependent agencies, utilities, and liquor stores.
Source: U.S. Census Bureau, State & Local Government Finances 2020

City Government Revenue by Source

Source	2020 ($000)	2020 ($ per capita)	2020 (%)
General Revenue			
From Federal Government	3,815	36	1.8
From State Government	34,694	332	16.2
From Local Governments	6,968	67	3.3
Taxes			
Property	59,674	571	27.9
Sales and Gross Receipts	474	5	0.2
Personal Income	0	0	0.0
Corporate Income	0	0	0.0
Motor Vehicle License	0	0	0.0
Other Taxes	3,011	29	1.4
Current Charges	43,321	414	20.3
Liquor Store	0	0	0.0
Utility	45,340	434	21.2

Source: U.S. Census Bureau, State & Local Government Finances 2020

City Government Expenditures by Function

Function	2020 ($000)	2020 ($ per capita)	2020 (%)
General Direct Expenditures			
Air Transportation	0	0	0.0
Corrections	0	0	0.0
Education	0	0	0.0
Employment Security Administration	0	0	0.0
Financial Administration	2,080	19	1.0
Fire Protection	25,938	248	12.0
General Public Buildings	1,158	11	0.5
Governmental Administration, Other	4,404	42	2.0
Health	437	4	0.2
Highways	34,483	329	15.9
Hospitals	0	0	0.0
Housing and Community Development	949	9	0.4
Interest on General Debt	8,874	84	4.1
Judicial and Legal	1,173	11	0.5
Libraries	0	0	0.0
Parking	2,658	25	1.2
Parks and Recreation	15,836	151	7.3
Police Protection	28,363	271	13.1
Public Welfare	0	0	0.0
Sewerage	24,848	237	11.5
Solid Waste Management	5,787	55	2.7
Veterans' Services	0	0	0.0
Liquor Store	0	0	0.0
Utility	45,937	439	21.2

Source: U.S. Census Bureau, State & Local Government Finances 2020

TAXES

State Corporate Income Tax Rates

State	Tax Rate (%)	Income Brackets ($)	Num. of Brackets	Financial Institution Tax Rate (%)[a]	Federal Income Tax Ded.
Wisconsin	7.9	Flat rate	1	7.9	No

Note: Tax rates as of January 1, 2023; (a) Rates listed are the corporate income tax rate applied to financial institutions or excise taxes based on income. Some states have other taxes based upon the value of deposits or shares.
Source: Federation of Tax Administrators, State Corporate Income Tax Rates, January 1, 2023

State Individual Income Tax Rates

State	Tax Rate (%)	Income Brackets ($)	Personal Exemptions ($)			Standard Ded. ($)	
			Single	Married	Depend.	Single	Married
Wisconsin (a)	3.54 - 7.65	13,810 - 304,170 (y)	700	1,400	700	12,760	23,620 (z)

Note: Tax rates as of January 1, 2023; Local- and county-level taxes are not included; Federal income tax is not deductible on state income tax returns; (a) 16 states have statutory provision for automatically adjusting to the rate of inflation the dollar values of the income tax brackets, standard deductions, and/or personal exemptions. Oregon does not index the income brackets for $125,000 and over; (y) The Wisconsin income brackets reported are for single individuals. For married taxpayers filing jointly, the same tax rates apply income brackets ranging from $18,420, to $405,550; (z) Alabama standard deduction is phased out for incomes over $25,000. Rhode Island exemptions & standard deductions phased out for incomes over $233,750; Wisconsin standard deduciton phases out for income over $16,989.
Source: Federation of Tax Administrators, State Individual Income Tax Rates, January 1, 2023

Various State Sales and Excise Tax Rates

State	State Sales Tax (%)	Gasoline[1] ($/gal.)	Cigarette[2] ($/pack)	Spirits[3] ($/gal.)	Wine[4] ($/gal.)	Beer[5] ($/gal.)	Recreational Marijuana (%)
Wisconsin	5	0.329	2.52	3.25	0.25	0.06	Not legal

Note: All tax rates as of January 1, 2023; (1) The American Petroleum Institute has developed a methodology for determining the average tax rate on a gallon of fuel. Rates may include any of the following: excise taxes, environmental fees, storage tank fees, other fees or taxes, general sales tax, and local taxes; (2) The federal excise tax of $1.0066 per pack and local taxes are not included; (3) Rates are those applicable to off-premise sales of 40% alcohol by volume (a.b.v.) distilled spirits in 750ml containers. Local excise taxes are excluded; (4) Rates are those applicable to off-premise sales of 11% a.b.v. non-carbonated wine in 750ml containers; (5) Rates are those applicable to off-premise sales of 4.7% a.b.v. beer in 12 ounce containers.
Source: Tax Foundation, 2023 Facts & Figures: How Does Your State Compare?

State Business Tax Climate Index Rankings

State	Overall Rank	Corporate Tax Rank	Individual Income Tax Rank	Sales Tax Rank	Property Tax Rank	Unemployment Insurance Tax Rank
Wisconsin	27	31	38	7	15	31

Note: The index is a measure of how each state's tax laws affect economic performance. The lower the rank, the more favorable a state's tax system is for business. States without a given tax are given a ranking of 1. The scores/rankings for the District of Columbia do not affect other states. The 2023 index represents the tax climate as of July 1, 2022.
Source: Tax Foundation, State Business Tax Climate Index 2023

TRANSPORTATION

Means of Transportation to Work

Area	Car/Truck/Van		Public Transportation			Bicycle	Walked	Other Means	Worked at Home
	Drove Alone	Car-pooled	Bus	Subway	Railroad				
City	77.7	10.7	1.1	0.0	0.0	0.2	2.3	1.1	6.9
MSA[1]	81.4	7.6	0.5	0.0	0.0	0.1	1.8	0.8	7.8
U.S.	73.2	8.6	2.0	1.6	0.5	0.5	2.5	1.5	9.7

Note: Figures are percentages and cover workers 16 years of age and older; (1) Figures cover the Green Bay, WI Metropolitan Statistical Area
Source: U.S. Census Bureau, 2017-2021 American Community Survey 5-Year Estimates

Travel Time to Work

Area	Less Than 10 Minutes	10 to 19 Minutes	20 to 29 Minutes	30 to 44 Minutes	45 to 59 Minutes	60 to 89 Minutes	90 Minutes or More
City	18.2	48.6	19.5	8.5	2.8	1.3	1.1
MSA[1]	17.9	40.4	21.9	13.0	3.6	1.7	1.4
U.S.	12.4	28.5	21.0	20.9	8.2	6.2	2.9

Note: Note: Figures are percentages and include workers 16 years old and over; (1) Figures cover the Green Bay, WI Metropolitan Statistical Area
Source: U.S. Census Bureau, 2017-2021 American Community Survey 5-Year Estimates

Key Congestion Measures

Measure	1990	2000	2010	2015	2020
Annual Hours of Delay, Total (000)	n/a	n/a	n/a	3,394	1,805
Annual Hours of Delay, Per Auto Commuter	n/a	n/a	n/a	15	8
Annual Congestion Cost, Per Auto Commuter ($)	n/a	n/a	n/a	318	182

Note: n/a not available
Source: Texas A&M Transportation Institute, 2021 Urban Mobility Report

Freeway Travel Time Index

Measure	1985	1990	1995	2000	2005	2010	2015	2020
Urban Area Index[1]	n/a	n/a	n/a	n/a	n/a	n/a	1.05	1.03
Urban Area Rank[1,2]	n/a	n/a	n/a	n/a	n/a	n/a	n/a	n/a

Note: Freeway Travel Time Index—the ratio of travel time in the peak period to the travel time at free-flow conditions. For example, a value of 1.30 indicates a 20-minute free-flow trip takes 26 minutes in the peak (20 minutes x 1.30 = 26 minutes); (1) Covers the Green Bay WI urban area; (2) Rank is based on 101 larger urban areas (#1 = highest travel time index); n/a not available
Source: Texas A&M Transportation Institute, 2021 Urban Mobility Report

Public Transportation

Agency Name / Mode of Transportation	Vehicles Operated in Maximum Service[1]	Annual Unlinked Passenger Trips[2] (in thous.)	Annual Passenger Miles[3] (in thous.)
Green Bay Metro			
Bus (directly operated)	16	495.4	1,579.7
Demand Response (purchased transportation)	12	28.5	169.2

Note: (1) Number of revenue vehicles operated by the given mode and type of service to meet the annual maximum service requirement. This is the revenue vehicle count during the peak season of the year; on the week and day that maximum service is provided. Vehicles operated in maximum service (VOMS) exclude atypical days and one-time special events; (2) Number of passengers who boarded public transportation vehicles. Passengers are counted each time they board a vehicle no matter how many vehicles they use to travel from their origin to their destination. (3) Sum of the distances ridden by all passengers during the entire fiscal year.
Source: Federal Transit Administration, National Transit Database, 2021

Air Transportation

Airport Name and Code / Type of Service	Passenger Airlines[1]	Passenger Enplanements	Freight Carriers[2]	Freight (lbs)
Austin-Bergstrom International (GRB)				
Domestic service (U.S. carriers - 2022)	17	301,082	3	65,448
International service (U.S. carriers - 2021)	0	0	0	0

Note: (1) Includes all U.S.-based major, minor and commuter airlines that carried at least one passenger during the year; (2) Includes all U.S.-based airlines and freight carriers that transported at least one pound of freight during the year.
Source: Bureau of Transportation Statistics, The Intermodal Transportation Database, Air Carriers: T-100 Domestic Market (U.S. Carriers), 2022; Bureau of Transportation Statistics, The Intermodal Transportation Database, Air Carriers: T-100 International Market (U.S. Carriers), 2021

BUSINESSES

Major Business Headquarters

Company Name	Industry	Rankings	
		Fortune[1]	Forbes[2]
Schreiber Foods	Food, drink & tobacco	-	103

Note: (1) Companies that produce a 10-K are ranked 1 to 500 based on 2021 revenue; (2) All private companies with at least $2 billion in annual revenue through the end of their most current fiscal year are ranked 1 to 246; companies listed are headquartered in the city; dashes indicate no ranking
Source: Fortune, "Fortune 500," 2022; Forbes, "America's Largest Private Companies," 2022

Living Environment

COST OF LIVING

Cost of Living Index

Composite Index	Groceries	Housing	Utilities	Trans-portation	Health Care	Misc. Goods/ Services
89.9	92.3	78.4	95.1	93.8	97.8	94.7

Note: The Cost of Living Index measures regional differences in the cost of consumer goods and services, excluding taxes and non-consumer expenditures, for professional and managerial households in the top income quintile. It is based on more than 50,000 prices covering almost 60 different items for which prices are collected three times a year by chambers of commerce, economic development organizations or university applied economic centers in each participating urban area. The numbers shown should be read as a percentage above or below the national average of 100. For example, a value of 115.4 in the groceries column indicates that grocery prices are 15.4% higher than the national average. Small differences in the index numbers should not be interpreted as significant; Figures cover the Green Bay WI urban area.
Source: The Council for Community and Economic Research, Cost of Living Index, 2022

Grocery Prices

Area[1]	T-Bone Steak ($/pound)	Frying Chicken ($/pound)	Whole Milk ($/half gal.)	Eggs ($/dozen)	Orange Juice ($/64 oz.)	Coffee ($/11.5 oz.)
City[2]	15.09	1.55	2.25	1.74	3.86	4.01
Avg.	13.81	1.59	2.43	2.25	3.85	4.95
Min.	10.17	0.90	1.51	1.30	2.90	3.46
Max.	19.35	3.30	4.32	4.32	5.31	8.59

*Note: (1) Values for the local area are compared with the average, minimum and maximum values for all 286 areas in the Cost of Living Index; (2) Figures cover the Green Bay WI urban area; **T-Bone Steak** (price per pound); **Frying Chicken** (price per pound, whole fryer); **Whole Milk** (half gallon carton); **Eggs** (price per dozen, Grade A, large); **Orange Juice** (64 oz. Tropicana or Florida Natural); **Coffee** (11.5 oz. can, vacuum-packed, Maxwell House, Hills Bros, or Folgers).*
Source: The Council for Community and Economic Research, Cost of Living Index, 2022

Housing and Utility Costs

Area[1]	New Home Price ($)	Apartment Rent ($/month)	All Electric ($/month)	Part Electric ($/month)	Other Energy ($/month)	Telephone ($/month)
City[2]	382,340	881	-	83.06	80.95	186.93
Avg.	450,913	1,371	176.41	99.93	76.96	190.22
Min.	229,283	546	100.84	31.56	27.15	174.27
Max.	2,434,977	4,569	356.86	249.59	272.24	208.31

*Note: (1) Values for the local area are compared with the average, minimum and maximum values for all 286 areas in the Cost of Living Index; (2) Figures cover the Green Bay WI urban area; **New Home Price** (2,400 sf living area, 8,000 sf lot, in urban area with full utilities); **Apartment Rent** (950 sf 2 bedroom/1.5 or 2 bath, unfurnished, excluding all utilities except water); **All Electric** (average monthly cost for an all-electric home); **Part Electric** (average monthly cost for a part-electric home); **Other Energy** (average monthly cost for natural gas, fuel oil, coal, wood, and any other forms of energy except electricity); **Telephone** (price includes the base monthly rate plus taxes and fees for three lines of mobile phone service).*
Source: The Council for Community and Economic Research, Cost of Living Index, 2022

Health Care, Transportation, and Other Costs

Area[1]	Doctor ($/visit)	Dentist ($/visit)	Optometrist ($/visit)	Gasoline ($/gallon)	Beauty Salon ($/visit)	Men's Shirt ($)
City[2]	152.75	98.67	75.78	3.45	27.46	26.90
Avg.	124.91	107.77	117.66	3.86	43.31	34.21
Min.	36.61	58.25	51.79	2.90	22.18	13.05
Max.	250.21	162.58	371.96	5.54	85.61	63.54

*Note: (1) Values for the local area are compared with the average, minimum and maximum values for all 286 areas in the Cost of Living Index; (2) Figures cover the Green Bay WI urban area; **Doctor** (general practitioners routine exam of an established patient); **Dentist** (adult teeth cleaning and periodic oral examination); **Optometrist** (full vision eye exam for established adult patient); **Gasoline** (one gallon regular unleaded, national brand, including all taxes, cash price at self-service pump if available); **Beauty Salon** (woman's shampoo, trim, and blow-dry); **Men's Shirt** (cotton/polyester dress shirt, pinpoint weave, long sleeves).*
Source: The Council for Community and Economic Research, Cost of Living Index, 2022

HOUSING

Homeownership Rate

Area	2015 (%)	2016 (%)	2017 (%)	2018 (%)	2019 (%)	2020 (%)	2021 (%)	2022 (%)
MSA[1]	n/a	n/a	n/a	n/a	n/a	n/a	n/a	n/a
U.S.	63.7	63.4	63.9	64.4	64.6	66.6	65.5	65.8

Note: (1) Figures cover the Green Bay, WI Metropolitan Statistical Area; n/a not available
Source: U.S. Census Bureau, Housing Vacancies and Homeownership Annual Statistics: 2015-2022

House Price Index (HPI)

Area	National Ranking[2]	Quarterly Change (%)	One-Year Change (%)	Five-Year Change (%)	Since 1991Q1 (%)
MSA[1]	25	3.83	17.89	59.68	250.27
U.S.[3]	–	0.34	8.41	58.44	289.08

Note: The HPI is a weighted repeat sales index. It measures average price changes in repeat sales or refinancings on the same properties. This information is obtained by reviewing repeat mortgage transactions on single-family properties whose mortgages have been purchased or securitized by Fannie Mae or Freddie Mac since January 1975; (1) Figures cover the Green Bay, WI Metropolitan Statistical Area; (2) Rankings are based on annual percentage change for all metro areas containing at least 15,000 transactions over the last 10 years and ranges from 1 to 257; (3) figures based on a weighted average of Census Division estimates using a seasonally adjusted, purchase-only index; all figures are for the period ending December 31, 2022
Source: Federal Housing Finance Agency, Change in FHFA Metropolitan Area House Price Indexes, 2022Q4

Median Single-Family Home Prices

Area	2020	2021	2022p	Percent Change 2021 to 2022
MSA[1]	204.2	234.5	259.4	10.6
U.S. Average	300.2	357.1	392.6	9.9

Note: Figures are median sales prices of existing single-family homes in thousands of dollars; (p) preliminary; (1) Figures cover the Green Bay, WI Metropolitan Statistical Area
Source: National Association of Realtors, Median Sales Price of Existing Single-Family Homes for Metropolitan Areas, 4th Quarter 2022

Qualifying Income Based on Median Sales Price of Existing Single-Family Homes

Area	With 5% Down ($)	With 10% Down ($)	With 20% Down ($)
MSA[1]	77,788	73,694	65,506
U.S. Average	112,234	106,237	94,513

Note: Figures are preliminary; Qualifying income is based on a mortgage rate of 6.77%. Monthly principal and interest payment is limited to 25% of income; (1) Figures cover the Green Bay, WI Metropolitan Statistical Area
Source: National Association of Realtors, Qualifying Income Based on Median Sales Price of Existing Single-Family Homes for Metropolitan Areas, 4th Quarter 2022

Home Value

Area	Under $100,000	$100,000 -$199,999	$200,000 -$299,999	$300,000 -$399,999	$400,000 -$499,999	$500,000 -$999,999	$1,000,000 or more	Median ($)
City	17.2	57.2	16.1	5.1	2.4	1.8	0.2	151,000
MSA[1]	12.8	41.4	26.0	10.9	4.6	3.6	0.7	188,800
U.S.	16.2	24.2	20.1	13.6	8.3	13.6	4.1	244,900

Note: Figures are percentages except for median and cover owner-occupied housing units; (1) Figures cover the Green Bay, WI Metropolitan Statistical Area
Source: U.S. Census Bureau, 2017-2021 American Community Survey 5-Year Estimates

Year Housing Structure Built

Area	2020 or Later	2010 -2019	2000 -2009	1990 -1999	1980 -1989	1970 -1979	1960 -1969	1950 -1959	1940 -1949	Before 1940	Median Year
City	0.1	2.3	7.0	10.4	12.0	18.6	12.9	15.6	6.5	14.7	1970
MSA[1]	<0.1	7.5	13.4	16.3	11.6	15.4	9.8	9.5	4.3	12.3	1979
U.S.	0.2	7.3	13.6	13.6	13.2	14.8	10.3	10.0	4.7	12.2	1979

Note: Figures are percentages except for Median Year; Note: (1) Figures cover the Green Bay, WI Metropolitan Statistical Area
Source: U.S. Census Bureau, 2017-2021 American Community Survey 5-Year Estimates

Gross Monthly Rent

Area	Under $500	$500 -$999	$1,000 -$1,499	$1,500 -$1,999	$2,000 -$2,499	$2,500 -$2,999	$3,000 and up	Median ($)
City	9.1	66.5	22.1	1.8	0.2	0.0	0.2	805
MSA[1]	6.8	64.8	24.4	2.9	0.3	0.3	0.4	851
U.S.	8.1	30.5	30.8	16.8	7.3	3.1	3.5	1,163

Note: Figures are percentages except for median; Gross rent is the contract rent plus the estimated average monthly cost of utilities (electricity, gas, and water and sewer) and fuels (oil, coal, kerosene, wood, etc.) if these are paid by the renter (or paid for the renter by someone else); (1) Figures cover the Green Bay, WI Metropolitan Statistical Area
Source: U.S. Census Bureau, 2017-2021 American Community Survey 5-Year Estimates

HEALTH

Health Risk Factors

Category	MSA[1] (%)	U.S. (%)
Adults aged 18–64 who have any kind of health care coverage	n/a	90.9
Adults who reported being in good or better health	n/a	85.2
Adults who have been told they have high blood cholesterol	n/a	35.7
Adults who have been told they have high blood pressure	n/a	32.4
Adults who are current smokers	n/a	14.4
Adults who currently use e-cigarettes	n/a	6.7
Adults who currently use chewing tobacco, snuff, or snus	n/a	3.5
Adults who are heavy drinkers[2]	n/a	6.3
Adults who are binge drinkers[3]	n/a	15.4
Adults who are overweight (BMI 25.0 - 29.9)	n/a	34.4
Adults who are obese (BMI 30.0 - 99.8)	n/a	33.9
Adults who participated in any physical activities in the past month	n/a	76.3

Note: (1) Figures for the Green Bay, WI Metropolitan Statistical Area were not available.
(2) Heavy drinkers are classified as adult men having more than 14 drinks per week and adult women having more than 7 drinks per week; (3) Binge drinkers are classified as males having five or more drinks on one occasion or females having four or more drinks on one occasion
Source: Centers for Disease Control and Prevention, Behaviorial Risk Factor Surveillance System, SMART: Selected Metropolitan Area Risk Trends, 2021

Acute and Chronic Health Conditions

Category	MSA[1] (%)	U.S. (%)
Adults who have ever been told they had a heart attack	n/a	4.0
Adults who have ever been told they have angina or coronary heart disease	n/a	3.8
Adults who have ever been told they had a stroke	n/a	3.0
Adults who have ever been told they have asthma	n/a	14.9
Adults who have ever been told they have arthritis	n/a	25.8
Adults who have ever been told they have diabetes[2]	n/a	10.9
Adults who have ever been told they had skin cancer	n/a	6.6
Adults who have ever been told they had any other types of cancer	n/a	7.5
Adults who have ever been told they have COPD	n/a	6.1
Adults who have ever been told they have kidney disease	n/a	3.0
Adults who have ever been told they have a form of depression	n/a	20.5

Note: (1) Figures for the Green Bay, WI Metropolitan Statistical Area were not available.
(2) Figures do not include pregnancy-related, borderline, or pre-diabetes
Source: Centers for Disease Control and Prevention, Behaviorial Risk Factor Surveillance System, SMART: Selected Metropolitan Area Risk Trends, 2021

Health Screening and Vaccination Rates

Category	MSA[1] (%)	U.S. (%)
Adults who have ever been tested for HIV	n/a	34.9
Adults who have had their blood cholesterol checked within the last five years	n/a	85.2
Adults aged 65+ who have had flu shot within the past year	n/a	68.6
Adults aged 65+ who have ever had a pneumonia vaccination	n/a	71.0

Note: (1) Figures for the Green Bay, WI Metropolitan Statistical Area were not available.
Source: Centers for Disease Control and Prevention, Behaviorial Risk Factor Surveillance System, SMART: Selected Metropolitan Area Risk Trends, 2021

Disability Status

Category	MSA[1] (%)	U.S. (%)
Adults who reported being deaf	n/a	7.2
Are you blind or have serious difficulty seeing, even when wearing glasses?	n/a	4.8
Are you limited in any way in any of your usual activities due to arthritis?	n/a	11.1
Do you have difficulty doing errands alone?	n/a	7.0
Do you have difficulty dressing or bathing?	n/a	3.6
Do you have serious difficulty concentrating/remembering/making decisions?	n/a	12.1
Do you have serious difficulty walking or climbing stairs?	n/a	12.8

Note: (1) Figures for the Green Bay, WI Metropolitan Statistical Area were not available.
Source: Centers for Disease Control and Prevention, Behaviorial Risk Factor Surveillance System, SMART: Selected Metropolitan Area Risk Trends, 2021

Mortality Rates for the Top 10 Causes of Death in the U.S.

ICD-10[a] Sub-Chapter	ICD-10[a] Code	Crude Mortality Rate[1] per 100,000 population	
		County[2]	U.S.
Malignant neoplasms	C00-C97	168.5	182.6
Ischaemic heart diseases	I20-I25	146.2	113.1
Other forms of heart disease	I30-I51	52.2	64.4
Other degenerative diseases of the nervous system	G30-G31	41.8	51.0
Cerebrovascular diseases	I60-I69	30.7	47.8
Other external causes of accidental injury	W00-X59	53.3	46.4
Chronic lower respiratory diseases	J40-J47	26.7	45.7
Organic, including symptomatic, mental disorders	F01-F09	50.5	35.9
Hypertensive diseases	I10-I15	17.4	35.0
Diabetes mellitus	E10-E14	17.5	29.6

Note: (a) ICD-10 = International Classification of Diseases 10th Revision; (1) Crude mortality rates are a three-year average covering 2019-2021; (2) Figures cover Brown County.
Source: Centers for Disease Control and Prevention, National Center for Health Statistics. National Vital Statistics System, Mortality 2018-2021 on CDC WONDER Online Database

Mortality Rates for Selected Causes of Death

ICD-10[a] Sub-Chapter	ICD-10[a] Code	Crude Mortality Rate[1] per 100,000 population	
		County[2]	U.S.
Assault	X85-Y09	2.5	7.0
Diseases of the liver	K70-K76	14.3	19.8
Human immunodeficiency virus (HIV) disease	B20-B24	Suppressed	1.5
Influenza and pneumonia	J09-J18	10.8	14.7
Intentional self-harm	X60-X84	16.0	14.3
Malnutrition	E40-E46	2.8	4.3
Obesity and other hyperalimentation	E65-E68	Unreliable	3.0
Renal failure	N17-N19	11.1	15.7
Transport accidents	V01-V99	8.8	13.6
Viral hepatitis	B15-B19	Suppressed	1.2

Note: (a) ICD-10 = International Classification of Diseases 10th Revision; (1) Crude mortality rates are a three-year average covering 2019-2021; (2) Figures cover Brown County; Data are suppressed when the data meet the criteria for confidentiality constraints; Crude mortality rates are flagged as unreliable when the rate would be calculated with a numerator of 20 or less.
Source: Centers for Disease Control and Prevention, National Center for Health Statistics. National Vital Statistics System, Mortality 2018-2021 on CDC WONDER Online Database

Health Insurance Coverage

Area	With Health Insurance	With Private Health Insurance	With Public Health Insurance	Without Health Insurance	Population Under Age 19 Without Health Insurance
City	91.7	64.2	36.7	8.3	5.5
MSA[1]	94.9	74.8	31.6	5.1	3.7
U.S.	91.2	67.8	35.4	8.8	5.3

Note: Figures are percentages that cover the civilian noninstitutionalized population; (1) Figures cover the Green Bay, WI Metropolitan Statistical Area
Source: U.S. Census Bureau, 2017-2021 American Community Survey 5-Year Estimates

Number of Medical Professionals

Area	MDs[3]	DOs[3,4]	Dentists	Podiatrists	Chiropractors	Optometrists
County[1] (number)	682	75	218	8	134	50
County[1] (rate[2])	253.8	27.9	80.9	3.0	49.7	18.5
U.S. (rate[2])	289.3	23.5	72.5	6.2	28.7	17.4

Note: Data as of 2021 unless noted; (1) Data covers Brown County; (2) Rate per 100,000 population; (3) Data as of 2020 and includes all active, non-federal physicians; (4) Doctor of Osteopathic Medicine
Source: U.S. Department of Health and Human Services, Health Resources and Services Administration, Bureau of Health Professions, Area Resource File (ARF) 2021-2022

EDUCATION

Public School District Statistics

District Name	Schls	Pupils	Pupil/ Teacher Ratio	Minority Pupils[1] (%)	LEP/ELL[2] (%)	IEP[3] (%)
Ashwaubenon School District	5	3,257	15.0	24.8	2.1	11.4
Green Bay Area PSD	43	19,166	13.1	60.0	20.7	15.1
Howard-Suamico School District	9	5,879	14.4	13.8	1.6	11.8

Note: Table includes school districts with 2,000 or more students; (1) Percentage of students that are not non-Hispanic white; (2) Percentage of students that are Limited English Proficient or English Language Learners (2018-19); (3) Percentage of students that have an Individualized Education Program (2019-20).
Source: U.S. Department of Education, National Center for Education Statistics, Common Core of Data, Local Education Agency (School District) Universe Survey: School Year 2021-2022

Highest Level of Education

Area	Less than H.S.	H.S. Diploma	Some College, No Deg.	Associate Degree	Bachelor's Degree	Master's Degree	Prof. School Degree	Doctorate Degree
City	12.2	31.3	19.7	11.7	18.3	5.0	0.9	0.8
MSA[1]	7.5	31.5	19.1	12.8	20.5	6.3	1.4	0.8
U.S.	11.1	26.5	20.0	8.7	20.6	9.3	2.2	1.5

Note: Figures cover persons age 25 and over; (1) Figures cover the Green Bay, WI Metropolitan Statistical Area
Source: U.S. Census Bureau, 2017-2021 American Community Survey 5-Year Estimates

Educational Attainment by Race

Area	High School Graduate or Higher (%)					Bachelor's Degree or Higher (%)				
	Total	White	Black	Asian	Hisp.[2]	Total	White	Black	Asian	Hisp.[2]
City	87.8	90.7	76.5	75.1	57.7	25.1	27.0	16.9	26.0	9.3
MSA[1]	92.5	94.3	76.4	83.4	61.7	29.1	29.8	19.0	47.3	13.4
U.S.	88.9	91.4	87.2	87.6	71.2	33.7	35.5	23.3	55.6	18.4

Note: Figures shown cover persons 25 years old and over; (1) Figures cover the Green Bay, WI Metropolitan Statistical Area; (2) People of Hispanic origin can be of any race
Source: U.S. Census Bureau, 2017-2021 American Community Survey 5-Year Estimates

School Enrollment by Grade and Control

Area	Preschool (%)		Kindergarten (%)		Grades 1 - 4 (%)		Grades 5 - 8 (%)		Grades 9 - 12 (%)	
	Public	Private	Public	Private	Public	Private	Public	Private	Public	Private
City	70.8	29.2	87.5	12.5	87.8	12.2	84.9	15.1	91.3	8.7
MSA[1]	67.1	32.9	86.7	13.3	88.4	11.6	86.7	13.3	91.8	8.2
U.S.	58.8	41.2	86.3	13.7	88.3	11.7	88.6	11.4	89.4	10.6

Note: Figures shown cover persons 3 years old and over; (1) Figures cover the Green Bay, WI Metropolitan Statistical Area
Source: U.S. Census Bureau, 2017-2021 American Community Survey 5-Year Estimates

Higher Education

Four-Year Colleges			Two-Year Colleges			Medical Schools[1]	Law Schools[2]	Voc/ Tech[3]
Public	Private Non-profit	Private For-profit	Public	Private Non-profit	Private For-profit			
1	2	1	1	0	0	0	0	2

Note: Figures cover institutions located within the Green Bay, WI Metropolitan Statistical Area and include main campuses only; (1) includes schools accredited by the Liaison Committee on Medical Education and the American Osteopathic Association's Commission on Osteopathic College Accreditation; (2) includes ABA-accredited schools, schools with provisional ABA accreditation, and state accredited schools; (3) includes all schools with programs that are less than 2 years.
Source: National Center for Education Statistics, Integrated Postsecondary Education System (IPEDS), 2021-22; Wikipedia, List of Medical Schools in the United States, accessed April 10, 2023; Wikipedia, List of Law Schools in the United States, accessed April 10, 2023

EMPLOYERS

Major Employers

Company Name	Industry
American Foods Group	Food manufacturing
APAC Customer Services	Business management
Associated Bank	Financial services
Aurora Health Care	Healthcare
Bellin Health	Healthcare
Georgia-Pacific	Paper manufacturing
Green Bay Packaging	Paper manufacturing
Green Bay Packers	NFL franchise
H.J. Martin and Son	Interior design
JBS	Food manufacturing
Nicolet National Bank	Financial services
Procter & Gamble Paper Products	Paper manufacturing
Schreiber Foods	Food manufacturing
Schwabe North America	Health products
St. Mary's Hospital Medical Center	Healthcare
St. Vincent Hospital	Healthcare
Wal-Mart Stores	Retail
Wisconsin Public Service	Utilities

Note: Companies shown are located within the Green Bay, WI Metropolitan Statistical Area.
Source: Hoovers.com; Wikipedia

PUBLIC SAFETY

Crime Rate

Area	Total Crime	Violent Crime Rate				Property Crime Rate		
		Murder	Rape[3]	Robbery	Aggrav. Assault	Burglary	Larceny -Theft	Motor Vehicle Theft
City	2,056.4	5.7	67.8	43.0	410.9	196.8	1,222.2	109.9
Suburbs[1]	816.1	0.9	22.7	3.2	54.1	122.4	580.0	32.8
Metro[2]	1,216.1	2.5	37.3	16.0	169.2	146.4	787.1	57.6
U.S.	2,356.7	6.5	38.4	73.9	279.7	314.2	1,398.0	246.0

Note: Figures are crimes per 100,000 population; (1) All areas within the metro area that are located outside the city limits; (2) Figures cover the Green Bay, WI Metropolitan Statistical Area; (3) All figures shown were reported using the revised Uniform Crime Reporting (UCR) definition of rape; Due to the transition to the National Incident-Based Reporting System (NIBRS), limited city and metro area data was released for 2021.
Source: FBI Uniform Crime Reports, 2020

Hate Crimes

Area	Number of Quarters Reported	Number of Incidents per Bias Motivation					
		Race/Ethnicity/ Ancestry	Religion	Sexual Orientation	Disability	Gender	Gender Identity
City	4	2	0	0	1	0	0
U.S.	4	5,227	1,244	1,110	130	75	266

Note: Due to the transition to the National Incident-Based Reporting System (NIBRS), limited crime data was released for 2021.
Source: Federal Bureau of Investigation, Hate Crime Statistics 2020

Identity Theft Consumer Reports

Area	Reports	Reports per 100,000 Population	Rank[2]
MSA[1]	362	113	340
U.S.	1,108,609	339	-

Note: (1) Figures cover the Green Bay, WI Metropolitan Statistical Area; (2) Rank ranges from 1 to 391 where 1 indicates greatest number of identity theft reports per 100,000 population
Source: Federal Trade Commission, Consumer Sentinel Network Data Book 2022

Fraud and Other Consumer Reports

Area	Reports	Reports per 100,000 Population	Rank[2]
MSA[1]	1,994	622	338
U.S.	4,064,520	1,245	-

Note: (1) Figures cover the Green Bay, WI Metropolitan Statistical Area; (2) Rank ranges from 1 to 391 where 1 indicates greatest number of fraud and other consumer reports per 100,000 population
Source: Federal Trade Commission, Consumer Sentinel Network Data Book 2022

POLITICS

2020 Presidential Election Results

Area	Biden	Trump	Jorgensen	Hawkins	Other
Brown County	45.5	52.7	1.3	0.0	0.5
U.S.	51.3	46.8	1.2	0.3	0.5

Note: Results are percentages and may not add to 100% due to rounding
Source: Dave Leip's Atlas of U.S. Presidential Elections

SPORTS

Professional Sports Teams

Team Name	League	Year Established
Green Bay Packers	National Football League (NFL)	1921

Note: Includes teams located in the Green Bay, WI Metropolitan Statistical Area.
Source: Wikipedia, Major Professional Sports Teams of the United States and Canada, April 12, 2023

CLIMATE

Average and Extreme Temperatures

Temperature	Jan	Feb	Mar	Apr	May	Jun	Jul	Aug	Sep	Oct	Nov	Dec	Yr.
Extreme High (°F)	50	55	77	89	91	98	99	99	95	88	72	62	99
Average High (°F)	23	27	38	54	67	76	81	78	70	58	42	28	54
Average Temp. (°F)	15	19	29	44	55	65	70	68	59	48	34	21	44
Average Low (°F)	6	10	21	34	44	53	58	56	48	38	26	13	34
Extreme Low (°F)	-31	-26	-29	7	21	32	40	38	24	15	-9	-27	-31

Note: Figures cover the years 1949-1990
Source: National Climatic Data Center, International Station Meteorological Climate Summary, 9/96

Average Precipitation/Snowfall/Humidity

Precip./Humidity	Jan	Feb	Mar	Apr	May	Jun	Jul	Aug	Sep	Oct	Nov	Dec	Yr.
Avg. Precip. (in.)	1.1	1.1	1.9	2.6	2.9	3.2	3.3	3.3	3.2	2.2	2.0	1.4	28.3
Avg. Snowfall (in.)	11	8	9	2	Tr	0	0	0	Tr	Tr	5	11	46
Avg. Rel. Hum. 6am (%)	77	79	81	79	79	82	86	90	89	85	82	80	83
Avg. Rel. Hum. 3pm (%)	68	65	63	54	52	55	55	58	59	59	67	71	60

Note: Figures cover the years 1949-1990; Tr = Trace amounts (<0.05 in. of rain; <0.5 in. of snow)
Source: National Climatic Data Center, International Station Meteorological Climate Summary, 9/96

Weather Conditions

Temperature			Daytime Sky			Precipitation		
5°F & below	32°F & below	90°F & above	Clear	Partly cloudy	Cloudy	0.01 inch or more precip.	0.1 inch or more snow/ice	Thunder-storms
39	163	7	86	125	154	120	40	33

Note: Figures are average number of days per year and cover the years 1949-1990
Source: National Climatic Data Center, International Station Meteorological Climate Summary, 9/96

HAZARDOUS WASTE

Superfund Sites

The Green Bay, WI metro area is home to three sites on the EPA's Superfund National Priorities List: **Algoma Municipal Landfill** (final); **Better Brite Plating Co. Chrome and Zinc Shops** (final); **Fox River Nrda/Pcb Releases** (proposed). There are a total of 1,165 Superfund sites with a status of proposed or final on the list in the U.S. *U.S. Environmental Protection Agency, National Priorities List, April 12, 2023*

AIR QUALITY

Air Quality Trends: Ozone

	1990	1995	2000	2005	2010	2015	2018	2019	2020	2021
MSA[1]	n/a	n/a	n/a	n/a	n/a	n/a	n/a	n/a	n/a	n/a
U.S.	0.087	0.089	0.081	0.080	0.072	0.067	0.069	0.065	0.065	0.067

Note: (1) Data covers the Green Bay, WI Metropolitan Statistical Area; n/a not available. The values shown are the composite ozone concentration averages among trend sites based on the highest fourth daily maximum 8-hour concentration in parts per million. These trends are based on sites having an adequate record of monitoring data during the trend period. Data from exceptional events are included.
Source: U.S. Environmental Protection Agency, Air Quality Monitoring Information, "Air Quality Trends by City, 1990-2021"

Air Quality Index

Area	Percent of Days when Air Quality was...[2]					AQI Statistics[2]	
	Good	Moderate	Unhealthy for Sensitive Groups	Unhealthy	Very Unhealthy	Maximum	Median
MSA[1]	73.4	25.2	1.4	0.0	0.0	125	40

Note: (1) Data covers the Green Bay, WI Metropolitan Statistical Area; (2) Based on 365 days with AQI data in 2021. Air Quality Index (AQI) is an index for reporting daily air quality. EPA calculates the AQI for five major air pollutants regulated by the Clean Air Act: ground-level ozone, particle pollution (aka particulate matter), carbon monoxide, sulfur dioxide, and nitrogen dioxide. The AQI runs from 0 to 500. The higher the AQI value, the greater the level of air pollution and the greater the health concern. There are six AQI categories: "Good" AQI is between 0 and 50. Air quality is considered satisfactory; "Moderate" AQI is between 51 and 100. Air quality is acceptable; "Unhealthy for Sensitive Groups" When AQI values are between 101 and 150, members of sensitive groups may experience health effects; "Unhealthy" When AQI values are between 151 and 200 everyone may begin to experience health effects; "Very Unhealthy" AQI values between 201 and 300 trigger a health alert; "Hazardous" AQI values over 300 trigger warnings of emergency conditions (not shown).
Source: U.S. Environmental Protection Agency, Air Quality Index Report, 2021

Air Quality Index Pollutants

Area	Percent of Days when AQI Pollutant was...[2]					
	Carbon Monoxide	Nitrogen Dioxide	Ozone	Sulfur Dioxide	Particulate Matter 2.5	Particulate Matter 10
MSA[1]	0.0	0.0	48.8	(3)	51.2	0.0

Note: (1) Data covers the Green Bay, WI Metropolitan Statistical Area; (2) Based on 365 days with AQI data in 2021. The Air Quality Index (AQI) is an index for reporting daily air quality. EPA calculates the AQI for five major air pollutants regulated by the Clean Air Act: ground-level ozone, particle pollution (also known as particulate matter), carbon monoxide, sulfur dioxide, and nitrogen dioxide. The AQI runs from 0 to 500. The higher the AQI value, the greater the level of air pollution and the greater the health concern; (3) Sulfur dioxide is no longer included in this table (as of December 8, 2021) because SO_2 concentrations tend to be very localized and not necessarily representative of broad geographical areas like counties and CBSAs.
Source: U.S. Environmental Protection Agency, Air Quality Index Report, 2021

Maximum Air Pollutant Concentrations: Particulate Matter, Ozone, CO and Lead

	Particulate Matter 10 (ug/m^3)	Particulate Matter 2.5 Wtd AM (ug/m^3)	Particulate Matter 2.5 24-Hr (ug/m^3)	Ozone (ppm)	Carbon Monoxide (ppm)	Lead (ug/m^3)
MSA[1] Level	n/a	8.7	26	0.068	n/a	n/a
NAAQS[2]	150	15	35	0.075	9	0.15
Met NAAQS[2]	n/a	Yes	Yes	Yes	n/a	n/a

Note: (1) Data covers the Green Bay, WI Metropolitan Statistical Area; Data from exceptional events are included; (2) National Ambient Air Quality Standards; ppm = parts per million; ug/m^3 = micrograms per cubic meter; n/a not available.
Concentrations: Particulate Matter 10 (coarse particulate)—highest second maximum 24-hour concentration; Particulate Matter 2.5 Wtd AM (fine particulate)—highest weighted annual mean concentration; Particulate Matter 2.5 24-Hour (fine particulate)—highest 98th percentile 24-hour concentration; Ozone—highest fourth daily maximum 8-hour concentration; Carbon Monoxide—highest second maximum non-overlapping 8-hour concentration; Lead—maximum running 3-month average
Source: U.S. Environmental Protection Agency, Air Quality Monitoring Information, "Air Quality Statistics by City, 2021"

Maximum Air Pollutant Concentrations: Nitrogen Dioxide and Sulfur Dioxide

	Nitrogen Dioxide AM (ppb)	Nitrogen Dioxide 1-Hr (ppb)	Sulfur Dioxide AM (ppb)	Sulfur Dioxide 1-Hr (ppb)	Sulfur Dioxide 24-Hr (ppb)
MSA[1] Level	n/a	n/a	n/a	5	n/a
NAAQS[2]	53	100	30	75	140
Met NAAQS[2]	n/a	n/a	n/a	Yes	n/a

Note: (1) Data covers the Green Bay, WI Metropolitan Statistical Area; Data from exceptional events are included; (2) National Ambient Air Quality Standards; ppm = parts per million; ug/m^3 = micrograms per cubic meter; n/a not available.
Concentrations: Nitrogen Dioxide AM—highest arithmetic mean concentration; Nitrogen Dioxide 1-Hr—highest 98th percentile 1-hour daily maximum concentration; Sulfur Dioxide AM—highest annual mean concentration; Sulfur Dioxide 1-Hr—highest 99th percentile 1-hour daily maximum concentration; Sulfur Dioxide 24-Hr—highest second maximum 24-hour concentration
Source: U.S. Environmental Protection Agency, Air Quality Monitoring Information, "Air Quality Statistics by City, 2021"

Indianapolis, Indiana

Background

Indianapolis sits within the boundaries of the Northern manufacturing belt and the midwestern Corn Belt, and its economy reflects both influences. On one side lies the Indianapolis industrial sector, including transportation, airplane and truck parts, paper and rubber products, and computer software. On the other side lies agriculture. Indianapolis is a leading grain market, as well as the largest meat-processing center outside of Chicago.

Despite pollution and other problems of urban decay in the late twentieth century, Indianapolis has made significant strides, completing dozens of major downtown projects, including Dolphin Adventure at the Indianapolis Zoo, Eiteljorg Museum of American Indians and Western Art expansion, Eli Lilly and Company Insulin Finishing Building, the Indianapolis Museum of Art expansion, and Circle Centre, a retail and entertainment complex that draws one million visitors a month. The city's IndyGo's $96 million Red Line bus rapid transit project was completed in in 2019.

Known as the "Crossroads of America," Indianapolis is bisected by more interstate highways than any other city in the nation, making it accessible from many locations and within a day's drive of half the country's population. As a result, the city is a popular choice for conventions and offers excellent facilities at the Indiana Convention Center & RCA Dome. The Indianapolis Artsgarden, offering more than 300 free performances and exhibits each year, is linked to the Convention Center by a skywalk, and is a world-class venue for the arts.

The city is home to one of the finest children's museums in the United States, and its 85 parks offer many outdoor activities.

Indianapolis has been called the rising food star of the Midwest, with top-notch restaurants in the Fletcher Place neighborhood and a number of city chefs and restaurateurs as recent semifinalists in the James Beard Foundation Awards. Microbreweries are a staple in the city, with more than 50 craft brewers. In 2022, the city boasted more than 70 farmers markets.

Known as the "Racing Capital of the World," Indianapolis hosts the world's three biggest single-day sporting events at the world-famous Indianapolis Motor Speedway: Indy 500; Brickyard 400; and SAP United States Grand Prix. The National Collegiate Athletic Association is also in Indianapolis, as is the NCAA Hall of Champions. Housing divisions of both Indiana and Purdue Universities make for a lively learning center.

Indianapolis's Conseco Fieldhouse hosted the Big Ten college basketball tournament from 2008 through 2012. The city hosted the Women's NCAA basketball tournament Final Fours in 2011 and 2016, and the 2012 Super Bowl.

The Indianapolis Art Museum is one of the largest general museums in the United States. Collections include works of Gaugin, Seurat, and Turner. The museum has integrated its galleries with other properties on its campus, including the Virginia B. Fairbanks Art & Nature Park and the Oldfields-Lilly House.

Indianapolis was initially planned by Alexander Ralston, the American engineer who assisted French architect Pierre L'Enfant in planning Washington, D.C. Thus, like the nation's capital, Indianapolis is laid out on a mile-square grid and is easily navigable. Its centerpiece is Monument Circle, home of the 284-foot Soldiers and Sailors Monument, with a 32-story panoramic view of the Indianapolis skyline.

Indianapolis has a temperate climate, with very warm summers and no dry season. Very cold winter weather sometime occurs with continental polar air from northern latitudes. In the summer, tropical air from the Gulf of Mexico brings warm temperatures and moderate humidity.

Rankings

General Rankings

- *Insider* listed 23 places in the U.S. that travel industry trends reveal would be popular destinations in 2023. This year the list trends towards cultural and historical happenings, sports events, wellness experiences and invigorating outdoor escapes. According to the website insider.com Indianapolis is a place to visit in 2023. *Insider, "23 of the Best Places You Should Travel to in the U.S. in 2023," December 17, 2022*

Business/Finance Rankings

- Based on metro area social media reviews, the employment opinion group Glassdoor surveyed 50 of the most populous U.S. metro areas and equally weighed cost of living, hiring opportunity, and job satisfaction to compose a list of "25 Best Cities for Jobs." Median pay and home value, and number of active job openings were also factored in. The Indianapolis metro area was ranked #3 in overall job satisfaction. *www.glassdoor.com, "Best Cities for Jobs," February 25, 2020*

- The Brookings Institution ranked the nation's largest cities based on income inequality. Indianapolis was ranked #72 (#1 = greatest inequality). Criteria: the "95/20 ratio," a figure representing the income at which a household earns more than 95 percent of all other households, divided by the income at which a household earns more than only 20 percent of all other households. *Brookings Institution, "Household Income Inequality, Largest Cities of 97 Large U.S. Metro Areas, 2014-2016," February 5, 2018*

- The Brookings Institution ranked the 100 largest metro areas in the U.S. based on income inequality. Indianapolis was ranked #58 (#1 = greatest inequality). Criteria: the "95/20 ratio," a figure representing the income at which a household earns more than 95 percent of all other households, divided by the income at which a household earns more than only 20 percent of all other households. *Brookings Institution, "Household Income Inequality, 100 Largest U.S. Metro Areas, 2014-2016," February 5, 2018*

- Indianapolis was identified as one of America's most frugal metro areas by *Coupons.com*. The city ranked #17 out of 25. Criteria: digital coupon usage. *Coupons.com, "America's Most Frugal Cities of 2017," March 22, 2018*

- Indianapolis was identified as one of the happiest cities to work in by CareerBliss.com, an online community for career advancement. The city ranked #7 out of 10. Criteria: an employee's relationship with his or her boss and co-workers; daily tasks; general work environment; compensation; opportunities for advancement; company culture and job reputation; and resources. *Businesswire.com, "CareerBliss Happiest Cities to Work 2019," February 12, 2019*

- The Indianapolis metro area appeared on the Milken Institute "2022 Best Performing Cities" list. Rank: #77 out of 200 large metro areas (population over 250,000). Criteria: job growth; wage and salary growth; high-tech output growth; housing affordability; household broadband access. *Milken Institute, "Best-Performing Cities 2022," March 28, 2022*

- *Forbes* ranked the 200 most populous metro areas to determine the nation's "Best Places for Business and Careers." The Indianapolis metro area was ranked #58. Criteria: costs (business and living); job growth (past and projected); income growth; quality of life; educational attainment (college and high school); projected economic growth; cultural and leisure opportunities; workplace tolerance laws; net migration patterns. *Forbes, "The Best Places for Business and Careers 2019: Seattle Still On Top," October 30, 2019*

Education Rankings

- Personal finance website *WalletHub* analyzed the 150 largest U.S. metropolitan statistical areas to determine where the most educated Americans are putting their degrees to work. Criteria: education levels; percentage of workers with degrees; education quality and attainment gap; public school quality rankings; quality and enrollment of each metro area's universities. Indianapolis was ranked #67 (#1 = most educated city). *www.WalletHub.com, "Most & Least Educated Cities in America," July 18, 2022*

- Indianapolis was selected as one of America's most literate cities. The city ranked #43 out of the 84 largest U.S. cities. Criteria: number of booksellers; library resources; Internet resources; educational attainment; periodical publishing resources; newspaper circulation. *Central Connecticut State University, "America's Most Literate Cities, 2018," February 2019*

Environmental Rankings

- Indianapolis was highlighted as one of the 25 metro areas most polluted by year-round particle pollution (Annual PM 2.5) in the U.S. during 2019 through 2021. The area ranked #10. *American Lung Association, "State of the Air 2023," April 19, 2023*

Food/Drink Rankings

- The U.S. Chamber of Commerce Foundation conducted an in-depth study on local food truck regulations, surveyed 288 food truck owners, and ranked 20 major American cities based on how friendly they are for operating a food truck. The compiled index assessed the following: procedures for obtaining permits and licenses; complying with restrictions; and financial obligations associated with operating a food truck. Indianapolis ranked #5 overall (1 being the best). *www.foodtrucknation.us, "Food Truck Nation," March 20, 2018*

Health/Fitness Rankings

- For each of the 100 largest cities in the United States, the American Fitness Index®, compiled in partnership between the American College of Sports Medicine and the Elevance Health Foundation, evaluated community infrastructure and 34 health behaviors including preventive health, levels of chronic disease conditions, food insecurity, sleep quality, pedestrian safety, air quality, and community/environment resources that support physical activity. Indianapolis ranked #97 for "community fitness." *americanfitnessindex.org, "2022 ACSM American Fitness Index Summary Report," July 12, 2022*

- The Indianapolis metro area was identified as one of the worst cities for bed bugs in America by pest control company Orkin. The area ranked #7 out of 50 based on the number of bed bug treatments Orkin performed from December 2021 to November 2022. *Orkin, "The Windy City Can't Blow Bed Bugs Away: Chicago Ranks #1 For Third Consecutive Year On Orkin's Bed Bug Cities List," January 9, 2023*

- Indianapolis was identified as a "2022 Spring Allergy Capital." The area ranked #63 out of 100. Three groups of factors were used to identify the most challenging cities for people with allergies during the spring season: annual spring pollen scores; over the counter allergy medicine use; number of board-certified allergy specialists. *Asthma and Allergy Foundation of America, "Spring Allergy Capitals 2022," March 2, 2022*

- Indianapolis was identified as a "2022 Fall Allergy Capital." The area ranked #67 out of 100. Three groups of factors were used to identify the most challenging cities for people with allergies during the fall season: annual fall pollen scores; over the counter allergy medicine use; number of board-certified allergy specialists. *Asthma and Allergy Foundation of America, "Fall Allergy Capitals 2022," March 2, 2022*

- Indianapolis was identified as a "2022 Asthma Capital." The area ranked #29 out of the nation's 100 largest metropolitan areas. Criteria: estimated asthma prevalence; asthma-related mortality; and ER visits due to asthma. Risk factors analyzed but not factored in the rankings: annual pollen score; annual air quality; public smoking laws; access to board-certified asthma specialists; rescue and controller medication use; uninsured rate; poverty rate. *Asthma and Allergy Foundation of America, "Asthma Capitals 2022: The Most Challenging Places to Live With Asthma," September 14, 2022*

Real Estate Rankings

- *WalletHub* compared the most populated U.S. cities to determine which had the best markets for real estate agents. Indianapolis ranked #94 where demand was high and pay was the best. Criteria: sales per agent; annual median wage for real-estate agents; monthly average starting salary for real estate agents; real estate job density and competition; unemployment rate; home turnover rate; housing-market health index; and other relevant metrics. *www.WalletHub.com, "2021 Best Places to Be a Real Estate Agent," May 12, 2021*

- Indianapolis was ranked #14 out of 235 metro areas in terms of housing affordability in 2022 by the National Association of Home Builders (#1 = most affordable). Criteria: the share of homes sold in that area affordable to a family earning the local median income, based on standard mortgage underwriting criteria. *National Association of Home Builders®, NAHB-Wells Fargo Housing Opportunity Index, 4th Quarter 2022*

Safety Rankings

- Allstate ranked the 200 largest cities in America in terms of driver safety. Indianapolis ranked #75. Criteria: internal property damage claims over a two-year period from January 2016 to December 2017. The report helps increase the importance of safety and awareness behind the wheel. *Allstate, "Allstate America's Best Drivers Report, 2019" June 24, 2019*

- The National Insurance Crime Bureau ranked 390 metro areas in the U.S. in terms of per capita rates of vehicle theft. The Indianapolis metro area ranked #67 (#1 = highest rate). Criteria: number of vehicle theft offenses per 100,000 inhabitants in 2021. *National Insurance Crime Bureau, "Hot Spots 2021," September 1, 2022*

Seniors/Retirement Rankings

- From its Best Cities for Successful Aging indexes, the Milken Institute generated rankings for metropolitan areas, weighing data in nine categories—health care, wellness, living arrangements, transportation and convenience, financial characteristics, education, employment, community engagement, and overall livability. The Indianapolis metro area was ranked #44 overall in the large metro area category. *Milken Institute, "Best Cities for Successful Aging, 2017" March 14, 2017*

Sports/Recreation Rankings

- Indianapolis was chosen as one of America's best cities for bicycling. The city ranked #30 out of 50. Criteria: cycling infrastructure that is safe and friendly for all ages; energy and bike culture. The editors evaluated cities with populations of 100,000 or more. *Bicycling, "The 50 Best Bike Cities in America," October 10, 2018*

Women/Minorities Rankings

- Personal finance website *WalletHub* compared more than 180 U.S. cities across two key dimensions, "Hispanic Business-Friendliness" and "Hispanic Purchasing Power," to arrive at the most favorable conditions for Hispanic entrepreneurs. Indianapolis was ranked #121 out of 182. Criteria includes: share of Hispanic-Owned Businesses; Hispanic entrepreneurship rate to median annual income of Hispanics; Small Business-Friendliness score; cost of living; and number of Hispanics with at least a bachelor's degree. *WalletHub.com, "2019's Best Cities for Hispanic Entrepreneurs," May 1, 2019*

Miscellaneous Rankings

- The watchdog site, Charity Navigator, conducted a study of charities in major markets both to analyze statistical differences in their financial, accountability, and transparency practices and to track year-to-year variations in individual philanthropic communities. The Indianapolis metro area was ranked #29 among the 30 metro markets in the rating category of Overall Score. *www.charitynavigator.org, "2017 Metro Market Study," May 1, 2017*

- *WalletHub* compared the 150 most populated U.S. cities to determine their operating efficiency. A "Quality of Services" score was constructed for each city and then divided by the total budget per capita to reveal which were managed the best. Indianapolis ranked #64. Criteria: financial stability; economy; education; safety; health; infrastructure and pollution. *www.WalletHub.com, "2022's Best- & Worst-Run Cities in America," June 21, 2022*

- Indianapolis was selected as one of "America's Friendliest Cities." The city ranked #6 in the "Friendliest" category. Respondents to an online survey were asked to rate 38 top urban destinations in the United States as to general friendliness, as well as manners, politeness and warm disposition. *Travel + Leisure, "America's Friendliest Cities," October 20, 2017*

Business Environment

DEMOGRAPHICS

Population Growth

Area	1990 Census	2000 Census	2010 Census	2020 Census	Population Growth (%) 1990-2020	Population Growth (%) 2010-2020
City	730,993	781,870	820,445	887,642	21.4	8.2
MSA[1]	1,294,217	1,525,104	1,756,241	2,111,040	63.1	20.2
U.S.	248,709,873	281,421,906	308,745,538	331,449,281	33.3	7.4

Note: (1) Figures cover the Indianapolis-Carmel-Anderson, IN Metropolitan Statistical Area
Source: U.S. Census Bureau, 1990 Census, 2000 Census, 2010 Census, 2020 Census

Race

Area	White Alone[2] (%)	Black Alone[2] (%)	Asian Alone[2] (%)	AIAN[3] Alone[2] (%)	NHOPI[4] Alone[2] (%)	Other Race Alone[2] (%)	Two or More Races (%)
City	52.0	27.9	4.3	0.5	0.0	7.7	7.5
MSA[1]	69.6	15.0	3.9	0.4	0.0	4.5	6.6
U.S.	61.6	12.4	6.0	1.1	0.2	8.4	10.2

Note: (1) Figures cover the Indianapolis-Carmel-Anderson, IN Metropolitan Statistical Area; (2) Alone is defined as not being in combination with one or more other races; (3) American Indian and Alaska Native; (4) Native Hawaiian and Other Pacific Islander
Source: U.S. Census Bureau, 2020 Census

Hispanic or Latino Origin

Area	Total (%)	Mexican (%)	Puerto Rican (%)	Cuban (%)	Other (%)
City	10.8	7.3	0.7	0.2	2.6
MSA[1]	7.1	4.6	0.6	0.1	1.8
U.S.	18.4	11.2	1.8	0.7	4.7

Note: Persons of Hispanic or Latino origin can be of any race; (1) Figures cover the Indianapolis-Carmel-Anderson, IN Metropolitan Statistical Area
Source: U.S. Census Bureau, 2017-2021 American Community Survey 5-Year Estimates

Age

Area	Under Age 5	Age 5–19	Age 20–34	Age 35–44	Age 45–54	Age 55–64	Age 65–74	Age 75–84	Age 85+	Median Age
City	6.6	20.2	24.0	13.4	11.3	11.8	7.9	3.5	1.3	34.5
MSA[1]	6.2	20.7	20.2	13.5	12.5	12.5	8.8	4.1	1.5	37.0
U.S.	5.6	19.2	20.2	12.7	12.4	13.1	10.0	4.9	1.9	38.8

Note: (1) Figures cover the Indianapolis-Carmel-Anderson, IN Metropolitan Statistical Area
Source: U.S. Census Bureau, 2020 Census

Disability by Age

Area	All Ages	Under 18 Years Old	18 to 64 Years Old	65 Years and Over
City	13.5	5.3	12.4	35.5
MSA[1]	12.3	4.8	10.8	32.9
U.S.	12.6	4.4	10.3	33.4

Note: Figures show percent of the civilian noninstitutionalized population that reported having a disability. Disability status is determined from six types of difficulty: vision, hearing, cognitive, ambulatory, self-care, and independent living. For children under 5 years old, hearing and vision difficulty are used to determine disability status. For children between the ages of 5 and 14, disability status is determined from hearing, vision, cognitive, ambulatory, and self-care difficulties. For people aged 15 years and older, they are considered to have a disability if they have difficulty with any one of the six difficulty types; Note: (1) Figures cover the Indianapolis-Carmel-Anderson, IN Metropolitan Statistical Area
Source: U.S. Census Bureau, 2017-2021 American Community Survey 5-Year Estimates

Ancestry

Area	German	Irish	English	American	Italian	Polish	French[2]	Scottish	Dutch
City	12.8	8.2	7.0	4.9	2.0	1.5	1.6	1.5	0.9
MSA[1]	16.6	9.6	9.5	8.1	2.5	1.7	1.7	1.7	1.2
U.S.	12.8	9.6	8.1	5.7	5.0	2.7	2.2	1.6	1.1

Note: Figures are the percentage of the total population reporting a particular ancestry. The nine most commonly reported ancestries in the U.S. are shown. Figures include multiple ancestries (e.g. if a person reported being Irish and Italian, they were included in both columns); (1) Figures cover the Indianapolis-Carmel-Anderson, IN Metropolitan Statistical Area; (2) Excludes Basque
Source: U.S. Census Bureau, 2017-2021 American Community Survey 5-Year Estimates

Foreign-born Population

Area	Any Foreign Country	Asia	Mexico	Europe	Caribbean	Central America[2]	South America	Africa	Canada
City	10.0	3.0	2.8	0.5	0.5	0.9	0.4	1.9	0.1
MSA[1]	7.3	2.7	1.6	0.6	0.2	0.5	0.4	1.2	0.1
U.S.	13.6	4.2	3.3	1.5	1.4	1.1	1.1	0.8	0.2

Note: (1) Figures cover the Indianapolis-Carmel-Anderson, IN Metropolitan Statistical Area; (2) Excludes Mexico.
Source: U.S. Census Bureau, 2017-2021 American Community Survey 5-Year Estimates

Household Size

Area	Persons in Household (%)							Average Household Size
	One	Two	Three	Four	Five	Six	Seven or More	
City	36.9	32.2	13.0	9.7	5.1	1.9	1.2	2.50
MSA[1]	29.3	34.1	14.8	12.9	5.9	1.9	1.1	2.50
U.S.	28.1	33.8	15.5	12.9	6.0	2.3	1.4	2.60

Note: (1) Figures cover the Indianapolis-Carmel-Anderson, IN Metropolitan Statistical Area
Source: U.S. Census Bureau, 2017-2021 American Community Survey 5-Year Estimates

Household Relationships

Area	House-holder	Opposite-sex Spouse	Same-sex Spouse	Opposite-sex Unmarried Partner	Same-sex Unmarried Partner	Child[2]	Grand-child	Other Relatives	Non-relatives
City	40.7	14.0	0.3	3.4	0.3	28.6	2.5	4.5	3.9
MSA[1]	39.2	17.9	0.2	2.8	0.2	29.6	2.1	3.5	2.8
U.S.	38.3	17.5	0.2	2.5	0.2	28.3	2.4	4.8	3.4

Note: Figures are percent of the total population; (1) Figures cover the Indianapolis-Carmel-Anderson, IN Metropolitan Statistical Area; (2) Includes biological, adopted, and stepchildren of the householder
Source: U.S. Census Bureau, 2020 Census

Gender

Area	Males	Females	Males per 100 Females
City	430,358	457,284	94.1
MSA[1]	1,033,439	1,077,601	95.9
U.S.	162,685,811	168,763,470	96.4

Note: (1) Figures cover the Indianapolis-Carmel-Anderson, IN Metropolitan Statistical Area
Source: U.S. Census Bureau, 2020 Census

Marital Status

Area	Never Married	Now Married[2]	Separated	Widowed	Divorced
City	41.8	39.4	1.7	4.8	12.3
MSA[1]	33.0	49.2	1.3	4.9	11.5
U.S.	33.8	48.0	1.8	5.6	10.8

Note: Figures are percentages and cover the population 15 years of age and older; (1) Figures cover the Indianapolis-Carmel-Anderson, IN Metropolitan Statistical Area; (2) Excludes separated
Source: U.S. Census Bureau, 2017-2021 American Community Survey 5-Year Estimates

Religious Groups by Family

Area	Catholic	Baptist	Methodist	LDS[2]	Pentecostal	Lutheran	Islam	Adventist	Other
MSA[1]	11.5	6.2	3.3	0.7	1.3	1.1	1.1	1.0	17.4
U.S.	18.7	7.3	3.0	2.0	1.8	1.7	1.3	1.3	11.6

Note: Figures are the number of adherents as a percentage of the total population and cover the eight largest religious groups in the U.S; (1) Figures cover the Indianapolis-Carmel-Anderson, IN Metropolitan Statistical Area; (2) Church of Jesus Christ of Latter-day Saints
Sources: 2020 U.S. Religion Census, Association of Statisticians of American Religious Bodies; The Association of Religion Data Archives (ARDA)

Religious Groups by Tradition

Area	Catholic	Evangelical Protestant	Mainline Protestant	Black Protestant	Islam	Judaism	Hinduism	Orthodox	Buddhism
MSA[1]	11.5	16.8	7.6	4.2	1.1	0.4	0.2	0.3	0.1
U.S.	18.7	16.5	5.2	2.3	1.3	0.6	0.4	0.4	0.3

Note: Figures are the number of adherents as a percentage of the total population; (1) Figures cover the Indianapolis-Carmel-Anderson, IN Metropolitan Statistical Area
Sources: 2020 U.S. Religion Census, Association of Statisticians of American Religious Bodies; The Association of Religion Data Archives (ARDA)

ECONOMY

Gross Metropolitan Product

Area	2020	2021	2022	2023	Rank[2]
MSA[1]	146.9	163.9	178.6	190.0	28

Note: Figures are in billions of dollars; (1) Figures cover the Indianapolis-Carmel-Anderson, IN Metropolitan Statistical Area; (2) Rank is based on 2021 data and ranges from 1 to 381
Source: U.S. Conference of Mayors, U.S. Metro Economies: U.S. Metros Compared to Global and State Economies, June 2022

Economic Growth

Area	2018-20 (%)	2021 (%)	2022 (%)	2023 (%)	Rank[2]
MSA[1]	-0.2	7.3	3.2	3.1	155
U.S.	-0.6	5.7	3.1	2.9	–

Note: Figures are real gross metropolitan product (GMP) growth rates and represent average annual percent change; (1) Figures cover the Indianapolis-Carmel-Anderson, IN Metropolitan Statistical Area; (2) Rank is based on 2020 2-year average annual percent change and ranges from 1 to 381
Source: U.S. Conference of Mayors, U.S. Metro Economies: U.S. Metros Compared to Global and State Economies, June 2022

Metropolitan Area Exports

Area	2016	2017	2018	2019	2020	2021	Rank[2]
MSA[1]	9,655.4	10,544.2	11,069.9	11,148.7	11,100.4	12,740.4	30

Note: Figures are in millions of dollars; (1) Figures cover the Indianapolis-Carmel-Anderson, IN Metropolitan Statistical Area; (2) Rank is based on 2021 data and ranges from 1 to 388
Source: U.S. Department of Commerce, International Trade Administration, Office of Trade and Economic Analysis, Industry and Analysis, Exports by Metropolitan Area, data extracted March 16, 2023

Building Permits

Area	Single-Family			Multi-Family			Total		
	2021	2022	Pct. Chg.	2021	2022	Pct. Chg.	2021	2022	Pct. Chg.
City	1,221	1,099	-10.0	968	1,011	4.4	2,189	2,110	-3.6
MSA[1]	10,159	8,578	-15.6	3,292	4,915	49.3	13,451	13,493	0.3
U.S.	1,115,400	975,600	-12.5	621,600	689,500	10.9	1,737,000	1,665,100	-4.1

Note: (1) Figures cover the Indianapolis-Carmel-Anderson, IN Metropolitan Statistical Area; Figures represent new, privately-owned housing units authorized (unadjusted data); All permit data are based on estimates with imputation
Source: U.S. Census Bureau, Manufacturing, Mining, and Construction Statistics, Building Permits, 2021, 2022

Bankruptcy Filings

Area	Business Filings			Nonbusiness Filings		
	2021	2022	% Chg.	2021	2022	% Chg.
Marion County	45	37	-17.8	2,705	2,399	-11.3
U.S.	14,347	13,481	-6.0	399,269	374,240	-6.3

Note: Business filings include Chapter 7, Chapter 9, Chapter 11, Chapter 12, Chapter 13, Chapter 15, and Section 304; Nonbusiness filings include Chapter 7, Chapter 11, and Chapter 13
Source: Administrative Office of the U.S. Courts, Business and Nonbusiness Bankruptcy, County Cases Commenced by Chapter of the Bankruptcy Code, During the 12-Month Period Ending December 31, 2021 and Business and Nonbusiness Bankruptcy, County Cases Commenced by Chapter of the Bankruptcy Code, During the 12-Month Period Ending December 31, 2022

Housing Vacancy Rates

Area	Gross Vacancy Rate[2] (%)			Year-Round Vacancy Rate[3] (%)			Rental Vacancy Rate[4] (%)			Homeowner Vacancy Rate[5] (%)		
	2020	2021	2022	2020	2021	2022	2020	2021	2022	2020	2021	2022
MSA[1]	7.3	6.2	7.7	7.0	6.1	7.2	10.4	8.2	11.0	0.8	0.7	1.0
U.S.	10.6	10.8	10.5	8.2	8.4	8.2	6.3	6.1	5.8	1.0	0.9	0.8

Note: (1) Figures cover the Indianapolis-Carmel-Anderson, IN Metropolitan Statistical Area; (2) The percentage of the total housing inventory that is vacant; (3) The percentage of the housing inventory (excluding seasonal units) that is year-round vacant; (4) The percentage of rental inventory that is vacant for rent; (5) The percentage of homeowner inventory that is vacant for sale
Source: U.S. Census Bureau, Housing Vacancies and Homeownership Annual Statistics: 2020, 2021, 2022

INCOME

Income

Area	Per Capita ($)	Median Household ($)	Average Household ($)
City	31,538	54,321	75,792
MSA[1]	36,867	67,330	92,858
U.S.	37,638	69,021	97,196

Note: (1) Figures cover the Indianapolis-Carmel-Anderson, IN Metropolitan Statistical Area
Source: U.S. Census Bureau, 2017-2021 American Community Survey 5-Year Estimates

Household Income Distribution

Area	Percent of Households Earning							
	Under $15,000	$15,000 -$24,999	$25,000 -$34,999	$35,000 -$49,999	$50,000 -$74,999	$75,000 -$99,999	$100,000 -$149,999	$150,000 and up
City	12.1	9.6	9.9	14.5	18.8	11.9	12.9	10.4
MSA[1]	8.6	7.4	8.3	12.1	18.4	13.4	16.2	15.6
U.S.	9.4	7.8	8.2	11.4	16.8	12.8	16.3	17.3

Note: (1) Figures cover the Indianapolis-Carmel-Anderson, IN Metropolitan Statistical Area
Source: U.S. Census Bureau, 2017-2021 American Community Survey 5-Year Estimates

Poverty Rate

Area	All Ages	Under 18 Years Old	18 to 64 Years Old	65 Years and Over
City	16.4	23.3	14.9	10.5
MSA[1]	11.1	15.0	10.2	7.7
U.S.	12.6	17.0	11.8	9.6

Note: Figures are percentage of people whose income during the past 12 months was below the poverty level;
(1) Figures cover the Indianapolis-Carmel-Anderson, IN Metropolitan Statistical Area
Source: U.S. Census Bureau, 2017-2021 American Community Survey 5-Year Estimates

EMPLOYMENT

Labor Force and Employment

Area	Civilian Labor Force			Workers Employed		
	Dec. 2021	Dec. 2022	% Chg.	Dec. 2021	Dec. 2022	% Chg.
City	450,127	464,032	3.1	441,617	452,513	2.5
MSA[1]	1,076,300	1,110,642	3.2	1,060,871	1,086,712	2.4
U.S.	161,696,000	164,224,000	1.6	155,732,000	158,872,000	2.0

Note: Data is not seasonally adjusted and covers workers 16 years of age and older; (1) Figures cover the Indianapolis-Carmel-Anderson, IN Metropolitan Statistical Area
Source: Bureau of Labor Statistics, Local Area Unemployment Statistics

Unemployment Rate

Area	2022											
	Jan.	Feb.	Mar.	Apr.	May	Jun.	Jul.	Aug.	Sep.	Oct.	Nov.	Dec.
City	2.7	3.0	3.0	2.5	2.8	3.5	3.8	3.4	2.4	2.9	3.0	2.5
MSA[1]	2.2	2.5	2.5	2.0	2.4	3.0	3.3	2.8	2.1	2.6	2.6	2.2
U.S.	4.4	4.1	3.8	3.3	3.4	3.8	3.8	3.8	3.3	3.4	3.4	3.3

Note: Data is not seasonally adjusted and covers workers 16 years of age and older; (1) Figures cover the Indianapolis-Carmel-Anderson, IN Metropolitan Statistical Area
Source: Bureau of Labor Statistics, Local Area Unemployment Statistics

Average Wages

Occupation	$/Hr.	Occupation	$/Hr.
Accountants and Auditors	38.48	Maintenance and Repair Workers	23.30
Automotive Mechanics	24.17	Marketing Managers	65.78
Bookkeepers	21.02	Network and Computer Systems Admin.	42.49
Carpenters	26.70	Nurses, Licensed Practical	27.80
Cashiers	12.72	Nurses, Registered	38.68
Computer Programmers	55.30	Nursing Assistants	16.97
Computer Systems Analysts	46.41	Office Clerks, General	20.15
Computer User Support Specialists	25.93	Physical Therapists	45.55
Construction Laborers	23.51	Physicians	161.40
Cooks, Restaurant	14.76	Plumbers, Pipefitters and Steamfitters	33.28
Customer Service Representatives	20.25	Police and Sheriff's Patrol Officers	32.70
Dentists	98.07	Postal Service Mail Carriers	27.71
Electricians	31.79	Real Estate Sales Agents	32.61
Engineers, Electrical	46.72	Retail Salespersons	15.60
Fast Food and Counter Workers	12.43	Sales Representatives, Technical/Scientific	52.85
Financial Managers	70.85	Secretaries, Exc. Legal/Medical/Executive	20.15
First-Line Supervisors of Office Workers	32.23	Security Guards	16.75
General and Operations Managers	62.85	Surgeons	185.56
Hairdressers/Cosmetologists	15.39	Teacher Assistants, Exc. Postsecondary*	14.25
Home Health and Personal Care Aides	14.07	Teachers, Secondary School, Exc. Sp. Ed.*	30.46
Janitors and Cleaners	15.71	Telemarketers	17.62
Landscaping/Groundskeeping Workers	17.19	Truck Drivers, Heavy/Tractor-Trailer	26.92
Lawyers	74.02	Truck Drivers, Light/Delivery Services	23.09
Maids and Housekeeping Cleaners	14.20	Waiters and Waitresses	13.35

Note: Wage data covers the Indianapolis-Carmel-Anderson, IN Metropolitan Statistical Area; (*) Hourly wages were calculated from annual wage data based on a 40 hour work week; n/a not available.
Source: Bureau of Labor Statistics, Metro Area Occupational Employment & Wage Estimates, May 2022

Employment by Industry

Sector	MSA[1]		U.S.
	Number of Employees	Percent of Total	Percent of Total
Construction	60,300	5.2	5.0
Private Education and Health Services	173,000	14.9	16.1
Financial Activities	76,800	6.6	5.9
Government	140,000	12.1	14.5
Information	12,600	1.1	2.0
Leisure and Hospitality	104,500	9.0	10.3
Manufacturing	96,100	8.3	8.4
Mining and Logging	800	0.1	0.4
Other Services	45,200	3.9	3.7
Professional and Business Services	192,800	16.6	14.7
Retail Trade	104,300	9.0	10.2
Transportation, Warehousing, and Utilities	96,000	8.3	4.9
Wholesale Trade	55,800	4.8	3.9

Note: Figures are non-farm employment as of December 2022. Figures are not seasonally adjusted and include workers 16 years of age and older; (1) Figures cover the Indianapolis-Carmel-Anderson, IN Metropolitan Statistical Area
Source: Bureau of Labor Statistics, Current Employment Statistics, Employment, Hours, and Earnings

Employment by Occupation

Occupation Classification	City (%)	MSA[1] (%)	U.S. (%)
Management, Business, Science, and Arts	38.2	41.8	40.3
Natural Resources, Construction, and Maintenance	7.1	7.4	8.7
Production, Transportation, and Material Moving	17.9	15.0	13.1
Sales and Office	20.9	21.2	20.9
Service	15.9	14.6	17.0

Note: Figures cover employed civilians 16 years of age and older; (1) Figures cover the Indianapolis-Carmel-Anderson, IN Metropolitan Statistical Area
Source: U.S. Census Bureau, 2017-2021 American Community Survey 5-Year Estimates

Occupations with Greatest Projected Employment Growth: 2022 – 2024

Occupation[1]	2022 Employment	2024 Projected Employment	Numeric Employment Change	Percent Employment Change
Laborers and Freight, Stock, and Material Movers, Hand	98,000	103,790	5,790	5.9
Retail Salespersons	87,130	89,970	2,840	3.3
Stockers and Order Fillers	53,700	56,260	2,560	4.8
Heavy and Tractor-Trailer Truck Drivers	57,980	59,970	1,990	3.4
General and Operations Managers	57,130	59,100	1,970	3.4
Cooks, Restaurant	27,050	28,980	1,930	7.1
Industrial Truck and Tractor Operators	26,810	28,690	1,880	7.0
Fast Food and Counter Workers	90,910	92,670	1,760	1.9
Janitors and Cleaners, Except Maids and Housekeeping Cleaners	49,870	51,520	1,650	3.3
Light Truck or Delivery Services Drivers	25,930	27,450	1,520	5.9

Note: Projections cover Indiana; (1) Sorted by numeric employment change
Source: www.projectionscentral.com, State Occupational Projections, 2022–2024 Short-Term Projections

Fastest-Growing Occupations: 2022 – 2024

Occupation[1]	2022 Employment	2024 Projected Employment	Numeric Employment Change	Percent Employment Change
Travel Agents	910	1,000	90	9.9
Nurse Practitioners	6,630	7,280	650	9.8
Information Security Analysts (SOC 2018)	1,710	1,870	160	9.4
Data Scientists	2,170	2,370	200	9.2
Web Developers	1,560	1,690	130	8.3
Logisticians	2,580	2,790	210	8.1
Software Developers	13,210	14,280	1,070	8.1
Veterinarians	1,980	2,130	150	7.6
Veterinary Assistants and Laboratory Animal Caretakers	2,630	2,830	200	7.6
Veterinary Technologists and Technicians	2,700	2,900	200	7.4

Note: Projections cover Indiana; (1) Sorted by percent employment change and excludes occupations with numeric employment change less than 50
Source: www.projectionscentral.com, State Occupational Projections, 2022–2024 Short-Term Projections

CITY FINANCES

City Government Finances

Component	2020 ($000)	2020 ($ per capita)
Total Revenues	4,368,218	4,984
Total Expenditures	4,295,937	4,902
Debt Outstanding	6,034,227	6,885
Cash and Securities[1]	3,349,454	3,822

Note: (1) Cash and security holdings of a government at the close of its fiscal year, including those of its dependent agencies, utilities, and liquor stores.
Source: U.S. Census Bureau, State & Local Government Finances 2020

City Government Revenue by Source

Source	2020 ($000)	2020 ($ per capita)	2020 (%)
General Revenue			
From Federal Government	66,501	76	1.5
From State Government	532,185	607	12.2
From Local Governments	26,365	30	0.6
Taxes			
Property	526,813	601	12.1
Sales and Gross Receipts	77,989	89	1.8
Personal Income	511,046	583	11.7
Corporate Income	0	0	0.0
Motor Vehicle License	2,703	3	0.1
Other Taxes	42,304	48	1.0
Current Charges	1,844,168	2,104	42.2
Liquor Store	0	0	0.0
Utility	573,028	654	13.1

Source: U.S. Census Bureau, State & Local Government Finances 2020

City Government Expenditures by Function

Function	2020 ($000)	2020 ($ per capita)	2020 (%)
General Direct Expenditures			
Air Transportation	199,609	227	4.6
Corrections	135,511	154	3.2
Education	0	0	0.0
Employment Security Administration	0	0	0.0
Financial Administration	30,818	35	0.7
Fire Protection	158,620	181	3.7
General Public Buildings	0	0	0.0
Governmental Administration, Other	21,479	24	0.5
Health	181,821	207	4.2
Highways	218,631	249	5.1
Hospitals	1,372,735	1,566	32.0
Housing and Community Development	122,386	139	2.8
Interest on General Debt	161,605	184	3.8
Judicial and Legal	112,880	128	2.6
Libraries	0	0	0.0
Parking	7,610	8	0.2
Parks and Recreation	92,713	105	2.2
Police Protection	246,637	281	5.7
Public Welfare	0	0	0.0
Sewerage	327,474	373	7.6
Solid Waste Management	87,841	100	2.0
Veterans' Services	0	0	0.0
Liquor Store	0	0	0.0
Utility	759,353	866	17.7

Source: U.S. Census Bureau, State & Local Government Finances 2020

TAXES

State Corporate Income Tax Rates

State	Tax Rate (%)	Income Brackets ($)	Num. of Brackets	Financial Institution Tax Rate (%)[a]	Federal Income Tax Ded.
Indiana	4.9	Flat rate	1	4.9	No

Note: Tax rates as of January 1, 2023; (a) Rates listed are the corporate income tax rate applied to financial institutions or excise taxes based on income. Some states have other taxes based upon the value of deposits or shares.
Source: Federation of Tax Administrators, State Corporate Income Tax Rates, January 1, 2023

State Individual Income Tax Rates

State	Tax Rate (%)	Income Brackets ($)	Personal Exemptions ($)			Standard Ded. ($)	
			Single	Married	Depend.	Single	Married
Indiana	3.15	Flat rate	1,000	2,000	2,500 (j)	–	–

Note: Tax rates as of January 1, 2023; Local- and county-level taxes are not included; Federal income tax is not deductible on state income tax returns; (j) In Indiana, includes an additional exemption of $1,500 for each dependent child.
Source: Federation of Tax Administrators, State Individual Income Tax Rates, January 1, 2023

Various State Sales and Excise Tax Rates

State	State Sales Tax (%)	Gasoline[1] ($/gal.)	Cigarette[2] ($/pack)	Spirits[3] ($/gal.)	Wine[4] ($/gal.)	Beer[5] ($/gal.)	Recreational Marijuana (%)
Indiana	7	0.516	0.995	2.68	0.47	0.12	Not legal

Note: All tax rates as of January 1, 2023; (1) The American Petroleum Institute has developed a methodology for determining the average tax rate on a gallon of fuel. Rates may include any of the following: excise taxes, environmental fees, storage tank fees, other fees or taxes, general sales tax, and local taxes; (2) The federal excise tax of $1.0066 per pack and local taxes are not included; (3) Rates are those applicable to off-premise sales of 40% alcohol by volume (a.b.v.) distilled spirits in 750ml containers. Local excise taxes are excluded; (4) Rates are those applicable to off-premise sales of 11% a.b.v. non-carbonated wine in 750ml containers; (5) Rates are those applicable to off-premise sales of 4.7% a.b.v. beer in 12 ounce containers.
Source: Tax Foundation, 2023 Facts & Figures: How Does Your State Compare?

State Business Tax Climate Index Rankings

State	Overall Rank	Corporate Tax Rank	Individual Income Tax Rank	Sales Tax Rank	Property Tax Rank	Unemployment Insurance Tax Rank
Indiana	9	11	15	19	2	27

Note: The index is a measure of how each state's tax laws affect economic performance. The lower the rank, the more favorable a state's tax system is for business. States without a given tax are given a ranking of 1. The scores/rankings for the District of Columbia do not affect other states. The 2023 index represents the tax climate as of July 1, 2022.
Source: Tax Foundation, State Business Tax Climate Index 2023

TRANSPORTATION

Means of Transportation to Work

Area	Car/Truck/Van		Public Transportation			Bicycle	Walked	Other Means	Worked at Home
	Drove Alone	Car-pooled	Bus	Subway	Railroad				
City	77.6	9.3	1.6	0.0	0.0	0.4	1.9	0.9	8.4
MSA[1]	78.7	8.2	0.7	0.0	0.0	0.2	1.4	0.9	9.8
U.S.	73.2	8.6	2.0	1.6	0.5	0.5	2.5	1.5	9.7

Note: Figures are percentages and cover workers 16 years of age and older; (1) Figures cover the Indianapolis-Carmel-Anderson, IN Metropolitan Statistical Area
Source: U.S. Census Bureau, 2017-2021 American Community Survey 5-Year Estimates

Travel Time to Work

Area	Less Than 10 Minutes	10 to 19 Minutes	20 to 29 Minutes	30 to 44 Minutes	45 to 59 Minutes	60 to 89 Minutes	90 Minutes or More
City	9.5	30.4	28.8	22.7	4.3	2.4	1.8
MSA[1]	11.4	27.7	23.9	24.5	7.4	3.4	1.7
U.S.	12.4	28.5	21.0	20.9	8.2	6.2	2.9

Note: Note: Figures are percentages and include workers 16 years old and over; (1) Figures cover the Indianapolis-Carmel-Anderson, IN Metropolitan Statistical Area
Source: U.S. Census Bureau, 2017-2021 American Community Survey 5-Year Estimates

Key Congestion Measures

Measure	1990	2000	2010	2015	2020
Annual Hours of Delay, Total (000)	12,169	21,747	35,485	41,413	23,362
Annual Hours of Delay, Per Auto Commuter	28	39	42	46	26
Annual Congestion Cost, Per Auto Commuter ($)	440	593	768	828	487

Note: Covers the Indianapolis IN urban area
Source: Texas A&M Transportation Institute, 2021 Urban Mobility Report

Freeway Travel Time Index

Measure	1985	1990	1995	2000	2005	2010	2015	2020
Urban Area Index[1]	1.09	1.11	1.14	1.17	1.17	1.17	1.18	1.06
Urban Area Rank[1,2]	36	42	41	36	49	41	41	75

Note: Freeway Travel Time Index—the ratio of travel time in the peak period to the travel time at free-flow conditions. For example, a value of 1.30 indicates a 20-minute free-flow trip takes 26 minutes in the peak (20 minutes x 1.30 = 26 minutes); (1) Covers the Indianapolis IN urban area; (2) Rank is based on 101 larger urban areas (#1 = highest travel time index)
Source: Texas A&M Transportation Institute, 2021 Urban Mobility Report

Public Transportation

Agency Name / Mode of Transportation	Vehicles Operated in Maximum Service[1]	Annual Unlinked Passenger Trips[2] (in thous.)	Annual Passenger Miles[3] (in thous.)
Indianapolis and Marion County Public Transportation (IndyGo)			
Bus (directly operated)	126	4,163.8	19,030.3
Bus (purchased transportation)	1	4.4	8.5
Bus Rapid Transit (directly operated)	16	866.4	3,135.9
Demand Response (purchased transportation)	39	137.6	1,792.2
Demand Response - Taxi	51	25.6	324.2
Demand Response - Transportation Network Company	51	6.2	64.5

Note: (1) Number of revenue vehicles operated by the given mode and type of service to meet the annual maximum service requirement. This is the revenue vehicle count during the peak season of the year; on the week and day that maximum service is provided. Vehicles operated in maximum service (VOMS) exclude atypical days and one-time special events; (2) Number of passengers who boarded public transportation vehicles. Passengers are counted each time they board a vehicle no matter how many vehicles they use to travel from their origin to their destination. (3) Sum of the distances ridden by all passengers during the entire fiscal year.
Source: Federal Transit Administration, National Transit Database, 2021

Air Transportation

Airport Name and Code / Type of Service	Passenger Airlines[1]	Passenger Enplanements	Freight Carriers[2]	Freight (lbs)
Indianapolis International (IND)				
Domestic service (U.S. carriers - 2022)	31	4,175,259	14	1,154,246,929
International service (U.S. carriers - 2021)	7	11,421	3	76,158,434

Note: (1) Includes all U.S.-based major, minor and commuter airlines that carried at least one passenger during the year; (2) Includes all U.S.-based airlines and freight carriers that transported at least one pound of freight during the year.
Source: Bureau of Transportation Statistics, The Intermodal Transportation Database, Air Carriers: T-100 Domestic Market (U.S. Carriers), 2022; Bureau of Transportation Statistics, The Intermodal Transportation Database, Air Carriers: T-100 International Market (U.S. Carriers), 2021

BUSINESSES

Major Business Headquarters

Company Name	Industry	Rankings	
		Fortune[1]	Forbes[2]
Elevance Health	Health care, insurance and managed care	20	-
EliLilly	Pharmaceuticals	122	-

Note: (1) Companies that produce a 10-K are ranked 1 to 500 based on 2021 revenue; (2) All private companies with at least $2 billion in annual revenue through the end of their most current fiscal year are ranked 1 to 246; companies listed are headquartered in the city; dashes indicate no ranking
Source: Fortune, "Fortune 500," 2022; Forbes, "America's Largest Private Companies," 2022

Fastest-Growing Businesses

According to *Inc.*, Indianapolis is home to five of America's 500 fastest-growing private companies: **Ink Staffing** (#51); **US Hydrovac** (#393); **Kennected** (#438); **Market Wagon** (#450); **Lucidia IT** (#482). Criteria: must be an independent, privately-held, for-profit, U.S. corporation, proprietorship or partnership as of December 31, 2021; revenues must be at least $100,000 in 2018 and $2 million in 2021; must have four-year operating/sales history. *Inc., "America's 500 Fastest-Growing Private Companies," 2022*

Living Environment

COST OF LIVING

Cost of Living Index

Composite Index	Groceries	Housing	Utilities	Trans- portation	Health Care	Misc. Goods/ Services
92.5	96.6	82.8	107.7	92.6	88.1	95.2

Note: The Cost of Living Index measures regional differences in the cost of consumer goods and services, excluding taxes and non-consumer expenditures, for professional and managerial households in the top income quintile. It is based on more than 50,000 prices covering almost 60 different items for which prices are collected three times a year by chambers of commerce, economic development organizations or university applied economic centers in each participating urban area. The numbers shown should be read as a percentage above or below the national average of 100. For example, a value of 115.4 in the groceries column indicates that grocery prices are 15.4% higher than the national average. Small differences in the index numbers should not be interpreted as significant; Figures cover the Indianapolis IN urban area.
Source: The Council for Community and Economic Research, Cost of Living Index, 2022

Grocery Prices

Area[1]	T-Bone Steak ($/pound)	Frying Chicken ($/pound)	Whole Milk ($/half gal.)	Eggs ($/dozen)	Orange Juice ($/64 oz.)	Coffee ($/11.5 oz.)
City[2]	14.69	1.70	2.12	1.99	3.50	4.75
Avg.	13.81	1.59	2.43	2.25	3.85	4.95
Min.	10.17	0.90	1.51	1.30	2.90	3.46
Max.	19.35	3.30	4.32	4.32	5.31	8.59

*Note: (1) Values for the local area are compared with the average, minimum and maximum values for all 286 areas in the Cost of Living Index; (2) Figures cover the Indianapolis IN urban area; **T-Bone Steak** (price per pound); **Frying Chicken** (price per pound, whole fryer); **Whole Milk** (half gallon carton); **Eggs** (price per dozen, Grade A, large); **Orange Juice** (64 oz. Tropicana or Florida Natural); **Coffee** (11.5 oz. can, vacuum-packed, Maxwell House, Hills Bros, or Folgers).*
Source: The Council for Community and Economic Research, Cost of Living Index, 2022

Housing and Utility Costs

Area[1]	New Home Price ($)	Apartment Rent ($/month)	All Electric ($/month)	Part Electric ($/month)	Other Energy ($/month)	Telephone ($/month)
City[2]	340,588	1,325	-	111.24	89.87	188.71
Avg.	450,913	1,371	176.41	99.93	76.96	190.22
Min.	229,283	546	100.84	31.56	27.15	174.27
Max.	2,434,977	4,569	356.86	249.59	272.24	208.31

*Note: (1) Values for the local area are compared with the average, minimum and maximum values for all 286 areas in the Cost of Living Index; (2) Figures cover the Indianapolis IN urban area; **New Home Price** (2,400 sf living area, 8,000 sf lot, in urban area with full utilities); **Apartment Rent** (950 sf 2 bedroom/1.5 or 2 bath, unfurnished, excluding all utilities except water); **All Electric** (average monthly cost for an all-electric home); **Part Electric** (average monthly cost for a part-electric home); **Other Energy** (average monthly cost for natural gas, fuel oil, coal, wood, and any other forms of energy except electricity); **Telephone** (price includes the base monthly rate plus taxes and fees for three lines of mobile phone service).*
Source: The Council for Community and Economic Research, Cost of Living Index, 2022

Health Care, Transportation, and Other Costs

Area[1]	Doctor ($/visit)	Dentist ($/visit)	Optometrist ($/visit)	Gasoline ($/gallon)	Beauty Salon ($/visit)	Men's Shirt ($)
City[2]	97.22	99.33	68.63	3.65	39.23	42.46
Avg.	124.91	107.77	117.66	3.86	43.31	34.21
Min.	36.61	58.25	51.79	2.90	22.18	13.05
Max.	250.21	162.58	371.96	5.54	85.61	63.54

*Note: (1) Values for the local area are compared with the average, minimum and maximum values for all 286 areas in the Cost of Living Index; (2) Figures cover the Indianapolis IN urban area; **Doctor** (general practitioners routine exam of an established patient); **Dentist** (adult teeth cleaning and periodic oral examination); **Optometrist** (full vision eye exam for established adult patient); **Gasoline** (one gallon regular unleaded, national brand, including all taxes, cash price at self-service pump if available); **Beauty Salon** (woman's shampoo, trim, and blow-dry); **Men's Shirt** (cotton/polyester dress shirt, pinpoint weave, long sleeves).*
Source: The Council for Community and Economic Research, Cost of Living Index, 2022

HOUSING

Homeownership Rate

Area	2015 (%)	2016 (%)	2017 (%)	2018 (%)	2019 (%)	2020 (%)	2021 (%)	2022 (%)
MSA[1]	64.6	63.9	63.9	64.3	66.2	70.0	70.1	68.8
U.S.	63.7	63.4	63.9	64.4	64.6	66.6	65.5	65.8

Note: (1) Figures cover the Indianapolis-Carmel-Anderson, IN Metropolitan Statistical Area
Source: U.S. Census Bureau, Housing Vacancies and Homeownership Annual Statistics: 2015-2022

House Price Index (HPI)

Area	National Ranking[2]	Quarterly Change (%)	One-Year Change (%)	Five-Year Change (%)	Since 1991Q1 (%)
MSA[1]	99	-1.53	12.29	62.22	209.62
U.S.[3]	–	0.34	8.41	58.44	289.08

Note: The HPI is a weighted repeat sales index. It measures average price changes in repeat sales or refinancings on the same properties. This information is obtained by reviewing repeat mortgage transactions on single-family properties whose mortgages have been purchased or securitized by Fannie Mae or Freddie Mac since January 1975; (1) Figures cover the Indianapolis-Carmel-Anderson, IN Metropolitan Statistical Area; (2) Rankings are based on annual percentage change for all metro areas containing at least 15,000 transactions over the last 10 years and ranges from 1 to 257; (3) figures based on a weighted average of Census Division estimates using a seasonally adjusted, purchase-only index; all figures are for the period ending December 31, 2022
Source: Federal Housing Finance Agency, Change in FHFA Metropolitan Area House Price Indexes, 2022Q4

Median Single-Family Home Prices

Area	2020	2021	2022[p]	Percent Change 2021 to 2022
MSA[1]	227.6	260.5	294.6	13.1
U.S. Average	300.2	357.1	392.6	9.9

Note: Figures are median sales prices of existing single-family homes in thousands of dollars; (p) preliminary; (1) Figures cover the Indianapolis-Carmel-Anderson, IN Metropolitan Statistical Area
Source: National Association of Realtors, Median Sales Price of Existing Single-Family Homes for Metropolitan Areas, 4th Quarter 2022

Qualifying Income Based on Median Sales Price of Existing Single-Family Homes

Area	With 5% Down ($)	With 10% Down ($)	With 20% Down ($)
MSA[1]	88,917	84,238	74,878
U.S. Average	112,234	106,237	94,513

Note: Figures are preliminary; Qualifying income is based on a mortgage rate of 6.77%. Monthly principal and interest payment is limited to 25% of income; (1) Figures cover the Indianapolis-Carmel-Anderson, IN Metropolitan Statistical Area
Source: National Association of Realtors, Qualifying Income Based on Median Sales Price of Existing Single-Family Homes for Metropolitan Areas, 4th Quarter 2022

Home Value

Area	Under $100,000	$100,000 -$199,999	$200,000 -$299,999	$300,000 -$399,999	$400,000 -$499,999	$500,000 -$999,999	$1,000,000 or more	Median ($)
City	23.7	43.7	17.7	7.2	3.1	3.9	0.7	156,300
MSA[1]	17.1	37.2	22.1	11.7	5.5	5.6	0.9	186,700
U.S.	16.2	24.2	20.1	13.6	8.3	13.6	4.1	244,900

Note: Figures are percentages except for median and cover owner-occupied housing units; (1) Figures cover the Indianapolis-Carmel-Anderson, IN Metropolitan Statistical Area
Source: U.S. Census Bureau, 2017-2021 American Community Survey 5-Year Estimates

Year Housing Structure Built

Area	2020 or Later	2010 -2019	2000 -2009	1990 -1999	1980 -1989	1970 -1979	1960 -1969	1950 -1959	1940 -1949	Before 1940	Median Year
City	0.1	5.0	9.2	12.5	11.5	12.9	13.6	12.8	6.2	16.3	1971
MSA[1]	0.2	8.8	14.9	16.3	10.3	12.1	10.6	10.1	4.5	12.3	1980
U.S.	0.2	7.3	13.6	13.6	13.2	14.8	10.3	10.0	4.7	12.2	1979

Note: Figures are percentages except for Median Year; Note: (1) Figures cover the Indianapolis-Carmel-Anderson, IN Metropolitan Statistical Area
Source: U.S. Census Bureau, 2017-2021 American Community Survey 5-Year Estimates

Gross Monthly Rent

Area	Under $500	$500 -$999	$1,000 -$1,499	$1,500 -$1,999	$2,000 -$2,499	$2,500 -$2,999	$3,000 and up	Median ($)
City	6.0	49.3	34.3	7.9	1.7	0.4	0.4	962
MSA[1]	5.7	46.0	35.5	9.7	2.0	0.5	0.6	987
U.S.	8.1	30.5	30.8	16.8	7.3	3.1	3.5	1,163

Note: Figures are percentages except for median; Gross rent is the contract rent plus the estimated average monthly cost of utilities (electricity, gas, and water and sewer) and fuels (oil, coal, kerosene, wood, etc.) if these are paid by the renter (or paid for the renter by someone else); (1) Figures cover the Indianapolis-Carmel-Anderson, IN Metropolitan Statistical Area
Source: U.S. Census Bureau, 2017-2021 American Community Survey 5-Year Estimates

HEALTH

Health Risk Factors

Category	MSA[1] (%)	U.S. (%)
Adults aged 18–64 who have any kind of health care coverage	90.9	90.9
Adults who reported being in good or better health	85.2	85.2
Adults who have been told they have high blood cholesterol	35.2	35.7
Adults who have been told they have high blood pressure	32.4	32.4
Adults who are current smokers	15.6	14.4
Adults who currently use e-cigarettes	8.6	6.7
Adults who currently use chewing tobacco, snuff, or snus	2.8	3.5
Adults who are heavy drinkers[2]	6.0	6.3
Adults who are binge drinkers[3]	15.5	15.4
Adults who are overweight (BMI 25.0 - 29.9)	33.2	34.4
Adults who are obese (BMI 30.0 - 99.8)	34.8	33.9
Adults who participated in any physical activities in the past month	74.9	76.3

Note: (1) Figures cover the Indianapolis-Carmel-Anderson, IN Metropolitan Statistical Area; (2) Heavy drinkers are classified as adult men having more than 14 drinks per week and adult women having more than 7 drinks per week; (3) Binge drinkers are classified as males having five or more drinks on one occasion or females having four or more drinks on one occasion
Source: Centers for Disease Control and Prevention, Behaviorial Risk Factor Surveillance System, SMART: Selected Metropolitan Area Risk Trends, 2021

Acute and Chronic Health Conditions

Category	MSA[1] (%)	U.S. (%)
Adults who have ever been told they had a heart attack	4.2	4.0
Adults who have ever been told they have angina or coronary heart disease	3.8	3.8
Adults who have ever been told they had a stroke	2.7	3.0
Adults who have ever been told they have asthma	14.3	14.9
Adults who have ever been told they have arthritis	26.2	25.8
Adults who have ever been told they have diabetes[2]	11.6	10.9
Adults who have ever been told they had skin cancer	7.0	6.6
Adults who have ever been told they had any other types of cancer	7.3	7.5
Adults who have ever been told they have COPD	6.9	6.1
Adults who have ever been told they have kidney disease	3.7	3.0
Adults who have ever been told they have a form of depression	23.4	20.5

Note: (1) Figures cover the Indianapolis-Carmel-Anderson, IN Metropolitan Statistical Area; (2) Figures do not include pregnancy-related, borderline, or pre-diabetes
Source: Centers for Disease Control and Prevention, Behaviorial Risk Factor Surveillance System, SMART: Selected Metropolitan Area Risk Trends, 2021

Health Screening and Vaccination Rates

Category	MSA[1] (%)	U.S. (%)
Adults who have ever been tested for HIV	36.1	34.9
Adults who have had their blood cholesterol checked within the last five years	85.4	85.2
Adults aged 65+ who have had flu shot within the past year	70.3	68.6
Adults aged 65+ who have ever had a pneumonia vaccination	77.1	71.0

Note: (1) Figures cover the Indianapolis-Carmel-Anderson, IN Metropolitan Statistical Area.
Source: Centers for Disease Control and Prevention, Behaviorial Risk Factor Surveillance System, SMART: Selected Metropolitan Area Risk Trends, 2021

Disability Status

Category	MSA[1] (%)	U.S. (%)
Adults who reported being deaf	4.9	7.2
Are you blind or have serious difficulty seeing, even when wearing glasses?	4.7	4.8
Are you limited in any way in any of your usual activities due to arthritis?	9.7	11.1
Do you have difficulty doing errands alone?	6.9	7.0
Do you have difficulty dressing or bathing?	2.9	3.6
Do you have serious difficulty concentrating/remembering/making decisions?	11.5	12.1
Do you have serious difficulty walking or climbing stairs?	12.8	12.8

Note: (1) Figures cover the Indianapolis-Carmel-Anderson, IN Metropolitan Statistical Area.
Source: Centers for Disease Control and Prevention, Behaviorial Risk Factor Surveillance System, SMART: Selected Metropolitan Area Risk Trends, 2021

Mortality Rates for the Top 10 Causes of Death in the U.S.

ICD-10[a] Sub-Chapter	ICD-10[a] Code	Crude Mortality Rate[1] per 100,000 population	
		County[2]	U.S.
Malignant neoplasms	C00-C97	175.0	182.6
Ischaemic heart diseases	I20-I25	85.4	113.1
Other forms of heart disease	I30-I51	63.0	64.4
Other degenerative diseases of the nervous system	G30-G31	39.5	51.0
Cerebrovascular diseases	I60-I69	40.1	47.8
Other external causes of accidental injury	W00-X59	77.5	46.4
Chronic lower respiratory diseases	J40-J47	55.4	45.7
Organic, including symptomatic, mental disorders	F01-F09	33.5	35.9
Hypertensive diseases	I10-I15	34.9	35.0
Diabetes mellitus	E10-E14	32.9	29.6

Note: (a) ICD-10 = International Classification of Diseases 10th Revision; (1) Crude mortality rates are a three-year average covering 2019-2021; (2) Figures cover Marion County.
Source: Centers for Disease Control and Prevention, National Center for Health Statistics. National Vital Statistics System, Mortality 2018-2021 on CDC WONDER Online Database

Mortality Rates for Selected Causes of Death

ICD-10[a] Sub-Chapter	ICD-10[a] Code	Crude Mortality Rate[1] per 100,000 population	
		County[2]	U.S.
Assault	X85-Y09	22.6	7.0
Diseases of the liver	K70-K76	19.5	19.8
Human immunodeficiency virus (HIV) disease	B20-B24	2.2	1.5
Influenza and pneumonia	J09-J18	9.6	14.7
Intentional self-harm	X60-X84	14.4	14.3
Malnutrition	E40-E46	6.5	4.3
Obesity and other hyperalimentation	E65-E68	2.4	3.0
Renal failure	N17-N19	19.7	15.7
Transport accidents	V01-V99	16.7	13.6
Viral hepatitis	B15-B19	1.3	1.2

Note: (a) ICD-10 = International Classification of Diseases 10th Revision; (1) Crude mortality rates are a three-year average covering 2019-2021; (2) Figures cover Marion County; Data are suppressed when the data meet the criteria for confidentiality constraints; Crude mortality rates are flagged as unreliable when the rate would be calculated with a numerator of 20 or less.
Source: Centers for Disease Control and Prevention, National Center for Health Statistics. National Vital Statistics System, Mortality 2018-2021 on CDC WONDER Online Database

Health Insurance Coverage

Area	With Health Insurance	With Private Health Insurance	With Public Health Insurance	Without Health Insurance	Population Under Age 19 Without Health Insurance
City	90.2	62.4	37.4	9.8	6.3
MSA[1]	92.4	71.4	31.8	7.6	5.2
U.S.	91.2	67.8	35.4	8.8	5.3

Note: Figures are percentages that cover the civilian noninstitutionalized population; (1) Figures cover the Indianapolis-Carmel-Anderson, IN Metropolitan Statistical Area
Source: U.S. Census Bureau, 2017-2021 American Community Survey 5-Year Estimates

Number of Medical Professionals

Area	MDs[3]	DOs[3,4]	Dentists	Podiatrists	Chiropractors	Optometrists
County[1] (number)	4,407	212	893	62	163	203
County[1] (rate[2])	451.2	21.7	92.0	6.4	16.8	20.9
U.S. (rate[2])	289.3	23.5	72.5	6.2	28.7	17.4

Note: Data as of 2021 unless noted; (1) Data covers Marion County; (2) Rate per 100,000 population; (3) Data as of 2020 and includes all active, non-federal physicians; (4) Doctor of Osteopathic Medicine
Source: U.S. Department of Health and Human Services, Health Resources and Services Administration, Bureau of Health Professions, Area Resource File (ARF) 2021-2022

Best Hospitals

According to *U.S. News,* the Indianapolis-Carmel-Anderson, IN metro area is home to one of the best hospitals in the U.S.: **Indiana University Health Medical Center** (1 adult specialty and 10 pediatric specialties). The hospital listed was nationally ranked in at least one of 15 adult or 10 pediatric specialties. The number of specialties shown cover the parent hospital. Only 164 U.S. hospitals performed well enough to be nationally ranked in one or more specialties. Twenty hospitals in the U.S. made the Honor Roll. The Best Hospitals Honor Roll takes both the national rankings and the procedure and condition ratings into account. Hospitals received points if they were nationally ranked in one of the 15 adult specialties—the higher they ranked, the more points they got—and how many ratings of "high performing" they earned in the 17 procedures and conditions. *U.S. News Online, "America's Best Hospitals 2022-23"*

According to *U.S. News,* the Indianapolis-Carmel-Anderson, IN metro area is home to one of the best children's hospitals in the U.S.: **Riley Hospital for Children at IU Health** (10 pediatric specialties). The hospital listed was highly ranked in at least one of 10 pediatric specialties. Eighty-six children's hospitals in the U.S. were nationally ranked in at least one specialty. Hospitals received points for being ranked in a specialty, and the 10 hospitals with the most points across the 10 specialties make up the Honor Roll. *U.S. News Online, "America's Best Children's Hospitals 2022-23"*

EDUCATION

Public School District Statistics

District Name	Schls	Pupils	Pupil/ Teacher Ratio	Minority Pupils[1] (%)	LEP/ELL[2] (%)	IEP[3] (%)
Franklin Township Com Sch Corp	11	11,139	36.9	38.7	5.4	18.7
Indiana Connections Academy	1	6,255	33.5	24.8	1.0	17.5
Indianapolis Public Schools	57	22,115	13.4	78.9	19.0	21.9
M S D Decatur Township	9	6,681	16.6	43.8	7.0	18.4
M S D Lawrence Township	17	16,247	17.4	81.1	14.8	13.6
M S D Pike Township	13	10,928	16.0	93.0	17.7	15.9
M S D Warren Township	15	11,801	15.3	83.0	8.9	17.2
M S D Washington Township	14	10,901	14.7	71.3	14.3	17.5
M S D Wayne Township	19	16,343	14.4	75.6	17.5	14.2
Perry Township Schools	17	16,603	16.8	62.3	26.8	16.3

Note: Table includes school districts with 2,000 or more students; (1) Percentage of students that are not non-Hispanic white; (2) Percentage of students that are Limited English Proficient or English Language Learners (2018-19); (3) Percentage of students that have an Individualized Education Program (2019-20).
Source: U.S. Department of Education, National Center for Education Statistics, Common Core of Data, Local Education Agency (School District) Universe Survey: School Year 2021-2022

Best High Schools

According to *U.S. News,* Indianapolis is home to one of the top 500 high schools in the U.S.: **Herron High School** (#318). Nearly 18,000 public, magnet and charter schools were ranked based on their performance on state assessments and how well they prepare students for college. *U.S. News & World Report, "Best High Schools 2022"*

Highest Level of Education

Area	Less than H.S.	H.S. Diploma	Some College, No Deg.	Associate Degree	Bachelor's Degree	Master's Degree	Prof. School Degree	Doctorate Degree
City	13.3	27.3	18.8	7.6	21.1	8.2	2.3	1.2
MSA[1]	9.4	27.3	18.9	8.0	23.2	9.4	2.3	1.3
U.S.	11.1	26.5	20.0	8.7	20.6	9.3	2.2	1.5

Note: Figures cover persons age 25 and over; (1) Figures cover the Indianapolis-Carmel-Anderson, IN Metropolitan Statistical Area
Source: U.S. Census Bureau, 2017-2021 American Community Survey 5-Year Estimates

Educational Attainment by Race

Area	High School Graduate or Higher (%)					Bachelor's Degree or Higher (%)				
	Total	White	Black	Asian	Hisp.[2]	Total	White	Black	Asian	Hisp.[2]
City	86.7	89.7	85.3	70.5	60.6	32.9	38.4	20.9	44.3	15.8
MSA[1]	90.6	92.5	86.5	81.0	67.3	36.3	38.5	22.9	55.5	21.3
U.S.	88.9	91.4	87.2	87.6	71.2	33.7	35.5	23.3	55.6	18.4

Note: Figures shown cover persons 25 years old and over; (1) Figures cover the Indianapolis-Carmel-Anderson, IN Metropolitan Statistical Area; (2) People of Hispanic origin can be of any race
Source: U.S. Census Bureau, 2017-2021 American Community Survey 5-Year Estimates

School Enrollment by Grade and Control

Area	Preschool (%)		Kindergarten (%)		Grades 1 - 4 (%)		Grades 5 - 8 (%)		Grades 9 - 12 (%)	
	Public	Private	Public	Private	Public	Private	Public	Private	Public	Private
City	58.5	41.5	86.4	13.6	83.9	16.1	84.2	15.8	87.5	12.5
MSA[1]	52.2	47.8	87.2	12.8	86.8	13.2	87.0	13.0	88.4	11.6
U.S.	58.8	41.2	86.3	13.7	88.3	11.7	88.6	11.4	89.4	10.6

Note: Figures shown cover persons 3 years old and over; (1) Figures cover the Indianapolis-Carmel-Anderson, IN Metropolitan Statistical Area
Source: U.S. Census Bureau, 2017-2021 American Community Survey 5-Year Estimates

Higher Education

Four-Year Colleges			Two-Year Colleges			Medical Schools[1]	Law Schools[2]	Voc/ Tech[3]
Public	Private Non-profit	Private For-profit	Public	Private Non-profit	Private For-profit			
1	10	2	1	0	5	2	1	10

Note: Figures cover institutions located within the Indianapolis-Carmel-Anderson, IN Metropolitan Statistical Area and include main campuses only; (1) includes schools accredited by the Liaison Committee on Medical Education and the American Osteopathic Association's Commission on Osteopathic College Accreditation; (2) includes ABA-accredited schools, schools with provisional ABA accreditation, and state accredited schools; (3) includes all schools with programs that are less than 2 years.
Source: National Center for Education Statistics, Integrated Postsecondary Education System (IPEDS), 2021-22; Wikipedia, List of Medical Schools in the United States, accessed April 10, 2023; Wikipedia, List of Law Schools in the United States, accessed April 10, 2023

According to *U.S. News & World Report*, the Indianapolis-Carmel-Anderson, IN metro area is home to one of the top 100 liberal arts colleges in the U.S.: **DePauw University** (#45 tie). The indicators used to capture academic quality fall into a number of categories: assessment by administrators at peer institutions; retention of students; faculty resources; student selectivity; financial resources; alumni giving; high school counselor ratings of colleges; and graduation rate. *U.S. News & World Report, "America's Best Colleges 2023"*

According to *U.S. News & World Report*, the Indianapolis-Carmel-Anderson, IN metro area is home to one of the top 100 law schools in the U.S.: **Indiana University—Indianapolis (McKinney)** (#98 tie). The rankings are based on a weighted average of 12 measures of quality: peer assessment score; assessment score by lawyers/judges; median LSAT scores; median undergrad GPA; acceptance rate; employment rates for graduates; placement success; bar passage rate; faculty resources; expenditures per student; student/faculty ratio; and library resources. *U.S. News & World Report, "America's Best Graduate Schools, Law, 2023"*

According to *U.S. News & World Report*, the Indianapolis-Carmel-Anderson, IN metro area is home to one of the top 75 medical schools for research in the U.S.: **Indiana University—Indianapolis** (#41 tie). The rankings are based on a weighted average of 11 measures of quality: quality assessment; peer assessment score; assessment score by residency directors; research activity; total research activity; average research activity per faculty member; student selectivity; median MCAT total score; median undergraduate GPA; acceptance rate; and faculty resources. *U.S. News & World Report, "America's Best Graduate Schools, Medical, 2023"*

EMPLOYERS

Major Employers

Company Name	Industry
Allison Transmission	Motor vehicle parts & accessories
Ameritech	Local and long distance telephone
Apple American Indiana	Restaurant/family chain
Automotive Components Holdings	Steering mechanisms, motor vehicle
Celadon Trucking Service	Trucking, except local
CNO Financial Group	Insurance services
Communikty Hospitals of Indiana	General medical & surgical hospitals
Conseco Variable Ins Company	Life insurance
Defense Finance and Accounting Services	Accounting, auditing, & bookkeeping
Eli Lilly and Company	Pharmaceutical preparations
Family & Social Svcs Admin	Administration of social and human resources
Federal Express Corporation	Air cargo carrier
GEICO	Auto insurance
Hewlett-Packard Co.	Computer terminals
Indiana Department of Transportation	Regulation administration of transportation
Indiana Police State	General government, state government
Liberty Mutual	Insurance services
Meridian Citizens Mutual Ins Company	Fire, marine & casualty insurance
Methodist Hospital	General medical & surgical hospitals
Navient	Financial services
Rolls Royce Corporation	Aircraft engines & engine parts
St. Vincent Hospital and Healthcare Ctr	General medical & surgical hospitals
The Health Hospital of Marion County	General medical & surgical hospitals
Trustees of indiana University	University
United States Postal Service	U.S. postal service

Note: Companies shown are located within the Indianapolis-Carmel-Anderson, IN Metropolitan Statistical Area.
Source: Hoovers.com; Wikipedia

Best Companies to Work For

Elevance Health (formerly Anthem), headquartered in Indianapolis, is among "The 100 Best Companies to Work For." To pick the best companies, *Fortune* partnered with the Great Place to Work Institute. Two-thirds of a company's score is based on the results of the Institute's Trust Index survey, which is sent to a random sample of employees from each company. The questions related to attitudes about management's credibility, job satisfaction, and camaraderie. The other third of the scoring is based on the company's responses to the Institute's Culture Audit, which includes detailed questions about pay and benefit programs, and a series of open-ended questions about hiring practices, internal communication, training, recognition programs, and diversity efforts. Any company that is at least five years old with more than 1,000 U.S. employees is eligible. *Fortune, "The 100 Best Companies to Work For," 2023*

Elevance Health (formerly Anthem), headquartered in Indianapolis, is among "Fortune's Best Workplaces for Women." To pick the best companies, *Fortune* partnered with the Great Place to Work Institute. To be considered for the list, companies must be Great Place To Work-Certified. Companies must also employ at least 50 women, at least 20% of their non-executive managers must be female, and at least one executive must be female. To determine the Best Workplaces for Women, Great Place To Work measured the differences in women's survey responses to those of their peers and assesses the impact of demographics and roles on the quality and consistency of women's experiences. Great Place To Work also analyzed the gender balance of each workplace, how it compared to each company's industry, and patterns in representation as women rise from front-line positions to the board of directors. *Fortune, "Best Workplaces for Women," 2022*

Elevance Health (formerly Anthem), headquartered in Indianapolis, is among "Best Workplaces in Health Care." To determine the Best Workplaces in Health Care list, Great Place To Work analyzed the survey responses of over 161,000 employees from Great Place To Work-Certified companies in the health care industry. Survey data analysis and company-provided datapoints are then factored into a combined score to compare and rank the companies that create the most consistently positive experience for all employees in this industry. *Fortune, "Best Workplaces in Health Care," 2022*

Resultant, headquartered in Indianapolis, is among the "100 Best Places to Work in IT." To qualify, companies had to have a minimum of 100 total employees and five IT employees. The best places to work were selected based on DEI (diversity, equity, and inclusion) practices; IT turnover, promotions, and growth; IT retention and engagement programs; remote/hybrid working; benefits and perks (such as elder care and child care, flextime, and reimbursement for college tuition); and training and career development opportunities. *Computerworld, "Best Places to Work in IT," 2023*

PUBLIC SAFETY

Crime Rate

Area	Total Crime	Violent Crime Rate				Property Crime Rate		
		Murder	Rape[3]	Robbery	Aggrav. Assault	Burglary	Larceny -Theft	Motor Vehicle Theft
City	4,440.6	24.3	64.3	243.2	538.9	580.6	2,376.9	612.5
Suburbs[1]	n/a	n/a	n/a	n/a	n/a	n/a	n/a	n/a
Metro[2]	n/a	n/a	n/a	n/a	n/a	n/a	n/a	n/a
U.S.	2,356.7	6.5	38.4	73.9	279.7	314.2	1,398.0	246.0

Note: Figures are crimes per 100,000 population; (1) All areas within the metro area that are located outside the city limits; (2) Figures cover the Indianapolis-Carmel-Anderson, IN Metropolitan Statistical Area; n/a not available; (3) All figures shown were reported using the revised Uniform Crime Reporting (UCR) definition of rape; Due to the transition to the National Incident-Based Reporting System (NIBRS), limited city and metro area data was released for 2021.
Source: FBI Uniform Crime Reports, 2020

Hate Crimes

Area	Number of Quarters Reported	Number of Incidents per Bias Motivation					
		Race/Ethnicity/ Ancestry	Religion	Sexual Orientation	Disability	Gender	Gender Identity
City[1]	4	18	0	6	0	0	0
U.S.	4	5,227	1,244	1,110	130	75	266

Note: (1) Figures include one incident reported with more than one bias motivation; Due to the transition to the National Incident-Based Reporting System (NIBRS), limited crime data was released for 2021.
Source: Federal Bureau of Investigation, Hate Crime Statistics 2020

Identity Theft Consumer Reports

Area	Reports	Reports per 100,000 Population	Rank[2]
MSA[1]	5,389	263	93
U.S.	1,108,609	339	-

Note: (1) Figures cover the Indianapolis-Carmel-Anderson, IN Metropolitan Statistical Area; (2) Rank ranges from 1 to 391 where 1 indicates greatest number of identity theft reports per 100,000 population
Source: Federal Trade Commission, Consumer Sentinel Network Data Book 2022

Fraud and Other Consumer Reports

Area	Reports	Reports per 100,000 Population	Rank[2]
MSA[1]	20,830	1,016	91
U.S.	4,064,520	1,245	-

Note: (1) Figures cover the Indianapolis-Carmel-Anderson, IN Metropolitan Statistical Area; (2) Rank ranges from 1 to 391 where 1 indicates greatest number of fraud and other consumer reports per 100,000 population
Source: Federal Trade Commission, Consumer Sentinel Network Data Book 2022

POLITICS

2020 Presidential Election Results

Area	Biden	Trump	Jorgensen	Hawkins	Other
Marion County	63.3	34.3	1.8	0.1	0.4
U.S.	51.3	46.8	1.2	0.3	0.5

Note: Results are percentages and may not add to 100% due to rounding
Source: Dave Leip's Atlas of U.S. Presidential Elections

SPORTS

Professional Sports Teams

Team Name	League	Year Established
Indiana Pacers	National Basketball Association (NBA)	1967
Indianapolis Colts	National Football League (NFL)	1984

Note: Includes teams located in the Indianapolis-Carmel-Anderson, IN Metropolitan Statistical Area.
Source: Wikipedia, Major Professional Sports Teams of the United States and Canada, April 12, 2023

CLIMATE

Average and Extreme Temperatures

Temperature	Jan	Feb	Mar	Apr	May	Jun	Jul	Aug	Sep	Oct	Nov	Dec	Yr.
Extreme High (°F)	71	72	85	89	93	102	104	102	100	90	81	74	104
Average High (°F)	35	39	50	63	73	82	85	84	78	66	51	39	62
Average Temp. (°F)	27	31	41	52	63	72	76	73	67	55	43	31	53
Average Low (°F)	18	22	31	41	52	61	65	63	55	44	33	23	42
Extreme Low (°F)	-22	-21	-7	18	28	39	48	41	34	20	-2	-23	-23

Note: Figures cover the years 1948-1990
Source: National Climatic Data Center, International Station Meteorological Climate Summary, 9/96

Average Precipitation/Snowfall/Humidity

Precip./Humidity	Jan	Feb	Mar	Apr	May	Jun	Jul	Aug	Sep	Oct	Nov	Dec	Yr.
Avg. Precip. (in.)	2.8	2.5	3.6	3.6	4.0	3.9	4.3	3.4	2.9	2.6	3.3	3.3	40.2
Avg. Snowfall (in.)	7	6	4	1	Tr	0	0	0	0	Tr	2	5	25
Avg. Rel. Hum. 7am (%)	81	81	79	77	79	80	84	87	87	85	83	83	82
Avg. Rel. Hum. 4pm (%)	68	64	59	53	53	53	56	56	53	53	63	70	59

Note: Figures cover the years 1948-1990; Tr = Trace amounts (<0.05 in. of rain; <0.5 in. of snow)
Source: National Climatic Data Center, International Station Meteorological Climate Summary, 9/96

Weather Conditions

Temperature			Daytime Sky			Precipitation		
10°F & below	32°F & below	90°F & above	Clear	Partly cloudy	Cloudy	0.01 inch or more precip.	0.1 inch or more snow/ice	Thunder-storms
19	119	19	83	128	154	127	24	43

Note: Figures are average number of days per year and cover the years 1948-1990
Source: National Climatic Data Center, International Station Meteorological Climate Summary, 9/96

HAZARDOUS WASTE

Superfund Sites

The Indianapolis-Carmel-Anderson, IN metro area is home to six sites on the EPA's Superfund National Priorities List: **Broadway Street Corridor Groundwater Contamination** (final); **Envirochem Corp.** (final); **Keystone Corridor Ground Water Contamination** (final); **Northside Sanitary Landfill, Inc** (final); **Pike and Mulberry Streets PCE Plume** (final); **Reilly Tar & Chemical Corp. (Indianapolis Plant)** (final). There are a total of 1,165 Superfund sites with a status of proposed or final on the list in the U.S. *U.S. Environmental Protection Agency, National Priorities List, April 12, 2023*

AIR QUALITY

Air Quality Trends: Ozone

	1990	1995	2000	2005	2010	2015	2018	2019	2020	2021
MSA[1]	0.085	0.095	0.081	0.081	0.070	0.065	0.076	0.066	0.065	0.067
U.S.	0.087	0.089	0.081	0.080	0.072	0.067	0.069	0.065	0.065	0.067

Note: (1) Data covers the Indianapolis-Carmel-Anderson, IN Metropolitan Statistical Area. The values shown are the composite ozone concentration averages among trend sites based on the highest fourth daily maximum 8-hour concentration in parts per million. These trends are based on sites having an adequate record of monitoring data during the trend period. Data from exceptional events are included.
Source: U.S. Environmental Protection Agency, Air Quality Monitoring Information, "Air Quality Trends by City, 1990-2021"

Air Quality Index

Area	Percent of Days when Air Quality was...[2]					AQI Statistics[2]	
	Good	Moderate	Unhealthy for Sensitive Groups	Unhealthy	Very Unhealthy	Maximum	Median
MSA[1]	42.2	55.9	1.9	0.0	0.0	114	53

Note: (1) Data covers the Indianapolis-Carmel-Anderson, IN Metropolitan Statistical Area; (2) Based on 365 days with AQI data in 2021. Air Quality Index (AQI) is an index for reporting daily air quality. EPA calculates the AQI for five major air pollutants regulated by the Clean Air Act: ground-level ozone, particle pollution (aka particulate matter), carbon monoxide, sulfur dioxide, and nitrogen dioxide. The AQI runs from 0 to 500. The higher the AQI value, the greater the level of air pollution and the greater the health concern. There are six AQI categories: "Good" AQI is between 0 and 50. Air quality is considered satisfactory; "Moderate" AQI is between 51 and 100. Air quality is acceptable; "Unhealthy for Sensitive Groups" When AQI values are between 101 and 150, members of sensitive groups may experience health effects; "Unhealthy" When AQI values are between 151 and 200 everyone may begin to experience health effects; "Very Unhealthy" AQI values between 201 and 300 trigger a health alert; "Hazardous" AQI values over 300 trigger warnings of emergency conditions (not shown).
Source: U.S. Environmental Protection Agency, Air Quality Index Report, 2021

Air Quality Index Pollutants

Area	Percent of Days when AQI Pollutant was...[2]					
	Carbon Monoxide	Nitrogen Dioxide	Ozone	Sulfur Dioxide	Particulate Matter 2.5	Particulate Matter 10
MSA[1]	0.0	2.2	25.5	(3)	72.3	0.0

Note: (1) Data covers the Indianapolis-Carmel-Anderson, IN Metropolitan Statistical Area; (2) Based on 365 days with AQI data in 2021. The Air Quality Index (AQI) is an index for reporting daily air quality. EPA calculates the AQI for five major air pollutants regulated by the Clean Air Act: ground-level ozone, particle pollution (also known as particulate matter), carbon monoxide, sulfur dioxide, and nitrogen dioxide. The AQI runs from 0 to 500. The higher the AQI value, the greater the level of air pollution and the greater the health concern; (3) Sulfur dioxide is no longer included in this table (as of December 8, 2021) because SO_2 concentrations tend to be very localized and not necessarily representative of broad geographical areas like counties and CBSAs.
Source: U.S. Environmental Protection Agency, Air Quality Index Report, 2021

Maximum Air Pollutant Concentrations: Particulate Matter, Ozone, CO and Lead

	Particulate Matter 10 (ug/m³)	Particulate Matter 2.5 Wtd AM (ug/m³)	Particulate Matter 2.5 24-Hr (ug/m³)	Ozone (ppm)	Carbon Monoxide (ppm)	Lead (ug/m³)
MSA[1] Level	55	12.6	32	0.067	2	n/a
NAAQS[2]	150	15	35	0.075	9	0.15
Met NAAQS[2]	Yes	Yes	Yes	Yes	Yes	n/a

Note: (1) Data covers the Indianapolis-Carmel-Anderson, IN Metropolitan Statistical Area; Data from exceptional events are included; (2) National Ambient Air Quality Standards; ppm = parts per million; ug/m³ = micrograms per cubic meter; n/a not available.
Concentrations: Particulate Matter 10 (coarse particulate)—highest second maximum 24-hour concentration; Particulate Matter 2.5 Wtd AM (fine particulate)—highest weighted annual mean concentration; Particulate Matter 2.5 24-Hour (fine particulate)—highest 98th percentile 24-hour concentration; Ozone—highest fourth daily maximum 8-hour concentration; Carbon Monoxide—highest second maximum non-overlapping 8-hour concentration; Lead—maximum running 3-month average
Source: U.S. Environmental Protection Agency, Air Quality Monitoring Information, "Air Quality Statistics by City, 2021"

Maximum Air Pollutant Concentrations: Nitrogen Dioxide and Sulfur Dioxide

	Nitrogen Dioxide AM (ppb)	Nitrogen Dioxide 1-Hr (ppb)	Sulfur Dioxide AM (ppb)	Sulfur Dioxide 1-Hr (ppb)	Sulfur Dioxide 24-Hr (ppb)
MSA[1] Level	12	40	n/a	3	n/a
NAAQS[2]	53	100	30	75	140
Met NAAQS[2]	Yes	Yes	n/a	Yes	n/a

Note: (1) Data covers the Indianapolis-Carmel-Anderson, IN Metropolitan Statistical Area; Data from exceptional events are included; (2) National Ambient Air Quality Standards; ppm = parts per million; ug/m³ = micrograms per cubic meter; n/a not available.
Concentrations: Nitrogen Dioxide AM—highest arithmetic mean concentration; Nitrogen Dioxide 1-Hr—highest 98th percentile 1-hour daily maximum concentration; Sulfur Dioxide AM—highest annual mean concentration; Sulfur Dioxide 1-Hr—highest 99th percentile 1-hour daily maximum concentration; Sulfur Dioxide 24-Hr—highest second maximum 24-hour concentration
Source: U.S. Environmental Protection Agency, Air Quality Monitoring Information, "Air Quality Statistics by City, 2021"

Kansas City, Missouri

Background

Kansas City lies on the western boundary of the state. With its sister city of the same name on the other side of the Kansas/Missouri border, both Kansas Cities make up the greater Kansas City metropolitan area.

The territory of the Kansa (or Kaw) tribe received intermittent visits from white settlers during the eighteenth and nineteenth centuries. In 1724, a fort was built in the general vicinity, and in 1804, Meriwether Lewis and William Clark explored the area on behalf of President Jefferson for the Louisiana Purchase. In 1821, the site was a trading post established by François Chouteau, who established the American Fur Company.

A combination of gold prospectors passing through on their way to California, via steamboat, rail, and coach, and the migration of would-be settlers to California and the Southwest stimulated economic activity in Kansas City during the 1800s. Three major trails—Santa Fe, California, and Oregon—all originated in Jackson County.

It was in this solid Midwestern city that the jazz clubs on 18th Street and Vine gave birth to the careers of Charlie Parker and Count Basie. Today a new generation of artists upholds Kansas City's reputation for great jazz, performing in dozens of clubs featuring live jazz nightly.

Kansas City is also home to more than 100 barbecue restaurants in the metropolitan area and each fall hosts what it claims is the world's biggest barbecue contest.

As one might expect from the heartland of America, Kansas City's major industries are hard wheat and cattle. This is not how to picture all of Kansas City, however. Downtown Kansas City continues to transform its skyline by incorporating modern skyscrapers among the more traditional nineteenth-century buildings. The city boasts over 100 parks and playgrounds, suburban areas with an above-average living standard, European statues that line wide stretching boulevards, and a foreign trade zone where foreign countries can store their goods free of import duties. It offers something for everyone, from cultural and sporting events to casinos and gaming, from hot barbecue to even hotter jazz. The Sprint Center arena is a world class home for major league sports, concerts, and events.

In 2019, the USDA opened two federal research labs in the Kansas City area. The Stowers Institute for Medical Research, adjacent to the University of Missouri-Kansas City main campus, and National Bio and Agro-Defense Facility (NBAF) in Manhattan Kansas, two hours from Kansas City.

The Kansas City International Airport is a modern and growing transportation hub. A new airport terminal opened in 2023, the largest infrastructure project in the city's history. The historic Union Station's restored grand hall, with its 95-foot ceilings, shares space with the Science City Museum, theaters, restaurants, and shops.

The city maintains its own symphony, lyric opera, and ballet. It boasts dozens of museums and art galleries, many with free admission. The Kansas City Zoo offers over 200 acres of exhibits, including the Orangutan Primadome and a penguin exhibit. Visitors to the Harley-Davidson plant can see how a "Hog" is built; other attractions include the Children's Peace Pavilion, the Kansas City Renaissance Festival, and Fiesta Hispana, a yearly celebration of Hispanic heritage.

The NFL's Kansas City Chiefs won Super Bowl LIV in 2020 and again in 2023. Also in 2020, the Sprint Center was renamed T-Mobile Center, poised to host future NBA and NHL franchises.

The National Weather Service office at Kansas City is very near the geographical center of the United States. The gently rolling terrain with no topographic impediments allows a free sweep of air from all directions, often creating conflict between warm, moist air from the Gulf of Mexico and cold polar air from the north. The summer season is characterized by warm days, mild nights, and moderate humidity. Winters are not severely cold, and sizeable snowfalls are rare.

Rankings

General Rankings

- *Insider* listed 23 places in the U.S. that travel industry trends reveal would be popular destinations in 2023. This year the list trends towards cultural and historical happenings, sports events, wellness experiences and invigorating outdoor escapes. According to the website insider.com Kansas City is a place to visit in 2023. *Insider, "23 of the Best Places You Should Travel to in the U.S. in 2023," December 17, 2022*

Business/Finance Rankings

- Based on metro area social media reviews, the employment opinion group Glassdoor surveyed 50 of the most populous U.S. metro areas and equally weighed cost of living, hiring opportunity, and job satisfaction to compose a list of "25 Best Cities for Jobs." Median pay and home value, and number of active job openings were also factored in. The Kansas City metro area was ranked #11 in overall job satisfaction. *www.glassdoor.com, "Best Cities for Jobs," February 25, 2020*

- The Brookings Institution ranked the nation's largest cities based on income inequality. Kansas City was ranked #77 (#1 = greatest inequality). Criteria: the "95/20 ratio," a figure representing the income at which a household earns more than 95 percent of all other households, divided by the income at which a household earns more than only 20 percent of all other households. *Brookings Institution, "Household Income Inequality, Largest Cities of 97 Large U.S. Metro Areas, 2014-2016," February 5, 2018*

- The Brookings Institution ranked the 100 largest metro areas in the U.S. based on income inequality. Kansas City was ranked #81 (#1 = greatest inequality). Criteria: the "95/20 ratio," a figure representing the income at which a household earns more than 95 percent of all other households, divided by the income at which a household earns more than only 20 percent of all other households. *Brookings Institution, "Household Income Inequality, 100 Largest U.S. Metro Areas, 2014-2016," February 5, 2018*

- Payscale.com ranked the 32 largest metro areas in terms of wage growth. The Kansas City metro area ranked #9. Criteria: quarterly changes in private industry employee and education professional wage growth from the previous year. *PayScale, "Wage Trends by Metro Area-1st Quarter," April 20, 2023*

- Kansas City was identified as one of America's most frugal metro areas by *Coupons.com*. The city ranked #18 out of 25. Criteria: digital coupon usage. *Coupons.com, "America's Most Frugal Cities of 2017," March 22, 2018*

- The Kansas City metro area appeared on the Milken Institute "2022 Best Performing Cities" list. Rank: #65 out of 200 large metro areas (population over 250,000). Criteria: job growth; wage and salary growth; high-tech output growth; housing affordability; household broadband access. *Milken Institute, "Best-Performing Cities 2022," March 28, 2022*

- *Forbes* ranked the 200 most populous metro areas to determine the nation's "Best Places for Business and Careers." The Kansas City metro area was ranked #51. Criteria: costs (business and living); job growth (past and projected); income growth; quality of life; educational attainment (college and high school); projected economic growth; cultural and leisure opportunities; workplace tolerance laws; net migration patterns. *Forbes, "The Best Places for Business and Careers 2019: Seattle Still On Top," October 30, 2019*

Culture/Performing Arts Rankings

- Kansas City was selected as one of the 25 best cities for moviemakers in North America. Great film cities are places where filmmaking dreams can come true, that offer more creative space, lower costs, and great outdoor locations. NYC & LA were intentionally excluded. Criteria: longstanding reputations as film-friendly communities; film community and culture; affordability; and quality of life. The city was ranked #24. *MovieMaker Magazine, "Best Places to Live and Work as a Moviemaker, 2023," January 18, 2023*

Education Rankings

- Personal finance website *WalletHub* analyzed the 150 largest U.S. metropolitan statistical areas to determine where the most educated Americans are putting their degrees to work. Criteria: education levels; percentage of workers with degrees; education quality and attainment gap; public school quality rankings; quality and enrollment of each metro area's universities. Kansas City was ranked #40 (#1 = most educated city). *www.WalletHub.com, "Most & Least Educated Cities in America," July 18, 2022*

- Kansas City was selected as one of the best cities for post grads by *Rent.com*. The city ranked among the top 10. Criteria: jobs per capita; unemployment rate; mean annual income; cost of living; rental inventory. *Rent.com, "Best Cities for College Grads," December 11, 2018*

- Kansas City was selected as one of America's most literate cities. The city ranked #20 out of the 84 largest U.S. cities. Criteria: number of booksellers; library resources; Internet resources; educational attainment; periodical publishing resources; newspaper circulation. *Central Connecticut State University, "America's Most Literate Cities, 2018," February 2019*

Environmental Rankings

- The U.S. Conference of Mayors and Walmart Stores sponsor the Mayors' Climate Protection Awards Program which recognize mayors for outstanding and innovative practices that address the climate crisis: increase energy efficiency in their cities, reduce carbon emissions and expand renewable energy. Kansas City received First Place Honors in the large city category. *U.S. Conference of Mayors, "2022 Mayors' Climate Protection Awards," June 3, 2022*

Food/Drink Rankings

- Kauffman Stadium was selected as one of PETA's "Top 10 Vegan-Friendly Ballparks" for 2019. The park ranked #9. *People for the Ethical Treatment of Animals, "Top 10 Vegan-Friendly Ballparks," May 23, 2019*

Health/Fitness Rankings

- For each of the 100 largest cities in the United States, the American Fitness Index®, compiled in partnership between the American College of Sports Medicine and the Elevance Health Foundation, evaluated community infrastructure and 34 health behaviors including preventive health, levels of chronic disease conditions, food insecurity, sleep quality, pedestrian safety, air quality, and community/environment resources that support physical activity. Kansas City ranked #88 for "community fitness." *americanfitnessindex.org, "2022 ACSM American Fitness Index Summary Report," July 12, 2022*

- Kansas City was identified as a "2022 Spring Allergy Capital." The area ranked #75 out of 100. Three groups of factors were used to identify the most challenging cities for people with allergies during the spring season: annual spring pollen scores; over the counter allergy medicine use; number of board-certified allergy specialists. *Asthma and Allergy Foundation of America, "Spring Allergy Capitals 2022," March 2, 2022*

- Kansas City was identified as a "2022 Fall Allergy Capital." The area ranked #68 out of 100. Three groups of factors were used to identify the most challenging cities for people with allergies during the fall season: annual fall pollen scores; over the counter allergy medicine use; number of board-certified allergy specialists. *Asthma and Allergy Foundation of America, "Fall Allergy Capitals 2022," March 2, 2022*

- Kansas City was identified as a "2022 Asthma Capital." The area ranked #53 out of the nation's 100 largest metropolitan areas. Criteria: estimated asthma prevalence; asthma-related mortality; and ER visits due to asthma. Risk factors analyzed but not factored in the rankings: annual pollen score; annual air quality; public smoking laws; access to board-certified asthma specialists; rescue and controller medication use; uninsured rate; poverty rate. *Asthma and Allergy Foundation of America, "Asthma Capitals 2022: The Most Challenging Places to Live With Asthma," September 14, 2022*

Real Estate Rankings

- *WalletHub* compared the most populated U.S. cities to determine which had the best markets for real estate agents. Kansas City ranked #26 where demand was high and pay was the best. Criteria: sales per agent; annual median wage for real-estate agents; monthly average starting salary for real estate agents; real estate job density and competition; unemployment rate; home turnover rate; housing-market health index; and other relevant metrics. *www.WalletHub.com, "2021 Best Places to Be a Real Estate Agent," May 12, 2021*

- Kansas City was ranked #77 out of 235 metro areas in terms of housing affordability in 2022 by the National Association of Home Builders (#1 = most affordable). Criteria: the share of homes sold in that area affordable to a family earning the local median income, based on standard mortgage underwriting criteria. *National Association of Home Builders®, NAHB-Wells Fargo Housing Opportunity Index, 4th Quarter 2022*

Safety Rankings

- To identify the most dangerous cities in America, *24/7 Wall St.* focused on violent crime categories—murder, non-negligent manslaughter, rape, robbery, and aggravated assault—as reported for every 100,000 residents using data from the FBI's 2020 annual Uniform Crime Report. For cities with populations over 25,000, Kansas City was ranked #15. *247wallst.com, "America's Most Dangerous Cities" November 12, 2021*

- Allstate ranked the 200 largest cities in America in terms of driver safety. Kansas City ranked #37. Criteria: internal property damage claims over a two-year period from January 2016 to December 2017. The report helps increase the importance of safety and awareness behind the wheel. *Allstate, "Allstate America's Best Drivers Report, 2019" June 24, 2019*

- Kansas City was identified as one of the most dangerous cities in America by NeighborhoodScout. The city ranked #25 out of 100 (#1 = most dangerous). Criteria: number of violent crimes per 1,000 residents. The editors evaluated cities with 25,000 or more residents. *NeighborhoodScout.com, "2023 Top 100 Most Dangerous Cities in the U.S.," January 12, 2023*

Seniors/Retirement Rankings

- From its Best Cities for Successful Aging indexes, the Milken Institute generated rankings for metropolitan areas, weighing data in nine categories—health care, wellness, living arrangements, transportation and convenience, financial characteristics, education, employment, community engagement, and overall livability. The Kansas City metro area was ranked #26 overall in the large metro area category. *Milken Institute, "Best Cities for Successful Aging, 2017" March 14, 2017*

Women/Minorities Rankings

- Personal finance website *WalletHub* compared more than 180 U.S. cities across two key dimensions, "Hispanic Business-Friendliness" and "Hispanic Purchasing Power," to arrive at the most favorable conditions for Hispanic entrepreneurs. Kansas City was ranked #84 out of 182. Criteria includes: share of Hispanic-Owned Businesses; Hispanic entrepreneurship rate to median annual income of Hispanics; Small Business-Friendliness score; cost of living; and number of Hispanics with at least a bachelor's degree. *WalletHub.com, "2019's Best Cities for Hispanic Entrepreneurs," May 1, 2019*

Miscellaneous Rankings

- Despite the freedom to now travel internationally, plugged-in travel influencers and experts continue to rediscover their local regions. Kansas City appeared on a *Forbes* list of places in the U.S. that provide solace as well as local inspiration. Whether it be quirky things to see and do, delicious take out, outdoor exploring and daytrips, these places are must-see destinations. *Forbes, "The Best Places To Travel In The U.S. In 2023, According To The Experts," April 13, 2023*

- *MoveHub* ranked 446 hipster cities across 20 countries, using its new and improved *alternative* Hipster Index and Kansas City came out as #38 among the top 50. Criteria: population over 150,000; number of vintage boutiques; density of tattoo parlors; vegan places to eat; coffee shops; and density of vinyl record stores. *www.movehub.com, "The Hipster Index: Brighton Pips Portland to Global Top Spot," July 28, 2021*

- The watchdog site, Charity Navigator, conducted a study of charities in major markets both to analyze statistical differences in their financial, accountability, and transparency practices and to track year-to-year variations in individual philanthropic communities. The Kansas City metro area was ranked #9 among the 30 metro markets in the rating category of Overall Score. *www.charitynavigator.org, "2017 Metro Market Study," May 1, 2017*

- *WalletHub* compared the 150 most populated U.S. cities to determine their operating efficiency. A "Quality of Services" score was constructed for each city and then divided by the total budget per capita to reveal which were managed the best. Kansas City ranked #106. Criteria: financial stability; economy; education; safety; health; infrastructure and pollution. *www.WalletHub.com, "2022's Best- & Worst-Run Cities in America," June 21, 2022*

- Kansas City was selected as one of "America's Friendliest Cities." The city ranked #16 in the "Friendliest" category. Respondents to an online survey were asked to rate 38 top urban destinations in the United States as to general friendliness, as well as manners, politeness and warm disposition. *Travel + Leisure, "America's Friendliest Cities," October 20, 2017*

Business Environment

DEMOGRAPHICS

Population Growth

Area	1990 Census	2000 Census	2010 Census	2020 Census	Population Growth (%)	
					1990-2020	2010-2020
City	434,967	441,545	459,787	508,090	16.8	10.5
MSA[1]	1,636,528	1,836,038	2,035,334	2,192,035	33.9	7.7
U.S.	248,709,873	281,421,906	308,745,538	331,449,281	33.3	7.4

Note: (1) Figures cover the Kansas City, MO-KS Metropolitan Statistical Area
Source: U.S. Census Bureau, 1990 Census, 2000 Census, 2010 Census, 2020 Census

Race

Area	White Alone[2] (%)	Black Alone[2] (%)	Asian Alone[2] (%)	AIAN[3] Alone[2] (%)	NHOPI[4] Alone[2] (%)	Other Race Alone[2] (%)	Two or More Races (%)
City	55.3	26.1	3.1	0.6	0.3	5.5	9.0
MSA[1]	70.9	12.0	3.1	0.6	0.2	4.2	9.0
U.S.	61.6	12.4	6.0	1.1	0.2	8.4	10.2

Note: (1) Figures cover the Kansas City, MO-KS Metropolitan Statistical Area; (2) Alone is defined as not being in combination with one or more other races; (3) American Indian and Alaska Native; (4) Native Hawaiian and Other Pacific Islander
Source: U.S. Census Bureau, 2020 Census

Hispanic or Latino Origin

Area	Total (%)	Mexican (%)	Puerto Rican (%)	Cuban (%)	Other (%)
City	10.7	7.7	0.4	0.4	2.2
MSA[1]	9.4	7.0	0.4	0.2	1.8
U.S.	18.4	11.2	1.8	0.7	4.7

Note: Persons of Hispanic or Latino origin can be of any race; (1) Figures cover the Kansas City, MO-KS Metropolitan Statistical Area
Source: U.S. Census Bureau, 2017-2021 American Community Survey 5-Year Estimates

Age

Area	Percent of Population									Median Age
	Under Age 5	Age 5–19	Age 20–34	Age 35–44	Age 45–54	Age 55–64	Age 65–74	Age 75–84	Age 85+	
City	6.2	18.5	25.0	13.6	11.4	11.9	8.2	3.7	1.5	35.1
MSA[1]	6.1	20.2	19.9	13.4	12.1	12.8	9.3	4.4	1.7	37.7
U.S.	5.6	19.2	20.2	12.7	12.4	13.1	10.0	4.9	1.9	38.8

Note: (1) Figures cover the Kansas City, MO-KS Metropolitan Statistical Area
Source: U.S. Census Bureau, 2020 Census

Disability by Age

Area	All Ages	Under 18 Years Old	18 to 64 Years Old	65 Years and Over
City	12.5	3.9	11.1	34.2
MSA[1]	11.7	4.0	9.9	32.2
U.S.	12.6	4.4	10.3	33.4

Note: Figures show percent of the civilian noninstitutionalized population that reported having a disability. Disability status is determined from six types of difficulty: vision, hearing, cognitive, ambulatory, self-care, and independent living. For children under 5 years old, hearing and vision difficulty are used to determine disability status. For children between the ages of 5 and 14, disability status is determined from hearing, vision, cognitive, ambulatory, and self-care difficulties. For people aged 15 years and older, they are considered to have a disability if they have difficulty with any one of the six difficulty types; Note: (1) Figures cover the Kansas City, MO-KS Metropolitan Statistical Area
Source: U.S. Census Bureau, 2017-2021 American Community Survey 5-Year Estimates

Ancestry

Area	German	Irish	English	American	Italian	Polish	French[2]	Scottish	Dutch
City	15.2	10.1	8.1	4.1	3.6	1.7	1.7	1.4	0.8
MSA[1]	19.9	12.3	11.1	4.9	3.2	1.6	2.1	1.9	1.2
U.S.	12.8	9.6	8.1	5.7	5.0	2.7	2.2	1.6	1.1

Note: Figures are the percentage of the total population reporting a particular ancestry. The nine most commonly reported ancestries in the U.S. are shown. Figures include multiple ancestries (e.g. if a person reported being Irish and Italian, they were included in both columns); (1) Figures cover the Kansas City, MO-KS Metropolitan Statistical Area; (2) Excludes Basque
Source: U.S. Census Bureau, 2017-2021 American Community Survey 5-Year Estimates

Foreign-born Population

| Area | Any Foreign Country | Percent of Population Born in | | | | | | | |
		Asia	Mexico	Europe	Caribbean	Central America[2]	South America	Africa	Canada
City	8.0	2.3	2.2	0.5	0.6	0.6	0.3	1.3	0.1
MSA[1]	6.8	2.3	2.0	0.5	0.2	0.6	0.2	0.8	0.1
U.S.	13.6	4.2	3.3	1.5	1.4	1.1	1.1	0.8	0.2

Note: (1) Figures cover the Kansas City, MO-KS Metropolitan Statistical Area; (2) Excludes Mexico.
Source: U.S. Census Bureau, 2017-2021 American Community Survey 5-Year Estimates

Household Size

| Area | Persons in Household (%) | | | | | | | Average Household Size |
	One	Two	Three	Four	Five	Six	Seven or More	
City	36.8	32.1	12.8	10.8	4.5	2.0	1.1	2.30
MSA[1]	29.1	34.4	14.3	13.1	5.7	2.1	1.2	2.50
U.S.	28.1	33.8	15.5	12.9	6.0	2.3	1.4	2.60

Note: (1) Figures cover the Kansas City, MO-KS Metropolitan Statistical Area
Source: U.S. Census Bureau, 2017-2021 American Community Survey 5-Year Estimates

Household Relationships

Area	House-holder	Opposite-sex Spouse	Same-sex Spouse	Opposite-sex Unmarried Partner	Same-sex Unmarried Partner	Child[2]	Grand-child	Other Relatives	Non-relatives
City	42.6	14.5	0.3	3.3	0.3	27.2	2.3	4.0	3.8
MSA[1]	39.6	18.4	0.2	2.6	0.2	29.4	2.0	3.3	2.7
U.S.	38.3	17.5	0.2	2.5	0.2	28.3	2.4	4.8	3.4

Note: Figures are percent of the total population; (1) Figures cover the Kansas City, MO-KS Metropolitan Statistical Area; (2) Includes biological, adopted, and stepchildren of the householder
Source: U.S. Census Bureau, 2020 Census

Gender

Area	Males	Females	Males per 100 Females
City	247,776	260,314	95.2
MSA[1]	1,076,104	1,115,931	96.4
U.S.	162,685,811	168,763,470	96.4

Note: (1) Figures cover the Kansas City, MO-KS Metropolitan Statistical Area
Source: U.S. Census Bureau, 2020 Census

Marital Status

Area	Never Married	Now Married[2]	Separated	Widowed	Divorced
City	39.3	40.6	2.0	4.8	13.3
MSA[1]	30.8	50.5	1.5	5.0	12.1
U.S.	33.8	48.0	1.8	5.6	10.8

Note: Figures are percentages and cover the population 15 years of age and older; (1) Figures cover the Kansas City, MO-KS Metropolitan Statistical Area; (2) Excludes separated
Source: U.S. Census Bureau, 2017-2021 American Community Survey 5-Year Estimates

Religious Groups by Family

Area	Catholic	Baptist	Methodist	LDS[2]	Pentecostal	Lutheran	Islam	Adventist	Other
MSA[1]	11.3	9.1	5.0	1.6	2.7	1.7	1.0	1.0	12.1
U.S.	18.7	7.3	3.0	2.0	1.8	1.7	1.3	1.3	11.6

Note: Figures are the number of adherents as a percentage of the total population and cover the eight largest religious groups in the U.S; (1) Figures cover the Kansas City, MO-KS Metropolitan Statistical Area; (2) Church of Jesus Christ of Latter-day Saints
Sources: 2020 U.S. Religion Census, Association of Statisticians of American Religious Bodies; The Association of Religion Data Archives (ARDA)

Religious Groups by Tradition

Area	Catholic	Evangelical Protestant	Mainline Protestant	Black Protestant	Islam	Judaism	Hinduism	Orthodox	Buddhism
MSA[1]	11.3	19.1	7.1	3.6	1.0	0.3	0.4	0.1	0.2
U.S.	18.7	16.5	5.2	2.3	1.3	0.6	0.4	0.4	0.3

Note: Figures are the number of adherents as a percentage of the total population; (1) Figures cover the Kansas City, MO-KS Metropolitan Statistical Area
Sources: 2020 U.S. Religion Census, Association of Statisticians of American Religious Bodies; The Association of Religion Data Archives (ARDA)

ECONOMY

Gross Metropolitan Product

Area	2020	2021	2022	2023	Rank[2]
MSA[1]	142.5	154.3	165.9	176.9	32

Note: Figures are in billions of dollars; (1) Figures cover the Kansas City, MO-KS Metropolitan Statistical Area; (2) Rank is based on 2021 data and ranges from 1 to 381
Source: U.S. Conference of Mayors, U.S. Metro Economies: U.S. Metros Compared to Global and State Economies, June 2022

Economic Growth

Area	2018-20 (%)	2021 (%)	2022 (%)	2023 (%)	Rank[2]
MSA[1]	0.0	4.0	1.7	3.5	140
U.S.	-0.6	5.7	3.1	2.9	—

Note: Figures are real gross metropolitan product (GMP) growth rates and represent average annual percent change; (1) Figures cover the Kansas City, MO-KS Metropolitan Statistical Area; (2) Rank is based on 2020 2-year average annual percent change and ranges from 1 to 381
Source: U.S. Conference of Mayors, U.S. Metro Economies: U.S. Metros Compared to Global and State Economies, June 2022

Metropolitan Area Exports

Area	2016	2017	2018	2019	2020	2021	Rank[2]
MSA[1]	6,709.8	7,015.0	7,316.9	7,652.6	7,862.7	9,177.6	38

Note: Figures are in millions of dollars; (1) Figures cover the Kansas City, MO-KS Metropolitan Statistical Area; (2) Rank is based on 2021 data and ranges from 1 to 388
Source: U.S. Department of Commerce, International Trade Administration, Office of Trade and Economic Analysis, Industry and Analysis, Exports by Metropolitan Area, data extracted March 16, 2023

Building Permits

Area	Single-Family			Multi-Family			Total		
	2021	2022	Pct. Chg.	2021	2022	Pct. Chg.	2021	2022	Pct. Chg.
City	890	746	-16.2	1,448	1,241	-14.3	2,338	1,987	-15.0
MSA[1]	7,051	5,204	-26.2	4,203	6,015	43.1	11,254	11,219	-0.3
U.S.	1,115,400	975,600	-12.5	621,600	689,500	10.9	1,737,000	1,665,100	-4.1

Note: (1) Figures cover the Kansas City, MO-KS Metropolitan Statistical Area; Figures represent new, privately-owned housing units authorized (unadjusted data); All permit data are based on estimates with imputation
Source: U.S. Census Bureau, Manufacturing, Mining, and Construction Statistics, Building Permits, 2021, 2022

Bankruptcy Filings

Area	Business Filings			Nonbusiness Filings		
	2021	2022	% Chg.	2021	2022	% Chg.
Jackson County	22	16	-27.3	1,027	1,037	1.0
U.S.	14,347	13,481	-6.0	399,269	374,240	-6.3

Note: Business filings include Chapter 7, Chapter 9, Chapter 11, Chapter 12, Chapter 13, Chapter 15, and Section 304; Nonbusiness filings include Chapter 7, Chapter 11, and Chapter 13
Source: Administrative Office of the U.S. Courts, Business and Nonbusiness Bankruptcy, County Cases Commenced by Chapter of the Bankruptcy Code, During the 12-Month Period Ending December 31, 2021 and Business and Nonbusiness Bankruptcy, County Cases Commenced by Chapter of the Bankruptcy Code, During the 12-Month Period Ending December 31, 2022

Housing Vacancy Rates

Area	Gross Vacancy Rate[2] (%)			Year-Round Vacancy Rate[3] (%)			Rental Vacancy Rate[4] (%)			Homeowner Vacancy Rate[5] (%)		
	2020	2021	2022	2020	2021	2022	2020	2021	2022	2020	2021	2022
MSA[1]	9.1	8.3	7.1	9.1	8.2	7.1	9.4	8.9	7.8	0.7	1.2	0.6
U.S.	10.6	10.8	10.5	8.2	8.4	8.2	6.3	6.1	5.8	1.0	0.9	0.8

Note: (1) Figures cover the Kansas City, MO-KS Metropolitan Statistical Area; (2) The percentage of the total housing inventory that is vacant; (3) The percentage of the housing inventory (excluding seasonal units) that is year-round vacant; (4) The percentage of rental inventory that is vacant for rent; (5) The percentage of homeowner inventory that is vacant for sale
Source: U.S. Census Bureau, Housing Vacancies and Homeownership Annual Statistics: 2020, 2021, 2022

INCOME

Income

Area	Per Capita ($)	Median Household ($)	Average Household ($)
City	35,352	60,042	81,577
MSA[1]	39,175	73,299	96,817
U.S.	37,638	69,021	97,196

Note: (1) Figures cover the Kansas City, MO-KS Metropolitan Statistical Area
Source: U.S. Census Bureau, 2017-2021 American Community Survey 5-Year Estimates

Household Income Distribution

Area	Percent of Households Earning							
	Under $15,000	$15,000 -$24,999	$25,000 -$34,999	$35,000 -$49,999	$50,000 -$74,999	$75,000 -$99,999	$100,000 -$149,999	$150,000 and up
City	11.4	8.8	9.6	12.7	17.2	12.7	15.2	12.3
MSA[1]	7.5	6.9	8.1	11.4	17.1	13.9	18.1	17.0
U.S.	9.4	7.8	8.2	11.4	16.8	12.8	16.3	17.3

Note: (1) Figures cover the Kansas City, MO-KS Metropolitan Statistical Area
Source: U.S. Census Bureau, 2017-2021 American Community Survey 5-Year Estimates

Poverty Rate

Area	All Ages	Under 18 Years Old	18 to 64 Years Old	65 Years and Over
City	15.0	22.2	13.4	10.1
MSA[1]	9.8	13.5	9.0	7.0
U.S.	12.6	17.0	11.8	9.6

Note: Figures are percentage of people whose income during the past 12 months was below the poverty level;
(1) Figures cover the Kansas City, MO-KS Metropolitan Statistical Area
Source: U.S. Census Bureau, 2017-2021 American Community Survey 5-Year Estimates

EMPLOYMENT

Labor Force and Employment

Area	Civilian Labor Force			Workers Employed		
	Dec. 2021	Dec. 2022	% Chg.	Dec. 2021	Dec. 2022	% Chg.
City	257,158	258,850	0.7	247,609	252,172	1.8
MSA[1]	1,138,286	1,149,586	1.0	1,105,453	1,121,442	1.4
U.S.	161,696,000	164,224,000	1.6	155,732,000	158,872,000	2.0

Note: Data is not seasonally adjusted and covers workers 16 years of age and older; (1) Figures cover the Kansas City, MO-KS Metropolitan Statistical Area
Source: Bureau of Labor Statistics, Local Area Unemployment Statistics

Unemployment Rate

Area	2022											
	Jan.	Feb.	Mar.	Apr.	May	Jun.	Jul.	Aug.	Sep.	Oct.	Nov.	Dec.
City	4.3	4.3	4.1	3.1	3.2	2.6	3.4	3.4	2.2	2.7	2.7	2.6
MSA[1]	3.4	3.7	3.3	2.4	2.7	2.6	3.2	3.1	2.2	2.6	2.5	2.4
U.S.	4.4	4.1	3.8	3.3	3.4	3.8	3.8	3.8	3.3	3.4	3.4	3.3

Note: Data is not seasonally adjusted and covers workers 16 years of age and older; (1) Figures cover the Kansas City, MO-KS Metropolitan Statistical Area
Source: Bureau of Labor Statistics, Local Area Unemployment Statistics

Average Wages

Occupation	$/Hr.	Occupation	$/Hr.
Accountants and Auditors	37.26	Maintenance and Repair Workers	22.59
Automotive Mechanics	22.90	Marketing Managers	68.75
Bookkeepers	22.32	Network and Computer Systems Admin.	42.01
Carpenters	28.49	Nurses, Licensed Practical	26.30
Cashiers	13.42	Nurses, Registered	36.82
Computer Programmers	32.32	Nursing Assistants	17.33
Computer Systems Analysts	43.98	Office Clerks, General	20.48
Computer User Support Specialists	28.08	Physical Therapists	44.96
Construction Laborers	22.55	Physicians	104.46
Cooks, Restaurant	15.09	Plumbers, Pipefitters and Steamfitters	31.93
Customer Service Representatives	19.33	Police and Sheriff's Patrol Officers	29.20
Dentists	85.61	Postal Service Mail Carriers	27.63
Electricians	32.19	Real Estate Sales Agents	26.48
Engineers, Electrical	49.54	Retail Salespersons	16.44
Fast Food and Counter Workers	13.01	Sales Representatives, Technical/Scientific	53.53
Financial Managers	74.13	Secretaries, Exc. Legal/Medical/Executive	19.21
First-Line Supervisors of Office Workers	31.26	Security Guards	18.98
General and Operations Managers	52.71	Surgeons	119.29
Hairdressers/Cosmetologists	19.13	Teacher Assistants, Exc. Postsecondary*	15.24
Home Health and Personal Care Aides	13.99	Teachers, Secondary School, Exc. Sp. Ed.*	28.68
Janitors and Cleaners	16.10	Telemarketers	20.21
Landscaping/Groundskeeping Workers	17.47	Truck Drivers, Heavy/Tractor-Trailer	26.24
Lawyers	70.16	Truck Drivers, Light/Delivery Services	22.59
Maids and Housekeeping Cleaners	14.27	Waiters and Waitresses	15.86

Note: Wage data covers the Kansas City, MO-KS Metropolitan Statistical Area; (*) Hourly wages were calculated from annual wage data based on a 40 hour work week; n/a not available.
Source: Bureau of Labor Statistics, Metro Area Occupational Employment & Wage Estimates, May 2022

Employment by Industry

Sector	MSA[1]		U.S.
	Number of Employees	Percent of Total	Percent of Total
Construction, Mining, and Logging	57,700	5.1	5.4
Private Education and Health Services	164,800	14.5	16.1
Financial Activities	79,900	7.0	5.9
Government	146,300	12.9	14.5
Information	16,900	1.5	2.0
Leisure and Hospitality	109,800	9.7	10.3
Manufacturing	86,500	7.6	8.4
Other Services	45,000	4.0	3.7
Professional and Business Services	193,900	17.1	14.7
Retail Trade	111,100	9.8	10.2
Transportation, Warehousing, and Utilities	71,200	6.3	4.9
Wholesale Trade	52,300	4.6	3.9

Note: Figures are non-farm employment as of December 2022. Figures are not seasonally adjusted and include workers 16 years of age and older; (1) Figures cover the Kansas City, MO-KS Metropolitan Statistical Area
Source: Bureau of Labor Statistics, Current Employment Statistics, Employment, Hours, and Earnings

Employment by Occupation

Occupation Classification	City (%)	MSA[1] (%)	U.S. (%)
Management, Business, Science, and Arts	42.3	42.5	40.3
Natural Resources, Construction, and Maintenance	6.3	7.7	8.7
Production, Transportation, and Material Moving	13.3	13.2	13.1
Sales and Office	21.5	21.7	20.9
Service	16.6	14.9	17.0

Note: Figures cover employed civilians 16 years of age and older; (1) Figures cover the Kansas City, MO-KS Metropolitan Statistical Area
Source: U.S. Census Bureau, 2017-2021 American Community Survey 5-Year Estimates

Occupations with Greatest Projected Employment Growth: 2022 – 2024

Occupation[1]	2022 Employment	2024 Projected Employment	Numeric Employment Change	Percent Employment Change
Home Health and Personal Care Aides	80,580	84,180	3,600	4.5
Stockers and Order Fillers	58,060	60,440	2,380	4.1
General and Operations Managers	86,320	88,430	2,110	2.4
Cooks, Restaurant	30,940	33,020	2,080	6.7
Registered Nurses	73,620	74,860	1,240	1.7
Laborers and Freight, Stock, and Material Movers, Hand	42,770	43,710	940	2.2
Maintenance and Repair Workers, General	38,300	39,130	830	2.2
Janitors and Cleaners, Except Maids and Housekeeping Cleaners	45,160	45,960	800	1.8
Industrial Truck and Tractor Operators	13,420	14,180	760	5.7
Waiters and Waitresses	41,390	42,140	750	1.8

Note: Projections cover Missouri; (1) Sorted by numeric employment change
Source: www.projectionscentral.com, State Occupational Projections, 2022–2024 Short-Term Projections

Fastest-Growing Occupations: 2022 – 2024

Occupation[1]	2022 Employment	2024 Projected Employment	Numeric Employment Change	Percent Employment Change
Nurse Practitioners	7,420	8,030	610	8.2
Logisticians	2,520	2,710	190	7.5
Ushers, Lobby Attendants, and Ticket Takers	2,670	2,860	190	7.1
Computer Numerically Controlled Tool Programmers	740	790	50	6.8
Cooks, Restaurant	30,940	33,020	2,080	6.7
Information Security Analysts (SOC 2018)	2,110	2,250	140	6.6
Operations Research Analysts	980	1,040	60	6.1
Fitness Trainers and Aerobics Instructors	7,500	7,940	440	5.9
Weighers, Measurers, Checkers, and Samplers, Recordkeeping	850	900	50	5.9
Physical Therapist Assistants	2,230	2,360	130	5.8

Note: Projections cover Missouri; (1) Sorted by percent employment change and excludes occupations with numeric employment change less than 50
Source: www.projectionscentral.com, State Occupational Projections, 2022–2024 Short-Term Projections

CITY FINANCES

City Government Finances

Component	2020 ($000)	2020 ($ per capita)
Total Revenues	2,073,732	4,187
Total Expenditures	2,151,882	4,344
Debt Outstanding	4,724,916	9,539
Cash and Securities[1]	3,578,346	7,224

Note: (1) Cash and security holdings of a government at the close of its fiscal year, including those of its dependent agencies, utilities, and liquor stores.
Source: U.S. Census Bureau, State & Local Government Finances 2020

City Government Revenue by Source

Source	2020 ($000)	2020 ($ per capita)	2020 (%)
General Revenue			
From Federal Government	71,494	144	3.4
From State Government	45,972	93	2.2
From Local Governments	8,869	18	0.4
Taxes			
Property	164,786	333	7.9
Sales and Gross Receipts	348,634	704	16.8
Personal Income	244,896	494	11.8
Corporate Income	46,012	93	2.2
Motor Vehicle License	6,389	13	0.3
Other Taxes	10,049	20	0.5
Current Charges	491,312	992	23.7
Liquor Store	0	0	0.0
Utility	169,505	342	8.2

Source: U.S. Census Bureau, State & Local Government Finances 2020

City Government Expenditures by Function

Function	2020 ($000)	2020 ($ per capita)	2020 (%)
General Direct Expenditures			
Air Transportation	303,764	613	14.1
Corrections	0	0	0.0
Education	0	0	0.0
Employment Security Administration	0	0	0.0
Financial Administration	19,649	39	0.9
Fire Protection	186,292	376	8.7
General Public Buildings	0	0	0.0
Governmental Administration, Other	57,818	116	2.7
Health	56,668	114	2.6
Highways	64,721	130	3.0
Hospitals	0	0	0.0
Housing and Community Development	76,199	153	3.5
Interest on General Debt	126,205	254	5.9
Judicial and Legal	14,597	29	0.7
Libraries	0	0	0.0
Parking	4,776	9	0.2
Parks and Recreation	83,650	168	3.9
Police Protection	236,614	477	11.0
Public Welfare	12,390	25	0.6
Sewerage	239,399	483	11.1
Solid Waste Management	0	0	0.0
Veterans' Services	0	0	0.0
Liquor Store	0	0	0.0
Utility	107,992	218	5.0

Source: U.S. Census Bureau, State & Local Government Finances 2020

TAXES

State Corporate Income Tax Rates

State	Tax Rate (%)	Income Brackets ($)	Num. of Brackets	Financial Institution Tax Rate (%)[a]	Federal Income Tax Ded.
Missouri	4.0	Flat rate	1	4.48	Yes (h)

Note: Tax rates as of January 1, 2023; (a) Rates listed are the corporate income tax rate applied to financial institutions or excise taxes based on income. Some states have other taxes based upon the value of deposits or shares; (h) 50% of the federal income tax is deductible.
Source: Federation of Tax Administrators, State Corporate Income Tax Rates, January 1, 2023

State Individual Income Tax Rates

State	Tax Rate (%)	Income Brackets ($)	Personal Exemptions ($)			Standard Ded. ($)	
			Single	Married	Depend.	Single	Married
Missouri (a)	0.0 - 4.95	1,207 - 8,449	(d)	(d)	(d)	13,850	27,700 (d)

Note: Tax rates as of January 1, 2023; Local- and county-level taxes are not included; (a) 16 states have statutory provision for automatically adjusting to the rate of inflation the dollar values of the income tax brackets, standard deductions, and/or personal exemptions. Oregon does not index the income brackets for $125,000 and over; (d) These states use the personal exemption/standard deduction amounts provided in the federal Internal Revenue Code.
Source: Federation of Tax Administrators, State Individual Income Tax Rates, January 1, 2023

Various State Sales and Excise Tax Rates

State	State Sales Tax (%)	Gasoline[1] ($/gal.)	Cigarette[2] ($/pack)	Spirits[3] ($/gal.)	Wine[4] ($/gal.)	Beer[5] ($/gal.)	Recreational Marijuana (%)
Missouri	4.225	0.2242	0.17	2.00	0.42	0.06	(j)

Note: All tax rates as of January 1, 2023; (1) The American Petroleum Institute has developed a methodology for determining the average tax rate on a gallon of fuel. Rates may include any of the following: excise taxes, environmental fees, storage tank fees, other fees or taxes, general sales tax, and local taxes; (2) The federal excise tax of $1.0066 per pack and local taxes are not included; (3) Rates are those applicable to off-premise sales of 40% alcohol by volume (a.b.v.) distilled spirits in 750ml containers. Local excise taxes are excluded; (4) Rates are those applicable to off-premise sales of 11% a.b.v. non-carbonated wine in 750ml containers; (5) Rates are those applicable to off-premise sales of 4.7% a.b.v. beer in 12 ounce containers; (j) 6% excise tax (retail price)
Source: Tax Foundation, 2023 Facts & Figures: How Does Your State Compare?

State Business Tax Climate Index Rankings

State	Overall Rank	Corporate Tax Rank	Individual Income Tax Rank	Sales Tax Rank	Property Tax Rank	Unemployment Insurance Tax Rank
Missouri	11	3	21	26	7	4

Note: The index is a measure of how each state's tax laws affect economic performance. The lower the rank, the more favorable a state's tax system is for business. States without a given tax are given a ranking of 1. The scores/rankings for the District of Columbia do not affect other states. The 2023 index represents the tax climate as of July 1, 2022.
Source: Tax Foundation, State Business Tax Climate Index 2023

TRANSPORTATION

Means of Transportation to Work

Area	Car/Truck/Van		Public Transportation			Bicycle	Walked	Other Means	Worked at Home
	Drove Alone	Car-pooled	Bus	Subway	Railroad				
City	77.2	7.4	2.2	0.0	0.0	0.2	1.7	1.5	9.8
MSA[1]	79.0	7.3	0.7	0.0	0.0	0.1	1.1	1.0	10.6
U.S.	73.2	8.6	2.0	1.6	0.5	2.5	1.5		9.7

Note: Figures are percentages and cover workers 16 years of age and older; (1) Figures cover the Kansas City, MO-KS Metropolitan Statistical Area
Source: U.S. Census Bureau, 2017-2021 American Community Survey 5-Year Estimates

Travel Time to Work

Area	Less Than 10 Minutes	10 to 19 Minutes	20 to 29 Minutes	30 to 44 Minutes	45 to 59 Minutes	60 to 89 Minutes	90 Minutes or More
City	11.6	33.4	27.9	20.3	4.0	1.7	1.2
MSA[1]	12.3	30.6	25.5	21.6	6.3	2.5	1.3
U.S.	12.4	28.5	21.0	20.9	8.2	6.2	2.9

Note: Note: Figures are percentages and include workers 16 years old and over; (1) Figures cover the Kansas City, MO-KS Metropolitan Statistical Area
Source: U.S. Census Bureau, 2017-2021 American Community Survey 5-Year Estimates

Key Congestion Measures

Measure	1990	2000	2010	2015	2020
Annual Hours of Delay, Total (000)	16,432	29,273	40,503	47,011	35,061
Annual Hours of Delay, Per Auto Commuter	26	34	40	45	34
Annual Congestion Cost, Per Auto Commuter ($)	544	730	802	861	694

Note: Covers the Kansas City MO-KS urban area
Source: Texas A&M Transportation Institute, 2021 Urban Mobility Report

Freeway Travel Time Index

Measure	1985	1990	1995	2000	2005	2010	2015	2020
Urban Area Index[1]	1.06	1.10	1.11	1.13	1.14	1.14	1.15	1.10
Urban Area Rank[1,2]	53	47	66	72	73	71	67	29

Note: Freeway Travel Time Index—the ratio of travel time in the peak period to the travel time at free-flow conditions. For example, a value of 1.30 indicates a 20-minute free-flow trip takes 26 minutes in the peak (20 minutes x 1.30 = 26 minutes); (1) Covers the Kansas City MO-KS urban area; (2) Rank is based on 101 larger urban areas (#1 = highest travel time index)
Source: Texas A&M Transportation Institute, 2021 Urban Mobility Report

Public Transportation

Agency Name / Mode of Transportation	Vehicles Operated in Maximum Service[1]	Annual Unlinked Passenger Trips[2] (in thous.)	Annual Passenger Miles[3] (in thous.)
Kansas City Area Transportation Authority (KCATA)			
Bus (directly operated)	105	8,431.3	30,995.2
Bus Rapid Transit (directly operated)	6	707.1	1,943.2
Demand Response (directly operated)	9	43.4	134.9
Demand Response (purchased transportation)	22	59.2	428.3
Demand Response - Taxi	59	195.6	1,541.5
Vanpool (purchased transportation)	19	31.7	1,108.0

Note: (1) Number of revenue vehicles operated by the given mode and type of service to meet the annual maximum service requirement. This is the revenue vehicle count during the peak season of the year; on the week and day that maximum service is provided. Vehicles operated in maximum service (VOMS) exclude atypical days and one-time special events; (2) Number of passengers who boarded public transportation vehicles. Passengers are counted each time they board a vehicle no matter how many vehicles they use to travel from their origin to their destination. (3) Sum of the distances ridden by all passengers during the entire fiscal year.
Source: Federal Transit Administration, National Transit Database, 2021

Air Transportation

Airport Name and Code / Type of Service	Passenger Airlines[1]	Passenger Enplanements	Freight Carriers[2]	Freight (lbs)
Kansas City International (MCI)				
Domestic service (U.S. carriers - 2022)	25	4,765,132	20	126,523,980
International service (U.S. carriers - 2021)	5	8,551	1	2,515

Note: (1) Includes all U.S.-based major, minor and commuter airlines that carried at least one passenger during the year; (2) Includes all U.S.-based airlines and freight carriers that transported at least one pound of freight during the year.
Source: Bureau of Transportation Statistics, The Intermodal Transportation Database, Air Carriers: T-100 Domestic Market (U.S. Carriers), 2022; Bureau of Transportation Statistics, The Intermodal Transportation Database, Air Carriers: T-100 International Market (U.S. Carriers), 2021

BUSINESSES

Major Business Headquarters

Company Name	Industry	Rankings Fortune[1]	Rankings Forbes[2]
Burns & McDonnell	Construction	-	232
Hallmark Cards	Media	-	154
JE Dunn Construction Group	Construction	-	113

Note: (1) Companies that produce a 10-K are ranked 1 to 500 based on 2021 revenue; (2) All private companies with at least $2 billion in annual revenue through the end of their most current fiscal year are ranked 1 to 246; companies listed are headquartered in the city; dashes indicate no ranking
Source: Fortune, "Fortune 500," 2022; Forbes, "America's Largest Private Companies," 2022

Fastest-Growing Businesses

According to *Inc.*, Kansas City is home to two of America's 500 fastest-growing private companies: **CrowdPharm** (#134); **Hawaiian Bros Island Grill** (#203). Criteria: must be an independent, privately-held, for-profit, U.S. corporation, proprietorship or partnership as of December 31, 2021; revenues must be at least $100,000 in 2018 and $2 million in 2021; must have four-year operating/sales history. *Inc., "America's 500 Fastest-Growing Private Companies," 2022*

Living Environment

COST OF LIVING

Cost of Living Index

Composite Index	Groceries	Housing	Utilities	Trans-portation	Health Care	Misc. Goods/ Services
94.9	92.3	102.6	102.0	86.2	88.2	91.1

Note: The Cost of Living Index measures regional differences in the cost of consumer goods and services, excluding taxes and non-consumer expenditures, for professional and managerial households in the top income quintile. It is based on more than 50,000 prices covering almost 60 different items for which prices are collected three times a year by chambers of commerce, economic development organizations or university applied economic centers in each participating urban area. The numbers shown should be read as a percentage above or below the national average of 100. For example, a value of 115.4 in the groceries column indicates that grocery prices are 15.4% higher than the national average. Small differences in the index numbers should not be interpreted as significant; Figures cover the Kansas City MO-KS urban area.
Source: The Council for Community and Economic Research, Cost of Living Index, 2022

Grocery Prices

Area[1]	T-Bone Steak ($/pound)	Frying Chicken ($/pound)	Whole Milk ($/half gal.)	Eggs ($/dozen)	Orange Juice ($/64 oz.)	Coffee ($/11.5 oz.)
City[2]	13.21	1.90	2.42	2.03	3.44	4.53
Avg.	13.81	1.59	2.43	2.25	3.85	4.95
Min.	10.17	0.90	1.51	1.30	2.90	3.46
Max.	19.35	3.30	4.32	4.32	5.31	8.59

*Note: (1) Values for the local area are compared with the average, minimum and maximum values for all 286 areas in the Cost of Living Index; (2) Figures cover the Kansas City MO-KS urban area; **T-Bone Steak** (price per pound); **Frying Chicken** (price per pound, whole fryer); **Whole Milk** (half gallon carton); **Eggs** (price per dozen, Grade A, large); **Orange Juice** (64 oz. Tropicana or Florida Natural); **Coffee** (11.5 oz. can, vacuum-packed, Maxwell House, Hills Bros, or Folgers).*
Source: The Council for Community and Economic Research, Cost of Living Index, 2022

Housing and Utility Costs

Area[1]	New Home Price ($)	Apartment Rent ($/month)	All Electric ($/month)	Part Electric ($/month)	Other Energy ($/month)	Telephone ($/month)
City[2]	439,207	1,471	-	98.92	78.39	198.58
Avg.	450,913	1,371	176.41	99.93	76.96	190.22
Min.	229,283	546	100.84	31.56	27.15	174.27
Max.	2,434,977	4,569	356.86	249.59	272.24	208.31

*Note: (1) Values for the local area are compared with the average, minimum and maximum values for all 286 areas in the Cost of Living Index; (2) Figures cover the Kansas City MO-KS urban area; **New Home Price** (2,400 sf living area, 8,000 sf lot, in urban area with full utilities); **Apartment Rent** (950 sf 2 bedroom/1.5 or 2 bath, unfurnished, excluding all utilities except water); **All Electric** (average monthly cost for an all-electric home); **Part Electric** (average monthly cost for a part-electric home); **Other Energy** (average monthly cost for natural gas, fuel oil, coal, wood, and any other forms of energy except electricity); **Telephone** (price includes the base monthly rate plus taxes and fees for three lines of mobile phone service).*
Source: The Council for Community and Economic Research, Cost of Living Index, 2022

Health Care, Transportation, and Other Costs

Area[1]	Doctor ($/visit)	Dentist ($/visit)	Optometrist ($/visit)	Gasoline ($/gallon)	Beauty Salon ($/visit)	Men's Shirt ($)
City[2]	90.64	101.00	89.60	3.40	33.07	36.41
Avg.	124.91	107.77	117.66	3.86	43.31	34.21
Min.	36.61	58.25	51.79	2.90	22.18	13.05
Max.	250.21	162.58	371.96	5.54	85.61	63.54

*Note: (1) Values for the local area are compared with the average, minimum and maximum values for all 286 areas in the Cost of Living Index; (2) Figures cover the Kansas City MO-KS urban area; **Doctor** (general practitioners routine exam of an established patient); **Dentist** (adult teeth cleaning and periodic oral examination); **Optometrist** (full vision eye exam for established adult patient); **Gasoline** (one gallon regular unleaded, national brand, including all taxes, cash price at self-service pump if available); **Beauty Salon** (woman's shampoo, trim, and blow-dry); **Men's Shirt** (cotton/polyester dress shirt, pinpoint weave, long sleeves).*
Source: The Council for Community and Economic Research, Cost of Living Index, 2022

HOUSING

Homeownership Rate

Area	2015 (%)	2016 (%)	2017 (%)	2018 (%)	2019 (%)	2020 (%)	2021 (%)	2022 (%)
MSA[1]	65.0	62.4	62.4	64.3	65.0	66.7	63.8	63.8
U.S.	63.7	63.4	63.9	64.4	64.6	66.6	65.5	65.8

Note: (1) Figures cover the Kansas City, MO-KS Metropolitan Statistical Area
Source: U.S. Census Bureau, Housing Vacancies and Homeownership Annual Statistics: 2015-2022

House Price Index (HPI)

Area	National Ranking[2]	Quarterly Change (%)	One-Year Change (%)	Five-Year Change (%)	Since 1991Q1 (%)
MSA[1]	102	-0.14	12.17	58.36	257.00
U.S.[3]	–	0.34	8.41	58.44	289.08

Note: The HPI is a weighted repeat sales index. It measures average price changes in repeat sales or refinancings on the same properties. This information is obtained by reviewing repeat mortgage transactions on single-family properties whose mortgages have been purchased or securitized by Fannie Mae or Freddie Mac since January 1975; (1) Figures cover the Kansas City, MO-KS Metropolitan Statistical Area; (2) Rankings are based on annual percentage change for all metro areas containing at least 15,000 transactions over the last 10 years and ranges from 1 to 257; (3) figures based on a weighted average of Census Division estimates using a seasonally adjusted, purchase-only index; all figures are for the period ending December 31, 2022
Source: Federal Housing Finance Agency, Change in FHFA Metropolitan Area House Price Indexes, 2022Q4

Median Single-Family Home Prices

Area	2020	2021	2022[p]	Percent Change 2021 to 2022
MSA[1]	237.4	279.2	309.5	10.9
U.S. Average	300.2	357.1	392.6	9.9

Note: Figures are median sales prices of existing single-family homes in thousands of dollars; (p) preliminary; (1) Figures cover the Kansas City, MO-KS Metropolitan Statistical Area
Source: National Association of Realtors, Median Sales Price of Existing Single-Family Homes for Metropolitan Areas, 4th Quarter 2022

Qualifying Income Based on Median Sales Price of Existing Single-Family Homes

Area	With 5% Down ($)	With 10% Down ($)	With 20% Down ($)
MSA[1]	89,217	84,521	75,130
U.S. Average	112,234	106,237	94,513

Note: Figures are preliminary; Qualifying income is based on a mortgage rate of 6.77%. Monthly principal and interest payment is limited to 25% of income; (1) Figures cover the Kansas City, MO-KS Metropolitan Statistical Area
Source: National Association of Realtors, Qualifying Income Based on Median Sales Price of Existing Single-Family Homes for Metropolitan Areas, 4th Quarter 2022

Home Value

Area	Under $100,000	$100,000 -$199,999	$200,000 -$299,999	$300,000 -$399,999	$400,000 -$499,999	$500,000 -$999,999	$1,000,000 or more	Median ($)
City	23.0	34.6	21.2	11.4	4.1	4.8	0.8	175,400
MSA[1]	15.2	31.5	24.6	14.0	6.8	6.8	1.1	211,900
U.S.	16.2	24.2	20.1	13.6	8.3	13.6	4.1	244,900

Note: Figures are percentages except for median and cover owner-occupied housing units; (1) Figures cover the Kansas City, MO-KS Metropolitan Statistical Area
Source: U.S. Census Bureau, 2017-2021 American Community Survey 5-Year Estimates

Year Housing Structure Built

Area	2020 or Later	2010 -2019	2000 -2009	1990 -1999	1980 -1989	1970 -1979	1960 -1969	1950 -1959	1940 -1949	Before 1940	Median Year
City	0.2	6.9	9.8	9.2	8.9	11.8	12.5	13.4	5.9	21.3	1968
MSA[1]	0.2	7.1	13.3	14.1	12.0	14.7	11.7	11.0	4.3	11.7	1978
U.S.	0.2	7.3	13.6	13.6	13.2	14.8	10.3	10.0	4.7	12.2	1979

Note: Figures are percentages except for Median Year; Note: (1) Figures cover the Kansas City, MO-KS Metropolitan Statistical Area
Source: U.S. Census Bureau, 2017-2021 American Community Survey 5-Year Estimates

Gross Monthly Rent

Area	Under $500	$500 -$999	$1,000 -$1,499	$1,500 -$1,999	$2,000 -$2,499	$2,500 -$2,999	$3,000 and up	Median ($)
City	7.2	39.0	38.6	11.6	2.4	0.7	0.5	1,040
MSA[1]	6.5	38.5	38.5	11.8	3.0	0.8	0.9	1,052
U.S.	8.1	30.5	30.8	16.8	7.3	3.1	3.5	1,163

Note: Figures are percentages except for median; Gross rent is the contract rent plus the estimated average monthly cost of utilities (electricity, gas, and water and sewer) and fuels (oil, coal, kerosene, wood, etc.) if these are paid by the renter (or paid for the renter by someone else); (1) Figures cover the Kansas City, MO-KS Metropolitan Statistical Area
Source: U.S. Census Bureau, 2017-2021 American Community Survey 5-Year Estimates

HEALTH

Health Risk Factors

Category	MSA[1] (%)	U.S. (%)
Adults aged 18–64 who have any kind of health care coverage	90.1	90.9
Adults who reported being in good or better health	86.0	85.2
Adults who have been told they have high blood cholesterol	37.9	35.7
Adults who have been told they have high blood pressure	32.7	32.4
Adults who are current smokers	14.6	14.4
Adults who currently use e-cigarettes	7.0	6.7
Adults who currently use chewing tobacco, snuff, or snus	3.5	3.5
Adults who are heavy drinkers[2]	6.2	6.3
Adults who are binge drinkers[3]	18.6	15.4
Adults who are overweight (BMI 25.0 - 29.9)	34.0	34.4
Adults who are obese (BMI 30.0 - 99.8)	36.3	33.9
Adults who participated in any physical activities in the past month	78.6	76.3

Note: (1) Figures cover the Kansas City, MO-KS Metropolitan Statistical Area; (2) Heavy drinkers are classified as adult men having more than 14 drinks per week and adult women having more than 7 drinks per week; (3) Binge drinkers are classified as males having five or more drinks on one occasion or females having four or more drinks on one occasion
Source: Centers for Disease Control and Prevention, Behaviorial Risk Factor Surveillance System, SMART: Selected Metropolitan Area Risk Trends, 2021

Acute and Chronic Health Conditions

Category	MSA[1] (%)	U.S. (%)
Adults who have ever been told they had a heart attack	3.5	4.0
Adults who have ever been told they have angina or coronary heart disease	4.0	3.8
Adults who have ever been told they had a stroke	3.2	3.0
Adults who have ever been told they have asthma	14.2	14.9
Adults who have ever been told they have arthritis	26.8	25.8
Adults who have ever been told they have diabetes[2]	10.5	10.9
Adults who have ever been told they had skin cancer	6.8	6.6
Adults who have ever been told they had any other types of cancer	7.9	7.5
Adults who have ever been told they have COPD	6.3	6.1
Adults who have ever been told they have kidney disease	2.6	3.0
Adults who have ever been told they have a form of depression	19.6	20.5

Note: (1) Figures cover the Kansas City, MO-KS Metropolitan Statistical Area; (2) Figures do not include pregnancy-related, borderline, or pre-diabetes
Source: Centers for Disease Control and Prevention, Behaviorial Risk Factor Surveillance System, SMART: Selected Metropolitan Area Risk Trends, 2021

Health Screening and Vaccination Rates

Category	MSA[1] (%)	U.S. (%)
Adults who have ever been tested for HIV	36.6	34.9
Adults who have had their blood cholesterol checked within the last five years	88.5	85.2
Adults aged 65+ who have had flu shot within the past year	70.6	68.6
Adults aged 65+ who have ever had a pneumonia vaccination	76.0	71.0

Note: (1) Figures cover the Kansas City, MO-KS Metropolitan Statistical Area.
Source: Centers for Disease Control and Prevention, Behaviorial Risk Factor Surveillance System, SMART: Selected Metropolitan Area Risk Trends, 2021

Disability Status

Category	MSA[1] (%)	U.S. (%)
Adults who reported being deaf	6.4	7.2
Are you blind or have serious difficulty seeing, even when wearing glasses?	3.8	4.8
Are you limited in any way in any of your usual activities due to arthritis?	10.4	11.1
Do you have difficulty doing errands alone?	6.4	7.0
Do you have difficulty dressing or bathing?	2.6	3.6
Do you have serious difficulty concentrating/remembering/making decisions?	12.0	12.1
Do you have serious difficulty walking or climbing stairs?	12.0	12.8

Note: (1) Figures cover the Kansas City, MO-KS Metropolitan Statistical Area.
Source: Centers for Disease Control and Prevention, Behaviorial Risk Factor Surveillance System, SMART: Selected Metropolitan Area Risk Trends, 2021

Mortality Rates for the Top 10 Causes of Death in the U.S.

ICD-10[a] Sub-Chapter	ICD-10[a] Code	Crude Mortality Rate[1] per 100,000 population	
		County[2]	U.S.
Malignant neoplasms	C00-C97	191.8	182.6
Ischaemic heart diseases	I20-I25	100.0	113.1
Other forms of heart disease	I30-I51	69.7	64.4
Other degenerative diseases of the nervous system	G30-G31	46.1	51.0
Cerebrovascular diseases	I60-I69	45.1	47.8
Other external causes of accidental injury	W00-X59	50.9	46.4
Chronic lower respiratory diseases	J40-J47	49.7	45.7
Organic, including symptomatic, mental disorders	F01-F09	48.1	35.9
Hypertensive diseases	I10-I15	35.8	35.0
Diabetes mellitus	E10-E14	26.0	29.6

Note: (a) ICD-10 = International Classification of Diseases 10th Revision; (1) Crude mortality rates are a three-year average covering 2019-2021; (2) Figures cover Jackson County.
Source: Centers for Disease Control and Prevention, National Center for Health Statistics. National Vital Statistics System, Mortality 2018-2021 on CDC WONDER Online Database

Mortality Rates for Selected Causes of Death

ICD-10[a] Sub-Chapter	ICD-10[a] Code	Crude Mortality Rate[1] per 100,000 population	
		County[2]	U.S.
Assault	X85-Y09	24.6	7.0
Diseases of the liver	K70-K76	21.2	19.8
Human immunodeficiency virus (HIV) disease	B20-B24	2.5	1.5
Influenza and pneumonia	J09-J18	12.6	14.7
Intentional self-harm	X60-X84	20.7	14.3
Malnutrition	E40-E46	6.1	4.3
Obesity and other hyperalimentation	E65-E68	1.6	3.0
Renal failure	N17-N19	23.9	15.7
Transport accidents	V01-V99	16.6	13.6
Viral hepatitis	B15-B19	Unreliable	1.2

Note: (a) ICD-10 = International Classification of Diseases 10th Revision; (1) Crude mortality rates are a three-year average covering 2019-2021; (2) Figures cover Jackson County; Data are suppressed when the data meet the criteria for confidentiality constraints; Crude mortality rates are flagged as unreliable when the rate would be calculated with a numerator of 20 or less.
Source: Centers for Disease Control and Prevention, National Center for Health Statistics. National Vital Statistics System, Mortality 2018-2021 on CDC WONDER Online Database

Health Insurance Coverage

Area	With Health Insurance	With Private Health Insurance	With Public Health Insurance	Without Health Insurance	Population Under Age 19 Without Health Insurance
City	88.2	68.9	28.9	11.8	6.9
MSA[1]	90.9	74.8	27.2	9.1	5.6
U.S.	91.2	67.8	35.4	8.8	5.3

Note: Figures are percentages that cover the civilian noninstitutionalized population; (1) Figures cover the Kansas City, MO-KS Metropolitan Statistical Area
Source: U.S. Census Bureau, 2017-2021 American Community Survey 5-Year Estimates

Number of Medical Professionals

Area	MDs[3]	DOs[3,4]	Dentists	Podiatrists	Chiropractors	Optometrists
County[1] (number)	2,255	424	659	46	341	145
County[1] (rate[2])	314.4	59.1	91.9	6.4	47.6	20.2
U.S. (rate[2])	289.3	23.5	72.5	6.2	28.7	17.4

Note: Data as of 2021 unless noted; (1) Data covers Jackson County; (2) Rate per 100,000 population; (3) Data as of 2020 and includes all active, non-federal physicians; (4) Doctor of Osteopathic Medicine
Source: U.S. Department of Health and Human Services, Health Resources and Services Administration, Bureau of Health Professions, Area Resource File (ARF) 2021-2022

Best Hospitals

According to *U.S. News,* the Kansas City, MO-KS metro area is home to two of the best hospitals in the U.S.: **Saint Luke's Mid America Heart Institute** (1 adult specialty); **University of Kansas Hospital** (8 adult specialties). The hospitals listed were nationally ranked in at least one of 15 adult or 10 pediatric specialties. The number of specialties shown cover the parent hospital. Only 164 U.S. hospitals performed well enough to be nationally ranked in one or more specialties. Twenty hospitals in the U.S. made the Honor Roll. The Best Hospitals Honor Roll takes both the national rankings and the procedure and condition ratings into account. Hospitals received points if they were nationally ranked in one of the 15 adult specialties—the higher they ranked, the more points they got—and how many ratings of "high performing" they earned in the 17 procedures and conditions. *U.S. News Online, "America's Best Hospitals 2022-23"*

According to *U.S. News,* the Kansas City, MO-KS metro area is home to one of the best children's hospitals in the U.S.: **Children's Mercy Kansas City Hospital** (10 pediatric specialties). The hospital listed was highly ranked in at least one of 10 pediatric specialties. Eighty-six children's hospitals in the U.S. were nationally ranked in at least one specialty. Hospitals received points for being ranked in a specialty, and the 10 hospitals with the most points across the 10 specialties make up the Honor Roll. *U.S. News Online, "America's Best Children's Hospitals 2022-23"*

EDUCATION

Public School District Statistics

District Name	Schls	Pupils	Pupil/ Teacher Ratio	Minority Pupils[1] (%)	LEP/ELL[2] (%)	IEP[3] (%)
Center 58	8	2,524	11.1	82.8	4.5	15.3
Hickman Mills C-1	12	5,177	12.9	90.3	6.9	13.5
Kansas City 33	35	14,094	16.0	89.3	22.8	12.5
North Kansas City 74	34	19,875	13.2	46.4	6.5	13.0
Park Hill	20	11,991	13.6	34.9	4.5	10.9

Note: Table includes school districts with 2,000 or more students; (1) Percentage of students that are not non-Hispanic white; (2) Percentage of students that are Limited English Proficient or English Language Learners (2018-19); (3) Percentage of students that have an Individualized Education Program (2019-20).
Source: U.S. Department of Education, National Center for Education Statistics, Common Core of Data, Local Education Agency (School District) Universe Survey: School Year 2021-2022

Best High Schools

According to *U.S. News,* Kansas City is home to two of the top 500 high schools in the U.S.: **Lincoln College Prep.** (#263); **Ewing Marion Kauffman High School** (#431). Nearly 18,000 public, magnet and charter schools were ranked based on their performance on state assessments and how well they prepare students for college. *U.S. News & World Report, "Best High Schools 2022"*

Highest Level of Education

Area	Less than H.S.	H.S. Diploma	Some College, No Deg.	Associate Degree	Bachelor's Degree	Master's Degree	Prof. School Degree	Doctorate Degree
City	9.0	24.9	22.2	7.4	23.0	9.8	2.6	1.2
MSA[1]	7.3	25.1	21.6	8.0	23.8	10.6	2.4	1.3
U.S.	11.1	26.5	20.0	8.7	20.6	9.3	2.2	1.5

Note: Figures cover persons age 25 and over; (1) Figures cover the Kansas City, MO-KS Metropolitan Statistical Area
Source: U.S. Census Bureau, 2017-2021 American Community Survey 5-Year Estimates

Educational Attainment by Race

Area	High School Graduate or Higher (%)					Bachelor's Degree or Higher (%)				
	Total	White	Black	Asian	Hisp.[2]	Total	White	Black	Asian	Hisp.[2]
City	91.0	93.9	88.6	86.1	71.3	36.5	45.2	16.9	48.4	19.0
MSA[1]	92.7	94.3	89.8	88.2	72.4	38.0	40.9	20.4	56.2	19.1
U.S.	88.9	91.4	87.2	87.6	71.2	33.7	35.5	23.3	55.6	18.4

Note: Figures shown cover persons 25 years old and over; (1) Figures cover the Kansas City, MO-KS Metropolitan Statistical Area; (2) People of Hispanic origin can be of any race
Source: U.S. Census Bureau, 2017-2021 American Community Survey 5-Year Estimates

School Enrollment by Grade and Control

Area	Preschool (%)		Kindergarten (%)		Grades 1 - 4 (%)		Grades 5 - 8 (%)		Grades 9 - 12 (%)	
	Public	Private	Public	Private	Public	Private	Public	Private	Public	Private
City	55.9	44.1	86.9	13.1	87.6	12.4	88.5	11.5	83.8	16.2
MSA[1]	59.2	40.8	88.2	11.8	88.3	11.7	89.5	10.5	88.8	11.2
U.S.	58.8	41.2	86.3	13.7	88.3	11.7	88.6	11.4	89.4	10.6

Note: Figures shown cover persons 3 years old and over; (1) Figures cover the Kansas City, MO-KS Metropolitan Statistical Area
Source: U.S. Census Bureau, 2017-2021 American Community Survey 5-Year Estimates

Higher Education

Four-Year Colleges			Two-Year Colleges			Medical Schools[1]	Law Schools[2]	Voc/ Tech[3]
Public	Private Non-profit	Private For-profit	Public	Private Non-profit	Private For-profit			
1	17	4	3	0	3	3	1	10

Note: Figures cover institutions located within the Kansas City, MO-KS Metropolitan Statistical Area and include main campuses only; (1) includes schools accredited by the Liaison Committee on Medical Education and the American Osteopathic Association's Commission on Osteopathic College Accreditation; (2) includes ABA-accredited schools, schools with provisional ABA accreditation, and state accredited schools; (3) includes all schools with programs that are less than 2 years.
Source: National Center for Education Statistics, Integrated Postsecondary Education System (IPEDS), 2021-22; Wikipedia, List of Medical Schools in the United States, accessed April 10, 2023; Wikipedia, List of Law Schools in the United States, accessed April 10, 2023

According to *U.S. News & World Report,* the Kansas City, MO-KS metro area is home to one of the top 75 medical schools for research in the U.S.: **University of Kansas Medical Center** (#64 tie). The rankings are based on a weighted average of 11 measures of quality: quality assessment; peer assessment score; assessment score by residency directors; research activity; total research activity; average research activity per faculty member; student selectivity; median MCAT total score; median undergraduate GPA; acceptance rate; and faculty resources. *U.S. News & World Report, "America's Best Graduate Schools, Medical, 2023"*

EMPLOYERS

Major Employers

Company Name	Industry
B&V Baker Guam JV	Engineering services
Black and Veatch Corp	Engineering services
DST Systems	Data processing
Embarq Corporation	Telephone communications
Ford Motor Company	Automobile assembly
Hallmark Cards	Greeting cards
HCA Midwest Division	Hospital management
Honeywell International	Search & navigation equipment
Internal Revenue Service	Taxation department, government
North Kansas City Hospital	General medical & surgical hospitals
Park University	Colleges & universities
Performance Contracting	Drywall
St. Lukes Hospital of Kansas	General medical & surgical hospitals
United Auto Workers	Labor union
University of Kansas	Medical centers
University of Missouri System	General medical & surgical hospitals

Note: Companies shown are located within the Kansas City, MO-KS Metropolitan Statistical Area.
Source: Hoovers.com; Wikipedia

Best Companies to Work For

Complete Technology Services, headquartered in Kansas City, is among the "100 Best Places to Work in IT." To qualify, companies had to have a minimum of 100 total employees and five IT employees. The best places to work were selected based on DEI (diversity, equity, and inclusion) practices; IT turnover, promotions, and growth; IT retention and engagement programs; remote/hybrid working; benefits and perks (such as elder care and child care, flextime, and reimbursement for college tuition); and training and career development opportunities. *Computerworld, "Best Places to Work in IT," 2023*

PUBLIC SAFETY

Crime Rate

Area	Total Crime	Violent Crime Rate				Property Crime Rate		
		Murder	Rape[3]	Robbery	Aggrav. Assault	Burglary	Larceny -Theft	Motor Vehicle Theft
City	5,705.4	35.2	76.5	257.3	1,216.8	615.2	2,595.1	909.2
Suburbs[1]	n/a	n/a	n/a	n/a	n/a	n/a	n/a	n/a
Metro[2]	n/a	n/a	n/a	n/a	n/a	n/a	n/a	n/a
U.S.	2,356.7	6.5	38.4	73.9	279.7	314.2	1,398.0	246.0

Note: Figures are crimes per 100,000 population; (1) All areas within the metro area that are located outside the city limits; (2) Figures cover the Kansas City, MO-KS Metropolitan Statistical Area; n/a not available; (3) All figures shown were reported using the revised Uniform Crime Reporting (UCR) definition of rape; Due to the transition to the National Incident-Based Reporting System (NIBRS), limited city and metro area data was released for 2021.
Source: FBI Uniform Crime Reports, 2020

Hate Crimes

Area	Number of Quarters Reported	Number of Incidents per Bias Motivation					
		Race/Ethnicity/ Ancestry	Religion	Sexual Orientation	Disability	Gender	Gender Identity
City[1]	4	34	5	7	0	1	2
U.S.	4	5,227	1,244	1,110	130	75	266

Note: (1) Figures include one incident reported with more than one bias motivation; Due to the transition to the National Incident-Based Reporting System (NIBRS), limited crime data was released for 2021.
Source: Federal Bureau of Investigation, Hate Crime Statistics 2020

Identity Theft Consumer Reports

Area	Reports	Reports per 100,000 Population	Rank[2]
MSA[1]	4,886	228	129
U.S.	1,108,609	339	-

Note: (1) Figures cover the Kansas City, MO-KS Metropolitan Statistical Area; (2) Rank ranges from 1 to 391 where 1 indicates greatest number of identity theft reports per 100,000 population
Source: Federal Trade Commission, Consumer Sentinel Network Data Book 2022

Fraud and Other Consumer Reports

Area	Reports	Reports per 100,000 Population	Rank[2]
MSA[1]	19,496	909	142
U.S.	4,064,520	1,245	-

Note: (1) Figures cover the Kansas City, MO-KS Metropolitan Statistical Area; (2) Rank ranges from 1 to 391 where 1 indicates greatest number of fraud and other consumer reports per 100,000 population
Source: Federal Trade Commission, Consumer Sentinel Network Data Book 2022

POLITICS

2020 Presidential Election Results

Area	Biden	Trump	Jorgensen	Hawkins	Other
Jackson County	59.8	37.9	1.4	0.4	0.5
U.S.	51.3	46.8	1.2	0.3	0.5

Note: Results are percentages and may not add to 100% due to rounding
Source: Dave Leip's Atlas of U.S. Presidential Elections

SPORTS

Professional Sports Teams

Team Name	League	Year Established
Kansas City Chiefs	National Football League (NFL)	1963
Kansas City Royals	Major League Baseball (MLB)	1969
Sporting Kansas City	Major League Soccer (MLS)	1996

Note: Includes teams located in the Kansas City, MO-KS Metropolitan Statistical Area.
Source: Wikipedia, Major Professional Sports Teams of the United States and Canada, April 12, 2023

CLIMATE

Average and Extreme Temperatures

Temperature	Jan	Feb	Mar	Apr	May	Jun	Jul	Aug	Sep	Oct	Nov	Dec	Yr.
Extreme High (°F)	69	76	86	93	92	105	107	109	102	92	82	70	109
Average High (°F)	35	40	54	65	74	84	90	87	79	66	52	39	64
Average Temp. (°F)	26	31	44	55	64	74	79	77	68	56	43	30	54
Average Low (°F)	17	22	34	44	54	63	69	66	58	45	34	21	44
Extreme Low (°F)	-17	-19	-10	12	30	42	54	43	33	21	1	-23	-23

Note: Figures cover the years 1972-1990
Source: National Climatic Data Center, International Station Meteorological Climate Summary, 9/96

Average Precipitation/Snowfall/Humidity

Precip./Humidity	Jan	Feb	Mar	Apr	May	Jun	Jul	Aug	Sep	Oct	Nov	Dec	Yr.
Avg. Precip. (in.)	1.1	1.2	2.8	3.0	5.5	4.1	3.8	4.1	4.9	3.6	2.1	1.6	38.1
Avg. Snowfall (in.)	6	5	3	1	0	0	0	0	0	Tr	1	5	21
Avg. Rel. Hum. 6am (%)	76	77	78	77	82	84	84	86	86	80	79	78	80
Avg. Rel. Hum. 3pm (%)	58	59	54	50	54	54	51	53	53	51	57	60	54

Note: Figures cover the years 1972-1990; Tr = Trace amounts (<0.05 in. of rain; <0.5 in. of snow)
Source: National Climatic Data Center, International Station Meteorological Climate Summary, 9/96

Weather Conditions

Temperature			Daytime Sky			Precipitation		
10°F & below	32°F & below	90°F & above	Clear	Partly cloudy	Cloudy	0.01 inch or more precip.	0.1 inch or more snow/ice	Thunder-storms
22	110	39	112	134	119	103	17	51

Note: Figures are average number of days per year and cover the years 1972-1990
Source: National Climatic Data Center, International Station Meteorological Climate Summary, 9/96

HAZARDOUS WASTE

Superfund Sites

The Kansas City, MO-KS metro area is home to six sites on the EPA's Superfund National Priorities List: **Armour Road** (final); **Chemical Commodities, Inc.** (final); **Conservation Chemical Co.** (final); **Doepke Disposal (Holliday)** (final); **Lake City Army Ammunition Plant (Northwest Lagoon)** (final); **Lee Chemical** (final). There are a total of 1,165 Superfund sites with a status of proposed or final on the list in the U.S. *U.S. Environmental Protection Agency, National Priorities List, April 12, 2023*

AIR QUALITY

Air Quality Trends: Ozone

	1990	1995	2000	2005	2010	2015	2018	2019	2020	2021
MSA[1]	0.075	0.095	0.087	0.082	0.067	0.063	0.072	0.061	0.064	0.067
U.S.	0.087	0.089	0.081	0.087	0.069	0.072	0.069	0.065	0.065	0.067

Note: (1) Data covers the Kansas City, MO-KS Metropolitan Statistical Area. The values shown are the composite ozone concentration averages among trend sites based on the highest fourth daily maximum 8-hour concentration in parts per million. These trends are based on sites having an adequate record of monitoring data during the trend period. Data from exceptional events are included.
Source: U.S. Environmental Protection Agency, Air Quality Monitoring Information, "Air Quality Trends by City, 1990-2021"

Air Quality Index

Area	Percent of Days when Air Quality was...[2]					AQI Statistics[2]	
	Good	Moderate	Unhealthy for Sensitive Groups	Unhealthy	Very Unhealthy	Maximum	Median
MSA[1]	52.9	43.6	3.6	0.0	0.0	147	50

Note: (1) Data covers the Kansas City, MO-KS Metropolitan Statistical Area; (2) Based on 365 days with AQI data in 2021. Air Quality Index (AQI) is an index for reporting daily air quality. EPA calculates the AQI for five major air pollutants regulated by the Clean Air Act: ground-level ozone, particle pollution (aka particulate matter), carbon monoxide, sulfur dioxide, and nitrogen dioxide. The AQI runs from 0 to 500. The higher the AQI value, the greater the level of air pollution and the greater the health concern. There are six AQI categories: "Good" AQI is between 0 and 50. Air quality is considered satisfactory; "Moderate" AQI is between 51 and 100. Air quality is acceptable; "Unhealthy for Sensitive Groups" When AQI values are between 101 and 150, members of sensitive groups may experience health effects; "Unhealthy" When AQI values are between 151 and 200 everyone may begin to experience health effects; "Very Unhealthy" AQI values between 201 and 300 trigger a health alert; "Hazardous" AQI values over 300 trigger warnings of emergency conditions (not shown).
Source: U.S. Environmental Protection Agency, Air Quality Index Report, 2021

Air Quality Index Pollutants

Area	Percent of Days when AQI Pollutant was...[2]					
	Carbon Monoxide	Nitrogen Dioxide	Ozone	Sulfur Dioxide	Particulate Matter 2.5	Particulate Matter 10
MSA[1]	0.0	0.3	38.6	(3)	50.1	11.0

Note: (1) Data covers the Kansas City, MO-KS Metropolitan Statistical Area; (2) Based on 365 days with AQI data in 2021. The Air Quality Index (AQI) is an index for reporting daily air quality. EPA calculates the AQI for five major air pollutants regulated by the Clean Air Act: ground-level ozone, particle pollution (also known as particulate matter), carbon monoxide, sulfur dioxide, and nitrogen dioxide. The AQI runs from 0 to 500. The higher the AQI value, the greater the level of air pollution and the greater the health concern; (3) Sulfur dioxide is no longer included in this table (as of December 8, 2021) because SO_2 concentrations tend to be very localized and not necessarily representative of broad geographical areas like counties and CBSAs.
Source: U.S. Environmental Protection Agency, Air Quality Index Report, 2021

Maximum Air Pollutant Concentrations: Particulate Matter, Ozone, CO and Lead

	Particulate Matter 10 (ug/m³)	Particulate Matter 2.5 Wtd AM (ug/m³)	Particulate Matter 2.5 24-Hr (ug/m³)	Ozone (ppm)	Carbon Monoxide (ppm)	Lead (ug/m³)
MSA[1] Level	103	11.2	31	0.071	1	n/a
NAAQS[2]	150	15	35	0.075	9	0.15
Met NAAQS[2]	Yes	Yes	Yes	Yes	Yes	n/a

Note: (1) Data covers the Kansas City, MO-KS Metropolitan Statistical Area; Data from exceptional events are included; (2) National Ambient Air Quality Standards; ppm = parts per million; ug/m³ = micrograms per cubic meter; n/a not available.
Concentrations: Particulate Matter 10 (coarse particulate)—highest second maximum 24-hour concentration; Particulate Matter 2.5 Wtd AM (fine particulate)—highest weighted annual mean concentration; Particulate Matter 2.5 24-Hour (fine particulate)—highest 98th percentile 24-hour concentration; Ozone—highest fourth daily maximum 8-hour concentration; Carbon Monoxide—highest second maximum non-overlapping 8-hour concentration; Lead—maximum running 3-month average
Source: U.S. Environmental Protection Agency, Air Quality Monitoring Information, "Air Quality Statistics by City, 2021"

Maximum Air Pollutant Concentrations: Nitrogen Dioxide and Sulfur Dioxide

	Nitrogen Dioxide AM (ppb)	Nitrogen Dioxide 1-Hr (ppb)	Sulfur Dioxide AM (ppb)	Sulfur Dioxide 1-Hr (ppb)	Sulfur Dioxide 24-Hr (ppb)
MSA[1] Level	10	44	n/a	9	n/a
NAAQS[2]	53	100	30	75	140
Met NAAQS[2]	Yes	Yes	n/a	Yes	n/a

Note: (1) Data covers the Kansas City, MO-KS Metropolitan Statistical Area; Data from exceptional events are included; (2) National Ambient Air Quality Standards; ppm = parts per million; ug/m³ = micrograms per cubic meter; n/a not available.
Concentrations: Nitrogen Dioxide AM—highest arithmetic mean concentration; Nitrogen Dioxide 1-Hr—highest 98th percentile 1-hour daily maximum concentration; Sulfur Dioxide AM—highest annual mean concentration; Sulfur Dioxide 1-Hr—highest 99th percentile 1-hour daily maximum concentration; Sulfur Dioxide 24-Hr—highest second maximum 24-hour concentration
Source: U.S. Environmental Protection Agency, Air Quality Monitoring Information, "Air Quality Statistics by City, 2021"

Lincoln, Nebraska

Background

Lincoln, the capital of Nebraska and the seat of Lancaster County is in the southeastern part of the state. It is a thriving and multifaceted city with a fascinating history and a dynamic and expanding contemporary economy and cultural life. Lincoln today is the second-largest city in Nebraska.

The site first attracted the attention of settlers in 1856 when commercial explorers found saline deposits on the banks of the Salt Creek, what is today known as Capitol Beach Lake. Salt was the center of the first major commercial activity in the city, with two large salt "boilers," Cox and Peckham, supplying this vital resource to farmers and townspeople in a wide stretch of the Plains region. Captain W.T. Donovan came to the area as a salt company representative, settling there permanently in 1867. He named the town Lancaster, after his home in Pennsylvania, which also became the county name.

Omaha was the capital of Nebraska but, with statehood, a drive began to move the capital south of the Platte River. The new capital, called Capitol City, was sited at Lancaster. State Senator J.H.N. Patrick proposed changing the name to Lincoln, largely because he thought it would discourage Democratic support, and Lincoln it became.

In the 1880s—a dynamic period of Lincoln's early economic growth—William Jennings Bryan came to town as a lawyer and budding politician and two years later was elected to the U.S. Congress. Another Lincoln luminary from this period was General John J. Pershing, who was an instructor in military science at the recently established University of Nebraska.

Lincoln was designated a "refugee-friendly" city by the U.S. Department of State in the 1970s and is home to over 30,000 immigrants and refugees from about 150 different countries. In 2021 the city's school district served about 2,400 immigrant or refugee families. Lincoln's bilingual liaisons help families who speak 130 languages.

The city's downtown is a modern entertainment, commercial, and office center, with the historic Haymarket District on its west edge. The state capitol building, designed by Bertram Grosvenor Goodhue in 1919, is of international repute; its modernist central white stone column, visible from surrounding prairie hilltops for miles, still uniquely defines the Lincoln skyline. In addition to recent downtown restoration and improved flood control, a major renovation to downtown's historic Atrium was completed in 2022, now a spectacular office space for new and existing businesses.

Lincoln is also a city of parks, with 133 at last count, including a children's zoo and wilderness park, with more than half of them designated as neighborhood and mini parks.

The University of Nebraska is city's largest institution of higher learning, and its football team attracts crowds of 90,000 to Memorial Stadium. The University of Nebraska is a major hub of cultural activity in the city and is the site of the State Museum of Natural History. Nebraska Wesleyan University and Union College are also located in Lincoln.

The city offers rich cultural resources that draw on its increasingly cosmopolitan character, as well as on the rural traditions of the state. The Lied Center for Performing Arts, on the University of Nebraska's downtown campus, features a full range of musical and dramatic performances, and the city hosts the Nebraska State Fair in early September. In 2010, Lincoln hosted the Special Olympics USA National Games.

The University of Nebraska, city government, and Bryan Health are top employers in Lincoln, with the city's public schools, metal finishing, construction, and book publishing all important industries.

The joint County-City Building houses the mayor's office, the city council, Lancaster County commissioner's office; county, district, and juvenile courts, and the judicial center is connected to the County-City Building by elevated walkways.

The climate in Lincoln is characterized by the robust and dramatic range of the Great Plains area. Most precipitation falls April through September, and thunderstorms are predominant in the summer months. Lincoln lies in a valley that affords considerable protection against tornadoes, although more than 25 Federal Signal warning sirens throughout the city are still tested every Wednesday morning, except in the winter months.

Rankings

General Rankings

- For its "Best for Vets: Places to Live 2019" rankings, *Military Times* evaluated 599 cities (83 large, 234 medium, 282 small) and compared the locations across three broad categories: veteran and military culture/services; economic indicators; and livability factors such as health, crime, traffic, and school quality. Lincoln ranked #12 out of the top 25, in the large city category (population of more than 250,000). Data points more specific to veterans and the military weighed more heavily than others. *rebootcamp.militarytimes.com, "Military Times Best Places to Live 2019," September 10, 2018*

- In their ninth annual survey, Livability.com looked at data for more than 2,300 mid-sized U.S. cities to determine the rankings for Livability's "Top 100 Best Places to Live" in 2022. Lincoln ranked #54. Criteria: housing and economy; social and civic engagement; education; demographics; health care options; transportation & infrastructure; and community amenities. *Livability.com, "Top 100 Best Places to Live 2022" July 19, 2022*

Business/Finance Rankings

- Lincoln was the #11-ranked city for savers, according to a study by the finance site GOBankingRates, which considered the prospects for people trying to save money. Criteria: average monthly cost of grocery items; median home listing price; median rent; median income; transportation costs; gas prices; and the cost of eating out for an inexpensive and mid-range meal in 100 U.S. cities. *www.gobankingrates.com, "The 20 Best (and Worst) Places to Live If You're Trying to Save Money," August 27, 2019*

- Lincoln was ranked #11 among 100 U.S. cities for most difficult conditions for savers, according to a study by the finance site GOBankingRates. Criteria: average monthly cost of grocery items; median home listing price; median rent; median income; transportation costs; gas prices; and the cost of eating out for an inexpensive and mid-range meal. *www.gobankingrates.com, "The 20 Best (and Worst) Places to Live If You're Trying to Save Money," August 27, 2019*

- The Lincoln metro area appeared on the Milken Institute "2022 Best Performing Cities" list. Rank: #26 out of 200 large metro areas (population over 250,000). Criteria: job growth; wage and salary growth; high-tech output growth; housing affordability; household broadband access. *Milken Institute, "Best-Performing Cities 2022," March 28, 2022*

- *Forbes* ranked the 200 most populous metro areas to determine the nation's "Best Places for Business and Careers." The Lincoln metro area was ranked #36. Criteria: costs (business and living); job growth (past and projected); income growth; quality of life; educational attainment (college and high school); projected economic growth; cultural and leisure opportunities; workplace tolerance laws; net migration patterns. *Forbes, "The Best Places for Business and Careers 2019: Seattle Still On Top," October 30, 2019*

Children/Family Rankings

- Lincoln was selected as one of the most playful cities in the U.S. by KaBOOM! The organization's Playful City USA initiative honors cities and towns across the nation that have made their communities more playable. Criteria: pledging to integrate play as a solution to challenges in their communities; making it easy for children to get active and balanced play; creating more family-friendly and innovative communities as a result. *KaBOOM! National Campaign for Play, "2017 Playful City USA Communities"*

- Lincoln was selected as one of the best cities for newlyweds by *Rent.com*. The city ranked #8 of 15. Criteria: cost of living; availability of affordable rental inventory; annual household income; activities and restaurant options; percentage of married couples; concentration of millennials; safety. *Rent.com, "The 15 Best Cities for Newlyweds," December 11, 2018*

Dating/Romance Rankings

- Lincoln was selected as one of the most romantic cities in the U.S. by video-rental kiosk company Redbox. The city ranked #8 out of 20. Criteria: number of romance-related rentals in 2016. *Redbox, "20 Most Romantic Cities," February 6, 2017*

Education Rankings

- Lincoln was selected as one of America's most literate cities. The city ranked #18 out of the 84 largest U.S. cities. Criteria: number of booksellers; library resources; Internet resources; educational attainment; periodical publishing resources; newspaper circulation. *Central Connecticut State University, "America's Most Literate Cities, 2018," February 2019*

Environmental Rankings

- Lincoln was highlighted as one of the cleanest metro areas for ozone air pollution in the U.S. during 2019 through 2021. The list represents cities with no monitored ozone air pollution in unhealthful ranges. *American Lung Association, "State of the Air 2023," April 19, 2023*

- Lincoln was highlighted as one of the top 25 cleanest metro areas for year-round particle pollution (Annual PM 2.5) in the U.S. during 2019 through 2021. The area ranked #22. *American Lung Association, "State of the Air 2023," April 19, 2023*

- Lincoln was highlighted as one of the top 59 cleanest metro areas for short-term particle pollution (24-hour PM 2.5) in the U.S. during 2019 through 2021. Monitors in these cities reported no days with unhealthful PM 2.5 levels. *American Lung Association, "State of the Air 2023," April 19, 2023*

Health/Fitness Rankings

- For each of the 100 largest cities in the United States, the American Fitness Index®, compiled in partnership between the American College of Sports Medicine and the Elevance Health Foundation, evaluated community infrastructure and 34 health behaviors including preventive health, levels of chronic disease conditions, food insecurity, sleep quality, pedestrian safety, air quality, and community/environment resources that support physical activity. Lincoln ranked #16 for "community fitness." *americanfitnessindex.org, "2022 ACSM American Fitness Index Summary Report," July 12, 2022*

- The Lincoln metro area was identified as one of the worst cities for bed bugs in America by pest control company Orkin. The area ranked #50 out of 50 based on the number of bed bug treatments Orkin performed from December 2021 to November 2022. *Orkin, "The Windy City Can't Blow Bed Bugs Away: Chicago Ranks #1 For Third Consecutive Year On Orkin's Bed Bug Cities List," January 9, 2023*

Real Estate Rankings

- *WalletHub* compared the most populated U.S. cities to determine which had the best markets for real estate agents. Lincoln ranked #32 where demand was high and pay was the best. Criteria: sales per agent; annual median wage for real-estate agents; monthly average starting salary for real estate agents; real estate job density and competition; unemployment rate; home turnover rate; housing-market health index; and other relevant metrics. *www.WalletHub.com, "2021 Best Places to Be a Real Estate Agent," May 12, 2021*

Safety Rankings

- Allstate ranked the 200 largest cities in America in terms of driver safety. Lincoln ranked #21. Criteria: internal property damage claims over a two-year period from January 2016 to December 2017. The report helps increase the importance of safety and awareness behind the wheel. *Allstate, "Allstate America's Best Drivers Report, 2019" June 24, 2019*

- The National Insurance Crime Bureau ranked 390 metro areas in the U.S. in terms of per capita rates of vehicle theft. The Lincoln metro area ranked #225 (#1 = highest rate). Criteria: number of vehicle theft offenses per 100,000 inhabitants in 2021. *National Insurance Crime Bureau, "Hot Spots 2021," September 1, 2022*

Seniors/Retirement Rankings

- From its Best Cities for Successful Aging indexes, the Milken Institute generated rankings for metropolitan areas, weighing data in nine categories—health care, wellness, living arrangements, transportation and convenience, financial characteristics, education, employment, community engagement, and overall livability. The Lincoln metro area was ranked #35 overall in the small metro area category. *Milken Institute, "Best Cities for Successful Aging, 2017" March 14, 2017*

- Lincoln made the 2022 *Forbes* list of "25 Best Places to Retire." Criteria, focused on overall affordability as well as quality of life indicators, include: housing/living costs compared to the national average and state taxes; air quality; crime rates; home price appreciation; risk associated with climate-change/natural hazards; availability of medical care; bikeability; walkability; healthy living. *Forbes.com, "The Best Places to Retire in 2022," May 13, 2022*

Sports/Recreation Rankings

- Lincoln was chosen as one of America's best cities for bicycling. The city ranked #35 out of 50. Criteria: cycling infrastructure that is safe and friendly for all ages; energy and bike culture. The editors evaluated cities with populations of 100,000 or more. *Bicycling, "The 50 Best Bike Cities in America," October 10, 2018*

Women/Minorities Rankings

- Personal finance website *WalletHub* compared more than 180 U.S. cities across two key dimensions, "Hispanic Business-Friendliness" and "Hispanic Purchasing Power," to arrive at the most favorable conditions for Hispanic entrepreneurs. Lincoln was ranked #106 out of 182. Criteria includes: share of Hispanic-Owned Businesses; Hispanic entrepreneurship rate to median annual income of Hispanics; Small Business-Friendliness score; cost of living; and number of Hispanics with at least a bachelor's degree. *WalletHub.com, "2019's Best Cities for Hispanic Entrepreneurs," May 1, 2019*

Miscellaneous Rankings

- *WalletHub* compared the 150 most populated U.S. cities to determine their operating efficiency. A "Quality of Services" score was constructed for each city and then divided by the total budget per capita to reveal which were managed the best. Lincoln ranked #6. Criteria: financial stability; economy; education; safety; health; infrastructure and pollution. *www.WalletHub.com, "2022's Best- & Worst-Run Cities in America," June 21, 2022*

Business Environment

DEMOGRAPHICS

Population Growth

Area	1990 Census	2000 Census	2010 Census	2020 Census	Population Growth (%) 1990-2020	Population Growth (%) 2010-2020
City	193,629	225,581	258,379	291,082	50.3	12.7
MSA[1]	229,091	266,787	302,157	340,217	48.5	12.6
U.S.	248,709,873	281,421,906	308,745,538	331,449,281	33.3	7.4

Note: (1) Figures cover the Lincoln, NE Metropolitan Statistical Area
Source: U.S. Census Bureau, 1990 Census, 2000 Census, 2010 Census, 2020 Census

Race

Area	White Alone[2] (%)	Black Alone[2] (%)	Asian Alone[2] (%)	AIAN[3] Alone[2] (%)	NHOPI[4] Alone[2] (%)	Other Race Alone[2] (%)	Two or More Races (%)
City	78.7	4.7	4.8	0.9	0.1	3.5	7.5
MSA[1]	80.8	4.1	4.2	0.8	0.1	3.1	6.9
U.S.	61.6	12.4	6.0	1.1	0.2	8.4	10.2

Note: (1) Figures cover the Lincoln, NE Metropolitan Statistical Area; (2) Alone is defined as not being in combination with one or more other races; (3) American Indian and Alaska Native; (4) Native Hawaiian and Other Pacific Islander
Source: U.S. Census Bureau, 2020 Census

Hispanic or Latino Origin

Area	Total (%)	Mexican (%)	Puerto Rican (%)	Cuban (%)	Other (%)
City	8.1	5.5	0.4	0.2	2.0
MSA[1]	7.2	4.9	0.3	0.2	1.7
U.S.	18.4	11.2	1.8	0.7	4.7

Note: Persons of Hispanic or Latino origin can be of any race; (1) Figures cover the Lincoln, NE Metropolitan Statistical Area
Source: U.S. Census Bureau, 2017-2021 American Community Survey 5-Year Estimates

Age

Area	Under Age 5	Age 5–19	Age 20–34	Age 35–44	Age 45–54	Age 55–64	Age 65–74	Age 75–84	Age 85+	Median Age
City	6.0	20.5	24.9	12.9	10.4	10.8	8.8	3.9	1.7	34.0
MSA[1]	6.0	20.9	23.4	12.9	10.6	11.4	9.1	4.1	1.7	34.8
U.S.	5.6	19.2	20.2	12.7	12.4	13.1	10.0	4.9	1.9	38.8

Note: (1) Figures cover the Lincoln, NE Metropolitan Statistical Area
Source: U.S. Census Bureau, 2020 Census

Disability by Age

Area	All Ages	Under 18 Years Old	18 to 64 Years Old	65 Years and Over
City	10.7	4.4	8.9	30.0
MSA[1]	10.7	4.1	8.8	30.4
U.S.	12.6	4.4	10.3	33.4

Note: Figures show percent of the civilian noninstitutionalized population that reported having a disability. Disability status is determined from six types of difficulty: vision, hearing, cognitive, ambulatory, self-care, and independent living. For children under 5 years old, hearing and vision difficulty are used to determine disability status. For children between the ages of 5 and 14, disability status is determined from hearing, vision, cognitive, ambulatory, and self-care difficulties. For people aged 15 years and older, they are considered to have a disability if they have difficulty with any one of the six difficulty types; Note: (1) Figures cover the Lincoln, NE Metropolitan Statistical Area
Source: U.S. Census Bureau, 2017-2021 American Community Survey 5-Year Estimates

Ancestry

Area	German	Irish	English	American	Italian	Polish	French[2]	Scottish	Dutch
City	31.5	11.5	8.9	3.3	2.0	2.4	1.8	1.4	1.6
MSA[1]	32.9	11.3	8.7	3.6	1.9	2.3	1.8	1.3	1.8
U.S.	12.8	9.6	8.1	5.7	5.0	2.7	2.2	1.6	1.1

Note: Figures are the percentage of the total population reporting a particular ancestry. The nine most commonly reported ancestries in the U.S. are shown. Figures include multiple ancestries (e.g. if a person reported being Irish and Italian, they were included in both columns); (1) Figures cover the Lincoln, NE Metropolitan Statistical Area; (2) Excludes Basque
Source: U.S. Census Bureau, 2017-2021 American Community Survey 5-Year Estimates

Foreign-born Population

Area	Any Foreign Country	Percent of Population Born in							
		Asia	Mexico	Europe	Caribbean	Central America[2]	South America	Africa	Canada
City	9.1	4.9	1.3	1.0	0.4	0.5	0.3	0.8	0.1
MSA[1]	8.0	4.2	1.1	0.9	0.3	0.4	0.2	0.7	0.1
U.S.	13.6	4.2	3.3	1.5	1.4	1.1	1.1	0.8	0.2

Note: (1) Figures cover the Lincoln, NE Metropolitan Statistical Area; (2) Excludes Mexico.
Source: U.S. Census Bureau, 2017-2021 American Community Survey 5-Year Estimates

Household Size

Area	Persons in Household (%)							Average Household Size
	One	Two	Three	Four	Five	Six	Seven or More	
City	31.6	33.8	13.8	11.9	5.5	2.5	0.9	2.40
MSA[1]	29.9	35.2	13.6	12.0	5.6	2.5	1.1	2.40
U.S.	28.1	33.8	15.5	12.9	6.0	2.3	1.4	2.60

Note: (1) Figures cover the Lincoln, NE Metropolitan Statistical Area
Source: U.S. Census Bureau, 2017-2021 American Community Survey 5-Year Estimates

Household Relationships

Area	House-holder	Opposite-sex Spouse	Same-sex Spouse	Opposite-sex Unmarried Partner	Same-sex Unmarried Partner	Child[2]	Grand-child	Other Relatives	Non-relatives
City	40.1	16.9	0.2	2.8	0.1	26.6	1.1	2.7	4.6
MSA[1]	39.5	17.9	0.2	2.6	0.1	27.2	1.1	2.6	4.1
U.S.	38.3	17.5	0.2	2.5	0.2	28.3	2.4	4.8	3.4

Note: Figures are percent of the total population; (1) Figures cover the Lincoln, NE Metropolitan Statistical Area; (2) Includes biological, adopted, and stepchildren of the householder
Source: U.S. Census Bureau, 2020 Census

Gender

Area	Males	Females	Males per 100 Females
City	145,790	145,292	100.3
MSA[1]	170,718	169,499	100.7
U.S.	162,685,811	168,763,470	96.4

Note: (1) Figures cover the Lincoln, NE Metropolitan Statistical Area
Source: U.S. Census Bureau, 2020 Census

Marital Status

Area	Never Married	Now Married[2]	Separated	Widowed	Divorced
City	39.7	45.3	0.9	4.0	10.1
MSA[1]	37.3	48.1	0.8	4.1	9.7
U.S.	33.8	48.0	1.8	5.6	10.8

Note: Figures are percentages and cover the population 15 years of age and older; (1) Figures cover the Lincoln, NE Metropolitan Statistical Area; (2) Excludes separated
Source: U.S. Census Bureau, 2017-2021 American Community Survey 5-Year Estimates

Religious Groups by Family

Area	Catholic	Baptist	Methodist	LDS[2]	Pentecostal	Lutheran	Islam	Adventist	Other
MSA[1]	13.2	1.0	5.7	1.2	3.1	9.1	0.1	1.8	10.0
U.S.	18.7	7.3	3.0	2.0	1.8	1.7	1.3	1.3	11.6

Note: Figures are the number of adherents as a percentage of the total population and cover the eight largest religious groups in the U.S; (1) Figures cover the Lincoln, NE Metropolitan Statistical Area; (2) Church of Jesus Christ of Latter-day Saints
Sources: 2020 U.S. Religion Census, Association of Statisticians of American Religious Bodies; The Association of Religion Data Archives (ARDA)

Religious Groups by Tradition

Area	Catholic	Evangelical Protestant	Mainline Protestant	Black Protestant	Islam	Judaism	Hinduism	Orthodox	Buddhism
MSA[1]	13.2	16.6	12.9	0.3	0.1	0.1	0.1	0.1	0.1
U.S.	18.7	16.5	5.2	2.3	1.3	0.6	0.4	0.4	0.3

Note: Figures are the number of adherents as a percentage of the total population; (1) Figures cover the Lincoln, NE Metropolitan Statistical Area
Sources: 2020 U.S. Religion Census, Association of Statisticians of American Religious Bodies; The Association of Religion Data Archives (ARDA)

ECONOMY

Gross Metropolitan Product

Area	2020	2021	2022	2023	Rank[2]
MSA[1]	21.2	23.8	25.4	26.9	129

Note: Figures are in billions of dollars; (1) Figures cover the Lincoln, NE Metropolitan Statistical Area; (2) Rank is based on 2021 data and ranges from 1 to 381
Source: U.S. Conference of Mayors, U.S. Metro Economies: U.S. Metros Compared to Global and State Economies, June 2022

Economic Growth

Area	2018-20 (%)	2021 (%)	2022 (%)	2023 (%)	Rank[2]
MSA[1]	0.1	5.0	0.9	2.8	131
U.S.	-0.6	5.7	3.1	2.9	

Note: Figures are real gross metropolitan product (GMP) growth rates and represent average annual percent change; (1) Figures cover the Lincoln, NE Metropolitan Statistical Area; (2) Rank is based on 2020 2-year average annual percent change and ranges from 1 to 381
Source: U.S. Conference of Mayors, U.S. Metro Economies: U.S. Metros Compared to Global and State Economies, June 2022

Metropolitan Area Exports

Area	2016	2017	2018	2019	2020	2021	Rank[2]
MSA[1]	796.9	860.9	885.6	807.0	726.3	872.6	171

Note: Figures are in millions of dollars; (1) Figures cover the Lincoln, NE Metropolitan Statistical Area; (2) Rank is based on 2021 data and ranges from 1 to 388
Source: U.S. Department of Commerce, International Trade Administration, Office of Trade and Economic Analysis, Industry and Analysis, Exports by Metropolitan Area, data extracted March 16, 2023

Building Permits

Area	Single-Family			Multi-Family			Total		
	2021	2022	Pct. Chg.	2021	2022	Pct. Chg.	2021	2022	Pct. Chg.
City	1,093	943	-13.7	1,227	2,179	77.6	2,320	3,122	34.6
MSA[1]	1,378	1,132	-17.9	1,229	2,217	80.4	2,607	3,349	28.5
U.S.	1,115,400	975,600	-12.5	621,600	689,500	10.9	1,737,000	1,665,100	-4.1

Note: (1) Figures cover the Lincoln, NE Metropolitan Statistical Area; Figures represent new, privately-owned housing units authorized (unadjusted data); All permit data are based on estimates with imputation
Source: U.S. Census Bureau, Manufacturing, Mining, and Construction Statistics, Building Permits, 2021, 2022

Bankruptcy Filings

Area	Business Filings			Nonbusiness Filings		
	2021	2022	% Chg.	2021	2022	% Chg.
Lancaster County	6	14	133.3	430	304	-29.3
U.S.	14,347	13,481	-6.0	399,269	374,240	-6.3

Note: Business filings include Chapter 7, Chapter 9, Chapter 11, Chapter 12, Chapter 13, Chapter 15, and Section 304; Nonbusiness filings include Chapter 7, Chapter 11, and Chapter 13
Source: Administrative Office of the U.S. Courts, Business and Nonbusiness Bankruptcy, County Cases Commenced by Chapter of the Bankruptcy Code, During the 12-Month Period Ending December 31, 2021 and Business and Nonbusiness Bankruptcy, County Cases Commenced by Chapter of the Bankruptcy Code, During the 12-Month Period Ending December 31, 2022

Housing Vacancy Rates

Area	Gross Vacancy Rate[2] (%)			Year-Round Vacancy Rate[3] (%)			Rental Vacancy Rate[4] (%)			Homeowner Vacancy Rate[5] (%)		
	2020	2021	2022	2020	2021	2022	2020	2021	2022	2020	2021	2022
MSA[1]	n/a	n/a	n/a	n/a	n/a	n/a	n/a	n/a	n/a	n/a	n/a	n/a
U.S.	10.6	10.8	10.5	8.2	8.4	8.2	6.3	6.1	5.8	1.0	0.9	0.8

Note: (1) Figures cover the Lincoln, NE Metropolitan Statistical Area; (2) The percentage of the total housing inventory that is vacant; (3) The percentage of the housing inventory (excluding seasonal units) that is year-round vacant; (4) The percentage of rental inventory that is vacant for rent; (5) The percentage of homeowner inventory that is vacant for sale; n/a not available
Source: U.S. Census Bureau, Housing Vacancies and Homeownership Annual Statistics: 2020, 2021, 2022

INCOME

Income

Area	Per Capita ($)	Median Household ($)	Average Household ($)
City	33,955	62,566	83,225
MSA[1]	35,055	65,508	87,123
U.S.	37,638	69,021	97,196

Note: (1) Figures cover the Lincoln, NE Metropolitan Statistical Area
Source: U.S. Census Bureau, 2017-2021 American Community Survey 5-Year Estimates

Household Income Distribution

Area	Percent of Households Earning							
	Under $15,000	$15,000 -$24,999	$25,000 -$34,999	$35,000 -$49,999	$50,000 -$74,999	$75,000 -$99,999	$100,000 -$149,999	$150,000 and up
City	8.4	7.9	9.8	13.0	20.2	12.4	16.1	12.0
MSA[1]	7.8	7.5	9.4	12.6	19.7	12.8	17.1	13.1
U.S.	9.4	7.8	8.2	11.4	16.8	12.8	16.3	17.3

Note: (1) Figures cover the Lincoln, NE Metropolitan Statistical Area
Source: U.S. Census Bureau, 2017-2021 American Community Survey 5-Year Estimates

Poverty Rate

Area	All Ages	Under 18 Years Old	18 to 64 Years Old	65 Years and Over
City	13.0	13.5	14.4	6.1
MSA[1]	11.8	11.9	13.1	5.9
U.S.	12.6	17.0	11.8	9.6

Note: Figures are percentage of people whose income during the past 12 months was below the poverty level;
(1) Figures cover the Lincoln, NE Metropolitan Statistical Area
Source: U.S. Census Bureau, 2017-2021 American Community Survey 5-Year Estimates

EMPLOYMENT

Labor Force and Employment

Area	Civilian Labor Force			Workers Employed		
	Dec. 2021	Dec. 2022	% Chg.	Dec. 2021	Dec. 2022	% Chg.
City	161,763	164,641	1.8	159,144	161,093	1.2
MSA[1]	188,166	191,439	1.7	185,143	187,374	1.2
U.S.	161,696,000	164,224,000	1.6	155,732,000	158,872,000	2.0

Note: Data is not seasonally adjusted and covers workers 16 years of age and older; (1) Figures cover the
Lincoln, NE Metropolitan Statistical Area
Source: Bureau of Labor Statistics, Local Area Unemployment Statistics

Unemployment Rate

Area	2022											
	Jan.	Feb.	Mar.	Apr.	May	Jun.	Jul.	Aug.	Sep.	Oct.	Nov.	Dec.
City	2.3	2.1	2.2	1.8	1.9	2.4	2.3	2.1	1.9	2.1	2.1	2.2
MSA[1]	2.3	2.1	2.1	1.8	1.9	2.4	2.3	2.1	1.9	2.0	2.1	2.1
U.S.	4.4	4.1	3.8	3.3	3.4	3.8	3.8	3.8	3.3	3.4	3.4	3.3

Note: Data is not seasonally adjusted and covers workers 16 years of age and older; (1) Figures cover the
Lincoln, NE Metropolitan Statistical Area
Source: Bureau of Labor Statistics, Local Area Unemployment Statistics

Average Wages

Occupation	$/Hr.	Occupation	$/Hr.
Accountants and Auditors	33.19	Maintenance and Repair Workers	21.04
Automotive Mechanics	25.66	Marketing Managers	49.76
Bookkeepers	21.09	Network and Computer Systems Admin.	40.83
Carpenters	22.21	Nurses, Licensed Practical	24.46
Cashiers	12.89	Nurses, Registered	35.52
Computer Programmers	42.91	Nursing Assistants	16.53
Computer Systems Analysts	38.01	Office Clerks, General	16.75
Computer User Support Specialists	25.23	Physical Therapists	44.49
Construction Laborers	19.61	Physicians	131.40
Cooks, Restaurant	15.58	Plumbers, Pipefitters and Steamfitters	25.79
Customer Service Representatives	17.91	Police and Sheriff's Patrol Officers	33.34
Dentists	73.53	Postal Service Mail Carriers	27.48
Electricians	25.71	Real Estate Sales Agents	19.09
Engineers, Electrical	47.33	Retail Salespersons	15.39
Fast Food and Counter Workers	12.48	Sales Representatives, Technical/Scientific	43.72
Financial Managers	61.87	Secretaries, Exc. Legal/Medical/Executive	19.78
First-Line Supervisors of Office Workers	26.83	Security Guards	14.91
General and Operations Managers	47.07	Surgeons	n/a
Hairdressers/Cosmetologists	17.83	Teacher Assistants, Exc. Postsecondary*	12.27
Home Health and Personal Care Aides	14.17	Teachers, Secondary School, Exc. Sp. Ed.*	28.33
Janitors and Cleaners	14.69	Telemarketers	13.08
Landscaping/Groundskeeping Workers	16.86	Truck Drivers, Heavy/Tractor-Trailer	35.10
Lawyers	56.01	Truck Drivers, Light/Delivery Services	21.50
Maids and Housekeeping Cleaners	13.97	Waiters and Waitresses	14.17

Note: Wage data covers the Lincoln, NE Metropolitan Statistical Area; (*) Hourly wages were calculated from
annual wage data based on a 40 hour work week; n/a not available.
Source: Bureau of Labor Statistics, Metro Area Occupational Employment & Wage Estimates, May 2022

Employment by Industry

Sector	MSA[1]		U.S.
	Number of Employees	Percent of Total	Percent of Total
Construction, Mining, and Logging	10,600	5.5	5.4
Private Education and Health Services	30,200	15.7	16.1
Financial Activities	10,800	5.6	5.9
Government	42,400	22.1	14.5
Information	3,600	1.9	2.0
Leisure and Hospitality	18,100	9.4	10.3
Manufacturing	14,800	7.7	8.4
Other Services	7,400	3.9	3.7
Professional and Business Services	19,700	10.3	14.7
Retail Trade	18,900	9.8	10.2
Transportation, Warehousing, and Utilities	11,200	5.8	4.9
Wholesale Trade	4,200	2.2	3.9

Note: Figures are non-farm employment as of December 2022. Figures are not seasonally adjusted and include workers 16 years of age and older; (1) Figures cover the Lincoln, NE Metropolitan Statistical Area
Source: Bureau of Labor Statistics, Current Employment Statistics, Employment, Hours, and Earnings

Employment by Occupation

Occupation Classification	City (%)	MSA[1] (%)	U.S. (%)
Management, Business, Science, and Arts	42.0	42.3	40.3
Natural Resources, Construction, and Maintenance	7.4	8.0	8.7
Production, Transportation, and Material Moving	11.8	11.9	13.1
Sales and Office	21.7	21.2	20.9
Service	17.2	16.6	17.0

Note: Figures cover employed civilians 16 years of age and older; (1) Figures cover the Lincoln, NE Metropolitan Statistical Area
Source: U.S. Census Bureau, 2017-2021 American Community Survey 5-Year Estimates

Occupations with Greatest Projected Employment Growth: 2022 – 2024

Occupation[1]	2022 Employment	2024 Projected Employment	Numeric Employment Change	Percent Employment Change
Fast Food and Counter Workers	30,020	30,710	690	2.3
Registered Nurses	28,100	28,770	670	2.4
Retail Salespersons	27,690	28,240	550	2.0
Cooks, Restaurant	6,920	7,460	540	7.8
Software Developers and Software Quality Assurance Analysts and Testers	11,020	11,510	490	4.4
Carpenters	10,710	11,200	490	4.6
Laborers and Freight, Stock, and Material Movers, Hand	20,000	20,490	490	2.5
Home Health and Personal Care Aides	12,470	12,930	460	3.7
Waiters and Waitresses	13,830	14,260	430	3.1
Electricians	6,420	6,850	430	6.7

Note: Projections cover Nebraska; (1) Sorted by numeric employment change
Source: www.projectionscentral.com, State Occupational Projections, 2022–2024 Short-Term Projections

Fastest-Growing Occupations: 2022 – 2024

Occupation[1]	2022 Employment	2024 Projected Employment	Numeric Employment Change	Percent Employment Change
First-Line Supervisors of Gambling Services Workers	60	240	180	300.0
Gaming Dealers	120	480	360	300.0
Gaming Managers	30	90	60	200.0
Gaming Cage Workers	30	90	60	200.0
Gaming Surveillance Officers and Gaming Investigators	30	80	50	166.7
Gaming Change Persons and Booth Cashiers	60	110	50	83.3
Gaming and Sports Book Writers and Runners	420	470	50	11.9
Fitness Trainers and Aerobics Instructors	3,400	3,750	350	10.3
Nurse Practitioners	1,770	1,910	140	7.9
Cooks, Restaurant	6,920	7,460	540	7.8

Note: Projections cover Nebraska; (1) Sorted by percent employment change and excludes occupations with numeric employment change less than 50
Source: www.projectionscentral.com, State Occupational Projections, 2022–2024 Short-Term Projections

CITY FINANCES

City Government Finances

Component	2020 ($000)	2020 ($ per capita)
Total Revenues	510,737	1,767
Total Expenditures	456,496	1,579
Debt Outstanding	62,678	217
Cash and Securities[1]	651,535	2,254

Note: (1) Cash and security holdings of a government at the close of its fiscal year, including those of its dependent agencies, utilities, and liquor stores.
Source: U.S. Census Bureau, State & Local Government Finances 2020

City Government Revenue by Source

Source	2020 ($000)	2020 ($ per capita)	2020 (%)
General Revenue			
From Federal Government	42,020	145	8.2
From State Government	28,072	97	5.5
From Local Governments	2,283	8	0.4
Taxes			
Property	82,542	286	16.2
Sales and Gross Receipts	79,516	275	15.6
Personal Income	0	0	0.0
Corporate Income	0	0	0.0
Motor Vehicle License	6,257	22	1.2
Other Taxes	59,198	205	11.6
Current Charges	104,401	361	20.4
Liquor Store	0	0	0.0
Utility	63,799	221	12.5

Source: U.S. Census Bureau, State & Local Government Finances 2020

City Government Expenditures by Function

Function	2020 ($000)	2020 ($ per capita)	2020 (%)
General Direct Expenditures			
Air Transportation	0	0	0.0
Corrections	0	0	0.0
Education	0	0	0.0
Employment Security Administration	0	0	0.0
Financial Administration	6,048	20	1.3
Fire Protection	30,558	105	6.7
General Public Buildings	1,209	4	0.3
Governmental Administration, Other	7,863	27	1.7
Health	22,150	76	4.9
Highways	72,942	252	16.0
Hospitals	0	0	0.0
Housing and Community Development	6,347	22	1.4
Interest on General Debt	2,507	8	0.5
Judicial and Legal	0	0	0.0
Libraries	5,855	20	1.3
Parking	7,464	25	1.6
Parks and Recreation	17,565	60	3.8
Police Protection	47,797	165	10.5
Public Welfare	8,990	31	2.0
Sewerage	34,613	119	7.6
Solid Waste Management	10,695	37	2.3
Veterans' Services	0	0	0.0
Liquor Store	0	0	0.0
Utility	109,381	378	24.0

Source: U.S. Census Bureau, State & Local Government Finances 2020

TAXES

State Corporate Income Tax Rates

State	Tax Rate (%)	Income Brackets ($)	Num. of Brackets	Financial Institution Tax Rate (%)[a]	Federal Income Tax Ded.
Nebraska	5.58 - 7.5	100,000	2	(a)	No

Note: Tax rates as of January 1, 2023; (a) Rates listed are the corporate income tax rate applied to financial institutions or excise taxes based on income. Some states have other taxes based upon the value of deposits or shares.
Source: Federation of Tax Administrators, State Corporate Income Tax Rates, January 1, 2023

State Individual Income Tax Rates

State	Tax Rate (%)	Income Brackets ($)	Personal Exemptions ($)			Standard Ded. ($)	
			Single	Married	Depend.	Single	Married
Nebraska (a)	2.46 - 6.64 (bb)	3,700 - 35,730 (b)	157	314	157 (c)	7,900	15,800

Note: Tax rates as of January 1, 2023; Local- and county-level taxes are not included; Federal income tax is not deductible on state income tax returns; (a) 16 states have statutory provision for automatically adjusting to the rate of inflation the dollar values of the income tax brackets, standard deductions, and/or personal exemptions. Oregon does not index the income brackets for $125,000 and over; (b) For joint returns, taxes are twice the tax on half the couple's income; (c) The personal exemption takes the form of a tax credit instead of a deduction; (bb) Louisiana tax rates may be adjusted down if revenue trigger is met on April 1st. Iowa is phasing-in a flat rate by 2027, while Nebraska and South Carolina is phasing-in a reduced top rate by 2027.
Source: Federation of Tax Administrators, State Individual Income Tax Rates, January 1, 2023

Various State Sales and Excise Tax Rates

State	State Sales Tax (%)	Gasoline[1] ($/gal.)	Cigarette[2] ($/pack)	Spirits[3] ($/gal.)	Wine[4] ($/gal.)	Beer[5] ($/gal.)	Recreational Marijuana (%)
Nebraska	5.5	0.257	0.64	3.75	0.95	0.31	Not legal

Note: All tax rates as of January 1, 2023; (1) The American Petroleum Institute has developed a methodology for determining the average tax rate on a gallon of fuel. Rates may include any of the following: excise taxes, environmental fees, storage tank fees, other fees or taxes, general sales tax, and local taxes; (2) The federal excise tax of $1.0066 per pack and local taxes are not included; (3) Rates are those applicable to off-premise sales of 40% alcohol by volume (a.b.v.) distilled spirits in 750ml containers. Local excise taxes are excluded; (4) Rates are those applicable to off-premise sales of 11% a.b.v. non-carbonated wine in 750ml containers; (5) Rates are those applicable to off-premise sales of 4.7% a.b.v. beer in 12 ounce containers.
Source: Tax Foundation, 2023 Facts & Figures: How Does Your State Compare?

State Business Tax Climate Index Rankings

State	Overall Rank	Corporate Tax Rank	Individual Income Tax Rank	Sales Tax Rank	Property Tax Rank	Unemployment Insurance Tax Rank
Nebraska	29	30	32	9	39	11

Note: The index is a measure of how each state's tax laws affect economic performance. The lower the rank, the more favorable a state's tax system is for business. States without a given tax are given a ranking of 1. The scores/rankings for the District of Columbia do not affect other states. The 2023 index represents the tax climate as of July 1, 2022.
Source: Tax Foundation, State Business Tax Climate Index 2023

TRANSPORTATION

Means of Transportation to Work

Area	Car/Truck/Van		Public Transportation			Bicycle	Walked	Other Means	Worked at Home
	Drove Alone	Car-pooled	Bus	Subway	Railroad				
City	78.2	9.1	1.0	0.0	0.0	0.8	3.3	0.7	7.0
MSA[1]	78.5	8.9	0.8	0.0	0.0	0.8	3.2	0.7	7.2
U.S.	73.2	8.6	2.0	1.6	0.5	0.5	2.5	1.5	9.7

Note: Figures are percentages and cover workers 16 years of age and older; (1) Figures cover the Lincoln, NE Metropolitan Statistical Area
Source: U.S. Census Bureau, 2017-2021 American Community Survey 5-Year Estimates

Travel Time to Work

Area	Less Than 10 Minutes	10 to 19 Minutes	20 to 29 Minutes	30 to 44 Minutes	45 to 59 Minutes	60 to 89 Minutes	90 Minutes or More
City	16.7	44.7	22.8	9.9	2.6	2.1	1.2
MSA[1]	16.9	41.6	23.5	11.6	3.0	2.2	1.3
U.S.	12.4	28.5	21.0	20.9	8.2	6.2	2.9

Note: Note: Figures are percentages and include workers 16 years old and over; (1) Figures cover the Lincoln, NE Metropolitan Statistical Area
Source: U.S. Census Bureau, 2017-2021 American Community Survey 5-Year Estimates

Key Congestion Measures

Measure	1990	2000	2010	2015	2020
Annual Hours of Delay, Total (000)	n/a	n/a	n/a	4,612	2,054
Annual Hours of Delay, Per Auto Commuter	n/a	n/a	n/a	16	7
Annual Congestion Cost, Per Auto Commuter ($)	n/a	n/a	n/a	330	153

Note: n/a not available
Source: Texas A&M Transportation Institute, 2021 Urban Mobility Report

Freeway Travel Time Index

Measure	1985	1990	1995	2000	2005	2010	2015	2020
Urban Area Index[1]	n/a	n/a	n/a	n/a	n/a	n/a	1.09	1.03
Urban Area Rank[1,2]	n/a	n/a	n/a	n/a	n/a	n/a	n/a	n/a

Note: Freeway Travel Time Index—the ratio of travel time in the peak period to the travel time at free-flow conditions. For example, a value of 1.30 indicates a 20-minute free-flow trip takes 26 minutes in the peak (20 minutes x 1.30 = 26 minutes); (1) Covers the Lincoln NE urban area; (2) Rank is based on 101 larger urban areas (#1 = highest travel time index); n/a not available
Source: Texas A&M Transportation Institute, 2021 Urban Mobility Report

Public Transportation

Agency Name / Mode of Transportation	Vehicles Operated in Maximum Service[1]	Annual Unlinked Passenger Trips[2] (in thous.)	Annual Passenger Miles[3] (in thous.)
StarTran			
Bus (directly operated)	56	1,701.8	5,042.4
Demand Response (directly operated)	17	64.1	580.3

Note: (1) Number of revenue vehicles operated by the given mode and type of service to meet the annual maximum service requirement. This is the revenue vehicle count during the peak season of the year; on the week and day that maximum service is provided. Vehicles operated in maximum service (VOMS) exclude atypical days and one-time special events; (2) Number of passengers who boarded public transportation vehicles. Passengers are counted each time they board a vehicle no matter how many vehicles they use to travel from their origin to their destination. (3) Sum of the distances ridden by all passengers during the entire fiscal year.
Source: Federal Transit Administration, National Transit Database, 2021

Air Transportation

Airport Name and Code / Type of Service	Passenger Airlines[1]	Passenger Enplanements	Freight Carriers[2]	Freight (lbs)
Lincoln Municipal (LNK)				
Domestic service (U.S. carriers - 2022)	18	93,914	4	79,218
International service (U.S. carriers - 2021)	0	0	0	0

Note: (1) Includes all U.S.-based major, minor and commuter airlines that carried at least one passenger during the year; (2) Includes all U.S.-based airlines and freight carriers that transported at least one pound of freight during the year.
Source: Bureau of Transportation Statistics, The Intermodal Transportation Database, Air Carriers: T-100 Domestic Market (U.S. Carriers), 2022; Bureau of Transportation Statistics, The Intermodal Transportation Database, Air Carriers: T-100 International Market (U.S. Carriers), 2021

BUSINESSES

Major Business Headquarters

Company Name	Industry	Rankings	
		Fortune[1]	Forbes[2]
No companies listed	-	-	-

Note: (1) Companies that produce a 10-K are ranked 1 to 500 based on 2021 revenue; (2) All private companies with at least $2 billion in annual revenue through the end of their most current fiscal year are ranked 1 to 246; companies listed are headquartered in the city; dashes indicate no ranking
Source: Fortune, "Fortune 500," 2022; Forbes, "America's Largest Private Companies," 2022

Living Environment

COST OF LIVING

Cost of Living Index

Composite Index	Groceries	Housing	Utilities	Trans- portation	Health Care	Misc. Goods/ Services
91.7	94.2	79.9	85.8	98.1	108.1	98.0

Note: The Cost of Living Index measures regional differences in the cost of consumer goods and services, excluding taxes and non-consumer expenditures, for professional and managerial households in the top income quintile. It is based on more than 50,000 prices covering almost 60 different items for which prices are collected three times a year by chambers of commerce, economic development organizations or university applied economic centers in each participating urban area. The numbers shown should be read as a percentage above or below the national average of 100. For example, a value of 115.4 in the groceries column indicates that grocery prices are 15.4% higher than the national average. Small differences in the index numbers should not be interpreted as significant; Figures cover the Lincoln NE urban area.
Source: The Council for Community and Economic Research, Cost of Living Index, 2022

Grocery Prices

Area[1]	T-Bone Steak ($/pound)	Frying Chicken ($/pound)	Whole Milk ($/half gal.)	Eggs ($/dozen)	Orange Juice ($/64 oz.)	Coffee ($/11.5 oz.)
City[2]	13.05	1.58	2.23	1.79	3.20	4.97
Avg.	13.81	1.59	2.43	2.25	3.85	4.95
Min.	10.17	0.90	1.51	1.30	2.90	3.46
Max.	19.35	3.30	4.32	4.32	5.31	8.59

Note: (1) Values for the local area are compared with the average, minimum and maximum values for all 286 areas in the Cost of Living Index; (2) Figures cover the Lincoln NE urban area; T-Bone Steak (price per pound); Frying Chicken (price per pound, whole fryer); Whole Milk (half gallon carton); Eggs (price per dozen, Grade A, large); Orange Juice (64 oz. Tropicana or Florida Natural); Coffee (11.5 oz. can, vacuum-packed, Maxwell House, Hills Bros, or Folgers).
Source: The Council for Community and Economic Research, Cost of Living Index, 2022

Housing and Utility Costs

Area[1]	New Home Price ($)	Apartment Rent ($/month)	All Electric ($/month)	Part Electric ($/month)	Other Energy ($/month)	Telephone ($/month)
City[2]	359,724	1,066	-	63.75	64.03	199.14
Avg.	450,913	1,371	176.41	99.93	76.96	190.22
Min.	229,283	546	100.84	31.56	27.15	174.27
Max.	2,434,977	4,569	356.86	249.59	272.24	208.31

Note: (1) Values for the local area are compared with the average, minimum and maximum values for all 286 areas in the Cost of Living Index; (2) Figures cover the Lincoln NE urban area; New Home Price (2,400 sf living area, 8,000 sf lot, in urban area with full utilities); Apartment Rent (950 sf 2 bedroom/1.5 or 2 bath, unfurnished, excluding all utilities except water); All Electric (average monthly cost for an all-electric home); Part Electric (average monthly cost for a part-electric home); Other Energy (average monthly cost for natural gas, fuel oil, coal, wood, and any other forms of energy except electricity); Telephone (price includes the base monthly rate plus taxes and fees for three lines of mobile phone service).
Source: The Council for Community and Economic Research, Cost of Living Index, 2022

Health Care, Transportation, and Other Costs

Area[1]	Doctor ($/visit)	Dentist ($/visit)	Optometrist ($/visit)	Gasoline ($/gallon)	Beauty Salon ($/visit)	Men's Shirt ($)
City[2]	157.42	104.71	103.26	3.64	38.48	50.37
Avg.	124.91	107.77	117.66	3.86	43.31	34.21
Min.	36.61	58.25	51.79	2.90	22.18	13.05
Max.	250.21	162.58	371.96	5.54	85.61	63.54

Note: (1) Values for the local area are compared with the average, minimum and maximum values for all 286 areas in the Cost of Living Index; (2) Figures cover the Lincoln NE urban area; Doctor (general practitioners routine exam of an established patient); Dentist (adult teeth cleaning and periodic oral examination); Optometrist (full vision eye exam for established adult patient); Gasoline (one gallon regular unleaded, national brand, including all taxes, cash price at self-service pump if available); Beauty Salon (woman's shampoo, trim, and blow-dry); Men's Shirt (cotton/polyester dress shirt, pinpoint weave, long sleeves).
Source: The Council for Community and Economic Research, Cost of Living Index, 2022

HOUSING

Homeownership Rate

Area	2015 (%)	2016 (%)	2017 (%)	2018 (%)	2019 (%)	2020 (%)	2021 (%)	2022 (%)
MSA[1]	n/a	n/a	n/a	n/a	n/a	n/a	n/a	n/a
U.S.	63.7	63.4	63.9	64.4	64.6	66.6	65.5	65.8

Note: (1) Figures cover the Lincoln, NE Metropolitan Statistical Area; n/a not available
Source: U.S. Census Bureau, Housing Vacancies and Homeownership Annual Statistics: 2015-2022

House Price Index (HPI)

Area	National Ranking[2]	Quarterly Change (%)	One-Year Change (%)	Five-Year Change (%)	Since 1991Q1 (%)
MSA[1]	107	0.03	12.01	49.08	257.46
U.S.[3]	–	0.34	8.41	58.44	289.08

Note: The HPI is a weighted repeat sales index. It measures average price changes in repeat sales or refinancings on the same properties. This information is obtained by reviewing repeat mortgage transactions on single-family properties whose mortgages have been purchased or securitized by Fannie Mae or Freddie Mac since January 1975; (1) Figures cover the Lincoln, NE Metropolitan Statistical Area; (2) Rankings are based on annual percentage change for all metro areas containing at least 15,000 transactions over the last 10 years and ranges from 1 to 257; (3) figures based on a weighted average of Census Division estimates using a seasonally adjusted, purchase-only index; all figures are for the period ending December 31, 2022
Source: Federal Housing Finance Agency, Change in FHFA Metropolitan Area House Price Indexes, 2022Q4

Median Single-Family Home Prices

Area	2020	2021	2022[p]	Percent Change 2021 to 2022
MSA[1]	219.8	245.1	273.1	11.4
U.S. Average	300.2	357.1	392.6	9.9

Note: Figures are median sales prices of existing single-family homes in thousands of dollars; (p) preliminary; (1) Figures cover the Lincoln, NE Metropolitan Statistical Area
Source: National Association of Realtors, Median Sales Price of Existing Single-Family Homes for Metropolitan Areas, 4th Quarter 2022

Qualifying Income Based on Median Sales Price of Existing Single-Family Homes

Area	With 5% Down ($)	With 10% Down ($)	With 20% Down ($)
MSA[1]	80,780	76,528	68,025
U.S. Average	112,234	106,237	94,513

Note: Figures are preliminary; Qualifying income is based on a mortgage rate of 6.77%. Monthly principal and interest payment is limited to 25% of income; (1) Figures cover the Lincoln, NE Metropolitan Statistical Area
Source: National Association of Realtors, Qualifying Income Based on Median Sales Price of Existing Single-Family Homes for Metropolitan Areas, 4th Quarter 2022

Home Value

Area	Under $100,000	$100,000 -$199,999	$200,000 -$299,999	$300,000 -$399,999	$400,000 -$499,999	$500,000 -$999,999	$1,000,000 or more	Median ($)
City	9.6	42.9	27.9	11.1	4.5	3.2	0.7	193,800
MSA[1]	9.4	39.9	27.0	12.5	5.5	4.7	0.9	202,300
U.S.	16.2	24.2	20.1	13.6	8.3	13.6	4.1	244,900

Note: Figures are percentages except for median and cover owner-occupied housing units; (1) Figures cover the Lincoln, NE Metropolitan Statistical Area
Source: U.S. Census Bureau, 2017-2021 American Community Survey 5-Year Estimates

Year Housing Structure Built

Area	2020 or Later	2010 -2019	2000 -2009	1990 -1999	1980 -1989	1970 -1979	1960 -1969	1950 -1959	1940 -1949	Before 1940	Median Year
City	0.1	10.3	13.1	14.2	10.4	15.4	9.4	10.7	3.4	13.0	1979
MSA[1]	0.1	10.1	13.5	14.2	10.1	15.6	9.6	9.8	3.3	13.7	1979
U.S.	0.2	7.3	13.6	13.6	13.2	14.8	10.3	10.0	4.7	12.2	1979

Note: Figures are percentages except for Median Year; Note: (1) Figures cover the Lincoln, NE Metropolitan Statistical Area
Source: U.S. Census Bureau, 2017-2021 American Community Survey 5-Year Estimates

Gross Monthly Rent

Area	Under $500	$500 -$999	$1,000 -$1,499	$1,500 -$1,999	$2,000 -$2,499	$2,500 -$2,999	$3,000 and up	Median ($)
City	6.2	53.4	30.1	7.6	1.4	0.3	1.1	920
MSA[1]	6.5	53.2	30.0	7.4	1.5	0.3	1.1	918
U.S.	8.1	30.5	30.8	16.8	7.3	3.1	3.5	1,163

Note: Figures are percentages except for median; Gross rent is the contract rent plus the estimated average monthly cost of utilities (electricity, gas, and water and sewer) and fuels (oil, coal, kerosene, wood, etc.) if these are paid by the renter (or paid for the renter by someone else); (1) Figures cover the Lincoln, NE Metropolitan Statistical Area
Source: U.S. Census Bureau, 2017-2021 American Community Survey 5-Year Estimates

HEALTH

Health Risk Factors

Category	MSA[1] (%)	U.S. (%)
Adults aged 18–64 who have any kind of health care coverage	93.1	90.9
Adults who reported being in good or better health	88.2	85.2
Adults who have been told they have high blood cholesterol	31.9	35.7
Adults who have been told they have high blood pressure	28.8	32.4
Adults who are current smokers	12.5	14.4
Adults who currently use e-cigarettes	9.0	6.7
Adults who currently use chewing tobacco, snuff, or snus	3.5	3.5
Adults who are heavy drinkers[2]	6.8	6.3
Adults who are binge drinkers[3]	21.4	15.4
Adults who are overweight (BMI 25.0 - 29.9)	33.5	34.4
Adults who are obese (BMI 30.0 - 99.8)	32.4	33.9
Adults who participated in any physical activities in the past month	81.9	76.3

Note: (1) Figures cover the Lincoln, NE Metropolitan Statistical Area; (2) Heavy drinkers are classified as adult men having more than 14 drinks per week and adult women having more than 7 drinks per week; (3) Binge drinkers are classified as males having five or more drinks on one occasion or females having four or more drinks on one occasion
Source: Centers for Disease Control and Prevention, Behaviorial Risk Factor Surveillance System, SMART: Selected Metropolitan Area Risk Trends, 2021

Acute and Chronic Health Conditions

Category	MSA[1] (%)	U.S. (%)
Adults who have ever been told they had a heart attack	2.5	4.0
Adults who have ever been told they have angina or coronary heart disease	3.1	3.8
Adults who have ever been told they had a stroke	2.5	3.0
Adults who have ever been told they have asthma	12.8	14.9
Adults who have ever been told they have arthritis	20.6	25.8
Adults who have ever been told they have diabetes[2]	8.2	10.9
Adults who have ever been told they had skin cancer	5.8	6.6
Adults who have ever been told they had any other types of cancer	4.9	7.5
Adults who have ever been told they have COPD	4.9	6.1
Adults who have ever been told they have kidney disease	2.7	3.0
Adults who have ever been told they have a form of depression	18.5	20.5

Note: (1) Figures cover the Lincoln, NE Metropolitan Statistical Area; (2) Figures do not include pregnancy-related, borderline, or pre-diabetes
Source: Centers for Disease Control and Prevention, Behaviorial Risk Factor Surveillance System, SMART: Selected Metropolitan Area Risk Trends, 2021

Health Screening and Vaccination Rates

Category	MSA[1] (%)	U.S. (%)
Adults who have ever been tested for HIV	28.4	34.9
Adults who have had their blood cholesterol checked within the last five years	84.1	85.2
Adults aged 65+ who have had flu shot within the past year	75.1	68.6
Adults aged 65+ who have ever had a pneumonia vaccination	78.3	71.0

Note: (1) Figures cover the Lincoln, NE Metropolitan Statistical Area.
Source: Centers for Disease Control and Prevention, Behaviorial Risk Factor Surveillance System, SMART: Selected Metropolitan Area Risk Trends, 2021

Disability Status

Category	MSA[1] (%)	U.S. (%)
Adults who reported being deaf	8.0	7.2
Are you blind or have serious difficulty seeing, even when wearing glasses?	2.7	4.8
Are you limited in any way in any of your usual activities due to arthritis?	8.6	11.1
Do you have difficulty doing errands alone?	3.9	7.0
Do you have difficulty dressing or bathing?	1.3	3.6
Do you have serious difficulty concentrating/remembering/making decisions?	8.9	12.1
Do you have serious difficulty walking or climbing stairs?	9.1	12.8

Note: (1) Figures cover the Lincoln, NE Metropolitan Statistical Area.
Source: Centers for Disease Control and Prevention, Behaviorial Risk Factor Surveillance System, SMART: Selected Metropolitan Area Risk Trends, 2021

Mortality Rates for the Top 10 Causes of Death in the U.S.

ICD-10[a] Sub-Chapter	ICD-10[a] Code	Crude Mortality Rate[1] per 100,000 population	
		County[2]	U.S.
Malignant neoplasms	C00-C97	145.7	182.6
Ischaemic heart diseases	I20-I25	64.6	113.1
Other forms of heart disease	I30-I51	58.7	64.4
Other degenerative diseases of the nervous system	G30-G31	54.8	51.0
Cerebrovascular diseases	I60-I69	36.0	47.8
Other external causes of accidental injury	W00-X59	29.2	46.4
Chronic lower respiratory diseases	J40-J47	46.7	45.7
Organic, including symptomatic, mental disorders	F01-F09	27.2	35.9
Hypertensive diseases	I10-I15	31.9	35.0
Diabetes mellitus	E10-E14	22.7	29.6

Note: (a) ICD-10 = International Classification of Diseases 10th Revision; (1) Crude mortality rates are a three-year average covering 2019-2021; (2) Figures cover Lancaster County.
Source: Centers for Disease Control and Prevention, National Center for Health Statistics. National Vital Statistics System, Mortality 2018-2021 on CDC WONDER Online Database

Mortality Rates for Selected Causes of Death

ICD-10[a] Sub-Chapter	ICD-10[a] Code	Crude Mortality Rate[1] per 100,000 population	
		County[2]	U.S.
Assault	X85-Y09	2.8	7.0
Diseases of the liver	K70-K76	15.6	19.8
Human immunodeficiency virus (HIV) disease	B20-B24	Suppressed	1.5
Influenza and pneumonia	J09-J18	9.6	14.7
Intentional self-harm	X60-X84	13.1	14.3
Malnutrition	E40-E46	7.3	4.3
Obesity and other hyperalimentation	E65-E68	2.9	3.0
Renal failure	N17-N19	11.5	15.7
Transport accidents	V01-V99	7.9	13.6
Viral hepatitis	B15-B19	Suppressed	1.2

Note: (a) ICD-10 = International Classification of Diseases 10th Revision; (1) Crude mortality rates are a three-year average covering 2019-2021; (2) Figures cover Lancaster County; Data are suppressed when the data meet the criteria for confidentiality constraints; Crude mortality rates are flagged as unreliable when the rate would be calculated with a numerator of 20 or less.
Source: Centers for Disease Control and Prevention, National Center for Health Statistics. National Vital Statistics System, Mortality 2018-2021 on CDC WONDER Online Database

Health Insurance Coverage

Area	With Health Insurance	With Private Health Insurance	With Public Health Insurance	Without Health Insurance	Population Under Age 19 Without Health Insurance
City	92.6	77.1	26.4	7.4	4.9
MSA[1]	93.1	78.1	26.2	6.9	4.7
U.S.	91.2	67.8	35.4	8.8	5.3

Note: Figures are percentages that cover the civilian noninstitutionalized population; (1) Figures cover the Lincoln, NE Metropolitan Statistical Area
Source: U.S. Census Bureau, 2017-2021 American Community Survey 5-Year Estimates

Number of Medical Professionals

Area	MDs[3]	DOs[3,4]	Dentists	Podiatrists	Chiropractors	Optometrists
County[1] (number)	722	42	333	18	153	69
County[1] (rate[2])	223.6	13.0	102.6	5.5	47.1	21.3
U.S. (rate[2])	289.3	23.5	72.5	6.2	28.7	17.4

Note: Data as of 2021 unless noted; (1) Data covers Lancaster County; (2) Rate per 100,000 population; (3) Data as of 2020 and includes all active, non-federal physicians; (4) Doctor of Osteopathic Medicine
Source: U.S. Department of Health and Human Services, Health Resources and Services Administration, Bureau of Health Professions, Area Resource File (ARF) 2021-2022

EDUCATION

Public School District Statistics

District Name	Schls	Pupils	Pupil/ Teacher Ratio	Minority Pupils[1] (%)	LEP/ELL[2] (%)	IEP[3] (%)
Lincoln Public Schools	74	41,747	13.5	37.1	7.5	17.8

Note: Table includes school districts with 2,000 or more students; (1) Percentage of students that are not non-Hispanic white; (2) Percentage of students that are Limited English Proficient or English Language Learners (2018-19); (3) Percentage of students that have an Individualized Education Program (2019-20).
Source: U.S. Department of Education, National Center for Education Statistics, Common Core of Data, Local Education Agency (School District) Universe Survey: School Year 2021-2022

Highest Level of Education

Area	Less than H.S.	H.S. Diploma	Some College, No Deg.	Associate Degree	Bachelor's Degree	Master's Degree	Prof. School Degree	Doctorate Degree
City	7.1	20.7	20.9	11.2	25.3	9.8	2.2	2.8
MSA[1]	6.6	21.4	20.7	11.7	25.1	9.8	2.1	2.6
U.S.	11.1	26.5	20.0	8.7	20.6	9.3	2.2	1.5

Note: Figures cover persons age 25 and over; (1) Figures cover the Lincoln, NE Metropolitan Statistical Area
Source: U.S. Census Bureau, 2017-2021 American Community Survey 5-Year Estimates

Educational Attainment by Race

Area	High School Graduate or Higher (%)					Bachelor's Degree or Higher (%)				
	Total	White	Black	Asian	Hisp.[2]	Total	White	Black	Asian	Hisp.[2]
City	92.9	95.0	87.1	79.8	69.0	40.1	41.7	26.6	43.7	19.9
MSA[1]	93.4	95.2	87.1	79.5	69.3	39.6	40.9	26.6	43.4	20.1
U.S.	88.9	91.4	87.2	87.6	71.2	33.7	35.5	23.3	55.6	18.4

Note: Figures shown cover persons 25 years old and over; (1) Figures cover the Lincoln, NE Metropolitan Statistical Area; (2) People of Hispanic origin can be of any race
Source: U.S. Census Bureau, 2017-2021 American Community Survey 5-Year Estimates

School Enrollment by Grade and Control

Area	Preschool (%)		Kindergarten (%)		Grades 1 - 4 (%)		Grades 5 - 8 (%)		Grades 9 - 12 (%)	
	Public	Private	Public	Private	Public	Private	Public	Private	Public	Private
City	50.3	49.7	73.0	27.0	83.5	16.5	83.1	16.9	87.0	13.0
MSA[1]	49.5	50.5	74.6	25.4	81.6	18.4	83.9	16.1	87.2	12.8
U.S.	58.8	41.2	86.3	13.7	88.3	11.7	88.6	11.4	89.4	10.6

Note: Figures shown cover persons 3 years old and over; (1) Figures cover the Lincoln, NE Metropolitan Statistical Area
Source: U.S. Census Bureau, 2017-2021 American Community Survey 5-Year Estimates

Higher Education

Four-Year Colleges			Two-Year Colleges			Medical Schools[1]	Law Schools[2]	Voc/ Tech[3]
Public	Private Non-profit	Private For-profit	Public	Private Non-profit	Private For-profit			
1	4	0	1	0	5	0	1	0

Note: Figures cover institutions located within the Lincoln, NE Metropolitan Statistical Area and include main campuses only; (1) includes schools accredited by the Liaison Committee on Medical Education and the American Osteopathic Association's Commission on Osteopathic College Accreditation; (2) includes ABA-accredited schools, schools with provisional ABA accreditation, and state accredited schools; (3) includes all schools with programs that are less than 2 years.
Source: National Center for Education Statistics, Integrated Postsecondary Education System (IPEDS), 2021-22; Wikipedia, List of Medical Schools in the United States, accessed April 10, 2023; Wikipedia, List of Law Schools in the United States, accessed April 10, 2023

According to *U.S. News & World Report,* the Lincoln, NE metro area is home to one of the top 200 national universities in the U.S.: **University of Nebraska — Lincoln** (#151 tie). The indicators used to capture academic quality fall into a number of categories: assessment by administrators at peer institutions; retention of students; faculty resources; student selectivity; financial resources; alumni giving; high school counselor ratings of colleges; and graduation rate. *U.S. News & World Report, "America's Best Colleges 2023"*

According to *U.S. News & World Report,* the Lincoln, NE metro area is home to one of the top 100 law schools in the U.S.: **University of Nebraska—Lincoln** (#78 tie). The rankings are based on a weighted average of 12 measures of quality: peer assessment score; assessment score by lawyers/judges; median LSAT scores; median undergrad GPA; acceptance rate; employment rates for graduates; placement success; bar passage rate; faculty resources; expenditures per student; student/faculty ratio; and library resources. *U.S. News & World Report, "America's Best Graduate Schools, Law, 2023"*

EMPLOYERS

Major Employers

Company Name	Industry
Bank of the West	Financial services
Cargill Meat Solutions	Food processing
CHI Health Bergan Mercy	Healthcare
CHI Health Saint Elizabeth	Healthcare
Con Agra Foods Inc	Food manufacturing
Creighton University	Education
First Data	Commerce
Health & Human Svc Dept	Government
JBS USA	Food processing
Methodist Hospital	Healthcare
Mutual of Omaha Insurance Co	Insurance
Nebraska Medical Center	Healthcare
Nebraska Medicine	Healthcare
Offutt AFB	U.S. military
Pay Pal	Payment services
Smithfield Farmland	Agriculture
Tyson Fresh Meats	Food processing
Union Pacific Railroad Co	Railroad
University of NE Medical Ctr	Healthcare
University of Nebraska	Education
West Corp	Communications

Note: Companies shown are located within the Lincoln, NE Metropolitan Statistical Area.
Source: Hoovers.com; Wikipedia

PUBLIC SAFETY

Crime Rate

Area	Total Crime	Violent Crime Rate				Property Crime Rate		
		Murder	Rape[3]	Robbery	Aggrav. Assault	Burglary	Larceny -Theft	Motor Vehicle Theft
City	3,133.7	1.7	110.9	57.0	213.3	339.4	2,255.4	155.9
Suburbs[1]	1,017.1	0.0	77.9	0.0	41.1	119.0	705.4	73.6
Metro[2]	2,843.7	1.5	106.4	49.2	189.7	309.2	2,043.0	144.7
U.S.	2,510.4	5.1	42.6	81.8	250.4	340.5	1,569.2	220.8

Note: Figures are crimes per 100,000 population; (1) All areas within the metro area that are located outside the city limits; (2) Figures cover the Lincoln, NE Metropolitan Statistical Area; (3) All figures shown were reported using the revised Uniform Crime Reporting (UCR) definition of rape; Due to the transition to the National Incident-Based Reporting System (NIBRS), limited city and metro area data was released for 2021.
Source: FBI Uniform Crime Reports, 2019 (data for 2020 was not available)

Hate Crimes

Area	Number of Quarters Reported	Number of Incidents per Bias Motivation					
		Race/Ethnicity/ Ancestry	Religion	Sexual Orientation	Disability	Gender	Gender Identity
City	3	17	5	3	0	0	0
U.S.	4	5,227	1,244	1,110	130	75	266

Note: Due to the transition to the National Incident-Based Reporting System (NIBRS), limited crime data was released for 2021.
Source: Federal Bureau of Investigation, Hate Crime Statistics 2020

Identity Theft Consumer Reports

Area	Reports	Reports per 100,000 Population	Rank[2]
MSA[1]	370	111	343
U.S.	1,108,609	339	-

Note: (1) Figures cover the Lincoln, NE Metropolitan Statistical Area; (2) Rank ranges from 1 to 391 where 1 indicates greatest number of identity theft reports per 100,000 population
Source: Federal Trade Commission, Consumer Sentinel Network Data Book 2022

Fraud and Other Consumer Reports

Area	Reports	Reports per 100,000 Population	Rank[2]
MSA[1]	2,156	647	324
U.S.	4,064,520	1,245	-

Note: (1) Figures cover the Lincoln, NE Metropolitan Statistical Area; (2) Rank ranges from 1 to 391 where 1 indicates greatest number of fraud and other consumer reports per 100,000 population
Source: Federal Trade Commission, Consumer Sentinel Network Data Book 2022

POLITICS

2020 Presidential Election Results

Area	Biden	Trump	Jorgensen	Hawkins	Other
Lancaster County	52.3	44.6	2.4	0.0	0.7
U.S.	51.3	46.8	1.2	0.3	0.5

Note: Results are percentages and may not add to 100% due to rounding
Source: Dave Leip's Atlas of U.S. Presidential Elections

SPORTS

Professional Sports Teams

Team Name	League	Year Established

No teams are located in the metro area
Source: Wikipedia, Major Professional Sports Teams of the United States and Canada, April 12, 2023

CLIMATE

Average and Extreme Temperatures

Temperature	Jan	Feb	Mar	Apr	May	Jun	Jul	Aug	Sep	Oct	Nov	Dec	Yr.
Extreme High (°F)	73	77	89	97	99	107	108	107	101	93	82	69	108
Average High (°F)	33	38	50	64	74	85	89	86	78	66	49	36	62
Average Temp. (°F)	22	28	39	52	62	73	78	75	66	53	38	26	51
Average Low (°F)	11	16	27	39	50	60	66	64	53	40	27	16	39
Extreme Low (°F)	-33	-24	-19	3	24	39	45	39	26	11	-5	-27	-33

Note: Figures cover the years 1948-1995
Source: National Climatic Data Center, International Station Meteorological Climate Summary, 9/96

Average Precipitation/Snowfall/Humidity

Precip./Humidity	Jan	Feb	Mar	Apr	May	Jun	Jul	Aug	Sep	Oct	Nov	Dec	Yr.
Avg. Precip. (in.)	0.8	0.8	2.4	2.9	4.1	3.7	3.7	3.4	3.1	1.9	1.4	0.9	29.1
Avg. Snowfall (in.)	6	5	6	1	Tr	0	0	0	Tr	Tr	3	6	27
Avg. Rel. Hum. 6am (%)	78	81	81	80	83	83	83	86	84	80	80	80	82
Avg. Rel. Hum. 3pm (%)	61	60	55	47	51	49	48	51	49	46	54	60	53

Note: Figures cover the years 1948-1995; Tr = Trace amounts (<0.05 in. of rain; <0.5 in. of snow)
Source: National Climatic Data Center, International Station Meteorological Climate Summary, 9/96

Weather Conditions

Temperature			Daytime Sky			Precipitation		
5°F & below	32°F & below	90°F & above	Clear	Partly cloudy	Cloudy	0.01 inch or more precip.	0.1 inch or more snow/ice	Thunder-storms
25	145	40	108	135	122	94	19	46

Note: Figures are average number of days per year and cover the years 1948-1995
Source: National Climatic Data Center, International Station Meteorological Climate Summary, 9/96

HAZARDOUS WASTE

Superfund Sites

The Lincoln, NE metro area has no sites on the EPA's Superfund Final National Priorities List. There are a total of 1,165 Superfund sites with a status of proposed or final on the list in the U.S. *U.S. Environmental Protection Agency, National Priorities List, April 12, 2023*

AIR QUALITY

Air Quality Trends: Ozone

	1990	1995	2000	2005	2010	2015	2018	2019	2020	2021
MSA[1]	0.057	0.060	0.057	0.056	0.050	0.061	0.062	0.056	0.054	0.059
U.S.	0.087	0.089	0.081	0.080	0.072	0.067	0.069	0.065	0.065	0.067

Note: (1) Data covers the Lincoln, NE Metropolitan Statistical Area. The values shown are the composite ozone concentration averages among trend sites based on the highest fourth daily maximum 8-hour concentration in parts per million. These trends are based on sites having an adequate record of monitoring data during the trend period. Data from exceptional events are included.
Source: U.S. Environmental Protection Agency, Air Quality Monitoring Information, "Air Quality Trends by City, 1990-2021"

Air Quality Index

Area	Percent of Days when Air Quality was...[2]					AQI Statistics[2]	
	Good	Moderate	Unhealthy for Sensitive Groups	Unhealthy	Very Unhealthy	Maximum	Median
MSA[1]	93.1	6.9	0.0	0.0	0.0	84	35

Note: (1) Data covers the Lincoln, NE Metropolitan Statistical Area; (2) Based on 276 days with AQI data in 2021. Air Quality Index (AQI) is an index for reporting daily air quality. EPA calculates the AQI for five major air pollutants regulated by the Clean Air Act: ground-level ozone, particle pollution (aka particulate matter), carbon monoxide, sulfur dioxide, and nitrogen dioxide. The AQI runs from 0 to 500. The higher the AQI value, the greater the level of air pollution and the greater the health concern. There are six AQI categories: "Good" AQI is between 0 and 50. Air quality is considered satisfactory; "Moderate" AQI is between 51 and 100. Air quality is acceptable; "Unhealthy for Sensitive Groups" When AQI values are between 101 and 150, members of sensitive groups may experience health effects; "Unhealthy" When AQI values are between 151 and 200 everyone may begin to experience health effects; "Very Unhealthy" AQI values between 201 and 300 trigger a health alert; "Hazardous" AQI values over 300 trigger warnings of emergency conditions (not shown).
Source: U.S. Environmental Protection Agency, Air Quality Index Report, 2021

Air Quality Index Pollutants

Area	Percent of Days when AQI Pollutant was...[2]					
	Carbon Monoxide	Nitrogen Dioxide	Ozone	Sulfur Dioxide	Particulate Matter 2.5	Particulate Matter 10
MSA[1]	0.0	0.0	78.6	(3)	21.4	0.0

Note: (1) Data covers the Lincoln, NE Metropolitan Statistical Area; (2) Based on 276 days with AQI data in 2021. The Air Quality Index (AQI) is an index for reporting daily air quality. EPA calculates the AQI for five major air pollutants regulated by the Clean Air Act: ground-level ozone, particle pollution (also known as particulate matter), carbon monoxide, sulfur dioxide, and nitrogen dioxide. The AQI runs from 0 to 500. The higher the AQI value, the greater the level of air pollution and the greater the health concern; (3) Sulfur dioxide is no longer included in this table (as of December 8, 2021) because SO$_2$ concentrations tend to be very localized and not necessarily representative of broad geographical areas like counties and CBSAs.
Source: U.S. Environmental Protection Agency, Air Quality Index Report, 2021

Maximum Air Pollutant Concentrations: Particulate Matter, Ozone, CO and Lead

	Particulate Matter 10 (ug/m^3)	Particulate Matter 2.5 Wtd AM (ug/m^3)	Particulate Matter 2.5 24-Hr (ug/m^3)	Ozone (ppm)	Carbon Monoxide (ppm)	Lead (ug/m^3)
MSA[1] Level	n/a	7.1	21	0.059	n/a	n/a
NAAQS[2]	150	15	35	0.075	9	0.15
Met NAAQS[2]	n/a	Yes	Yes	Yes	n/a	n/a

Note: (1) Data covers the Lincoln, NE Metropolitan Statistical Area; Data from exceptional events are included; (2) National Ambient Air Quality Standards; ppm = parts per million; ug/m^3 = micrograms per cubic meter; n/a not available.
Concentrations: Particulate Matter 10 (coarse particulate)—highest second maximum 24-hour concentration; Particulate Matter 2.5 Wtd AM (fine particulate)—highest weighted annual mean concentration; Particulate Matter 2.5 24-Hour (fine particulate)—highest 98th percentile 24-hour concentration; Ozone—highest fourth daily maximum 8-hour concentration; Carbon Monoxide—highest second maximum non-overlapping 8-hour concentration; Lead—maximum running 3-month average
Source: U.S. Environmental Protection Agency, Air Quality Monitoring Information, "Air Quality Statistics by City, 2021"

Maximum Air Pollutant Concentrations: Nitrogen Dioxide and Sulfur Dioxide

	Nitrogen Dioxide AM (ppb)	Nitrogen Dioxide 1-Hr (ppb)	Sulfur Dioxide AM (ppb)	Sulfur Dioxide 1-Hr (ppb)	Sulfur Dioxide 24-Hr (ppb)
MSA[1] Level	n/a	n/a	n/a	n/a	n/a
NAAQS[2]	53	100	30	75	140
Met NAAQS[2]	n/a	n/a	n/a	n/a	n/a

Note: (1) Data covers the Lincoln, NE Metropolitan Statistical Area; Data from exceptional events are included; (2) National Ambient Air Quality Standards; ppm = parts per million; ug/m^3 = micrograms per cubic meter; n/a not available.
Concentrations: Nitrogen Dioxide AM—highest arithmetic mean concentration; Nitrogen Dioxide 1-Hr—highest 98th percentile 1-hour daily maximum concentration; Sulfur Dioxide AM—highest annual mean concentration; Sulfur Dioxide 1-Hr—highest 99th percentile 1-hour daily maximum concentration; Sulfur Dioxide 24-Hr—highest second maximum 24-hour concentration
Source: U.S. Environmental Protection Agency, Air Quality Monitoring Information, "Air Quality Statistics by City, 2021"

Little Rock, Arkansas

Background

Little Rock is the capital of Arkansas and the most populous city in the state. It is located along the banks of the Arkansas River and marks the point where the flat Mississippi Delta ends and the foothills of the Quachita Mountains begin. The city is best known for its place in the history of the United States Civil Rights Movement and for its connection to former President William Jefferson Clinton, who served as the Governor of Arkansas before being elected our forty-second President.

The area that is now Little Rock was originally inhabited by Native American tribes including the Quapaw, Choctaw, and Cherokee, but the first Europeans in the area were Spanish, who passed through in the mid-sixteenth century. The city got its name from a rock formation on the southern side of the Arkansas River that was a landmark for river crossings. When French explorer Jean-Baptiste Benard de la Harpe arrived in the area in 1722, he called the area *Le petite roche*, or "the little rock," and the nickname stuck. La Harpe built a trading post on the site, but it would be more than 100 years before the city officially incorporated in 1831. When Arkansas became the 25th American state in 1836, Little Rock was chosen as its capital.

Initially the city grew quickly, but many projects, including the railroad between Little Rock and Memphis, were put on hold during the Civil War. Post-war reconstruction brought a wealth of new development and by the turn of the century, its transformation from a small, sleepy frontier town to a thriving, modern city was complete. After the Great Depression ended in the early 1930s, residents began to move out to the suburbs and new roads were built to accommodate the city's changing layout.

In 1957 the city was thrown into the national spotlight with Little Rock Nine—nine African American students who enrolled in the all-white Central High School, claiming it was their right, based on the U.S. Supreme Court's ruling on *Brown v. Board of Education*. Governor Orval Faubus sent the National Guard to prevent the students from entering the school, but they were eventually admitted under the protection of the U.S. Army sent by President Eisenhower.

Little Rock was brought to national prominence again in 1992 when Governor Bill Clinton started his presidential election campaign, and again when he gave his election-night acceptance speech from the steps of the Old State House in downtown Little Rock. Clinton has since solidified his link to the city through the William J. Clinton Presidential Center and Park.

Today, the city has a diverse economy built upon manufacturing, education, healthcare, and commercial trade. Many major corporations have headquarters in the city. The Little Rock Port is part of a comprehensive industrial business zone on the Arkansas River. In 2016, Little Rock joined "What Works Cities," a national initiative to help American cities enhance their use of data, improve services, and engage residents. In 2021, the city received the organization's silver certification, based on data governance, open data and results-driven contracting.

The Pulaski County Pedestrian and Bicycle Bridge, at 3,463 feet, is the world's longest bridge for pedestrians and bicyclists only. Prominent charitable organization Heifer International has its world headquarters in Little Rock. The city's Dickey-Stephens Park, a 7,000-seat baseball park, is home to minor league team Arkansas Travelers.

Attractions in Little Rock include the MacArthur Museum of Arkansas Military History, the Arkansas Museum of Discovery, and the Old State House Museum. In addition, the William J. Clinton Presidential Center and Park houses the Clinton Presidential Library and the headquarters of the Clinton Foundation. A section of downtown's Main Street, called Creative Corridor, combines the arts, entertainment, business, and culture, and is home to the Arkansas Repertory Theatre, Arkansas Symphony Orchestra, and Ballet Arkansas. Other cultural attractions in Little Rock include the Arkansas Arts Center, the Robinson Center Music Hall, and Wildwood Center for the Performing Arts. The city's major institutions of higher learning are the University of Arkansas at Little Rock and the University of Arkansas for Medical Sciences.

Little Rock has a humid subtropical climate, typical of the southern United States. Summers are generally hot, while winters are cooler; high humidity persists all year round. Rainfall can be heavy at times during the spring and fall but the city rarely receives any snow. The highest temperature recorded is 114 degrees. A deadly tornado touched down 10 miles west of the city in 2014, when powerful storms killed 16 people in three states. In April of 2017, a deadly flood devastated the city.

Rankings

Business/Finance Rankings

- The Brookings Institution ranked the nation's largest cities based on income inequality. Little Rock was ranked #19 (#1 = greatest inequality). Criteria: the "95/20 ratio," a figure representing the income at which a household earns more than 95 percent of all other households, divided by the income at which a household earns more than only 20 percent of all other households. *Brookings Institution, "Household Income Inequality, Largest Cities of 97 Large U.S. Metro Areas, 2014-2016," February 5, 2018*

- The Brookings Institution ranked the 100 largest metro areas in the U.S. based on income inequality. Little Rock was ranked #48 (#1 = greatest inequality). Criteria: the "95/20 ratio," a figure representing the income at which a household earns more than 95 percent of all other households, divided by the income at which a household earns more than only 20 percent of all other households. *Brookings Institution, "Household Income Inequality, 100 Largest U.S. Metro Areas, 2014-2016," February 5, 2018*

- The Little Rock metro area appeared on the Milken Institute "2022 Best Performing Cities" list. Rank: #126 out of 200 large metro areas (population over 250,000). Criteria: job growth; wage and salary growth; high-tech output growth; housing affordability; household broadband access. *Milken Institute, "Best-Performing Cities 2022," March 28, 2022*

- *Forbes* ranked the 200 most populous metro areas to determine the nation's "Best Places for Business and Careers." The Little Rock metro area was ranked #132. Criteria: costs (business and living); job growth (past and projected); income growth; quality of life; educational attainment (college and high school); projected economic growth; cultural and leisure opportunities; workplace tolerance laws; net migration patterns. *Forbes, "The Best Places for Business and Careers 2019: Seattle Still On Top," October 30, 2019*

Education Rankings

- Personal finance website *WalletHub* analyzed the 150 largest U.S. metropolitan statistical areas to determine where the most educated Americans are putting their degrees to work. Criteria: education levels; percentage of workers with degrees; education quality and attainment gap; public school quality rankings; quality and enrollment of each metro area's universities. Little Rock was ranked #80 (#1 = most educated city). *www.WalletHub.com, "Most & Least Educated Cities in America," July 18, 2022*

Health/Fitness Rankings

- Little Rock was identified as a "2022 Spring Allergy Capital." The area ranked #48 out of 100. Three groups of factors were used to identify the most challenging cities for people with allergies during the spring season: annual spring pollen scores; over the counter allergy medicine use; number of board-certified allergy specialists. *Asthma and Allergy Foundation of America, "Spring Allergy Capitals 2022," March 2, 2022*

- Little Rock was identified as a "2022 Fall Allergy Capital." The area ranked #45 out of 100. Three groups of factors were used to identify the most challenging cities for people with allergies during the fall season: annual fall pollen scores; over the counter allergy medicine use; number of board-certified allergy specialists. *Asthma and Allergy Foundation of America, "Fall Allergy Capitals 2022," March 2, 2022*

- Little Rock was identified as a "2022 Asthma Capital." The area ranked #93 out of the nation's 100 largest metropolitan areas. Criteria: estimated asthma prevalence; asthma-related mortality; and ER visits due to asthma. Risk factors analyzed but not factored in the rankings: annual pollen score; annual air quality; public smoking laws; access to board-certified asthma specialists; rescue and controller medication use; uninsured rate; poverty rate. *Asthma and Allergy Foundation of America, "Asthma Capitals 2022: The Most Challenging Places to Live With Asthma," September 14, 2022*

Real Estate Rankings

- *WalletHub* compared the most populated U.S. cities to determine which had the best markets for real estate agents. Little Rock ranked #119 where demand was high and pay was the best. Criteria: sales per agent; annual median wage for real-estate agents; monthly average starting salary for real estate agents; real estate job density and competition; unemployment rate; home turnover rate; housing-market health index; and other relevant metrics. *www.WalletHub.com, "2021 Best Places to Be a Real Estate Agent," May 12, 2021*

Safety Rankings

- To identify the most dangerous cities in America, *24/7 Wall St.* focused on violent crime categories—murder, non-negligent manslaughter, rape, robbery, and aggravated assault—as reported for every 100,000 residents using data from the FBI's 2020 annual Uniform Crime Report. For cities with populations over 25,000, Little Rock was ranked #6. *247wallst.com, "America's Most Dangerous Cities" November 12, 2021*

- Statistics drawn from the FBI's Uniform Crime Report were used to rank the cities where violent crime rose the most year over year from 2019 to 2020. Only cities with 25,000 or more residents were included. *24/7 Wall St.* found that Little Rock placed #7 of those with a notable surge in incidents of violent crime. *247wallst.com, "American Cities Where Crime Is Soaring," March 4, 2022*

- Allstate ranked the 200 largest cities in America in terms of driver safety. Little Rock ranked #112. Criteria: internal property damage claims over a two-year period from January 2016 to December 2017. The report helps increase the importance of safety and awareness behind the wheel. *Allstate, "Allstate America's Best Drivers Report, 2019" June 24, 2019*

- Little Rock was identified as one of the most dangerous cities in America by NeighborhoodScout. The city ranked #9 out of 100 (#1 = most dangerous). Criteria: number of violent crimes per 1,000 residents. The editors evaluated cities with 25,000 or more residents. *NeighborhoodScout.com, "2023 Top 100 Most Dangerous Cities in the U.S.," January 12, 2023*

- The National Insurance Crime Bureau ranked 390 metro areas in the U.S. in terms of per capita rates of vehicle theft. The Little Rock metro area ranked #37 (#1 = highest rate). Criteria: number of vehicle theft offenses per 100,000 inhabitants in 2021. *National Insurance Crime Bureau, "Hot Spots 2021," September 1, 2022*

Seniors/Retirement Rankings

- From its Best Cities for Successful Aging indexes, the Milken Institute generated rankings for metropolitan areas, weighing data in nine categories—health care, wellness, living arrangements, transportation and convenience, financial characteristics, education, employment, community engagement, and overall livability. The Little Rock metro area was ranked #47 overall in the large metro area category. *Milken Institute, "Best Cities for Successful Aging, 2017" March 14, 2017*

Women/Minorities Rankings

- Personal finance website *WalletHub* compared more than 180 U.S. cities across two key dimensions, "Hispanic Business-Friendliness" and "Hispanic Purchasing Power," to arrive at the most favorable conditions for Hispanic entrepreneurs. Little Rock was ranked #135 out of 182. Criteria includes: share of Hispanic-Owned Businesses; Hispanic entrepreneurship rate to median annual income of Hispanics; Small Business-Friendliness score; cost of living; and number of Hispanics with at least a bachelor's degree. *WalletHub.com, "2019's Best Cities for Hispanic Entrepreneurs," May 1, 2019*

Miscellaneous Rankings

- *WalletHub* compared the 150 most populated U.S. cities to determine their operating efficiency. A "Quality of Services" score was constructed for each city and then divided by the total budget per capita to reveal which were managed the best. Little Rock ranked #63. Criteria: financial stability; economy; education; safety; health; infrastructure and pollution. *www.WalletHub.com, "2022's Best- & Worst-Run Cities in America," June 21, 2022*

Business Environment

DEMOGRAPHICS

Population Growth

Area	1990 Census	2000 Census	2010 Census	2020 Census	Population Growth (%) 1990-2020	Population Growth (%) 2010-2020
City	177,519	183,133	193,524	202,591	14.1	4.7
MSA[1]	535,034	610,518	699,757	748,031	39.8	6.9
U.S.	248,709,873	281,421,906	308,745,538	331,449,281	33.3	7.4

Note: (1) Figures cover the Little Rock-North Little Rock-Conway, AR Metropolitan Statistical Area
Source: U.S. Census Bureau, 1990 Census, 2000 Census, 2010 Census, 2020 Census

Race

Area	White Alone[2] (%)	Black Alone[2] (%)	Asian Alone[2] (%)	AIAN[3] Alone[2] (%)	NHOPI[4] Alone[2] (%)	Other Race Alone[2] (%)	Two or More Races (%)
City	43.5	40.6	3.5	0.6	0.0	6.0	5.7
MSA[1]	64.0	23.2	1.8	0.6	0.1	3.7	6.6
U.S.	61.6	12.4	6.0	1.1	0.2	8.4	10.2

Note: (1) Figures cover the Little Rock-North Little Rock-Conway, AR Metropolitan Statistical Area; (2) Alone is defined as not being in combination with one or more other races; (3) American Indian and Alaska Native; (4) Native Hawaiian and Other Pacific Islander
Source: U.S. Census Bureau, 2020 Census

Hispanic or Latino Origin

Area	Total (%)	Mexican (%)	Puerto Rican (%)	Cuban (%)	Other (%)
City	7.8	4.7	0.2	0.3	2.5
MSA[1]	5.5	3.7	0.2	0.1	1.5
U.S.	18.4	11.2	1.8	0.7	4.7

Note: Persons of Hispanic or Latino origin can be of any race; (1) Figures cover the Little Rock-North Little Rock-Conway, AR Metropolitan Statistical Area
Source: U.S. Census Bureau, 2017-2021 American Community Survey 5-Year Estimates

Age

Area	Percent of Population Under Age 5	Age 5–19	Age 20–34	Age 35–44	Age 45–54	Age 55–64	Age 65–74	Age 75–84	Age 85+	Median Age
City	6.0	18.7	22.1	13.5	11.8	12.2	9.7	4.3	1.8	37.2
MSA[1]	5.9	19.9	20.2	13.1	12.0	12.7	10.0	4.7	1.6	38.0
U.S.	5.6	19.2	20.2	12.7	12.4	13.1	10.0	4.9	1.9	38.8

Note: (1) Figures cover the Little Rock-North Little Rock-Conway, AR Metropolitan Statistical Area
Source: U.S. Census Bureau, 2020 Census

Disability by Age

Area	All Ages	Under 18 Years Old	18 to 64 Years Old	65 Years and Over
City	13.2	4.7	11.6	34.5
MSA[1]	15.6	5.8	13.8	38.4
U.S.	12.6	4.4	10.3	33.4

Note: Figures show percent of the civilian noninstitutionalized population that reported having a disability. Disability status is determined from six types of difficulty: vision, hearing, cognitive, ambulatory, self-care, and independent living. For children under 5 years old, hearing and vision difficulty are used to determine disability status. For children between the ages of 5 and 14, disability status is determined from hearing, vision, cognitive, ambulatory, and self-care difficulties. For people aged 15 years and older, they are considered to have a disability if they have difficulty with any one of the six difficulty types; Note: (1) Figures cover the Little Rock-North Little Rock-Conway, AR Metropolitan Statistical Area
Source: U.S. Census Bureau, 2017-2021 American Community Survey 5-Year Estimates

Ancestry

Area	German	Irish	English	American	Italian	Polish	French[2]	Scottish	Dutch
City	7.3	6.2	8.8	5.2	1.4	0.9	1.5	1.6	0.4
MSA[1]	8.9	8.8	9.6	7.1	1.5	0.8	1.5	1.8	0.7
U.S.	12.8	9.6	8.1	5.7	5.0	2.7	2.2	1.6	1.1

Note: Figures are the percentage of the total population reporting a particular ancestry. The nine most commonly reported ancestries in the U.S. are shown. Figures include multiple ancestries (e.g. if a person reported being Irish and Italian, they were included in both columns); (1) Figures cover the Little Rock-North Little Rock-Conway, AR Metropolitan Statistical Area; (2) Excludes Basque
Source: U.S. Census Bureau, 2017-2021 American Community Survey 5-Year Estimates

Foreign-born Population

Area	Percent of Population Born in								
	Any Foreign Country	Asia	Mexico	Europe	Caribbean	Central America[2]	South America	Africa	Canada
City	7.1	2.6	1.7	0.5	0.1	1.1	0.4	0.4	0.1
MSA[1]	4.2	1.4	1.2	0.4	0.1	0.6	0.2	0.2	0.1
U.S.	13.6	4.2	3.3	1.5	1.4	1.1	1.1	0.8	0.2

Note: (1) Figures cover the Little Rock-North Little Rock-Conway, AR Metropolitan Statistical Area;
(2) Excludes Mexico.
Source: U.S. Census Bureau, 2017-2021 American Community Survey 5-Year Estimates

Household Size

Area	Persons in Household (%)							Average Household Size
	One	Two	Three	Four	Five	Six	Seven or More	
City	37.7	31.9	13.8	9.9	4.5	1.5	0.8	2.30
MSA[1]	30.3	34.4	15.8	11.7	5.2	1.7	0.8	2.50
U.S.	28.1	33.8	15.5	12.9	6.0	2.3	1.4	2.60

Note: (1) Figures cover the Little Rock-North Little Rock-Conway, AR Metropolitan Statistical Area
Source: U.S. Census Bureau, 2017-2021 American Community Survey 5-Year Estimates

Household Relationships

Area	House-holder	Opposite-sex Spouse	Same-sex Spouse	Opposite-sex Unmarried Partner	Same-sex Unmarried Partner	Child[2]	Grand-child	Other Relatives	Non-relatives
City	43.5	14.5	0.3	2.4	0.3	27.1	2.3	3.9	3.1
MSA[1]	40.8	17.7	0.2	2.3	0.2	27.9	2.6	3.6	2.7
U.S.	38.3	17.5	0.2	2.5	0.2	28.3	2.4	4.8	3.4

Note: Figures are percent of the total population; (1) Figures cover the Little Rock-North Little Rock-Conway, AR Metropolitan Statistical Area; (2) Includes biological, adopted, and stepchildren of the householder
Source: U.S. Census Bureau, 2020 Census

Gender

Area	Males	Females	Males per 100 Females
City	96,018	106,573	90.1
MSA[1]	361,694	386,337	93.6
U.S.	162,685,811	168,763,470	96.4

Note: (1) Figures cover the Little Rock-North Little Rock-Conway, AR Metropolitan Statistical Area
Source: U.S. Census Bureau, 2020 Census

Marital Status

Area	Never Married	Now Married[2]	Separated	Widowed	Divorced
City	38.2	40.4	1.8	5.6	14.1
MSA[1]	30.6	48.1	1.9	5.8	13.6
U.S.	33.8	48.0	1.8	5.6	10.8

Note: Figures are percentages and cover the population 15 years of age and older; (1) Figures cover the Little Rock-North Little Rock-Conway, AR Metropolitan Statistical Area; (2) Excludes separated
Source: U.S. Census Bureau, 2017-2021 American Community Survey 5-Year Estimates

Religious Groups by Family

Area	Catholic	Baptist	Methodist	LDS[2]	Pentecostal	Lutheran	Islam	Adventist	Other
MSA[1]	4.9	23.5	6.2	0.8	3.7	0.4	0.4	1.0	13.6
U.S.	18.7	7.3	3.0	2.0	1.8	1.7	1.3	1.3	11.6

Note: Figures are the number of adherents as a percentage of the total population and cover the eight largest religious groups in the U.S; (1) Figures cover the Little Rock-North Little Rock-Conway, AR Metropolitan Statistical Area; (2) Church of Jesus Christ of Latter-day Saints
Sources: 2020 U.S. Religion Census, Association of Statisticians of American Religious Bodies; The Association of Religion Data Archives (ARDA)

Religious Groups by Tradition

Area	Catholic	Evangelical Protestant	Mainline Protestant	Black Protestant	Islam	Judaism	Hinduism	Orthodox	Buddhism
MSA[1]	4.9	32.1	6.6	8.5	0.4	0.1	<0.1	0.1	0.1
U.S.	18.7	16.5	5.2	2.3	1.3	0.6	0.4	0.4	0.3

Note: Figures are the number of adherents as a percentage of the total population; (1) Figures cover the Little Rock-North Little Rock-Conway, AR Metropolitan Statistical Area
Sources: 2020 U.S. Religion Census, Association of Statisticians of American Religious Bodies; The Association of Religion Data Archives (ARDA)

ECONOMY

Gross Metropolitan Product

Area	2020	2021	2022	2023	Rank[2]
MSA[1]	38.6	42.3	45.8	48.0	81

Note: Figures are in billions of dollars; (1) Figures cover the Little Rock-North Little Rock-Conway, AR Metropolitan Statistical Area; (2) Rank is based on 2021 data and ranges from 1 to 381
Source: U.S. Conference of Mayors, U.S. Metro Economies: U.S. Metros Compared to Global and State Economies, June 2022

Economic Growth

Area	2018-20 (%)	2021 (%)	2022 (%)	2023 (%)	Rank[2]
MSA[1]	-0.6	5.2	2.2	1.9	182
U.S.	-0.6	5.7	3.1	2.9	–

Note: Figures are real gross metropolitan product (GMP) growth rates and represent average annual percent change; (1) Figures cover the Little Rock-North Little Rock-Conway, AR Metropolitan Statistical Area; (2) Rank is based on 2020 2-year average annual percent change and ranges from 1 to 381
Source: U.S. Conference of Mayors, U.S. Metro Economies: U.S. Metros Compared to Global and State Economies, June 2022

Metropolitan Area Exports

Area	2016	2017	2018	2019	2020	2021	Rank[2]
MSA[1]	1,871.0	2,146.1	1,607.4	1,642.5	n/a	1,370.6	132

Note: Figures are in millions of dollars; (1) Figures cover the Little Rock-North Little Rock-Conway, AR Metropolitan Statistical Area; (2) Rank is based on 2021 data and ranges from 1 to 388
Source: U.S. Department of Commerce, International Trade Administration, Office of Trade and Economic Analysis, Industry and Analysis, Exports by Metropolitan Area, data extracted March 16, 2023

Building Permits

Area	Single-Family			Multi-Family			Total		
	2021	2022	Pct. Chg.	2021	2022	Pct. Chg.	2021	2022	Pct. Chg.
City	666	377	-43.4	460	644	40.0	1,126	1,021	-9.3
MSA[1]	2,505	1,863	-25.6	1,130	1,475	30.5	3,635	3,338	-8.2
U.S.	1,115,400	975,600	-12.5	621,600	689,500	10.9	1,737,000	1,665,100	-4.1

Note: (1) Figures cover the Little Rock-North Little Rock-Conway, AR Metropolitan Statistical Area; Figures represent new, privately-owned housing units authorized (unadjusted data); All permit data are based on estimates with imputation
Source: U.S. Census Bureau, Manufacturing, Mining, and Construction Statistics, Building Permits, 2021, 2022

Bankruptcy Filings

Area	Business Filings			Nonbusiness Filings		
	2021	2022	% Chg.	2021	2022	% Chg.
Pulaski County	23	19	-17.4	1,157	1,352	16.9
U.S.	14,347	13,481	-6.0	399,269	374,240	-6.3

Note: Business filings include Chapter 7, Chapter 9, Chapter 11, Chapter 12, Chapter 13, Chapter 15, and Section 304; Nonbusiness filings include Chapter 7, Chapter 11, and Chapter 13
Source: Administrative Office of the U.S. Courts, Business and Nonbusiness Bankruptcy, County Cases Commenced by Chapter of the Bankruptcy Code, During the 12-Month Period Ending December 31, 2021 and Business and Nonbusiness Bankruptcy, County Cases Commenced by Chapter of the Bankruptcy Code, During the 12-Month Period Ending December 31, 2022

Housing Vacancy Rates

Area	Gross Vacancy Rate[2] (%)			Year-Round Vacancy Rate[3] (%)			Rental Vacancy Rate[4] (%)			Homeowner Vacancy Rate[5] (%)		
	2020	2021	2022	2020	2021	2022	2020	2021	2022	2020	2021	2022
MSA[1]	9.4	11.4	9.4	9.1	11.2	9.2	9.1	10.0	11.4	1.3	1.2	0.7
U.S.	10.6	10.8	10.5	8.2	8.4	8.2	6.3	6.1	5.8	1.0	0.9	0.8

Note: (1) Figures cover the Little Rock-North Little Rock-Conway, AR Metropolitan Statistical Area; (2) The percentage of the total housing inventory that is vacant; (3) The percentage of the housing inventory (excluding seasonal units) that is year-round vacant; (4) The percentage of rental inventory that is vacant for rent; (5) The percentage of homeowner inventory that is vacant for sale
Source: U.S. Census Bureau, Housing Vacancies and Homeownership Annual Statistics: 2020, 2021, 2022

INCOME

Income

Area	Per Capita ($)	Median Household ($)	Average Household ($)
City	39,141	56,928	89,748
MSA[1]	33,523	58,441	81,542
U.S.	37,638	69,021	97,196

Note: (1) Figures cover the Little Rock-North Little Rock-Conway, AR Metropolitan Statistical Area
Source: U.S. Census Bureau, 2017-2021 American Community Survey 5-Year Estimates

Household Income Distribution

Area	Percent of Households Earning							
	Under $15,000	$15,000 -$24,999	$25,000 -$34,999	$35,000 -$49,999	$50,000 -$74,999	$75,000 -$99,999	$100,000 -$149,999	$150,000 and up
City	11.5	10.1	10.4	13.4	16.2	11.5	12.3	14.4
MSA[1]	11.0	9.2	10.1	13.3	17.5	12.4	14.9	11.6
U.S.	9.4	7.8	8.2	11.4	16.8	12.8	16.3	17.3

Note: (1) Figures cover the Little Rock-North Little Rock-Conway, AR Metropolitan Statistical Area
Source: U.S. Census Bureau, 2017-2021 American Community Survey 5-Year Estimates

Poverty Rate

Area	All Ages	Under 18 Years Old	18 to 64 Years Old	65 Years and Over
City	15.6	22.9	14.2	9.2
MSA[1]	14.0	18.8	13.4	9.1
U.S.	12.6	17.0	11.8	9.6

Note: Figures are percentage of people whose income during the past 12 months was below the poverty level;
(1) Figures cover the Little Rock-North Little Rock-Conway, AR Metropolitan Statistical Area
Source: U.S. Census Bureau, 2017-2021 American Community Survey 5-Year Estimates

EMPLOYMENT

Labor Force and Employment

Area	Civilian Labor Force			Workers Employed		
	Dec. 2021	Dec. 2022	% Chg.	Dec. 2021	Dec. 2022	% Chg.
City	95,576	95,929	0.4	92,287	93,043	0.8
MSA[1]	350,674	353,640	0.8	341,122	343,843	0.8
U.S.	161,696,000	164,224,000	1.6	155,732,000	158,872,000	2.0

Note: Data is not seasonally adjusted and covers workers 16 years of age and older; (1) Figures cover the
Little Rock-North Little Rock-Conway, AR Metropolitan Statistical Area
Source: Bureau of Labor Statistics, Local Area Unemployment Statistics

Unemployment Rate

Area	2022											
	Jan.	Feb.	Mar.	Apr.	May	Jun.	Jul.	Aug.	Sep.	Oct.	Nov.	Dec.
City	4.3	4.2	3.7	3.8	3.6	4.1	4.6	3.9	3.9	3.3	3.2	3.0
MSA[1]	3.8	3.8	3.3	3.2	3.2	3.7	4.0	3.5	3.5	2.8	2.9	2.8
U.S.	4.4	4.1	3.8	3.3	3.4	3.8	3.8	3.8	3.3	3.4	3.4	3.3

Note: Data is not seasonally adjusted and covers workers 16 years of age and older; (1) Figures cover the
Little Rock-North Little Rock-Conway, AR Metropolitan Statistical Area
Source: Bureau of Labor Statistics, Local Area Unemployment Statistics

Average Wages

Occupation	$/Hr.	Occupation	$/Hr.
Accountants and Auditors	34.54	Maintenance and Repair Workers	18.37
Automotive Mechanics	21.76	Marketing Managers	51.80
Bookkeepers	20.43	Network and Computer Systems Admin.	38.74
Carpenters	20.73	Nurses, Licensed Practical	23.12
Cashiers	12.61	Nurses, Registered	34.48
Computer Programmers	39.86	Nursing Assistants	15.09
Computer Systems Analysts	36.35	Office Clerks, General	17.64
Computer User Support Specialists	22.91	Physical Therapists	44.50
Construction Laborers	17.13	Physicians	90.44
Cooks, Restaurant	14.00	Plumbers, Pipefitters and Steamfitters	22.44
Customer Service Representatives	18.06	Police and Sheriff's Patrol Officers	23.08
Dentists	85.98	Postal Service Mail Carriers	26.80
Electricians	21.91	Real Estate Sales Agents	n/a
Engineers, Electrical	46.55	Retail Salespersons	14.90
Fast Food and Counter Workers	12.41	Sales Representatives, Technical/Scientific	44.97
Financial Managers	56.25	Secretaries, Exc. Legal/Medical/Executive	18.48
First-Line Supervisors of Office Workers	26.41	Security Guards	15.34
General and Operations Managers	41.68	Surgeons	n/a
Hairdressers/Cosmetologists	13.73	Teacher Assistants, Exc. Postsecondary*	14.46
Home Health and Personal Care Aides	12.92	Teachers, Secondary School, Exc. Sp. Ed.*	25.70
Janitors and Cleaners	13.43	Telemarketers	n/a
Landscaping/Groundskeeping Workers	15.21	Truck Drivers, Heavy/Tractor-Trailer	26.45
Lawyers	50.96	Truck Drivers, Light/Delivery Services	22.85
Maids and Housekeeping Cleaners	12.84	Waiters and Waitresses	13.89

Note: Wage data covers the Little Rock-North Little Rock-Conway, AR Metropolitan Statistical Area;
(*) Hourly wages were calculated from annual wage data based on a 40 hour work week; n/a not available.
Source: Bureau of Labor Statistics, Metro Area Occupational Employment & Wage Estimates, May 2022

Employment by Industry

Sector	MSA[1]		U.S.
	Number of Employees	Percent of Total	Percent of Total
Construction, Mining, and Logging	19,200	4.9	5.4
Private Education and Health Services	63,000	16.2	16.1
Financial Activities	24,900	6.4	5.9
Government	69,600	17.9	14.5
Information	5,700	1.5	2.0
Leisure and Hospitality	33,500	8.6	10.3
Manufacturing	19,900	5.1	8.4
Other Services	25,500	6.6	3.7
Professional and Business Services	47,800	12.3	14.7
Retail Trade	39,600	10.2	10.2
Transportation, Warehousing, and Utilities	22,500	5.8	4.9
Wholesale Trade	18,000	4.6	3.9

Note: Figures are non-farm employment as of December 2022. Figures are not seasonally adjusted and include workers 16 years of age and older; (1) Figures cover the Little Rock-North Little Rock-Conway, AR Metropolitan Statistical Area
Source: Bureau of Labor Statistics, Current Employment Statistics, Employment, Hours, and Earnings

Employment by Occupation

Occupation Classification	City (%)	MSA[1] (%)	U.S. (%)
Management, Business, Science, and Arts	47.3	40.8	40.3
Natural Resources, Construction, and Maintenance	4.9	8.4	8.7
Production, Transportation, and Material Moving	10.0	12.5	13.1
Sales and Office	22.1	22.5	20.9
Service	15.7	15.8	17.0

Note: Figures cover employed civilians 16 years of age and older; (1) Figures cover the Little Rock-North Little Rock-Conway, AR Metropolitan Statistical Area
Source: U.S. Census Bureau, 2017-2021 American Community Survey 5-Year Estimates

Occupations with Greatest Projected Employment Growth: 2022 – 2024

Occupation[1]	2022 Employment	2024 Projected Employment	Numeric Employment Change	Percent Employment Change
Fast Food and Counter Workers	36,020	37,440	1,420	3.9
General and Operations Managers	29,660	30,970	1,310	4.4
Retail Salespersons	34,310	35,400	1,090	3.2
Insurance Sales Agents	9,270	10,340	1,070	11.5
Laborers and Freight, Stock, and Material Movers, Hand	29,100	30,110	1,010	3.5
Cooks, Restaurant	11,010	11,990	980	8.9
Heavy and Tractor-Trailer Truck Drivers	37,530	38,450	920	2.5
Insurance Claims and Policy Processing Clerks	7,660	8,550	890	11.6
Claims Adjusters, Examiners, and Investigators	7,740	8,620	880	11.4
Stockers and Order Fillers	21,740	22,590	850	3.9

Note: Projections cover Arkansas; (1) Sorted by numeric employment change
Source: www.projectionscentral.com, State Occupational Projections, 2022–2024 Short-Term Projections

Fastest-Growing Occupations: 2022 – 2024

Occupation[1]	2022 Employment	2024 Projected Employment	Numeric Employment Change	Percent Employment Change
Fundraisers	1,930	2,530	600	31.1
Insurance Underwriters	1,530	1,740	210	13.7
Insurance Claims and Policy Processing Clerks	7,660	8,550	890	11.6
Insurance Sales Agents	9,270	10,340	1,070	11.5
Claims Adjusters, Examiners, and Investigators	7,740	8,620	880	11.4
Nurse Practitioners	2,650	2,930	280	10.6
Meeting, Convention, and Event Planners	720	790	70	9.7
Community and Social Service Specialists, All Other	730	800	70	9.6
Logisticians	1,380	1,510	130	9.4
Statisticians	530	580	50	9.4

Note: Projections cover Arkansas; (1) Sorted by percent employment change and excludes occupations with numeric employment change less than 50
Source: www.projectionscentral.com, State Occupational Projections, 2022–2024 Short-Term Projections

CITY FINANCES

City Government Finances

Component	2020 ($000)	2020 ($ per capita)
Total Revenues	542,412	2,749
Total Expenditures	489,413	2,480
Debt Outstanding	624,349	3,164
Cash and Securities[1]	466,657	2,365

Note: (1) Cash and security holdings of a government at the close of its fiscal year, including those of its dependent agencies, utilities, and liquor stores.
Source: U.S. Census Bureau, State & Local Government Finances 2020

City Government Revenue by Source

Source	2020 ($000)	2020 ($ per capita)	2020 (%)
General Revenue			
From Federal Government	11,707	59	2.2
From State Government	22,542	114	4.2
From Local Governments	59,507	302	11.0
Taxes			
Property	58,697	297	10.8
Sales and Gross Receipts	131,051	664	24.2
Personal Income	0	0	0.0
Corporate Income	0	0	0.0
Motor Vehicle License	0	0	0.0
Other Taxes	10,385	53	1.9
Current Charges	187,777	952	34.6
Liquor Store	0	0	0.0
Utility	0	0	0.0

Source: U.S. Census Bureau, State & Local Government Finances 2020

City Government Expenditures by Function

Function	2020 ($000)	2020 ($ per capita)	2020 (%)
General Direct Expenditures			
Air Transportation	36,501	185	7.5
Corrections	0	0	0.0
Education	0	0	0.0
Employment Security Administration	0	0	0.0
Financial Administration	11,373	57	2.3
Fire Protection	53,765	272	11.0
General Public Buildings	1,002	5	0.2
Governmental Administration, Other	7,121	36	1.5
Health	33,382	169	6.8
Highways	32,480	164	6.6
Hospitals	0	0	0.0
Housing and Community Development	7,815	39	1.6
Interest on General Debt	19,626	99	4.0
Judicial and Legal	5,797	29	1.2
Libraries	2,501	12	0.5
Parking	1,561	7	0.3
Parks and Recreation	46,803	237	9.6
Police Protection	81,306	412	16.6
Public Welfare	0	0	0.0
Sewerage	57,225	290	11.7
Solid Waste Management	17,845	90	3.6
Veterans' Services	0	0	0.0
Liquor Store	0	0	0.0
Utility	0	0	0.0

Source: U.S. Census Bureau, State & Local Government Finances 2020

TAXES

State Corporate Income Tax Rates

State	Tax Rate (%)	Income Brackets ($)	Num. of Brackets	Financial Institution Tax Rate (%)[a]	Federal Income Tax Ded.
Arkansas	1.0 - 5.1	3,000 - 26,000	5	1.0 - 5.1	No

Note: Tax rates as of January 1, 2023; (a) Rates listed are the corporate income tax rate applied to financial institutions or excise taxes based on income. Some states have other taxes based upon the value of deposits or shares.
Source: Federation of Tax Administrators, State Corporate Income Tax Rates, January 1, 2023

State Individual Income Tax Rates

State	Tax Rate (%)	Income Brackets ($)	Personal Exemptions ($)			Standard Ded. ($)	
			Single	Married	Depend.	Single	Married
Arkansas (a)	2.0 - 4.9 (f)	4,300 - 8,501	29	58	29 (c)	2,270	4,540

Note: Tax rates as of January 1, 2023; Local- and county-level taxes are not included; Federal income tax is not deductible on state income tax returns; (a) 16 states have statutory provision for automatically adjusting to the rate of inflation the dollar values of the income tax brackets, standard deductions, and/or personal exemptions. Oregon does not index the income brackets for $125,000 and over; (c) The personal exemption takes the form of a tax credit instead of a deduction; (f) Arkansas has separate brackets for taxpayers with income under $84,500.
Source: Federation of Tax Administrators, State Individual Income Tax Rates, January 1, 2023

Various State Sales and Excise Tax Rates

State	State Sales Tax (%)	Gasoline[1] ($/gal.)	Cigarette[2] ($/pack)	Spirits[3] ($/gal.)	Wine[4] ($/gal.)	Beer[5] ($/gal.)	Recreational Marijuana (%)
Arkansas	6.5	0.248	1.15	8.01	1.41	0.35	Not legal

Note: All tax rates as of January 1, 2023; (1) The American Petroleum Institute has developed a methodology for determining the average tax rate on a gallon of fuel. Rates may include any of the following: excise taxes, environmental fees, storage tank fees, other fees or taxes, general sales tax, and local taxes; (2) The federal excise tax of $1.0066 per pack and local taxes are not included; (3) Rates are those applicable to off-premise sales of 40% alcohol by volume (a.b.v.) distilled spirits in 750ml containers. Local excise taxes are excluded; (4) Rates are those applicable to off-premise sales of 11% a.b.v. non-carbonated wine in 750ml containers; (5) Rates are those applicable to off-premise sales of 4.7% a.b.v. beer in 12 ounce containers.
Source: Tax Foundation, 2023 Facts & Figures: How Does Your State Compare?

State Business Tax Climate Index Rankings

State	Overall Rank	Corporate Tax Rank	Individual Income Tax Rank	Sales Tax Rank	Property Tax Rank	Unemployment Insurance Tax Rank
Arkansas	40	29	37	45	27	20

Note: The index is a measure of how each state's tax laws affect economic performance. The lower the rank, the more favorable a state's tax system is for business. States without a given tax are given a ranking of 1. The scores/rankings for the District of Columbia do not affect other states. The 2023 index represents the tax climate as of July 1, 2022.
Source: Tax Foundation, State Business Tax Climate Index 2023

TRANSPORTATION

Means of Transportation to Work

Area	Car/Truck/Van		Public Transportation			Bicycle	Walked	Other Means	Worked at Home
	Drove Alone	Car-pooled	Bus	Subway	Railroad				
City	78.5	9.7	0.7	0.0	0.0	0.2	1.8	1.5	7.7
MSA[1]	81.6	9.4	0.4	0.0	0.0	0.1	1.1	1.1	6.3
U.S.	73.2	8.6	2.0	1.6	0.5	0.5	2.5	1.5	9.7

Note: Figures are percentages and cover workers 16 years of age and older; (1) Figures cover the Little Rock-North Little Rock-Conway, AR Metropolitan Statistical Area
Source: U.S. Census Bureau, 2017-2021 American Community Survey 5-Year Estimates

Travel Time to Work

Area	Less Than 10 Minutes	10 to 19 Minutes	20 to 29 Minutes	30 to 44 Minutes	45 to 59 Minutes	60 to 89 Minutes	90 Minutes or More
City	15.4	45.3	23.6	11.0	2.3	1.5	0.9
MSA[1]	13.0	32.7	22.6	20.4	7.0	2.9	1.4
U.S.	12.4	28.5	21.0	20.9	8.2	6.2	2.9

Note: Note: Figures are percentages and include workers 16 years old and over; (1) Figures cover the Little Rock-North Little Rock-Conway, AR Metropolitan Statistical Area
Source: U.S. Census Bureau, 2017-2021 American Community Survey 5-Year Estimates

Key Congestion Measures

Measure	1990	2000	2010	2015	2020
Annual Hours of Delay, Total (000)	2,637	7,628	16,142	17,871	14,655
Annual Hours of Delay, Per Auto Commuter	11	27	35	40	33
Annual Congestion Cost, Per Auto Commuter ($)	201	437	737	751	665

Note: Covers the Little Rock AR urban area
Source: Texas A&M Transportation Institute, 2021 Urban Mobility Report

Freeway Travel Time Index

Measure	1985	1990	1995	2000	2005	2010	2015	2020
Urban Area Index[1]	1.03	1.04	1.06	1.10	1.12	1.14	1.13	1.10
Urban Area Rank[1,2]	89	94	93	85	86	71	83	29

Note: Freeway Travel Time Index—the ratio of travel time in the peak period to the travel time at free-flow conditions. For example, a value of 1.30 indicates a 20-minute free-flow trip takes 26 minutes in the peak (20 minutes x 1.30 = 26 minutes); (1) Covers the Little Rock AR urban area; (2) Rank is based on 101 larger urban areas (#1 = highest travel time index)
Source: Texas A&M Transportation Institute, 2021 Urban Mobility Report

Public Transportation

Agency Name / Mode of Transportation	Vehicles Operated in Maximum Service[1]	Annual Unlinked Passenger Trips[2] (in thous.)	Annual Passenger Miles[3] (in thous.)
Central Arkansas Transit Authority (CATA)			
Bus (directly operated)	34	1,210.8	5,824.2
Demand Response (directly operated)	21	97.9	491.4
Demand Response (purchased transportation)	9	30.1	205.4
Streetcar Rail (directly operated)	2	22.8	58.8
Vanpool (purchased transportation)	5	7.3	347.1

Note: (1) Number of revenue vehicles operated by the given mode and type of service to meet the annual maximum service requirement. This is the revenue vehicle count during the peak season of the year; on the week and day that maximum service is provided. Vehicles operated in maximum service (VOMS) exclude atypical days and one-time special events; (2) Number of passengers who boarded public transportation vehicles. Passengers are counted each time they board a vehicle no matter how many vehicles they use to travel from their origin to their destination. (3) Sum of the distances ridden by all passengers during the entire fiscal year.
Source: Federal Transit Administration, National Transit Database, 2021

Air Transportation

Airport Name and Code / Type of Service	Passenger Airlines[1]	Passenger Enplanements	Freight Carriers[2]	Freight (lbs)
Little Rock National Airport (LIT)				
Domestic service (U.S. carriers - 2022)	21	983,164	12	14,745,748
International service (U.S. carriers - 2021)	1	8	1	3,520

Note: (1) Includes all U.S.-based major, minor and commuter airlines that carried at least one passenger during the year; (2) Includes all U.S.-based airlines and freight carriers that transported at least one pound of freight during the year.
Source: Bureau of Transportation Statistics, The Intermodal Transportation Database, Air Carriers: T-100 Domestic Market (U.S. Carriers), 2022; Bureau of Transportation Statistics, The Intermodal Transportation Database, Air Carriers: T-100 International Market (U.S. Carriers), 2021

BUSINESSES

Major Business Headquarters

Company Name	Industry	Rankings	
		Fortune[1]	Forbes[2]
Dillard's	General merchandiser	488	-

Note: (1) Companies that produce a 10-K are ranked 1 to 500 based on 2021 revenue; (2) All private companies with at least $2 billion in annual revenue through the end of their most current fiscal year are ranked 1 to 246; companies listed are headquartered in the city; dashes indicate no ranking
Source: Fortune, "Fortune 500," 2022; Forbes, "America's Largest Private Companies," 2022

Fastest-Growing Businesses

According to *Initiative for a Competitive Inner City (ICIC)*, Little Rock is home to one of America's 100 fastest-growing "inner city" companies: **MHP/Team SI** (#30). Criteria for inclusion: company must be headquartered in or have 51 percent or more of its physical operations in an economically distressed urban area; must be an independent, for-profit corporation, partnership or proprietorship; must have 10 or more employees and have a five-year sales history that includes sales of at least $200,000 in the base year and at least $1 million in the current year with no decrease in sales over the two most recent years. Companies were ranked overall by revenue growth over the five-year period between 2017 and 2021. *Initiative for a Competitive Inner City (ICIC), "Inner City 100 Companies," 2022*

Living Environment

COST OF LIVING

Cost of Living Index

Composite Index	Groceries	Housing	Utilities	Trans-portation	Health Care	Misc. Goods/ Services
95.6	94.7	83.3	102.0	92.2	78.4	108.0

Note: The Cost of Living Index measures regional differences in the cost of consumer goods and services, excluding taxes and non-consumer expenditures, for professional and managerial households in the top income quintile. It is based on more than 50,000 prices covering almost 60 different items for which prices are collected three times a year by chambers of commerce, economic development organizations or university applied economic centers in each participating urban area. The numbers shown should be read as a percentage above or below the national average of 100. For example, a value of 115.4 in the groceries column indicates that grocery prices are 15.4% higher than the national average. Small differences in the index numbers should not be interpreted as significant; Figures cover the Little Rock-North Little Rock AR urban area.
Source: The Council for Community and Economic Research, Cost of Living Index, 2022

Grocery Prices

Area[1]	T-Bone Steak ($/pound)	Frying Chicken ($/pound)	Whole Milk ($/half gal.)	Eggs ($/dozen)	Orange Juice ($/64 oz.)	Coffee ($/11.5 oz.)
City[2]	12.30	1.41	2.12	2.08	3.74	3.90
Avg.	13.81	1.59	2.43	2.25	3.85	4.95
Min.	10.17	0.90	1.51	1.30	2.90	3.46
Max.	19.35	3.30	4.32	4.32	5.31	8.59

*Note: (1) Values for the local area are compared with the average, minimum and maximum values for all 286 areas in the Cost of Living Index; (2) Figures cover the Little Rock-North Little Rock AR urban area; **T-Bone Steak** (price per pound); **Frying Chicken** (price per pound, whole fryer); **Whole Milk** (half gallon carton); **Eggs** (price per dozen, Grade A, large); **Orange Juice** (64 oz. Tropicana or Florida Natural); **Coffee** (11.5 oz. can, vacuum-packed, Maxwell House, Hills Bros, or Folgers).*
Source: The Council for Community and Economic Research, Cost of Living Index, 2022

Housing and Utility Costs

Area[1]	New Home Price ($)	Apartment Rent ($/month)	All Electric ($/month)	Part Electric ($/month)	Other Energy ($/month)	Telephone ($/month)
City[2]	395,450	946	-	81.77	91.69	204.44
Avg.	450,913	1,371	176.41	99.93	76.96	190.22
Min.	229,283	546	100.84	31.56	27.15	174.27
Max.	2,434,977	4,569	356.86	249.59	272.24	208.31

*Note: (1) Values for the local area are compared with the average, minimum and maximum values for all 286 areas in the Cost of Living Index; (2) Figures cover the Little Rock-North Little Rock AR urban area; **New Home Price** (2,400 sf living area, 8,000 sf lot, in urban area with full utilities); **Apartment Rent** (950 sf 2 bedroom/1.5 or 2 bath, unfurnished, excluding all utilities except water); **All Electric** (average monthly cost for an all-electric home); **Part Electric** (average monthly cost for a part-electric home); **Other Energy** (average monthly cost for natural gas, fuel oil, coal, wood, and any other forms of energy except electricity); **Telephone** (price includes the base monthly rate plus taxes and fees for three lines of mobile phone service).*
Source: The Council for Community and Economic Research, Cost of Living Index, 2022

Health Care, Transportation, and Other Costs

Area[1]	Doctor ($/visit)	Dentist ($/visit)	Optometrist ($/visit)	Gasoline ($/gallon)	Beauty Salon ($/visit)	Men's Shirt ($)
City[2]	116.78	58.25	94.06	3.52	52.55	37.55
Avg.	124.91	107.77	117.66	3.86	43.31	34.21
Min.	36.61	58.25	51.79	2.90	22.18	13.05
Max.	250.21	162.58	371.96	5.54	85.61	63.54

*Note: (1) Values for the local area are compared with the average, minimum and maximum values for all 286 areas in the Cost of Living Index; (2) Figures cover the Little Rock-North Little Rock AR urban area; **Doctor** (general practitioners routine exam of an established patient); **Dentist** (adult teeth cleaning and periodic oral examination); **Optometrist** (full vision eye exam for established adult patient); **Gasoline** (one gallon regular unleaded, national brand, including all taxes, cash price at self-service pump if available); **Beauty Salon** (woman's shampoo, trim, and blow-dry); **Men's Shirt** (cotton/polyester dress shirt, pinpoint weave, long sleeves).*
Source: The Council for Community and Economic Research, Cost of Living Index, 2022

HOUSING

Homeownership Rate

Area	2015 (%)	2016 (%)	2017 (%)	2018 (%)	2019 (%)	2020 (%)	2021 (%)	2022 (%)
MSA[1]	65.8	64.9	61.0	62.2	65.0	67.7	64.6	64.4
U.S.	63.7	63.4	63.9	64.4	64.6	66.6	65.5	65.8

Note: (1) Figures cover the Little Rock-North Little Rock-Conway, AR Metropolitan Statistical Area
Source: U.S. Census Bureau, Housing Vacancies and Homeownership Annual Statistics: 2015-2022

House Price Index (HPI)

Area	National Ranking[2]	Quarterly Change (%)	One-Year Change (%)	Five-Year Change (%)	Since 1991Q1 (%)
MSA[1]	119	0.21	11.59	41.21	196.34
U.S.[3]	–	0.34	8.41	58.44	289.08

Note: The HPI is a weighted repeat sales index. It measures average price changes in repeat sales or refinancings on the same properties. This information is obtained by reviewing repeat mortgage transactions on single-family properties whose mortgages have been purchased or securitized by Fannie Mae or Freddie Mac since January 1975; (1) Figures cover the Little Rock-North Little Rock-Conway, AR Metropolitan Statistical Area; (2) Rankings are based on annual percentage change for all metro areas containing at least 15,000 transactions over the last 10 years and ranges from 1 to 257; (3) figures based on a weighted average of Census Division estimates using a seasonally adjusted, purchase-only index; all figures are for the period ending December 31, 2022
Source: Federal Housing Finance Agency, Change in FHFA Metropolitan Area House Price Indexes, 2022Q4

Median Single-Family Home Prices

Area	2020	2021	2022p	Percent Change 2021 to 2022
MSA[1]	166.9	184.6	205.6	11.4
U.S. Average	300.2	357.1	392.6	9.9

Note: Figures are median sales prices of existing single-family homes in thousands of dollars; (p) preliminary; (1) Figures cover the Little Rock-North Little Rock-Conway, AR Metropolitan Statistical Area
Source: National Association of Realtors, Median Sales Price of Existing Single-Family Homes for Metropolitan Areas, 4th Quarter 2022

Qualifying Income Based on Median Sales Price of Existing Single-Family Homes

Area	With 5% Down ($)	With 10% Down ($)	With 20% Down ($)
MSA[1]	61,273	58,048	51,598
U.S. Average	112,234	106,237	94,513

Note: Figures are preliminary; Qualifying income is based on a mortgage rate of 6.77%. Monthly principal and interest payment is limited to 25% of income; (1) Figures cover the Little Rock-North Little Rock-Conway, AR Metropolitan Statistical Area
Source: National Association of Realtors, Qualifying Income Based on Median Sales Price of Existing Single-Family Homes for Metropolitan Areas, 4th Quarter 2022

Home Value

Area	Under $100,000	$100,000 -$199,999	$200,000 -$299,999	$300,000 -$399,999	$400,000 -$499,999	$500,000 -$999,999	$1,000,000 or more	Median ($)
City	22.0	33.4	17.9	11.1	5.5	8.4	1.6	179,500
MSA[1]	23.2	39.9	20.4	8.5	3.2	4.0	0.8	164,200
U.S.	16.2	24.2	20.1	13.6	8.3	13.6	4.1	244,900

Note: Figures are percentages except for median and cover owner-occupied housing units; (1) Figures cover the Little Rock-North Little Rock-Conway, AR Metropolitan Statistical Area
Source: U.S. Census Bureau, 2017-2021 American Community Survey 5-Year Estimates

Year Housing Structure Built

Area	2020 or Later	2010 -2019	2000 -2009	1990 -1999	1980 -1989	1970 -1979	1960 -1969	1950 -1959	1940 -1949	Before 1940	Median Year
City	0.0	8.0	11.4	12.3	13.7	18.5	13.8	9.4	5.1	7.8	1978
MSA[1]	0.3	12.0	17.4	16.6	14.0	15.9	10.0	6.8	3.2	3.8	1987
U.S.	0.2	7.3	13.6	13.6	13.2	14.8	10.3	10.0	4.7	12.2	1979

Note: Figures are percentages except for Median Year; Note: (1) Figures cover the Little Rock-North Little Rock-Conway, AR Metropolitan Statistical Area
Source: U.S. Census Bureau, 2017-2021 American Community Survey 5-Year Estimates

Gross Monthly Rent

Area	Under $500	$500 -$999	$1,000 -$1,499	$1,500 -$1,999	$2,000 -$2,499	$2,500 -$2,999	$3,000 and up	Median ($)
City	7.8	49.3	33.3	6.7	1.4	0.7	0.8	940
MSA[1]	8.1	55.9	29.1	5.3	0.9	0.4	0.4	893
U.S.	8.1	30.5	30.8	16.8	7.3	3.1	3.5	1,163

Note: Figures are percentages except for median; Gross rent is the contract rent plus the estimated average monthly cost of utilities (electricity, gas, and water and sewer) and fuels (oil, coal, kerosene, wood, etc.) if these are paid by the renter (or paid for the renter by someone else); (1) Figures cover the Little Rock-North Little Rock-Conway, AR Metropolitan Statistical Area
Source: U.S. Census Bureau, 2017-2021 American Community Survey 5-Year Estimates

HEALTH

Health Risk Factors

Category	MSA[1] (%)	U.S. (%)
Adults aged 18–64 who have any kind of health care coverage	90.8	90.9
Adults who reported being in good or better health	82.3	85.2
Adults who have been told they have high blood cholesterol	34.1	35.7
Adults who have been told they have high blood pressure	40.6	32.4
Adults who are current smokers	20.5	14.4
Adults who currently use e-cigarettes	6.3	6.7
Adults who currently use chewing tobacco, snuff, or snus	2.9	3.5
Adults who are heavy drinkers[2]	7.7	6.3
Adults who are binge drinkers[3]	11.7	15.4
Adults who are overweight (BMI 25.0 - 29.9)	32.0	34.4
Adults who are obese (BMI 30.0 - 99.8)	41.7	33.9
Adults who participated in any physical activities in the past month	76.7	76.3

Note: (1) Figures cover the Little Rock-North Little Rock-Conway, AR Metropolitan Statistical Area; (2) Heavy drinkers are classified as adult men having more than 14 drinks per week and adult women having more than 7 drinks per week; (3) Binge drinkers are classified as males having five or more drinks on one occasion or females having four or more drinks on one occasion
Source: Centers for Disease Control and Prevention, Behaviorial Risk Factor Surveillance System, SMART: Selected Metropolitan Area Risk Trends, 2021

Acute and Chronic Health Conditions

Category	MSA[1] (%)	U.S. (%)
Adults who have ever been told they had a heart attack	3.6	4.0
Adults who have ever been told they have angina or coronary heart disease	4.9	3.8
Adults who have ever been told they had a stroke	3.7	3.0
Adults who have ever been told they have asthma	16.1	14.9
Adults who have ever been told they have arthritis	30.9	25.8
Adults who have ever been told they have diabetes[2]	10.4	10.9
Adults who have ever been told they had skin cancer	6.9	6.6
Adults who have ever been told they had any other types of cancer	8.7	7.5
Adults who have ever been told they have COPD	8.1	6.1
Adults who have ever been told they have kidney disease	3.6	3.0
Adults who have ever been told they have a form of depression	21.8	20.5

Note: (1) Figures cover the Little Rock-North Little Rock-Conway, AR Metropolitan Statistical Area; (2) Figures do not include pregnancy-related, borderline, or pre-diabetes
Source: Centers for Disease Control and Prevention, Behaviorial Risk Factor Surveillance System, SMART: Selected Metropolitan Area Risk Trends, 2021

Health Screening and Vaccination Rates

Category	MSA[1] (%)	U.S. (%)
Adults who have ever been tested for HIV	35.3	34.9
Adults who have had their blood cholesterol checked within the last five years	86.8	85.2
Adults aged 65+ who have had flu shot within the past year	70.2	68.6
Adults aged 65+ who have ever had a pneumonia vaccination	72.6	71.0

Note: (1) Figures cover the Little Rock-North Little Rock-Conway, AR Metropolitan Statistical Area.
Source: Centers for Disease Control and Prevention, Behaviorial Risk Factor Surveillance System, SMART: Selected Metropolitan Area Risk Trends, 2021

Disability Status

Category	MSA[1] (%)	U.S. (%)
Adults who reported being deaf	8.6	7.2
Are you blind or have serious difficulty seeing, even when wearing glasses?	5.4	4.8
Are you limited in any way in any of your usual activities due to arthritis?	14.4	11.1
Do you have difficulty doing errands alone?	7.3	7.0
Do you have difficulty dressing or bathing?	4.7	3.6
Do you have serious difficulty concentrating/remembering/making decisions?	14.8	12.1
Do you have serious difficulty walking or climbing stairs?	15.5	12.8

Note: (1) Figures cover the Little Rock-North Little Rock-Conway, AR Metropolitan Statistical Area.
Source: Centers for Disease Control and Prevention, Behaviorial Risk Factor Surveillance System, SMART: Selected Metropolitan Area Risk Trends, 2021

Mortality Rates for the Top 10 Causes of Death in the U.S.

ICD-10[a] Sub-Chapter	ICD-10[a] Code	Crude Mortality Rate[1] per 100,000 population	
		County[2]	U.S.
Malignant neoplasms	C00-C97	187.4	182.6
Ischaemic heart diseases	I20-I25	121.1	113.1
Other forms of heart disease	I30-I51	51.2	64.4
Other degenerative diseases of the nervous system	G30-G31	98.6	51.0
Cerebrovascular diseases	I60-I69	53.1	47.8
Other external causes of accidental injury	W00-X59	45.8	46.4
Chronic lower respiratory diseases	J40-J47	54.2	45.7
Organic, including symptomatic, mental disorders	F01-F09	18.0	35.9
Hypertensive diseases	I10-I15	43.5	35.0
Diabetes mellitus	E10-E14	54.3	29.6

Note: (a) ICD-10 = International Classification of Diseases 10th Revision; (1) Crude mortality rates are a three-year average covering 2019-2021; (2) Figures cover Pulaski County.
Source: Centers for Disease Control and Prevention, National Center for Health Statistics. National Vital Statistics System, Mortality 2018-2021 on CDC WONDER Online Database

Mortality Rates for Selected Causes of Death

ICD-10[a] Sub-Chapter	ICD-10[a] Code	Crude Mortality Rate[1] per 100,000 population	
		County[2]	U.S.
Assault	X85-Y09	20.1	7.0
Diseases of the liver	K70-K76	22.1	19.8
Human immunodeficiency virus (HIV) disease	B20-B24	4.0	1.5
Influenza and pneumonia	J09-J18	14.2	14.7
Intentional self-harm	X60-X84	16.3	14.3
Malnutrition	E40-E46	6.4	4.3
Obesity and other hyperalimentation	E65-E68	5.2	3.0
Renal failure	N17-N19	22.1	15.7
Transport accidents	V01-V99	21.8	13.6
Viral hepatitis	B15-B19	1.9	1.2

Note: (a) ICD-10 = International Classification of Diseases 10th Revision; (1) Crude mortality rates are a three-year average covering 2019-2021; (2) Figures cover Pulaski County; Data are suppressed when the data meet the criteria for confidentiality constraints; Crude mortality rates are flagged as unreliable when the rate would be calculated with a numerator of 20 or less.
Source: Centers for Disease Control and Prevention, National Center for Health Statistics. National Vital Statistics System, Mortality 2018-2021 on CDC WONDER Online Database

Health Insurance Coverage

Area	With Health Insurance	With Private Health Insurance	With Public Health Insurance	Without Health Insurance	Population Under Age 19 Without Health Insurance
City	91.3	63.9	38.7	8.7	4.4
MSA[1]	92.3	66.2	39.1	7.7	4.3
U.S.	91.2	67.8	35.4	8.8	5.3

Note: Figures are percentages that cover the civilian noninstitutionalized population; (1) Figures cover the Little Rock-North Little Rock-Conway, AR Metropolitan Statistical Area
Source: U.S. Census Bureau, 2017-2021 American Community Survey 5-Year Estimates

Number of Medical Professionals

Area	MDs[3]	DOs[3,4]	Dentists	Podiatrists	Chiropractors	Optometrists
County[1] (number)	2,965	61	309	19	88	87
County[1] (rate[2])	743.0	15.3	77.7	4.8	22.1	21.9
U.S. (rate[2])	289.3	23.5	72.5	6.2	28.7	17.4

Note: Data as of 2021 unless noted; (1) Data covers Pulaski County; (2) Rate per 100,000 population; (3) Data as of 2020 and includes all active, non-federal physicians; (4) Doctor of Osteopathic Medicine
Source: U.S. Department of Health and Human Services, Health Resources and Services Administration, Bureau of Health Professions, Area Resource File (ARF) 2021-2022

Best Hospitals

According to *U.S. News,* the Little Rock-North Little Rock-Conway, AR metro area is home to one of the best children's hospitals in the U.S.: **Arkansas Children's Hospital** (7 pediatric specialties). The hospital listed was highly ranked in at least one of 10 pediatric specialties. Eighty-six children's hospitals in the U.S. were nationally ranked in at least one specialty. Hospitals received points for being ranked in a specialty, and the 10 hospitals with the most points across the 10 specialties make up the Honor Roll. *U.S. News Online, "America's Best Children's Hospitals 2022-23"*

EDUCATION

Public School District Statistics

District Name	Schls	Pupils	Pupil/ Teacher Ratio	Minority Pupils[1] (%)	LEP/ELL[2] (%)	IEP[3] (%)
Arkansas Virtual Academy	3	3,855	16.1	33.2	1.7	16.5
Estem High Charter	5	3,052	14.3	80.4	4.2	10.9
Lisa Academy Charter	8	3,469	13.3	78.7	16.2	11.4
Little Rock School District	42	22,054	14.6	80.6	13.0	16.7
Pulaski Co. Spec. School Dist.	26	11,709	12.6	61.9	5.5	15.6

Note: Table includes school districts with 2,000 or more students; (1) Percentage of students that are not non-Hispanic white; (2) Percentage of students that are Limited English Proficient or English Language Learners (2018-19); (3) Percentage of students that have an Individualized Education Program (2019-20).
Source: U.S. Department of Education, National Center for Education Statistics, Common Core of Data, Local Education Agency (School District) Universe Survey: School Year 2021-2022

Highest Level of Education

Area	Less than H.S.	H.S. Diploma	Some College, No Deg.	Associate Degree	Bachelor's Degree	Master's Degree	Prof. School Degree	Doctorate Degree
City	8.1	21.7	19.8	6.4	25.3	11.8	4.3	2.8
MSA[1]	8.4	29.1	22.2	8.3	19.9	8.6	2.2	1.4
U.S.	11.1	26.5	20.0	8.7	20.6	9.3	2.2	1.5

Note: Figures cover persons age 25 and over; (1) Figures cover the Little Rock-North Little Rock-Conway, AR Metropolitan Statistical Area
Source: U.S. Census Bureau, 2017-2021 American Community Survey 5-Year Estimates

Educational Attainment by Race

Area	High School Graduate or Higher (%)					Bachelor's Degree or Higher (%)				
	Total	White	Black	Asian	Hisp.[2]	Total	White	Black	Asian	Hisp.[2]
City	91.9	94.1	90.0	87.5	67.6	44.1	57.8	25.7	61.9	13.0
MSA[1]	91.6	92.8	90.2	87.1	70.1	32.1	34.4	24.8	51.1	15.5
U.S.	88.9	91.4	87.2	87.6	71.2	33.7	35.5	23.3	55.6	18.4

Note: Figures shown cover persons 25 years old and over; (1) Figures cover the Little Rock-North Little Rock-Conway, AR Metropolitan Statistical Area; (2) People of Hispanic origin can be of any race
Source: U.S. Census Bureau, 2017-2021 American Community Survey 5-Year Estimates

School Enrollment by Grade and Control

Area	Preschool (%)		Kindergarten (%)		Grades 1 - 4 (%)		Grades 5 - 8 (%)		Grades 9 - 12 (%)	
	Public	Private	Public	Private	Public	Private	Public	Private	Public	Private
City	67.9	32.1	88.9	11.1	78.3	21.7	79.1	20.9	76.2	23.8
MSA[1]	70.5	29.5	90.1	9.9	87.0	13.0	86.6	13.4	86.4	13.6
U.S.	58.8	41.2	86.3	13.7	88.3	11.7	88.6	11.4	89.4	10.6

Note: Figures shown cover persons 3 years old and over; (1) Figures cover the Little Rock-North Little Rock-Conway, AR Metropolitan Statistical Area
Source: U.S. Census Bureau, 2017-2021 American Community Survey 5-Year Estimates

Higher Education

Four-Year Colleges			Two-Year Colleges			Medical Schools[1]	Law Schools[2]	Voc/ Tech[3]
Public	Private Non-profit	Private For-profit	Public	Private Non-profit	Private For-profit			
4	4	1	1	2	0	1	1	12

Note: Figures cover institutions located within the Little Rock-North Little Rock-Conway, AR Metropolitan Statistical Area and include main campuses only; (1) includes schools accredited by the Liaison Committee on Medical Education and the American Osteopathic Association's Commission on Osteopathic College Accreditation; (2) includes ABA-accredited schools, schools with provisional ABA accreditation, and state accredited schools; (3) includes all schools with programs that are less than 2 years.
Source: National Center for Education Statistics, Integrated Postsecondary Education System (IPEDS), 2021-22; Wikipedia, List of Medical Schools in the United States, accessed April 10, 2023; Wikipedia, List of Law Schools in the United States, accessed April 10, 2023

According to *U.S. News & World Report*, the Little Rock-North Little Rock-Conway, AR metro area is home to one of the top 75 medical schools for research in the U.S.: **University of Arkansas for Medical Sciences** (#74 tie). The rankings are based on a weighted average of 11 measures of quality: quality assessment; peer assessment score; assessment score by residency directors; research activity; total research activity; average research activity per faculty member; student selectivity; median MCAT total score; median undergraduate GPA; acceptance rate; and faculty resources. *U.S. News & World Report, "America's Best Graduate Schools, Medical, 2023"*

EMPLOYERS

Major Employers

Company Name	Industry
Arkansas Blue Cross and Blue Shield	Hospitals and medical service plans
Arkansas Childrens Hospital	Specialty hospitals, except psychiatric
Baptist Health Systems	General medical & surgical hospitals
Dassault Falcon Jet Corp	Aviation and or aeronautical engineering
Dept of Highway and Trans Arkansas	Regulation, administration of transportation
Dept of Finance & Admin Arkansas	Finance, taxation, and monetary policy
Fidelity Information Systems	Data processing services
Loreal USA	Toilet preparations
Mountaire Farms	Broiler, fryer and roaster chickens
Pulaski County	General practice, attorney
St. Vincent Health System	Medical services organization
United States Dept of Veteran Affairs	General medical & surgical hospitals
University of Arkansas System	Colleges & universities
Valor Telecommunications	Voice telephone communications
Veterans Health Administration	Administration of veterans affairs

Note: Companies shown are located within the Little Rock-North Little Rock-Conway, AR Metropolitan Statistical Area.
Source: Hoovers.com; Wikipedia

PUBLIC SAFETY

Crime Rate

Area	Total Crime	Violent Crime Rate				Property Crime Rate		
		Murder	Rape[3]	Robbery	Aggrav. Assault	Burglary	Larceny -Theft	Motor Vehicle Theft
City	6,707.0	24.8	99.1	190.2	1,535.8	772.4	3,572.3	512.4
Suburbs[1]	3,185.5	8.9	56.1	52.4	493.6	457.2	1,830.0	287.2
Metro[2]	4,117.3	13.1	67.5	88.9	769.4	540.6	2,291.0	346.8
U.S.	2,356.7	6.5	38.4	73.9	279.7	314.2	1,398.0	246.0

Note: Figures are crimes per 100,000 population; (1) All areas within the metro area that are located outside the city limits; (2) Figures cover the Little Rock-North Little Rock-Conway, AR Metropolitan Statistical Area; (3) All figures shown were reported using the revised Uniform Crime Reporting (UCR) definition of rape; Due to the transition to the National Incident-Based Reporting System (NIBRS), limited city and metro area data was released for 2021.
Source: FBI Uniform Crime Reports, 2020

Hate Crimes

Area	Number of Quarters Reported	Number of Incidents per Bias Motivation					
		Race/Ethnicity/ Ancestry	Religion	Sexual Orientation	Disability	Gender	Gender Identity
City	4	0	0	0	0	0	0
U.S.	4	5,227	1,244	1,110	130	75	266

Note: Due to the transition to the National Incident-Based Reporting System (NIBRS), limited crime data was released for 2021.
Source: Federal Bureau of Investigation, Hate Crime Statistics 2020

Identity Theft Consumer Reports

Area	Reports	Reports per 100,000 Population	Rank[2]
MSA[1]	1,890	255	98
U.S.	1,108,609	339	-

Note: (1) Figures cover the Little Rock-North Little Rock-Conway, AR Metropolitan Statistical Area; (2) Rank ranges from 1 to 391 where 1 indicates greatest number of identity theft reports per 100,000 population
Source: Federal Trade Commission, Consumer Sentinel Network Data Book 2022

Fraud and Other Consumer Reports

Area	Reports	Reports per 100,000 Population	Rank[2]
MSA[1]	8,047	1,087	68
U.S.	4,064,520	1,245	-

Note: (1) Figures cover the Little Rock-North Little Rock-Conway, AR Metropolitan Statistical Area; (2) Rank ranges from 1 to 391 where 1 indicates greatest number of fraud and other consumer reports per 100,000 population
Source: Federal Trade Commission, Consumer Sentinel Network Data Book 2022

POLITICS

2020 Presidential Election Results

Area	Biden	Trump	Jorgensen	Hawkins	Other
Pulaski County	60.0	37.5	1.0	0.3	1.3
U.S.	51.3	46.8	1.2	0.3	0.5

Note: Results are percentages and may not add to 100% due to rounding
Source: Dave Leip's Atlas of U.S. Presidential Elections

SPORTS

Professional Sports Teams

Team Name	League	Year Established

No teams are located in the metro area
Source: Wikipedia, Major Professional Sports Teams of the United States and Canada, April 12, 2023

CLIMATE

Average and Extreme Temperatures

Temperature	Jan	Feb	Mar	Apr	May	Jun	Jul	Aug	Sep	Oct	Nov	Dec	Yr.
Extreme High (°F)	83	85	91	95	98	105	112	108	103	97	86	80	112
Average High (°F)	50	54	63	73	81	89	92	91	85	75	62	53	73
Average Temp. (°F)	40	45	53	63	71	79	82	81	74	63	52	43	62
Average Low (°F)	30	34	42	51	60	68	72	70	63	51	41	34	51
Extreme Low (°F)	-4	-5	17	28	40	46	54	52	38	29	17	-1	-5

Note: Figures cover the years 1948-1990
Source: National Climatic Data Center, International Station Meteorological Climate Summary, 9/96

Average Precipitation/Snowfall/Humidity

Precip./Humidity	Jan	Feb	Mar	Apr	May	Jun	Jul	Aug	Sep	Oct	Nov	Dec	Yr.
Avg. Precip. (in.)	4.1	4.2	4.9	5.2	5.4	3.6	3.5	3.2	3.8	3.5	4.8	4.5	50.7
Avg. Snowfall (in.)	3	2	1	Tr	0	0	0	0	0	0	Tr	1	5
Avg. Rel. Hum. 6am (%)	80	80	78	81	86	86	87	88	87	86	82	80	84
Avg. Rel. Hum. 3pm (%)	57	54	50	50	53	52	54	52	52	48	52	57	53

Note: Figures cover the years 1948-1990; Tr = Trace amounts (<0.05 in. of rain; <0.5 in. of snow)
Source: National Climatic Data Center, International Station Meteorological Climate Summary, 9/96

Weather Conditions

Temperature			Daytime Sky			Precipitation		
10°F & below	32°F & below	90°F & above	Clear	Partly cloudy	Cloudy	0.01 inch or more precip.	0.1 inch or more snow/ice	Thunder-storms
1	57	73	110	142	113	104	4	57

Note: Figures are average number of days per year and cover the years 1948-1990
Source: National Climatic Data Center, International Station Meteorological Climate Summary, 9/96

HAZARDOUS WASTE

Superfund Sites

The Little Rock-North Little Rock-Conway, AR metro area has no sites on the EPA's Superfund Final National Priorities List. There are a total of 1,165 Superfund sites with a status of proposed or final on the list in the U.S. *U.S. Environmental Protection Agency, National Priorities List, April 12, 2023*

AIR QUALITY

Air Quality Trends: Ozone

	1990	1995	2000	2005	2010	2015	2018	2019	2020	2021
MSA[1]	0.080	0.086	0.090	0.083	0.072	0.063	0.066	0.059	0.062	0.066
U.S.	0.087	0.089	0.081	0.080	0.072	0.067	0.069	0.065	0.065	0.067

Note: (1) Data covers the Little Rock-North Little Rock-Conway, AR Metropolitan Statistical Area. The values shown are the composite ozone concentration averages among trend sites based on the highest fourth daily maximum 8-hour concentration in parts per million. These trends are based on sites having an adequate record of monitoring data during the trend period. Data from exceptional events are included.
Source: U.S. Environmental Protection Agency, Air Quality Monitoring Information, "Air Quality Trends by City, 1990-2021"

Air Quality Index

Area	Percent of Days when Air Quality was...[2]					AQI Statistics[2]	
	Good	Moderate	Unhealthy for Sensitive Groups	Unhealthy	Very Unhealthy	Maximum	Median
MSA[1]	58.4	41.1	0.5	0.0	0.0	112	47

Note: (1) Data covers the Little Rock-North Little Rock-Conway, AR Metropolitan Statistical Area; (2) Based on 365 days with AQI data in 2021. Air Quality Index (AQI) is an index for reporting daily air quality. EPA calculates the AQI for five major air pollutants regulated by the Clean Air Act: ground-level ozone, particle pollution (aka particulate matter), carbon monoxide, sulfur dioxide, and nitrogen dioxide. The AQI runs from 0 to 500. The higher the AQI value, the greater the level of air pollution and the greater the health concern. There are six AQI categories: "Good" AQI is between 0 and 50. Air quality is considered satisfactory; "Moderate" AQI is between 51 and 100. Air quality is acceptable; "Unhealthy for Sensitive Groups" When AQI values are between 101 and 150, members of sensitive groups may experience health effects; "Unhealthy" When AQI values are between 151 and 200 everyone may begin to experience health effects; "Very Unhealthy" AQI values between 201 and 300 trigger a health alert; "Hazardous" AQI values over 300 trigger warnings of emergency conditions (not shown).
Source: U.S. Environmental Protection Agency, Air Quality Index Report, 2021

Air Quality Index Pollutants

Area	Percent of Days when AQI Pollutant was...[2]					
	Carbon Monoxide	Nitrogen Dioxide	Ozone	Sulfur Dioxide	Particulate Matter 2.5	Particulate Matter 10
MSA[1]	0.0	1.6	27.9	(3)	70.4	0.0

Note: (1) Data covers the Little Rock-North Little Rock-Conway, AR Metropolitan Statistical Area; (2) Based on 365 days with AQI data in 2021. The Air Quality Index (AQI) is an index for reporting daily air quality. EPA calculates the AQI for five major air pollutants regulated by the Clean Air Act: ground-level ozone, particle pollution (also known as particulate matter), carbon monoxide, sulfur dioxide, and nitrogen dioxide. The AQI runs from 0 to 500. The higher the AQI value, the greater the level of air pollution and the greater the health concern; (3) Sulfur dioxide is no longer included in this table (as of December 8, 2021) because SO_2 concentrations tend to be very localized and not necessarily representative of broad geographical areas like counties and CBSAs.
Source: U.S. Environmental Protection Agency, Air Quality Index Report, 2021

Maximum Air Pollutant Concentrations: Particulate Matter, Ozone, CO and Lead

	Particulate Matter 10 (ug/m^3)	Particulate Matter 2.5 Wtd AM (ug/m^3)	Particulate Matter 2.5 24-Hr (ug/m^3)	Ozone (ppm)	Carbon Monoxide (ppm)	Lead (ug/m^3)
MSA[1] Level	32	9.7	25	0.067	1	n/a
NAAQS[2]	150	15	35	0.075	9	0.15
Met NAAQS[2]	Yes	Yes	Yes	Yes	Yes	n/a

Note: (1) Data covers the Little Rock-North Little Rock-Conway, AR Metropolitan Statistical Area; Data from exceptional events are included; (2) National Ambient Air Quality Standards; ppm = parts per million; ug/m^3 = micrograms per cubic meter; n/a not available.
Concentrations: Particulate Matter 10 (coarse particulate)—highest second maximum 24-hour concentration; Particulate Matter 2.5 Wtd AM (fine particulate)—highest weighted annual mean concentration; Particulate Matter 2.5 24-Hour (fine particulate)—highest 98th percentile 24-hour concentration; Ozone—highest fourth daily maximum 8-hour concentration; Carbon Monoxide—highest second maximum non-overlapping 8-hour concentration; Lead—maximum running 3-month average
Source: U.S. Environmental Protection Agency, Air Quality Monitoring Information, "Air Quality Statistics by City, 2021"

Maximum Air Pollutant Concentrations: Nitrogen Dioxide and Sulfur Dioxide

	Nitrogen Dioxide AM (ppb)	Nitrogen Dioxide 1-Hr (ppb)	Sulfur Dioxide AM (ppb)	Sulfur Dioxide 1-Hr (ppb)	Sulfur Dioxide 24-Hr (ppb)
MSA[1] Level	7	38	n/a	6	n/a
NAAQS[2]	53	100	30	75	140
Met NAAQS[2]	Yes	Yes	n/a	Yes	n/a

Note: (1) Data covers the Little Rock-North Little Rock-Conway, AR Metropolitan Statistical Area; Data from exceptional events are included; (2) National Ambient Air Quality Standards; ppm = parts per million; ug/m^3 = micrograms per cubic meter; n/a not available.
Concentrations: Nitrogen Dioxide AM—highest arithmetic mean concentration; Nitrogen Dioxide 1-Hr—highest 98th percentile 1-hour daily maximum concentration; Sulfur Dioxide AM—highest annual mean concentration; Sulfur Dioxide 1-Hr—highest 99th percentile 1-hour daily maximum concentration; Sulfur Dioxide 24-Hr—highest second maximum 24-hour concentration
Source: U.S. Environmental Protection Agency, Air Quality Monitoring Information, "Air Quality Statistics by City, 2021"

Madison, Wisconsin

Background

Madison was selected as Wisconsin's territorial capital in 1836 before construction of the city began in 1838. Despite repeated threats to move the capital elsewhere by members of the legislature, it has maintained its status. It was named for President James Madison in 1836 and incorporated into a village in 1856. When Wisconsin attained statehood in 1848, the University of Wisconsin (one of the largest in the country) was established.

Most of the city, including its business center, is situated on an isthmus between Lake Mendota and Lake Minona in the south-central part of the state. Two other lakes, Kengonsa and Waubesa, lie to the south. By ordinance, the city's skyline is dominated by the capitol dome, which weighs 2,500 tons.

Madison serves as the trade center of a rich agricultural and dairy region. Food processing is a major industry. Batteries, dairy equipment, and machine tools are produced there as well.

Wisconsin state government and the University of Wisconsin-Madison remain the two largest Madison employers. Madison continues to evolve from a government-based economy to consumer services and a base for high-tech, particularly in the health, biotech, and advertising sectors. Beginning in the early 1990s, the city experienced a steady economic boom fostered by the development of high-tech companies and UW-Madison working with local businesses and entrepreneurs to transfer the results of academic research into real-world applications, especially bio-tech applications. UW-Madison recently began offering fully online degrees. Businesses are attracted to Madison's skill base, taking advantage of the area's high level of education.

The city has received numerous awards, beginning in 1948 when it was named Best Place to Live in America by *Life* magazine. Although Madison is a progressive, eclectic city, it also offers the atmosphere of a small town with many picturesque communities, four lakes, and over 200 parks. There are a total of 29,000 acres designated for recreational use, including 46 miles of hiking trails, over 150 miles of bicycle trails, 92 miles of shoreline for swimming and boating, and 20 golf courses. The city claims to be the bike capital of the Midwest, with more bikes than cars and more than 200 miles of scenic biking and hiking trails.

Madison's many restaurants boast a large variety of ethnic food, from Greek and Italian to Japanese, Mexican, and Middle Eastern, as well as many brew pubs.

Cultural life in Madison has long had a center in the downtown, at the Madison Civic Center and its associated sites. Project Overture renovated and redeveloped a variety of cultural venues, including the Madison Museum of Contemporary Art with innovative design and sculpture-garden rooftop. A 2,250-seat hall houses the Madison Symphony Orchestra, whose old home, the Oscar Meyer Theater, is used by groups such as the CTM Family Theatre and the Wisconsin Chamber group. Keeping the goal of architectural integration in mind, facades of nearby buildings have been refurbished and preserved.

In 2018, Forward Madison FC became the city's first professional soccer team.

Another major attraction in Madison is the Olbrich Botanical Gardens, with 16 acres of outdoor display gardens, including sunken, perennial, rose, rock, herb, and wildflower gardens. Over 250,000 visitors a year enjoy the gardens, which include a lush, tropical conservatory filled with exotic plants, bright flowers, a rushing waterfall, and free-flying birds.

Madison is home to many institutions of higher learning, including the University of Wisconsin-Madison, Edgewood College, Herzing College, Lakeland College, and Madison Media Institute.

The area has the typical continental climate of interior North America with a large annual temperature range and frequent short-period temperature changes. The city lies in the path of the frequent cyclones and anticyclones that move eastward over this area during fall, winter, and spring. The most frequent air masses are of polar origin, with occasional influxes of arctic air affecting the area during the winter months. Summers are pleasant, with only occasional periods of extreme heat or high humidity.

Rankings

General Rankings

- *US News & World Report* conducted a survey of more than 3,600 people and analyzed the 150 largest metropolitan areas to determine what matters most when selecting where to settle down. Madison ranked #17 out of the top 25 as having the best combination of desirable factors. Criteria: cost of living; quality of life and education; net migration; job market; desirability; and other factors. *money.usnews.com, "The 25 Best Places to Live in the U.S. in 2022-2023," May 17, 2022*

- Madison was selected as one of the best places to live in the United States by *Money* magazine. The city ranked #40 out of 50. This year's list focused on cities that would be welcoming to a broader group of people and with populations of at least 20,000. Beginning with a pool of 1,370 candidates, editors looked at 350 data points, organized into the these nine categories: income and personal finance, cost of living, economic opportunity, housing market, fun and amenities, health and safety, education, diversity, and quality of life. *Money, "The 50 Best Places to Live in the U.S. in 2022-2023" September 29, 2022*

- In their ninth annual survey, Livability.com looked at data for more than 2,300 mid-sized U.S. cities to determine the rankings for Livability's "Top 100 Best Places to Live" in 2022. Madison ranked #1. Criteria: housing and economy; social and civic engagement; education; demographics; health care options; transportation & infrastructure; and community amenities. *Livability.com, "Top 100 Best Places to Live 2022" July 19, 2022*

Business/Finance Rankings

- According to *Business Insider*, the Madison metro area is a prime place to run a startup or move an existing business to. The area ranked #13. More than 300 metro areas were analyzed for factors that were of top concern to new business owners. Data was based on the 2019 U.S. Census Bureau American Community Survey, statistics from the CDC, Bureau of Labor Statistics employment report, and University of Chicago analysis. Criteria: business formations; percentage of vaccinated population; percentage of households with internet subscriptions; median household income; and share of work that can be done from home. *www.businessinsider.com, "The 20 Best Cities for Starting a Business in 2022 Include Baltimore, Boulder, and Boston," January 5, 2022*

- The Brookings Institution ranked the nation's largest cities based on income inequality. Madison was ranked #86 (#1 = greatest inequality). Criteria: the "95/20 ratio," a figure representing the income at which a household earns more than 95 percent of all other households, divided by the income at which a household earns more than only 20 percent of all other households. *Brookings Institution, "Household Income Inequality, Largest Cities of 97 Large U.S. Metro Areas, 2014-2016," February 5, 2018*

- The Brookings Institution ranked the 100 largest metro areas in the U.S. based on income inequality. Madison was ranked #95 (#1 = greatest inequality). Criteria: the "95/20 ratio," a figure representing the income at which a household earns more than 95 percent of all other households, divided by the income at which a household earns more than only 20 percent of all other households. *Brookings Institution, "Household Income Inequality, 100 Largest U.S. Metro Areas, 2014-2016," February 5, 2018*

- Livability.com rated Madison as #10 of ten cities where new college grads' job prospects are brightest. Criteria included: number of 22- to 29-year olds; good job opportunities; affordable housing options; public transportation users; educational attainment; variety of fun things to do. *Livability.com, "2018 Top 10 Best Cities for Recent College Grads," April 26, 2018*

- The Madison metro area appeared on the Milken Institute "2022 Best Performing Cities" list. Rank: #50 out of 200 large metro areas (population over 250,000). Criteria: job growth; wage and salary growth; high-tech output growth; housing affordability; household broadband access. *Milken Institute, "Best-Performing Cities 2022," March 28, 2022*

- *Forbes* ranked the 200 most populous metro areas to determine the nation's "Best Places for Business and Careers." The Madison metro area was ranked #57. Criteria: costs (business and living); job growth (past and projected); income growth; quality of life; educational attainment (college and high school); projected economic growth; cultural and leisure opportunities; workplace tolerance laws; net migration patterns. *Forbes, "The Best Places for Business and Careers 2019: Seattle Still On Top," October 30, 2019*

Dating/Romance Rankings

- Madison was ranked #15 out of 25 cities that stood out for inspiring romance and attracting diners on the website OpenTable.com. Criteria: percentage of people who dined out on Valentine's Day in 2018; percentage of romantic restaurants as rated by OpenTable diner reviews; and percentage of tables seated for two. *OpenTable, "25 Most Romantic Cities in America for 2019," February 7, 2019*

- Madison was selected as one of America's best cities for singles by the readers of *Travel + Leisure* in their annual "America's Favorite Cities" survey. Criteria included good-looking locals, cool shopping, an active bar scene and hipster-magnet coffee bars. *Travel + Leisure, "Best Cities in America for Singles," July 21, 2017*

Education Rankings

- Personal finance website *WalletHub* analyzed the 150 largest U.S. metropolitan statistical areas to determine where the most educated Americans are putting their degrees to work. Criteria: education levels; percentage of workers with degrees; education quality and attainment gap; public school quality rankings; quality and enrollment of each metro area's universities. Madison was ranked #4 (#1 = most educated city). *www.WalletHub.com, "Most & Least Educated Cities in America," July 18, 2022*

- Madison was selected as one of America's most literate cities. The city ranked #10 out of the 84 largest U.S. cities. Criteria: number of booksellers; library resources; Internet resources; educational attainment; periodical publishing resources; newspaper circulation. *Central Connecticut State University, "America's Most Literate Cities, 2018," February 2019*

Health/Fitness Rankings

- For each of the 100 largest cities in the United States, the American Fitness Index®, compiled in partnership between the American College of Sports Medicine and the Elevance Health Foundation, evaluated community infrastructure and 34 health behaviors including preventive health, levels of chronic disease conditions, food insecurity, sleep quality, pedestrian safety, air quality, and community/environment resources that support physical activity. Madison ranked #2 for "community fitness." *americanfitnessindex.org, "2022 ACSM American Fitness Index Summary Report," July 12, 2022*

- Madison was identified as a "2022 Spring Allergy Capital." The area ranked #89 out of 100. Three groups of factors were used to identify the most challenging cities for people with allergies during the spring season: annual spring pollen scores; over the counter allergy medicine use; number of board-certified allergy specialists. *Asthma and Allergy Foundation of America, "Spring Allergy Capitals 2022," March 2, 2022*

- Madison was identified as a "2022 Fall Allergy Capital." The area ranked #86 out of 100. Three groups of factors were used to identify the most challenging cities for people with allergies during the fall season: annual fall pollen scores; over the counter allergy medicine use; number of board-certified allergy specialists. *Asthma and Allergy Foundation of America, "Fall Allergy Capitals 2022," March 2, 2022*

- Madison was identified as a "2022 Asthma Capital." The area ranked #96 out of the nation's 100 largest metropolitan areas. Criteria: estimated asthma prevalence; asthma-related mortality; and ER visits due to asthma. Risk factors analyzed but not factored in the rankings: annual pollen score; annual air quality; public smoking laws; access to board-certified asthma specialists; rescue and controller medication use; uninsured rate; poverty rate. *Asthma and Allergy Foundation of America, "Asthma Capitals 2022: The Most Challenging Places to Live With Asthma," September 14, 2022*

Real Estate Rankings

- *WalletHub* compared the most populated U.S. cities to determine which had the best markets for real estate agents. Madison ranked #60 where demand was high and pay was the best. Criteria: sales per agent; annual median wage for real-estate agents; monthly average starting salary for real estate agents; real estate job density and competition; unemployment rate; home turnover rate; housing-market health index; and other relevant metrics. *www.WalletHub.com, "2021 Best Places to Be a Real Estate Agent," May 12, 2021*

- Madison was ranked #71 out of 235 metro areas in terms of housing affordability in 2022 by the National Association of Home Builders (#1 = most affordable). Criteria: the share of homes sold in that area affordable to a family earning the local median income, based on standard mortgage underwriting criteria. *National Association of Home Builders®, NAHB-Wells Fargo Housing Opportunity Index, 4th Quarter 2022*

Safety Rankings

- Allstate ranked the 200 largest cities in America in terms of driver safety. Madison ranked #11. Criteria: internal property damage claims over a two-year period from January 2016 to December 2017. The report helps increase the importance of safety and awareness behind the wheel. *Allstate, "Allstate America's Best Drivers Report, 2019" June 24, 2019*

- The National Insurance Crime Bureau ranked 390 metro areas in the U.S. in terms of per capita rates of vehicle theft. The Madison metro area ranked #208 (#1 = highest rate). Criteria: number of vehicle theft offenses per 100,000 inhabitants in 2021. *National Insurance Crime Bureau, "Hot Spots 2021," September 1, 2022*

Seniors/Retirement Rankings

- From its Best Cities for Successful Aging indexes, the Milken Institute generated rankings for metropolitan areas, weighing data in nine categories—health care, wellness, living arrangements, transportation and convenience, financial characteristics, education, employment, community engagement, and overall livability. The Madison metro area was ranked #2 overall in the large metro area category. *Milken Institute, "Best Cities for Successful Aging, 2017" March 14, 2017*

- Madison made the 2022 *Forbes* list of "25 Best Places to Retire." Criteria, focused on overall affordability as well as quality of life indicators, include: housing/living costs compared to the national average and state taxes; air quality; crime rates; home price appreciation; risk associated with climate-change/natural hazards; availability of medical care; bikeability; walkability; healthy living. *Forbes.com, "The Best Places to Retire in 2022," May 13, 2022*

Sports/Recreation Rankings

- Madison was chosen as one of America's best cities for bicycling. The city ranked #8 out of 50. Criteria: cycling infrastructure that is safe and friendly for all ages; energy and bike culture. The editors evaluated cities with populations of 100,000 or more. *Bicycling, "The 50 Best Bike Cities in America," October 10, 2018*

Women/Minorities Rankings

- Personal finance website *WalletHub* compared more than 180 U.S. cities across two key dimensions, "Hispanic Business-Friendliness" and "Hispanic Purchasing Power," to arrive at the most favorable conditions for Hispanic entrepreneurs. Madison was ranked #100 out of 182. Criteria includes: share of Hispanic-Owned Businesses; Hispanic entrepreneurship rate to median annual income of Hispanics; Small Business-Friendliness score; cost of living; and number of Hispanics with at least a bachelor's degree. *WalletHub.com, "2019's Best Cities for Hispanic Entrepreneurs," May 1, 2019*

Miscellaneous Rankings

- *MoveHub* ranked 446 hipster cities across 20 countries, using its new and improved *alternative* Hipster Index and Madison came out as #30 among the top 50. Criteria: population over 150,000; number of vintage boutiques; density of tattoo parlors; vegan places to eat; coffee shops; and density of vinyl record stores. *www.movehub.com, "The Hipster Index: Brighton Pips Portland to Global Top Spot," July 28, 2021*

- Madison was selected as a 2022 Digital Cities Survey winner. The city ranked #6 in the large city (250,000 to 499,999 population) category. The survey examined and assessed how city governments are utilizing technology to continue innovation, engage with residents, and persevere through the challenges of the pandemic. Survey questions focused on ten initiatives: cybersecurity; citizen experience; disaster recovery; business intelligence; IT personnel; data governance; business automation; IT governance; infrastructure modernization; and broadband connectivity. *Center for Digital Government, "2022 Digital Cities Survey," November 10, 2022*

- *WalletHub* compared the 150 most populated U.S. cities to determine their operating efficiency. A "Quality of Services" score was constructed for each city and then divided by the total budget per capita to reveal which were managed the best. Madison ranked #24. Criteria: financial stability; economy; education; safety; health; infrastructure and pollution. *www.WalletHub.com, "2022's Best-& Worst-Run Cities in America," June 21, 2022*

Business Environment

DEMOGRAPHICS

Population Growth

Area	1990 Census	2000 Census	2010 Census	2020 Census	Population Growth (%) 1990-2020	Population Growth (%) 2010-2020
City	193,451	208,054	233,209	269,840	39.5	15.7
MSA[1]	432,323	501,774	568,593	680,796	57.5	19.7
U.S.	248,709,873	281,421,906	308,745,538	331,449,281	33.3	7.4

Note: (1) Figures cover the Madison, WI Metropolitan Statistical Area
Source: U.S. Census Bureau, 1990 Census, 2000 Census, 2010 Census, 2020 Census

Race

Area	White Alone[2] (%)	Black Alone[2] (%)	Asian Alone[2] (%)	AIAN[3] Alone[2] (%)	NHOPI[4] Alone[2] (%)	Other Race Alone[2] (%)	Two or More Races (%)
City	71.0	7.4	9.5	0.5	0.1	3.8	7.8
MSA[1]	80.2	4.7	5.4	0.4	0.0	2.9	6.4
U.S.	61.6	12.4	6.0	1.1	0.2	8.4	10.2

Note: (1) Figures cover the Madison, WI Metropolitan Statistical Area; (2) Alone is defined as not being in combination with one or more other races; (3) American Indian and Alaska Native; (4) Native Hawaiian and Other Pacific Islander
Source: U.S. Census Bureau, 2020 Census

Hispanic or Latino Origin

Area	Total (%)	Mexican (%)	Puerto Rican (%)	Cuban (%)	Other (%)
City	7.8	4.5	0.7	0.2	2.4
MSA[1]	6.1	3.7	0.5	0.1	1.7
U.S.	18.4	11.2	1.8	0.7	4.7

Note: Persons of Hispanic or Latino origin can be of any race; (1) Figures cover the Madison, WI Metropolitan Statistical Area
Source: U.S. Census Bureau, 2017-2021 American Community Survey 5-Year Estimates

Age

Area	Under Age 5	Age 5–19	Age 20–34	Age 35–44	Age 45–54	Age 55–64	Age 65–74	Age 75–84	Age 85+	Median Age
City	5.0	16.4	33.7	12.6	9.4	9.6	8.1	3.5	1.6	32.0
MSA[1]	5.3	18.3	23.6	13.3	11.5	12.3	9.6	4.2	1.8	36.9
U.S.	5.6	19.2	20.2	12.7	12.4	13.1	10.0	4.9	1.9	38.8

Note: (1) Figures cover the Madison, WI Metropolitan Statistical Area
Source: U.S. Census Bureau, 2020 Census

Disability by Age

Area	All Ages	Under 18 Years Old	18 to 64 Years Old	65 Years and Over
City	8.3	4.4	6.4	25.0
MSA[1]	8.9	4.2	6.9	24.6
U.S.	12.6	4.4	10.3	33.4

Note: Figures show percent of the civilian noninstitutionalized population that reported having a disability. Disability status is determined from six types of difficulty: vision, hearing, cognitive, ambulatory, self-care, and independent living. For children under 5 years old, hearing and vision difficulty are used to determine disability status. For children between the ages of 5 and 14, disability status is determined from hearing, vision, cognitive, ambulatory, and self-care difficulties. For people aged 15 years and older, they are considered to have a disability if they have difficulty with any one of the six difficulty types; Note: (1) Figures cover the Madison, WI Metropolitan Statistical Area
Source: U.S. Census Bureau, 2017-2021 American Community Survey 5-Year Estimates

Ancestry

Area	German	Irish	English	American	Italian	Polish	French[2]	Scottish	Dutch
City	29.4	12.0	8.8	2.0	4.0	5.5	2.4	1.8	1.8
MSA[1]	35.2	12.9	9.1	2.7	3.6	5.1	2.5	1.6	1.7
U.S.	12.8	9.6	8.1	5.7	5.0	2.7	2.2	1.6	1.1

Note: Figures are the percentage of the total population reporting a particular ancestry. The nine most commonly reported ancestries in the U.S. are shown. Figures include multiple ancestries (e.g. if a person reported being Irish and Italian, they were included in both columns); (1) Figures cover the Madison, WI Metropolitan Statistical Area; (2) Excludes Basque
Source: U.S. Census Bureau, 2017-2021 American Community Survey 5-Year Estimates

Foreign-born Population

Area	Percent of Population Born in								
	Any Foreign Country	Asia	Mexico	Europe	Caribbean	Central America[2]	South America	Africa	Canada
City	12.0	6.2	1.4	1.6	0.2	0.3	1.0	1.0	0.3
MSA[1]	7.6	3.5	1.2	1.0	0.1	0.2	0.6	0.6	0.2
U.S.	13.6	4.2	3.3	1.1	1.4	1.1	1.1	0.8	0.2

Note: (1) Figures cover the Madison, WI Metropolitan Statistical Area; (2) Excludes Mexico.
Source: U.S. Census Bureau, 2017-2021 American Community Survey 5-Year Estimates

Household Size

Area	Persons in Household (%)							Average Household Size
	One	Two	Three	Four	Five	Six	Seven or More	
City	37.7	35.3	12.4	9.4	3.5	1.0	0.6	2.20
MSA[1]	31.5	36.8	13.7	11.4	4.4	1.4	0.8	2.30
U.S.	28.1	33.8	15.5	12.9	6.0	2.3	1.4	2.60

Note: (1) Figures cover the Madison, WI Metropolitan Statistical Area
Source: U.S. Census Bureau, 2017-2021 American Community Survey 5-Year Estimates

Household Relationships

Area	House-holder	Opposite-sex Spouse	Same-sex Spouse	Opposite-sex Unmarried Partner	Same-sex Unmarried Partner	Child[2]	Grand-child	Other Relatives	Non-relatives
City	44.8	14.5	0.4	3.8	0.3	19.7	0.7	2.4	8.2
MSA[1]	42.2	18.6	0.3	3.3	0.2	25.0	0.8	2.1	4.5
U.S.	38.3	17.5	0.2	2.5	0.2	28.3	2.4	4.8	3.4

Note: Figures are percent of the total population; (1) Figures cover the Madison, WI Metropolitan Statistical Area; (2) Includes biological, adopted, and stepchildren of the householder
Source: U.S. Census Bureau, 2020 Census

Gender

Area	Males	Females	Males per 100 Females
City	133,922	135,918	98.5
MSA[1]	338,757	342,039	99.0
U.S.	162,685,811	168,763,470	96.4

Note: (1) Figures cover the Madison, WI Metropolitan Statistical Area
Source: U.S. Census Bureau, 2020 Census

Marital Status

Area	Never Married	Now Married[2]	Separated	Widowed	Divorced
City	50.3	37.2	0.7	3.3	8.5
MSA[1]	37.1	48.2	0.8	4.1	9.9
U.S.	33.8	48.0	1.8	5.6	10.8

Note: Figures are percentages and cover the population 15 years of age and older; (1) Figures cover the Madison, WI Metropolitan Statistical Area; (2) Excludes separated
Source: U.S. Census Bureau, 2017-2021 American Community Survey 5-Year Estimates

Religious Groups by Family

Area	Catholic	Baptist	Methodist	LDS[2]	Pentecostal	Lutheran	Islam	Adventist	Other
MSA[1]	14.4	0.5	2.0	0.7	0.2	9.2	1.2	0.7	8.4
U.S.	18.7	7.3	3.0	2.0	1.8	1.7	1.3	1.3	11.6

Note: Figures are the number of adherents as a percentage of the total population and cover the eight largest religious groups in the U.S; (1) Figures cover the Madison, WI Metropolitan Statistical Area; (2) Church of Jesus Christ of Latter-day Saints
Sources: 2020 U.S. Religion Census, Association of Statisticians of American Religious Bodies; The Association of Religion Data Archives (ARDA)

Religious Groups by Tradition

Area	Catholic	Evangelical Protestant	Mainline Protestant	Black Protestant	Islam	Judaism	Hinduism	Orthodox	Buddhism
MSA[1]	14.4	8.0	10.6	0.2	1.2	0.4	0.1	0.1	0.9
U.S.	18.7	16.5	5.2	2.3	1.3	0.6	0.4	0.4	0.3

Note: Figures are the number of adherents as a percentage of the total population; (1) Figures cover the Madison, WI Metropolitan Statistical Area
Sources: 2020 U.S. Religion Census, Association of Statisticians of American Religious Bodies; The Association of Religion Data Archives (ARDA)

ECONOMY

Gross Metropolitan Product

Area	2020	2021	2022	2023	Rank[2]
MSA[1]	51.5	56.1	60.8	64.9	63

Note: Figures are in billions of dollars; (1) Figures cover the Madison, WI Metropolitan Statistical Area; (2) Rank is based on 2021 data and ranges from 1 to 381
Source: U.S. Conference of Mayors, U.S. Metro Economies: U.S. Metros Compared to Global and State Economies, June 2022

Economic Growth

Area	2018-20 (%)	2021 (%)	2022 (%)	2023 (%)	Rank[2]
MSA[1]	0.1	4.4	2.7	3.7	132
U.S.	-0.6	5.7	3.1	2.9	–

Note: Figures are real gross metropolitan product (GMP) growth rates and represent average annual percent change; (1) Figures cover the Madison, WI Metropolitan Statistical Area; (2) Rank is based on 2020 2-year average annual percent change and ranges from 1 to 381
Source: U.S. Conference of Mayors, U.S. Metro Economies: U.S. Metros Compared to Global and State Economies, June 2022

Metropolitan Area Exports

Area	2016	2017	2018	2019	2020	2021	Rank[2]
MSA[1]	2,204.8	2,187.7	2,460.2	2,337.6	2,450.5	2,756.3	89

Note: Figures are in millions of dollars; (1) Figures cover the Madison, WI Metropolitan Statistical Area; (2) Rank is based on 2021 data and ranges from 1 to 388
Source: U.S. Department of Commerce, International Trade Administration, Office of Trade and Economic Analysis, Industry and Analysis, Exports by Metropolitan Area, data extracted March 16, 2023

Building Permits

Area	Single-Family			Multi-Family			Total		
	2021	2022	Pct. Chg.	2021	2022	Pct. Chg.	2021	2022	Pct. Chg.
City	327	314	-4.0	3,299	2,046	-38.0	3,626	2,360	-34.9
MSA[1]	1,737	1,530	-11.9	5,457	4,049	-25.8	7,194	5,579	-22.4
U.S.	1,115,400	975,600	-12.5	621,600	689,500	10.9	1,737,000	1,665,100	-4.1

Note: (1) Figures cover the Madison, WI Metropolitan Statistical Area; Figures represent new, privately-owned housing units authorized (unadjusted data); All permit data are based on estimates with imputation
Source: U.S. Census Bureau, Manufacturing, Mining, and Construction Statistics, Building Permits, 2021, 2022

Bankruptcy Filings

Area	Business Filings			Nonbusiness Filings		
	2021	2022	% Chg.	2021	2022	% Chg.
Dane County	26	10	-61.5	436	383	-12.2
U.S.	14,347	13,481	-6.0	399,269	374,240	-6.3

Note: Business filings include Chapter 7, Chapter 9, Chapter 11, Chapter 12, Chapter 13, Chapter 15, and Section 304; Nonbusiness filings include Chapter 7, Chapter 11, and Chapter 13
Source: Administrative Office of the U.S. Courts, Business and Nonbusiness Bankruptcy, County Cases Commenced by Chapter of the Bankruptcy Code, During the 12-Month Period Ending December 31, 2021 and Business and Nonbusiness Bankruptcy, County Cases Commenced by Chapter of the Bankruptcy Code, During the 12-Month Period Ending December 31, 2022

Housing Vacancy Rates

Area	Gross Vacancy Rate[2] (%)			Year-Round Vacancy Rate[3] (%)			Rental Vacancy Rate[4] (%)			Homeowner Vacancy Rate[5] (%)		
	2020	2021	2022	2020	2021	2022	2020	2021	2022	2020	2021	2022
MSA[1]	n/a	n/a	n/a	n/a	n/a	n/a	n/a	n/a	n/a	n/a	n/a	n/a
U.S.	10.6	10.8	10.5	8.2	8.4	8.2	6.3	6.1	5.8	1.0	0.9	0.8

Note: (1) Figures cover the Madison, WI Metropolitan Statistical Area; (2) The percentage of the total housing inventory that is vacant; (3) The percentage of the housing inventory (excluding seasonal units) that is year-round vacant; (4) The percentage of rental inventory that is vacant for rent; (5) The percentage of homeowner inventory that is vacant for sale; n/a not available
Source: U.S. Census Bureau, Housing Vacancies and Homeownership Annual Statistics: 2020, 2021, 2022

INCOME

Income

Area	Per Capita ($)	Median Household ($)	Average Household ($)
City	42,693	70,466	94,746
MSA[1]	43,359	77,519	100,891
U.S.	37,638	69,021	97,196

Note: (1) Figures cover the Madison, WI Metropolitan Statistical Area
Source: U.S. Census Bureau, 2017-2021 American Community Survey 5-Year Estimates

Household Income Distribution

Area	Percent of Households Earning							
	Under $15,000	$15,000 -$24,999	$25,000 -$34,999	$35,000 -$49,999	$50,000 -$74,999	$75,000 -$99,999	$100,000 -$149,999	$150,000 and up
City	10.0	6.8	7.5	11.0	17.5	14.1	16.9	16.0
MSA[1]	6.9	6.0	6.7	11.1	17.7	14.3	18.9	18.3
U.S.	9.4	7.8	8.2	11.4	16.8	12.8	16.3	17.3

Note: (1) Figures cover the Madison, WI Metropolitan Statistical Area
Source: U.S. Census Bureau, 2017-2021 American Community Survey 5-Year Estimates

Poverty Rate

Area	All Ages	Under 18 Years Old	18 to 64 Years Old	65 Years and Over
City	16.6	13.0	19.2	7.1
MSA[1]	10.1	9.0	11.5	5.8
U.S.	12.6	17.0	11.8	9.6

Note: Figures are percentage of people whose income during the past 12 months was below the poverty level;
(1) Figures cover the Madison, WI Metropolitan Statistical Area
Source: U.S. Census Bureau, 2017-2021 American Community Survey 5-Year Estimates

EMPLOYMENT

Labor Force and Employment

Area	Civilian Labor Force			Workers Employed		
	Dec. 2021	Dec. 2022	% Chg.	Dec. 2021	Dec. 2022	% Chg.
City	162,642	161,298	-0.8	160,375	158,871	-0.9
MSA[1]	400,355	395,887	-1.1	393,718	389,430	-1.1
U.S.	161,696,000	164,224,000	1.6	155,732,000	158,872,000	2.0

Note: Data is not seasonally adjusted and covers workers 16 years of age and older; (1) Figures cover the Madison, WI Metropolitan Statistical Area
Source: Bureau of Labor Statistics, Local Area Unemployment Statistics

Unemployment Rate

Area	2022											
	Jan.	Feb.	Mar.	Apr.	May	Jun.	Jul.	Aug.	Sep.	Oct.	Nov.	Dec.
City	1.9	2.0	2.0	1.9	2.2	2.8	2.5	2.4	2.6	2.2	2.0	1.5
MSA[1]	2.3	2.5	2.4	2.1	2.2	2.8	2.5	2.5	2.6	2.2	2.0	1.6
U.S.	4.4	4.1	3.8	3.3	3.4	3.8	3.8	3.8	3.3	3.4	3.4	3.3

Note: Data is not seasonally adjusted and covers workers 16 years of age and older; (1) Figures cover the Madison, WI Metropolitan Statistical Area
Source: Bureau of Labor Statistics, Local Area Unemployment Statistics

Average Wages

Occupation	$/Hr.	Occupation	$/Hr.
Accountants and Auditors	37.27	Maintenance and Repair Workers	22.80
Automotive Mechanics	24.24	Marketing Managers	70.25
Bookkeepers	22.60	Network and Computer Systems Admin.	43.19
Carpenters	27.63	Nurses, Licensed Practical	25.83
Cashiers	14.13	Nurses, Registered	41.46
Computer Programmers	56.02	Nursing Assistants	18.71
Computer Systems Analysts	44.74	Office Clerks, General	20.66
Computer User Support Specialists	29.94	Physical Therapists	43.49
Construction Laborers	23.76	Physicians	152.61
Cooks, Restaurant	16.05	Plumbers, Pipefitters and Steamfitters	35.91
Customer Service Representatives	20.72	Police and Sheriff's Patrol Officers	35.34
Dentists	83.83	Postal Service Mail Carriers	27.00
Electricians	34.25	Real Estate Sales Agents	33.85
Engineers, Electrical	46.88	Retail Salespersons	16.03
Fast Food and Counter Workers	12.42	Sales Representatives, Technical/Scientific	36.52
Financial Managers	72.88	Secretaries, Exc. Legal/Medical/Executive	21.15
First-Line Supervisors of Office Workers	33.73	Security Guards	17.01
General and Operations Managers	65.92	Surgeons	n/a
Hairdressers/Cosmetologists	17.32	Teacher Assistants, Exc. Postsecondary*	16.63
Home Health and Personal Care Aides	14.89	Teachers, Secondary School, Exc. Sp. Ed.*	29.79
Janitors and Cleaners	16.04	Telemarketers	n/a
Landscaping/Groundskeeping Workers	18.73	Truck Drivers, Heavy/Tractor-Trailer	25.52
Lawyers	66.28	Truck Drivers, Light/Delivery Services	20.60
Maids and Housekeeping Cleaners	14.97	Waiters and Waitresses	15.98

Note: Wage data covers the Madison, WI Metropolitan Statistical Area; (*) Hourly wages were calculated from annual wage data based on a 40 hour work week; n/a not available.
Source: Bureau of Labor Statistics, Metro Area Occupational Employment & Wage Estimates, May 2022

Employment by Industry

Sector	MSA[1]		U.S.
	Number of Employees	Percent of Total	Percent of Total
Construction, Mining, and Logging	20,200	4.8	5.4
Private Education and Health Services	51,400	12.3	16.1
Financial Activities	24,400	5.8	5.9
Government	90,900	21.7	14.5
Information	19,300	4.6	2.0
Leisure and Hospitality	33,300	7.9	10.3
Manufacturing	39,100	9.3	8.4
Other Services	21,000	5.0	3.7
Professional and Business Services	52,700	12.6	14.7
Retail Trade	39,900	9.5	10.2
Transportation, Warehousing, and Utilities	11,800	2.8	4.9
Wholesale Trade	15,400	3.7	3.9

Note: Figures are non-farm employment as of December 2022. Figures are not seasonally adjusted and include workers 16 years of age and older; (1) Figures cover the Madison, WI Metropolitan Statistical Area
Source: Bureau of Labor Statistics, Current Employment Statistics, Employment, Hours, and Earnings

Employment by Occupation

Occupation Classification	City (%)	MSA[1] (%)	U.S. (%)
Management, Business, Science, and Arts	56.0	50.5	40.3
Natural Resources, Construction, and Maintenance	4.0	6.5	8.7
Production, Transportation, and Material Moving	8.1	10.7	13.1
Sales and Office	16.8	18.4	20.9
Service	15.1	14.0	17.0

Note: Figures cover employed civilians 16 years of age and older; (1) Figures cover the Madison, WI Metropolitan Statistical Area
Source: U.S. Census Bureau, 2017-2021 American Community Survey 5-Year Estimates

Occupations with Greatest Projected Employment Growth: 2022 – 2024

Occupation[1]	2022 Employment	2024 Projected Employment	Numeric Employment Change	Percent Employment Change
Laborers and Freight, Stock, and Material Movers, Hand	64,310	67,940	3,630	5.6
Maids and Housekeeping Cleaners	22,820	26,320	3,500	15.3
Fast Food and Counter Workers	58,230	61,720	3,490	6.0
Farmworkers and Laborers, Crop, Nursery, and Greenhouse	48,090	51,190	3,100	6.4
Cooks, Restaurant	23,140	25,660	2,520	10.9
Childcare Workers	14,930	17,390	2,460	16.5
Industrial Truck and Tractor Operators	17,330	19,540	2,210	12.8
Home Health and Personal Care Aides	75,480	77,560	2,080	2.8
Waiters and Waitresses	34,590	36,650	2,060	6.0
Stockers and Order Fillers	47,340	48,990	1,650	3.5

Note: Projections cover Wisconsin; (1) Sorted by numeric employment change
Source: www.projectionscentral.com, State Occupational Projections, 2022–2024 Short-Term Projections

Fastest-Growing Occupations: 2022 – 2024

Occupation[1]	2022 Employment	2024 Projected Employment	Numeric Employment Change	Percent Employment Change
Personal Care and Service Workers, All Other	140	240	100	71.4
Ushers, Lobby Attendants, and Ticket Takers	1,350	1,630	280	20.7
Childcare Workers	14,930	17,390	2,460	16.5
Maids and Housekeeping Cleaners	22,820	26,320	3,500	15.3
Industrial Truck and Tractor Operators	17,330	19,540	2,210	12.8
Reservation and Transportation Ticket Agents and Travel Clerks	1,000	1,120	120	12.0
Travel Agents	820	910	90	11.0
Cooks, Restaurant	23,140	25,660	2,520	10.9
Medical Scientists, Except Epidemiologists	1,360	1,500	140	10.3
Athletes and Sports Competitors	580	640	60	10.3

Note: Projections cover Wisconsin; (1) Sorted by percent employment change and excludes occupations with numeric employment change less than 50
Source: www.projectionscentral.com, State Occupational Projections, 2022–2024 Short-Term Projections

CITY FINANCES

City Government Finances

Component	2020 ($000)	2020 ($ per capita)
Total Revenues	616,551	2,374
Total Expenditures	651,051	2,507
Debt Outstanding	1,003,653	3,865
Cash and Securities[1]	741,463	2,855

Note: (1) Cash and security holdings of a government at the close of its fiscal year, including those of its dependent agencies, utilities, and liquor stores.
Source: U.S. Census Bureau, State & Local Government Finances 2020

City Government Revenue by Source

Source	2020 ($000)	2020 ($ per capita)	2020 (%)
General Revenue			
From Federal Government	34,910	134	5.7
From State Government	78,206	301	12.7
From Local Governments	16,018	62	2.6
Taxes			
Property	255,410	984	41.4
Sales and Gross Receipts	19,021	73	3.1
Personal Income	0	0	0.0
Corporate Income	0	0	0.0
Motor Vehicle License	0	0	0.0
Other Taxes	8,922	34	1.4
Current Charges	112,271	432	18.2
Liquor Store	0	0	0.0
Utility	52,229	201	8.5

Source: U.S. Census Bureau, State & Local Government Finances 2020

City Government Expenditures by Function

Function	2020 ($000)	2020 ($ per capita)	2020 (%)
General Direct Expenditures			
Air Transportation	0	0	0.0
Corrections	0	0	0.0
Education	0	0	0.0
Employment Security Administration	0	0	0.0
Financial Administration	6,776	26	1.0
Fire Protection	57,538	221	8.8
General Public Buildings	2,644	10	0.4
Governmental Administration, Other	19,349	74	3.0
Health	16,935	65	2.6
Highways	88,909	342	13.7
Hospitals	0	0	0.0
Housing and Community Development	57,241	220	8.8
Interest on General Debt	27,704	106	4.3
Judicial and Legal	3,025	11	0.5
Libraries	26,549	102	4.1
Parking	12,632	48	1.9
Parks and Recreation	69,141	266	10.6
Police Protection	80,193	308	12.3
Public Welfare	0	0	0.0
Sewerage	43,960	169	6.8
Solid Waste Management	15,150	58	2.3
Veterans' Services	0	0	0.0
Liquor Store	0	0	0.0
Utility	91,369	351	14.0

Source: U.S. Census Bureau, State & Local Government Finances 2020

TAXES

State Corporate Income Tax Rates

State	Tax Rate (%)	Income Brackets ($)	Num. of Brackets	Financial Institution Tax Rate (%)[a]	Federal Income Tax Ded.
Wisconsin	7.9	Flat rate	1	7.9	No

Note: Tax rates as of January 1, 2023; (a) Rates listed are the corporate income tax rate applied to financial institutions or excise taxes based on income. Some states have other taxes based upon the value of deposits or shares.
Source: Federation of Tax Administrators, State Corporate Income Tax Rates, January 1, 2023

State Individual Income Tax Rates

State	Tax Rate (%)	Income Brackets ($)	Personal Exemptions ($)			Standard Ded. ($)	
			Single	Married	Depend.	Single	Married
Wisconsin (a)	3.54 - 7.65	13,810 - 304,170 (y)	700	1,400	700	12,760	23,620 (z)

Note: Tax rates as of January 1, 2023; Local- and county-level taxes are not included; Federal income tax is not deductible on state income tax returns; (a) 16 states have statutory provision for automatically adjusting to the rate of inflation the dollar values of the income tax brackets, standard deductions, and/or personal exemptions. Oregon does not index the income brackets for $125,000 and over; (y) The Wisconsin income brackets reported are for single individuals. For married taxpayers filing jointly, the same tax rates apply income brackets ranging from $18,420, to $405,550; (z) Alabama standard deduction is phased out for incomes over $25,000. Rhode Island exemptions & standard deductions phased out for incomes over $233,750; Wisconsin standard deduciton phases out for income over $16,989.
Source: Federation of Tax Administrators, State Individual Income Tax Rates, January 1, 2023

Various State Sales and Excise Tax Rates

State	State Sales Tax (%)	Gasoline[1] ($/gal.)	Cigarette[2] ($/pack)	Spirits[3] ($/gal.)	Wine[4] ($/gal.)	Beer[5] ($/gal.)	Recreational Marijuana (%)
Wisconsin	5	0.329	2.52	3.25	0.25	0.06	Not legal

Note: All tax rates as of January 1, 2023; (1) The American Petroleum Institute has developed a methodology for determining the average tax rate on a gallon of fuel. Rates may include any of the following: excise taxes, environmental fees, storage tank fees, other fees or taxes, general sales tax, and local taxes; (2) The federal excise tax of $1.0066 per pack and local taxes are not included; (3) Rates are those applicable to off-premise sales of 40% alcohol by volume (a.b.v.) distilled spirits in 750ml containers. Local excise taxes are excluded; (4) Rates are those applicable to off-premise sales of 11% a.b.v. non-carbonated wine in 750ml containers; (5) Rates are those applicable to off-premise sales of 4.7% a.b.v. beer in 12 ounce containers.
Source: Tax Foundation, 2023 Facts & Figures: How Does Your State Compare?

State Business Tax Climate Index Rankings

State	Overall Rank	Corporate Tax Rank	Individual Income Tax Rank	Sales Tax Rank	Property Tax Rank	Unemployment Insurance Tax Rank
Wisconsin	27	31	38	7	15	31

Note: The index is a measure of how each state's tax laws affect economic performance. The lower the rank, the more favorable a state's tax system is for business. States without a given tax are given a ranking of 1. The scores/rankings for the District of Columbia do not affect other states. The 2023 index represents the tax climate as of July 1, 2022.
Source: Tax Foundation, State Business Tax Climate Index 2023

TRANSPORTATION

Means of Transportation to Work

Area	Car/Truck/Van		Public Transportation			Bicycle	Walked	Other Means	Worked at Home
	Drove Alone	Car-pooled	Bus	Subway	Railroad				
City	60.5	6.6	7.0	0.0	0.1	3.6	8.9	1.3	12.1
MSA[1]	71.0	6.5	3.3	0.0	0.0	1.8	4.9	1.0	11.5
U.S.	73.2	8.6	2.0	1.6	0.5	0.5	2.5	1.5	9.7

Note: Figures are percentages and cover workers 16 years of age and older; (1) Figures cover the Madison, WI Metropolitan Statistical Area
Source: U.S. Census Bureau, 2017-2021 American Community Survey 5-Year Estimates

Travel Time to Work

Area	Less Than 10 Minutes	10 to 19 Minutes	20 to 29 Minutes	30 to 44 Minutes	45 to 59 Minutes	60 to 89 Minutes	90 Minutes or More
City	14.9	39.6	24.8	15.1	3.0	1.8	0.8
MSA[1]	15.9	32.2	24.8	18.2	5.3	2.5	1.1
U.S.	12.4	28.5	21.0	20.9	8.2	6.2	2.9

Note: Note: Figures are percentages and include workers 16 years old and over; (1) Figures cover the Madison, WI Metropolitan Statistical Area
Source: U.S. Census Bureau, 2017-2021 American Community Survey 5-Year Estimates

Key Congestion Measures

Measure	1990	2000	2010	2015	2020
Annual Hours of Delay, Total (000)	2,448	4,474	8,637	10,435	7,945
Annual Hours of Delay, Per Auto Commuter	17	23	33	37	28
Annual Congestion Cost, Per Auto Commuter ($)	268	377	576	641	514

Note: Covers the Madison WI urban area
Source: Texas A&M Transportation Institute, 2021 Urban Mobility Report

Freeway Travel Time Index

Measure	1985	1990	1995	2000	2005	2010	2015	2020
Urban Area Index[1]	1.08	1.08	1.09	1.11	1.14	1.14	1.15	1.05
Urban Area Rank[1,2]	40	62	77	79	73	71	67	85

Note: Freeway Travel Time Index—the ratio of travel time in the peak period to the travel time at free-flow conditions. For example, a value of 1.30 indicates a 20-minute free-flow trip takes 26 minutes in the peak (20 minutes x 1.30 = 26 minutes); (1) Covers the Madison WI urban area; (2) Rank is based on 101 larger urban areas (#1 = highest travel time index)
Source: Texas A&M Transportation Institute, 2021 Urban Mobility Report

Public Transportation

Agency Name / Mode of Transportation	Vehicles Operated in Maximum Service[1]	Annual Unlinked Passenger Trips[2] (in thous.)	Annual Passenger Miles[3] (in thous.)
Metro Transit System (Metro)			
Bus (directly operated)	139	5,390.0	18,811.2
Demand Response - Taxi	23	68.0	415.9

Note: (1) Number of revenue vehicles operated by the given mode and type of service to meet the annual maximum service requirement. This is the revenue vehicle count during the peak season of the year; on the week and day that maximum service is provided. Vehicles operated in maximum service (VOMS) exclude atypical days and one-time special events; (2) Number of passengers who boarded public transportation vehicles. Passengers are counted each time they board a vehicle no matter how many vehicles they use to travel from their origin to their destination. (3) Sum of the distances ridden by all passengers during the entire fiscal year.
Source: Federal Transit Administration, National Transit Database, 2021

Air Transportation

Airport Name and Code / Type of Service	Passenger Airlines[1]	Passenger Enplanements	Freight Carriers[2]	Freight (lbs)
Dane County Regional-Truax Field (MSN)				
Domestic service (U.S. carriers - 2022)	23	916,070	8	24,914,144
International service (U.S. carriers - 2021)	1	223	0	0

Note: (1) Includes all U.S.-based major, minor and commuter airlines that carried at least one passenger during the year; (2) Includes all U.S.-based airlines and freight carriers that transported at least one pound of freight during the year.
Source: Bureau of Transportation Statistics, The Intermodal Transportation Database, Air Carriers: T-100 Domestic Market (U.S. Carriers), 2022; Bureau of Transportation Statistics, The Intermodal Transportation Database, Air Carriers: T-100 International Market (U.S. Carriers), 2021

BUSINESSES

Major Business Headquarters

Company Name	Industry	Rankings	
		Fortune[1]	Forbes[2]
American Family Insurance Group	Insurance, property and casualty (stock)	251	-

Note: (1) Companies that produce a 10-K are ranked 1 to 500 based on 2021 revenue; (2) All private companies with at least $2 billion in annual revenue through the end of their most current fiscal year are ranked 1 to 246; companies listed are headquartered in the city; dashes indicate no ranking
Source: Fortune, "Fortune 500," 2022; Forbes, "America's Largest Private Companies," 2022

Fastest-Growing Businesses

According to *Inc.*, Madison is home to one of America's 500 fastest-growing private companies: **Lost Boys Interactive** (#494). Criteria: must be an independent, privately-held, for-profit, U.S. corporation, proprietorship or partnership as of December 31, 2021; revenues must be at least $100,000 in 2018 and $2 million in 2021; must have four-year operating/sales history. *Inc., "America's 500 Fastest-Growing Private Companies," 2022*

According to Deloitte, Madison is home to one of North America's 500 fastest-growing high-technology companies: **Exact Sciences Corporation** (#432). Companies are ranked by percentage growth in revenue over a four-year period. Criteria for inclusion: company must be headquartered within North America; must own proprietary intellectual property or technology that is sold to customers in products that contributes to a significant portion of the company's operating revenue; must have been in business for a minumum of four years with 2018 operating revenues of at least $50,000 USD/CD and 2021 operating revenues of at least $5 million USD/CD. *Deloitte, 2022 Technology Fast 500*[TM]

Living Environment

COST OF LIVING

Cost of Living Index

Composite Index	Groceries	Housing	Utilities	Trans-portation	Health Care	Misc. Goods/ Services
102.9	101.7	100.1	109.0	97.3	123.5	102.7

Note: The Cost of Living Index measures regional differences in the cost of consumer goods and services, excluding taxes and non-consumer expenditures, for professional and managerial households in the top income quintile. It is based on more than 50,000 prices covering almost 60 different items for which prices are collected three times a year by chambers of commerce, economic development organizations or university applied economic centers in each participating urban area. The numbers shown should be read as a percentage above or below the national average of 100. For example, a value of 115.4 in the groceries column indicates that grocery prices are 15.4% higher than the national average. Small differences in the index numbers should not be interpreted as significant; Figures cover the Madison WI urban area.
Source: The Council for Community and Economic Research, Cost of Living Index, 2022

Grocery Prices

Area[1]	T-Bone Steak ($/pound)	Frying Chicken ($/pound)	Whole Milk ($/half gal.)	Eggs ($/dozen)	Orange Juice ($/64 oz.)	Coffee ($/11.5 oz.)
City[2]	16.50	1.80	2.27	1.88	3.60	5.26
Avg.	13.81	1.59	2.43	2.25	3.85	4.95
Min.	10.17	0.90	1.51	1.30	2.90	3.46
Max.	19.35	3.30	4.32	4.32	5.31	8.59

*Note: (1) Values for the local area are compared with the average, minimum and maximum values for all 286 areas in the Cost of Living Index; (2) Figures cover the Madison WI urban area; **T-Bone Steak** (price per pound); **Frying Chicken** (price per pound, whole fryer); **Whole Milk** (half gallon carton); **Eggs** (price per dozen, Grade A, large); **Orange Juice** (64 oz. Tropicana or Florida Natural); **Coffee** (11.5 oz. can, vacuum-packed, Maxwell House, Hills Bros, or Folgers).*
Source: The Council for Community and Economic Research, Cost of Living Index, 2022

Housing and Utility Costs

Area[1]	New Home Price ($)	Apartment Rent ($/month)	All Electric ($/month)	Part Electric ($/month)	Other Energy ($/month)	Telephone ($/month)
City[2]	475,954	1,205	-	114.02	94.46	183.66
Avg.	450,913	1,371	176.41	99.93	76.96	190.22
Min.	229,283	546	100.84	31.56	27.15	174.27
Max.	2,434,977	4,569	356.86	249.59	272.24	208.31

*Note: (1) Values for the local area are compared with the average, minimum and maximum values for all 286 areas in the Cost of Living Index; (2) Figures cover the Madison WI urban area; **New Home Price** (2,400 sf living area, 8,000 sf lot, in urban area with full utilities); **Apartment Rent** (950 sf 2 bedroom/1.5 or 2 bath, unfurnished, excluding all utilities except water); **All Electric** (average monthly cost for an all-electric home); **Part Electric** (average monthly cost for a part-electric home); **Other Energy** (average monthly cost for natural gas, fuel oil, coal, wood, and any other forms of energy except electricity); **Telephone** (price includes the base monthly rate plus taxes and fees for three lines of mobile phone service).*
Source: The Council for Community and Economic Research, Cost of Living Index, 2022

Health Care, Transportation, and Other Costs

Area[1]	Doctor ($/visit)	Dentist ($/visit)	Optometrist ($/visit)	Gasoline ($/gallon)	Beauty Salon ($/visit)	Men's Shirt ($)
City[2]	207.78	115.45	65.67	3.59	54.45	43.08
Avg.	124.91	107.77	117.66	3.86	43.31	34.21
Min.	36.61	58.25	51.79	2.90	22.18	13.05
Max.	250.21	162.58	371.96	5.54	85.61	63.54

*Note: (1) Values for the local area are compared with the average, minimum and maximum values for all 286 areas in the Cost of Living Index; (2) Figures cover the Madison WI urban area; **Doctor** (general practitioners routine exam of an established patient); **Dentist** (adult teeth cleaning and periodic oral examination); **Optometrist** (full vision eye exam for established adult patient); **Gasoline** (one gallon regular unleaded, national brand, including all taxes, cash price at self-service pump if available); **Beauty Salon** (woman's shampoo, trim, and blow-dry); **Men's Shirt** (cotton/polyester dress shirt, pinpoint weave, long sleeves).*
Source: The Council for Community and Economic Research, Cost of Living Index, 2022

HOUSING

Homeownership Rate

Area	2015 (%)	2016 (%)	2017 (%)	2018 (%)	2019 (%)	2020 (%)	2021 (%)	2022 (%)
MSA[1]	n/a	n/a	n/a	n/a	n/a	n/a	n/a	n/a
U.S.	63.7	63.4	63.9	64.4	64.6	66.6	65.5	65.8

Note: (1) Figures cover the Madison, WI Metropolitan Statistical Area; n/a not available
Source: U.S. Census Bureau, Housing Vacancies and Homeownership Annual Statistics: 2015-2022

House Price Index (HPI)

Area	National Ranking[2]	Quarterly Change (%)	One-Year Change (%)	Five-Year Change (%)	Since 1991Q1 (%)
MSA[1]	121	-1.67	11.52	45.50	303.94
U.S.[3]	–	0.34	8.41	58.44	289.08

Note: The HPI is a weighted repeat sales index. It measures average price changes in repeat sales or refinancings on the same properties. This information is obtained by reviewing repeat mortgage transactions on single-family properties whose mortgages have been purchased or securitized by Fannie Mae or Freddie Mac since January 1975; (1) Figures cover the Madison, WI Metropolitan Statistical Area; (2) Rankings are based on annual percentage change for all metro areas containing at least 15,000 transactions over the last 10 years and ranges from 1 to 257; (3) figures based on a weighted average of Census Division estimates using a seasonally adjusted, purchase-only index; all figures are for the period ending December 31, 2022
Source: Federal Housing Finance Agency, Change in FHFA Metropolitan Area House Price Indexes, 2022Q4

Median Single-Family Home Prices

Area	2020	2021	2022[p]	Percent Change 2021 to 2022
MSA[1]	326.4	361.5	392.7	8.6
U.S. Average	300.2	357.1	392.6	9.9

Note: Figures are median sales prices of existing single-family homes in thousands of dollars; (p) preliminary; (1) Figures cover the Madison, WI Metropolitan Statistical Area
Source: National Association of Realtors, Median Sales Price of Existing Single-Family Homes for Metropolitan Areas, 4th Quarter 2022

Qualifying Income Based on Median Sales Price of Existing Single-Family Homes

Area	With 5% Down ($)	With 10% Down ($)	With 20% Down ($)
MSA[1]	113,690	107,706	95,739
U.S. Average	112,234	106,237	94,513

Note: Figures are preliminary; Qualifying income is based on a mortgage rate of 6.77%. Monthly principal and interest payment is limited to 25% of income; (1) Figures cover the Madison, WI Metropolitan Statistical Area
Source: National Association of Realtors, Qualifying Income Based on Median Sales Price of Existing Single-Family Homes for Metropolitan Areas, 4th Quarter 2022

Home Value

Area	Under $100,000	$100,000 -$199,999	$200,000 -$299,999	$300,000 -$399,999	$400,000 -$499,999	$500,000 -$999,999	$1,000,000 or more	Median ($)
City	3.4	18.6	35.0	22.5	10.9	8.3	1.3	277,800
MSA[1]	5.1	20.5	30.8	21.7	10.9	9.4	1.6	277,400
U.S.	16.2	24.2	20.1	13.6	8.3	13.6	4.1	244,900

Note: Figures are percentages except for median and cover owner-occupied housing units; (1) Figures cover the Madison, WI Metropolitan Statistical Area
Source: U.S. Census Bureau, 2017-2021 American Community Survey 5-Year Estimates

Year Housing Structure Built

Area	2020 or Later	2010 -2019	2000 -2009	1990 -1999	1980 -1989	1970 -1979	1960 -1969	1950 -1959	1940 -1949	Before 1940	Median Year
City	0.1	10.1	13.5	12.8	9.8	13.7	11.8	9.4	4.5	14.2	1977
MSA[1]	0.2	9.4	15.4	15.5	10.7	14.3	9.5	7.6	3.5	13.9	1981
U.S.	0.2	7.3	13.6	13.6	13.2	14.8	10.3	10.0	4.7	12.2	1979

Note: Figures are percentages except for Median Year; Note: (1) Figures cover the Madison, WI Metropolitan Statistical Area
Source: U.S. Census Bureau, 2017-2021 American Community Survey 5-Year Estimates

Gross Monthly Rent

Area	Under $500	$500 -$999	$1,000 -$1,499	$1,500 -$1,999	$2,000 -$2,499	$2,500 -$2,999	$3,000 and up	Median ($)
City	4.2	25.0	44.1	17.9	5.5	1.6	1.7	1,212
MSA[1]	4.5	31.5	41.8	15.7	4.3	1.1	1.2	1,143
U.S.	8.1	30.5	30.8	16.8	7.3	3.1	3.5	1,163

Note: Figures are percentages except for median; Gross rent is the contract rent plus the estimated average monthly cost of utilities (electricity, gas, and water and sewer) and fuels (oil, coal, kerosene, wood, etc.) if these are paid by the renter (or paid for the renter by someone else); (1) Figures cover the Madison, WI Metropolitan Statistical Area
Source: U.S. Census Bureau, 2017-2021 American Community Survey 5-Year Estimates

HEALTH

Health Risk Factors

Category	MSA[1] (%)	U.S. (%)
Adults aged 18–64 who have any kind of health care coverage	n/a	90.9
Adults who reported being in good or better health	n/a	85.2
Adults who have been told they have high blood cholesterol	n/a	35.7
Adults who have been told they have high blood pressure	n/a	32.4
Adults who are current smokers	n/a	14.4
Adults who currently use e-cigarettes	n/a	6.7
Adults who currently use chewing tobacco, snuff, or snus	n/a	3.5
Adults who are heavy drinkers[2]	n/a	6.3
Adults who are binge drinkers[3]	n/a	15.4
Adults who are overweight (BMI 25.0 - 29.9)	n/a	34.4
Adults who are obese (BMI 30.0 - 99.8)	n/a	33.9
Adults who participated in any physical activities in the past month	n/a	76.3

Note: (1) Figures for the Madison, WI Metropolitan Statistical Area were not available.
(2) Heavy drinkers are classified as adult men having more than 14 drinks per week and adult women having more than 7 drinks per week; (3) Binge drinkers are classified as males having five or more drinks on one occasion or females having four or more drinks on one occasion
Source: Centers for Disease Control and Prevention, Behaviorial Risk Factor Surveillance System, SMART: Selected Metropolitan Area Risk Trends, 2021

Acute and Chronic Health Conditions

Category	MSA[1] (%)	U.S. (%)
Adults who have ever been told they had a heart attack	n/a	4.0
Adults who have ever been told they have angina or coronary heart disease	n/a	3.8
Adults who have ever been told they had a stroke	n/a	3.0
Adults who have ever been told they have asthma	n/a	14.9
Adults who have ever been told they have arthritis	n/a	25.8
Adults who have ever been told they have diabetes[2]	n/a	10.9
Adults who have ever been told they had skin cancer	n/a	6.6
Adults who have ever been told they had any other types of cancer	n/a	7.5
Adults who have ever been told they have COPD	n/a	6.1
Adults who have ever been told they have kidney disease	n/a	3.0
Adults who have ever been told they have a form of depression	n/a	20.5

Note: (1) Figures for the Madison, WI Metropolitan Statistical Area were not available.
(2) Figures do not include pregnancy-related, borderline, or pre-diabetes
Source: Centers for Disease Control and Prevention, Behaviorial Risk Factor Surveillance System, SMART: Selected Metropolitan Area Risk Trends, 2021

Health Screening and Vaccination Rates

Category	MSA[1] (%)	U.S. (%)
Adults who have ever been tested for HIV	n/a	34.9
Adults who have had their blood cholesterol checked within the last five years	n/a	85.2
Adults aged 65+ who have had flu shot within the past year	n/a	68.6
Adults aged 65+ who have ever had a pneumonia vaccination	n/a	71.0

Note: (1) Figures for the Madison, WI Metropolitan Statistical Area were not available.
Source: Centers for Disease Control and Prevention, Behaviorial Risk Factor Surveillance System, SMART: Selected Metropolitan Area Risk Trends, 2021

Disability Status

Category	MSA[1] (%)	U.S. (%)
Adults who reported being deaf	n/a	7.2
Are you blind or have serious difficulty seeing, even when wearing glasses?	n/a	4.8
Are you limited in any way in any of your usual activities due to arthritis?	n/a	11.1
Do you have difficulty doing errands alone?	n/a	7.0
Do you have difficulty dressing or bathing?	n/a	3.6
Do you have serious difficulty concentrating/remembering/making decisions?	n/a	12.1
Do you have serious difficulty walking or climbing stairs?	n/a	12.8

Note: (1) Figures for the Madison, WI Metropolitan Statistical Area were not available.
Source: Centers for Disease Control and Prevention, Behaviorial Risk Factor Surveillance System, SMART: Selected Metropolitan Area Risk Trends, 2021

Mortality Rates for the Top 10 Causes of Death in the U.S.

ICD-10[a] Sub-Chapter	ICD-10[a] Code	Crude Mortality Rate[1] per 100,000 population	
		County[2]	U.S.
Malignant neoplasms	C00-C97	141.3	182.6
Ischaemic heart diseases	I20-I25	66.5	113.1
Other forms of heart disease	I30-I51	48.4	64.4
Other degenerative diseases of the nervous system	G30-G31	36.8	51.0
Cerebrovascular diseases	I60-I69	30.5	47.8
Other external causes of accidental injury	W00-X59	65.7	46.4
Chronic lower respiratory diseases	J40-J47	22.1	45.7
Organic, including symptomatic, mental disorders	F01-F09	42.7	35.9
Hypertensive diseases	I10-I15	15.0	35.0
Diabetes mellitus	E10-E14	13.6	29.6

Note: (a) ICD-10 = International Classification of Diseases 10th Revision; (1) Crude mortality rates are a three-year average covering 2019-2021; (2) Figures cover Dane County.
Source: Centers for Disease Control and Prevention, National Center for Health Statistics. National Vital Statistics System, Mortality 2018-2021 on CDC WONDER Online Database

Mortality Rates for Selected Causes of Death

ICD-10[a] Sub-Chapter	ICD-10[a] Code	Crude Mortality Rate[1] per 100,000 population	
		County[2]	U.S.
Assault	X85-Y09	2.2	7.0
Diseases of the liver	K70-K76	10.9	19.8
Human immunodeficiency virus (HIV) disease	B20-B24	Suppressed	1.5
Influenza and pneumonia	J09-J18	6.6	14.7
Intentional self-harm	X60-X84	11.8	14.3
Malnutrition	E40-E46	1.4	4.3
Obesity and other hyperalimentation	E65-E68	2.2	3.0
Renal failure	N17-N19	7.5	15.7
Transport accidents	V01-V99	7.6	13.6
Viral hepatitis	B15-B19	Suppressed	1.2

Note: (a) ICD-10 = International Classification of Diseases 10th Revision; (1) Crude mortality rates are a three-year average covering 2019-2021; (2) Figures cover Dane County; Data are suppressed when the data meet the criteria for confidentiality constraints; Crude mortality rates are flagged as unreliable when the rate would be calculated with a numerator of 20 or less.
Source: Centers for Disease Control and Prevention, National Center for Health Statistics. National Vital Statistics System, Mortality 2018-2021 on CDC WONDER Online Database

Health Insurance Coverage

Area	With Health Insurance	With Private Health Insurance	With Public Health Insurance	Without Health Insurance	Population Under Age 19 Without Health Insurance
City	96.0	82.9	23.3	4.0	2.4
MSA[1]	96.1	83.0	25.6	3.9	2.4
U.S.	91.2	67.8	35.4	8.8	5.3

Note: Figures are percentages that cover the civilian noninstitutionalized population; (1) Figures cover the Madison, WI Metropolitan Statistical Area
Source: U.S. Census Bureau, 2017-2021 American Community Survey 5-Year Estimates

Number of Medical Professionals

Area	MDs[3]	DOs[3,4]	Dentists	Podiatrists	Chiropractors	Optometrists
County[1] (number)	3,458	116	414	27	254	118
County[1] (rate[2])	615.0	20.6	73.4	4.8	45.0	20.9
U.S. (rate[2])	289.3	23.5	72.5	6.2	28.7	17.4

Note: Data as of 2021 unless noted; (1) Data covers Dane County; (2) Rate per 100,000 population; (3) Data as of 2020 and includes all active, non-federal physicians; (4) Doctor of Osteopathic Medicine
Source: U.S. Department of Health and Human Services, Health Resources and Services Administration, Bureau of Health Professions, Area Resource File (ARF) 2021-2022

Best Hospitals

According to *U.S. News,* the Madison, WI metro area is home to one of the best hospitals in the U.S.: **UW Health University Hospital** (4 adult specialties and 1 pediatric specialty). The hospital listed was nationally ranked in at least one of 15 adult or 10 pediatric specialties. The number of specialties shown cover the parent hospital. Only 164 U.S. hospitals performed well enough to be nationally ranked in one or more specialties. Twenty hospitals in the U.S. made the Honor Roll. The Best Hospitals Honor Roll takes both the national rankings and the procedure and condition ratings into account. Hospitals received points if they were nationally ranked in one of the 15 adult specialties—the higher they ranked, the more points they got—and how many ratings of "high performing" they earned in the 17 procedures and conditions. *U.S. News Online, "America's Best Hospitals 2022-23"*

According to *U.S. News,* the Madison, WI metro area is home to one of the best children's hospitals in the U.S.: **American Family Children's Hospital** (1 pediatric specialty). The hospital listed was highly ranked in at least one of 10 pediatric specialties. Eighty-six children's hospitals in the U.S. were nationally ranked in at least one specialty. Hospitals received points for being ranked in a specialty, and the 10 hospitals with the most points across the 10 specialties make up the Honor Roll. *U.S. News Online, "America's Best Children's Hospitals 2022-23"*

EDUCATION

Public School District Statistics

District Name	Schls	Pupils	Pupil/ Teacher Ratio	Minority Pupils[1] (%)	LEP/ELL[2] (%)	IEP[3] (%)
Madison Metropolitan SD	54	25,497	12.1	59.2	19.9	14.3

Note: Table includes school districts with 2,000 or more students; (1) Percentage of students that are not non-Hispanic white; (2) Percentage of students that are Limited English Proficient or English Language Learners (2018-19); (3) Percentage of students that have an Individualized Education Program (2019-20). Source: U.S. Department of Education, National Center for Education Statistics, Common Core of Data, Local Education Agency (School District) Universe Survey: School Year 2021-2022

Highest Level of Education

Area	Less than H.S.	H.S. Diploma	Some College, No Deg.	Associate Degree	Bachelor's Degree	Master's Degree	Prof. School Degree	Doctorate Degree
City	4.4	14.2	15.4	7.5	32.5	15.9	4.2	5.9
MSA[1]	4.3	20.6	17.5	9.8	28.8	12.3	3.1	3.5
U.S.	11.1	26.5	20.0	8.7	20.6	9.3	2.2	1.5

Note: Figures cover persons age 25 and over; (1) Figures cover the Madison, WI Metropolitan Statistical Area Source: U.S. Census Bureau, 2017-2021 American Community Survey 5-Year Estimates

Educational Attainment by Race

Area	High School Graduate or Higher (%)					Bachelor's Degree or Higher (%)				
	Total	White	Black	Asian	Hisp.[2]	Total	White	Black	Asian	Hisp.[2]
City	95.6	97.2	88.8	92.4	79.2	58.5	60.9	24.7	70.9	40.0
MSA[1]	95.7	96.8	90.1	90.5	77.2	47.7	48.1	25.2	68.5	30.6
U.S.	88.9	91.4	87.2	87.6	71.2	33.7	35.5	23.3	55.6	18.4

Note: Figures shown cover persons 25 years old and over; (1) Figures cover the Madison, WI Metropolitan Statistical Area; (2) People of Hispanic origin can be of any race Source: U.S. Census Bureau, 2017-2021 American Community Survey 5-Year Estimates

School Enrollment by Grade and Control

Area	Preschool (%)		Kindergarten (%)		Grades 1 - 4 (%)		Grades 5 - 8 (%)		Grades 9 - 12 (%)	
	Public	Private	Public	Private	Public	Private	Public	Private	Public	Private
City	51.2	48.8	87.9	12.1	88.7	11.3	88.1	11.9	90.6	9.4
MSA[1]	67.4	32.6	88.0	12.0	89.6	10.4	90.2	9.8	94.3	5.7
U.S.	58.8	41.2	86.3	13.7	88.3	11.7	88.6	11.4	89.4	10.6

Note: Figures shown cover persons 3 years old and over; (1) Figures cover the Madison, WI Metropolitan Statistical Area Source: U.S. Census Bureau, 2017-2021 American Community Survey 5-Year Estimates

Higher Education

Four-Year Colleges			Two-Year Colleges			Medical Schools[1]	Law Schools[2]	Voc/ Tech[3]
Public	Private Non-profit	Private For-profit	Public	Private Non-profit	Private For-profit			
2	2	0	0	0	0	1	1	4

Note: Figures cover institutions located within the Madison, WI Metropolitan Statistical Area and include main campuses only; (1) includes schools accredited by the Liaison Committee on Medical Education and the American Osteopathic Association's Commission on Osteopathic College Accreditation; (2) includes ABA-accredited schools, schools with provisional ABA accreditation, and state accredited schools; (3) includes all schools with programs that are less than 2 years. Source: National Center for Education Statistics, Integrated Postsecondary Education System (IPEDS), 2021-22; Wikipedia, List of Medical Schools in the United States, accessed April 10, 2023; Wikipedia, List of Law Schools in the United States, accessed April 10, 2023

According to *U.S. News & World Report,* the Madison, WI metro area is home to one of the top 200 national universities in the U.S.: **University of Wisconsin—Madison** (#38 tie). The indicators used to capture academic quality fall into a number of categories: assessment by administrators at peer institutions; retention of students; faculty resources; student selectivity; financial resources; alumni giving; high school counselor ratings of colleges; and graduation rate. *U.S. News & World Report, "America's Best Colleges 2023"*

According to *U.S. News & World Report,* the Madison, WI metro area is home to one of the top 100 law schools in the U.S.: **University of Wisconsin—Madison** (#43 tie). The rankings are based on a weighted average of 12 measures of quality: peer assessment score; assessment score by lawyers/judges; median LSAT scores; median undergrad GPA; acceptance rate; employment rates for graduates; placement success; bar passage rate; faculty resources; expenditures per student; student/faculty ratio; and library resources. *U.S. News & World Report, "America's Best Graduate Schools, Law, 2023"*

According to *U.S. News & World Report,* the Madison, WI metro area is home to one of the top 75 medical schools for research in the U.S.: **University of Wisconsin—Madison** (#37 tie). The rankings are based on a weighted average of 11 measures of quality: quality assessment; peer assessment score; assessment score by residency directors; research activity; total research activity; average research activity per faculty member; student selectivity; median MCAT total score; median undergraduate GPA; acceptance rate; and faculty resources. *U.S. News & World Report, "America's Best Graduate Schools, Medical, 2023"*

According to *U.S. News & World Report,* the Madison, WI metro area is home to one of the top 75 business schools in the U.S.: **University of Wisconsin—Madison** (#47 tie). The rankings are based on a weighted average of the following nine measures: quality assessment; peer assessment; recruiter assessment; placement success; mean starting salary and bonus; student selectivity; mean GMAT and GRE scores; mean undergraduate GPA; and acceptance rate. *U.S. News & World Report, "America's Best Graduate Schools, Business, 2023"*

EMPLOYERS

Major Employers

Company Name	Industry
American Family Mutual Insurance Co.	Fire, marine, & casualty insurance
Community Living Alliance	Social services for the handicapped
Covence Laboratories	Druggists preparations
CUNA Mutual Insurance Society	Telephone communication, except radio
Kraft Foods Global	Luncheon meat from purchased meat
University of Wisconsin Hospitals	General medical & surgical hospitals
Veterans Health Administration	General medical & surgical hospitals
WI Dept of Workforce Development	Administration of social & manpower programs
Wisconsin Department of Administration	Administration of general economic programs
Wisconsin Department of Health Services	Administration of public health programs
Wisconsin Department of Natural Resources	Land, mineral, & wildlife conservation
Wisconsin Department of Transportation	Regulation, administration of transportation
Wisconsin Dept of Natural Resources	Land, mineral, & wildlife conservation
Wisconsin Physicians Srvc Ins Corp	Hospital & medical services plans

Note: Companies shown are located within the Madison, WI Metropolitan Statistical Area.
Source: Hoovers.com; Wikipedia

PUBLIC SAFETY

Crime Rate

Area	Total Crime	Violent Crime Rate				Property Crime Rate		
		Murder	Rape[3]	Robbery	Aggrav. Assault	Burglary	Larceny -Theft	Motor Vehicle Theft
City	3,099.3	3.8	28.2	62.8	225.7	497.5	2,034.7	246.6
Suburbs[1]	1,304.6	1.7	21.3	17.4	85.0	157.7	930.9	90.6
Metro[2]	2,007.2	2.5	24.0	35.2	140.1	290.7	1,363.0	151.7
U.S.	2,356.7	6.5	38.4	73.9	279.7	314.2	1,398.0	246.0

Note: Figures are crimes per 100,000 population; (1) All areas within the metro area that are located outside the city limits; (2) Figures cover the Madison, WI Metropolitan Statistical Area; (3) All figures shown were reported using the revised Uniform Crime Reporting (UCR) definition of rape; Due to the transition to the National Incident-Based Reporting System (NIBRS), limited city and metro area data was released for 2021.
Source: FBI Uniform Crime Reports, 2020

Hate Crimes

Area	Number of Quarters Reported	Number of Incidents per Bias Motivation					
		Race/Ethnicity/ Ancestry	Religion	Sexual Orientation	Disability	Gender	Gender Identity
City	4	4	0	1	0	0	0
U.S.	4	5,227	1,244	1,110	130	75	266

Note: Due to the transition to the National Incident-Based Reporting System (NIBRS), limited crime data was released for 2021.
Source: Federal Bureau of Investigation, Hate Crime Statistics 2020

Identity Theft Consumer Reports

Area	Reports	Reports per 100,000 Population	Rank[2]
MSA[1]	1,020	154	247
U.S.	1,108,609	339	-

Note: (1) Figures cover the Madison, WI Metropolitan Statistical Area; (2) Rank ranges from 1 to 391 where 1 indicates greatest number of identity theft reports per 100,000 population
Source: Federal Trade Commission, Consumer Sentinel Network Data Book 2022

Fraud and Other Consumer Reports

Area	Reports	Reports per 100,000 Population	Rank[2]
MSA[1]	5,622	852	177
U.S.	4,064,520	1,245	-

Note: (1) Figures cover the Madison, WI Metropolitan Statistical Area; (2) Rank ranges from 1 to 391 where 1 indicates greatest number of fraud and other consumer reports per 100,000 population
Source: Federal Trade Commission, Consumer Sentinel Network Data Book 2022

POLITICS

2020 Presidential Election Results

Area	Biden	Trump	Jorgensen	Hawkins	Other
Dane County	75.5	22.9	1.1	0.1	0.6
U.S.	51.3	46.8	1.2	0.3	0.5

Note: Results are percentages and may not add to 100% due to rounding
Source: Dave Leip's Atlas of U.S. Presidential Elections

SPORTS

Professional Sports Teams

Team Name	League	Year Established

No teams are located in the metro area
Source: Wikipedia, Major Professional Sports Teams of the United States and Canada, April 12, 2023

CLIMATE

Average and Extreme Temperatures

Temperature	Jan	Feb	Mar	Apr	May	Jun	Jul	Aug	Sep	Oct	Nov	Dec	Yr.
Extreme High (°F)	56	61	82	94	93	101	104	102	99	90	76	62	104
Average High (°F)	26	30	42	58	70	79	84	81	72	61	44	30	57
Average Temp. (°F)	17	21	32	46	57	67	72	69	61	50	36	23	46
Average Low (°F)	8	12	22	35	45	54	59	57	49	38	27	14	35
Extreme Low (°F)	-37	-28	-29	0	19	31	36	35	25	13	-8	-25	-37

Note: Figures cover the years 1948-1990
Source: National Climatic Data Center, International Station Meteorological Climate Summary, 9/96

Average Precipitation/Snowfall/Humidity

Precip./Humidity	Jan	Feb	Mar	Apr	May	Jun	Jul	Aug	Sep	Oct	Nov	Dec	Yr.
Avg. Precip. (in.)	1.1	1.1	2.1	2.9	3.2	3.8	3.9	3.9	3.0	2.3	2.0	1.7	31.1
Avg. Snowfall (in.)	10	7	9	2	Tr	0	0	0	Tr	Tr	4	11	42
Avg. Rel. Hum. 6am (%)	78	80	81	80	79	81	85	89	90	85	84	82	83
Avg. Rel. Hum. 3pm (%)	66	63	59	50	50	51	53	55	55	54	64	69	57

Note: Figures cover the years 1948-1990; Tr = Trace amounts (<0.05 in. of rain; <0.5 in. of snow)
Source: National Climatic Data Center, International Station Meteorological Climate Summary, 9/96

Weather Conditions

Temperature			Daytime Sky			Precipitation		
5°F & below	32°F & below	90°F & above	Clear	Partly cloudy	Cloudy	0.01 inch or more precip.	0.1 inch or more snow/ice	Thunder-storms
35	161	14	88	119	158	118	38	40

Note: Figures are average number of days per year and cover the years 1948-1990
Source: National Climatic Data Center, International Station Meteorological Climate Summary, 9/96

HAZARDOUS WASTE

Superfund Sites

The Madison, WI metro area is home to four sites on the EPA's Superfund National Priorities List: **City Disposal Corp. Landfill** (final); **Hagen Farm** (final); **Madison Metropolitan Sewerage District Lagoons** (final); **Refuse Hideaway Landfill** (final). There are a total of 1,165 Superfund sites with a status of proposed or final on the list in the U.S. *U.S. Environmental Protection Agency, National Priorities List, April 12, 2023*

AIR QUALITY

Air Quality Trends: Ozone

	1990	1995	2000	2005	2010	2015	2018	2019	2020	2021
MSA[1]	0.077	0.084	0.072	0.079	0.062	0.064	0.066	0.059	0.070	0.066
U.S.	0.087	0.089	0.081	0.080	0.072	0.067	0.069	0.065	0.065	0.067

Note: (1) Data covers the Madison, WI Metropolitan Statistical Area. The values shown are the composite ozone concentration averages among trend sites based on the highest fourth daily maximum 8-hour concentration in parts per million. These trends are based on sites having an adequate record of monitoring data during the trend period. Data from exceptional events are included.
Source: U.S. Environmental Protection Agency, Air Quality Monitoring Information, "Air Quality Trends by City, 1990-2021"

Air Quality Index

Area	Percent of Days when Air Quality was...[2]					AQI Statistics[2]	
	Good	Moderate	Unhealthy for Sensitive Groups	Unhealthy	Very Unhealthy	Maximum	Median
MSA[1]	67.1	32.6	0.3	0.0	0.0	101	42

Note: (1) Data covers the Madison, WI Metropolitan Statistical Area; (2) Based on 365 days with AQI data in 2021. Air Quality Index (AQI) is an index for reporting daily air quality. EPA calculates the AQI for five major air pollutants regulated by the Clean Air Act: ground-level ozone, particle pollution (aka particulate matter), carbon monoxide, sulfur dioxide, and nitrogen dioxide. The AQI runs from 0 to 500. The higher the AQI value, the greater the level of air pollution and the greater the health concern. There are six AQI categories: "Good" AQI is between 0 and 50. Air quality is considered satisfactory; "Moderate" AQI is between 51 and 100. Air quality is acceptable; "Unhealthy for Sensitive Groups" When AQI values are between 101 and 150, members of sensitive groups may experience health effects; "Unhealthy" When AQI values are between 151 and 200 everyone may begin to experience health effects; "Very Unhealthy" AQI values between 201 and 300 trigger a health alert; "Hazardous" AQI values over 300 trigger warnings of emergency conditions (not shown).
Source: U.S. Environmental Protection Agency, Air Quality Index Report, 2021

Air Quality Index Pollutants

Area	Percent of Days when AQI Pollutant was...[2]					
	Carbon Monoxide	Nitrogen Dioxide	Ozone	Sulfur Dioxide	Particulate Matter 2.5	Particulate Matter 10
MSA[1]	0.0	0.0	39.2	(3)	60.8	0.0

Note: (1) Data covers the Madison, WI Metropolitan Statistical Area; (2) Based on 365 days with AQI data in 2021. The Air Quality Index (AQI) is an index for reporting daily air quality. EPA calculates the AQI for five major air pollutants regulated by the Clean Air Act: ground-level ozone, particle pollution (also known as particulate matter), carbon monoxide, sulfur dioxide, and nitrogen dioxide. The AQI runs from 0 to 500. The higher the AQI value, the greater the level of air pollution and the greater the health concern; (3) Sulfur dioxide is no longer included in this table (as of December 8, 2021) because SO_2 concentrations tend to be very localized and not necessarily representative of broad geographical areas like counties and CBSAs.
Source: U.S. Environmental Protection Agency, Air Quality Index Report, 2021

Maximum Air Pollutant Concentrations: Particulate Matter, Ozone, CO and Lead

	Particulate Matter 10 (ug/m³)	Particulate Matter 2.5 Wtd AM (ug/m³)	Particulate Matter 2.5 24-Hr (ug/m³)	Ozone (ppm)	Carbon Monoxide (ppm)	Lead (ug/m³)
MSA[1] Level	49	9.5	27	0.066	n/a	n/a
NAAQS[2]	150	15	35	0.075	9	0.15
Met NAAQS[2]	Yes	Yes	Yes	Yes	n/a	n/a

Note: (1) Data covers the Madison, WI Metropolitan Statistical Area; Data from exceptional events are included; (2) National Ambient Air Quality Standards; ppm = parts per million; ug/m³ = micrograms per cubic meter; n/a not available.
Concentrations: Particulate Matter 10 (coarse particulate)—highest second maximum 24-hour concentration; Particulate Matter 2.5 Wtd AM (fine particulate)—highest weighted annual mean concentration; Particulate Matter 2.5 24-Hour (fine particulate)—highest 98th percentile 24-hour concentration; Ozone—highest fourth daily maximum 8-hour concentration; Carbon Monoxide—highest second maximum non-overlapping 8-hour concentration; Lead—maximum running 3-month average
Source: U.S. Environmental Protection Agency, Air Quality Monitoring Information, "Air Quality Statistics by City, 2021"

Maximum Air Pollutant Concentrations: Nitrogen Dioxide and Sulfur Dioxide

	Nitrogen Dioxide AM (ppb)	Nitrogen Dioxide 1-Hr (ppb)	Sulfur Dioxide AM (ppb)	Sulfur Dioxide 1-Hr (ppb)	Sulfur Dioxide 24-Hr (ppb)
MSA[1] Level	n/a	n/a	n/a	2	n/a
NAAQS[2]	53	100	30	75	140
Met NAAQS[2]	n/a	n/a	n/a	Yes	n/a

Note: (1) Data covers the Madison, WI Metropolitan Statistical Area; Data from exceptional events are included; (2) National Ambient Air Quality Standards; ppm = parts per million; ug/m³ = micrograms per cubic meter; n/a not available.
Concentrations: Nitrogen Dioxide AM—highest arithmetic mean concentration; Nitrogen Dioxide 1-Hr—highest 98th percentile 1-hour daily maximum concentration; Sulfur Dioxide AM—highest annual mean concentration; Sulfur Dioxide 1-Hr—highest 99th percentile 1-hour daily maximum concentration; Sulfur Dioxide 24-Hr—highest second maximum 24-hour concentration
Source: U.S. Environmental Protection Agency, Air Quality Monitoring Information, "Air Quality Statistics by City, 2021"

Milwaukee, Wisconsin

Background

Many people associate Milwaukee with beer, likely due to the 1970s television show *Laverne and Shirley*, where main characters worked in a Milwaukee brewery, and to the large influx of German immigrants during the 1840s who left an indelible mark upon the city. However, there is a lot more to Wisconsin's largest city than beer.

Milwaukee originally began as a trading post for French fur traders. Its favorable location on the western shore of Lake Michigan and at the confluence of the Milwaukee, Menomonee, and Kinnickinnic rivers made the site a natural meeting place. In 1818, Solomon Laurent Juneau, a son-in-law of a French fur trader, became Milwaukee's first founder and permanent white settler.

During the 1840s, Milwaukee saw a wave of German immigrants hit its shores. Many of these exiles were unsuccessful revolutionaries in the overthrow of the German monarchy. Despite their lack of success back home, however, they had considerable influence in the new country, including political, with three socialist mayors; economical, with Pabst and Schlitz breweries located in Milwaukee; and cultural, with the Goethe House cultural resource center located in the central library of the Milwaukee Public Library system.

Today, Milwaukee is diverse in many ways. The city is home to more than a dozen nationalities, including Irish, Mexican, Serbian, Scandinavian, Polish, Italian, German, and Puerto Rican, as well as a large and thriving African American population. And while the brewing industry does remain a major employer in the city that was once the number one producer of beer worldwide, Milwaukee's economy has widely diversified in recent years, with headquarters of six Fortune 500 companies. Prominent industries in Milwaukee today include healthcare, financial services, education, and manufacturing.

Culture and entertainment thrive in Milwaukee. The Milwaukee Public Museum features exhibits devoted to science, technology, and natural history, and includes the first IMAX(r) theater in Wisconsin. The city is home to the Florentine Opera Company, the Milwaukee Symphony Orchestra, the Milwaukee Ballet, the Milwaukee Repertory Theater, and the Milwaukee Shakespeare Company. The annual lakefront music festival Summerfest is considered the largest music festival in the world with nearly a million people attending yearly. The Milwaukee Art Museum is known worldwide with the breathtaking Quadracci Pavilion designed by Santiago Calatrava. Discovery World, the city's largest science museum, is known for its high-tech, hands-on exhibits.

The city is home to numerous colleges and universities, including Marquette University and the University of Wisconsin-Milwaukee.

Milwaukee introduced The Hop in 2018—a modern, free electric streetcar system, and reports an average of 575 riders daily. In 2019, the city partnered with Bublr Bikes to improve access to biking and bike share. They added 250 bikes—17 of them adaptive for all abilities—and more bike stations throughout the city.

Milwaukee is home to two professional sports teams, the Brewers of Major League Baseball and the Bucks of the National Basketball Association. Both have fielded highly competitive teams in recent years, each featuring a central, Most Valuable Player award-winning star, Christian Yelich and Giannis Antetokounmpo, respectively. In addition, Milwaukee is considered a home market for the popular Green Bay Packers football team, who play a little over an hour away. Among college sports, Marquette University's men's basketball team, the Golden Eagles, is a popular draw, playing in the competitive Big East conference.

Fiserv Forum, a multi-purpose arena and home of the NBA Milwaukee Bucks, opened in 2018. In 2021, it hosted its first NBA Finals game.

Milwaukee has a continental climate, and its weather is quite changeable. Temperatures vary widely through the year. In winter, arctic air masses from Canada bring frigid winter temperatures, while in summer high temperatures occur with brisk, hot winds from the southwest. Lake Michigan mitigates these extremes, as do the other Great Lakes; in late autumn and winter, the coldest air masses from the northwest are often warmed by the lakes before they can reach the city.

Rankings

General Rankings

- Milwaukee was selected as one of the best places in the world that are "under the radar, ahead of the curve, and ready for exploring" by *National Geographic Travel* editors. The list reflects 25 of the most extraordinary and inspiring destinations that also support local communities and ecosystems. These timeless must-see sites for 2023, are framed by the five categories of Culture, Family, Adventure, Community, and Nature. *www.nationalgeographic.com/travel, "Best of the World, 25 Breathtaking Places And Experiences for 2023," October 26, 2022*

Business/Finance Rankings

- Based on metro area social media reviews, the employment opinion group Glassdoor surveyed 50 of the most populous U.S. metro areas and equally weighed cost of living, hiring opportunity, and job satisfaction to compose a list of "25 Best Cities for Jobs." Median pay and home value, and number of active job openings were also factored in. The Milwaukee metro area was ranked #19 in overall job satisfaction. *www.glassdoor.com, "Best Cities for Jobs," February 25, 2020*

- The Brookings Institution ranked the nation's largest cities based on income inequality. Milwaukee was ranked #46 (#1 = greatest inequality). Criteria: the "95/20 ratio," a figure representing the income at which a household earns more than 95 percent of all other households, divided by the income at which a household earns more than only 20 percent of all other households. *Brookings Institution, "Household Income Inequality, Largest Cities of 97 Large U.S. Metro Areas, 2014-2016," February 5, 2018*

- The Brookings Institution ranked the 100 largest metro areas in the U.S. based on income inequality. Milwaukee was ranked #17 (#1 = greatest inequality). Criteria: the "95/20 ratio," a figure representing the income at which a household earns more than 95 percent of all other households, divided by the income at which a household earns more than only 20 percent of all other households. *Brookings Institution, "Household Income Inequality, 100 Largest U.S. Metro Areas, 2014-2016," February 5, 2018*

- Payscale.com ranked the 32 largest metro areas in terms of wage growth. The Milwaukee metro area ranked #18. Criteria: quarterly changes in private industry employee and education professional wage growth from the previous year. *PayScale, "Wage Trends by Metro Area-1st Quarter," April 20, 2023*

- The Milwaukee metro area appeared on the Milken Institute "2022 Best Performing Cities" list. Rank: #147 out of 200 large metro areas (population over 250,000). Criteria: job growth; wage and salary growth; high-tech output growth; housing affordability; household broadband access. *Milken Institute, "Best-Performing Cities 2022," March 28, 2022*

- *Forbes* ranked the 200 most populous metro areas to determine the nation's "Best Places for Business and Careers." The Milwaukee metro area was ranked #89. Criteria: costs (business and living); job growth (past and projected); income growth; quality of life; educational attainment (college and high school); projected economic growth; cultural and leisure opportunities; workplace tolerance laws; net migration patterns. *Forbes, "The Best Places for Business and Careers 2019: Seattle Still On Top," October 30, 2019*

Education Rankings

- Personal finance website *WalletHub* analyzed the 150 largest U.S. metropolitan statistical areas to determine where the most educated Americans are putting their degrees to work. Criteria: education levels; percentage of workers with degrees; education quality and attainment gap; public school quality rankings; quality and enrollment of each metro area's universities. Milwaukee was ranked #59 (#1 = most educated city). *www.WalletHub.com, "Most & Least Educated Cities in America, " July 18, 2022*

- Milwaukee was selected as one of America's most literate cities. The city ranked #40 out of the 84 largest U.S. cities. Criteria: number of booksellers; library resources; Internet resources; educational attainment; periodical publishing resources; newspaper circulation. *Central Connecticut State University, "America's Most Literate Cities, 2018," February 2019*

Environmental Rankings

- The U.S. Environmental Protection Agency (EPA) released its list of mid-size U.S. metropolitan areas with the most ENERGY STAR certified buildings in 2022. The Milwaukee metro area was ranked #8 out of 10. *U.S. Environmental Protection Agency, "2023 Energy Star Top Cities," April 26, 2023*

Health/Fitness Rankings

- For each of the 100 largest cities in the United States, the American Fitness Index®, compiled in partnership between the American College of Sports Medicine and the Elevance Health Foundation, evaluated community infrastructure and 34 health behaviors including preventive health, levels of chronic disease conditions, food insecurity, sleep quality, pedestrian safety, air quality, and community/environment resources that support physical activity. Milwaukee ranked #32 for "community fitness." *americanfitnessindex.org, "2022 ACSM American Fitness Index Summary Report," July 12, 2022*

- The Milwaukee metro area was identified as one of the worst cities for bed bugs in America by pest control company Orkin. The area ranked #40 out of 50 based on the number of bed bug treatments Orkin performed from December 2021 to November 2022. *Orkin, "The Windy City Can't Blow Bed Bugs Away: Chicago Ranks #1 For Third Consecutive Year On Orkin's Bed Bug Cities List," January 9, 2023*

- Milwaukee was identified as a "2022 Spring Allergy Capital." The area ranked #86 out of 100. Three groups of factors were used to identify the most challenging cities for people with allergies during the spring season: annual spring pollen scores; over the counter allergy medicine use; number of board-certified allergy specialists. *Asthma and Allergy Foundation of America, "Spring Allergy Capitals 2022," March 2, 2022*

- Milwaukee was identified as a "2022 Fall Allergy Capital." The area ranked #84 out of 100. Three groups of factors were used to identify the most challenging cities for people with allergies during the fall season: annual fall pollen scores; over the counter allergy medicine use; number of board-certified allergy specialists. *Asthma and Allergy Foundation of America, "Fall Allergy Capitals 2022," March 2, 2022*

- Milwaukee was identified as a "2022 Asthma Capital." The area ranked #48 out of the nation's 100 largest metropolitan areas. Criteria: estimated asthma prevalence; asthma-related mortality; and ER visits due to asthma. Risk factors analyzed but not factored in the rankings: annual pollen score; annual air quality; public smoking laws; access to board-certified asthma specialists; rescue and controller medication use; uninsured rate; poverty rate. *Asthma and Allergy Foundation of America, "Asthma Capitals 2022: The Most Challenging Places to Live With Asthma," September 14, 2022*

Real Estate Rankings

- *WalletHub* compared the most populated U.S. cities to determine which had the best markets for real estate agents. Milwaukee ranked #92 where demand was high and pay was the best. Criteria: sales per agent; annual median wage for real-estate agents; monthly average starting salary for real estate agents; real estate job density and competition; unemployment rate; home turnover rate; housing-market health index; and other relevant metrics. *www.WalletHub.com, "2021 Best Places to Be a Real Estate Agent," May 12, 2021*

- The Milwaukee metro area was identified as one of the nations's 20 hottest housing markets in 2023. Criteria: listing views as an indicator of demand and number of days on the market as an indicator of pace. The area ranked #15. *Realtor.com, "January 2023 Top 20 Hottest Housing Markets," February 23, 2023*

- Milwaukee was ranked #19 in the top 20 out of the 100 largest metro areas in terms of house price appreciation in 2022 (#1 = highest rate). *Federal Housing Finance Agency, House Price Index, 4th Quarter 2022*

- Milwaukee was ranked #54 out of 235 metro areas in terms of housing affordability in 2022 by the National Association of Home Builders (#1 = most affordable). Criteria: the share of homes sold in that area affordable to a family earning the local median income, based on standard mortgage underwriting criteria. *National Association of Home Builders®, NAHB-Wells Fargo Housing Opportunity Index, 4th Quarter 2022*

Safety Rankings

- To identify the most dangerous cities in America, *24/7 Wall St.* focused on violent crime categories—murder, non-negligent manslaughter, rape, robbery, and aggravated assault—as reported for every 100,000 residents using data from the FBI's 2020 annual Uniform Crime Report. For cities with populations over 25,000, Milwaukee was ranked #13. *247wallst.com, "America's Most Dangerous Cities" November 12, 2021*

- Statistics drawn from the FBI's Uniform Crime Report were used to rank the cities where violent crime rose the most year over year from 2019 to 2020. Only cities with 25,000 or more residents were included. *24/7 Wall St.* found that Milwaukee placed #15 of those with a notable surge in incidents of violent crime. *247wallst.com, "American Cities Where Crime Is Soaring," March 4, 2022*

- Allstate ranked the 200 largest cities in America in terms of driver safety. Milwaukee ranked #61. Criteria: internal property damage claims over a two-year period from January 2016 to December 2017. The report helps increase the importance of safety and awareness behind the wheel. *Allstate, "Allstate America's Best Drivers Report, 2019" June 24, 2019*

- Milwaukee was identified as one of the most dangerous cities in America by NeighborhoodScout. The city ranked #13 out of 100 (#1 = most dangerous). Criteria: number of violent crimes per 1,000 residents. The editors evaluated cities with 25,000 or more residents. *NeighborhoodScout.com, "2023 Top 100 Most Dangerous Cities in the U.S.," January 12, 2023*

- The National Insurance Crime Bureau ranked 390 metro areas in the U.S. in terms of per capita rates of vehicle theft. The Milwaukee metro area ranked #8 (#1 = highest rate). Criteria: number of vehicle theft offenses per 100,000 inhabitants in 2021. *National Insurance Crime Bureau, "Hot Spots 2021," September 1, 2022*

Seniors/Retirement Rankings

- From its Best Cities for Successful Aging indexes, the Milken Institute generated rankings for metropolitan areas, weighing data in nine categories—health care, wellness, living arrangements, transportation and convenience, financial characteristics, education, employment, community engagement, and overall livability. The Milwaukee metro area was ranked #33 overall in the large metro area category. *Milken Institute, "Best Cities for Successful Aging, 2017" March 14, 2017*

Sports/Recreation Rankings

- Milwaukee was chosen as one of America's best cities for bicycling. The city ranked #36 out of 50. Criteria: cycling infrastructure that is safe and friendly for all ages; energy and bike culture. The editors evaluated cities with populations of 100,000 or more. *Bicycling, "The 50 Best Bike Cities in America," October 10, 2018*

Women/Minorities Rankings

- *Women's Health*, together with the site Yelp, identified the 15 "Wellthiest" spots in the U.S. Milwaukee appeared among the top for happiest, healthiest, outdoorsiest and Zen-iest. *Women's Health, "The 15 Wellthiest Cities in the U.S." July 5, 2017*

- Personal finance website *WalletHub* compared more than 180 U.S. cities across two key dimensions, "Hispanic Business-Friendliness" and "Hispanic Purchasing Power," to arrive at the most favorable conditions for Hispanic entrepreneurs. Milwaukee was ranked #165 out of 182. Criteria includes: share of Hispanic-Owned Businesses; Hispanic entrepreneurship rate to median annual income of Hispanics; Small Business-Friendliness score; cost of living; and number of Hispanics with at least a bachelor's degree. *WalletHub.com, "2019's Best Cities for Hispanic Entrepreneurs," May 1, 2019*

Miscellaneous Rankings

- The watchdog site, Charity Navigator, conducted a study of charities in major markets both to analyze statistical differences in their financial, accountability, and transparency practices and to track year-to-year variations in individual philanthropic communities. The Milwaukee metro area was ranked #12 among the 30 metro markets in the rating category of Overall Score. *www.charitynavigator.org, "2017 Metro Market Study," May 1, 2017*

- *WalletHub* compared the 150 most populated U.S. cities to determine their operating efficiency. A "Quality of Services" score was constructed for each city and then divided by the total budget per capita to reveal which were managed the best. Milwaukee ranked #123. Criteria: financial stability; economy; education; safety; health; infrastructure and pollution. *www.WalletHub.com, "2022's Best- & Worst-Run Cities in America," June 21, 2022*

- Milwaukee was selected as one of "America's Friendliest Cities." The city ranked #10 in the "Friendliest" category. Respondents to an online survey were asked to rate 38 top urban destinations in the United States as to general friendliness, as well as manners, politeness and warm disposition. *Travel + Leisure, "America's Friendliest Cities," October 20, 2017*

Business Environment

DEMOGRAPHICS

Population Growth

Area	1990 Census	2000 Census	2010 Census	2020 Census	Population Growth (%) 1990-2020	Population Growth (%) 2010-2020
City	628,095	596,974	594,833	577,222	-8.1	-3.0
MSA[1]	1,432,149	1,500,741	1,555,908	1,574,731	10.0	1.2
U.S.	248,709,873	281,421,906	308,745,538	331,449,281	33.3	7.4

Note: (1) Figures cover the Milwaukee-Waukesha, WI Metropolitan Statistical Area
Source: U.S. Census Bureau, 1990 Census, 2000 Census, 2010 Census, 2020 Census

Race

Area	White Alone[2] (%)	Black Alone[2] (%)	Asian Alone[2] (%)	AIAN[3] Alone[2] (%)	NHOPI[4] Alone[2] (%)	Other Race Alone[2] (%)	Two or More Races (%)
City	36.1	38.6	5.2	0.9	0.0	9.0	10.1
MSA[1]	66.7	16.3	4.2	0.6	0.0	4.6	7.6
U.S.	61.6	12.4	6.0	1.1	0.2	8.4	10.2

Note: (1) Figures cover the Milwaukee-Waukesha, WI Metropolitan Statistical Area; (2) Alone is defined as not being in combination with one or more other races; (3) American Indian and Alaska Native; (4) Native Hawaiian and Other Pacific Islander
Source: U.S. Census Bureau, 2020 Census

Hispanic or Latino Origin

Area	Total (%)	Mexican (%)	Puerto Rican (%)	Cuban (%)	Other (%)
City	19.9	13.4	4.9	0.2	1.4
MSA[1]	11.3	7.5	2.6	0.2	1.1
U.S.	18.4	11.2	1.8	0.7	4.7

Note: Persons of Hispanic or Latino origin can be of any race; (1) Figures cover the Milwaukee-Waukesha, WI Metropolitan Statistical Area
Source: U.S. Census Bureau, 2017-2021 American Community Survey 5-Year Estimates

Age

Area	Under Age 5	Age 5–19	Age 20–34	Age 35–44	Age 45–54	Age 55–64	Age 65–74	Age 75–84	Age 85+	Median Age
City	6.8	21.9	25.6	12.6	10.8	10.8	7.3	2.9	1.3	32.1
MSA[1]	5.8	19.6	19.9	12.6	12.0	13.5	9.7	4.6	2.1	38.5
U.S.	5.6	19.2	20.2	12.7	12.4	13.1	10.0	4.9	1.9	38.8

Note: (1) Figures cover the Milwaukee-Waukesha, WI Metropolitan Statistical Area
Source: U.S. Census Bureau, 2020 Census

Disability by Age

Area	All Ages	Under 18 Years Old	18 to 64 Years Old	65 Years and Over
City	12.5	5.0	11.6	36.6
MSA[1]	11.0	3.9	8.9	29.8
U.S.	12.6	4.4	10.3	33.4

Note: Figures show percent of the civilian noninstitutionalized population that reported having a disability. Disability status is determined from six types of difficulty: vision, hearing, cognitive, ambulatory, self-care, and independent living. For children under 5 years old, hearing and vision difficulty are used to determine disability status. For children between the ages of 5 and 14, disability status is determined from hearing, vision, cognitive, ambulatory, and self-care difficulties. For people aged 15 years and older, they are considered to have a disability if they have difficulty with any one of the six difficulty types; Note: (1) Figures cover the Milwaukee-Waukesha, WI Metropolitan Statistical Area
Source: U.S. Census Bureau, 2017-2021 American Community Survey 5-Year Estimates

Ancestry

Area	German	Irish	English	American	Italian	Polish	French[2]	Scottish	Dutch
City	15.1	5.6	2.1	1.3	2.5	5.9	1.2	0.4	0.6
MSA[1]	31.9	9.5	4.6	2.1	4.2	10.3	2.2	0.9	1.2
U.S.	12.8	9.6	8.1	5.7	5.0	2.7	2.2	1.6	1.1

Note: Figures are the percentage of the total population reporting a particular ancestry. The nine most commonly reported ancestries in the U.S. are shown. Figures include multiple ancestries (e.g. if a person reported being Irish and Italian, they were included in both columns); (1) Figures cover the Milwaukee-Waukesha, WI Metropolitan Statistical Area; (2) Excludes Basque
Source: U.S. Census Bureau, 2017-2021 American Community Survey 5-Year Estimates

Foreign-born Population

Area	Any Foreign Country	Percent of Population Born in							
		Asia	Mexico	Europe	Caribbean	Central America[2]	South America	Africa	Canada
City	10.1	2.8	4.9	0.7	0.4	0.3	0.2	0.8	0.1
MSA[1]	7.5	2.8	2.3	1.2	0.2	0.2	0.3	0.4	0.1
U.S.	13.6	4.2	3.3	1.4	1.1	1.1	1.1	0.8	0.2

Note: (1) Figures cover the Milwaukee-Waukesha, WI Metropolitan Statistical Area; (2) Excludes Mexico.
Source: U.S. Census Bureau, 2017-2021 American Community Survey 5-Year Estimates

Household Size

Area	Persons in Household (%)							Average Household Size
	One	Two	Three	Four	Five	Six	Seven or More	
City	37.8	28.9	13.7	10.0	5.7	2.4	1.5	2.50
MSA[1]	32.3	34.4	13.8	11.6	5.3	1.8	0.9	2.40
U.S.	28.1	33.8	15.5	12.9	6.0	2.3	1.4	2.60

Note: (1) Figures cover the Milwaukee-Waukesha, WI Metropolitan Statistical Area
Source: U.S. Census Bureau, 2017-2021 American Community Survey 5-Year Estimates

Household Relationships

Area	House-holder	Opposite-sex Spouse	Same-sex Spouse	Opposite-sex Unmarried Partner	Same-sex Unmarried Partner	Child[2]	Grand-child	Other Relatives	Non-relatives
City	40.8	10.2	0.2	3.6	0.2	30.2	2.7	4.9	4.4
MSA[1]	41.3	17.5	0.2	2.9	0.2	28.7	1.6	3.1	2.7
U.S.	38.3	17.5	0.2	2.5	0.2	28.3	2.4	4.8	3.4

Note: Figures are percent of the total population; (1) Figures cover the Milwaukee-Waukesha, WI Metropolitan Statistical Area; (2) Includes biological, adopted, and stepchildren of the householder
Source: U.S. Census Bureau, 2020 Census

Gender

Area	Males	Females	Males per 100 Females
City	278,386	298,836	93.2
MSA[1]	766,278	808,453	94.8
U.S.	162,685,811	168,763,470	96.4

Note: (1) Figures cover the Milwaukee-Waukesha, WI Metropolitan Statistical Area
Source: U.S. Census Bureau, 2020 Census

Marital Status

Area	Never Married	Now Married[2]	Separated	Widowed	Divorced
City	54.4	29.4	1.9	4.4	9.9
MSA[1]	37.4	46.2	1.1	5.1	10.1
U.S.	33.8	48.0	1.8	5.6	10.8

Note: Figures are percentages and cover the population 15 years of age and older; (1) Figures cover the Milwaukee-Waukesha, WI Metropolitan Statistical Area; (2) Excludes separated
Source: U.S. Census Bureau, 2017-2021 American Community Survey 5-Year Estimates

Religious Groups by Family

Area	Catholic	Baptist	Methodist	LDS[2]	Pentecostal	Lutheran	Islam	Adventist	Other
MSA[1]	24.5	3.0	1.0	0.4	2.8	9.1	2.8	0.9	10.7
U.S.	18.7	7.3	3.0	2.0	1.8	1.7	1.3	1.3	11.6

Note: Figures are the number of adherents as a percentage of the total population and cover the eight largest religious groups in the U.S; (1) Figures cover the Milwaukee-Waukesha, WI Metropolitan Statistical Area; (2) Church of Jesus Christ of Latter-day Saints
Sources: 2020 U.S. Religion Census, Association of Statisticians of American Religious Bodies; The Association of Religion Data Archives (ARDA)

Religious Groups by Tradition

Area	Catholic	Evangelical Protestant	Mainline Protestant	Black Protestant	Islam	Judaism	Hinduism	Orthodox	Buddhism
MSA[1]	24.5	16.3	5.4	3.3	2.8	0.4	0.4	0.5	0.4
U.S.	18.7	16.5	5.2	2.3	1.3	0.6	0.4	0.4	0.3

Note: Figures are the number of adherents as a percentage of the total population; (1) Figures cover the Milwaukee-Waukesha, WI Metropolitan Statistical Area
Sources: 2020 U.S. Religion Census, Association of Statisticians of American Religious Bodies; The Association of Religion Data Archives (ARDA)

ECONOMY

Gross Metropolitan Product

Area	2020	2021	2022	2023	Rank[2]
MSA[1]	102.4	110.1	119.2	126.3	38

Note: Figures are in billions of dollars; (1) Figures cover the Milwaukee-Waukesha, WI Metropolitan Statistical Area; (2) Rank is based on 2021 data and ranges from 1 to 381
Source: U.S. Conference of Mayors, U.S. Metro Economies: U.S. Metros Compared to Global and State Economies, June 2022

Economic Growth

Area	2018-20 (%)	2021 (%)	2022 (%)	2023 (%)	Rank[2]
MSA[1]	-1.8	3.1	2.5	2.8	271
U.S.	-0.6	5.7	3.1	2.9	–

Note: Figures are real gross metropolitan product (GMP) growth rates and represent average annual percent change; (1) Figures cover the Milwaukee-Waukesha, WI Metropolitan Statistical Area; (2) Rank is based on 2020 2-year average annual percent change and ranges from 1 to 381
Source: U.S. Conference of Mayors, U.S. Metro Economies: U.S. Metros Compared to Global and State Economies, June 2022

Metropolitan Area Exports

Area	2016	2017	2018	2019	2020	2021	Rank[2]
MSA[1]	7,256.2	7,279.1	7,337.6	6,896.3	6,624.0	7,282.8	46

Note: Figures are in millions of dollars; (1) Figures cover the Milwaukee-Waukesha, WI Metropolitan Statistical Area; (2) Rank is based on 2021 data and ranges from 1 to 388
Source: U.S. Department of Commerce, International Trade Administration, Office of Trade and Economic Analysis, Industry and Analysis, Exports by Metropolitan Area, data extracted March 16, 2023

Building Permits

Area	Single-Family			Multi-Family			Total		
	2021	2022	Pct. Chg.	2021	2022	Pct. Chg.	2021	2022	Pct. Chg.
City	28	42	50.0	176	134	-23.9	204	176	-13.7
MSA[1]	1,779	1,557	-12.5	1,150	1,609	39.9	2,929	3,166	8.1
U.S.	1,115,400	975,600	-12.5	621,600	689,500	10.9	1,737,000	1,665,100	-4.1

Note: (1) Figures cover the Milwaukee-Waukesha, WI Metropolitan Statistical Area; Figures represent new, privately-owned housing units authorized (unadjusted data); All permit data are based on estimates with imputation
Source: U.S. Census Bureau, Manufacturing, Mining, and Construction Statistics, Building Permits, 2021, 2022

Bankruptcy Filings

Area	Business Filings			Nonbusiness Filings		
	2021	2022	% Chg.	2021	2022	% Chg.
Milwaukee County	20	20	0.0	3,237	2,957	-8.6
U.S.	14,347	13,481	-6.0	399,269	374,240	-6.3

Note: Business filings include Chapter 7, Chapter 9, Chapter 11, Chapter 12, Chapter 13, Chapter 15, and Section 304; Nonbusiness filings include Chapter 7, Chapter 11, and Chapter 13
Source: Administrative Office of the U.S. Courts, Business and Nonbusiness Bankruptcy, County Cases Commenced by Chapter of the Bankruptcy Code, During the 12-Month Period Ending December 31, 2021 and Business and Nonbusiness Bankruptcy, County Cases Commenced by Chapter of the Bankruptcy Code, During the 12-Month Period Ending December 31, 2022

Housing Vacancy Rates

Area	Gross Vacancy Rate[2] (%)			Year-Round Vacancy Rate[3] (%)			Rental Vacancy Rate[4] (%)			Homeowner Vacancy Rate[5] (%)		
	2020	2021	2022	2020	2021	2022	2020	2021	2022	2020	2021	2022
MSA[1]	6.6	5.2	5.2	6.3	5.1	5.1	4.6	2.2	5.9	0.6	0.5	0.1
U.S.	10.6	10.8	10.5	8.2	8.4	8.2	6.3	6.1	5.8	1.0	0.9	0.8

Note: (1) Figures cover the Milwaukee-Waukesha, WI Metropolitan Statistical Area; (2) The percentage of the total housing inventory that is vacant; (3) The percentage of the housing inventory (excluding seasonal units) that is year-round vacant; (4) The percentage of rental inventory that is vacant for rent; (5) The percentage of homeowner inventory that is vacant for sale
Source: U.S. Census Bureau, Housing Vacancies and Homeownership Annual Statistics: 2020, 2021, 2022

INCOME

Income

Area	Per Capita ($)	Median Household ($)	Average Household ($)
City	25,564	45,318	61,529
MSA[1]	38,930	67,448	92,423
U.S.	37,638	69,021	97,196

Note: (1) Figures cover the Milwaukee-Waukesha, WI Metropolitan Statistical Area
Source: U.S. Census Bureau, 2017-2021 American Community Survey 5-Year Estimates

Household Income Distribution

Area	Percent of Households Earning							
	Under $15,000	$15,000 -$24,999	$25,000 -$34,999	$35,000 -$49,999	$50,000 -$74,999	$75,000 -$99,999	$100,000 -$149,999	$150,000 and up
City	16.5	11.5	11.7	14.6	17.8	11.6	10.5	5.8
MSA[1]	9.4	7.8	8.5	11.8	17.1	13.2	16.7	15.5
U.S.	9.4	7.8	8.2	11.4	16.8	12.8	16.3	17.3

Note: (1) Figures cover the Milwaukee-Waukesha, WI Metropolitan Statistical Area
Source: U.S. Census Bureau, 2017-2021 American Community Survey 5-Year Estimates

Poverty Rate

Area	All Ages	Under 18 Years Old	18 to 64 Years Old	65 Years and Over
City	24.1	33.4	21.6	15.9
MSA[1]	12.6	17.7	11.6	9.0
U.S.	12.6	17.0	11.8	9.6

Note: Figures are percentage of people whose income during the past 12 months was below the poverty level;
(1) Figures cover the Milwaukee-Waukesha, WI Metropolitan Statistical Area
Source: U.S. Census Bureau, 2017-2021 American Community Survey 5-Year Estimates

EMPLOYMENT

Labor Force and Employment

Area	Civilian Labor Force			Workers Employed		
	Dec. 2021	Dec. 2022	% Chg.	Dec. 2021	Dec. 2022	% Chg.
City	272,797	266,036	-2.5	262,401	257,421	-1.9
MSA[1]	817,582	799,375	-2.2	796,196	780,437	-2.0
U.S.	161,696,000	164,224,000	1.6	155,732,000	158,872,000	2.0

Note: Data is not seasonally adjusted and covers workers 16 years of age and older; (1) Figures cover the
Milwaukee-Waukesha, WI Metropolitan Statistical Area
Source: Bureau of Labor Statistics, Local Area Unemployment Statistics

Unemployment Rate

Area	2022											
	Jan.	Feb.	Mar.	Apr.	May	Jun.	Jul.	Aug.	Sep.	Oct.	Nov.	Dec.
City	4.8	5.1	5.0	5.0	4.9	5.4	5.5	5.5	4.8	4.6	4.1	3.2
MSA[1]	3.4	3.7	3.6	3.5	3.4	4.0	4.0	3.9	3.6	3.3	3.0	2.4
U.S.	4.4	4.1	3.8	3.3	3.4	3.8	3.8	3.8	3.3	3.4	3.4	3.3

Note: Data is not seasonally adjusted and covers workers 16 years of age and older; (1) Figures cover the
Milwaukee-Waukesha, WI Metropolitan Statistical Area
Source: Bureau of Labor Statistics, Local Area Unemployment Statistics

Average Wages

Occupation	$/Hr.	Occupation	$/Hr.
Accountants and Auditors	38.84	Maintenance and Repair Workers	22.70
Automotive Mechanics	25.28	Marketing Managers	68.47
Bookkeepers	22.52	Network and Computer Systems Admin.	46.07
Carpenters	27.42	Nurses, Licensed Practical	26.39
Cashiers	13.47	Nurses, Registered	39.44
Computer Programmers	48.26	Nursing Assistants	17.93
Computer Systems Analysts	47.82	Office Clerks, General	19.83
Computer User Support Specialists	27.77	Physical Therapists	45.40
Construction Laborers	24.14	Physicians	104.93
Cooks, Restaurant	15.78	Plumbers, Pipefitters and Steamfitters	35.62
Customer Service Representatives	21.30	Police and Sheriff's Patrol Officers	35.72
Dentists	86.72	Postal Service Mail Carriers	27.42
Electricians	36.15	Real Estate Sales Agents	24.00
Engineers, Electrical	46.03	Retail Salespersons	16.36
Fast Food and Counter Workers	12.08	Sales Representatives, Technical/Scientific	39.18
Financial Managers	74.52	Secretaries, Exc. Legal/Medical/Executive	20.72
First-Line Supervisors of Office Workers	33.87	Security Guards	16.44
General and Operations Managers	68.48	Surgeons	n/a
Hairdressers/Cosmetologists	18.97	Teacher Assistants, Exc. Postsecondary*	16.86
Home Health and Personal Care Aides	13.83	Teachers, Secondary School, Exc. Sp. Ed.*	33.03
Janitors and Cleaners	15.71	Telemarketers	16.38
Landscaping/Groundskeeping Workers	17.75	Truck Drivers, Heavy/Tractor-Trailer	26.40
Lawyers	80.34	Truck Drivers, Light/Delivery Services	21.54
Maids and Housekeeping Cleaners	14.73	Waiters and Waitresses	15.68

Note: Wage data covers the Milwaukee-Waukesha, WI Metropolitan Statistical Area; (*) Hourly wages were
calculated from annual wage data based on a 40 hour work week; n/a not available.
Source: Bureau of Labor Statistics, Metro Area Occupational Employment & Wage Estimates, May 2022

Employment by Industry

Sector	MSA[1]		U.S.
	Number of Employees	Percent of Total	Percent of Total
Construction	33,700	3.9	5.0
Private Education and Health Services	173,700	20.3	16.1
Financial Activities	51,100	6.0	5.9
Government	82,400	9.6	14.5
Information	12,400	1.4	2.0
Leisure and Hospitality	72,300	8.4	10.3
Manufacturing	115,900	13.5	8.4
Mining and Logging	500	0.1	0.4
Other Services	44,200	5.2	3.7
Professional and Business Services	119,000	13.9	14.7
Retail Trade	76,700	8.9	10.2
Transportation, Warehousing, and Utilities	36,300	4.2	4.9
Wholesale Trade	39,100	4.6	3.9

Note: Figures are non-farm employment as of December 2022. Figures are not seasonally adjusted and include workers 16 years of age and older; (1) Figures cover the Milwaukee-Waukesha, WI Metropolitan Statistical Area
Source: Bureau of Labor Statistics, Current Employment Statistics, Employment, Hours, and Earnings

Employment by Occupation

Occupation Classification	City (%)	MSA[1] (%)	U.S. (%)
Management, Business, Science, and Arts	32.7	42.0	40.3
Natural Resources, Construction, and Maintenance	6.1	6.3	8.7
Production, Transportation, and Material Moving	20.1	15.0	13.1
Sales and Office	18.7	20.6	20.9
Service	22.4	16.1	17.0

Note: Figures cover employed civilians 16 years of age and older; (1) Figures cover the Milwaukee-Waukesha, WI Metropolitan Statistical Area
Source: U.S. Census Bureau, 2017-2021 American Community Survey 5-Year Estimates

Occupations with Greatest Projected Employment Growth: 2022 – 2024

Occupation[1]	2022 Employment	2024 Projected Employment	Numeric Employment Change	Percent Employment Change
Laborers and Freight, Stock, and Material Movers, Hand	64,310	67,940	3,630	5.6
Maids and Housekeeping Cleaners	22,820	26,320	3,500	15.3
Fast Food and Counter Workers	58,230	61,720	3,490	6.0
Farmworkers and Laborers, Crop, Nursery, and Greenhouse	48,090	51,190	3,100	6.4
Cooks, Restaurant	23,140	25,660	2,520	10.9
Childcare Workers	14,930	17,390	2,460	16.5
Industrial Truck and Tractor Operators	17,330	19,540	2,210	12.8
Home Health and Personal Care Aides	75,480	77,560	2,080	2.8
Waiters and Waitresses	34,590	36,650	2,060	6.0
Stockers and Order Fillers	47,340	48,990	1,650	3.5

Note: Projections cover Wisconsin; (1) Sorted by numeric employment change
Source: www.projectionscentral.com, State Occupational Projections, 2022–2024 Short-Term Projections

Fastest-Growing Occupations: 2022 – 2024

Occupation[1]	2022 Employment	2024 Projected Employment	Numeric Employment Change	Percent Employment Change
Personal Care and Service Workers, All Other	140	240	100	71.4
Ushers, Lobby Attendants, and Ticket Takers	1,350	1,630	280	20.7
Childcare Workers	14,930	17,390	2,460	16.5
Maids and Housekeeping Cleaners	22,820	26,320	3,500	15.3
Industrial Truck and Tractor Operators	17,330	19,540	2,210	12.8
Reservation and Transportation Ticket Agents and Travel Clerks	1,000	1,120	120	12.0
Travel Agents	820	910	90	11.0
Cooks, Restaurant	23,140	25,660	2,520	10.9
Medical Scientists, Except Epidemiologists	1,360	1,500	140	10.3
Athletes and Sports Competitors	580	640	60	10.3

Note: Projections cover Wisconsin; (1) Sorted by percent employment change and excludes occupations with numeric employment change less than 50
Source: www.projectionscentral.com, State Occupational Projections, 2022–2024 Short-Term Projections

CITY FINANCES

City Government Finances

Component	2020 ($000)	2020 ($ per capita)
Total Revenues	1,129,334	1,914
Total Expenditures	1,410,307	2,390
Debt Outstanding	1,905,259	3,228
Cash and Securities[1]	693,312	1,175

Note: (1) Cash and security holdings of a government at the close of its fiscal year, including those of its dependent agencies, utilities, and liquor stores.
Source: U.S. Census Bureau, State & Local Government Finances 2020

City Government Revenue by Source

Source	2020 ($000)	2020 ($ per capita)	2020 (%)
General Revenue			
From Federal Government	47,887	81	4.2
From State Government	289,169	490	25.6
From Local Governments	49,712	84	4.4
Taxes			
Property	321,364	545	28.5
Sales and Gross Receipts	0	0	0.0
Personal Income	0	0	0.0
Corporate Income	0	0	0.0
Motor Vehicle License	6,279	11	0.6
Other Taxes	18,502	31	1.6
Current Charges	239,127	405	21.2
Liquor Store	0	0	0.0
Utility	80,166	136	7.1

Source: U.S. Census Bureau, State & Local Government Finances 2020

City Government Expenditures by Function

Function	2020 ($000)	2020 ($ per capita)	2020 (%)
General Direct Expenditures			
Air Transportation	0	0	0.0
Corrections	8,971	15	0.6
Education	0	0	0.0
Employment Security Administration	0	0	0.0
Financial Administration	93,036	157	6.6
Fire Protection	119,237	202	8.5
General Public Buildings	34,474	58	2.4
Governmental Administration, Other	145,886	247	10.3
Health	24,049	40	1.7
Highways	154,345	261	10.9
Hospitals	0	0	0.0
Housing and Community Development	27,810	47	2.0
Interest on General Debt	93,639	158	6.6
Judicial and Legal	25,353	43	1.8
Libraries	33,798	57	2.4
Parking	25,841	43	1.8
Parks and Recreation	3,343	5	0.2
Police Protection	307,794	521	21.8
Public Welfare	0	0	0.0
Sewerage	110,060	186	7.8
Solid Waste Management	43,701	74	3.1
Veterans' Services	0	0	0.0
Liquor Store	0	0	0.0
Utility	104,932	177	7.4

Source: U.S. Census Bureau, State & Local Government Finances 2020

TAXES

State Corporate Income Tax Rates

State	Tax Rate (%)	Income Brackets ($)	Num. of Brackets	Financial Institution Tax Rate (%)[a]	Federal Income Tax Ded.
Wisconsin	7.9	Flat rate	1	7.9	No

Note: Tax rates as of January 1, 2023; (a) Rates listed are the corporate income tax rate applied to financial institutions or excise taxes based on income. Some states have other taxes based upon the value of deposits or shares.
Source: Federation of Tax Administrators, State Corporate Income Tax Rates, January 1, 2023

State Individual Income Tax Rates

State	Tax Rate (%)	Income Brackets ($)	Personal Exemptions ($)			Standard Ded. ($)	
			Single	Married	Depend.	Single	Married
Wisconsin (a)	3.54 - 7.65	13,810 - 304,170 (y)	700	1,400	700	12,760	23,620 (z)

Note: Tax rates as of January 1, 2023; Local- and county-level taxes are not included; Federal income tax is not deductible on state income tax returns; (a) 16 states have statutory provision for automatically adjusting to the rate of inflation the dollar values of the income tax brackets, standard deductions, and/or personal exemptions. Oregon does not index the income brackets for $125,000 and over; (y) The Wisconsin income brackets reported are for single individuals. For married taxpayers filing jointly, the same tax rates apply income brackets ranging from $18,420, to $405,550; (z) Alabama standard deduction is phased out for incomes over $25,000. Rhode Island exemptions & standard deductions phased out for incomes over $233,750; Wisconsin standard deduciton phases out for income over $16,989.
Source: Federation of Tax Administrators, State Individual Income Tax Rates, January 1, 2023

Various State Sales and Excise Tax Rates

State	State Sales Tax (%)	Gasoline[1] ($/gal.)	Cigarette[2] ($/pack)	Spirits[3] ($/gal.)	Wine[4] ($/gal.)	Beer[5] ($/gal.)	Recreational Marijuana (%)
Wisconsin	5	0.329	2.52	3.25	0.25	0.06	Not legal

Note: All tax rates as of January 1, 2023; (1) The American Petroleum Institute has developed a methodology for determining the average tax rate on a gallon of fuel. Rates may include any of the following: excise taxes, environmental fees, storage tank fees, other fees or taxes, general sales tax, and local taxes; (2) The federal excise tax of $1.0066 per pack and local taxes are not included; (3) Rates are those applicable to off-premise sales of 40% alcohol by volume (a.b.v.) distilled spirits in 750ml containers. Local excise taxes are excluded; (4) Rates are those applicable to off-premise sales of 11% a.b.v. non-carbonated wine in 750ml containers; (5) Rates are those applicable to off-premise sales of 4.7% a.b.v. beer in 12 ounce containers.
Source: Tax Foundation, 2023 Facts & Figures: How Does Your State Compare?

State Business Tax Climate Index Rankings

State	Overall Rank	Corporate Tax Rank	Individual Income Tax Rank	Sales Tax Rank	Property Tax Rank	Unemployment Insurance Tax Rank
Wisconsin	27	31	38	7	15	31

Note: The index is a measure of how each state's tax laws affect economic performance. The lower the rank, the more favorable a state's tax system is for business. States without a given tax are given a ranking of 1. The scores/rankings for the District of Columbia do not affect other states. The 2023 index represents the tax climate as of July 1, 2022.
Source: Tax Foundation, State Business Tax Climate Index 2023

TRANSPORTATION

Means of Transportation to Work

Area	Car/Truck/Van		Public Transportation			Bicycle	Walked	Other Means	Worked at Home
	Drove Alone	Car-pooled	Bus	Subway	Railroad				
City	71.2	9.5	5.8	0.0	0.0	0.6	4.1	1.0	7.7
MSA[1]	77.4	7.1	2.4	0.0	0.0	0.4	2.3	0.8	9.5
U.S.	73.2	8.6	2.0	1.6	0.5	0.5	2.5	1.5	9.7

Note: Figures are percentages and cover workers 16 years of age and older; (1) Figures cover the Milwaukee-Waukesha, WI Metropolitan Statistical Area
Source: U.S. Census Bureau, 2017-2021 American Community Survey 5-Year Estimates

Travel Time to Work

Area	Less Than 10 Minutes	10 to 19 Minutes	20 to 29 Minutes	30 to 44 Minutes	45 to 59 Minutes	60 to 89 Minutes	90 Minutes or More
City	10.4	36.6	26.1	19.1	3.5	2.7	1.7
MSA[1]	12.1	32.1	25.7	21.2	5.0	2.5	1.4
U.S.	12.4	28.5	21.0	20.9	8.2	6.2	2.9

Note: Note: Figures are percentages and include workers 16 years old and over; (1) Figures cover the Milwaukee-Waukesha, WI Metropolitan Statistical Area
Source: U.S. Census Bureau, 2017-2021 American Community Survey 5-Year Estimates

Key Congestion Measures

Measure	1990	2000	2010	2015	2020
Annual Hours of Delay, Total (000)	17,556	26,505	33,479	37,896	24,340
Annual Hours of Delay, Per Auto Commuter	26	33	40	44	29
Annual Congestion Cost, Per Auto Commuter ($)	742	843	845	884	602

Note: Covers the Milwaukee WI urban area
Source: Texas A&M Transportation Institute, 2021 Urban Mobility Report

Freeway Travel Time Index

Measure	1985	1990	1995	2000	2005	2010	2015	2020
Urban Area Index[1]	1.08	1.12	1.14	1.15	1.16	1.16	1.17	1.07
Urban Area Rank[1,2]	40	35	41	53	57	54	46	57

Note: Freeway Travel Time Index—the ratio of travel time in the peak period to the travel time at free-flow conditions. For example, a value of 1.30 indicates a 20-minute free-flow trip takes 26 minutes in the peak (20 minutes x 1.30 = 26 minutes); (1) Covers the Milwaukee WI urban area; (2) Rank is based on 101 larger urban areas (#1 = highest travel time index)
Source: Texas A&M Transportation Institute, 2021 Urban Mobility Report

Public Transportation

Agency Name / Mode of Transportation	Vehicles Operated in Maximum Service[1]	Annual Unlinked Passenger Trips[2] (in thous.)	Annual Passenger Miles[3] (in thous.)
Milwaukee County Transit System (MCTS)			
Bus (purchased transportation)	306	15,728.8	50,839.6
Demand Response (purchased transportation)	62	269.6	1,743.3

Note: (1) Number of revenue vehicles operated by the given mode and type of service to meet the annual maximum service requirement. This is the revenue vehicle count during the peak season of the year; on the week and day that maximum service is provided. Vehicles operated in maximum service (VOMS) exclude atypical days and one-time special events; (2) Number of passengers who boarded public transportation vehicles. Passengers are counted each time they board a vehicle no matter how many vehicles they use to travel from their origin to their destination. (3) Sum of the distances ridden by all passengers during the entire fiscal year.
Source: Federal Transit Administration, National Transit Database, 2021

Air Transportation

Airport Name and Code / Type of Service	Passenger Airlines[1]	Passenger Enplanements	Freight Carriers[2]	Freight (lbs)
General Mitchell International (MKE)				
Domestic service (U.S. carriers - 2022)	26	2,646,748	13	69,246,832
International service (U.S. carriers - 2021)	5	7,342	0	0

Note: (1) Includes all U.S.-based major, minor and commuter airlines that carried at least one passenger during the year; (2) Includes all U.S.-based airlines and freight carriers that transported at least one pound of freight during the year.
Source: Bureau of Transportation Statistics, The Intermodal Transportation Database, Air Carriers: T-100 Domestic Market (U.S. Carriers), 2022; Bureau of Transportation Statistics, The Intermodal Transportation Database, Air Carriers: T-100 International Market (U.S. Carriers), 2021

BUSINESSES

Major Business Headquarters

Company Name	Industry	Rankings	
		Fortune[1]	Forbes[2]
ManpowerGroup	Temporary help	167	-
Northwestern Mutual	Insurance, life and health (mutual)	97	-
Rockwell Automation	Electronics, electrical equip.	472	-
WEC Energy Group	Utilities, gas and electric	416	-

Note: (1) Companies that produce a 10-K are ranked 1 to 500 based on 2021 revenue; (2) All private companies with at least $2 billion in annual revenue through the end of their most current fiscal year are ranked 1 to 246; companies listed are headquartered in the city; dashes indicate no ranking
Source: Fortune, "Fortune 500," 2022; Forbes, "America's Largest Private Companies," 2022

Living Environment

COST OF LIVING

Cost of Living Index

Composite Index	Groceries	Housing	Utilities	Trans-portation	Health Care	Misc. Goods/ Services
99.6	97.1	100.0	107.6	93.3	117.6	97.3

Note: The Cost of Living Index measures regional differences in the cost of consumer goods and services, excluding taxes and non-consumer expenditures, for professional and managerial households in the top income quintile. It is based on more than 50,000 prices covering almost 60 different items for which prices are collected three times a year by chambers of commerce, economic development organizations or university applied economic centers in each participating urban area. The numbers shown should be read as a percentage above or below the national average of 100. For example, a value of 115.4 in the groceries column indicates that grocery prices are 15.4% higher than the national average. Small differences in the index numbers should not be interpreted as significant; Figures cover the Milwaukee-Waukesha WI urban area.
Source: The Council for Community and Economic Research, Cost of Living Index, 2022

Grocery Prices

Area[1]	T-Bone Steak ($/pound)	Frying Chicken ($/pound)	Whole Milk ($/half gal.)	Eggs ($/dozen)	Orange Juice ($/64 oz.)	Coffee ($/11.5 oz.)
City[2]	15.29	1.57	2.52	2.18	3.77	4.12
Avg.	13.81	1.59	2.43	2.25	3.85	4.95
Min.	10.17	0.90	1.51	1.30	2.90	3.46
Max.	19.35	3.30	4.32	4.32	5.31	8.59

*Note: (1) Values for the local area are compared with the average, minimum and maximum values for all 286 areas in the Cost of Living Index; (2) Figures cover the Milwaukee-Waukesha WI urban area; **T-Bone Steak** (price per pound); **Frying Chicken** (price per pound, whole fryer); **Whole Milk** (half gallon carton); **Eggs** (price per dozen, Grade A, large); **Orange Juice** (64 oz. Tropicana or Florida Natural); **Coffee** (11.5 oz. can, vacuum-packed, Maxwell House, Hills Bros, or Folgers).*
Source: The Council for Community and Economic Research, Cost of Living Index, 2022

Housing and Utility Costs

Area[1]	New Home Price ($)	Apartment Rent ($/month)	All Electric ($/month)	Part Electric ($/month)	Other Energy ($/month)	Telephone ($/month)
City[2]	432,791	1,481	-	104.40	98.25	186.18
Avg.	450,913	1,371	176.41	99.93	76.96	190.22
Min.	229,283	546	100.84	31.56	27.15	174.27
Max.	2,434,977	4,569	356.86	249.59	272.24	208.31

*Note: (1) Values for the local area are compared with the average, minimum and maximum values for all 286 areas in the Cost of Living Index; (2) Figures cover the Milwaukee-Waukesha WI urban area; **New Home Price** (2,400 sf living area, 8,000 sf lot, in urban area with full utilities); **Apartment Rent** (950 sf 2 bedroom/1.5 or 2 bath, unfurnished, excluding all utilities except water); **All Electric** (average monthly cost for an all-electric home); **Part Electric** (average monthly cost for a part-electric home); **Other Energy** (average monthly cost for natural gas, fuel oil, coal, wood, and any other forms of energy except electricity); **Telephone** (price includes the base monthly rate plus taxes and fees for three lines of mobile phone service).*
Source: The Council for Community and Economic Research, Cost of Living Index, 2022

Health Care, Transportation, and Other Costs

Area[1]	Doctor ($/visit)	Dentist ($/visit)	Optometrist ($/visit)	Gasoline ($/gallon)	Beauty Salon ($/visit)	Men's Shirt ($)
City[2]	181.86	123.58	75.00	3.66	37.70	33.64
Avg.	124.91	107.77	117.66	3.86	43.31	34.21
Min.	36.61	58.25	51.79	2.90	22.18	13.05
Max.	250.21	162.58	371.96	5.54	85.61	63.54

*Note: (1) Values for the local area are compared with the average, minimum and maximum values for all 286 areas in the Cost of Living Index; (2) Figures cover the Milwaukee-Waukesha WI urban area; **Doctor** (general practitioners routine exam of an established patient); **Dentist** (adult teeth cleaning and periodic oral examination); **Optometrist** (full vision eye exam for established adult patient); **Gasoline** (one gallon regular unleaded, national brand, including all taxes, cash price at self-service pump if available); **Beauty Salon** (woman's shampoo, trim, and blow-dry); **Men's Shirt** (cotton/polyester dress shirt, pinpoint weave, long sleeves).*
Source: The Council for Community and Economic Research, Cost of Living Index, 2022

HOUSING

Homeownership Rate

Area	2015 (%)	2016 (%)	2017 (%)	2018 (%)	2019 (%)	2020 (%)	2021 (%)	2022 (%)
MSA[1]	57.0	60.4	63.9	62.3	56.9	58.5	56.8	57.3
U.S.	63.7	63.4	63.9	64.4	64.6	66.6	65.5	65.8

Note: (1) Figures cover the Milwaukee-Waukesha, WI Metropolitan Statistical Area
Source: U.S. Census Bureau, Housing Vacancies and Homeownership Annual Statistics: 2015-2022

House Price Index (HPI)

Area	National Ranking[2]	Quarterly Change (%)	One-Year Change (%)	Five-Year Change (%)	Since 1991Q1 (%)
MSA[1]	134	-1.54	11.11	45.94	239.44
U.S.[3]	–	0.34	8.41	58.44	289.08

Note: The HPI is a weighted repeat sales index. It measures average price changes in repeat sales or refinancings on the same properties. This information is obtained by reviewing repeat mortgage transactions on single-family properties whose mortgages have been purchased or securitized by Fannie Mae or Freddie Mac since January 1975; (1) Figures cover the Milwaukee-Waukesha-West Allis, WI Metropolitan Statistical Area; (2) Rankings are based on annual percentage change for all metro areas containing at least 15,000 transactions over the last 10 years and ranges from 1 to 257; (3) figures based on a weighted average of Census Division estimates using a seasonally adjusted, purchase-only index; all figures are for the period ending December 31, 2022
Source: Federal Housing Finance Agency, Change in FHFA Metropolitan Area House Price Indexes, 2022Q4

Median Single-Family Home Prices

Area	2020	2021	2022[p]	Percent Change 2021 to 2022
MSA[1]	291.3	319.0	345.3	8.2
U.S. Average	300.2	357.1	392.6	9.9

Note: Figures are median sales prices of existing single-family homes in thousands of dollars; (p) preliminary; (1) Figures cover the Milwaukee-Waukesha, WI Metropolitan Statistical Area
Source: National Association of Realtors, Median Sales Price of Existing Single-Family Homes for Metropolitan Areas, 4th Quarter 2022

Qualifying Income Based on Median Sales Price of Existing Single-Family Homes

Area	With 5% Down ($)	With 10% Down ($)	With 20% Down ($)
MSA[1]	100,227	94,951	84,401
U.S. Average	112,234	106,237	94,513

Note: Figures are preliminary; Qualifying income is based on a mortgage rate of 6.77%. Monthly principal and interest payment is limited to 25% of income; (1) Figures cover the Milwaukee-Waukesha, WI Metropolitan Statistical Area
Source: National Association of Realtors, Qualifying Income Based on Median Sales Price of Existing Single-Family Homes for Metropolitan Areas, 4th Quarter 2022

Home Value

Area	Under $100,000	$100,000 -$199,999	$200,000 -$299,999	$300,000 -$399,999	$400,000 -$499,999	$500,000 -$999,999	$1,000,000 or more	Median ($)
City	30.6	48.6	14.1	3.3	1.2	1.8	0.5	135,600
MSA[1]	10.6	29.0	27.8	16.4	7.5	7.4	1.2	235,100
U.S.	16.2	24.2	20.1	13.6	8.3	13.6	4.1	244,900

Note: Figures are percentages except for median and cover owner-occupied housing units; (1) Figures cover the Milwaukee-Waukesha, WI Metropolitan Statistical Area
Source: U.S. Census Bureau, 2017-2021 American Community Survey 5-Year Estimates

Year Housing Structure Built

Area	2020 or Later	2010 -2019	2000 -2009	1990 -1999	1980 -1989	1970 -1979	1960 -1969	1950 -1959	1940 -1949	Before 1940	Median Year
City	0.1	2.6	3.5	3.3	4.1	8.7	11.4	19.5	10.4	36.5	1952
MSA[1]	0.1	4.2	8.2	10.9	7.8	12.9	11.5	15.7	6.9	21.8	1965
U.S.	0.2	7.3	13.6	13.6	13.2	14.8	10.3	10.0	4.7	12.2	1979

Note: Figures are percentages except for Median Year; Note: (1) Figures cover the Milwaukee-Waukesha, WI Metropolitan Statistical Area
Source: U.S. Census Bureau, 2017-2021 American Community Survey 5-Year Estimates

Gross Monthly Rent

Area	Under $500	$500 -$999	$1,000 -$1,499	$1,500 -$1,999	$2,000 -$2,499	$2,500 -$2,999	$3,000 and up	Median ($)
City	7.7	55.0	28.4	6.3	1.6	0.6	0.4	910
MSA[1]	6.9	48.0	32.3	9.1	2.4	0.7	0.5	963
U.S.	8.1	30.5	30.8	16.8	7.3	3.1	3.5	1,163

Note: Figures are percentages except for median; Gross rent is the contract rent plus the estimated average monthly cost of utilities (electricity, gas, and water and sewer) and fuels (oil, coal, kerosene, wood, etc.) if these are paid by the renter (or paid for the renter by someone else); (1) Figures cover the Milwaukee-Waukesha, WI Metropolitan Statistical Area
Source: U.S. Census Bureau, 2017-2021 American Community Survey 5-Year Estimates

HEALTH

Health Risk Factors

Category	MSA[1] (%)	U.S. (%)
Adults aged 18–64 who have any kind of health care coverage	94.9	90.9
Adults who reported being in good or better health	85.9	85.2
Adults who have been told they have high blood cholesterol	36.5	35.7
Adults who have been told they have high blood pressure	34.0	32.4
Adults who are current smokers	14.1	14.4
Adults who currently use e-cigarettes	5.1	6.7
Adults who currently use chewing tobacco, snuff, or snus	2.4	3.5
Adults who are heavy drinkers[2]	8.9	6.3
Adults who are binge drinkers[3]	23.6	15.4
Adults who are overweight (BMI 25.0 - 29.9)	33.3	34.4
Adults who are obese (BMI 30.0 - 99.8)	35.6	33.9
Adults who participated in any physical activities in the past month	82.1	76.3

Note: (1) Figures cover the Milwaukee-Waukesha-West Allis, WI Metropolitan Statistical Area; (2) Heavy drinkers are classified as adult men having more than 14 drinks per week and adult women having more than 7 drinks per week; (3) Binge drinkers are classified as males having five or more drinks on one occasion or females having four or more drinks on one occasion
Source: Centers for Disease Control and Prevention, Behaviorial Risk Factor Surveillance System, SMART: Selected Metropolitan Area Risk Trends, 2021

Acute and Chronic Health Conditions

Category	MSA[1] (%)	U.S. (%)
Adults who have ever been told they had a heart attack	3.8	4.0
Adults who have ever been told they have angina or coronary heart disease	3.8	3.8
Adults who have ever been told they had a stroke	4.9	3.0
Adults who have ever been told they have asthma	15.7	14.9
Adults who have ever been told they have arthritis	28.3	25.8
Adults who have ever been told they have diabetes[2]	9.6	10.9
Adults who have ever been told they had skin cancer	5.0	6.6
Adults who have ever been told they had any other types of cancer	6.1	7.5
Adults who have ever been told they have COPD	6.6	6.1
Adults who have ever been told they have kidney disease	3.2	3.0
Adults who have ever been told they have a form of depression	18.4	20.5

Note: (1) Figures cover the Milwaukee-Waukesha-West Allis, WI Metropolitan Statistical Area; (2) Figures do not include pregnancy-related, borderline, or pre-diabetes
Source: Centers for Disease Control and Prevention, Behaviorial Risk Factor Surveillance System, SMART: Selected Metropolitan Area Risk Trends, 2021

Health Screening and Vaccination Rates

Category	MSA[1] (%)	U.S. (%)
Adults who have ever been tested for HIV	34.9	34.9
Adults who have had their blood cholesterol checked within the last five years	85.6	85.2
Adults aged 65+ who have had flu shot within the past year	71.9	68.6
Adults aged 65+ who have ever had a pneumonia vaccination	69.7	71.0

Note: (1) Figures cover the Milwaukee-Waukesha-West Allis, WI Metropolitan Statistical Area.
Source: Centers for Disease Control and Prevention, Behaviorial Risk Factor Surveillance System, SMART: Selected Metropolitan Area Risk Trends, 2021

Disability Status

Category	MSA[1] (%)	U.S. (%)
Adults who reported being deaf	6.1	7.2
Are you blind or have serious difficulty seeing, even when wearing glasses?	3.4	4.8
Are you limited in any way in any of your usual activities due to arthritis?	12.5	11.1
Do you have difficulty doing errands alone?	7.3	7.0
Do you have difficulty dressing or bathing?	4.0	3.6
Do you have serious difficulty concentrating/remembering/making decisions?	11.8	12.1
Do you have serious difficulty walking or climbing stairs?	13.5	12.8

Note: (1) Figures cover the Milwaukee-Waukesha-West Allis, WI Metropolitan Statistical Area.
Source: Centers for Disease Control and Prevention, Behaviorial Risk Factor Surveillance System, SMART: Selected Metropolitan Area Risk Trends, 2021

Mortality Rates for the Top 10 Causes of Death in the U.S.

ICD-10[a] Sub-Chapter	ICD-10[a] Code	Crude Mortality Rate[1] per 100,000 population	
		County[2]	U.S.
Malignant neoplasms	C00-C97	177.5	182.6
Ischaemic heart diseases	I20-I25	121.2	113.1
Other forms of heart disease	I30-I51	58.6	64.4
Other degenerative diseases of the nervous system	G30-G31	32.1	51.0
Cerebrovascular diseases	I60-I69	44.0	47.8
Other external causes of accidental injury	W00-X59	92.7	46.4
Chronic lower respiratory diseases	J40-J47	39.3	45.7
Organic, including symptomatic, mental disorders	F01-F09	50.2	35.9
Hypertensive diseases	I10-I15	35.3	35.0
Diabetes mellitus	E10-E14	29.9	29.6

Note: (a) ICD-10 = International Classification of Diseases 10th Revision; (1) Crude mortality rates are a three-year average covering 2019-2021; (2) Figures cover Milwaukee County.
Source: Centers for Disease Control and Prevention, National Center for Health Statistics. National Vital Statistics System, Mortality 2018-2021 on CDC WONDER Online Database

Mortality Rates for Selected Causes of Death

ICD-10[a] Sub-Chapter	ICD-10[a] Code	Crude Mortality Rate[1] per 100,000 population	
		County[2]	U.S.
Assault	X85-Y09	19.4	7.0
Diseases of the liver	K70-K76	16.7	19.8
Human immunodeficiency virus (HIV) disease	B20-B24	1.4	1.5
Influenza and pneumonia	J09-J18	10.6	14.7
Intentional self-harm	X60-X84	13.4	14.3
Malnutrition	E40-E46	5.0	4.3
Obesity and other hyperalimentation	E65-E68	3.5	3.0
Renal failure	N17-N19	15.9	15.7
Transport accidents	V01-V99	12.3	13.6
Viral hepatitis	B15-B19	1.5	1.2

Note: (a) ICD-10 = International Classification of Diseases 10th Revision; (1) Crude mortality rates are a three-year average covering 2019-2021; (2) Figures cover Milwaukee County; Data are suppressed when the data meet the criteria for confidentiality constraints; Crude mortality rates are flagged as unreliable when the rate would be calculated with a numerator of 20 or less.
Source: Centers for Disease Control and Prevention, National Center for Health Statistics. National Vital Statistics System, Mortality 2018-2021 on CDC WONDER Online Database

Health Insurance Coverage

Area	With Health Insurance	With Private Health Insurance	With Public Health Insurance	Without Health Insurance	Population Under Age 19 Without Health Insurance
City	90.6	54.1	44.8	9.4	3.5
MSA[1]	94.3	71.8	34.1	5.7	2.8
U.S.	91.2	67.8	35.4	8.8	5.3

Note: Figures are percentages that cover the civilian noninstitutionalized population; (1) Figures cover the Milwaukee-Waukesha, WI Metropolitan Statistical Area
Source: U.S. Census Bureau, 2017-2021 American Community Survey 5-Year Estimates

Number of Medical Professionals

Area	MDs[3]	DOs[3,4]	Dentists	Podiatrists	Chiropractors	Optometrists
County[1] (number)	3,643	208	817	66	196	107
County[1] (rate[2])	388.3	22.2	88.0	7.1	21.1	11.5
U.S. (rate[2])	289.3	23.5	72.5	6.2	28.7	17.4

Note: Data as of 2021 unless noted; (1) Data covers Milwaukee County; (2) Rate per 100,000 population; (3) Data as of 2020 and includes all active, non-federal physicians; (4) Doctor of Osteopathic Medicine
Source: U.S. Department of Health and Human Services, Health Resources and Services Administration, Bureau of Health Professions, Area Resource File (ARF) 2021-2022

Best Hospitals

According to *U.S. News,* the Milwaukee-Waukesha, WI metro area is home to two of the best hospitals in the U.S.: **Aurora St. Luke's Medical Center** (1 adult specialty); **Froedtert Hospital and the Medical College of Wisconsin** (3 adult specialties). The hospitals listed were nationally ranked in at least one of 15 adult or 10 pediatric specialties. The number of specialties shown cover the parent hospital. Only 164 U.S. hospitals performed well enough to be nationally ranked in one or more specialties. Twenty hospitals in the U.S. made the Honor Roll. The Best Hospitals Honor Roll takes both the national rankings and the procedure and condition ratings into account. Hospitals received points if they were nationally ranked in one of the 15 adult specialties—the higher they ranked, the more points they got—and how many ratings of "high performing" they earned in the 17 procedures and conditions. *U.S. News Online, "America's Best Hospitals 2022-23"*

According to *U.S. News,* the Milwaukee-Waukesha, WI metro area is home to one of the best children's hospitals in the U.S.: **Children's Wisconsin Hospital** (8 pediatric specialties). The hospital listed was highly ranked in at least one of 10 pediatric specialties. Eighty-six children's hospitals in the U.S. were nationally ranked in at least one specialty. Hospitals received points for being ranked in a specialty, and the 10 hospitals with the most points across the 10 specialties make up the Honor Roll. *U.S. News Online, "America's Best Children's Hospitals 2022-23"*

EDUCATION

Public School District Statistics

District Name	Schls	Pupils	Pupil/ Teacher Ratio	Minority Pupils[1] (%)	LEP/ELL[2] (%)	IEP[3] (%)
Milwaukee School District	156	69,115	16.2	90.4	11.9	20.1

Note: Table includes school districts with 2,000 or more students; (1) Percentage of students that are not non-Hispanic white; (2) Percentage of students that are Limited English Proficient or English Language Learners (2018-19); (3) Percentage of students that have an Individualized Education Program (2019-20). Source: U.S. Department of Education, National Center for Education Statistics, Common Core of Data, Local Education Agency (School District) Universe Survey: School Year 2021-2022

Best High Schools

According to *U.S. News,* Milwaukee is home to one of the top 500 high schools in the U.S.: **Carmen High School of Science and Technology** (#476). Nearly 18,000 public, magnet and charter schools were ranked based on their performance on state assessments and how well they prepare students for college. *U.S. News & World Report, "Best High Schools 2022"*

Highest Level of Education

Area	Less than H.S.	H.S. Diploma	Some College, No Deg.	Associate Degree	Bachelor's Degree	Master's Degree	Prof. School Degree	Doctorate Degree
City	15.1	30.9	21.1	7.4	16.3	6.7	1.4	1.0
MSA[1]	7.9	26.1	19.7	8.9	24.3	9.4	2.3	1.5
U.S.	11.1	26.5	20.0	8.7	20.6	9.3	2.2	1.5

Note: Figures cover persons age 25 and over; (1) Figures cover the Milwaukee-Waukesha, WI Metropolitan Statistical Area Source: U.S. Census Bureau, 2017-2021 American Community Survey 5-Year Estimates

Educational Attainment by Race

Area	High School Graduate or Higher (%)					Bachelor's Degree or Higher (%)				
	Total	White	Black	Asian	Hisp.[2]	Total	White	Black	Asian	Hisp.[2]
City	84.9	90.5	84.9	74.8	64.4	25.5	37.6	13.5	32.7	10.8
MSA[1]	92.1	95.2	85.9	86.1	71.0	37.4	42.3	15.1	53.3	16.6
U.S.	88.9	91.4	87.2	87.6	71.2	33.7	35.5	23.3	55.6	18.4

Note: Figures shown cover persons 25 years old and over; (1) Figures cover the Milwaukee-Waukesha, WI Metropolitan Statistical Area; (2) People of Hispanic origin can be of any race Source: U.S. Census Bureau, 2017-2021 American Community Survey 5-Year Estimates

School Enrollment by Grade and Control

Area	Preschool (%)		Kindergarten (%)		Grades 1 - 4 (%)		Grades 5 - 8 (%)		Grades 9 - 12 (%)	
	Public	Private	Public	Private	Public	Private	Public	Private	Public	Private
City	74.3	25.7	77.9	22.1	75.8	24.2	74.5	25.5	81.4	18.6
MSA[1]	58.0	42.0	78.8	21.2	79.9	20.1	79.6	20.4	85.4	14.6
U.S.	58.8	41.2	86.3	13.7	88.3	11.7	88.6	11.4	89.4	10.6

Note: Figures shown cover persons 3 years old and over; (1) Figures cover the Milwaukee-Waukesha, WI Metropolitan Statistical Area Source: U.S. Census Bureau, 2017-2021 American Community Survey 5-Year Estimates

Higher Education

Four-Year Colleges			Two-Year Colleges			Medical Schools[1]	Law Schools[2]	Voc/ Tech[3]
Public	Private Non-profit	Private For-profit	Public	Private Non-profit	Private For-profit			
2	16	1	2	0	2	1	1	3

Note: Figures cover institutions located within the Milwaukee-Waukesha, WI Metropolitan Statistical Area and include main campuses only; (1) includes schools accredited by the Liaison Committee on Medical Education and the American Osteopathic Association's Commission on Osteopathic College Accreditation; (2) includes ABA-accredited schools, schools with provisional ABA accreditation, and state accredited schools; (3) includes all schools with programs that are less than 2 years.
Source: National Center for Education Statistics, Integrated Postsecondary Education System (IPEDS), 2021-22; Wikipedia, List of Medical Schools in the United States, accessed April 10, 2023; Wikipedia, List of Law Schools in the United States, accessed April 10, 2023

According to *U.S. News & World Report*, the Milwaukee-Waukesha, WI metro area is home to one of the top 200 national universities in the U.S.: **Marquette University** (#83 tie). The indicators used to capture academic quality fall into a number of categories: assessment by administrators at peer institutions; retention of students; faculty resources; student selectivity; financial resources; alumni giving; high school counselor ratings of colleges; and graduation rate. *U.S. News & World Report, "America's Best Colleges 2023"*

EMPLOYERS

Major Employers

Company Name	Industry
Ascension Wisconsin	Health care system
Aurora Health	Health care system
Children's Hospital of Wisconsin	Pediatric health care services
Froedtert Health	Health care services
GE Healthcare Technologies	Medical imaging & information systems
Kohl's	Department stores
Kroger Co./Roundy's	Food distributor & retailer
Medical College of Wisconsin	Medical school
Northwestern Mutual	Life insurance & investment services
ProHealth Care Inc.	Health care system
Quad/Graphics	Commercial printing and print mgmt
WEC Energy	Electric & natural gas utility

Note: Companies shown are located within the Milwaukee-Waukesha, WI Metropolitan Statistical Area.
Source: Hoovers.com; Wikipedia

Best Companies to Work For

Baird, headquartered in Milwaukee, is among "The 100 Best Companies to Work For." To pick the best companies, *Fortune* partnered with the Great Place to Work Institute. Two-thirds of a company's score is based on the results of the Institute's Trust Index survey, which is sent to a random sample of employees from each company. The questions related to attitudes about management's credibility, job satisfaction, and camaraderie. The other third of the scoring is based on the company's responses to the Institute's Culture Audit, which includes detailed questions about pay and benefit programs, and a series of open-ended questions about hiring practices, internal communication, training, recognition programs, and diversity efforts. Any company that is at least five years old with more than 1,000 U.S. employees is eligible. *Fortune, "The 100 Best Companies to Work For," 2023*

Baird, headquartered in Milwaukee, is among "Fortune's Best Workplaces for Women." To pick the best companies, *Fortune* partnered with the Great Place to Work Institute. To be considered for the list, companies must be Great Place To Work-Certified. Companies must also employ at least 50 women, at least 20% of their non-executive managers must be female, and at least one executive must be female. To determine the Best Workplaces for Women, Great Place To Work measured the differences in women's survey responses to those of their peers and assesses the impact of demographics and roles on the quality and consistency of women's experiences. Great Place To Work also analyzed the gender balance of each workplace, how it compared to each company's industry, and patterns in representation as women rise from front-line positions to the board of directors. *Fortune, "Best Workplaces for Women," 2022*

Baird, headquartered in Milwaukee, is among "Fortune's Best Workplaces for Parents." To pick the best companies, *Fortune* partnered with the Great Place to Work Institute. To be considered for the list, companies must be Great Place To Work-Certified and have at least 50 responses from parents in the US. The survey enables employees to share confidential quantitative and qualitative feedback about their organization's culture by responding to 60 statements on a 5-point scale and answering two open-ended questions. Collectively, these statements describe a great employee experience, defined by high levels of trust, respect, credibility, fairness, pride, and camaraderie. In addition, companies provide organizational data like size, location, industry, demographics, roles, and levels; and provide information about parental leave, adoption, flexible schedule, childcare and dependent health care benefits. *Fortune, "Best Workplaces for Parents," 2022*

PUBLIC SAFETY

Crime Rate

Area	Total Crime	Violent Crime Rate				Property Crime Rate		
		Murder	Rape[3]	Robbery	Aggrav. Assault	Burglary	Larceny -Theft	Motor Vehicle Theft
City	4,325.4	32.4	73.2	326.8	1,164.5	578.5	1,388.2	761.8
Suburbs[1]	1,624.3	1.5	20.3	29.8	78.2	114.7	1,274.1	105.6
Metro[2]	2,634.0	13.1	40.0	140.8	484.3	288.1	1,316.8	350.9
U.S.	2,356.7	6.5	38.4	73.9	279.7	314.2	1,398.0	246.0

Note: Figures are crimes per 100,000 population; (1) All areas within the metro area that are located outside the city limits; (2) Figures cover the Milwaukee-Waukesha-West Allis, WI Metropolitan Statistical Area; (3) All figures shown were reported using the revised Uniform Crime Reporting (UCR) definition of rape; Due to the transition to the National Incident-Based Reporting System (NIBRS), limited city and metro area data was released for 2021.
Source: FBI Uniform Crime Reports, 2020

Hate Crimes

Area	Number of Quarters Reported	Number of Incidents per Bias Motivation					
		Race/Ethnicity/ Ancestry	Religion	Sexual Orientation	Disability	Gender	Gender Identity
City	4	1	1	0	0	0	0
U.S.	4	5,227	1,244	1,110	130	75	266

Note: Due to the transition to the National Incident-Based Reporting System (NIBRS), limited crime data was released for 2021.
Source: Federal Bureau of Investigation, Hate Crime Statistics 2020

Identity Theft Consumer Reports

Area	Reports	Reports per 100,000 Population	Rank[2]
MSA[1]	3,765	239	118
U.S.	1,108,609	339	-

Note: (1) Figures cover the Milwaukee-Waukesha, WI Metropolitan Statistical Area; (2) Rank ranges from 1 to 391 where 1 indicates greatest number of identity theft reports per 100,000 population
Source: Federal Trade Commission, Consumer Sentinel Network Data Book 2022

Fraud and Other Consumer Reports

Area	Reports	Reports per 100,000 Population	Rank[2]
MSA[1]	15,162	962	114
U.S.	4,064,520	1,245	-

Note: (1) Figures cover the Milwaukee-Waukesha, WI Metropolitan Statistical Area; (2) Rank ranges from 1 to 391 where 1 indicates greatest number of fraud and other consumer reports per 100,000 population
Source: Federal Trade Commission, Consumer Sentinel Network Data Book 2022

POLITICS

2020 Presidential Election Results

Area	Biden	Trump	Jorgensen	Hawkins	Other
Milwaukee County	69.1	29.3	0.9	0.0	0.7
U.S.	51.3	46.8	1.2	0.3	0.5

Note: Results are percentages and may not add to 100% due to rounding
Source: Dave Leip's Atlas of U.S. Presidential Elections

SPORTS

Professional Sports Teams

Team Name	League	Year Established
Milwaukee Brewers	Major League Baseball (MLB)	1970
Milwaukee Bucks	National Basketball Association (NBA)	1968

Note: Includes teams located in the Milwaukee-Waukesha, WI Metropolitan Statistical Area.
Source: Wikipedia, Major Professional Sports Teams of the United States and Canada, April 12, 2023

CLIMATE

Average and Extreme Temperatures

Temperature	Jan	Feb	Mar	Apr	May	Jun	Jul	Aug	Sep	Oct	Nov	Dec	Yr.
Extreme High (°F)	60	65	82	91	92	101	101	103	98	89	77	63	103
Average High (°F)	27	31	40	54	65	76	80	79	71	60	45	32	55
Average Temp. (°F)	20	24	33	45	55	66	71	70	62	51	38	25	47
Average Low (°F)	12	16	26	36	45	55	62	61	53	42	30	18	38
Extreme Low (°F)	-26	-19	-10	12	21	36	40	44	28	18	-5	-20	-26

Note: Figures cover the years 1948-1990
Source: National Climatic Data Center, International Station Meteorological Climate Summary, 9/96

Average Precipitation/Snowfall/Humidity

Precip./Humidity	Jan	Feb	Mar	Apr	May	Jun	Jul	Aug	Sep	Oct	Nov	Dec	Yr.
Avg. Precip. (in.)	1.6	1.4	2.6	3.3	2.9	3.4	3.6	3.4	2.9	2.3	2.3	2.2	32.0
Avg. Snowfall (in.)	13	10	9	2	Tr	0	0	0	0	Tr	3	11	49
Avg. Rel. Hum. 6am (%)	76	77	78	78	77	79	82	86	86	82	80	80	80
Avg. Rel. Hum. 3pm (%)	68	66	64	58	58	58	59	62	61	61	66	70	63

Note: Figures cover the years 1948-1990; Tr = Trace amounts (<0.05 in. of rain; <0.5 in. of snow)
Source: National Climatic Data Center, International Station Meteorological Climate Summary, 9/96

Weather Conditions

Temperature			Daytime Sky			Precipitation		
5°F & below	32°F & below	90°F & above	Clear	Partly cloudy	Cloudy	0.01 inch or more precip.	0.1 inch or more snow/ice	Thunder-storms
22	141	10	90	118	157	126	38	35

Note: Figures are average number of days per year and cover the years 1948-1990
Source: National Climatic Data Center, International Station Meteorological Climate Summary, 9/96

HAZARDOUS WASTE

Superfund Sites

The Milwaukee-Waukesha, WI metro area is home to five sites on the EPA's Superfund National Priorities List: **Amcast Industrial Corporation** (final); **Lauer I Sanitary Landfill** (final); **Master Disposal Service Landfill** (final); **Moss-American Co., Inc. (Kerr-Mcgee Oil Co.)** (final); **Muskego Sanitary Landfill** (final). There are a total of 1,165 Superfund sites with a status of proposed or final on the list in the U.S. *U.S. Environmental Protection Agency, National Priorities List, April 12, 2023*

AIR QUALITY

Air Quality Trends: Ozone

	1990	1995	2000	2005	2010	2015	2018	2019	2020	2021
MSA[1]	0.095	0.106	0.082	0.092	0.079	0.069	0.073	0.066	0.074	0.072
U.S.	0.087	0.089	0.081	0.080	0.072	0.067	0.069	0.065	0.065	0.067

Note: (1) Data covers the Milwaukee-Waukesha, WI Metropolitan Statistical Area. The values shown are the composite ozone concentration averages among trend sites based on the highest fourth daily maximum 8-hour concentration in parts per million. These trends are based on sites having an adequate record of monitoring data during the trend period. Data from exceptional events are included.
Source: U.S. Environmental Protection Agency, Air Quality Monitoring Information, "Air Quality Trends by City, 1990-2021"

Air Quality Index

Area	Percent of Days when Air Quality was...[2]					AQI Statistics[2]	
	Good	Moderate	Unhealthy for Sensitive Groups	Unhealthy	Very Unhealthy	Maximum	Median
MSA[1]	57.3	39.5	3.3	0.0	0.0	129	47

Note: (1) Data covers the Milwaukee-Waukesha, WI Metropolitan Statistical Area; (2) Based on 365 days with AQI data in 2021. Air Quality Index (AQI) is an index for reporting daily air quality. EPA calculates the AQI for five major air pollutants regulated by the Clean Air Act: ground-level ozone, particle pollution (aka particulate matter), carbon monoxide, sulfur dioxide, and nitrogen dioxide. The AQI runs from 0 to 500. The higher the AQI value, the greater the level of air pollution and the greater the health concern. There are six AQI categories: "Good" AQI is between 0 and 50. Air quality is considered satisfactory; "Moderate" AQI is between 51 and 100. Air quality is acceptable; "Unhealthy for Sensitive Groups" When AQI values are between 101 and 150, members of sensitive groups may experience health effects; "Unhealthy" When AQI values are between 151 and 200 everyone may begin to experience health effects; "Very Unhealthy" AQI values between 201 and 300 trigger a health alert; "Hazardous" AQI values over 300 trigger warnings of emergency conditions (not shown).
Source: U.S. Environmental Protection Agency, Air Quality Index Report, 2021

Air Quality Index Pollutants

Area	Percent of Days when AQI Pollutant was...[2]					
	Carbon Monoxide	Nitrogen Dioxide	Ozone	Sulfur Dioxide	Particulate Matter 2.5	Particulate Matter 10
MSA[1]	0.0	1.4	52.3	(3)	43.6	2.7

Note: (1) Data covers the Milwaukee-Waukesha, WI Metropolitan Statistical Area; (2) Based on 365 days with AQI data in 2021. The Air Quality Index (AQI) is an index for reporting daily air quality. EPA calculates the AQI for five major air pollutants regulated by the Clean Air Act: ground-level ozone, particle pollution (also known as particulate matter), carbon monoxide, sulfur dioxide, and nitrogen dioxide. The AQI runs from 0 to 500. The higher the AQI value, the greater the level of air pollution and the greater the health concern; (3) Sulfur dioxide is no longer included in this table (as of December 8, 2021) because SO_2 concentrations tend to be very localized and not necessarily representative of broad geographical areas like counties and CBSAs.
Source: U.S. Environmental Protection Agency, Air Quality Index Report, 2021

Maximum Air Pollutant Concentrations: Particulate Matter, Ozone, CO and Lead

	Particulate Matter 10 (ug/m^3)	Particulate Matter 2.5 Wtd AM (ug/m^3)	Particulate Matter 2.5 24-Hr (ug/m^3)	Ozone (ppm)	Carbon Monoxide (ppm)	Lead (ug/m^3)
MSA[1] Level	70	10.2	27	0.073	1	n/a
NAAQS[2]	150	15	35	0.075	9	0.15
Met NAAQS[2]	Yes	Yes	Yes	Yes	Yes	n/a

Note: (1) Data covers the Milwaukee-Waukesha, WI Metropolitan Statistical Area; Data from exceptional events are included; (2) National Ambient Air Quality Standards; ppm = parts per million; ug/m^3 = micrograms per cubic meter; n/a = not available.
Concentrations: Particulate Matter 10 (coarse particulate)—highest second maximum 24-hour concentration; Particulate Matter 2.5 Wtd AM (fine particulate)—highest weighted annual mean concentration; Particulate Matter 2.5 24-Hour (fine particulate)—highest 98th percentile 24-hour concentration; Ozone—highest fourth daily maximum 8-hour concentration; Carbon Monoxide—highest second maximum non-overlapping 8-hour concentration; Lead—maximum running 3-month average
Source: U.S. Environmental Protection Agency, Air Quality Monitoring Information, "Air Quality Statistics by City, 2021"

Maximum Air Pollutant Concentrations: Nitrogen Dioxide and Sulfur Dioxide

	Nitrogen Dioxide AM (ppb)	Nitrogen Dioxide 1-Hr (ppb)	Sulfur Dioxide AM (ppb)	Sulfur Dioxide 1-Hr (ppb)	Sulfur Dioxide 24-Hr (ppb)
MSA[1] Level	13	42	n/a	n/a	n/a
NAAQS[2]	53	100	30	75	140
Met NAAQS[2]	Yes	Yes	n/a	n/a	n/a

Note: (1) Data covers the Milwaukee-Waukesha, WI Metropolitan Statistical Area; Data from exceptional events are included; (2) National Ambient Air Quality Standards; ppm = parts per million; ug/m^3 = micrograms per cubic meter; n/a not available.
Concentrations: Nitrogen Dioxide AM—highest arithmetic mean concentration; Nitrogen Dioxide 1-Hr—highest 98th percentile 1-hour daily maximum concentration; Sulfur Dioxide AM—highest annual mean concentration; Sulfur Dioxide 1-Hr—highest 99th percentile 1-hour daily maximum concentration; Sulfur Dioxide 24-Hr—highest second maximum 24-hour concentration
Source: U.S. Environmental Protection Agency, Air Quality Monitoring Information, "Air Quality Statistics by City, 2021"

Minneapolis, Minnesota

Background

Minneapolis is a vibrant, cosmopolitan city that boasts sunlit skyscrapers and sparkling lakes, as well as theater, museums, and abundant recreation. Known for performing and visual arts, education, finance, advertising, and manufacturing, Minneapolis is also a hub of trade, industry, transportation and finance for the Upper Midwest.

In 1680, a French Franciscan priest, Father Louis Hennepin, was the area's first white man to arrive on the scene. In 1819, Fort Snelling was established to protect fur traders from the Sioux and Chippewa tribes. In 1848, two towns, St. Anthony (later named St. Paul), and Minneapolis, grew simultaneously, thus forming the metropolitan area known today as the Twin Cities. A tide of Swedish, German, and Norwegian immigrants came in the late nineteenth century, giving the city a decidedly Scandinavian flavor. Its many lakes gave Minneapolis its name, which comes from the Dakota word "minne," or "of the waters," and the Greek "polis," or city.

Minneapolis's traditional industries are lumber and flour milling. Since the 1950s, technology, including electronics, computers, and other related science industries, has played a vital role in the city's economy, as has printing and advertising. Ten Fortune 500 companies are based in Minneapolis, including UnitedHealth Group, Target, Best Buy, and 3M.

The city's economy is fueled by an influx of urban dwellers and rapid growth of rental units to house them. The Pillsbury A-Mill Apartment Complex, and the 26 Story Apartment Building are just two of the city's multi-million-dollar housing projects.

The U.S. Bank Stadium was funded by NFL tenant Minnesota Vikings, and the state. During construction of the stadium—built on the site of the old Metrodome—the team played its 2014 and 2015 seasons in the TCF Bank Stadium at the University of Minnesota. Called "Minnesota's biggest-ever public works project," the stadium opened in 2016 with 66,000 seats, and expanded to 70,000 for the 2018 Super Bowl.

Minneapolis has the fourth-highest percentage of LGBTQ individuals behind San Francisco, Seattle, and Atlanta. In 2013, the city was among 25 U.S. cities to receive the highest possible score from the Human Rights Campaign. In contrast, the city has experienced continued unrest in the wake of the 2020 death of African American George Floyd at the hands of Minneapolis police.

Well-known for its cultural and artistic offerings, Minneapolis occupies more theater seats per capita than any U.S. city outside of New York. The Minneapolis Institute of Arts has more than 100,000 pieces of art with renovated African Art galleries. A Michael Graves-designed wing holds contemporary and modern works. Other area attractions include the Science Museum of Minnesota, the Minneapolis Zoo, and the Charles A. Lindbergh Historic Site.

More than five miles of downtown Minneapolis are connected by comfortable, climate-controlled glass "skyways" one flight above ground.

Minneapolis is home to award-winning restaurants and chefs. Many Minneapolis-based chefs have won James Beard Foundation Awards, causing the city to be recognized as a flourishing food mecca.

Minneapolis is a major transportation hub. The Minneapolis-St. Paul International Airport reported more than 25 million travelers and $15.9 billion in revenue in 2021.

The city also hosts a Northstar Corridor commuter line between downtown and Big Lake on existing railroad tracks, and a Green Line linking downtown, the University of Minnesota, and downtown St. Paul. Old rail lines and bridges within the city have been converted for bicycles and pedestrians.

Minneapolis is located at the confluence of the Mississippi and Minnesota rivers. Numerous lakes mark the surrounding region, with 22 within the city park system. The climate is predominantly continental, with extreme swings in seasonal temperatures. Blizzards, freezing rain, tornadoes, wind, and hailstorms do occur. Due to the spring snow melt and excessive rain, the Mississippi River sees its share of floods.

Rankings

General Rankings

- The human resources consulting firm Mercer ranked 231 major cities worldwide in terms of overall quality of life. Minneapolis ranked #61. Criteria: political, social, economic, and socio-cultural factors; medical and health considerations; schools and education; public services and transportation; recreation; consumer goods; housing; and natural environment. *Mercer, "Mercer 2019 Quality of Living Survey," March 13, 2019*

- In their ninth annual survey, Livability.com looked at data for more than 2,300 mid-sized U.S. cities to determine the rankings for Livability's "Top 100 Best Places to Live" in 2022. Minneapolis ranked #6. Criteria: housing and economy; social and civic engagement; education; demographics; health care options; transportation & infrastructure; and community amenities. *Livability.com, "Top 100 Best Places to Live 2022" July 19, 2022*

Business/Finance Rankings

- Based on metro area social media reviews, the employment opinion group Glassdoor surveyed 50 of the most populous U.S. metro areas and equally weighed cost of living, hiring opportunity, and job satisfaction to compose a list of "25 Best Cities for Jobs." Median pay and home value, and number of active job openings were also factored in. The Minneapolis metro area was ranked #21 in overall job satisfaction. *www.glassdoor.com, "Best Cities for Jobs," February 25, 2020*

- The Brookings Institution ranked the nation's largest cities based on income inequality. Minneapolis was ranked #31 (#1 = greatest inequality). Criteria: the "95/20 ratio," a figure representing the income at which a household earns more than 95 percent of all other households, divided by the income at which a household earns more than only 20 percent of all other households. *Brookings Institution, "Household Income Inequality, Largest Cities of 97 Large U.S. Metro Areas, 2014-2016," February 5, 2018*

- The Brookings Institution ranked the 100 largest metro areas in the U.S. based on income inequality. Minneapolis was ranked #85 (#1 = greatest inequality). Criteria: the "95/20 ratio," a figure representing the income at which a household earns more than 95 percent of all other households, divided by the income at which a household earns more than only 20 percent of all other households. *Brookings Institution, "Household Income Inequality, 100 Largest U.S. Metro Areas, 2014-2016," February 5, 2018*

- Payscale.com ranked the 32 largest metro areas in terms of wage growth. The Minneapolis metro area ranked #24. Criteria: quarterly changes in private industry employee and education professional wage growth from the previous year. *PayScale, "Wage Trends by Metro Area-1st Quarter," April 20, 2023*

- The Minneapolis metro area was identified as one of the most debt-ridden places in America by the finance site Credit.com. The metro area was ranked #22. Criteria: residents' average credit card debt as well as median income. *Credit.com, "25 Cities With the Most Credit Card Debt," February 28, 2018*

- The Minneapolis metro area appeared on the Milken Institute "2022 Best Performing Cities" list. Rank: #119 out of 200 large metro areas (population over 250,000). Criteria: job growth; wage and salary growth; high-tech output growth; housing affordability; household broadband access. *Milken Institute, "Best-Performing Cities 2022," March 28, 2022*

- *Forbes* ranked the 200 most populous metro areas to determine the nation's "Best Places for Business and Careers." The Minneapolis metro area was ranked #32. Criteria: costs (business and living); job growth (past and projected); income growth; quality of life; educational attainment (college and high school); projected economic growth; cultural and leisure opportunities; workplace tolerance laws; net migration patterns. *Forbes, "The Best Places for Business and Careers 2019: Seattle Still On Top," October 30, 2019*

- Mercer Human Resources Consulting ranked 227 cities worldwide in terms of cost-of-living. Minneapolis ranked #83 (the lower the ranking, the higher the cost-of-living). The survey measured the comparative cost of over 200 items (such as housing, food, clothing, domestic supplies, transportation, and recreation/entertainment) in each location. *Mercer, "2022 Cost of Living City Ranking," June 29, 2022*

Education Rankings

- Personal finance website *WalletHub* analyzed the 150 largest U.S. metropolitan statistical areas to determine where the most educated Americans are putting their degrees to work. Criteria: education levels; percentage of workers with degrees; education quality and attainment gap; public school quality rankings; quality and enrollment of each metro area's universities. Minneapolis was ranked #19 (#1 = most educated city). *www.WalletHub.com, "Most & Least Educated Cities in America," July 18, 2022*

- Minneapolis was selected as one of the best cities for post grads by *Rent.com*. The city ranked among the top 10. Criteria: jobs per capita; unemployment rate; mean annual income; cost of living; rental inventory. *Rent.com, "Best Cities for College Grads," December 11, 2018*

- Minneapolis was selected as one of America's most literate cities. The city ranked #4 out of the 84 largest U.S. cities. Criteria: number of booksellers; library resources; Internet resources; educational attainment; periodical publishing resources; newspaper circulation. *Central Connecticut State University, "America's Most Literate Cities, 2018," February 2019*

Environmental Rankings

- Niche compiled a list of the nation's snowiest cities, based on the National Oceanic and Atmospheric Administration's 30-year average snowfall data. Among cities with a population of at least 50,000, Minneapolis ranked #24. *Niche.com, Top 25 Snowiest Cities in America, December 10, 2018*

- Sperling's BestPlaces assessed the 50 largest metropolitan areas of the United States for the likelihood of dangerously extreme weather events or earthquakes. In general the Southeast and South-Central regions have the highest risk of weather extremes and earthquakes, while the Pacific Northwest enjoys the lowest risk. Of the least risky metropolitan areas, the Minneapolis metro area was ranked #7. *www.bestplaces.net, "Avoid Natural Disasters: BestPlaces Reveals The Top 10 Safest Places to Live," October 25, 2017*

- The U.S. Environmental Protection Agency (EPA) released its list of U.S. metropolitan areas with the most ENERGY STAR certified buildings in 2022. The Minneapolis metro area was ranked #16 out of 25. *U.S. Environmental Protection Agency, "2023 Energy Star Top Cities," April 26, 2023*

Food/Drink Rankings

- The U.S. Chamber of Commerce Foundation conducted an in-depth study on local food truck regulations, surveyed 288 food truck owners, and ranked 20 major American cities based on how friendly they are for operating a food truck. The compiled index assessed the following: procedures for obtaining permits and licenses; complying with restrictions; and financial obligations associated with operating a food truck. Minneapolis ranked #16 overall (1 being the best). *www.foodtrucknation.us, "Food Truck Nation," March 20, 2018*

- Target Field was selected as one of PETA's "Top 10 Vegan-Friendly Ballparks" for 2019. The park ranked #3. *People for the Ethical Treatment of Animals, "Top 10 Vegan-Friendly Ballparks," May 23, 2019*

Health/Fitness Rankings

- For each of the 100 largest cities in the United States, the American Fitness Index®, compiled in partnership between the American College of Sports Medicine and the Elevance Health Foundation, evaluated community infrastructure and 34 health behaviors including preventive health, levels of chronic disease conditions, food insecurity, sleep quality, pedestrian safety, air quality, and community/environment resources that support physical activity. Minneapolis ranked #3 for "community fitness." *americanfitnessindex.org, "2022 ACSM American Fitness Index Summary Report," July 12, 2022*

- Minneapolis was identified as a "2022 Spring Allergy Capital." The area ranked #84 out of 100. Three groups of factors were used to identify the most challenging cities for people with allergies during the spring season: annual spring pollen scores; over the counter allergy medicine use; number of board-certified allergy specialists. *Asthma and Allergy Foundation of America, "Spring Allergy Capitals 2022," March 2, 2022*

- Minneapolis was identified as a "2022 Fall Allergy Capital." The area ranked #82 out of 100. Three groups of factors were used to identify the most challenging cities for people with allergies during the fall season: annual fall pollen scores; over the counter allergy medicine use; number of board-certified allergy specialists. *Asthma and Allergy Foundation of America, "Fall Allergy Capitals 2022," March 2, 2022*

- Minneapolis was identified as a "2022 Asthma Capital." The area ranked #55 out of the nation's 100 largest metropolitan areas. Criteria: estimated asthma prevalence; asthma-related mortality; and ER visits due to asthma. Risk factors analyzed but not factored in the rankings: annual pollen score; annual air quality; public smoking laws; access to board-certified asthma specialists; rescue and controller medication use; uninsured rate; poverty rate. *Asthma and Allergy Foundation of America, "Asthma Capitals 2022: The Most Challenging Places to Live With Asthma," September 14, 2022*

Real Estate Rankings

- *WalletHub* compared the most populated U.S. cities to determine which had the best markets for real estate agents. Minneapolis ranked #96 where demand was high and pay was the best. Criteria: sales per agent; annual median wage for real-estate agents; monthly average starting salary for real estate agents; real estate job density and competition; unemployment rate; home turnover rate; housing-market health index; and other relevant metrics. *www.WalletHub.com, "2021 Best Places to Be a Real Estate Agent," May 12, 2021*

- Minneapolis was ranked #69 out of 235 metro areas in terms of housing affordability in 2022 by the National Association of Home Builders (#1 = most affordable). Criteria: the share of homes sold in that area affordable to a family earning the local median income, based on standard mortgage underwriting criteria. *National Association of Home Builders®, NAHB-Wells Fargo Housing Opportunity Index, 4th Quarter 2022*

Safety Rankings

- To identify the most dangerous cities in America, *24/7 Wall St.* focused on violent crime categories—murder, non-negligent manslaughter, rape, robbery, and aggravated assault—as reported for every 100,000 residents using data from the FBI's 2020 annual Uniform Crime Report. For cities with populations over 25,000, Minneapolis was ranked #48. *247wallst.com, "America's Most Dangerous Cities" November 12, 2021*

- Statistics drawn from the FBI's Uniform Crime Report were used to rank the cities where violent crime rose the most year over year from 2019 to 2020. Only cities with 25,000 or more residents were included. *24/7 Wall St.* found that Minneapolis placed #21 of those with a notable surge in incidents of violent crime. *247wallst.com, "American Cities Where Crime Is Soaring," March 4, 2022*

- Allstate ranked the 200 largest cities in America in terms of driver safety. Minneapolis ranked #137. Criteria: internal property damage claims over a two-year period from January 2016 to December 2017. The report helps increase the importance of safety and awareness behind the wheel. *Allstate, "Allstate America's Best Drivers Report, 2019" June 24, 2019*

- Minneapolis was identified as one of the most dangerous cities in America by NeighborhoodScout. The city ranked #36 out of 100 (#1 = most dangerous). Criteria: number of violent crimes per 1,000 residents. The editors evaluated cities with 25,000 or more residents. *NeighborhoodScout.com, "2023 Top 100 Most Dangerous Cities in the U.S.," January 12, 2023*

Seniors/Retirement Rankings

- From its Best Cities for Successful Aging indexes, the Milken Institute generated rankings for metropolitan areas, weighing data in nine categories—health care, wellness, living arrangements, transportation and convenience, financial characteristics, education, employment, community engagement, and overall livability. The Minneapolis metro area was ranked #14 overall in the large metro area category. *Milken Institute, "Best Cities for Successful Aging, 2017" March 14, 2017*

Sports/Recreation Rankings

- Minneapolis was chosen as one of America's best cities for bicycling. The city ranked #4 out of 50. Criteria: cycling infrastructure that is safe and friendly for all ages; energy and bike culture. The editors evaluated cities with populations of 100,000 or more. *Bicycling, "The 50 Best Bike Cities in America," October 10, 2018*

Transportation Rankings

- Business Insider presented an AllTransit Performance Score ranking of public transportation in major U.S. cities and towns, with populations over 250,000, in which Minneapolis earned the #12-ranked "Transit Score," awarded for frequency of service, access to jobs, quality and number of stops, and affordability. *www.businessinsider.com, "The 17 Major U.S. Cities with the Best Public Transportation," April 17, 2018*

Women/Minorities Rankings

- Minneapolis was selected as one of the queerest cities in America by *The Advocate*. The city ranked #22 out of 25. Criteria, among many: Trans Pride parades/festivals; gay rugby teams; lesbian bars; LGBTQ centers; theater screenings of "Moonlight"; LGBTQ-inclusive nondiscrimination ordinances; and gay bowling teams. *The Advocate, "Queerest Cities in America 2017" January 12, 2017*

- Personal finance website *WalletHub* compared more than 180 U.S. cities across two key dimensions, "Hispanic Business-Friendliness" and "Hispanic Purchasing Power," to arrive at the most favorable conditions for Hispanic entrepreneurs. Minneapolis was ranked #131 out of 182. Criteria includes: share of Hispanic-Owned Businesses; Hispanic entrepreneurship rate to median annual income of Hispanics; Small Business-Friendliness score; cost of living; and number of Hispanics with at least a bachelor's degree. *WalletHub.com, "2019's Best Cities for Hispanic Entrepreneurs," May 1, 2019*

Miscellaneous Rankings

- *MoveHub* ranked 446 hipster cities across 20 countries, using its new and improved *alternative* Hipster Index and Minneapolis came out as #13 among the top 50. Criteria: population over 150,000; number of vintage boutiques; density of tattoo parlors; vegan places to eat; coffee shops; and density of vinyl record stores. *www.movehub.com, "The Hipster Index: Brighton Pips Portland to Global Top Spot," July 28, 2021*

- The watchdog site, Charity Navigator, conducted a study of charities in major markets both to analyze statistical differences in their financial, accountability, and transparency practices and to track year-to-year variations in individual philanthropic communities. The Minneapolis metro area was ranked #8 among the 30 metro markets in the rating category of Overall Score. *www.charitynavigator.org, "2017 Metro Market Study," May 1, 2017*

- *WalletHub* compared the 150 most populated U.S. cities to determine their operating efficiency. A "Quality of Services" score was constructed for each city and then divided by the total budget per capita to reveal which were managed the best. Minneapolis ranked #117. Criteria: financial stability; economy; education; safety; health; infrastructure and pollution. *www.WalletHub.com, "2022's Best- & Worst-Run Cities in America," June 21, 2022*

- Minneapolis was selected as one of "America's Friendliest Cities." The city ranked #18 in the "Friendliest" category. Respondents to an online survey were asked to rate 38 top urban destinations in the United States as to general friendliness, as well as manners, politeness and warm disposition. *Travel + Leisure, "America's Friendliest Cities," October 20, 2017*

- The National Alliance to End Homelessness listed the 25 most populous metro areas with the highest rate of homelessness. The Minneapolis metro area had a high rate of homelessness. Criteria: number of homeless people per 10,000 population in 2016. *National Alliance to End Homelessness, "Homelessness in the 25 Most Populous U.S. Metro Areas," September 1, 2017*

Business Environment

DEMOGRAPHICS

Population Growth

Area	1990 Census	2000 Census	2010 Census	2020 Census	Population Growth (%) 1990-2020	Population Growth (%) 2010-2020
City	368,383	382,618	382,578	429,954	16.7	12.4
MSA[1]	2,538,834	2,968,806	3,279,833	3,690,261	45.4	12.5
U.S.	248,709,873	281,421,906	308,745,538	331,449,281	33.3	7.4

Note: (1) Figures cover the Minneapolis-St. Paul-Bloomington, MN-WI Metropolitan Statistical Area
Source: U.S. Census Bureau, 1990 Census, 2000 Census, 2010 Census, 2020 Census

Race

Area	White Alone[2] (%)	Black Alone[2] (%)	Asian Alone[2] (%)	AIAN[3] Alone[2] (%)	NHOPI[4] Alone[2] (%)	Other Race Alone[2] (%)	Two or More Races (%)
City	59.5	19.1	5.8	1.7	0.0	5.9	8.0
MSA[1]	73.0	9.1	7.2	0.8	0.0	3.3	6.6
U.S.	61.6	12.4	6.0	1.1	0.2	8.4	10.2

Note: (1) Figures cover the Minneapolis-St. Paul-Bloomington, MN-WI Metropolitan Statistical Area;
(2) Alone is defined as not being in combination with one or more other races; (3) American Indian and Alaska Native; (4) Native Hawaiian and Other Pacific Islander
Source: U.S. Census Bureau, 2020 Census

Hispanic or Latino Origin

Area	Total (%)	Mexican (%)	Puerto Rican (%)	Cuban (%)	Other (%)
City	9.8	5.3	0.5	0.2	3.8
MSA[1]	6.1	3.8	0.4	0.1	1.8
U.S.	18.4	11.2	1.8	0.7	4.7

Note: Persons of Hispanic or Latino origin can be of any race; (1) Figures cover the Minneapolis-St. Paul-Bloomington, MN-WI Metropolitan Statistical Area
Source: U.S. Census Bureau, 2017-2021 American Community Survey 5-Year Estimates

Age

Area	Under Age 5	Age 5–19	Age 20–34	Age 35–44	Age 45–54	Age 55–64	Age 65–74	Age 75–84	Age 85+	Median Age
City	5.6	16.1	32.8	14.7	10.3	9.7	7.1	2.6	1.0	32.6
MSA[1]	6.1	19.8	20.5	13.7	12.3	13.0	8.9	4.1	1.7	37.5
U.S.	5.6	19.2	20.2	12.7	12.4	13.1	10.0	4.9	1.9	38.8

Note: (1) Figures cover the Minneapolis-St. Paul-Bloomington, MN-WI Metropolitan Statistical Area
Source: U.S. Census Bureau, 2020 Census

Disability by Age

Area	All Ages	Under 18 Years Old	18 to 64 Years Old	65 Years and Over
City	11.0	4.9	9.8	32.2
MSA[1]	10.0	3.9	8.2	28.5
U.S.	12.6	4.4	10.3	33.4

Note: Figures show percent of the civilian noninstitutionalized population that reported having a disability. Disability status is determined from six types of difficulty: vision, hearing, cognitive, ambulatory, self-care, and independent living. For children under 5 years old, hearing and vision difficulty are used to determine disability status. For children between the ages of 5 and 14, disability status is determined from hearing, vision, cognitive, ambulatory, and self-care difficulties. For people aged 15 years and older, they are considered to have a disability if they have difficulty with any one of the six difficulty types; Note: (1) Figures cover the Minneapolis-St. Paul-Bloomington, MN-WI Metropolitan Statistical Area
Source: U.S. Census Bureau, 2017-2021 American Community Survey 5-Year Estimates

Ancestry

Area	German	Irish	English	American	Italian	Polish	French[2]	Scottish	Dutch
City	20.9	10.5	6.5	1.9	2.6	3.9	2.7	1.4	1.3
MSA[1]	28.1	10.9	6.3	3.0	2.6	4.1	3.2	1.2	1.4
U.S.	12.8	9.6	8.1	5.7	5.0	2.7	2.2	1.6	1.1

Note: Figures are the percentage of the total population reporting a particular ancestry. The nine most commonly reported ancestries in the U.S. are shown. Figures include multiple ancestries (e.g. if a person reported being Irish and Italian, they were included in both columns); (1) Figures cover the Minneapolis-St. Paul-Bloomington, MN-WI Metropolitan Statistical Area; (2) Excludes Basque
Source: U.S. Census Bureau, 2017-2021 American Community Survey 5-Year Estimates

Foreign-born Population

Area	Any Foreign Country	Percent of Population Born in							
		Asia	Mexico	Europe	Caribbean	Central America[2]	South America	Africa	Canada
City	14.8	3.7	1.8	1.2	0.3	0.4	1.5	5.8	0.3
MSA[1]	10.7	4.1	1.1	1.0	0.1	0.4	0.6	3.0	0.2
U.S.	13.6	4.2	3.3	1.4	1.1	0.4	1.1	0.8	0.2

Note: (1) Figures cover the Minneapolis-St. Paul-Bloomington, MN-WI Metropolitan Statistical Area;
(2) Excludes Mexico.
Source: U.S. Census Bureau, 2017-2021 American Community Survey 5-Year Estimates

Household Size

Area	Persons in Household (%)							Average Household Size
	One	Two	Three	Four	Five	Six	Seven or More	
City	40.4	31.6	11.6	9.6	3.5	1.7	1.5	2.20
MSA[1]	28.1	34.2	14.7	13.6	5.9	2.1	1.4	2.50
U.S.	28.1	33.8	15.5	12.9	6.0	2.3	1.4	2.60

Note: (1) Figures cover the Minneapolis-St. Paul-Bloomington, MN-WI Metropolitan Statistical Area
Source: U.S. Census Bureau, 2017-2021 American Community Survey 5-Year Estimates

Household Relationships

Area	House-holder	Opposite-sex Spouse	Same-sex Spouse	Opposite-sex Unmarried Partner	Same-sex Unmarried Partner	Child[2]	Grand-child	Other Relatives	Non-relatives
City	43.7	12.0	0.6	3.9	0.5	22.1	1.1	3.5	8.0
MSA[1]	38.9	18.7	0.2	2.8	0.2	29.4	1.2	3.3	3.3
U.S.	38.3	17.5	0.2	2.5	0.2	28.3	2.4	4.8	3.4

Note: Figures are percent of the total population; (1) Figures cover the Minneapolis-St. Paul-Bloomington,
MN-WI Metropolitan Statistical Area; (2) Includes biological, adopted, and stepchildren of the householder
Source: U.S. Census Bureau, 2020 Census

Gender

Area	Males	Females	Males per 100 Females
City	216,381	213,573	101.3
MSA[1]	1,824,100	1,866,161	97.7
U.S.	162,685,811	168,763,470	96.4

Note: (1) Figures cover the Minneapolis-St. Paul-Bloomington, MN-WI Metropolitan Statistical Area
Source: U.S. Census Bureau, 2020 Census

Marital Status

Area	Never Married	Now Married[2]	Separated	Widowed	Divorced
City	51.2	34.3	1.4	3.0	10.1
MSA[1]	33.7	51.0	1.0	4.1	10.1
U.S.	33.8	48.0	1.8	5.6	10.8

Note: Figures are percentages and cover the population 15 years of age and older; (1) Figures cover the
Minneapolis-St. Paul-Bloomington, MN-WI Metropolitan Statistical Area; (2) Excludes separated
Source: U.S. Census Bureau, 2017-2021 American Community Survey 5-Year Estimates

Religious Groups by Family

Area	Catholic	Baptist	Methodist	LDS[2]	Pentecostal	Lutheran	Islam	Adventist	Other
MSA[1]	19.8	0.8	1.4	0.5	2.5	10.7	2.9	0.7	7.4
U.S.	18.7	7.3	3.0	2.0	1.8	1.7	1.3	1.3	11.6

Note: Figures are the number of adherents as a percentage of the total population and cover the eight largest
religious groups in the U.S; (1) Figures cover the Minneapolis-St. Paul-Bloomington, MN-WI Metropolitan
Statistical Area; (2) Church of Jesus Christ of Latter-day Saints
Sources: 2020 U.S. Religion Census, Association of Statisticians of American Religious Bodies; The
Association of Religion Data Archives (ARDA)

Religious Groups by Tradition

Area	Catholic	Evangelical Protestant	Mainline Protestant	Black Protestant	Islam	Judaism	Hinduism	Orthodox	Buddhism
MSA[1]	19.8	10.6	10.3	0.5	2.9	0.6	0.2	0.3	0.3
U.S.	18.7	16.5	5.2	2.3	1.3	0.6	0.4	0.4	0.3

Note: Figures are the number of adherents as a percentage of the total population; (1) Figures cover the
Minneapolis-St. Paul-Bloomington, MN-WI Metropolitan Statistical Area
Sources: 2020 U.S. Religion Census, Association of Statisticians of American Religious Bodies; The
Association of Religion Data Archives (ARDA)

ECONOMY

Gross Metropolitan Product

Area	2020	2021	2022	2023	Rank[2]
MSA[1]	270.7	298.9	324.7	344.9	15

Note: Figures are in billions of dollars; (1) Figures cover the Minneapolis-St. Paul-Bloomington, MN-WI Metropolitan Statistical Area; (2) Rank is based on 2021 data and ranges from 1 to 381
Source: U.S. Conference of Mayors, U.S. Metro Economies: U.S. Metros Compared to Global and State Economies, June 2022

Economic Growth

Area	2018-20 (%)	2021 (%)	2022 (%)	2023 (%)	Rank[2]
MSA[1]	-1.9	5.9	2.8	3.0	276
U.S.	-0.6	5.7	3.1	2.9	—

Note: Figures are real gross metropolitan product (GMP) growth rates and represent average annual percent change; (1) Figures cover the Minneapolis-St. Paul-Bloomington, MN-WI Metropolitan Statistical Area; (2) Rank is based on 2020 2-year average annual percent change and ranges from 1 to 381
Source: U.S. Conference of Mayors, U.S. Metro Economies: U.S. Metros Compared to Global and State Economies, June 2022

Metropolitan Area Exports

Area	2016	2017	2018	2019	2020	2021	Rank[2]
MSA[1]	18,329.2	19,070.9	20,016.2	18,633.0	17,109.5	21,098.8	21

Note: Figures are in millions of dollars; (1) Figures cover the Minneapolis-St. Paul-Bloomington, MN-WI Metropolitan Statistical Area; (2) Rank is based on 2021 data and ranges from 1 to 388
Source: U.S. Department of Commerce, International Trade Administration, Office of Trade and Economic Analysis, Industry and Analysis, Exports by Metropolitan Area, data extracted March 16, 2023

Building Permits

Area	Single-Family			Multi-Family			Total		
	2021	2022	Pct. Chg.	2021	2022	Pct. Chg.	2021	2022	Pct. Chg.
City	63	55	-12.7	3,119	3,626	16.3	3,182	3,681	15.7
MSA[1]	11,734	9,114	-22.3	14,343	14,611	1.9	26,077	23,725	-9.0
U.S.	1,115,400	975,600	-12.5	621,600	689,500	10.9	1,737,000	1,665,100	-4.1

Note: (1) Figures cover the Minneapolis-St. Paul-Bloomington, MN-WI Metropolitan Statistical Area; Figures represent new, privately-owned housing units authorized (unadjusted data); All permit data are based on estimates with imputation
Source: U.S. Census Bureau, Manufacturing, Mining, and Construction Statistics, Building Permits, 2021, 2022

Bankruptcy Filings

Area	Business Filings			Nonbusiness Filings		
	2021	2022	% Chg.	2021	2022	% Chg.
Hennepin County	52	55	5.8	1,240	1,200	-3.2
U.S.	14,347	13,481	-6.0	399,269	374,240	-6.3

Note: Business filings include Chapter 7, Chapter 9, Chapter 11, Chapter 12, Chapter 13, Chapter 15, and Section 304; Nonbusiness filings include Chapter 7, Chapter 11, and Chapter 13
Source: Administrative Office of the U.S. Courts, Business and Nonbusiness Bankruptcy, County Cases Commenced by Chapter of the Bankruptcy Code, During the 12-Month Period Ending December 31, 2021 and Business and Nonbusiness Bankruptcy, County Cases Commenced by Chapter of the Bankruptcy Code, During the 12-Month Period Ending December 31, 2022

Housing Vacancy Rates

Area	Gross Vacancy Rate[2] (%)			Year-Round Vacancy Rate[3] (%)			Rental Vacancy Rate[4] (%)			Homeowner Vacancy Rate[5] (%)		
	2020	2021	2022	2020	2021	2022	2020	2021	2022	2020	2021	2022
MSA[1]	4.7	5.3	4.8	3.7	4.6	4.5	4.0	4.9	6.7	0.5	0.6	0.8
U.S.	10.6	10.8	10.5	8.2	8.4	8.2	6.3	6.1	5.8	1.0	0.9	0.8

Note: (1) Figures cover the Minneapolis-St. Paul-Bloomington, MN-WI Metropolitan Statistical Area; (2) The percentage of the total housing inventory that is vacant; (3) The percentage of the housing inventory (excluding seasonal units) that is year-round vacant; (4) The percentage of rental inventory that is vacant for rent; (5) The percentage of homeowner inventory that is vacant for sale
Source: U.S. Census Bureau, Housing Vacancies and Homeownership Annual Statistics: 2020, 2021, 2022

INCOME

Income

Area	Per Capita ($)	Median Household ($)	Average Household ($)
City	43,925	70,099	99,741
MSA[1]	45,301	87,397	114,491
U.S.	37,638	69,021	97,196

Note: (1) Figures cover the Minneapolis-St. Paul-Bloomington, MN-WI Metropolitan Statistical Area
Source: U.S. Census Bureau, 2017-2021 American Community Survey 5-Year Estimates

Household Income Distribution

Area	Percent of Households Earning							
	Under $15,000	$15,000 -$24,999	$25,000 -$34,999	$35,000 -$49,999	$50,000 -$74,999	$75,000 -$99,999	$100,000 -$149,999	$150,000 and up
City	11.3	7.1	7.5	11.0	16.1	12.6	15.9	18.5
MSA[1]	6.1	5.2	6.1	9.7	16.0	13.7	20.2	23.2
U.S.	9.4	7.8	8.2	11.4	16.8	12.8	16.3	17.3

Note: (1) Figures cover the Minneapolis-St. Paul-Bloomington, MN-WI Metropolitan Statistical Area
Source: U.S. Census Bureau, 2017-2021 American Community Survey 5-Year Estimates

Poverty Rate

Area	All Ages	Under 18 Years Old	18 to 64 Years Old	65 Years and Over
City	17.0	21.2	16.3	13.6
MSA[1]	8.1	10.1	7.7	6.8
U.S.	12.6	17.0	11.8	9.6

Note: Figures are percentage of people whose income during the past 12 months was below the poverty level;
(1) Figures cover the Minneapolis-St. Paul-Bloomington, MN-WI Metropolitan Statistical Area
Source: U.S. Census Bureau, 2017-2021 American Community Survey 5-Year Estimates

EMPLOYMENT

Labor Force and Employment

Area	Civilian Labor Force			Workers Employed		
	Dec. 2021	Dec. 2022	% Chg.	Dec. 2021	Dec. 2022	% Chg.
City	241,913	246,063	1.7	235,948	240,094	1.8
MSA[1]	1,991,752	2,028,489	1.8	1,943,478	1,975,295	1.6
U.S.	161,696,000	164,224,000	1.6	155,732,000	158,872,000	2.0

Note: Data is not seasonally adjusted and covers workers 16 years of age and older; (1) Figures cover the
Minneapolis-St. Paul-Bloomington, MN-WI Metropolitan Statistical Area
Source: Bureau of Labor Statistics, Local Area Unemployment Statistics

Unemployment Rate

Area	2022											
	Jan.	Feb.	Mar.	Apr.	May	Jun.	Jul.	Aug.	Sep.	Oct.	Nov.	Dec.
City	3.0	2.2	2.4	1.5	1.7	2.4	2.2	2.3	2.0	1.9	2.0	2.4
MSA[1]	3.0	2.4	2.6	1.5	1.6	2.2	2.0	2.2	1.9	1.7	1.9	2.6
U.S.	4.4	4.1	3.8	3.3	3.4	3.8	3.8	3.8	3.3	3.4	3.4	3.3

Note: Data is not seasonally adjusted and covers workers 16 years of age and older; (1) Figures cover the
Minneapolis-St. Paul-Bloomington, MN-WI Metropolitan Statistical Area
Source: Bureau of Labor Statistics, Local Area Unemployment Statistics

Average Wages

Occupation	$/Hr.	Occupation	$/Hr.
Accountants and Auditors	41.61	Maintenance and Repair Workers	25.64
Automotive Mechanics	26.35	Marketing Managers	78.99
Bookkeepers	24.93	Network and Computer Systems Admin.	46.85
Carpenters	31.05	Nurses, Licensed Practical	27.70
Cashiers	14.83	Nurses, Registered	44.32
Computer Programmers	56.92	Nursing Assistants	22.36
Computer Systems Analysts	51.73	Office Clerks, General	22.34
Computer User Support Specialists	30.92	Physical Therapists	43.60
Construction Laborers	27.61	Physicians	145.35
Cooks, Restaurant	17.93	Plumbers, Pipefitters and Steamfitters	39.07
Customer Service Representatives	22.61	Police and Sheriff's Patrol Officers	39.69
Dentists	93.89	Postal Service Mail Carriers	27.77
Electricians	37.09	Real Estate Sales Agents	n/a
Engineers, Electrical	50.35	Retail Salespersons	17.68
Fast Food and Counter Workers	14.79	Sales Representatives, Technical/Scientific	47.57
Financial Managers	76.74	Secretaries, Exc. Legal/Medical/Executive	23.29
First-Line Supervisors of Office Workers	34.96	Security Guards	18.79
General and Operations Managers	56.37	Surgeons	176.40
Hairdressers/Cosmetologists	20.87	Teacher Assistants, Exc. Postsecondary*	18.50
Home Health and Personal Care Aides	15.64	Teachers, Secondary School, Exc. Sp. Ed.*	31.91
Janitors and Cleaners	17.94	Telemarketers	22.98
Landscaping/Groundskeeping Workers	19.96	Truck Drivers, Heavy/Tractor-Trailer	28.77
Lawyers	83.25	Truck Drivers, Light/Delivery Services	23.50
Maids and Housekeeping Cleaners	17.58	Waiters and Waitresses	13.34

Note: Wage data covers the Minneapolis-St. Paul-Bloomington, MN-WI Metropolitan Statistical Area;
(*) Hourly wages were calculated from annual wage data based on a 40 hour work week; n/a not available.
Source: Bureau of Labor Statistics, Metro Area Occupational Employment & Wage Estimates, May 2022

Employment by Industry

Sector	MSA[1]		U.S.
	Number of Employees	Percent of Total	Percent of Total
Construction, Mining, and Logging	79,800	4.1	5.4
Private Education and Health Services	352,500	18.0	16.1
Financial Activities	149,800	7.6	5.9
Government	245,000	12.5	14.5
Information	30,200	1.5	2.0
Leisure and Hospitality	174,900	8.9	10.3
Manufacturing	205,400	10.5	8.4
Other Services	70,100	3.6	3.7
Professional and Business Services	301,500	15.4	14.7
Retail Trade	183,100	9.3	10.2
Transportation, Warehousing, and Utilities	84,300	4.3	4.9
Wholesale Trade	84,500	4.3	3.9

Note: Figures are non-farm employment as of December 2022. Figures are not seasonally adjusted and include workers 16 years of age and older; (1) Figures cover the Minneapolis-St. Paul-Bloomington, MN-WI Metropolitan Statistical Area
Source: Bureau of Labor Statistics, Current Employment Statistics, Employment, Hours, and Earnings

Employment by Occupation

Occupation Classification	City (%)	MSA[1] (%)	U.S. (%)
Management, Business, Science, and Arts	54.2	46.6	40.3
Natural Resources, Construction, and Maintenance	3.3	6.5	8.7
Production, Transportation, and Material Moving	9.1	12.2	13.1
Sales and Office	17.7	20.1	20.9
Service	15.8	14.5	17.0

Note: Figures cover employed civilians 16 years of age and older; (1) Figures cover the Minneapolis-St. Paul-Bloomington, MN-WI Metropolitan Statistical Area
Source: U.S. Census Bureau, 2017-2021 American Community Survey 5-Year Estimates

Occupations with Greatest Projected Employment Growth: 2022 – 2024

Occupation[1]	2022 Employment	2024 Projected Employment	Numeric Employment Change	Percent Employment Change
Home Health and Personal Care Aides	116,020	120,600	4,580	3.9
Cooks, Restaurant	23,930	25,800	1,870	7.8
Software Developers and Software Quality Assurance Analysts and Testers	48,010	49,650	1,640	3.4
General and Operations Managers	68,530	70,150	1,620	2.4
Fast Food and Counter Workers	63,160	64,720	1,560	2.5
Retail Salespersons	76,640	77,760	1,120	1.5
Stockers and Order Fillers	38,470	39,540	1,070	2.8
Registered Nurses	72,140	73,200	1,060	1.5
Waiters and Waitresses	36,730	37,740	1,010	2.7
Market Research Analysts and Marketing Specialists	22,780	23,760	980	4.3

Note: Projections cover Minnesota; (1) Sorted by numeric employment change
Source: www.projectionscentral.com, State Occupational Projections, 2022–2024 Short-Term Projections

Fastest-Growing Occupations: 2022 – 2024

Occupation[1]	2022 Employment	2024 Projected Employment	Numeric Employment Change	Percent Employment Change
Nurse Practitioners	4,810	5,250	440	9.1
Flight Attendants	2,780	3,020	240	8.6
Cooks, Restaurant	23,930	25,800	1,870	7.8
Statisticians	970	1,040	70	7.2
Dental Laboratory Technicians	690	740	50	7.2
Logisticians	2,720	2,910	190	7.0
Computer Numerically Controlled Tool Programmers	1,080	1,150	70	6.5
Physician Assistants	3,280	3,490	210	6.4
Medical and Health Services Managers	9,790	10,400	610	6.2
Operations Research Analysts	2,420	2,560	140	5.8

Note: Projections cover Minnesota; (1) Sorted by percent employment change and excludes occupations with numeric employment change less than 50
Source: www.projectionscentral.com, State Occupational Projections, 2022–2024 Short-Term Projections

CITY FINANCES

City Government Finances

Component	2020 ($000)	2020 ($ per capita)
Total Revenues	1,414,336	3,292
Total Expenditures	1,362,979	3,173
Debt Outstanding	2,694,974	6,273
Cash and Securities[1]	2,846,062	6,625

Note: (1) Cash and security holdings of a government at the close of its fiscal year, including those of its dependent agencies, utilities, and liquor stores.
Source: U.S. Census Bureau, State & Local Government Finances 2020

City Government Revenue by Source

Source	2020 ($000)	2020 ($ per capita)	2020 (%)
General Revenue			
From Federal Government	30,850	72	2.2
From State Government	157,497	367	11.1
From Local Governments	0	0	0.0
Taxes			
Property	353,456	823	25.0
Sales and Gross Receipts	128,896	300	9.1
Personal Income	0	0	0.0
Corporate Income	0	0	0.0
Motor Vehicle License	0	0	0.0
Other Taxes	47,916	112	3.4
Current Charges	437,087	1,017	30.9
Liquor Store	0	0	0.0
Utility	83,288	194	5.9

Source: U.S. Census Bureau, State & Local Government Finances 2020

City Government Expenditures by Function

Function	2020 ($000)	2020 ($ per capita)	2020 (%)
General Direct Expenditures			
Air Transportation	0	0	0.0
Corrections	0	0	0.0
Education	0	0	0.0
Employment Security Administration	0	0	0.0
Financial Administration	23,643	55	1.7
Fire Protection	69,300	161	5.1
General Public Buildings	8,744	20	0.6
Governmental Administration, Other	13,547	31	1.0
Health	27,791	64	2.0
Highways	71,092	165	5.2
Hospitals	0	0	0.0
Housing and Community Development	144,304	335	10.6
Interest on General Debt	137,778	320	10.1
Judicial and Legal	17,387	40	1.3
Libraries	0	0	0.0
Parking	49,501	115	3.6
Parks and Recreation	131,553	306	9.7
Police Protection	181,165	421	13.3
Public Welfare	0	0	0.0
Sewerage	135,658	315	10.0
Solid Waste Management	40,908	95	3.0
Veterans' Services	0	0	0.0
Liquor Store	0	0	0.0
Utility	108,187	251	7.9

Source: U.S. Census Bureau, State & Local Government Finances 2020

TAXES

State Corporate Income Tax Rates

State	Tax Rate (%)	Income Brackets ($)	Num. of Brackets	Financial Institution Tax Rate (%)[a]	Federal Income Tax Ded.
Minnesota	9.8 (l)	Flat rate	1	9.8 (l)	No

Note: Tax rates as of January 1, 2023; (a) Rates listed are the corporate income tax rate applied to financial institutions or excise taxes based on income. Some states have other taxes based upon the value of deposits or shares; (l) In addition, Minnesota levies a 5.8% tentative minimum tax on Alternative Minimum Taxable Income. Minnesota also imposes a surtax ranging up to $11,570.
Source: Federation of Tax Administrators, State Corporate Income Tax Rates, January 1, 2023

State Individual Income Tax Rates

| State | Tax Rate (%) | Income Brackets ($) | Personal Exemptions ($) | | | Standard Ded. ($) | |
			Single	Married	Depend.	Single	Married
Minnesota (a)	5.35 - 9.85	30,070 - 183,341 (n)	(d)	(d)	4,450	13,850	27,700 (d)

Note: Tax rates as of January 1, 2023; Local- and county-level taxes are not included; Federal income tax is not deductible on state income tax returns; (a) 16 states have statutory provision for automatically adjusting to the rate of inflation the dollar values of the income tax brackets, standard deductions, and/or personal exemptions. Oregon does not index the income brackets for $125,000 and over; (d) These states use the personal exemption/standard deduction amounts provided in the federal Internal Revenue Code; (n) The income brackets reported for Minnesota are for single individuals. For married couples filing jointly, the same tax rates apply to income brackets ranging from $43,950 to $304,971.
Source: Federation of Tax Administrators, State Individual Income Tax Rates, January 1, 2023

Various State Sales and Excise Tax Rates

State	State Sales Tax (%)	Gasoline[1] ($/gal.)	Cigarette[2] ($/pack)	Spirits[3] ($/gal.)	Wine[4] ($/gal.)	Beer[5] ($/gal.)	Recreational Marijuana (%)
Minnesota	6.875	0.306	3.732	8.70	1.24	0.47	Not legal

Note: All tax rates as of January 1, 2023; (1) The American Petroleum Institute has developed a methodology for determining the average tax rate on a gallon of fuel. Rates may include any of the following: excise taxes, environmental fees, storage tank fees, other fees or taxes, general sales tax, and local taxes; (2) The federal excise tax of $1.0066 per pack and local taxes are not included; (3) Rates are those applicable to off-premise sales of 40% alcohol by volume (a.b.v.) distilled spirits in 750ml containers. Local excise taxes are excluded; (4) Rates are those applicable to off-premise sales of 11% a.b.v. non-carbonated wine in 750ml containers; (5) Rates are those applicable to off-premise sales of 4.7% a.b.v. beer in 12 ounce containers.
Source: Tax Foundation, 2023 Facts & Figures: How Does Your State Compare?

State Business Tax Climate Index Rankings

State	Overall Rank	Corporate Tax Rank	Individual Income Tax Rank	Sales Tax Rank	Property Tax Rank	Unemployment Insurance Tax Rank
Minnesota	45	43	43	29	31	34

Note: The index is a measure of how each state's tax laws affect economic performance. The lower the rank, the more favorable a state's tax system is for business. States without a given tax are given a ranking of 1. The scores/rankings for the District of Columbia do not affect other states. The 2023 index represents the tax climate as of July 1, 2022.
Source: Tax Foundation, State Business Tax Climate Index 2023

TRANSPORTATION

Means of Transportation to Work

| Area | Car/Truck/Van | | Public Transportation | | | Bicycle | Walked | Other Means | Worked at Home |
	Drove Alone	Car-pooled	Bus	Subway	Railroad				
City	56.4	6.3	8.6	0.6	0.2	2.9	6.6	2.6	15.8
MSA[1]	72.1	7.4	3.2	0.1	0.1	0.6	2.1	1.3	13.1
U.S.	73.2	8.6	2.0	1.6	0.5	0.5	2.5	1.5	9.7

Note: Figures are percentages and cover workers 16 years of age and older; (1) Figures cover the Minneapolis-St. Paul-Bloomington, MN-WI Metropolitan Statistical Area
Source: U.S. Census Bureau, 2017-2021 American Community Survey 5-Year Estimates

Travel Time to Work

Area	Less Than 10 Minutes	10 to 19 Minutes	20 to 29 Minutes	30 to 44 Minutes	45 to 59 Minutes	60 to 89 Minutes	90 Minutes or More
City	7.9	32.6	30.2	20.9	4.5	2.7	1.1
MSA[1]	10.6	28.0	25.2	23.2	7.7	4.0	1.4
U.S.	12.4	28.5	21.0	20.9	8.2	6.2	2.9

Note: Note: Figures are percentages and include workers 16 years old and over; (1) Figures cover the Minneapolis-St. Paul-Bloomington, MN-WI Metropolitan Statistical Area
Source: U.S. Census Bureau, 2017-2021 American Community Survey 5-Year Estimates

Key Congestion Measures

Measure	1990	2000	2010	2015	2020
Annual Hours of Delay, Total (000)	26,330	68,767	84,317	99,730	59,835
Annual Hours of Delay, Per Auto Commuter	24	47	47	53	32
Annual Congestion Cost, Per Auto Commuter ($)	477	935	910	995	620

Note: Covers the Minneapolis-St. Paul MN-WI urban area
Source: Texas A&M Transportation Institute, 2021 Urban Mobility Report

Freeway Travel Time Index

Measure	1985	1990	1995	2000	2005	2010	2015	2020
Urban Area Index[1]	1.10	1.14	1.21	1.27	1.28	1.25	1.25	1.11
Urban Area Rank[1,2]	27	26	16	10	14	21	24	20

Note: Freeway Travel Time Index—the ratio of travel time in the peak period to the travel time at free-flow conditions. For example, a value of 1.30 indicates a 20-minute free-flow trip takes 26 minutes in the peak (20 minutes x 1.30 = 26 minutes); (1) Covers the Minneapolis-St. Paul MN-WI urban area; (2) Rank is based on 101 larger urban areas (#1 = highest travel time index)
Source: Texas A&M Transportation Institute, 2021 Urban Mobility Report

Public Transportation

Agency Name / Mode of Transportation	Vehicles Operated in Maximum Service[1]	Annual Unlinked Passenger Trips[2] (in thous.)	Annual Passenger Miles[3] (in thous.)
Metro Transit			
Bus (directly operated)	490	22,137.1	93,379.2
Commuter Rail (purchased transportation)	10	50.4	1,245.8
Light Rail (directly operated)	75	10,673.6	42,399.6

Note: (1) Number of revenue vehicles operated by the given mode and type of service to meet the annual maximum service requirement. This is the revenue vehicle count during the peak season of the year; on the week and day that maximum service is provided. Vehicles operated in maximum service (VOMS) exclude atypical days and one-time special events; (2) Number of passengers who boarded public transportation vehicles. Passengers are counted each time they board a vehicle no matter how many vehicles they use to travel from their origin to their destination. (3) Sum of the distances ridden by all passengers during the entire fiscal year.
Source: Federal Transit Administration, National Transit Database, 2021

Air Transportation

Airport Name and Code / Type of Service	Passenger Airlines[1]	Passenger Enplanements	Freight Carriers[2]	Freight (lbs)
Minneapolis-St. Paul International (MSP)				
Domestic service (U.S. carriers - 2022)	35	14,176,543	19	179,880,065
International service (U.S. carriers - 2021)	6	340,122	3	11,255,361

Note: (1) Includes all U.S.-based major, minor and commuter airlines that carried at least one passenger during the year; (2) Includes all U.S.-based airlines and freight carriers that transported at least one pound of freight during the year.
Source: Bureau of Transportation Statistics, The Intermodal Transportation Database, Air Carriers: T-100 Domestic Market (U.S. Carriers), 2022; Bureau of Transportation Statistics, The Intermodal Transportation Database, Air Carriers: T-100 International Market (U.S. Carriers), 2021

BUSINESSES

Major Business Headquarters

Company Name	Industry	Rankings Fortune[1]	Rankings Forbes[2]
Ameriprise Financial	Diversified financials	277	-
Cargill	Food & drink	-	1
General Mills	Food consumer products	201	-
Mortenson	Construction	-	115
Ryan Companies	Construction	-	139
Target	General merchandisers	32	-
Thrivent Financial	Not-for-profit financial services	351	-
U.S. Bancorp	Commercial banks	150	-
Xcel Energy	Utilities, gas and electric	278	-

Note: (1) Companies that produce a 10-K are ranked 1 to 500 based on 2021 revenue; (2) All private companies with at least $2 billion in annual revenue through the end of their most current fiscal year are ranked 1 to 246; companies listed are headquartered in the city; dashes indicate no ranking
Source: Fortune, "Fortune 500," 2022; Forbes, "America's Largest Private Companies," 2022

Fastest-Growing Businesses

According to *Inc.*, Minneapolis is home to five of America's 500 fastest-growing private companies: **Franchise Ramp** (#49); **Branch** (#220); **The Stable** (#329); **Bold Orange Company** (#470); **Kwikly Dental Staffing** (#491). Criteria: must be an independent, privately-held, for-profit, U.S. corporation, proprietorship or partnership as of December 31, 2021; revenues must be at least $100,000 in 2018 and $2 million in 2021; must have four-year operating/sales history. *Inc., "America's 500 Fastest-Growing Private Companies," 2022*

According to Deloitte, Minneapolis is home to two of North America's 500 fastest-growing high-technology companies: **Branch** (#69); **Total Expert** (#494). Companies are ranked by percentage growth in revenue over a four-year period. Criteria for inclusion: company must be headquartered within North America; must own proprietary intellectual property or technology that is sold to customers in products that contributes to a significant portion of the company's operating revenue; must have been in business for a minumum of four years with 2018 operating revenues of at least $50,000 USD/CD and 2021 operating revenues of at least $5 million USD/CD. *Deloitte, 2022 Technology Fast 500*[TM]

Living Environment

COST OF LIVING

Cost of Living Index

Composite Index	Groceries	Housing	Utilities	Trans-portation	Health Care	Misc. Goods/Services
98.9	95.0	91.6	99.6	104.2	102.4	104.8

Note: The Cost of Living Index measures regional differences in the cost of consumer goods and services, excluding taxes and non-consumer expenditures, for professional and managerial households in the top income quintile. It is based on more than 50,000 prices covering almost 60 different items for which prices are collected three times a year by chambers of commerce, economic development organizations or university applied economic centers in each participating urban area. The numbers shown should be read as a percentage above or below the national average of 100. For example, a value of 115.4 in the groceries column indicates that grocery prices are 15.4% higher than the national average. Small differences in the index numbers should not be interpreted as significant; Figures cover the Minneapolis MN urban area.
Source: The Council for Community and Economic Research, Cost of Living Index, 2022

Grocery Prices

Area[1]	T-Bone Steak ($/pound)	Frying Chicken ($/pound)	Whole Milk ($/half gal.)	Eggs ($/dozen)	Orange Juice ($/64 oz.)	Coffee ($/11.5 oz.)
City[2]	14.32	1.95	2.28	1.83	3.78	4.69
Avg.	13.81	1.59	2.43	2.25	3.85	4.95
Min.	10.17	0.90	1.51	1.30	2.90	3.46
Max.	19.35	3.30	4.32	4.32	5.31	8.59

*Note: (1) Values for the local area are compared with the average, minimum and maximum values for all 286 areas in the Cost of Living Index; (2) Figures cover the Minneapolis MN urban area; **T-Bone Steak** (price per pound); **Frying Chicken** (price per pound, whole fryer); **Whole Milk** (half gallon carton); **Eggs** (price per dozen, Grade A, large); **Orange Juice** (64 oz. Tropicana or Florida Natural); **Coffee** (11.5 oz. can, vacuum-packed, Maxwell House, Hills Bros, or Folgers).*
Source: The Council for Community and Economic Research, Cost of Living Index, 2022

Housing and Utility Costs

Area[1]	New Home Price ($)	Apartment Rent ($/month)	All Electric ($/month)	Part Electric ($/month)	Other Energy ($/month)	Telephone ($/month)
City[2]	404,076	1,318	-	102.55	74.40	188.30
Avg.	450,913	1,371	176.41	99.93	76.96	190.22
Min.	229,283	546	100.84	31.56	27.15	174.27
Max.	2,434,977	4,569	356.86	249.59	272.24	208.31

*Note: (1) Values for the local area are compared with the average, minimum and maximum values for all 286 areas in the Cost of Living Index; (2) Figures cover the Minneapolis MN urban area; **New Home Price** (2,400 sf living area, 8,000 sf lot, in urban area with full utilities); **Apartment Rent** (950 sf 2 bedroom/1.5 or 2 bath, unfurnished, excluding all utilities except water); **All Electric** (average monthly cost for an all-electric home); **Part Electric** (average monthly cost for a part-electric home); **Other Energy** (average monthly cost for natural gas, fuel oil, coal, wood, and any other forms of energy except electricity); **Telephone** (price includes the base monthly rate plus taxes and fees for three lines of mobile phone service).*
Source: The Council for Community and Economic Research, Cost of Living Index, 2022

Health Care, Transportation, and Other Costs

Area[1]	Doctor ($/visit)	Dentist ($/visit)	Optometrist ($/visit)	Gasoline ($/gallon)	Beauty Salon ($/visit)	Men's Shirt ($)
City[2]	161.06	88.15	100.90	3.94	37.88	35.74
Avg.	124.91	107.77	117.66	3.86	43.31	34.21
Min.	36.61	58.25	51.79	2.90	22.18	13.05
Max.	250.21	162.58	371.96	5.54	85.61	63.54

*Note: (1) Values for the local area are compared with the average, minimum and maximum values for all 286 areas in the Cost of Living Index; (2) Figures cover the Minneapolis MN urban area; **Doctor** (general practitioners routine exam of an established patient); **Dentist** (adult teeth cleaning and periodic oral examination); **Optometrist** (full vision eye exam for established adult patient); **Gasoline** (one gallon regular unleaded, national brand, including all taxes, cash price at self-service pump if available); **Beauty Salon** (woman's shampoo, trim, and blow-dry); **Men's Shirt** (cotton/polyester dress shirt, pinpoint weave, long sleeves).*
Source: The Council for Community and Economic Research, Cost of Living Index, 2022

HOUSING

Homeownership Rate

Area	2015 (%)	2016 (%)	2017 (%)	2018 (%)	2019 (%)	2020 (%)	2021 (%)	2022 (%)
MSA[1]	67.9	69.1	70.1	67.8	70.2	73.0	75.0	73.0
U.S.	63.7	63.4	63.9	64.4	64.6	66.6	65.5	65.8

Note: (1) Figures cover the Minneapolis-St. Paul-Bloomington, MN-WI Metropolitan Statistical Area
Source: U.S. Census Bureau, Housing Vacancies and Homeownership Annual Statistics: 2015-2022

House Price Index (HPI)

Area	National Ranking[2]	Quarterly Change (%)	One-Year Change (%)	Five-Year Change (%)	Since 1991Q1 (%)
MSA[1]	239	-1.83	6.08	41.05	273.41
U.S.[3]	–	0.34	8.41	58.44	289.08

Note: The HPI is a weighted repeat sales index. It measures average price changes in repeat sales or refinancings on the same properties. This information is obtained by reviewing repeat mortgage transactions on single-family properties whose mortgages have been purchased or securitized by Fannie Mae or Freddie Mac since January 1975; (1) Figures cover the Minneapolis-St. Paul-Bloomington, MN-WI Metropolitan Statistical Area; (2) Rankings are based on annual percentage change for all metro areas containing at least 15,000 transactions over the last 10 years and ranges from 1 to 257; (3) figures based on a weighted average of Census Division estimates using a seasonally adjusted, purchase-only index; all figures are for the period ending December 31, 2022
Source: Federal Housing Finance Agency, Change in FHFA Metropolitan Area House Price Indexes, 2022Q4

Median Single-Family Home Prices

Area	2020	2021	2022p	Percent Change 2021 to 2022
MSA[1]	315.2	354.8	375.4	5.8
U.S. Average	300.2	357.1	392.6	9.9

Note: Figures are median sales prices of existing single-family homes in thousands of dollars; (p) preliminary; (1) Figures cover the Minneapolis-St. Paul-Bloomington, MN-WI Metropolitan Statistical Area
Source: National Association of Realtors, Median Sales Price of Existing Single-Family Homes for Metropolitan Areas, 4th Quarter 2022

Qualifying Income Based on Median Sales Price of Existing Single-Family Homes

Area	With 5% Down ($)	With 10% Down ($)	With 20% Down ($)
MSA[1]	109,382	103,625	92,111
U.S. Average	112,234	106,237	94,513

Note: Figures are preliminary; Qualifying income is based on a mortgage rate of 6.77%. Monthly principal and interest payment is limited to 25% of income; (1) Figures cover the Minneapolis-St. Paul-Bloomington, MN-WI Metropolitan Statistical Area
Source: National Association of Realtors, Qualifying Income Based on Median Sales Price of Existing Single-Family Homes for Metropolitan Areas, 4th Quarter 2022

Home Value

Area	Under $100,000	$100,000 -$199,999	$200,000 -$299,999	$300,000 -$399,999	$400,000 -$499,999	$500,000 -$999,999	$1,000,000 or more	Median ($)
City	4.2	19.5	31.1	20.3	9.7	12.6	2.5	284,400
MSA[1]	4.6	17.1	32.2	21.8	11.2	11.4	1.7	287,600
U.S.	16.2	24.2	20.1	13.6	8.3	13.6	4.1	244,900

Note: Figures are percentages except for median and cover owner-occupied housing units; (1) Figures cover the Minneapolis-St. Paul-Bloomington, MN-WI Metropolitan Statistical Area
Source: U.S. Census Bureau, 2017-2021 American Community Survey 5-Year Estimates

Year Housing Structure Built

Area	2020 or Later	2010 -2019	2000 -2009	1990 -1999	1980 -1989	1970 -1979	1960 -1969	1950 -1959	1940 -1949	Before 1940	Median Year
City	<0.1	7.3	6.3	4.0	6.8	8.2	7.5	9.0	6.9	43.9	1949
MSA[1]	0.2	7.0	13.5	13.9	14.2	14.3	9.8	9.5	3.7	13.8	1979
U.S.	0.2	7.3	13.6	13.6	13.2	14.8	10.3	10.0	4.7	12.2	1979

Note: Figures are percentages except for Median Year; Note: (1) Figures cover the Minneapolis-St. Paul-Bloomington, MN-WI Metropolitan Statistical Area
Source: U.S. Census Bureau, 2017-2021 American Community Survey 5-Year Estimates

Gross Monthly Rent

Area	Under $500	$500 -$999	$1,000 -$1,499	$1,500 -$1,999	$2,000 -$2,499	$2,500 -$2,999	$3,000 and up	Median ($)
City	10.9	27.0	33.1	17.8	7.4	2.0	1.9	1,159
MSA[1]	8.1	24.0	37.9	20.4	6.3	1.7	1.6	1,207
U.S.	8.1	30.5	30.8	16.8	7.3	3.1	3.5	1,163

Note: Figures are percentages except for median; Gross rent is the contract rent plus the estimated average monthly cost of utilities (electricity, gas, and water and sewer) and fuels (oil, coal, kerosene, wood, etc.) if these are paid by the renter (or paid for the renter by someone else); (1) Figures cover the Minneapolis-St. Paul-Bloomington, MN-WI Metropolitan Statistical Area
Source: U.S. Census Bureau, 2017-2021 American Community Survey 5-Year Estimates

HEALTH

Health Risk Factors

Category	MSA[1] (%)	U.S. (%)
Adults aged 18–64 who have any kind of health care coverage	94.2	90.9
Adults who reported being in good or better health	88.8	85.2
Adults who have been told they have high blood cholesterol	31.1	35.7
Adults who have been told they have high blood pressure	27.9	32.4
Adults who are current smokers	12.0	14.4
Adults who currently use e-cigarettes	5.8	6.7
Adults who currently use chewing tobacco, snuff, or snus	2.7	3.5
Adults who are heavy drinkers[2]	7.4	6.3
Adults who are binge drinkers[3]	18.0	15.4
Adults who are overweight (BMI 25.0 - 29.9)	34.5	34.4
Adults who are obese (BMI 30.0 - 99.8)	31.1	33.9
Adults who participated in any physical activities in the past month	82.1	76.3

Note: (1) Figures cover the Minneapolis-St. Paul-Bloomington, MN-WI Metropolitan Statistical Area;
(2) Heavy drinkers are classified as adult men having more than 14 drinks per week and adult women having
more than 7 drinks per week; (3) Binge drinkers are classified as males having five or more drinks on one
occasion or females having four or more drinks on one occasion
Source: Centers for Disease Control and Prevention, Behaviorial Risk Factor Surveillance System, SMART:
Selected Metropolitan Area Risk Trends, 2021

Acute and Chronic Health Conditions

Category	MSA[1] (%)	U.S. (%)
Adults who have ever been told they had a heart attack	3.3	4.0
Adults who have ever been told they have angina or coronary heart disease	3.4	3.8
Adults who have ever been told they had a stroke	2.2	3.0
Adults who have ever been told they have asthma	12.9	14.9
Adults who have ever been told they have arthritis	20.7	25.8
Adults who have ever been told they have diabetes[2]	8.5	10.9
Adults who have ever been told they had skin cancer	6.1	6.6
Adults who have ever been told they had any other types of cancer	6.8	7.5
Adults who have ever been told they have COPD	3.8	6.1
Adults who have ever been told they have kidney disease	2.7	3.0
Adults who have ever been told they have a form of depression	20.2	20.5

Note: (1) Figures cover the Minneapolis-St. Paul-Bloomington, MN-WI Metropolitan Statistical Area; (2)
Figures do not include pregnancy-related, borderline, or pre-diabetes
Source: Centers for Disease Control and Prevention, Behaviorial Risk Factor Surveillance System, SMART:
Selected Metropolitan Area Risk Trends, 2021

Health Screening and Vaccination Rates

Category	MSA[1] (%)	U.S. (%)
Adults who have ever been tested for HIV	33.3	34.9
Adults who have had their blood cholesterol checked within the last five years	85.4	85.2
Adults aged 65+ who have had flu shot within the past year	73.3	68.6
Adults aged 65+ who have ever had a pneumonia vaccination	70.1	71.0

Note: (1) Figures cover the Minneapolis-St. Paul-Bloomington, MN-WI Metropolitan Statistical Area.
Source: Centers for Disease Control and Prevention, Behaviorial Risk Factor Surveillance System, SMART:
Selected Metropolitan Area Risk Trends, 2021

Disability Status

Category	MSA[1] (%)	U.S. (%)
Adults who reported being deaf	5.2	7.2
Are you blind or have serious difficulty seeing, even when wearing glasses?	2.5	4.8
Are you limited in any way in any of your usual activities due to arthritis?	7.8	11.1
Do you have difficulty doing errands alone?	5.2	7.0
Do you have difficulty dressing or bathing?	2.6	3.6
Do you have serious difficulty concentrating/remembering/making decisions?	9.7	12.1
Do you have serious difficulty walking or climbing stairs?	9.1	12.8

Note: (1) Figures cover the Minneapolis-St. Paul-Bloomington, MN-WI Metropolitan Statistical Area.
Source: Centers for Disease Control and Prevention, Behaviorial Risk Factor Surveillance System, SMART:
Selected Metropolitan Area Risk Trends, 2021

Mortality Rates for the Top 10 Causes of Death in the U.S.

ICD-10[a] Sub-Chapter	ICD-10[a] Code	Crude Mortality Rate[1] per 100,000 population	
		County[2]	U.S.
Malignant neoplasms	C00-C97	153.7	182.6
Ischaemic heart diseases	I20-I25	54.3	113.1
Other forms of heart disease	I30-I51	42.8	64.4
Other degenerative diseases of the nervous system	G30-G31	41.3	51.0
Cerebrovascular diseases	I60-I69	37.7	47.8
Other external causes of accidental injury	W00-X59	56.9	46.4
Chronic lower respiratory diseases	J40-J47	28.2	45.7
Organic, including symptomatic, mental disorders	F01-F09	51.2	35.9
Hypertensive diseases	I10-I15	26.0	35.0
Diabetes mellitus	E10-E14	21.8	29.6

Note: (a) ICD-10 = International Classification of Diseases 10th Revision; (1) Crude mortality rates are a three-year average covering 2019-2021; (2) Figures cover Hennepin County.
Source: Centers for Disease Control and Prevention, National Center for Health Statistics. National Vital Statistics System, Mortality 2018-2021 on CDC WONDER Online Database

Mortality Rates for Selected Causes of Death

ICD-10[a] Sub-Chapter	ICD-10[a] Code	Crude Mortality Rate[1] per 100,000 population	
		County[2]	U.S.
Assault	X85-Y09	6.1	7.0
Diseases of the liver	K70-K76	18.0	19.8
Human immunodeficiency virus (HIV) disease	B20-B24	1.1	1.5
Influenza and pneumonia	J09-J18	6.9	14.7
Intentional self-harm	X60-X84	11.9	14.3
Malnutrition	E40-E46	1.8	4.3
Obesity and other hyperalimentation	E65-E68	2.5	3.0
Renal failure	N17-N19	7.2	15.7
Transport accidents	V01-V99	6.3	13.6
Viral hepatitis	B15-B19	1.1	1.2

Note: (a) ICD-10 = International Classification of Diseases 10th Revision; (1) Crude mortality rates are a three-year average covering 2019-2021; (2) Figures cover Hennepin County; Data are suppressed when the data meet the criteria for confidentiality constraints; Crude mortality rates are flagged as unreliable when the rate would be calculated with a numerator of 20 or less.
Source: Centers for Disease Control and Prevention, National Center for Health Statistics. National Vital Statistics System, Mortality 2018-2021 on CDC WONDER Online Database

Health Insurance Coverage

Area	With Health Insurance	With Private Health Insurance	With Public Health Insurance	Without Health Insurance	Population Under Age 19 Without Health Insurance
City	93.9	68.8	33.0	6.1	3.1
MSA[1]	95.7	77.9	29.9	4.3	2.8
U.S.	91.2	67.8	35.4	8.8	5.3

Note: Figures are percentages that cover the civilian noninstitutionalized population; (1) Figures cover the Minneapolis-St. Paul-Bloomington, MN-WI Metropolitan Statistical Area
Source: U.S. Census Bureau, 2017-2021 American Community Survey 5-Year Estimates

Number of Medical Professionals

Area	MDs[3]	DOs[3,4]	Dentists	Podiatrists	Chiropractors	Optometrists
County[1] (number)	6,816	308	1,312	66	977	274
County[1] (rate[2])	532.0	24.0	103.5	5.2	77.1	21.6
U.S. (rate[2])	289.3	23.5	72.5	6.2	28.7	17.4

Note: Data as of 2021 unless noted; (1) Data covers Hennepin County; (2) Rate per 100,000 population; (3) Data as of 2020 and includes all active, non-federal physicians; (4) Doctor of Osteopathic Medicine
Source: U.S. Department of Health and Human Services, Health Resources and Services Administration, Bureau of Health Professions, Area Resource File (ARF) 2021-2022

Best Hospitals

According to *U.S. News,* the Minneapolis-St. Paul-Bloomington, MN-WI metro area is home to two of the best hospitals in the U.S.: **Abbott Northwestern Hospital** (1 adult specialty); **M Health Fairview University of Minnesota Medical Center** (1 adult specialty and 1 pediatric specialty). The hospitals listed were nationally ranked in at least one of 15 adult or 10 pediatric specialties. The number of specialties shown cover the parent hospital. Only 164 U.S. hospitals performed well enough to be nationally ranked in one or more specialties. Twenty hospitals in the U.S. made the Honor Roll. The Best Hospitals Honor Roll takes both the national rankings and the procedure and condition ratings into account. Hospitals received points if they were nationally ranked in one of the 15 adult specialties—the higher they ranked, the more points they got—and how many ratings of "high performing" they earned in the 17 procedures and conditions. *U.S. News Online, "America's Best Hospitals 2022-23"*

According to *U.S. News,* the Minneapolis-St. Paul-Bloomington, MN-WI metro area is home to two of the best children's hospitals in the U.S.: **Children's Minnesota Hospital** (1 pediatric specialty); **M Health Fairview Masonic Children's Hospital** (1 pediatric specialty). The hospitals listed were highly ranked in at least one of 10 pediatric specialties. Eighty-six children's hospitals in the U.S. were nationally ranked in at least one specialty. Hospitals received points for being ranked in a specialty, and the 10 hospitals with the most points across the 10 specialties make up the Honor Roll. *U.S. News Online, "America's Best Children's Hospitals 2022-23"*

EDUCATION

Public School District Statistics

District Name	Schls	Pupils	Pupil/ Teacher Ratio	Minority Pupils[1] (%)	LEP/ELL[2] (%)	IEP[3] (%)
Minneapolis Public School District	97	30,115	14.3	61.5	19.9	18.9
Minnesota Transitions Charter	9	4,893	22.0	38.7	10.2	16.0

Note: Table includes school districts with 2,000 or more students; (1) Percentage of students that are not non-Hispanic white; (2) Percentage of students that are Limited English Proficient or English Language Learners (2018-19); (3) Percentage of students that have an Individualized Education Program (2019-20). Source: U.S. Department of Education, National Center for Education Statistics, Common Core of Data, Local Education Agency (School District) Universe Survey: School Year 2021-2022

Highest Level of Education

Area	Less than H.S.	H.S. Diploma	Some College, No Deg.	Associate Degree	Bachelor's Degree	Master's Degree	Prof. School Degree	Doctorate Degree
City	9.3	14.2	16.4	7.4	31.7	14.5	3.9	2.5
MSA[1]	6.0	20.5	19.4	10.6	28.3	10.9	2.6	1.7
U.S.	11.1	26.5	20.0	8.7	20.6	9.3	2.2	1.5

Note: Figures cover persons age 25 and over; (1) Figures cover the Minneapolis-St. Paul-Bloomington, MN-WI Metropolitan Statistical Area Source: U.S. Census Bureau, 2017-2021 American Community Survey 5-Year Estimates

Educational Attainment by Race

Area	High School Graduate or Higher (%)					Bachelor's Degree or Higher (%)				
	Total	White	Black	Asian	Hisp.[2]	Total	White	Black	Asian	Hisp.[2]
City	90.7	96.7	74.7	84.7	66.1	52.6	63.7	17.2	57.3	25.6
MSA[1]	94.0	96.6	82.8	82.7	73.9	43.5	46.1	23.6	46.0	24.1
U.S.	88.9	91.4	87.2	87.6	71.2	33.7	35.5	23.3	55.6	18.4

Note: Figures shown cover persons 25 years old and over; (1) Figures cover the Minneapolis-St. Paul-Bloomington, MN-WI Metropolitan Statistical Area; (2) People of Hispanic origin can be of any race Source: U.S. Census Bureau, 2017-2021 American Community Survey 5-Year Estimates

School Enrollment by Grade and Control

Area	Preschool (%)		Kindergarten (%)		Grades 1 - 4 (%)		Grades 5 - 8 (%)		Grades 9 - 12 (%)	
	Public	Private	Public	Private	Public	Private	Public	Private	Public	Private
City	55.0	45.0	85.0	15.0	87.3	12.7	88.9	11.1	90.7	9.3
MSA[1]	61.4	38.6	87.3	12.7	89.0	11.0	89.6	10.4	91.6	8.4
U.S.	58.8	41.2	86.3	13.7	88.3	11.7	88.6	11.4	89.4	10.6

Note: Figures shown cover persons 3 years old and over; (1) Figures cover the Minneapolis-St. Paul-Bloomington, MN-WI Metropolitan Statistical Area Source: U.S. Census Bureau, 2017-2021 American Community Survey 5-Year Estimates

Higher Education

Four-Year Colleges			Two-Year Colleges			Medical Schools[1]	Law Schools[2]	Voc/ Tech[3]
Public	Private Non-profit	Private For-profit	Public	Private Non-profit	Private For-profit			
3	21	5	10	0	0	1	3	7

Note: Figures cover institutions located within the Minneapolis-St. Paul-Bloomington, MN-WI Metropolitan Statistical Area and include main campuses only; (1) includes schools accredited by the Liaison Committee on Medical Education and the American Osteopathic Association's Commission on Osteopathic College Accreditation; (2) includes ABA-accredited schools, schools with provisional ABA accreditation, and state accredited schools; (3) includes all schools with programs that are less than 2 years. Source: National Center for Education Statistics, Integrated Postsecondary Education System (IPEDS), 2021-22; Wikipedia, List of Medical Schools in the United States, accessed April 10, 2023; Wikipedia, List of Law Schools in the United States, accessed April 10, 2023

According to *U.S. News & World Report,* the Minneapolis-St. Paul-Bloomington, MN-WI metro area is home to two of the top 200 national universities in the U.S.: **University of Minnesota—Twin Cities** (#62 tie); **University of St. Thomas (MN)** (#137 tie). The indicators used to capture academic quality fall into a number of categories: assessment by administrators at peer institutions; retention of students; faculty resources; student selectivity; financial resources; alumni giving; high school counselor ratings of colleges; and graduation rate. *U.S. News & World Report, "America's Best Colleges 2023"*

According to *U.S. News & World Report,* the Minneapolis-St. Paul-Bloomington, MN-WI metro area is home to three of the top 100 liberal arts colleges in the U.S.: **Carleton College** (#6 tie); **Macalester College** (#27 tie); **St. Olaf College** (#63 tie). The indicators used to capture academic quality fall into a number of categories: assessment by administrators at peer institutions; retention of students; faculty resources; student selectivity; financial resources; alumni giving; high school counselor ratings of colleges; and graduation rate. *U.S. News & World Report, "America's Best Colleges 2023"*

According to *U.S. News & World Report,* the Minneapolis-St. Paul-Bloomington, MN-WI metro area is home to one of the top 100 law schools in the U.S.: **University of Minnesota** (#21 tie). The rankings are based on a weighted average of 12 measures of quality: peer assessment score; assessment score by lawyers/judges; median LSAT scores; median undergrad GPA; acceptance rate; employment rates for graduates; placement success; bar passage rate; faculty resources; expenditures per student; student/faculty ratio; and library resources. *U.S. News & World Report, "America's Best Graduate Schools, Law, 2023"*

According to *U.S. News & World Report,* the Minneapolis-St. Paul-Bloomington, MN-WI metro area is home to one of the top 75 medical schools for research in the U.S.: **University of Minnesota** (#43 tie). The rankings are based on a weighted average of 11 measures of quality: quality assessment; peer assessment score; assessment score by residency directors; research activity; total research activity; average research activity per faculty member; student selectivity; median MCAT total score; median undergraduate GPA; acceptance rate; and faculty resources. *U.S. News & World Report, "America's Best Graduate Schools, Medical, 2023"*

According to *U.S. News & World Report,* the Minneapolis-St. Paul-Bloomington, MN-WI metro area is home to one of the top 75 business schools in the U.S.: **University of Minnesota—Twin Cities (Carlson)** (#33 tie). The rankings are based on a weighted average of the following nine measures: quality assessment; peer assessment; recruiter assessment; placement success; mean starting salary and bonus; student selectivity; mean GMAT and GRE scores; mean undergraduate GPA; and acceptance rate. *U.S. News & World Report, "America's Best Graduate Schools, Business, 2023"*

EMPLOYERS

Major Employers

Company Name	Industry
3M Company	Adhesives, sealants
Ameriprise Financial	Investment advice
Anderson Corporation	Millwork
Aware Integrated	Hospital & medical services plans
Bethesda Healtheast Hospital	General medical & surgical hospitals
Carlson Holdings	Hotels & motels
City of Minneapolis	Municipal government
County of Hennepin	County government
Hennepin County	County government
Honeywell International	Aircraft engines & engine parts
Lawson Software	Application computer software
Medtronic	Electromedical equipment
Minnesota Department of Human Services	Family services agency
Minnesota Department of Transportation	Regulation, administration of transportation
North Memorial Hospital	General medical & surgical hospitals
Regents of the University of Minnesota	Specialty outpatient clinics, nec
Rosemount Apple Valley and Eagan	Personal service agents, brokers, & bureaus
St. Paul Fire & Marine Insurance Company	Fire, marine, & casualty insurance
Thomson Legal Regulatory	Books, publishing & printing
United Parcel Service	Package delivery services
Wells Fargo	Mortgage bankers
West Publishing Corporation	Data base information retrieval

Note: Companies shown are located within the Minneapolis-St. Paul-Bloomington, MN-WI Metropolitan Statistical Area.
Source: Hoovers.com; Wikipedia

Best Companies to Work For

Target Corporation, headquartered in Minneapolis, is among "The 100 Best Companies to Work For." To pick the best companies, *Fortune* partnered with the Great Place to Work Institute. Two-thirds of a company's score is based on the results of the Institute's Trust Index survey, which is sent to a random sample of employees from each company. The questions related to attitudes about management's credibility, job satisfaction, and camaraderie. The other third of the scoring is based on the company's responses to the Institute's Culture Audit, which includes detailed questions about pay and benefit programs, and a series of open-ended questions about hiring practices, internal communication, training, recognition programs, and diversity efforts. Any company that is at least five years old with more than 1,000 U.S. employees is eligible. *Fortune, "The 100 Best Companies to Work For," 2023*

Ceridian HCM, headquartered in Minneapolis, is among the "100 Best Places to Work in IT." To qualify, companies had to have a minimum of 100 total employees and five IT employees. The best places to work were selected based on DEI (diversity, equity, and inclusion) practices; IT turnover, promotions, and growth; IT retention and engagement programs; remote/hybrid working; benefits and perks (such as elder care and child care, flextime, and reimbursement for college tuition); and training and career development opportunities. *Computerworld, "Best Places to Work in IT," 2023*

PUBLIC SAFETY

Crime Rate

Area	Total Crime	Violent Crime Rate				Property Crime Rate		
		Murder	Rape[3]	Robbery	Aggrav. Assault	Burglary	Larceny -Theft	Motor Vehicle Theft
City	5,713.0	18.2	83.0	409.5	644.2	899.8	2,747.1	911.3
Suburbs[1]	n/a	n/a	n/a	n/a	n/a	n/a	n/a	n/a
Metro[2]	n/a	n/a	n/a	n/a	n/a	n/a	n/a	n/a
U.S.	2,356.7	6.5	38.4	73.9	279.7	314.2	1,398.0	246.0

Note: Figures are crimes per 100,000 population; (1) All areas within the metro area that are located outside the city limits; (2) Figures cover the Minneapolis-St. Paul-Bloomington, MN-WI Metropolitan Statistical Area; n/a not available; (3) All figures shown were reported using the revised Uniform Crime Reporting (UCR) definition of rape; Due to the transition to the National Incident-Based Reporting System (NIBRS), limited city and metro area data was released for 2021.
Source: FBI Uniform Crime Reports, 2020

Hate Crimes

Area	Number of Quarters Reported	Number of Incidents per Bias Motivation					
		Race/Ethnicity/ Ancestry	Religion	Sexual Orientation	Disability	Gender	Gender Identity
City	4	18	4	5	0	0	0
U.S.	4	5,227	1,244	1,110	130	75	266

Note: Due to the transition to the National Incident-Based Reporting System (NIBRS), limited crime data was released for 2021.
Source: Federal Bureau of Investigation, Hate Crime Statistics 2020

Identity Theft Consumer Reports

Area	Reports	Reports per 100,000 Population	Rank[2]
MSA[1]	5,622	156	243
U.S.	1,108,609	339	-

Note: (1) Figures cover the Minneapolis-St. Paul-Bloomington, MN-WI Metropolitan Statistical Area; (2) Rank ranges from 1 to 391 where 1 indicates greatest number of identity theft reports per 100,000 population
Source: Federal Trade Commission, Consumer Sentinel Network Data Book 2022

Fraud and Other Consumer Reports

Area	Reports	Reports per 100,000 Population	Rank[2]
MSA[1]	31,097	862	171
U.S.	4,064,520	1,245	-

Note: (1) Figures cover the Minneapolis-St. Paul-Bloomington, MN-WI Metropolitan Statistical Area; (2) Rank ranges from 1 to 391 where 1 indicates greatest number of fraud and other consumer reports per 100,000 population
Source: Federal Trade Commission, Consumer Sentinel Network Data Book 2022

POLITICS

2020 Presidential Election Results

Area	Biden	Trump	Jorgensen	Hawkins	Other
Hennepin County	70.5	27.2	1.0	0.3	1.0
U.S.	51.3	46.8	1.2	0.3	0.5

Note: Results are percentages and may not add to 100% due to rounding
Source: Dave Leip's Atlas of U.S. Presidential Elections

SPORTS

Professional Sports Teams

Team Name	League	Year Established
Minnesota Timberwolves	National Basketball Association (NBA)	1989
Minnesota Twins	Major League Baseball (MLB)	1961
Minnesota United FC	Major League Soccer (MLS)	2017
Minnesota Vikings	National Football League (NFL)	1961
Minnesota Wild	National Hockey League (NHL)	2000

Note: Includes teams located in the Minneapolis-St. Paul-Bloomington, MN-WI Metropolitan Statistical Area.
Source: Wikipedia, Major Professional Sports Teams of the United States and Canada, April 12, 2023

CLIMATE

Average and Extreme Temperatures

Temperature	Jan	Feb	Mar	Apr	May	Jun	Jul	Aug	Sep	Oct	Nov	Dec	Yr.
Extreme High (°F)	57	60	83	95	96	102	105	101	98	89	74	63	105
Average High (°F)	21	27	38	56	69	79	84	81	71	59	41	26	54
Average Temp. (°F)	12	18	30	46	59	69	74	71	61	50	33	19	45
Average Low (°F)	3	9	21	36	48	58	63	61	50	39	25	11	35
Extreme Low (°F)	-34	-28	-32	2	18	37	43	39	26	15	-17	-29	-34

Note: Figures cover the years 1948-1990
Source: National Climatic Data Center, International Station Meteorological Climate Summary, 9/96

Average Precipitation/Snowfall/Humidity

Precip./Humidity	Jan	Feb	Mar	Apr	May	Jun	Jul	Aug	Sep	Oct	Nov	Dec	Yr.
Avg. Precip. (in.)	0.8	0.8	1.9	2.2	3.1	4.0	3.8	3.6	2.5	1.9	1.4	1.0	27.1
Avg. Snowfall (in.)	11	9	12	3	Tr	0	0	0	Tr	Tr	7	10	52
Avg. Rel. Hum. 6am (%)	75	76	77	75	75	79	81	84	85	81	80	79	79
Avg. Rel. Hum. 3pm (%)	64	62	58	48	47	50	50	52	53	52	62	68	55

Note: Figures cover the years 1948-1990; Tr = Trace amounts (<0.05 in. of rain; <0.5 in. of snow)
Source: National Climatic Data Center, International Station Meteorological Climate Summary, 9/96

Weather Conditions

Temperature			Daytime Sky			Precipitation		
5°F & below	32°F & below	90°F & above	Clear	Partly cloudy	Cloudy	0.01 inch or more precip.	0.1 inch or more snow/ice	Thunder-storms
45	156	16	93	125	147	113	41	37

Note: Figures are average number of days per year and cover the years 1948-1990
Source: National Climatic Data Center, International Station Meteorological Climate Summary, 9/96

HAZARDOUS WASTE

Superfund Sites

The Minneapolis-St. Paul-Bloomington, MN-WI metro area is home to 16 sites on the EPA's Superfund National Priorities List: **Baytown Township Ground Water Plume** (final); **FMC Corp. (Fridley Plant)** (final); **Freeway Sanitary Landfill** (final); **General Mills/Henkel Corp.** (final); **Highway 100 and County Road 3 Groundwater Plume** (final); **Joslyn Manufacturing & Supply Co.** (final); **Koppers Coke** (final); **Kurt Manufacturing Co.** (final); **Macgillis & Gibbs Co./Bell Lumber & Pole Co.** (final); **Naval Industrial Reserve Ordnance Plant** (final); **New Brighton/Arden Hills/Tcaap (USARMY)** (final); **Oakdale Dump** (final); **Reilly Tar & Chemical Corp. (Saint Louis Park Plant)** (final); **South Andover Site** (final); **South Minneapolis Residential Soil Contamination** (final); **Southeast Hennepin Area Groundwater and Vapor** (final). There are a total of 1,165 Superfund sites with a status of proposed or final on the list in the U.S. *U.S. Environmental Protection Agency, National Priorities List, April 12, 2023*

AIR QUALITY

Air Quality Trends: Ozone

	1990	1995	2000	2005	2010	2015	2018	2019	2020	2021
MSA[1]	0.068	0.084	0.065	0.074	0.066	0.061	0.065	0.059	0.060	0.067
U.S.	0.087	0.089	0.081	0.080	0.072	0.067	0.069	0.065	0.065	0.067

Note: (1) Data covers the Minneapolis-St. Paul-Bloomington, MN-WI Metropolitan Statistical Area. The values shown are the composite ozone concentration averages among trend sites based on the highest fourth daily maximum 8-hour concentration in parts per million. These trends are based on sites having an adequate record of monitoring data during the trend period. Data from exceptional events are included.
Source: U.S. Environmental Protection Agency, Air Quality Monitoring Information, "Air Quality Trends by City, 1990-2021"

Air Quality Index

Area	Percent of Days when Air Quality was...[2]					AQI Statistics[2]	
	Good	Moderate	Unhealthy for Sensitive Groups	Unhealthy	Very Unhealthy	Maximum	Median
MSA[1]	63.0	34.8	1.4	0.8	0.0	182	44

Note: (1) Data covers the Minneapolis-St. Paul-Bloomington, MN-WI Metropolitan Statistical Area; (2) Based on 365 days with AQI data in 2021. Air Quality Index (AQI) is an index for reporting daily air quality. EPA calculates the AQI for five major air pollutants regulated by the Clean Air Act: ground-level ozone, particle pollution (aka particulate matter), carbon monoxide, sulfur dioxide, and nitrogen dioxide. The AQI runs from 0 to 500. The higher the AQI value, the greater the level of air pollution and the greater the health concern. There are six AQI categories: "Good" AQI is between 0 and 50. Air quality is considered satisfactory; "Moderate" AQI is between 51 and 100. Air quality is acceptable; "Unhealthy for Sensitive Groups" When AQI values are between 101 and 150, members of sensitive groups may experience health effects; "Unhealthy" When AQI values are between 151 and 200 everyone may begin to experience health effects; "Very Unhealthy" AQI values between 201 and 300 trigger a health alert; "Hazardous" AQI values over 300 trigger warnings of emergency conditions (not shown).
Source: U.S. Environmental Protection Agency, Air Quality Index Report, 2021

Air Quality Index Pollutants

Area	Percent of Days when AQI Pollutant was...[2]					
	Carbon Monoxide	Nitrogen Dioxide	Ozone	Sulfur Dioxide	Particulate Matter 2.5	Particulate Matter 10
MSA[1]	0.0	3.3	47.7	(3)	41.1	7.9

Note: (1) Data covers the Minneapolis-St. Paul-Bloomington, MN-WI Metropolitan Statistical Area; (2) Based on 365 days with AQI data in 2021. The Air Quality Index (AQI) is an index for reporting daily air quality. EPA calculates the AQI for five major air pollutants regulated by the Clean Air Act: ground-level ozone, particle pollution (also known as particulate matter), carbon monoxide, sulfur dioxide, and nitrogen dioxide. The AQI runs from 0 to 500. The higher the AQI value, the greater the level of air pollution and the greater the health concern; (3) Sulfur dioxide is no longer included in this table (as of December 8, 2021) because SO_2 concentrations tend to be very localized and not necessarily representative of broad geographical areas like counties and CBSAs.
Source: U.S. Environmental Protection Agency, Air Quality Index Report, 2021

Maximum Air Pollutant Concentrations: Particulate Matter, Ozone, CO and Lead

	Particulate Matter 10 (ug/m^3)	Particulate Matter 2.5 Wtd AM (ug/m^3)	Particulate Matter 2.5 24-Hr (ug/m^3)	Ozone (ppm)	Carbon Monoxide (ppm)	Lead (ug/m^3)
MSA[1] Level	115	8.8	30	0.07	2	0.08
NAAQS[2]	150	15	35	0.075	9	0.15
Met NAAQS[2]	Yes	Yes	Yes	Yes	Yes	Yes

Note: (1) Data covers the Minneapolis-St. Paul-Bloomington, MN-WI Metropolitan Statistical Area; Data from exceptional events are included; (2) National Ambient Air Quality Standards; ppm = parts per million; ug/m^3 = micrograms per cubic meter; n/a not available.
Concentrations: Particulate Matter 10 (coarse particulate)—highest second maximum 24-hour concentration; Particulate Matter 2.5 Wtd AM (fine particulate)—highest weighted annual mean concentration; Particulate Matter 2.5 24-Hour (fine particulate)—highest 98th percentile 24-hour concentration; Ozone—highest fourth daily maximum 8-hour concentration; Carbon Monoxide—highest second maximum non-overlapping 8-hour concentration; Lead—maximum running 3-month average
Source: U.S. Environmental Protection Agency, Air Quality Monitoring Information, "Air Quality Statistics by City, 2021"

Maximum Air Pollutant Concentrations: Nitrogen Dioxide and Sulfur Dioxide

	Nitrogen Dioxide AM (ppb)	Nitrogen Dioxide 1-Hr (ppb)	Sulfur Dioxide AM (ppb)	Sulfur Dioxide 1-Hr (ppb)	Sulfur Dioxide 24-Hr (ppb)
MSA[1] Level	8	38	n/a	14	n/a
NAAQS[2]	53	100	30	75	140
Met NAAQS[2]	Yes	Yes	n/a	Yes	n/a

Note: (1) Data covers the Minneapolis-St. Paul-Bloomington, MN-WI Metropolitan Statistical Area; Data from exceptional events are included; (2) National Ambient Air Quality Standards; ppm = parts per million; ug/m^3 = micrograms per cubic meter; n/a not available.
Concentrations: Nitrogen Dioxide AM—highest arithmetic mean concentration; Nitrogen Dioxide 1-Hr—highest 98th percentile 1-hour daily maximum concentration; Sulfur Dioxide AM—highest annual mean concentration; Sulfur Dioxide 1-Hr—highest 99th percentile 1-hour daily maximum concentration; Sulfur Dioxide 24-Hr—highest second maximum 24-hour concentration
Source: U.S. Environmental Protection Agency, Air Quality Monitoring Information, "Air Quality Statistics by City, 2021"

Oklahoma City, Oklahoma

Background

The 1992 film *Far and Away*, directed by Ron Howard, shows Tom Cruise charging away on his horse to claim land in the Oklahoma Territory. That dramatic scene depicted a true event from the great Oklahoma land run of 1889. A pistol was fired from the Oklahoma Station house of the Santa Fe Railroad and 10,000 homesteaders raced away to stake land claims in central Oklahoma territory. Overnight, Oklahoma City (or OKC) had been founded.

The town grew quickly along the tracks of the Santa Fe Railroad. Soon it became a distribution center for the territory's crops and livestock. Today, the city still functions as a major transportation center for the state's farm produce and livestock industry. By 1910 the city had become the state capital, which also furthered growth. But in 1928, growth went through the ceiling when oil was discovered within the city limits, forever changing the economic face of Oklahoma City from one of livestock and feed to one of livestock, feed, and oil.

After World War II, Oklahoma City, like many other cities, entered industry, most notably aircraft and related industries. The Tinker Air Force Base and the Federal Aviation Administration's Mike Monroney Aeronautical Center—home to the largest concentration of Dept. of Transportation personnel outside of Washington, D.C.—have made Oklahoma City a leading aviation center and, combined, employ more than 30,000 federal and civil contract workers. Major economic sectors for the Greater Oklahoma City region—the geographic center of the continent—also include energy, bioscience, and logistics.

The area caters to a Western lifestyle. The town is the home of the National Cowboy and Western Heritage Museum, with its famous 18-foot-tall sculpture, "End of the Trail," by James Earle Fraser. The Oklahoma History Center, affiliated with the Smithsonian Institute, occupies a 215,000 square foot building on an 18-acre campus. The Red Earth Museum features 1,400 items of Native American art and a research center. To the north of Oklahoma City's Capitol building is the Tribal Flag Plaza, displaying the 39 native tribal flags of Oklahoma. Each September the State Fair is held in Oklahoma City, and each January the International Finals Rodeo is held at the State Fair Park. If swinging a bat is more your style than riding a bronco, there's the National Softball Hall of Fame and Museum.

In the mid-1960s, Oklahoma City hired famous architect I.M. Pei to redesign its downtown area. Taking inspiration from the Tivoli Gardens of Copenhagen, the downtown boasts the Myriad Gardens, a 12-acre recreational park with gardens, and amphitheater. The seven-story Crystal Bridge Tropical Conservatory was completely restored and reopened in 2022.

The city is also home to the Oklahoma City Thunder, a team that's become a leading NBA contender in recent years, often making the playoffs.

A national tragedy occurred in Oklahoma City on April 19, 1995, when a terrorist truck bomb destroyed part of the Alfred P. Murray Federal Building in the downtown area, killing 168 people and injuring more than 500. In the face of such tragedy, the world marveled at how Oklahoma City and the state of Oklahoma carried itself with dignity and generosity. The Oklahoma City National Memorial commemorates those people whose lives were ended or forever changed on that day.

Oklahoma City's weather is changeable. There are pronounced daily and seasonal temperature changes and considerable variation in seasonal and annual precipitation. Summers are long and usually hot, while winters are comparatively mild and short. The city is in Tornado Alley, which is frequently visited in the springtime by violent thunderstorms producing damaging winds, large hail, and tornadoes.

Rankings

General Rankings

- For its "Best for Vets: Places to Live 2019" rankings, *Military Times* evaluated 599 cities (83 large, 234 medium, 282 small) and compared the locations across three broad categories: veteran and military culture/services; economic indicators; and livability factors such as health, crime, traffic, and school quality. Oklahoma City ranked #6 out of the top 25, in the large city category (population of more than 250,000). Data points more specific to veterans and the military weighed more heavily than others. *rebootcamp.militarytimes.com, "Military Times Best Places to Live 2019," September 10, 2018*

- The Oklahoma City metro area was identified as one of America's fastest-growing areas in terms of population and business growth by *MagnifyMoney*. The area ranked #31 out of 35. The 100 most populous metro areas in the U.S. were evaluated on their change from 2011 to 2016 in the following categories: people and housing; workforce and employment opportunities; growing industry. *www.businessinsider.com, "The 35 Cities in the US with the Biggest Influx of People, the Most Work Opportunities, and the Hottest Business Growth," August 12, 2018*

Business/Finance Rankings

- Oklahoma City was the #2-ranked city for savers, according to a study by the finance site GOBankingRates, which considered the prospects for people trying to save money. Criteria: average monthly cost of grocery items; median home listing price; median rent; median income; transportation costs; gas prices; and the cost of eating out for an inexpensive and mid-range meal in 100 U.S. cities. *www.gobankingrates.com, "The 20 Best (and Worst) Places to Live If You're Trying to Save Money," August 27, 2019*

- Oklahoma City was ranked #2 among 100 U.S. cities for most difficult conditions for savers, according to a study by the finance site GOBankingRates. Criteria: average monthly cost of grocery items; median home listing price; median rent; median income; transportation costs; gas prices; and the cost of eating out for an inexpensive and mid-range meal. *www.gobankingrates.com, "The 20 Best (and Worst) Places to Live If You're Trying to Save Money," August 27, 2019*

- Based on metro area social media reviews, the employment opinion group Glassdoor surveyed 50 of the most populous U.S. metro areas and equally weighed cost of living, hiring opportunity, and job satisfaction to compose a list of "25 Best Cities for Jobs." Median pay and home value, and number of active job openings were also factored in. The Oklahoma City metro area was ranked #12 in overall job satisfaction. *www.glassdoor.com, "Best Cities for Jobs," February 25, 2020*

- The Brookings Institution ranked the nation's largest cities based on income inequality. Oklahoma City was ranked #70 (#1 = greatest inequality). Criteria: the "95/20 ratio," a figure representing the income at which a household earns more than 95 percent of all other households, divided by the income at which a household earns more than only 20 percent of all other households. *Brookings Institution, "Household Income Inequality, Largest Cities of 97 Large U.S. Metro Areas, 2014-2016," February 5, 2018*

- The Brookings Institution ranked the 100 largest metro areas in the U.S. based on income inequality. Oklahoma City was ranked #47 (#1 = greatest inequality). Criteria: the "95/20 ratio," a figure representing the income at which a household earns more than 95 percent of all other households, divided by the income at which a household earns more than only 20 percent of all other households. *Brookings Institution, "Household Income Inequality, 100 Largest U.S. Metro Areas, 2014-2016," February 5, 2018*

- For its annual survey of the "Cheapest U.S. Cities to Live In," Kiplinger applied Cost of Living Index statistics developed by the Council for Community and Economic Research to U.S. Census Bureau population and median household income data for 265 urban areas. Only areas with at least 50,000 residents were considered. In the resulting ranking, Oklahoma City ranked #11. *Kiplinger.com, "The 25 Cheapest Places to Live: U.S. Cities Edition," April 3, 2023*

- The Oklahoma City metro area appeared on the Milken Institute "2022 Best Performing Cities" list. Rank: #142 out of 200 large metro areas (population over 250,000). Criteria: job growth; wage and salary growth; high-tech output growth; housing affordability; household broadband access. *Milken Institute, "Best-Performing Cities 2022," March 28, 2022*

- *Forbes* ranked the 200 most populous metro areas to determine the nation's "Best Places for Business and Careers." The Oklahoma City metro area was ranked #54. Criteria: costs (business and living); job growth (past and projected); income growth; quality of life; educational attainment (college and high school); projected economic growth; cultural and leisure opportunities; workplace tolerance laws; net migration patterns. *Forbes, "The Best Places for Business and Careers 2019: Seattle Still On Top," October 30, 2019*

Dating/Romance Rankings

- Oklahoma City was ranked #18 out of 25 cities that stood out for inspiring romance and attracting diners on the website OpenTable.com. Criteria: percentage of people who dined out on Valentine's Day in 2018; percentage of romantic restaurants as rated by OpenTable diner reviews; and percentage of tables seated for two. *OpenTable, "25 Most Romantic Cities in America for 2019," February 7, 2019*

Education Rankings

- Personal finance website *WalletHub* analyzed the 150 largest U.S. metropolitan statistical areas to determine where the most educated Americans are putting their degrees to work. Criteria: education levels; percentage of workers with degrees; education quality and attainment gap; public school quality rankings; quality and enrollment of each metro area's universities. Oklahoma City was ranked #84 (#1 = most educated city). *www.WalletHub.com, "Most & Least Educated Cities in America," July 18, 2022*

- Oklahoma City was selected as one of America's most literate cities. The city ranked #48 out of the 84 largest U.S. cities. Criteria: number of booksellers; library resources; Internet resources; educational attainment; periodical publishing resources; newspaper circulation. *Central Connecticut State University, "America's Most Literate Cities, 2018," February 2019*

Environmental Rankings

- Sperling's BestPlaces assessed the 50 largest metropolitan areas of the United States for the likelihood of dangerously extreme weather events or earthquakes. In general the Southeast and South-Central regions have the highest risk of weather extremes and earthquakes, while the Pacific Northwest enjoys the lowest risk. Of the most risky metropolitan areas, the Oklahoma City metro area was ranked #3. *www.bestplaces.net, "Avoid Natural Disasters: BestPlaces Reveals The Top 10 Safest Places to Live," October 25, 2017*

Health/Fitness Rankings

- For each of the 100 largest cities in the United States, the American Fitness Index®, compiled in partnership between the American College of Sports Medicine and the Elevance Health Foundation, evaluated community infrastructure and 34 health behaviors including preventive health, levels of chronic disease conditions, food insecurity, sleep quality, pedestrian safety, air quality, and community/environment resources that support physical activity. Oklahoma City ranked #100 for "community fitness." *americanfitnessindex.org, "2022 ACSM American Fitness Index Summary Report," July 12, 2022*

- Oklahoma City was identified as a "2022 Spring Allergy Capital." The area ranked #6 out of 100. Three groups of factors were used to identify the most challenging cities for people with allergies during the spring season: annual spring pollen scores; over the counter allergy medicine use; number of board-certified allergy specialists. *Asthma and Allergy Foundation of America, "Spring Allergy Capitals 2022," March 2, 2022*

- Oklahoma City was identified as a "2022 Fall Allergy Capital." The area ranked #5 out of 100. Three groups of factors were used to identify the most challenging cities for people with allergies during the fall season: annual fall pollen scores; over the counter allergy medicine use; number of board-certified allergy specialists. *Asthma and Allergy Foundation of America, "Fall Allergy Capitals 2022," March 2, 2022*

- Oklahoma City was identified as a "2022 Asthma Capital." The area ranked #73 out of the nation's 100 largest metropolitan areas. Criteria: estimated asthma prevalence; asthma-related mortality; and ER visits due to asthma. Risk factors analyzed but not factored in the rankings: annual pollen score; annual air quality; public smoking laws; access to board-certified asthma specialists; rescue and controller medication use; uninsured rate; poverty rate. *Asthma and Allergy Foundation of America, "Asthma Capitals 2022: The Most Challenging Places to Live With Asthma," September 14, 2022*

Real Estate Rankings

- *WalletHub* compared the most populated U.S. cities to determine which had the best markets for real estate agents. Oklahoma City ranked #126 where demand was high and pay was the best. Criteria: sales per agent; annual median wage for real-estate agents; monthly average starting salary for real estate agents; real estate job density and competition; unemployment rate; home turnover rate; housing-market health index; and other relevant metrics. *www.WalletHub.com, "2021 Best Places to Be a Real Estate Agent," May 12, 2021*

- Oklahoma City was ranked #50 out of 235 metro areas in terms of housing affordability in 2022 by the National Association of Home Builders (#1 = most affordable). Criteria: the share of homes sold in that area affordable to a family earning the local median income, based on standard mortgage underwriting criteria. *National Association of Home Builders®, NAHB-Wells Fargo Housing Opportunity Index, 4th Quarter 2022*

Safety Rankings

- Allstate ranked the 200 largest cities in America in terms of driver safety. Oklahoma City ranked #45. Criteria: internal property damage claims over a two-year period from January 2016 to December 2017. The report helps increase the importance of safety and awareness behind the wheel. *Allstate, "Allstate America's Best Drivers Report, 2019" June 24, 2019*

- The National Insurance Crime Bureau ranked 390 metro areas in the U.S. in terms of per capita rates of vehicle theft. The Oklahoma City metro area ranked #74 (#1 = highest rate). Criteria: number of vehicle theft offenses per 100,000 inhabitants in 2021. *National Insurance Crime Bureau, "Hot Spots 2021," September 1, 2022*

Seniors/Retirement Rankings

- From its Best Cities for Successful Aging indexes, the Milken Institute generated rankings for metropolitan areas, weighing data in nine categories—health care, wellness, living arrangements, transportation and convenience, financial characteristics, education, employment, community engagement, and overall livability. The Oklahoma City metro area was ranked #28 overall in the large metro area category. *Milken Institute, "Best Cities for Successful Aging, 2017" March 14, 2017*

Women/Minorities Rankings

- Personal finance website *WalletHub* compared more than 180 U.S. cities across two key dimensions, "Hispanic Business-Friendliness" and "Hispanic Purchasing Power," to arrive at the most favorable conditions for Hispanic entrepreneurs. Oklahoma City was ranked #16 out of 182. Criteria includes: share of Hispanic-Owned Businesses; Hispanic entrepreneurship rate to median annual income of Hispanics; Small Business-Friendliness score; cost of living; and number of Hispanics with at least a bachelor's degree. *WalletHub.com, "2019's Best Cities for Hispanic Entrepreneurs," May 1, 2019*

Miscellaneous Rankings

- Despite the freedom to now travel internationally, plugged-in travel influencers and experts continue to rediscover their local regions. Oklahoma City appeared on a *Forbes* list of places in the U.S. that provide solace as well as local inspiration. Whether it be quirky things to see and do, delicious take out, outdoor exploring and daytrips, these places are must-see destinations. *Forbes, "The Best Places To Travel In The U.S. In 2023, According To The Experts," April 13, 2023*

- *WalletHub* compared the 150 most populated U.S. cities to determine their operating efficiency. A "Quality of Services" score was constructed for each city and then divided by the total budget per capita to reveal which were managed the best. Oklahoma City ranked #8. Criteria: financial stability; economy; education; safety; health; infrastructure and pollution. *www.WalletHub.com, "2022's Best- & Worst-Run Cities in America," June 21, 2022*

Business Environment

DEMOGRAPHICS

Population Growth

Area	1990 Census	2000 Census	2010 Census	2020 Census	Population Growth (%)	
					1990-2020	2010-2020
City	445,065	506,132	579,999	681,054	53.0	17.4
MSA[1]	971,042	1,095,421	1,252,987	1,425,695	46.8	13.8
U.S.	248,709,873	281,421,906	308,745,538	331,449,281	33.3	7.4

Note: (1) Figures cover the Oklahoma City, OK Metropolitan Statistical Area
Source: U.S. Census Bureau, 1990 Census, 2000 Census, 2010 Census, 2020 Census

Race

Area	White Alone[2] (%)	Black Alone[2] (%)	Asian Alone[2] (%)	AIAN[3] Alone[2] (%)	NHOPI[4] Alone[2] (%)	Other Race Alone[2] (%)	Two or More Races (%)
City	53.6	14.0	4.6	3.4	0.2	11.1	13.1
MSA[1]	62.5	10.3	3.3	4.0	0.1	7.2	12.6
U.S.	61.6	12.4	6.0	1.1	0.2	8.4	10.2

Note: (1) Figures cover the Oklahoma City, OK Metropolitan Statistical Area; (2) Alone is defined as not being in combination with one or more other races; (3) American Indian and Alaska Native; (4) Native Hawaiian and Other Pacific Islander
Source: U.S. Census Bureau, 2020 Census

Hispanic or Latino Origin

Area	Total (%)	Mexican (%)	Puerto Rican (%)	Cuban (%)	Other (%)
City	19.9	16.1	0.4	0.1	3.3
MSA[1]	13.9	10.9	0.4	0.1	2.5
U.S.	18.4	11.2	1.8	0.7	4.7

Note: Persons of Hispanic or Latino origin can be of any race; (1) Figures cover the Oklahoma City, OK Metropolitan Statistical Area
Source: U.S. Census Bureau, 2017-2021 American Community Survey 5-Year Estimates

Age

Area	Percent of Population									Median Age
	Under Age 5	Age 5–19	Age 20–34	Age 35–44	Age 45–54	Age 55–64	Age 65–74	Age 75–84	Age 85+	
City	6.7	20.7	22.7	13.9	11.2	11.4	8.3	3.8	1.5	34.9
MSA[1]	6.2	21.0	21.6	13.4	11.3	12.0	8.9	4.2	1.6	35.8
U.S.	5.6	19.2	20.2	12.7	12.4	13.1	10.0	4.9	1.9	38.8

Note: (1) Figures cover the Oklahoma City, OK Metropolitan Statistical Area
Source: U.S. Census Bureau, 2020 Census

Disability by Age

Area	All Ages	Under 18 Years Old	18 to 64 Years Old	65 Years and Over
City	13.1	4.3	11.9	36.6
MSA[1]	14.0	4.5	12.4	38.4
U.S.	12.6	4.4	10.3	33.4

Note: Figures show percent of the civilian noninstitutionalized population that reported having a disability. Disability status is determined from six types of difficulty: vision, hearing, cognitive, ambulatory, self-care, and independent living. For children under 5 years old, hearing and vision difficulty are used to determine disability status. For children between the ages of 5 and 14, disability status is determined from hearing, vision, cognitive, ambulatory, and self-care difficulties. For people aged 15 years and older, they are considered to have a disability if they have difficulty with any one of the six difficulty types; Note: (1) Figures cover the Oklahoma City, OK Metropolitan Statistical Area
Source: U.S. Census Bureau, 2017-2021 American Community Survey 5-Year Estimates

Ancestry

Area	German	Irish	English	American	Italian	Polish	French[2]	Scottish	Dutch
City	10.0	7.8	7.7	5.7	1.8	0.7	1.3	1.6	0.9
MSA[1]	11.6	8.9	9.1	7.0	1.8	0.8	1.5	1.8	1.0
U.S.	12.8	9.6	8.1	5.7	5.0	2.7	2.2	1.6	1.1

Note: Figures are the percentage of the total population reporting a particular ancestry. The nine most commonly reported ancestries in the U.S. are shown. Figures include multiple ancestries (e.g. if a person reported being Irish and Italian, they were included in both columns); (1) Figures cover the Oklahoma City, OK Metropolitan Statistical Area; (2) Excludes Basque
Source: U.S. Census Bureau, 2017-2021 American Community Survey 5-Year Estimates

Foreign-born Population

Area	Any Foreign Country	Percent of Population Born in							
		Asia	Mexico	Europe	Caribbean	Central America[2]	South America	Africa	Canada
City	11.6	3.2	5.3	0.5	0.2	1.2	0.4	0.6	0.2
MSA[1]	7.9	2.3	3.3	0.4	0.1	0.8	0.3	0.5	0.2
U.S.	13.6	4.2	3.3	1.5	1.4	1.1	1.1	0.8	0.2

Note: (1) Figures cover the Oklahoma City, OK Metropolitan Statistical Area; (2) Excludes Mexico.
Source: U.S. Census Bureau, 2017-2021 American Community Survey 5-Year Estimates

Household Size

Area	Persons in Household (%)							Average Household Size
	One	Two	Three	Four	Five	Six	Seven or More	
City	31.4	31.8	15.1	11.6	6.5	2.5	1.1	2.50
MSA[1]	28.6	33.5	15.8	12.3	6.3	2.5	1.1	2.50
U.S.	28.1	33.8	15.5	12.9	6.0	2.3	1.4	2.60

Note: (1) Figures cover the Oklahoma City, OK Metropolitan Statistical Area
Source: U.S. Census Bureau, 2017-2021 American Community Survey 5-Year Estimates

Household Relationships

Area	House-holder	Opposite-sex Spouse	Same-sex Spouse	Opposite-sex Unmarried Partner	Same-sex Unmarried Partner	Child[2]	Grand-child	Other Relatives	Non-relatives
City	39.4	16.6	0.2	2.6	0.2	29.4	2.3	4.3	3.1
MSA[1]	38.8	17.7	0.2	2.4	0.2	29.0	2.3	3.8	3.1
U.S.	38.3	17.5	0.2	2.5	0.2	28.3	2.4	4.8	3.4

Note: Figures are percent of the total population; (1) Figures cover the Oklahoma City, OK Metropolitan Statistical Area; (2) Includes biological, adopted, and stepchildren of the householder
Source: U.S. Census Bureau, 2020 Census

Gender

Area	Males	Females	Males per 100 Females
City	335,613	345,441	97.2
MSA[1]	702,324	723,371	97.1
U.S.	162,685,811	168,763,470	96.4

Note: (1) Figures cover the Oklahoma City, OK Metropolitan Statistical Area
Source: U.S. Census Bureau, 2020 Census

Marital Status

Area	Never Married	Now Married[2]	Separated	Widowed	Divorced
City	33.3	46.6	2.1	5.3	12.7
MSA[1]	31.4	49.2	1.8	5.4	12.3
U.S.	33.8	48.0	1.8	5.6	10.8

Note: Figures are percentages and cover the population 15 years of age and older; (1) Figures cover the Oklahoma City, OK Metropolitan Statistical Area; (2) Excludes separated
Source: U.S. Census Bureau, 2017-2021 American Community Survey 5-Year Estimates

Religious Groups by Family

Area	Catholic	Baptist	Methodist	LDS[2]	Pentecostal	Lutheran	Islam	Adventist	Other
MSA[1]	10.0	16.6	6.2	1.3	3.9	0.6	0.6	0.9	21.4
U.S.	18.7	7.3	3.0	2.0	1.8	1.7	1.3	1.3	11.6

Note: Figures are the number of adherents as a percentage of the total population and cover the eight largest religious groups in the U.S; (1) Figures cover the Oklahoma City, OK Metropolitan Statistical Area; (2) Church of Jesus Christ of Latter-day Saints
Sources: 2020 U.S. Religion Census, Association of Statisticians of American Religious Bodies; The Association of Religion Data Archives (ARDA)

Religious Groups by Tradition

Area	Catholic	Evangelical Protestant	Mainline Protestant	Black Protestant	Islam	Judaism	Hinduism	Orthodox	Buddhism
MSA[1]	10.0	38.7	7.1	2.2	0.6	0.1	0.4	0.1	0.4
U.S.	18.7	16.5	5.2	2.3	1.3	0.6	0.4	0.4	0.3

Note: Figures are the number of adherents as a percentage of the total population; (1) Figures cover the Oklahoma City, OK Metropolitan Statistical Area
Sources: 2020 U.S. Religion Census, Association of Statisticians of American Religious Bodies; The Association of Religion Data Archives (ARDA)

ECONOMY

Gross Metropolitan Product

Area	2020	2021	2022	2023	Rank[2]
MSA[1]	74.4	81.6	92.9	98.2	49

Note: Figures are in billions of dollars; (1) Figures cover the Oklahoma City, OK Metropolitan Statistical Area; (2) Rank is based on 2021 data and ranges from 1 to 381
Source: U.S. Conference of Mayors, U.S. Metro Economies: U.S. Metros Compared to Global and State Economies, June 2022

Economic Growth

Area	2018-20 (%)	2021 (%)	2022 (%)	2023 (%)	Rank[2]
MSA[1]	-2.2	2.3	4.2	4.8	307
U.S.	-0.6	5.7	3.1	2.9	–

Note: Figures are real gross metropolitan product (GMP) growth rates and represent average annual percent change; (1) Figures cover the Oklahoma City, OK Metropolitan Statistical Area; (2) Rank is based on 2020 2-year average annual percent change and ranges from 1 to 381
Source: U.S. Conference of Mayors, U.S. Metro Economies: U.S. Metros Compared to Global and State Economies, June 2022

Metropolitan Area Exports

Area	2016	2017	2018	2019	2020	2021	Rank[2]
MSA[1]	1,260.0	1,278.8	1,489.4	1,434.5	1,326.6	1,773.2	116

Note: Figures are in millions of dollars; (1) Figures cover the Oklahoma City, OK Metropolitan Statistical Area; (2) Rank is based on 2021 data and ranges from 1 to 388
Source: U.S. Department of Commerce, International Trade Administration, Office of Trade and Economic Analysis, Industry and Analysis, Exports by Metropolitan Area, data extracted March 16, 2023

Building Permits

Area	Single-Family			Multi-Family			Total		
	2021	2022	Pct. Chg.	2021	2022	Pct. Chg.	2021	2022	Pct. Chg.
City	4,127	3,298	-20.1	140	260	85.7	4,267	3,558	-16.6
MSA[1]	7,637	5,971	-21.8	443	940	112.2	8,080	6,911	-14.5
U.S.	1,115,400	975,600	-12.5	621,600	689,500	10.9	1,737,000	1,665,100	-4.1

Note: (1) Figures cover the Oklahoma City, OK Metropolitan Statistical Area; Figures represent new, privately-owned housing units authorized (unadjusted data); All permit data are based on estimates with imputation
Source: U.S. Census Bureau, Manufacturing, Mining, and Construction Statistics, Building Permits, 2021, 2022

Bankruptcy Filings

Area	Business Filings			Nonbusiness Filings		
	2021	2022	% Chg.	2021	2022	% Chg.
Oklahoma County	52	50	-3.8	1,424	1,199	-15.8
U.S.	14,347	13,481	-6.0	399,269	374,240	-6.3

Note: Business filings include Chapter 7, Chapter 9, Chapter 11, Chapter 12, Chapter 13, Chapter 15, and Section 304; Nonbusiness filings include Chapter 7, Chapter 11, and Chapter 13
Source: Administrative Office of the U.S. Courts, Business and Nonbusiness Bankruptcy, County Cases Commenced by Chapter of the Bankruptcy Code, During the 12-Month Period Ending December 31, 2021 and Business and Nonbusiness Bankruptcy, County Cases Commenced by Chapter of the Bankruptcy Code, During the 12-Month Period Ending December 31, 2022

Housing Vacancy Rates

Area	Gross Vacancy Rate[2] (%)			Year-Round Vacancy Rate[3] (%)			Rental Vacancy Rate[4] (%)			Homeowner Vacancy Rate[5] (%)		
	2020	2021	2022	2020	2021	2022	2020	2021	2022	2020	2021	2022
MSA[1]	7.5	6.1	8.6	7.3	6.0	8.5	6.4	5.7	10.6	0.9	0.8	0.9
U.S.	10.6	10.8	10.5	8.2	8.4	8.2	6.3	6.1	5.8	1.0	0.9	0.8

Note: (1) Figures cover the Oklahoma City, OK Metropolitan Statistical Area; (2) The percentage of the total housing inventory that is vacant; (3) The percentage of the housing inventory (excluding seasonal units) that is year-round vacant; (4) The percentage of rental inventory that is vacant for rent; (5) The percentage of homeowner inventory that is vacant for sale
Source: U.S. Census Bureau, Housing Vacancies and Homeownership Annual Statistics: 2020, 2021, 2022

INCOME

Income

Area	Per Capita ($)	Median Household ($)	Average Household ($)
City	33,162	59,679	81,931
MSA[1]	34,136	63,351	85,884
U.S.	37,638	69,021	97,196

Note: (1) Figures cover the Oklahoma City, OK Metropolitan Statistical Area
Source: U.S. Census Bureau, 2017-2021 American Community Survey 5-Year Estimates

Household Income Distribution

Area	Percent of Households Earning							
	Under $15,000	$15,000 -$24,999	$25,000 -$34,999	$35,000 -$49,999	$50,000 -$74,999	$75,000 -$99,999	$100,000 -$149,999	$150,000 and up
City	10.7	7.7	9.6	13.9	18.7	12.8	14.6	12.1
MSA[1]	9.4	7.9	9.1	13.0	18.6	13.4	15.6	12.8
U.S.	9.4	7.8	8.2	11.4	16.8	12.8	16.3	17.3

Note: (1) Figures cover the Oklahoma City, OK Metropolitan Statistical Area
Source: U.S. Census Bureau, 2017-2021 American Community Survey 5-Year Estimates

Poverty Rate

Area	All Ages	Under 18 Years Old	18 to 64 Years Old	65 Years and Over
City	14.9	21.5	13.6	8.4
MSA[1]	13.6	18.6	12.9	7.8
U.S.	12.6	17.0	11.8	9.6

Note: Figures are percentage of people whose income during the past 12 months was below the poverty level;
(1) Figures cover the Oklahoma City, OK Metropolitan Statistical Area
Source: U.S. Census Bureau, 2017-2021 American Community Survey 5-Year Estimates

EMPLOYMENT

Labor Force and Employment

Area	Civilian Labor Force			Workers Employed		
	Dec. 2021	Dec. 2022	% Chg.	Dec. 2021	Dec. 2022	% Chg.
City	327,538	333,291	1.8	320,689	324,655	1.2
MSA[1]	699,178	711,592	1.8	685,472	694,168	1.3
U.S.	161,696,000	164,224,000	1.6	155,732,000	158,872,000	2.0

Note: Data is not seasonally adjusted and covers workers 16 years of age and older; (1) Figures cover the Oklahoma City, OK Metropolitan Statistical Area
Source: Bureau of Labor Statistics, Local Area Unemployment Statistics

Unemployment Rate

Area	2022											
	Jan.	Feb.	Mar.	Apr.	May	Jun.	Jul.	Aug.	Sep.	Oct.	Nov.	Dec.
City	2.9	3.0	2.9	2.7	2.8	3.4	3.0	3.3	3.2	3.4	2.9	2.6
MSA[1]	2.8	2.9	2.7	2.6	2.7	3.2	2.9	3.1	3.1	3.3	2.8	2.4
U.S.	4.4	4.1	3.8	3.3	3.4	3.8	3.8	3.8	3.3	3.4	3.4	3.3

Note: Data is not seasonally adjusted and covers workers 16 years of age and older; (1) Figures cover the Oklahoma City, OK Metropolitan Statistical Area
Source: Bureau of Labor Statistics, Local Area Unemployment Statistics

Average Wages

Occupation	$/Hr.	Occupation	$/Hr.
Accountants and Auditors	37.21	Maintenance and Repair Workers	18.75
Automotive Mechanics	22.78	Marketing Managers	64.04
Bookkeepers	20.87	Network and Computer Systems Admin.	41.84
Carpenters	21.48	Nurses, Licensed Practical	23.45
Cashiers	12.66	Nurses, Registered	37.19
Computer Programmers	43.42	Nursing Assistants	14.90
Computer Systems Analysts	43.52	Office Clerks, General	16.78
Computer User Support Specialists	26.61	Physical Therapists	44.06
Construction Laborers	19.08	Physicians	126.14
Cooks, Restaurant	14.94	Plumbers, Pipefitters and Steamfitters	24.68
Customer Service Representatives	18.11	Police and Sheriff's Patrol Officers	33.22
Dentists	84.37	Postal Service Mail Carriers	27.22
Electricians	27.58	Real Estate Sales Agents	n/a
Engineers, Electrical	47.89	Retail Salespersons	15.14
Fast Food and Counter Workers	11.19	Sales Representatives, Technical/Scientific	39.45
Financial Managers	64.38	Secretaries, Exc. Legal/Medical/Executive	18.26
First-Line Supervisors of Office Workers	30.11	Security Guards	15.95
General and Operations Managers	48.66	Surgeons	n/a
Hairdressers/Cosmetologists	17.09	Teacher Assistants, Exc. Postsecondary*	11.92
Home Health and Personal Care Aides	12.14	Teachers, Secondary School, Exc. Sp. Ed.*	27.00
Janitors and Cleaners	13.56	Telemarketers	18.98
Landscaping/Groundskeeping Workers	16.15	Truck Drivers, Heavy/Tractor-Trailer	24.66
Lawyers	53.26	Truck Drivers, Light/Delivery Services	20.54
Maids and Housekeeping Cleaners	12.31	Waiters and Waitresses	12.33

Note: Wage data covers the Oklahoma City, OK Metropolitan Statistical Area; (*) Hourly wages were calculated from annual wage data based on a 40 hour work week; n/a not available.
Source: Bureau of Labor Statistics, Metro Area Occupational Employment & Wage Estimates, May 2022

Employment by Industry

Sector	MSA[1]		U.S.
	Number of Employees	Percent of Total	Percent of Total
Construction	33,900	4.9	5.0
Private Education and Health Services	105,700	15.4	16.1
Financial Activities	36,800	5.4	5.9
Government	129,200	18.8	14.5
Information	5,900	0.9	2.0
Leisure and Hospitality	77,100	11.2	10.3
Manufacturing	35,500	5.2	8.4
Mining and Logging	11,100	1.6	0.4
Other Services	29,000	4.2	3.7
Professional and Business Services	91,400	13.3	14.7
Retail Trade	71,300	10.4	10.2
Transportation, Warehousing, and Utilities	35,500	5.2	4.9
Wholesale Trade	23,200	3.4	3.9

Note: Figures are non-farm employment as of December 2022. Figures are not seasonally adjusted and include workers 16 years of age and older; (1) Figures cover the Oklahoma City, OK Metropolitan Statistical Area
Source: Bureau of Labor Statistics, Current Employment Statistics, Employment, Hours, and Earnings

Employment by Occupation

Occupation Classification	City (%)	MSA[1] (%)	U.S. (%)
Management, Business, Science, and Arts	38.5	39.3	40.3
Natural Resources, Construction, and Maintenance	9.9	10.0	8.7
Production, Transportation, and Material Moving	12.7	12.2	13.1
Sales and Office	21.9	22.1	20.9
Service	17.0	16.5	17.0

Note: Figures cover employed civilians 16 years of age and older; (1) Figures cover the Oklahoma City, OK Metropolitan Statistical Area
Source: U.S. Census Bureau, 2017-2021 American Community Survey 5-Year Estimates

Occupations with Greatest Projected Employment Growth: 2022 – 2024

Occupation[1]	2022 Employment	2024 Projected Employment	Numeric Employment Change	Percent Employment Change
Laborers and Freight, Stock, and Material Movers, Hand	34,240	35,720	1,480	4.3
Cooks, Restaurant	19,010	20,280	1,270	6.7
Stockers and Order Fillers	16,770	17,590	820	4.9
Light Truck or Delivery Services Drivers	12,400	13,170	770	6.2
Cashiers	42,800	43,500	700	1.6
Retail Salespersons	48,810	49,390	580	1.2
General and Operations Managers	25,640	26,200	560	2.2
Home Health and Personal Care Aides	13,440	13,950	510	3.8
Waiters and Waitresses	27,150	27,640	490	1.8
Heavy and Tractor-Trailer Truck Drivers	28,040	28,530	490	1.7

Note: Projections cover Oklahoma; (1) Sorted by numeric employment change
Source: www.projectionscentral.com, State Occupational Projections, 2022–2024 Short-Term Projections

Fastest-Growing Occupations: 2022 – 2024

Occupation[1]	2022 Employment	2024 Projected Employment	Numeric Employment Change	Percent Employment Change
Roustabouts, Oil and Gas	3,100	3,360	260	8.4
Rotary Drill Operators, Oil and Gas	1,830	1,980	150	8.2
Information Security Analysts (SOC 2018)	800	860	60	7.5
Cooks, Restaurant	19,010	20,280	1,270	6.7
Service Unit Operators, Oil, Gas, and Mining	2,110	2,250	140	6.6
Light Truck or Delivery Services Drivers	12,400	13,170	770	6.2
Nurse Practitioners	2,310	2,450	140	6.1
Physical Therapist Assistants	1,550	1,630	80	5.2
Fitness Trainers and Aerobics Instructors	4,610	4,850	240	5.2
Medical and Health Services Managers	7,950	8,350	400	5.0

Note: Projections cover Oklahoma; (1) Sorted by percent employment change and excludes occupations with numeric employment change less than 50
Source: www.projectionscentral.com, State Occupational Projections, 2022–2024 Short-Term Projections

CITY FINANCES

City Government Finances

Component	2020 ($000)	2020 ($ per capita)
Total Revenues	1,592,400	2,431
Total Expenditures	1,413,994	2,159
Debt Outstanding	2,282,455	3,484
Cash and Securities[1]	3,074,686	4,694

Note: (1) Cash and security holdings of a government at the close of its fiscal year, including those of its dependent agencies, utilities, and liquor stores.
Source: U.S. Census Bureau, State & Local Government Finances 2020

City Government Revenue by Source

Source	2020 ($000)	2020 ($ per capita)	2020 (%)
General Revenue			
From Federal Government	48,386	74	3.0
From State Government	63,414	97	4.0
From Local Governments	33,871	52	2.1
Taxes			
Property	126,497	193	7.9
Sales and Gross Receipts	566,586	865	35.6
Personal Income	0	0	0.0
Corporate Income	0	0	0.0
Motor Vehicle License	0	0	0.0
Other Taxes	72,971	111	4.6
Current Charges	275,064	420	17.3
Liquor Store	0	0	0.0
Utility	183,671	280	11.5

Source: U.S. Census Bureau, State & Local Government Finances 2020

City Government Expenditures by Function

Function	2020 ($000)	2020 ($ per capita)	2020 (%)
General Direct Expenditures			
Air Transportation	89,198	136	6.3
Corrections	0	0	0.0
Education	0	0	0.0
Employment Security Administration	0	0	0.0
Financial Administration	10,496	16	0.7
Fire Protection	163,589	249	11.6
General Public Buildings	0	0	0.0
Governmental Administration, Other	14,170	21	1.0
Health	4,875	7	0.3
Highways	117,119	178	8.3
Hospitals	0	0	0.0
Housing and Community Development	24,138	36	1.7
Interest on General Debt	37,776	57	2.7
Judicial and Legal	18,665	28	1.3
Libraries	0	0	0.0
Parking	5,821	8	0.4
Parks and Recreation	218,706	333	15.5
Police Protection	205,552	313	14.5
Public Welfare	0	0	0.0
Sewerage	36,228	55	2.6
Solid Waste Management	51,039	77	3.6
Veterans' Services	0	0	0.0
Liquor Store	0	0	0.0
Utility	365,781	558	25.9

Source: U.S. Census Bureau, State & Local Government Finances 2020

TAXES

State Corporate Income Tax Rates

State	Tax Rate (%)	Income Brackets ($)	Num. of Brackets	Financial Institution Tax Rate (%)[a]	Federal Income Tax Ded.
Oklahoma	4.0	Flat rate	1	4.0	No

Note: Tax rates as of January 1, 2023; (a) Rates listed are the corporate income tax rate applied to financial institutions or excise taxes based on income. Some states have other taxes based upon the value of deposits or shares.
Source: Federation of Tax Administrators, State Corporate Income Tax Rates, January 1, 2023

State Individual Income Tax Rates

State	Tax Rate (%)	Income Brackets ($)	Personal Exemptions ($)			Standard Ded. ($)	
			Single	Married	Depend.	Single	Married
Oklahoma	0.25 - 4.75	1,000 - 7,200 (v)	1,000	2,000	1,000	6,350	12,700

Note: Tax rates as of January 1, 2023; Local- and county-level taxes are not included; Federal income tax is not deductible on state income tax returns; (v) The income brackets reported for Oklahoma are for single persons. For married persons filing jointly, the same tax rates apply to income brackets ranging from $2,000, to $12,200.
Source: Federation of Tax Administrators, State Individual Income Tax Rates, January 1, 2023

Various State Sales and Excise Tax Rates

State	State Sales Tax (%)	Gasoline[1] ($/gal.)	Cigarette[2] ($/pack)	Spirits[3] ($/gal.)	Wine[4] ($/gal.)	Beer[5] ($/gal.)	Recreational Marijuana (%)
Oklahoma	4.5	0.20	2.03	5.56	0.72	0.40	Not legal

Note: All tax rates as of January 1, 2023; (1) The American Petroleum Institute has developed a methodology for determining the average tax rate on a gallon of fuel. Rates may include any of the following: excise taxes, environmental fees, storage tank fees, other fees or taxes, general sales tax, and local taxes; (2) The federal excise tax of $1.0066 per pack and local taxes are not included; (3) Rates are those applicable to off-premise sales of 40% alcohol by volume (a.b.v.) distilled spirits in 750ml containers. Local excise taxes are excluded; (4) Rates are those applicable to off-premise sales of 11% a.b.v. non-carbonated wine in 750ml containers; (5) Rates are those applicable to off-premise sales of 4.7% a.b.v. beer in 12 ounce containers.
Source: Tax Foundation, 2023 Facts & Figures: How Does Your State Compare?

State Business Tax Climate Index Rankings

State	Overall Rank	Corporate Tax Rank	Individual Income Tax Rank	Sales Tax Rank	Property Tax Rank	Unemployment Insurance Tax Rank
Oklahoma	23	4	31	39	30	1

Note: The index is a measure of how each state's tax laws affect economic performance. The lower the rank, the more favorable a state's tax system is for business. States without a given tax are given a ranking of 1. The scores/rankings for the District of Columbia do not affect other states. The 2023 index represents the tax climate as of July 1, 2022.
Source: Tax Foundation, State Business Tax Climate Index 2023

TRANSPORTATION

Means of Transportation to Work

Area	Car/Truck/Van		Public Transportation			Bicycle	Walked	Other Means	Worked at Home
	Drove Alone	Car-pooled	Bus	Subway	Railroad				
City	80.0	9.7	0.4	0.0	0.0	0.2	1.6	1.4	6.8
MSA[1]	80.6	9.1	0.3	0.0	0.0	0.3	1.6	1.2	7.0
U.S.	73.2	8.6	2.0	1.6	0.5	0.5	2.5	1.5	9.7

Note: Figures are percentages and cover workers 16 years of age and older; (1) Figures cover the Oklahoma City, OK Metropolitan Statistical Area
Source: U.S. Census Bureau, 2017-2021 American Community Survey 5-Year Estimates

Travel Time to Work

Area	Less Than 10 Minutes	10 to 19 Minutes	20 to 29 Minutes	30 to 44 Minutes	45 to 59 Minutes	60 to 89 Minutes	90 Minutes or More
City	10.5	36.0	29.0	18.2	3.5	1.4	1.4
MSA[1]	11.9	32.3	25.4	20.6	5.7	2.5	1.6
U.S.	12.4	28.5	21.0	20.9	8.2	6.2	2.9

Note: Note: Figures are percentages and include workers 16 years old and over; (1) Figures cover the Oklahoma City, OK Metropolitan Statistical Area
Source: U.S. Census Bureau, 2017-2021 American Community Survey 5-Year Estimates

Key Congestion Measures

Measure	1990	2000	2010	2015	2020
Annual Hours of Delay, Total (000)	8,518	22,189	32,864	40,393	30,057
Annual Hours of Delay, Per Auto Commuter	17	36	43	47	35
Annual Congestion Cost, Per Auto Commuter ($)	314	618	727	826	656

Note: Covers the Oklahoma City OK urban area
Source: Texas A&M Transportation Institute, 2021 Urban Mobility Report

Freeway Travel Time Index

Measure	1985	1990	1995	2000	2005	2010	2015	2020
Urban Area Index[1]	1.06	1.08	1.11	1.16	1.18	1.18	1.19	1.12
Urban Area Rank[1,2]	53	62	66	43	41	38	38	10

Note: Freeway Travel Time Index—the ratio of travel time in the peak period to the travel time at free-flow conditions. For example, a value of 1.30 indicates a 20-minute free-flow trip takes 26 minutes in the peak (20 minutes x 1.30 = 26 minutes); (1) Covers the Oklahoma City OK urban area; (2) Rank is based on 101 larger urban areas (#1 = highest travel time index)
Source: Texas A&M Transportation Institute, 2021 Urban Mobility Report

Public Transportation

Agency Name / Mode of Transportation	Vehicles Operated in Maximum Service[1]	Annual Unlinked Passenger Trips[2] (in thous.)	Annual Passenger Miles[3] (in thous.)
Central Oklahoma Transportation & Parking Authority (COTPA)			
Bus (directly operated)	49	1,846.1	8,977.4
Demand Response (directly operated)	17	43.9	365.4
Streetcar Rail (purchased transportation)	5	246.3	687.5

Note: (1) Number of revenue vehicles operated by the given mode and type of service to meet the annual maximum service requirement. This is the revenue vehicle count during the peak season of the year; on the week and day that maximum service is provided. Vehicles operated in maximum service (VOMS) exclude atypical days and one-time special events; (2) Number of passengers who boarded public transportation vehicles. Passengers are counted each time they board a vehicle no matter how many vehicles they use to travel from their origin to their destination. (3) Sum of the distances ridden by all passengers during the entire fiscal year.
Source: Federal Transit Administration, National Transit Database, 2021

Air Transportation

Airport Name and Code / Type of Service	Passenger Airlines[1]	Passenger Enplanements	Freight Carriers[2]	Freight (lbs)
Will Rogers World Airport (OKC)				
Domestic service (U.S. carriers - 2022)	26	1,927,889	12	29,239,822
International service (U.S. carriers - 2021)	0	0	0	0

Note: (1) Includes all U.S.-based major, minor and commuter airlines that carried at least one passenger during the year; (2) Includes all U.S.-based airlines and freight carriers that transported at least one pound of freight during the year.
Source: Bureau of Transportation Statistics, The Intermodal Transportation Database, Air Carriers: T-100 Domestic Market (U.S. Carriers), 2022; Bureau of Transportation Statistics, The Intermodal Transportation Database, Air Carriers: T-100 International Market (U.S. Carriers), 2021

BUSINESSES

Major Business Headquarters

Company Name	Industry	Rankings	
		Fortune[1]	Forbes[2]
Continental Resources	Oil & gas operations	-	87
Devon Energy	Petroleum exploration	309	-
Hobby Lobby Stores	Retailing	-	71
Love's Travel Stops & Country Stores	Convenience stores & gas stations	-	10

Note: (1) Companies that produce a 10-K are ranked 1 to 500 based on 2021 revenue; (2) All private companies with at least $2 billion in annual revenue through the end of their most current fiscal year are ranked 1 to 246; companies listed are headquartered in the city; dashes indicate no ranking
Source: Fortune, "Fortune 500," 2022; Forbes, "America's Largest Private Companies," 2022

Living Environment

COST OF LIVING

Cost of Living Index

Composite Index	Groceries	Housing	Utilities	Trans-portation	Health Care	Misc. Goods/ Services
83.9	91.1	71.0	94.4	90.8	100.6	84.4

Note: The Cost of Living Index measures regional differences in the cost of consumer goods and services, excluding taxes and non-consumer expenditures, for professional and managerial households in the top income quintile. It is based on more than 50,000 prices covering almost 60 different items for which prices are collected three times a year by chambers of commerce, economic development organizations or university applied economic centers in each participating urban area. The numbers shown should be read as a percentage above or below the national average of 100. For example, a value of 115.4 in the groceries column indicates that grocery prices are 15.4% higher than the national average. Small differences in the index numbers should not be interpreted as significant; Figures cover the Oklahoma City OK urban area.
Source: The Council for Community and Economic Research, Cost of Living Index, 2022

Grocery Prices

Area[1]	T-Bone Steak ($/pound)	Frying Chicken ($/pound)	Whole Milk ($/half gal.)	Eggs ($/dozen)	Orange Juice ($/64 oz.)	Coffee ($/11.5 oz.)
City[2]	12.72	1.51	2.34	2.04	3.32	4.72
Avg.	13.81	1.59	2.43	2.25	3.85	4.95
Min.	10.17	0.90	1.51	1.30	2.90	3.46
Max.	19.35	3.30	4.32	4.32	5.31	8.59

*Note: (1) Values for the local area are compared with the average, minimum and maximum values for all 286 areas in the Cost of Living Index; (2) Figures cover the Oklahoma City OK urban area; **T-Bone Steak** (price per pound); **Frying Chicken** (price per pound, whole fryer); **Whole Milk** (half gallon carton); **Eggs** (price per dozen, Grade A, large); **Orange Juice** (64 oz. Tropicana or Florida Natural); **Coffee** (11.5 oz. can, vacuum-packed, Maxwell House, Hills Bros, or Folgers).*
Source: The Council for Community and Economic Research, Cost of Living Index, 2022

Housing and Utility Costs

Area[1]	New Home Price ($)	Apartment Rent ($/month)	All Electric ($/month)	Part Electric ($/month)	Other Energy ($/month)	Telephone ($/month)
City[2]	333,325	860	-	90.04	66.60	195.02
Avg.	450,913	1,371	176.41	99.93	76.96	190.22
Min.	229,283	546	100.84	31.56	27.15	174.27
Max.	2,434,977	4,569	356.86	249.59	272.24	208.31

*Note: (1) Values for the local area are compared with the average, minimum and maximum values for all 286 areas in the Cost of Living Index; (2) Figures cover the Oklahoma City OK urban area; **New Home Price** (2,400 sf living area, 8,000 sf lot, in urban area with full utilities); **Apartment Rent** (950 sf 2 bedroom/1.5 or 2 bath, unfurnished, excluding all utilities except water); **All Electric** (average monthly cost for an all-electric home); **Part Electric** (average monthly cost for a part-electric home); **Other Energy** (average monthly cost for natural gas, fuel oil, coal, wood, and any other forms of energy except electricity); **Telephone** (price includes the base monthly rate plus taxes and fees for three lines of mobile phone service).*
Source: The Council for Community and Economic Research, Cost of Living Index, 2022

Health Care, Transportation, and Other Costs

Area[1]	Doctor ($/visit)	Dentist ($/visit)	Optometrist ($/visit)	Gasoline ($/gallon)	Beauty Salon ($/visit)	Men's Shirt ($)
City[2]	111.16	120.92	115.53	3.36	43.00	21.10
Avg.	124.91	107.77	117.66	3.86	43.31	34.21
Min.	36.61	58.25	51.79	2.90	22.18	13.05
Max.	250.21	162.58	371.96	5.54	85.61	63.54

*Note: (1) Values for the local area are compared with the average, minimum and maximum values for all 286 areas in the Cost of Living Index; (2) Figures cover the Oklahoma City OK urban area; **Doctor** (general practitioners routine exam of an established patient); **Dentist** (adult teeth cleaning and periodic oral examination); **Optometrist** (full vision eye exam for established adult patient); **Gasoline** (one gallon regular unleaded, national brand, including all taxes, cash price at self-service pump if available); **Beauty Salon** (woman's shampoo, trim, and blow-dry); **Men's Shirt** (cotton/polyester dress shirt, pinpoint weave, long sleeves).*
Source: The Council for Community and Economic Research, Cost of Living Index, 2022

HOUSING

Homeownership Rate

Area	2015 (%)	2016 (%)	2017 (%)	2018 (%)	2019 (%)	2020 (%)	2021 (%)	2022 (%)
MSA[1]	61.4	63.1	64.7	64.6	64.3	68.3	61.9	64.8
U.S.	63.7	63.4	63.9	64.4	64.6	66.6	65.5	65.8

Note: (1) Figures cover the Oklahoma City, OK Metropolitan Statistical Area
Source: U.S. Census Bureau, Housing Vacancies and Homeownership Annual Statistics: 2015-2022

House Price Index (HPI)

Area	National Ranking[2]	Quarterly Change (%)	One-Year Change (%)	Five-Year Change (%)	Since 1991Q1 (%)
MSA[1]	97	0.36	12.37	49.27	260.86
U.S.[3]	–	0.34	8.41	58.44	289.08

Note: The HPI is a weighted repeat sales index. It measures average price changes in repeat sales or refinancings on the same properties. This information is obtained by reviewing repeat mortgage transactions on single-family properties whose mortgages have been purchased or securitized by Fannie Mae or Freddie Mac since January 1975; (1) Figures cover the Oklahoma City, OK Metropolitan Statistical Area; (2) Rankings are based on annual percentage change for all metro areas containing at least 15,000 transactions over the last 10 years and ranges from 1 to 257; (3) figures based on a weighted average of Census Division estimates using a seasonally adjusted, purchase-only index; all figures are for the period ending December 31, 2022
Source: Federal Housing Finance Agency, Change in FHFA Metropolitan Area House Price Indexes, 2022Q4

Median Single-Family Home Prices

Area	2020	2021	2022[p]	Percent Change 2021 to 2022
MSA[1]	174.9	194.2	223.4	15.0
U.S. Average	300.2	357.1	392.6	9.9

Note: Figures are median sales prices of existing single-family homes in thousands of dollars; (p) preliminary; (1) Figures cover the Oklahoma City, OK Metropolitan Statistical Area
Source: National Association of Realtors, Median Sales Price of Existing Single-Family Homes for Metropolitan Areas, 4th Quarter 2022

Qualifying Income Based on Median Sales Price of Existing Single-Family Homes

Area	With 5% Down ($)	With 10% Down ($)	With 20% Down ($)
MSA[1]	66,479	62,980	55,982
U.S. Average	112,234	106,237	94,513

Note: Figures are preliminary; Qualifying income is based on a mortgage rate of 6.77%. Monthly principal and interest payment is limited to 25% of income; (1) Figures cover the Oklahoma City, OK Metropolitan Statistical Area
Source: National Association of Realtors, Qualifying Income Based on Median Sales Price of Existing Single-Family Homes for Metropolitan Areas, 4th Quarter 2022

Home Value

Area	Under $100,000	$100,000 -$199,999	$200,000 -$299,999	$300,000 -$399,999	$400,000 -$499,999	$500,000 -$999,999	$1,000,000 or more	Median ($)
City	23.1	38.5	21.4	8.2	3.8	3.8	1.2	168,900
MSA[1]	21.7	39.2	20.6	9.0	4.1	4.1	1.2	169,300
U.S.	16.2	24.2	20.1	13.6	8.3	13.6	4.1	244,900

Note: Figures are percentages except for median and cover owner-occupied housing units; (1) Figures cover the Oklahoma City, OK Metropolitan Statistical Area
Source: U.S. Census Bureau, 2017-2021 American Community Survey 5-Year Estimates

Year Housing Structure Built

Area	2020 or Later	2010 -2019	2000 -2009	1990 -1999	1980 -1989	1970 -1979	1960 -1969	1950 -1959	1940 -1949	Before 1940	Median Year
City	0.3	12.0	13.4	9.9	14.2	15.9	11.5	10.0	5.0	7.9	1980
MSA[1]	0.3	11.8	14.7	11.0	14.3	16.8	11.4	9.2	4.6	5.9	1981
U.S.	0.2	7.3	13.6	13.6	13.2	14.8	10.3	10.0	4.7	12.2	1979

Note: Figures are percentages except for Median Year; Note: (1) Figures cover the Oklahoma City, OK Metropolitan Statistical Area
Source: U.S. Census Bureau, 2017-2021 American Community Survey 5-Year Estimates

Gross Monthly Rent

Area	Under $500	$500 -$999	$1,000 -$1,499	$1,500 -$1,999	$2,000 -$2,499	$2,500 -$2,999	$3,000 and up	Median ($)
City	6.5	51.2	32.1	7.8	1.6	0.4	0.4	933
MSA[1]	6.8	50.2	32.3	8.0	1.6	0.5	0.6	937
U.S.	8.1	30.5	30.8	16.8	7.3	3.1	3.5	1,163

Note: Figures are percentages except for median; Gross rent is the contract rent plus the estimated average monthly cost of utilities (electricity, gas, and water and sewer) and fuels (oil, coal, kerosene, wood, etc.) if these are paid by the renter (or paid for the renter by someone else); (1) Figures cover the Oklahoma City, OK Metropolitan Statistical Area
Source: U.S. Census Bureau, 2017-2021 American Community Survey 5-Year Estimates

HEALTH

Health Risk Factors

Category	MSA[1] (%)	U.S. (%)
Adults aged 18–64 who have any kind of health care coverage	85.3	90.9
Adults who reported being in good or better health	81.3	85.2
Adults who have been told they have high blood cholesterol	37.6	35.7
Adults who have been told they have high blood pressure	36.6	32.4
Adults who are current smokers	14.1	14.4
Adults who currently use e-cigarettes	9.6	6.7
Adults who currently use chewing tobacco, snuff, or snus	5.0	3.5
Adults who are heavy drinkers[2]	3.3	6.3
Adults who are binge drinkers[3]	12.4	15.4
Adults who are overweight (BMI 25.0 - 29.9)	32.4	34.4
Adults who are obese (BMI 30.0 - 99.8)	37.5	33.9
Adults who participated in any physical activities in the past month	74.1	76.3

Note: (1) Figures cover the Oklahoma City, OK Metropolitan Statistical Area; (2) Heavy drinkers are classified as adult men having more than 14 drinks per week and adult women having more than 7 drinks per week; (3) Binge drinkers are classified as males having five or more drinks on one occasion or females having four or more drinks on one occasion
Source: Centers for Disease Control and Prevention, Behaviorial Risk Factor Surveillance System, SMART: Selected Metropolitan Area Risk Trends, 2021

Acute and Chronic Health Conditions

Category	MSA[1] (%)	U.S. (%)
Adults who have ever been told they had a heart attack	4.0	4.0
Adults who have ever been told they have angina or coronary heart disease	4.7	3.8
Adults who have ever been told they had a stroke	3.5	3.0
Adults who have ever been told they have asthma	16.5	14.9
Adults who have ever been told they have arthritis	25.1	25.8
Adults who have ever been told they have diabetes[2]	11.4	10.9
Adults who have ever been told they had skin cancer	5.3	6.6
Adults who have ever been told they had any other types of cancer	7.1	7.5
Adults who have ever been told they have COPD	6.8	6.1
Adults who have ever been told they have kidney disease	2.8	3.0
Adults who have ever been told they have a form of depression	23.7	20.5

Note: (1) Figures cover the Oklahoma City, OK Metropolitan Statistical Area; (2) Figures do not include pregnancy-related, borderline, or pre-diabetes
Source: Centers for Disease Control and Prevention, Behaviorial Risk Factor Surveillance System, SMART: Selected Metropolitan Area Risk Trends, 2021

Health Screening and Vaccination Rates

Category	MSA[1] (%)	U.S. (%)
Adults who have ever been tested for HIV	32.2	34.9
Adults who have had their blood cholesterol checked within the last five years	83.3	85.2
Adults aged 65+ who have had flu shot within the past year	71.3	68.6
Adults aged 65+ who have ever had a pneumonia vaccination	79.1	71.0

Note: (1) Figures cover the Oklahoma City, OK Metropolitan Statistical Area.
Source: Centers for Disease Control and Prevention, Behaviorial Risk Factor Surveillance System, SMART: Selected Metropolitan Area Risk Trends, 2021

Disability Status

Category	MSA[1] (%)	U.S. (%)
Adults who reported being deaf	9.7	7.2
Are you blind or have serious difficulty seeing, even when wearing glasses?	5.5	4.8
Are you limited in any way in any of your usual activities due to arthritis?	11.3	11.1
Do you have difficulty doing errands alone?	6.8	7.0
Do you have difficulty dressing or bathing?	4.6	3.6
Do you have serious difficulty concentrating/remembering/making decisions?	13.1	12.1
Do you have serious difficulty walking or climbing stairs?	15.5	12.8

Note: (1) Figures cover the Oklahoma City, OK Metropolitan Statistical Area.
Source: Centers for Disease Control and Prevention, Behaviorial Risk Factor Surveillance System, SMART: Selected Metropolitan Area Risk Trends, 2021

Mortality Rates for the Top 10 Causes of Death in the U.S.

ICD-10[a] Sub-Chapter	ICD-10[a] Code	Crude Mortality Rate[1] per 100,000 population	
		County[2]	U.S.
Malignant neoplasms	C00-C97	182.5	182.6
Ischaemic heart diseases	I20-I25	129.4	113.1
Other forms of heart disease	I30-I51	48.2	64.4
Other degenerative diseases of the nervous system	G30-G31	64.7	51.0
Cerebrovascular diseases	I60-I69	41.4	47.8
Other external causes of accidental injury	W00-X59	57.2	46.4
Chronic lower respiratory diseases	J40-J47	59.2	45.7
Organic, including symptomatic, mental disorders	F01-F09	30.5	35.9
Hypertensive diseases	I10-I15	69.6	35.0
Diabetes mellitus	E10-E14	36.3	29.6

Note: (a) ICD-10 = International Classification of Diseases 10th Revision; (1) Crude mortality rates are a three-year average covering 2019-2021; (2) Figures cover Oklahoma County.
Source: Centers for Disease Control and Prevention, National Center for Health Statistics. National Vital Statistics System, Mortality 2018-2021 on CDC WONDER Online Database

Mortality Rates for Selected Causes of Death

ICD-10[a] Sub-Chapter	ICD-10[a] Code	Crude Mortality Rate[1] per 100,000 population	
		County[2]	U.S.
Assault	X85-Y09	12.2	7.0
Diseases of the liver	K70-K76	20.9	19.8
Human immunodeficiency virus (HIV) disease	B20-B24	3.4	1.5
Influenza and pneumonia	J09-J18	11.3	14.7
Intentional self-harm	X60-X84	21.5	14.3
Malnutrition	E40-E46	3.6	4.3
Obesity and other hyperalimentation	E65-E68	2.5	3.0
Renal failure	N17-N19	11.1	15.7
Transport accidents	V01-V99	14.6	13.6
Viral hepatitis	B15-B19	2.2	1.2

Note: (a) ICD-10 = International Classification of Diseases 10th Revision; (1) Crude mortality rates are a three-year average covering 2019-2021; (2) Figures cover Oklahoma County; Data are suppressed when the data meet the criteria for confidentiality constraints; Crude mortality rates are flagged as unreliable when the rate would be calculated with a numerator of 20 or less.
Source: Centers for Disease Control and Prevention, National Center for Health Statistics. National Vital Statistics System, Mortality 2018-2021 on CDC WONDER Online Database

Health Insurance Coverage

Area	With Health Insurance	With Private Health Insurance	With Public Health Insurance	Without Health Insurance	Population Under Age 19 Without Health Insurance
City	85.6	64.7	32.3	14.4	7.5
MSA[1]	87.4	68.4	31.5	12.6	6.9
U.S.	91.2	67.8	35.4	8.8	5.3

Note: Figures are percentages that cover the civilian noninstitutionalized population; (1) Figures cover the Oklahoma City, OK Metropolitan Statistical Area
Source: U.S. Census Bureau, 2017-2021 American Community Survey 5-Year Estimates

Number of Medical Professionals

Area	MDs[3]	DOs[3,4]	Dentists	Podiatrists	Chiropractors	Optometrists
County[1] (number)	3,373	343	871	42	231	164
County[1] (rate[2])	423.1	43.0	109.1	5.3	28.9	20.5
U.S. (rate[2])	289.3	23.5	72.5	6.2	28.7	17.4

Note: Data as of 2021 unless noted; (1) Data covers Oklahoma County; (2) Rate per 100,000 population; (3) Data as of 2020 and includes all active, non-federal physicians; (4) Doctor of Osteopathic Medicine
Source: U.S. Department of Health and Human Services, Health Resources and Services Administration, Bureau of Health Professions, Area Resource File (ARF) 2021-2022

Best Hospitals

According to *U.S. News,* the Oklahoma City, OK metro area is home to one of the best children's hospitals in the U.S.: **Oklahoma Children's Hospital OU Health** (2 pediatric specialties). The hospital listed was highly ranked in at least one of 10 pediatric specialties. Eighty-six children's hospitals in the U.S. were nationally ranked in at least one specialty. Hospitals received points for being ranked in a specialty, and the 10 hospitals with the most points across the 10 specialties make up the Honor Roll. *U.S. News Online, "America's Best Children's Hospitals 2022-23"*

EDUCATION

Public School District Statistics

District Name	Schls	Pupils	Pupil/Teacher Ratio	Minority Pupils[1] (%)	LEP/ELL[2] (%)	IEP[3] (%)
Epic Blended Learning Charter	6	15,177	28.1	56.7	1.8	15.4
Epic One On One Charter School	3	23,155	26.2	43.3	0.4	19.2
Oklahoma City	59	32,086	14.3	88.3	34.3	15.1
Santa Fe South (charter)	7	3,694	17.5	98.5	44.8	11.4
Western Heights	8	2,748	15.6	85.4	24.5	13.7

Note: Table includes school districts with 2,000 or more students; (1) Percentage of students that are not non-Hispanic white; (2) Percentage of students that are Limited English Proficient or English Language Learners (2018-19); (3) Percentage of students that have an Individualized Education Program (2019-20). Source: U.S. Department of Education, National Center for Education Statistics, Common Core of Data, Local Education Agency (School District) Universe Survey: School Year 2021-2022

Best High Schools

According to *U.S. News*, Oklahoma City is home to two of the top 500 high schools in the U.S.: **Harding Charter Preparatory High School** (#115); **Classen High School of Advanced Studies** (#145). Nearly 18,000 public, magnet and charter schools were ranked based on their performance on state assessments and how well they prepare students for college. *U.S. News & World Report, "Best High Schools 2022"*

Highest Level of Education

Area	Less than H.S.	H.S. Diploma	Some College, No Deg.	Associate Degree	Bachelor's Degree	Master's Degree	Prof. School Degree	Doctorate Degree
City	12.5	24.6	22.5	8.1	20.5	8.0	2.6	1.2
MSA[1]	10.2	26.4	22.9	8.1	20.7	8.1	2.2	1.4
U.S.	11.1	26.5	20.0	8.7	20.6	9.3	2.2	1.5

Note: Figures cover persons age 25 and over; (1) Figures cover the Oklahoma City, OK Metropolitan Statistical Area
Source: U.S. Census Bureau, 2017-2021 American Community Survey 5-Year Estimates

Educational Attainment by Race

Area	High School Graduate or Higher (%)					Bachelor's Degree or Higher (%)				
	Total	White	Black	Asian	Hisp.[2]	Total	White	Black	Asian	Hisp.[2]
City	87.5	89.5	91.2	80.6	57.6	32.3	35.4	24.3	42.3	10.4
MSA[1]	89.8	91.3	91.6	83.3	62.2	32.4	34.4	24.0	47.2	13.2
U.S.	88.9	91.4	87.2	87.6	71.2	33.7	35.5	23.3	55.6	18.4

Note: Figures shown cover persons 25 years old and over; (1) Figures cover the Oklahoma City, OK Metropolitan Statistical Area; (2) People of Hispanic origin can be of any race
Source: U.S. Census Bureau, 2017-2021 American Community Survey 5-Year Estimates

School Enrollment by Grade and Control

Area	Preschool (%)		Kindergarten (%)		Grades 1 - 4 (%)		Grades 5 - 8 (%)		Grades 9 - 12 (%)	
	Public	Private	Public	Private	Public	Private	Public	Private	Public	Private
City	70.9	29.1	87.6	12.4	89.5	10.5	88.2	11.8	88.1	11.9
MSA[1]	71.5	28.5	87.9	12.1	89.2	10.8	88.8	11.2	89.1	10.9
U.S.	58.8	41.2	86.3	13.7	88.3	11.7	88.6	11.4	89.4	10.6

Note: Figures shown cover persons 3 years old and over; (1) Figures cover the Oklahoma City, OK Metropolitan Statistical Area
Source: U.S. Census Bureau, 2017-2021 American Community Survey 5-Year Estimates

Higher Education

Four-Year Colleges			Two-Year Colleges			Medical Schools[1]	Law Schools[2]	Voc/Tech[3]
Public	Private Non-profit	Private For-profit	Public	Private Non-profit	Private For-profit			
6	6	0	6	1	0	1	2	10

Note: Figures cover institutions located within the Oklahoma City, OK Metropolitan Statistical Area and include main campuses only; (1) includes schools accredited by the Liaison Committee on Medical Education and the American Osteopathic Association's Commission on Osteopathic College Accreditation; (2) includes ABA-accredited schools, schools with provisional ABA accreditation, and state accredited schools; (3) includes all schools with programs that are less than 2 years.
Source: National Center for Education Statistics, Integrated Postsecondary Education System (IPEDS), 2021-22; Wikipedia, List of Medical Schools in the United States, accessed April 10, 2023; Wikipedia, List of Law Schools in the United States, accessed April 10, 2023

According to *U.S. News & World Report*, the Oklahoma City, OK metro area is home to one of the top 200 national universities in the U.S.: **University of Oklahoma** (#127 tie). The indicators used to capture academic quality fall into a number of categories: assessment by administrators at peer institutions; retention of students; faculty resources; student selectivity; financial resources; alumni giving; high school counselor ratings of colleges; and graduation rate. *U.S. News & World Report, "America's Best Colleges 2023"*

According to *U.S. News & World Report,* the Oklahoma City, OK metro area is home to one of the top 100 law schools in the U.S.: **University of Oklahoma** (#88 tie). The rankings are based on a weighted average of 12 measures of quality: peer assessment score; assessment score by lawyers/judges; median LSAT scores; median undergrad GPA; acceptance rate; employment rates for graduates; placement success; bar passage rate; faculty resources; expenditures per student; student/faculty ratio; and library resources. *U.S. News & World Report, "America's Best Graduate Schools, Law, 2023"*

According to *U.S. News & World Report,* the Oklahoma City, OK metro area is home to one of the top 75 medical schools for research in the U.S.: **University of Oklahoma** (#74 tie). The rankings are based on a weighted average of 11 measures of quality: quality assessment; peer assessment score; assessment score by residency directors; research activity; total research activity; average research activity per faculty member; student selectivity; median MCAT total score; median undergraduate GPA; acceptance rate; and faculty resources. *U.S. News & World Report, "America's Best Graduate Schools, Medical, 2023"*

EMPLOYERS

Major Employers

Company Name	Industry
AT&T	Telecommunications
Chesapeake Energy Corp	Oil & gas
City of Oklahoma City	Municipal government
Devon Energy Corp	Oil & gas
FAA Mike Monroney Aeronautical Center	Aerospace
Hobby Lobby Stores	Wholesale & retail
INTEGRIS Health	Health care
Mercy Health Center	Health care
Norman Regional Hospital	Health care
OGE Energy Corp	Utility
Oklahoma City Community College	Education
OU Medical Center	Health care
Sonic Corp	Wholesale & retail
SSM Health Care of Oklahoma	Health care
State of Oklahoma	State government
The Boeing Company	Aerospace
Tinker Air Force Base	U.S. military
University of Central Oklahoma	Higher education
University of Oklahoma - Norman	Higher education
University of Oklahoma Health Sci Ctr	Higher education

Note: Companies shown are located within the Oklahoma City, OK Metropolitan Statistical Area.
Source: Hoovers.com; Wikipedia

Best Companies to Work For

American Fidelity, headquartered in Oklahoma City, is among the "100 Best Places to Work in IT." To qualify, companies had to have a minimum of 100 total employees and five IT employees. The best places to work were selected based on DEI (diversity, equity, and inclusion) practices; IT turnover, promotions, and growth; IT retention and engagement programs; remote/hybrid working; benefits and perks (such as elder care and child care, flextime, and reimbursement for college tuition); and training and career development opportunities. *Computerworld, "Best Places to Work in IT," 2023*

PUBLIC SAFETY

Crime Rate

Area	Total Crime	Violent Crime Rate				Property Crime Rate		
		Murder	Rape[3]	Robbery	Aggrav. Assault	Burglary	Larceny -Theft	Motor Vehicle Theft
City	4,621.5	9.5	84.2	123.1	509.1	881.3	2,444.3	569.9
Suburbs[1]	2,313.8	6.3	37.1	28.2	177.5	392.7	1,432.3	239.8
Metro[2]	3,387.0	7.8	59.0	72.3	331.7	619.4	1,902.9	393.3
U.S.	2,356.7	6.5	38.4	73.9	279.7	314.2	1,398.0	246.0

Note: Figures are crimes per 100,000 population; (1) All areas within the metro area that are located outside the city limits; (2) Figures cover the Oklahoma City, OK Metropolitan Statistical Area; (3) All figures shown were reported using the revised Uniform Crime Reporting (UCR) definition of rape; Due to the transition to the National Incident-Based Reporting System (NIBRS), limited city and metro area data was released for 2021.
Source: FBI Uniform Crime Reports, 2020

Hate Crimes

Area	Number of Quarters Reported	Number of Incidents per Bias Motivation					
		Race/Ethnicity/ Ancestry	Religion	Sexual Orientation	Disability	Gender	Gender Identity
City	4	3	1	0	1	0	0
U.S.	4	5,227	1,244	1,110	130	75	266

Note: Due to the transition to the National Incident-Based Reporting System (NIBRS), limited crime data was released for 2021.
Source: Federal Bureau of Investigation, Hate Crime Statistics 2020

Identity Theft Consumer Reports

Area	Reports	Reports per 100,000 Population	Rank[2]
MSA[1]	2,725	195	174
U.S.	1,108,609	339	-

Note: (1) Figures cover the Oklahoma City, OK Metropolitan Statistical Area; (2) Rank ranges from 1 to 391 where 1 indicates greatest number of identity theft reports per 100,000 population
Source: Federal Trade Commission, Consumer Sentinel Network Data Book 2022

Fraud and Other Consumer Reports

Area	Reports	Reports per 100,000 Population	Rank[2]
MSA[1]	11,891	851	178
U.S.	4,064,520	1,245	-

Note: (1) Figures cover the Oklahoma City, OK Metropolitan Statistical Area; (2) Rank ranges from 1 to 391 where 1 indicates greatest number of fraud and other consumer reports per 100,000 population
Source: Federal Trade Commission, Consumer Sentinel Network Data Book 2022

POLITICS

2020 Presidential Election Results

Area	Biden	Trump	Jorgensen	Hawkins	Other
Oklahoma County	48.1	49.2	1.8	0.0	0.9
U.S.	51.3	46.8	1.2	0.3	0.5

Note: Results are percentages and may not add to 100% due to rounding
Source: Dave Leip's Atlas of U.S. Presidential Elections

SPORTS

Professional Sports Teams

Team Name	League	Year Established
Oklahoma City Thunder	National Basketball Association (NBA)	2008

Note: Includes teams located in the Oklahoma City, OK Metropolitan Statistical Area.
Source: Wikipedia, Major Professional Sports Teams of the United States and Canada, April 12, 2023

CLIMATE

Average and Extreme Temperatures

Temperature	Jan	Feb	Mar	Apr	May	Jun	Jul	Aug	Sep	Oct	Nov	Dec	Yr.
Extreme High (°F)	80	84	93	100	104	105	109	110	104	96	87	86	110
Average High (°F)	47	52	61	72	79	87	93	92	84	74	60	50	71
Average Temp. (°F)	36	41	50	60	69	77	82	81	73	62	49	40	60
Average Low (°F)	26	30	38	49	58	66	71	70	62	51	38	29	49
Extreme Low (°F)	-4	-3	1	20	32	47	53	51	36	22	11	-8	-8

Note: Figures cover the years 1948-1990
Source: National Climatic Data Center, International Station Meteorological Climate Summary, 9/96

Average Precipitation/Snowfall/Humidity

Precip./Humidity	Jan	Feb	Mar	Apr	May	Jun	Jul	Aug	Sep	Oct	Nov	Dec	Yr.
Avg. Precip. (in.)	1.2	1.5	2.5	2.8	5.6	4.4	2.8	2.5	3.5	3.1	1.6	1.3	32.8
Avg. Snowfall (in.)	3	3	2	Tr	0	0	0	0	0	Tr	1	2	10
Avg. Rel. Hum. 6am (%)	78	78	76	77	84	84	81	81	82	79	78	77	80
Avg. Rel. Hum. 3pm (%)	53	52	47	46	52	51	46	44	47	46	48	52	49

Note: Figures cover the years 1948-1990; Tr = Trace amounts (<0.05 in. of rain; <0.5 in. of snow)
Source: National Climatic Data Center, International Station Meteorological Climate Summary, 9/96

Weather Conditions

Temperature			Daytime Sky			Precipitation		
10°F & below	32°F & below	90°F & above	Clear	Partly cloudy	Cloudy	0.01 inch or more precip.	0.1 inch or more snow/ice	Thunder-storms
5	79	70	124	131	110	80	8	50

Note: Figures are average number of days per year and cover the years 1948-1990
Source: National Climatic Data Center, International Station Meteorological Climate Summary, 9/96

HAZARDOUS WASTE

Superfund Sites

The Oklahoma City, OK metro area is home to two sites on the EPA's Superfund National Priorities List: **Eagle Industries** (final); **Hardage/Criner** (final). There are a total of 1,165 Superfund sites with a status of proposed or final on the list in the U.S. *U.S. Environmental Protection Agency, National Priorities List, April 12, 2023*

AIR QUALITY

Air Quality Trends: Ozone

	1990	1995	2000	2005	2010	2015	2018	2019	2020	2021
MSA[1]	0.080	0.087	0.083	0.077	0.071	0.067	0.072	0.065	0.066	0.068
U.S.	0.087	0.089	0.081	0.080	0.072	0.067	0.069	0.065	0.065	0.067

Note: (1) Data covers the Oklahoma City, OK Metropolitan Statistical Area. The values shown are the composite ozone concentration averages among trend sites based on the highest fourth daily maximum 8-hour concentration in parts per million. These trends are based on sites having an adequate record of monitoring data during the trend period. Data from exceptional events are included.
Source: U.S. Environmental Protection Agency, Air Quality Monitoring Information, "Air Quality Trends by City, 1990-2021"

Air Quality Index

Area	Percent of Days when Air Quality was...[2]					AQI Statistics[2]	
	Good	Moderate	Unhealthy for Sensitive Groups	Unhealthy	Very Unhealthy	Maximum	Median
MSA[1]	48.2	49.0	2.7	0.0	0.0	140	51

Note: (1) Data covers the Oklahoma City, OK Metropolitan Statistical Area; (2) Based on 365 days with AQI data in 2021. Air Quality Index (AQI) is an index for reporting daily air quality. EPA calculates the AQI for five major air pollutants regulated by the Clean Air Act: ground-level ozone, particle pollution (aka particulate matter), carbon monoxide, sulfur dioxide, and nitrogen dioxide. The AQI runs from 0 to 500. The higher the AQI value, the greater the level of air pollution and the greater the health concern. There are six AQI categories: "Good" AQI is between 0 and 50. Air quality is considered satisfactory; "Moderate" AQI is between 51 and 100. Air quality is acceptable; "Unhealthy for Sensitive Groups" When AQI values are between 101 and 150, members of sensitive groups may experience health effects; "Unhealthy" When AQI values are between 151 and 200 everyone may begin to experience health effects; "Very Unhealthy" AQI values between 201 and 300 trigger a health alert; "Hazardous" AQI values over 300 trigger warnings of emergency conditions (not shown).
Source: U.S. Environmental Protection Agency, Air Quality Index Report, 2021

Air Quality Index Pollutants

Area	Percent of Days when AQI Pollutant was...[2]					
	Carbon Monoxide	Nitrogen Dioxide	Ozone	Sulfur Dioxide	Particulate Matter 2.5	Particulate Matter 10
MSA[1]	0.0	3.0	41.6	(3)	54.8	0.5

Note: (1) Data covers the Oklahoma City, OK Metropolitan Statistical Area; (2) Based on 365 days with AQI data in 2021. The Air Quality Index (AQI) is an index for reporting daily air quality. EPA calculates the AQI for five major air pollutants regulated by the Clean Air Act: ground-level ozone, particle pollution (also known as particulate matter), carbon monoxide, sulfur dioxide, and nitrogen dioxide. The AQI runs from 0 to 500. The higher the AQI value, the greater the level of air pollution and the greater the health concern; (3) Sulfur dioxide is no longer included in this table (as of December 8, 2021) because SO_2 concentrations tend to be very localized and not necessarily representative of broad geographical areas like counties and CBSAs.
Source: U.S. Environmental Protection Agency, Air Quality Index Report, 2021

Maximum Air Pollutant Concentrations: Particulate Matter, Ozone, CO and Lead

	Particulate Matter 10 (ug/m³)	Particulate Matter 2.5 Wtd AM (ug/m³)	Particulate Matter 2.5 24-Hr (ug/m³)	Ozone (ppm)	Carbon Monoxide (ppm)	Lead (ug/m³)
MSA[1] Level	64	11.2	28	0.07	1	n/a
NAAQS[2]	150	15	35	0.075	9	0.15
Met NAAQS[2]	Yes	Yes	Yes	Yes	Yes	n/a

Note: (1) Data covers the Oklahoma City, OK Metropolitan Statistical Area; Data from exceptional events are included; (2) National Ambient Air Quality Standards; ppm = parts per million; ug/m³ = micrograms per cubic meter; n/a not available.
Concentrations: Particulate Matter 10 (coarse particulate)—highest second maximum 24-hour concentration; Particulate Matter 2.5 Wtd AM (fine particulate)—highest weighted annual mean concentration; Particulate Matter 2.5 24-Hour (fine particulate)—highest 98th percentile 24-hour concentration; Ozone—highest fourth daily maximum 8-hour concentration; Carbon Monoxide—highest second maximum non-overlapping 8-hour concentration; Lead—maximum running 3-month average
Source: U.S. Environmental Protection Agency, Air Quality Monitoring Information, "Air Quality Statistics by City, 2021"

Maximum Air Pollutant Concentrations: Nitrogen Dioxide and Sulfur Dioxide

	Nitrogen Dioxide AM (ppb)	Nitrogen Dioxide 1-Hr (ppb)	Sulfur Dioxide AM (ppb)	Sulfur Dioxide 1-Hr (ppb)	Sulfur Dioxide 24-Hr (ppb)
MSA[1] Level	13	47	n/a	1	n/a
NAAQS[2]	53	100	30	75	140
Met NAAQS[2]	Yes	Yes	n/a	Yes	n/a

Note: (1) Data covers the Oklahoma City, OK Metropolitan Statistical Area; Data from exceptional events are included; (2) National Ambient Air Quality Standards; ppm = parts per million; ug/m³ = micrograms per cubic meter; n/a not available.
Concentrations: Nitrogen Dioxide AM—highest arithmetic mean concentration; Nitrogen Dioxide 1-Hr—highest 98th percentile 1-hour daily maximum concentration; Sulfur Dioxide AM—highest annual mean concentration; Sulfur Dioxide 1-Hr—highest 99th percentile 1-hour daily maximum concentration; Sulfur Dioxide 24-Hr—highest second maximum 24-hour concentration
Source: U.S. Environmental Protection Agency, Air Quality Monitoring Information, "Air Quality Statistics by City, 2021"

Omaha, Nebraska

Background

Omaha's central location in the heartland of the United States has been important to its strong economy. Located on the western banks of the Missouri River, the city has been a significant agricultural and transportation center since its establishment in 1854. In its earliest history, Omaha was a trading center and "Gateway to the West." From these roots, Omaha has seen steady growth.

Of the nearly 20,000 businesses located in the metropolitan area, five are Fortune 500 companies, including Mutual of Omaha, Union Pacific Railroad, and Berkshire Hathaway, which is owned by the "Oracle of Omaha" Warren Buffet, recognized as one of the richest men in the world.

The headquarters of insurance companies, direct response/telemarketing centers and other national and international firms call Omaha home. The city is also a regional service and trade center with these segments comprising nearly 60 percent of metro area employment.

Omaha is large enough to offer a variety of cosmopolitan attractions, yet small enough to provide a relaxed lifestyle. Recreational activities abound, and residents enjoy a low cost of living, outstanding health care and a low crime rate.

The Omaha metropolitan area is served by several public and private school systems, and offers 11 colleges and universities, including Gallup University. Gallup's Riverfront Campus opened in 2013 and houses Gallup Poll Service, Gallup Performance Management Systems, and an international management education program.

The community also has access to excellent cultural programs, including the professional Omaha Symphony, Omaha Theater Ballet, and Opera Omaha. Performances by these groups and other touring companies are held in the magnificent Orpheum Theater, a restored 1920s vaudeville venue. The Bemis Center for Contemporary Arts, the largest urban artist colony in the world, plays host to artists from all over the world.

Omaha is home to world-famous Father Flanagan's Boys and Girls Town, and the award-winning Henry Doorly Zoo, which includes the world's largest indoor rainforest and a collection of rare white tigers. Other attractions include the Strategic Air & Space Museum and the birthplaces of Malcom X and former President Gerald R. Ford.

Omaha celebrated its 150th birthday in 2004 and continues to devote much effort to new projects. The acreage fronting the Missouri River, is home to a 2,700-foot bridge with a 506-foot span across the river connecting nearly 150 miles of trails in Nebraska and Iowa. The Midwestern headquarters for the National Park Service is in Omaha, the first building in Nebraska to be rated tops under the Leadership in Energy and Environmental Design system, or LEED. The nearby Riverfront Place is a six-acre urban neighborhood that includes residential units, commercial space, a public plaza, riverfront access, and connections to miles of walking trails.

Omaha's weather shows the usual contrasts of a continental climate, with cold, dry winters and warm summers. Situated between two climatic zones, the humid east and the dry west, fluctuation between these zones results in weather characteristic of either, or combinations of both. Most precipitation falls between April and September in the form of severe thunderstorms or evening lightning shows.

Rankings

General Rankings

- For its "Best for Vets: Places to Live 2019" rankings, *Military Times* evaluated 599 cities (83 large, 234 medium, 282 small) and compared the locations across three broad categories: veteran and military culture/services; economic indicators; and livability factors such as health, crime, traffic, and school quality. Omaha ranked #9 out of the top 25, in the large city category (population of more than 250,000). Data points more specific to veterans and the military weighed more heavily than others. *rebootcamp.militarytimes.com, "Military Times Best Places to Live 2019," September 10, 2018*

- The Omaha metro area was identified as one of America's fastest-growing areas in terms of population and business growth by *MagnifyMoney*. The area ranked #33 out of 35. The 100 most populous metro areas in the U.S. were evaluated on their change from 2011 to 2016 in the following categories: people and housing; workforce and employment opportunities; growing industry. *www.businessinsider.com, "The 35 Cities in the US with the Biggest Influx of People, the Most Work Opportunities, and the Hottest Business Growth," August 12, 2018*

- In their ninth annual survey, Livability.com looked at data for more than 2,300 mid-sized U.S. cities to determine the rankings for Livability's "Top 100 Best Places to Live" in 2022. Omaha ranked #20. Criteria: housing and economy; social and civic engagement; education; demographics; health care options; transportation & infrastructure; and community amenities. *Livability.com, "Top 100 Best Places to Live 2022" July 19, 2022*

Business/Finance Rankings

- Omaha was the #8-ranked city for savers, according to a study by the finance site GOBankingRates, which considered the prospects for people trying to save money. Criteria: average monthly cost of grocery items; median home listing price; median rent; median income; transportation costs; gas prices; and the cost of eating out for an inexpensive and mid-range meal in 100 U.S. cities. *www.gobankingrates.com, "The 20 Best (and Worst) Places to Live If You're Trying to Save Money," August 27, 2019*

- Omaha was ranked #8 among 100 U.S. cities for most difficult conditions for savers, according to a study by the finance site GOBankingRates. Criteria: average monthly cost of grocery items; median home listing price; median rent; median income; transportation costs; gas prices; and the cost of eating out for an inexpensive and mid-range meal. *www.gobankingrates.com, "The 20 Best (and Worst) Places to Live If You're Trying to Save Money," August 27, 2019*

- The Brookings Institution ranked the nation's largest cities based on income inequality. Omaha was ranked #67 (#1 = greatest inequality). Criteria: the "95/20 ratio," a figure representing the income at which a household earns more than 95 percent of all other households, divided by the income at which a household earns more than only 20 percent of all other households. *Brookings Institution, "Household Income Inequality, Largest Cities of 97 Large U.S. Metro Areas, 2014-2016," February 5, 2018*

- The Brookings Institution ranked the 100 largest metro areas in the U.S. based on income inequality. Omaha was ranked #90 (#1 = greatest inequality). Criteria: the "95/20 ratio," a figure representing the income at which a household earns more than 95 percent of all other households, divided by the income at which a household earns more than only 20 percent of all other households. *Brookings Institution, "Household Income Inequality, 100 Largest U.S. Metro Areas, 2014-2016," February 5, 2018*

- Omaha was cited as one of America's top metros for total major capital investment facility projects in 2022. The area ranked #3 in the mid-sized metro area category (population 200,000 to 1 million). *Site Selection, "Top Metros of 2022," March 2023*

- The Omaha metro area appeared on the Milken Institute "2022 Best Performing Cities" list. Rank: #60 out of 200 large metro areas (population over 250,000). Criteria: job growth; wage and salary growth; high-tech output growth; housing affordability; household broadband access. *Milken Institute, "Best-Performing Cities 2022," March 28, 2022*

- *Forbes* ranked the 200 most populous metro areas to determine the nation's "Best Places for Business and Careers." The Omaha metro area was ranked #38. Criteria: costs (business and living); job growth (past and projected); income growth; quality of life; educational attainment (college and high school); projected economic growth; cultural and leisure opportunities; workplace tolerance laws; net migration patterns. *Forbes, "The Best Places for Business and Careers 2019: Seattle Still On Top," October 30, 2019*

Dating/Romance Rankings

- Omaha was ranked #19 out of 25 cities that stood out for inspiring romance and attracting diners on the website OpenTable.com. Criteria: percentage of people who dined out on Valentine's Day in 2018; percentage of romantic restaurants as rated by OpenTable diner reviews; and percentage of tables seated for two. *OpenTable, "25 Most Romantic Cities in America for 2019," February 7, 2019*

Education Rankings

- Personal finance website *WalletHub* analyzed the 150 largest U.S. metropolitan statistical areas to determine where the most educated Americans are putting their degrees to work. Criteria: education levels; percentage of workers with degrees; education quality and attainment gap; public school quality rankings; quality and enrollment of each metro area's universities. Omaha was ranked #41 (#1 = most educated city). *www.WalletHub.com, "Most & Least Educated Cities in America, " July 18, 2022*

- Omaha was selected as one of America's most literate cities. The city ranked #39 out of the 84 largest U.S. cities. Criteria: number of booksellers; library resources; Internet resources; educational attainment; periodical publishing resources; newspaper circulation. *Central Connecticut State University, "America's Most Literate Cities, 2018," February 2019*

Health/Fitness Rankings

- For each of the 100 largest cities in the United States, the American Fitness Index®, compiled in partnership between the American College of Sports Medicine and the Elevance Health Foundation, evaluated community infrastructure and 34 health behaviors including preventive health, levels of chronic disease conditions, food insecurity, sleep quality, pedestrian safety, air quality, and community/environment resources that support physical activity. Omaha ranked #44 for "community fitness." *americanfitnessindex.org, "2022 ACSM American Fitness Index Summary Report," July 12, 2022*

- The Omaha metro area was identified as one of the worst cities for bed bugs in America by pest control company Orkin. The area ranked #32 out of 50 based on the number of bed bug treatments Orkin performed from December 2021 to November 2022. *Orkin, "The Windy City Can't Blow Bed Bugs Away: Chicago Ranks #1 For Third Consecutive Year On Orkin's Bed Bug Cities List," January 9, 2023*

- Omaha was identified as a "2022 Spring Allergy Capital." The area ranked #76 out of 100. Three groups of factors were used to identify the most challenging cities for people with allergies during the spring season: annual spring pollen scores; over the counter allergy medicine use; number of board-certified allergy specialists. *Asthma and Allergy Foundation of America, "Spring Allergy Capitals 2022," March 2, 2022*

- Omaha was identified as a "2022 Fall Allergy Capital." The area ranked #69 out of 100. Three groups of factors were used to identify the most challenging cities for people with allergies during the fall season: annual fall pollen scores; over the counter allergy medicine use; number of board-certified allergy specialists. *Asthma and Allergy Foundation of America, "Fall Allergy Capitals 2022," March 2, 2022*

- Omaha was identified as a "2022 Asthma Capital." The area ranked #32 out of the nation's 100 largest metropolitan areas. Criteria: estimated asthma prevalence; asthma-related mortality; and ER visits due to asthma. Risk factors analyzed but not factored in the rankings: annual pollen score; annual air quality; public smoking laws; access to board-certified asthma specialists; rescue and controller medication use; uninsured rate; poverty rate. *Asthma and Allergy Foundation of America, "Asthma Capitals 2022: The Most Challenging Places to Live With Asthma," September 14, 2022*

Real Estate Rankings

- *WalletHub* compared the most populated U.S. cities to determine which had the best markets for real estate agents. Omaha ranked #42 where demand was high and pay was the best. Criteria: sales per agent; annual median wage for real-estate agents; monthly average starting salary for real estate agents; real estate job density and competition; unemployment rate; home turnover rate; housing-market health index; and other relevant metrics. *www.WalletHub.com, "2021 Best Places to Be a Real Estate Agent," May 12, 2021*

Safety Rankings

- Allstate ranked the 200 largest cities in America in terms of driver safety. Omaha ranked #33. Criteria: internal property damage claims over a two-year period from January 2016 to December 2017. The report helps increase the importance of safety and awareness behind the wheel. *Allstate, "Allstate America's Best Drivers Report, 2019" June 24, 2019*

Seniors/Retirement Rankings

- From its Best Cities for Successful Aging indexes, the Milken Institute generated rankings for metropolitan areas, weighing data in nine categories—health care, wellness, living arrangements, transportation and convenience, financial characteristics, education, employment, community engagement, and overall livability. The Omaha metro area was ranked #7 overall in the large metro area category. *Milken Institute, "Best Cities for Successful Aging, 2017" March 14, 2017*

Sports/Recreation Rankings

- Omaha was chosen as one of America's best cities for bicycling. The city ranked #45 out of 50. Criteria: cycling infrastructure that is safe and friendly for all ages; energy and bike culture. The editors evaluated cities with populations of 100,000 or more. *Bicycling, "The 50 Best Bike Cities in America," October 10, 2018*

Women/Minorities Rankings

- Personal finance website *WalletHub* compared more than 180 U.S. cities across two key dimensions, "Hispanic Business-Friendliness" and "Hispanic Purchasing Power," to arrive at the most favorable conditions for Hispanic entrepreneurs. Omaha was ranked #108 out of 182. Criteria includes: share of Hispanic-Owned Businesses; Hispanic entrepreneurship rate to median annual income of Hispanics; Small Business-Friendliness score; cost of living; and number of Hispanics with at least a bachelor's degree. *WalletHub.com, "2019's Best Cities for Hispanic Entrepreneurs," May 1, 2019*

Miscellaneous Rankings

- *WalletHub* compared the 150 most populated U.S. cities to determine their operating efficiency. A "Quality of Services" score was constructed for each city and then divided by the total budget per capita to reveal which were managed the best. Omaha ranked #68. Criteria: financial stability; economy; education; safety; health; infrastructure and pollution. *www.WalletHub.com, "2022's Best-& Worst-Run Cities in America," June 21, 2022*

Business Environment

DEMOGRAPHICS

Population Growth

Area	1990 Census	2000 Census	2010 Census	2020 Census	Population Growth (%) 1990-2020	Population Growth (%) 2010-2020
City	371,972	390,007	408,958	486,051	30.7	18.9
MSA[1]	685,797	767,041	865,350	967,604	41.1	11.8
U.S.	248,709,873	281,421,906	308,745,538	331,449,281	33.3	7.4

Note: (1) Figures cover the Omaha-Council Bluffs, NE-IA Metropolitan Statistical Area
Source: U.S. Census Bureau, 1990 Census, 2000 Census, 2010 Census, 2020 Census

Race

Area	White Alone[2] (%)	Black Alone[2] (%)	Asian Alone[2] (%)	AIAN[3] Alone[2] (%)	NHOPI[4] Alone[2] (%)	Other Race Alone[2] (%)	Two or More Races (%)
City	65.5	12.4	4.6	1.1	0.1	7.2	9.1
MSA[1]	74.9	7.7	3.5	0.8	0.1	5.0	8.0
U.S.	61.6	12.4	6.0	1.1	0.2	8.4	10.2

Note: (1) Figures cover the Omaha-Council Bluffs, NE-IA Metropolitan Statistical Area; (2) Alone is defined as not being in combination with one or more other races; (3) American Indian and Alaska Native; (4) Native Hawaiian and Other Pacific Islander
Source: U.S. Census Bureau, 2020 Census

Hispanic or Latino Origin

Area	Total (%)	Mexican (%)	Puerto Rican (%)	Cuban (%)	Other (%)
City	14.5	10.9	0.5	0.2	2.9
MSA[1]	11.0	8.2	0.5	0.1	2.1
U.S.	18.4	11.2	1.8	0.7	4.7

Note: Persons of Hispanic or Latino origin can be of any race; (1) Figures cover the Omaha-Council Bluffs, NE-IA Metropolitan Statistical Area
Source: U.S. Census Bureau, 2017-2021 American Community Survey 5-Year Estimates

Age

Area	Percent of Population Under Age 5	Age 5–19	Age 20–34	Age 35–44	Age 45–54	Age 55–64	Age 65–74	Age 75–84	Age 85+	Median Age
City	6.6	20.7	23.1	13.0	11.0	11.7	8.4	3.8	1.6	34.7
MSA[1]	6.6	21.5	20.4	13.4	11.5	12.2	8.8	4.0	1.6	36.0
U.S.	5.6	19.2	20.2	12.7	12.4	13.1	10.0	4.9	1.9	38.8

Note: (1) Figures cover the Omaha-Council Bluffs, NE-IA Metropolitan Statistical Area
Source: U.S. Census Bureau, 2020 Census

Disability by Age

Area	All Ages	Under 18 Years Old	18 to 64 Years Old	65 Years and Over
City	10.9	3.6	9.6	30.9
MSA[1]	11.0	3.6	9.5	31.4
U.S.	12.6	4.4	10.3	33.4

Note: Figures show percent of the civilian noninstitutionalized population that reported having a disability. Disability status is determined from six types of difficulty: vision, hearing, cognitive, ambulatory, self-care, and independent living. For children under 5 years old, hearing and vision difficulty are used to determine disability status. For children between the ages of 5 and 14, disability status is determined from hearing, vision, cognitive, ambulatory, and self-care difficulties. For people aged 15 years and older, they are considered to have a disability if they have difficulty with any one of the six difficulty types; Note: (1) Figures cover the Omaha-Council Bluffs, NE-IA Metropolitan Statistical Area
Source: U.S. Census Bureau, 2017-2021 American Community Survey 5-Year Estimates

Ancestry

Area	German	Irish	English	American	Italian	Polish	French[2]	Scottish	Dutch
City	24.7	13.0	7.8	3.0	4.0	3.5	1.9	1.6	1.4
MSA[1]	28.3	13.1	9.1	3.5	3.9	3.7	1.9	1.5	1.6
U.S.	12.8	9.6	8.1	5.7	5.0	2.7	2.2	1.6	1.1

Note: Figures are the percentage of the total population reporting a particular ancestry. The nine most commonly reported ancestries in the U.S. are shown. Figures include multiple ancestries (e.g. if a person reported being Irish and Italian, they were included in both columns); (1) Figures cover the Omaha-Council Bluffs, NE-IA Metropolitan Statistical Area; (2) Excludes Basque
Source: U.S. Census Bureau, 2017-2021 American Community Survey 5-Year Estimates

Foreign-born Population

Area	Any Foreign Country	Asia	Mexico	Europe	Caribbean	Central America[2]	South America	Africa	Canada
City	10.8	3.3	3.4	0.7	0.1	1.2	0.4	1.5	0.2
MSA[1]	7.6	2.5	2.4	0.6	0.1	0.7	0.3	1.0	0.1
U.S.	13.6	4.2	3.3	1.5	1.1	1.4	1.1	0.8	0.2

Note: (1) Figures cover the Omaha-Council Bluffs, NE-IA Metropolitan Statistical Area; (2) Excludes Mexico.
Source: U.S. Census Bureau, 2017-2021 American Community Survey 5-Year Estimates

Household Size

Area	One	Two	Three	Four	Five	Six	Seven or More	Average Household Size
City	33.6	31.6	13.7	10.8	6.2	2.5	1.6	2.40
MSA[1]	28.9	33.6	14.6	12.3	6.6	2.5	1.5	2.50
U.S.	28.1	33.8	15.5	12.9	6.0	2.3	1.4	2.60

Note: (1) Figures cover the Omaha-Council Bluffs, NE-IA Metropolitan Statistical Area
Source: U.S. Census Bureau, 2017-2021 American Community Survey 5-Year Estimates

Household Relationships

Area	House-holder	Opposite-sex Spouse	Same-sex Spouse	Opposite-sex Unmarried Partner	Same-sex Unmarried Partner	Child[2]	Grand-child	Other Relatives	Non-relatives
City	39.8	16.0	0.2	2.8	0.2	29.6	1.8	3.7	3.6
MSA[1]	38.8	18.4	0.2	2.6	0.1	30.6	1.6	3.1	2.8
U.S.	38.3	17.5	0.2	2.5	0.2	28.3	2.4	4.8	3.4

Note: Figures are percent of the total population; (1) Figures cover the Omaha-Council Bluffs, NE-IA Metropolitan Statistical Area; (2) Includes biological, adopted, and stepchildren of the householder
Source: U.S. Census Bureau, 2020 Census

Gender

Area	Males	Females	Males per 100 Females
City	239,675	246,376	97.3
MSA[1]	478,627	488,977	97.9
U.S.	162,685,811	168,763,470	96.4

Note: (1) Figures cover the Omaha-Council Bluffs, NE-IA Metropolitan Statistical Area
Source: U.S. Census Bureau, 2020 Census

Marital Status

Area	Never Married	Now Married[2]	Separated	Widowed	Divorced
City	37.2	45.6	1.4	4.8	11.1
MSA[1]	32.2	51.3	1.2	4.7	10.7
U.S.	33.8	48.0	1.8	5.6	10.8

Note: Figures are percentages and cover the population 15 years of age and older; (1) Figures cover the Omaha-Council Bluffs, NE-IA Metropolitan Statistical Area; (2) Excludes separated
Source: U.S. Census Bureau, 2017-2021 American Community Survey 5-Year Estimates

Religious Groups by Family

Area	Catholic	Baptist	Methodist	LDS[2]	Pentecostal	Lutheran	Islam	Adventist	Other
MSA[1]	19.9	2.8	2.8	1.6	1.0	6.1	0.2	1.0	9.0
U.S.	18.7	7.3	3.0	2.0	1.8	1.7	1.3	1.3	11.6

Note: Figures are the number of adherents as a percentage of the total population and cover the eight largest religious groups in the U.S; (1) Figures cover the Omaha-Council Bluffs, NE-IA Metropolitan Statistical Area; (2) Church of Jesus Christ of Latter-day Saints
Sources: 2020 U.S. Religion Census, Association of Statisticians of American Religious Bodies; The Association of Religion Data Archives (ARDA)

Religious Groups by Tradition

Area	Catholic	Evangelical Protestant	Mainline Protestant	Black Protestant	Islam	Judaism	Hinduism	Orthodox	Buddhism
MSA[1]	19.9	10.8	7.9	1.5	0.2	0.3	1.0	0.2	0.2
U.S.	18.7	16.5	5.2	2.3	1.3	0.6	0.4	0.4	0.3

Note: Figures are the number of adherents as a percentage of the total population; (1) Figures cover the Omaha-Council Bluffs, NE-IA Metropolitan Statistical Area
Sources: 2020 U.S. Religion Census, Association of Statisticians of American Religious Bodies; The Association of Religion Data Archives (ARDA)

ECONOMY

Gross Metropolitan Product

Area	2020	2021	2022	2023	Rank[2]
MSA[1]	69.1	77.9	83.2	88.2	50

Note: Figures are in billions of dollars; (1) Figures cover the Omaha-Council Bluffs, NE-IA Metropolitan Statistical Area; (2) Rank is based on 2021 data and ranges from 1 to 381
Source: U.S. Conference of Mayors, U.S. Metro Economies: U.S. Metros Compared to Global and State Economies, June 2022

Economic Growth

Area	2018-20 (%)	2021 (%)	2022 (%)	2023 (%)	Rank[2]
MSA[1]	0.2	5.3	0.8	3.0	127
U.S.	-0.6	5.7	3.1	2.9	–

Note: Figures are real gross metropolitan product (GMP) growth rates and represent average annual percent change; (1) Figures cover the Omaha-Council Bluffs, NE-IA Metropolitan Statistical Area; (2) Rank is based on 2020 2-year average annual percent change and ranges from 1 to 381
Source: U.S. Conference of Mayors, U.S. Metro Economies: U.S. Metros Compared to Global and State Economies, June 2022

Metropolitan Area Exports

Area	2016	2017	2018	2019	2020	2021	Rank[2]
MSA[1]	3,509.7	3,756.2	4,371.6	3,725.7	3,852.5	4,595.1	64

Note: Figures are in millions of dollars; (1) Figures cover the Omaha-Council Bluffs, NE-IA Metropolitan Statistical Area; (2) Rank is based on 2021 data and ranges from 1 to 388
Source: U.S. Department of Commerce, International Trade Administration, Office of Trade and Economic Analysis, Industry and Analysis, Exports by Metropolitan Area, data extracted March 16, 2023

Building Permits

Area	Single-Family			Multi-Family			Total		
	2021	2022	Pct. Chg.	2021	2022	Pct. Chg.	2021	2022	Pct. Chg.
City	1,620	1,217	-24.9	1,547	2,552	65.0	3,167	3,769	19.0
MSA[1]	3,677	2,651	-27.9	2,705	3,469	28.2	6,382	6,120	-4.1
U.S.	1,115,400	975,600	-12.5	621,600	689,500	10.9	1,737,000	1,665,100	-4.1

Note: (1) Figures cover the Omaha-Council Bluffs, NE-IA Metropolitan Statistical Area; Figures represent new, privately-owned housing units authorized (unadjusted data); All permit data are based on estimates with imputation
Source: U.S. Census Bureau, Manufacturing, Mining, and Construction Statistics, Building Permits, 2021, 2022

Bankruptcy Filings

Area	Business Filings			Nonbusiness Filings		
	2021	2022	% Chg.	2021	2022	% Chg.
Douglas County	20	21	5.0	807	628	-22.2
U.S.	14,347	13,481	-6.0	399,269	374,240	-6.3

Note: Business filings include Chapter 7, Chapter 9, Chapter 11, Chapter 12, Chapter 13, Chapter 15, and Section 304; Nonbusiness filings include Chapter 7, Chapter 11, and Chapter 13
Source: Administrative Office of the U.S. Courts, Business and Nonbusiness Bankruptcy, County Cases Commenced by Chapter of the Bankruptcy Code, During the 12-Month Period Ending December 31, 2021 and Business and Nonbusiness Bankruptcy, County Cases Commenced by Chapter of the Bankruptcy Code, During the 12-Month Period Ending December 31, 2022

Housing Vacancy Rates

Area	Gross Vacancy Rate[2] (%)			Year-Round Vacancy Rate[3] (%)			Rental Vacancy Rate[4] (%)			Homeowner Vacancy Rate[5] (%)		
	2020	2021	2022	2020	2021	2022	2020	2021	2022	2020	2021	2022
MSA[1]	5.6	6.0	5.4	5.3	5.7	5.0	6.5	5.1	4.2	0.5	0.7	0.8
U.S.	10.6	10.8	10.5	8.2	8.4	8.2	6.3	6.1	5.8	1.0	0.9	0.8

Note: (1) Figures cover the Omaha-Council Bluffs, NE-IA Metropolitan Statistical Area; (2) The percentage of the total housing inventory that is vacant; (3) The percentage of the housing inventory (excluding seasonal units) that is year-round vacant; (4) The percentage of rental inventory that is vacant for rent; (5) The percentage of homeowner inventory that is vacant for sale
Source: U.S. Census Bureau, Housing Vacancies and Homeownership Annual Statistics: 2020, 2021, 2022

INCOME

Income

Area	Per Capita ($)	Median Household ($)	Average Household ($)
City	36,749	65,359	90,389
MSA[1]	38,289	73,757	97,122
U.S.	37,638	69,021	97,196

Note: (1) Figures cover the Omaha-Council Bluffs, NE-IA Metropolitan Statistical Area
Source: U.S. Census Bureau, 2017-2021 American Community Survey 5-Year Estimates

Household Income Distribution

Area	Percent of Households Earning							
	Under $15,000	$15,000 -$24,999	$25,000 -$34,999	$35,000 -$49,999	$50,000 -$74,999	$75,000 -$99,999	$100,000 -$149,999	$150,000 and up
City	9.5	7.3	8.4	12.5	18.9	13.7	15.5	14.1
MSA[1]	7.6	6.5	7.7	11.3	17.7	14.2	18.5	16.4
U.S.	9.4	7.8	8.2	11.4	16.8	12.8	16.3	17.3

Note: (1) Figures cover the Omaha-Council Bluffs, NE-IA Metropolitan Statistical Area
Source: U.S. Census Bureau, 2017-2021 American Community Survey 5-Year Estimates

Poverty Rate

Area	All Ages	Under 18 Years Old	18 to 64 Years Old	65 Years and Over
City	12.1	15.7	11.4	8.4
MSA[1]	9.3	11.2	9.0	7.1
U.S.	12.6	17.0	11.8	9.6

Note: Figures are percentage of people whose income during the past 12 months was below the poverty level;
(1) Figures cover the Omaha-Council Bluffs, NE-IA Metropolitan Statistical Area
Source: U.S. Census Bureau, 2017-2021 American Community Survey 5-Year Estimates

EMPLOYMENT

Labor Force and Employment

Area	Civilian Labor Force			Workers Employed		
	Dec. 2021	Dec. 2022	% Chg.	Dec. 2021	Dec. 2022	% Chg.
City	250,414	253,695	1.3	244,895	246,725	0.7
MSA[1]	502,000	508,654	1.3	490,956	495,693	1.0
U.S.	161,696,000	164,224,000	1.6	155,732,000	158,872,000	2.0

Note: Data is not seasonally adjusted and covers workers 16 years of age and older; (1) Figures cover the
Omaha-Council Bluffs, NE-IA Metropolitan Statistical Area
Source: Bureau of Labor Statistics, Local Area Unemployment Statistics

Unemployment Rate

Area	2022											
	Jan.	Feb.	Mar.	Apr.	May	Jun.	Jul.	Aug.	Sep.	Oct.	Nov.	Dec.
City	2.9	2.8	2.7	2.3	2.3	2.9	3.1	2.7	2.4	2.6	2.5	2.7
MSA[1]	2.9	2.7	2.6	2.1	2.1	2.7	2.7	2.5	2.2	2.4	2.4	2.5
U.S.	4.4	4.1	3.8	3.3	3.4	3.8	3.8	3.8	3.3	3.4	3.4	3.3

Note: Data is not seasonally adjusted and covers workers 16 years of age and older; (1) Figures cover the
Omaha-Council Bluffs, NE-IA Metropolitan Statistical Area
Source: Bureau of Labor Statistics, Local Area Unemployment Statistics

Average Wages

Occupation	$/Hr.	Occupation	$/Hr.
Accountants and Auditors	36.79	Maintenance and Repair Workers	22.11
Automotive Mechanics	24.01	Marketing Managers	58.09
Bookkeepers	22.22	Network and Computer Systems Admin.	44.11
Carpenters	22.88	Nurses, Licensed Practical	25.44
Cashiers	13.40	Nurses, Registered	36.18
Computer Programmers	45.89	Nursing Assistants	17.53
Computer Systems Analysts	44.58	Office Clerks, General	18.19
Computer User Support Specialists	26.48	Physical Therapists	43.62
Construction Laborers	20.49	Physicians	142.86
Cooks, Restaurant	15.05	Plumbers, Pipefitters and Steamfitters	32.29
Customer Service Representatives	18.92	Police and Sheriff's Patrol Officers	34.43
Dentists	78.54	Postal Service Mail Carriers	27.42
Electricians	27.41	Real Estate Sales Agents	29.75
Engineers, Electrical	47.76	Retail Salespersons	16.07
Fast Food and Counter Workers	12.76	Sales Representatives, Technical/Scientific	41.32
Financial Managers	65.55	Secretaries, Exc. Legal/Medical/Executive	19.89
First-Line Supervisors of Office Workers	28.58	Security Guards	17.42
General and Operations Managers	47.42	Surgeons	158.30
Hairdressers/Cosmetologists	21.04	Teacher Assistants, Exc. Postsecondary*	13.94
Home Health and Personal Care Aides	14.54	Teachers, Secondary School, Exc. Sp. Ed.*	28.50
Janitors and Cleaners	15.19	Telemarketers	13.51
Landscaping/Groundskeeping Workers	17.69	Truck Drivers, Heavy/Tractor-Trailer	32.23
Lawyers	59.74	Truck Drivers, Light/Delivery Services	21.83
Maids and Housekeeping Cleaners	14.69	Waiters and Waitresses	15.36

Note: Wage data covers the Omaha-Council Bluffs, NE-IA Metropolitan Statistical Area; (*) Hourly wages
were calculated from annual wage data based on a 40 hour work week; n/a not available.
Source: Bureau of Labor Statistics, Metro Area Occupational Employment & Wage Estimates, May 2022

Employment by Industry

Sector	MSA[1]		U.S.
	Number of Employees	Percent of Total	Percent of Total
Construction, Mining, and Logging	31,800	6.3	5.4
Private Education and Health Services	82,100	16.3	16.1
Financial Activities	42,000	8.3	5.9
Government	67,000	13.3	14.5
Information	10,200	2.0	2.0
Leisure and Hospitality	49,000	9.7	10.3
Manufacturing	35,000	6.9	8.4
Other Services	19,300	3.8	3.7
Professional and Business Services	71,900	14.2	14.7
Retail Trade	53,100	10.5	10.2
Transportation, Warehousing, and Utilities	26,700	5.3	4.9
Wholesale Trade	16,700	3.3	3.9

Note: Figures are non-farm employment as of December 2022. Figures are not seasonally adjusted and include workers 16 years of age and older; (1) Figures cover the Omaha-Council Bluffs, NE-IA Metropolitan Statistical Area
Source: Bureau of Labor Statistics, Current Employment Statistics, Employment, Hours, and Earnings

Employment by Occupation

Occupation Classification	City (%)	MSA[1] (%)	U.S. (%)
Management, Business, Science, and Arts	42.2	42.6	40.3
Natural Resources, Construction, and Maintenance	7.9	8.6	8.7
Production, Transportation, and Material Moving	12.3	12.0	13.1
Sales and Office	21.7	21.5	20.9
Service	16.0	15.4	17.0

Note: Figures cover employed civilians 16 years of age and older; (1) Figures cover the Omaha-Council Bluffs, NE-IA Metropolitan Statistical Area
Source: U.S. Census Bureau, 2017-2021 American Community Survey 5-Year Estimates

Occupations with Greatest Projected Employment Growth: 2022 – 2024

Occupation[1]	2022 Employment	2024 Projected Employment	Numeric Employment Change	Percent Employment Change
Fast Food and Counter Workers	30,020	30,710	690	2.3
Registered Nurses	28,100	28,770	670	2.4
Retail Salespersons	27,690	28,240	550	2.0
Cooks, Restaurant	6,920	7,460	540	7.8
Software Developers and Software Quality Assurance Analysts and Testers	11,020	11,510	490	4.4
Carpenters	10,710	11,200	490	4.6
Laborers and Freight, Stock, and Material Movers, Hand	20,000	20,490	490	2.5
Home Health and Personal Care Aides	12,470	12,930	460	3.7
Waiters and Waitresses	13,830	14,260	430	3.1
Electricians	6,420	6,850	430	6.7

Note: Projections cover Nebraska; (1) Sorted by numeric employment change
Source: www.projectionscentral.com, State Occupational Projections, 2022–2024 Short-Term Projections

Fastest-Growing Occupations: 2022 – 2024

Occupation[1]	2022 Employment	2024 Projected Employment	Numeric Employment Change	Percent Employment Change
First-Line Supervisors of Gambling Services Workers	60	240	180	300.0
Gaming Dealers	120	480	360	300.0
Gaming Managers	30	90	60	200.0
Gaming Cage Workers	30	90	60	200.0
Gaming Surveillance Officers and Gaming Investigators	30	80	50	166.7
Gaming Change Persons and Booth Cashiers	60	110	50	83.3
Gaming and Sports Book Writers and Runners	420	470	50	11.9
Fitness Trainers and Aerobics Instructors	3,400	3,750	350	10.3
Nurse Practitioners	1,770	1,910	140	7.9
Cooks, Restaurant	6,920	7,460	540	7.8

Note: Projections cover Nebraska; (1) Sorted by percent employment change and excludes occupations with numeric employment change less than 50
Source: www.projectionscentral.com, State Occupational Projections, 2022–2024 Short-Term Projections

CITY FINANCES

City Government Finances

Component	2020 ($000)	2020 ($ per capita)
Total Revenues	811,217	1,696
Total Expenditures	738,637	1,545
Debt Outstanding	1,417,289	2,964
Cash and Securities[1]	445,394	931

Note: (1) Cash and security holdings of a government at the close of its fiscal year, including those of its dependent agencies, utilities, and liquor stores.
Source: U.S. Census Bureau, State & Local Government Finances 2020

City Government Revenue by Source

Source	2020 ($000)	2020 ($ per capita)	2020 (%)
General Revenue			
From Federal Government	24,284	51	3.0
From State Government	58,471	122	7.2
From Local Governments	6,982	15	0.9
Taxes			
Property	178,931	374	22.1
Sales and Gross Receipts	170,073	356	21.0
Personal Income	0	0	0.0
Corporate Income	0	0	0.0
Motor Vehicle License	37,978	79	4.7
Other Taxes	87,396	183	10.8
Current Charges	244,369	511	30.1
Liquor Store	0	0	0.0
Utility	0	0	0.0

Source: U.S. Census Bureau, State & Local Government Finances 2020

City Government Expenditures by Function

Function	2020 ($000)	2020 ($ per capita)	2020 (%)
General Direct Expenditures			
Air Transportation	0	0	0.0
Corrections	0	0	0.0
Education	0	0	0.0
Employment Security Administration	0	0	0.0
Financial Administration	0	0	0.0
Fire Protection	111,079	232	15.0
General Public Buildings	13,189	27	1.8
Governmental Administration, Other	7,920	16	1.1
Health	0	0	0.0
Highways	129,829	271	17.6
Hospitals	0	0	0.0
Housing and Community Development	0	0	0.0
Interest on General Debt	51,115	106	6.9
Judicial and Legal	4,939	10	0.7
Libraries	16,265	34	2.2
Parking	7,008	14	0.9
Parks and Recreation	30,538	63	4.1
Police Protection	154,407	322	20.9
Public Welfare	0	0	0.0
Sewerage	125,105	261	16.9
Solid Waste Management	20,207	42	2.7
Veterans' Services	0	0	0.0
Liquor Store	0	0	0.0
Utility	0	0	0.0

Source: U.S. Census Bureau, State & Local Government Finances 2020

TAXES

State Corporate Income Tax Rates

State	Tax Rate (%)	Income Brackets ($)	Num. of Brackets	Financial Institution Tax Rate (%)[a]	Federal Income Tax Ded.
Nebraska	5.58 - 7.5	100,000	2	(a)	No

Note: Tax rates as of January 1, 2023; (a) Rates listed are the corporate income tax rate applied to financial institutions or excise taxes based on income. Some states have other taxes based upon the value of deposits or shares.
Source: Federation of Tax Administrators, State Corporate Income Tax Rates, January 1, 2023

State Individual Income Tax Rates

State	Tax Rate (%)	Income Brackets ($)	Personal Exemptions ($)			Standard Ded. ($)	
			Single	Married	Depend.	Single	Married
Nebraska (a)	2.46 - 6.64 (bb)	3,700 - 35,730 (b)	157	314	157 (c)	7,900	15,800

Note: Tax rates as of January 1, 2023; Local- and county-level taxes are not included; Federal income tax is not deductible on state income tax returns; (a) 16 states have statutory provision for automatically adjusting to the rate of inflation the dollar values of the income tax brackets, standard deductions, and/or personal exemptions. Oregon does not index the income brackets for $125,000 and over; (b) For joint returns, taxes are twice the tax on half the couple's income; (c) The personal exemption takes the form of a tax credit instead of a deduction; (bb) Louisiana tax rates may be adjusted down if revenue trigger is met on April 1st. Iowa is phasing-in a flat rate by 2027, while Nebraska and South Carolina is phasing-in a reduced top rate by 2027.
Source: Federation of Tax Administrators, State Individual Income Tax Rates, January 1, 2023

Various State Sales and Excise Tax Rates

State	State Sales Tax (%)	Gasoline[1] ($/gal.)	Cigarette[2] ($/pack)	Spirits[3] ($/gal.)	Wine[4] ($/gal.)	Beer[5] ($/gal.)	Recreational Marijuana (%)
Nebraska	5.5	0.257	0.64	3.75	0.95	0.31	Not legal

Note: All tax rates as of January 1, 2023; (1) The American Petroleum Institute has developed a methodology for determining the average tax rate on a gallon of fuel. Rates may include any of the following: excise taxes, environmental fees, storage tank fees, other fees or taxes, general sales tax, and local taxes; (2) The federal excise tax of $1.0066 per pack and local taxes are not included; (3) Rates are those applicable to off-premise sales of 40% alcohol by volume (a.b.v.) distilled spirits in 750ml containers. Local excise taxes are excluded; (4) Rates are those applicable to off-premise sales of 11% a.b.v. non-carbonated wine in 750ml containers; (5) Rates are those applicable to off-premise sales of 4.7% a.b.v. beer in 12 ounce containers.
Source: Tax Foundation, 2023 Facts & Figures: How Does Your State Compare?

State Business Tax Climate Index Rankings

State	Overall Rank	Corporate Tax Rank	Individual Income Tax Rank	Sales Tax Rank	Property Tax Rank	Unemployment Insurance Tax Rank
Nebraska	29	30	32	9	39	11

Note: The index is a measure of how each state's tax laws affect economic performance. The lower the rank, the more favorable a state's tax system is for business. States without a given tax are given a ranking of 1. The scores/rankings for the District of Columbia do not affect other states. The 2023 index represents the tax climate as of July 1, 2022.
Source: Tax Foundation, State Business Tax Climate Index 2023

TRANSPORTATION

Means of Transportation to Work

Area	Car/Truck/Van		Public Transportation			Bicycle	Walked	Other Means	Worked at Home
	Drove Alone	Car-pooled	Bus	Subway	Railroad				
City	77.2	8.9	1.3	0.0	0.0	0.2	2.1	1.0	9.3
MSA[1]	79.5	8.0	0.7	0.0	0.0	0.1	1.7	1.0	9.0
U.S.	73.2	8.6	2.0	1.6	0.5	0.5	2.5	1.5	9.7

Note: Figures are percentages and cover workers 16 years of age and older; (1) Figures cover the Omaha-Council Bluffs, NE-IA Metropolitan Statistical Area
Source: U.S. Census Bureau, 2017-2021 American Community Survey 5-Year Estimates

Travel Time to Work

Area	Less Than 10 Minutes	10 to 19 Minutes	20 to 29 Minutes	30 to 44 Minutes	45 to 59 Minutes	60 to 89 Minutes	90 Minutes or More
City	14.5	41.2	26.7	12.4	2.5	1.9	0.9
MSA[1]	14.1	36.1	27.3	16.0	3.6	1.9	1.1
U.S.	12.4	28.5	21.0	20.9	8.2	6.2	2.9

Note: Note: Figures are percentages and include workers 16 years old and over; (1) Figures cover the Omaha-Council Bluffs, NE-IA Metropolitan Statistical Area
Source: U.S. Census Bureau, 2017-2021 American Community Survey 5-Year Estimates

Key Congestion Measures

Measure	1990	2000	2010	2015	2020
Annual Hours of Delay, Total (000)	4,364	9,694	14,864	17,796	9,777
Annual Hours of Delay, Per Auto Commuter	15	26	32	36	19
Annual Congestion Cost, Per Auto Commuter ($)	297	494	599	663	377

Note: Covers the Omaha NE-IA urban area
Source: Texas A&M Transportation Institute, 2021 Urban Mobility Report

Freeway Travel Time Index

Measure	1985	1990	1995	2000	2005	2010	2015	2020
Urban Area Index[1]	1.05	1.08	1.10	1.13	1.15	1.16	1.16	1.05
Urban Area Rank[1,2]	64	62	72	72	68	54	57	85

Note: Freeway Travel Time Index—the ratio of travel time in the peak period to the travel time at free-flow conditions. For example, a value of 1.30 indicates a 20-minute free-flow trip takes 26 minutes in the peak (20 minutes x 1.30 = 26 minutes); (1) Covers the Omaha NE-IA urban area; (2) Rank is based on 101 larger urban areas (#1 = highest travel time index)
Source: Texas A&M Transportation Institute, 2021 Urban Mobility Report

Public Transportation

Agency Name / Mode of Transportation	Vehicles Operated in Maximum Service[1]	Annual Unlinked Passenger Trips[2] (in thous.)	Annual Passenger Miles[3] (in thous.)
Transit Authority of Omaha (MAT)			
Bus (directly operated)	81	2,084.2	6,970.4
Demand Response (directly operated)	25	70.8	374.9

Note: (1) Number of revenue vehicles operated by the given mode and type of service to meet the annual maximum service requirement. This is the revenue vehicle count during the peak season of the year; on the week and day that maximum service is provided. Vehicles operated in maximum service (VOMS) exclude atypical days and one-time special events; (2) Number of passengers who boarded public transportation vehicles. Passengers are counted each time they board a vehicle no matter how many vehicles they use to travel from their origin to their destination. (3) Sum of the distances ridden by all passengers during the entire fiscal year.
Source: Federal Transit Administration, National Transit Database, 2021

Air Transportation

Airport Name and Code / Type of Service	Passenger Airlines[1]	Passenger Enplanements	Freight Carriers[2]	Freight (lbs)
Eppley Airfield (OMA)				
Domestic service (U.S. carriers - 2022)	27	2,203,424	15	64,156,017
International service (U.S. carriers - 2021)	0	0	0	0

Note: (1) Includes all U.S.-based major, minor and commuter airlines that carried at least one passenger during the year; (2) Includes all U.S.-based airlines and freight carriers that transported at least one pound of freight during the year.
Source: Bureau of Transportation Statistics, The Intermodal Transportation Database, Air Carriers: T-100 Domestic Market (U.S. Carriers), 2022; Bureau of Transportation Statistics, The Intermodal Transportation Database, Air Carriers: T-100 International Market (U.S. Carriers), 2021

BUSINESSES

Major Business Headquarters

Company Name	Industry	Rankings Fortune[1]	Rankings Forbes[2]
Berkshire Hathaway	Insurance, property and casualty (stock)	7	-
Kiewit	Construction	-	33
Mutual of Omaha Insurance	Insurance, life and health (stock)	324	-
Peter Kiewit Sons'	Engineering, construction	313	-
Scoular	Food, drink & tobacco	-	48
Tenaska	Multicompany	-	18
Union Pacific	Railroads	163	-

Note: (1) Companies that produce a 10-K are ranked 1 to 500 based on 2021 revenue; (2) All private companies with at least $2 billion in annual revenue through the end of their most current fiscal year are ranked 1 to 246; companies listed are headquartered in the city; dashes indicate no ranking
Source: Fortune, "Fortune 500," 2022; Forbes, "America's Largest Private Companies," 2022

Fastest-Growing Businesses

According to *Inc.*, Omaha is home to one of America's 500 fastest-growing private companies: **Viking Industrial Painting** (#389). Criteria: must be an independent, privately-held, for-profit, U.S. corporation, proprietorship or partnership as of December 31, 2021; revenues must be at least $100,000 in 2018 and $2 million in 2021; must have four-year operating/sales history. *Inc., "America's 500 Fastest-Growing Private Companies," 2022*

Living Environment

COST OF LIVING

Cost of Living Index

Composite Index	Groceries	Housing	Utilities	Trans- portation	Health Care	Misc. Goods/ Services
92.5	96.5	84.0	94.0	102.9	96.8	94.0

Note: The Cost of Living Index measures regional differences in the cost of consumer goods and services, excluding taxes and non-consumer expenditures, for professional and managerial households in the top income quintile. It is based on more than 50,000 prices covering almost 60 different items for which prices are collected three times a year by chambers of commerce, economic development organizations or university applied economic centers in each participating urban area. The numbers shown should be read as a percentage above or below the national average of 100. For example, a value of 115.4 in the groceries column indicates that grocery prices are 15.4% higher than the national average. Small differences in the index numbers should not be interpreted as significant; Figures cover the Omaha NE urban area.
Source: The Council for Community and Economic Research, Cost of Living Index, 2022

Grocery Prices

Area[1]	T-Bone Steak ($/pound)	Frying Chicken ($/pound)	Whole Milk ($/half gal.)	Eggs ($/dozen)	Orange Juice ($/64 oz.)	Coffee ($/11.5 oz.)
City[2]	15.11	1.71	2.00	1.72	3.59	5.20
Avg.	13.81	1.59	2.43	2.25	3.85	4.95
Min.	10.17	0.90	1.51	1.30	2.90	3.46
Max.	19.35	3.30	4.32	4.32	5.31	8.59

*Note: (1) Values for the local area are compared with the average, minimum and maximum values for all 286 areas in the Cost of Living Index; (2) Figures cover the Omaha NE urban area; **T-Bone Steak** (price per pound); **Frying Chicken** (price per pound, whole fryer); **Whole Milk** (half gallon carton); **Eggs** (price per dozen, Grade A, large); **Orange Juice** (64 oz. Tropicana or Florida Natural); **Coffee** (11.5 oz. can, vacuum-packed, Maxwell House, Hills Bros, or Folgers).*
Source: The Council for Community and Economic Research, Cost of Living Index, 2022

Housing and Utility Costs

Area[1]	New Home Price ($)	Apartment Rent ($/month)	All Electric ($/month)	Part Electric ($/month)	Other Energy ($/month)	Telephone ($/month)
City[2]	350,853	1,290	-	92.74	60.25	198.80
Avg.	450,913	1,371	176.41	99.93	76.96	190.22
Min.	229,283	546	100.84	31.56	27.15	174.27
Max.	2,434,977	4,569	356.86	249.59	272.24	208.31

*Note: (1) Values for the local area are compared with the average, minimum and maximum values for all 286 areas in the Cost of Living Index; (2) Figures cover the Omaha NE urban area; **New Home Price** (2,400 sf living area, 8,000 sf lot, in urban area with full utilities); **Apartment Rent** (950 sf 2 bedroom/1.5 or 2 bath, unfurnished, excluding all utilities except water); **All Electric** (average monthly cost for an all-electric home); **Part Electric** (average monthly cost for a part-electric home); **Other Energy** (average monthly cost for natural gas, fuel oil, coal, wood, and any other forms of energy except electricity); **Telephone** (price includes the base monthly rate plus taxes and fees for three lines of mobile phone service).*
Source: The Council for Community and Economic Research, Cost of Living Index, 2022

Health Care, Transportation, and Other Costs

Area[1]	Doctor ($/visit)	Dentist ($/visit)	Optometrist ($/visit)	Gasoline ($/gallon)	Beauty Salon ($/visit)	Men's Shirt ($)
City[2]	140.67	89.91	120.78	3.75	30.74	28.27
Avg.	124.91	107.77	117.66	3.86	43.31	34.21
Min.	36.61	58.25	51.79	2.90	22.18	13.05
Max.	250.21	162.58	371.96	5.54	85.61	63.54

*Note: (1) Values for the local area are compared with the average, minimum and maximum values for all 286 areas in the Cost of Living Index; (2) Figures cover the Omaha NE urban area; **Doctor** (general practitioners routine exam of an established patient); **Dentist** (adult teeth cleaning and periodic oral examination); **Optometrist** (full vision eye exam for established adult patient); **Gasoline** (one gallon regular unleaded, national brand, including all taxes, cash price at self-service pump if available); **Beauty Salon** (woman's shampoo, trim, and blow-dry); **Men's Shirt** (cotton/polyester dress shirt, pinpoint weave, long sleeves).*
Source: The Council for Community and Economic Research, Cost of Living Index, 2022

HOUSING

Homeownership Rate

Area	2015 (%)	2016 (%)	2017 (%)	2018 (%)	2019 (%)	2020 (%)	2021 (%)	2022 (%)
MSA[1]	69.6	69.2	65.5	67.8	66.9	68.6	68.6	67.9
U.S.	63.7	63.4	63.9	64.4	64.6	66.6	65.5	65.8

Note: (1) Figures cover the Omaha-Council Bluffs, NE-IA Metropolitan Statistical Area
Source: U.S. Census Bureau, Housing Vacancies and Homeownership Annual Statistics: 2015-2022

House Price Index (HPI)

Area	National Ranking[2]	Quarterly Change (%)	One-Year Change (%)	Five-Year Change (%)	Since 1991Q1 (%)
MSA[1]	161	-0.79	10.26	51.61	252.12
U.S.[3]	–	0.34	8.41	58.44	289.08

Note: The HPI is a weighted repeat sales index. It measures average price changes in repeat sales or refinancings on the same properties. This information is obtained by reviewing repeat mortgage transactions on single-family properties whose mortgages have been purchased or securitized by Fannie Mae or Freddie Mac since January 1975; (1) Figures cover the Omaha-Council Bluffs, NE-IA Metropolitan Statistical Area; (2) Rankings are based on annual percentage change for all metro areas containing at least 15,000 transactions over the last 10 years and ranges from 1 to 257; (3) figures based on a weighted average of Census Division estimates using a seasonally adjusted, purchase-only index; all figures are for the period ending December 31, 2022
Source: Federal Housing Finance Agency, Change in FHFA Metropolitan Area House Price Indexes, 2022Q4

Median Single-Family Home Prices

Area	2020	2021	2022p	Percent Change 2021 to 2022
MSA[1]	220.6	242.0	272.6	12.6
U.S. Average	300.2	357.1	392.6	9.9

Note: Figures are median sales prices of existing single-family homes in thousands of dollars; (p) preliminary; (1) Figures cover the Omaha-Council Bluffs, NE-IA Metropolitan Statistical Area
Source: National Association of Realtors, Median Sales Price of Existing Single-Family Homes for Metropolitan Areas, 4th Quarter 2022

Qualifying Income Based on Median Sales Price of Existing Single-Family Homes

Area	With 5% Down ($)	With 10% Down ($)	With 20% Down ($)
MSA[1]	79,942	75,734	67,320
U.S. Average	112,234	106,237	94,513

Note: Figures are preliminary; Qualifying income is based on a mortgage rate of 6.77%. Monthly principal and interest payment is limited to 25% of income; (1) Figures cover the Omaha-Council Bluffs, NE-IA Metropolitan Statistical Area
Source: National Association of Realtors, Qualifying Income Based on Median Sales Price of Existing Single-Family Homes for Metropolitan Areas, 4th Quarter 2022

Home Value

Area	Under $100,000	$100,000 -$199,999	$200,000 -$299,999	$300,000 -$399,999	$400,000 -$499,999	$500,000 -$999,999	$1,000,000 or more	Median ($)
City	15.7	42.7	23.3	9.7	4.0	3.9	0.7	177,700
MSA[1]	13.4	38.4	24.8	12.5	5.4	4.7	0.8	195,000
U.S.	16.2	24.2	20.1	13.6	8.3	13.6	4.1	244,900

Note: Figures are percentages except for median and cover owner-occupied housing units; (1) Figures cover the Omaha-Council Bluffs, NE-IA Metropolitan Statistical Area
Source: U.S. Census Bureau, 2017-2021 American Community Survey 5-Year Estimates

Year Housing Structure Built

Area	2020 or Later	2010 -2019	2000 -2009	1990 -1999	1980 -1989	1970 -1979	1960 -1969	1950 -1959	1940 -1949	Before 1940	Median Year
City	0.1	5.1	8.3	12.4	10.9	15.1	14.4	10.9	4.6	18.3	1971
MSA[1]	0.3	9.0	14.4	12.5	9.8	14.1	11.7	8.4	3.5	16.3	1977
U.S.	0.2	7.3	13.6	13.6	13.2	14.8	10.3	10.0	4.7	12.2	1979

Note: Figures are percentages except for Median Year; Note: (1) Figures cover the Omaha-Council Bluffs, NE-IA Metropolitan Statistical Area
Source: U.S. Census Bureau, 2017-2021 American Community Survey 5-Year Estimates

Gross Monthly Rent

Area	Under $500	$500 -$999	$1,000 -$1,499	$1,500 -$1,999	$2,000 -$2,499	$2,500 -$2,999	$3,000 and up	Median ($)
City	5.4	44.7	36.8	10.2	1.6	0.4	0.9	999
MSA[1]	6.4	43.7	36.5	10.2	1.7	0.5	1.2	1,000
U.S.	8.1	30.5	30.8	16.8	7.3	3.1	3.5	1,163

Note: Figures are percentages except for median; Gross rent is the contract rent plus the estimated average monthly cost of utilities (electricity, gas, and water and sewer) and fuels (oil, coal, kerosene, wood, etc.) if these are paid by the renter (or paid for the renter by someone else); (1) Figures cover the Omaha-Council Bluffs, NE-IA Metropolitan Statistical Area
Source: U.S. Census Bureau, 2017-2021 American Community Survey 5-Year Estimates

HEALTH

Health Risk Factors

Category	MSA[1] (%)	U.S. (%)
Adults aged 18–64 who have any kind of health care coverage	89.3	90.9
Adults who reported being in good or better health	86.7	85.2
Adults who have been told they have high blood cholesterol	35.4	35.7
Adults who have been told they have high blood pressure	30.4	32.4
Adults who are current smokers	13.0	14.4
Adults who currently use e-cigarettes	6.6	6.7
Adults who currently use chewing tobacco, snuff, or snus	3.2	3.5
Adults who are heavy drinkers[2]	7.2	6.3
Adults who are binge drinkers[3]	19.9	15.4
Adults who are overweight (BMI 25.0 - 29.9)	34.7	34.4
Adults who are obese (BMI 30.0 - 99.8)	35.0	33.9
Adults who participated in any physical activities in the past month	77.0	76.3

Note: (1) Figures cover the Omaha-Council Bluffs, NE-IA Metropolitan Statistical Area; (2) Heavy drinkers are classified as adult men having more than 14 drinks per week and adult women having more than 7 drinks per week; (3) Binge drinkers are classified as males having five or more drinks on one occasion or females having four or more drinks on one occasion
Source: Centers for Disease Control and Prevention, Behaviorial Risk Factor Surveillance System, SMART: Selected Metropolitan Area Risk Trends, 2021

Acute and Chronic Health Conditions

Category	MSA[1] (%)	U.S. (%)
Adults who have ever been told they had a heart attack	2.9	4.0
Adults who have ever been told they have angina or coronary heart disease	3.0	3.8
Adults who have ever been told they had a stroke	2.5	3.0
Adults who have ever been told they have asthma	13.0	14.9
Adults who have ever been told they have arthritis	23.5	25.8
Adults who have ever been told they have diabetes[2]	9.7	10.9
Adults who have ever been told they had skin cancer	6.2	6.6
Adults who have ever been told they had any other types of cancer	6.7	7.5
Adults who have ever been told they have COPD	5.7	6.1
Adults who have ever been told they have kidney disease	2.4	3.0
Adults who have ever been told they have a form of depression	18.6	20.5

Note: (1) Figures cover the Omaha-Council Bluffs, NE-IA Metropolitan Statistical Area; (2) Figures do not include pregnancy-related, borderline, or pre-diabetes
Source: Centers for Disease Control and Prevention, Behaviorial Risk Factor Surveillance System, SMART: Selected Metropolitan Area Risk Trends, 2021

Health Screening and Vaccination Rates

Category	MSA[1] (%)	U.S. (%)
Adults who have ever been tested for HIV	28.1	34.9
Adults who have had their blood cholesterol checked within the last five years	83.8	85.2
Adults aged 65+ who have had flu shot within the past year	72.4	68.6
Adults aged 65+ who have ever had a pneumonia vaccination	76.9	71.0

Note: (1) Figures cover the Omaha-Council Bluffs, NE-IA Metropolitan Statistical Area.
Source: Centers for Disease Control and Prevention, Behaviorial Risk Factor Surveillance System, SMART: Selected Metropolitan Area Risk Trends, 2021

Disability Status

Category	MSA[1] (%)	U.S. (%)
Adults who reported being deaf	5.7	7.2
Are you blind or have serious difficulty seeing, even when wearing glasses?	3.2	4.8
Are you limited in any way in any of your usual activities due to arthritis?	9.5	11.1
Do you have difficulty doing errands alone?	6.6	7.0
Do you have difficulty dressing or bathing?	2.9	3.6
Do you have serious difficulty concentrating/remembering/making decisions?	10.9	12.1
Do you have serious difficulty walking or climbing stairs?	11.3	12.8

Note: (1) Figures cover the Omaha-Council Bluffs, NE-IA Metropolitan Statistical Area.
Source: Centers for Disease Control and Prevention, Behaviorial Risk Factor Surveillance System, SMART: Selected Metropolitan Area Risk Trends, 2021

Mortality Rates for the Top 10 Causes of Death in the U.S.

ICD-10[a] Sub-Chapter	ICD-10[a] Code	Crude Mortality Rate[1] per 100,000 population	
		County[2]	U.S.
Malignant neoplasms	C00-C97	160.8	182.6
Ischaemic heart diseases	I20-I25	55.1	113.1
Other forms of heart disease	I30-I51	59.2	64.4
Other degenerative diseases of the nervous system	G30-G31	51.3	51.0
Cerebrovascular diseases	I60-I69	38.8	47.8
Other external causes of accidental injury	W00-X59	29.3	46.4
Chronic lower respiratory diseases	J40-J47	43.3	45.7
Organic, including symptomatic, mental disorders	F01-F09	31.5	35.9
Hypertensive diseases	I10-I15	36.2	35.0
Diabetes mellitus	E10-E14	27.9	29.6

Note: (a) ICD-10 = International Classification of Diseases 10th Revision; (1) Crude mortality rates are a three-year average covering 2019-2021; (2) Figures cover Douglas County.
Source: Centers for Disease Control and Prevention, National Center for Health Statistics. National Vital Statistics System, Mortality 2018-2021 on CDC WONDER Online Database

Mortality Rates for Selected Causes of Death

ICD-10[a] Sub-Chapter	ICD-10[a] Code	Crude Mortality Rate[1] per 100,000 population	
		County[2]	U.S.
Assault	X85-Y09	6.0	7.0
Diseases of the liver	K70-K76	17.4	19.8
Human immunodeficiency virus (HIV) disease	B20-B24	1.4	1.5
Influenza and pneumonia	J09-J18	11.6	14.7
Intentional self-harm	X60-X84	14.2	14.3
Malnutrition	E40-E46	4.8	4.3
Obesity and other hyperalimentation	E65-E68	3.9	3.0
Renal failure	N17-N19	10.2	15.7
Transport accidents	V01-V99	9.0	13.6
Viral hepatitis	B15-B19	Unreliable	1.2

Note: (a) ICD-10 = International Classification of Diseases 10th Revision; (1) Crude mortality rates are a three-year average covering 2019-2021; (2) Figures cover Douglas County; Data are suppressed when the data meet the criteria for confidentiality constraints; Crude mortality rates are flagged as unreliable when the rate would be calculated with a numerator of 20 or less.
Source: Centers for Disease Control and Prevention, National Center for Health Statistics. National Vital Statistics System, Mortality 2018-2021 on CDC WONDER Online Database

Health Insurance Coverage

Area	With Health Insurance	With Private Health Insurance	With Public Health Insurance	Without Health Insurance	Population Under Age 19 Without Health Insurance
City	89.7	70.8	28.7	10.3	7.0
MSA[1]	92.3	75.4	27.6	7.7	5.0
U.S.	91.2	67.8	35.4	8.8	5.3

Note: Figures are percentages that cover the civilian noninstitutionalized population; (1) Figures cover the Omaha-Council Bluffs, NE-IA Metropolitan Statistical Area
Source: U.S. Census Bureau, 2017-2021 American Community Survey 5-Year Estimates

Number of Medical Professionals

Area	MDs[3]	DOs[3,4]	Dentists	Podiatrists	Chiropractors	Optometrists
County[1] (number)	3,202	152	593	29	247	127
County[1] (rate[2])	547.3	26.0	101.4	5.0	42.2	21.7
U.S. (rate[2])	289.3	23.5	72.5	6.2	28.7	17.4

Note: Data as of 2021 unless noted; (1) Data covers Douglas County; (2) Rate per 100,000 population; (3) Data as of 2020 and includes all active, non-federal physicians; (4) Doctor of Osteopathic Medicine
Source: U.S. Department of Health and Human Services, Health Resources and Services Administration, Bureau of Health Professions, Area Resource File (ARF) 2021-2022

Best Hospitals

According to *U.S. News,* the Omaha-Council Bluffs, NE-IA metro area is home to one of the best children's hospitals in the U.S.: **Children's Hospital and Medical Center** (2 pediatric specialties). The hospital listed was highly ranked in at least one of 10 pediatric specialties. Eighty-six children's hospitals in the U.S. were nationally ranked in at least one specialty. Hospitals received points for being ranked in a specialty, and the 10 hospitals with the most points across the 10 specialties make up the Honor Roll. *U.S. News Online, "America's Best Children's Hospitals 2022-23"*

EDUCATION

Public School District Statistics

District Name	Schls	Pupils	Pupil/ Teacher Ratio	Minority Pupils[1] (%)	LEP/ELL[2] (%)	IEP[3] (%)
Millard Public Schools	36	23,762	15.8	25.4	2.2	12.0
Omaha Public Schools	111	51,626	15.0	76.6	17.4	19.8
Westside Community Schools	14	6,221	14.0	32.6	2.2	11.8

Note: Table includes school districts with 2,000 or more students; (1) Percentage of students that are not non-Hispanic white; (2) Percentage of students that are Limited English Proficient or English Language Learners (2018-19); (3) Percentage of students that have an Individualized Education Program (2019-20). Source: U.S. Department of Education, National Center for Education Statistics, Common Core of Data, Local Education Agency (School District) Universe Survey: School Year 2021-2022

Best High Schools

According to *U.S. News*, Omaha is home to one of the top 500 high schools in the U.S.: **Elkhorn South High School** (#236). Nearly 18,000 public, magnet and charter schools were ranked based on their performance on state assessments and how well they prepare students for college. *U.S. News & World Report, "Best High Schools 2022"*

Highest Level of Education

Area	Less than H.S.	H.S. Diploma	Some College, No Deg.	Associate Degree	Bachelor's Degree	Master's Degree	Prof. School Degree	Doctorate Degree
City	9.7	21.7	22.0	7.8	24.9	9.1	3.1	1.6
MSA[1]	7.7	23.1	22.0	9.4	24.3	9.6	2.4	1.4
U.S.	11.1	26.5	20.0	8.7	20.6	9.3	2.2	1.5

Note: Figures cover persons age 25 and over; (1) Figures cover the Omaha-Council Bluffs, NE-IA Metropolitan Statistical Area Source: U.S. Census Bureau, 2017-2021 American Community Survey 5-Year Estimates

Educational Attainment by Race

Area	High School Graduate or Higher (%)					Bachelor's Degree or Higher (%)				
	Total	White	Black	Asian	Hisp.[2]	Total	White	Black	Asian	Hisp.[2]
City	90.3	93.1	87.9	72.2	60.3	38.7	42.8	17.7	49.8	13.8
MSA[1]	92.3	94.2	88.8	75.9	66.1	37.7	39.7	20.5	49.0	17.3
U.S.	88.9	91.4	87.2	87.6	71.2	33.7	35.5	23.3	55.6	18.4

Note: Figures shown cover persons 25 years old and over; (1) Figures cover the Omaha-Council Bluffs, NE-IA Metropolitan Statistical Area; (2) People of Hispanic origin can be of any race Source: U.S. Census Bureau, 2017-2021 American Community Survey 5-Year Estimates

School Enrollment by Grade and Control

Area	Preschool (%)		Kindergarten (%)		Grades 1 - 4 (%)		Grades 5 - 8 (%)		Grades 9 - 12 (%)	
	Public	Private	Public	Private	Public	Private	Public	Private	Public	Private
City	52.7	47.3	81.2	18.8	82.9	17.1	83.3	16.7	83.2	16.8
MSA[1]	57.9	42.1	83.0	17.0	85.1	14.9	85.4	14.6	85.4	14.6
U.S.	58.8	41.2	86.3	13.7	88.3	11.7	88.6	11.4	89.4	10.6

Note: Figures shown cover persons 3 years old and over; (1) Figures cover the Omaha-Council Bluffs, NE-IA Metropolitan Statistical Area Source: U.S. Census Bureau, 2017-2021 American Community Survey 5-Year Estimates

Higher Education

Four-Year Colleges			Two-Year Colleges			Medical Schools[1]	Law Schools[2]	Voc/ Tech[3]
Public	Private Non-profit	Private For-profit	Public	Private Non-profit	Private For-profit			
2	6	0	2	0	4	2	1	0

Note: Figures cover institutions located within the Omaha-Council Bluffs, NE-IA Metropolitan Statistical Area and include main campuses only; (1) includes schools accredited by the Liaison Committee on Medical Education and the American Osteopathic Association's Commission on Osteopathic College Accreditation; (2) includes ABA-accredited schools, schools with provisional ABA accreditation, and state accredited schools; (3) includes all schools with programs that are less than 2 years. Source: National Center for Education Statistics, Integrated Postsecondary Education System (IPEDS), 2021-22; Wikipedia, List of Medical Schools in the United States, accessed April 10, 2023; Wikipedia, List of Law Schools in the United States, accessed April 10, 2023

According to *U.S. News & World Report,* the Omaha-Council Bluffs, NE-IA metro area is home to one of the top 200 national universities in the U.S.: **Creighton University** (#115 tie). The indicators used to capture academic quality fall into a number of categories: assessment by administrators at peer institutions; retention of students; faculty resources; student selectivity; financial resources; alumni giving; high school counselor ratings of colleges; and graduation rate. *U.S. News & World Report, "America's Best Colleges 2023"*

According to *U.S. News & World Report,* the Omaha-Council Bluffs, NE-IA metro area is home to one of the top 75 medical schools for research in the U.S.: **University of Nebraska Medical Center** (#53 tie). The rankings are based on a weighted average of 11 measures of quality: quality assessment; peer assessment score; assessment score by residency directors; research activity; total research activity; average research activity per faculty member; student selectivity; median MCAT total score; median undergraduate GPA; acceptance rate; and faculty resources. *U.S. News & World Report, "America's Best Graduate Schools, Medical, 2023"*

EMPLOYERS

Major Employers

Company Name	Industry
Alegent Health	General medical & surgical hospitals
City of Omaha	Municipal government
Creighton St. Joseph Reg Healthcare Sys	General medical & surgical hospitals
Creighton University	Colleges & universities
Drivers Management	Truck driver services
First Data Resources	Data processing service
Harveys Iowa Management Company	Casino hotels
Kiewit Offshore Services	Fabricated structural metal
Metropolitan Community College	Community college
Mutual of Omaha Insurance Company	Life insurance
Nebraska Furniture Mart	Furniture stores
Omaha Public Power District	Electric services
The Archbishop Bergan Mercy Hospital	General medical & surgical hospitals
The Nebraska Medical Center	General medical & surgical hospitals
The Pacesetter Corporation	General remodeling, single-family houses
Tyson Foods	Meats & meat products
Valmont Industries	Irrigation equipment, self-propelled

Note: Companies shown are located within the Omaha-Council Bluffs, NE-IA Metropolitan Statistical Area. Source: Hoovers.com; Wikipedia

Best Companies to Work For

Mutual of Omaha, headquartered in Omaha, is among "The 100 Best Companies to Work For." To pick the best companies, *Fortune* partnered with the Great Place to Work Institute. Two-thirds of a company's score is based on the results of the Institute's Trust Index survey, which is sent to a random sample of employees from each company. The questions related to attitudes about management's credibility, job satisfaction, and camaraderie. The other third of the scoring is based on the company's responses to the Institute's Culture Audit, which includes detailed questions about pay and benefit programs, and a series of open-ended questions about hiring practices, internal communication, training, recognition programs, and diversity efforts. Any company that is at least five years old with more than 1,000 U.S. employees is eligible. *Fortune, "The 100 Best Companies to Work For," 2023*

Mutual of Omaha, headquartered in Omaha, is among "Fortune's Best Workplaces for Women." To pick the best companies, *Fortune* partnered with the Great Place to Work Institute. To be considered for the list, companies must be Great Place To Work-Certified. Companies must also employ at least 50 women, at least 20% of their non-executive managers must be female, and at least one executive must be female. To determine the Best Workplaces for Women, Great Place To Work measured the differences in women's survey responses to those of their peers and assesses the impact of demographics and roles on the quality and consistency of women's experiences. Great Place To Work also analyzed the gender balance of each workplace, how it compared to each company's industry, and patterns in representation as women rise from front-line positions to the board of directors. *Fortune, "Best Workplaces for Women," 2022*

Fusion Medical Staffing; Prime Time Healthcare, headquartered in Omaha, are among "Best Workplaces in Health Care." To determine the Best Workplaces in Health Care list, Great Place To Work analyzed the survey responses of over 161,000 employees from Great Place To Work-Certified companies in the health care industry. Survey data analysis and company-provided datapoints are then factored into a combined score to compare and rank the companies that create the most consistently positive experience for all employees in this industry. *Fortune, "Best Workplaces in Health Care," 2022*

PUBLIC SAFETY

Crime Rate

Area	Total Crime	Violent Crime Rate				Property Crime Rate		
		Murder	Rape[3]	Robbery	Aggrav. Assault	Burglary	Larceny -Theft	Motor Vehicle Theft
City	3,805.8	7.7	73.1	96.6	453.9	316.7	2,227.2	630.7
Suburbs[1]	1,602.2	1.5	37.1	23.2	163.9	191.7	977.7	207.1
Metro[2]	2,710.6	4.6	55.2	60.1	309.8	254.6	1,606.2	420.2
U.S.	2,356.7	6.5	38.4	73.9	279.7	314.2	1,398.0	246.0

Note: Figures are crimes per 100,000 population; (1) All areas within the metro area that are located outside the city limits; (2) Figures cover the Omaha-Council Bluffs, NE-IA Metropolitan Statistical Area; (3) All figures shown were reported using the revised Uniform Crime Reporting (UCR) definition of rape; Due to the transition to the National Incident-Based Reporting System (NIBRS), limited city and metro area data was released for 2021.
Source: FBI Uniform Crime Reports, 2020

Hate Crimes

Area	Number of Quarters Reported	Number of Incidents per Bias Motivation					
		Race/Ethnicity/ Ancestry	Religion	Sexual Orientation	Disability	Gender	Gender Identity
City	4	1	6	2	0	0	0
U.S.	4	5,227	1,244	1,110	130	75	266

Note: Due to the transition to the National Incident-Based Reporting System (NIBRS), limited crime data was released for 2021.
Source: Federal Bureau of Investigation, Hate Crime Statistics 2020

Identity Theft Consumer Reports

Area	Reports	Reports per 100,000 Population	Rank[2]
MSA[1]	1,222	130	297
U.S.	1,108,609	339	-

Note: (1) Figures cover the Omaha-Council Bluffs, NE-IA Metropolitan Statistical Area; (2) Rank ranges from 1 to 391 where 1 indicates greatest number of identity theft reports per 100,000 population
Source: Federal Trade Commission, Consumer Sentinel Network Data Book 2022

Fraud and Other Consumer Reports

Area	Reports	Reports per 100,000 Population	Rank[2]
MSA[1]	7,818	832	193
U.S.	4,064,520	1,245	-

Note: (1) Figures cover the Omaha-Council Bluffs, NE-IA Metropolitan Statistical Area; (2) Rank ranges from 1 to 391 where 1 indicates greatest number of fraud and other consumer reports per 100,000 population
Source: Federal Trade Commission, Consumer Sentinel Network Data Book 2022

POLITICS

2020 Presidential Election Results

Area	Biden	Trump	Jorgensen	Hawkins	Other
Douglas County	54.4	43.1	2.0	0.0	0.6
U.S.	51.3	46.8	1.2	0.3	0.5

Note: Results are percentages and may not add to 100% due to rounding
Source: Dave Leip's Atlas of U.S. Presidential Elections

SPORTS

Professional Sports Teams

Team Name	League	Year Established

No teams are located in the metro area
Source: Wikipedia, Major Professional Sports Teams of the United States and Canada, April 12, 2023

CLIMATE

Average and Extreme Temperatures

Temperature	Jan	Feb	Mar	Apr	May	Jun	Jul	Aug	Sep	Oct	Nov	Dec	Yr.
Extreme High (°F)	67	77	89	97	98	105	110	107	103	95	80	69	110
Average High (°F)	31	37	48	64	74	84	88	85	77	66	49	36	62
Average Temp. (°F)	22	27	38	52	63	73	77	75	66	54	39	27	51
Average Low (°F)	11	17	27	40	52	61	66	64	54	42	29	17	40
Extreme Low (°F)	-23	-21	-16	5	27	38	44	43	25	13	-9	-23	-23

Note: Figures cover the years 1948-1992
Source: National Climatic Data Center, International Station Meteorological Climate Summary, 9/96

Average Precipitation/Snowfall/Humidity

Precip./Humidity	Jan	Feb	Mar	Apr	May	Jun	Jul	Aug	Sep	Oct	Nov	Dec	Yr.
Avg. Precip. (in.)	0.8	0.9	2.0	2.8	4.3	4.0	3.7	3.8	3.4	2.1	1.5	0.9	30.1
Avg. Snowfall (in.)	7	6	7	1	Tr	0	0	0	Tr	Tr	3	6	29
Avg. Rel. Hum. 6am (%)	78	80	79	77	80	82	84	86	85	81	79	80	81
Avg. Rel. Hum. 3pm (%)	61	59	54	46	49	50	51	53	51	47	55	61	53

Note: Figures cover the years 1948-1992; Tr = Trace amounts (<0.05 in. of rain; <0.5 in. of snow)
Source: National Climatic Data Center, International Station Meteorological Climate Summary, 9/96

Weather Conditions

Temperature			Daytime Sky			Precipitation		
5°F & below	32°F & below	90°F & above	Clear	Partly cloudy	Cloudy	0.01 inch or more precip.	0.1 inch or more snow/ice	Thunder-storms
23	139	35	100	142	123	97	20	46

Note: Figures are average number of days per year and cover the years 1948-1992.
Source: National Climatic Data Center, International Station Meteorological Climate Summary, 9/96

HAZARDOUS WASTE

Superfund Sites

The Omaha-Council Bluffs, NE-IA metro area is home to three sites on the EPA's Superfund National Priorities List: **Nebraska Ordnance Plant (Former)** (final); **Old Hwy 275 and N 288th Street** (final); **Omaha Lead** (final). There are a total of 1,165 Superfund sites with a status of proposed or final on the list in the U.S. *U.S. Environmental Protection Agency, National Priorities List, April 12, 2023*

AIR QUALITY

Air Quality Trends: Ozone

	1990	1995	2000	2005	2010	2015	2018	2019	2020	2021
MSA[1]	0.054	0.075	0.063	0.069	0.058	0.055	0.063	0.050	0.055	0.055
U.S.	0.087	0.089	0.081	0.080	0.072	0.067	0.069	0.065	0.065	0.067

Note: (1) Data covers the Omaha-Council Bluffs, NE-IA Metropolitan Statistical Area. The values shown are the composite ozone concentration averages among trend sites based on the highest fourth daily maximum 8-hour concentration in parts per million. These trends are based on sites having an adequate record of monitoring data during the trend period. Data from exceptional events are included.
Source: U.S. Environmental Protection Agency, Air Quality Monitoring Information, "Air Quality Trends by City, 1990-2021"

Air Quality Index

Area	Percent of Days when Air Quality was...[2]					AQI Statistics[2]	
	Good	Moderate	Unhealthy for Sensitive Groups	Unhealthy	Very Unhealthy	Maximum	Median
MSA[1]	72.9	25.8	1.4	0.0	0.0	150	42

Note: (1) Data covers the Omaha-Council Bluffs, NE-IA Metropolitan Statistical Area; (2) Based on 365 days with AQI data in 2021. Air Quality Index (AQI) is an index for reporting daily air quality. EPA calculates the AQI for five major air pollutants regulated by the Clean Air Act: ground-level ozone, particle pollution (aka particulate matter), carbon monoxide, sulfur dioxide, and nitrogen dioxide. The AQI runs from 0 to 500. The higher the AQI value, the greater the level of air pollution and the greater the health concern. There are six AQI categories: "Good" AQI is between 0 and 50. Air quality is considered satisfactory; "Moderate" AQI is between 51 and 100. Air quality is acceptable; "Unhealthy for Sensitive Groups" When AQI values are between 101 and 150, members of sensitive groups may experience health effects; "Unhealthy" When AQI values are between 151 and 200 everyone may begin to experience health effects; "Very Unhealthy" AQI values between 201 and 300 trigger a health alert; "Hazardous" AQI values over 300 trigger warnings of emergency conditions (not shown).
Source: U.S. Environmental Protection Agency, Air Quality Index Report, 2021

Air Quality Index Pollutants

Area	Percent of Days when AQI Pollutant was...[2]					
	Carbon Monoxide	Nitrogen Dioxide	Ozone	Sulfur Dioxide	Particulate Matter 2.5	Particulate Matter 10
MSA[1]	0.0	0.0	53.4	(3)	38.4	8.2

Note: (1) Data covers the Omaha-Council Bluffs, NE-IA Metropolitan Statistical Area; (2) Based on 365 days with AQI data in 2021. The Air Quality Index (AQI) is an index for reporting daily air quality. EPA calculates the AQI for five major air pollutants regulated by the Clean Air Act: ground-level ozone, particle pollution (also known as particulate matter), carbon monoxide, sulfur dioxide, and nitrogen dioxide. The AQI runs from 0 to 500. The higher the AQI value, the greater the level of air pollution and the greater the health concern; (3) Sulfur dioxide is no longer included in this table (as of December 8, 2021) because SO_2 concentrations tend to be very localized and not necessarily representative of broad geographical areas like counties and CBSAs.
Source: U.S. Environmental Protection Agency, Air Quality Index Report, 2021

Maximum Air Pollutant Concentrations: Particulate Matter, Ozone, CO and Lead

	Particulate Matter 10 (ug/m^3)	Particulate Matter 2.5 Wtd AM (ug/m^3)	Particulate Matter 2.5 24-Hr (ug/m^3)	Ozone (ppm)	Carbon Monoxide (ppm)	Lead (ug/m^3)
MSA[1] Level	70	8.9	26	0.066	1	0.09
NAAQS[2]	150	15	35	0.075	9	0.15
Met NAAQS[2]	Yes	Yes	Yes	Yes	Yes	Yes

Note: (1) Data covers the Omaha-Council Bluffs, NE-IA Metropolitan Statistical Area; Data from exceptional events are included; (2) National Ambient Air Quality Standards; ppm = parts per million; ug/m^3 = micrograms per cubic meter; n/a not available.
Concentrations: Particulate Matter 10 (coarse particulate)—highest second maximum 24-hour concentration; Particulate Matter 2.5 Wtd AM (fine particulate)—highest weighted annual mean concentration; Particulate Matter 2.5 24-Hour (fine particulate)—highest 98th percentile 24-hour concentration; Ozone—highest fourth daily maximum 8-hour concentration; Carbon Monoxide—highest second maximum non-overlapping 8-hour concentration; Lead—maximum running 3-month average
Source: U.S. Environmental Protection Agency, Air Quality Monitoring Information, "Air Quality Statistics by City, 2021"

Maximum Air Pollutant Concentrations: Nitrogen Dioxide and Sulfur Dioxide

	Nitrogen Dioxide AM (ppb)	Nitrogen Dioxide 1-Hr (ppb)	Sulfur Dioxide AM (ppb)	Sulfur Dioxide 1-Hr (ppb)	Sulfur Dioxide 24-Hr (ppb)
MSA[1] Level	n/a	n/a	n/a	48	n/a
NAAQS[2]	53	100	30	75	140
Met NAAQS[2]	n/a	n/a	n/a	Yes	n/a

Note: (1) Data covers the Omaha-Council Bluffs, NE-IA Metropolitan Statistical Area; Data from exceptional events are included; (2) National Ambient Air Quality Standards; ppm = parts per million; ug/m^3 = micrograms per cubic meter; n/a not available.
Concentrations: Nitrogen Dioxide AM—highest arithmetic mean concentration; Nitrogen Dioxide 1-Hr—highest 98th percentile 1-hour daily maximum concentration; Sulfur Dioxide AM—highest annual mean concentration; Sulfur Dioxide 1-Hr—highest 99th percentile 1-hour daily maximum concentration; Sulfur Dioxide 24-Hr—highest second maximum 24-hour concentration
Source: U.S. Environmental Protection Agency, Air Quality Monitoring Information, "Air Quality Statistics by City, 2021"

Rochester, Minnesota

Background

Rochester, Minnesota is often characterized as a medical mecca, based on the city's history of major breakthroughs in modern medicine. Before Dr. William Mayo arrived in 1864, as an examining physician for Civil War draftees, Rochester was a transportation hub for the wheat markets of southeastern Minnesota. Rochester's destiny was determined when a pioneer of medicine, a determined Sister of St. Francis, and a devastating tornado converged on the evening of August 21, 1883.

Dr. William Worrall (W.W.) Mayo had been schooled in Manchester England, migrated to the U.S., and completed his medical training in Indiana. In 1864, he and his young family settled in Rochester and, following the Civil War, set up a medical practice.

When a deadly tornado hit Rochester on August 21, 1883, killing dozens and injuring hundreds, the Mayos (father and two sons, Will and Charlie) and other Rochester physicians called upon the Sisters of St. Francis who worked tirelessly with the Drs. Mayo. In 1889, they established St. Mary's Hospital, in spite of the Mayos' insistence that Rochester was too small for such a hospital. In 1914, St. Mary's Hospital would become the Mayo Clinic which today is a medical model of integrated medicine consisting of teamwork, pooled knowledge, and resources among physicians, used throughout the world. Dr. Mayo personally trained his students, thinking that the best way to learn medicine is by studying large numbers of cases and by hands-on experience, known today as residency training, a standard in medical education.

The Mayo Clinic is still a world pioneer, making Rochester a medical destination, and employing over 30,000 in Rochester alone. Additional Mayo facilities have been established in Arizona and Florida. The Mayo Clinic is the largest not-for-profit medical practice in the world. In 1973, Mayo opened its medical school, the most selective in the country and today, the Mayo Clinic offers history and art tours.

IBM was a mainstay of Rochester's economy for years, employing over 8,000 employees in its heyday. IBM's nickname "Big Blue" was based on the Rochester facility, which is constructed of blue panels designed to reflect the Minnesota sky. The building was dedicated in 1958 and was the largest IBM facility under one roof in the world. In 1990, the National Building Museum acknowledged the facility for its historic significance and innovation. In 2016, IBM consolidated, and in 2018, the property was sold and renamed the Rochester Technology Campus.

The History Center of Olmsted County offers an impressive variety of programs, including research facilities and rare collections. Venues include tours of the historic 38-room, Mayowood Mansion and gardens—once the home of the Mayo family. Much of the architecture was the handiwork of W. W. Mayo himself.

The oldest cultural arts institution in the community, Rochester Symphony Orchestra & Chorale was founded in 1919 as a professional performing arts organization. Its earliest ensemble—the Lawler-Dodge Orchestra—was founded in 1912 as a volunteer orchestra, driven by Daisy Plummer, wife of world-famous Mayo Clinic physician, Dr. Henry Plummer, and directed by Harold Cooke. The Orchestra performed in the former Chateau Theatre where they played background music for silent movies.

The Rochester Downtown Alliance created the Summer Market and Music Festival, and STYLE, the Runway Experience. StyleICE is a unique celebration in which local downtown bars produce an all-ice experience. Everything from glasses to couches is created out of ice and features special lighting effects and live music. In 2019, a new, state-of-the-art movie theater opened its doors in the city.

Minnesota has one of the most extensive state park systems in the nation. Likewise, Rochester's city park system is large, with more than 100 sites covering five square miles. The city also maintains 85 miles of paved trails in addition to state trails such as the Douglas State Trail. The nearest state park is Whitewater State Park.

Rochester features a humid continental climate with four distinct seasons. Summers are very warm, and winters are very cold. Rochester sees an annual average of 30 inches of rainfall and 48 inches of snowfall. Significant snow accumulation is common during the winter months. Spring and fall are transitional, with a warming trend during the spring and a cooling trend during the fall. It is not uncommon to see snowfall during early spring and late fall.

Rankings

General Rankings

- In their ninth annual survey, Livability.com looked at data for more than 2,300 mid-sized U.S. cities to determine the rankings for Livability's "Top 100 Best Places to Live" in 2022. Rochester ranked #3. Criteria: housing and economy; social and civic engagement; education; demographics; health care options; transportation & infrastructure; and community amenities. *Livability.com, "Top 100 Best Places to Live 2022" July 19, 2022*

Business/Finance Rankings

- The Rochester metro area appeared on the Milken Institute "2022 Best Performing Cities" list. Rank: #50 out of 201 small metro areas (population over 60,000). Criteria: job growth; wage and salary growth; high-tech output growth; housing affordability; household broadband access. *Milken Institute, "Best-Performing Cities 2022," March 28, 2022*

- *Forbes* ranked 203 smaller metro areas (population under 268,000) to determine the nation's "Best Small Places for Business and Careers." The Rochester metro area was ranked #37. Criteria: costs (business and living); job growth (past and projected); income growth; quality of life; educational attainment (college and high school); projected economic growth; cultural and leisure opportunities; workplace tolerance laws; net migration patterns. *Forbes, "The Best Small Places for Business and Careers 2019," October 30, 2019*

Environmental Rankings

- Rochester was highlighted as one of the cleanest metro areas for ozone air pollution in the U.S. during 2019 through 2021. The list represents cities with no monitored ozone air pollution in unhealthful ranges. *American Lung Association, "State of the Air 2023," April 19, 2023*

- Rochester was highlighted as one of the top 25 cleanest metro areas for year-round particle pollution (Annual PM 2.5) in the U.S. during 2019 through 2021. The area ranked #19. *American Lung Association, "State of the Air 2023," April 19, 2023*

Safety Rankings

- The National Insurance Crime Bureau ranked 390 metro areas in the U.S. in terms of per capita rates of vehicle theft. The Rochester metro area ranked #327 (#1 = highest rate). Criteria: number of vehicle theft offenses per 100,000 inhabitants in 2021. *National Insurance Crime Bureau, "Hot Spots 2021," September 1, 2022*

Seniors/Retirement Rankings

- From its Best Cities for Successful Aging indexes, the Milken Institute generated rankings for metropolitan areas, weighing data in nine categories—health care, wellness, living arrangements, transportation and convenience, financial characteristics, education, employment, community engagement, and overall livability. The Rochester metro area was ranked #24 overall in the small metro area category. *Milken Institute, "Best Cities for Successful Aging, 2017" March 14, 2017*

- Rochester made the 2022 *Forbes* list of "25 Best Places to Retire." Criteria, focused on overall affordability as well as quality of life indicators, include: housing/living costs compared to the national average and state taxes; air quality; home price appreciation; risk associated with climate-change/natural hazards; availability of medical care; bikeability; walkability; healthy living. *Forbes.com, "The Best Places to Retire in 2022," May 13, 2022*

Business Environment

DEMOGRAPHICS

Population Growth

Area	1990 Census	2000 Census	2010 Census	2020 Census	Population Growth (%) 1990-2020	Population Growth (%) 2010-2020
City	74,151	85,806	106,769	121,395	63.7	13.7
MSA[1]	141,945	163,618	186,011	226,329	59.4	21.7
U.S.	248,709,873	281,421,906	308,745,538	331,449,281	33.3	7.4

Note: (1) Figures cover the Rochester, MN Metropolitan Statistical Area
Source: U.S. Census Bureau, 1990 Census, 2000 Census, 2010 Census, 2020 Census

Race

Area	White Alone[2] (%)	Black Alone[2] (%)	Asian Alone[2] (%)	AIAN[3] Alone[2] (%)	NHOPI[4] Alone[2] (%)	Other Race Alone[2] (%)	Two or More Races (%)
City	73.2	8.9	7.9	0.4	0.1	2.9	6.6
MSA[1]	82.3	5.1	4.7	0.3	0.0	2.2	5.4
U.S.	61.6	12.4	6.0	1.1	0.2	8.4	10.2

Note: (1) Figures cover the Rochester, MN Metropolitan Statistical Area; (2) Alone is defined as not being in combination with one or more other races; (3) American Indian and Alaska Native; (4) Native Hawaiian and Other Pacific Islander
Source: U.S. Census Bureau, 2020 Census

Hispanic or Latino Origin

Area	Total (%)	Mexican (%)	Puerto Rican (%)	Cuban (%)	Other (%)
City	5.8	3.7	0.6	0.1	1.4
MSA[1]	4.7	2.9	0.4	0.1	1.3
U.S.	18.4	11.2	1.8	0.7	4.7

Note: Persons of Hispanic or Latino origin can be of any race; (1) Figures cover the Rochester, MN Metropolitan Statistical Area
Source: U.S. Census Bureau, 2017-2021 American Community Survey 5-Year Estimates

Age

Area	Percent of Population Under Age 5	Age 5–19	Age 20–34	Age 35–44	Age 45–54	Age 55–64	Age 65–74	Age 75–84	Age 85+	Median Age
City	6.5	18.6	23.3	13.4	10.5	11.9	8.5	5.0	2.3	36.0
MSA[1]	6.2	19.8	19.3	13.2	11.2	13.4	9.4	5.3	2.3	38.4
U.S.	5.6	19.2	20.2	12.7	12.4	13.1	10.0	4.9	1.9	38.8

Note: (1) Figures cover the Rochester, MN Metropolitan Statistical Area
Source: U.S. Census Bureau, 2020 Census

Disability by Age

Area	All Ages	Under 18 Years Old	18 to 64 Years Old	65 Years and Over
City	10.3	4.2	7.9	30.7
MSA[1]	10.0	3.8	7.6	28.6
U.S.	12.6	4.4	10.3	33.4

Note: Figures show percent of the civilian noninstitutionalized population that reported having a disability. Disability status is determined from six types of difficulty: vision, hearing, cognitive, ambulatory, self-care, and independent living. For children under 5 years old, hearing and vision difficulty are used to determine disability status. For children between the ages of 5 and 14, disability status is determined from hearing, vision, cognitive, ambulatory, and self-care difficulties. For people aged 15 years and older, they are considered to have a disability if they have difficulty with any one of the six difficulty types; Note: (1) Figures cover the Rochester, MN Metropolitan Statistical Area
Source: U.S. Census Bureau, 2017-2021 American Community Survey 5-Year Estimates

Ancestry

Area	German	Irish	English	American	Italian	Polish	French[2]	Scottish	Dutch
City	28.7	10.2	6.7	3.1	1.5	2.9	1.8	1.3	1.6
MSA[1]	34.2	11.0	6.8	3.4	1.3	2.8	1.9	1.2	1.9
U.S.	12.8	9.6	8.1	5.7	5.0	2.7	2.2	1.6	1.1

Note: Figures are the percentage of the total population reporting a particular ancestry. The nine most commonly reported ancestries in the U.S. are shown. Figures include multiple ancestries (e.g. if a person reported being Irish and Italian, they were included in both columns); (1) Figures cover the Rochester, MN Metropolitan Statistical Area; (2) Excludes Basque
Source: U.S. Census Bureau, 2017-2021 American Community Survey 5-Year Estimates

Foreign-born Population

Area	Any Foreign Country	Asia	Mexico	Europe	Caribbean	Central America[2]	South America	Africa	Canada
City	13.6	5.4	1.0	1.7	0.1	0.2	0.5	4.5	0.2
MSA[1]	8.5	3.2	0.7	1.1	0.1	0.2	0.4	2.4	0.2
U.S.	13.6	4.2	3.3	1.5	1.1	1.1	1.1	0.8	0.2

Note: (1) Figures cover the Rochester, MN Metropolitan Statistical Area; (2) Excludes Mexico.
Source: U.S. Census Bureau, 2017-2021 American Community Survey 5-Year Estimates

Household Size

Area	Persons in Household (%) One	Two	Three	Four	Five	Six	Seven or More	Average Household Size
City	31.0	34.8	13.1	12.2	5.5	1.9	1.4	2.40
MSA[1]	27.4	36.9	13.3	13.1	6.1	1.9	1.2	2.50
U.S.	28.1	33.8	15.5	12.9	6.0	2.3	1.4	2.60

Note: (1) Figures cover the Rochester, MN Metropolitan Statistical Area
Source: U.S. Census Bureau, 2017-2021 American Community Survey 5-Year Estimates

Household Relationships

Area	House-holder	Opposite-sex Spouse	Same-sex Spouse	Opposite-sex Unmarried Partner	Same-sex Unmarried Partner	Child[2]	Grand-child	Other Relatives	Non-relatives
City	41.1	18.5	0.2	2.8	0.1	27.8	0.9	2.8	3.3
MSA[1]	40.1	20.5	0.1	2.7	0.1	28.9	1.0	2.2	2.5
U.S.	38.3	17.5	0.2	2.5	0.2	28.3	2.4	4.8	3.4

Note: Figures are percent of the total population; (1) Figures cover the Rochester, MN Metropolitan Statistical Area; (2) Includes biological, adopted, and stepchildren of the householder
Source: U.S. Census Bureau, 2020 Census

Gender

Area	Males	Females	Males per 100 Females
City	58,643	62,752	93.5
MSA[1]	111,433	114,896	97.0
U.S.	162,685,811	168,763,470	96.4

Note: (1) Figures cover the Rochester, MN Metropolitan Statistical Area
Source: U.S. Census Bureau, 2020 Census

Marital Status

Area	Never Married	Now Married[2]	Separated	Widowed	Divorced
City	33.3	51.7	1.2	4.7	9.2
MSA[1]	29.0	56.0	0.9	4.7	9.3
U.S.	33.8	48.0	1.8	5.6	10.8

Note: Figures are percentages and cover the population 15 years of age and older; (1) Figures cover the Rochester, MN Metropolitan Statistical Area; (2) Excludes separated
Source: U.S. Census Bureau, 2017-2021 American Community Survey 5-Year Estimates

Religious Groups by Family

Area	Catholic	Baptist	Methodist	LDS[2]	Pentecostal	Lutheran	Islam	Adventist	Other
MSA[1]	15.6	0.4	2.8	1.5	1.9	19.3	1.0	0.7	10.1
U.S.	18.7	7.3	3.0	2.0	1.8	1.7	1.3	1.3	11.6

Note: Figures are the number of adherents as a percentage of the total population and cover the eight largest religious groups in the U.S; (1) Figures cover the Rochester, MN Metropolitan Statistical Area; (2) Church of Jesus Christ of Latter-day Saints
Sources: 2020 U.S. Religion Census, Association of Statisticians of American Religious Bodies; The Association of Religion Data Archives (ARDA)

Religious Groups by Tradition

Area	Catholic	Evangelical Protestant	Mainline Protestant	Black Protestant	Islam	Judaism	Hinduism	Orthodox	Buddhism
MSA[1]	15.6	15.0	19.1	n/a	1.0	0.1	0.1	0.2	0.2
U.S.	18.7	16.5	5.2	2.3	1.3	0.6	0.4	0.4	0.3

Note: Figures are the number of adherents as a percentage of the total population; (1) Figures cover the Rochester, MN Metropolitan Statistical Area
Sources: 2020 U.S. Religion Census, Association of Statisticians of American Religious Bodies; The Association of Religion Data Archives (ARDA)

ECONOMY

Gross Metropolitan Product

Area	2020	2021	2022	2023	Rank[2]
MSA[1]	14.2	15.8	17.1	18.1	178

Note: Figures are in billions of dollars; (1) Figures cover the Rochester, MN Metropolitan Statistical Area; (2) Rank is based on 2021 data and ranges from 1 to 381
Source: U.S. Conference of Mayors, U.S. Metro Economies: U.S. Metros Compared to Global and State Economies, June 2022

Economic Growth

Area	2018-20 (%)	2021 (%)	2022 (%)	2023 (%)	Rank[2]
MSA[1]	-0.9	6.6	2.9	2.5	209
U.S.	-0.6	5.7	3.1	2.9	–

Note: Figures are real gross metropolitan product (GMP) growth rates and represent average annual percent change; (1) Figures cover the Rochester, MN Metropolitan Statistical Area; (2) Rank is based on 2020 2-year average annual percent change and ranges from 1 to 381
Source: U.S. Conference of Mayors, U.S. Metro Economies: U.S. Metros Compared to Global and State Economies, June 2022

Metropolitan Area Exports

Area	2016	2017	2018	2019	2020	2021	Rank[2]
MSA[1]	398.0	495.3	537.6	390.1	194.0	224.9	292

Note: Figures are in millions of dollars; (1) Figures cover the Rochester, MN Metropolitan Statistical Area; (2) Rank is based on 2021 data and ranges from 1 to 388
Source: U.S. Department of Commerce, International Trade Administration, Office of Trade and Economic Analysis, Industry and Analysis, Exports by Metropolitan Area, data extracted March 16, 2023

Building Permits

Area	Single-Family			Multi-Family			Total		
	2021	2022	Pct. Chg.	2021	2022	Pct. Chg.	2021	2022	Pct. Chg.
City	251	234	-6.8	374	847	126.5	625	1,081	73.0
MSA[1]	721	641	-11.1	414	1,080	160.9	1,135	1,721	51.6
U.S.	1,115,400	975,600	-12.5	621,600	689,500	10.9	1,737,000	1,665,100	-4.1

Note: (1) Figures cover the Rochester, MN Metropolitan Statistical Area; Figures represent new, privately-owned housing units authorized (unadjusted data); All permit data are based on estimates with imputation
Source: U.S. Census Bureau, Manufacturing, Mining, and Construction Statistics, Building Permits, 2021, 2022

Bankruptcy Filings

Area	Business Filings			Nonbusiness Filings		
	2021	2022	% Chg.	2021	2022	% Chg.
Olmsted County	0	1	n/a	90	119	32.2
U.S.	14,347	13,481	-6.0	399,269	374,240	-6.3

Note: Business filings include Chapter 7, Chapter 9, Chapter 11, Chapter 12, Chapter 13, Chapter 15, and Section 304; Nonbusiness filings include Chapter 7, Chapter 11, and Chapter 13
Source: Administrative Office of the U.S. Courts, Business and Nonbusiness Bankruptcy, County Cases Commenced by Chapter of the Bankruptcy Code, During the 12-Month Period Ending December 31, 2021 and Business and Nonbusiness Bankruptcy, County Cases Commenced by Chapter of the Bankruptcy Code, During the 12-Month Period Ending December 31, 2022

Housing Vacancy Rates

Area	Gross Vacancy Rate[2] (%)			Year-Round Vacancy Rate[3] (%)			Rental Vacancy Rate[4] (%)			Homeowner Vacancy Rate[5] (%)		
	2020	2021	2022	2020	2021	2022	2020	2021	2022	2020	2021	2022
MSA[1]	n/a	n/a	n/a	n/a	n/a	n/a	n/a	n/a	n/a	n/a	n/a	n/a
U.S.	10.6	10.8	10.5	8.2	8.4	8.2	6.3	6.1	5.8	1.0	0.9	0.8

Note: (1) Figures cover the Rochester, MN Metropolitan Statistical Area; (2) The percentage of the total housing inventory that is vacant; (3) The percentage of the housing inventory (excluding seasonal units) that is year-round vacant; (4) The percentage of rental inventory that is vacant for rent; (5) The percentage of homeowner inventory that is vacant for sale; n/a not available
Source: U.S. Census Bureau, Housing Vacancies and Homeownership Annual Statistics: 2020, 2021, 2022

INCOME

Income

Area	Per Capita ($)	Median Household ($)	Average Household ($)
City	43,827	79,159	106,381
MSA[1]	42,841	80,865	106,479
U.S.	37,638	69,021	97,196

Note: (1) Figures cover the Rochester, MN Metropolitan Statistical Area
Source: U.S. Census Bureau, 2017-2021 American Community Survey 5-Year Estimates

Household Income Distribution

Area	Percent of Households Earning							
	Under $15,000	$15,000 -$24,999	$25,000 -$34,999	$35,000 -$49,999	$50,000 -$74,999	$75,000 -$99,999	$100,000 -$149,999	$150,000 and up
City	6.9	6.3	5.8	10.4	18.0	13.9	18.8	19.9
MSA[1]	6.2	6.0	6.4	10.1	17.8	14.0	20.1	19.5
U.S.	9.4	7.8	8.2	11.4	16.8	12.8	16.3	17.3

Note: (1) Figures cover the Rochester, MN Metropolitan Statistical Area
Source: U.S. Census Bureau, 2017-2021 American Community Survey 5-Year Estimates

Poverty Rate

Area	All Ages	Under 18 Years Old	18 to 64 Years Old	65 Years and Over
City	8.7	9.6	8.9	6.4
MSA[1]	7.4	8.6	7.4	6.0
U.S.	12.6	17.0	11.8	9.6

Note: Figures are percentage of people whose income during the past 12 months was below the poverty level;
(1) Figures cover the Rochester, MN Metropolitan Statistical Area
Source: U.S. Census Bureau, 2017-2021 American Community Survey 5-Year Estimates

EMPLOYMENT

Labor Force and Employment

Area	Civilian Labor Force			Workers Employed		
	Dec. 2021	Dec. 2022	% Chg.	Dec. 2021	Dec. 2022	% Chg.
City	67,368	68,064	1.0	65,967	66,601	1.0
MSA[1]	126,103	127,371	1.0	123,345	124,243	0.7
U.S.	161,696,000	164,224,000	1.6	155,732,000	158,872,000	2.0

Note: Data is not seasonally adjusted and covers workers 16 years of age and older; (1) Figures cover the Rochester, MN Metropolitan Statistical Area
Source: Bureau of Labor Statistics, Local Area Unemployment Statistics

Unemployment Rate

Area	2022											
	Jan.	Feb.	Mar.	Apr.	May	Jun.	Jul.	Aug.	Sep.	Oct.	Nov.	Dec.
City	2.6	2.0	2.1	1.2	1.3	1.9	1.7	1.8	1.6	1.5	1.6	2.1
MSA[1]	3.0	2.3	2.4	1.3	1.3	1.9	1.7	1.8	1.5	1.4	1.6	2.5
U.S.	4.4	4.1	3.8	3.3	3.4	3.8	3.8	3.8	3.3	3.4	3.4	3.3

Note: Data is not seasonally adjusted and covers workers 16 years of age and older; (1) Figures cover the Rochester, MN Metropolitan Statistical Area
Source: Bureau of Labor Statistics, Local Area Unemployment Statistics

Average Wages

Occupation	$/Hr.	Occupation	$/Hr.
Accountants and Auditors	39.00	Maintenance and Repair Workers	23.54
Automotive Mechanics	23.13	Marketing Managers	62.16
Bookkeepers	22.86	Network and Computer Systems Admin.	48.04
Carpenters	28.86	Nurses, Licensed Practical	25.78
Cashiers	14.39	Nurses, Registered	43.30
Computer Programmers	43.06	Nursing Assistants	19.09
Computer Systems Analysts	50.23	Office Clerks, General	21.24
Computer User Support Specialists	31.25	Physical Therapists	41.61
Construction Laborers	25.20	Physicians	143.61
Cooks, Restaurant	16.86	Plumbers, Pipefitters and Steamfitters	37.05
Customer Service Representatives	20.61	Police and Sheriff's Patrol Officers	34.21
Dentists	83.58	Postal Service Mail Carriers	27.15
Electricians	33.41	Real Estate Sales Agents	n/a
Engineers, Electrical	51.22	Retail Salespersons	16.90
Fast Food and Counter Workers	14.09	Sales Representatives, Technical/Scientific	35.30
Financial Managers	65.15	Secretaries, Exc. Legal/Medical/Executive	21.71
First-Line Supervisors of Office Workers	31.71	Security Guards	17.79
General and Operations Managers	51.56	Surgeons	156.35
Hairdressers/Cosmetologists	19.51	Teacher Assistants, Exc. Postsecondary*	17.00
Home Health and Personal Care Aides	15.54	Teachers, Secondary School, Exc. Sp. Ed.*	31.98
Janitors and Cleaners	18.28	Telemarketers	n/a
Landscaping/Groundskeeping Workers	18.74	Truck Drivers, Heavy/Tractor-Trailer	26.90
Lawyers	57.71	Truck Drivers, Light/Delivery Services	21.79
Maids and Housekeeping Cleaners	15.90	Waiters and Waitresses	12.51

Note: Wage data covers the Rochester, MN Metropolitan Statistical Area; (*) Hourly wages were calculated from annual wage data based on a 40 hour work week; n/a not available.
Source: Bureau of Labor Statistics, Metro Area Occupational Employment & Wage Estimates, May 2022

Employment by Industry

Sector	MSA[1]		U.S.
	Number of Employees	Percent of Total	Percent of Total
Construction, Mining, and Logging	4,900	4.0	5.4
Private Education and Health Services	53,300	43.3	16.1
Financial Activities	2,900	2.4	5.9
Government	12,900	10.5	14.5
Information	1,100	0.9	2.0
Leisure and Hospitality	10,500	8.5	10.3
Manufacturing	9,700	7.9	8.4
Other Services	3,700	3.0	3.7
Professional and Business Services	6,600	5.4	14.7
Retail Trade	12,200	9.9	10.2
Transportation, Warehousing, and Utilities	2,600	2.1	4.9
Wholesale Trade	2,600	2.1	3.9

Note: Figures are non-farm employment as of December 2022. Figures are not seasonally adjusted and include workers 16 years of age and older; (1) Figures cover the Rochester, MN Metropolitan Statistical Area
Source: Bureau of Labor Statistics, Current Employment Statistics, Employment, Hours, and Earnings

Employment by Occupation

Occupation Classification	City (%)	MSA[1] (%)	U.S. (%)
Management, Business, Science, and Arts	54.0	48.8	40.3
Natural Resources, Construction, and Maintenance	5.0	7.7	8.7
Production, Transportation, and Material Moving	8.4	10.7	13.1
Sales and Office	16.4	17.3	20.9
Service	16.3	15.5	17.0

Note: Figures cover employed civilians 16 years of age and older; (1) Figures cover the Rochester, MN Metropolitan Statistical Area
Source: U.S. Census Bureau, 2017-2021 American Community Survey 5-Year Estimates

Occupations with Greatest Projected Employment Growth: 2022 – 2024

Occupation[1]	2022 Employment	2024 Projected Employment	Numeric Employment Change	Percent Employment Change
Home Health and Personal Care Aides	116,020	120,600	4,580	3.9
Cooks, Restaurant	23,930	25,800	1,870	7.8
Software Developers and Software Quality Assurance Analysts and Testers	48,010	49,650	1,640	3.4
General and Operations Managers	68,530	70,150	1,620	2.4
Fast Food and Counter Workers	63,160	64,720	1,560	2.5
Retail Salespersons	76,640	77,760	1,120	1.5
Stockers and Order Fillers	38,470	39,540	1,070	2.8
Registered Nurses	72,140	73,200	1,060	1.5
Waiters and Waitresses	36,730	37,740	1,010	2.7
Market Research Analysts and Marketing Specialists	22,780	23,760	980	4.3

Note: Projections cover Minnesota; (1) Sorted by numeric employment change
Source: www.projectionscentral.com, State Occupational Projections, 2022–2024 Short-Term Projections

Fastest-Growing Occupations: 2022 – 2024

Occupation[1]	2022 Employment	2024 Projected Employment	Numeric Employment Change	Percent Employment Change
Nurse Practitioners	4,810	5,250	440	9.1
Flight Attendants	2,780	3,020	240	8.6
Cooks, Restaurant	23,930	25,800	1,870	7.8
Statisticians	970	1,040	70	7.2
Dental Laboratory Technicians	690	740	50	7.2
Logisticians	2,720	2,910	190	7.0
Computer Numerically Controlled Tool Programmers	1,080	1,150	70	6.5
Physician Assistants	3,280	3,490	210	6.4
Medical and Health Services Managers	9,790	10,400	610	6.2
Operations Research Analysts	2,420	2,560	140	5.8

Note: Projections cover Minnesota; (1) Sorted by percent employment change and excludes occupations with numeric employment change less than 50
Source: www.projectionscentral.com, State Occupational Projections, 2022–2024 Short-Term Projections

CITY FINANCES

City Government Finances

Component	2020 ($000)	2020 ($ per capita)
Total Revenues	583,681	4,908
Total Expenditures	522,116	4,390
Debt Outstanding	2,867,930	24,113
Cash and Securities[1]	2,811,165	23,636

Note: (1) Cash and security holdings of a government at the close of its fiscal year, including those of its dependent agencies, utilities, and liquor stores.
Source: U.S. Census Bureau, State & Local Government Finances 2020

City Government Revenue by Source

Source	2020 ($000)	2020 ($ per capita)	2020 (%)
General Revenue			
From Federal Government	5,689	48	1.0
From State Government	39,958	336	6.8
From Local Governments	4,700	40	0.8
Taxes			
Property	73,978	622	12.7
Sales and Gross Receipts	31,572	265	5.4
Personal Income	0	0	0.0
Corporate Income	0	0	0.0
Motor Vehicle License	0	0	0.0
Other Taxes	4,423	37	0.8
Current Charges	97,504	820	16.7
Liquor Store	0	0	0.0
Utility	211,934	1,782	36.3

Source: U.S. Census Bureau, State & Local Government Finances 2020

City Government Expenditures by Function

Function	2020 ($000)	2020 ($ per capita)	2020 (%)
General Direct Expenditures			
Air Transportation	6,304	53	1.2
Corrections	0	0	0.0
Education	0	0	0.0
Employment Security Administration	0	0	0.0
Financial Administration	3,561	29	0.7
Fire Protection	18,602	156	3.6
General Public Buildings	0	0	0.0
Governmental Administration, Other	840	7	0.2
Health	0	0	0.0
Highways	36,152	304	6.9
Hospitals	0	0	0.0
Housing and Community Development	561	4	0.1
Interest on General Debt	116,490	979	22.3
Judicial and Legal	0	0	0.0
Libraries	8,958	75	1.7
Parking	4,238	35	0.8
Parks and Recreation	25,671	215	4.9
Police Protection	38,123	320	7.3
Public Welfare	0	0	0.0
Sewerage	18,055	151	3.5
Solid Waste Management	0	0	0.0
Veterans' Services	0	0	0.0
Liquor Store	0	0	0.0
Utility	192,288	1,616	36.8

Source: U.S. Census Bureau, State & Local Government Finances 2020

TAXES

State Corporate Income Tax Rates

State	Tax Rate (%)	Income Brackets ($)	Num. of Brackets	Financial Institution Tax Rate (%)[a]	Federal Income Tax Ded.
Minnesota	9.8 (l)	Flat rate	1	9.8 (l)	No

Note: Tax rates as of January 1, 2023; (a) Rates listed are the corporate income tax rate applied to financial institutions or excise taxes based on income. Some states have other taxes based upon the value of deposits or shares; (l) In addition, Minnesota levies a 5.8% tentative minimum tax on Alternative Minimum Taxable Income. Minnesota also imposes a surtax ranging up to $11,570.
Source: Federation of Tax Administrators, State Corporate Income Tax Rates, January 1, 2023

State Individual Income Tax Rates

State	Tax Rate (%)	Income Brackets ($)	Personal Exemptions ($)			Standard Ded. ($)	
			Single	Married	Depend.	Single	Married
Minnesota (a)	5.35 - 9.85	30,070 - 183,341 (n)	(d)	(d)	4,450	13,850	27,700 (d)

Note: Tax rates as of January 1, 2023; Local- and county-level taxes are not included; Federal income tax is not deductible on state income tax returns; (a) 16 states have statutory provision for automatically adjusting to the rate of inflation the dollar values of the income tax brackets, standard deductions, and/or personal exemptions. Oregon does not index the income brackets for $125,000 and over; (d) These states use the personal exemption/standard deduction amounts provided in the federal Internal Revenue Code; (n) The income brackets reported for Minnesota are for single individuals. For married couples filing jointly, the same tax rates apply to income brackets ranging from $43,950 to $304,971.
Source: Federation of Tax Administrators, State Individual Income Tax Rates, January 1, 2023

Various State Sales and Excise Tax Rates

State	State Sales Tax (%)	Gasoline[1] ($/gal.)	Cigarette[2] ($/pack)	Spirits[3] ($/gal.)	Wine[4] ($/gal.)	Beer[5] ($/gal.)	Recreational Marijuana (%)
Minnesota	6.875	0.306	3.732	8.70	1.24	0.47	Not legal

Note: All tax rates as of January 1, 2023; (1) The American Petroleum Institute has developed a methodology for determining the average tax rate on a gallon of fuel. Rates may include any of the following: excise taxes, environmental fees, storage tank fees, other fees or taxes, general sales tax, and local taxes; (2) The federal excise tax of $1.0066 per pack and local taxes are not included; (3) Rates are those applicable to off-premise sales of 40% alcohol by volume (a.b.v.) distilled spirits in 750ml containers. Local excise taxes are excluded; (4) Rates are those applicable to off-premise sales of 11% a.b.v. non-carbonated wine in 750ml containers; (5) Rates are those applicable to off-premise sales of 4.7% a.b.v. beer in 12 ounce containers.
Source: Tax Foundation, 2023 Facts & Figures: How Does Your State Compare?

State Business Tax Climate Index Rankings

State	Overall Rank	Corporate Tax Rank	Individual Income Tax Rank	Sales Tax Rank	Property Tax Rank	Unemployment Insurance Tax Rank
Minnesota	45	43	43	29	31	34

Note: The index is a measure of how each state's tax laws affect economic performance. The lower the rank, the more favorable a state's tax system is for business. States without a given tax are given a ranking of 1. The scores/rankings for the District of Columbia do not affect other states. The 2023 index represents the tax climate as of July 1, 2022.
Source: Tax Foundation, State Business Tax Climate Index 2023

TRANSPORTATION

Means of Transportation to Work

Area	Car/Truck/Van		Public Transportation			Bicycle	Walked	Other Means	Worked at Home
	Drove Alone	Car-pooled	Bus	Subway	Railroad				
City	67.8	11.9	5.4	0.0	0.0	0.8	4.2	1.2	8.8
MSA[1]	71.2	11.0	3.4	0.0	0.0	0.5	3.5	1.0	9.4
U.S.	73.2	8.6	2.0	1.6	0.5	0.5	2.5	1.5	9.7

Note: Figures are percentages and cover workers 16 years of age and older; (1) Figures cover the Rochester, MN Metropolitan Statistical Area
Source: U.S. Census Bureau, 2017-2021 American Community Survey 5-Year Estimates

Travel Time to Work

Area	Less Than 10 Minutes	10 to 19 Minutes	20 to 29 Minutes	30 to 44 Minutes	45 to 59 Minutes	60 to 89 Minutes	90 Minutes or More
City	17.7	55.5	14.1	6.5	2.8	2.2	1.2
MSA[1]	18.1	41.7	18.6	12.6	4.3	2.9	1.9
U.S.	12.4	28.5	21.0	20.9	8.2	6.2	2.9

Note: Note: Figures are percentages and include workers 16 years old and over; (1) Figures cover the Rochester, MN Metropolitan Statistical Area
Source: U.S. Census Bureau, 2017-2021 American Community Survey 5-Year Estimates

Key Congestion Measures

Measure	1990	2000	2010	2015	2020
Annual Hours of Delay, Total (000)	n/a	n/a	n/a	2,253	1,692
Annual Hours of Delay, Per Auto Commuter	n/a	n/a	n/a	19	14
Annual Congestion Cost, Per Auto Commuter ($)	n/a	n/a	n/a	386	313

Note: n/a not available
Source: Texas A&M Transportation Institute, 2021 Urban Mobility Report

Freeway Travel Time Index

Measure	1985	1990	1995	2000	2005	2010	2015	2020
Urban Area Index[1]	n/a	n/a	n/a	n/a	n/a	n/a	1.10	1.07
Urban Area Rank[1,2]	n/a	n/a	n/a	n/a	n/a	n/a	n/a	n/a

Note: Freeway Travel Time Index—the ratio of travel time in the peak period to the travel time at free-flow conditions. For example, a value of 1.30 indicates a 20-minute free-flow trip takes 26 minutes in the peak (20 minutes x 1.30 = 26 minutes); (1) Covers the Rochester MN urban area; (2) Rank is based on 101 larger urban areas (#1 = highest travel time index); n/a not available
Source: Texas A&M Transportation Institute, 2021 Urban Mobility Report

Public Transportation

Agency Name / Mode of Transportation	Vehicles Operated in Maximum Service[1]	Annual Unlinked Passenger Trips[2] (in thous.)	Annual Passenger Miles[3] (in thous.)
City of Rochester Public Transportation			
Bus (purchased transportation)	42	743.8	2,729.9
Demand Response (purchased transportation)	5	17.5	97.0
Demand Response - Taxi	4	5.8	32.1

Note: (1) Number of revenue vehicles operated by the given mode and type of service to meet the annual maximum service requirement. This is the revenue vehicle count during the peak season of the year; on the week and day that maximum service is provided. Vehicles operated in maximum service (VOMS) exclude atypical days and one-time special events; (2) Number of passengers who boarded public transportation vehicles. Passengers are counted each time they board a vehicle no matter how many vehicles they use to travel from their origin to their destination. (3) Sum of the distances ridden by all passengers during the entire fiscal year.
Source: Federal Transit Administration, National Transit Database, 2021

Air Transportation

Airport Name and Code / Type of Service	Passenger Airlines[1]	Passenger Enplanements	Freight Carriers[2]	Freight (lbs)
Rochester International Airport (RST)				
Domestic service (U.S. carriers - 2022)	8	84,415	4	10,260,793
International service (U.S. carriers - 2021)	0	0	0	0

Note: (1) Includes all U.S.-based major, minor and commuter airlines that carried at least one passenger during the year; (2) Includes all U.S.-based airlines and freight carriers that transported at least one pound of freight during the year.
Source: Bureau of Transportation Statistics, The Intermodal Transportation Database, Air Carriers: T-100 Domestic Market (U.S. Carriers), 2022; Bureau of Transportation Statistics, The Intermodal Transportation Database, Air Carriers: T-100 International Market (U.S. Carriers), 2021

BUSINESSES

Major Business Headquarters

Company Name	Industry	Rankings	
		Fortune[1]	Forbes[2]
No companies listed	-	-	-

Note: (1) Companies that produce a 10-K are ranked 1 to 500 based on 2021 revenue; (2) All private companies with at least $2 billion in annual revenue through the end of their most current fiscal year are ranked 1 to 246; companies listed are headquartered in the city; dashes indicate no ranking
Source: Fortune, "Fortune 500," 2022; Forbes, "America's Largest Private Companies," 2022

Living Environment

COST OF LIVING

Cost of Living Index

Composite Index	Groceries	Housing	Utilities	Trans-portation	Health Care	Misc. Goods/Services
n/a	n/a	n/a	n/a	n/a	n/a	n/a

Note: The Cost of Living Index measures regional differences in the cost of consumer goods and services, excluding taxes and non-consumer expenditures, for professional and managerial households in the top income quintile. It is based on more than 50,000 prices covering almost 60 different items for which prices are collected three times a year by chambers of commerce, economic development organizations or university applied economic centers in each participating urban area. The numbers shown should be read as a percentage above or below the national average of 100. For example, a value of 115.4 in the groceries column indicates that grocery prices are 15.4% higher than the national average. Small differences in the index numbers should not be interpreted as significant; n/a not available.
Source: The Council for Community and Economic Research, Cost of Living Index, 2022

Grocery Prices

Area[1]	T-Bone Steak ($/pound)	Frying Chicken ($/pound)	Whole Milk ($/half gal.)	Eggs ($/dozen)	Orange Juice ($/64 oz.)	Coffee ($/11.5 oz.)
City[2]	n/a	n/a	n/a	n/a	n/a	n/a
Avg.	13.81	1.59	2.43	2.25	3.85	4.95
Min.	10.17	0.90	1.51	1.30	2.90	3.46
Max.	19.35	3.30	4.32	4.32	5.31	8.59

*Note: (1) Values for the local area are compared with the average, minimum and maximum values for all 286 areas in the Cost of Living Index; (2) Figures cover the Rochester MN urban area; n/a not available; **T-Bone Steak** (price per pound); **Frying Chicken** (price per pound, whole fryer); **Whole Milk** (half gallon carton); **Eggs** (price per dozen, Grade A, large); **Orange Juice** (64 oz. Tropicana or Florida Natural); **Coffee** (11.5 oz. can, vacuum-packed, Maxwell House, Hills Bros, or Folgers).*
Source: The Council for Community and Economic Research, Cost of Living Index, 2022

Housing and Utility Costs

Area[1]	New Home Price ($)	Apartment Rent ($/month)	All Electric ($/month)	Part Electric ($/month)	Other Energy ($/month)	Telephone ($/month)
City[2]	n/a	n/a	n/a	n/a	n/a	n/a
Avg.	450,913	1,371	176.41	99.93	76.96	190.22
Min.	229,283	546	100.84	31.56	27.15	174.27
Max.	2,434,977	4,569	356.86	249.59	272.24	208.31

*Note: (1) Values for the local area are compared with the average, minimum and maximum values for all 286 areas in the Cost of Living Index; (2) Figures cover the Rochester MN urban area; n/a not available; **New Home Price** (2,400 sf living area, 8,000 sf lot, in urban area with full utilities); **Apartment Rent** (950 sf 2 bedroom/1.5 or 2 bath, unfurnished, excluding all utilities except water); **All Electric** (average monthly cost for an all-electric home); **Part Electric** (average monthly cost for a part-electric home); **Other Energy** (average monthly cost for natural gas, fuel oil, coal, wood, and any other forms of energy except electricity); **Telephone** (price includes the base monthly rate plus taxes and fees for three lines of mobile phone service).*
Source: The Council for Community and Economic Research, Cost of Living Index, 2022

Health Care, Transportation, and Other Costs

Area[1]	Doctor ($/visit)	Dentist ($/visit)	Optometrist ($/visit)	Gasoline ($/gallon)	Beauty Salon ($/visit)	Men's Shirt ($)
City[2]	n/a	n/a	n/a	n/a	n/a	n/a
Avg.	124.91	107.77	117.66	3.86	43.31	34.21
Min.	36.61	58.25	51.79	2.90	22.18	13.05
Max.	250.21	162.58	371.96	5.54	85.61	63.54

*Note: (1) Values for the local area are compared with the average, minimum and maximum values for all 286 areas in the Cost of Living Index; (2) Figures cover the Rochester MN urban area; n/a not available; **Doctor** (general practitioners routine exam of an established patient); **Dentist** (adult teeth cleaning and periodic oral examination); **Optometrist** (full vision eye exam for established adult patient); **Gasoline** (one gallon regular unleaded, national brand, including all taxes, cash price at self-service pump if available); **Beauty Salon** (woman's shampoo, trim, and blow-dry); **Men's Shirt** (cotton/polyester dress shirt, pinpoint weave, long sleeves).*
Source: The Council for Community and Economic Research, Cost of Living Index, 2022

HOUSING

Homeownership Rate

Area	2015 (%)	2016 (%)	2017 (%)	2018 (%)	2019 (%)	2020 (%)	2021 (%)	2022 (%)
MSA[1]	n/a	n/a	n/a	n/a	n/a	n/a	n/a	n/a
U.S.	63.7	63.4	63.9	64.4	64.6	66.6	65.5	65.8

Note: (1) Figures cover the Rochester, MN Metropolitan Statistical Area; n/a not available
Source: U.S. Census Bureau, Housing Vacancies and Homeownership Annual Statistics: 2015-2022

House Price Index (HPI)

Area	National Ranking[2]	Quarterly Change (%)	One-Year Change (%)	Five-Year Change (%)	Since 1991Q1 (%)
MSA[1]	234	-3.55	6.25	42.75	234.69
U.S.[3]	–	0.34	8.41	58.44	289.08

Note: The HPI is a weighted repeat sales index. It measures average price changes in repeat sales or refinancings on the same properties. This information is obtained by reviewing repeat mortgage transactions on single-family properties whose mortgages have been purchased or securitized by Fannie Mae or Freddie Mac since January 1975; (1) Figures cover the Rochester, MN Metropolitan Statistical Area; (2) Rankings are based on annual percentage change for all metro areas containing at least 15,000 transactions over the last 10 years and ranges from 1 to 257; (3) figures based on a weighted average of Census Division estimates using a seasonally adjusted, purchase-only index; all figures are for the period ending December 31, 2022
Source: Federal Housing Finance Agency, Change in FHFA Metropolitan Area House Price Indexes, 2022Q4

Median Single-Family Home Prices

Area	2020	2021	2022p	Percent Change 2021 to 2022
MSA[1]	n/a	n/a	n/a	n/a
U.S. Average	300.2	357.1	392.6	9.9

Note: Figures are median sales prices of existing single-family homes in thousands of dollars; (p) preliminary; n/a not available; (1) Figures cover the Rochester, MN Metropolitan Statistical Area
Source: National Association of Realtors, Median Sales Price of Existing Single-Family Homes for Metropolitan Areas, 4th Quarter 2022

Qualifying Income Based on Median Sales Price of Existing Single-Family Homes

Area	With 5% Down ($)	With 10% Down ($)	With 20% Down ($)
MSA[1]	n/a	n/a	n/a
U.S. Average	112,234	106,237	94,513

Note: Figures are preliminary; Qualifying income is based on a mortgage rate of 6.77%. Monthly principal and interest payment is limited to 25% of income; n/a not available; (1) Figures cover the Rochester, MN Metropolitan Statistical Area
Source: National Association of Realtors, Qualifying Income Based on Median Sales Price of Existing Single-Family Homes for Metropolitan Areas, 4th Quarter 2022

Home Value

Area	Under $100,000	$100,000 -$199,999	$200,000 -$299,999	$300,000 -$399,999	$400,000 -$499,999	$500,000 -$999,999	$1,000,000 or more	Median ($)
City	5.8	30.7	30.8	16.9	8.6	6.8	0.5	236,400
MSA[1]	9.2	29.8	26.8	16.1	8.6	8.3	1.2	234,700
U.S.	16.2	24.2	20.1	13.6	8.3	13.6	4.1	244,900

Note: Figures are percentages except for median and cover owner-occupied housing units; (1) Figures cover the Rochester, MN Metropolitan Statistical Area
Source: U.S. Census Bureau, 2017-2021 American Community Survey 5-Year Estimates

Year Housing Structure Built

Area	2020 or Later	2010 -2019	2000 -2009	1990 -1999	1980 -1989	1970 -1979	1960 -1969	1950 -1959	1940 -1949	Before 1940	Median Year
City	0.4	12.3	18.0	14.4	12.0	12.5	10.0	8.8	3.4	8.1	1986
MSA[1]	0.3	9.6	17.9	14.4	10.8	13.2	9.0	7.6	3.4	13.8	1983
U.S.	0.2	7.3	13.6	13.6	13.2	14.8	10.3	10.0	4.7	12.2	1979

Note: Figures are percentages except for Median Year; Note: (1) Figures cover the Rochester, MN Metropolitan Statistical Area
Source: U.S. Census Bureau, 2017-2021 American Community Survey 5-Year Estimates

Gross Monthly Rent

Area	Under $500	$500 -$999	$1,000 -$1,499	$1,500 -$1,999	$2,000 -$2,499	$2,500 -$2,999	$3,000 and up	Median ($)
City	7.8	34.8	32.6	17.7	3.4	1.3	2.4	1,120
MSA[1]	10.2	39.0	30.7	14.7	2.8	1.0	1.8	1,013
U.S.	8.1	30.5	30.8	16.8	7.3	3.1	3.5	1,163

Note: Figures are percentages except for median; Gross rent is the contract rent plus the estimated average monthly cost of utilities (electricity, gas, and water and sewer) and fuels (oil, coal, kerosene, wood, etc.) if these are paid by the renter (or paid for the renter by someone else); (1) Figures cover the Rochester, MN Metropolitan Statistical Area
Source: U.S. Census Bureau, 2017-2021 American Community Survey 5-Year Estimates

HEALTH

Health Risk Factors

Category	MSA[1] (%)	U.S. (%)
Adults aged 18–64 who have any kind of health care coverage	n/a	90.9
Adults who reported being in good or better health	n/a	85.2
Adults who have been told they have high blood cholesterol	n/a	35.7
Adults who have been told they have high blood pressure	n/a	32.4
Adults who are current smokers	n/a	14.4
Adults who currently use e-cigarettes	n/a	6.7
Adults who currently use chewing tobacco, snuff, or snus	n/a	3.5
Adults who are heavy drinkers[2]	n/a	6.3
Adults who are binge drinkers[3]	n/a	15.4
Adults who are overweight (BMI 25.0 - 29.9)	n/a	34.4
Adults who are obese (BMI 30.0 - 99.8)	n/a	33.9
Adults who participated in any physical activities in the past month	n/a	76.3

Note: (1) Figures for the Rochester, MN Metropolitan Statistical Area were not available.
(2) Heavy drinkers are classified as adult men having more than 14 drinks per week and adult women having more than 7 drinks per week; (3) Binge drinkers are classified as males having five or more drinks on one occasion or females having four or more drinks on one occasion
Source: Centers for Disease Control and Prevention, Behaviorial Risk Factor Surveillance System, SMART: Selected Metropolitan Area Risk Trends, 2021

Acute and Chronic Health Conditions

Category	MSA[1] (%)	U.S. (%)
Adults who have ever been told they had a heart attack	n/a	4.0
Adults who have ever been told they have angina or coronary heart disease	n/a	3.8
Adults who have ever been told they had a stroke	n/a	3.0
Adults who have ever been told they have asthma	n/a	14.9
Adults who have ever been told they have arthritis	n/a	25.8
Adults who have ever been told they have diabetes[2]	n/a	10.9
Adults who have ever been told they had skin cancer	n/a	6.6
Adults who have ever been told they had any other types of cancer	n/a	7.5
Adults who have ever been told they have COPD	n/a	6.1
Adults who have ever been told they have kidney disease	n/a	3.0
Adults who have ever been told they have a form of depression	n/a	20.5

Note: (1) Figures for the Rochester, MN Metropolitan Statistical Area were not available.
(2) Figures do not include pregnancy-related, borderline, or pre-diabetes
Source: Centers for Disease Control and Prevention, Behaviorial Risk Factor Surveillance System, SMART: Selected Metropolitan Area Risk Trends, 2021

Health Screening and Vaccination Rates

Category	MSA[1] (%)	U.S. (%)
Adults who have ever been tested for HIV	n/a	34.9
Adults who have had their blood cholesterol checked within the last five years	n/a	85.2
Adults aged 65+ who have had flu shot within the past year	n/a	68.6
Adults aged 65+ who have ever had a pneumonia vaccination	n/a	71.0

Note: (1) Figures for the Rochester, MN Metropolitan Statistical Area were not available.
Source: Centers for Disease Control and Prevention, Behaviorial Risk Factor Surveillance System, SMART: Selected Metropolitan Area Risk Trends, 2021

Disability Status

Category	MSA[1] (%)	U.S. (%)
Adults who reported being deaf	n/a	7.2
Are you blind or have serious difficulty seeing, even when wearing glasses?	n/a	4.8
Are you limited in any way in any of your usual activities due to arthritis?	n/a	11.1
Do you have difficulty doing errands alone?	n/a	7.0
Do you have difficulty dressing or bathing?	n/a	3.6
Do you have serious difficulty concentrating/remembering/making decisions?	n/a	12.1
Do you have serious difficulty walking or climbing stairs?	n/a	12.8

Note: (1) Figures for the Rochester, MN Metropolitan Statistical Area were not available.
Source: Centers for Disease Control and Prevention, Behaviorial Risk Factor Surveillance System, SMART: Selected Metropolitan Area Risk Trends, 2021

Mortality Rates for the Top 10 Causes of Death in the U.S.

ICD-10[a] Sub-Chapter	ICD-10[a] Code	Crude Mortality Rate[1] per 100,000 population	
		County[2]	U.S.
Malignant neoplasms	C00-C97	155.9	182.6
Ischaemic heart diseases	I20-I25	95.0	113.1
Other forms of heart disease	I30-I51	41.0	64.4
Other degenerative diseases of the nervous system	G30-G31	69.9	51.0
Cerebrovascular diseases	I60-I69	30.4	47.8
Other external causes of accidental injury	W00-X59	40.3	46.4
Chronic lower respiratory diseases	J40-J47	29.3	45.7
Organic, including symptomatic, mental disorders	F01-F09	52.2	35.9
Hypertensive diseases	I10-I15	37.2	35.0
Diabetes mellitus	E10-E14	10.8	29.6

Note: (a) ICD-10 = International Classification of Diseases 10th Revision; (1) Crude mortality rates are a three-year average covering 2019-2021; (2) Figures cover Olmsted County.
Source: Centers for Disease Control and Prevention, National Center for Health Statistics. National Vital Statistics System, Mortality 2018-2021 on CDC WONDER Online Database

Mortality Rates for Selected Causes of Death

ICD-10[a] Sub-Chapter	ICD-10[a] Code	Crude Mortality Rate[1] per 100,000 population	
		County[2]	U.S.
Assault	X85-Y09	Unreliable	7.0
Diseases of the liver	K70-K76	12.1	19.8
Human immunodeficiency virus (HIV) disease	B20-B24	Suppressed	1.5
Influenza and pneumonia	J09-J18	5.6	14.7
Intentional self-harm	X60-X84	12.5	14.3
Malnutrition	E40-E46	Suppressed	4.3
Obesity and other hyperalimentation	E65-E68	Suppressed	3.0
Renal failure	N17-N19	5.4	15.7
Transport accidents	V01-V99	8.3	13.6
Viral hepatitis	B15-B19	Suppressed	1.2

Note: (a) ICD-10 = International Classification of Diseases 10th Revision; (1) Crude mortality rates are a three-year average covering 2019-2021; (2) Figures cover Olmsted County; Data are suppressed when the data meet the criteria for confidentiality constraints; Crude mortality rates are flagged as unreliable when the rate would be calculated with a numerator of 20 or less.
Source: Centers for Disease Control and Prevention, National Center for Health Statistics. National Vital Statistics System, Mortality 2018-2021 on CDC WONDER Online Database

Health Insurance Coverage

Area	With Health Insurance	With Private Health Insurance	With Public Health Insurance	Without Health Insurance	Population Under Age 19 Without Health Insurance
City	96.2	79.1	30.9	3.8	2.0
MSA[1]	95.7	79.6	30.8	4.3	3.3
U.S.	91.2	67.8	35.4	8.8	5.3

Note: Figures are percentages that cover the civilian noninstitutionalized population; (1) Figures cover the Rochester, MN Metropolitan Statistical Area
Source: U.S. Census Bureau, 2017-2021 American Community Survey 5-Year Estimates

Number of Medical Professionals

Area	MDs[3]	DOs[3,4]	Dentists	Podiatrists	Chiropractors	Optometrists
County[1] (number)	4,027	75	205	11	72	37
County[1] (rate[2])	2,470.7	46.0	125.4	6.7	44.1	22.6
U.S. (rate[2])	289.3	23.5	72.5	6.2	28.7	17.4

Note: Data as of 2021 unless noted; (1) Data covers Olmsted County; (2) Rate per 100,000 population; (3) Data as of 2020 and includes all active, non-federal physicians; (4) Doctor of Osteopathic Medicine
Source: U.S. Department of Health and Human Services, Health Resources and Services Administration, Bureau of Health Professions, Area Resource File (ARF) 2021-2022

Best Hospitals

According to *U.S. News,* the Rochester, MN metro area is home to one of the best hospitals in the U.S.: **Mayo Clinic** (Honor Roll/14 adult specialties and 10 pediatric specialties). The hospital listed was nationally ranked in at least one of 15 adult or 10 pediatric specialties. The number of specialties shown cover the parent hospital. Only 164 U.S. hospitals performed well enough to be nationally ranked in one or more specialties. Twenty hospitals in the U.S. made the Honor Roll. The Best Hospitals Honor Roll takes both the national rankings and the procedure and condition ratings into account. Hospitals received points if they were nationally ranked in one of the 15 adult specialties—the higher they ranked, the more points they got—and how many ratings of "high performing" they earned in the 17 procedures and conditions. *U.S. News Online, "America's Best Hospitals 2022-23"*

According to *U.S. News,* the Rochester, MN metro area is home to one of the best children's hospitals in the U.S.: **Mayo Clinic Children's Center** (10 pediatric specialties). The hospital listed was highly ranked in at least one of 10 pediatric specialties. Eighty-six children's hospitals in the U.S. were nationally ranked in at least one specialty. Hospitals received points for being ranked in a specialty, and the 10 hospitals with the most points across the 10 specialties make up the Honor Roll. *U.S. News Online, "America's Best Children's Hospitals 2022-23"*

EDUCATION

Public School District Statistics

District Name	Schls	Pupils	Pupil/ Teacher Ratio	Minority Pupils[1] (%)	LEP/ELL[2] (%)	IEP[3] (%)
Rochester Public School District	47	17,617	21.0	45.4	10.4	18.1

Note: Table includes school districts with 2,000 or more students; (1) Percentage of students that are not non-Hispanic white; (2) Percentage of students that are Limited English Proficient or English Language Learners (2018-19); (3) Percentage of students that have an Individualized Education Program (2019-20). Source: U.S. Department of Education, National Center for Education Statistics, Common Core of Data, Local Education Agency (School District) Universe Survey: School Year 2021-2022

Highest Level of Education

Area	Less than H.S.	H.S. Diploma	Some College, No Deg.	Associate Degree	Bachelor's Degree	Master's Degree	Prof. School Degree	Doctorate Degree
City	5.6	18.6	15.8	11.3	26.6	13.1	5.2	3.6
MSA[1]	5.3	23.2	17.8	12.6	23.9	10.6	4.1	2.4
U.S.	11.1	26.5	20.0	8.7	20.6	9.3	2.2	1.5

Note: Figures cover persons age 25 and over; (1) Figures cover the Rochester, MN Metropolitan Statistical Area Source: U.S. Census Bureau, 2017-2021 American Community Survey 5-Year Estimates

Educational Attainment by Race

Area	High School Graduate or Higher (%)					Bachelor's Degree or Higher (%)				
	Total	White	Black	Asian	Hisp.[2]	Total	White	Black	Asian	Hisp.[2]
City	94.4	96.8	70.6	88.5	76.7	48.7	49.9	19.9	61.8	33.6
MSA[1]	94.7	96.1	71.8	88.1	77.4	41.0	41.1	19.5	59.6	31.3
U.S.	88.9	91.4	87.2	87.6	71.2	33.7	35.5	23.3	55.6	18.4

Note: Figures shown cover persons 25 years old and over; (1) Figures cover the Rochester, MN Metropolitan Statistical Area; (2) People of Hispanic origin can be of any race Source: U.S. Census Bureau, 2017-2021 American Community Survey 5-Year Estimates

School Enrollment by Grade and Control

Area	Preschool (%)		Kindergarten (%)		Grades 1 - 4 (%)		Grades 5 - 8 (%)		Grades 9 - 12 (%)	
	Public	Private	Public	Private	Public	Private	Public	Private	Public	Private
City	52.1	47.9	90.2	9.8	90.8	9.2	88.0	12.0	89.3	10.7
MSA[1]	63.8	36.2	91.4	8.6	90.6	9.4	89.8	10.2	91.2	8.8
U.S.	58.8	41.2	86.3	13.7	88.3	11.7	88.6	11.4	89.4	10.6

Note: Figures shown cover persons 3 years old and over; (1) Figures cover the Rochester, MN Metropolitan Statistical Area Source: U.S. Census Bureau, 2017-2021 American Community Survey 5-Year Estimates

Higher Education

Four-Year Colleges			Two-Year Colleges			Medical Schools[1]	Law Schools[2]	Voc/ Tech[3]
Public	Private Non-profit	Private For-profit	Public	Private Non-profit	Private For-profit			
1	1	0	1	0	0	1	0	1

Note: Figures cover institutions located within the Rochester, MN Metropolitan Statistical Area and include main campuses only; (1) includes schools accredited by the Liaison Committee on Medical Education and the American Osteopathic Association's Commission on Osteopathic College Accreditation; (2) includes ABA-accredited schools, schools with provisional ABA accreditation, and state accredited schools; (3) includes all schools with programs that are less than 2 years. Source: National Center for Education Statistics, Integrated Postsecondary Education System (IPEDS), 2021-22; Wikipedia, List of Medical Schools in the United States, accessed April 10, 2023; Wikipedia, List of Law Schools in the United States, accessed April 10, 2023

According to *U.S. News & World Report,* the Rochester, MN metro area is home to one of the top 75 medical schools for research in the U.S.: **Mayo Clinic School of Medicine (Alix)** (#14 tie). The rankings are based on a weighted average of 11 measures of quality: quality assessment; peer assessment score; assessment score by residency directors; research activity; total research activity; average research activity per faculty member; student selectivity; median MCAT total score; median undergraduate GPA; acceptance rate; and faculty resources. *U.S. News & World Report, "America's Best Graduate Schools, Medical, 2023"*

EMPLOYERS

Major Employers

Company Name	Industry
Benchmark Electronics	Contract mfg/design/engineering
Cardinal of Minnesota	Res. services/dev. disabilities
Charter Communications	Cable & other pay television services
City of Rochester	Municipal government
Crenlo	Fabricated metal
Federal Medical Center	Corrections/medical
Halcon	Furniture manufacturer
Hiawatha Homes	Res. services/dev. disabilities
IBM	Electronics
Interstate Hotels & Resorts	Hotel/restaurant services
Kemps	Food processing
Mayo Clinic	Healthcare
McNeilus Steel	Steel fabrication
McNeilus Truck	Mobile concrete mixers, garbage trucks
Olmstead County	Government
Olmstead Medical Center	Healthcare
Pace Dairy	Food processing
RCTC	Post-secondary education
Reichel Foods	Refrigerated lunch & snacks
Rochester Meat Company	Meat processor
Rochester Medical Corp	Medical device manufacturer
Rochester Public Schools	Education
Samaritan Bethany	Health care of the aging
Seneca Food	Food processing
Think Bank	Banking and financial services

Note: Companies shown are located within the Rochester, MN Metropolitan Statistical Area.
Source: Hoovers.com; Wikipedia

PUBLIC SAFETY

Crime Rate

Area	Total Crime	Violent Crime Rate				Property Crime Rate		
		Murder	Rape[3]	Robbery	Aggrav. Assault	Burglary	Larceny -Theft	Motor Vehicle Theft
City	2,172.3	4.2	61.5	36.6	147.1	275.9	1,519.1	128.0
Suburbs[1]	824.5	1.0	36.1	2.9	75.1	191.3	456.7	61.5
Metro[2]	1,552.4	2.7	49.8	21.1	114.0	237.0	1,030.4	97.4
U.S.	2,356.7	6.5	38.4	73.9	279.7	314.2	1,398.0	246.0

Note: Figures are crimes per 100,000 population; (1) All areas within the metro area that are located outside the city limits; (2) Figures cover the Rochester, MN Metropolitan Statistical Area; (3) All figures shown were reported using the revised Uniform Crime Reporting (UCR) definition of rape; Due to the transition to the National Incident-Based Reporting System (NIBRS), limited city and metro area data was released for 2021.
Source: FBI Uniform Crime Reports, 2020

Hate Crimes

Area	Number of Quarters Reported	Number of Incidents per Bias Motivation					
		Race/Ethnicity/ Ancestry	Religion	Sexual Orientation	Disability	Gender	Gender Identity
City	4	3	0	0	0	0	0
U.S.	4	5,227	1,244	1,110	130	75	266

Note: Due to the transition to the National Incident-Based Reporting System (NIBRS), limited crime data was released for 2021.
Source: Federal Bureau of Investigation, Hate Crime Statistics 2020

Identity Theft Consumer Reports

Area	Reports	Reports per 100,000 Population	Rank[2]
MSA[1]	248	113	341
U.S.	1,108,609	339	-

Note: (1) Figures cover the Rochester, MN Metropolitan Statistical Area; (2) Rank ranges from 1 to 391 where 1 indicates greatest number of identity theft reports per 100,000 population
Source: Federal Trade Commission, Consumer Sentinel Network Data Book 2022

Fraud and Other Consumer Reports

Area	Reports	Reports per 100,000 Population	Rank[2]
MSA[1]	1,444	657	322
U.S.	4,064,520	1,245	-

Note: (1) Figures cover the Rochester, MN Metropolitan Statistical Area; (2) Rank ranges from 1 to 391 where 1 indicates greatest number of fraud and other consumer reports per 100,000 population
Source: Federal Trade Commission, Consumer Sentinel Network Data Book 2022

POLITICS

2020 Presidential Election Results

Area	Biden	Trump	Jorgensen	Hawkins	Other
Olmsted County	54.2	43.4	1.2	0.3	0.9
U.S.	51.3	46.8	1.2	0.3	0.5

Note: Results are percentages and may not add to 100% due to rounding
Source: Dave Leip's Atlas of U.S. Presidential Elections

SPORTS

Professional Sports Teams

Team Name	League	Year Established

No teams are located in the metro area
Source: Wikipedia, Major Professional Sports Teams of the United States and Canada, April 12, 2023

CLIMATE

Average and Extreme Temperatures

Temperature	Jan	Feb	Mar	Apr	May	Jun	Jul	Aug	Sep	Oct	Nov	Dec	Yr.
Extreme High (°F)	55	63	79	91	92	101	102	100	97	90	74	62	102
Average High (°F)	21	26	38	55	68	78	82	79	70	59	40	26	54
Average Temp. (°F)	12	18	29	45	57	67	71	69	60	48	32	19	44
Average Low (°F)	3	8	20	34	46	56	60	58	48	38	24	10	34
Extreme Low (°F)	-40	-29	-31	5	21	35	42	35	23	11	-20	-33	-40

Note: Figures cover the years 1948-1995
Source: National Climatic Data Center, International Station Meteorological Climate Summary, 9/96

Average Precipitation/Snowfall/Humidity

Precip./Humidity	Jan	Feb	Mar	Apr	May	Jun	Jul	Aug	Sep	Oct	Nov	Dec	Yr.
Avg. Precip. (in.)	0.8	0.8	1.8	2.8	3.4	4.0	4.2	3.9	3.1	2.0	1.7	1.0	29.4
Avg. Snowfall (in.)	9	8	10	4	Tr	0	0	0	Tr	1	6	10	47
Avg. Rel. Hum. 6am (%)	80	81	82	80	80	82	86	88	87	82	83	83	83
Avg. Rel. Hum. 3pm (%)	72	68	65	54	52	53	56	57	56	54	66	74	61

Note: Figures cover the years 1948-1995; Tr = Trace amounts (<0.05 in. of rain; <0.5 in. of snow)
Source: National Climatic Data Center, International Station Meteorological Climate Summary, 9/96

Weather Conditions

Temperature			Daytime Sky			Precipitation		
5°F & below	32°F & below	90°F & above	Clear	Partly cloudy	Cloudy	0.01 inch or more precip.	0.1 inch or more snow/ice	Thunder-storms
46	165	9	87	126	152	114	40	41

Note: Figures are average number of days per year and cover the years 1948-1995
Source: National Climatic Data Center, International Station Meteorological Climate Summary, 9/96

HAZARDOUS WASTE

Superfund Sites

The Rochester, MN metro area has no sites on the EPA's Superfund Final National Priorities List. There are a total of 1,165 Superfund sites with a status of proposed or final on the list in the U.S. *U.S. Environmental Protection Agency, National Priorities List, April 12, 2023*

AIR QUALITY

Air Quality Trends: Ozone

	1990	1995	2000	2005	2010	2015	2018	2019	2020	2021
MSA[1]	n/a	n/a	n/a	n/a	n/a	n/a	n/a	n/a	n/a	n/a
U.S.	0.087	0.089	0.081	0.080	0.072	0.067	0.069	0.065	0.065	0.067

Note: (1) Data covers the Rochester, MN Metropolitan Statistical Area; n/a not available. The values shown are the composite ozone concentration averages among trend sites based on the highest fourth daily maximum 8-hour concentration in parts per million. These trends are based on sites having an adequate record of monitoring data during the trend period. Data from exceptional events are included.
Source: U.S. Environmental Protection Agency, Air Quality Monitoring Information, "Air Quality Trends by City, 1990-2021"

Air Quality Index

Area	Percent of Days when Air Quality was...[2]					AQI Statistics[2]	
	Good	Moderate	Unhealthy for Sensitive Groups	Unhealthy	Very Unhealthy	Maximum	Median
MSA[1]	83.4	16.1	0.6	0.0	0.0	125	36

Note: (1) Data covers the Rochester, MN Metropolitan Statistical Area; (2) Based on 361 days with AQI data in 2021. Air Quality Index (AQI) is an index for reporting daily air quality. EPA calculates the AQI for five major air pollutants regulated by the Clean Air Act: ground-level ozone, particle pollution (aka particulate matter), carbon monoxide, sulfur dioxide, and nitrogen dioxide. The AQI runs from 0 to 500. The higher the AQI value, the greater the level of air pollution and the greater the health concern. There are six AQI categories: "Good" AQI is between 0 and 50. Air quality is considered satisfactory; "Moderate" AQI is between 51 and 100. Air quality is acceptable; "Unhealthy for Sensitive Groups" When AQI values are between 101 and 150, members of sensitive groups may experience health effects; "Unhealthy" When AQI values are between 151 and 200 everyone may begin to experience health effects; "Very Unhealthy" AQI values between 201 and 300 trigger a health alert; "Hazardous" AQI values over 300 trigger warnings of emergency conditions (not shown).
Source: U.S. Environmental Protection Agency, Air Quality Index Report, 2021

Air Quality Index Pollutants

Area	Percent of Days when AQI Pollutant was...[2]					
	Carbon Monoxide	Nitrogen Dioxide	Ozone	Sulfur Dioxide	Particulate Matter 2.5	Particulate Matter 10
MSA[1]	0.0	0.0	61.5	(3)	38.5	0.0

Note: (1) Data covers the Rochester, MN Metropolitan Statistical Area; (2) Based on 361 days with AQI data in 2021. The Air Quality Index (AQI) is an index for reporting daily air quality. EPA calculates the AQI for five major air pollutants regulated by the Clean Air Act: ground-level ozone, particle pollution (also known as particulate matter), carbon monoxide, sulfur dioxide, and nitrogen dioxide. The AQI runs from 0 to 500. The higher the AQI value, the greater the level of air pollution and the greater the health concern; (3) Sulfur dioxide is no longer included in this table (as of December 8, 2021) because SO_2 concentrations tend to be very localized and not necessarily representative of broad geographical areas like counties and CBSAs.
Source: U.S. Environmental Protection Agency, Air Quality Index Report, 2021

Maximum Air Pollutant Concentrations: Particulate Matter, Ozone, CO and Lead

	Particulate Matter 10 (ug/m³)	Particulate Matter 2.5 Wtd AM (ug/m³)	Particulate Matter 2.5 24-Hr (ug/m³)	Ozone (ppm)	Carbon Monoxide (ppm)	Lead (ug/m³)
MSA[1] Level	n/a	n/a	n/a	0.067	n/a	n/a
NAAQS[2]	150	15	35	0.075	9	0.15
Met NAAQS[2]	n/a	n/a	n/a	Yes	n/a	n/a

Note: (1) Data covers the Rochester, MN Metropolitan Statistical Area; Data from exceptional events are included; (2) National Ambient Air Quality Standards; ppm = parts per million; ug/m³ = micrograms per cubic meter; n/a not available.
Concentrations: Particulate Matter 10 (coarse particulate)—highest second maximum 24-hour concentration; Particulate Matter 2.5 Wtd AM (fine particulate)—highest weighted annual mean concentration; Particulate Matter 2.5 24-Hour (fine particulate)—highest 98th percentile 24-hour concentration; Ozone—highest fourth daily maximum 8-hour concentration; Carbon Monoxide—highest second maximum non-overlapping 8-hour concentration; Lead—maximum running 3-month average
Source: U.S. Environmental Protection Agency, Air Quality Monitoring Information, "Air Quality Statistics by City, 2021"

Maximum Air Pollutant Concentrations: Nitrogen Dioxide and Sulfur Dioxide

	Nitrogen Dioxide AM (ppb)	Nitrogen Dioxide 1-Hr (ppb)	Sulfur Dioxide AM (ppb)	Sulfur Dioxide 1-Hr (ppb)	Sulfur Dioxide 24-Hr (ppb)
MSA[1] Level	n/a	n/a	n/a	n/a	n/a
NAAQS[2]	53	100	30	75	140
Met NAAQS[2]	n/a	n/a	n/a	n/a	n/a

Note: (1) Data covers the Rochester, MN Metropolitan Statistical Area; Data from exceptional events are included; (2) National Ambient Air Quality Standards; ppm = parts per million; ug/m³ = micrograms per cubic meter; n/a not available.
Concentrations: Nitrogen Dioxide AM—highest arithmetic mean concentration; Nitrogen Dioxide 1-Hr—highest 98th percentile 1-hour daily maximum concentration; Sulfur Dioxide AM—highest annual mean concentration; Sulfur Dioxide 1-Hr—highest 99th percentile 1-hour daily maximum concentration; Sulfur Dioxide 24-Hr—highest second maximum 24-hour concentration
Source: U.S. Environmental Protection Agency, Air Quality Monitoring Information, "Air Quality Statistics by City, 2021"

Saint Louis, Missouri

Background

St. Louis, the second-largest city in Missouri, the "Gateway to the West," is known for a skyline dominated by the Gateway Arch, which was built in 1965 as a monument to President Thomas Jefferson's vision of a continental United States.

St. Louis began as an inland river trading post for French settlers from New Orleans. Founder Pierre Laclade was granted exclusive rights by the Louisiana government to trade with the tribes of the region. The site was rich with wildlife, including raccoon, beaver, muskrat, otter, and bear, making for an active fur trade. In 1827, John Jacob Astor started a profitable fur business called the American Fur Company.

After the Civil War, St. Louis experienced an industrial and cultural boom. The city's industries included iron, steel, leather, and food, and it became a center for Hegelian thought, based on German philosopher Hegel, thanks to the large influx of German immigrants.

World War I, the Depression, and Prohibition all contributed to St. Louis's economic decline which started in the 1950s and continued through the 1970s. Since the 1980s, however, St. Louis has been prospering and today, its diverse economy includes the service, manufacturing, trade, transportation, and tourism industries, and it is home to eight Fortune 500 companies. Major companies with significant operations in the city include Nestle, Wells Fargo, and Boeing.

Major research universities include Saint Louis University and Washington University in St. Louis, and the Washington University Medical Center neighborhood is home to many medical and pharmaceutical institutions, giving the city the nickname Biobelt of the Midwest.

The city's attractions include The St. Louis Walk of Fame honoring its rich musical tradition and legendary sons and daughters Chuck Berry, Tina Turner, Miles Davis, and Scott Joplin. The St. Louis Art Museum houses more than 30,000 pieces of art. The Black World History Museum honors such notable African American Missourians as George Washington Carver, Dred and Harriet Scott, musician Clark Terry, and others.

Other historical sites include the 630-foot, stainless steel Gateway Arch, Daniel Boone Home, Lewis and Clark State Historic Site, and Ulysses S. Grant National Historic Site. Children enjoy the St. Louis Zoo, St. Louis Children's Aquarium, St. Louis Science Center, and Worldways Children's Museum with interactive cultural exhibits.

St. Louis operates more than 100 parks and is home to the Missouri Botanical Garden, which is among the top three botanical gardens worldwide. The city also hosts Laumeier Sculpture Park, Gateway International Raceway, and the Soulard Farmers Market and surrounding historical neighborhood offering dining options ranging from Cajun to continental.

St. Loius is home to Major League Baseball's St. Louis Cardinals, and National Hockey League's St. Louis Blues. The St. Louis SC of Major League Soccer begins play this year. The U.S. Chess Championship, which began in 1845, has been held at the St. Louis Chess Club since 2009.

St. Louis is situated at the confluence of the Missouri and Mississippi rivers, near the geographical center of the United States. It experiences the four seasons without the hardship of prolonged periods of extreme heat or high humidity. Winters are brisk, stimulating, and seldom severe. Thunderstorms, which occur between 40 and 50 days a year, are generally not severe.

Rankings

General Rankings

- The human resources consulting firm Mercer ranked 231 major cities worldwide in terms of overall quality of life. Saint Louis ranked #70. Criteria: political, social, economic, and socio-cultural factors; medical and health considerations; schools and education; public services and transportation; recreation; consumer goods; housing; and natural environment. *Mercer, "Mercer 2019 Quality of Living Survey," March 13, 2019*

Business/Finance Rankings

- Based on metro area social media reviews, the employment opinion group Glassdoor surveyed 50 of the most populous U.S. metro areas and equally weighed cost of living, hiring opportunity, and job satisfaction to compose a list of "25 Best Cities for Jobs." Median pay and home value, and number of active job openings were also factored in. The Saint Louis metro area was ranked #6 in overall job satisfaction. *www.glassdoor.com, "Best Cities for Jobs," February 25, 2020*

- The Brookings Institution ranked the nation's largest cities based on income inequality. Saint Louis was ranked #18 (#1 = greatest inequality). Criteria: the "95/20 ratio," a figure representing the income at which a household earns more than 95 percent of all other households, divided by the income at which a household earns more than only 20 percent of all other households. *Brookings Institution, "Household Income Inequality, Largest Cities of 97 Large U.S. Metro Areas, 2014-2016," February 5, 2018*

- The Brookings Institution ranked the 100 largest metro areas in the U.S. based on income inequality. Saint Louis was ranked #65 (#1 = greatest inequality). Criteria: the "95/20 ratio," a figure representing the income at which a household earns more than 95 percent of all other households, divided by the income at which a household earns more than only 20 percent of all other households. *Brookings Institution, "Household Income Inequality, 100 Largest U.S. Metro Areas, 2014-2016," February 5, 2018*

- Payscale.com ranked the 32 largest metro areas in terms of wage growth. The Saint Louis metro area ranked #5. Criteria: quarterly changes in private industry employee and education professional wage growth from the previous year. *PayScale, "Wage Trends by Metro Area-1st Quarter," April 20, 2023*

- The Saint Louis metro area was identified as one of the most debt-ridden places in America by the finance site Credit.com. The metro area was ranked #20. Criteria: residents' average credit card debt as well as median income. *Credit.com, "25 Cities With the Most Credit Card Debt," February 28, 2018*

- For its annual survey of the "Cheapest U.S. Cities to Live In," Kiplinger applied Cost of Living Index statistics developed by the Council for Community and Economic Research to U.S. Census Bureau population and median household income data for 265 urban areas. Only areas with at least 50,000 residents were considered. In the resulting ranking, Saint Louis ranked #23. *Kiplinger.com, "The 25 Cheapest Places to Live: U.S. Cities Edition," April 3, 2023*

- Saint Louis was identified as one of America's most frugal metro areas by *Coupons.com*. The city ranked #23 out of 25. Criteria: digital coupon usage. *Coupons.com, "America's Most Frugal Cities of 2017," March 22, 2018*

- The Saint Louis metro area appeared on the Milken Institute "2022 Best Performing Cities" list. Rank: #149 out of 200 large metro areas (population over 250,000). Criteria: job growth; wage and salary growth; high-tech output growth; housing affordability; household broadband access. *Milken Institute, "Best-Performing Cities 2022," March 28, 2022*

- *Forbes* ranked the 200 most populous metro areas to determine the nation's "Best Places for Business and Careers." The Saint Louis metro area was ranked #70. Criteria: costs (business and living); job growth (past and projected); income growth; quality of life; educational attainment (college and high school); projected economic growth; cultural and leisure opportunities; workplace tolerance laws; net migration patterns. *Forbes, "The Best Places for Business and Careers 2019: Seattle Still On Top," October 30, 2019*

- Mercer Human Resources Consulting ranked 227 cities worldwide in terms of cost-of-living. Saint Louis ranked #101 (the lower the ranking, the higher the cost-of-living). The survey measured the comparative cost of over 200 items (such as housing, food, clothing, domestic supplies, transportation, and recreation/entertainment) in each location. *Mercer, "2022 Cost of Living City Ranking," June 29, 2022*

Education Rankings

- Personal finance website *WalletHub* analyzed the 150 largest U.S. metropolitan statistical areas to determine where the most educated Americans are putting their degrees to work. Criteria: education levels; percentage of workers with degrees; education quality and attainment gap; public school quality rankings; quality and enrollment of each metro area's universities. Saint Louis was ranked #45 (#1 = most educated city). *www.WalletHub.com, "Most & Least Educated Cities in America," July 18, 2022*

- Saint Louis was selected as one of America's most literate cities. The city ranked #12 out of the 84 largest U.S. cities. Criteria: number of booksellers; library resources; Internet resources; educational attainment; periodical publishing resources; newspaper circulation. *Central Connecticut State University, "America's Most Literate Cities, 2018," February 2019*

Food/Drink Rankings

- The U.S. Chamber of Commerce Foundation conducted an in-depth study on local food truck regulations, surveyed 288 food truck owners, and ranked 20 major American cities based on how friendly they are for operating a food truck. The compiled index assessed the following: procedures for obtaining permits and licenses; complying with restrictions; and financial obligations associated with operating a food truck. Saint Louis ranked #12 overall (1 being the best). *www.foodtrucknation.us, "Food Truck Nation," March 20, 2018*

Health/Fitness Rankings

- For each of the 100 largest cities in the United States, the American Fitness Index®, compiled in partnership between the American College of Sports Medicine and the Elevance Health Foundation, evaluated community infrastructure and 34 health behaviors including preventive health, levels of chronic disease conditions, food insecurity, sleep quality, pedestrian safety, air quality, and community/environment resources that support physical activity. Saint Louis ranked #70 for "community fitness." *americanfitnessindex.org, "2022 ACSM American Fitness Index Summary Report," July 12, 2022*

- The Saint Louis metro area was identified as one of the worst cities for bed bugs in America by pest control company Orkin. The area ranked #25 out of 50 based on the number of bed bug treatments Orkin performed from December 2021 to November 2022. *Orkin, "The Windy City Can't Blow Bed Bugs Away: Chicago Ranks #1 For Third Consecutive Year On Orkin's Bed Bug Cities List," January 9, 2023*

- Saint Louis was identified as a "2022 Spring Allergy Capital." The area ranked #25 out of 100. Three groups of factors were used to identify the most challenging cities for people with allergies during the spring season: annual spring pollen scores; over the counter allergy medicine use; number of board-certified allergy specialists. *Asthma and Allergy Foundation of America, "Spring Allergy Capitals 2022," March 2, 2022*

- Saint Louis was identified as a "2022 Fall Allergy Capital." The area ranked #36 out of 100. Three groups of factors were used to identify the most challenging cities for people with allergies during the fall season: annual fall pollen scores; over the counter allergy medicine use; number of board-certified allergy specialists. *Asthma and Allergy Foundation of America, "Fall Allergy Capitals 2022," March 2, 2022*

- Saint Louis was identified as a "2022 Asthma Capital." The area ranked #14 out of the nation's 100 largest metropolitan areas. Criteria: estimated asthma prevalence; asthma-related mortality; and ER visits due to asthma. Risk factors analyzed but not factored in the rankings: annual pollen score; annual air quality; public smoking laws; access to board-certified asthma specialists; rescue and controller medication use; uninsured rate; poverty rate. *Asthma and Allergy Foundation of America, "Asthma Capitals 2022: The Most Challenging Places to Live With Asthma," September 14, 2022*

Real Estate Rankings

- *WalletHub* compared the most populated U.S. cities to determine which had the best markets for real estate agents. Saint Louis ranked #146 where demand was high and pay was the best. Criteria: sales per agent; annual median wage for real-estate agents; monthly average starting salary for real estate agents; real estate job density and competition; unemployment rate; home turnover rate; housing-market health index; and other relevant metrics. *www.WalletHub.com, "2021 Best Places to Be a Real Estate Agent," May 12, 2021*

- Saint Louis was ranked #40 out of 235 metro areas in terms of housing affordability in 2022 by the National Association of Home Builders (#1 = most affordable). Criteria: the share of homes sold in that area affordable to a family earning the local median income, based on standard mortgage underwriting criteria. *National Association of Home Builders®, NAHB-Wells Fargo Housing Opportunity Index, 4th Quarter 2022*

Safety Rankings

- To identify the most dangerous cities in America, *24/7 Wall St.* focused on violent crime categories—murder, non-negligent manslaughter, rape, robbery, and aggravated assault—as reported for every 100,000 residents using data from the FBI's 2020 annual Uniform Crime Report. For cities with populations over 25,000, Saint Louis was ranked #5. *247wallst.com, "America's Most Dangerous Cities" November 12, 2021*

- Allstate ranked the 200 largest cities in America in terms of driver safety. Saint Louis ranked #115. Criteria: internal property damage claims over a two-year period from January 2016 to December 2017. The report helps increase the importance of safety and awareness behind the wheel. *Allstate, "Allstate America's Best Drivers Report, 2019" June 24, 2019*

- Saint Louis was identified as one of the most dangerous cities in America by NeighborhoodScout. The city ranked #23 out of 100 (#1 = most dangerous). Criteria: number of violent crimes per 1,000 residents. The editors evaluated cities with 25,000 or more residents. *NeighborhoodScout.com, "2023 Top 100 Most Dangerous Cities in the U.S.," January 12, 2023*

Seniors/Retirement Rankings

- From its Best Cities for Successful Aging indexes, the Milken Institute generated rankings for metropolitan areas, weighing data in nine categories—health care, wellness, living arrangements, transportation and convenience, financial characteristics, education, employment, community engagement, and overall livability. The Saint Louis metro area was ranked #27 overall in the large metro area category. *Milken Institute, "Best Cities for Successful Aging, 2017" March 14, 2017*

Women/Minorities Rankings

- Saint Louis was selected as one of the queerest cities in America by *The Advocate*. The city ranked #11 out of 25. Criteria, among many: Trans Pride parades/festivals; gay rugby teams; lesbian bars; LGBTQ centers; theater screenings of "Moonlight"; LGBTQ-inclusive nondiscrimination ordinances; and gay bowling teams. *The Advocate, "Queerest Cities in America 2017" January 12, 2017*

- Personal finance website *WalletHub* compared more than 180 U.S. cities across two key dimensions, "Hispanic Business-Friendliness" and "Hispanic Purchasing Power," to arrive at the most favorable conditions for Hispanic entrepreneurs. Saint Louis was ranked #59 out of 182. Criteria includes: share of Hispanic-Owned Businesses; Hispanic entrepreneurship rate to median annual income of Hispanics; Small Business-Friendliness score; cost of living; and number of Hispanics with at least a bachelor's degree. *WalletHub.com, "2019's Best Cities for Hispanic Entrepreneurs," May 1, 2019*

Miscellaneous Rankings

- *MoveHub* ranked 446 hipster cities across 20 countries, using its new and improved *alternative* Hipster Index and Saint Louis came out as #34 among the top 50. Criteria: population over 150,000; number of vintage boutiques; density of tattoo parlors; vegan places to eat; coffee shops; and density of vinyl record stores. *www.movehub.com, "The Hipster Index: Brighton Pips Portland to Global Top Spot," July 28, 2021*

- In its roundup of St. Patrick's Day parades "Gayot" listed the best festivals and parades of all things Irish. The festivities in Saint Louis as among the best in North America. *www.gayot.com, "Best St. Patrick's Day Parades," March 2023*

- The watchdog site, Charity Navigator, conducted a study of charities in major markets both to analyze statistical differences in their financial, accountability, and transparency practices and to track year-to-year variations in individual philanthropic communities. The Saint Louis metro area was ranked #3 among the 30 metro markets in the rating category of Overall Score. *www.charitynavigator.org, "2017 Metro Market Study," May 1, 2017*

- *WalletHub* compared the 150 most populated U.S. cities to determine their operating efficiency. A "Quality of Services" score was constructed for each city and then divided by the total budget per capita to reveal which were managed the best. Saint Louis ranked #133. Criteria: financial stability; economy; education; safety; health; infrastructure and pollution. *www.WalletHub.com, "2022's Best- & Worst-Run Cities in America," June 21, 2022*

- The National Alliance to End Homelessness listed the 25 most populous metro areas with the highest rate of homelessness. The Saint Louis metro area had a high rate of homelessness. Criteria: number of homeless people per 10,000 population in 2016. *National Alliance to End Homelessness, "Homelessness in the 25 Most Populous U.S. Metro Areas," September 1, 2017*

Business Environment

DEMOGRAPHICS

Population Growth

Area	1990 Census	2000 Census	2010 Census	2020 Census	Population Growth (%)	
					1990-2020	2010-2020
City	396,685	348,189	319,294	301,578	-24.0	-5.5
MSA[1]	2,580,897	2,698,687	2,812,896	2,820,253	9.3	0.3
U.S.	248,709,873	281,421,906	308,745,538	331,449,281	33.3	7.4

Note: (1) Figures cover the St. Louis, MO-IL Metropolitan Statistical Area
Source: U.S. Census Bureau, 1990 Census, 2000 Census, 2010 Census, 2020 Census

Race

Area	White Alone[2] (%)	Black Alone[2] (%)	Asian Alone[2] (%)	AIAN[3] Alone[2] (%)	NHOPI[4] Alone[2] (%)	Other Race Alone[2] (%)	Two or More Races (%)
City	43.9	43.0	4.1	0.3	0.0	2.6	6.1
MSA[1]	71.2	18.0	2.9	0.3	0.0	1.6	6.0
U.S.	61.6	12.4	6.0	1.1	0.2	8.4	10.2

Note: (1) Figures cover the St. Louis, MO-IL Metropolitan Statistical Area; (2) Alone is defined as not being in combination with one or more other races; (3) American Indian and Alaska Native; (4) Native Hawaiian and Other Pacific Islander
Source: U.S. Census Bureau, 2020 Census

Hispanic or Latino Origin

Area	Total (%)	Mexican (%)	Puerto Rican (%)	Cuban (%)	Other (%)
City	4.2	2.5	0.2	0.2	1.3
MSA[1]	3.2	2.0	0.3	0.1	0.9
U.S.	18.4	11.2	1.8	0.7	4.7

Note: Persons of Hispanic or Latino origin can be of any race; (1) Figures cover the St. Louis, MO-IL Metropolitan Statistical Area
Source: U.S. Census Bureau, 2017-2021 American Community Survey 5-Year Estimates

Age

Area	Percent of Population									Median Age
	Under Age 5	Age 5–19	Age 20–34	Age 35–44	Age 45–54	Age 55–64	Age 65–74	Age 75–84	Age 85+	
City	5.3	15.1	28.8	13.6	10.9	12.8	8.7	3.4	1.4	35.4
MSA[1]	5.6	18.9	19.4	12.6	12.1	14.1	10.3	5.0	2.1	39.7
U.S.	5.6	19.2	20.2	12.7	12.4	13.1	10.0	4.9	1.9	38.8

Note: (1) Figures cover the St. Louis, MO-IL Metropolitan Statistical Area
Source: U.S. Census Bureau, 2020 Census

Disability by Age

Area	All Ages	Under 18 Years Old	18 to 64 Years Old	65 Years and Over
City	15.4	6.2	13.3	38.5
MSA[1]	13.0	4.7	10.8	32.4
U.S.	12.6	4.4	10.3	33.4

Note: Figures show percent of the civilian noninstitutionalized population that reported having a disability. Disability status is determined from six types of difficulty: vision, hearing, cognitive, ambulatory, self-care, and independent living. For children under 5 years old, hearing and vision difficulty are used to determine disability status. For children between the ages of 5 and 14, disability status is determined from hearing, vision, cognitive, ambulatory, and self-care difficulties. For people aged 15 years and older, they are considered to have a disability if they have difficulty with any one of the six difficulty types; Note: (1) Figures cover the St. Louis, MO-IL Metropolitan Statistical Area
Source: U.S. Census Bureau, 2017-2021 American Community Survey 5-Year Estimates

Ancestry

Area	German	Irish	English	American	Italian	Polish	French[2]	Scottish	Dutch
City	15.7	9.7	5.4	4.4	4.0	1.7	2.3	1.2	0.8
MSA[1]	26.1	12.9	8.6	5.4	4.6	2.3	3.0	1.5	1.0
U.S.	12.8	9.6	8.1	5.7	5.0	2.7	2.2	1.6	1.1

Note: Figures are the percentage of the total population reporting a particular ancestry. The nine most commonly reported ancestries in the U.S. are shown. Figures include multiple ancestries (e.g. if a person reported being Irish and Italian, they were included in both columns); (1) Figures cover the St. Louis, MO-IL Metropolitan Statistical Area; (2) Excludes Basque
Source: U.S. Census Bureau, 2017-2021 American Community Survey 5-Year Estimates

Foreign-born Population

Area	Any Foreign Country	Asia	Mexico	Europe	Caribbean	Central America[2]	South America	Africa	Canada
City	6.8	2.8	0.7	1.2	0.2	0.3	0.2	1.3	0.1
MSA[1]	4.8	2.2	0.5	1.1	0.1	0.2	0.2	0.5	0.1
U.S.	13.6	4.2	3.3	1.5	1.4	1.1	1.1	0.8	0.2

Note: (1) Figures cover the St. Louis, MO-IL Metropolitan Statistical Area; (2) Excludes Mexico.
Source: U.S. Census Bureau, 2017-2021 American Community Survey 5-Year Estimates

Household Size

Area	One	Two	Three	Four	Five	Six	Seven or More	Average Household Size
City	46.3	30.2	10.8	7.4	3.2	1.0	1.1	2.10
MSA[1]	30.6	34.5	15.0	12.2	5.2	1.6	0.9	2.40
U.S.	28.1	33.8	15.5	12.9	6.0	2.3	1.4	2.60

Note: (1) Figures cover the St. Louis, MO-IL Metropolitan Statistical Area
Source: U.S. Census Bureau, 2017-2021 American Community Survey 5-Year Estimates

Household Relationships

Area	House-holder	Opposite-sex Spouse	Same-sex Spouse	Opposite-sex Unmarried Partner	Same-sex Unmarried Partner	Child[2]	Grand-child	Other Relatives	Non-relatives
City	48.0	10.3	0.4	3.7	0.4	22.5	2.6	4.0	4.3
MSA[1]	40.8	18.2	0.2	2.6	0.2	28.5	2.2	3.0	2.4
U.S.	38.3	17.5	0.2	2.5	0.2	28.3	2.4	4.8	3.4

Note: Figures are percent of the total population; (1) Figures cover the St. Louis, MO-IL Metropolitan Statistical Area; (2) Includes biological, adopted, and stepchildren of the householder
Source: U.S. Census Bureau, 2020 Census

Gender

Area	Males	Females	Males per 100 Females
City	147,340	154,238	95.5
MSA[1]	1,369,631	1,450,622	94.4
U.S.	162,685,811	168,763,470	96.4

Note: (1) Figures cover the St. Louis, MO-IL Metropolitan Statistical Area
Source: U.S. Census Bureau, 2020 Census

Marital Status

Area	Never Married	Now Married[2]	Separated	Widowed	Divorced
City	48.8	30.7	2.9	5.2	12.3
MSA[1]	32.2	48.7	1.7	5.9	11.4
U.S.	33.8	48.0	1.8	5.6	10.8

Note: Figures are percentages and cover the population 15 years of age and older; (1) Figures cover the St. Louis, MO-IL Metropolitan Statistical Area; (2) Excludes separated
Source: U.S. Census Bureau, 2017-2021 American Community Survey 5-Year Estimates

Religious Groups by Family

Area	Catholic	Baptist	Methodist	LDS[2]	Pentecostal	Lutheran	Islam	Adventist	Other
MSA[1]	21.2	8.6	2.9	0.7	1.4	3.2	1.3	0.8	11.1
U.S.	18.7	7.3	3.0	2.0	1.8	1.7	1.3	1.3	11.6

Note: Figures are the number of adherents as a percentage of the total population and cover the eight largest religious groups in the U.S; (1) Figures cover the St. Louis, MO-IL Metropolitan Statistical Area; (2) Church of Jesus Christ of Latter-day Saints
Sources: 2020 U.S. Religion Census, Association of Statisticians of American Religious Bodies; The Association of Religion Data Archives (ARDA)

Religious Groups by Tradition

Area	Catholic	Evangelical Protestant	Mainline Protestant	Black Protestant	Islam	Judaism	Hinduism	Orthodox	Buddhism
MSA[1]	21.2	16.1	5.7	3.9	1.3	0.6	0.2	0.2	0.3
U.S.	18.7	16.5	5.2	2.3	1.3	0.6	0.4	0.4	0.3

Note: Figures are the number of adherents as a percentage of the total population; (1) Figures cover the St. Louis, MO-IL Metropolitan Statistical Area
Sources: 2020 U.S. Religion Census, Association of Statisticians of American Religious Bodies; The Association of Religion Data Archives (ARDA)

ECONOMY

Gross Metropolitan Product

Area	2020	2021	2022	2023	Rank[2]
MSA[1]	171.5	187.7	201.8	212.8	23

Note: Figures are in billions of dollars; (1) Figures cover the St. Louis, MO-IL Metropolitan Statistical Area;
(2) Rank is based on 2021 data and ranges from 1 to 381
Source: U.S. Conference of Mayors, U.S. Metro Economies: U.S. Metros Compared to Global and State
Economies, June 2022

Economic Growth

Area	2018-20 (%)	2021 (%)	2022 (%)	2023 (%)	Rank[2]
MSA[1]	-1.2	5.3	1.6	2.0	232
U.S.	-0.6	5.7	3.1	2.9	—

Note: Figures are real gross metropolitan product (GMP) growth rates and represent average annual percent
change; (1) Figures cover the St. Louis, MO-IL Metropolitan Statistical Area; (2) Rank is based on 2020 2-year
average annual percent change and ranges from 1 to 381
Source: U.S. Conference of Mayors, U.S. Metro Economies: U.S. Metros Compared to Global and State
Economies, June 2022

Metropolitan Area Exports

Area	2016	2017	2018	2019	2020	2021	Rank[2]
MSA[1]	8,346.5	9,662.9	10,866.8	10,711.1	9,089.4	10,486.1	34

Note: Figures are in millions of dollars; (1) Figures cover the St. Louis, MO-IL Metropolitan Statistical Area;
(2) Rank is based on 2021 data and ranges from 1 to 388
Source: U.S. Department of Commerce, International Trade Administration, Office of Trade and Economic
Analysis, Industry and Analysis, Exports by Metropolitan Area, data extracted March 16, 2023

Building Permits

Area	Single-Family			Multi-Family			Total		
	2021	2022	Pct. Chg.	2021	2022	Pct. Chg.	2021	2022	Pct. Chg.
City	146	122	-16.4	809	1,054	30.3	955	1,176	23.1
MSA[1]	5,716	4,743	-17.0	2,610	4,388	68.1	8,326	9,131	9.7
U.S.	1,115,400	975,600	-12.5	621,600	689,500	10.9	1,737,000	1,665,100	-4.1

Note: (1) Figures cover the St. Louis, MO-IL Metropolitan Statistical Area; Figures represent new,
privately-owned housing units authorized (unadjusted data); All permit data are based on estimates with
imputation
Source: U.S. Census Bureau, Manufacturing, Mining, and Construction Statistics, Building Permits, 2021,
2022

Bankruptcy Filings

Area	Business Filings			Nonbusiness Filings		
	2021	2022	% Chg.	2021	2022	% Chg.
Saint Louis city County	12	15	25.0	1,395	1,247	-10.6
U.S.	14,347	13,481	-6.0	399,269	374,240	-6.3

Note: Business filings include Chapter 7, Chapter 9, Chapter 11, Chapter 12, Chapter 13, Chapter 15, and
Section 304; Nonbusiness filings include Chapter 7, Chapter 11, and Chapter 13
Source: Administrative Office of the U.S. Courts, Business and Nonbusiness Bankruptcy, County Cases
Commenced by Chapter of the Bankruptcy Code, During the 12-Month Period Ending December 31, 2021 and
Business and Nonbusiness Bankruptcy, County Cases Commenced by Chapter of the Bankruptcy Code, During
the 12-Month Period Ending December 31, 2022

Housing Vacancy Rates

Area	Gross Vacancy Rate[2] (%)			Year-Round Vacancy Rate[3] (%)			Rental Vacancy Rate[4] (%)			Homeowner Vacancy Rate[5] (%)		
	2020	2021	2022	2020	2021	2022	2020	2021	2022	2020	2021	2022
MSA[1]	6.4	7.0	7.2	6.3	7.0	7.1	5.3	6.5	6.8	0.7	0.5	1.4
U.S.	10.6	10.8	10.5	8.2	8.4	8.2	6.3	6.1	5.8	1.0	0.9	0.8

Note: (1) Figures cover the St. Louis, MO-IL Metropolitan Statistical Area; (2) The percentage of the total
housing inventory that is vacant; (3) The percentage of the housing inventory (excluding seasonal units) that is
year-round vacant; (4) The percentage of rental inventory that is vacant for rent; (5) The percentage of
homeowner inventory that is vacant for sale
Source: U.S. Census Bureau, Housing Vacancies and Homeownership Annual Statistics: 2020, 2021, 2022

INCOME

Income

Area	Per Capita ($)	Median Household ($)	Average Household ($)
City	33,326	48,751	68,681
MSA[1]	39,168	69,635	94,953
U.S.	37,638	69,021	97,196

Note: (1) Figures cover the St. Louis, MO-IL Metropolitan Statistical Area
Source: U.S. Census Bureau, 2017-2021 American Community Survey 5-Year Estimates

Household Income Distribution

Area	Percent of Households Earning							
	Under $15,000	$15,000 -$24,999	$25,000 -$34,999	$35,000 -$49,999	$50,000 -$74,999	$75,000 -$99,999	$100,000 -$149,999	$150,000 and up
City	17.0	10.3	10.7	12.9	17.5	10.5	12.1	8.9
MSA[1]	8.6	7.4	8.1	11.8	17.5	13.5	16.9	16.3
U.S.	9.4	7.8	8.2	11.4	16.8	12.8	16.3	17.3

Note: (1) Figures cover the St. Louis, MO-IL Metropolitan Statistical Area
Source: U.S. Census Bureau, 2017-2021 American Community Survey 5-Year Estimates

Poverty Rate

Area	All Ages	Under 18 Years Old	18 to 64 Years Old	65 Years and Over
City	19.6	27.3	18.3	15.4
MSA[1]	10.5	14.4	9.9	7.7
U.S.	12.6	17.0	11.8	9.6

Note: Figures are percentage of people whose income during the past 12 months was below the poverty level;
(1) Figures cover the St. Louis, MO-IL Metropolitan Statistical Area
Source: U.S. Census Bureau, 2017-2021 American Community Survey 5-Year Estimates

EMPLOYMENT

Labor Force and Employment

Area	Civilian Labor Force			Workers Employed		
	Dec. 2021	Dec. 2022	% Chg.	Dec. 2021	Dec. 2022	% Chg.
City	150,418	149,690	-0.5	143,212	145,026	1.3
MSA[1]	1,460,514	1,459,027	-0.1	1,407,703	1,422,207	1.0
U.S.	161,696,000	164,224,000	1.6	155,732,000	158,872,000	2.0

Note: Data is not seasonally adjusted and covers workers 16 years of age and older; (1) Figures cover the St. Louis, MO-IL Metropolitan Statistical Area
Source: Bureau of Labor Statistics, Local Area Unemployment Statistics

Unemployment Rate

Area	2022											
	Jan.	Feb.	Mar.	Apr.	May	Jun.	Jul.	Aug.	Sep.	Oct.	Nov.	Dec.
City	5.4	5.0	4.9	3.6	3.8	3.3	4.1	4.1	2.5	3.0	3.2	3.1
MSA[1]	4.3	3.7	3.7	2.9	3.2	2.8	3.2	3.3	2.3	2.7	2.7	2.5
U.S.	4.4	4.1	3.8	3.3	3.4	3.8	3.8	3.8	3.3	3.4	3.4	3.3

Note: Data is not seasonally adjusted and covers workers 16 years of age and older; (1) Figures cover the St. Louis, MO-IL Metropolitan Statistical Area
Source: Bureau of Labor Statistics, Local Area Unemployment Statistics

Average Wages

Occupation	$/Hr.	Occupation	$/Hr.
Accountants and Auditors	37.46	Maintenance and Repair Workers	24.01
Automotive Mechanics	23.04	Marketing Managers	64.07
Bookkeepers	23.29	Network and Computer Systems Admin.	45.06
Carpenters	29.99	Nurses, Licensed Practical	26.06
Cashiers	13.92	Nurses, Registered	36.14
Computer Programmers	39.08	Nursing Assistants	16.41
Computer Systems Analysts	49.69	Office Clerks, General	20.76
Computer User Support Specialists	30.84	Physical Therapists	44.14
Construction Laborers	27.50	Physicians	142.81
Cooks, Restaurant	15.55	Plumbers, Pipefitters and Steamfitters	35.55
Customer Service Representatives	20.00	Police and Sheriff's Patrol Officers	29.89
Dentists	n/a	Postal Service Mail Carriers	27.22
Electricians	33.40	Real Estate Sales Agents	23.21
Engineers, Electrical	50.08	Retail Salespersons	17.00
Fast Food and Counter Workers	13.40	Sales Representatives, Technical/Scientific	48.57
Financial Managers	72.89	Secretaries, Exc. Legal/Medical/Executive	19.80
First-Line Supervisors of Office Workers	31.51	Security Guards	17.68
General and Operations Managers	54.93	Surgeons	n/a
Hairdressers/Cosmetologists	18.85	Teacher Assistants, Exc. Postsecondary*	15.52
Home Health and Personal Care Aides	13.32	Teachers, Secondary School, Exc. Sp. Ed.*	29.12
Janitors and Cleaners	16.09	Telemarketers	18.25
Landscaping/Groundskeeping Workers	17.58	Truck Drivers, Heavy/Tractor-Trailer	26.27
Lawyers	68.34	Truck Drivers, Light/Delivery Services	22.92
Maids and Housekeeping Cleaners	14.77	Waiters and Waitresses	16.19

Note: Wage data covers the St. Louis, MO-IL Metropolitan Statistical Area; (*) Hourly wages were calculated from annual wage data based on a 40 hour work week; n/a not available.
Source: Bureau of Labor Statistics, Metro Area Occupational Employment & Wage Estimates, May 2022

Employment by Industry

Sector	MSA[1]		U.S.
	Number of Employees	Percent of Total	Percent of Total
Construction, Mining, and Logging	71,100	5.0	5.4
Private Education and Health Services	264,200	18.6	16.1
Financial Activities	97,900	6.9	5.9
Government	154,700	10.9	14.5
Information	28,300	2.0	2.0
Leisure and Hospitality	141,700	10.0	10.3
Manufacturing	118,300	8.3	8.4
Other Services	54,200	3.8	3.7
Professional and Business Services	220,700	15.5	14.7
Retail Trade	136,900	9.6	10.2
Transportation, Warehousing, and Utilities	67,100	4.7	4.9
Wholesale Trade	68,500	4.8	3.9

Note: Figures are non-farm employment as of December 2022. Figures are not seasonally adjusted and include workers 16 years of age and older; (1) Figures cover the St. Louis, MO-IL Metropolitan Statistical Area
Source: Bureau of Labor Statistics, Current Employment Statistics, Employment, Hours, and Earnings

Employment by Occupation

Occupation Classification	City (%)	MSA[1] (%)	U.S. (%)
Management, Business, Science, and Arts	45.4	42.7	40.3
Natural Resources, Construction, and Maintenance	4.7	7.6	8.7
Production, Transportation, and Material Moving	11.3	12.5	13.1
Sales and Office	18.2	21.3	20.9
Service	20.3	15.9	17.0

Note: Figures cover employed civilians 16 years of age and older; (1) Figures cover the St. Louis, MO-IL Metropolitan Statistical Area
Source: U.S. Census Bureau, 2017-2021 American Community Survey 5-Year Estimates

Occupations with Greatest Projected Employment Growth: 2022 – 2024

Occupation[1]	2022 Employment	2024 Projected Employment	Numeric Employment Change	Percent Employment Change
Home Health and Personal Care Aides	80,580	84,180	3,600	4.5
Stockers and Order Fillers	58,060	60,440	2,380	4.1
General and Operations Managers	86,320	88,430	2,110	2.4
Cooks, Restaurant	30,940	33,020	2,080	6.7
Registered Nurses	73,620	74,860	1,240	1.7
Laborers and Freight, Stock, and Material Movers, Hand	42,770	43,710	940	2.2
Maintenance and Repair Workers, General	38,300	39,130	830	2.2
Janitors and Cleaners, Except Maids and Housekeeping Cleaners	45,160	45,960	800	1.8
Industrial Truck and Tractor Operators	13,420	14,180	760	5.7
Waiters and Waitresses	41,390	42,140	750	1.8

Note: Projections cover Missouri; (1) Sorted by numeric employment change
Source: www.projectionscentral.com, State Occupational Projections, 2022–2024 Short-Term Projections

Fastest-Growing Occupations: 2022 – 2024

Occupation[1]	2022 Employment	2024 Projected Employment	Numeric Employment Change	Percent Employment Change
Nurse Practitioners	7,420	8,030	610	8.2
Logisticians	2,520	2,710	190	7.5
Ushers, Lobby Attendants, and Ticket Takers	2,670	2,860	190	7.1
Computer Numerically Controlled Tool Programmers	740	790	50	6.8
Cooks, Restaurant	30,940	33,020	2,080	6.7
Information Security Analysts (SOC 2018)	2,110	2,250	140	6.6
Operations Research Analysts	980	1,040	60	6.1
Fitness Trainers and Aerobics Instructors	7,500	7,940	440	5.9
Weighers, Measurers, Checkers, and Samplers, Recordkeeping	850	900	50	5.9
Physical Therapist Assistants	2,230	2,360	130	5.8

Note: Projections cover Missouri; (1) Sorted by percent employment change and excludes occupations with numeric employment change less than 50
Source: www.projectionscentral.com, State Occupational Projections, 2022–2024 Short-Term Projections

CITY FINANCES

City Government Finances

Component	2020 ($000)	2020 ($ per capita)
Total Revenues	1,125,508	3,745
Total Expenditures	1,096,079	3,647
Debt Outstanding	1,588,039	5,283
Cash and Securities[1]	777,190	2,586

Note: (1) Cash and security holdings of a government at the close of its fiscal year, including those of its dependent agencies, utilities, and liquor stores.
Source: U.S. Census Bureau, State & Local Government Finances 2020

City Government Revenue by Source

Source	2020 ($000)	2020 ($ per capita)	2020 (%)
General Revenue			
From Federal Government	7,151	24	0.6
From State Government	116,082	386	10.3
From Local Governments	0	0	0.0
Taxes			
Property	103,511	344	9.2
Sales and Gross Receipts	290,111	965	25.8
Personal Income	175,760	585	15.6
Corporate Income	42,361	141	3.8
Motor Vehicle License	1,385	5	0.1
Other Taxes	32,841	109	2.9
Current Charges	265,365	883	23.6
Liquor Store	0	0	0.0
Utility	52,338	174	4.7

Source: U.S. Census Bureau, State & Local Government Finances 2020

City Government Expenditures by Function

Function	2020 ($000)	2020 ($ per capita)	2020 (%)
General Direct Expenditures			
Air Transportation	138,076	459	12.6
Corrections	52,426	174	4.8
Education	0	0	0.0
Employment Security Administration	0	0	0.0
Financial Administration	21,110	70	1.9
Fire Protection	90,617	301	8.3
General Public Buildings	15,497	51	1.4
Governmental Administration, Other	17,363	57	1.6
Health	44,401	147	4.1
Highways	30,190	100	2.8
Hospitals	0	0	0.0
Housing and Community Development	35,083	116	3.2
Interest on General Debt	74,557	248	6.8
Judicial and Legal	35,288	117	3.2
Libraries	0	0	0.0
Parking	12,245	40	1.1
Parks and Recreation	22,660	75	2.1
Police Protection	217,560	723	19.8
Public Welfare	0	0	0.0
Sewerage	2,367	7	0.2
Solid Waste Management	17,266	57	1.6
Veterans' Services	0	0	0.0
Liquor Store	0	0	0.0
Utility	52,818	175	4.8

Source: U.S. Census Bureau, State & Local Government Finances 2020

TAXES

State Corporate Income Tax Rates

State	Tax Rate (%)	Income Brackets ($)	Num. of Brackets	Financial Institution Tax Rate (%)[a]	Federal Income Tax Ded.
Missouri	4.0	Flat rate	1	4.48	Yes (h)

Note: Tax rates as of January 1, 2023; (a) Rates listed are the corporate income tax rate applied to financial institutions or excise taxes based on income. Some states have other taxes based upon the value of deposits or shares; (h) 50% of the federal income tax is deductible.
Source: Federation of Tax Administrators, State Corporate Income Tax Rates, January 1, 2023

State Individual Income Tax Rates

State	Tax Rate (%)	Income Brackets ($)	Personal Exemptions ($)			Standard Ded. ($)	
			Single	Married	Depend.	Single	Married
Missouri (a)	0.0 - 4.95	1,207 - 8,449	(d)	(d)	(d)	13,850	27,700 (d)

Note: Tax rates as of January 1, 2023; Local- and county-level taxes are not included; (a) 16 states have statutory provision for automatically adjusting to the rate of inflation the dollar values of the income tax brackets, standard deductions, and/or personal exemptions. Oregon does not index the income brackets for $125,000 and over; (d) These states use the personal exemption/standard deduction amounts provided in the federal Internal Revenue Code.
Source: Federation of Tax Administrators, State Individual Income Tax Rates, January 1, 2023

Various State Sales and Excise Tax Rates

State	State Sales Tax (%)	Gasoline[1] ($/gal.)	Cigarette[2] ($/pack)	Spirits[3] ($/gal.)	Wine[4] ($/gal.)	Beer[5] ($/gal.)	Recreational Marijuana (%)
Missouri	4.225	0.2242	0.17	2.00	0.42	0.06	(j)

Note: All tax rates as of January 1, 2023; (1) The American Petroleum Institute has developed a methodology for determining the average tax rate on a gallon of fuel. Rates may include any of the following: excise taxes, environmental fees, storage tank fees, other fees or taxes, general sales tax, and local taxes; (2) The federal excise tax of $1.0066 per pack and local taxes are not included; (3) Rates are those applicable to off-premise sales of 40% alcohol by volume (a.b.v.) distilled spirits in 750ml containers. Local excise taxes are excluded; (4) Rates are those applicable to off-premise sales of 11% a.b.v. non-carbonated wine in 750ml containers; (5) Rates are those applicable to off-premise sales of 4.7% a.b.v. beer in 12 ounce containers; (j) 6% excise tax (retail price)
Source: Tax Foundation, 2023 Facts & Figures: How Does Your State Compare?

State Business Tax Climate Index Rankings

State	Overall Rank	Corporate Tax Rank	Individual Income Tax Rank	Sales Tax Rank	Property Tax Rank	Unemployment Insurance Tax Rank
Missouri	11	3	21	26	7	4

Note: The index is a measure of how each state's tax laws affect economic performance. The lower the rank, the more favorable a state's tax system is for business. States without a given tax are given a ranking of 1. The scores/rankings for the District of Columbia do not affect other states. The 2023 index represents the tax climate as of July 1, 2022.
Source: Tax Foundation, State Business Tax Climate Index 2023

TRANSPORTATION

Means of Transportation to Work

Area	Car/Truck/Van		Public Transportation			Bicycle	Walked	Other Means	Worked at Home
	Drove Alone	Car-pooled	Bus	Subway	Railroad				
City	69.9	6.6	5.8	0.4	0.1	0.9	4.4	1.4	10.5
MSA[1]	79.2	6.7	1.4	0.2	0.1	0.2	1.6	1.0	9.8
U.S.	73.2	8.6	2.0	1.6	0.5	0.5	2.5	1.5	9.7

Note: Figures are percentages and cover workers 16 years of age and older; (1) Figures cover the St. Louis, MO-IL Metropolitan Statistical Area
Source: U.S. Census Bureau, 2017-2021 American Community Survey 5-Year Estimates

Travel Time to Work

Area	Less Than 10 Minutes	10 to 19 Minutes	20 to 29 Minutes	30 to 44 Minutes	45 to 59 Minutes	60 to 89 Minutes	90 Minutes or More
City	9.2	35.2	26.5	19.7	4.3	2.9	2.1
MSA[1]	11.0	27.3	24.4	24.0	7.9	3.8	1.7
U.S.	12.4	28.5	21.0	20.9	8.2	6.2	2.9

Note: Note: Figures are percentages and include workers 16 years old and over; (1) Figures cover the St. Louis, MO-IL Metropolitan Statistical Area
Source: U.S. Census Bureau, 2017-2021 American Community Survey 5-Year Estimates

Key Congestion Measures

Measure	1990	2000	2010	2015	2020
Annual Hours of Delay, Total (000)	25,229	47,642	62,483	69,729	51,115
Annual Hours of Delay, Per Auto Commuter	24	39	43	45	33
Annual Congestion Cost, Per Auto Commuter ($)	609	861	899	925	719

Note: Covers the St. Louis MO-IL urban area
Source: Texas A&M Transportation Institute, 2021 Urban Mobility Report

Freeway Travel Time Index

Measure	1985	1990	1995	2000	2005	2010	2015	2020
Urban Area Index[1]	1.07	1.09	1.13	1.15	1.16	1.16	1.15	1.08
Urban Area Rank[1,2]	48	56	47	53	57	54	67	44

Note: Freeway Travel Time Index—the ratio of travel time in the peak period to the travel time at free-flow conditions. For example, a value of 1.30 indicates a 20-minute free-flow trip takes 26 minutes in the peak (20 minutes x 1.30 = 26 minutes); (1) Covers the St. Louis MO-IL urban area; (2) Rank is based on 101 larger urban areas (#1 = highest travel time index)
Source: Texas A&M Transportation Institute, 2021 Urban Mobility Report

Public Transportation

Agency Name / Mode of Transportation	Vehicles Operated in Maximum Service[1]	Annual Unlinked Passenger Trips[2] (in thous.)	Annual Passenger Miles[3] (in thous.)
Bi-State Development Agency (METRO)			
Bus (directly operated)	317	11,499.1	61,478.7
Demand Response (directly operated)	102	411.5	4,785.5
Light Rail (directly operated)	42	5,472.1	37,347.1

Note: (1) Number of revenue vehicles operated by the given mode and type of service to meet the annual maximum service requirement. This is the revenue vehicle count during the peak season of the year; on the week and day that maximum service is provided. Vehicles operated in maximum service (VOMS) exclude atypical days and one-time special events; (2) Number of passengers who boarded public transportation vehicles. Passengers are counted each time they board a vehicle no matter how many vehicles they use to travel from their origin to their destination. (3) Sum of the distances ridden by all passengers during the entire fiscal year.
Source: Federal Transit Administration, National Transit Database, 2021

Air Transportation

Airport Name and Code / Type of Service	Passenger Airlines[1]	Passenger Enplanements	Freight Carriers[2]	Freight (lbs)
Lambert-St. Louis International (STL)				
Domestic service (U.S. carriers - 2022)	30	6,518,657	16	95,265,490
International service (U.S. carriers - 2021)	7	100,389	2	400,978

Note: (1) Includes all U.S.-based major, minor and commuter airlines that carried at least one passenger during the year; (2) Includes all U.S.-based airlines and freight carriers that transported at least one pound of freight during the year.
Source: Bureau of Transportation Statistics, The Intermodal Transportation Database, Air Carriers: T-100 Domestic Market (U.S. Carriers), 2022; Bureau of Transportation Statistics, The Intermodal Transportation Database, Air Carriers: T-100 International Market (U.S. Carriers), 2021

BUSINESSES

Major Business Headquarters

Company Name	Industry	Rankings Fortune[1]	Rankings Forbes[2]
Alberici	Construction	-	209
Ameren	Utilities, gas and electric	500	-
Arco Construction	Construction	-	145
Centene	Health care, insurance and managed care	26	-
Clayco Construction	Construction	-	105
Edward Jones	Diversified financials	-	31
Emerson Electric	Electronics, electrical equip.	199	-
Enterprise Holdings	Services	-	9
Graybar Electric	Wholesalers, diversified	399	55
McCarthy Holdings	Construction	-	127
Schnuck Markets	Food markets	-	179
World Wide Technology	Technology hardware & equipment	-	27

Note: (1) Companies that produce a 10-K are ranked 1 to 500 based on 2021 revenue; (2) All private companies with at least $2 billion in annual revenue through the end of their most current fiscal year are ranked 1 to 246; companies listed are headquartered in the city; dashes indicate no ranking
Source: Fortune, "Fortune 500," 2022; Forbes, "America's Largest Private Companies," 2022

Living Environment

COST OF LIVING

Cost of Living Index

Composite Index	Groceries	Housing	Utilities	Trans-portation	Health Care	Misc. Goods/ Services
86.3	97.3	74.3	93.4	90.2	88.6	88.0

Note: The Cost of Living Index measures regional differences in the cost of consumer goods and services, excluding taxes and non-consumer expenditures, for professional and managerial households in the top income quintile. It is based on more than 50,000 prices covering almost 60 different items for which prices are collected three times a year by chambers of commerce, economic development organizations or university applied economic centers in each participating urban area. The numbers shown should be read as a percentage above or below the national average of 100. For example, a value of 115.4 in the groceries column indicates that grocery prices are 15.4% higher than the national average. Small differences in the index numbers should not be interpreted as significant; Figures cover the St. Louis MO-IL urban area.
Source: The Council for Community and Economic Research, Cost of Living Index, 2022

Grocery Prices

Area[1]	T-Bone Steak ($/pound)	Frying Chicken ($/pound)	Whole Milk ($/half gal.)	Eggs ($/dozen)	Orange Juice ($/64 oz.)	Coffee ($/11.5 oz.)
City[2]	17.61	1.85	1.97	2.17	3.66	4.65
Avg.	13.81	1.59	2.43	2.25	3.85	4.95
Min.	10.17	0.90	1.51	1.30	2.90	3.46
Max.	19.35	3.30	4.32	4.32	5.31	8.59

*Note: (1) Values for the local area are compared with the average, minimum and maximum values for all 286 areas in the Cost of Living Index; (2) Figures cover the St. Louis MO-IL urban area; **T-Bone Steak** (price per pound); **Frying Chicken** (price per pound, whole fryer); **Whole Milk** (half gallon carton); **Eggs** (price per dozen, Grade A, large); **Orange Juice** (64 oz. Tropicana or Florida Natural); **Coffee** (11.5 oz. can, vacuum-packed, Maxwell House, Hills Bros, or Folgers).*
Source: The Council for Community and Economic Research, Cost of Living Index, 2022

Housing and Utility Costs

Area[1]	New Home Price ($)	Apartment Rent ($/month)	All Electric ($/month)	Part Electric ($/month)	Other Energy ($/month)	Telephone ($/month)
City[2]	339,758	981	-	80.89	68.47	201.40
Avg.	450,913	1,371	176.41	99.93	76.96	190.22
Min.	229,283	546	100.84	31.56	27.15	174.27
Max.	2,434,977	4,569	356.86	249.59	272.24	208.31

*Note: (1) Values for the local area are compared with the average, minimum and maximum values for all 286 areas in the Cost of Living Index; (2) Figures cover the St. Louis MO-IL urban area; **New Home Price** (2,400 sf living area, 8,000 sf lot, in urban area with full utilities); **Apartment Rent** (950 sf 2 bedroom/1.5 or 2 bath, unfurnished, excluding all utilities except water); **All Electric** (average monthly cost for an all-electric home); **Part Electric** (average monthly cost for a part-electric home); **Other Energy** (average monthly cost for natural gas, fuel oil, coal, wood, and any other forms of energy except electricity); **Telephone** (price includes the base monthly rate plus taxes and fees for three lines of mobile phone service).*
Source: The Council for Community and Economic Research, Cost of Living Index, 2022

Health Care, Transportation, and Other Costs

Area[1]	Doctor ($/visit)	Dentist ($/visit)	Optometrist ($/visit)	Gasoline ($/gallon)	Beauty Salon ($/visit)	Men's Shirt ($)
City[2]	86.89	101.96	85.05	3.81	39.83	21.57
Avg.	124.91	107.77	117.66	3.86	43.31	34.21
Min.	36.61	58.25	51.79	2.90	22.18	13.05
Max.	250.21	162.58	371.96	5.54	85.61	63.54

*Note: (1) Values for the local area are compared with the average, minimum and maximum values for all 286 areas in the Cost of Living Index; (2) Figures cover the St. Louis MO-IL urban area; **Doctor** (general practitioners routine exam of an established patient); **Dentist** (adult teeth cleaning and periodic oral examination); **Optometrist** (full vision eye exam for established adult patient); **Gasoline** (one gallon regular unleaded, national brand, including all taxes, cash price at self-service pump if available); **Beauty Salon** (woman's shampoo, trim, and blow-dry); **Men's Shirt** (cotton/polyester dress shirt, pinpoint weave, long sleeves).*
Source: The Council for Community and Economic Research, Cost of Living Index, 2022

HOUSING

Homeownership Rate

Area	2015 (%)	2016 (%)	2017 (%)	2018 (%)	2019 (%)	2020 (%)	2021 (%)	2022 (%)
MSA[1]	68.7	66.4	65.6	65.8	68.1	71.1	73.8	69.9
U.S.	63.7	63.4	63.9	64.4	64.6	66.6	65.5	65.8

Note: (1) Figures cover the St. Louis, MO-IL Metropolitan Statistical Area
Source: U.S. Census Bureau, Housing Vacancies and Homeownership Annual Statistics: 2015-2022

House Price Index (HPI)

Area	National Ranking[2]	Quarterly Change (%)	One-Year Change (%)	Five-Year Change (%)	Since 1991Q1 (%)
MSA[1]	190	-0.80	9.10	40.60	193.95
U.S.[3]	–	0.34	8.41	58.44	289.08

Note: The HPI is a weighted repeat sales index. It measures average price changes in repeat sales or refinancings on the same properties. This information is obtained by reviewing repeat mortgage transactions on single-family properties whose mortgages have been purchased or securitized by Fannie Mae or Freddie Mac since January 1975; (1) Figures cover the St. Louis, MO-IL Metropolitan Statistical Area; (2) Rankings are based on annual percentage change for all metro areas containing at least 15,000 transactions over the last 10 years and ranges from 1 to 257; (3) figures based on a weighted average of Census Division estimates using a seasonally adjusted, purchase-only index; all figures are for the period ending December 31, 2022
Source: Federal Housing Finance Agency, Change in FHFA Metropolitan Area House Price Indexes, 2022Q4

Median Single-Family Home Prices

Area	2020	2021	2022p	Percent Change 2021 to 2022
MSA[1]	205.8	226.1	245.3	8.5
U.S. Average	300.2	357.1	392.6	9.9

Note: Figures are median sales prices of existing single-family homes in thousands of dollars; (p) preliminary; (1) Figures cover the St. Louis, MO-IL Metropolitan Statistical Area
Source: National Association of Realtors, Median Sales Price of Existing Single-Family Homes for Metropolitan Areas, 4th Quarter 2022

Qualifying Income Based on Median Sales Price of Existing Single-Family Homes

Area	With 5% Down ($)	With 10% Down ($)	With 20% Down ($)
MSA[1]	71,505	67,742	60,215
U.S. Average	112,234	106,237	94,513

Note: Figures are preliminary; Qualifying income is based on a mortgage rate of 6.77%. Monthly principal and interest payment is limited to 25% of income; (1) Figures cover the St. Louis, MO-IL Metropolitan Statistical Area
Source: National Association of Realtors, Qualifying Income Based on Median Sales Price of Existing Single-Family Homes for Metropolitan Areas, 4th Quarter 2022

Home Value

Area	Under $100,000	$100,000 -$199,999	$200,000 -$299,999	$300,000 -$399,999	$400,000 -$499,999	$500,000 -$999,999	$1,000,000 or more	Median ($)
City	29.9	36.3	17.8	8.4	3.4	3.4	0.9	153,200
MSA[1]	20.0	33.1	22.7	12.1	5.2	5.7	1.2	189,600
U.S.	16.2	24.2	20.1	13.6	8.3	13.6	4.1	244,900

Note: Figures are percentages except for median and cover owner-occupied housing units; (1) Figures cover the St. Louis, MO-IL Metropolitan Statistical Area
Source: U.S. Census Bureau, 2017-2021 American Community Survey 5-Year Estimates

Year Housing Structure Built

Area	2020 or Later	2010 -2019	2000 -2009	1990 -1999	1980 -1989	1970 -1979	1960 -1969	1950 -1959	1940 -1949	Before 1940	Median Year
City	<0.1	2.4	4.0	3.0	3.2	4.4	6.5	10.2	8.1	58.2	<1940
MSA[1]	0.2	5.3	11.4	12.1	11.1	13.0	12.6	12.6	5.5	16.2	1972
U.S.	0.2	7.3	13.6	13.6	13.2	14.8	10.3	10.0	4.7	12.2	1979

Note: Figures are percentages except for Median Year; Note: (1) Figures cover the St. Louis, MO-IL Metropolitan Statistical Area
Source: U.S. Census Bureau, 2017-2021 American Community Survey 5-Year Estimates

Gross Monthly Rent

Area	Under $500	$500 -$999	$1,000 -$1,499	$1,500 -$1,999	$2,000 -$2,499	$2,500 -$2,999	$3,000 and up	Median ($)
City	10.6	54.3	26.8	6.1	1.7	0.3	0.2	873
MSA[1]	7.9	47.8	33.0	7.6	2.1	0.6	1.1	952
U.S.	8.1	30.5	30.8	16.8	7.3	3.1	3.5	1,163

Note: Figures are percentages except for median; Gross rent is the contract rent plus the estimated average monthly cost of utilities (electricity, gas, and water and sewer) and fuels (oil, coal, kerosene, wood, etc.) if these are paid by the renter (or paid for the renter by someone else); (1) Figures cover the St. Louis, MO-IL Metropolitan Statistical Area
Source: U.S. Census Bureau, 2017-2021 American Community Survey 5-Year Estimates

HEALTH

Health Risk Factors

Category	MSA[1] (%)	U.S. (%)
Adults aged 18–64 who have any kind of health care coverage	92.1	90.9
Adults who reported being in good or better health	85.5	85.2
Adults who have been told they have high blood cholesterol	33.2	35.7
Adults who have been told they have high blood pressure	34.1	32.4
Adults who are current smokers	15.5	14.4
Adults who currently use e-cigarettes	7.0	6.7
Adults who currently use chewing tobacco, snuff, or snus	2.7	3.5
Adults who are heavy drinkers[2]	6.7	6.3
Adults who are binge drinkers[3]	16.4	15.4
Adults who are overweight (BMI 25.0 - 29.9)	30.7	34.4
Adults who are obese (BMI 30.0 - 99.8)	37.8	33.9
Adults who participated in any physical activities in the past month	75.2	76.3

Note: (1) Figures cover the St. Louis, MO-IL Metropolitan Statistical Area; (2) Heavy drinkers are classified as adult men having more than 14 drinks per week and adult women having more than 7 drinks per week; (3) Binge drinkers are classified as males having five or more drinks on one occasion or females having four or more drinks on one occasion
Source: Centers for Disease Control and Prevention, Behaviorial Risk Factor Surveillance System, SMART: Selected Metropolitan Area Risk Trends, 2021

Acute and Chronic Health Conditions

Category	MSA[1] (%)	U.S. (%)
Adults who have ever been told they had a heart attack	4.1	4.0
Adults who have ever been told they have angina or coronary heart disease	4.2	3.8
Adults who have ever been told they had a stroke	3.6	3.0
Adults who have ever been told they have asthma	13.9	14.9
Adults who have ever been told they have arthritis	26.9	25.8
Adults who have ever been told they have diabetes[2]	12.2	10.9
Adults who have ever been told they had skin cancer	7.1	6.6
Adults who have ever been told they had any other types of cancer	7.5	7.5
Adults who have ever been told they have COPD	6.9	6.1
Adults who have ever been told they have kidney disease	2.3	3.0
Adults who have ever been told they have a form of depression	21.5	20.5

Note: (1) Figures cover the St. Louis, MO-IL Metropolitan Statistical Area; (2) Figures do not include pregnancy-related, borderline, or pre-diabetes
Source: Centers for Disease Control and Prevention, Behaviorial Risk Factor Surveillance System, SMART: Selected Metropolitan Area Risk Trends, 2021

Health Screening and Vaccination Rates

Category	MSA[1] (%)	U.S. (%)
Adults who have ever been tested for HIV	33.7	34.9
Adults who have had their blood cholesterol checked within the last five years	86.6	85.2
Adults aged 65+ who have had flu shot within the past year	73.7	68.6
Adults aged 65+ who have ever had a pneumonia vaccination	75.4	71.0

Note: (1) Figures cover the St. Louis, MO-IL Metropolitan Statistical Area.
Source: Centers for Disease Control and Prevention, Behaviorial Risk Factor Surveillance System, SMART: Selected Metropolitan Area Risk Trends, 2021

Disability Status

Category	MSA[1] (%)	U.S. (%)
Adults who reported being deaf	7.9	7.2
Are you blind or have serious difficulty seeing, even when wearing glasses?	5.7	4.8
Are you limited in any way in any of your usual activities due to arthritis?	12.2	11.1
Do you have difficulty doing errands alone?	9.3	7.0
Do you have difficulty dressing or bathing?	4.8	3.6
Do you have serious difficulty concentrating/remembering/making decisions?	12.8	12.1
Do you have serious difficulty walking or climbing stairs?	14.3	12.8

Note: (1) Figures cover the St. Louis, MO-IL Metropolitan Statistical Area.
Source: Centers for Disease Control and Prevention, Behaviorial Risk Factor Surveillance System, SMART: Selected Metropolitan Area Risk Trends, 2021

Mortality Rates for the Top 10 Causes of Death in the U.S.

ICD-10[a] Sub-Chapter	ICD-10[a] Code	Crude Mortality Rate[1] per 100,000 population	
		County[2]	U.S.
Malignant neoplasms	C00-C97	191.8	182.6
Ischaemic heart diseases	I20-I25	127.3	113.1
Other forms of heart disease	I30-I51	56.4	64.4
Other degenerative diseases of the nervous system	G30-G31	34.1	51.0
Cerebrovascular diseases	I60-I69	55.3	47.8
Other external causes of accidental injury	W00-X59	109.9	46.4
Chronic lower respiratory diseases	J40-J47	36.7	45.7
Organic, including symptomatic, mental disorders	F01-F09	22.0	35.9
Hypertensive diseases	I10-I15	63.9	35.0
Diabetes mellitus	E10-E14	29.8	29.6

Note: (a) ICD-10 = International Classification of Diseases 10th Revision; (1) Crude mortality rates are a three-year average covering 2019-2021; (2) Figures cover St. Louis city.
Source: Centers for Disease Control and Prevention, National Center for Health Statistics. National Vital Statistics System, Mortality 2018-2021 on CDC WONDER Online Database

Mortality Rates for Selected Causes of Death

ICD-10[a] Sub-Chapter	ICD-10[a] Code	Crude Mortality Rate[1] per 100,000 population	
		County[2]	U.S.
Assault	X85-Y09	53.2	7.0
Diseases of the liver	K70-K76	17.5	19.8
Human immunodeficiency virus (HIV) disease	B20-B24	3.8	1.5
Influenza and pneumonia	J09-J18	13.2	14.7
Intentional self-harm	X60-X84	13.2	14.3
Malnutrition	E40-E46	6.2	4.3
Obesity and other hyperalimentation	E65-E68	3.3	3.0
Renal failure	N17-N19	25.1	15.7
Transport accidents	V01-V99	19.3	13.6
Viral hepatitis	B15-B19	Unreliable	1.2

Note: (a) ICD-10 = International Classification of Diseases 10th Revision; (1) Crude mortality rates are a three-year average covering 2019-2021; (2) Figures cover St. Louis city; Data are suppressed when the data meet the criteria for confidentiality constraints; Crude mortality rates are flagged as unreliable when the rate would be calculated with a numerator of 20 or less.
Source: Centers for Disease Control and Prevention, National Center for Health Statistics. National Vital Statistics System, Mortality 2018-2021 on CDC WONDER Online Database

Health Insurance Coverage

Area	With Health Insurance	With Private Health Insurance	With Public Health Insurance	Without Health Insurance	Population Under Age 19 Without Health Insurance
City	89.5	62.6	35.2	10.5	4.3
MSA[1]	93.7	74.5	30.5	6.3	3.4
U.S.	91.2	67.8	35.4	8.8	5.3

Note: Figures are percentages that cover the civilian noninstitutionalized population; (1) Figures cover the St. Louis, MO-IL Metropolitan Statistical Area
Source: U.S. Census Bureau, 2017-2021 American Community Survey 5-Year Estimates

Number of Medical Professionals

Area	MDs[3]	DOs[3,4]	Dentists	Podiatrists	Chiropractors	Optometrists
County[1] (number)	3,674	106	185	14	62	57
County[1] (rate[2])	1,222.5	35.3	63.1	4.8	21.1	19.4
U.S. (rate[2])	289.3	23.5	72.5	6.2	28.7	17.4

Note: Data as of 2021 unless noted; (1) Data covers St. Louis City County; (2) Rate per 100,000 population; (3) Data as of 2020 and includes all active, non-federal physicians; (4) Doctor of Osteopathic Medicine
Source: U.S. Department of Health and Human Services, Health Resources and Services Administration, Bureau of Health Professions, Area Resource File (ARF) 2021-2022

Best Hospitals

According to *U.S. News,* the St. Louis, MO-IL metro area is home to two of the best hospitals in the U.S.: **Barnes-Jewish Hospital** (Honor Roll/11 adult specialties); **Siteman Cancer Center at Barnes-Jewish Hospital** (Honor Roll/11 adult specialties). The hospitals listed were nationally ranked in at least one of 15 adult or 10 pediatric specialties. The number of specialties shown cover the parent hospital. Only 164 U.S. hospitals performed well enough to be nationally ranked in one or more specialties. Twenty hospitals in the U.S. made the Honor Roll. The Best Hospitals Honor Roll takes both the national rankings and the procedure and condition ratings into account. Hospitals received points if they were nationally ranked in one of the 15 adult specialties—the higher they ranked, the more points they got—and how many ratings of "high performing" they earned in the 17 procedures and conditions. *U.S. News Online, "America's Best Hospitals 2022-23"*

According to *U.S. News,* the St. Louis, MO-IL metro area is home to two of the best children's hospitals in the U.S.: **St. Louis Children's Hospital-Washington University** (10 pediatric specialties); **SSM Health Cardinal Glennon Children's Hospital-St. Louis University** (3 pediatric specialties). The hospitals listed were highly ranked in at least one of 10 pediatric specialties. Eighty-six children's hospitals in the U.S. were nationally ranked in at least one specialty. Hospitals received points for being ranked in a specialty, and the 10 hospitals with the most points across the 10 specialties make up the Honor Roll. *U.S. News Online, "America's Best Children's Hospitals 2022-23"*

EDUCATION

Public School District Statistics

District Name	Schls	Pupils	Pupil/ Teacher Ratio	Minority Pupils[1] (%)	LEP/ELL[2] (%)	IEP[3] (%)
Affton 101	4	2,588	15.0	26.8	9.3	15.4
Confluence Academies	6	2,570	11.9	94.9	8.2	10.7
Kipp St Louis Public Schools	6	2,624	12.3	99.2	1.8	11.2
Ladue	8	4,382	13.1	43.7	5.2	12.2
Lindbergh Schools	10	7,402	15.8	16.7	4.5	15.0
Mehlville R-IX	18	10,162	13.7	20.3	10.3	16.7
Normandy Schools Collaborative	7	2,865	15.0	98.7	1.9	12.7
Ritenour	10	6,316	14.8	77.8	11.6	16.6
Riverview Gardens	13	5,327	18.0	98.9	0.7	14.4
St. Louis City	67	18,747	12.4	87.5	9.5	14.5

Note: Table includes school districts with 2,000 or more students; (1) Percentage of students that are not non-Hispanic white; (2) Percentage of students that are Limited English Proficient or English Language Learners (2018-19); (3) Percentage of students that have an Individualized Education Program (2019-20).
Source: U.S. Department of Education, National Center for Education Statistics, Common Core of Data, Local Education Agency (School District) Universe Survey: School Year 2021-2022

Best High Schools

According to *U.S. News,* Saint Louis is home to two of the top 500 high schools in the U.S.: **Metro Academic and Classical High School** (#220); **Ladue Horton Watkins High School** (#387). Nearly 18,000 public, magnet and charter schools were ranked based on their performance on state assessments and how well they prepare students for college. *U.S. News & World Report, "Best High Schools 2022"*

Highest Level of Education

Area	Less than H.S.	H.S. Diploma	Some College, No Deg.	Associate Degree	Bachelor's Degree	Master's Degree	Prof. School Degree	Doctorate Degree
City	10.8	24.4	20.3	6.5	21.3	11.3	3.2	2.2
MSA[1]	7.2	25.7	21.7	9.2	21.5	10.9	2.2	1.6
U.S.	11.1	26.5	20.0	8.7	20.6	9.3	2.2	1.5

Note: Figures cover persons age 25 and over; (1) Figures cover the St. Louis, MO-IL Metropolitan Statistical Area
Source: U.S. Census Bureau, 2017-2021 American Community Survey 5-Year Estimates

Educational Attainment by Race

Area	High School Graduate or Higher (%)					Bachelor's Degree or Higher (%)				
	Total	White	Black	Asian	Hisp.[2]	Total	White	Black	Asian	Hisp.[2]
City	89.2	94.4	83.1	87.1	79.1	38.0	53.9	16.6	57.9	36.7
MSA[1]	92.8	94.2	87.5	90.8	82.3	36.2	38.6	20.4	68.0	31.3
U.S.	88.9	91.4	87.2	87.6	71.2	33.7	35.5	23.3	55.6	18.4

Note: Figures shown cover persons 25 years old and over; (1) Figures cover the St. Louis, MO-IL Metropolitan Statistical Area; (2) People of Hispanic origin can be of any race
Source: U.S. Census Bureau, 2017-2021 American Community Survey 5-Year Estimates

School Enrollment by Grade and Control

Area	Preschool (%)		Kindergarten (%)		Grades 1 - 4 (%)		Grades 5 - 8 (%)		Grades 9 - 12 (%)	
	Public	Private	Public	Private	Public	Private	Public	Private	Public	Private
City	56.8	43.2	73.9	26.1	82.9	17.1	78.8	21.2	80.6	19.4
MSA[1]	53.6	46.4	80.8	19.2	83.8	16.2	82.7	17.3	85.1	14.9
U.S.	58.8	41.2	86.3	13.7	88.3	11.7	88.6	11.4	89.4	10.6

Note: Figures shown cover persons 3 years old and over; (1) Figures cover the St. Louis, MO-IL Metropolitan Statistical Area
Source: U.S. Census Bureau, 2017-2021 American Community Survey 5-Year Estimates

Higher Education

Four-Year Colleges			Two-Year Colleges			Medical Schools[1]	Law Schools[2]	Voc/ Tech[3]
Public	Private Non-profit	Private For-profit	Public	Private Non-profit	Private For-profit			
3	23	4	7	0	4	2	2	14

Note: Figures cover institutions located within the St. Louis, MO-IL Metropolitan Statistical Area and include main campuses only; (1) includes schools accredited by the Liaison Committee on Medical Education and the American Osteopathic Association's Commission on Osteopathic College Accreditation; (2) includes ABA-accredited schools, schools with provisional ABA accreditation, and state accredited schools; (3) includes all schools with programs that are less than 2 years.
Source: National Center for Education Statistics, Integrated Postsecondary Education System (IPEDS), 2021-22; Wikipedia, List of Medical Schools in the United States, accessed April 10, 2023; Wikipedia, List of Law Schools in the United States, accessed April 10, 2023

According to *U.S. News & World Report*, the St. Louis, MO-IL metro area is home to two of the top 200 national universities in the U.S.: **Washington University in St. Louis** (#15 tie); **Saint Louis University** (#105 tie). The indicators used to capture academic quality fall into a number of categories: assessment by administrators at peer institutions; retention of students; faculty resources; student selectivity; financial resources; alumni giving; high school counselor ratings of colleges; and graduation rate. *U.S. News & World Report, "America's Best Colleges 2023"*

According to *U.S. News & World Report*, the St. Louis, MO-IL metro area is home to one of the top 100 liberal arts colleges in the U.S.: **Principia College** (#51 tie). The indicators used to capture academic quality fall into a number of categories: assessment by administrators at peer institutions; retention of students; faculty resources; student selectivity; financial resources; alumni giving; high school counselor ratings of colleges; and graduation rate. *U.S. News & World Report, "America's Best Colleges 2023"*

According to *U.S. News & World Report*, the St. Louis, MO-IL metro area is home to two of the top 100 law schools in the U.S.: **Washington University in St. Louis** (#16); **Saint Louis University** (#98 tie). The rankings are based on a weighted average of 12 measures of quality: peer assessment score; assessment score by lawyers/judges; median LSAT scores; median undergrad GPA; acceptance rate; employment rates for graduates; placement success; bar passage rate; faculty resources; expenditures per student; student/faculty ratio; and library resources. *U.S. News & World Report, "America's Best Graduate Schools, Law, 2023"*

According to *U.S. News & World Report*, the St. Louis, MO-IL metro area is home to two of the top 75 medical schools for research in the U.S.: **Washington University in St. Louis** (#11 tie); **Saint Louis University** (#73). The rankings are based on a weighted average of 11 measures of quality: quality assessment; peer assessment score; assessment score by residency directors; research activity; total research activity; average research activity per faculty member; student selectivity; median MCAT total score; median undergraduate GPA; acceptance rate; and faculty resources. *U.S. News & World Report, "America's Best Graduate Schools, Medical, 2023"*

According to *U.S. News & World Report*, the St. Louis, MO-IL metro area is home to one of the top 75 business schools in the U.S.: **Washington University in St. Louis (Olin)** (#29 tie). The rankings are based on a weighted average of the following nine measures: quality assessment; peer assessment; recruiter assessment; placement success; mean starting salary and bonus; student selectivity; mean GMAT and GRE scores; mean undergraduate GPA; and acceptance rate. *U.S. News & World Report, "America's Best Graduate Schools, Business, 2023"*

EMPLOYERS

Major Employers

Company Name	Industry
Barnes Jewish Hospital	Healthcare
BJC Healthcare	Healthcare
Boeing Defense	Space & Security
City of Saint Louis	Municipal government
Defense Finance and Accounting Service	Federal government
Mercy	Healthcare
Saint Louis University	Colleges and universities
SSM Health	Healthcare
Wal-Mart Stores	Retail
Washington University on St. Louis	College and universities

Note: Companies shown are located within the St. Louis, MO-IL Metropolitan Statistical Area.
Source: Hoovers.com; Wikipedia

Best Companies to Work For

Edward Jones; World Wide Technology, headquartered in Saint Louis, are among "The 100 Best Companies to Work For." To pick the best companies, *Fortune* partnered with the Great Place to Work Institute. Two-thirds of a company's score is based on the results of the Institute's Trust Index survey, which is sent to a random sample of employees from each company. The questions related to attitudes about management's credibility, job satisfaction, and camaraderie. The other third of the scoring is based on the company's responses to the Institute's Culture Audit, which includes detailed questions about pay and benefit programs, and a series of open-ended questions about hiring practices, internal communication, training, recognition programs, and diversity efforts. Any company that is at least five years old with more than 1,000 U.S. employees is eligible. *Fortune, "The 100 Best Companies to Work For," 2023*

Edward Jones, headquartered in Saint Louis, is among "Fortune's Best Workplaces for Women." To pick the best companies, *Fortune* partnered with the Great Place to Work Institute. To be considered for the list, companies must be Great Place To Work-Certified. Companies must also employ at least 50 women, at least 20% of their non-executive managers must be female, and at least one executive must be female. To determine the Best Workplaces for Women, Great Place To Work measured the differences in women's survey responses to those of their peers and assesses the impact of demographics and roles on the quality and consistency of women's experiences. Great Place To Work also analyzed the gender balance of each workplace, how it compared to each company's industry, and patterns in representation as women rise from front-line positions to the board of directors. *Fortune, "Best Workplaces for Women," 2022*

Centene Corporation, headquartered in Saint Louis, is among "Best Workplaces in Health Care." To determine the Best Workplaces in Health Care list, Great Place To Work analyzed the survey responses of over 161,000 employees from Great Place To Work-Certified companies in the health care industry. Survey data analysis and company-provided datapoints are then factored into a combined score to compare and rank the companies that create the most consistently positive experience for all employees in this industry. *Fortune, "Best Workplaces in Health Care," 2022*

Connectria, headquartered in Saint Louis, is among the "100 Best Places to Work in IT." To qualify, companies had to have a minimum of 100 total employees and five IT employees. The best places to work were selected based on DEI (diversity, equity, and inclusion) practices; IT turnover, promotions, and growth; IT retention and engagement programs; remote/hybrid working; benefits and perks (such as elder care and child care, flextime, and reimbursement for college tuition); and training and career development opportunities. *Computerworld, "Best Places to Work in IT," 2023*

PUBLIC SAFETY

Crime Rate

Area	Total Crime	Violent Crime Rate				Property Crime Rate		
		Murder	Rape[3]	Robbery	Aggrav. Assault	Burglary	Larceny -Theft	Motor Vehicle Theft
City	7,846.6	88.1	78.4	416.2	1,433.5	855.2	3,895.8	1,079.3
Suburbs[1]	n/a	5.6	29.6	39.0	241.8	262.7	n/a	283.8
Metro[2]	n/a	14.3	34.8	79.2	368.7	325.8	n/a	368.6
U.S.	2,356.7	6.5	38.4	73.9	279.7	314.2	1,398.0	246.0

Note: Figures are crimes per 100,000 population; (1) All areas within the metro area that are located outside the city limits; (2) Figures cover the St. Louis, MO-IL Metropolitan Statistical Area; (3) All figures shown were reported using the revised Uniform Crime Reporting (UCR) definition of rape; Due to the transition to the National Incident-Based Reporting System (NIBRS), limited city and metro area data was released for 2021.
Source: FBI Uniform Crime Reports, 2020

Hate Crimes

Area	Number of Quarters Reported	Number of Incidents per Bias Motivation					
		Race/Ethnicity/ Ancestry	Religion	Sexual Orientation	Disability	Gender	Gender Identity
City	2	1	0	0	0	0	0
U.S.	4	5,227	1,244	1,110	130	75	266

Note: Due to the transition to the National Incident-Based Reporting System (NIBRS), limited crime data was released for 2021.
Source: Federal Bureau of Investigation, Hate Crime Statistics 2020

Identity Theft Consumer Reports

Area	Reports	Reports per 100,000 Population	Rank[2]
MSA[1]	8,205	292	75
U.S.	1,108,609	339	-

Note: (1) Figures cover the St. Louis, MO-IL Metropolitan Statistical Area; (2) Rank ranges from 1 to 391 where 1 indicates greatest number of identity theft reports per 100,000 population
Source: Federal Trade Commission, Consumer Sentinel Network Data Book 2022

Fraud and Other Consumer Reports

Area	Reports	Reports per 100,000 Population	Rank[2]
MSA[1]	32,168	1,146	51
U.S.	4,064,520	1,245	-

Note: (1) Figures cover the St. Louis, MO-IL Metropolitan Statistical Area; (2) Rank ranges from 1 to 391 where 1 indicates greatest number of fraud and other consumer reports per 100,000 population
Source: Federal Trade Commission, Consumer Sentinel Network Data Book 2022

POLITICS

2020 Presidential Election Results

Area	Biden	Trump	Jorgensen	Hawkins	Other
St. Louis City	81.9	16.0	1.1	0.4	0.5
U.S.	51.3	46.8	1.2	0.3	0.5

Note: Results are percentages and may not add to 100% due to rounding
Source: Dave Leip's Atlas of U.S. Presidential Elections

SPORTS

Professional Sports Teams

Team Name	League	Year Established
Saint Louis Blues	National Hockey League (NHL)	1967
Saint Louis Cardinals	Major League Baseball (MLB)	1882
St. Louis City SC	Major League Soccer (MLS)	2023

Note: Includes teams located in the St. Louis, MO-IL Metropolitan Statistical Area.
Source: Wikipedia, Major Professional Sports Teams of the United States and Canada, April 12, 2023

CLIMATE

Average and Extreme Temperatures

Temperature	Jan	Feb	Mar	Apr	May	Jun	Jul	Aug	Sep	Oct	Nov	Dec	Yr.
Extreme High (°F)	77	83	89	93	98	105	115	107	104	94	85	76	115
Average High (°F)	39	43	54	67	76	85	89	87	80	69	54	42	66
Average Temp. (°F)	30	34	44	56	66	75	79	78	70	59	45	34	56
Average Low (°F)	21	25	34	46	55	65	69	67	59	48	36	26	46
Extreme Low (°F)	-18	-10	-5	22	31	43	51	47	36	23	1	-16	-18

Note: Figures cover the years 1945-1990
Source: National Climatic Data Center, International Station Meteorological Climate Summary, 9/96

Average Precipitation/Snowfall/Humidity

Precip./Humidity	Jan	Feb	Mar	Apr	May	Jun	Jul	Aug	Sep	Oct	Nov	Dec	Yr.
Avg. Precip. (in.)	1.9	2.2	3.4	3.4	3.8	4.0	3.8	2.9	2.9	2.8	3.0	2.6	36.8
Avg. Snowfall (in.)	6	4	4	Tr	0	0	0	0	0	Tr	1	4	20
Avg. Rel. Hum. 6am (%)	80	81	80	78	81	82	84	86	87	83	81	81	82
Avg. Rel. Hum. 3pm (%)	62	59	54	49	51	51	51	52	50	50	56	63	54

Note: Figures cover the years 1945-1990; Tr = Trace amounts (<0.05 in. of rain; <0.5 in. of snow)
Source: National Climatic Data Center, International Station Meteorological Climate Summary, 9/96

Weather Conditions

Temperature			Daytime Sky			Precipitation		
10°F & below	32°F & below	90°F & above	Clear	Partly cloudy	Cloudy	0.01 inch or more precip.	0.1 inch or more snow/ice	Thunder-storms
13	100	43	97	138	130	109	14	46

Note: Figures are average number of days per year and cover the years 1945-1990
Source: National Climatic Data Center, International Station Meteorological Climate Summary, 9/96

HAZARDOUS WASTE

Superfund Sites

The St. Louis, MO-IL metro area is home to 11 sites on the EPA's Superfund National Priorities List: **Chemetco** (final); **Circle Smelting Corp.** (proposed); **Ellisville Site** (final); **Jennison-Wright Corporation** (final); **Minker/Stout/Romaine Creek** (final); **Nl Industries/Taracorp Lead Smelter** (final); **Oak Grove Village Well** (final); **Old American Zinc Plant** (final); **Riverfront** (final); **Sauget Area 1** (proposed); **Sauget Area 2** (proposed). There are a total of 1,165 Superfund sites with a status of proposed or final on the list in the U.S. *U.S. Environmental Protection Agency, National Priorities List, April 12, 2023*

AIR QUALITY

Air Quality Trends: Ozone

	1990	1995	2000	2005	2010	2015	2018	2019	2020	2021
MSA[1]	0.077	0.084	0.074	0.078	0.069	0.067	0.072	0.066	0.066	0.067
U.S.	0.087	0.089	0.081	0.080	0.072	0.067	0.069	0.065	0.065	0.067

Note: (1) Data covers the St. Louis, MO-IL Metropolitan Statistical Area. The values shown are the composite ozone concentration averages among trend sites based on the highest fourth daily maximum 8-hour concentration in parts per million. These trends are based on sites having an adequate record of monitoring data during the trend period. Data from exceptional events are included.
Source: U.S. Environmental Protection Agency, Air Quality Monitoring Information, "Air Quality Trends by City, 1990-2021"

Air Quality Index

Area	Percent of Days when Air Quality was...[2]					AQI Statistics[2]	
	Good	Moderate	Unhealthy for Sensitive Groups	Unhealthy	Very Unhealthy	Maximum	Median
MSA[1]	38.1	57.8	3.6	0.5	0.0	187	55

Note: (1) Data covers the St. Louis, MO-IL Metropolitan Statistical Area; (2) Based on 365 days with AQI data in 2021. Air Quality Index (AQI) is an index for reporting daily air quality. EPA calculates the AQI for five major air pollutants regulated by the Clean Air Act: ground-level ozone, particle pollution (aka particulate matter), carbon monoxide, sulfur dioxide, and nitrogen dioxide. The AQI runs from 0 to 500. The higher the AQI value, the greater the level of air pollution and the greater the health concern. There are six AQI categories: "Good" AQI is between 0 and 50. Air quality is considered satisfactory; "Moderate" AQI is between 51 and 100. Air quality is acceptable; "Unhealthy for Sensitive Groups" When AQI values are between 101 and 150, members of sensitive groups may experience health effects; "Unhealthy" When AQI values are between 151 and 200 everyone may begin to experience health effects; "Very Unhealthy" AQI values between 201 and 300 trigger a health alert; "Hazardous" AQI values over 300 trigger warnings of emergency conditions (not shown).
Source: U.S. Environmental Protection Agency, Air Quality Index Report, 2021

Air Quality Index Pollutants

Area	Percent of Days when AQI Pollutant was...[2]					
	Carbon Monoxide	Nitrogen Dioxide	Ozone	Sulfur Dioxide	Particulate Matter 2.5	Particulate Matter 10
MSA[1]	0.0	0.5	25.8	(3)	70.1	3.6

Note: (1) Data covers the St. Louis, MO-IL Metropolitan Statistical Area; (2) Based on 365 days with AQI data in 2021. The Air Quality Index (AQI) is an index for reporting daily air quality. EPA calculates the AQI for five major air pollutants regulated by the Clean Air Act: ground-level ozone, particle pollution (also known as particulate matter), carbon monoxide, sulfur dioxide, and nitrogen dioxide. The AQI runs from 0 to 500. The higher the AQI value, the greater the level of air pollution and the greater the health concern; (3) Sulfur dioxide is no longer included in this table (as of December 8, 2021) because SO_2 concentrations tend to be very localized and not necessarily representative of broad geographical areas like counties and CBSAs.
Source: U.S. Environmental Protection Agency, Air Quality Index Report, 2021

Maximum Air Pollutant Concentrations: Particulate Matter, Ozone, CO and Lead

	Particulate Matter 10 (ug/m^3)	Particulate Matter 2.5 Wtd AM (ug/m^3)	Particulate Matter 2.5 24-Hr (ug/m^3)	Ozone (ppm)	Carbon Monoxide (ppm)	Lead (ug/m^3)
MSA[1] Level	161	10	23	0.073	1	0.06
NAAQS[2]	150	15	35	0.075	9	0.15
Met NAAQS[2]	No	Yes	Yes	Yes	Yes	Yes

Note: (1) Data covers the St. Louis, MO-IL Metropolitan Statistical Area; Data from exceptional events are included; (2) National Ambient Air Quality Standards; ppm = parts per million; ug/m^3 = micrograms per cubic meter; n/a not available.
Concentrations: Particulate Matter 10 (coarse particulate)—highest second maximum 24-hour concentration; Particulate Matter 2.5 Wtd AM (fine particulate)—highest weighted annual mean concentration; Particulate Matter 2.5 24-Hour (fine particulate)—highest 98th percentile 24-hour concentration; Ozone—highest fourth daily maximum 8-hour concentration; Carbon Monoxide—highest second maximum non-overlapping 8-hour concentration; Lead—maximum running 3-month average
Source: U.S. Environmental Protection Agency, Air Quality Monitoring Information, "Air Quality Statistics by City, 2021"

Maximum Air Pollutant Concentrations: Nitrogen Dioxide and Sulfur Dioxide

	Nitrogen Dioxide AM (ppb)	Nitrogen Dioxide 1-Hr (ppb)	Sulfur Dioxide AM (ppb)	Sulfur Dioxide 1-Hr (ppb)	Sulfur Dioxide 24-Hr (ppb)
MSA[1] Level	10	46	n/a	34	n/a
NAAQS[2]	53	100	30	75	140
Met NAAQS[2]	Yes	Yes	n/a	Yes	n/a

Note: (1) Data covers the St. Louis, MO-IL Metropolitan Statistical Area; Data from exceptional events are included; (2) National Ambient Air Quality Standards; ppm = parts per million; ug/m³ = micrograms per cubic meter; n/a not available.
Concentrations: Nitrogen Dioxide AM—highest arithmetic mean concentration; Nitrogen Dioxide 1-Hr—highest 98th percentile 1-hour daily maximum concentration; Sulfur Dioxide AM—highest annual mean concentration; Sulfur Dioxide 1-Hr—highest 99th percentile 1-hour daily maximum concentration; Sulfur Dioxide 24-Hr—highest second maximum 24-hour concentration
Source: U.S. Environmental Protection Agency, Air Quality Monitoring Information, "Air Quality Statistics by City, 2021"

Sioux Falls, South Dakota

Background

Sioux Falls, in southeastern South Dakota, is named for the falls on the Big Sioux River where it is located. It is the seat of Minnehaha County and overlaps Lincoln County. Sioux Falls is a Great Plains city, rich in history and scenic attractions, a dynamic economic center, and a splendid family town, offering an extensive range of outdoor activities.

The city was founded prior to the Civil War by settlers who were attracted by the nearby stone quarries and the possibility of harnessing the river for waterpower. Many Scottish, English, and Norwegian immigrants came to the area and used their skills as stonecutters. The community was incorporated as a village in 1877 and as a city in 1883.

At the city's popular Falls Park, the remains of a water-driven mill testify to the importance of the river. The city has preserved much of its early architectural charm, and five separate historical districts with buildings of considerable interest, including the R.F. Pettigrew home, residence of the state's first U.S. senator, and the Minnehaha County Courthouse.

Sioux Falls's restoration "Phillips to the Falls" program connected the park to the rest of downtown by extending Phillips Avenue north to Falls Park and expanding the park to the south.

Sioux Falls offers one of the Midwest's most dynamic business environments, partly due to the lack of a state corporate income tax, and is home to industry leaders in agri-business, distribution and trade, financial services, high-tech manufacturing, health care, retail, and tourism. The city embarked on a 2022-2026 capital program to replace, rehabilitate, and expand street and utility infrastructure and invest in the park system and entertainment venues, at a cost of $812 million.

The city is at the heart of a large agricultural and stock-raising area, producing corn and soybeans, and serving as a regional center for stockyards and meat-packing plants. Industries in Sioux Falls also produce computer components, electronics, and artificial flowers. Some of the nation's leading credit card operations are based in the city, employment opportunities are varied and abundant, and the city's unemployment rate is generally half that of the state.

Amazon's new five-story, 3-million-square-foot distribution center opened in the city in 2022, bringing with it 1,000 full time jobs. Other major employees include Tyson Foods and Sioux City Schools.

Air travel is available through the Sioux Falls Regional Airport, which connects conveniently to major air hubs.

Sioux Falls is an important center of higher education, home to the University of South Dakota, Dakota State University, South Dakota State University, Northern State University, Augustana College, National American University, Colorado Technical University at Sioux Falls, and Southeast Technical Institute. The Federal Earth Resource Observation System operates a major data collection and analysis site nearby.

The city and its environs are home to a variety of recreation, such as the Catfish Bay Water Ski & Stage Show, Empire Golf Sport Dome, Great Bear Recreation Park, Huset's Speedway, and Wild Water West, the state's largest water and amusement park. The Downtown River Greenway Project recently celebrated completion of its riverfront trail connection to Chris Larsen Park, providing users with over 12 miles of continuous trail.

The modern Washington Pavilion of Arts and Science in the Sioux Falls historic downtown district features a performing arts space, a domed Omni theater, a science museum, and display areas for the city's Fine Arts Center. The Sioux Falls Jazz and Blues Festival celebrated its 30th anniversary in 2021.

The climate is continental with frequent weather changes, a result of differing, usually cold, air masses, which move in rapidly. During the late fall and winter, cold fronts accompanied by strong, gusty winds can cause temperatures to drop significantly during a 24-hour period. Rainfall is heavier during the spring and summer, and thunderstorms are frequent. Summer daytime temperatures can be high, but the nights are usually comfortable.

Rankings

General Rankings

- In their ninth annual survey, Livability.com looked at data for more than 2,300 mid-sized U.S. cities to determine the rankings for Livability's "Top 100 Best Places to Live" in 2022. Sioux Falls ranked #38. Criteria: housing and economy; social and civic engagement; education; demographics; health care options; transportation & infrastructure; and community amenities. *Livability.com, "Top 100 Best Places to Live 2022" July 19, 2022*

Business/Finance Rankings

- The Sioux Falls metro area appeared on the Milken Institute "2022 Best Performing Cities" list. Rank: #7 out of 201 small metro areas (population over 60,000). Criteria: job growth; wage and salary growth; high-tech output growth; housing affordability; household broadband access. *Milken Institute, "Best-Performing Cities 2022," March 28, 2022*

- *Forbes* ranked 203 smaller metro areas (population under 268,000) to determine the nation's "Best Small Places for Business and Careers." The Sioux Falls metro area was ranked #1. Criteria: costs (business and living); job growth (past and projected); income growth; quality of life; educational attainment (college and high school); projected economic growth; cultural and leisure opportunities; workplace tolerance laws; net migration patterns. *Forbes, "The Best Small Places for Business and Careers 2019," October 30, 2019*

Dating/Romance Rankings

- Sioux Falls was selected as one of the most romantic cities in the U.S. by video-rental kiosk company Redbox. The city ranked #7 out of 20. Criteria: number of romance-related rentals in 2016. *Redbox, "20 Most Romantic Cities," February 6, 2017*

Real Estate Rankings

- *WalletHub* compared the most populated U.S. cities to determine which had the best markets for real estate agents. Sioux Falls ranked #23 where demand was high and pay was the best. Criteria: sales per agent; annual median wage for real-estate agents; monthly average starting salary for real estate agents; real estate job density and competition; unemployment rate; home turnover rate; housing-market health index; and other relevant metrics. *www.WalletHub.com, "2021 Best Places to Be a Real Estate Agent," May 12, 2021*

Safety Rankings

- Allstate ranked the 200 largest cities in America in terms of driver safety. Sioux Falls ranked #72. Criteria: internal property damage claims over a two-year period from January 2016 to December 2017. The report helps increase the importance of safety and awareness behind the wheel. *Allstate, "Allstate America's Best Drivers Report, 2019" June 24, 2019*

- The National Insurance Crime Bureau ranked 390 metro areas in the U.S. in terms of per capita rates of vehicle theft. The Sioux Falls metro area ranked #36 (#1 = highest rate). Criteria: number of vehicle theft offenses per 100,000 inhabitants in 2021. *National Insurance Crime Bureau, "Hot Spots 2021," September 1, 2022*

Seniors/Retirement Rankings

- From its Best Cities for Successful Aging indexes, the Milken Institute generated rankings for metropolitan areas, weighing data in nine categories—health care, wellness, living arrangements, transportation and convenience, financial characteristics, education, employment, community engagement, and overall livability. The Sioux Falls metro area was ranked #5 overall in the small metro area category. *Milken Institute, "Best Cities for Successful Aging, 2017" March 14, 2017*

- Sioux Falls made the 2022 *Forbes* list of "25 Best Places to Retire." Criteria, focused on overall affordability as well as quality of life indicators, include: housing/living costs compared to the national average and state taxes; air quality; crime rates; home price appreciation; risk associated with climate-change/natural hazards; availability of medical care; bikeability; walkability; healthy living. *Forbes.com, "The Best Places to Retire in 2022," May 13, 2022*

Women/Minorities Rankings

- *Women's Health*, together with the site Yelp, identified the 15 "Wellthiest" spots in the U.S. Sioux Falls appeared among the top for happiest, healthiest, outdoorsiest and Zen-iest. *Women's Health, "The 15 Wellthiest Cities in the U.S." July 5, 2017*

- Personal finance website *WalletHub* compared more than 180 U.S. cities across two key dimensions, "Hispanic Business-Friendliness" and "Hispanic Purchasing Power," to arrive at the most favorable conditions for Hispanic entrepreneurs. Sioux Falls was ranked #19 out of 182. Criteria includes: share of Hispanic-Owned Businesses; Hispanic entrepreneurship rate to median annual income of Hispanics; Small Business-Friendliness score; cost of living; and number of Hispanics with at least a bachelor's degree. *WalletHub.com, "2019's Best Cities for Hispanic Entrepreneurs," May 1, 2019*

Miscellaneous Rankings

- The financial planning site SmartAsset has compiled its annual study on the best places for Halloween in the U.S. for 2022. 146 cities were compared to determine that Sioux Falls ranked #19 out of 35 for still being able to enjoy the festivities despite COVID-19. Metrics included: safety, family-friendliness, percentage of children in the population, concentration of candy and costume shops, weather and COVID infection rates. *www.smartasset.com, "2022 Edition-Best Places to Celebrate Halloween," October 19, 2022*

- *WalletHub* compared the 150 most populated U.S. cities to determine their operating efficiency. A "Quality of Services" score was constructed for each city and then divided by the total budget per capita to reveal which were managed the best. Sioux Falls ranked #17. Criteria: financial stability; economy; education; safety; health; infrastructure and pollution. *www.WalletHub.com, "2022's Best-& Worst-Run Cities in America," June 21, 2022*

Business Environment

DEMOGRAPHICS

Population Growth

Area	1990 Census	2000 Census	2010 Census	2020 Census	Population Growth (%)	
					1990-2020	2010-2020
City	102,262	123,975	153,888	192,517	88.3	25.1
MSA[1]	153,500	187,093	228,261	276,730	80.3	21.2
U.S.	248,709,873	281,421,906	308,745,538	331,449,281	33.3	7.4

Note: (1) Figures cover the Sioux Falls, SD Metropolitan Statistical Area
Source: U.S. Census Bureau, 1990 Census, 2000 Census, 2010 Census, 2020 Census

Race

Area	White Alone[2] (%)	Black Alone[2] (%)	Asian Alone[2] (%)	AIAN[3] Alone[2] (%)	NHOPI[4] Alone[2] (%)	Other Race Alone[2] (%)	Two or More Races (%)
City	79.0	6.3	2.8	2.7	0.0	2.9	6.1
MSA[1]	83.4	4.6	2.0	2.2	0.0	2.3	5.5
U.S.	61.6	12.4	6.0	1.1	0.2	8.4	10.2

Note: (1) Figures cover the Sioux Falls, SD Metropolitan Statistical Area; (2) Alone is defined as not being in combination with one or more other races; (3) American Indian and Alaska Native; (4) Native Hawaiian and Other Pacific Islander
Source: U.S. Census Bureau, 2020 Census

Hispanic or Latino Origin

Area	Total (%)	Mexican (%)	Puerto Rican (%)	Cuban (%)	Other (%)
City	5.5	2.6	0.3	0.1	2.6
MSA[1]	4.6	2.3	0.2	0.1	2.1
U.S.	18.4	11.2	1.8	0.7	4.7

Note: Persons of Hispanic or Latino origin can be of any race; (1) Figures cover the Sioux Falls, SD Metropolitan Statistical Area
Source: U.S. Census Bureau, 2017-2021 American Community Survey 5-Year Estimates

Age

Area	Percent of Population									Median Age
	Under Age 5	Age 5–19	Age 20–34	Age 35–44	Age 45–54	Age 55–64	Age 65–74	Age 75–84	Age 85+	
City	7.0	19.8	22.7	13.8	10.7	11.4	8.7	4.0	1.8	35.3
MSA[1]	7.0	20.9	20.5	13.8	11.1	11.9	8.8	4.0	1.7	36.0
U.S.	5.6	19.2	20.2	12.7	12.4	13.1	10.0	4.9	1.9	38.8

Note: (1) Figures cover the Sioux Falls, SD Metropolitan Statistical Area
Source: U.S. Census Bureau, 2020 Census

Disability by Age

Area	All Ages	Under 18 Years Old	18 to 64 Years Old	65 Years and Over
City	10.1	3.4	9.0	28.9
MSA[1]	9.9	3.2	8.7	28.5
U.S.	12.6	4.4	10.3	33.4

Note: Figures show percent of the civilian noninstitutionalized population that reported having a disability. Disability status is determined from six types of difficulty: vision, hearing, cognitive, ambulatory, self-care, and independent living. For children under 5 years old, hearing and vision difficulty are used to determine disability status. For children between the ages of 5 and 14, disability status is determined from hearing, vision, cognitive, ambulatory, and self-care difficulties. For people aged 15 years and older, they are considered to have a disability if they have difficulty with any one of the six difficulty types; Note: (1) Figures cover the Sioux Falls, SD Metropolitan Statistical Area
Source: U.S. Census Bureau, 2017-2021 American Community Survey 5-Year Estimates

Ancestry

Area	German	Irish	English	American	Italian	Polish	French[2]	Scottish	Dutch
City	33.6	10.9	6.5	4.2	1.6	1.5	1.8	0.9	6.1
MSA[1]	35.2	10.4	6.1	5.2	1.4	1.4	1.8	0.9	6.4
U.S.	12.8	9.6	8.1	5.7	5.0	2.7	2.2	1.6	1.1

Note: Figures are the percentage of the total population reporting a particular ancestry. The nine most commonly reported ancestries in the U.S. are shown. Figures include multiple ancestries (e.g. if a person reported being Irish and Italian, they were included in both columns); (1) Figures cover the Sioux Falls, SD Metropolitan Statistical Area; (2) Excludes Basque
Source: U.S. Census Bureau, 2017-2021 American Community Survey 5-Year Estimates

Foreign-born Population

Area	Any Foreign Country	Percent of Population Born in							
		Asia	Mexico	Europe	Caribbean	Central America[2]	South America	Africa	Canada
City	8.7	2.1	0.5	1.1	0.1	1.1	0.1	3.4	0.1
MSA[1]	6.5	1.5	0.5	0.9	0.1	0.8	0.1	2.4	0.1
U.S.	13.6	4.2	1.5	1.4	1.1	1.1	0.1	0.8	0.2

Note: (1) Figures cover the Sioux Falls, SD Metropolitan Statistical Area; (2) Excludes Mexico.
Source: U.S. Census Bureau, 2017-2021 American Community Survey 5-Year Estimates

Household Size

Area	Persons in Household (%)							Average Household Size
	One	Two	Three	Four	Five	Six	Seven or More	
City	32.3	33.4	14.1	11.2	6.1	1.8	1.0	2.40
MSA[1]	28.8	34.5	14.6	12.2	6.8	2.0	1.1	2.50
U.S.	28.1	33.8	15.5	12.9	6.0	2.3	1.4	2.60

Note: (1) Figures cover the Sioux Falls, SD Metropolitan Statistical Area
Source: U.S. Census Bureau, 2017-2021 American Community Survey 5-Year Estimates

Household Relationships

Area	House-holder	Opposite-sex Spouse	Same-sex Spouse	Opposite-sex Unmarried Partner	Same-sex Unmarried Partner	Child[2]	Grand-child	Other Relatives	Non-relatives
City	40.7	18.0	0.1	3.2	0.1	28.4	1.1	2.7	3.1
MSA[1]	39.5	19.4	0.1	2.9	0.1	29.8	1.1	2.3	2.6
U.S.	38.3	17.5	0.2	2.5	0.2	28.3	2.4	4.8	3.4

Note: Figures are percent of the total population; (1) Figures cover the Sioux Falls, SD Metropolitan Statistical Area; (2) Includes biological, adopted, and stepchildren of the householder
Source: U.S. Census Bureau, 2020 Census

Gender

Area	Males	Females	Males per 100 Females
City	95,676	96,841	98.8
MSA[1]	138,437	138,293	100.1
U.S.	162,685,811	168,763,470	96.4

Note: (1) Figures cover the Sioux Falls, SD Metropolitan Statistical Area
Source: U.S. Census Bureau, 2020 Census

Marital Status

Area	Never Married	Now Married[2]	Separated	Widowed	Divorced
City	34.5	48.6	1.2	4.3	11.4
MSA[1]	30.6	53.2	1.0	4.4	10.8
U.S.	33.8	48.0	1.8	5.6	10.8

Note: Figures are percentages and cover the population 15 years of age and older; (1) Figures cover the Sioux Falls, SD Metropolitan Statistical Area; (2) Excludes separated
Source: U.S. Census Bureau, 2017-2021 American Community Survey 5-Year Estimates

Religious Groups by Family

Area	Catholic	Baptist	Methodist	LDS[2]	Pentecostal	Lutheran	Islam	Adventist	Other
MSA[1]	13.1	0.7	2.9	0.7	1.7	16.4	0.1	0.6	20.3
U.S.	18.7	7.3	3.0	2.0	1.8	1.7	1.3	1.3	11.6

Note: Figures are the number of adherents as a percentage of the total population and cover the eight largest religious groups in the U.S; (1) Figures cover the Sioux Falls, SD Metropolitan Statistical Area; (2) Church of Jesus Christ of Latter-day Saints
Sources: 2020 U.S. Religion Census, Association of Statisticians of American Religious Bodies; The Association of Religion Data Archives (ARDA)

Religious Groups by Tradition

Area	Catholic	Evangelical Protestant	Mainline Protestant	Black Protestant	Islam	Judaism	Hinduism	Orthodox	Buddhism
MSA[1]	13.1	21.0	20.2	0.1	0.1	n/a	n/a	0.8	<0.1
U.S.	18.7	16.5	5.2	2.3	1.3	0.6	0.4	0.4	0.3

Note: Figures are the number of adherents as a percentage of the total population; (1) Figures cover the Sioux Falls, SD Metropolitan Statistical Area
Sources: 2020 U.S. Religion Census, Association of Statisticians of American Religious Bodies; The Association of Religion Data Archives (ARDA)

ECONOMY

Gross Metropolitan Product

Area	2020	2021	2022	2023	Rank[2]
MSA[1]	23.4	26.6	28.7	30.6	118

Note: Figures are in billions of dollars; (1) Figures cover the Sioux Falls, SD Metropolitan Statistical Area; (2) Rank is based on 2021 data and ranges from 1 to 381
Source: U.S. Conference of Mayors, U.S. Metro Economies: U.S. Metros Compared to Global and State Economies, June 2022

Economic Growth

Area	2018-20 (%)	2021 (%)	2022 (%)	2023 (%)	Rank[2]
MSA[1]	0.4	7.1	1.9	3.7	111
U.S.	-0.6	5.7	3.1	2.9	–

Note: Figures are real gross metropolitan product (GMP) growth rates and represent average annual percent change; (1) Figures cover the Sioux Falls, SD Metropolitan Statistical Area; (2) Rank is based on 2020 2-year average annual percent change and ranges from 1 to 381
Source: U.S. Conference of Mayors, U.S. Metro Economies: U.S. Metros Compared to Global and State Economies, June 2022

Metropolitan Area Exports

Area	2016	2017	2018	2019	2020	2021	Rank[2]
MSA[1]	334.3	386.8	400.0	431.5	524.9	547.3	207

Note: Figures are in millions of dollars; (1) Figures cover the Sioux Falls, SD Metropolitan Statistical Area; (2) Rank is based on 2021 data and ranges from 1 to 388
Source: U.S. Department of Commerce, International Trade Administration, Office of Trade and Economic Analysis, Industry and Analysis, Exports by Metropolitan Area, data extracted March 16, 2023

Building Permits

Area	Single-Family			Multi-Family			Total		
	2021	2022	Pct. Chg.	2021	2022	Pct. Chg.	2021	2022	Pct. Chg.
City	1,313	1,036	-21.1	1,819	3,429	88.5	3,132	4,465	42.6
MSA[1]	1,893	1,626	-14.1	2,093	3,928	87.7	3,986	5,554	39.3
U.S.	1,115,400	975,600	-12.5	621,600	689,500	10.9	1,737,000	1,665,100	-4.1

Note: (1) Figures cover the Sioux Falls, SD Metropolitan Statistical Area; Figures represent new, privately-owned housing units authorized (unadjusted data); All permit data are based on estimates with imputation
Source: U.S. Census Bureau, Manufacturing, Mining, and Construction Statistics, Building Permits, 2021, 2022

Bankruptcy Filings

Area	Business Filings			Nonbusiness Filings		
	2021	2022	% Chg.	2021	2022	% Chg.
Minnehaha County	7	6	-14.3	221	201	-9.0
U.S.	14,347	13,481	-6.0	399,269	374,240	-6.3

Note: Business filings include Chapter 7, Chapter 9, Chapter 11, Chapter 12, Chapter 13, Chapter 15, and Section 304; Nonbusiness filings include Chapter 7, Chapter 11, and Chapter 13
Source: Administrative Office of the U.S. Courts, Business and Nonbusiness Bankruptcy, County Cases Commenced by Chapter of the Bankruptcy Code, During the 12-Month Period Ending December 31, 2021 and Business and Nonbusiness Bankruptcy, County Cases Commenced by Chapter of the Bankruptcy Code, During the 12-Month Period Ending December 31, 2022

Housing Vacancy Rates

Area	Gross Vacancy Rate[2] (%)			Year-Round Vacancy Rate[3] (%)			Rental Vacancy Rate[4] (%)			Homeowner Vacancy Rate[5] (%)		
	2020	2021	2022	2020	2021	2022	2020	2021	2022	2020	2021	2022
MSA[1]	n/a	n/a	n/a	n/a	n/a	n/a	n/a	n/a	n/a	n/a	n/a	n/a
U.S.	10.6	10.8	10.5	8.2	8.4	8.2	6.3	6.1	5.8	1.0	0.9	0.8

Note: (1) Figures cover the Sioux Falls, SD Metropolitan Statistical Area; (2) The percentage of the total housing inventory that is vacant; (3) The percentage of the housing inventory (excluding seasonal units) that is year-round vacant; (4) The percentage of rental inventory that is vacant for rent; (5) The percentage of homeowner inventory that is vacant for sale; n/a not available
Source: U.S. Census Bureau, Housing Vacancies and Homeownership Annual Statistics: 2020, 2021, 2022

INCOME

Income

Area	Per Capita ($)	Median Household ($)	Average Household ($)
City	36,430	66,761	87,676
MSA[1]	37,200	72,547	92,236
U.S.	37,638	69,021	97,196

Note: (1) Figures cover the Sioux Falls, SD Metropolitan Statistical Area
Source: U.S. Census Bureau, 2017-2021 American Community Survey 5-Year Estimates

Household Income Distribution

Area	Percent of Households Earning							
	Under $15,000	$15,000 -$24,999	$25,000 -$34,999	$35,000 -$49,999	$50,000 -$74,999	$75,000 -$99,999	$100,000 -$149,999	$150,000 and up
City	7.3	7.4	9.7	12.4	19.1	15.0	17.1	11.9
MSA[1]	6.2	6.7	8.7	11.8	18.7	15.7	18.9	13.3
U.S.	9.4	7.8	8.2	11.4	16.8	12.8	16.3	17.3

Note: (1) Figures cover the Sioux Falls, SD Metropolitan Statistical Area
Source: U.S. Census Bureau, 2017-2021 American Community Survey 5-Year Estimates

Poverty Rate

Area	All Ages	Under 18 Years Old	18 to 64 Years Old	65 Years and Over
City	9.5	10.6	9.6	6.8
MSA[1]	7.9	8.5	8.0	6.3
U.S.	12.6	17.0	11.8	9.6

Note: Figures are percentage of people whose income during the past 12 months was below the poverty level;
(1) Figures cover the Sioux Falls, SD Metropolitan Statistical Area
Source: U.S. Census Bureau, 2017-2021 American Community Survey 5-Year Estimates

EMPLOYMENT

Labor Force and Employment

Area	Civilian Labor Force			Workers Employed		
	Dec. 2021	Dec. 2022	% Chg.	Dec. 2021	Dec. 2022	% Chg.
City	109,388	111,832	2.2	106,662	109,520	2.7
MSA[1]	159,168	162,847	2.3	155,392	159,650	2.7
U.S.	161,696,000	164,224,000	1.6	155,732,000	158,872,000	2.0

Note: Data is not seasonally adjusted and covers workers 16 years of age and older; (1) Figures cover the Sioux Falls, SD Metropolitan Statistical Area
Source: Bureau of Labor Statistics, Local Area Unemployment Statistics

Unemployment Rate

Area	2022											
	Jan.	Feb.	Mar.	Apr.	May	Jun.	Jul.	Aug.	Sep.	Oct.	Nov.	Dec.
City	2.6	2.8	2.4	2.0	1.9	2.1	1.7	2.0	1.6	1.9	1.8	2.1
MSA[1]	2.5	2.7	2.3	1.9	1.9	2.1	1.7	2.0	1.5	1.8	1.7	2.0
U.S.	4.4	4.1	3.8	3.3	3.4	3.8	3.8	3.8	3.3	3.4	3.4	3.3

Note: Data is not seasonally adjusted and covers workers 16 years of age and older; (1) Figures cover the Sioux Falls, SD Metropolitan Statistical Area
Source: Bureau of Labor Statistics, Local Area Unemployment Statistics

Average Wages

Occupation	$/Hr.	Occupation	$/Hr.
Accountants and Auditors	36.65	Maintenance and Repair Workers	20.54
Automotive Mechanics	24.92	Marketing Managers	66.13
Bookkeepers	19.54	Network and Computer Systems Admin.	35.57
Carpenters	20.96	Nurses, Licensed Practical	22.26
Cashiers	13.46	Nurses, Registered	30.18
Computer Programmers	31.23	Nursing Assistants	15.47
Computer Systems Analysts	41.70	Office Clerks, General	15.70
Computer User Support Specialists	21.59	Physical Therapists	41.62
Construction Laborers	18.01	Physicians	n/a
Cooks, Restaurant	15.46	Plumbers, Pipefitters and Steamfitters	25.38
Customer Service Representatives	18.54	Police and Sheriff's Patrol Officers	31.52
Dentists	69.39	Postal Service Mail Carriers	27.07
Electricians	26.54	Real Estate Sales Agents	n/a
Engineers, Electrical	46.30	Retail Salespersons	18.12
Fast Food and Counter Workers	13.18	Sales Representatives, Technical/Scientific	57.97
Financial Managers	76.40	Secretaries, Exc. Legal/Medical/Executive	17.76
First-Line Supervisors of Office Workers	28.08	Security Guards	16.09
General and Operations Managers	71.87	Surgeons	n/a
Hairdressers/Cosmetologists	19.15	Teacher Assistants, Exc. Postsecondary*	12.99
Home Health and Personal Care Aides	15.27	Teachers, Secondary School, Exc. Sp. Ed.*	24.57
Janitors and Cleaners	15.35	Telemarketers	n/a
Landscaping/Groundskeeping Workers	16.41	Truck Drivers, Heavy/Tractor-Trailer	26.46
Lawyers	60.68	Truck Drivers, Light/Delivery Services	21.01
Maids and Housekeeping Cleaners	13.76	Waiters and Waitresses	13.23

Note: Wage data covers the Sioux Falls, SD Metropolitan Statistical Area; (*) Hourly wages were calculated from annual wage data based on a 40 hour work week; n/a not available.
Source: Bureau of Labor Statistics, Metro Area Occupational Employment & Wage Estimates, May 2022

Employment by Industry

Sector	MSA[1]		U.S.
	Number of Employees	Percent of Total	Percent of Total
Construction, Mining, and Logging	9,800	5.8	5.4
Private Education and Health Services	36,400	21.6	16.1
Financial Activities	15,300	9.1	5.9
Government	15,300	9.1	14.5
Information	2,600	1.5	2.0
Leisure and Hospitality	16,000	9.5	10.3
Manufacturing	14,700	8.7	8.4
Other Services	6,600	3.9	3.7
Professional and Business Services	16,500	9.8	14.7
Retail Trade	20,000	11.8	10.2
Transportation, Warehousing, and Utilities	6,400	3.8	4.9
Wholesale Trade	9,200	5.5	3.9

Note: Figures are non-farm employment as of December 2022. Figures are not seasonally adjusted and include workers 16 years of age and older; (1) Figures cover the Sioux Falls, SD Metropolitan Statistical Area
Source: Bureau of Labor Statistics, Current Employment Statistics, Employment, Hours, and Earnings

Employment by Occupation

Occupation Classification	City (%)	MSA[1] (%)	U.S. (%)
Management, Business, Science, and Arts	38.8	39.6	40.3
Natural Resources, Construction, and Maintenance	7.9	9.0	8.7
Production, Transportation, and Material Moving	14.4	13.8	13.1
Sales and Office	22.4	22.0	20.9
Service	16.6	15.6	17.0

Note: Figures cover employed civilians 16 years of age and older; (1) Figures cover the Sioux Falls, SD Metropolitan Statistical Area
Source: U.S. Census Bureau, 2017-2021 American Community Survey 5-Year Estimates

Occupations with Greatest Projected Employment Growth: 2022 – 2024

Occupation[1]	2022 Employment	2024 Projected Employment	Numeric Employment Change	Percent Employment Change
Registered Nurses	13,750	14,190	440	3.2
Fast Food and Counter Workers	14,010	14,420	410	2.9
Stockers and Order Fillers	8,340	8,690	350	4.2
Retail Salespersons	14,700	15,000	300	2.0
Sales Representatives, Wholesale and Manufacturing, Except Technical and Scientific Products	5,660	5,950	290	5.1
Janitors and Cleaners, Except Maids and Housekeeping Cleaners	9,620	9,860	240	2.5
Heavy and Tractor-Trailer Truck Drivers	7,790	8,030	240	3.1
Software Developers and Software Quality Assurance Analysts and Testers	2,770	3,000	230	8.3
Carpenters	5,950	6,180	230	3.9
Laborers and Freight, Stock, and Material Movers, Hand	5,860	6,080	220	3.8

Note: Projections cover South Dakota; (1) Sorted by numeric employment change
Source: www.projectionscentral.com, State Occupational Projections, 2022–2024 Short-Term Projections

Fastest-Growing Occupations: 2022 – 2024

Occupation[1]	2022 Employment	2024 Projected Employment	Numeric Employment Change	Percent Employment Change
Wind Turbine Service Technicians	260	310	50	19.2
Nurse Practitioners	620	700	80	12.9
Information Security Analysts (SOC 2018)	490	540	50	10.2
Industrial Machinery Mechanics	1,170	1,270	100	8.5
Software Developers and Software Quality Assurance Analysts and Testers	2,770	3,000	230	8.3
Cooks, Restaurant	1,720	1,860	140	8.1
Industrial Engineers	640	690	50	7.8
Market Research Analysts and Marketing Specialists	1,200	1,290	90	7.5
Mobile Heavy Equipment Mechanics, Except Engines	680	730	50	7.4
Farm Equipment Mechanics and Service Technicians	1,200	1,280	80	6.7

Note: Projections cover South Dakota; (1) Sorted by percent employment change and excludes occupations with numeric employment change less than 50
Source: www.projectionscentral.com, State Occupational Projections, 2022–2024 Short-Term Projections

CITY FINANCES

City Government Finances

Component	2020 ($000)	2020 ($ per capita)
Total Revenues	409,965	2,231
Total Expenditures	335,073	1,823
Debt Outstanding	220,123	1,198
Cash and Securities[1]	312,281	1,699

Note: (1) Cash and security holdings of a government at the close of its fiscal year, including those of its dependent agencies, utilities, and liquor stores.
Source: U.S. Census Bureau, State & Local Government Finances 2020

City Government Revenue by Source

Source	2020 ($000)	2020 ($ per capita)	2020 (%)
General Revenue			
From Federal Government	23,851	130	5.8
From State Government	9,080	49	2.2
From Local Governments	337	2	0.1
Taxes			
Property	66,576	362	16.2
Sales and Gross Receipts	151,095	822	36.9
Personal Income	0	0	0.0
Corporate Income	0	0	0.0
Motor Vehicle License	0	0	0.0
Other Taxes	10,859	59	2.6
Current Charges	59,032	321	14.4
Liquor Store	0	0	0.0
Utility	44,020	240	10.7

Source: U.S. Census Bureau, State & Local Government Finances 2020

City Government Expenditures by Function

Function	2020 ($000)	2020 ($ per capita)	2020 (%)
General Direct Expenditures			
Air Transportation	0	0	0.0
Corrections	0	0	0.0
Education	0	0	0.0
Employment Security Administration	0	0	0.0
Financial Administration	3,042	16	0.9
Fire Protection	30,967	168	9.2
General Public Buildings	3,559	19	1.1
Governmental Administration, Other	5,326	29	1.6
Health	12,888	70	3.8
Highways	77,788	423	23.2
Hospitals	0	0	0.0
Housing and Community Development	17,493	95	5.2
Interest on General Debt	8,386	45	2.5
Judicial and Legal	1,844	10	0.6
Libraries	8,230	44	2.5
Parking	1,638	8	0.5
Parks and Recreation	27,162	147	8.1
Police Protection	37,355	203	11.1
Public Welfare	0	0	0.0
Sewerage	25,487	138	7.6
Solid Waste Management	10,198	55	3.0
Veterans' Services	0	0	0.0
Liquor Store	0	0	0.0
Utility	46,326	252	13.8

Source: U.S. Census Bureau, State & Local Government Finances 2020

TAXES

State Corporate Income Tax Rates

State	Tax Rate (%)	Income Brackets ($)	Num. of Brackets	Financial Institution Tax Rate (%)[a]	Federal Income Tax Ded.
South Dakota	None	–	–	6.0-0.25 (b)	No

Note: Tax rates as of January 1, 2023; (a) Rates listed are the corporate income tax rate applied to financial institutions or excise taxes based on income. Some states have other taxes based upon the value of deposits or shares; (b) Minimum tax is $800 in California, $250 in District of Columbia, $50 in Arizona and North Dakota (banks), $400 ($100 banks) in Rhode Island, $200 per location in South Dakota (banks), $100 in Utah, $300 in Vermont.
Source: Federation of Tax Administrators, State Corporate Income Tax Rates, January 1, 2023

State Individual Income Tax Rates

State	Tax Rate (%)	Income Brackets ($)	Personal Exemptions ($)			Standard Ded. ($)	
			Single	Married	Depend.	Single	Married
South Dakota				– No state income tax –			

Note: Tax rates as of January 1, 2023; Local- and county-level taxes are not included
Source: Federation of Tax Administrators, State Individual Income Tax Rates, January 1, 2023

Various State Sales and Excise Tax Rates

State	State Sales Tax (%)	Gasoline[1] ($/gal.)	Cigarette[2] ($/pack)	Spirits[3] ($/gal.)	Wine[4] ($/gal.)	Beer[5] ($/gal.)	Recreational Marijuana (%)
South Dakota	4.5	0.30	1.53	4.87	1.41	0.27	Not legal

Note: All tax rates as of January 1, 2023; (1) The American Petroleum Institute has developed a methodology for determining the average tax rate on a gallon of fuel. Rates may include any of the following: excise taxes, environmental fees, storage tank fees, other fees or taxes, general sales tax, and local taxes; (2) The federal excise tax of $1.0066 per pack and local taxes are not included; (3) Rates are those applicable to off-premise sales of 40% alcohol by volume (a.b.v.) distilled spirits in 750ml containers. Local excise taxes are excluded; (4) Rates are those applicable to off-premise sales of 11% a.b.v. non-carbonated wine in 750ml containers; (5) Rates are those applicable to off-premise sales of 4.7% a.b.v. beer in 12 ounce containers.
Source: Tax Foundation, 2023 Facts & Figures: How Does Your State Compare?

State Business Tax Climate Index Rankings

State	Overall Rank	Corporate Tax Rank	Individual Income Tax Rank	Sales Tax Rank	Property Tax Rank	Unemployment Insurance Tax Rank
South Dakota	2	1	1	34	14	37

Note: The index is a measure of how each state's tax laws affect economic performance. The lower the rank, the more favorable a state's tax system is for business. States without a given tax are given a ranking of 1. The scores/rankings for the District of Columbia do not affect other states. The 2023 index represents the tax climate as of July 1, 2022.
Source: Tax Foundation, State Business Tax Climate Index 2023

TRANSPORTATION

Means of Transportation to Work

Area	Car/Truck/Van		Public Transportation			Bicycle	Walked	Other Means	Worked at Home
	Drove Alone	Car-pooled	Bus	Subway	Railroad				
City	81.7	7.8	0.6	0.0	0.0	0.3	2.1	0.7	6.8
MSA[1]	81.7	7.6	0.5	0.0	0.0	0.3	1.9	0.6	7.4
U.S.	73.2	8.6	2.0	1.6	0.5	0.5	2.5	1.5	9.7

Note: Figures are percentages and cover workers 16 years of age and older; (1) Figures cover the Sioux Falls, SD Metropolitan Statistical Area
Source: U.S. Census Bureau, 2017-2021 American Community Survey 5-Year Estimates

Travel Time to Work

Area	Less Than 10 Minutes	10 to 19 Minutes	20 to 29 Minutes	30 to 44 Minutes	45 to 59 Minutes	60 to 89 Minutes	90 Minutes or More
City	16.7	51.6	22.0	5.8	1.7	1.2	1.0
MSA[1]	16.8	43.8	24.1	10.0	2.6	1.4	1.2
U.S.	12.4	28.5	21.0	20.9	8.2	6.2	2.9

Note: Note: Figures are percentages and include workers 16 years old and over; (1) Figures cover the Sioux Falls, SD Metropolitan Statistical Area
Source: U.S. Census Bureau, 2017-2021 American Community Survey 5-Year Estimates

Key Congestion Measures

Measure	1990	2000	2010	2015	2020
Annual Hours of Delay, Total (000)	n/a	n/a	n/a	3,176	1,708
Annual Hours of Delay, Per Auto Commuter	n/a	n/a	n/a	18	9
Annual Congestion Cost, Per Auto Commuter ($)	n/a	n/a	n/a	366	206

Note: n/a not available
Source: Texas A&M Transportation Institute, 2021 Urban Mobility Report

Freeway Travel Time Index

Measure	1985	1990	1995	2000	2005	2010	2015	2020
Urban Area Index[1]	n/a	n/a	n/a	n/a	n/a	n/a	1.05	1.03
Urban Area Rank[1,2]	n/a	n/a	n/a	n/a	n/a	n/a	n/a	n/a

Note: Freeway Travel Time Index—the ratio of travel time in the peak period to the travel time at free-flow conditions. For example, a value of 1.30 indicates a 20-minute free-flow trip takes 26 minutes in the peak (20 minutes x 1.30 = 26 minutes); (1) Covers the Sioux Falls SD urban area; (2) Rank is based on 101 larger urban areas (#1 = highest travel time index); n/a not available
Source: Texas A&M Transportation Institute, 2021 Urban Mobility Report

Public Transportation

Agency Name / Mode of Transportation	Vehicles Operated in Maximum Service[1]	Annual Unlinked Passenger Trips[2] (in thous.)	Annual Passenger Miles[3] (in thous.)
Sioux Falls Transit			
Bus (directly operated)	16	389.8	1,629.4
Demand Response (directly operated)	16	50.7	376.7

Note: (1) Number of revenue vehicles operated by the given mode and type of service to meet the annual maximum service requirement. This is the revenue vehicle count during the peak season of the year; on the week and day that maximum service is provided. Vehicles operated in maximum service (VOMS) exclude atypical days and one-time special events; (2) Number of passengers who boarded public transportation vehicles. Passengers are counted each time they board a vehicle no matter how many vehicles they use to travel from their origin to their destination. (3) Sum of the distances ridden by all passengers during the entire fiscal year.
Source: Federal Transit Administration, National Transit Database, 2021

Air Transportation

Airport Name and Code / Type of Service	Passenger Airlines[1]	Passenger Enplanements	Freight Carriers[2]	Freight (lbs)
Joe Foss Field (FSD)				
Domestic service (U.S. carriers - 2022)	20	605,679	7	37,585,024
International service (U.S. carriers - 2021)	0	0	1	18,953,179

Note: (1) Includes all U.S.-based major, minor and commuter airlines that carried at least one passenger during the year; (2) Includes all U.S.-based airlines and freight carriers that transported at least one pound of freight during the year.
Source: Bureau of Transportation Statistics, The Intermodal Transportation Database, Air Carriers: T-100 Domestic Market (U.S. Carriers), 2022; Bureau of Transportation Statistics, The Intermodal Transportation Database, Air Carriers: T-100 International Market (U.S. Carriers), 2021

BUSINESSES

Major Business Headquarters

Company Name	Industry	Rankings	
		Fortune[1]	Forbes[2]
No companies listed	-	-	-

Note: (1) Companies that produce a 10-K are ranked 1 to 500 based on 2021 revenue; (2) All private companies with at least $2 billion in annual revenue through the end of their most current fiscal year are ranked 1 to 246; companies listed are headquartered in the city; dashes indicate no ranking
Source: Fortune, "Fortune 500," 2022; Forbes, "America's Largest Private Companies," 2022

Living Environment

COST OF LIVING

Cost of Living Index

Composite Index	Groceries	Housing	Utilities	Trans-portation	Health Care	Misc. Goods/ Services
91.5	94.2	93.3	83.6	86.2	103.8	90.3

Note: The Cost of Living Index measures regional differences in the cost of consumer goods and services, excluding taxes and non-consumer expenditures, for professional and managerial households in the top income quintile. It is based on more than 50,000 prices covering almost 60 different items for which prices are collected three times a year by chambers of commerce, economic development organizations or university applied economic centers in each participating urban area. The numbers shown should be read as a percentage above or below the national average of 100. For example, a value of 115.4 in the groceries column indicates that grocery prices are 15.4% higher than the national average. Small differences in the index numbers should not be interpreted as significant; Figures cover the Sioux Falls SD urban area.
Source: The Council for Community and Economic Research, Cost of Living Index, 2022

Grocery Prices

Area[1]	T-Bone Steak ($/pound)	Frying Chicken ($/pound)	Whole Milk ($/half gal.)	Eggs ($/dozen)	Orange Juice ($/64 oz.)	Coffee ($/11.5 oz.)
City[2]	12.85	1.47	2.61	2.26	3.63	5.53
Avg.	13.81	1.59	2.43	2.25	3.85	4.95
Min.	10.17	0.90	1.51	1.30	2.90	3.46
Max.	19.35	3.30	4.32	4.32	5.31	8.59

*Note: (1) Values for the local area are compared with the average, minimum and maximum values for all 286 areas in the Cost of Living Index; (2) Figures cover the Sioux Falls SD urban area; **T-Bone Steak** (price per pound); **Frying Chicken** (price per pound, whole fryer); **Whole Milk** (half gallon carton); **Eggs** (price per dozen, Grade A, large); **Orange Juice** (64 oz. Tropicana or Florida Natural); **Coffee** (11.5 oz. can, vacuum-packed, Maxwell House, Hills Bros, or Folgers).*
Source: The Council for Community and Economic Research, Cost of Living Index, 2022

Housing and Utility Costs

Area[1]	New Home Price ($)	Apartment Rent ($/month)	All Electric ($/month)	Part Electric ($/month)	Other Energy ($/month)	Telephone ($/month)
City[2]	450,933	1,111	-	84.19	47.87	182.72
Avg.	450,913	1,371	176.41	99.93	76.96	190.22
Min.	229,283	546	100.84	31.56	27.15	174.27
Max.	2,434,977	4,569	356.86	249.59	272.24	208.31

*Note: (1) Values for the local area are compared with the average, minimum and maximum values for all 286 areas in the Cost of Living Index; (2) Figures cover the Sioux Falls SD urban area; **New Home Price** (2,400 sf living area, 8,000 sf lot, in urban area with full utilities); **Apartment Rent** (950 sf 2 bedroom/1.5 or 2 bath, unfurnished, excluding all utilities except water); **All Electric** (average monthly cost for an all-electric home); **Part Electric** (average monthly cost for a part-electric home); **Other Energy** (average monthly cost for natural gas, fuel oil, coal, wood, and any other forms of energy except electricity); **Telephone** (price includes the base monthly rate plus taxes and fees for three lines of mobile phone service).*
Source: The Council for Community and Economic Research, Cost of Living Index, 2022

Health Care, Transportation, and Other Costs

Area[1]	Doctor ($/visit)	Dentist ($/visit)	Optometrist ($/visit)	Gasoline ($/gallon)	Beauty Salon ($/visit)	Men's Shirt ($)
City[2]	164.33	103.08	126.50	3.57	33.33	24.13
Avg.	124.91	107.77	117.66	3.86	43.31	34.21
Min.	36.61	58.25	51.79	2.90	22.18	13.05
Max.	250.21	162.58	371.96	5.54	85.61	63.54

*Note: (1) Values for the local area are compared with the average, minimum and maximum values for all 286 areas in the Cost of Living Index; (2) Figures cover the Sioux Falls SD urban area; **Doctor** (general practitioners routine exam of an established patient); **Dentist** (adult teeth cleaning and periodic oral examination); **Optometrist** (full vision eye exam for established adult patient); **Gasoline** (one gallon regular unleaded, national brand, including all taxes, cash price at self-service pump if available); **Beauty Salon** (woman's shampoo, trim, and blow-dry); **Men's Shirt** (cotton/polyester dress shirt, pinpoint weave, long sleeves).*
Source: The Council for Community and Economic Research, Cost of Living Index, 2022

HOUSING

Homeownership Rate

Area	2015 (%)	2016 (%)	2017 (%)	2018 (%)	2019 (%)	2020 (%)	2021 (%)	2022 (%)
MSA[1]	n/a	n/a	n/a	n/a	n/a	n/a	n/a	n/a
U.S.	63.7	63.4	63.9	64.4	64.6	66.6	65.5	65.8

Note: (1) Figures cover the Sioux Falls, SD Metropolitan Statistical Area; n/a not available
Source: U.S. Census Bureau, Housing Vacancies and Homeownership Annual Statistics: 2015-2022

House Price Index (HPI)

Area	National Ranking[2]	Quarterly Change (%)	One-Year Change (%)	Five-Year Change (%)	Since 1991Q1 (%)
MSA[1]	92	-1.20	12.49	55.67	315.04
U.S.[3]	–	0.34	8.41	58.44	289.08

Note: The HPI is a weighted repeat sales index. It measures average price changes in repeat sales or refinancings on the same properties. This information is obtained by reviewing repeat mortgage transactions on single-family properties whose mortgages have been purchased or securitized by Fannie Mae or Freddie Mac since January 1975; (1) Figures cover the Sioux Falls, SD Metropolitan Statistical Area; (2) Rankings are based on annual percentage change for all metro areas containing at least 15,000 transactions over the last 10 years and ranges from 1 to 257; (3) figures based on a weighted average of Census Division estimates using a seasonally adjusted, purchase-only index; all figures are for the period ending December 31, 2022
Source: Federal Housing Finance Agency, Change in FHFA Metropolitan Area House Price Indexes, 2022Q4

Median Single-Family Home Prices

Area	2020	2021	2022[p]	Percent Change 2021 to 2022
MSA[1]	236.3	269.5	314.3	16.6
U.S. Average	300.2	357.1	392.6	9.9

Note: Figures are median sales prices of existing single-family homes in thousands of dollars; (p) preliminary; (1) Figures cover the Sioux Falls, SD Metropolitan Statistical Area
Source: National Association of Realtors, Median Sales Price of Existing Single-Family Homes for Metropolitan Areas, 4th Quarter 2022

Qualifying Income Based on Median Sales Price of Existing Single-Family Homes

Area	With 5% Down ($)	With 10% Down ($)	With 20% Down ($)
MSA[1]	89,426	84,719	75,306
U.S. Average	112,234	106,237	94,513

Note: Figures are preliminary; Qualifying income is based on a mortgage rate of 6.77%. Monthly principal and interest payment is limited to 25% of income; (1) Figures cover the Sioux Falls, SD Metropolitan Statistical Area
Source: National Association of Realtors, Qualifying Income Based on Median Sales Price of Existing Single-Family Homes for Metropolitan Areas, 4th Quarter 2022

Home Value

Area	Under $100,000	$100,000 -$199,999	$200,000 -$299,999	$300,000 -$399,999	$400,000 -$499,999	$500,000 -$999,999	$1,000,000 or more	Median ($)
City	10.1	32.4	31.9	12.6	6.1	5.6	1.3	218,600
MSA[1]	11.0	31.1	29.9	14.0	6.4	6.5	1.2	221,500
U.S.	16.2	24.2	20.1	13.6	8.3	13.6	4.1	244,900

Note: Figures are percentages except for median and cover owner-occupied housing units; (1) Figures cover the Sioux Falls, SD Metropolitan Statistical Area
Source: U.S. Census Bureau, 2017-2021 American Community Survey 5-Year Estimates

Year Housing Structure Built

Area	2020 or Later	2010 -2019	2000 -2009	1990 -1999	1980 -1989	1970 -1979	1960 -1969	1950 -1959	1940 -1949	Before 1940	Median Year
City	0.3	17.8	17.9	14.7	9.7	12.1	7.0	8.3	3.1	9.1	1990
MSA[1]	0.2	16.0	18.0	14.9	8.7	12.7	6.7	7.4	3.2	12.2	1989
U.S.	0.2	7.3	13.6	13.6	13.2	14.8	10.3	10.0	4.7	12.2	1979

Note: Figures are percentages except for Median Year; Note: (1) Figures cover the Sioux Falls, SD Metropolitan Statistical Area
Source: U.S. Census Bureau, 2017-2021 American Community Survey 5-Year Estimates

Gross Monthly Rent

Area	Under $500	$500 -$999	$1,000 -$1,499	$1,500 -$1,999	$2,000 -$2,499	$2,500 -$2,999	$3,000 and up	Median ($)
City	6.2	58.7	27.7	5.7	0.6	0.4	0.8	892
MSA[1]	7.0	57.8	27.5	5.8	0.8	0.3	0.7	889
U.S.	8.1	30.5	30.8	16.8	7.3	3.1	3.5	1,163

Note: Figures are percentages except for median; Gross rent is the contract rent plus the estimated average monthly cost of utilities (electricity, gas, and water and sewer) and fuels (oil, coal, kerosene, wood, etc.) if these are paid by the renter (or paid for the renter by someone else); (1) Figures cover the Sioux Falls, SD Metropolitan Statistical Area
Source: U.S. Census Bureau, 2017-2021 American Community Survey 5-Year Estimates

HEALTH

Health Risk Factors

Category	MSA[1] (%)	U.S. (%)
Adults aged 18–64 who have any kind of health care coverage	91.9	90.9
Adults who reported being in good or better health	88.9	85.2
Adults who have been told they have high blood cholesterol	33.9	35.7
Adults who have been told they have high blood pressure	28.0	32.4
Adults who are current smokers	11.6	14.4
Adults who currently use e-cigarettes	6.3	6.7
Adults who currently use chewing tobacco, snuff, or snus	5.8	3.5
Adults who are heavy drinkers[2]	4.4	6.3
Adults who are binge drinkers[3]	20.6	15.4
Adults who are overweight (BMI 25.0 - 29.9)	33.9	34.4
Adults who are obese (BMI 30.0 - 99.8)	36.3	33.9
Adults who participated in any physical activities in the past month	80.2	76.3

Note: (1) Figures cover the Sioux Falls, SD Metropolitan Statistical Area; (2) Heavy drinkers are classified as adult men having more than 14 drinks per week and adult women having more than 7 drinks per week; (3) Binge drinkers are classified as males having five or more drinks on one occasion or females having four or more drinks on one occasion
Source: Centers for Disease Control and Prevention, Behaviorial Risk Factor Surveillance System, SMART: Selected Metropolitan Area Risk Trends, 2021

Acute and Chronic Health Conditions

Category	MSA[1] (%)	U.S. (%)
Adults who have ever been told they had a heart attack	4.2	4.0
Adults who have ever been told they have angina or coronary heart disease	3.7	3.8
Adults who have ever been told they had a stroke	n/a	3.0
Adults who have ever been told they have asthma	13.3	14.9
Adults who have ever been told they have arthritis	22.0	25.8
Adults who have ever been told they have diabetes[2]	10.0	10.9
Adults who have ever been told they had skin cancer	6.4	6.6
Adults who have ever been told they had any other types of cancer	7.9	7.5
Adults who have ever been told they have COPD	3.7	6.1
Adults who have ever been told they have kidney disease	3.2	3.0
Adults who have ever been told they have a form of depression	17.4	20.5

Note: (1) Figures cover the Sioux Falls, SD Metropolitan Statistical Area; (2) Figures do not include pregnancy-related, borderline, or pre-diabetes
Source: Centers for Disease Control and Prevention, Behaviorial Risk Factor Surveillance System, SMART: Selected Metropolitan Area Risk Trends, 2021

Health Screening and Vaccination Rates

Category	MSA[1] (%)	U.S. (%)
Adults who have ever been tested for HIV	29.1	34.9
Adults who have had their blood cholesterol checked within the last five years	81.8	85.2
Adults aged 65+ who have had flu shot within the past year	79.4	68.6
Adults aged 65+ who have ever had a pneumonia vaccination	75.9	71.0

Note: (1) Figures cover the Sioux Falls, SD Metropolitan Statistical Area.
Source: Centers for Disease Control and Prevention, Behaviorial Risk Factor Surveillance System, SMART: Selected Metropolitan Area Risk Trends, 2021

Disability Status

Category	MSA[1] (%)	U.S. (%)
Adults who reported being deaf	6.4	7.2
Are you blind or have serious difficulty seeing, even when wearing glasses?	2.6	4.8
Are you limited in any way in any of your usual activities due to arthritis?	7.5	11.1
Do you have difficulty doing errands alone?	6.1	7.0
Do you have difficulty dressing or bathing?	n/a	3.6
Do you have serious difficulty concentrating/remembering/making decisions?	11.4	12.1
Do you have serious difficulty walking or climbing stairs?	8.0	12.8

Note: (1) Figures cover the Sioux Falls, SD Metropolitan Statistical Area.
Source: Centers for Disease Control and Prevention, Behaviorial Risk Factor Surveillance System, SMART: Selected Metropolitan Area Risk Trends, 2021

Mortality Rates for the Top 10 Causes of Death in the U.S.

ICD-10[a] Sub-Chapter	ICD-10[a] Code	Crude Mortality Rate[1] per 100,000 population	
		County[2]	U.S.
Malignant neoplasms	C00-C97	184.7	182.6
Ischaemic heart diseases	I20-I25	90.9	113.1
Other forms of heart disease	I30-I51	27.3	64.4
Other degenerative diseases of the nervous system	G30-G31	57.0	51.0
Cerebrovascular diseases	I60-I69	41.2	47.8
Other external causes of accidental injury	W00-X59	47.0	46.4
Chronic lower respiratory diseases	J40-J47	41.4	45.7
Organic, including symptomatic, mental disorders	F01-F09	18.5	35.9
Hypertensive diseases	I10-I15	49.0	35.0
Diabetes mellitus	E10-E14	17.6	29.6

Note: (a) ICD-10 = International Classification of Diseases 10th Revision; (1) Crude mortality rates are a three-year average covering 2019-2021; (2) Figures cover Minnehaha County.
Source: Centers for Disease Control and Prevention, National Center for Health Statistics. National Vital Statistics System, Mortality 2018-2021 on CDC WONDER Online Database

Mortality Rates for Selected Causes of Death

ICD-10[a] Sub-Chapter	ICD-10[a] Code	Crude Mortality Rate[1] per 100,000 population	
		County[2]	U.S.
Assault	X85-Y09	3.4	7.0
Diseases of the liver	K70-K76	22.9	19.8
Human immunodeficiency virus (HIV) disease	B20-B24	Suppressed	1.5
Influenza and pneumonia	J09-J18	12.0	14.7
Intentional self-harm	X60-X84	16.5	14.3
Malnutrition	E40-E46	12.6	4.3
Obesity and other hyperalimentation	E65-E68	Suppressed	3.0
Renal failure	N17-N19	5.9	15.7
Transport accidents	V01-V99	13.7	13.6
Viral hepatitis	B15-B19	Suppressed	1.2

Note: (a) ICD-10 = International Classification of Diseases 10th Revision; (1) Crude mortality rates are a three-year average covering 2019-2021; (2) Figures cover Minnehaha County; Data are suppressed when the data meet the criteria for confidentiality constraints; Crude mortality rates are flagged as unreliable when the rate would be calculated with a numerator of 20 or less.
Source: Centers for Disease Control and Prevention, National Center for Health Statistics. National Vital Statistics System, Mortality 2018-2021 on CDC WONDER Online Database

Health Insurance Coverage

Area	With Health Insurance	With Private Health Insurance	With Public Health Insurance	Without Health Insurance	Population Under Age 19 Without Health Insurance
City	92.0	77.5	26.1	8.0	5.2
MSA[1]	92.8	79.1	25.2	7.2	4.7
U.S.	91.2	67.8	35.4	8.8	5.3

Note: Figures are percentages that cover the civilian noninstitutionalized population; (1) Figures cover the Sioux Falls, SD Metropolitan Statistical Area
Source: U.S. Census Bureau, 2017-2021 American Community Survey 5-Year Estimates

Number of Medical Professionals

Area	MDs[3]	DOs[3,4]	Dentists	Podiatrists	Chiropractors	Optometrists
County[1] (number)	729	47	112	11	116	38
County[1] (rate[2])	369.1	23.8	56.1	5.5	58.1	19.0
U.S. (rate[2])	289.3	23.5	72.5	6.2	28.7	17.4

Note: Data as of 2021 unless noted; (1) Data covers Minnehaha County; (2) Rate per 100,000 population; (3) Data as of 2020 and includes all active, non-federal physicians; (4) Doctor of Osteopathic Medicine
Source: U.S. Department of Health and Human Services, Health Resources and Services Administration, Bureau of Health Professions, Area Resource File (ARF) 2021-2022

Best Hospitals

According to *U.S. News,* the Sioux Falls, SD metro area is home to one of the best hospitals in the U.S.: **Sanford USD Medical Center** (1 adult specialty). The hospital listed was nationally ranked in at least one of 15 adult or 10 pediatric specialties. The number of specialties shown cover the parent hospital. Only 164 U.S. hospitals performed well enough to be nationally ranked in one or more specialties. Twenty hospitals in the U.S. made the Honor Roll. The Best Hospitals Honor Roll takes both the national rankings and the procedure and condition ratings into account. Hospitals received points if they were nationally ranked in one of the 15 adult specialties—the higher they ranked, the more points they got—and how many ratings of "high performing" they earned in the 17 procedures and conditions. *U.S. News Online, "America's Best Hospitals 2022-23"*

EDUCATION

Public School District Statistics

District Name	Schls	Pupils	Pupil/ Teacher Ratio	Minority Pupils[1] (%)	LEP/ELL[2] (%)	IEP[3] (%)
Sioux Falls School District 49-5	45	24,957	15.1	41.4	10.2	15.6

Note: Table includes school districts with 2,000 or more students; (1) Percentage of students that are not non-Hispanic white; (2) Percentage of students that are Limited English Proficient or English Language Learners (2018-19); (3) Percentage of students that have an Individualized Education Program (2019-20).
Source: U.S. Department of Education, National Center for Education Statistics, Common Core of Data, Local Education Agency (School District) Universe Survey: School Year 2021-2022

Highest Level of Education

Area	Less than H.S.	H.S. Diploma	Some College, No Deg.	Associate Degree	Bachelor's Degree	Master's Degree	Prof. School Degree	Doctorate Degree
City	6.7	24.6	20.5	12.2	24.3	8.3	2.4	1.0
MSA[1]	6.3	25.7	20.2	13.0	24.1	7.8	2.0	1.0
U.S.	11.1	26.5	20.0	8.7	20.6	9.3	2.2	1.5

Note: Figures cover persons age 25 and over; (1) Figures cover the Sioux Falls, SD Metropolitan Statistical Area
Source: U.S. Census Bureau, 2017-2021 American Community Survey 5-Year Estimates

Educational Attainment by Race

Area	High School Graduate or Higher (%)					Bachelor's Degree or Higher (%)				
	Total	White	Black	Asian	Hisp.[2]	Total	White	Black	Asian	Hisp.[2]
City	93.3	95.3	83.9	74.3	73.5	36.0	37.9	20.0	44.2	17.9
MSA[1]	93.7	95.1	84.5	75.7	73.0	34.8	36.1	19.6	44.4	18.6
U.S.	88.9	91.4	87.2	87.6	71.2	33.7	35.5	23.3	55.6	18.4

Note: Figures shown cover persons 25 years old and over; (1) Figures cover the Sioux Falls, SD Metropolitan Statistical Area; (2) People of Hispanic origin can be of any race
Source: U.S. Census Bureau, 2017-2021 American Community Survey 5-Year Estimates

School Enrollment by Grade and Control

Area	Preschool (%)		Kindergarten (%)		Grades 1 - 4 (%)		Grades 5 - 8 (%)		Grades 9 - 12 (%)	
	Public	Private	Public	Private	Public	Private	Public	Private	Public	Private
City	53.8	46.2	92.3	7.7	86.4	13.6	88.8	11.2	84.6	15.4
MSA[1]	56.2	43.8	91.6	8.4	87.3	12.7	90.0	10.0	87.1	12.9
U.S.	58.8	41.2	86.3	13.7	88.3	11.7	88.6	11.4	89.4	10.6

Note: Figures shown cover persons 3 years old and over; (1) Figures cover the Sioux Falls, SD Metropolitan Statistical Area
Source: U.S. Census Bureau, 2017-2021 American Community Survey 5-Year Estimates

Higher Education

Four-Year Colleges			Two-Year Colleges			Medical Schools[1]	Law Schools[2]	Voc/ Tech[3]
Public	Private Non-profit	Private For-profit	Public	Private Non-profit	Private For-profit			
0	3	0	1	2	0	1	0	1

Note: Figures cover institutions located within the Sioux Falls, SD Metropolitan Statistical Area and include main campuses only; (1) includes schools accredited by the Liaison Committee on Medical Education and the American Osteopathic Association's Commission on Osteopathic College Accreditation; (2) includes ABA-accredited schools, schools with provisional ABA accreditation, and state accredited schools; (3) includes all schools with programs that are less than 2 years.
Source: National Center for Education Statistics, Integrated Postsecondary Education System (IPEDS), 2021-22; Wikipedia, List of Medical Schools in the United States, accessed April 10, 2023; Wikipedia, List of Law Schools in the United States, accessed April 10, 2023

EMPLOYERS

Major Employers

Company Name	Industry
Avera Health	Health care
Billion Automotive	Auto dealership
Capital One	Financial/credit card processing
CIGNA	Mail order pharmacy
Citi	Credit card processing
City of Sioux Falls	Municipal government
Department of Veterans Affairs	Government medical facilities
Esurance	Insurance service center
Evangelical Lutheran Good Samaritan	Health care
First Premier Bank/Premier Bankcard	Financial/credit card processing
Hy-Vee Food Stores	Retail grocery
John Morrell & Co.	Meat processing
Lewis Drug	Retail pharmacy
LifeScape	Health care
Midcontinent Communications	Telecommunications/cable services
Minnehaha County	Government
Raven Industries	Manufacturing
Sammons Financial Group/Midland National	Insurance
Sanford Health	Health care
Sioux Falls School District 49-5	Education
StarMark Cabinetry	Manufacturing
United States Postal Service	U.S. postal service
USGS EROS Data Center/SGT	Satellite info processing
Wal-Mart and Sam's Club	Retail & wholesale
Wells Fargo	Financial/credit card/student loans

Note: Companies shown are located within the Sioux Falls, SD Metropolitan Statistical Area.
Source: Hoovers.com; Wikipedia

PUBLIC SAFETY

Crime Rate

Area	Total Crime	Violent Crime Rate				Property Crime Rate		
		Murder	Rape[3]	Robbery	Aggrav. Assault	Burglary	Larceny -Theft	Motor Vehicle Theft
City	3,729.0	6.9	51.8	54.4	484.6	365.1	2,273.0	493.1
Suburbs[1]	1,410.7	2.3	31.5	8.2	172.8	462.4	597.9	135.5
Metro[2]	3,001.8	5.5	45.4	39.9	386.8	395.6	1,747.6	381.0
U.S.	2,356.7	6.5	38.4	73.9	279.7	314.2	1,398.0	246.0

Note: Figures are crimes per 100,000 population; (1) All areas within the metro area that are located outside the city limits; (2) Figures cover the Sioux Falls, SD Metropolitan Statistical Area; (3) All figures shown were reported using the revised Uniform Crime Reporting (UCR) definition of rape; Due to the transition to the National Incident-Based Reporting System (NIBRS), limited city and metro area data was released for 2021.
Source: FBI Uniform Crime Reports, 2020

Hate Crimes

Area	Number of Quarters Reported	Number of Incidents per Bias Motivation					
		Race/Ethnicity/ Ancestry	Religion	Sexual Orientation	Disability	Gender	Gender Identity
City	4	1	0	0	0	0	0
U.S.	4	5,227	1,244	1,110	130	75	266

Note: Due to the transition to the National Incident-Based Reporting System (NIBRS), limited crime data was released for 2021.
Source: Federal Bureau of Investigation, Hate Crime Statistics 2020

Identity Theft Consumer Reports

Area	Reports	Reports per 100,000 Population	Rank[2]
MSA[1]	300	113	339
U.S.	1,108,609	339	-

Note: (1) Figures cover the Sioux Falls, SD Metropolitan Statistical Area; (2) Rank ranges from 1 to 391 where 1 indicates greatest number of identity theft reports per 100,000 population
Source: Federal Trade Commission, Consumer Sentinel Network Data Book 2022

Fraud and Other Consumer Reports

Area	Reports	Reports per 100,000 Population	Rank[2]
MSA[1]	1,615	611	347
U.S.	4,064,520	1,245	-

Note: (1) Figures cover the Sioux Falls, SD Metropolitan Statistical Area; (2) Rank ranges from 1 to 391 where 1 indicates greatest number of fraud and other consumer reports per 100,000 population
Source: Federal Trade Commission, Consumer Sentinel Network Data Book 2022

POLITICS

2020 Presidential Election Results

Area	Biden	Trump	Jorgensen	Hawkins	Other
Minnehaha County	43.8	53.3	2.8	0.0	0.0
U.S.	51.3	46.8	1.2	0.3	0.5

Note: Results are percentages and may not add to 100% due to rounding
Source: Dave Leip's Atlas of U.S. Presidential Elections

SPORTS

Professional Sports Teams

Team Name	League	Year Established

No teams are located in the metro area
Source: Wikipedia, Major Professional Sports Teams of the United States and Canada, April 12, 2023

CLIMATE

Average and Extreme Temperatures

Temperature	Jan	Feb	Mar	Apr	May	Jun	Jul	Aug	Sep	Oct	Nov	Dec	Yr.
Extreme High (°F)	66	70	88	94	104	110	110	109	104	94	76	62	110
Average High (°F)	25	30	41	59	71	80	86	84	74	62	43	29	57
Average Temp. (°F)	15	20	32	47	59	69	75	72	62	50	33	20	46
Average Low (°F)	5	10	22	35	47	57	62	60	49	38	23	10	35
Extreme Low (°F)	-36	-31	-23	4	17	33	38	34	22	9	-17	-28	-36

Note: Figures cover the years 1932-1990
Source: National Climatic Data Center, International Station Meteorological Climate Summary, 9/96

Average Precipitation/Snowfall/Humidity

Precip./Humidity	Jan	Feb	Mar	Apr	May	Jun	Jul	Aug	Sep	Oct	Nov	Dec	Yr.
Avg. Precip. (in.)	0.6	0.8	1.6	2.4	3.3	3.9	2.8	3.2	2.8	1.5	1.0	0.7	24.6
Avg. Snowfall (in.)	7	8	9	2	0	0	0	0	Tr	Tr	5	7	38
Avg. Rel. Hum. 6am (%)	n/a	n/a	n/a	n/a	n/a	n/a	n/a	n/a	n/a	n/a	n/a	n/a	n/a
Avg. Rel. Hum. 3pm (%)	n/a	n/a	n/a	n/a	n/a	n/a	n/a	n/a	n/a	n/a	n/a	n/a	n/a

Note: Figures cover the years 1932-1990; Tr = Trace amounts (<0.05 in. of rain; <0.5 in. of snow)
Source: National Climatic Data Center, International Station Meteorological Climate Summary, 9/96

Weather Conditions

Temperature			Daytime Sky			Precipitation		
5°F & below	32°F & below	90°F & above	Clear	Partly cloudy	Cloudy	0.01 inch or more precip.	0.1 inch or more snow/ice	Thunder-storms
n/a	n/a	n/a	95	136	134	n/a	n/a	n/a

Note: Figures are average number of days per year and cover the years 1932-1990
Source: National Climatic Data Center, International Station Meteorological Climate Summary, 9/96

HAZARDOUS WASTE

Superfund Sites

The Sioux Falls, SD metro area has no sites on the EPA's Superfund Final National Priorities List. There are a total of 1,165 Superfund sites with a status of proposed or final on the list in the U.S. *U.S. Environmental Protection Agency, National Priorities List, April 12, 2023*

AIR QUALITY

Air Quality Trends: Ozone

	1990	1995	2000	2005	2010	2015	2018	2019	2020	2021
MSA[1]	n/a	n/a	n/a	n/a	n/a	n/a	n/a	n/a	n/a	n/a
U.S.	0.087	0.089	0.081	0.080	0.072	0.067	0.069	0.065	0.065	0.067

Note: (1) Data covers the Sioux Falls, SD Metropolitan Statistical Area; n/a not available. The values shown are the composite ozone concentration averages among trend sites based on the highest fourth daily maximum 8-hour concentration in parts per million. These trends are based on sites having an adequate record of monitoring data during the trend period. Data from exceptional events are included.
Source: U.S. Environmental Protection Agency, Air Quality Monitoring Information, "Air Quality Trends by City, 1990-2021"

Air Quality Index

Area	Percent of Days when Air Quality was...[2]					AQI Statistics[2]	
	Good	Moderate	Unhealthy for Sensitive Groups	Unhealthy	Very Unhealthy	Maximum	Median
MSA[1]	81.7	16.9	0.9	0.6	0.0	182	36

Note: (1) Data covers the Sioux Falls, SD Metropolitan Statistical Area; (2) Based on 349 days with AQI data in 2021. Air Quality Index (AQI) is an index for reporting daily air quality. EPA calculates the AQI for five major air pollutants regulated by the Clean Air Act: ground-level ozone, particle pollution (aka particulate matter), carbon monoxide, sulfur dioxide, and nitrogen dioxide. The AQI runs from 0 to 500. The higher the AQI value, the greater the level of air pollution and the greater the health concern. There are six AQI categories: "Good" AQI is between 0 and 50. Air quality is considered satisfactory; "Moderate" AQI is between 51 and 100. Air quality is acceptable; "Unhealthy for Sensitive Groups" When AQI values are between 101 and 150, members of sensitive groups may experience health effects; "Unhealthy" When AQI values are between 151 and 200 everyone may begin to experience health effects; "Very Unhealthy" AQI values between 201 and 300 trigger a health alert; "Hazardous" AQI values over 300 trigger warnings of emergency conditions (not shown).
Source: U.S. Environmental Protection Agency, Air Quality Index Report, 2021

Air Quality Index Pollutants

Area	Percent of Days when AQI Pollutant was...[2]					
	Carbon Monoxide	Nitrogen Dioxide	Ozone	Sulfur Dioxide	Particulate Matter 2.5	Particulate Matter 10
MSA[1]	0.0	4.6	65.9	(3)	22.3	7.2

Note: (1) Data covers the Sioux Falls, SD Metropolitan Statistical Area; (2) Based on 349 days with AQI data in 2021. The Air Quality Index (AQI) is an index for reporting daily air quality. EPA calculates the AQI for five major air pollutants regulated by the Clean Air Act: ground-level ozone, particle pollution (also known as particulate matter), carbon monoxide, sulfur dioxide, and nitrogen dioxide. The AQI runs from 0 to 500. The higher the AQI value, the greater the level of air pollution and the greater the health concern; (3) Sulfur dioxide is no longer included in this table (as of December 8, 2021) because SO_2 concentrations tend to be very localized and not necessarily representative of broad geographical areas like counties and CBSAs.
Source: U.S. Environmental Protection Agency, Air Quality Index Report, 2021

Maximum Air Pollutant Concentrations: Particulate Matter, Ozone, CO and Lead

	Particulate Matter 10 (ug/m³)	Particulate Matter 2.5 Wtd AM (ug/m³)	Particulate Matter 2.5 24-Hr (ug/m³)	Ozone (ppm)	Carbon Monoxide (ppm)	Lead (ug/m³)
MSA[1] Level	110	n/a	n/a	0.065	1	n/a
NAAQS[2]	150	15	35	0.075	9	0.15
Met NAAQS[2]	Yes	n/a	n/a	Yes	Yes	n/a

Note: (1) Data covers the Sioux Falls, SD Metropolitan Statistical Area; Data from exceptional events are included; (2) National Ambient Air Quality Standards; ppm = parts per million; ug/m³ = micrograms per cubic meter; n/a not available.
Concentrations: Particulate Matter 10 (coarse particulate)—highest second maximum 24-hour concentration; Particulate Matter 2.5 Wtd AM (fine particulate)—highest weighted annual mean concentration; Particulate Matter 2.5 24-Hour (fine particulate)—highest 98th percentile 24-hour concentration; Ozone—highest fourth daily maximum 8-hour concentration; Carbon Monoxide—highest second maximum non-overlapping 8-hour concentration; Lead—maximum running 3-month average
Source: U.S. Environmental Protection Agency, Air Quality Monitoring Information, "Air Quality Statistics by City, 2021"

Maximum Air Pollutant Concentrations: Nitrogen Dioxide and Sulfur Dioxide

	Nitrogen Dioxide AM (ppb)	Nitrogen Dioxide 1-Hr (ppb)	Sulfur Dioxide AM (ppb)	Sulfur Dioxide 1-Hr (ppb)	Sulfur Dioxide 24-Hr (ppb)
MSA[1] Level	n/a	n/a	n/a	n/a	n/a
NAAQS[2]	53	100	30	75	140
Met NAAQS[2]	n/a	n/a	n/a	n/a	n/a

Note: (1) Data covers the Sioux Falls, SD Metropolitan Statistical Area; Data from exceptional events are included; (2) National Ambient Air Quality Standards; ppm = parts per million; ug/m³ = micrograms per cubic meter; n/a not available.
Concentrations: Nitrogen Dioxide AM—highest arithmetic mean concentration; Nitrogen Dioxide 1-Hr—highest 98th percentile 1-hour daily maximum concentration; Sulfur Dioxide AM—highest annual mean concentration; Sulfur Dioxide 1-Hr—highest 99th percentile 1-hour daily maximum concentration; Sulfur Dioxide 24-Hr—highest second maximum 24-hour concentration
Source: U.S. Environmental Protection Agency, Air Quality Monitoring Information, "Air Quality Statistics by City, 2021"

Springfield, Illinois

Background

Springfield, Illinois is located the Midwest region of the United States. It was visited in the early 1800s by hunter and sugar maker Robert Pullman who traveled with a small team to unexplored areas north of his home and discovered Sugar Creek with an abundance of sugar maple trees and rich soil. He built a cabin in the area in October 1817 and returned to his home in southern Illinois the following spring with the maple sugar and furs he had harvested.

After Illinois entered the Union in 1818, Elisha Kelly from North Carolina discovered the Sugar Creek area and relocated there with family and friends. They named the area Calhoun in honor of Senator John C. Calhoun of South Carolina. In 1821 businessman Elijah Iles relocated his family there from Missouri and opened the first general store. Calhoun was renamed Springfield in 1832 after Springfield, Massachusetts, a thriving town that Iles aspired to.

Abraham Lincoln, although known as Springfield's most prominent citizen, was born in Hodgenville, Kentucky in 1809. He moved to the Springfield area in 1831, and to the city proper in 1837 where he practiced law and politics. Lincoln's famous farewell speech, and one of his earliest published speeches, his Lyceum address, was delivered in Springfield in January of 1838; the next year, Springfield became the capital of Illinois due to Lincoln's efforts.

In 1852, Springfield connected with the railroad system which led to its economic expansion. After Lincoln became President of the United States in 1861, Springfield became a training area for the Civil War, and Confederate prisoner camp. By 1900 Springfield emerged as a major player in the coal and farming industries, and a hub for the Illinois railroad.

Another celebrity resident of Springfield is architect Frank Lloyd Wright, who built the Dana Thomas House for the silver mine heiress Susan Lawrence Dana in 1902. This 12,000 square foot, 35-room house is the best-preserved example of Lloyd's "Prairie" houses. The Dana Thomas House has the largest known collection of Wright's site-specific furniture and glass art throughout its 16 levels. It has been thoroughly renovated and is currently a museum.

Today, Springfield's economy is diversified and growing. Major business sectors include government, healthcare, education, insurance, and finance.

In 2014, the city became home to a new business incubator, Innovate Springfield which, in 2018, became part of a nationwide innovation network.

Springfield is an American history buff's dream for all things Lincoln; his home and law office are open to the public and listed as National Historic sites. The Abraham Lincoln Presidential Library and Museum, built in 2005, houses the original Gettysburg Address and the largest collection of Lincoln biographical works. The nearby Capitol Building is where Lincoln served in the House of Representatives and where mourners passed his body as it laid in state in 1865. Just a short walk from the Capitol is Oak Ridge Cemetery where Lincoln and his immediate family are buried at Lincoln's Tomb. More recently, former President Obama announced both his candidacy for the presidency and his choice for running mate Joe Biden at the State Capitol building in Springfield.

Two popular annual events hosted by the city are the Old Capitol Art Fair and the Route 66 Film Festival. Springfield is home to the Hoogland Center for the Arts, Springfield Theatre Center, Springfield Ballet Company, Illinois Symphony Orchestra, and the Springfield Municipal Opera. The Illinois state legislature adopted a resolution proclaiming Springfield the "Chili Capital of the Civilized World."

Springfield's climate is typically continental with cold winters, warm summers, and frequent fluctuations in temperature and humidity. The moderate temperatures of spring and fall are pleasant. The city was hit by two tornadoes in 2006.

Rankings

Business/Finance Rankings

- The Springfield metro area appeared on the Milken Institute "2022 Best Performing Cities" list. Rank: #145 out of 201 small metro areas (population over 60,000). Criteria: job growth; wage and salary growth; high-tech output growth; housing affordability; household broadband access. *Milken Institute, "Best-Performing Cities 2022," March 28, 2022*

- *Forbes* ranked 203 smaller metro areas (population under 268,000) to determine the nation's "Best Small Places for Business and Careers." The Springfield metro area was ranked #34. Criteria: costs (business and living); job growth (past and projected); income growth; quality of life; educational attainment (college and high school); projected economic growth; cultural and leisure opportunities; workplace tolerance laws; net migration patterns. *Forbes, "The Best Small Places for Business and Careers 2019," October 30, 2019*

Environmental Rankings

- Springfield was highlighted as one of the cleanest metro areas for ozone air pollution in the U.S. during 2019 through 2021. The list represents cities with no monitored ozone air pollution in unhealthful ranges. *American Lung Association, "State of the Air 2023," April 19, 2023*

- Springfield was highlighted as one of the top 59 cleanest metro areas for short-term particle pollution (24-hour PM 2.5) in the U.S. during 2019 through 2021. Monitors in these cities reported no days with unhealthful PM 2.5 levels. *American Lung Association, "State of the Air 2023," April 19, 2023*

Real Estate Rankings

- The Springfield metro area was identified as one of the nations's 20 hottest housing markets in 2023. Criteria: listing views as an indicator of demand and number of days on the market as an indicator of pace. The area ranked #19. *Realtor.com, "January 2023 Top 20 Hottest Housing Markets," February 23, 2023*

- The Springfield metro area was identified as one of the 20 most affordable housing markets in the U.S. in 2022. The area ranked #12 out of 186 markets. Criteria: qualification for a mortgage loan with a 10 percent down payment on a typical home. *National Association of Realtors®, Qualifying Income Based on Sales Price of Existing Single-Family Homes for Metropolitan Areas, 2022*

- Springfield was ranked #20 out of 235 metro areas in terms of housing affordability in 2022 by the National Association of Home Builders (#1 = most affordable). Criteria: the share of homes sold in that area affordable to a family earning the local median income, based on standard mortgage underwriting criteria. *National Association of Home Builders®, NAHB-Wells Fargo Housing Opportunity Index, 4th Quarter 2022*

Safety Rankings

- Statistics drawn from the FBI's Uniform Crime Report were used to rank the cities where violent crime rose the most year over year from 2019 to 2020. Only cities with 25,000 or more residents were included. *24/7 Wall St.* found that Springfield placed #46 of those with a notable surge in incidents of violent crime. *247wallst.com, "American Cities Where Crime Is Soaring," March 4, 2022*

- The National Insurance Crime Bureau ranked 390 metro areas in the U.S. in terms of per capita rates of vehicle theft. The Springfield metro area ranked #112 (#1 = highest rate). Criteria: number of vehicle theft offenses per 100,000 inhabitants in 2021. *National Insurance Crime Bureau, "Hot Spots 2021," September 1, 2022*

Seniors/Retirement Rankings

- From its Best Cities for Successful Aging indexes, the Milken Institute generated rankings for metropolitan areas, weighing data in nine categories—health care, wellness, living arrangements, transportation and convenience, financial characteristics, education, employment, community engagement, and overall livability. The Springfield metro area was ranked #92 overall in the small metro area category. *Milken Institute, "Best Cities for Successful Aging, 2017" March 14, 2017*

Business Environment

DEMOGRAPHICS

Population Growth

Area	1990 Census	2000 Census	2010 Census	2020 Census	Population Growth (%) 1990-2020	Population Growth (%) 2010-2020
City	108,997	111,454	116,250	114,394	5.0	-1.6
MSA[1]	189,550	201,437	210,170	208,640	10.1	-0.7
U.S.	248,709,873	281,421,906	308,745,538	331,449,281	33.3	7.4

Note: (1) Figures cover the Springfield, IL Metropolitan Statistical Area
Source: U.S. Census Bureau, 1990 Census, 2000 Census, 2010 Census, 2020 Census

Race

Area	White Alone[2] (%)	Black Alone[2] (%)	Asian Alone[2] (%)	AIAN[3] Alone[2] (%)	NHOPI[4] Alone[2] (%)	Other Race Alone[2] (%)	Two or More Races (%)
City	68.9	20.4	2.9	0.3	0.0	1.1	6.4
MSA[1]	78.4	12.5	2.1	0.2	0.0	0.9	5.8
U.S.	61.6	12.4	6.0	1.1	0.2	8.4	10.2

Note: (1) Figures cover the Springfield, IL Metropolitan Statistical Area; (2) Alone is defined as not being in combination with one or more other races; (3) American Indian and Alaska Native; (4) Native Hawaiian and Other Pacific Islander
Source: U.S. Census Bureau, 2020 Census

Hispanic or Latino Origin

Area	Total (%)	Mexican (%)	Puerto Rican (%)	Cuban (%)	Other (%)
City	2.9	1.5	0.6	0.1	0.7
MSA[1]	2.4	1.4	0.4	0.1	0.5
U.S.	18.4	11.2	1.8	0.7	4.7

Note: Persons of Hispanic or Latino origin can be of any race; (1) Figures cover the Springfield, IL Metropolitan Statistical Area
Source: U.S. Census Bureau, 2017-2021 American Community Survey 5-Year Estimates

Age

Area	Under Age 5	Age 5–19	Age 20–34	Age 35–44	Age 45–54	Age 55–64	Age 65–74	Age 75–84	Age 85+	Median Age
City	5.8	17.6	19.4	12.2	11.6	14.1	11.5	5.5	2.4	40.7
MSA[1]	5.6	18.9	17.6	12.5	12.1	14.5	11.4	5.3	2.1	41.2
U.S.	5.6	19.2	20.2	12.7	12.4	13.1	10.0	4.9	1.9	38.8

Note: (1) Figures cover the Springfield, IL Metropolitan Statistical Area
Source: U.S. Census Bureau, 2020 Census

Disability by Age

Area	All Ages	Under 18 Years Old	18 to 64 Years Old	65 Years and Over
City	14.7	6.2	13.0	31.2
MSA[1]	13.7	6.2	11.6	30.4
U.S.	12.6	4.4	10.3	33.4

Note: Figures show percent of the civilian noninstitutionalized population that reported having a disability. Disability status is determined from six types of difficulty: vision, hearing, cognitive, ambulatory, self-care, and independent living. For children under 5 years old, hearing and vision difficulty are used to determine disability status. For children between the ages of 5 and 14, disability status is determined from hearing, vision, cognitive, ambulatory, and self-care difficulties. For people aged 15 years and older, they are considered to have a disability if they have difficulty with any one of the six difficulty types; Note: (1) Figures cover the Springfield, IL Metropolitan Statistical Area
Source: U.S. Census Bureau, 2017-2021 American Community Survey 5-Year Estimates

Ancestry

Area	German	Irish	English	American	Italian	Polish	French[2]	Scottish	Dutch
City	18.9	11.4	9.6	4.1	4.5	2.0	1.9	1.8	1.1
MSA[1]	21.5	12.5	10.9	5.1	4.8	1.9	2.2	1.9	1.3
U.S.	12.8	9.6	8.1	5.7	5.0	2.7	2.2	1.6	1.1

Note: Figures are the percentage of the total population reporting a particular ancestry. The nine most commonly reported ancestries in the U.S. are shown. Figures include multiple ancestries (e.g. if a person reported being Irish and Italian, they were included in both columns); (1) Figures cover the Springfield, IL Metropolitan Statistical Area; (2) Excludes Basque
Source: U.S. Census Bureau, 2017-2021 American Community Survey 5-Year Estimates

Foreign-born Population

Area	Any Foreign Country	Asia	Mexico	Europe	Caribbean	Central America[2]	South America	Africa	Canada
City	4.4	2.3	0.5	0.5	0.1	0.1	0.2	0.6	0.0
MSA[1]	2.9	1.5	0.3	0.4	0.1	0.0	0.2	0.3	0.0
U.S.	13.6	4.2	3.3	1.5	1.4	1.1	1.1	0.8	0.2

Note: (1) Figures cover the Springfield, IL Metropolitan Statistical Area; (2) Excludes Mexico.
Source: U.S. Census Bureau, 2017-2021 American Community Survey 5-Year Estimates

Household Size

Area	One	Two	Three	Four	Five	Six	Seven or More	Average Household Size
City	39.4	32.5	12.4	9.6	3.8	1.3	1.0	2.20
MSA[1]	33.8	35.4	13.4	10.5	4.6	1.3	0.9	2.30
U.S.	28.1	33.8	15.5	12.9	6.0	2.3	1.4	2.60

Note: (1) Figures cover the Springfield, IL Metropolitan Statistical Area
Source: U.S. Census Bureau, 2017-2021 American Community Survey 5-Year Estimates

Household Relationships

Area	Householder	Opposite-sex Spouse	Same-sex Spouse	Opposite-sex Unmarried Partner	Same-sex Unmarried Partner	Child[2]	Grandchild	Other Relatives	Non-relatives
City	44.8	15.5	0.2	3.2	0.2	25.7	1.9	2.8	2.8
MSA[1]	42.9	18.2	0.2	3.0	0.2	27.2	1.8	2.4	2.4
U.S.	38.3	17.5	0.2	2.5	0.2	28.3	2.4	4.8	3.4

Note: Figures are percent of the total population; (1) Figures cover the Springfield, IL Metropolitan Statistical Area; (2) Includes biological, adopted, and stepchildren of the householder
Source: U.S. Census Bureau, 2020 Census

Gender

Area	Males	Females	Males per 100 Females
City	54,215	60,179	90.1
MSA[1]	100,412	108,228	92.8
U.S.	162,685,811	168,763,470	96.4

Note: (1) Figures cover the Springfield, IL Metropolitan Statistical Area
Source: U.S. Census Bureau, 2020 Census

Marital Status

Area	Never Married	Now Married[2]	Separated	Widowed	Divorced
City	37.6	39.5	1.6	6.2	15.1
MSA[1]	32.4	46.6	1.3	6.1	13.6
U.S.	33.8	48.0	1.8	5.6	10.8

Note: Figures are percentages and cover the population 15 years of age and older; (1) Figures cover the Springfield, IL Metropolitan Statistical Area; (2) Excludes separated
Source: U.S. Census Bureau, 2017-2021 American Community Survey 5-Year Estimates

Religious Groups by Family

Area	Catholic	Baptist	Methodist	LDS[2]	Pentecostal	Lutheran	Islam	Adventist	Other
MSA[1]	15.2	4.7	4.3	0.5	1.5	4.7	0.5	0.8	14.6
U.S.	18.7	7.3	3.0	2.0	1.8	1.7	1.3	1.3	11.6

Note: Figures are the number of adherents as a percentage of the total population and cover the eight largest religious groups in the U.S; (1) Figures cover the Springfield, IL Metropolitan Statistical Area; (2) Church of Jesus Christ of Latter-day Saints
Sources: 2020 U.S. Religion Census, Association of Statisticians of American Religious Bodies; The Association of Religion Data Archives (ARDA)

Religious Groups by Tradition

Area	Catholic	Evangelical Protestant	Mainline Protestant	Black Protestant	Islam	Judaism	Hinduism	Orthodox	Buddhism
MSA[1]	15.2	19.0	7.7	2.4	0.5	0.2	0.3	0.1	<0.1
U.S.	18.7	16.5	5.2	2.3	1.3	0.6	0.4	0.4	0.3

Note: Figures are the number of adherents as a percentage of the total population; (1) Figures cover the Springfield, IL Metropolitan Statistical Area
Sources: 2020 U.S. Religion Census, Association of Statisticians of American Religious Bodies; The Association of Religion Data Archives (ARDA)

ECONOMY

Gross Metropolitan Product

Area	2020	2021	2022	2023	Rank[2]
MSA[1]	11.7	13.1	13.8	14.6	196

Note: Figures are in billions of dollars; (1) Figures cover the Springfield, IL Metropolitan Statistical Area; (2) Rank is based on 2021 data and ranges from 1 to 381
Source: U.S. Conference of Mayors, U.S. Metro Economies: U.S. Metros Compared to Global and State Economies, June 2022

Economic Growth

Area	2018-20 (%)	2021 (%)	2022 (%)	2023 (%)	Rank[2]
MSA[1]	-3.3	9.4	0.6	2.6	346
U.S.	-0.6	5.7	3.1	2.9	—

Note: Figures are real gross metropolitan product (GMP) growth rates and represent average annual percent change; (1) Figures cover the Springfield, IL Metropolitan Statistical Area; (2) Rank is based on 2020 2-year average annual percent change and ranges from 1 to 381
Source: U.S. Conference of Mayors, U.S. Metro Economies: U.S. Metros Compared to Global and State Economies, June 2022

Metropolitan Area Exports

Area	2016	2017	2018	2019	2020	2021	Rank[2]
MSA[1]	88.3	107.5	91.2	99.8	90.5	98.9	351

Note: Figures are in millions of dollars; (1) Figures cover the Springfield, IL Metropolitan Statistical Area; (2) Rank is based on 2021 data and ranges from 1 to 388
Source: U.S. Department of Commerce, International Trade Administration, Office of Trade and Economic Analysis, Industry and Analysis, Exports by Metropolitan Area, data extracted March 16, 2023

Building Permits

Area	Single-Family			Multi-Family			Total		
	2021	2022	Pct. Chg.	2021	2022	Pct. Chg.	2021	2022	Pct. Chg.
City	137	55	-59.9	87	10	-88.5	224	65	-71.0
MSA[1]	239	146	-38.9	93	64	-31.2	332	210	-36.7
U.S.	1,115,400	975,600	-12.5	621,600	689,500	10.9	1,737,000	1,665,100	-4.1

Note: (1) Figures cover the Springfield, IL Metropolitan Statistical Area; Figures represent new, privately-owned housing units authorized (unadjusted data); All permit data are based on estimates with imputation
Source: U.S. Census Bureau, Manufacturing, Mining, and Construction Statistics, Building Permits, 2021, 2022

Bankruptcy Filings

Area	Business Filings			Nonbusiness Filings		
	2021	2022	% Chg.	2021	2022	% Chg.
Sangamon County	6	5	-16.7	221	186	-15.8
U.S.	14,347	13,481	-6.0	399,269	374,240	-6.3

Note: Business filings include Chapter 7, Chapter 9, Chapter 11, Chapter 12, Chapter 13, Chapter 15, and Section 304; Nonbusiness filings include Chapter 7, Chapter 11, and Chapter 13
Source: Administrative Office of the U.S. Courts, Business and Nonbusiness Bankruptcy, County Cases Commenced by Chapter of the Bankruptcy Code, During the 12-Month Period Ending December 31, 2021 and Business and Nonbusiness Bankruptcy, County Cases Commenced by Chapter of the Bankruptcy Code, During the 12-Month Period Ending December 31, 2022

Housing Vacancy Rates

Area	Gross Vacancy Rate[2] (%)			Year-Round Vacancy Rate[3] (%)			Rental Vacancy Rate[4] (%)			Homeowner Vacancy Rate[5] (%)		
	2020	2021	2022	2020	2021	2022	2020	2021	2022	2020	2021	2022
MSA[1]	n/a	n/a	n/a	n/a	n/a	n/a	n/a	n/a	n/a	n/a	n/a	n/a
U.S.	10.6	10.8	10.5	8.2	8.4	8.2	6.3	6.1	5.8	1.0	0.9	0.8

Note: (1) Figures cover the Springfield, IL Metropolitan Statistical Area; (2) The percentage of the total housing inventory that is vacant; (3) The percentage of the housing inventory (excluding seasonal units) that is year-round vacant; (4) The percentage of rental inventory that is vacant for rent; (5) The percentage of homeowner inventory that is vacant for sale; n/a not available
Source: U.S. Census Bureau, Housing Vacancies and Homeownership Annual Statistics: 2020, 2021, 2022

INCOME

Income

Area	Per Capita ($)	Median Household ($)	Average Household ($)
City	35,851	57,596	79,460
MSA[1]	37,961	66,999	87,390
U.S.	37,638	69,021	97,196

Note: (1) Figures cover the Springfield, IL Metropolitan Statistical Area
Source: U.S. Census Bureau, 2017-2021 American Community Survey 5-Year Estimates

Household Income Distribution

Area	Percent of Households Earning							
	Under $15,000	$15,000 -$24,999	$25,000 -$34,999	$35,000 -$49,999	$50,000 -$74,999	$75,000 -$99,999	$100,000 -$149,999	$150,000 and up
City	13.8	9.1	9.7	11.9	16.0	13.3	15.0	11.2
MSA[1]	10.4	7.9	8.4	11.5	16.2	14.1	18.0	13.7
U.S.	9.4	7.8	8.2	11.4	16.8	12.8	16.3	17.3

Note: (1) Figures cover the Springfield, IL Metropolitan Statistical Area
Source: U.S. Census Bureau, 2017-2021 American Community Survey 5-Year Estimates

Poverty Rate

Area	All Ages	Under 18 Years Old	18 to 64 Years Old	65 Years and Over
City	18.5	28.2	17.6	9.2
MSA[1]	13.6	20.0	13.2	7.3
U.S.	12.6	17.0	11.8	9.6

Note: Figures are percentage of people whose income during the past 12 months was below the poverty level;
(1) Figures cover the Springfield, IL Metropolitan Statistical Area
Source: U.S. Census Bureau, 2017-2021 American Community Survey 5-Year Estimates

EMPLOYMENT

Labor Force and Employment

Area	Civilian Labor Force			Workers Employed		
	Dec. 2021	Dec. 2022	% Chg.	Dec. 2021	Dec. 2022	% Chg.
City	55,434	55,938	0.9	53,040	53,888	1.6
MSA[1]	103,907	105,050	1.1	99,703	101,310	1.6
U.S.	161,696,000	164,224,000	1.6	155,732,000	158,872,000	2.0

Note: Data is not seasonally adjusted and covers workers 16 years of age and older; (1) Figures cover the
Springfield, IL Metropolitan Statistical Area
Source: Bureau of Labor Statistics, Local Area Unemployment Statistics

Unemployment Rate

Area	2022											
	Jan.	Feb.	Mar.	Apr.	May	Jun.	Jul.	Aug.	Sep.	Oct.	Nov.	Dec.
City	5.3	5.0	4.6	4.9	5.2	4.6	4.8	4.9	4.3	4.5	4.3	3.7
MSA[1]	5.1	4.8	4.5	4.6	4.7	4.2	4.3	4.3	3.8	3.9	3.9	3.6
U.S.	4.4	4.1	3.8	3.3	3.4	3.8	3.8	3.8	3.3	3.4	3.4	3.3

Note: Data is not seasonally adjusted and covers workers 16 years of age and older; (1) Figures cover the
Springfield, IL Metropolitan Statistical Area
Source: Bureau of Labor Statistics, Local Area Unemployment Statistics

Average Wages

Occupation	$/Hr.	Occupation	$/Hr.
Accountants and Auditors	37.41	Maintenance and Repair Workers	23.40
Automotive Mechanics	23.85	Marketing Managers	62.68
Bookkeepers	22.33	Network and Computer Systems Admin.	36.92
Carpenters	28.27	Nurses, Licensed Practical	25.11
Cashiers	13.91	Nurses, Registered	37.80
Computer Programmers	43.32	Nursing Assistants	17.22
Computer Systems Analysts	48.50	Office Clerks, General	20.11
Computer User Support Specialists	26.48	Physical Therapists	46.06
Construction Laborers	30.22	Physicians	146.21
Cooks, Restaurant	16.03	Plumbers, Pipefitters and Steamfitters	38.31
Customer Service Representatives	19.00	Police and Sheriff's Patrol Officers	34.84
Dentists	72.48	Postal Service Mail Carriers	26.37
Electricians	35.32	Real Estate Sales Agents	26.10
Engineers, Electrical	47.34	Retail Salespersons	16.08
Fast Food and Counter Workers	13.61	Sales Representatives, Technical/Scientific	39.68
Financial Managers	64.09	Secretaries, Exc. Legal/Medical/Executive	20.55
First-Line Supervisors of Office Workers	30.02	Security Guards	17.77
General and Operations Managers	52.04	Surgeons	n/a
Hairdressers/Cosmetologists	18.76	Teacher Assistants, Exc. Postsecondary*	15.04
Home Health and Personal Care Aides	14.39	Teachers, Secondary School, Exc. Sp. Ed.*	30.36
Janitors and Cleaners	16.63	Telemarketers	n/a
Landscaping/Groundskeeping Workers	18.70	Truck Drivers, Heavy/Tractor-Trailer	24.23
Lawyers	61.68	Truck Drivers, Light/Delivery Services	23.13
Maids and Housekeeping Cleaners	16.39	Waiters and Waitresses	14.77

Note: Wage data covers the Springfield, IL Metropolitan Statistical Area; (*) Hourly wages were calculated
from annual wage data based on a 40 hour work week; n/a not available.
Source: Bureau of Labor Statistics, Metro Area Occupational Employment & Wage Estimates, May 2022

Employment by Industry

Sector	MSA[1]		U.S.
	Number of Employees	Percent of Total	Percent of Total
Construction, Mining, and Logging	3,700	3.4	5.4
Private Education and Health Services	21,000	19.2	16.1
Financial Activities	6,100	5.6	5.9
Government	26,400	24.1	14.5
Information	2,200	2.0	2.0
Leisure and Hospitality	10,500	9.6	10.3
Manufacturing	3,600	3.3	8.4
Other Services	6,000	5.5	3.7
Professional and Business Services	12,500	11.4	14.7
Retail Trade	11,900	10.9	10.2
Transportation, Warehousing, and Utilities	2,500	2.3	4.9
Wholesale Trade	3,200	2.9	3.9

Note: Figures are non-farm employment as of December 2022. Figures are not seasonally adjusted and include workers 16 years of age and older; (1) Figures cover the Springfield, IL Metropolitan Statistical Area
Source: Bureau of Labor Statistics, Current Employment Statistics, Employment, Hours, and Earnings

Employment by Occupation

Occupation Classification	City (%)	MSA[1] (%)	U.S. (%)
Management, Business, Science, and Arts	43.4	44.0	40.3
Natural Resources, Construction, and Maintenance	5.0	6.8	8.7
Production, Transportation, and Material Moving	10.6	10.5	13.1
Sales and Office	21.8	21.7	20.9
Service	19.2	17.1	17.0

Note: Figures cover employed civilians 16 years of age and older; (1) Figures cover the Springfield, IL Metropolitan Statistical Area
Source: U.S. Census Bureau, 2017-2021 American Community Survey 5-Year Estimates

Occupations with Greatest Projected Employment Growth: 2022 – 2024

Occupation[1]	2022 Employment	2024 Projected Employment	Numeric Employment Change	Percent Employment Change
Laborers and Freight, Stock, and Material Movers, Hand	197,270	205,510	8,240	4.2
Fast Food and Counter Workers	144,440	149,210	4,770	3.3
Cooks, Restaurant	42,630	46,710	4,080	9.6
Home Health and Personal Care Aides	100,160	104,050	3,890	3.9
Waiters and Waitresses	73,770	77,220	3,450	4.7
Heavy and Tractor-Trailer Truck Drivers	76,720	79,980	3,260	4.2
General and Operations Managers	126,240	129,310	3,070	2.4
Software Developers and Software Quality Assurance Analysts and Testers	67,670	70,440	2,770	4.1
Light Truck or Delivery Services Drivers	64,670	67,340	2,670	4.1
Stockers and Order Fillers	80,950	83,070	2,120	2.6

Note: Projections cover Illinois; (1) Sorted by numeric employment change
Source: www.projectionscentral.com, State Occupational Projections, 2022–2024 Short-Term Projections

Fastest-Growing Occupations: 2022 – 2024

Occupation[1]	2022 Employment	2024 Projected Employment	Numeric Employment Change	Percent Employment Change
Gaming Service Workers, All Other	150	220	70	46.7
Gaming Dealers	1,200	1,740	540	45.0
First-Line Supervisors of Gambling Services Workers	380	540	160	42.1
Gaming Change Persons and Booth Cashiers	340	480	140	41.2
Gaming Cage Workers	220	300	80	36.4
Hotel, Motel, and Resort Desk Clerks	6,430	7,520	1,090	17.0
Ushers, Lobby Attendants, and Ticket Takers	3,830	4,350	520	13.6
Lodging Managers	820	910	90	11.0
Baggage Porters and Bellhops	1,200	1,330	130	10.8
Cooks, Restaurant	42,630	46,710	4,080	9.6

Note: Projections cover Illinois; (1) Sorted by percent employment change and excludes occupations with numeric employment change less than 50
Source: www.projectionscentral.com, State Occupational Projections, 2022–2024 Short-Term Projections

CITY FINANCES

City Government Finances

Component	2020 ($000)	2020 ($ per capita)
Total Revenues	429,253	3,758
Total Expenditures	449,865	3,938
Debt Outstanding	1,455,832	12,745
Cash and Securities[1]	260,417	2,280

Note: (1) Cash and security holdings of a government at the close of its fiscal year, including those of its dependent agencies, utilities, and liquor stores.
Source: U.S. Census Bureau, State & Local Government Finances 2020

City Government Revenue by Source

Source	2020 ($000)	2020 ($ per capita)	2020 (%)
General Revenue			
From Federal Government	9,795	86	2.3
From State Government	52,262	458	12.2
From Local Governments	1,582	14	0.4
Taxes			
Property	28,987	254	6.8
Sales and Gross Receipts	61,596	539	14.3
Personal Income	0	0	0.0
Corporate Income	0	0	0.0
Motor Vehicle License	0	0	0.0
Other Taxes	1,420	12	0.3
Current Charges	22,749	199	5.3
Liquor Store	0	0	0.0
Utility	245,937	2,153	57.3

Source: U.S. Census Bureau, State & Local Government Finances 2020

City Government Expenditures by Function

Function	2020 ($000)	2020 ($ per capita)	2020 (%)
General Direct Expenditures			
Air Transportation	0	0	0.0
Corrections	0	0	0.0
Education	0	0	0.0
Employment Security Administration	0	0	0.0
Financial Administration	2,423	21	0.5
Fire Protection	40,614	355	9.0
General Public Buildings	2,243	19	0.5
Governmental Administration, Other	6,858	60	1.5
Health	0	0	0.0
Highways	35,373	309	7.9
Hospitals	0	0	0.0
Housing and Community Development	9,232	80	2.1
Interest on General Debt	4,569	40	1.0
Judicial and Legal	0	0	0.0
Libraries	3,794	33	0.8
Parking	717	6	0.2
Parks and Recreation	2,855	25	0.6
Police Protection	51,502	450	11.4
Public Welfare	0	0	0.0
Sewerage	7,269	63	1.6
Solid Waste Management	0	0	0.0
Veterans' Services	0	0	0.0
Liquor Store	0	0	0.0
Utility	245,361	2,148	54.5

Source: U.S. Census Bureau, State & Local Government Finances 2020

TAXES

State Corporate Income Tax Rates

State	Tax Rate (%)	Income Brackets ($)	Num. of Brackets	Financial Institution Tax Rate (%)[a]	Federal Income Tax Ded.
Illinois	9.5 (g)	Flat rate	1	9.5 (g)	No

Note: Tax rates as of January 1, 2023; (a) Rates listed are the corporate income tax rate applied to financial institutions or excise taxes based on income. Some states have other taxes based upon the value of deposits or shares; (g) The Illinois rate of 9.5% is the sum of a corporate income tax rate of 7.0% plus a replacement tax of 2.5%.
Source: Federation of Tax Administrators, State Corporate Income Tax Rates, January 1, 2023

State Individual Income Tax Rates

State	Tax Rate (%)	Income Brackets ($)	Personal Exemptions ($) Single	Married	Depend.	Standard Ded. ($) Single	Married
Illinois (a)	4.95	Flat rate	2,425	4,850	2,425	–	–

Note: Tax rates as of January 1, 2023; Local- and county-level taxes are not included; Federal income tax is not deductible on state income tax returns; (a) 16 states have statutory provision for automatically adjusting to the rate of inflation the dollar values of the income tax brackets, standard deductions, and/or personal exemptions. Oregon does not index the income brackets for $125,000 and over.
Source: Federation of Tax Administrators, State Individual Income Tax Rates, January 1, 2023

Various State Sales and Excise Tax Rates

State	State Sales Tax (%)	Gasoline[1] ($/gal.)	Cigarette[2] ($/pack)	Spirits[3] ($/gal.)	Wine[4] ($/gal.)	Beer[5] ($/gal.)	Recreational Marijuana (%)
Illinois	6.25	0.654	2.98	8.55	1.39	0.23	(f)

Note: All tax rates as of January 1, 2023; (1) The American Petroleum Institute has developed a methodology for determining the average tax rate on a gallon of fuel. Rates may include any of the following: excise taxes, environmental fees, storage tank fees, other fees or taxes, general sales tax, and local taxes; (2) The federal excise tax of $1.0066 per pack and local taxes are not included; (3) Rates are those applicable to off-premise sales of 40% alcohol by volume (a.b.v.) distilled spirits in 750ml containers. Local excise taxes are excluded; (4) Rates are those applicable to off-premise sales of 11% a.b.v. non-carbonated wine in 750ml containers; (5) Rates are those applicable to off-premise sales of 4.7% a.b.v. beer in 12 ounce containers; (f) 7% excise tax of value at wholesale level; 10% tax on cannabis flower or products with less than 35% THC; 20% tax on products infused with cannabis, such as edible products; 25% tax on any product with a THC concentration higher than 35%
Source: Tax Foundation, 2023 Facts & Figures: How Does Your State Compare?

State Business Tax Climate Index Rankings

State	Overall Rank	Corporate Tax Rank	Individual Income Tax Rank	Sales Tax Rank	Property Tax Rank	Unemployment Insurance Tax Rank
Illinois	36	38	13	38	44	43

Note: The index is a measure of how each state's tax laws affect economic performance. The lower the rank, the more favorable a state's tax system is for business. States without a given tax are given a ranking of 1. The scores/rankings for the District of Columbia do not affect other states. The 2023 index represents the tax climate as of July 1, 2022.
Source: Tax Foundation, State Business Tax Climate Index 2023

TRANSPORTATION

Means of Transportation to Work

Area	Car/Truck/Van Drove Alone	Car-pooled	Public Transportation Bus	Subway	Railroad	Bicycle	Walked	Other Means	Worked at Home
City	79.6	6.4	1.6	0.1	0.0	0.5	1.6	1.7	8.7
MSA[1]	81.6	6.4	0.9	0.1	0.0	0.4	1.4	1.3	8.0
U.S.	73.2	8.6	2.0	1.6	0.5	0.5	2.5	1.5	9.7

Note: Figures are percentages and cover workers 16 years of age and older; (1) Figures cover the Springfield, IL Metropolitan Statistical Area
Source: U.S. Census Bureau, 2017-2021 American Community Survey 5-Year Estimates

Travel Time to Work

Area	Less Than 10 Minutes	10 to 19 Minutes	20 to 29 Minutes	30 to 44 Minutes	45 to 59 Minutes	60 to 89 Minutes	90 Minutes or More
City	17.4	53.1	17.9	6.3	1.8	2.3	1.3
MSA[1]	15.0	43.3	23.5	11.8	2.5	2.1	1.8
U.S.	12.4	28.5	21.0	20.9	8.2	6.2	2.9

Note: Note: Figures are percentages and include workers 16 years old and over; (1) Figures cover the Springfield, IL Metropolitan Statistical Area
Source: U.S. Census Bureau, 2017-2021 American Community Survey 5-Year Estimates

Key Congestion Measures

Measure	1990	2000	2010	2015	2020
Annual Hours of Delay, Total (000)	n/a	n/a	n/a	2,489	1,669
Annual Hours of Delay, Per Auto Commuter	n/a	n/a	n/a	14	9
Annual Congestion Cost, Per Auto Commuter ($)	n/a	n/a	n/a	297	214

Note: n/a not available
Source: Texas A&M Transportation Institute, 2021 Urban Mobility Report

Freeway Travel Time Index

Measure	1985	1990	1995	2000	2005	2010	2015	2020
Urban Area Index[1]	n/a	n/a	n/a	n/a	n/a	n/a	1.06	1.05
Urban Area Rank[1,2]	n/a	n/a	n/a	n/a	n/a	n/a	n/a	n/a

Note: Freeway Travel Time Index—the ratio of travel time in the peak period to the travel time at free-flow conditions. For example, a value of 1.30 indicates a 20-minute free-flow trip takes 26 minutes in the peak (20 minutes x 1.30 = 26 minutes); (1) Covers the Springfield IL urban area; (2) Rank is based on 101 larger urban areas (#1 = highest travel time index); n/a not available
Source: Texas A&M Transportation Institute, 2021 Urban Mobility Report

Public Transportation

Agency Name / Mode of Transportation	Vehicles Operated in Maximum Service[1]	Annual Unlinked Passenger Trips[2] (in thous.)	Annual Passenger Miles[3] (in thous.)
Springfield Mass Transit District (SMTD)			
Bus (directly operated)	48	973.8	3,576.7
Demand Response (directly operated)	15	63.4	338.8

Note: (1) Number of revenue vehicles operated by the given mode and type of service to meet the annual maximum service requirement. This is the revenue vehicle count during the peak season of the year; on the week and day that maximum service is provided. Vehicles operated in maximum service (VOMS) exclude atypical days and one-time special events; (2) Number of passengers who boarded public transportation vehicles. Passengers are counted each time they board a vehicle no matter how many vehicles they use to travel from their origin to their destination. (3) Sum of the distances ridden by all passengers during the entire fiscal year.
Source: Federal Transit Administration, National Transit Database, 2021

Air Transportation

Airport Name and Code / Type of Service	Passenger Airlines[1]	Passenger Enplanements	Freight Carriers[2]	Freight (lbs)
Capital Airport (SPI)				
Domestic service (U.S. carriers - 2022)	7	72,466	1	1,325
International service (U.S. carriers - 2021)	0	0	0	0

Note: (1) Includes all U.S.-based major, minor and commuter airlines that carried at least one passenger during the year; (2) Includes all U.S.-based airlines and freight carriers that transported at least one pound of freight during the year.
Source: Bureau of Transportation Statistics, The Intermodal Transportation Database, Air Carriers: T-100 Domestic Market (U.S. Carriers), 2022; Bureau of Transportation Statistics, The Intermodal Transportation Database, Air Carriers: T-100 International Market (U.S. Carriers), 2021

BUSINESSES

Major Business Headquarters

Company Name	Industry	Rankings	
		Fortune[1]	Forbes[2]
No companies listed	-	-	-

Note: (1) Companies that produce a 10-K are ranked 1 to 500 based on 2021 revenue; (2) All private companies with at least $2 billion in annual revenue through the end of their most current fiscal year are ranked 1 to 246; companies listed are headquartered in the city; dashes indicate no ranking
Source: Fortune, "Fortune 500," 2022; Forbes, "America's Largest Private Companies," 2022

Living Environment

COST OF LIVING

Cost of Living Index

Composite Index	Groceries	Housing	Utilities	Trans-portation	Health Care	Misc. Goods/ Services
93.1	96.5	89.3	102.1	104.6	98.3	88.6

Note: The Cost of Living Index measures regional differences in the cost of consumer goods and services, excluding taxes and non-consumer expenditures, for professional and managerial households in the top income quintile. It is based on more than 50,000 prices covering almost 60 different items for which prices are collected three times a year by chambers of commerce, economic development organizations or university applied economic centers in each participating urban area. The numbers shown should be read as a percentage above or below the national average of 100. For example, a value of 115.4 in the groceries column indicates that grocery prices are 15.4% higher than the national average. Small differences in the index numbers should not be interpreted as significant; Figures cover the Springfield IL urban area.
Source: The Council for Community and Economic Research, Cost of Living Index, 2022

Grocery Prices

Area[1]	T-Bone Steak ($/pound)	Frying Chicken ($/pound)	Whole Milk ($/half gal.)	Eggs ($/dozen)	Orange Juice ($/64 oz.)	Coffee ($/11.5 oz.)
City[2]	14.11	2.05	1.85	1.54	3.88	4.88
Avg.	13.81	1.59	2.43	2.25	3.85	4.95
Min.	10.17	0.90	1.51	1.30	2.90	3.46
Max.	19.35	3.30	4.32	4.32	5.31	8.59

Note: (1) Values for the local area are compared with the average, minimum and maximum values for all 286 areas in the Cost of Living Index; (2) Figures cover the Springfield IL urban area; **T-Bone Steak** (price per pound); **Frying Chicken** (price per pound, whole fryer); **Whole Milk** (half gallon carton); **Eggs** (price per dozen, Grade A, large); **Orange Juice** (64 oz. Tropicana or Florida Natural); **Coffee** (11.5 oz. can, vacuum-packed, Maxwell House, Hills Bros, or Folgers).
Source: The Council for Community and Economic Research, Cost of Living Index, 2022

Housing and Utility Costs

Area[1]	New Home Price ($)	Apartment Rent ($/month)	All Electric ($/month)	Part Electric ($/month)	Other Energy ($/month)	Telephone ($/month)
City[2]	408,667	1,152	-	91.51	94.77	185.67
Avg.	450,913	1,371	176.41	99.93	76.96	190.22
Min.	229,283	546	100.84	31.56	27.15	174.27
Max.	2,434,977	4,569	356.86	249.59	272.24	208.31

Note: (1) Values for the local area are compared with the average, minimum and maximum values for all 286 areas in the Cost of Living Index; (2) Figures cover the Springfield IL urban area; **New Home Price** (2,400 sf living area, 8,000 sf lot, in urban area with full utilities); **Apartment Rent** (950 sf 2 bedroom/1.5 or 2 bath, unfurnished, excluding all utilities except water); **All Electric** (average monthly cost for an all-electric home); **Part Electric** (average monthly cost for a part-electric home); **Other Energy** (average monthly cost for natural gas, fuel oil, coal, wood, and any other forms of energy except electricity); **Telephone** (price includes the base monthly rate plus taxes and fees for three lines of mobile phone service).
Source: The Council for Community and Economic Research, Cost of Living Index, 2022

Health Care, Transportation, and Other Costs

Area[1]	Doctor ($/visit)	Dentist ($/visit)	Optometrist ($/visit)	Gasoline ($/gallon)	Beauty Salon ($/visit)	Men's Shirt ($)
City[2]	120.00	103.33	123.00	3.95	28.33	17.09
Avg.	124.91	107.77	117.66	3.86	43.31	34.21
Min.	36.61	58.25	51.79	2.90	22.18	13.05
Max.	250.21	162.58	371.96	5.54	85.61	63.54

Note: (1) Values for the local area are compared with the average, minimum and maximum values for all 286 areas in the Cost of Living Index; (2) Figures cover the Springfield IL urban area; **Doctor** (general practitioners routine exam of an established patient); **Dentist** (adult teeth cleaning and periodic oral examination); **Optometrist** (full vision eye exam for established adult patient); **Gasoline** (one gallon regular unleaded, national brand, including all taxes, cash price at self-service pump if available); **Beauty Salon** (woman's shampoo, trim, and blow-dry); **Men's Shirt** (cotton/polyester dress shirt, pinpoint weave, long sleeves).
Source: The Council for Community and Economic Research, Cost of Living Index, 2022

HOUSING

Homeownership Rate

Area	2015 (%)	2016 (%)	2017 (%)	2018 (%)	2019 (%)	2020 (%)	2021 (%)	2022 (%)
MSA[1]	n/a	n/a	n/a	n/a	n/a	n/a	n/a	n/a
U.S.	63.7	63.4	63.9	64.4	64.6	66.6	65.5	65.8

Note: (1) Figures cover the Springfield, IL Metropolitan Statistical Area; n/a not available
Source: U.S. Census Bureau, Housing Vacancies and Homeownership Annual Statistics: 2015-2022

House Price Index (HPI)

Area	National Ranking[2]	Quarterly Change (%)	One-Year Change (%)	Five-Year Change (%)	Since 1991Q1 (%)
MSA[1]	158	-0.16	10.38	29.11	125.30
U.S.[3]	–	0.34	8.41	58.44	289.08

Note: The HPI is a weighted repeat sales index. It measures average price changes in repeat sales or refinancings on the same properties. This information is obtained by reviewing repeat mortgage transactions on single-family properties whose mortgages have been purchased or securitized by Fannie Mae or Freddie Mac since January 1975; (1) Figures cover the Springfield, IL Metropolitan Statistical Area; (2) Rankings are based on annual percentage change for all metro areas containing at least 15,000 transactions over the last 10 years and ranges from 1 to 257; (3) figures based on a weighted average of Census Division estimates using a seasonally adjusted, purchase-only index; all figures are for the period ending December 31, 2022
Source: Federal Housing Finance Agency, Change in FHFA Metropolitan Area House Price Indexes, 2022Q4

Median Single-Family Home Prices

Area	2020	2021	2022[p]	Percent Change 2021 to 2022
MSA[1]	148.0	146.7	157.0	7.0
U.S. Average	300.2	357.1	392.6	9.9

Note: Figures are median sales prices of existing single-family homes in thousands of dollars; (p) preliminary; (1) Figures cover the Springfield, IL Metropolitan Statistical Area
Source: National Association of Realtors, Median Sales Price of Existing Single-Family Homes for Metropolitan Areas, 4th Quarter 2022

Qualifying Income Based on Median Sales Price of Existing Single-Family Homes

Area	With 5% Down ($)	With 10% Down ($)	With 20% Down ($)
MSA[1]	48,587	46,030	40,916
U.S. Average	112,234	106,237	94,513

Note: Figures are preliminary; Qualifying income is based on a mortgage rate of 6.77%. Monthly principal and interest payment is limited to 25% of income; (1) Figures cover the Springfield, IL Metropolitan Statistical Area
Source: National Association of Realtors, Qualifying Income Based on Median Sales Price of Existing Single-Family Homes for Metropolitan Areas, 4th Quarter 2022

Home Value

Area	Under $100,000	$100,000 -$199,999	$200,000 -$299,999	$300,000 -$399,999	$400,000 -$499,999	$500,000 -$999,999	$1,000,000 or more	Median ($)
City	34.4	38.8	15.9	6.3	2.4	1.9	0.4	132,900
MSA[1]	29.8	38.6	19.5	7.3	2.4	2.0	0.4	148,000
U.S.	16.2	24.2	20.1	13.6	8.3	13.6	4.1	244,900

Note: Figures are percentages except for median and cover owner-occupied housing units; (1) Figures cover the Springfield, IL Metropolitan Statistical Area
Source: U.S. Census Bureau, 2017-2021 American Community Survey 5-Year Estimates

Year Housing Structure Built

Area	2020 or Later	2010 -2019	2000 -2009	1990 -1999	1980 -1989	1970 -1979	1960 -1969	1950 -1959	1940 -1949	Before 1940	Median Year
City	<0.1	3.0	8.6	13.0	8.8	17.4	12.6	10.8	6.0	19.7	1971
MSA[1]	<0.1	4.3	10.0	13.2	8.7	17.3	11.7	11.0	6.0	17.8	1972
U.S.	0.2	7.3	13.6	13.6	13.2	14.8	10.3	10.0	4.7	12.2	1979

Note: Figures are percentages except for Median Year; Note: (1) Figures cover the Springfield, IL Metropolitan Statistical Area
Source: U.S. Census Bureau, 2017-2021 American Community Survey 5-Year Estimates

Gross Monthly Rent

Area	Under $500	$500 -$999	$1,000 -$1,499	$1,500 -$1,999	$2,000 -$2,499	$2,500 -$2,999	$3,000 and up	Median ($)
City	10.6	58.7	23.8	4.8	0.9	0.8	0.4	852
MSA[1]	10.4	57.4	25.5	4.8	0.8	0.6	0.5	857
U.S.	8.1	30.5	30.8	16.8	7.3	3.1	3.5	1,163

Note: Figures are percentages except for median; Gross rent is the contract rent plus the estimated average monthly cost of utilities (electricity, gas, and water and sewer) and fuels (oil, coal, kerosene, wood, etc.) if these are paid by the renter (or paid for the renter by someone else); (1) Figures cover the Springfield, IL Metropolitan Statistical Area
Source: U.S. Census Bureau, 2017-2021 American Community Survey 5-Year Estimates

HEALTH

Health Risk Factors

Category	MSA[1] (%)	U.S. (%)
Adults aged 18–64 who have any kind of health care coverage	n/a	90.9
Adults who reported being in good or better health	n/a	85.2
Adults who have been told they have high blood cholesterol	n/a	35.7
Adults who have been told they have high blood pressure	n/a	32.4
Adults who are current smokers	n/a	14.4
Adults who currently use e-cigarettes	n/a	6.7
Adults who currently use chewing tobacco, snuff, or snus	n/a	3.5
Adults who are heavy drinkers[2]	n/a	6.3
Adults who are binge drinkers[3]	n/a	15.4
Adults who are overweight (BMI 25.0 - 29.9)	n/a	34.4
Adults who are obese (BMI 30.0 - 99.8)	n/a	33.9
Adults who participated in any physical activities in the past month	n/a	76.3

Note: (1) Figures for the Springfield, IL Metropolitan Statistical Area were not available.
(2) Heavy drinkers are classified as adult men having more than 14 drinks per week and adult women having more than 7 drinks per week; (3) Binge drinkers are classified as males having five or more drinks on one occasion or females having four or more drinks on one occasion
Source: Centers for Disease Control and Prevention, Behaviorial Risk Factor Surveillance System, SMART: Selected Metropolitan Area Risk Trends, 2021

Acute and Chronic Health Conditions

Category	MSA[1] (%)	U.S. (%)
Adults who have ever been told they had a heart attack	n/a	4.0
Adults who have ever been told they have angina or coronary heart disease	n/a	3.8
Adults who have ever been told they had a stroke	n/a	3.0
Adults who have ever been told they have asthma	n/a	14.9
Adults who have ever been told they have arthritis	n/a	25.8
Adults who have ever been told they have diabetes[2]	n/a	10.9
Adults who have ever been told they had skin cancer	n/a	6.6
Adults who have ever been told they had any other types of cancer	n/a	7.5
Adults who have ever been told they have COPD	n/a	6.1
Adults who have ever been told they have kidney disease	n/a	3.0
Adults who have ever been told they have a form of depression	n/a	20.5

Note: (1) Figures for the Springfield, IL Metropolitan Statistical Area were not available.
(2) Figures do not include pregnancy-related, borderline, or pre-diabetes
Source: Centers for Disease Control and Prevention, Behaviorial Risk Factor Surveillance System, SMART: Selected Metropolitan Area Risk Trends, 2021

Health Screening and Vaccination Rates

Category	MSA[1] (%)	U.S. (%)
Adults who have ever been tested for HIV	n/a	34.9
Adults who have had their blood cholesterol checked within the last five years	n/a	85.2
Adults aged 65+ who have had flu shot within the past year	n/a	68.6
Adults aged 65+ who have ever had a pneumonia vaccination	n/a	71.0

Note: (1) Figures for the Springfield, IL Metropolitan Statistical Area were not available.
Source: Centers for Disease Control and Prevention, Behaviorial Risk Factor Surveillance System, SMART: Selected Metropolitan Area Risk Trends, 2021

Disability Status

Category	MSA[1] (%)	U.S. (%)
Adults who reported being deaf	n/a	7.2
Are you blind or have serious difficulty seeing, even when wearing glasses?	n/a	4.8
Are you limited in any way in any of your usual activities due to arthritis?	n/a	11.1
Do you have difficulty doing errands alone?	n/a	7.0
Do you have difficulty dressing or bathing?	n/a	3.6
Do you have serious difficulty concentrating/remembering/making decisions?	n/a	12.1
Do you have serious difficulty walking or climbing stairs?	n/a	12.8

Note: (1) Figures for the Springfield, IL Metropolitan Statistical Area were not available.
Source: Centers for Disease Control and Prevention, Behaviorial Risk Factor Surveillance System, SMART: Selected Metropolitan Area Risk Trends, 2021

Mortality Rates for the Top 10 Causes of Death in the U.S.

ICD-10[a] Sub-Chapter	ICD-10[a] Code	Crude Mortality Rate[1] per 100,000 population	
		County[2]	U.S.
Malignant neoplasms	C00-C97	221.0	182.6
Ischaemic heart diseases	I20-I25	121.6	113.1
Other forms of heart disease	I30-I51	78.9	64.4
Other degenerative diseases of the nervous system	G30-G31	38.2	51.0
Cerebrovascular diseases	I60-I69	41.3	47.8
Other external causes of accidental injury	W00-X59	54.9	46.4
Chronic lower respiratory diseases	J40-J47	55.5	45.7
Organic, including symptomatic, mental disorders	F01-F09	50.7	35.9
Hypertensive diseases	I10-I15	34.6	35.0
Diabetes mellitus	E10-E14	25.0	29.6

Note: (a) ICD-10 = International Classification of Diseases 10th Revision; (1) Crude mortality rates are a three-year average covering 2019-2021; (2) Figures cover Sangamon County.
Source: Centers for Disease Control and Prevention, National Center for Health Statistics. National Vital Statistics System, Mortality 2018-2021 on CDC WONDER Online Database

Mortality Rates for Selected Causes of Death

ICD-10[a] Sub-Chapter	ICD-10[a] Code	Crude Mortality Rate[1] per 100,000 population	
		County[2]	U.S.
Assault	X85-Y09	6.9	7.0
Diseases of the liver	K70-K76	23.3	19.8
Human immunodeficiency virus (HIV) disease	B20-B24	Suppressed	1.5
Influenza and pneumonia	J09-J18	19.7	14.7
Intentional self-harm	X60-X84	15.3	14.3
Malnutrition	E40-E46	4.5	4.3
Obesity and other hyperalimentation	E65-E68	Unreliable	3.0
Renal failure	N17-N19	19.7	15.7
Transport accidents	V01-V99	12.0	13.6
Viral hepatitis	B15-B19	Suppressed	1.2

Note: (a) ICD-10 = International Classification of Diseases 10th Revision; (1) Crude mortality rates are a three-year average covering 2019-2021; (2) Figures cover Sangamon County; Data are suppressed when the data meet the criteria for confidentiality constraints; Crude mortality rates are flagged as unreliable when the rate would be calculated with a numerator of 20 or less.
Source: Centers for Disease Control and Prevention, National Center for Health Statistics. National Vital Statistics System, Mortality 2018-2021 on CDC WONDER Online Database

Health Insurance Coverage

Area	With Health Insurance	With Private Health Insurance	With Public Health Insurance	Without Health Insurance	Population Under Age 19 Without Health Insurance
City	95.7	69.7	41.8	4.3	1.4
MSA[1]	96.2	74.4	37.3	3.8	1.4
U.S.	91.2	67.8	35.4	8.8	5.3

Note: Figures are percentages that cover the civilian noninstitutionalized population; (1) Figures cover the Springfield, IL Metropolitan Statistical Area
Source: U.S. Census Bureau, 2017-2021 American Community Survey 5-Year Estimates

Number of Medical Professionals

Area	MDs[3]	DOs[3,4]	Dentists	Podiatrists	Chiropractors	Optometrists
County[1] (number)	1,263	47	168	11	76	42
County[1] (rate[2])	644.3	24.0	86.3	5.6	39.0	21.6
U.S. (rate[2])	289.3	23.5	72.5	6.2	28.7	17.4

Note: Data as of 2021 unless noted; (1) Data covers Sangamon County; (2) Rate per 100,000 population; (3) Data as of 2020 and includes all active, non-federal physicians; (4) Doctor of Osteopathic Medicine
Source: U.S. Department of Health and Human Services, Health Resources and Services Administration, Bureau of Health Professions, Area Resource File (ARF) 2021-2022

EDUCATION

Public School District Statistics

District Name	Schls	Pupils	Pupil/ Teacher Ratio	Minority Pupils[1] (%)	LEP/ELL[2] (%)	IEP[3] (%)
Springfield SD 186	35	13,070	12.7	62.2	1.1	22.9

Note: Table includes school districts with 2,000 or more students; (1) Percentage of students that are not non-Hispanic white; (2) Percentage of students that are Limited English Proficient or English Language Learners (2018-19); (3) Percentage of students that have an Individualized Education Program (2019-20).
Source: U.S. Department of Education, National Center for Education Statistics, Common Core of Data, Local Education Agency (School District) Universe Survey: School Year 2021-2022

Highest Level of Education

Area	Less than H.S.	H.S. Diploma	Some College, No Deg.	Associate Degree	Bachelor's Degree	Master's Degree	Prof. School Degree	Doctorate Degree
City	8.7	26.6	22.1	8.2	20.2	9.6	3.5	1.2
MSA[1]	7.1	28.0	22.7	8.8	20.3	9.4	2.6	1.1
U.S.	11.1	26.5	20.0	8.7	20.6	9.3	2.2	1.5

Note: Figures cover persons age 25 and over; (1) Figures cover the Springfield, IL Metropolitan Statistical Area
Source: U.S. Census Bureau, 2017-2021 American Community Survey 5-Year Estimates

Educational Attainment by Race

Area	High School Graduate or Higher (%)					Bachelor's Degree or Higher (%)				
	Total	White	Black	Asian	Hisp.[2]	Total	White	Black	Asian	Hisp.[2]
City	91.3	93.6	80.0	94.0	86.8	34.4	37.2	14.3	69.9	43.3
MSA[1]	92.9	94.4	80.8	90.9	89.3	33.4	34.8	15.5	68.2	42.6
U.S.	88.9	91.4	87.2	87.6	71.2	33.7	35.5	23.3	55.6	18.4

Note: Figures shown cover persons 25 years old and over; (1) Figures cover the Springfield, IL Metropolitan Statistical Area; (2) People of Hispanic origin can be of any race
Source: U.S. Census Bureau, 2017-2021 American Community Survey 5-Year Estimates

School Enrollment by Grade and Control

Area	Preschool (%)		Kindergarten (%)		Grades 1 - 4 (%)		Grades 5 - 8 (%)		Grades 9 - 12 (%)	
	Public	Private	Public	Private	Public	Private	Public	Private	Public	Private
City	53.6	46.4	80.8	19.2	80.5	19.5	86.1	13.9	86.8	13.2
MSA[1]	58.6	41.4	85.1	14.9	85.1	14.9	89.7	10.3	90.4	9.6
U.S.	58.8	41.2	86.3	13.7	88.3	11.7	88.6	11.4	89.4	10.6

Note: Figures shown cover persons 3 years old and over; (1) Figures cover the Springfield, IL Metropolitan Statistical Area
Source: U.S. Census Bureau, 2017-2021 American Community Survey 5-Year Estimates

Higher Education

Four-Year Colleges			Two-Year Colleges			Medical Schools[1]	Law Schools[2]	Voc/ Tech[3]
Public	Private Non-profit	Private For-profit	Public	Private Non-profit	Private For-profit			
1	1	0	1	0	0	1	0	3

Note: Figures cover institutions located within the Springfield, IL Metropolitan Statistical Area and include main campuses only; (1) includes schools accredited by the Liaison Committee on Medical Education and the American Osteopathic Association's Commission on Osteopathic College Accreditation; (2) includes ABA-accredited schools, schools with provisional ABA accreditation, and state accredited schools; (3) includes all schools with programs that are less than 2 years.
Source: National Center for Education Statistics, Integrated Postsecondary Education System (IPEDS), 2021-22; Wikipedia, List of Medical Schools in the United States, accessed April 10, 2023; Wikipedia, List of Law Schools in the United States, accessed April 10, 2023

EMPLOYERS

Major Employers

Company Name	Industry
BlueCross BlueShield of Illinois	Insurance
Horace Mann Insurance Company	Insurance
Illinois National Guard	U.S. military
Memorial Health System	Healthcare
Southern Illinois University School of Med.	Education
Springfield Clinic	Healthcare
Springfield School District #186	Education
St. John's Medical	Healthcare
State of Illinois	State government
U.S. Postal Service	Government/postal service
University of Illinois at Springfield	Education

Note: Companies shown are located within the Springfield, IL Metropolitan Statistical Area.
Source: Hoovers.com; Wikipedia

PUBLIC SAFETY

Crime Rate

Area	Total Crime	Violent Crime Rate				Property Crime Rate		
		Murder	Rape[3]	Robbery	Aggrav. Assault	Burglary	Larceny -Theft	Motor Vehicle Theft
City	n/a	9.7	88.7	171.2	676.8	822.6	n/a	223.0
Suburbs[1]	n/a	1.1	36.1	21.9	259.1	349.8	n/a	122.4
Metro[2]	n/a	5.8	65.2	104.7	490.8	612.0	n/a	178.2
U.S.	2,356.7	6.5	38.4	73.9	279.7	314.2	1,398.0	246.0

Note: Figures are crimes per 100,000 population; (1) All areas within the metro area that are located outside the city limits; (2) Figures cover the Springfield, IL Metropolitan Statistical Area; (3) All figures shown were reported using the revised Uniform Crime Reporting (UCR) definition of rape; Due to the transition to the National Incident-Based Reporting System (NIBRS), limited city and metro area data was released for 2021.
Source: FBI Uniform Crime Reports, 2020

Hate Crimes

Area	Number of Quarters Reported	Number of Incidents per Bias Motivation					
		Race/Ethnicity/ Ancestry	Religion	Sexual Orientation	Disability	Gender	Gender Identity
City	4	2	0	0	0	0	0
U.S.	4	5,227	1,244	1,110	130	75	266

Note: Due to the transition to the National Incident-Based Reporting System (NIBRS), limited crime data was released for 2021.
Source: Federal Bureau of Investigation, Hate Crime Statistics 2020

Identity Theft Consumer Reports

Area	Reports	Reports per 100,000 Population	Rank[2]
MSA[1]	407	195	173
U.S.	1,108,609	339	-

Note: (1) Figures cover the Springfield, IL Metropolitan Statistical Area; (2) Rank ranges from 1 to 391 where 1 indicates greatest number of identity theft reports per 100,000 population
Source: Federal Trade Commission, Consumer Sentinel Network Data Book 2022

Fraud and Other Consumer Reports

Area	Reports	Reports per 100,000 Population	Rank[2]
MSA[1]	1,654	794	220
U.S.	4,064,520	1,245	-

Note: (1) Figures cover the Springfield, IL Metropolitan Statistical Area; (2) Rank ranges from 1 to 391 where 1 indicates greatest number of fraud and other consumer reports per 100,000 population
Source: Federal Trade Commission, Consumer Sentinel Network Data Book 2022

POLITICS

2020 Presidential Election Results

Area	Biden	Trump	Jorgensen	Hawkins	Other
Sangamon County	46.5	50.9	1.4	0.6	0.6
U.S.	51.3	46.8	1.2	0.3	0.5

Note: Results are percentages and may not add to 100% due to rounding
Source: Dave Leip's Atlas of U.S. Presidential Elections

SPORTS

Professional Sports Teams

Team Name	League	Year Established

No teams are located in the metro area
Source: Wikipedia, Major Professional Sports Teams of the United States and Canada, April 12, 2023

CLIMATE

Average and Extreme Temperatures

Temperature	Jan	Feb	Mar	Apr	May	Jun	Jul	Aug	Sep	Oct	Nov	Dec	Yr.
Extreme High (°F)	73	78	91	90	101	104	112	108	101	93	83	74	112
Average High (°F)	35	38	50	63	74	84	88	85	79	67	51	38	63
Average Temp. (°F)	27	30	41	53	64	73	78	75	68	57	43	31	54
Average Low (°F)	19	22	32	43	53	63	67	65	57	46	34	24	44
Extreme Low (°F)	-21	-24	-12	17	28	40	48	43	32	13	-3	-21	-24

Note: Figures cover the years 1948-1995
Source: National Climatic Data Center, International Station Meteorological Climate Summary, 9/96

Average Precipitation/Snowfall/Humidity

Precip./Humidity	Jan	Feb	Mar	Apr	May	Jun	Jul	Aug	Sep	Oct	Nov	Dec	Yr.
Avg. Precip. (in.)	1.8	1.7	3.1	3.6	3.8	3.9	3.3	3.1	3.3	2.6	2.4	2.1	34.9
Avg. Snowfall (in.)	6	6	4	1	Tr	0	0	0	0	Tr	1	5	21
Avg. Rel. Hum. 6am (%)	80	81	81	79	81	82	85	89	87	83	82	82	83
Avg. Rel. Hum. 3pm (%)	67	65	59	52	51	51	54	56	50	50	60	69	57

Note: Figures cover the years 1948-1995; Tr = Trace amounts (<0.05 in. of rain; <0.5 in. of snow)
Source: National Climatic Data Center, International Station Meteorological Climate Summary, 9/96

Weather Conditions

Temperature			Daytime Sky			Precipitation		
10°F & below	32°F & below	90°F & above	Clear	Partly cloudy	Cloudy	0.01 inch or more precip.	0.1 inch or more snow/ice	Thunderstorms
19	111	34	96	126	143	111	18	49

Note: Figures are average number of days per year and cover the years 1948-1995
Source: National Climatic Data Center, International Station Meteorological Climate Summary, 9/96

HAZARDOUS WASTE

Superfund Sites

The Springfield, IL metro area has no sites on the EPA's Superfund Final National Priorities List. There are a total of 1,165 Superfund sites with a status of proposed or final on the list in the U.S. *U.S. Environmental Protection Agency, National Priorities List, April 12, 2023*

AIR QUALITY

Air Quality Trends: Ozone

	1990	1995	2000	2005	2010	2015	2018	2019	2020	2021
MSA[1]	n/a	n/a	n/a	n/a	n/a	n/a	n/a	n/a	n/a	n/a
U.S.	0.087	0.089	0.081	0.080	0.072	0.067	0.069	0.065	0.065	0.067

Note: (1) Data covers the Springfield, IL Metropolitan Statistical Area; n/a not available. The values shown are the composite ozone concentration averages among trend sites based on the highest fourth daily maximum 8-hour concentration in parts per million. These trends are based on sites having an adequate record of monitoring data during the trend period. Data from exceptional events are included.
Source: U.S. Environmental Protection Agency, Air Quality Monitoring Information, "Air Quality Trends by City, 1990-2021"

Air Quality Index

Area	Percent of Days when Air Quality was...[2]					AQI Statistics[2]	
	Good	Moderate	Unhealthy for Sensitive Groups	Unhealthy	Very Unhealthy	Maximum	Median
MSA[1]	80.7	19.3	0.0	0.0	0.0	97	38

Note: (1) Data covers the Springfield, IL Metropolitan Statistical Area; (2) Based on 362 days with AQI data in 2021. Air Quality Index (AQI) is an index for reporting daily air quality. EPA calculates the AQI for five major air pollutants regulated by the Clean Air Act: ground-level ozone, particle pollution (aka particulate matter), carbon monoxide, sulfur dioxide, and nitrogen dioxide. The AQI runs from 0 to 500. The higher the AQI value, the greater the level of air pollution and the greater the health concern. There are six AQI categories: "Good" AQI is between 0 and 50. Air quality is considered satisfactory; "Moderate" AQI is between 51 and 100. Air quality is acceptable; "Unhealthy for Sensitive Groups" When AQI values are between 101 and 150, members of sensitive groups may experience health effects; "Unhealthy" When AQI values are between 151 and 200 everyone may begin to experience health effects; "Very Unhealthy" AQI values between 201 and 300 trigger a health alert; "Hazardous" AQI values over 300 trigger warnings of emergency conditions (not shown).
Source: U.S. Environmental Protection Agency, Air Quality Index Report, 2021

Air Quality Index Pollutants

Area	Percent of Days when AQI Pollutant was...[2]					
	Carbon Monoxide	Nitrogen Dioxide	Ozone	Sulfur Dioxide	Particulate Matter 2.5	Particulate Matter 10
MSA[1]	0.0	0.0	43.1	(3)	56.9	0.0

Note: (1) Data covers the Springfield, IL Metropolitan Statistical Area; (2) Based on 362 days with AQI data in 2021. The Air Quality Index (AQI) is an index for reporting daily air quality. EPA calculates the AQI for five major air pollutants regulated by the Clean Air Act: ground-level ozone, particle pollution (also known as particulate matter), carbon monoxide, sulfur dioxide, and nitrogen dioxide. The AQI runs from 0 to 500. The higher the AQI value, the greater the level of air pollution and the greater the health concern; (3) Sulfur dioxide is no longer included in this table (as of December 8, 2021) because SO_2 concentrations tend to be very localized and not necessarily representative of broad geographical areas like counties and CBSAs.
Source: U.S. Environmental Protection Agency, Air Quality Index Report, 2021

Maximum Air Pollutant Concentrations: Particulate Matter, Ozone, CO and Lead

	Particulate Matter 10 (ug/m^3)	Particulate Matter 2.5 Wtd AM (ug/m^3)	Particulate Matter 2.5 24-Hr (ug/m^3)	Ozone (ppm)	Carbon Monoxide (ppm)	Lead (ug/m^3)
MSA[1] Level	n/a	8.7	22	0.057	n/a	n/a
NAAQS[2]	150	15	35	0.075	9	0.15
Met NAAQS[2]	n/a	Yes	Yes	Yes	n/a	n/a

Note: (1) Data covers the Springfield, IL Metropolitan Statistical Area; Data from exceptional events are included; (2) National Ambient Air Quality Standards; ppm = parts per million; ug/m^3 = micrograms per cubic meter; n/a not available.
Concentrations: Particulate Matter 10 (coarse particulate)—highest second maximum 24-hour concentration; Particulate Matter 2.5 Wtd AM (fine particulate)—highest weighted annual mean concentration; Particulate Matter 2.5 24-Hour (fine particulate)—highest 98th percentile 24-hour concentration; Ozone—highest fourth daily maximum 8-hour concentration; Carbon Monoxide—highest second maximum non-overlapping 8-hour concentration; Lead—maximum running 3-month average
Source: U.S. Environmental Protection Agency, Air Quality Monitoring Information, "Air Quality Statistics by City, 2021"

Maximum Air Pollutant Concentrations: Nitrogen Dioxide and Sulfur Dioxide

	Nitrogen Dioxide AM (ppb)	Nitrogen Dioxide 1-Hr (ppb)	Sulfur Dioxide AM (ppb)	Sulfur Dioxide 1-Hr (ppb)	Sulfur Dioxide 24-Hr (ppb)
MSA[1] Level	n/a	n/a	n/a	n/a	n/a
NAAQS[2]	53	100	30	75	140
Met NAAQS[2]	n/a	n/a	n/a	n/a	n/a

Note: (1) Data covers the Springfield, IL Metropolitan Statistical Area; Data from exceptional events are included; (2) National Ambient Air Quality Standards; ppm = parts per million; ug/m^3 = micrograms per cubic meter; n/a not available.
Concentrations: Nitrogen Dioxide AM—highest arithmetic mean concentration; Nitrogen Dioxide 1-Hr—highest 98th percentile 1-hour daily maximum concentration; Sulfur Dioxide AM—highest annual mean concentration; Sulfur Dioxide 1-Hr—highest 99th percentile 1-hour daily maximum concentration; Sulfur Dioxide 24-Hr—highest second maximum 24-hour concentration
Source: U.S. Environmental Protection Agency, Air Quality Monitoring Information, "Air Quality Statistics by City, 2021"

Tulsa, Oklahoma

Background

The city of Tulsa stands at the intersection of Tulsa, Osage, Rogers, and Wagoner counties, in north-east Oklahoma. On the Arkansas River, Tulsa sits between the Osage Hills and the foothills of the Ozark Mountains.

Tulsa was first settled by Creek Indians in 1828. In 1848, Lewis Perryman established the first trading post at the new settlement, and his son George developed a regular mail station at the site in 1878, which came to be called Tulsa, likely from the Talsi (or Talasi) branch of the Creek Tribe. In 2020, the U.S. Supreme Court ruled that that city was indeed Native American land.

Originally a cattle and dry goods trading center used by ranchers scattered throughout the area, Tulsa was integrated into a wider trade area in 1882 when the Frisco Railroad brought a line into the town. This facilitated new settlers to move into the area and allowed "Tulsey Town," as it was called, to transport cattle throughout the nation. Tulsa was incorporated as a town on January 18, 1898.

Oil was first discovered in the area in 1901 at Red Fork. In 1905, a huge strike—the world's largest at the time—was made at Glenn Pool. Since then, Tulsa's fortune has been tied to the oil industry. Oklahoma achieved statehood two years after the Glenn Pool strike, and by 1920 the city was well-known as the "Oil Capital of the World." During this boom period, many of Tulsa's historic buildings were constructed, which explains the city's extraordinary art deco influence in its down-town architecture. The influx of wealthy easterners left parts of the city resembling New York and Philadelphia.

Oil naturally fueled the growth of aviation, and Tulsa was an early aviation center. By the beginning of the Second World War, many of the nation's pilots were being trained at Spartan School of Aeronautics in the city, and Douglas Aircraft in 1942 sited a major plant there. In later years, both McDonnell-Douglas and Rockwell International based aviation and space technology operations in Tulsa.

Today, Tulsa is home to American Airlines' Maintenance & Engineering Center, one of the world's largest such commercial centers. Work began in 2021 on a $550 million major renovation to the center which will take seven years to complete. The first additions—a new hangar and base support building—are now complete.

The city is home to Lufthansa Technik who announced plans to more than double their employees in the next few years. Major employers in the city include Imperial, Vanguard Car Rental, BOK Financial Corporation, Samson Resources, and Saint Francis Health System.

The city's location in the center of the nation makes it a hub for logistics, with its busy Tulsa International Airport and Tulsa Port of Catoosa, a 445-mile navigation system that links Tulsa to the Mississippi, making Tulsa a major inland ice-free port, with a designated foreign trade zone, and a 2,000-acre industrial park that includes an Amazon distribution center.

Tulsa is part of the Oklahoma-South Kansas Unmanned Aerial Systems (drone) industry cluster. It is ranked as the third most drone-friendly state. In 2021, Tulsa announced a new Geeenwood Entrepreneurship Incubator at Moton, providing financing, space, training, networking, and resources for aspiring entrepreneurs.

The city hosts a broad range of cultural and recreational activities, including the Gilcrease Museum, holder of the world's largest collection of art and artifacts of the American West, and Philbrook Museum of Art. Many cultural activities are sponsored by the city's several universities, including a branch of Oklahoma State University. Discovery Lab just opened a new 50,000 sq-ft. facility with state-of-the-art exhibit experiences, education opportunities with on-site educators.

The city is host to Tulsa Rose Gardens, Municipal Rose Gardens—built by the Works Progress Administration and opened in 1934—and Tulsa Zoo. A new casino opened in 2022.

The city's Cox Business Convention Center includes an assembly hall, the state's largest ballroom, and 34 meeting rooms. The BOK (Bank of Oklahoma) Center is a multi-purpose arena that plays host to the Tulsa Oilers ice hockey team. Minor league baseball team, Tulsa Drillers, play in ONEOK Field, as do the Tulsa Roughnecks FC soccer team. The University of Tulsa's men's basketball team hosts the competitive Golden Hurricane team, and Oral Roberts University's boasts men's basketball team, the Golden Eagles.

Tulsa's weather is continental and generally mild, with unpredictable amounts of precipitation. Winters for the region bordering on the Great Plains are comparatively short and mild.

Rankings

General Rankings

- Tulsa was selected as one of the best places to live in America by *Outside Magazine.* Criteria centered on diversity; sustainability; outdoor equity; and affordability. Local experts shared highlights from hands-on experience in each location. *Outside Magazine, "The 20 Most Livable Towns and Cities in America," October 15, 2021*

Business/Finance Rankings

- Tulsa was the #5-ranked city for savers, according to a study by the finance site GOBankingRates, which considered the prospects for people trying to save money. Criteria: average monthly cost of grocery items; median home listing price; median rent; median income; transportation costs; gas prices; and the cost of eating out for an inexpensive and mid-range meal in 100 U.S. cities. *www.gobankingrates.com, "The 20 Best (and Worst) Places to Live If You're Trying to Save Money," August 27, 2019*

- Tulsa was ranked #5 among 100 U.S. cities for most difficult conditions for savers, according to a study by the finance site GOBankingRates. Criteria: average monthly cost of grocery items; median home listing price; median rent; median income; transportation costs; gas prices; and the cost of eating out for an inexpensive and mid-range meal. *www.gobankingrates.com, "The 20 Best (and Worst) Places to Live If You're Trying to Save Money," August 27, 2019*

- The Brookings Institution ranked the nation's largest cities based on income inequality. Tulsa was ranked #42 (#1 = greatest inequality). Criteria: the "95/20 ratio," a figure representing the income at which a household earns more than 95 percent of all other households, divided by the income at which a household earns more than only 20 percent of all other households. *Brookings Institution, "Household Income Inequality, Largest Cities of 97 Large U.S. Metro Areas, 2014-2016," February 5, 2018*

- The Brookings Institution ranked the 100 largest metro areas in the U.S. based on income inequality. Tulsa was ranked #44 (#1 = greatest inequality). Criteria: the "95/20 ratio," a figure representing the income at which a household earns more than 95 percent of all other households, divided by the income at which a household earns more than only 20 percent of all other households. *Brookings Institution, "Household Income Inequality, 100 Largest U.S. Metro Areas, 2014-2016," February 5, 2018*

- The Tulsa metro area appeared on the Milken Institute "2022 Best Performing Cities" list. Rank: #169 out of 200 large metro areas (population over 250,000). Criteria: job growth; wage and salary growth; high-tech output growth; housing affordability; household broadband access. *Milken Institute, "Best-Performing Cities 2022," March 28, 2022*

- *Forbes* ranked the 200 most populous metro areas to determine the nation's "Best Places for Business and Careers." The Tulsa metro area was ranked #120. Criteria: costs (business and living); job growth (past and projected); income growth; quality of life; educational attainment (college and high school); projected economic growth; cultural and leisure opportunities; workplace tolerance laws; net migration patterns. *Forbes, "The Best Places for Business and Careers 2019: Seattle Still On Top," October 30, 2019*

Culture/Performing Arts Rankings

- Tulsa was selected as one of the 25 best cities for moviemakers in North America. Great film cities are places where filmmaking dreams can come true, that offer more creative space, lower costs, and great outdoor locations. NYC & LA were intentionally excluded. Criteria: longstanding reputations as film-friendly communities; film community and culture; affordability; and quality of life. The city was ranked #19. *MovieMaker Magazine, "Best Places to Live and Work as a Moviemaker, 2023," January 18, 2023*

Dating/Romance Rankings

- Tulsa was ranked #24 out of 25 cities that stood out for inspiring romance and attracting diners on the website OpenTable.com. Criteria: percentage of people who dined out on Valentine's Day in 2018; percentage of romantic restaurants as rated by OpenTable diner reviews; and percentage of tables seated for two. *OpenTable, "25 Most Romantic Cities in America for 2019," February 7, 2019*

Education Rankings

- Personal finance website *WalletHub* analyzed the 150 largest U.S. metropolitan statistical areas to determine where the most educated Americans are putting their degrees to work. Criteria: education levels; percentage of workers with degrees; education quality and attainment gap; public school quality rankings; quality and enrollment of each metro area's universities. Tulsa was ranked #110 (#1 = most educated city). *www.WalletHub.com, "Most & Least Educated Cities in America, " July 18, 2022*

- Tulsa was selected as one of America's most literate cities. The city ranked #24 out of the 84 largest U.S. cities. Criteria: number of booksellers; library resources; Internet resources; educational attainment; periodical publishing resources; newspaper circulation. *Central Connecticut State University, "America's Most Literate Cities, 2018," February 2019*

Health/Fitness Rankings

- For each of the 100 largest cities in the United States, the American Fitness Index®, compiled in partnership between the American College of Sports Medicine and the Elevance Health Foundation, evaluated community infrastructure and 34 health behaviors including preventive health, levels of chronic disease conditions, food insecurity, sleep quality, pedestrian safety, air quality, and community/environment resources that support physical activity. Tulsa ranked #98 for "community fitness." *americanfitnessindex.org, "2022 ACSM American Fitness Index Summary Report," July 12, 2022*

- Tulsa was identified as a "2022 Spring Allergy Capital." The area ranked #24 out of 100. Three groups of factors were used to identify the most challenging cities for people with allergies during the spring season: annual spring pollen scores; over the counter allergy medicine use; number of board-certified allergy specialists. *Asthma and Allergy Foundation of America, "Spring Allergy Capitals 2022," March 2, 2022*

- Tulsa was identified as a "2022 Fall Allergy Capital." The area ranked #21 out of 100. Three groups of factors were used to identify the most challenging cities for people with allergies during the fall season: annual fall pollen scores; over the counter allergy medicine use; number of board-certified allergy specialists. *Asthma and Allergy Foundation of America, "Fall Allergy Capitals 2022," March 2, 2022*

- Tulsa was identified as a "2022 Asthma Capital." The area ranked #57 out of the nation's 100 largest metropolitan areas. Criteria: estimated asthma prevalence; asthma-related mortality; and ER visits due to asthma. Risk factors analyzed but not factored in the rankings: annual pollen score; annual air quality; public smoking laws; access to board-certified asthma specialists; rescue and controller medication use; uninsured rate; poverty rate. *Asthma and Allergy Foundation of America, "Asthma Capitals 2022: The Most Challenging Places to Live With Asthma," September 14, 2022*

Real Estate Rankings

- *WalletHub* compared the most populated U.S. cities to determine which had the best markets for real estate agents. Tulsa ranked #66 where demand was high and pay was the best. Criteria: sales per agent; annual median wage for real-estate agents; monthly average starting salary for real estate agents; real estate job density and competition; unemployment rate; home turnover rate; housing-market health index; and other relevant metrics. *www.WalletHub.com, "2021 Best Places to Be a Real Estate Agent," May 12, 2021*

- Tulsa was ranked #15 in the top 20 out of the 100 largest metro areas in terms of house price appreciation in 2022 (#1 = highest rate). *Federal Housing Finance Agency, House Price Index, 4th Quarter 2022*

- Tulsa was ranked #67 out of 235 metro areas in terms of housing affordability in 2022 by the National Association of Home Builders (#1 = most affordable). Criteria: the share of homes sold in that area affordable to a family earning the local median income, based on standard mortgage underwriting criteria. *National Association of Home Builders®, NAHB-Wells Fargo Housing Opportunity Index, 4th Quarter 2022*

Safety Rankings

- Allstate ranked the 200 largest cities in America in terms of driver safety. Tulsa ranked #51. Criteria: internal property damage claims over a two-year period from January 2016 to December 2017. The report helps increase the importance of safety and awareness behind the wheel. *Allstate, "Allstate America's Best Drivers Report, 2019" June 24, 2019*

- Tulsa was identified as one of the most dangerous cities in America by NeighborhoodScout. The city ranked #66 out of 100 (#1 = most dangerous). Criteria: number of violent crimes per 1,000 residents. The editors evaluated cities with 25,000 or more residents. *NeighborhoodScout.com, "2023 Top 100 Most Dangerous Cities in the U.S.," January 12, 2023*

- The National Insurance Crime Bureau ranked 390 metro areas in the U.S. in terms of per capita rates of vehicle theft. The Tulsa metro area ranked #15 (#1 = highest rate). Criteria: number of vehicle theft offenses per 100,000 inhabitants in 2021. *National Insurance Crime Bureau, "Hot Spots 2021," September 1, 2022*

Seniors/Retirement Rankings

- From its Best Cities for Successful Aging indexes, the Milken Institute generated rankings for metropolitan areas, weighing data in nine categories—health care, wellness, living arrangements, transportation and convenience, financial characteristics, education, employment, community engagement, and overall livability. The Tulsa metro area was ranked #57 overall in the large metro area category. *Milken Institute, "Best Cities for Successful Aging, 2017" March 14, 2017*

Women/Minorities Rankings

- Personal finance website *WalletHub* compared more than 180 U.S. cities across two key dimensions, "Hispanic Business-Friendliness" and "Hispanic Purchasing Power," to arrive at the most favorable conditions for Hispanic entrepreneurs. Tulsa was ranked #33 out of 182. Criteria includes: share of Hispanic-Owned Businesses; Hispanic entrepreneurship rate to median annual income of Hispanics; Small Business-Friendliness score; cost of living; and number of Hispanics with at least a bachelor's degree. *WalletHub.com, "2019's Best Cities for Hispanic Entrepreneurs," May 1, 2019*

Miscellaneous Rankings

- Tulsa was selected as a 2022 Digital Cities Survey winner. The city ranked #10 in the large city (250,000 to 499,999 population) category. The survey examined and assessed how city governments are utilizing technology to continue innovation, engage with residents, and persevere through the challenges of the pandemic. Survey questions focused on ten initiatives: cybersecurity; citizen experience; disaster recovery; business intelligence; IT personnel; data governance; business automation; IT governance; infrastructure modernization; and broadband connectivity. *Center for Digital Government, "2022 Digital Cities Survey," November 10, 2022*

- *WalletHub* compared the 150 most populated U.S. cities to determine their operating efficiency. A "Quality of Services" score was constructed for each city and then divided by the total budget per capita to reveal which were managed the best. Tulsa ranked #37. Criteria: financial stability; economy; education; safety; health; infrastructure and pollution. *www.WalletHub.com, "2022's Best-& Worst-Run Cities in America," June 21, 2022*

Business Environment

DEMOGRAPHICS

Population Growth

Area	1990 Census	2000 Census	2010 Census	2020 Census	Population Growth (%) 1990-2020	Population Growth (%) 2010-2020
City	367,241	393,049	391,906	413,066	12.5	5.4
MSA[1]	761,019	859,532	937,478	1,015,331	33.4	8.3
U.S.	248,709,873	281,421,906	308,745,538	331,449,281	33.3	7.4

Note: (1) Figures cover the Tulsa, OK Metropolitan Statistical Area
Source: U.S. Census Bureau, 1990 Census, 2000 Census, 2010 Census, 2020 Census

Race

Area	White Alone[2] (%)	Black Alone[2] (%)	Asian Alone[2] (%)	AIAN[3] Alone[2] (%)	NHOPI[4] Alone[2] (%)	Other Race Alone[2] (%)	Two or More Races (%)
City	51.8	14.9	3.5	5.2	0.2	9.8	14.6
MSA[1]	61.3	7.9	2.8	8.1	0.1	5.4	14.2
U.S.	61.6	12.4	6.0	1.1	0.2	8.4	10.2

Note: (1) Figures cover the Tulsa, OK Metropolitan Statistical Area; (2) Alone is defined as not being in combination with one or more other races; (3) American Indian and Alaska Native; (4) Native Hawaiian and Other Pacific Islander
Source: U.S. Census Bureau, 2020 Census

Hispanic or Latino Origin

Area	Total (%)	Mexican (%)	Puerto Rican (%)	Cuban (%)	Other (%)
City	17.1	13.4	0.6	0.1	3.0
MSA[1]	10.5	8.1	0.4	0.1	1.9
U.S.	18.4	11.2	1.8	0.7	4.7

Note: Persons of Hispanic or Latino origin can be of any race; (1) Figures cover the Tulsa, OK Metropolitan Statistical Area
Source: U.S. Census Bureau, 2017-2021 American Community Survey 5-Year Estimates

Age

Area	Under Age 5	Age 5–19	Age 20–34	Age 35–44	Age 45–54	Age 55–64	Age 65–74	Age 75–84	Age 85+	Median Age
City	6.5	19.8	22.5	12.9	11.1	11.8	9.0	4.3	2.0	35.8
MSA[1]	6.2	20.6	19.6	12.8	11.8	12.7	9.7	4.9	1.8	37.6
U.S.	5.6	19.2	20.2	12.7	12.4	13.1	10.0	4.9	1.9	38.8

Note: (1) Figures cover the Tulsa, OK Metropolitan Statistical Area
Source: U.S. Census Bureau, 2020 Census

Disability by Age

Area	All Ages	Under 18 Years Old	18 to 64 Years Old	65 Years and Over
City	14.2	4.7	13.1	34.6
MSA[1]	14.7	4.8	13.1	37.4
U.S.	12.6	4.4	10.3	33.4

Note: Figures show percent of the civilian noninstitutionalized population that reported having a disability. Disability status is determined from six types of difficulty: vision, hearing, cognitive, ambulatory, self-care, and independent living. For children under 5 years old, hearing and vision difficulty are used to determine disability status. For children between the ages of 5 and 14, disability status is determined from hearing, vision, cognitive, ambulatory, and self-care difficulties. For people aged 15 years and older, they are considered to have a disability if they have difficulty with any one of the six difficulty types; Note: (1) Figures cover the Tulsa, OK Metropolitan Statistical Area
Source: U.S. Census Bureau, 2017-2021 American Community Survey 5-Year Estimates

Ancestry

Area	German	Irish	English	American	Italian	Polish	French[2]	Scottish	Dutch
City	10.8	8.7	9.3	5.4	2.0	0.9	1.9	2.0	0.8
MSA[1]	12.6	10.2	9.9	5.6	1.9	0.9	2.0	2.0	1.1
U.S.	12.8	9.6	8.1	5.7	5.0	2.7	2.2	1.6	1.1

Note: Figures are the percentage of the total population reporting a particular ancestry. The nine most commonly reported ancestries in the U.S. are shown. Figures include multiple ancestries (e.g. if a person reported being Irish and Italian, they were included in both columns); (1) Figures cover the Tulsa, OK Metropolitan Statistical Area; (2) Excludes Basque
Source: U.S. Census Bureau, 2017-2021 American Community Survey 5-Year Estimates

Foreign-born Population

Area	Any Foreign Country	Asia	Mexico	Europe	Caribbean	Central America[2]	South America	Africa	Canada
City	11.0	2.6	5.2	0.6	0.2	1.0	0.5	0.6	0.1
MSA[1]	6.7	1.9	2.8	0.5	0.1	0.5	0.3	0.3	0.1
U.S.	13.6	4.2	3.3	1.5	1.4	1.1	1.1	0.8	0.2

Note: (1) Figures cover the Tulsa, OK Metropolitan Statistical Area; (2) Excludes Mexico.
Source: U.S. Census Bureau, 2017-2021 American Community Survey 5-Year Estimates

Household Size

Area	One	Two	Three	Four	Five	Six	Seven or More	Average Household Size
City	35.6	32.3	13.2	10.4	5.1	2.3	1.2	2.40
MSA[1]	28.9	33.8	15.2	12.2	6.0	2.6	1.3	2.60
U.S.	28.1	33.8	15.5	12.9	6.0	2.3	1.4	2.60

Note: (1) Figures cover the Tulsa, OK Metropolitan Statistical Area
Source: U.S. Census Bureau, 2017-2021 American Community Survey 5-Year Estimates

Household Relationships

Area	Householder	Opposite-sex Spouse	Same-sex Spouse	Opposite-sex Unmarried Partner	Same-sex Unmarried Partner	Child[2]	Grandchild	Other Relatives	Non-relatives
City	41.6	14.8	0.2	2.9	0.2	27.8	2.3	4.3	3.4
MSA[1]	39.1	18.2	0.2	2.4	0.1	29.0	2.6	3.9	2.7
U.S.	38.3	17.5	0.2	2.5	0.2	28.3	2.4	4.8	3.4

Note: Figures are percent of the total population; (1) Figures cover the Tulsa, OK Metropolitan Statistical Area; (2) Includes biological, adopted, and stepchildren of the householder
Source: U.S. Census Bureau, 2020 Census

Gender

Area	Males	Females	Males per 100 Females
City	201,814	211,252	95.5
MSA[1]	499,555	515,776	96.9
U.S.	162,685,811	168,763,470	96.4

Note: (1) Figures cover the Tulsa, OK Metropolitan Statistical Area
Source: U.S. Census Bureau, 2020 Census

Marital Status

Area	Never Married	Now Married[2]	Separated	Widowed	Divorced
City	35.0	42.4	2.4	5.7	14.4
MSA[1]	29.1	49.8	1.9	6.1	13.0
U.S.	33.8	48.0	1.8	5.6	10.8

Note: Figures are percentages and cover the population 15 years of age and older; (1) Figures cover the Tulsa, OK Metropolitan Statistical Area; (2) Excludes separated
Source: U.S. Census Bureau, 2017-2021 American Community Survey 5-Year Estimates

Religious Groups by Family

Area	Catholic	Baptist	Methodist	LDS[2]	Pentecostal	Lutheran	Islam	Adventist	Other
MSA[1]	5.6	15.5	7.7	1.2	2.5	0.5	0.5	1.2	22.2
U.S.	18.7	7.3	3.0	2.0	1.8	1.7	1.3	1.3	11.6

Note: Figures are the number of adherents as a percentage of the total population and cover the eight largest religious groups in the U.S; (1) Figures cover the Tulsa, OK Metropolitan Statistical Area; (2) Church of Jesus Christ of Latter-day Saints
Sources: 2020 U.S. Religion Census, Association of Statisticians of American Religious Bodies; The Association of Religion Data Archives (ARDA)

Religious Groups by Tradition

Area	Catholic	Evangelical Protestant	Mainline Protestant	Black Protestant	Islam	Judaism	Hinduism	Orthodox	Buddhism
MSA[1]	5.6	37.8	8.6	1.7	0.5	0.2	0.1	0.1	<0.1
U.S.	18.7	16.5	5.2	2.3	1.3	0.6	0.4	0.4	0.3

Note: Figures are the number of adherents as a percentage of the total population; (1) Figures cover the Tulsa, OK Metropolitan Statistical Area
Sources: 2020 U.S. Religion Census, Association of Statisticians of American Religious Bodies; The Association of Religion Data Archives (ARDA)

ECONOMY

Gross Metropolitan Product

Area	2020	2021	2022	2023	Rank[2]
MSA[1]	53.7	58.3	65.1	68.5	59

Note: Figures are in billions of dollars; (1) Figures cover the Tulsa, OK Metropolitan Statistical Area; (2) Rank is based on 2021 data and ranges from 1 to 381
Source: U.S. Conference of Mayors, U.S. Metro Economies: U.S. Metros Compared to Global and State Economies, June 2022

Economic Growth

Area	2018-20 (%)	2021 (%)	2022 (%)	2023 (%)	Rank[2]
MSA[1]	-1.7	1.1	3.1	3.5	266
U.S.	-0.6	5.7	3.1	2.9	—

Note: Figures are real gross metropolitan product (GMP) growth rates and represent average annual percent change; (1) Figures cover the Tulsa, OK Metropolitan Statistical Area; (2) Rank is based on 2020 2-year average annual percent change and ranges from 1 to 381
Source: U.S. Conference of Mayors, U.S. Metro Economies: U.S. Metros Compared to Global and State Economies, June 2022

Metropolitan Area Exports

Area	2016	2017	2018	2019	2020	2021	Rank[2]
MSA[1]	2,363.0	2,564.7	3,351.7	3,399.2	2,567.8	3,064.8	81

Note: Figures are in millions of dollars; (1) Figures cover the Tulsa, OK Metropolitan Statistical Area; (2) Rank is based on 2021 data and ranges from 1 to 388
Source: U.S. Department of Commerce, International Trade Administration, Office of Trade and Economic Analysis, Industry and Analysis, Exports by Metropolitan Area, data extracted March 16, 2023

Building Permits

Area	Single-Family			Multi-Family			Total		
	2021	2022	Pct. Chg.	2021	2022	Pct. Chg.	2021	2022	Pct. Chg.
City	652	452	-30.7	165	369	123.6	817	821	0.5
MSA[1]	4,354	3,843	-11.7	566	1,280	126.1	4,920	5,123	4.1
U.S.	1,115,400	975,600	-12.5	621,600	689,500	10.9	1,737,000	1,665,100	-4.1

Note: (1) Figures cover the Tulsa, OK Metropolitan Statistical Area; Figures represent new, privately-owned housing units authorized (unadjusted data); All permit data are based on estimates with imputation
Source: U.S. Census Bureau, Manufacturing, Mining, and Construction Statistics, Building Permits, 2021, 2022

Bankruptcy Filings

Area	Business Filings			Nonbusiness Filings		
	2021	2022	% Chg.	2021	2022	% Chg.
Tulsa County	30	51	70.0	874	758	-13.3
U.S.	14,347	13,481	-6.0	399,269	374,240	-6.3

Note: Business filings include Chapter 7, Chapter 9, Chapter 11, Chapter 12, Chapter 13, Chapter 15, and Section 304; Nonbusiness filings include Chapter 7, Chapter 11, and Chapter 13
Source: Administrative Office of the U.S. Courts, Business and Nonbusiness Bankruptcy, County Cases Commenced by Chapter of the Bankruptcy Code, During the 12-Month Period Ending December 31, 2021 and Business and Nonbusiness Bankruptcy, County Cases Commenced by Chapter of the Bankruptcy Code, During the 12-Month Period Ending December 31, 2022

Housing Vacancy Rates

Area	Gross Vacancy Rate[2] (%)			Year-Round Vacancy Rate[3] (%)			Rental Vacancy Rate[4] (%)			Homeowner Vacancy Rate[5] (%)		
	2020	2021	2022	2020	2021	2022	2020	2021	2022	2020	2021	2022
MSA[1]	9.4	11.0	8.9	8.8	10.0	8.5	8.6	5.3	5.6	0.8	1.5	0.7
U.S.	10.6	10.8	10.5	8.2	8.4	8.2	6.3	6.1	5.8	1.0	0.9	0.8

Note: (1) Figures cover the Tulsa, OK Metropolitan Statistical Area; (2) The percentage of the total housing inventory that is vacant; (3) The percentage of the housing inventory (excluding seasonal units) that is year-round vacant; (4) The percentage of rental inventory that is vacant for rent; (5) The percentage of homeowner inventory that is vacant for sale
Source: U.S. Census Bureau, Housing Vacancies and Homeownership Annual Statistics: 2020, 2021, 2022

INCOME

Income

Area	Per Capita ($)	Median Household ($)	Average Household ($)
City	33,492	52,438	79,727
MSA[1]	33,647	60,866	84,069
U.S.	37,638	69,021	97,196

Note: (1) Figures cover the Tulsa, OK Metropolitan Statistical Area
Source: U.S. Census Bureau, 2017-2021 American Community Survey 5-Year Estimates

Household Income Distribution

Area	Percent of Households Earning							
	Under $15,000	$15,000 -$24,999	$25,000 -$34,999	$35,000 -$49,999	$50,000 -$74,999	$75,000 -$99,999	$100,000 -$149,999	$150,000 and up
City	12.7	9.8	11.0	14.2	17.7	11.5	11.7	11.5
MSA[1]	9.6	8.5	9.9	13.1	18.6	12.8	15.3	12.2
U.S.	9.4	7.8	8.2	11.4	16.8	12.8	16.3	17.3

Note: (1) Figures cover the Tulsa, OK Metropolitan Statistical Area
Source: U.S. Census Bureau, 2017-2021 American Community Survey 5-Year Estimates

Poverty Rate

Area	All Ages	Under 18 Years Old	18 to 64 Years Old	65 Years and Over
City	18.0	26.8	16.7	8.8
MSA[1]	13.4	19.0	12.6	7.6
U.S.	12.6	17.0	11.8	9.6

Note: Figures are percentage of people whose income during the past 12 months was below the poverty level;
(1) Figures cover the Tulsa, OK Metropolitan Statistical Area
Source: U.S. Census Bureau, 2017-2021 American Community Survey 5-Year Estimates

EMPLOYMENT

Labor Force and Employment

Area	Civilian Labor Force			Workers Employed		
	Dec. 2021	Dec. 2022	% Chg.	Dec. 2021	Dec. 2022	% Chg.
City	194,312	199,027	2.4	189,673	193,469	2.0
MSA[1]	479,679	491,520	2.5	468,777	478,458	2.1
U.S.	161,696,000	164,224,000	1.6	155,732,000	158,872,000	2.0

Note: Data is not seasonally adjusted and covers workers 16 years of age and older; (1) Figures cover the Tulsa, OK Metropolitan Statistical Area
Source: Bureau of Labor Statistics, Local Area Unemployment Statistics

Unemployment Rate

Area	2022											
	Jan.	Feb.	Mar.	Apr.	May	Jun.	Jul.	Aug.	Sep.	Oct.	Nov.	Dec.
City	3.2	3.3	3.2	3.0	3.1	3.7	3.4	3.7	3.6	3.7	3.2	2.8
MSA[1]	3.1	3.3	3.1	2.9	3.0	3.6	3.3	3.4	3.4	3.5	3.0	2.7
U.S.	4.4	4.1	3.8	3.3	3.4	3.8	3.8	3.8	3.3	3.4	3.4	3.3

Note: Data is not seasonally adjusted and covers workers 16 years of age and older; (1) Figures cover the Tulsa, OK Metropolitan Statistical Area
Source: Bureau of Labor Statistics, Local Area Unemployment Statistics

Average Wages

Occupation	$/Hr.	Occupation	$/Hr.
Accountants and Auditors	39.68	Maintenance and Repair Workers	19.66
Automotive Mechanics	22.38	Marketing Managers	69.45
Bookkeepers	20.66	Network and Computer Systems Admin.	41.63
Carpenters	21.83	Nurses, Licensed Practical	24.26
Cashiers	12.73	Nurses, Registered	38.32
Computer Programmers	44.62	Nursing Assistants	15.05
Computer Systems Analysts	44.82	Office Clerks, General	17.16
Computer User Support Specialists	26.87	Physical Therapists	43.95
Construction Laborers	19.26	Physicians	78.82
Cooks, Restaurant	14.72	Plumbers, Pipefitters and Steamfitters	26.43
Customer Service Representatives	18.17	Police and Sheriff's Patrol Officers	26.48
Dentists	83.90	Postal Service Mail Carriers	27.22
Electricians	27.67	Real Estate Sales Agents	40.04
Engineers, Electrical	48.62	Retail Salespersons	15.59
Fast Food and Counter Workers	11.21	Sales Representatives, Technical/Scientific	38.20
Financial Managers	72.14	Secretaries, Exc. Legal/Medical/Executive	18.07
First-Line Supervisors of Office Workers	29.35	Security Guards	15.18
General and Operations Managers	51.65	Surgeons	n/a
Hairdressers/Cosmetologists	16.50	Teacher Assistants, Exc. Postsecondary*	12.67
Home Health and Personal Care Aides	12.65	Teachers, Secondary School, Exc. Sp. Ed.*	28.15
Janitors and Cleaners	14.02	Telemarketers	18.01
Landscaping/Groundskeeping Workers	15.90	Truck Drivers, Heavy/Tractor-Trailer	24.99
Lawyers	60.61	Truck Drivers, Light/Delivery Services	19.91
Maids and Housekeeping Cleaners	12.45	Waiters and Waitresses	11.71

Note: Wage data covers the Tulsa, OK Metropolitan Statistical Area; (*) Hourly wages were calculated from annual wage data based on a 40 hour work week; n/a not available.
Source: Bureau of Labor Statistics, Metro Area Occupational Employment & Wage Estimates, May 2022

Employment by Industry

Sector	MSA[1]		U.S.
	Number of Employees	Percent of Total	Percent of Total
Construction	24,200	5.3	5.0
Private Education and Health Services	73,600	16.0	16.1
Financial Activities	23,800	5.2	5.9
Government	58,400	12.7	14.5
Information	5,300	1.2	2.0
Leisure and Hospitality	46,300	10.1	10.3
Manufacturing	49,000	10.7	8.4
Mining and Logging	3,700	0.8	0.4
Other Services	20,600	4.5	3.7
Professional and Business Services	63,500	13.8	14.7
Retail Trade	50,500	11.0	10.2
Transportation, Warehousing, and Utilities	24,000	5.2	4.9
Wholesale Trade	16,800	3.7	3.9

Note: Figures are non-farm employment as of December 2022. Figures are not seasonally adjusted and include workers 16 years of age and older; (1) Figures cover the Tulsa, OK Metropolitan Statistical Area
Source: Bureau of Labor Statistics, Current Employment Statistics, Employment, Hours, and Earnings

Employment by Occupation

Occupation Classification	City (%)	MSA[1] (%)	U.S. (%)
Management, Business, Science, and Arts	37.6	37.5	40.3
Natural Resources, Construction, and Maintenance	9.3	9.8	8.7
Production, Transportation, and Material Moving	13.4	14.2	13.1
Sales and Office	22.0	22.2	20.9
Service	17.7	16.3	17.0

Note: Figures cover employed civilians 16 years of age and older; (1) Figures cover the Tulsa, OK Metropolitan Statistical Area
Source: U.S. Census Bureau, 2017-2021 American Community Survey 5-Year Estimates

Occupations with Greatest Projected Employment Growth: 2022 – 2024

Occupation[1]	2022 Employment	2024 Projected Employment	Numeric Employment Change	Percent Employment Change
Laborers and Freight, Stock, and Material Movers, Hand	34,240	35,720	1,480	4.3
Cooks, Restaurant	19,010	20,280	1,270	6.7
Stockers and Order Fillers	16,770	17,590	820	4.9
Light Truck or Delivery Services Drivers	12,400	13,170	770	6.2
Cashiers	42,800	43,500	700	1.6
Retail Salespersons	48,810	49,390	580	1.2
General and Operations Managers	25,640	26,200	560	2.2
Home Health and Personal Care Aides	13,440	13,950	510	3.8
Waiters and Waitresses	27,150	27,640	490	1.8
Heavy and Tractor-Trailer Truck Drivers	28,040	28,530	490	1.7

Note: Projections cover Oklahoma; (1) Sorted by numeric employment change
Source: www.projectionscentral.com, State Occupational Projections, 2022–2024 Short-Term Projections

Fastest-Growing Occupations: 2022 – 2024

Occupation[1]	2022 Employment	2024 Projected Employment	Numeric Employment Change	Percent Employment Change
Roustabouts, Oil and Gas	3,100	3,360	260	8.4
Rotary Drill Operators, Oil and Gas	1,830	1,980	150	8.2
Information Security Analysts (SOC 2018)	800	860	60	7.5
Cooks, Restaurant	19,010	20,280	1,270	6.7
Service Unit Operators, Oil, Gas, and Mining	2,110	2,250	140	6.6
Light Truck or Delivery Services Drivers	12,400	13,170	770	6.2
Nurse Practitioners	2,310	2,450	140	6.1
Physical Therapist Assistants	1,550	1,630	80	5.2
Fitness Trainers and Aerobics Instructors	4,610	4,850	240	5.2
Medical and Health Services Managers	7,950	8,350	400	5.0

Note: Projections cover Oklahoma; (1) Sorted by percent employment change and excludes occupations with numeric employment change less than 50
Source: www.projectionscentral.com, State Occupational Projections, 2022–2024 Short-Term Projections

CITY FINANCES

City Government Finances

Component	2020 ($000)	2020 ($ per capita)
Total Revenues	1,073,999	2,677
Total Expenditures	1,026,628	2,559
Debt Outstanding	1,514,008	3,774
Cash and Securities[1]	1,665,567	4,152

Note: (1) Cash and security holdings of a government at the close of its fiscal year, including those of its dependent agencies, utilities, and liquor stores.
Source: U.S. Census Bureau, State & Local Government Finances 2020

City Government Revenue by Source

Source	2020 ($000)	2020 ($ per capita)	2020 (%)
General Revenue			
From Federal Government	59,562	148	5.5
From State Government	12,145	30	1.1
From Local Governments	24,991	62	2.3
Taxes			
Property	84,830	211	7.9
Sales and Gross Receipts	354,813	884	33.0
Personal Income	0	0	0.0
Corporate Income	0	0	0.0
Motor Vehicle License	0	0	0.0
Other Taxes	9,429	24	0.9
Current Charges	277,731	692	25.9
Liquor Store	0	0	0.0
Utility	127,112	317	11.8

Source: U.S. Census Bureau, State & Local Government Finances 2020

City Government Expenditures by Function

Function	2020 ($000)	2020 ($ per capita)	2020 (%)
General Direct Expenditures			
Air Transportation	47,981	119	4.7
Corrections	0	0	0.0
Education	0	0	0.0
Employment Security Administration	0	0	0.0
Financial Administration	13,148	32	1.3
Fire Protection	85,416	212	8.3
General Public Buildings	0	0	0.0
Governmental Administration, Other	30,636	76	3.0
Health	77,213	192	7.5
Highways	141,035	351	13.7
Hospitals	0	0	0.0
Housing and Community Development	7,971	19	0.8
Interest on General Debt	35,684	88	3.5
Judicial and Legal	6,320	15	0.6
Libraries	0	0	0.0
Parking	5,539	13	0.5
Parks and Recreation	88,132	219	8.6
Police Protection	126,004	314	12.3
Public Welfare	18,735	46	1.8
Sewerage	150,228	374	14.6
Solid Waste Management	23,949	59	2.3
Veterans' Services	0	0	0.0
Liquor Store	0	0	0.0
Utility	161,980	403	15.8

Source: U.S. Census Bureau, State & Local Government Finances 2020

TAXES

State Corporate Income Tax Rates

State	Tax Rate (%)	Income Brackets ($)	Num. of Brackets	Financial Institution Tax Rate (%)[a]	Federal Income Tax Ded.
Oklahoma	4.0	Flat rate	1	4.0	No

Note: Tax rates as of January 1, 2023; (a) Rates listed are the corporate income tax rate applied to financial institutions or excise taxes based on income. Some states have other taxes based upon the value of deposits or shares.
Source: Federation of Tax Administrators, State Corporate Income Tax Rates, January 1, 2023

State Individual Income Tax Rates

State	Tax Rate (%)	Income Brackets ($)	Personal Exemptions ($)			Standard Ded. ($)	
			Single	Married	Depend.	Single	Married
Oklahoma	0.25 - 4.75	1,000 - 7,200 (v)	1,000	2,000	1,000	6,350	12,700

Note: Tax rates as of January 1, 2023; Local- and county-level taxes are not included; Federal income tax is not deductible on state income tax returns; (v) The income brackets reported for Oklahoma are for single persons. For married persons filing jointly, the same tax rates apply to income brackets ranging from $2,000, to $12,200.
Source: Federation of Tax Administrators, State Individual Income Tax Rates, January 1, 2023

Various State Sales and Excise Tax Rates

State	State Sales Tax (%)	Gasoline[1] ($/gal.)	Cigarette[2] ($/pack)	Spirits[3] ($/gal.)	Wine[4] ($/gal.)	Beer[5] ($/gal.)	Recreational Marijuana (%)
Oklahoma	4.5	0.20	2.03	5.56	0.72	0.40	Not legal

Note: All tax rates as of January 1, 2023; (1) The American Petroleum Institute has developed a methodology for determining the average tax rate on a gallon of fuel. Rates may include any of the following: excise taxes, environmental fees, storage tank fees, other fees or taxes, general sales tax, and local taxes; (2) The federal excise tax of $1.0066 per pack and local taxes are not included; (3) Rates are those applicable to off-premise sales of 40% alcohol by volume (a.b.v.) distilled spirits in 750ml containers. Local excise taxes are excluded; (4) Rates are those applicable to off-premise sales of 11% a.b.v. non-carbonated wine in 750ml containers; (5) Rates are those applicable to off-premise sales of 4.7% a.b.v. beer in 12 ounce containers.
Source: Tax Foundation, 2023 Facts & Figures: How Does Your State Compare?

State Business Tax Climate Index Rankings

State	Overall Rank	Corporate Tax Rank	Individual Income Tax Rank	Sales Tax Rank	Property Tax Rank	Unemployment Insurance Tax Rank
Oklahoma	23	4	31	39	30	1

Note: The index is a measure of how each state's tax laws affect economic performance. The lower the rank, the more favorable a state's tax system is for business. States without a given tax are given a ranking of 1. The scores/rankings for the District of Columbia do not affect other states. The 2023 index represents the tax climate as of July 1, 2022.
Source: Tax Foundation, State Business Tax Climate Index 2023

TRANSPORTATION

Means of Transportation to Work

Area	Car/Truck/Van		Public Transportation			Bicycle	Walked	Other Means	Worked at Home
	Drove Alone	Car-pooled	Bus	Subway	Railroad				
City	78.4	9.9	0.6	0.0	0.0	0.2	1.8	1.9	7.2
MSA[1]	80.7	9.1	0.3	0.0	0.0	0.1	1.3	1.3	7.1
U.S.	73.2	8.6	2.0	1.6	0.5	0.5	2.5	1.5	9.7

Note: Figures are percentages and cover workers 16 years of age and older; (1) Figures cover the Tulsa, OK Metropolitan Statistical Area
Source: U.S. Census Bureau, 2017-2021 American Community Survey 5-Year Estimates

Travel Time to Work

Area	Less Than 10 Minutes	10 to 19 Minutes	20 to 29 Minutes	30 to 44 Minutes	45 to 59 Minutes	60 to 89 Minutes	90 Minutes or More
City	14.2	44.9	26.3	10.1	1.9	1.4	1.2
MSA[1]	13.3	33.7	26.9	18.0	4.6	2.1	1.4
U.S.	12.4	28.5	21.0	20.9	8.2	6.2	2.9

Note: Note: Figures are percentages and include workers 16 years old and over; (1) Figures cover the Tulsa, OK Metropolitan Statistical Area
Source: U.S. Census Bureau, 2017-2021 American Community Survey 5-Year Estimates

Key Congestion Measures

Measure	1990	2000	2010	2015	2020
Annual Hours of Delay, Total (000)	7,681	14,079	20,116	23,868	14,440
Annual Hours of Delay, Per Auto Commuter	21	34	35	42	27
Annual Congestion Cost, Per Auto Commuter ($)	425	588	668	733	479

Note: Covers the Tulsa OK urban area
Source: Texas A&M Transportation Institute, 2021 Urban Mobility Report

Freeway Travel Time Index

Measure	1985	1990	1995	2000	2005	2010	2015	2020
Urban Area Index[1]	1.06	1.08	1.11	1.13	1.16	1.16	1.15	1.08
Urban Area Rank[1,2]	53	62	66	72	57	54	67	44

Note: Freeway Travel Time Index—the ratio of travel time in the peak period to the travel time at free-flow conditions. For example, a value of 1.30 indicates a 20-minute free-flow trip takes 26 minutes in the peak (20 minutes x 1.30 = 26 minutes); (1) Covers the Tulsa OK urban area; (2) Rank is based on 101 larger urban areas (#1 = highest travel time index)
Source: Texas A&M Transportation Institute, 2021 Urban Mobility Report

Public Transportation

Agency Name / Mode of Transportation	Vehicles Operated in Maximum Service[1]	Annual Unlinked Passenger Trips[2] (in thous.)	Annual Passenger Miles[3] (in thous.)
Metropolitan Tulsa Transit Authority (MTTA)			
Bus (directly operated)	51	1,245.1	6,574.1
Bus (purchased transportation)	16	36.6	256.2
Demand Response (purchased transportation)	21	69.5	675.9

Note: (1) Number of revenue vehicles operated by the given mode and type of service to meet the annual maximum service requirement. This is the revenue vehicle count during the peak season of the year; on the week and day that maximum service is provided. Vehicles operated in maximum service (VOMS) exclude atypical days and one-time special events; (2) Number of passengers who boarded public transportation vehicles. Passengers are counted each time they board a vehicle no matter how many vehicles they use to travel from their origin to their destination. (3) Sum of the distances ridden by all passengers during the entire fiscal year.
Source: Federal Transit Administration, National Transit Database, 2021

Air Transportation

Airport Name and Code / Type of Service	Passenger Airlines[1]	Passenger Enplanements	Freight Carriers[2]	Freight (lbs)
Tulsa International (TUL)				
Domestic service (U.S. carriers - 2022)	27	1,447,036	13	58,113,753
International service (U.S. carriers - 2021)	1	12	0	0

Note: (1) Includes all U.S.-based major, minor and commuter airlines that carried at least one passenger during the year; (2) Includes all U.S.-based airlines and freight carriers that transported at least one pound of freight during the year.
Source: Bureau of Transportation Statistics, The Intermodal Transportation Database, Air Carriers: T-100 Domestic Market (U.S. Carriers), 2022; Bureau of Transportation Statistics, The Intermodal Transportation Database, Air Carriers: T-100 International Market (U.S. Carriers), 2021

BUSINESSES

Major Business Headquarters

Company Name	Industry	Rankings	
		Fortune[1]	Forbes[2]
Oneok	Pipelines	224	-
QuikTrip	Convenience stores & gas stations	-	21
Williams	Energy	347	-

Note: (1) Companies that produce a 10-K are ranked 1 to 500 based on 2021 revenue; (2) All private companies with at least $2 billion in annual revenue through the end of their most current fiscal year are ranked 1 to 246; companies listed are headquartered in the city; dashes indicate no ranking
Source: Fortune, "Fortune 500," 2022; Forbes, "America's Largest Private Companies," 2022

Fastest-Growing Businesses

According to *Inc.*, Tulsa is home to one of America's 500 fastest-growing private companies: **Medefy** (#146). Criteria: must be an independent, privately-held, for-profit, U.S. corporation, proprietorship or partnership as of December 31, 2021; revenues must be at least $100,000 in 2018 and $2 million in 2021; must have four-year operating/sales history. *Inc., "America's 500 Fastest-Growing Private Companies," 2022*

Living Environment

COST OF LIVING

Cost of Living Index

Composite Index	Groceries	Housing	Utilities	Trans-portation	Health Care	Misc. Goods/ Services
87.4	92.9	68.0	94.3	91.0	97.9	96.7

Note: The Cost of Living Index measures regional differences in the cost of consumer goods and services, excluding taxes and non-consumer expenditures, for professional and managerial households in the top income quintile. It is based on more than 50,000 prices covering almost 60 different items for which prices are collected three times a year by chambers of commerce, economic development organizations or university applied economic centers in each participating urban area. The numbers shown should be read as a percentage above or below the national average of 100. For example, a value of 115.4 in the groceries column indicates that grocery prices are 15.4% higher than the national average. Small differences in the index numbers should not be interpreted as significant; Figures cover the Tulsa OK urban area.
Source: The Council for Community and Economic Research, Cost of Living Index, 2022

Grocery Prices

Area[1]	T-Bone Steak ($/pound)	Frying Chicken ($/pound)	Whole Milk ($/half gal.)	Eggs ($/dozen)	Orange Juice ($/64 oz.)	Coffee ($/11.5 oz.)
City[2]	13.52	1.46	2.57	1.97	3.57	4.66
Avg.	13.81	1.59	2.43	2.25	3.85	4.95
Min.	10.17	0.90	1.51	1.30	2.90	3.46
Max.	19.35	3.30	4.32	4.32	5.31	8.59

Note: (1) Values for the local area are compared with the average, minimum and maximum values for all 286 areas in the Cost of Living Index; (2) Figures cover the Tulsa OK urban area; T-Bone Steak (price per pound); Frying Chicken (price per pound, whole fryer); Whole Milk (half gallon carton); Eggs (price per dozen, Grade A, large); Orange Juice (64 oz. Tropicana or Florida Natural); Coffee (11.5 oz. can, vacuum-packed, Maxwell House, Hills Bros, or Folgers).
Source: The Council for Community and Economic Research, Cost of Living Index, 2022

Housing and Utility Costs

Area[1]	New Home Price ($)	Apartment Rent ($/month)	All Electric ($/month)	Part Electric ($/month)	Other Energy ($/month)	Telephone ($/month)
City[2]	313,413	852	-	90.90	68.43	190.79
Avg.	450,913	1,371	176.41	99.93	76.96	190.22
Min.	229,283	546	100.84	31.56	27.15	174.27
Max.	2,434,977	4,569	356.86	249.59	272.24	208.31

Note: (1) Values for the local area are compared with the average, minimum and maximum values for all 286 areas in the Cost of Living Index; (2) Figures cover the Tulsa OK urban area; New Home Price (2,400 sf living area, 8,000 sf lot, in urban area with full utilities); Apartment Rent (950 sf 2 bedroom/1.5 or 2 bath, unfurnished, excluding all utilities except water); All Electric (average monthly cost for an all-electric home); Part Electric (average monthly cost for a part-electric home); Other Energy (average monthly cost for natural gas, fuel oil, coal, wood, and any other forms of energy except electricity); Telephone (price includes the base monthly rate plus taxes and fees for three lines of mobile phone service).
Source: The Council for Community and Economic Research, Cost of Living Index, 2022

Health Care, Transportation, and Other Costs

Area[1]	Doctor ($/visit)	Dentist ($/visit)	Optometrist ($/visit)	Gasoline ($/gallon)	Beauty Salon ($/visit)	Men's Shirt ($)
City[2]	126.65	101.50	105.72	3.23	43.68	29.27
Avg.	124.91	107.77	117.66	3.86	43.31	34.21
Min.	36.61	58.25	51.79	2.90	22.18	13.05
Max.	250.21	162.58	371.96	5.54	85.61	63.54

Note: (1) Values for the local area are compared with the average, minimum and maximum values for all 286 areas in the Cost of Living Index; (2) Figures cover the Tulsa OK urban area; Doctor (general practitioners routine exam of an established patient); Dentist (adult teeth cleaning and periodic oral examination); Optometrist (full vision eye exam for established adult patient); Gasoline (one gallon regular unleaded, national brand, including all taxes, cash price at self-service pump if available); Beauty Salon (woman's shampoo, trim, and blow-dry); Men's Shirt (cotton/polyester dress shirt, pinpoint weave, long sleeves).
Source: The Council for Community and Economic Research, Cost of Living Index, 2022

HOUSING

Homeownership Rate

Area	2015 (%)	2016 (%)	2017 (%)	2018 (%)	2019 (%)	2020 (%)	2021 (%)	2022 (%)
MSA[1]	65.2	65.4	66.8	68.3	70.5	70.1	63.8	63.7
U.S.	63.7	63.4	63.9	64.4	64.6	66.6	65.5	65.8

Note: (1) Figures cover the Tulsa, OK Metropolitan Statistical Area
Source: U.S. Census Bureau, Housing Vacancies and Homeownership Annual Statistics: 2015-2022

House Price Index (HPI)

Area	National Ranking[2]	Quarterly Change (%)	One-Year Change (%)	Five-Year Change (%)	Since 1991Q1 (%)
MSA[1]	58	0.72	14.67	52.24	236.95
U.S.[3]	—	0.34	8.41	58.44	289.08

Note: The HPI is a weighted repeat sales index. It measures average price changes in repeat sales or refinancings on the same properties. This information is obtained by reviewing repeat mortgage transactions on single-family properties whose mortgages have been purchased or securitized by Fannie Mae or Freddie Mac since January 1975; (1) Figures cover the Tulsa, OK Metropolitan Statistical Area; (2) Rankings are based on annual percentage change for all metro areas containing at least 15,000 transactions over the last 10 years and ranges from 1 to 257; (3) figures based on a weighted average of Census Division estimates using a seasonally adjusted, purchase-only index; all figures are for the period ending December 31, 2022
Source: Federal Housing Finance Agency, Change in FHFA Metropolitan Area House Price Indexes, 2022Q4

Median Single-Family Home Prices

Area	2020	2021	2022p	Percent Change 2021 to 2022
MSA[1]	195.9	221.6	242.3	9.3
U.S. Average	300.2	357.1	392.6	9.9

Note: Figures are median sales prices of existing single-family homes in thousands of dollars; (p) preliminary; (1) Figures cover the Tulsa, OK Metropolitan Statistical Area
Source: National Association of Realtors, Median Sales Price of Existing Single-Family Homes for Metropolitan Areas, 4th Quarter 2022

Qualifying Income Based on Median Sales Price of Existing Single-Family Homes

Area	With 5% Down ($)	With 10% Down ($)	With 20% Down ($)
MSA[1]	71,595	67,827	60,290
U.S. Average	112,234	106,237	94,513

Note: Figures are preliminary; Qualifying income is based on a mortgage rate of 6.77%. Monthly principal and interest payment is limited to 25% of income; (1) Figures cover the Tulsa, OK Metropolitan Statistical Area
Source: National Association of Realtors, Qualifying Income Based on Median Sales Price of Existing Single-Family Homes for Metropolitan Areas, 4th Quarter 2022

Home Value

Area	Under $100,000	$100,000 -$199,999	$200,000 -$299,999	$300,000 -$399,999	$400,000 -$499,999	$500,000 -$999,999	$1,000,000 or more	Median ($)
City	28.0	36.9	15.4	8.2	4.4	5.5	1.5	151,500
MSA[1]	24.2	39.1	19.5	8.6	3.5	4.1	0.9	163,100
U.S.	16.2	24.2	20.1	13.6	8.3	13.6	4.1	244,900

Note: Figures are percentages except for median and cover owner-occupied housing units; (1) Figures cover the Tulsa, OK Metropolitan Statistical Area
Source: U.S. Census Bureau, 2017-2021 American Community Survey 5-Year Estimates

Year Housing Structure Built

Area	2020 or Later	2010 -2019	2000 -2009	1990 -1999	1980 -1989	1970 -1979	1960 -1969	1950 -1959	1940 -1949	Before 1940	Median Year
City	0.1	4.6	6.2	9.2	13.4	20.6	14.4	16.5	6.4	8.7	1972
MSA[1]	0.3	9.1	13.7	12.1	14.1	18.8	10.5	10.5	4.3	6.7	1980
U.S.	0.2	7.3	13.6	13.6	13.2	14.8	10.3	10.0	4.7	12.2	1979

Note: Figures are percentages except for Median Year; Note: (1) Figures cover the Tulsa, OK Metropolitan Statistical Area
Source: U.S. Census Bureau, 2017-2021 American Community Survey 5-Year Estimates

Gross Monthly Rent

Area	Under $500	$500 -$999	$1,000 -$1,499	$1,500 -$1,999	$2,000 -$2,499	$2,500 -$2,999	$3,000 and up	Median ($)
City	8.9	54.8	28.8	4.8	1.3	0.5	0.9	882
MSA[1]	8.7	51.9	30.3	6.3	1.6	0.4	0.8	909
U.S.	8.1	30.5	30.8	16.8	7.3	3.1	3.5	1,163

Note: Figures are percentages except for median; Gross rent is the contract rent plus the estimated average monthly cost of utilities (electricity, gas, and water and sewer) and fuels (oil, coal, kerosene, wood, etc.) if these are paid by the renter (or paid for the renter by someone else); (1) Figures cover the Tulsa, OK Metropolitan Statistical Area
Source: U.S. Census Bureau, 2017-2021 American Community Survey 5-Year Estimates

HEALTH

Health Risk Factors

Category	MSA[1] (%)	U.S. (%)
Adults aged 18–64 who have any kind of health care coverage	84.8	90.9
Adults who reported being in good or better health	81.4	85.2
Adults who have been told they have high blood cholesterol	36.9	35.7
Adults who have been told they have high blood pressure	36.5	32.4
Adults who are current smokers	15.2	14.4
Adults who currently use e-cigarettes	9.0	6.7
Adults who currently use chewing tobacco, snuff, or snus	5.1	3.5
Adults who are heavy drinkers[2]	4.0	6.3
Adults who are binge drinkers[3]	12.2	15.4
Adults who are overweight (BMI 25.0 - 29.9)	34.6	34.4
Adults who are obese (BMI 30.0 - 99.8)	37.3	33.9
Adults who participated in any physical activities in the past month	72.7	76.3

Note: (1) Figures cover the Tulsa, OK Metropolitan Statistical Area; (2) Heavy drinkers are classified as adult men having more than 14 drinks per week and adult women having more than 7 drinks per week; (3) Binge drinkers are classified as males having five or more drinks on one occasion or females having four or more drinks on one occasion
Source: Centers for Disease Control and Prevention, Behaviorial Risk Factor Surveillance System, SMART: Selected Metropolitan Area Risk Trends, 2021

Acute and Chronic Health Conditions

Category	MSA[1] (%)	U.S. (%)
Adults who have ever been told they had a heart attack	5.2	4.0
Adults who have ever been told they have angina or coronary heart disease	5.5	3.8
Adults who have ever been told they had a stroke	4.2	3.0
Adults who have ever been told they have asthma	15.2	14.9
Adults who have ever been told they have arthritis	24.5	25.8
Adults who have ever been told they have diabetes[2]	13.1	10.9
Adults who have ever been told they had skin cancer	5.7	6.6
Adults who have ever been told they had any other types of cancer	7.4	7.5
Adults who have ever been told they have COPD	6.7	6.1
Adults who have ever been told they have kidney disease	3.3	3.0
Adults who have ever been told they have a form of depression	24.7	20.5

Note: (1) Figures cover the Tulsa, OK Metropolitan Statistical Area; (2) Figures do not include pregnancy-related, borderline, or pre-diabetes
Source: Centers for Disease Control and Prevention, Behaviorial Risk Factor Surveillance System, SMART: Selected Metropolitan Area Risk Trends, 2021

Health Screening and Vaccination Rates

Category	MSA[1] (%)	U.S. (%)
Adults who have ever been tested for HIV	31.9	34.9
Adults who have had their blood cholesterol checked within the last five years	81.8	85.2
Adults aged 65+ who have had flu shot within the past year	69.9	68.6
Adults aged 65+ who have ever had a pneumonia vaccination	72.3	71.0

Note: (1) Figures cover the Tulsa, OK Metropolitan Statistical Area.
Source: Centers for Disease Control and Prevention, Behaviorial Risk Factor Surveillance System, SMART: Selected Metropolitan Area Risk Trends, 2021

Disability Status

Category	MSA[1] (%)	U.S. (%)
Adults who reported being deaf	8.0	7.2
Are you blind or have serious difficulty seeing, even when wearing glasses?	5.5	4.8
Are you limited in any way in any of your usual activities due to arthritis?	9.5	11.1
Do you have difficulty doing errands alone?	9.4	7.0
Do you have difficulty dressing or bathing?	4.0	3.6
Do you have serious difficulty concentrating/remembering/making decisions?	13.0	12.1
Do you have serious difficulty walking or climbing stairs?	16.1	12.8

Note: (1) Figures cover the Tulsa, OK Metropolitan Statistical Area.
Source: Centers for Disease Control and Prevention, Behaviorial Risk Factor Surveillance System, SMART: Selected Metropolitan Area Risk Trends, 2021

Mortality Rates for the Top 10 Causes of Death in the U.S.

ICD-10[a] Sub-Chapter	ICD-10[a] Code	Crude Mortality Rate[1] per 100,000 population	
		County[2]	U.S.
Malignant neoplasms	C00-C97	181.5	182.6
Ischaemic heart diseases	I20-I25	87.6	113.1
Other forms of heart disease	I30-I51	41.7	64.4
Other degenerative diseases of the nervous system	G30-G31	50.5	51.0
Cerebrovascular diseases	I60-I69	47.9	47.8
Other external causes of accidental injury	W00-X59	44.5	46.4
Chronic lower respiratory diseases	J40-J47	53.8	45.7
Organic, including symptomatic, mental disorders	F01-F09	29.4	35.9
Hypertensive diseases	I10-I15	161.4	35.0
Diabetes mellitus	E10-E14	24.6	29.6

Note: (a) ICD-10 = International Classification of Diseases 10th Revision; (1) Crude mortality rates are a three-year average covering 2019-2021; (2) Figures cover Tulsa County.
Source: Centers for Disease Control and Prevention, National Center for Health Statistics. National Vital Statistics System, Mortality 2018-2021 on CDC WONDER Online Database

Mortality Rates for Selected Causes of Death

ICD-10[a] Sub-Chapter	ICD-10[a] Code	Crude Mortality Rate[1] per 100,000 population	
		County[2]	U.S.
Assault	X85-Y09	10.5	7.0
Diseases of the liver	K70-K76	23.1	19.8
Human immunodeficiency virus (HIV) disease	B20-B24	2.0	1.5
Influenza and pneumonia	J09-J18	15.0	14.7
Intentional self-harm	X60-X84	20.7	14.3
Malnutrition	E40-E46	2.6	4.3
Obesity and other hyperalimentation	E65-E68	1.4	3.0
Renal failure	N17-N19	8.5	15.7
Transport accidents	V01-V99	15.3	13.6
Viral hepatitis	B15-B19	2.6	1.2

Note: (a) ICD-10 = International Classification of Diseases 10th Revision; (1) Crude mortality rates are a three-year average covering 2019-2021; (2) Figures cover Tulsa County; Data are suppressed when the data meet the criteria for confidentiality constraints; Crude mortality rates are flagged as unreliable when the rate would be calculated with a numerator of 20 or less.
Source: Centers for Disease Control and Prevention, National Center for Health Statistics. National Vital Statistics System, Mortality 2018-2021 on CDC WONDER Online Database

Health Insurance Coverage

Area	With Health Insurance	With Private Health Insurance	With Public Health Insurance	Without Health Insurance	Population Under Age 19 Without Health Insurance
City	83.3	58.7	35.8	16.7	8.7
MSA[1]	86.3	65.3	33.3	13.7	7.7
U.S.	91.2	67.8	35.4	8.8	5.3

Note: Figures are percentages that cover the civilian noninstitutionalized population; (1) Figures cover the Tulsa, OK Metropolitan Statistical Area
Source: U.S. Census Bureau, 2017-2021 American Community Survey 5-Year Estimates

Number of Medical Professionals

Area	MDs[3]	DOs[3,4]	Dentists	Podiatrists	Chiropractors	Optometrists
County[1] (number)	1,771	747	473	29	261	159
County[1] (rate[2])	264.3	111.5	70.3	4.3	38.8	23.6
U.S. (rate[2])	289.3	23.5	72.5	6.2	28.7	17.4

Note: Data as of 2021 unless noted; (1) Data covers Tulsa County; (2) Rate per 100,000 population; (3) Data as of 2020 and includes all active, non-federal physicians; (4) Doctor of Osteopathic Medicine
Source: U.S. Department of Health and Human Services, Health Resources and Services Administration, Bureau of Health Professions, Area Resource File (ARF) 2021-2022

EDUCATION

Public School District Statistics

District Name	Schls	Pupils	Pupil/ Teacher Ratio	Minority Pupils[1] (%)	LEP/ELL[2] (%)	IEP[3] (%)
Tulsa	69	33,211	16.9	77.8	21.1	16.4
Union	17	15,008	17.7	75.1	22.2	12.5

Note: Table includes school districts with 2,000 or more students; (1) Percentage of students that are not non-Hispanic white; (2) Percentage of students that are Limited English Proficient or English Language Learners (2018-19); (3) Percentage of students that have an Individualized Education Program (2019-20).
Source: U.S. Department of Education, National Center for Education Statistics, Common Core of Data, Local Education Agency (School District) Universe Survey: School Year 2021-2022

Best High Schools

According to *U.S. News,* Tulsa is home to one of the top 500 high schools in the U.S.: **Booker T. Washington High School** (#340). Nearly 18,000 public, magnet and charter schools were ranked based on their performance on state assessments and how well they prepare students for college. *U.S. News & World Report, "Best High Schools 2022"*

Highest Level of Education

Area	Less than H.S.	H.S. Diploma	Some College, No Deg.	Associate Degree	Bachelor's Degree	Master's Degree	Prof. School Degree	Doctorate Degree
City	12.1	25.3	22.1	8.0	20.7	7.7	2.7	1.3
MSA[1]	10.0	28.8	23.3	9.2	19.2	6.7	1.8	1.0
U.S.	11.1	26.5	20.0	8.7	20.6	9.3	2.2	1.5

Note: Figures cover persons age 25 and over; (1) Figures cover the Tulsa, OK Metropolitan Statistical Area
Source: U.S. Census Bureau, 2017-2021 American Community Survey 5-Year Estimates

Educational Attainment by Race

Area	High School Graduate or Higher (%)					Bachelor's Degree or Higher (%)				
	Total	White	Black	Asian	Hisp.[2]	Total	White	Black	Asian	Hisp.[2]
City	87.9	90.8	89.6	74.0	59.8	32.4	37.6	17.8	37.0	11.5
MSA[1]	90.0	91.7	90.1	76.7	65.8	28.7	31.1	19.6	34.9	14.0
U.S.	88.9	91.4	87.2	87.6	71.2	33.7	35.5	23.3	55.6	18.4

Note: Figures shown cover persons 25 years old and over; (1) Figures cover the Tulsa, OK Metropolitan Statistical Area; (2) People of Hispanic origin can be of any race
Source: U.S. Census Bureau, 2017-2021 American Community Survey 5-Year Estimates

School Enrollment by Grade and Control

Area	Preschool (%)		Kindergarten (%)		Grades 1 - 4 (%)		Grades 5 - 8 (%)		Grades 9 - 12 (%)	
	Public	Private	Public	Private	Public	Private	Public	Private	Public	Private
City	63.6	36.4	82.4	17.6	85.0	15.0	83.0	17.0	81.8	18.2
MSA[1]	66.3	33.7	85.2	14.8	86.1	13.9	86.5	13.5	85.9	14.1
U.S.	58.8	41.2	86.3	13.7	88.3	11.7	88.6	11.4	89.4	10.6

Note: Figures shown cover persons 3 years old and over; (1) Figures cover the Tulsa, OK Metropolitan Statistical Area
Source: U.S. Census Bureau, 2017-2021 American Community Survey 5-Year Estimates

Higher Education

Four-Year Colleges			Two-Year Colleges			Medical Schools[1]	Law Schools[2]	Voc/ Tech[3]
Public	Private Non-profit	Private For-profit	Public	Private Non-profit	Private For-profit			
3	3	1	3	2	3	1	1	6

Note: Figures cover institutions located within the Tulsa, OK Metropolitan Statistical Area and include main campuses only; (1) includes schools accredited by the Liaison Committee on Medical Education and the American Osteopathic Association's Commission on Osteopathic College Accreditation; (2) includes ABA-accredited schools, schools with provisional ABA accreditation, and state accredited schools; (3) includes all schools with programs that are less than 2 years.
Source: National Center for Education Statistics, Integrated Postsecondary Education System (IPEDS), 2021-22; Wikipedia, List of Medical Schools in the United States, accessed April 10, 2023; Wikipedia, List of Law Schools in the United States, accessed April 10, 2023

According to *U.S. News & World Report,* the Tulsa, OK metro area is home to one of the top 200 national universities in the U.S.: **University of Tulsa** (#137 tie). The indicators used to capture academic quality fall into a number of categories: assessment by administrators at peer institutions; retention of students; faculty resources; student selectivity; financial resources; alumni giving; high school counselor ratings of colleges; and graduation rate. *U.S. News & World Report, "America's Best Colleges 2023"*

EMPLOYERS

Major Employers

Company Name	Industry
AHS Hillcrest Medical Center	General medical & surgical hospitals
American Airlines	Airports, flying fields, & services
BlueCross BlueShield of Oklahoma	Hospital & medical services plans
Caprock Pipeline Company	Pipelines, natural gas
County of Tulsa	County government
Dollar Thrifty Automotive Group	Passenger car rental
GHS Health Maintenance Organization	Health insurance carriers
IBM	Computer related consulting services
IC of Oklahoma	Truck & bus bodies
Matrix Service	Oil & gas pipeline construction
ONEOK	Natural gas transmission
Saint Francis Health System	General medical & surgical hospitals
St. John Medical Center	General medical & surgical hospitals
State Farm Fire and Casualty Company	Fire, marine, & casualty insurance
The Bama Companies	Bread, cake & related products
The Boeing Company	Missile guidance systems & equipment
The NORDAM Group	Aircraft parts & equipment, nec
The Williams Companies	Natural gas transmission

Note: Companies shown are located within the Tulsa, OK Metropolitan Statistical Area.
Source: Hoovers.com; Wikipedia

Best Companies to Work For

Craft Health, headquartered in Tulsa, is among "Best Workplaces in Health Care." To determine the Best Workplaces in Health Care list, Great Place To Work analyzed the survey responses of over 161,000 employees from Great Place To Work-Certified companies in the health care industry. Survey data analysis and company-provided datapoints are then factored into a combined score to compare and rank the companies that create the most consistently positive experience for all employees in this industry. *Fortune, "Best Workplaces in Health Care," 2022*

PUBLIC SAFETY

Crime Rate

Area	Total Crime	Violent Crime Rate				Property Crime Rate		
		Murder	Rape[3]	Robbery	Aggrav. Assault	Burglary	Larceny -Theft	Motor Vehicle Theft
City	6,244.2	17.9	94.0	184.3	836.5	1,095.8	3,045.0	970.7
Suburbs[1]	2,005.9	3.6	31.0	21.9	174.2	380.7	1,150.1	244.3
Metro[2]	3,701.1	9.3	56.2	86.8	439.1	666.7	1,908.0	534.9
U.S.	2,356.7	6.5	38.4	73.9	279.7	314.2	1,398.0	246.0

Note: Figures are crimes per 100,000 population; (1) All areas within the metro area that are located outside the city limits; (2) Figures cover the Tulsa, OK Metropolitan Statistical Area; (3) All figures shown were reported using the revised Uniform Crime Reporting (UCR) definition of rape; Due to the transition to the National Incident-Based Reporting System (NIBRS), limited city and metro area data was released for 2021.
Source: FBI Uniform Crime Reports, 2020

Hate Crimes

Area	Number of Quarters Reported	Number of Incidents per Bias Motivation					
		Race/Ethnicity/ Ancestry	Religion	Sexual Orientation	Disability	Gender	Gender Identity
City	4	1	0	0	0	0	0
U.S.	4	5,227	1,244	1,110	130	75	266

Note: Due to the transition to the National Incident-Based Reporting System (NIBRS), limited crime data was released for 2021.
Source: Federal Bureau of Investigation, Hate Crime Statistics 2020

Identity Theft Consumer Reports

Area	Reports	Reports per 100,000 Population	Rank[2]
MSA[1]	1,784	179	195
U.S.	1,108,609	339	-

Note: (1) Figures cover the Tulsa, OK Metropolitan Statistical Area; (2) Rank ranges from 1 to 391 where 1 indicates greatest number of identity theft reports per 100,000 population
Source: Federal Trade Commission, Consumer Sentinel Network Data Book 2022

Fraud and Other Consumer Reports

Area	Reports	Reports per 100,000 Population	Rank[2]
MSA[1]	7,835	787	228
U.S.	4,064,520	1,245	-

Note: (1) Figures cover the Tulsa, OK Metropolitan Statistical Area; (2) Rank ranges from 1 to 391 where 1 indicates greatest number of fraud and other consumer reports per 100,000 population
Source: Federal Trade Commission, Consumer Sentinel Network Data Book 2022

POLITICS

2020 Presidential Election Results

Area	Biden	Trump	Jorgensen	Hawkins	Other
Tulsa County	40.9	56.5	1.8	0.0	0.8
U.S.	51.3	46.8	1.2	0.3	0.5

Note: Results are percentages and may not add to 100% due to rounding
Source: Dave Leip's Atlas of U.S. Presidential Elections

SPORTS

Professional Sports Teams

Team Name	League	Year Established

No teams are located in the metro area
Source: Wikipedia, Major Professional Sports Teams of the United States and Canada, April 12, 2023

CLIMATE

Average and Extreme Temperatures

Temperature	Jan	Feb	Mar	Apr	May	Jun	Jul	Aug	Sep	Oct	Nov	Dec	Yr.
Extreme High (°F)	79	86	96	102	96	103	112	110	105	98	85	80	112
Average High (°F)	46	52	61	72	80	88	93	93	85	74	61	50	71
Average Temp. (°F)	36	41	50	61	69	78	83	82	74	63	50	40	61
Average Low (°F)	25	30	38	50	59	68	72	70	63	51	39	29	50
Extreme Low (°F)	-6	-7	-3	22	35	49	51	52	35	26	10	-8	-8

Note: Figures cover the years 1948-1990
Source: National Climatic Data Center, International Station Meteorological Climate Summary, 9/96

Average Precipitation/Snowfall/Humidity

Precip./Humidity	Jan	Feb	Mar	Apr	May	Jun	Jul	Aug	Sep	Oct	Nov	Dec	Yr.
Avg. Precip. (in.)	1.6	1.9	3.2	3.7	5.6	4.3	3.4	3.0	4.1	3.5	2.6	1.9	38.9
Avg. Snowfall (in.)	3	2	2	Tr	0	0	0	0	0	Tr	1	2	10
Avg. Rel. Hum. 6am (%)	78	78	76	77	85	85	82	84	85	82	78	78	81
Avg. Rel. Hum. 3pm (%)	53	51	47	46	54	53	48	46	49	46	48	52	49

Note: Figures cover the years 1948-1990; Tr = Trace amounts (<0.05 in. of rain; <0.5 in. of snow)
Source: National Climatic Data Center, International Station Meteorological Climate Summary, 9/96

Weather Conditions

Temperature			Daytime Sky			Precipitation		
10°F & below	32°F & below	90°F & above	Clear	Partly cloudy	Cloudy	0.01 inch or more precip.	0.1 inch or more snow/ice	Thunderstorms
6	78	74	117	141	107	88	8	50

Note: Figures are average number of days per year and cover the years 1948-1990
Source: National Climatic Data Center, International Station Meteorological Climate Summary, 9/96

HAZARDOUS WASTE

Superfund Sites

The Tulsa, OK metro area is home to one site on the EPA's Superfund National Priorities List: **Henryetta Iron and Metal** (final). There are a total of 1,165 Superfund sites with a status of proposed or final on the list in the U.S. *U.S. Environmental Protection Agency, National Priorities List, April 12, 2023*

AIR QUALITY

Air Quality Trends: Ozone

	1990	1995	2000	2005	2010	2015	2018	2019	2020	2021
MSA[1]	0.086	0.091	0.081	0.072	0.069	0.061	0.067	0.062	0.061	0.063
U.S.	0.087	0.089	0.081	0.080	0.072	0.067	0.069	0.065	0.065	0.067

Note: (1) Data covers the Tulsa, OK Metropolitan Statistical Area. The values shown are the composite ozone concentration averages among trend sites based on the highest fourth daily maximum 8-hour concentration in parts per million. These trends are based on sites having an adequate record of monitoring data during the trend period. Data from exceptional events are included.
Source: U.S. Environmental Protection Agency, Air Quality Monitoring Information, "Air Quality Trends by City, 1990-2021"

Air Quality Index

Area	Percent of Days when Air Quality was...[2]					AQI Statistics[2]	
	Good	Moderate	Unhealthy for Sensitive Groups	Unhealthy	Very Unhealthy	Maximum	Median
MSA[1]	60.3	37.0	2.2	0.5	0.0	163	47

Note: (1) Data covers the Tulsa, OK Metropolitan Statistical Area; (2) Based on 365 days with AQI data in 2021. Air Quality Index (AQI) is an index for reporting daily air quality. EPA calculates the AQI for five major air pollutants regulated by the Clean Air Act: ground-level ozone, particle pollution (aka particulate matter), carbon monoxide, sulfur dioxide, and nitrogen dioxide. The AQI runs from 0 to 500. The higher the AQI value, the greater the level of air pollution and the greater the health concern. There are six AQI categories: "Good" AQI is between 0 and 50. Air quality is considered satisfactory; "Moderate" AQI is between 51 and 100. Air quality is acceptable; "Unhealthy for Sensitive Groups" When AQI values are between 101 and 150, members of sensitive groups may experience health effects; "Unhealthy" When AQI values are between 151 and 200 everyone may begin to experience health effects; "Very Unhealthy" AQI values between 201 and 300 trigger a health alert; "Hazardous" AQI values over 300 trigger warnings of emergency conditions (not shown).
Source: U.S. Environmental Protection Agency, Air Quality Index Report, 2021

Air Quality Index Pollutants

Area	Percent of Days when AQI Pollutant was...[2]					
	Carbon Monoxide	Nitrogen Dioxide	Ozone	Sulfur Dioxide	Particulate Matter 2.5	Particulate Matter 10
MSA[1]	0.0	0.0	52.9	(3)	46.3	0.8

Note: (1) Data covers the Tulsa, OK Metropolitan Statistical Area; (2) Based on 365 days with AQI data in 2021. The Air Quality Index (AQI) is an index for reporting daily air quality. EPA calculates the AQI for five major air pollutants regulated by the Clean Air Act: ground-level ozone, particle pollution (also known as particulate matter), carbon monoxide, sulfur dioxide, and nitrogen dioxide. The AQI runs from 0 to 500. The higher the AQI value, the greater the level of air pollution and the greater the health concern; (3) Sulfur dioxide is no longer included in this table (as of December 8, 2021) because SO_2 concentrations tend to be very localized and not necessarily representative of broad geographical areas like counties and CBSAs.
Source: U.S. Environmental Protection Agency, Air Quality Index Report, 2021

Maximum Air Pollutant Concentrations: Particulate Matter, Ozone, CO and Lead

	Particulate Matter 10 (ug/m^3)	Particulate Matter 2.5 Wtd AM (ug/m^3)	Particulate Matter 2.5 24-Hr (ug/m^3)	Ozone (ppm)	Carbon Monoxide (ppm)	Lead (ug/m^3)
MSA[1] Level	99	10.1	29	0.068	1	n/a
NAAQS[2]	150	15	35	0.075	9	0.15
Met NAAQS[2]	Yes	Yes	Yes	Yes	Yes	n/a

Note: (1) Data covers the Tulsa, OK Metropolitan Statistical Area; Data from exceptional events are included; (2) National Ambient Air Quality Standards; ppm = parts per million; ug/m^3 = micrograms per cubic meter; n/a not available.
Concentrations: Particulate Matter 10 (coarse particulate)—highest second maximum 24-hour concentration; Particulate Matter 2.5 Wtd AM (fine particulate)—highest weighted annual mean concentration; Particulate Matter 2.5 24-Hour (fine particulate)—highest 98th percentile 24-hour concentration; Ozone—highest fourth daily maximum 8-hour concentration; Carbon Monoxide—highest second maximum non-overlapping 8-hour concentration; Lead—maximum running 3-month average
Source: U.S. Environmental Protection Agency, Air Quality Monitoring Information, "Air Quality Statistics by City, 2021"

Maximum Air Pollutant Concentrations: Nitrogen Dioxide and Sulfur Dioxide

	Nitrogen Dioxide AM (ppb)	Nitrogen Dioxide 1-Hr (ppb)	Sulfur Dioxide AM (ppb)	Sulfur Dioxide 1-Hr (ppb)	Sulfur Dioxide 24-Hr (ppb)
MSA[1] Level	7	38	n/a	5	n/a
NAAQS[2]	53	100	30	75	140
Met NAAQS[2]	Yes	Yes	n/a	Yes	n/a

Note: (1) Data covers the Tulsa, OK Metropolitan Statistical Area; Data from exceptional events are included; (2) National Ambient Air Quality Standards; ppm = parts per million; ug/m^3 = micrograms per cubic meter; n/a not available.
Concentrations: Nitrogen Dioxide AM—highest arithmetic mean concentration; Nitrogen Dioxide 1-Hr—highest 98th percentile 1-hour daily maximum concentration; Sulfur Dioxide AM—highest annual mean concentration; Sulfur Dioxide 1-Hr—highest 99th percentile 1-hour daily maximum concentration; Sulfur Dioxide 24-Hr—highest second maximum 24-hour concentration
Source: U.S. Environmental Protection Agency, Air Quality Monitoring Information, "Air Quality Statistics by City, 2021"

Wichita, Kansas

Background

Lying in the southeastern plains of Kansas, Wichita took its name from a local Indian tribe. Starting in 1864, two white entrepreneurs, Jesse Chisholm and James R. Mead, struck up a lively trade in the area with the native people. Shortly after the tribe was relocated to Indian Territory in Oklahoma in 1867, white settlers planted roots around Chisholm's and Mead's trading post. Chisholm laid out a trail from the post to Texas, from which cowboys drove Longhorn cattle to the railhead of the Wichita and Southwestern Railroad, feeding the cows along the way.

In the 1880s, like many Plains-area cattle-shipping points, Wichita hosted dance halls, gambling, and saloons. Wyatt Earp served there as a lawman for a time. In 1886, the town officially became a city, having grown to over 20,000 in population, much of it due to eager speculation in prairie lands.

After the turn of the century, oil was discovered in the area, luring more people, and the city swelled to over 100,000 by 1930. Shortly after World War I, which saw great advancements in aviation, Wichita's first airplane factory was built, and the city became the country's leading manufacturer of aircraft. Walter H. Beech, Clyde V. Cessna, and Lloyd C. Stearman became famous members of the community for their early leadership in the industry.

Wichita is the largest and most dominant industrial city in the state. Oil rigs and aircraft factories kept the dire times of the Great Depression from Wichita, while much of the rest of the state was consumed by the Dust Bowl. During World War II, more airplanes rolled off the city's three assembly lines than in any other city in America. Steady aircraft industry growth continued until the 1980s, when a slump occurred. By the late 1990s, a revival of the industry was in full swing until the early 2000s when major layoffs again occurred. In 2013, Boeing closed its Wichita plant, but the void was filled by Spirit Aerosystems. Wichita, now accustomed to the cyclical nature of the aircraft industry, remains a major manufacturer of private and military aircraft, with Spirit, Airbus Americas Engineering, Cessna, Bombardier Learjet, and Hawker Beechcraft all in operation there.

Another important Wichita company is Koch Industries, which deals in chemicals, energy, and gas liquids, among other products. The city is headquarters to Cargill Beef; Koch and Cargill are the two largest privately held companies in the U.S. Other major industries in Wichita are healthcare and manufacturing. The city ranks #1 in all manufacturing jobs, and #3 in high-tech manufacturing jobs, namely in aerospace, IT systems, and energy sectors.

Transportation to and from Wichita is easy. The Wichita Dwight D. Eisenhower Airport is the largest in the state, and the city is also serviced by Colonel James Jabara Airport. Two railroad lines run freight service through the city and Wichita Bicycle Master Plan oversaw the city's new 149-mile Priority Bicycle Network.

Wichita State University, a public research institution, is the largest of the city's three universities and the third largest in the state behind Friends University, a private non-denominational Christian institution, and Newman University, a private Catholic school. All three schools feature sports teams, although Wichita State University is the only to compete at the Division I level. Wichita is also home to several minor league teams, including the Wind Surge (baseball), the Thunder (ice hockey), and the Force (indoor football).

Wichita has many acclaimed cultural institutions, including the Wichita Museum of Art, whose permanent collection features 7,000 objects, Ulrich Museum of Art, located at Wichita State, and Wichita Symphony Orchestra, the oldest professional symphony orchestra in Kansas. Since 1972, Wichita has hosted the River Festival, which features a host of events, and attracts nearly 400,000 people each year. The annual Wichita Black Arts Festival celebrates the cultural achievements of the city's African American community.

The climate in Wichita is continental but generally mild, punctuated occasionally by more intemperate weather conditions. Summers are usually warm and humid. Winters are usually mild, with brief periods of cold weather. Snowfall is light to moderate, with the ground rarely being covered for more than three days. Thunderstorms, occasionally severe, occur through the spring and summer months.

Rankings

Business/Finance Rankings

- Wichita was the #4-ranked city for savers, according to a study by the finance site GOBankingRates, which considered the prospects for people trying to save money. Criteria: average monthly cost of grocery items; median home listing price; median rent; median income; transportation costs; gas prices; and the cost of eating out for an inexpensive and mid-range meal in 100 U.S. cities. *www.gobankingrates.com, "The 20 Best (and Worst) Places to Live If You're Trying to Save Money," August 27, 2019*

- Wichita was ranked #4 among 100 U.S. cities for most difficult conditions for savers, according to a study by the finance site GOBankingRates. Criteria: average monthly cost of grocery items; median home listing price; median rent; median income; transportation costs; gas prices; and the cost of eating out for an inexpensive and mid-range meal. *www.gobankingrates.com, "The 20 Best (and Worst) Places to Live If You're Trying to Save Money," August 27, 2019*

- The Brookings Institution ranked the nation's largest cities based on income inequality. Wichita was ranked #76 (#1 = greatest inequality). Criteria: the "95/20 ratio," a figure representing the income at which a household earns more than 95 percent of all other households, divided by the income at which a household earns more than only 20 percent of all other households. *Brookings Institution, "Household Income Inequality, Largest Cities of 97 Large U.S. Metro Areas, 2014-2016," February 5, 2018*

- The Brookings Institution ranked the 100 largest metro areas in the U.S. based on income inequality. Wichita was ranked #84 (#1 = greatest inequality). Criteria: the "95/20 ratio," a figure representing the income at which a household earns more than 95 percent of all other households, divided by the income at which a household earns more than only 20 percent of all other households. *Brookings Institution, "Household Income Inequality, 100 Largest U.S. Metro Areas, 2014-2016," February 5, 2018*

- The Wichita metro area appeared on the Milken Institute "2022 Best Performing Cities" list. Rank: #130 out of 200 large metro areas (population over 250,000). Criteria: job growth; wage and salary growth; high-tech output growth; housing affordability; household broadband access. *Milken Institute, "Best-Performing Cities 2022," March 28, 2022*

- *Forbes* ranked the 200 most populous metro areas to determine the nation's "Best Places for Business and Careers." The Wichita metro area was ranked #119. Criteria: costs (business and living); job growth (past and projected); income growth; quality of life; educational attainment (college and high school); projected economic growth; cultural and leisure opportunities; workplace tolerance laws; net migration patterns. *Forbes, "The Best Places for Business and Careers 2019: Seattle Still On Top," October 30, 2019*

Education Rankings

- Personal finance website *WalletHub* analyzed the 150 largest U.S. metropolitan statistical areas to determine where the most educated Americans are putting their degrees to work. Criteria: education levels; percentage of workers with degrees; education quality and attainment gap; public school quality rankings; quality and enrollment of each metro area's universities. Wichita was ranked #93 (#1 = most educated city). *www.WalletHub.com, "Most & Least Educated Cities in America," July 18, 2022*

- Wichita was selected as one of America's most literate cities. The city ranked #63 out of the 84 largest U.S. cities. Criteria: number of booksellers; library resources; Internet resources; educational attainment; periodical publishing resources; newspaper circulation. *Central Connecticut State University, "America's Most Literate Cities, 2018," February 2019*

Health/Fitness Rankings

- For each of the 100 largest cities in the United States, the American Fitness Index®, compiled in partnership between the American College of Sports Medicine and the Elevance Health Foundation, evaluated community infrastructure and 34 health behaviors including preventive health, levels of chronic disease conditions, food insecurity, sleep quality, pedestrian safety, air quality, and community/environment resources that support physical activity. Wichita ranked #89 for "community fitness." *americanfitnessindex.org, "2022 ACSM American Fitness Index Summary Report," July 12, 2022*

- Wichita was identified as a "2022 Spring Allergy Capital." The area ranked #3 out of 100. Three groups of factors were used to identify the most challenging cities for people with allergies during the spring season: annual spring pollen scores; over the counter allergy medicine use; number of board-certified allergy specialists. *Asthma and Allergy Foundation of America, "Spring Allergy Capitals 2022," March 2, 2022*

- Wichita was identified as a "2022 Fall Allergy Capital." The area ranked #2 out of 100. Three groups of factors were used to identify the most challenging cities for people with allergies during the fall season: annual fall pollen scores; over the counter allergy medicine use; number of board-certified allergy specialists. *Asthma and Allergy Foundation of America, "Fall Allergy Capitals 2022," March 2, 2022*

- Wichita was identified as a "2022 Asthma Capital." The area ranked #23 out of the nation's 100 largest metropolitan areas. Criteria: estimated asthma prevalence; asthma-related mortality; and ER visits due to asthma. Risk factors analyzed but not factored in the rankings: annual pollen score; annual air quality; public smoking laws; access to board-certified asthma specialists; rescue and controller medication use; uninsured rate; poverty rate. *Asthma and Allergy Foundation of America, "Asthma Capitals 2022: The Most Challenging Places to Live With Asthma," September 14, 2022*

Real Estate Rankings

- *WalletHub* compared the most populated U.S. cities to determine which had the best markets for real estate agents. Wichita ranked #95 where demand was high and pay was the best. Criteria: sales per agent; annual median wage for real-estate agents; monthly average starting salary for real estate agents; real estate job density and competition; unemployment rate; home turnover rate; housing-market health index; and other relevant metrics. *www.WalletHub.com, "2021 Best Places to Be a Real Estate Agent," May 12, 2021*

- Wichita was ranked #54 out of 235 metro areas in terms of housing affordability in 2022 by the National Association of Home Builders (#1 = most affordable). Criteria: the share of homes sold in that area affordable to a family earning the local median income, based on standard mortgage underwriting criteria. *National Association of Home Builders®, NAHB-Wells Fargo Housing Opportunity Index, 4th Quarter 2022*

Safety Rankings

- Allstate ranked the 200 largest cities in America in terms of driver safety. Wichita ranked #24. Criteria: internal property damage claims over a two-year period from January 2016 to December 2017. The report helps increase the importance of safety and awareness behind the wheel. *Allstate, "Allstate America's Best Drivers Report, 2019" June 24, 2019*

- Wichita was identified as one of the most dangerous cities in America by NeighborhoodScout. The city ranked #54 out of 100 (#1 = most dangerous). Criteria: number of violent crimes per 1,000 residents. The editors evaluated cities with 25,000 or more residents. *NeighborhoodScout.com, "2023 Top 100 Most Dangerous Cities in the U.S.," January 12, 2023*

- The National Insurance Crime Bureau ranked 390 metro areas in the U.S. in terms of per capita rates of vehicle theft. The Wichita metro area ranked #26 (#1 = highest rate). Criteria: number of vehicle theft offenses per 100,000 inhabitants in 2021. *National Insurance Crime Bureau, "Hot Spots 2021," September 1, 2022*

Seniors/Retirement Rankings

- From its Best Cities for Successful Aging indexes, the Milken Institute generated rankings for metropolitan areas, weighing data in nine categories—health care, wellness, living arrangements, transportation and convenience, financial characteristics, education, employment, community engagement, and overall livability. The Wichita metro area was ranked #41 overall in the large metro area category. *Milken Institute, "Best Cities for Successful Aging, 2017" March 14, 2017*

Women/Minorities Rankings

- Personal finance website *WalletHub* compared more than 180 U.S. cities across two key dimensions, "Hispanic Business-Friendliness" and "Hispanic Purchasing Power," to arrive at the most favorable conditions for Hispanic entrepreneurs. Wichita was ranked #119 out of 182. Criteria includes: share of Hispanic-Owned Businesses; Hispanic entrepreneurship rate to median annual income of Hispanics; Small Business-Friendliness score; cost of living; and number of Hispanics with at least a bachelor's degree. *WalletHub.com, "2019's Best Cities for Hispanic Entrepreneurs," May 1, 2019*

Miscellaneous Rankings

- Wichita was selected as a 2022 Digital Cities Survey winner. The city ranked #9 in the large city (250,000 to 499,999 population) category. The survey examined and assessed how city governments are utilizing technology to continue innovation, engage with residents, and persevere through the challenges of the pandemic. Survey questions focused on ten initiatives: cybersecurity; citizen experience; disaster recovery; business intelligence; IT personnel; data governance; business automation; IT governance; infrastructure modernization; and broadband connectivity. *Center for Digital Government, "2022 Digital Cities Survey," November 10, 2022*

- The financial planning site SmartAsset has compiled its annual study on the best places for Halloween in the U.S. for 2022. 146 cities were compared to determine that Wichita ranked #29 out of 35 for still being able to enjoy the festivities despite COVID-19. Metrics included: safety, family-friendliness, percentage of children in the population, concentration of candy and costume shops, weather and COVID infection rates. *www.smartasset.com, "2022 Edition-Best Places to Celebrate Halloween," October 19, 2022*

- *WalletHub* compared the 150 most populated U.S. cities to determine their operating efficiency. A "Quality of Services" score was constructed for each city and then divided by the total budget per capita to reveal which were managed the best. Wichita ranked #50. Criteria: financial stability; economy; education; safety; health; infrastructure and pollution. *www.WalletHub.com, "2022's Best- & Worst-Run Cities in America," June 21, 2022*

Business Environment

DEMOGRAPHICS

Population Growth

Area	1990 Census	2000 Census	2010 Census	2020 Census	Population Growth (%) 1990-2020	Population Growth (%) 2010-2020
City	313,693	344,284	382,368	397,532	26.7	4.0
MSA[1]	511,111	571,166	623,061	647,610	26.7	3.9
U.S.	248,709,873	281,421,906	308,745,538	331,449,281	33.3	7.4

Note: (1) Figures cover the Wichita, KS Metropolitan Statistical Area
Source: U.S. Census Bureau, 1990 Census, 2000 Census, 2010 Census, 2020 Census

Race

Area	White Alone[2] (%)	Black Alone[2] (%)	Asian Alone[2] (%)	AIAN[3] Alone[2] (%)	NHOPI[4] Alone[2] (%)	Other Race Alone[2] (%)	Two or More Races (%)
City	63.4	11.0	5.1	1.3	0.1	7.4	11.7
MSA[1]	71.7	7.5	3.7	1.2	0.1	5.4	10.4
U.S.	61.6	12.4	6.0	1.1	0.2	8.4	10.2

Note: (1) Figures cover the Wichita, KS Metropolitan Statistical Area; (2) Alone is defined as not being in combination with one or more other races; (3) American Indian and Alaska Native; (4) Native Hawaiian and Other Pacific Islander
Source: U.S. Census Bureau, 2020 Census

Hispanic or Latino Origin

Area	Total (%)	Mexican (%)	Puerto Rican (%)	Cuban (%)	Other (%)
City	17.6	15.1	0.5	0.1	1.9
MSA[1]	13.6	11.5	0.4	0.1	1.6
U.S.	18.4	11.2	1.8	0.7	4.7

Note: Persons of Hispanic or Latino origin can be of any race; (1) Figures cover the Wichita, KS Metropolitan Statistical Area
Source: U.S. Census Bureau, 2017-2021 American Community Survey 5-Year Estimates

Age

Area	Under Age 5	Age 5–19	Age 20–34	Age 35–44	Age 45–54	Age 55–64	Age 65–74	Age 75–84	Age 85+	Median Age
City	6.3	21.0	21.7	12.4	11.1	12.4	9.1	4.1	1.8	35.7
MSA[1]	6.2	21.6	19.9	12.5	11.2	12.9	9.5	4.4	1.9	36.7
U.S.	5.6	19.2	20.2	12.7	12.4	13.1	10.0	4.9	1.9	38.8

Note: (1) Figures cover the Wichita, KS Metropolitan Statistical Area
Source: U.S. Census Bureau, 2020 Census

Disability by Age

Area	All Ages	Under 18 Years Old	18 to 64 Years Old	65 Years and Over
City	14.8	5.7	13.7	35.4
MSA[1]	14.5	5.8	12.9	35.7
U.S.	12.6	4.4	10.3	33.4

Note: Figures show percent of the civilian noninstitutionalized population that reported having a disability. Disability status is determined from six types of difficulty: vision, hearing, cognitive, ambulatory, self-care, and independent living. For children under 5 years old, hearing and vision difficulty are used to determine disability status. For children between the ages of 5 and 14, disability status is determined from hearing, vision, cognitive, ambulatory, and self-care difficulties. For people aged 15 years and older, they are considered to have a disability if they have difficulty with any one of the six difficulty types; Note: (1) Figures cover the Wichita, KS Metropolitan Statistical Area
Source: U.S. Census Bureau, 2017-2021 American Community Survey 5-Year Estimates

Ancestry

Area	German	Irish	English	American	Italian	Polish	French[2]	Scottish	Dutch
City	19.0	9.6	9.7	4.8	1.6	0.9	2.0	1.6	1.2
MSA[1]	21.4	9.9	10.0	5.7	1.7	0.9	2.0	1.8	1.3
U.S.	12.8	9.6	8.1	5.7	5.0	2.7	2.2	1.6	1.1

Note: Figures are the percentage of the total population reporting a particular ancestry. The nine most commonly reported ancestries in the U.S. are shown. Figures include multiple ancestries (e.g. if a person reported being Irish and Italian, they were included in both columns); (1) Figures cover the Wichita, KS Metropolitan Statistical Area; (2) Excludes Basque
Source: U.S. Census Bureau, 2017-2021 American Community Survey 5-Year Estimates

Foreign-born Population

Area	Percent of Population Born in								
	Any Foreign Country	Asia	Mexico	Europe	Caribbean	Central America[2]	South America	Africa	Canada
City	9.9	3.7	4.2	0.5	0.1	0.5	0.3	0.5	0.1
MSA[1]	7.3	2.7	2.9	0.5	0.1	0.4	0.2	0.4	0.1
U.S.	13.6	4.2	3.3	1.5	1.4	1.1	1.1	0.8	0.2

Note: (1) Figures cover the Wichita, KS Metropolitan Statistical Area; (2) Excludes Mexico.
Source: U.S. Census Bureau, 2017-2021 American Community Survey 5-Year Estimates

Household Size

Area	Persons in Household (%)							Average Household Size
	One	Two	Three	Four	Five	Six	Seven or More	
City	32.9	32.5	13.0	11.2	6.2	2.5	1.7	2.50
MSA[1]	29.8	33.5	13.9	11.8	6.7	2.6	1.8	2.60
U.S.	28.1	33.8	15.5	12.9	6.0	2.3	1.4	2.60

Note: (1) Figures cover the Wichita, KS Metropolitan Statistical Area
Source: U.S. Census Bureau, 2017-2021 American Community Survey 5-Year Estimates

Household Relationships

Area	House-holder	Opposite-sex Spouse	Same-sex Spouse	Opposite-sex Unmarried Partner	Same-sex Unmarried Partner	Child[2]	Grand-child	Other Relatives	Non-relatives
City	40.0	16.4	0.2	2.7	0.2	29.1	2.2	3.7	3.1
MSA[1]	39.0	18.2	0.1	2.4	0.1	29.8	2.1	3.2	2.6
U.S.	38.3	17.5	0.2	2.5	0.2	28.3	2.4	4.8	3.4

Note: Figures are percent of the total population; (1) Figures cover the Wichita, KS Metropolitan Statistical Area; (2) Includes biological, adopted, and stepchildren of the householder
Source: U.S. Census Bureau, 2020 Census

Gender

Area	Males	Females	Males per 100 Females
City	196,575	200,957	97.8
MSA[1]	321,349	326,261	98.5
U.S.	162,685,811	168,763,470	96.4

Note: (1) Figures cover the Wichita, KS Metropolitan Statistical Area
Source: U.S. Census Bureau, 2020 Census

Marital Status

Area	Never Married	Now Married[2]	Separated	Widowed	Divorced
City	33.7	45.6	1.9	5.0	13.8
MSA[1]	30.3	50.2	1.4	5.4	12.7
U.S.	33.8	48.0	1.8	5.6	10.8

Note: Figures are percentages and cover the population 15 years of age and older; (1) Figures cover the Wichita, KS Metropolitan Statistical Area; (2) Excludes separated
Source: U.S. Census Bureau, 2017-2021 American Community Survey 5-Year Estimates

Religious Groups by Family

Area	Catholic	Baptist	Methodist	LDS[2]	Pentecostal	Lutheran	Islam	Adventist	Other
MSA[1]	12.7	23.5	4.5	1.5	1.4	1.3	0.1	1.1	15.0
U.S.	18.7	7.3	3.0	2.0	1.8	1.7	1.3	1.3	11.6

Note: Figures are the number of adherents as a percentage of the total population and cover the eight largest religious groups in the U.S; (1) Figures cover the Wichita, KS Metropolitan Statistical Area; (2) Church of Jesus Christ of Latter-day Saints
Sources: 2020 U.S. Religion Census, Association of Statisticians of American Religious Bodies; The Association of Religion Data Archives (ARDA)

Religious Groups by Tradition

Area	Catholic	Evangelical Protestant	Mainline Protestant	Black Protestant	Islam	Judaism	Hinduism	Orthodox	Buddhism
MSA[1]	12.7	19.4	23.2	2.6	0.1	<0.1	0.1	0.2	0.5
U.S.	18.7	16.5	5.2	2.3	1.3	0.6	0.4	0.4	0.3

Note: Figures are the number of adherents as a percentage of the total population; (1) Figures cover the Wichita, KS Metropolitan Statistical Area
Sources: 2020 U.S. Religion Census, Association of Statisticians of American Religious Bodies; The Association of Religion Data Archives (ARDA)

ECONOMY

Gross Metropolitan Product

Area	2020	2021	2022	2023	Rank[2]
MSA[1]	36.7	40.2	44.0	47.1	83

Note: Figures are in billions of dollars; (1) Figures cover the Wichita, KS Metropolitan Statistical Area; (2) Rank is based on 2021 data and ranges from 1 to 381
Source: U.S. Conference of Mayors, U.S. Metro Economies: U.S. Metros Compared to Global and State Economies, June 2022

Economic Growth

Area	2018-20 (%)	2021 (%)	2022 (%)	2023 (%)	Rank[2]
MSA[1]	-2.0	4.3	2.9	4.1	286
U.S.	-0.6	5.7	3.1	2.9	—

Note: Figures are real gross metropolitan product (GMP) growth rates and represent average annual percent change; (1) Figures cover the Wichita, KS Metropolitan Statistical Area; (2) Rank is based on 2020 2-year average annual percent change and ranges from 1 to 381
Source: U.S. Conference of Mayors, U.S. Metro Economies: U.S. Metros Compared to Global and State Economies, June 2022

Metropolitan Area Exports

Area	2016	2017	2018	2019	2020	2021	Rank[2]
MSA[1]	3,054.9	3,299.2	3,817.0	3,494.7	2,882.1	3,615.3	74

Note: Figures are in millions of dollars; (1) Figures cover the Wichita, KS Metropolitan Statistical Area; (2) Rank is based on 2021 data and ranges from 1 to 388
Source: U.S. Department of Commerce, International Trade Administration, Office of Trade and Economic Analysis, Industry and Analysis, Exports by Metropolitan Area, data extracted March 16, 2023

Building Permits

Area	Single-Family			Multi-Family			Total		
	2021	2022	Pct. Chg.	2021	2022	Pct. Chg.	2021	2022	Pct. Chg.
City	760	787	3.6	368	276	-25.0	1,128	1,063	-5.8
MSA[1]	1,618	1,586	-2.0	766	1,264	65.0	2,384	2,850	19.5
U.S.	1,115,400	975,600	-12.5	621,600	689,500	10.9	1,737,000	1,665,100	-4.1

Note: (1) Figures cover the Wichita, KS Metropolitan Statistical Area; Figures represent new, privately-owned housing units authorized (unadjusted data); All permit data are based on estimates with imputation
Source: U.S. Census Bureau, Manufacturing, Mining, and Construction Statistics, Building Permits, 2021, 2022

Bankruptcy Filings

Area	Business Filings			Nonbusiness Filings		
	2021	2022	% Chg.	2021	2022	% Chg.
Sedgwick County	20	14	-30.0	760	658	-13.4
U.S.	14,347	13,481	-6.0	399,269	374,240	-6.3

Note: Business filings include Chapter 7, Chapter 9, Chapter 11, Chapter 12, Chapter 13, Chapter 15, and Section 304; Nonbusiness filings include Chapter 7, Chapter 11, and Chapter 13
Source: Administrative Office of the U.S. Courts, Business and Nonbusiness Bankruptcy, County Cases Commenced by Chapter of the Bankruptcy Code, During the 12-Month Period Ending December 31, 2021 and Business and Nonbusiness Bankruptcy, County Cases Commenced by Chapter of the Bankruptcy Code, During the 12-Month Period Ending December 31, 2022

Housing Vacancy Rates

Area	Gross Vacancy Rate[2] (%)			Year-Round Vacancy Rate[3] (%)			Rental Vacancy Rate[4] (%)			Homeowner Vacancy Rate[5] (%)		
	2020	2021	2022	2020	2021	2022	2020	2021	2022	2020	2021	2022
MSA[1]	n/a	n/a	n/a	n/a	n/a	n/a	n/a	n/a	n/a	n/a	n/a	n/a
U.S.	10.6	10.8	10.5	8.2	8.4	8.2	6.3	6.1	5.8	1.0	0.9	0.8

Note: (1) Figures cover the Wichita, KS Metropolitan Statistical Area; (2) The percentage of the total housing inventory that is vacant; (3) The percentage of the housing inventory (excluding seasonal units) that is year-round vacant; (4) The percentage of rental inventory that is vacant for rent; (5) The percentage of homeowner inventory that is vacant for sale; n/a not available
Source: U.S. Census Bureau, Housing Vacancies and Homeownership Annual Statistics: 2020, 2021, 2022

INCOME

Income

Area	Per Capita ($)	Median Household ($)	Average Household ($)
City	31,558	56,374	77,762
MSA[1]	32,124	61,445	81,209
U.S.	37,638	69,021	97,196

Note: (1) Figures cover the Wichita, KS Metropolitan Statistical Area
Source: U.S. Census Bureau, 2017-2021 American Community Survey 5-Year Estimates

Household Income Distribution

Area	Percent of Households Earning							
	Under $15,000	$15,000 -$24,999	$25,000 -$34,999	$35,000 -$49,999	$50,000 -$74,999	$75,000 -$99,999	$100,000 -$149,999	$150,000 and up
City	10.8	9.3	10.3	14.0	18.9	12.8	13.6	10.3
MSA[1]	9.2	8.6	9.1	13.4	19.6	13.4	15.5	11.0
U.S.	9.4	7.8	8.2	11.4	16.8	12.8	16.3	17.3

Note: (1) Figures cover the Wichita, KS Metropolitan Statistical Area
Source: U.S. Census Bureau, 2017-2021 American Community Survey 5-Year Estimates

Poverty Rate

Area	All Ages	Under 18 Years Old	18 to 64 Years Old	65 Years and Over
City	15.2	20.8	14.5	8.5
MSA[1]	12.6	16.7	12.0	7.6
U.S.	12.6	17.0	11.8	9.6

Note: Figures are percentage of people whose income during the past 12 months was below the poverty level;
(1) Figures cover the Wichita, KS Metropolitan Statistical Area
Source: U.S. Census Bureau, 2017-2021 American Community Survey 5-Year Estimates

EMPLOYMENT

Labor Force and Employment

Area	Civilian Labor Force			Workers Employed		
	Dec. 2021	Dec. 2022	% Chg.	Dec. 2021	Dec. 2022	% Chg.
City	190,708	192,293	0.8	184,998	186,223	0.7
MSA[1]	317,498	320,744	1.0	309,104	311,289	0.7
U.S.	161,696,000	164,224,000	1.6	155,732,000	158,872,000	2.0

Note: Data is not seasonally adjusted and covers workers 16 years of age and older; (1) Figures cover the Wichita, KS Metropolitan Statistical Area
Source: Bureau of Labor Statistics, Local Area Unemployment Statistics

Unemployment Rate

Area	2022											
	Jan.	Feb.	Mar.	Apr.	May	Jun.	Jul.	Aug.	Sep.	Oct.	Nov.	Dec.
City	3.7	3.6	3.6	2.8	3.2	3.5	4.1	3.8	3.1	3.2	3.1	3.2
MSA[1]	3.4	3.3	3.3	2.6	3.0	3.2	3.8	3.5	2.9	3.0	2.9	2.9
U.S.	4.4	4.1	3.8	3.3	3.4	3.8	3.8	3.8	3.3	3.4	3.4	3.3

Note: Data is not seasonally adjusted and covers workers 16 years of age and older; (1) Figures cover the Wichita, KS Metropolitan Statistical Area
Source: Bureau of Labor Statistics, Local Area Unemployment Statistics

Average Wages

Occupation	$/Hr.	Occupation	$/Hr.
Accountants and Auditors	36.01	Maintenance and Repair Workers	19.99
Automotive Mechanics	21.40	Marketing Managers	63.35
Bookkeepers	19.47	Network and Computer Systems Admin.	40.60
Carpenters	23.61	Nurses, Licensed Practical	23.92
Cashiers	12.22	Nurses, Registered	33.08
Computer Programmers	33.61	Nursing Assistants	15.61
Computer Systems Analysts	40.07	Office Clerks, General	14.16
Computer User Support Specialists	27.25	Physical Therapists	43.47
Construction Laborers	18.13	Physicians	100.53
Cooks, Restaurant	13.72	Plumbers, Pipefitters and Steamfitters	27.23
Customer Service Representatives	17.53	Police and Sheriff's Patrol Officers	25.83
Dentists	76.11	Postal Service Mail Carriers	26.65
Electricians	28.57	Real Estate Sales Agents	27.02
Engineers, Electrical	43.15	Retail Salespersons	15.34
Fast Food and Counter Workers	11.16	Sales Representatives, Technical/Scientific	51.87
Financial Managers	70.00	Secretaries, Exc. Legal/Medical/Executive	17.74
First-Line Supervisors of Office Workers	28.52	Security Guards	15.50
General and Operations Managers	46.78	Surgeons	n/a
Hairdressers/Cosmetologists	16.45	Teacher Assistants, Exc. Postsecondary*	14.41
Home Health and Personal Care Aides	12.10	Teachers, Secondary School, Exc. Sp. Ed.*	28.44
Janitors and Cleaners	14.45	Telemarketers	n/a
Landscaping/Groundskeeping Workers	15.78	Truck Drivers, Heavy/Tractor-Trailer	23.66
Lawyers	54.07	Truck Drivers, Light/Delivery Services	20.17
Maids and Housekeeping Cleaners	12.87	Waiters and Waitresses	14.48

Note: Wage data covers the Wichita, KS Metropolitan Statistical Area; (*) Hourly wages were calculated from annual wage data based on a 40 hour work week; n/a not available.
Source: Bureau of Labor Statistics, Metro Area Occupational Employment & Wage Estimates, May 2022

Employment by Industry

Sector	MSA[1]		U.S.
	Number of Employees	Percent of Total	Percent of Total
Construction, Mining, and Logging	17,800	5.7	5.4
Private Education and Health Services	46,100	14.9	16.1
Financial Activities	12,200	3.9	5.9
Government	44,300	14.3	14.5
Information	3,700	1.2	2.0
Leisure and Hospitality	33,600	10.8	10.3
Manufacturing	52,100	16.8	8.4
Other Services	11,500	3.7	3.7
Professional and Business Services	35,100	11.3	14.7
Retail Trade	31,900	10.3	10.2
Transportation, Warehousing, and Utilities	12,500	4.0	4.9
Wholesale Trade	9,500	3.1	3.9

Note: Figures are non-farm employment as of December 2022. Figures are not seasonally adjusted and include workers 16 years of age and older; (1) Figures cover the Wichita, KS Metropolitan Statistical Area
Source: Bureau of Labor Statistics, Current Employment Statistics, Employment, Hours, and Earnings

Employment by Occupation

Occupation Classification	City (%)	MSA[1] (%)	U.S. (%)
Management, Business, Science, and Arts	35.1	37.2	40.3
Natural Resources, Construction, and Maintenance	9.8	10.2	8.7
Production, Transportation, and Material Moving	15.7	15.3	13.1
Sales and Office	21.4	20.6	20.9
Service	18.0	16.6	17.0

Note: Figures cover employed civilians 16 years of age and older; (1) Figures cover the Wichita, KS Metropolitan Statistical Area
Source: U.S. Census Bureau, 2017-2021 American Community Survey 5-Year Estimates

Occupations with Greatest Projected Employment Growth: 2022 – 2024

Occupation[1]	2022 Employment	2024 Projected Employment	Numeric Employment Change	Percent Employment Change
Home Health and Personal Care Aides	23,840	24,950	1,110	4.7
Software Developers	11,820	12,750	930	7.9
Cooks, Restaurant	11,840	12,630	790	6.7
General and Operations Managers	23,870	24,530	660	2.8
Heavy and Tractor-Trailer Truck Drivers	24,940	25,530	590	2.4
Market Research Analysts and Marketing Specialists	9,210	9,750	540	5.9
Accountants and Auditors	14,020	14,530	510	3.6
Laborers and Freight, Stock, and Material Movers, Hand	24,120	24,620	500	2.1
Registered Nurses	30,550	31,000	450	1.5
Sales Representatives of Services, Except Advertising, Insurance, Financial Services, and Travel	12,330	12,770	440	3.6

Note: Projections cover Kansas; (1) Sorted by numeric employment change
Source: www.projectionscentral.com, State Occupational Projections, 2022–2024 Short-Term Projections

Fastest-Growing Occupations: 2022 – 2024

Occupation[1]	2022 Employment	2024 Projected Employment	Numeric Employment Change	Percent Employment Change
Ushers, Lobby Attendants, and Ticket Takers	820	940	120	14.6
Cargo and Freight Agents	680	760	80	11.8
Avionics Technicians	700	780	80	11.4
Aircraft Mechanics and Service Technicians	1,750	1,940	190	10.9
Aerospace Engineers	1,980	2,190	210	10.6
Aerospace Engineering and Operations Technicians	660	730	70	10.6
Hotel, Motel, and Resort Desk Clerks	2,530	2,780	250	9.9
Information Security Analysts (SOC 2018)	1,030	1,130	100	9.7
Lodging Managers	540	590	50	9.3
Computer Numerically Controlled Tool Programmers	670	730	60	9.0

Note: Projections cover Kansas; (1) Sorted by percent employment change and excludes occupations with numeric employment change less than 50
Source: www.projectionscentral.com, State Occupational Projections, 2022–2024 Short-Term Projections

CITY FINANCES

City Government Finances

Component	2020 ($000)	2020 ($ per capita)
Total Revenues	579,387	1,486
Total Expenditures	401,856	1,031
Debt Outstanding	2,854,083	7,319
Cash and Securities[1]	2,082,981	5,342

Note: (1) Cash and security holdings of a government at the close of its fiscal year, including those of its dependent agencies, utilities, and liquor stores.
Source: U.S. Census Bureau, State & Local Government Finances 2020

City Government Revenue by Source

Source	2020 ($000)	2020 ($ per capita)	2020 (%)
General Revenue			
From Federal Government	7,837	20	1.4
From State Government	27,031	69	4.7
From Local Governments	0	0	0.0
Taxes			
Property	134,668	345	23.2
Sales and Gross Receipts	69,458	178	12.0
Personal Income	0	0	0.0
Corporate Income	0	0	0.0
Motor Vehicle License	0	0	0.0
Other Taxes	47,511	122	8.2
Current Charges	142,367	365	24.6
Liquor Store	0	0	0.0
Utility	91,202	234	15.7

Source: U.S. Census Bureau, State & Local Government Finances 2020

City Government Expenditures by Function

Function	2020 ($000)	2020 ($ per capita)	2020 (%)
General Direct Expenditures			
Air Transportation	24,379	62	6.1
Corrections	0	0	0.0
Education	0	0	0.0
Employment Security Administration	0	0	0.0
Financial Administration	5,644	14	1.4
Fire Protection	48,044	123	12.0
General Public Buildings	4,752	12	1.2
Governmental Administration, Other	6,803	17	1.7
Health	1,854	4	0.5
Highways	34,020	87	8.5
Hospitals	0	0	0.0
Housing and Community Development	166	< 1	< 0.1
Interest on General Debt	17,181	44	4.3
Judicial and Legal	9,694	24	2.4
Libraries	9,466	24	2.4
Parking	1,637	4	0.4
Parks and Recreation	32,091	82	8.0
Police Protection	90,771	232	22.6
Public Welfare	319	< 1	< 0.1
Sewerage	43,409	111	10.8
Solid Waste Management	1,921	4	0.5
Veterans' Services	0	0	0.0
Liquor Store	0	0	0.0
Utility	58,054	148	14.4

Source: U.S. Census Bureau, State & Local Government Finances 2020

TAXES

State Corporate Income Tax Rates

State	Tax Rate (%)	Income Brackets ($)	Num. of Brackets	Financial Institution Tax Rate (%)[a]	Federal Income Tax Ded.
Kansas	4.0 (i)	Flat rate	1	2.25 (j)	No

Note: Tax rates as of January 1, 2023; (a) Rates listed are the corporate income tax rate applied to financial institutions or excise taxes based on income. Some states have other taxes based upon the value of deposits or shares; (i) In addition to the flat 4% corporate income tax, Kansas levies a 3.0% surtax on taxable income over $50,000. Banks pay a privilege tax of 2.25% of net income, plus a surtax of 2.125% (2.25% for savings and loans, trust companies, and federally chartered savings banks) on net income in excess of $25,000; (j) The state franchise tax on financial institutions is either (1) the sum of 1% of the Maine net income of the financial institution for the taxable year, plus 8¢ per $1,000 of the institution's Maine assets as of the end of its taxable year, or (2)39¢ per $1,000 of the institution's Maine assets as of the end of its taxable year.
Source: Federation of Tax Administrators, State Corporate Income Tax Rates, January 1, 2023

State Individual Income Tax Rates

State	Tax Rate (%)	Income Brackets ($)	Personal Exemptions ($)			Standard Ded. ($)	
			Single	Married	Depend.	Single	Married
Kansas	3.1 - 5.7	15,000 - 30,000 (b)	2,250	4,500	2,250	3,500	8,000

Note: Tax rates as of January 1, 2023; Local- and county-level taxes are not included; Federal income tax is not deductible on state income tax returns; (b) For joint returns, taxes are twice the tax on half the couple's income.
Source: Federation of Tax Administrators, State Individual Income Tax Rates, January 1, 2023

Various State Sales and Excise Tax Rates

State	State Sales Tax (%)	Gasoline[1] ($/gal,)	Cigarette[2] ($/pack)	Spirits[3] ($/gal.)	Wine[4] ($/gal.)	Beer[5] ($/gal.)	Recreational Marijuana (%)
Kansas	6.5	0.2403	1.29	2.50	0.30	0.18	Not legal

Note: All tax rates as of January 1, 2023; (1) The American Petroleum Institute has developed a methodology for determining the average tax rate on a gallon of fuel. Rates may include any of the following: excise taxes, environmental fees, storage tank fees, other fees or taxes, general sales tax, and local taxes; (2) The federal excise tax of $1.0066 per pack and local taxes are not included; (3) Rates are those applicable to off-premise sales of 40% alcohol by volume (a.b.v.) distilled spirits in 750ml containers. Local excise taxes are excluded; (4) Rates are those applicable to off-premise sales of 11% a.b.v. non-carbonated wine in 750ml containers; (5) Rates are those applicable to off-premise sales of 4.7% a.b.v. beer in 12 ounce containers.
Source: Tax Foundation, 2023 Facts & Figures: How Does Your State Compare?

State Business Tax Climate Index Rankings

State	Overall Rank	Corporate Tax Rank	Individual Income Tax Rank	Sales Tax Rank	Property Tax Rank	Unemployment Insurance Tax Rank
Kansas	25	21	22	25	17	15

Note: The index is a measure of how each state's tax laws affect economic performance. The lower the rank, the more favorable a state's tax system is for business. States without a given tax are given a ranking of 1. The scores/rankings for the District of Columbia do not affect other states. The 2023 index represents the tax climate as of July 1, 2022.
Source: Tax Foundation, State Business Tax Climate Index 2023

TRANSPORTATION

Means of Transportation to Work

Area	Car/Truck/Van		Public Transportation			Bicycle	Walked	Other Means	Worked at Home
	Drove Alone	Car-pooled	Bus	Subway	Railroad				
City	81.4	9.8	0.6	0.0	0.0	0.4	1.2	1.4	5.1
MSA[1]	82.2	8.7	0.4	0.0	0.0	0.3	1.5	1.3	5.6
U.S.	73.2	8.6	2.0	1.6	0.5	0.5	2.5	1.5	9.7

Note: Figures are percentages and cover workers 16 years of age and older; (1) Figures cover the Wichita, KS Metropolitan Statistical Area
Source: U.S. Census Bureau, 2017-2021 American Community Survey 5-Year Estimates

Travel Time to Work

Area	Less Than 10 Minutes	10 to 19 Minutes	20 to 29 Minutes	30 to 44 Minutes	45 to 59 Minutes	60 to 89 Minutes	90 Minutes or More
City	14.3	44.9	26.7	9.9	1.6	1.4	1.2
MSA[1]	16.1	37.2	26.2	15.1	2.7	1.5	1.3
U.S.	12.4	28.5	21.0	20.9	8.2	6.2	2.9

Note: Note: Figures are percentages and include workers 16 years old and over; (1) Figures cover the Wichita, KS Metropolitan Statistical Area
Source: U.S. Census Bureau, 2017-2021 American Community Survey 5-Year Estimates

Key Congestion Measures

Measure	1990	2000	2010	2015	2020
Annual Hours of Delay, Total (000)	3,702	5,994	8,917	10,498	7,423
Annual Hours of Delay, Per Auto Commuter	22	28	29	34	25
Annual Congestion Cost, Per Auto Commuter ($)	321	393	464	505	377

Note: Covers the Wichita KS urban area
Source: Texas A&M Transportation Institute, 2021 Urban Mobility Report

Freeway Travel Time Index

Measure	1985	1990	1995	2000	2005	2010	2015	2020
Urban Area Index[1]	1.08	1.11	1.13	1.14	1.16	1.14	1.14	1.09
Urban Area Rank[1,2]	40	42	47	62	57	71	79	40

Note: Freeway Travel Time Index—the ratio of travel time in the peak period to the travel time at free-flow conditions. For example, a value of 1.30 indicates a 20-minute free-flow trip takes 26 minutes in the peak (20 minutes x 1.30 = 26 minutes); (1) Covers the Wichita KS urban area; (2) Rank is based on 101 larger urban areas (#1 = highest travel time index)
Source: Texas A&M Transportation Institute, 2021 Urban Mobility Report

Public Transportation

Agency Name / Mode of Transportation	Vehicles Operated in Maximum Service[1]	Annual Unlinked Passenger Trips[2] (in thous.)	Annual Passenger Miles[3] (in thous.)
Wichita Transit (WT)			
Bus (directly operated)	43	768.9	4,135.2
Demand Response (directly operated)	22	73.7	711.2

Note: (1) Number of revenue vehicles operated by the given mode and type of service to meet the annual maximum service requirement. This is the revenue vehicle count during the peak season of the year; on the week and day that maximum service is provided. Vehicles operated in maximum service (VOMS) exclude atypical days and one-time special events; (2) Number of passengers who boarded public transportation vehicles. Passengers are counted each time they board a vehicle no matter how many vehicles they use to travel from their origin to their destination. (3) Sum of the distances ridden by all passengers during the entire fiscal year.
Source: Federal Transit Administration, National Transit Database, 2021

Air Transportation

Airport Name and Code / Type of Service	Passenger Airlines[1]	Passenger Enplanements	Freight Carriers[2]	Freight (lbs)
Wichita Mid-Continent Airport (ICT)				
Domestic service (U.S. carriers - 2022)	24	762,301	12	28,316,346
International service (U.S. carriers - 2021)	1	109	0	0

Note: (1) Includes all U.S.-based major, minor and commuter airlines that carried at least one passenger during the year; (2) Includes all U.S.-based airlines and freight carriers that transported at least one pound of freight during the year.
Source: Bureau of Transportation Statistics, The Intermodal Transportation Database, Air Carriers: T-100 Domestic Market (U.S. Carriers), 2022; Bureau of Transportation Statistics, The Intermodal Transportation Database, Air Carriers: T-100 International Market (U.S. Carriers), 2021

BUSINESSES

Major Business Headquarters

Company Name	Industry	Rankings	
		Fortune[1]	Forbes[2]
Koch Industries	Multicompany	-	2

Note: (1) Companies that produce a 10-K are ranked 1 to 500 based on 2021 revenue; (2) All private companies with at least $2 billion in annual revenue through the end of their most current fiscal year are ranked 1 to 246; companies listed are headquartered in the city; dashes indicate no ranking
Source: Fortune, "Fortune 500," 2022; Forbes, "America's Largest Private Companies," 2022

Living Environment

COST OF LIVING

Cost of Living Index

Composite Index	Groceries	Housing	Utilities	Trans-portation	Health Care	Misc. Goods/ Services
91.0	100.6	71.2	98.0	97.0	92.8	99.5

Note: The Cost of Living Index measures regional differences in the cost of consumer goods and services, excluding taxes and non-consumer expenditures, for professional and managerial households in the top income quintile. It is based on more than 50,000 prices covering almost 60 different items for which prices are collected three times a year by chambers of commerce, economic development organizations or university applied economic centers in each participating urban area. The numbers shown should be read as a percentage above or below the national average of 100. For example, a value of 115.4 in the groceries column indicates that grocery prices are 15.4% higher than the national average. Small differences in the index numbers should not be interpreted as significant; Figures cover the Wichita KS urban area.
Source: The Council for Community and Economic Research, Cost of Living Index, 2022

Grocery Prices

Area[1]	T-Bone Steak ($/pound)	Frying Chicken ($/pound)	Whole Milk ($/half gal.)	Eggs ($/dozen)	Orange Juice ($/64 oz.)	Coffee ($/11.5 oz.)
City[2]	13.71	1.63	2.05	1.95	4.15	4.95
Avg.	13.81	1.59	2.43	2.25	3.85	4.95
Min.	10.17	0.90	1.51	1.30	2.90	3.46
Max.	19.35	3.30	4.32	4.32	5.31	8.59

*Note: (1) Values for the local area are compared with the average, minimum and maximum values for all 286 areas in the Cost of Living Index; (2) Figures cover the Wichita KS urban area; **T-Bone Steak** (price per pound); **Frying Chicken** (price per pound, whole fryer); **Whole Milk** (half gallon carton); **Eggs** (price per dozen, Grade A, large); **Orange Juice** (64 oz. Tropicana or Florida Natural); **Coffee** (11.5 oz. can, vacuum-packed, Maxwell House, Hills Bros, or Folgers).*
Source: The Council for Community and Economic Research, Cost of Living Index, 2022

Housing and Utility Costs

Area[1]	New Home Price ($)	Apartment Rent ($/month)	All Electric ($/month)	Part Electric ($/month)	Other Energy ($/month)	Telephone ($/month)
City[2]	314,516	978	-	93.16	71.97	198.70
Avg.	450,913	1,371	176.41	99.93	76.96	190.22
Min.	229,283	546	100.84	31.56	27.15	174.27
Max.	2,434,977	4,569	356.86	249.59	272.24	208.31

*Note: (1) Values for the local area are compared with the average, minimum and maximum values for all 286 areas in the Cost of Living Index; (2) Figures cover the Wichita KS urban area; **New Home Price** (2,400 sf living area, 8,000 sf lot, in urban area with full utilities); **Apartment Rent** (950 sf 2 bedroom/1.5 or 2 bath, unfurnished, excluding all utilities except water); **All Electric** (average monthly cost for an all-electric home); **Part Electric** (average monthly cost for a part-electric home); **Other Energy** (average monthly cost for natural gas, fuel oil, coal, wood, and any other forms of energy except electricity); **Telephone** (price includes the base monthly rate plus taxes and fees for three lines of mobile phone service).*
Source: The Council for Community and Economic Research, Cost of Living Index, 2022

Health Care, Transportation, and Other Costs

Area[1]	Doctor ($/visit)	Dentist ($/visit)	Optometrist ($/visit)	Gasoline ($/gallon)	Beauty Salon ($/visit)	Men's Shirt ($)
City[2]	106.36	92.39	162.06	3.75	41.30	51.01
Avg.	124.91	107.77	117.66	3.86	43.31	34.21
Min.	36.61	58.25	51.79	2.90	22.18	13.05
Max.	250.21	162.58	371.96	5.54	85.61	63.54

*Note: (1) Values for the local area are compared with the average, minimum and maximum values for all 286 areas in the Cost of Living Index; (2) Figures cover the Wichita KS urban area; **Doctor** (general practitioners routine exam of an established patient); **Dentist** (adult teeth cleaning and periodic oral examination); **Optometrist** (full vision eye exam for established adult patient); **Gasoline** (one gallon regular unleaded, national brand, including all taxes, cash price at self-service pump if available); **Beauty Salon** (woman's shampoo, trim, and blow-dry); **Men's Shirt** (cotton/polyester dress shirt, pinpoint weave, long sleeves).*
Source: The Council for Community and Economic Research, Cost of Living Index, 2022

HOUSING

Homeownership Rate

Area	2015 (%)	2016 (%)	2017 (%)	2018 (%)	2019 (%)	2020 (%)	2021 (%)	2022 (%)
MSA[1]	n/a	n/a	n/a	n/a	n/a	n/a	n/a	n/a
U.S.	63.7	63.4	63.9	64.4	64.6	66.6	65.5	65.8

Note: (1) Figures cover the Wichita, KS Metropolitan Statistical Area; n/a not available
Source: U.S. Census Bureau, Housing Vacancies and Homeownership Annual Statistics: 2015-2022

House Price Index (HPI)

Area	National Ranking[2]	Quarterly Change (%)	One-Year Change (%)	Five-Year Change (%)	Since 1991Q1 (%)
MSA[1]	151	-1.84	10.63	47.99	197.78
U.S.[3]	–	0.34	8.41	58.44	289.08

Note: The HPI is a weighted repeat sales index. It measures average price changes in repeat sales or refinancings on the same properties. This information is obtained by reviewing repeat mortgage transactions on single-family properties whose mortgages have been purchased or securitized by Fannie Mae or Freddie Mac since January 1975; (1) Figures cover the Wichita, KS Metropolitan Statistical Area; (2) Rankings are based on annual percentage change for all metro areas containing at least 15,000 transactions over the last 10 years and ranges from 1 to 257; (3) figures based on a weighted average of Census Division estimates using a seasonally adjusted, purchase-only index; all figures are for the period ending December 31, 2022
Source: Federal Housing Finance Agency, Change in FHFA Metropolitan Area House Price Indexes, 2022Q4

Median Single-Family Home Prices

Area	2020	2021	2022p	Percent Change 2021 to 2022
MSA[1]	175.0	191.2	209.4	9.5
U.S. Average	300.2	357.1	392.6	9.9

Note: Figures are median sales prices of existing single-family homes in thousands of dollars; (p) preliminary; (1) Figures cover the Wichita, KS Metropolitan Statistical Area
Source: National Association of Realtors, Median Sales Price of Existing Single-Family Homes for Metropolitan Areas, 4th Quarter 2022

Qualifying Income Based on Median Sales Price of Existing Single-Family Homes

Area	With 5% Down ($)	With 10% Down ($)	With 20% Down ($)
MSA[1]	62,859	59,550	52,933
U.S. Average	112,234	106,237	94,513

Note: Figures are preliminary; Qualifying income is based on a mortgage rate of 6.77%. Monthly principal and interest payment is limited to 25% of income; (1) Figures cover the Wichita, KS Metropolitan Statistical Area
Source: National Association of Realtors, Qualifying Income Based on Median Sales Price of Existing Single-Family Homes for Metropolitan Areas, 4th Quarter 2022

Home Value

Area	Under $100,000	$100,000 -$199,999	$200,000 -$299,999	$300,000 -$399,999	$400,000 -$499,999	$500,000 -$999,999	$1,000,000 or more	Median ($)
City	31.2	39.6	17.3	6.7	2.2	2.7	0.3	145,300
MSA[1]	28.6	40.0	18.4	7.4	2.6	2.6	0.4	151,900
U.S.	16.2	24.2	20.1	13.6	8.3	13.6	4.1	244,900

Note: Figures are percentages except for median and cover owner-occupied housing units; (1) Figures cover the Wichita, KS Metropolitan Statistical Area
Source: U.S. Census Bureau, 2017-2021 American Community Survey 5-Year Estimates

Year Housing Structure Built

Area	2020 or Later	2010 -2019	2000 -2009	1990 -1999	1980 -1989	1970 -1979	1960 -1969	1950 -1959	1940 -1949	Before 1940	Median Year
City	0.1	5.9	9.9	12.2	12.3	13.1	9.8	18.6	8.0	10.2	1973
MSA[1]	0.1	6.7	11.8	13.5	12.4	13.1	8.8	16.4	6.5	10.7	1976
U.S.	0.2	7.3	13.6	13.6	13.2	14.8	10.3	10.0	4.7	12.2	1979

Note: Figures are percentages except for Median Year; Note: (1) Figures cover the Wichita, KS Metropolitan Statistical Area
Source: U.S. Census Bureau, 2017-2021 American Community Survey 5-Year Estimates

Gross Monthly Rent

Area	Under $500	$500 -$999	$1,000 -$1,499	$1,500 -$1,999	$2,000 -$2,499	$2,500 -$2,999	$3,000 and up	Median ($)
City	8.1	60.2	26.3	3.9	0.8	0.2	0.5	856
MSA[1]	8.8	57.8	26.3	5.4	0.9	0.4	0.5	868
U.S.	8.1	30.5	30.8	16.8	7.3	3.1	3.5	1,163

Note: Figures are percentages except for median; Gross rent is the contract rent plus the estimated average monthly cost of utilities (electricity, gas, and water and sewer) and fuels (oil, coal, kerosene, wood, etc.) if these are paid by the renter (or paid for the renter by someone else); (1) Figures cover the Wichita, KS Metropolitan Statistical Area
Source: U.S. Census Bureau, 2017-2021 American Community Survey 5-Year Estimates

HEALTH

Health Risk Factors

Category	MSA[1] (%)	U.S. (%)
Adults aged 18–64 who have any kind of health care coverage	86.1	90.9
Adults who reported being in good or better health	84.4	85.2
Adults who have been told they have high blood cholesterol	39.7	35.7
Adults who have been told they have high blood pressure	35.3	32.4
Adults who are current smokers	18.0	14.4
Adults who currently use e-cigarettes	7.8	6.7
Adults who currently use chewing tobacco, snuff, or snus	3.8	3.5
Adults who are heavy drinkers[2]	5.6	6.3
Adults who are binge drinkers[3]	15.7	15.4
Adults who are overweight (BMI 25.0 - 29.9)	32.2	34.4
Adults who are obese (BMI 30.0 - 99.8)	39.6	33.9
Adults who participated in any physical activities in the past month	74.8	76.3

Note: (1) Figures cover the Wichita, KS Metropolitan Statistical Area; (2) Heavy drinkers are classified as adult men having more than 14 drinks per week and adult women having more than 7 drinks per week; (3) Binge drinkers are classified as males having five or more drinks on one occasion or females having four or more drinks on one occasion
Source: Centers for Disease Control and Prevention, Behaviorial Risk Factor Surveillance System, SMART: Selected Metropolitan Area Risk Trends, 2021

Acute and Chronic Health Conditions

Category	MSA[1] (%)	U.S. (%)
Adults who have ever been told they had a heart attack	5.3	4.0
Adults who have ever been told they have angina or coronary heart disease	4.5	3.8
Adults who have ever been told they had a stroke	3.2	3.0
Adults who have ever been told they have asthma	16.0	14.9
Adults who have ever been told they have arthritis	27.8	25.8
Adults who have ever been told they have diabetes[2]	12.0	10.9
Adults who have ever been told they had skin cancer	5.7	6.6
Adults who have ever been told they had any other types of cancer	7.5	7.5
Adults who have ever been told they have COPD	6.4	6.1
Adults who have ever been told they have kidney disease	2.9	3.0
Adults who have ever been told they have a form of depression	20.8	20.5

Note: (1) Figures cover the Wichita, KS Metropolitan Statistical Area; (2) Figures do not include pregnancy-related, borderline, or pre-diabetes
Source: Centers for Disease Control and Prevention, Behaviorial Risk Factor Surveillance System, SMART: Selected Metropolitan Area Risk Trends, 2021

Health Screening and Vaccination Rates

Category	MSA[1] (%)	U.S. (%)
Adults who have ever been tested for HIV	31.9	34.9
Adults who have had their blood cholesterol checked within the last five years	81.7	85.2
Adults aged 65+ who have had flu shot within the past year	70.4	68.6
Adults aged 65+ who have ever had a pneumonia vaccination	73.4	71.0

Note: (1) Figures cover the Wichita, KS Metropolitan Statistical Area.
Source: Centers for Disease Control and Prevention, Behaviorial Risk Factor Surveillance System, SMART: Selected Metropolitan Area Risk Trends, 2021

Disability Status

Category	MSA[1] (%)	U.S. (%)
Adults who reported being deaf	7.0	7.2
Are you blind or have serious difficulty seeing, even when wearing glasses?	5.4	4.8
Are you limited in any way in any of your usual activities due to arthritis?	12.0	11.1
Do you have difficulty doing errands alone?	7.5	7.0
Do you have difficulty dressing or bathing?	3.2	3.6
Do you have serious difficulty concentrating/remembering/making decisions?	13.6	12.1
Do you have serious difficulty walking or climbing stairs?	13.8	12.8

Note: (1) Figures cover the Wichita, KS Metropolitan Statistical Area.
Source: Centers for Disease Control and Prevention, Behaviorial Risk Factor Surveillance System, SMART: Selected Metropolitan Area Risk Trends, 2021

Mortality Rates for the Top 10 Causes of Death in the U.S.

ICD-10[a] Sub-Chapter	ICD-10[a] Code	Crude Mortality Rate[1] per 100,000 population	
		County[2]	U.S.
Malignant neoplasms	C00-C97	180.0	182.6
Ischaemic heart diseases	I20-I25	126.4	113.1
Other forms of heart disease	I30-I51	54.9	64.4
Other degenerative diseases of the nervous system	G30-G31	63.0	51.0
Cerebrovascular diseases	I60-I69	44.4	47.8
Other external causes of accidental injury	W00-X59	53.0	46.4
Chronic lower respiratory diseases	J40-J47	57.7	45.7
Organic, including symptomatic, mental disorders	F01-F09	44.4	35.9
Hypertensive diseases	I10-I15	31.2	35.0
Diabetes mellitus	E10-E14	29.7	29.6

Note: (a) ICD-10 = International Classification of Diseases 10th Revision; (1) Crude mortality rates are a three-year average covering 2019-2021; (2) Figures cover Sedgwick County.
Source: Centers for Disease Control and Prevention, National Center for Health Statistics. National Vital Statistics System, Mortality 2018-2021 on CDC WONDER Online Database

Mortality Rates for Selected Causes of Death

ICD-10[a] Sub-Chapter	ICD-10[a] Code	Crude Mortality Rate[1] per 100,000 population	
		County[2]	U.S.
Assault	X85-Y09	9.7	7.0
Diseases of the liver	K70-K76	24.7	19.8
Human immunodeficiency virus (HIV) disease	B20-B24	1.3	1.5
Influenza and pneumonia	J09-J18	13.3	14.7
Intentional self-harm	X60-X84	20.1	14.3
Malnutrition	E40-E46	3.5	4.3
Obesity and other hyperalimentation	E65-E68	2.4	3.0
Renal failure	N17-N19	19.2	15.7
Transport accidents	V01-V99	14.5	13.6
Viral hepatitis	B15-B19	1.5	1.2

Note: (a) ICD-10 = International Classification of Diseases 10th Revision; (1) Crude mortality rates are a three-year average covering 2019-2021; (2) Figures cover Sedgwick County; Data are suppressed when the data meet the criteria for confidentiality constraints; Crude mortality rates are flagged as unreliable when the rate would be calculated with a numerator of 20 or less.
Source: Centers for Disease Control and Prevention, National Center for Health Statistics. National Vital Statistics System, Mortality 2018-2021 on CDC WONDER Online Database

Health Insurance Coverage

Area	With Health Insurance	With Private Health Insurance	With Public Health Insurance	Without Health Insurance	Population Under Age 19 Without Health Insurance
City	87.8	65.8	33.6	12.2	5.8
MSA[1]	89.8	70.6	31.6	10.2	5.2
U.S.	91.2	67.8	35.4	8.8	5.3

Note: Figures are percentages that cover the civilian noninstitutionalized population; (1) Figures cover the Wichita, KS Metropolitan Statistical Area
Source: U.S. Census Bureau, 2017-2021 American Community Survey 5-Year Estimates

Number of Medical Professionals

Area	MDs[3]	DOs[3,4]	Dentists	Podiatrists	Chiropractors	Optometrists
County[1] (number)	1,326	178	362	10	227	152
County[1] (rate[2])	252.9	34.0	69.1	1.9	43.3	29.0
U.S. (rate[2])	289.3	23.5	72.5	6.2	28.7	17.4

Note: Data as of 2021 unless noted; (1) Data covers Sedgwick County; (2) Rate per 100,000 population; (3) Data as of 2020 and includes all active, non-federal physicians; (4) Doctor of Osteopathic Medicine
Source: U.S. Department of Health and Human Services, Health Resources and Services Administration, Bureau of Health Professions, Area Resource File (ARF) 2021-2022

EDUCATION

Public School District Statistics

District Name	Schls	Pupils	Pupil/ Teacher Ratio	Minority Pupils[1] (%)	LEP/ELL[2] (%)	IEP[3] (%)
Wichita	88	46,657	10.2	69.6	17.3	15.8

Note: Table includes school districts with 2,000 or more students; (1) Percentage of students that are not non-Hispanic white; (2) Percentage of students that are Limited English Proficient or English Language Learners (2018-19); (3) Percentage of students that have an Individualized Education Program (2019-20).
Source: U.S. Department of Education, National Center for Education Statistics, Common Core of Data, Local Education Agency (School District) Universe Survey: School Year 2021-2022

Highest Level of Education

Area	Less than H.S.	H.S. Diploma	Some College, No Deg.	Associate Degree	Bachelor's Degree	Master's Degree	Prof. School Degree	Doctorate Degree
City	11.8	26.2	23.4	8.1	19.3	8.4	1.7	1.1
MSA[1]	9.8	26.5	23.8	8.8	20.1	8.5	1.5	1.0
U.S.	11.1	26.5	20.0	8.7	20.6	9.3	2.2	1.5

Note: Figures cover persons age 25 and over; (1) Figures cover the Wichita, KS Metropolitan Statistical Area
Source: U.S. Census Bureau, 2017-2021 American Community Survey 5-Year Estimates

Educational Attainment by Race

Area	High School Graduate or Higher (%)					Bachelor's Degree or Higher (%)				
	Total	White	Black	Asian	Hisp.[2]	Total	White	Black	Asian	Hisp.[2]
City	88.2	91.6	87.8	73.7	63.9	30.5	33.6	17.7	35.1	13.3
MSA[1]	90.2	92.8	87.6	74.2	66.9	31.1	33.0	19.0	35.5	16.4
U.S.	88.9	91.4	87.2	87.6	71.2	33.7	35.5	23.3	55.6	18.4

Note: Figures shown cover persons 25 years old and over; (1) Figures cover the Wichita, KS Metropolitan Statistical Area; (2) People of Hispanic origin can be of any race
Source: U.S. Census Bureau, 2017-2021 American Community Survey 5-Year Estimates

School Enrollment by Grade and Control

Area	Preschool (%)		Kindergarten (%)		Grades 1 - 4 (%)		Grades 5 - 8 (%)		Grades 9 - 12 (%)	
	Public	Private	Public	Private	Public	Private	Public	Private	Public	Private
City	62.8	37.2	84.4	15.6	86.4	13.6	83.7	16.3	84.5	15.5
MSA[1]	64.9	35.1	83.7	16.3	86.6	13.4	86.2	13.8	87.4	12.6
U.S.	58.8	41.2	86.3	13.7	88.3	11.7	88.6	11.4	89.4	10.6

Note: Figures shown cover persons 3 years old and over; (1) Figures cover the Wichita, KS Metropolitan Statistical Area
Source: U.S. Census Bureau, 2017-2021 American Community Survey 5-Year Estimates

Higher Education

Four-Year Colleges			Two-Year Colleges			Medical Schools[1]	Law Schools[2]	Voc/ Tech[3]
Public	Private Non-profit	Private For-profit	Public	Private Non-profit	Private For-profit			
1	4	0	2	0	2	1	0	4

Note: Figures cover institutions located within the Wichita, KS Metropolitan Statistical Area and include main campuses only; (1) includes schools accredited by the Liaison Committee on Medical Education and the American Osteopathic Association's Commission on Osteopathic College Accreditation; (2) includes ABA-accredited schools, schools with provisional ABA accreditation, and state accredited schools; (3) includes all schools with programs that are less than 2 years.
Source: National Center for Education Statistics, Integrated Postsecondary Education System (IPEDS), 2021-22; Wikipedia, List of Medical Schools in the United States, accessed April 10, 2023; Wikipedia, List of Law Schools in the United States, accessed April 10, 2023

EMPLOYERS

Major Employers

Company Name	Industry
AGCO Corporation	Agricultural equipment
Beechcraft Corp.	Aircraft
Boeing Defense, Space & Security	Aircraft modification
Bombardier Learjet	Aircraft
Cargill Meat Solutions	Meat products
Cessna Aircraft Company	Manufacturing
City of Wichita	Municipal government
Cox Communications	Broadband communications & entertainment company
Dillons Food Stores	Grocery stores
Koch Industries	Manufacturing, energy & commodities
McConnell Air Force Base	U.S. military
Robert J. Dole VA Medical Center	Veterans medical center
Sedgwick County	County government
Spirit AeroSystems	Manufacturing
State of Kansas	State government
U.S. Postal Service	Federal mail delivery service
Unified School District 260 Derby	Public elementary & secondary schools
Unified School District 261 Haysville	Public elementary & secondary schools
Unified School District 265 Goddard	Public elementary & secondary schools
Unified School District 490 El Dorado	Public elementary & secondary schools
United States Government	Federal government
USD 259 Wichita	Education
Via Christi Health	Healthcare
Wesley Medical Center	Health care
Wichita State University	Public higher education

Note: Companies shown are located within the Wichita, KS Metropolitan Statistical Area.
Source: Hoovers.com; Wikipedia

PUBLIC SAFETY

Crime Rate

Area	Total Crime	Violent Crime Rate				Property Crime Rate		
		Murder	Rape[3]	Robbery	Aggrav. Assault	Burglary	Larceny -Theft	Motor Vehicle Theft
City	6,462.8	9.0	94.1	118.2	919.8	686.3	4,044.6	590.9
Suburbs[1]	n/a	1.6	42.3	14.5	156.8	271.8	n/a	129.8
Metro[2]	n/a	6.1	74.0	77.9	623.3	525.2	n/a	411.7
U.S.	2,510.4	5.1	42.6	81.8	250.4	340.5	1,569.2	220.8

Note: Figures are crimes per 100,000 population; (1) All areas within the metro area that are located outside the city limits; (2) Figures cover the Wichita, KS Metropolitan Statistical Area; (3) All figures shown were reported using the revised Uniform Crime Reporting (UCR) definition of rape; Due to the transition to the National Incident-Based Reporting System (NIBRS), limited city and metro area data was released for 2021.
Source: FBI Uniform Crime Reports, 2019 (data for 2020 was not available)

Hate Crimes

Area	Number of Quarters Reported	Number of Incidents per Bias Motivation					
		Race/Ethnicity/ Ancestry	Religion	Sexual Orientation	Disability	Gender	Gender Identity
City	4	6	1	0	0	0	0
U.S.	4	5,227	1,244	1,110	130	75	266

Note: Due to the transition to the National Incident-Based Reporting System (NIBRS), limited crime data was released for 2021.
Source: Federal Bureau of Investigation, Hate Crime Statistics 2020

Identity Theft Consumer Reports

Area	Reports	Reports per 100,000 Population	Rank[2]
MSA[1]	1,340	209	156
U.S.	1,108,609	339	-

Note: (1) Figures cover the Wichita, KS Metropolitan Statistical Area; (2) Rank ranges from 1 to 391 where 1 indicates greatest number of identity theft reports per 100,000 population
Source: Federal Trade Commission, Consumer Sentinel Network Data Book 2022

Fraud and Other Consumer Reports

Area	Reports	Reports per 100,000 Population	Rank[2]
MSA[1]	5,160	807	214
U.S.	4,064,520	1,245	-

Note: (1) Figures cover the Wichita, KS Metropolitan Statistical Area; (2) Rank ranges from 1 to 391 where 1 indicates greatest number of fraud and other consumer reports per 100,000 population
Source: Federal Trade Commission, Consumer Sentinel Network Data Book 2022

POLITICS

2020 Presidential Election Results

Area	Biden	Trump	Jorgensen	Hawkins	Other
Sedgwick County	42.6	54.4	2.4	0.0	0.5
U.S.	51.3	46.8	1.2	0.3	0.5

Note: Results are percentages and may not add to 100% due to rounding
Source: Dave Leip's Atlas of U.S. Presidential Elections

SPORTS

Professional Sports Teams

Team Name	League	Year Established

No teams are located in the metro area
Source: Wikipedia, Major Professional Sports Teams of the United States and Canada, April 12, 2023

CLIMATE

Average and Extreme Temperatures

Temperature	Jan	Feb	Mar	Apr	May	Jun	Jul	Aug	Sep	Oct	Nov	Dec	Yr.
Extreme High (°F)	75	84	89	96	100	110	113	110	107	95	87	83	113
Average High (°F)	40	46	56	68	77	87	92	91	82	71	55	44	68
Average Temp. (°F)	30	35	45	57	66	76	81	80	71	59	45	34	57
Average Low (°F)	20	24	33	45	55	65	70	68	59	47	34	24	45
Extreme Low (°F)	-12	-21	-3	15	31	43	51	47	31	21	1	-16	-21

Note: Figures cover the years 1948-1990
Source: National Climatic Data Center, International Station Meteorological Climate Summary, 9/96

Average Precipitation/Snowfall/Humidity

Precip./Humidity	Jan	Feb	Mar	Apr	May	Jun	Jul	Aug	Sep	Oct	Nov	Dec	Yr.
Avg. Precip. (in.)	0.9	1.0	2.3	2.3	3.9	4.3	3.7	3.0	3.2	2.3	1.4	1.0	29.3
Avg. Snowfall (in.)	5	4	3	Tr	0	0	0	0	0	Tr	2	3	17
Avg. Rel. Hum. 6am (%)	78	79	77	78	83	83	78	79	82	80	79	79	80
Avg. Rel. Hum. 3pm (%)	56	54	48	46	51	47	42	43	47	47	51	56	49

Note: Figures cover the years 1948-1990; Tr = Trace amounts (<0.05 in. of rain; <0.5 in. of snow)
Source: National Climatic Data Center, International Station Meteorological Climate Summary, 9/96

Weather Conditions

Temperature			Daytime Sky			Precipitation		
10°F & below	32°F & below	90°F & above	Clear	Partly cloudy	Cloudy	0.01 inch or more precip.	0.1 inch or more snow/ice	Thunder-storms
13	110	63	117	132	116	87	13	54

Note: Figures are average number of days per year and cover the years 1948-1990
Source: National Climatic Data Center, International Station Meteorological Climate Summary, 9/96

HAZARDOUS WASTE

Superfund Sites

The Wichita, KS metro area is home to two sites on the EPA's Superfund National Priorities List: **57th and North Broadway Streets Site** (final); **Pester Refinery Co.** (final). There are a total of 1,165 Superfund sites with a status of proposed or final on the list in the U.S. *U.S. Environmental Protection Agency, National Priorities List, April 12, 2023*

AIR QUALITY

Air Quality Trends: Ozone

	1990	1995	2000	2005	2010	2015	2018	2019	2020	2021
MSA[1]	0.077	0.069	0.080	0.074	0.075	0.064	0.064	0.062	0.059	0.061
U.S.	0.087	0.089	0.081	0.080	0.072	0.067	0.069	0.065	0.065	0.067

Note: (1) Data covers the Wichita, KS Metropolitan Statistical Area. The values shown are the composite ozone concentration averages among trend sites based on the highest fourth daily maximum 8-hour concentration in parts per million. These trends are based on sites having an adequate record of monitoring data during the trend period. Data from exceptional events are included.
Source: U.S. Environmental Protection Agency, Air Quality Monitoring Information, "Air Quality Trends by City, 1990-2021"

Air Quality Index

Area	Percent of Days when Air Quality was...[2]					AQI Statistics[2]	
	Good	Moderate	Unhealthy for Sensitive Groups	Unhealthy	Very Unhealthy	Maximum	Median
MSA[1]	59.7	38.9	1.4	0.0	0.0	147	47

Note: (1) Data covers the Wichita, KS Metropolitan Statistical Area; (2) Based on 365 days with AQI data in 2021. Air Quality Index (AQI) is an index for reporting daily air quality. EPA calculates the AQI for five major air pollutants regulated by the Clean Air Act: ground-level ozone, particle pollution (aka particulate matter), carbon monoxide, sulfur dioxide, and nitrogen dioxide. The AQI runs from 0 to 500. The higher the AQI value, the greater the level of air pollution and the greater the health concern. There are six AQI categories: "Good" AQI is between 0 and 50. Air quality is considered satisfactory; "Moderate" AQI is between 51 and 100. Air quality is acceptable; "Unhealthy for Sensitive Groups" When AQI values are between 101 and 150, members of sensitive groups may experience health effects; "Unhealthy" When AQI values are between 151 and 200 everyone may begin to experience health effects; "Very Unhealthy" AQI values between 201 and 300 trigger a health alert; "Hazardous" AQI values over 300 trigger warnings of emergency conditions (not shown).
Source: U.S. Environmental Protection Agency, Air Quality Index Report, 2021

Air Quality Index Pollutants

Area	Percent of Days when AQI Pollutant was...[2]					
	Carbon Monoxide	Nitrogen Dioxide	Ozone	Sulfur Dioxide	Particulate Matter 2.5	Particulate Matter 10
MSA[1]	0.0	0.5	42.7	(3)	48.8	7.9

Note: (1) Data covers the Wichita, KS Metropolitan Statistical Area; (2) Based on 365 days with AQI data in 2021. The Air Quality Index (AQI) is an index for reporting daily air quality. EPA calculates the AQI for five major air pollutants regulated by the Clean Air Act: ground-level ozone, particle pollution (also known as particulate matter), carbon monoxide, sulfur dioxide, and nitrogen dioxide. The AQI runs from 0 to 500. The higher the AQI value, the greater the level of air pollution and the greater the health concern; (3) Sulfur dioxide is no longer included in this table (as of December 8, 2021) because SO$_2$ concentrations tend to be very localized and not necessarily representative of broad geographical areas like counties and CBSAs.
Source: U.S. Environmental Protection Agency, Air Quality Index Report, 2021

Maximum Air Pollutant Concentrations: Particulate Matter, Ozone, CO and Lead

	Particulate Matter 10 (ug/m^3)	Particulate Matter 2.5 Wtd AM (ug/m^3)	Particulate Matter 2.5 24-Hr (ug/m^3)	Ozone (ppm)	Carbon Monoxide (ppm)	Lead (ug/m^3)
MSA[1] Level	89	11.3	31	0.067	n/a	n/a
NAAQS[2]	150	15	35	0.075	9	0.15
Met NAAQS[2]	Yes	Yes	Yes	Yes	n/a	n/a

Note: (1) Data covers the Wichita, KS Metropolitan Statistical Area; Data from exceptional events are included; (2) National Ambient Air Quality Standards; ppm = parts per million; ug/m^3 = micrograms per cubic meter; n/a not available.
Concentrations: Particulate Matter 10 (coarse particulate)—highest second maximum 24-hour concentration; Particulate Matter 2.5 Wtd AM (fine particulate)—highest weighted annual mean concentration; Particulate Matter 2.5 24-Hour (fine particulate)—highest 98th percentile 24-hour concentration; Ozone—highest fourth daily maximum 8-hour concentration; Carbon Monoxide—highest second maximum non-overlapping 8-hour concentration; Lead—maximum running 3-month average
Source: U.S. Environmental Protection Agency, Air Quality Monitoring Information, "Air Quality Statistics by City, 2021"

Maximum Air Pollutant Concentrations: Nitrogen Dioxide and Sulfur Dioxide

	Nitrogen Dioxide AM (ppb)	Nitrogen Dioxide 1-Hr (ppb)	Sulfur Dioxide AM (ppb)	Sulfur Dioxide 1-Hr (ppb)	Sulfur Dioxide 24-Hr (ppb)
MSA[1] Level	7	39	n/a	4	n/a
NAAQS[2]	53	100	30	75	140
Met NAAQS[2]	Yes	Yes	n/a	Yes	n/a

Note: (1) Data covers the Wichita, KS Metropolitan Statistical Area; Data from exceptional events are included; (2) National Ambient Air Quality Standards; ppm = parts per million; ug/m^3 = micrograms per cubic meter; n/a not available.
Concentrations: Nitrogen Dioxide AM—highest arithmetic mean concentration; Nitrogen Dioxide 1-Hr—highest 98th percentile 1-hour daily maximum concentration; Sulfur Dioxide AM—highest annual mean concentration; Sulfur Dioxide 1-Hr—highest 99th percentile 1-hour daily maximum concentration; Sulfur Dioxide 24-Hr—highest second maximum 24-hour concentration
Source: U.S. Environmental Protection Agency, Air Quality Monitoring Information, "Air Quality Statistics by City, 2021"

Appendixes

Appendix A: Comparative Statistics

Table of Contents

Population Growth: City

Area	1990 Census	2000 Census	2010 Census	2020 Census	Population Growth (%)	
					1990-2020	2010-2020
Albuquerque, NM	388,375	448,607	545,852	564,559	45.4	3.4
Allentown, PA	105,066	106,632	118,032	125,845	19.8	6.6
Anchorage, AK	226,338	260,283	291,826	291,247	28.7	-0.2
Ann Arbor, MI	111,018	114,024	113,934	123,851	11.6	8.7
Athens, GA	86,561	100,266	115,452	127,315	47.1	10.3
Atlanta, GA	394,092	416,474	420,003	498,715	26.5	18.7
Austin, TX	499,053	656,562	790,390	961,855	92.7	21.7
Baltimore, MD	736,014	651,154	620,961	585,708	-20.4	-5.7
Boise City, ID	144,317	185,787	205,671	235,684	63.3	14.6
Boston, MA	574,283	589,141	617,594	675,647	17.7	9.4
Boulder, CO	87,737	94,673	97,385	108,250	23.4	11.2
Brownsville, TX	114,025	139,722	175,023	186,738	63.8	6.7
Cape Coral, FL	75,507	102,286	154,305	194,016	157.0	25.7
Cedar Rapids, IA	110,829	120,758	126,326	137,710	24.3	9.0
Charleston, SC	96,102	96,650	120,083	150,227	56.3	25.1
Charlotte, NC	428,283	540,828	731,424	874,579	104.2	19.6
Chicago, IL	2,783,726	2,896,016	2,695,598	2,746,388	-1.3	1.9
Cincinnati, OH	363,974	331,285	296,943	309,317	-15.0	4.2
Clarksville, TN	78,569	103,455	132,929	166,722	112.2	25.4
Cleveland, OH	505,333	478,403	396,815	372,624	-26.3	-6.1
College Station, TX	53,318	67,890	93,857	120,511	126.0	28.4
Colorado Springs, CO	283,798	360,890	416,427	478,961	68.8	15.0
Columbia, MO	71,069	84,531	108,500	126,254	77.6	16.4
Columbia, SC	115,475	116,278	129,272	136,632	18.3	5.7
Columbus, OH	648,656	711,470	787,033	905,748	39.6	15.1
Dallas, TX	1,006,971	1,188,580	1,197,816	1,304,379	29.5	8.9
Davenport, IA	95,705	98,359	99,685	101,724	6.3	2.0
Denver, CO	467,153	554,636	600,158	715,522	53.2	19.2
Des Moines, IA	193,569	198,682	203,433	214,133	10.6	5.3
Durham, NC	151,737	187,035	228,330	283,506	86.8	24.2
Edison, NJ	88,680	97,687	99,967	107,588	21.3	7.6
El Paso, TX	515,541	563,662	649,121	678,815	31.7	4.6
Fargo, ND	74,372	90,599	105,549	125,990	69.4	19.4
Fort Collins, CO	89,555	118,652	143,986	169,810	89.6	17.9
Fort Wayne, IN	205,671	205,727	253,691	263,886	28.3	4.0
Fort Worth, TX	448,311	534,694	741,206	918,915	105.0	24.0
Grand Rapids, MI	189,145	197,800	188,040	198,917	5.2	5.8
Greeley, CO	60,887	76,930	92,889	108,795	78.7	17.1
Green Bay, WI	96,466	102,313	104,057	107,395	11.3	3.2
Greensboro, NC	193,389	223,891	269,666	299,035	54.6	10.9
Honolulu, HI	376,465	371,657	337,256	350,964	-6.8	4.1
Houston, TX	1,697,610	1,953,631	2,099,451	2,304,580	35.8	9.8
Huntsville, AL	161,842	158,216	180,105	215,006	32.8	19.4
Indianapolis, IN	730,993	781,870	820,445	887,642	21.4	8.2
Jacksonville, FL	635,221	735,617	821,784	949,611	49.5	15.6
Kansas City, MO	434,967	441,545	459,787	508,090	16.8	10.5
Lafayette, LA	104,735	110,257	120,623	121,374	15.9	0.6
Las Cruces, NM	63,267	74,267	97,618	111,385	76.1	14.1
Las Vegas, NV	261,374	478,434	583,756	641,903	145.6	10.0
Lexington, KY	225,366	260,512	295,803	322,570	43.1	9.0
Lincoln, NE	193,629	225,581	258,379	291,082	50.3	12.7
Little Rock, AR	177,519	183,133	193,524	202,591	14.1	4.7
Los Angeles, CA	3,487,671	3,694,820	3,792,621	3,898,747	11.8	2.8
Louisville, KY	269,160	256,231	597,337	386,884	43.7	-35.2
Madison, WI	193,451	208,054	233,209	269,840	39.5	15.7

Table continued on following page.

Area	1990 Census	2000 Census	2010 Census	2020 Census	Population Growth (%)	
					1990-2020	2010-2020
Manchester, NH	99,567	107,006	109,565	115,644	16.1	5.5
Miami, FL	358,843	362,470	399,457	442,241	23.2	10.7
Midland, TX	89,358	94,996	111,147	132,524	48.3	19.2
Milwaukee, WI	628,095	596,974	594,833	577,222	-8.1	-3.0
Minneapolis, MN	368,383	382,618	382,578	429,954	16.7	12.4
Nashville, TN	488,364	545,524	601,222	689,447	41.2	14.7
New Haven, CT	130,474	123,626	129,779	134,023	2.7	3.3
New Orleans, LA	496,938	484,674	343,829	383,997	-22.7	11.7
New York, NY	7,322,552	8,008,278	8,175,133	8,804,190	20.2	7.7
Oklahoma City, OK	445,065	506,132	579,999	681,054	53.0	17.4
Omaha, NE	371,972	390,007	408,958	486,051	30.7	18.9
Orlando, FL	161,172	185,951	238,300	307,573	90.8	29.1
Philadelphia, PA	1,585,577	1,517,550	1,526,006	1,603,797	1.1	5.1
Phoenix, AZ	989,873	1,321,045	1,445,632	1,608,139	62.5	11.2
Pittsburgh, PA	369,785	334,563	305,704	302,971	-18.1	-0.9
Portland, OR	485,833	529,121	583,776	652,503	34.3	11.8
Providence, RI	160,734	173,618	178,042	190,934	18.8	7.2
Provo, UT	87,148	105,166	112,488	115,162	32.1	2.4
Raleigh, NC	226,841	276,093	403,892	467,665	106.2	15.8
Reno, NV	139,950	180,480	225,221	264,165	88.8	17.3
Richmond, VA	202,783	197,790	204,214	226,610	11.7	11.0
Rochester, MN	74,151	85,806	106,769	121,395	63.7	13.7
Sacramento, CA	368,923	407,018	466,488	524,943	42.3	12.5
St. Louis, MO	396,685	348,189	319,294	301,578	-24.0	-5.5
Salem, OR	112,046	136,924	154,637	175,535	56.7	13.5
Salt Lake City, UT	159,796	181,743	186,440	199,723	25.0	7.1
San Antonio, TX	997,258	1,144,646	1,327,407	1,434,625	43.9	8.1
San Diego, CA	1,111,048	1,223,400	1,307,402	1,386,932	24.8	6.1
San Francisco, CA	723,959	776,733	805,235	873,965	20.7	8.5
San Jose, CA	784,324	894,943	945,942	1,013,240	29.2	7.1
Santa Rosa, CA	123,297	147,595	167,815	178,127	44.5	6.1
Savannah, GA	138,038	131,510	136,286	147,780	7.1	8.4
Seattle, WA	516,262	563,374	608,660	737,015	42.8	21.1
Sioux Falls, SD	102,262	123,975	153,888	192,517	88.3	25.1
Springfield, IL	108,997	111,454	116,250	114,394	5.0	-1.6
Tampa, FL	279,960	303,447	335,709	384,959	37.5	14.7
Tucson, AZ	417,942	486,699	520,116	542,629	29.8	4.3
Tulsa, OK	367,241	393,049	391,906	413,066	12.5	5.4
Tuscaloosa, AL	81,075	77,906	90,468	99,600	22.8	10.1
Virginia Beach, VA	393,069	425,257	437,994	459,470	16.9	4.9
Washington, DC	606,900	572,059	601,723	689,545	13.6	14.6
Wichita, KS	313,693	344,284	382,368	397,532	26.7	4.0
Wilmington, NC	64,609	75,838	106,476	115,451	78.7	8.4
Winston-Salem, NC	168,139	185,776	229,617	249,545	48.4	8.7
Worcester, MA	169,759	172,648	181,045	206,518	21.7	14.1
U.S.	248,709,873	281,421,906	308,745,538	331,449,281	33.3	7.4

Source: U.S. Census Bureau, 1990 Census,, 2000 Census,, 2010 Census,, 2020 Census

Population Growth: Metro Area

Area	1990 Census	2000 Census	2010 Census	2020 Census	Population Growth (%)	
					1990-2020	2010-2020
Albuquerque, NM	599,416	729,649	887,077	916,528	52.9	3.3
Allentown, PA	686,666	740,395	821,173	861,889	25.5	5.0
Anchorage, AK	266,021	319,605	380,821	398,328	49.7	4.6
Ann Arbor, MI	282,937	322,895	344,791	372,258	31.6	8.0
Athens, GA	136,025	166,079	192,541	215,415	58.4	11.9
Atlanta, GA	3,069,411	4,247,981	5,268,860	6,089,815	98.4	15.6
Austin, TX	846,217	1,249,763	1,716,289	2,283,371	169.8	33.0
Baltimore, MD	2,382,172	2,552,994	2,710,489	2,844,510	19.4	4.9
Boise City, ID	319,596	464,840	616,561	764,718	139.3	24.0
Boston, MA	4,133,895	4,391,344	4,552,402	4,941,632	19.5	8.5
Boulder, CO	208,898	269,758	294,567	330,758	58.3	12.3
Brownsville, TX	260,120	335,227	406,220	421,017	61.9	3.6
Cape Coral, FL	335,113	440,888	618,754	760,822	127.0	23.0
Cedar Rapids, IA	210,640	237,230	257,940	276,520	31.3	7.2
Charleston, SC	506,875	549,033	664,607	799,636	57.8	20.3
Charlotte, NC	1,024,331	1,330,448	1,758,038	2,660,329	159.7	51.3
Chicago, IL	8,182,076	9,098,316	9,461,105	9,618,502	17.6	1.7
Cincinnati, OH	1,844,917	2,009,632	2,130,151	2,256,884	22.3	5.9
Clarksville, TN	189,277	232,000	273,949	320,535	69.3	17.0
Cleveland, OH	2,102,219	2,148,143	2,077,240	2,088,251	-0.7	0.5
College Station, TX	150,998	184,885	228,660	268,248	77.7	17.3
Colorado Springs, CO	409,482	537,484	645,613	755,105	84.4	17.0
Columbia, MO	122,010	145,666	172,786	210,864	72.8	22.0
Columbia, SC	548,325	647,158	767,598	829,470	51.3	8.1
Columbus, OH	1,405,176	1,612,694	1,836,536	2,138,926	52.2	16.5
Dallas, TX	3,989,294	5,161,544	6,371,773	7,637,387	91.4	19.9
Davenport, IA	368,151	376,019	379,690	384,324	4.4	1.2
Denver, CO	1,666,935	2,179,296	2,543,482	2,963,821	77.8	16.5
Des Moines, IA	416,346	481,394	569,633	709,466	70.4	24.5
Durham, NC	344,646	426,493	504,357	649,903	88.6	28.9
Edison, NJ	16,845,992	18,323,002	18,897,109	20,140,470	19.6	6.6
El Paso, TX	591,610	679,622	800,647	868,859	46.9	8.5
Fargo, ND	153,296	174,367	208,777	249,843	63.0	19.7
Fort Collins, CO	186,136	251,494	299,630	359,066	92.9	19.8
Fort Wayne, IN	354,435	390,156	416,257	419,601	18.4	0.8
Fort Worth, TX	3,989,294	5,161,544	6,371,773	7,637,387	91.4	19.9
Grand Rapids, MI	645,914	740,482	774,160	1,087,592	68.4	40.5
Greeley, CO	131,816	180,926	252,825	328,981	149.6	30.1
Green Bay, WI	243,698	282,599	306,241	328,268	34.7	7.2
Greensboro, NC	540,257	643,430	723,801	776,566	43.7	7.3
Honolulu, HI	836,231	876,156	953,207	1,016,508	21.6	6.6
Houston, TX	3,767,335	4,715,407	5,946,800	7,122,240	89.1	19.8
Huntsville, AL	293,047	342,376	417,593	491,723	67.8	17.8
Indianapolis, IN	1,294,217	1,525,104	1,756,241	2,111,040	63.1	20.2
Jacksonville, FL	925,213	1,122,750	1,345,596	1,605,848	73.6	19.3
Kansas City, MO	1,636,528	1,836,038	2,035,334	2,192,035	33.9	7.7
Lafayette, LA	208,740	239,086	273,738	478,384	129.2	74.8
Las Cruces, NM	135,510	174,682	209,233	219,561	62.0	4.9
Las Vegas, NV	741,459	1,375,765	1,951,269	2,265,461	205.5	16.1
Lexington, KY	348,428	408,326	472,099	516,811	48.3	9.5
Lincoln, NE	229,091	266,787	302,157	340,217	48.5	12.6
Little Rock, AR	535,034	610,518	699,757	748,031	39.8	6.9
Los Angeles, CA	11,273,720	12,365,627	12,828,837	13,200,998	17.1	2.9
Louisville, KY	1,055,973	1,161,975	1,283,566	1,285,439	21.7	0.1
Madison, WI	432,323	501,774	568,593	680,796	57.5	19.7

Table continued on following page.

Area	1990 Census	2000 Census	2010 Census	2020 Census	Population Growth (%)	
					1990-2020	2010-2020
Manchester, NH	336,073	380,841	400,721	422,937	25.8	5.5
Miami, FL	4,056,100	5,007,564	5,564,635	6,138,333	51.3	10.3
Midland, TX	106,611	116,009	136,872	175,220	64.4	28.0
Milwaukee, WI	1,432,149	1,500,741	1,555,908	1,574,731	10.0	1.2
Minneapolis, MN	2,538,834	2,968,806	3,279,833	3,690,261	45.4	12.5
Nashville, TN	1,048,218	1,311,789	1,589,934	1,989,519	89.8	25.1
New Haven, CT	804,219	824,008	862,477	864,835	7.5	0.3
New Orleans, LA	1,264,391	1,316,510	1,167,764	1,271,845	0.6	8.9
New York, NY	16,845,992	18,323,002	18,897,109	20,140,470	19.6	6.6
Oklahoma City, OK	971,042	1,095,421	1,252,987	1,425,695	46.8	13.8
Omaha, NE	685,797	767,041	865,350	967,604	41.1	11.8
Orlando, FL	1,224,852	1,644,561	2,134,411	2,673,376	118.3	25.3
Philadelphia, PA	5,435,470	5,687,147	5,965,343	6,245,051	14.9	4.7
Phoenix, AZ	2,238,480	3,251,876	4,192,887	4,845,832	116.5	15.6
Pittsburgh, PA	2,468,289	2,431,087	2,356,285	2,370,930	-3.9	0.6
Portland, OR	1,523,741	1,927,881	2,226,009	2,512,859	64.9	12.9
Providence, RI	1,509,789	1,582,997	1,600,852	1,676,579	11.0	4.7
Provo, UT	269,407	376,774	526,810	671,185	149.1	27.4
Raleigh, NC	541,081	797,071	1,130,490	1,413,982	161.3	25.1
Reno, NV	257,193	342,885	425,417	490,596	90.8	15.3
Richmond, VA	949,244	1,096,957	1,258,251	1,314,434	38.5	4.5
Rochester, MN	141,945	163,618	186,011	226,329	59.4	21.7
Sacramento, CA	1,481,126	1,796,857	2,149,127	2,397,382	61.9	11.6
St. Louis, MO	2,580,897	2,698,687	2,812,896	2,820,253	9.3	0.3
Salem, OR	278,024	347,214	390,738	433,353	55.9	10.9
Salt Lake City, UT	768,075	968,858	1,124,197	1,257,936	63.8	11.9
San Antonio, TX	1,407,745	1,711,703	2,142,508	2,558,143	81.7	19.4
San Diego, CA	2,498,016	2,813,833	3,095,313	3,298,634	32.1	6.6
San Francisco, CA	3,686,592	4,123,740	4,335,391	4,749,008	28.8	9.5
San Jose, CA	1,534,280	1,735,819	1,836,911	2,000,468	30.4	8.9
Santa Rosa, CA	388,222	458,614	483,878	488,863	25.9	1.0
Savannah, GA	258,060	293,000	347,611	404,798	56.9	16.5
Seattle, WA	2,559,164	3,043,878	3,439,809	4,018,762	57.0	16.8
Sioux Falls, SD	153,500	187,093	228,261	276,730	80.3	21.2
Springfield, IL	189,550	201,437	210,170	208,640	10.1	-0.7
Tampa, FL	2,067,959	2,395,997	2,783,243	3,175,275	53.5	14.1
Tucson, AZ	666,880	843,746	980,263	1,043,433	56.5	6.4
Tulsa, OK	761,019	859,532	937,478	1,015,331	33.4	8.3
Tuscaloosa, AL	176,123	192,034	219,461	268,674	52.5	22.4
Virginia Beach, VA	1,449,389	1,576,370	1,671,683	1,799,674	24.2	7.7
Washington, DC	4,122,914	4,796,183	5,582,170	6,385,162	54.9	14.4
Wichita, KS	511,111	571,166	623,061	647,610	26.7	3.9
Wilmington, NC	200,124	274,532	362,315	285,905	42.9	-21.1
Winston-Salem, NC	361,091	421,961	477,717	675,966	87.2	41.5
Worcester, MA	709,728	750,963	798,552	978,529	37.9	22.5
U.S.	248,709,873	281,421,906	308,745,538	331,449,281	33.3	7.4

Note: Figures cover the Metropolitan Statistical Area (MSA)
Source: U.S. Census Bureau, 1990 Census,, 2000 Census,, 2010 Census,, 2020 Census

Male/Female Ratio: City

City	Males	Females	Males per 100 Females
Albuquerque, NM	274,173	290,386	94.4
Allentown, PA	60,577	65,268	92.8
Anchorage, AK	147,894	143,353	103.2
Ann Arbor, MI	61,263	62,588	97.9
Athens, GA	59,963	67,352	89.0
Atlanta, GA	245,444	253,271	96.9
Austin, TX	485,739	476,116	102.0
Baltimore, MD	274,635	311,073	88.3
Boise City, ID	116,758	118,926	98.2
Boston, MA	319,326	356,321	89.6
Boulder, CO	55,982	52,268	107.1
Brownsville, TX	89,293	97,445	91.6
Cape Coral, FL	95,028	98,988	96.0
Cedar Rapids, IA	67,218	70,492	95.4
Charleston, SC	71,681	78,546	91.3
Charlotte, NC	421,316	453,263	93.0
Chicago, IL	1,332,725	1,413,663	94.3
Cincinnati, OH	149,736	159,581	93.8
Clarksville, TN	81,849	84,873	96.4
Cleveland, OH	180,991	191,633	94.4
College Station, TX	61,203	59,308	103.2
Colorado Springs, CO	236,731	242,230	97.7
Columbia, MO	60,766	65,488	92.8
Columbia, SC	67,155	69,477	96.7
Columbus, OH	441,869	463,879	95.3
Dallas, TX	647,963	656,416	98.7
Davenport, IA	49,751	51,973	95.7
Denver, CO	358,405	357,117	100.4
Des Moines, IA	105,618	108,515	97.3
Durham, NC	133,353	150,153	88.8
Edison, NJ	53,123	54,465	97.5
El Paso, TX	326,540	352,275	92.7
Fargo, ND	63,707	62,283	102.3
Fort Collins, CO	84,217	85,593	98.4
Fort Wayne, IN	128,678	135,208	95.2
Fort Worth, TX	449,923	468,992	95.9
Grand Rapids, MI	97,037	101,880	95.2
Greeley, CO	53,848	54,947	98.0
Green Bay, WI	53,407	53,988	98.9
Greensboro, NC	138,465	160,570	86.2
Honolulu, HI	172,783	178,181	97.0
Houston, TX	1,140,598	1,163,982	98.0
Huntsville, AL	104,200	110,806	94.0
Indianapolis, IN	430,358	457,284	94.1
Jacksonville, FL	459,204	490,407	93.6
Kansas City, MO	247,776	260,314	95.2
Lafayette, LA	58,213	63,161	92.2
Las Cruces, NM	53,571	57,814	92.7
Las Vegas, NV	317,700	324,203	98.0
Lexington, KY	155,876	166,694	93.5
Lincoln, NE	145,790	145,292	100.3
Little Rock, AR	96,018	106,573	90.1
Los Angeles, CA	1,925,675	1,973,072	97.6
Louisville, KY	186,813	200,071	93.4
Madison, WI	133,922	135,918	98.5

Table continued on following page.

City	Males	Females	Males per 100 Females
Manchester, NH	57,668	57,976	99.5
Miami, FL	218,706	223,535	97.8
Midland, TX	66,552	65,972	100.9
Milwaukee, WI	278,386	298,836	93.2
Minneapolis, MN	216,381	213,573	101.3
Nashville, TN	332,568	356,879	93.2
New Haven, CT	64,141	69,882	91.8
New Orleans, LA	181,171	202,826	89.3
New York, NY	4,184,548	4,619,642	90.6
Oklahoma City, OK	335,613	345,441	97.2
Omaha, NE	239,675	246,376	97.3
Orlando, FL	148,481	159,092	93.3
Philadelphia, PA	760,383	843,414	90.2
Phoenix, AZ	799,456	808,683	98.9
Pittsburgh, PA	148,157	154,814	95.7
Portland, OR	322,690	329,813	97.8
Providence, RI	92,861	98,073	94.7
Provo, UT	56,944	58,218	97.8
Raleigh, NC	224,994	242,671	92.7
Reno, NV	134,002	130,163	102.9
Richmond, VA	107,678	118,932	90.5
Rochester, MN	58,643	62,752	93.5
Sacramento, CA	255,987	268,956	95.2
St. Louis, MO	147,340	154,238	95.5
Salem, OR	87,574	87,961	99.6
Salt Lake City, UT	102,530	97,193	105.5
San Antonio, TX	699,905	734,720	95.3
San Diego, CA	694,107	692,825	100.2
San Francisco, CA	446,144	427,821	104.3
San Jose, CA	509,260	503,980	101.0
Santa Rosa, CA	86,767	91,360	95.0
Savannah, GA	69,878	77,902	89.7
Seattle, WA	371,247	365,768	101.5
Sioux Falls, SD	95,676	96,841	98.8
Springfield, IL	54,215	60,179	90.1
Tampa, FL	187,761	197,198	95.2
Tucson, AZ	269,110	273,519	98.4
Tulsa, OK	201,814	211,252	95.5
Tuscaloosa, AL	47,020	52,580	89.4
Virginia Beach, VA	224,059	235,411	95.2
Washington, DC	322,777	366,768	88.0
Wichita, KS	196,575	200,957	97.8
Wilmington, NC	54,189	61,262	88.5
Winston-Salem, NC	116,698	132,847	87.8
Worcester, MA	100,540	105,978	94.9
U.S.	162,685,811	168,763,470	96.4

Source: U.S. Census Bureau, 2020 Census

Male/Female Ratio: Metro Area

Metro Area	Males	Females	Males per 100 Females
Albuquerque, NM	449,092	467,436	96.1
Allentown, PA	419,780	442,109	94.9
Anchorage, AK	203,277	195,051	104.2
Ann Arbor, MI	182,825	189,433	96.5
Athens, GA	103,235	112,180	92.0
Atlanta, GA	2,933,974	3,155,841	93.0
Austin, TX	1,138,942	1,144,429	99.5
Baltimore, MD	1,365,439	1,479,071	92.3
Boise City, ID	380,892	383,826	99.2
Boston, MA	2,390,705	2,550,927	93.7
Boulder, CO	166,794	163,964	101.7
Brownsville, TX	203,223	217,794	93.3
Cape Coral, FL	371,444	389,378	95.4
Cedar Rapids, IA	136,845	139,675	98.0
Charleston, SC	389,850	409,786	95.1
Charlotte, NC	1,289,221	1,371,108	94.0
Chicago, IL	4,694,560	4,923,942	95.3
Cincinnati, OH	1,107,410	1,149,474	96.3
Clarksville, TN	159,552	160,983	99.1
Cleveland, OH	1,008,568	1,079,683	93.4
College Station, TX	134,329	133,919	100.3
Colorado Springs, CO	379,052	376,053	100.8
Columbia, MO	102,929	107,935	95.4
Columbia, SC	398,440	431,030	92.4
Columbus, OH	1,050,767	1,088,159	96.6
Dallas, TX	3,753,384	3,884,003	96.6
Davenport, IA	189,247	195,077	97.0
Denver, CO	1,481,349	1,482,472	99.9
Des Moines, IA	349,805	359,661	97.3
Durham, NC	312,256	337,647	92.5
Edison, NJ	9,693,702	10,446,768	92.8
El Paso, TX	422,688	446,171	94.7
Fargo, ND	125,674	124,169	101.2
Fort Collins, CO	177,804	181,262	98.1
Fort Wayne, IN	205,785	213,816	96.2
Fort Worth, TX	3,753,384	3,884,003	96.6
Grand Rapids, MI	540,561	547,031	98.8
Greeley, CO	164,843	164,138	100.4
Green Bay, WI	163,689	164,579	99.5
Greensboro, NC	370,483	406,083	91.2
Honolulu, HI	509,569	506,939	100.5
Houston, TX	3,505,374	3,616,866	96.9
Huntsville, AL	241,092	250,631	96.2
Indianapolis, IN	1,033,439	1,077,601	95.9
Jacksonville, FL	779,083	826,765	94.2
Kansas City, MO	1,076,104	1,115,931	96.4
Lafayette, LA	231,864	246,520	94.1
Las Cruces, NM	107,150	112,411	95.3
Las Vegas, NV	1,126,444	1,139,017	98.9
Lexington, KY	250,691	266,120	94.2
Lincoln, NE	170,718	169,499	100.7
Little Rock, AR	361,694	386,337	93.6
Los Angeles, CA	6,469,965	6,731,033	96.1
Louisville, KY	628,220	657,219	95.6
Madison, WI	338,757	342,039	99.0

Table continued on following page.

Metro Area	Males	Females	Males per 100 Females
Manchester, NH	209,879	213,058	98.5
Miami, FL	2,954,448	3,183,885	92.8
Midland, TX	88,457	86,763	102.0
Milwaukee, WI	766,278	808,453	94.8
Minneapolis, MN	1,824,100	1,866,161	97.7
Nashville, TN	968,381	1,021,138	94.8
New Haven, CT	415,391	449,444	92.4
New Orleans, LA	610,653	661,192	92.4
New York, NY	9,693,702	10,446,768	92.8
Oklahoma City, OK	702,324	723,371	97.1
Omaha, NE	478,627	488,977	97.9
Orlando, FL	1,296,256	1,377,120	94.1
Philadelphia, PA	3,015,319	3,229,732	93.4
Phoenix, AZ	2,395,320	2,450,512	97.7
Pittsburgh, PA	1,157,964	1,212,966	95.5
Portland, OR	1,240,947	1,271,912	97.6
Providence, RI	812,496	864,083	94.0
Provo, UT	336,952	334,233	100.8
Raleigh, NC	687,440	726,542	94.6
Reno, NV	247,924	242,672	102.2
Richmond, VA	632,849	681,585	92.8
Rochester, MN	111,433	114,896	97.0
Sacramento, CA	1,170,850	1,226,532	95.5
St. Louis, MO	1,369,631	1,450,622	94.4
Salem, OR	214,703	218,650	98.2
Salt Lake City, UT	632,295	625,641	101.1
San Antonio, TX	1,254,014	1,304,129	96.2
San Diego, CA	1,642,796	1,655,838	99.2
San Francisco, CA	2,344,775	2,404,233	97.5
San Jose, CA	1,007,254	993,214	101.4
Santa Rosa, CA	238,535	250,328	95.3
Savannah, GA	194,814	209,984	92.8
Seattle, WA	2,007,150	2,011,612	99.8
Sioux Falls, SD	138,437	138,293	100.1
Springfield, IL	100,412	108,228	92.8
Tampa, FL	1,535,385	1,639,890	93.6
Tucson, AZ	512,753	530,680	96.6
Tulsa, OK	499,555	515,776	96.9
Tuscaloosa, AL	127,913	140,761	90.9
Virginia Beach, VA	879,439	920,235	95.6
Washington, DC	3,091,711	3,293,451	93.9
Wichita, KS	321,349	326,261	98.5
Wilmington, NC	137,791	148,114	93.0
Winston-Salem, NC	324,467	351,499	92.3
Worcester, MA	482,355	496,174	97.2
U.S.	162,685,811	168,763,470	96.4

Note: Figures cover the Metropolitan Statistical Area (MSA)
Source: U.S. Census Bureau, 2020 Census

Race: City

City	White Alone[1] (%)	Black Alone[1] (%)	Asian Alone[1] (%)	AIAN[2] Alone[1] (%)	NHOPI[3] Alone[1] (%)	Other Race Alone[1] (%)	Two or More Races (%)
Albuquerque, NM	52.2	3.5	3.4	5.6	0.1	14.2	21.0
Allentown, PA	38.3	13.2	2.1	0.8	0.1	30.1	15.5
Anchorage, AK	56.5	5.0	9.5	8.1	3.4	3.5	14.0
Ann Arbor, MI	67.6	6.8	15.7	0.2	0.1	1.8	7.9
Athens, GA	58.1	24.7	3.9	0.5	0.1	6.1	6.7
Atlanta, GA	39.8	47.2	4.5	0.3	0.0	2.4	5.8
Austin, TX	54.7	7.3	9.0	1.0	0.1	11.9	16.1
Baltimore, MD	27.8	57.8	3.6	0.4	0.0	4.8	5.5
Boise City, ID	81.2	2.3	3.6	0.7	0.3	3.5	8.5
Boston, MA	47.1	20.6	11.3	0.4	0.1	10.1	10.5
Boulder, CO	78.8	1.3	6.4	0.6	0.1	4.7	8.1
Brownsville, TX	34.9	0.3	0.6	0.7	0.0	20.5	42.9
Cape Coral, FL	72.3	4.3	1.7	0.3	0.1	5.8	15.6
Cedar Rapids, IA	77.8	10.4	2.7	0.3	0.4	1.7	6.8
Charleston, SC	73.5	17.0	2.2	0.3	0.1	1.6	5.3
Charlotte, NC	41.7	33.1	7.1	0.6	0.1	9.6	7.9
Chicago, IL	35.9	29.2	7.0	1.3	0.0	15.8	10.8
Cincinnati, OH	47.7	40.6	2.5	0.3	0.1	3.0	5.8
Clarksville, TN	57.0	24.4	2.5	0.5	0.5	4.2	10.9
Cleveland, OH	34.5	48.4	2.8	0.4	0.0	6.3	7.6
College Station, TX	63.5	8.1	10.2	0.5	0.1	7.4	10.2
Colorado Springs, CO	70.3	5.9	3.4	1.1	0.3	6.2	12.8
Columbia, MO	72.5	11.9	5.6	0.3	0.1	2.2	7.4
Columbia, SC	50.7	38.5	3.1	0.3	0.1	2.3	5.1
Columbus, OH	53.2	28.6	6.2	0.4	0.0	4.3	7.2
Dallas, TX	36.1	23.3	3.7	1.2	0.1	19.5	16.2
Davenport, IA	74.1	12.0	2.2	0.4	0.0	2.6	8.7
Denver, CO	60.6	8.9	3.9	1.5	0.2	11.3	13.5
Des Moines, IA	64.5	11.7	6.8	0.7	0.1	6.6	9.6
Durham, NC	40.2	36.2	5.6	0.7	0.0	9.8	7.4
Edison, NJ	28.1	7.6	53.7	0.4	0.0	4.7	5.5
El Paso, TX	36.8	3.7	1.5	1.1	0.2	20.6	36.0
Fargo, ND	78.9	8.8	4.1	1.6	0.1	1.2	5.3
Fort Collins, CO	80.8	1.5	3.6	0.8	0.1	3.6	9.6
Fort Wayne, IN	65.0	15.3	5.8	0.5	0.0	5.6	7.8
Fort Worth, TX	44.9	19.6	5.2	0.9	0.1	14.2	15.1
Grand Rapids, MI	60.3	18.9	2.3	0.9	0.0	9.0	8.7
Greeley, CO	62.0	2.7	2.0	1.8	0.1	14.8	16.6
Green Bay, WI	66.6	5.5	4.4	4.4	0.1	8.4	10.6
Greensboro, NC	40.0	42.0	5.1	0.6	0.0	5.6	6.6
Honolulu, HI	16.4	1.7	52.9	0.2	9.2	1.3	18.2
Houston, TX	32.1	22.6	7.3	1.2	0.1	20.7	16.1
Huntsville, AL	56.6	29.3	2.5	0.7	0.1	3.4	7.3
Indianapolis, IN	52.0	27.9	4.3	0.5	0.0	7.7	7.5
Jacksonville, FL	50.1	30.6	5.1	0.4	0.1	4.6	9.1
Kansas City, MO	55.3	26.1	3.1	0.6	0.3	5.5	9.0
Lafayette, LA	58.1	30.7	2.6	0.4	0.0	2.3	5.8
Las Cruces, NM	51.9	2.7	1.9	2.3	0.1	16.6	24.5
Las Vegas, NV	46.0	12.9	7.2	1.1	0.7	17.0	15.0
Lexington, KY	68.3	14.9	4.2	0.3	0.0	5.2	7.1
Lincoln, NE	78.7	4.7	4.8	0.9	0.1	3.5	7.5
Little Rock, AR	43.5	40.6	3.5	0.6	0.0	6.0	5.7
Los Angeles, CA	34.9	8.6	11.9	1.7	0.2	29.5	13.3
Louisville, KY	66.3	17.5	3.5	0.3	0.1	4.2	8.0

Table continued on following page.

City	White Alone[1] (%)	Black Alone[1] (%)	Asian Alone[1] (%)	AIAN[2] Alone[1] (%)	NHOPI[3] Alone[1] (%)	Other Race Alone[1] (%)	Two or More Races (%)
Madison, WI	71.0	7.4	9.5	0.5	0.1	3.8	7.8
Manchester, NH	76.7	5.5	4.2	0.3	0.0	5.2	7.9
Miami, FL	30.2	12.9	1.4	0.4	0.0	14.3	40.7
Midland, TX	57.6	7.9	2.6	0.9	0.1	12.5	18.4
Milwaukee, WI	36.1	38.6	5.2	0.9	0.0	9.0	10.1
Minneapolis, MN	59.5	19.1	5.8	1.7	0.0	5.9	8.0
Nashville, TN	55.2	24.6	4.0	0.6	0.0	8.1	7.6
New Haven, CT	32.7	32.2	6.8	1.0	0.1	15.3	12.0
New Orleans, LA	32.9	54.2	2.8	0.3	0.0	3.2	6.4
New York, NY	34.1	22.1	15.7	1.0	0.1	17.0	10.1
Oklahoma City, OK	53.6	14.0	4.6	3.4	0.2	11.1	13.1
Omaha, NE	65.5	12.4	4.6	1.1	0.1	7.2	9.1
Orlando, FL	40.0	23.8	4.3	0.4	0.1	12.3	19.0
Philadelphia, PA	36.3	39.3	8.3	0.4	0.1	8.7	6.9
Phoenix, AZ	49.7	7.8	4.1	2.6	0.2	20.1	15.5
Pittsburgh, PA	62.7	22.8	6.5	0.2	0.0	1.8	5.9
Portland, OR	68.8	5.9	8.1	1.1	0.6	4.8	10.7
Providence, RI	37.7	13.5	6.1	1.5	0.1	26.9	14.2
Provo, UT	74.6	0.9	2.5	1.0	1.5	8.2	11.3
Raleigh, NC	53.3	26.3	5.0	0.6	0.1	7.5	7.4
Reno, NV	62.7	3.1	7.1	1.4	0.8	12.0	13.0
Richmond, VA	43.3	40.4	2.8	0.4	0.1	6.8	6.2
Rochester, MN	73.2	8.9	7.9	0.4	0.1	2.9	6.6
Sacramento, CA	34.8	13.2	19.9	1.4	1.6	15.3	13.8
St. Louis, MO	43.9	43.0	4.1	0.3	0.0	2.6	6.1
Salem, OR	69.1	1.7	3.2	1.7	1.4	10.9	12.1
Salt Lake City, UT	68.4	2.9	5.5	1.4	2.1	9.7	9.9
San Antonio, TX	44.3	7.2	3.3	1.2	0.1	16.7	27.1
San Diego, CA	46.4	5.9	17.9	0.9	0.4	14.1	14.4
San Francisco, CA	41.3	5.3	33.9	0.7	0.4	8.4	9.9
San Jose, CA	27.3	2.9	38.5	1.4	0.4	18.2	11.2
Santa Rosa, CA	55.7	2.3	6.1	2.3	0.6	19.1	13.9
Savannah, GA	37.9	49.1	3.8	0.3	0.2	3.1	5.5
Seattle, WA	61.3	7.0	17.1	0.7	0.3	3.2	10.5
Sioux Falls, SD	79.0	6.3	2.8	2.7	0.0	2.9	6.1
Springfield, IL	68.9	20.4	2.9	0.3	0.0	1.1	6.4
Tampa, FL	49.7	21.9	5.4	0.4	0.1	7.6	14.8
Tucson, AZ	54.5	5.6	3.2	2.9	0.3	15.2	18.3
Tulsa, OK	51.8	14.9	3.5	5.2	0.2	9.8	14.6
Tuscaloosa, AL	48.7	41.2	2.4	0.3	0.1	2.1	5.3
Virginia Beach, VA	60.7	18.6	7.5	0.4	0.2	3.0	9.6
Washington, DC	39.6	41.4	4.9	0.5	0.1	5.4	8.1
Wichita, KS	63.4	11.0	5.1	1.3	0.1	7.4	11.7
Wilmington, NC	70.9	16.5	1.6	0.4	0.1	3.9	6.6
Winston-Salem, NC	45.8	32.5	2.5	0.7	0.1	10.7	7.6
Worcester, MA	53.3	14.8	7.1	0.5	0.0	12.9	11.3
U.S.	61.6	12.4	6.0	1.1	0.2	8.4	10.2

Note: (1) Alone is defined as not being in combination with one or more other races; (2) American Indian and Alaska Native; (3) Native Hawaiian and Other Pacific Islander
Source: U.S. Census Bureau, 2020 Census

Race: Metro Area

Metro Area	White Alone[1] (%)	Black Alone[1] (%)	Asian Alone[1] (%)	AIAN[2] Alone[1] (%)	NHOPI[3] Alone[1] (%)	Other Race Alone[1] (%)	Two or More Races (%)
Albuquerque, NM	52.8	2.8	2.5	6.6	0.1	14.5	20.6
Allentown, PA	72.9	6.3	3.2	0.3	0.0	8.5	8.8
Anchorage, AK	62.1	3.9	7.3	7.7	2.6	3.0	13.3
Ann Arbor, MI	69.2	11.5	9.0	0.3	0.1	2.0	7.9
Athens, GA	67.0	17.9	3.6	0.4	0.0	4.7	6.3
Atlanta, GA	45.5	33.6	6.6	0.5	0.0	6.0	7.7
Austin, TX	57.3	7.0	7.1	0.9	0.1	11.1	16.5
Baltimore, MD	53.9	28.5	6.3	0.4	0.0	4.0	6.8
Boise City, ID	80.0	1.3	2.1	0.9	0.3	5.9	9.6
Boston, MA	68.4	7.4	8.7	0.3	0.0	6.9	8.4
Boulder, CO	77.4	1.0	5.0	0.8	0.1	5.8	10.0
Brownsville, TX	38.6	0.5	0.7	0.7	0.0	19.0	40.4
Cape Coral, FL	69.7	7.7	1.7	0.5	0.0	7.5	12.8
Cedar Rapids, IA	84.7	6.1	2.0	0.2	0.2	1.2	5.6
Charleston, SC	64.0	23.0	2.0	0.5	0.1	3.9	6.5
Charlotte, NC	59.5	21.9	4.3	0.6	0.1	6.4	7.2
Chicago, IL	54.0	16.4	7.1	0.9	0.0	11.3	10.2
Cincinnati, OH	76.7	12.1	3.0	0.3	0.1	2.1	5.7
Clarksville, TN	65.8	19.1	2.0	0.5	0.4	3.2	9.0
Cleveland, OH	68.9	19.6	2.6	0.2	0.0	2.6	6.0
College Station, TX	60.7	11.0	5.6	0.7	0.1	9.8	12.1
Colorado Springs, CO	71.3	5.8	3.0	1.0	0.4	5.8	12.7
Columbia, MO	77.7	9.3	3.8	0.3	0.1	1.8	7.1
Columbia, SC	55.7	32.4	2.3	0.4	0.1	3.1	6.0
Columbus, OH	70.1	15.7	4.9	0.3	0.0	2.7	6.3
Dallas, TX	48.9	16.0	7.9	1.0	0.1	12.2	13.9
Davenport, IA	78.2	8.3	2.4	0.4	0.0	3.2	7.5
Denver, CO	66.7	5.6	4.6	1.2	0.2	8.8	12.8
Des Moines, IA	79.8	5.6	4.3	0.4	0.1	3.2	6.7
Durham, NC	54.3	25.0	4.9	0.7	0.0	7.9	7.2
Edison, NJ	46.5	16.1	12.5	0.8	0.1	14.1	10.0
El Paso, TX	36.3	3.3	1.4	1.2	0.2	21.7	35.8
Fargo, ND	82.8	6.5	2.7	1.5	0.0	1.1	5.3
Fort Collins, CO	82.4	1.1	2.4	0.8	0.1	3.8	9.4
Fort Wayne, IN	73.7	10.6	4.4	0.4	0.0	4.0	6.8
Fort Worth, TX	48.9	16.0	7.9	1.0	0.1	12.2	13.9
Grand Rapids, MI	78.0	6.9	2.8	0.6	0.0	4.7	7.0
Greeley, CO	70.5	1.4	1.8	1.3	0.1	11.2	13.8
Green Bay, WI	81.8	2.6	2.7	2.5	0.0	3.8	6.6
Greensboro, NC	56.7	26.7	4.1	0.6	0.0	5.5	6.4
Honolulu, HI	18.5	2.0	43.0	0.2	10.0	1.7	24.5
Houston, TX	41.4	17.4	8.4	1.0	0.1	16.0	15.7
Huntsville, AL	65.0	21.4	2.5	0.7	0.1	2.9	7.3
Indianapolis, IN	69.6	15.0	3.9	0.4	0.0	4.5	6.6
Jacksonville, FL	61.6	21.2	4.2	0.4	0.1	3.6	8.8
Kansas City, MO	70.9	12.0	3.1	0.6	0.2	4.2	9.0
Lafayette, LA	65.8	24.5	1.9	0.4	0.0	2.3	5.1
Las Cruces, NM	47.5	1.9	1.2	1.9	0.1	20.1	27.4
Las Vegas, NV	44.9	12.7	10.5	1.0	0.9	15.4	14.7
Lexington, KY	74.9	11.1	2.9	0.3	0.0	4.2	6.6
Lincoln, NE	80.8	4.1	4.2	0.8	0.1	3.1	6.9
Little Rock, AR	64.0	23.2	1.8	0.6	0.1	3.7	6.6
Los Angeles, CA	35.2	6.4	16.7	1.5	0.3	25.2	14.7
Louisville, KY	72.7	14.8	2.5	0.3	0.1	2.9	6.8

Table continued on following page.

Metro Area	White Alone[1] (%)	Black Alone[1] (%)	Asian Alone[1] (%)	AIAN[2] Alone[1] (%)	NHOPI[3] Alone[1] (%)	Other Race Alone[1] (%)	Two or More Races (%)
Madison, WI	80.2	4.7	5.4	0.4	0.0	2.9	6.4
Manchester, NH	82.8	2.6	3.9	0.2	0.0	3.5	6.9
Miami, FL	39.6	19.5	2.7	0.4	0.0	9.7	28.1
Midland, TX	58.2	6.4	2.3	0.9	0.1	13.2	18.9
Milwaukee, WI	66.7	16.3	4.2	0.6	0.0	4.6	7.6
Minneapolis, MN	73.0	9.1	7.2	0.8	0.0	3.3	6.6
Nashville, TN	70.0	14.3	3.1	0.5	0.1	5.1	7.0
New Haven, CT	62.9	13.8	4.3	0.5	0.1	9.0	9.5
New Orleans, LA	50.3	33.3	2.9	0.5	0.0	4.8	8.1
New York, NY	46.5	16.1	12.5	0.8	0.1	14.1	10.0
Oklahoma City, OK	62.5	10.3	3.3	4.0	0.1	7.2	12.6
Omaha, NE	74.9	7.7	3.5	0.8	0.1	5.0	8.0
Orlando, FL	50.4	15.4	4.7	0.4	0.1	11.4	17.7
Philadelphia, PA	60.7	20.4	6.6	0.3	0.0	5.1	6.8
Phoenix, AZ	60.2	5.8	4.3	2.5	0.3	13.4	13.5
Pittsburgh, PA	82.7	8.4	2.9	0.1	0.0	0.9	4.9
Portland, OR	71.5	3.0	7.1	1.1	0.6	6.0	10.7
Providence, RI	73.9	5.2	3.1	0.6	0.0	8.0	9.1
Provo, UT	81.8	0.7	1.6	0.7	1.0	5.4	8.9
Raleigh, NC	60.1	18.3	7.0	0.6	0.0	6.4	7.6
Reno, NV	64.2	2.5	5.9	1.8	0.7	11.8	13.0
Richmond, VA	56.5	27.7	4.3	0.5	0.1	4.4	6.4
Rochester, MN	82.3	5.1	4.7	0.3	0.0	2.2	5.4
Sacramento, CA	52.5	7.0	14.9	1.1	0.9	10.4	13.2
St. Louis, MO	71.2	18.0	2.9	0.3	0.0	1.6	6.0
Salem, OR	69.6	1.1	2.1	2.0	1.0	12.2	12.0
Salt Lake City, UT	72.3	1.9	4.1	1.1	1.8	9.1	9.8
San Antonio, TX	50.3	7.1	2.9	1.1	0.2	14.0	24.4
San Diego, CA	49.5	4.7	12.5	1.2	0.5	15.8	15.8
San Francisco, CA	39.3	7.1	27.5	1.0	0.7	12.7	11.7
San Jose, CA	32.5	2.3	38.1	1.2	0.4	14.6	11.0
Santa Rosa, CA	62.7	1.6	4.7	1.8	0.4	15.3	13.5
Savannah, GA	55.6	30.8	3.1	0.4	0.1	3.4	6.6
Seattle, WA	60.1	6.1	15.4	1.1	1.1	5.3	11.0
Sioux Falls, SD	83.4	4.6	2.0	2.2	0.0	2.3	5.5
Springfield, IL	78.4	12.5	2.1	0.2	0.0	0.9	5.8
Tampa, FL	64.4	11.8	3.9	0.4	0.1	6.2	13.1
Tucson, AZ	60.7	3.8	3.0	3.3	0.2	12.2	16.7
Tulsa, OK	61.3	7.9	2.8	8.1	0.1	5.4	14.2
Tuscaloosa, AL	57.5	33.9	1.3	0.4	0.0	2.5	4.3
Virginia Beach, VA	54.0	30.3	4.1	0.4	0.2	2.9	8.1
Washington, DC	44.5	24.5	11.0	0.6	0.1	9.3	10.1
Wichita, KS	71.7	7.5	3.7	1.2	0.1	5.4	10.4
Wilmington, NC	75.6	12.2	1.3	0.5	0.1	3.8	6.4
Winston-Salem, NC	67.0	17.2	1.8	0.6	0.1	6.7	6.5
Worcester, MA	74.5	5.2	4.9	0.4	0.0	6.3	8.6
U.S.	61.6	12.4	6.0	1.1	0.2	8.4	10.2

Note: Figures cover the Metropolitan Statistical Area (MSA); (1) Alone is defined as not being in combination with one or more other races; (2) American Indian and Alaska Native; (3) Native Hawaiian & Other Pacific Islander
Source: U.S. Census Bureau, 2020 Census

Hispanic Origin: City

City	Hispanic or Latino (%)	Mexican (%)	Puerto Rican (%)	Cuban (%)	Other Hispanic or Latino (%)
Albuquerque, NM	49.8	29.7	0.7	0.4	19.0
Allentown, PA	54.5	2.6	27.6	0.8	23.5
Anchorage, AK	9.5	4.6	1.5	0.4	3.0
Ann Arbor, MI	4.6	2.4	0.3	0.3	1.7
Athens, GA	11.0	5.9	0.4	0.6	4.0
Atlanta, GA	5.0	1.9	0.8	0.3	2.0
Austin, TX	33.1	25.6	1.0	0.7	5.8
Baltimore, MD	5.6	1.1	0.8	0.3	3.3
Boise City, ID	8.8	6.4	0.5	0.1	1.9
Boston, MA	19.8	1.1	5.2	0.4	13.1
Boulder, CO	10.6	6.3	0.4	0.4	3.6
Brownsville, TX	94.7	90.5	0.2	0.1	3.8
Cape Coral, FL	23.2	1.7	4.9	9.7	7.0
Cedar Rapids, IA	4.4	3.2	0.2	0.1	1.0
Charleston, SC	4.2	1.9	0.6	0.1	1.6
Charlotte, NC	14.9	5.3	1.1	0.6	7.9
Chicago, IL	28.7	21.2	3.5	0.3	3.8
Cincinnati, OH	4.4	1.4	0.6	0.2	2.2
Clarksville, TN	11.7	5.6	3.0	0.4	2.8
Cleveland, OH	12.2	1.6	8.6	0.2	1.8
College Station, TX	17.7	12.8	0.7	0.2	4.1
Colorado Springs, CO	18.4	12.1	1.2	0.3	4.9
Columbia, MO	3.7	2.1	0.3	0.0	1.2
Columbia, SC	5.6	2.4	1.1	0.3	1.8
Columbus, OH	6.5	3.1	1.0	0.1	2.3
Dallas, TX	42.0	34.7	0.6	0.3	6.4
Davenport, IA	8.9	8.2	0.3	0.1	0.3
Denver, CO	29.4	22.6	0.7	0.3	5.9
Des Moines, IA	14.6	11.6	0.3	0.2	2.4
Durham, NC	13.2	6.4	0.9	0.3	5.7
Edison, NJ	10.8	1.4	2.8	0.7	6.0
El Paso, TX	81.6	76.9	1.0	0.2	3.5
Fargo, ND	3.2	2.0	0.3	0.0	0.9
Fort Collins, CO	12.6	9.0	0.5	0.1	3.0
Fort Wayne, IN	9.5	7.2	0.6	0.1	1.6
Fort Worth, TX	35.3	29.8	1.2	0.4	3.9
Grand Rapids, MI	15.7	9.6	1.6	0.3	4.1
Greeley, CO	40.3	33.0	0.9	0.1	6.3
Green Bay, WI	16.6	13.0	1.9	0.0	1.8
Greensboro, NC	8.4	4.5	1.1	0.2	2.6
Honolulu, HI	7.2	2.2	2.0	0.1	2.8
Houston, TX	44.5	30.3	0.7	0.8	12.8
Huntsville, AL	6.4	3.6	1.1	0.2	1.6
Indianapolis, IN	10.8	7.3	0.7	0.2	2.6
Jacksonville, FL	10.9	2.0	3.4	1.6	3.9
Kansas City, MO	10.7	7.7	0.4	0.4	2.2
Lafayette, LA	4.6	1.4	0.1	0.2	2.9
Las Cruces, NM	61.8	51.1	0.6	0.2	9.9
Las Vegas, NV	34.1	24.9	1.2	1.4	6.5
Lexington, KY	7.4	4.7	0.6	0.2	1.9
Lincoln, NE	8.1	5.5	0.4	0.2	2.0
Little Rock, AR	7.8	4.7	0.2	0.3	2.5
Los Angeles, CA	48.4	31.5	0.5	0.4	16.1
Louisville, KY	6.5	2.3	0.4	2.3	1.4
Madison, WI	7.8	4.5	0.7	0.2	2.4

Table continued on following page.

City	Hispanic or Latino (%)	Mexican (%)	Puerto Rican (%)	Cuban (%)	Other Hispanic or Latino (%)
Manchester, NH	11.0	1.6	3.9	0.1	5.4
Miami, FL	72.3	1.9	3.5	33.4	33.5
Midland, TX	46.5	42.5	0.5	1.0	2.5
Milwaukee, WI	19.9	13.4	4.9	0.2	1.4
Minneapolis, MN	9.8	5.3	0.5	0.2	3.8
Nashville, TN	10.6	5.9	0.6	0.4	3.8
New Haven, CT	30.3	5.3	16.5	0.4	8.1
New Orleans, LA	5.6	1.2	0.2	0.6	3.5
New York, NY	28.9	3.8	7.7	0.5	16.9
Oklahoma City, OK	19.9	16.1	0.4	0.1	3.3
Omaha, NE	14.5	10.9	0.5	0.2	2.9
Orlando, FL	34.2	1.8	15.8	3.0	13.6
Philadelphia, PA	15.4	1.3	8.7	0.3	5.1
Phoenix, AZ	42.7	37.9	0.7	0.4	3.8
Pittsburgh, PA	3.5	1.2	0.7	0.1	1.6
Portland, OR	10.3	7.0	0.5	0.4	2.3
Providence, RI	42.9	1.3	7.9	0.3	33.4
Provo, UT	17.8	11.3	0.7	0.2	5.6
Raleigh, NC	11.3	5.0	1.4	0.4	4.5
Reno, NV	23.3	17.8	0.7	0.3	4.6
Richmond, VA	7.3	1.3	0.8	0.3	4.9
Rochester, MN	5.8	3.7	0.6	0.1	1.4
Sacramento, CA	28.9	24.1	0.9	0.2	3.7
St. Louis, MO	4.2	2.5	0.2	0.2	1.3
Salem, OR	22.4	19.5	0.6	0.1	2.2
Salt Lake City, UT	19.9	14.2	0.4	0.3	5.0
San Antonio, TX	65.7	56.7	1.4	0.3	7.3
San Diego, CA	30.1	25.6	0.8	0.3	3.4
San Francisco, CA	15.4	7.8	0.7	0.3	6.7
San Jose, CA	31.0	26.0	0.5	0.2	4.3
Santa Rosa, CA	34.0	29.3	0.5	0.1	4.1
Savannah, GA	6.5	2.1	2.0	0.4	2.0
Seattle, WA	7.2	4.2	0.4	0.2	2.4
Sioux Falls, SD	5.5	2.6	0.3	0.1	2.6
Springfield, IL	2.9	1.5	0.6	0.1	0.7
Tampa, FL	26.2	3.1	6.9	8.0	8.3
Tucson, AZ	44.6	39.8	0.9	0.2	3.7
Tulsa, OK	17.1	13.4	0.6	0.1	3.0
Tuscaloosa, AL	4.4	2.5	0.6	0.3	0.9
Virginia Beach, VA	8.6	2.7	2.2	0.3	3.4
Washington, DC	11.3	1.9	0.9	0.5	8.0
Wichita, KS	17.6	15.1	0.5	0.1	1.9
Wilmington, NC	7.1	2.7	1.3	0.4	2.7
Winston-Salem, NC	16.2	9.7	1.5	0.2	4.8
Worcester, MA	23.9	0.8	14.7	0.3	8.1
U.S.	18.4	11.2	1.8	0.7	4.7

Note: Persons of Hispanic or Latino origin can be of any race
Source: U.S. Census Bureau, 2017-2021 American Community Survey 5-Year Estimates

Hispanic Origin: Metro Area

Metro Area	Hispanic or Latino (%)	Mexican (%)	Puerto Rican (%)	Cuban (%)	Other Hispanic or Latino (%)
Albuquerque, NM	49.7	29.0	0.7	0.4	19.7
Allentown, PA	18.4	1.3	9.3	0.4	7.3
Anchorage, AK	8.4	4.1	1.3	0.4	2.6
Ann Arbor, MI	5.0	2.8	0.5	0.2	1.5
Athens, GA	8.9	4.7	0.8	0.4	2.9
Atlanta, GA	11.0	5.5	1.1	0.4	3.9
Austin, TX	32.7	26.3	1.0	0.5	5.0
Baltimore, MD	6.2	1.4	1.0	0.2	3.6
Boise City, ID	14.1	11.5	0.5	0.1	2.0
Boston, MA	11.6	0.7	2.8	0.3	7.8
Boulder, CO	14.0	9.9	0.5	0.3	3.3
Brownsville, TX	90.0	86.0	0.3	0.1	3.6
Cape Coral, FL	22.6	5.4	4.6	5.7	6.8
Cedar Rapids, IA	3.2	2.4	0.1	0.0	0.7
Charleston, SC	5.9	2.7	0.8	0.1	2.3
Charlotte, NC	10.6	4.6	1.1	0.4	4.6
Chicago, IL	22.5	17.5	2.2	0.3	2.6
Cincinnati, OH	3.5	1.6	0.4	0.1	1.4
Clarksville, TN	9.3	4.7	2.4	0.2	2.0
Cleveland, OH	6.2	1.4	3.5	0.1	1.1
College Station, TX	25.7	21.8	0.4	0.3	3.1
Colorado Springs, CO	17.5	10.9	1.4	0.4	4.9
Columbia, MO	3.4	2.1	0.2	0.1	1.0
Columbia, SC	5.8	2.8	1.1	0.2	1.7
Columbus, OH	4.5	2.1	0.8	0.1	1.6
Dallas, TX	29.3	23.6	0.8	0.3	4.5
Davenport, IA	9.1	8.0	0.3	0.1	0.7
Denver, CO	23.4	17.5	0.6	0.2	5.0
Des Moines, IA	7.4	5.5	0.3	0.1	1.5
Durham, NC	11.3	5.9	0.8	0.3	4.3
Edison, NJ	24.8	2.9	5.9	0.8	15.3
El Paso, TX	82.9	78.1	0.9	0.2	3.6
Fargo, ND	3.4	2.4	0.3	0.0	0.7
Fort Collins, CO	12.0	8.8	0.4	0.2	2.6
Fort Wayne, IN	7.4	5.6	0.4	0.1	1.3
Fort Worth, TX	29.3	23.6	0.8	0.3	4.5
Grand Rapids, MI	9.9	6.8	0.9	0.3	1.9
Greeley, CO	30.0	24.5	0.5	0.2	4.8
Green Bay, WI	8.1	6.1	0.9	0.1	1.0
Greensboro, NC	8.8	5.7	1.0	0.2	1.9
Honolulu, HI	10.2	3.2	3.5	0.1	3.5
Houston, TX	37.9	27.3	0.7	0.7	9.2
Huntsville, AL	5.4	3.2	0.8	0.1	1.3
Indianapolis, IN	7.1	4.6	0.6	0.1	1.8
Jacksonville, FL	9.6	1.9	3.0	1.3	3.5
Kansas City, MO	9.4	7.0	0.4	0.2	1.8
Lafayette, LA	4.1	1.8	0.2	0.1	2.0
Las Cruces, NM	68.9	60.8	0.4	0.1	7.6
Las Vegas, NV	31.8	23.3	1.1	1.5	5.9
Lexington, KY	6.3	4.2	0.5	0.1	1.5
Lincoln, NE	7.2	4.9	0.3	0.2	1.7
Little Rock, AR	5.5	3.7	0.2	0.1	1.5
Los Angeles, CA	45.2	34.5	0.5	0.4	9.8
Louisville, KY	5.3	2.4	0.4	1.3	1.1
Madison, WI	6.1	3.7	0.5	0.1	1.7

Table continued on following page.

Metro Area	Hispanic or Latino (%)	Mexican (%)	Puerto Rican (%)	Cuban (%)	Other Hispanic or Latino (%)
Manchester, NH	7.4	1.1	2.5	0.2	3.5
Miami, FL	45.6	2.5	3.8	18.6	20.6
Midland, TX	46.3	42.7	0.4	0.9	2.3
Milwaukee, WI	11.3	7.5	2.6	0.2	1.1
Minneapolis, MN	6.1	3.8	0.4	0.1	1.8
Nashville, TN	7.7	4.3	0.6	0.3	2.5
New Haven, CT	19.2	2.2	10.6	0.4	6.0
New Orleans, LA	9.1	1.7	0.5	0.6	6.3
New York, NY	24.8	2.9	5.9	0.8	15.3
Oklahoma City, OK	13.9	10.9	0.4	0.1	2.5
Omaha, NE	11.0	8.2	0.5	0.1	2.1
Orlando, FL	31.8	2.8	15.0	2.5	11.5
Philadelphia, PA	9.9	1.9	4.6	0.3	3.2
Phoenix, AZ	31.5	27.1	0.7	0.3	3.4
Pittsburgh, PA	1.9	0.6	0.5	0.1	0.7
Portland, OR	12.5	9.4	0.4	0.3	2.4
Providence, RI	13.7	0.9	4.4	0.2	8.3
Provo, UT	12.1	7.5	0.3	0.1	4.1
Raleigh, NC	10.8	5.6	1.4	0.4	3.5
Reno, NV	25.1	19.3	0.7	0.4	4.6
Richmond, VA	6.7	1.6	1.0	0.2	3.8
Rochester, MN	4.7	2.9	0.4	0.1	1.3
Sacramento, CA	22.2	17.8	0.7	0.2	3.5
St. Louis, MO	3.2	2.0	0.3	0.1	0.9
Salem, OR	24.9	22.1	0.4	0.1	2.3
Salt Lake City, UT	18.5	13.1	0.5	0.2	4.7
San Antonio, TX	56.0	48.2	1.4	0.3	6.0
San Diego, CA	34.3	29.9	0.8	0.2	3.4
San Francisco, CA	22.0	14.1	0.7	0.2	7.0
San Jose, CA	26.2	21.5	0.5	0.2	4.1
Santa Rosa, CA	27.5	22.7	0.4	0.2	4.2
Savannah, GA	6.5	2.9	1.6	0.5	1.6
Seattle, WA	10.5	7.3	0.6	0.2	2.5
Sioux Falls, SD	4.6	2.3	0.2	0.1	2.1
Springfield, IL	2.4	1.4	0.4	0.1	0.5
Tampa, FL	20.5	3.7	6.3	4.3	6.3
Tucson, AZ	38.0	33.7	0.9	0.2	3.2
Tulsa, OK	10.5	8.1	0.4	0.1	1.9
Tuscaloosa, AL	3.8	2.4	0.3	0.2	0.9
Virginia Beach, VA	7.2	2.4	1.9	0.3	2.5
Washington, DC	16.2	2.3	1.2	0.3	12.4
Wichita, KS	13.6	11.5	0.4	0.1	1.6
Wilmington, NC	6.2	2.5	1.0	0.3	2.4
Winston-Salem, NC	10.8	6.7	1.1	0.2	2.8
Worcester, MA	12.3	0.9	7.2	0.2	4.0
U.S.	18.4	11.2	1.8	0.7	4.7

Note: Persons of Hispanic or Latino origin can be of any race; Figures cover the Metropolitan Statistical Area (MSA)
Source: U.S. Census Bureau, 2017-2021 American Community Survey 5-Year Estimates

Household Size: City

City	Persons in Household (%)							Average Household Size
	One	Two	Three	Four	Five	Six	Seven or More	
Albuquerque, NM	36.4	32.9	13.6	10.1	4.7	1.2	0.7	2.36
Allentown, PA	29.4	29.5	14.0	14.3	7.3	3.0	2.1	2.65
Anchorage, AK	26.8	32.9	15.5	13.5	6.2	2.6	2.1	2.68
Ann Arbor, MI	33.6	37.5	13.0	10.6	2.8	1.6	0.5	2.21
Athens, GA	34.2	34.4	14.9	11.1	3.4	1.1	0.6	2.22
Atlanta, GA	45.8	31.9	10.9	6.7	2.5	1.1	0.7	2.06
Austin, TX	34.7	33.7	14.3	10.4	4.2	1.5	0.8	2.28
Baltimore, MD	41.4	29.8	13.8	8.1	3.7	1.6	1.1	2.32
Boise City, ID	31.6	36.5	14.9	9.9	4.9	1.3	0.5	2.37
Boston, MA	36.2	32.7	15.1	9.4	3.9	1.6	0.9	2.30
Boulder, CO	35.7	35.9	13.9	10.5	2.7	0.4	0.5	2.21
Brownsville, TX	19.2	23.6	17.0	19.2	12.4	4.6	3.5	3.31
Cape Coral, FL	26.0	42.6	13.7	10.6	5.0	1.1	0.7	2.59
Cedar Rapids, IA	33.7	34.3	14.6	10.3	4.4	1.4	0.9	2.31
Charleston, SC	35.0	38.5	13.2	9.6	2.7	0.6	0.1	2.23
Charlotte, NC	34.1	31.7	15.0	11.9	4.6	1.5	0.9	2.47
Chicago, IL	38.2	29.5	13.5	10.0	4.9	2.1	1.4	2.41
Cincinnati, OH	44.5	30.2	11.4	8.4	3.0	1.3	0.8	2.11
Clarksville, TN	24.5	32.7	17.0	15.9	6.0	2.3	1.4	2.69
Cleveland, OH	46.0	27.9	12.0	7.3	3.7	1.7	1.0	2.15
College Station, TX	32.4	31.1	14.8	14.9	3.5	2.4	0.5	2.51
Colorado Springs, CO	27.5	36.0	15.0	12.4	5.5	2.2	1.1	2.48
Columbia, MO	35.6	31.7	13.7	11.1	5.7	1.2	0.7	2.33
Columbia, SC	39.1	32.6	13.4	8.9	4.0	1.4	0.2	2.19
Columbus, OH	35.8	32.6	13.3	10.1	4.8	1.7	1.3	2.32
Dallas, TX	36.3	29.5	13.1	10.3	6.4	2.4	1.6	2.49
Davenport, IA	34.3	35.7	13.1	9.1	5.0	1.7	0.8	2.36
Denver, CO	38.5	33.5	11.7	9.4	3.8	1.5	1.2	2.21
Des Moines, IA	34.8	30.5	14.3	10.8	5.1	2.5	1.6	2.40
Durham, NC	35.5	33.9	14.1	9.6	4.3	1.6	0.7	2.27
Edison, NJ	17.7	28.6	20.6	22.7	6.3	2.2	1.7	2.90
El Paso, TX	25.4	28.5	17.5	15.6	8.2	3.0	1.4	2.83
Fargo, ND	38.0	33.9	13.2	9.0	4.1	1.1	0.4	2.15
Fort Collins, CO	25.2	37.4	17.6	14.0	4.0	1.1	0.4	2.36
Fort Wayne, IN	32.8	32.7	14.1	10.8	5.6	2.6	1.1	2.42
Fort Worth, TX	26.6	29.4	16.5	14.6	7.5	3.1	2.0	2.81
Grand Rapids, MI	33.2	30.9	15.1	10.2	6.0	2.2	2.1	2.47
Greeley, CO	25.4	32.8	16.1	13.5	7.3	3.0	1.6	2.73
Green Bay, WI	34.9	32.2	13.5	10.6	5.5	1.5	1.3	2.36
Greensboro, NC	35.1	31.9	15.5	10.3	4.5	1.4	0.9	2.36
Honolulu, HI	34.9	30.4	14.1	10.5	4.9	2.1	2.8	2.54
Houston, TX	32.7	29.1	15.6	11.9	6.2	2.5	1.5	2.57
Huntsville, AL	36.6	34.9	14.4	8.5	3.9	0.8	0.5	2.21
Indianapolis, IN	36.8	32.2	12.9	9.7	5.1	1.8	1.1	2.46
Jacksonville, FL	32.2	32.8	16.3	10.7	5.1	1.6	0.9	2.50
Kansas City, MO	36.7	32.0	12.7	10.8	4.4	1.9	1.1	2.31
Lafayette, LA	33.6	36.0	14.1	8.6	4.7	1.5	1.1	2.30
Las Cruces, NM	31.9	31.4	15.8	12.6	5.5	1.6	0.7	2.46
Las Vegas, NV	30.2	31.3	15.5	12.1	6.1	2.7	1.7	2.65
Lexington, KY	33.0	34.2	14.3	11.4	4.2	1.7	0.8	2.30
Lincoln, NE	31.6	33.7	13.7	11.8	5.4	2.4	0.9	2.37
Little Rock, AR	37.6	31.8	13.8	9.9	4.4	1.4	0.7	2.33
Los Angeles, CA	30.5	28.5	15.4	13.1	6.7	2.9	2.5	2.75
Louisville, KY	33.8	32.9	15.1	10.7	4.9	1.4	0.9	2.39

Table continued on following page.

City	Persons in Household (%)							Average Household Size
	One	Two	Three	Four	Five	Six	Seven or More	
Madison, WI	37.7	35.2	12.4	9.4	3.4	1.0	0.5	2.16
Manchester, NH	33.9	33.2	15.8	10.3	3.5	1.9	1.0	2.32
Miami, FL	35.9	32.2	16.2	9.2	3.8	1.3	1.0	2.38
Midland, TX	26.8	28.2	17.2	15.2	8.2	2.8	1.3	2.57
Milwaukee, WI	37.7	28.8	13.7	10.0	5.7	2.3	1.5	2.45
Minneapolis, MN	40.4	31.6	11.5	9.5	3.4	1.7	1.5	2.24
Nashville, TN	35.2	33.3	14.5	9.6	4.6	1.4	1.1	2.34
New Haven, CT	36.7	29.1	16.1	9.0	5.3	2.0	1.4	2.48
New Orleans, LA	46.4	28.7	12.5	7.9	2.7	1.1	0.4	2.37
New York, NY	32.4	28.6	16.3	12.1	5.7	2.5	2.0	2.63
Oklahoma City, OK	31.3	31.8	15.1	11.6	6.4	2.5	1.0	2.49
Omaha, NE	33.6	31.6	13.6	10.7	6.1	2.5	1.6	2.44
Orlando, FL	32.8	33.5	16.0	10.8	4.3	1.3	1.0	2.53
Philadelphia, PA	37.1	29.4	14.9	10.2	4.8	1.8	1.3	2.40
Phoenix, AZ	27.9	30.0	15.2	13.0	7.4	3.6	2.7	2.71
Pittsburgh, PA	44.2	32.4	12.4	6.7	2.5	1.0	0.5	2.04
Portland, OR	34.9	35.2	13.7	10.3	3.5	1.2	0.8	2.26
Providence, RI	33.6	29.0	15.5	11.1	7.0	1.9	1.6	2.56
Provo, UT	15.1	34.8	17.3	14.9	7.2	6.9	3.4	3.10
Raleigh, NC	34.6	32.8	14.4	12.0	4.2	1.2	0.5	2.37
Reno, NV	31.9	34.0	14.6	11.2	5.3	1.4	1.2	2.37
Richmond, VA	42.4	33.0	12.0	7.6	2.8	1.3	0.5	2.19
Rochester, MN	31.0	34.7	13.0	12.2	5.5	1.9	1.4	2.40
Sacramento, CA	30.5	30.3	14.6	13.0	6.1	2.8	2.4	2.63
St. Louis, MO	46.2	30.2	10.8	7.3	3.2	0.9	1.0	2.08
Salem, OR	29.6	33.2	14.8	11.0	6.4	2.7	2.0	2.58
Salt Lake City, UT	38.2	32.7	11.9	9.3	4.1	1.9	1.7	2.32
San Antonio, TX	30.6	29.5	15.4	12.7	6.9	2.9	1.7	2.64
San Diego, CA	27.8	34.0	15.7	12.9	5.6	2.1	1.5	2.64
San Francisco, CA	36.5	32.9	13.9	10.1	3.6	1.4	1.3	2.34
San Jose, CA	19.7	28.9	18.8	17.9	8.0	3.2	3.2	3.08
Santa Rosa, CA	28.4	32.4	15.0	13.8	6.6	2.0	1.3	2.60
Savannah, GA	32.8	35.4	15.2	9.6	4.5	1.3	0.9	2.46
Seattle, WA	39.9	35.0	12.1	8.9	2.5	0.8	0.5	2.08
Sioux Falls, SD	32.2	33.4	14.0	11.2	6.1	1.8	1.0	2.37
Springfield, IL	39.3	32.5	12.3	9.5	3.8	1.2	1.0	2.18
Tampa, FL	35.9	31.1	15.6	10.7	4.2	1.5	0.6	2.41
Tucson, AZ	34.9	31.0	14.2	11.2	5.2	2.0	1.2	2.35
Tulsa, OK	35.5	32.2	13.2	10.4	5.0	2.2	1.1	2.41
Tuscaloosa, AL	37.2	32.9	14.0	9.9	3.8	1.3	0.6	2.45
Virginia Beach, VA	24.5	35.5	17.6	13.7	6.0	1.7	0.6	2.53
Washington, DC	45.4	30.6	11.6	7.3	3.1	1.0	0.6	2.08
Wichita, KS	32.8	32.4	13.0	11.2	6.2	2.5	1.7	2.51
Wilmington, NC	39.9	36.9	11.5	7.4	3.0	0.6	0.3	2.10
Winston-Salem, NC	36.0	31.7	14.7	9.3	4.6	2.4	1.0	2.43
Worcester, MA	34.9	28.3	17.0	11.9	4.4	2.1	1.0	2.40
U.S.	28.0	33.8	15.5	12.8	5.9	2.2	1.4	2.60

U.S. Census Bureau, 2017-2021 American Community Survey 5-Year Estimates

Household Size: Metro Area

Metro Area	Persons in Household (%)							Average Household Size
	One	Two	Three	Four	Five	Six	Seven or More	
Albuquerque, NM	32.3	34.7	14.2	10.7	5.1	1.7	1.0	2.49
Allentown, PA	26.5	35.6	15.2	13.6	5.8	1.9	1.1	2.52
Anchorage, AK	25.7	33.3	15.5	13.4	6.7	2.8	2.3	2.70
Ann Arbor, MI	29.9	36.6	14.7	11.7	4.2	1.8	0.8	2.39
Athens, GA	28.7	34.5	16.6	13.2	4.5	1.3	0.9	2.46
Atlanta, GA	26.7	31.7	17.0	14.2	6.2	2.4	1.4	2.69
Austin, TX	27.2	33.7	15.9	13.5	5.9	2.2	1.2	2.54
Baltimore, MD	29.1	32.7	16.1	12.9	5.6	2.0	1.1	2.55
Boise City, ID	24.7	36.0	15.3	12.5	6.5	3.1	1.6	2.67
Boston, MA	27.5	33.0	16.6	14.4	5.5	1.7	0.9	2.50
Boulder, CO	29.4	36.3	14.8	13.1	4.2	1.5	0.4	2.41
Brownsville, TX	20.4	26.8	16.4	17.5	10.4	4.9	3.3	3.21
Cape Coral, FL	28.6	44.2	11.5	8.8	4.6	1.3	0.7	2.49
Cedar Rapids, IA	29.5	36.6	14.1	11.9	5.1	1.6	0.9	2.41
Charleston, SC	28.7	36.1	16.2	11.8	4.9	1.4	0.7	2.50
Charlotte, NC	27.4	34.0	16.1	13.8	5.6	1.8	0.9	2.59
Chicago, IL	29.2	31.1	15.6	13.6	6.5	2.3	1.4	2.61
Cincinnati, OH	29.2	33.9	15.0	12.8	5.5	2.1	1.1	2.49
Clarksville, TN	25.1	33.1	17.6	13.9	6.1	2.5	1.3	2.68
Cleveland, OH	34.8	33.5	13.9	10.5	4.5	1.5	0.8	2.32
College Station, TX	30.8	32.6	14.6	12.7	5.3	2.6	1.1	2.56
Colorado Springs, CO	24.5	35.7	15.9	13.2	6.6	2.3	1.5	2.60
Columbia, MO	31.5	35.1	13.7	11.9	5.3	1.4	0.8	2.41
Columbia, SC	30.4	34.2	15.4	11.8	5.1	1.9	0.9	2.46
Columbus, OH	28.8	33.9	15.2	12.8	5.8	2.0	1.2	2.49
Dallas, TX	25.1	30.7	16.7	14.9	7.7	2.9	1.7	2.77
Davenport, IA	31.2	36.3	13.2	11.4	5.0	1.8	0.8	2.39
Denver, CO	28.4	34.4	15.0	13.1	5.3	2.2	1.3	2.51
Des Moines, IA	28.5	34.1	14.2	13.7	6.2	2.0	1.0	2.48
Durham, NC	30.7	36.0	15.0	11.2	4.8	1.4	0.7	2.40
Edison, NJ	28.0	29.5	17.0	14.4	6.4	2.5	1.9	2.71
El Paso, TX	23.6	27.7	17.7	16.2	9.1	3.6	1.7	2.94
Fargo, ND	33.2	33.8	13.9	11.2	5.4	1.4	0.8	2.33
Fort Collins, CO	24.8	39.8	15.7	12.2	4.9	1.4	0.8	2.38
Fort Wayne, IN	29.0	34.3	14.1	12.1	6.1	2.6	1.4	2.51
Fort Worth, TX	25.1	30.7	16.7	14.9	7.7	2.9	1.7	2.77
Grand Rapids, MI	25.0	34.3	15.2	14.3	7.2	2.4	1.4	2.61
Greeley, CO	20.1	34.4	16.3	15.8	8.1	3.2	1.6	2.84
Green Bay, WI	28.3	37.5	14.0	11.7	5.5	1.7	0.9	2.41
Greensboro, NC	30.0	34.5	16.1	11.5	4.9	1.8	0.9	2.47
Honolulu, HI	24.5	30.4	16.5	13.4	7.1	3.7	4.0	2.96
Houston, TX	24.2	29.6	17.2	15.7	8.0	3.0	1.8	2.83
Huntsville, AL	29.3	36.0	15.3	11.9	5.0	1.5	0.6	2.42
Indianapolis, IN	29.2	34.1	14.7	12.9	5.8	1.8	1.1	2.54
Jacksonville, FL	28.0	34.8	16.4	12.1	5.7	1.8	1.0	2.57
Kansas City, MO	29.1	34.4	14.3	13.0	5.7	2.0	1.2	2.50
Lafayette, LA	27.5	33.6	16.7	13.1	5.7	2.0	1.1	2.56
Las Cruces, NM	27.3	33.2	15.7	13.5	6.4	2.0	1.5	2.66
Las Vegas, NV	28.0	32.7	15.5	12.2	6.7	2.7	1.8	2.71
Lexington, KY	29.8	35.1	15.5	12.1	4.5	1.8	0.8	2.39
Lincoln, NE	29.9	35.2	13.6	12.0	5.6	2.4	1.0	2.41
Little Rock, AR	30.3	34.4	15.8	11.7	5.1	1.7	0.7	2.47
Los Angeles, CA	24.6	28.6	17.0	15.4	7.9	3.3	2.8	2.95
Louisville, KY	30.3	34.4	15.5	11.7	5.2	1.7	0.9	2.47

Table continued on following page.

Metro Area	Persons in Household (%)							Average Household Size
	One	Two	Three	Four	Five	Six	Seven or More	
Madison, WI	31.5	36.8	13.6	11.4	4.3	1.4	0.7	2.31
Manchester, NH	27.1	35.7	16.3	13.0	4.8	2.1	0.7	2.50
Miami, FL	28.0	32.4	17.0	13.3	5.9	2.0	1.1	2.68
Midland, TX	25.7	28.1	17.0	15.7	8.6	2.6	2.0	2.61
Milwaukee, WI	32.2	34.3	13.7	11.5	5.2	1.7	0.9	2.40
Minneapolis, MN	28.1	34.1	14.7	13.5	5.8	2.1	1.4	2.53
Nashville, TN	26.9	34.8	16.2	13.1	5.7	1.8	1.1	2.57
New Haven, CT	30.6	33.1	16.4	12.2	4.7	1.6	0.9	2.49
New Orleans, LA	34.1	32.0	15.3	11.2	4.6	1.6	0.9	2.52
New York, NY	28.0	29.5	17.0	14.4	6.4	2.5	1.9	2.71
Oklahoma City, OK	28.5	33.4	15.7	12.2	6.3	2.5	1.1	2.53
Omaha, NE	28.9	33.5	14.5	12.2	6.6	2.4	1.4	2.53
Orlando, FL	24.1	34.6	17.0	13.9	6.6	2.2	1.2	2.83
Philadelphia, PA	29.2	32.1	16.1	13.4	5.7	1.9	1.1	2.53
Phoenix, AZ	25.9	34.5	14.6	12.7	6.8	3.0	2.2	2.65
Pittsburgh, PA	33.7	35.3	14.1	10.7	4.1	1.2	0.5	2.27
Portland, OR	26.9	35.5	15.4	13.3	5.3	2.0	1.3	2.53
Providence, RI	29.6	33.1	16.7	12.7	5.1	1.6	0.8	2.46
Provo, UT	12.4	28.6	15.5	15.9	12.5	8.9	5.9	3.52
Raleigh, NC	25.4	34.1	16.6	14.8	5.9	1.9	0.9	2.61
Reno, NV	27.4	34.9	15.5	12.5	5.8	2.0	1.5	2.51
Richmond, VA	29.4	34.5	15.7	12.3	5.3	1.7	0.8	2.51
Rochester, MN	27.4	36.9	13.3	13.0	6.1	1.9	1.1	2.46
Sacramento, CA	24.6	32.9	15.9	14.7	6.9	2.7	1.9	2.73
St. Louis, MO	30.5	34.5	15.0	12.2	5.1	1.5	0.8	2.43
Salem, OR	25.3	34.1	15.2	12.4	7.4	3.3	2.0	2.74
Salt Lake City, UT	23.1	30.9	15.7	13.8	8.5	4.6	3.1	2.92
San Antonio, TX	26.2	30.9	16.2	14.0	7.5	3.0	1.8	2.74
San Diego, CA	24.0	32.8	16.8	14.6	6.8	2.7	1.9	2.81
San Francisco, CA	26.4	31.8	16.8	14.8	6.1	2.2	1.6	2.71
San Jose, CA	20.4	30.4	19.1	17.7	7.2	2.7	2.2	2.94
Santa Rosa, CA	26.9	35.1	14.8	13.7	6.1	1.9	1.1	2.56
Savannah, GA	27.9	36.7	15.8	12.1	4.8	1.5	0.9	2.56
Seattle, WA	27.2	33.9	16.0	13.9	5.4	1.9	1.3	2.53
Sioux Falls, SD	28.7	34.4	14.5	12.2	6.8	2.0	1.1	2.45
Springfield, IL	33.7	35.4	13.4	10.4	4.6	1.3	0.9	2.28
Tampa, FL	30.7	36.3	14.9	10.8	4.6	1.5	0.8	2.46
Tucson, AZ	30.7	35.4	13.4	11.3	5.2	2.3	1.3	2.41
Tulsa, OK	28.8	33.7	15.2	12.2	6.0	2.5	1.3	2.57
Tuscaloosa, AL	30.1	34.6	15.5	11.7	5.4	1.5	0.8	2.62
Virginia Beach, VA	27.8	34.4	16.9	12.5	5.5	1.8	0.8	2.49
Washington, DC	27.8	30.7	16.1	14.5	6.5	2.6	1.6	2.67
Wichita, KS	29.7	33.4	13.9	11.8	6.6	2.5	1.8	2.56
Wilmington, NC	33.6	36.4	14.4	10.1	3.6	1.2	0.4	2.30
Winston-Salem, NC	30.1	35.7	15.6	10.7	4.7	2.0	0.9	2.47
Worcester, MA	27.0	33.0	17.4	14.5	5.3	1.6	0.8	2.52
U.S.	28.0	33.8	15.5	12.8	5.9	2.2	1.4	2.60

Note: Figures cover the Metropolitan Statistical Area (MSA)
Source: U.S. Census Bureau, 2017-2021 American Community Survey 5-Year Estimates

Household Relationships: City

City	House-holder	Opposite-sex Spouse	Same-sex Spouse	Opposite-sex Unmarried Partner	Same-sex Unmarried Partner	Child[1]	Grand-child	Other Relatives	Non-relatives
Albuquerque, NM	42.1	15.1	0.3	3.4	0.3	27.0	2.5	4.6	3.2
Allentown, PA	36.3	11.6	0.2	3.7	0.2	30.6	3.2	6.8	4.1
Anchorage, AK	37.5	17.0	0.2	3.0	0.2	28.3	1.9	4.6	4.2
Ann Arbor, MI	40.3	13.3	0.3	2.4	0.2	17.1	0.5	1.6	11.5
Athens, GA	40.1	11.6	0.2	2.7	0.2	20.8	2.0	3.7	10.7
Atlanta, GA	45.7	10.4	0.5	3.1	0.6	20.7	2.1	3.9	5.9
Austin, TX	42.7	14.5	0.4	3.6	0.4	23.2	1.5	4.1	6.4
Baltimore, MD	42.9	9.6	0.3	3.3	0.3	24.9	3.7	5.8	6.1
Boise City, ID	41.4	17.8	0.2	3.2	0.2	24.7	1.3	2.9	5.4
Boston, MA	41.4	10.4	0.5	3.1	0.4	20.6	1.7	5.3	9.7
Boulder, CO	40.2	13.0	0.3	3.1	0.2	16.4	0.3	1.6	12.3
Brownsville, TX	30.8	15.0	0.1	1.4	0.1	36.7	4.7	8.3	1.6
Cape Coral, FL	39.5	21.2	0.3	3.2	0.1	25.5	2.1	4.8	2.8
Cedar Rapids, IA	42.2	16.7	0.2	3.5	0.2	26.8	1.3	2.9	3.4
Charleston, SC	45.0	17.0	0.3	3.1	0.2	21.8	1.4	2.7	5.3
Charlotte, NC	40.6	15.2	0.2	2.8	0.2	28.0	2.1	4.9	4.2
Chicago, IL	41.6	12.2	0.3	3.0	0.3	26.6	3.0	6.4	4.8
Cincinnati, OH	45.1	10.2	0.3	3.4	0.3	24.6	2.2	3.4	5.3
Clarksville, TN	36.6	16.9	0.2	2.5	0.1	31.2	2.4	3.9	3.5
Cleveland, OH	45.0	8.5	0.2	3.5	0.3	27.0	3.3	5.0	3.8
College Station, TX	35.2	11.2	0.2	1.8	0.1	19.7	0.7	2.7	13.7
Colorado Springs, CO	39.7	18.3	0.3	2.6	0.2	27.5	1.9	3.6	4.3
Columbia, MO	40.5	14.1	0.2	2.8	0.2	22.4	1.0	2.5	7.8
Columbia, SC	39.2	10.5	0.2	2.1	0.2	19.5	1.6	2.8	5.8
Columbus, OH	42.2	12.9	0.3	3.6	0.3	26.2	2.1	4.4	5.2
Dallas, TX	40.1	13.4	0.4	2.6	0.3	28.6	3.2	6.2	4.0
Davenport, IA	41.9	15.9	0.2	3.7	0.2	27.0	2.0	3.0	3.2
Denver, CO	44.4	14.0	0.5	4.1	0.4	22.3	1.9	4.4	5.9
Des Moines, IA	41.1	14.2	0.3	3.5	0.2	27.9	2.0	4.4	3.9
Durham, NC	42.0	14.8	0.4	2.9	0.3	24.6	1.8	4.4	4.6
Edison, NJ	34.3	21.2	0.1	1.1	0.1	32.2	1.4	6.8	1.9
El Paso, TX	35.9	15.8	0.2	1.8	0.1	32.7	3.9	6.4	2.0
Fargo, ND	44.5	15.5	0.1	3.6	0.2	23.5	0.7	2.5	5.0
Fort Collins, CO	39.9	16.0	0.2	3.3	0.2	22.1	0.9	2.4	9.0
Fort Wayne, IN	40.7	15.6	0.2	3.1	0.2	29.7	2.0	3.4	3.0
Fort Worth, TX	35.2	15.8	0.2	2.1	0.1	33.0	3.1	5.6	3.0
Grand Rapids, MI	40.2	13.1	0.3	3.6	0.3	26.1	2.1	4.0	6.6
Greeley, CO	34.9	15.8	0.2	2.5	0.1	29.4	2.6	5.0	5.1
Green Bay, WI	40.7	15.2	0.2	4.0	0.2	28.6	1.6	3.4	3.0
Greensboro, NC	40.9	13.6	0.2	2.6	0.2	26.4	2.0	4.1	3.6
Honolulu, HI	39.1	15.0	0.3	2.4	0.2	22.2	3.1	9.1	5.6
Houston, TX	38.9	14.0	0.3	2.4	0.2	29.5	2.9	6.5	3.6
Huntsville, AL	42.8	16.5	0.2	2.2	0.2	25.1	2.1	3.5	3.1
Indianapolis, IN	40.7	14.0	0.3	3.4	0.3	28.6	2.5	4.5	3.9
Jacksonville, FL	39.9	15.6	0.2	2.8	0.2	27.7	2.8	4.9	3.6
Kansas City, MO	42.6	14.5	0.3	3.3	0.3	27.2	2.3	4.0	3.8
Lafayette, LA	43.0	15.3	0.2	2.8	0.2	27.0	2.3	3.5	3.8
Las Cruces, NM	41.1	14.9	0.2	3.4	0.3	28.5	2.5	4.5	3.6
Las Vegas, NV	37.5	15.2	0.3	2.9	0.2	29.3	2.7	6.7	4.3
Lexington, KY	41.7	16.0	0.3	2.9	0.3	25.3	1.6	3.4	4.4
Lincoln, NE	40.1	16.9	0.2	2.8	0.1	26.6	1.1	2.7	4.6
Little Rock, AR	43.5	14.5	0.3	2.4	0.3	27.1	2.3	3.9	3.1
Los Angeles, CA	36.2	13.1	0.3	2.8	0.3	26.5	2.8	9.0	6.3
Louisville, KY	40.0	18.0	0.2	2.9	0.2	28.8	2.6	4.2	2.7
Madison, WI	44.8	14.5	0.4	3.8	0.3	19.7	0.7	2.4	8.2

Table continued on following page.

City	House-holder	Opposite-sex Spouse	Same-sex Spouse	Opposite-sex Unmarried Partner	Same-sex Unmarried Partner	Child[1]	Grand-child	Other Relatives	Non-relatives
Manchester, NH	42.5	14.9	0.3	4.3	0.2	24.3	1.6	4.3	4.7
Miami, FL	42.4	12.6	0.5	3.3	0.3	22.5	2.4	8.7	5.8
Midland, TX	36.4	18.5	0.1	2.1	0.1	31.9	3.0	4.2	2.5
Milwaukee, WI	40.8	10.2	0.2	3.6	0.2	30.2	2.7	4.9	4.4
Minneapolis, MN	43.7	12.0	0.6	3.9	0.5	22.1	1.1	3.5	8.0
Nashville, TN	42.1	14.3	0.3	3.0	0.3	24.0	1.9	4.7	5.7
New Haven, CT	39.0	9.4	0.3	2.9	0.2	27.0	2.5	5.0	5.7
New Orleans, LA	43.0	11.0	0.3	3.1	0.4	26.1	3.2	4.6	4.3
New York, NY	38.3	12.7	0.3	2.2	0.2	27.6	2.5	8.3	5.3
Oklahoma City, OK	39.4	16.6	0.2	2.6	0.2	29.4	2.3	4.3	3.1
Omaha, NE	39.8	16.0	0.2	2.8	0.2	29.6	1.8	3.7	3.6
Orlando, FL	41.7	13.7	0.5	3.5	0.4	26.1	2.0	5.9	5.0
Philadelphia, PA	41.0	10.9	0.3	3.1	0.3	26.8	3.6	5.9	5.2
Phoenix, AZ	36.3	14.4	0.3	3.1	0.3	30.2	2.9	6.6	4.2
Pittsburgh, PA	46.1	11.5	0.3	3.6	0.4	19.3	1.7	3.1	6.7
Portland, OR	43.2	14.9	0.7	4.4	0.6	21.2	1.1	3.7	7.2
Providence, RI	36.5	10.5	0.3	2.9	0.3	27.3	1.9	5.7	6.1
Provo, UT	29.6	15.9	0.1	0.6	0.0	25.7	1.6	4.0	12.7
Raleigh, NC	41.8	15.1	0.2	2.9	0.2	25.5	1.4	3.9	5.0
Reno, NV	41.1	15.2	0.3	3.8	0.2	24.8	1.7	4.7	5.7
Richmond, VA	45.2	10.4	0.4	4.0	0.4	20.8	2.1	4.3	7.4
Rochester, MN	41.1	18.5	0.2	2.8	0.1	27.8	0.9	2.8	3.3
Sacramento, CA	36.7	13.5	0.4	3.0	0.3	28.0	2.6	7.5	4.7
St. Louis, MO	48.0	10.3	0.4	3.7	0.4	22.5	2.6	4.0	4.3
Salem, OR	36.6	16.0	0.2	3.1	0.2	28.1	1.9	4.6	4.2
Salt Lake City, UT	42.3	13.9	0.5	3.4	0.4	22.1	1.7	4.2	7.6
San Antonio, TX	37.5	14.7	0.3	2.7	0.2	30.3	3.8	5.5	3.2
San Diego, CA	37.2	15.7	0.4	2.6	0.3	25.0	2.0	6.2	6.1
San Francisco, CA	42.6	13.6	0.8	3.3	0.6	17.6	1.3	6.8	10.3
San Jose, CA	32.4	17.1	0.2	1.9	0.1	28.6	2.3	9.8	6.1
Santa Rosa, CA	37.6	16.2	0.4	3.0	0.2	27.3	1.8	6.2	5.5
Savannah, GA	39.9	11.2	0.3	2.7	0.3	24.9	3.2	4.4	5.0
Seattle, WA	46.9	15.2	0.8	4.3	0.6	17.5	0.7	2.8	7.3
Sioux Falls, SD	40.7	18.0	0.1	3.2	0.1	28.4	1.1	2.7	3.1
Springfield, IL	44.8	15.5	0.2	3.2	0.2	25.7	1.9	2.8	2.8
Tampa, FL	40.9	13.8	0.3	3.2	0.3	25.8	2.3	4.9	4.5
Tucson, AZ	41.1	13.3	0.3	3.3	0.3	25.4	2.8	4.8	4.5
Tulsa, OK	41.6	14.8	0.2	2.9	0.2	27.8	2.3	4.3	3.4
Tuscaloosa, AL	41.0	10.6	0.1	2.1	0.1	21.3	2.4	3.5	8.7
Virginia Beach, VA	38.8	18.6	0.2	2.4	0.1	28.7	2.2	4.0	3.5
Washington, DC	45.3	10.3	0.6	3.1	0.5	20.4	2.4	4.2	7.1
Wichita, KS	40.0	16.4	0.2	2.7	0.2	29.1	2.2	3.7	3.1
Wilmington, NC	45.7	14.9	0.3	3.4	0.3	21.2	1.5	3.0	5.9
Winston-Salem, NC	40.9	14.6	0.2	2.5	0.2	28.1	2.4	4.3	2.7
Worcester, MA	38.3	12.2	0.3	2.8	0.2	26.3	1.7	5.7	5.3
U.S.	38.3	17.5	0.2	2.5	0.2	28.3	2.4	4.8	3.4

Note: Figures are percent of the total population; (1) Includes biological, adopted, and stepchildren of the householder
Source: U.S. Census Bureau, 2020 Census

Household Relationships: Metro Area

Metro Area	House-holder	Opposite-sex Spouse	Same-sex Spouse	Opposite-sex Unmarried Partner	Same-sex Unmarried Partner	Child[1]	Grand-child	Other Relatives	Non-relatives
Albuquerque, NM	40.1	16.3	0.3	3.1	0.3	27.7	3.1	4.6	2.9
Allentown, PA	38.8	18.7	0.2	2.9	0.1	28.2	2.0	4.1	2.5
Anchorage, AK	37.1	17.6	0.2	2.9	0.1	29.1	1.9	4.2	4.0
Ann Arbor, MI	39.7	17.0	0.3	2.4	0.2	24.3	1.3	2.5	5.8
Athens, GA	38.6	15.6	0.2	2.3	0.2	25.1	2.3	3.7	7.3
Atlanta, GA	37.1	16.7	0.2	2.1	0.2	30.4	2.7	5.7	3.5
Austin, TX	38.6	17.3	0.3	2.7	0.3	27.8	1.9	4.4	4.6
Baltimore, MD	38.7	16.8	0.2	2.4	0.2	28.7	2.5	4.8	3.5
Boise City, ID	36.6	19.5	0.2	2.5	0.1	29.7	1.9	3.5	3.8
Boston, MA	38.7	17.4	0.3	2.5	0.2	27.1	1.6	4.5	4.4
Boulder, CO	40.1	18.0	0.3	2.8	0.2	23.8	1.0	2.6	6.8
Brownsville, TX	31.5	15.3	0.1	1.7	0.1	36.1	5.2	7.4	1.7
Cape Coral, FL	41.8	20.9	0.3	3.0	0.2	22.4	1.8	4.4	3.3
Cedar Rapids, IA	40.9	19.3	0.1	3.0	0.1	27.9	1.2	2.3	2.5
Charleston, SC	39.9	18.1	0.2	2.4	0.1	27.3	2.6	3.8	3.5
Charlotte, NC	38.9	18.3	0.2	2.4	0.2	29.2	2.4	4.2	2.8
Chicago, IL	38.2	17.1	0.2	2.3	0.1	30.3	2.4	5.1	2.8
Cincinnati, OH	39.5	18.1	0.2	2.7	0.1	28.9	2.3	3.2	2.9
Clarksville, TN	36.7	18.2	0.2	2.2	0.1	30.5	2.5	3.6	3.0
Cleveland, OH	42.5	17.1	0.1	2.7	0.1	27.7	2.1	3.3	2.3
College Station, TX	36.9	14.6	0.1	2.0	0.1	24.7	1.9	3.5	8.3
Colorado Springs, CO	37.5	19.3	0.2	2.2	0.1	28.5	2.0	3.6	3.8
Columbia, MO	39.8	16.5	0.2	2.8	0.2	24.9	1.4	2.5	5.7
Columbia, SC	39.9	17.0	0.2	2.1	0.2	27.5	2.7	3.8	3.0
Columbus, OH	39.4	17.4	0.2	2.9	0.2	28.5	2.0	3.5	3.3
Dallas, TX	36.2	17.6	0.2	2.0	0.2	31.7	2.7	5.5	2.9
Davenport, IA	41.4	18.8	0.2	2.9	0.1	27.9	1.8	2.5	2.2
Denver, CO	39.4	17.9	0.3	2.9	0.2	27.4	1.9	4.4	4.3
Des Moines, IA	39.6	19.2	0.2	2.7	0.1	29.6	1.3	2.8	2.6
Durham, NC	40.3	17.2	0.3	2.5	0.2	25.1	1.9	3.8	3.9
Edison, NJ	36.8	15.8	0.2	2.0	0.2	29.7	2.1	7.1	4.1
El Paso, TX	34.2	15.8	0.2	1.7	0.1	33.5	4.2	6.5	1.8
Fargo, ND	41.5	17.7	0.1	3.2	0.1	27.0	0.7	2.2	3.9
Fort Collins, CO	40.2	19.4	0.2	2.8	0.2	24.0	1.2	2.7	6.0
Fort Wayne, IN	39.5	18.0	0.2	2.7	0.1	30.5	1.9	2.9	2.5
Fort Worth, TX	36.2	17.6	0.2	2.0	0.2	31.7	2.7	5.5	2.9
Grand Rapids, MI	37.3	19.0	0.1	2.5	0.1	29.6	1.7	2.9	3.5
Greeley, CO	34.6	19.3	0.1	2.2	0.1	31.5	2.4	4.6	3.6
Green Bay, WI	40.5	19.8	0.1	3.3	0.1	28.1	1.2	2.2	2.2
Greensboro, NC	40.2	17.1	0.2	2.4	0.2	27.4	2.3	3.9	2.6
Honolulu, HI	33.1	16.3	0.2	1.9	0.1	26.2	4.5	9.2	4.9
Houston, TX	35.2	17.1	0.2	2.0	0.1	32.7	2.8	6.1	2.6
Huntsville, AL	40.1	19.3	0.1	1.9	0.1	27.8	2.3	3.4	2.3
Indianapolis, IN	39.2	17.9	0.2	2.8	0.2	29.6	2.1	3.5	2.8
Jacksonville, FL	39.1	17.9	0.2	2.6	0.2	28.0	2.6	4.3	3.2
Kansas City, MO	39.6	18.4	0.2	2.6	0.2	29.4	2.0	3.3	2.7
Lafayette, LA	39.5	17.1	0.2	2.7	0.2	30.4	2.9	3.5	2.5
Las Cruces, NM	37.5	15.9	0.2	2.7	0.2	30.0	3.6	5.1	2.7
Las Vegas, NV	37.3	15.5	0.3	3.0	0.2	28.7	2.6	7.0	4.4
Lexington, KY	40.5	17.4	0.2	2.8	0.2	26.5	2.0	3.4	3.7
Lincoln, NE	39.5	17.9	0.2	2.6	0.1	27.2	1.1	2.6	4.1
Little Rock, AR	40.8	17.7	0.2	2.3	0.2	27.9	2.6	3.6	2.7
Los Angeles, CA	34.0	15.2	0.2	2.3	0.2	29.0	3.0	9.1	5.1
Louisville, KY	40.5	17.7	0.2	2.8	0.2	27.6	2.5	3.6	2.9
Madison, WI	42.2	18.6	0.3	3.3	0.2	25.0	0.8	2.1	4.5

Table continued on following page.

Metro Area	House-holder	Opposite-sex Spouse	Same-sex Spouse	Opposite-sex Unmarried Partner	Same-sex Unmarried Partner	Child[1]	Grand-child	Other Relatives	Non-relatives
Manchester, NH	39.7	19.2	0.3	3.2	0.1	27.2	1.6	3.5	3.2
Miami, FL	38.0	16.0	0.3	2.6	0.2	27.6	2.5	7.8	3.7
Midland, TX	35.8	18.6	0.1	2.0	0.1	32.3	3.2	4.4	2.6
Milwaukee, WI	41.3	17.5	0.2	2.9	0.2	28.7	1.6	3.1	2.7
Minneapolis, MN	38.9	18.7	0.2	2.8	0.2	29.4	1.2	3.3	3.3
Nashville, TN	38.8	18.2	0.2	2.4	0.2	28.1	2.2	4.1	3.8
New Haven, CT	39.7	16.5	0.2	2.6	0.2	28.1	2.0	4.4	2.9
New Orleans, LA	40.3	15.3	0.2	2.7	0.2	28.8	3.1	4.6	2.9
New York, NY	36.8	15.8	0.2	2.0	0.2	29.7	2.1	7.1	4.1
Oklahoma City, OK	38.8	17.7	0.2	2.4	0.2	29.0	2.3	3.8	3.1
Omaha, NE	38.8	18.4	0.2	2.6	0.1	30.6	1.6	3.1	2.8
Orlando, FL	37.0	17.0	0.3	2.7	0.2	28.4	2.4	6.0	4.2
Philadelphia, PA	38.7	16.9	0.2	2.5	0.2	29.2	2.5	4.4	3.0
Phoenix, AZ	36.9	17.2	0.2	2.8	0.2	29.0	2.5	5.4	3.7
Pittsburgh, PA	43.2	19.0	0.2	2.8	0.2	25.6	1.6	2.6	2.4
Portland, OR	39.0	18.1	0.4	3.2	0.3	26.7	1.6	4.2	4.9
Providence, RI	40.0	16.9	0.2	3.0	0.2	27.2	1.9	4.1	3.0
Provo, UT	28.0	18.8	0.1	0.7	0.0	39.0	2.1	4.0	4.8
Raleigh, NC	38.4	19.2	0.2	2.2	0.2	30.0	1.5	3.7	3.0
Reno, NV	39.5	17.2	0.2	3.4	0.2	26.1	2.1	5.0	4.9
Richmond, VA	39.5	17.3	0.2	2.5	0.2	27.7	2.4	4.0	3.3
Rochester, MN	40.1	20.5	0.1	2.7	0.1	28.9	1.0	2.2	2.5
Sacramento, CA	36.2	17.1	0.3	2.4	0.2	29.4	2.2	6.0	4.2
St. Louis, MO	40.8	18.2	0.2	2.6	0.2	28.5	2.2	3.0	2.4
Salem, OR	35.7	17.6	0.2	2.7	0.1	29.3	2.3	5.0	4.1
Salt Lake City, UT	34.0	17.4	0.3	2.1	0.2	32.4	2.5	5.3	4.4
San Antonio, TX	36.2	16.9	0.2	2.3	0.2	31.0	3.5	5.1	2.8
San Diego, CA	35.1	16.9	0.3	2.3	0.2	27.8	2.3	6.6	5.1
San Francisco, CA	36.7	17.0	0.4	2.3	0.3	26.3	1.8	6.9	5.9
San Jose, CA	33.8	18.4	0.2	1.8	0.1	28.3	1.9	7.9	5.6
Santa Rosa, CA	38.4	17.6	0.4	2.9	0.2	26.1	1.9	5.2	5.5
Savannah, GA	38.7	16.6	0.2	2.4	0.2	28.0	2.8	4.1	3.4
Seattle, WA	38.9	18.3	0.3	2.9	0.2	26.7	1.5	4.6	4.7
Sioux Falls, SD	39.5	19.4	0.1	2.9	0.1	29.8	1.1	2.3	2.6
Springfield, IL	42.9	18.2	0.2	3.0	0.2	27.2	1.8	2.4	2.4
Tampa, FL	41.2	17.6	0.3	3.1	0.2	25.5	2.2	4.6	3.4
Tucson, AZ	40.9	17.2	0.3	2.9	0.2	25.5	2.6	4.4	3.4
Tulsa, OK	39.1	18.2	0.2	2.4	0.1	29.0	2.6	3.9	2.7
Tuscaloosa, AL	39.8	15.2	0.1	1.9	0.1	26.5	3.2	3.9	4.5
Virginia Beach, VA	39.0	17.4	0.2	2.3	0.1	27.7	2.5	4.0	3.3
Washington, DC	37.0	17.3	0.3	2.0	0.2	29.3	2.0	5.9	4.4
Wichita, KS	39.0	18.2	0.1	2.4	0.1	29.8	2.1	3.2	2.6
Wilmington, NC	42.3	18.7	0.2	2.9	0.2	24.4	1.9	3.1	3.9
Winston-Salem, NC	40.9	18.6	0.2	2.3	0.1	27.5	2.4	3.7	2.2
Worcester, MA	38.6	17.9	0.2	2.9	0.1	28.1	1.7	4.0	3.1
U.S.	38.3	17.5	0.2	2.5	0.2	28.3	2.4	4.8	3.4

Note: Figures are percent of the total population; Figures cover the Metropolitan Statistical Area; (1) Includes biological, adopted, and stepchildren of the householder
Source: U.S. Census Bureau, 2020 Census

Age: City

City	Percent of Population									Median Age
	Under Age 5	Age 5–19	Age 20–34	Age 35–44	Age 45–54	Age 55–64	Age 65–74	Age 75–84	Age 85+	
Albuquerque, NM	5.1	18.6	21.8	13.2	11.7	12.7	10.2	4.9	1.9	38.2
Allentown, PA	6.8	21.0	23.3	12.4	11.4	11.6	7.8	3.9	1.7	34.2
Anchorage, AK	6.4	19.6	23.4	13.7	11.7	12.6	8.3	3.1	0.9	35.2
Ann Arbor, MI	3.9	15.5	42.4	9.6	7.8	8.1	7.3	3.6	1.7	27.9
Athens, GA	5.1	16.6	38.4	10.7	8.8	8.5	7.3	3.5	1.2	28.2
Atlanta, GA	4.9	15.5	33.3	14.3	11.2	9.5	6.8	3.3	1.3	33.1
Austin, TX	5.5	16.7	31.8	16.1	11.4	9.0	6.1	2.5	1.0	33.0
Baltimore, MD	5.5	16.6	27.0	13.1	10.7	12.6	8.9	4.0	1.6	35.5
Boise City, ID	5.1	18.4	23.4	13.6	11.7	12.0	9.5	4.5	1.8	37.1
Boston, MA	4.5	14.1	37.6	12.0	9.6	9.8	7.2	3.7	1.5	31.7
Boulder, CO	3.0	19.4	34.9	10.4	10.3	9.1	7.7	3.6	1.6	30.0
Brownsville, TX	6.6	25.8	20.0	12.3	12.0	10.1	7.9	3.8	1.5	32.9
Cape Coral, FL	4.5	16.6	14.9	11.3	13.4	16.0	14.5	6.8	2.1	47.2
Cedar Rapids, IA	6.3	19.1	22.5	13.0	11.2	12.0	8.9	4.6	2.4	36.4
Charleston, SC	5.6	14.6	28.5	13.9	10.3	11.2	9.7	4.4	1.8	35.7
Charlotte, NC	6.1	19.3	25.8	14.6	12.6	10.5	6.9	3.0	1.1	34.2
Chicago, IL	5.5	16.9	27.5	14.4	11.9	11.1	7.7	3.7	1.4	35.1
Cincinnati, OH	6.1	18.3	29.2	11.9	10.0	11.5	8.0	3.3	1.7	32.7
Clarksville, TN	8.3	21.9	28.4	13.0	9.9	9.2	5.8	2.5	0.8	29.9
Cleveland, OH	6.0	18.2	24.2	11.8	11.5	13.9	9.0	3.9	1.7	36.1
College Station, TX	5.4	24.3	43.8	8.4	6.3	5.2	3.8	2.1	0.6	22.5
Colorado Springs, CO	5.9	19.0	23.7	13.2	11.3	12.2	8.9	4.1	1.6	35.9
Columbia, MO	5.5	20.5	32.8	11.4	9.1	8.9	7.0	3.3	1.5	29.2
Columbia, SC	4.6	22.1	30.7	11.1	9.5	9.8	7.7	3.2	1.3	29.9
Columbus, OH	6.6	18.1	30.0	13.4	10.7	10.3	6.9	2.9	1.2	32.3
Dallas, TX	6.5	19.3	26.6	14.2	11.7	10.6	6.8	3.1	1.3	33.6
Davenport, IA	6.1	18.8	21.8	12.5	11.5	12.8	9.7	4.6	2.1	37.5
Denver, CO	5.4	15.5	31.0	15.8	11.1	9.4	7.4	3.2	1.3	34.1
Des Moines, IA	6.6	19.7	24.0	13.1	11.3	11.8	8.2	3.6	1.7	34.8
Durham, NC	6.0	17.6	28.2	13.9	11.1	10.4	8.1	3.4	1.3	33.9
Edison, NJ	5.3	19.7	18.1	16.5	13.3	12.2	8.9	4.2	1.9	39.0
El Paso, TX	5.9	21.7	21.9	11.9	11.9	11.9	8.6	4.3	1.9	35.4
Fargo, ND	6.2	17.8	30.1	13.0	9.7	10.3	7.7	3.5	1.8	32.5
Fort Collins, CO	4.4	19.4	31.1	12.7	10.2	9.5	7.7	3.4	1.6	31.7
Fort Wayne, IN	6.9	20.8	21.9	12.4	11.2	11.9	9.1	4.1	1.9	35.3
Fort Worth, TX	7.0	22.7	23.1	14.3	12.1	10.3	6.6	2.9	1.1	33.2
Grand Rapids, MI	6.4	18.1	31.1	12.2	9.3	10.1	7.3	3.4	2.1	31.7
Greeley, CO	6.9	22.5	25.0	12.3	10.2	9.8	7.9	3.9	1.6	31.9
Green Bay, WI	6.5	20.6	22.5	12.9	11.1	12.4	8.6	3.7	1.5	35.2
Greensboro, NC	5.5	20.0	24.9	12.1	11.5	11.3	8.7	4.2	1.8	34.7
Honolulu, HI	4.5	14.3	20.5	13.0	12.7	13.7	11.5	6.0	3.6	42.9
Houston, TX	6.6	19.7	25.1	14.3	11.6	10.7	7.3	3.4	1.3	34.2
Huntsville, AL	5.6	17.7	24.2	12.0	11.2	13.1	9.0	5.2	2.2	36.9
Indianapolis, IN	6.6	20.2	24.0	13.4	11.3	11.8	7.9	3.5	1.3	34.5
Jacksonville, FL	6.0	18.2	22.3	12.9	12.2	13.1	9.3	4.2	1.6	37.4
Kansas City, MO	6.2	18.5	25.0	13.6	11.4	11.9	8.2	3.7	1.5	35.1
Lafayette, LA	5.6	17.9	23.5	12.4	10.9	13.0	10.2	4.6	2.0	37.3
Las Cruces, NM	5.8	20.1	23.5	11.9	10.0	11.2	10.0	5.4	2.1	35.5
Las Vegas, NV	5.7	20.0	20.0	13.5	13.1	12.1	9.4	4.7	1.5	38.0
Lexington, KY	5.7	19.2	24.7	13.3	11.4	11.2	8.6	4.0	1.6	35.2
Lincoln, NE	6.0	20.5	24.9	12.9	10.4	10.8	8.8	3.9	1.7	34.0
Little Rock, AR	6.0	18.7	22.1	13.5	11.8	12.2	9.7	4.3	1.8	37.2
Los Angeles, CA	4.9	17.0	25.6	14.6	12.9	11.5	8.0	3.9	1.7	36.5
Louisville, KY	5.9	19.2	18.9	12.8	12.8	13.4	10.0	4.8	1.9	39.5

Table continued on following page.

City	Percent of Population									Median Age
	Under Age 5	Age 5–19	Age 20–34	Age 35–44	Age 45–54	Age 55–64	Age 65–74	Age 75–84	Age 85+	
Madison, WI	5.0	16.4	33.7	12.6	9.4	9.6	8.1	3.5	1.6	32.0
Manchester, NH	5.3	15.7	26.0	12.6	12.1	13.4	9.0	3.9	2.0	37.0
Miami, FL	4.8	13.6	24.0	15.0	13.5	12.4	8.8	5.5	2.5	39.7
Midland, TX	7.9	21.7	23.5	14.4	10.3	11.0	6.7	3.0	1.5	33.3
Milwaukee, WI	6.8	21.9	25.6	12.6	10.8	10.8	7.3	2.9	1.3	32.1
Minneapolis, MN	5.6	16.1	32.8	14.7	10.3	9.7	7.1	2.6	1.0	32.6
Nashville, TN	6.1	16.6	29.5	14.1	10.7	10.8	7.5	3.3	1.3	33.8
New Haven, CT	5.6	20.8	30.4	12.8	10.0	9.4	6.6	3.1	1.2	31.0
New Orleans, LA	5.5	17.5	24.9	14.0	11.1	12.3	9.4	3.9	1.5	36.2
New York, NY	5.4	16.7	24.8	13.9	12.2	12.0	8.7	4.4	1.9	36.8
Oklahoma City, OK	6.7	20.7	22.7	13.9	11.2	11.4	8.3	3.8	1.5	34.9
Omaha, NE	6.6	20.7	23.1	13.0	11.0	11.7	8.4	3.8	1.6	34.7
Orlando, FL	5.7	17.6	27.2	15.6	12.4	10.1	6.8	3.2	1.3	34.7
Philadelphia, PA	5.5	17.6	27.2	12.9	10.9	11.6	8.5	4.0	1.7	34.8
Phoenix, AZ	6.3	21.6	22.9	13.7	12.4	11.3	7.5	3.2	1.1	34.5
Pittsburgh, PA	4.4	14.5	34.3	11.5	8.8	11.1	9.1	4.2	2.0	33.0
Portland, OR	4.5	14.6	25.8	17.2	13.1	10.8	8.9	3.7	1.4	37.6
Providence, RI	5.6	21.3	29.4	12.4	10.4	9.8	6.6	3.0	1.4	30.9
Provo, UT	7.1	21.4	44.5	8.3	6.1	5.4	3.8	2.2	1.1	23.8
Raleigh, NC	5.5	18.5	28.0	14.0	12.1	10.1	7.0	3.3	1.4	33.7
Reno, NV	5.5	18.0	24.5	12.7	11.3	11.9	9.9	4.6	1.5	36.3
Richmond, VA	5.5	15.8	33.4	12.0	9.3	10.8	8.2	3.4	1.5	32.4
Rochester, MN	6.5	18.6	23.3	13.4	10.5	11.9	8.5	5.0	2.3	36.0
Sacramento, CA	5.9	18.8	24.6	14.1	11.5	11.2	8.5	3.7	1.6	35.4
St. Louis, MO	5.3	15.1	28.8	13.6	10.9	12.8	8.7	3.4	1.4	35.4
Salem, OR	5.9	20.3	21.7	13.6	11.5	11.2	9.6	4.5	1.8	36.3
Salt Lake City, UT	5.1	16.7	33.3	14.1	10.3	9.2	7.0	2.9	1.3	32.1
San Antonio, TX	6.1	20.6	23.4	13.0	11.8	11.4	8.2	3.9	1.6	34.9
San Diego, CA	5.0	16.8	26.7	14.2	11.9	11.3	8.3	4.0	1.7	35.8
San Francisco, CA	4.0	10.5	29.3	15.8	12.5	11.4	9.2	4.6	2.4	38.2
San Jose, CA	5.3	18.5	22.2	14.7	13.9	12.2	7.7	4.0	1.6	37.6
Santa Rosa, CA	5.1	18.5	19.4	13.7	12.1	12.5	10.9	5.4	2.5	39.9
Savannah, GA	5.8	18.4	28.0	12.2	10.2	11.2	8.6	4.0	1.6	33.5
Seattle, WA	4.4	12.6	33.1	16.0	11.8	9.7	7.7	3.3	1.5	35.0
Sioux Falls, SD	7.0	19.8	22.7	13.8	10.7	11.4	8.7	4.0	1.8	35.3
Springfield, IL	5.8	17.6	19.4	12.2	11.6	14.1	11.5	5.5	2.4	40.7
Tampa, FL	5.4	18.7	24.6	13.6	12.4	11.9	8.0	3.8	1.5	35.8
Tucson, AZ	5.3	18.2	24.8	12.0	10.9	12.1	9.9	4.8	1.9	36.2
Tulsa, OK	6.5	19.8	22.5	12.9	11.1	11.8	9.0	4.3	2.0	35.8
Tuscaloosa, AL	5.1	20.8	34.3	10.0	8.8	9.0	7.2	3.3	1.5	27.1
Virginia Beach, VA	5.8	18.6	22.4	13.3	11.8	12.9	9.1	4.4	1.7	37.1
Washington, DC	5.4	13.9	32.9	15.2	10.0	9.9	7.4	3.6	1.5	33.9
Wichita, KS	6.3	21.0	21.7	12.4	11.1	12.4	9.1	4.1	1.8	35.7
Wilmington, NC	4.3	15.1	27.2	11.8	11.0	12.1	10.8	5.7	2.3	37.8
Winston-Salem, NC	5.8	20.5	22.0	12.2	11.6	12.1	9.1	4.5	2.0	36.2
Worcester, MA	5.4	18.9	26.8	12.1	11.5	11.9	7.9	3.7	1.9	34.3
U.S.	5.6	19.2	20.2	12.7	12.4	13.1	10.0	4.9	1.9	38.8

Source: U.S. Census Bureau, 2020 Census

Age: Metro Area

Metro Area	Percent of Population									Median Age
	Under Age 5	Age 5–19	Age 20–34	Age 35–44	Age 45–54	Age 55–64	Age 65–74	Age 75–84	Age 85+	
Albuquerque, NM	5.1	19.2	19.8	12.6	11.7	13.4	11.0	5.2	1.8	39.4
Allentown, PA	5.0	18.5	18.2	11.8	12.9	14.6	11.0	5.6	2.5	41.9
Anchorage, AK	6.5	20.4	22.2	13.7	11.8	12.7	8.6	3.1	0.9	35.5
Ann Arbor, MI	4.7	17.5	28.4	11.6	11.3	11.6	9.1	4.1	1.6	34.5
Athens, GA	5.3	18.8	28.8	11.6	10.9	10.5	8.6	4.2	1.3	32.5
Atlanta, GA	5.7	20.6	20.9	13.7	13.8	12.1	8.3	3.7	1.2	36.9
Austin, TX	5.9	20.0	24.8	15.3	12.4	10.3	7.3	3.1	1.1	34.7
Baltimore, MD	5.6	18.8	20.5	13.0	12.4	13.6	9.6	4.7	1.9	38.6
Boise City, ID	5.9	21.8	19.7	13.4	11.9	11.7	9.5	4.6	1.6	36.9
Boston, MA	4.9	17.2	22.6	12.5	12.6	13.5	9.8	4.8	2.1	39.0
Boulder, CO	4.2	19.0	23.5	12.7	12.7	12.5	9.7	4.2	1.6	37.6
Brownsville, TX	6.5	25.3	19.3	12.0	11.9	10.6	8.6	4.3	1.6	34.0
Cape Coral, FL	4.3	15.4	15.4	10.1	11.0	14.7	16.4	9.7	3.0	49.7
Cedar Rapids, IA	5.9	19.9	19.1	12.8	11.9	13.2	9.7	5.1	2.2	38.8
Charleston, SC	5.8	18.6	21.4	13.5	11.8	12.6	10.0	4.6	1.5	37.8
Charlotte, NC	5.8	20.2	20.0	13.6	13.7	12.3	8.8	4.2	1.4	37.8
Chicago, IL	5.5	19.3	20.8	13.4	12.9	12.9	9.0	4.3	1.8	38.2
Cincinnati, OH	5.9	20.1	19.8	12.4	12.3	13.4	9.7	4.5	1.8	38.2
Clarksville, TN	7.9	21.3	25.4	12.4	10.7	10.6	7.3	3.3	1.1	31.8
Cleveland, OH	5.2	17.7	18.8	11.7	12.4	14.6	11.3	5.6	2.5	41.7
College Station, TX	5.9	22.0	32.3	10.5	8.8	9.1	6.8	3.3	1.3	27.5
Colorado Springs, CO	6.0	20.0	23.1	12.9	11.4	12.4	8.8	3.9	1.4	35.6
Columbia, MO	5.7	20.6	26.7	12.0	10.2	10.9	8.4	3.9	1.5	32.8
Columbia, SC	5.4	20.2	20.1	12.4	12.4	13.2	10.2	4.6	1.6	38.4
Columbus, OH	6.2	19.8	22.2	13.4	12.3	12.0	8.6	3.9	1.5	36.2
Dallas, TX	6.2	21.8	21.4	14.1	13.0	11.4	7.4	3.4	1.1	35.3
Davenport, IA	5.7	19.5	17.9	12.4	11.8	13.6	11.0	5.6	2.3	40.3
Denver, CO	5.5	18.8	23.0	14.7	12.6	11.7	8.5	3.7	1.4	36.6
Des Moines, IA	6.5	20.8	20.2	13.8	12.0	11.9	8.7	4.1	1.7	36.6
Durham, NC	5.2	18.4	23.1	12.7	12.1	12.3	9.9	4.6	1.6	37.4
Edison, NJ	5.4	18.0	21.5	13.3	12.8	13.0	9.2	4.7	2.1	38.7
El Paso, TX	6.1	22.6	22.4	12.1	11.8	11.5	8.0	3.9	1.7	34.2
Fargo, ND	6.7	19.9	25.7	13.7	10.4	10.7	7.7	3.5	1.7	33.5
Fort Collins, CO	4.6	18.5	23.6	12.9	11.0	12.4	10.5	4.8	1.8	37.4
Fort Wayne, IN	6.7	21.3	19.9	12.4	11.7	12.4	9.4	4.4	1.8	36.6
Fort Worth, TX	6.2	21.8	21.4	14.1	13.0	11.4	7.4	3.4	1.1	35.3
Grand Rapids, MI	6.1	20.6	21.8	12.5	11.5	12.5	8.9	4.3	1.8	36.2
Greeley, CO	6.9	22.6	21.3	13.9	11.6	11.1	8.0	3.4	1.2	34.5
Green Bay, WI	5.8	19.8	18.8	12.6	12.2	14.0	10.1	4.8	1.8	39.3
Greensboro, NC	5.3	19.6	19.9	11.7	12.9	13.2	10.2	5.1	1.9	39.4
Honolulu, HI	5.4	17.3	21.1	12.6	12.2	12.9	10.4	5.4	2.8	39.8
Houston, TX	6.5	22.1	21.0	14.3	12.7	11.4	7.7	3.3	1.1	35.3
Huntsville, AL	5.6	19.2	20.4	12.6	12.8	13.9	9.1	4.7	1.7	38.7
Indianapolis, IN	6.2	20.7	20.2	13.5	12.5	12.5	8.8	4.1	1.5	37.0
Jacksonville, FL	5.6	18.9	19.5	12.8	12.6	13.6	10.4	4.8	1.7	39.6
Kansas City, MO	6.1	20.2	19.9	13.4	12.1	12.8	9.3	4.4	1.7	37.7
Lafayette, LA	6.3	20.5	19.3	12.9	11.7	13.5	9.6	4.5	1.6	37.8
Las Cruces, NM	5.8	21.3	21.6	11.4	10.6	12.2	10.2	5.2	1.9	36.0
Las Vegas, NV	5.7	19.4	20.6	13.9	13.1	12.1	9.5	4.6	1.3	38.0
Lexington, KY	5.9	19.7	22.2	13.2	12.1	12.1	9.2	4.2	1.6	36.5
Lincoln, NE	6.0	20.9	23.4	12.9	10.6	11.4	9.1	4.1	1.7	34.8
Little Rock, AR	5.9	19.9	20.2	13.1	12.0	12.7	10.0	4.7	1.6	38.0
Los Angeles, CA	5.0	18.3	22.5	13.7	13.3	12.4	8.6	4.4	1.9	37.9
Louisville, KY	5.8	18.9	19.5	12.9	12.6	13.6	10.2	4.7	1.8	39.3

Table continued on following page.

Metro Area	Percent of Population									Median Age
	Under Age 5	Age 5–19	Age 20–34	Age 35–44	Age 45–54	Age 55–64	Age 65–74	Age 75–84	Age 85+	
Madison, WI	5.3	18.3	23.6	13.3	11.5	12.3	9.6	4.2	1.8	36.9
Manchester, NH	5.0	17.5	20.0	12.3	13.5	15.2	10.0	4.7	1.9	40.9
Miami, FL	4.8	17.1	18.7	13.0	13.8	13.7	10.2	6.0	2.6	42.1
Midland, TX	7.8	22.3	22.9	14.3	10.7	11.2	6.7	2.9	1.3	33.3
Milwaukee, WI	5.8	19.6	19.9	12.6	12.0	13.5	9.7	4.6	2.1	38.5
Minneapolis, MN	6.1	19.8	20.5	13.7	12.3	13.0	8.9	4.1	1.7	37.5
Nashville, TN	6.0	19.6	22.1	13.9	12.5	12.1	8.6	3.9	1.3	36.4
New Haven, CT	4.9	18.1	20.3	11.9	12.6	14.1	10.4	5.3	2.5	40.4
New Orleans, LA	5.7	18.9	20.3	13.3	11.9	13.4	10.3	4.6	1.7	38.6
New York, NY	5.4	18.0	21.5	13.3	12.8	13.0	9.2	4.7	2.1	38.7
Oklahoma City, OK	6.2	21.0	21.6	13.4	11.3	12.0	8.9	4.2	1.6	35.8
Omaha, NE	6.6	21.5	20.4	13.4	11.5	12.2	8.8	4.0	1.6	36.0
Orlando, FL	5.2	19.5	21.2	13.5	12.9	12.2	9.2	4.6	1.7	37.9
Philadelphia, PA	5.3	18.7	20.7	12.6	12.4	13.7	9.8	4.8	2.1	39.1
Phoenix, AZ	5.7	20.5	20.5	12.8	12.1	11.9	9.8	5.1	1.7	37.5
Pittsburgh, PA	4.9	16.3	19.3	11.8	12.1	14.9	12.0	5.9	2.8	42.9
Portland, OR	5.2	18.3	21.0	14.8	12.8	12.0	9.8	4.4	1.6	38.6
Providence, RI	4.8	17.9	20.0	12.1	12.8	14.5	10.6	5.2	2.4	40.8
Provo, UT	8.9	27.9	26.5	12.8	8.9	6.9	4.9	2.5	0.9	25.9
Raleigh, NC	5.8	21.0	20.5	14.3	13.8	11.7	8.0	3.6	1.2	36.8
Reno, NV	5.4	18.5	21.4	12.3	11.8	13.1	10.9	5.0	1.5	38.5
Richmond, VA	5.5	18.9	20.8	12.7	12.3	13.3	10.1	4.6	1.8	38.6
Rochester, MN	6.2	19.8	19.3	13.2	11.2	13.4	9.4	5.3	2.3	38.4
Sacramento, CA	5.6	19.8	20.3	13.2	12.1	12.7	9.8	4.8	2.0	38.2
St. Louis, MO	5.6	18.9	19.4	12.6	12.1	14.1	10.3	5.0	2.1	39.7
Salem, OR	5.9	20.8	20.0	12.7	11.3	11.9	10.4	5.1	1.9	37.4
Salt Lake City, UT	6.7	22.8	23.7	14.7	11.1	9.7	7.0	3.1	1.1	32.8
San Antonio, TX	6.1	21.4	21.0	13.2	12.2	11.8	8.7	4.1	1.5	36.0
San Diego, CA	5.3	18.5	23.2	13.4	12.2	12.2	9.0	4.3	1.9	37.1
San Francisco, CA	5.0	16.8	21.7	14.7	13.3	12.4	9.3	4.7	2.0	39.1
San Jose, CA	5.3	18.4	22.4	14.6	13.6	12.0	7.7	4.2	1.9	37.5
Santa Rosa, CA	4.6	17.3	18.2	12.9	12.2	14.2	12.7	5.8	2.3	42.6
Savannah, GA	5.9	19.7	22.5	13.0	11.7	12.2	9.3	4.3	1.5	36.3
Seattle, WA	5.7	17.9	22.7	14.9	12.7	12.1	8.5	3.9	1.5	37.2
Sioux Falls, SD	7.0	20.9	20.5	13.8	11.1	11.9	8.8	4.0	1.7	36.0
Springfield, IL	5.6	18.9	17.6	12.5	12.1	14.5	11.4	5.3	2.1	41.2
Tampa, FL	4.8	17.1	18.3	12.3	12.8	14.2	11.8	6.2	2.3	42.7
Tucson, AZ	4.9	17.8	19.8	11.5	10.9	13.1	12.7	6.8	2.4	41.2
Tulsa, OK	6.2	20.6	19.6	12.8	11.8	12.7	9.7	4.9	1.8	37.6
Tuscaloosa, AL	5.8	20.1	24.7	11.9	11.1	11.8	9.0	4.1	1.5	34.5
Virginia Beach, VA	5.8	18.8	22.2	12.5	11.5	13.4	9.5	4.6	1.7	37.3
Washington, DC	5.8	19.4	21.5	14.3	13.2	12.3	8.2	3.9	1.4	37.2
Wichita, KS	6.2	21.6	19.9	12.5	11.2	12.9	9.5	4.4	1.9	36.7
Wilmington, NC	4.8	16.9	20.5	12.7	12.6	13.3	11.7	5.7	2.0	41.1
Winston-Salem, NC	5.3	19.2	18.2	11.6	13.2	14.0	10.8	5.6	2.1	41.1
Worcester, MA	5.0	18.5	19.8	12.3	13.4	14.6	9.9	4.6	2.0	40.3
U.S.	5.6	19.2	20.2	12.7	12.4	13.1	10.0	4.9	1.9	38.8

Note: Figures cover the Metropolitan Statistical Area (MSA)
Source: U.S. Census Bureau, 2020 Census

Ancestry: City

City	German	Irish	English	American	Italian	Polish	French[1]	Scottish	Dutch
Albuquerque, NM	9.2	7.6	7.8	3.3	3.2	1.4	1.8	1.4	0.9
Allentown, PA	9.8	4.7	2.0	2.7	4.2	1.8	0.7	0.4	0.8
Anchorage, AK	13.8	9.4	8.5	3.6	3.2	2.0	2.3	1.9	1.3
Ann Arbor, MI	17.0	10.4	10.1	2.7	4.9	6.0	2.7	2.6	2.4
Athens, GA	8.4	8.2	9.8	3.5	3.4	1.5	2.0	2.8	0.8
Atlanta, GA	6.8	5.9	8.1	4.8	2.9	1.4	1.8	1.5	0.5
Austin, TX	10.9	8.3	8.7	2.9	3.0	1.8	2.4	2.1	0.7
Baltimore, MD	6.1	5.7	3.3	2.8	3.1	2.3	0.9	0.7	0.3
Boise City, ID	16.9	12.1	18.1	4.4	4.2	1.9	2.2	3.2	1.7
Boston, MA	4.8	13.1	4.9	2.2	7.2	2.1	1.8	1.1	0.4
Boulder, CO	16.2	11.5	11.4	2.4	6.0	3.6	2.4	3.3	1.3
Brownsville, TX	0.9	0.5	0.6	1.7	0.4	0.1	0.4	0.1	0.2
Cape Coral, FL	14.2	11.5	7.8	12.3	9.6	3.4	2.0	1.5	0.9
Cedar Rapids, IA	29.0	13.5	9.0	3.6	1.7	1.3	1.9	1.7	1.6
Charleston, SC	10.8	10.5	11.4	21.1	4.2	2.2	2.5	2.3	0.7
Charlotte, NC	8.0	6.9	7.0	4.8	3.4	1.5	1.3	1.7	0.5
Chicago, IL	7.3	7.3	2.8	2.1	3.9	5.2	0.9	0.7	0.5
Cincinnati, OH	17.3	9.4	6.2	3.5	3.8	1.6	1.4	1.1	0.9
Clarksville, TN	12.2	8.6	7.1	6.1	4.2	1.0	1.4	1.6	1.1
Cleveland, OH	9.5	8.5	3.2	2.2	4.6	3.9	0.9	0.6	0.5
College Station, TX	15.9	8.4	8.8	3.3	3.5	1.8	2.9	1.7	0.8
Colorado Springs, CO	17.7	10.6	11.4	4.2	4.7	2.2	2.7	2.7	1.4
Columbia, MO	24.6	12.0	11.0	4.4	3.6	2.2	1.9	2.3	1.2
Columbia, SC	9.6	6.9	7.7	5.5	3.3	1.1	1.9	1.9	0.6
Columbus, OH	15.2	10.2	6.9	4.0	4.9	2.1	1.3	1.6	0.8
Dallas, TX	5.1	4.2	5.1	4.2	1.7	0.8	1.2	1.1	0.4
Davenport, IA	27.7	15.3	7.5	3.4	2.2	2.0	1.5	1.6	1.6
Denver, CO	13.9	10.1	9.0	2.6	5.0	2.7	2.1	2.1	1.1
Des Moines, IA	19.1	11.9	8.2	3.1	3.6	1.2	1.5	1.2	2.3
Durham, NC	8.1	6.5	9.4	3.7	3.3	1.7	1.6	1.6	0.6
Edison, NJ	4.4	5.8	1.6	1.7	7.8	3.3	1.0	0.5	0.2
El Paso, TX	3.8	2.5	1.9	2.2	1.3	0.5	0.7	0.4	0.2
Fargo, ND	35.0	8.2	5.0	2.5	1.0	2.1	3.5	1.2	1.0
Fort Collins, CO	23.4	12.9	13.0	3.6	5.8	3.0	3.2	3.3	1.8
Fort Wayne, IN	23.1	9.4	7.8	5.5	2.3	2.2	2.7	1.6	1.1
Fort Worth, TX	7.2	6.1	6.5	4.2	1.8	1.0	1.3	1.5	0.7
Grand Rapids, MI	14.1	8.0	6.4	2.5	3.0	6.3	1.9	1.6	13.0
Greeley, CO	16.6	8.4	7.5	3.1	2.7	1.6	1.6	1.9	1.0
Green Bay, WI	28.7	8.5	4.3	4.1	2.1	8.0	3.6	1.0	2.6
Greensboro, NC	6.5	5.5	8.6	4.4	2.4	1.0	1.2	1.6	0.5
Honolulu, HI	4.4	3.1	3.2	1.4	1.7	0.8	0.8	0.6	0.2
Houston, TX	4.8	3.5	4.3	3.4	1.6	0.9	1.4	0.9	0.4
Huntsville, AL	9.4	8.9	10.6	10.2	2.3	1.2	1.8	1.9	0.9
Indianapolis, IN	12.8	8.2	7.0	4.9	2.0	1.5	1.6	1.5	0.9
Jacksonville, FL	7.5	7.6	6.5	5.7	3.7	1.4	1.3	1.5	0.6
Kansas City, MO	15.2	10.1	8.1	4.1	3.6	1.7	1.7	1.4	0.8
Lafayette, LA	8.0	5.4	5.9	5.9	3.6	0.3	16.2	1.0	0.4
Las Cruces, NM	7.0	5.8	6.4	2.6	1.9	1.0	1.2	1.1	0.8
Las Vegas, NV	8.5	7.3	6.2	3.2	5.2	1.8	1.6	1.3	0.7
Lexington, KY	13.1	11.0	12.1	8.2	3.1	1.6	1.6	2.6	1.1
Lincoln, NE	31.5	11.5	8.9	3.3	2.0	2.4	1.8	1.4	1.6
Little Rock, AR	7.3	6.2	8.8	5.2	1.4	0.9	1.5	1.6	0.4
Los Angeles, CA	3.8	3.6	3.1	3.9	2.7	1.4	1.1	0.7	0.4
Louisville, KY	15.2	11.5	9.3	6.5	2.6	1.1	1.7	1.6	0.9
Madison, WI	29.4	12.0	8.8	2.0	4.0	5.5	2.4	1.8	1.8
Manchester, NH	6.2	19.3	9.5	2.9	8.8	3.8	11.4	2.7	0.3

Table continued on following page.

City	German	Irish	English	American	Italian	Polish	French[1]	Scottish	Dutch
Miami, FL	1.8	1.3	1.0	2.7	2.5	0.7	0.9	0.2	0.2
Midland, TX	5.8	5.2	6.0	4.7	1.0	0.5	1.5	1.4	0.3
Milwaukee, WI	15.1	5.6	2.1	1.3	2.5	5.9	1.2	0.4	0.6
Minneapolis, MN	20.9	10.5	6.5	1.9	2.6	3.9	2.7	1.4	1.3
Nashville, TN	8.4	7.8	8.7	6.8	2.6	1.4	1.6	1.9	0.7
New Haven, CT	3.9	6.2	3.2	2.0	8.2	2.0	1.2	0.5	0.5
New Orleans, LA	6.1	5.7	4.9	2.2	3.7	0.9	5.2	1.0	0.4
New York, NY	2.9	4.4	1.9	3.8	6.1	2.3	0.8	0.5	0.3
Oklahoma City, OK	10.0	7.8	7.7	5.7	1.8	0.7	1.3	1.6	0.9
Omaha, NE	24.7	13.0	7.8	3.0	4.0	3.5	1.9	1.6	1.4
Orlando, FL	6.2	5.7	5.7	5.6	4.7	1.6	1.5	1.0	0.6
Philadelphia, PA	6.7	9.9	2.8	2.5	6.9	3.1	0.8	0.6	0.3
Phoenix, AZ	9.8	7.4	6.3	2.8	3.8	1.8	1.6	1.2	0.8
Pittsburgh, PA	17.9	13.8	5.4	3.0	12.1	6.7	1.4	1.3	0.5
Portland, OR	15.3	11.2	11.9	4.5	4.5	2.3	2.8	2.9	1.7
Providence, RI	3.7	8.0	3.9	2.1	6.9	1.4	2.9	0.8	0.3
Provo, UT	9.9	5.2	25.3	2.6	1.8	0.7	1.4	4.1	1.7
Raleigh, NC	9.0	8.1	10.4	8.4	3.9	2.0	1.7	2.3	0.9
Reno, NV	12.0	10.6	10.5	4.2	5.7	1.9	2.4	2.0	1.2
Richmond, VA	7.3	7.0	8.9	4.5	3.5	1.4	1.5	1.9	0.5
Rochester, MN	28.7	10.2	6.7	3.1	1.5	2.9	1.8	1.3	1.6
Sacramento, CA	6.6	5.9	5.5	1.8	3.5	1.0	1.5	1.1	0.6
St. Louis, MO	15.7	9.7	5.4	4.4	4.0	1.7	2.3	1.2	0.8
Salem, OR	16.9	9.3	11.1	3.6	2.9	1.4	2.7	2.5	1.8
Salt Lake City, UT	10.9	6.9	17.7	3.2	4.1	1.4	2.1	3.5	1.8
San Antonio, TX	7.0	4.3	4.0	3.2	1.8	1.0	1.4	0.8	0.3
San Diego, CA	8.3	7.1	6.2	2.3	4.2	1.8	1.7	1.4	0.7
San Francisco, CA	6.9	7.6	5.5	2.5	4.6	1.8	2.1	1.3	0.7
San Jose, CA	4.6	4.0	3.8	1.8	3.3	0.8	1.1	0.8	0.5
Santa Rosa, CA	11.1	9.8	9.6	2.5	6.6	1.6	2.8	1.7	1.1
Savannah, GA	6.5	7.6	5.4	4.0	3.1	1.5	1.6	1.3	0.6
Seattle, WA	14.4	11.0	11.1	2.3	4.5	2.6	3.0	2.8	1.3
Sioux Falls, SD	33.6	10.9	6.5	4.2	1.6	1.5	1.8	0.9	6.1
Springfield, IL	18.9	11.4	9.6	4.1	4.5	2.0	1.9	1.8	1.1
Tampa, FL	8.7	7.5	6.7	6.5	6.2	2.0	1.8	1.4	0.7
Tucson, AZ	11.1	8.1	7.4	2.8	3.5	1.9	1.8	1.5	0.8
Tulsa, OK	10.8	8.7	9.3	5.4	2.0	0.9	1.9	2.0	0.8
Tuscaloosa, AL	5.2	6.1	6.4	5.7	1.9	0.7	1.3	2.1	0.5
Virginia Beach, VA	11.3	10.7	10.1	7.8	5.6	2.1	2.2	2.2	0.8
Washington, DC	7.5	7.3	6.1	2.8	4.3	2.2	1.6	1.4	0.7
Wichita, KS	19.0	9.6	9.7	4.8	1.6	0.9	2.0	1.6	1.2
Wilmington, NC	10.2	9.4	11.7	4.7	5.3	2.0	1.8	2.7	0.8
Winston-Salem, NC	8.7	6.4	8.5	4.8	2.4	0.9	1.2	1.9	0.7
Worcester, MA	3.0	14.0	4.6	3.7	8.9	4.2	5.7	1.0	0.3
U.S.	12.8	9.6	8.1	5.7	5.0	2.7	2.2	1.6	1.1

Note: Figures are the percentage of the total population reporting a particular ancestry. The nine most commonly reported ancestries in the U.S. are shown. Figures include multiple ancestries (e.g. if a person reported being Irish and Italian, they were included in both columns); (1) Excludes Basque
Source: U.S. Census Bureau, 2017-2021 American Community Survey 5-Year Estimates

Ancestry: Metro Area

Metro Area	German	Irish	English	American	Italian	Polish	French[1]	Scottish	Dutch
Albuquerque, NM	9.2	7.2	7.7	3.9	3.1	1.3	1.7	1.5	0.7
Allentown, PA	22.8	12.8	6.1	4.9	11.8	4.9	1.4	1.0	1.8
Anchorage, AK	14.7	9.9	8.8	4.0	3.0	2.0	2.4	2.0	1.4
Ann Arbor, MI	18.3	10.6	10.8	5.9	4.6	6.3	2.9	2.7	2.0
Athens, GA	8.4	10.1	11.7	6.7	2.9	1.1	1.8	2.6	1.0
Atlanta, GA	6.5	6.4	8.0	8.0	2.6	1.2	1.3	1.6	0.6
Austin, TX	12.3	8.1	9.1	3.7	2.8	1.6	2.3	2.1	0.8
Baltimore, MD	14.3	11.3	8.0	4.6	5.9	3.8	1.4	1.5	0.6
Boise City, ID	16.4	10.2	17.6	4.9	3.5	1.4	2.4	2.9	1.9
Boston, MA	5.8	20.3	9.7	3.3	12.4	3.1	4.2	2.1	0.5
Boulder, CO	18.4	11.9	13.4	3.0	5.4	3.2	2.7	3.0	1.7
Brownsville, TX	1.9	1.1	1.8	1.9	0.5	0.2	0.5	0.3	0.1
Cape Coral, FL	13.5	10.7	8.4	12.5	7.8	3.1	2.1	1.7	1.1
Cedar Rapids, IA	32.6	14.2	9.1	4.1	1.7	1.1	2.2	1.9	2.0
Charleston, SC	10.1	9.5	10.6	11.8	3.9	1.8	2.1	2.3	0.6
Charlotte, NC	10.7	8.5	8.9	8.8	3.9	1.8	1.5	2.1	0.8
Chicago, IL	13.7	10.5	4.5	2.5	6.4	8.3	1.3	0.9	1.1
Cincinnati, OH	26.1	13.2	10.0	6.2	4.0	1.6	1.8	1.8	1.0
Clarksville, TN	11.8	8.8	8.3	7.4	3.2	1.1	1.4	1.7	1.0
Cleveland, OH	18.7	13.4	7.7	4.2	9.4	7.4	1.5	1.4	0.8
College Station, TX	13.5	7.6	7.6	3.8	2.8	1.8	2.4	1.6	0.7
Colorado Springs, CO	17.8	10.6	10.9	4.4	4.5	2.3	2.6	2.6	1.4
Columbia, MO	25.0	11.7	11.6	6.2	2.9	1.7	2.1	2.1	1.3
Columbia, SC	9.5	7.1	8.3	7.5	2.3	1.3	1.4	1.8	0.6
Columbus, OH	20.7	12.7	9.6	5.7	5.2	2.3	1.7	2.1	1.1
Dallas, TX	8.2	6.5	7.6	5.9	2.1	1.0	1.5	1.5	0.6
Davenport, IA	25.9	13.5	8.2	4.0	2.3	2.1	1.7	1.4	1.8
Denver, CO	17.1	10.7	10.5	3.3	5.0	2.4	2.4	2.2	1.4
Des Moines, IA	26.2	13.0	10.1	4.0	3.1	1.4	1.7	1.5	3.6
Durham, NC	9.3	8.0	11.1	5.4	3.5	1.8	1.7	2.1	0.7
Edison, NJ	6.0	8.9	2.9	4.0	11.6	3.7	0.9	0.6	0.5
El Paso, TX	3.5	2.3	1.8	2.2	1.2	0.5	0.6	0.4	0.2
Fargo, ND	35.4	7.8	4.8	2.5	1.1	2.2	3.1	1.1	1.1
Fort Collins, CO	25.2	13.1	14.1	4.1	5.2	2.8	3.2	3.4	2.1
Fort Wayne, IN	26.4	9.5	8.3	6.4	2.5	2.1	3.1	1.6	1.1
Fort Worth, TX	8.2	6.5	7.6	5.9	2.1	1.0	1.5	1.5	0.6
Grand Rapids, MI	18.8	9.5	8.9	3.4	3.0	6.3	2.5	1.7	18.0
Greeley, CO	20.5	10.1	9.7	4.1	3.7	1.9	1.9	1.8	1.4
Green Bay, WI	35.4	9.6	4.8	3.8	2.1	9.5	3.9	0.8	4.1
Greensboro, NC	8.5	7.0	9.4	7.3	2.4	1.1	1.3	2.1	0.8
Honolulu, HI	5.2	3.9	3.7	1.3	1.9	0.8	1.1	0.8	0.4
Houston, TX	7.3	5.0	5.8	3.8	2.0	1.1	1.9	1.1	0.6
Huntsville, AL	8.9	9.5	11.1	11.7	2.2	1.3	1.6	1.9	0.8
Indianapolis, IN	16.6	9.6	9.5	8.1	2.5	1.7	1.7	1.7	1.2
Jacksonville, FL	9.3	9.4	8.9	7.9	4.3	1.8	1.7	2.0	0.7
Kansas City, MO	19.9	12.3	11.1	4.9	3.2	1.6	2.1	1.9	1.2
Lafayette, LA	6.3	4.3	4.2	6.4	2.6	0.4	16.5	0.6	0.3
Las Cruces, NM	6.5	4.7	5.3	2.5	1.6	0.7	1.1	1.1	0.7
Las Vegas, NV	8.2	6.9	6.3	3.0	4.9	1.8	1.5	1.2	0.6
Lexington, KY	12.7	11.3	12.6	11.4	2.8	1.4	1.6	2.5	1.1
Lincoln, NE	32.9	11.3	8.7	3.6	1.9	2.3	1.8	1.3	1.8
Little Rock, AR	8.9	8.8	9.6	7.1	1.5	0.8	1.5	1.8	0.7
Los Angeles, CA	5.1	4.3	4.1	3.5	2.9	1.2	1.2	0.8	0.5
Louisville, KY	17.3	12.5	10.8	8.1	2.5	1.2	1.9	1.9	1.0
Madison, WI	35.2	12.9	9.1	2.7	3.6	5.1	2.5	1.6	1.7
Manchester, NH	8.0	20.7	13.9	3.3	9.8	4.0	11.2	3.3	0.7

Table continued on following page.

Metro Area	German	Irish	English	American	Italian	Polish	French[1]	Scottish	Dutch
Miami, FL	4.3	4.2	2.9	5.9	4.9	1.8	1.2	0.6	0.4
Midland, TX	6.0	5.0	5.7	5.0	1.2	0.5	1.4	1.2	0.2
Milwaukee, WI	31.9	9.5	4.6	2.1	4.2	10.3	2.2	0.9	1.2
Minneapolis, MN	28.1	10.9	6.3	3.0	2.6	4.1	3.2	1.2	1.4
Nashville, TN	9.9	9.3	11.1	10.2	2.7	1.3	1.7	2.1	0.8
New Haven, CT	7.5	14.2	7.1	2.9	19.9	5.4	3.0	1.0	0.5
New Orleans, LA	9.6	7.9	5.5	4.8	7.3	0.7	11.0	1.0	0.4
New York, NY	6.0	8.9	2.9	4.0	11.6	3.7	0.9	0.6	0.5
Oklahoma City, OK	11.6	8.9	9.1	7.0	1.8	0.8	1.5	1.8	1.0
Omaha, NE	28.3	13.1	9.1	3.5	3.9	3.7	1.9	1.5	1.6
Orlando, FL	8.1	7.2	6.5	8.2	5.1	1.8	1.7	1.2	0.7
Philadelphia, PA	14.1	17.4	7.4	3.2	12.4	4.7	1.2	1.2	0.7
Phoenix, AZ	12.5	8.6	8.6	3.8	4.4	2.3	1.9	1.6	1.0
Pittsburgh, PA	25.1	17.0	8.6	3.3	15.2	8.1	1.6	1.9	1.0
Portland, OR	16.4	10.5	11.7	4.6	3.7	1.8	2.7	2.7	1.7
Providence, RI	4.5	17.2	10.7	3.2	13.1	3.4	8.6	1.5	0.4
Provo, UT	10.0	4.9	29.5	4.2	2.2	0.5	1.6	4.3	1.5
Raleigh, NC	9.9	9.1	11.6	8.2	4.6	2.1	1.8	2.4	0.8
Reno, NV	12.5	10.6	10.9	3.8	6.2	1.8	2.6	2.0	1.2
Richmond, VA	9.0	7.9	11.7	6.7	3.8	1.5	1.5	1.9	0.7
Rochester, MN	34.2	11.0	6.8	3.4	1.3	2.8	1.9	1.2	1.9
Sacramento, CA	10.1	7.9	8.7	2.6	4.7	1.2	1.9	1.6	0.9
St. Louis, MO	26.1	12.9	8.6	5.4	4.6	2.3	3.0	1.5	1.0
Salem, OR	16.9	9.0	10.6	3.7	2.8	1.2	2.6	2.3	1.8
Salt Lake City, UT	9.7	5.7	21.7	4.0	2.9	0.9	1.9	3.6	1.7
San Antonio, TX	10.0	5.7	5.8	3.6	2.1	1.4	1.7	1.2	0.4
San Diego, CA	8.9	7.4	6.7	2.7	4.1	1.7	1.8	1.4	0.8
San Francisco, CA	7.3	7.0	6.2	2.3	4.4	1.4	1.8	1.4	0.7
San Jose, CA	5.8	4.7	4.7	2.0	3.7	1.1	1.3	0.9	0.6
Santa Rosa, CA	12.8	12.2	10.9	2.5	8.3	1.7	3.1	2.5	1.2
Savannah, GA	9.1	9.9	8.7	7.4	3.5	1.4	1.7	1.7	0.6
Seattle, WA	13.8	9.4	10.1	3.0	3.5	1.8	2.6	2.5	1.3
Sioux Falls, SD	35.2	10.4	6.1	5.2	1.4	1.4	1.8	0.9	6.4
Springfield, IL	21.5	12.5	10.9	5.1	4.8	1.9	2.2	1.9	1.3
Tampa, FL	11.6	10.3	8.5	8.6	7.3	2.9	2.4	1.7	0.9
Tucson, AZ	13.1	8.9	9.1	3.3	3.9	2.3	2.1	1.9	1.0
Tulsa, OK	12.6	10.2	9.9	5.6	1.9	0.9	2.0	2.0	1.1
Tuscaloosa, AL	5.0	6.5	6.9	10.9	1.5	0.4	0.9	1.9	0.5
Virginia Beach, VA	9.5	8.8	9.8	8.5	4.0	1.7	1.8	1.7	0.7
Washington, DC	9.0	8.4	7.5	4.0	4.2	2.1	1.5	1.5	0.7
Wichita, KS	21.4	9.9	10.0	5.7	1.7	0.9	2.0	1.8	1.3
Wilmington, NC	11.3	10.8	12.1	5.8	5.6	2.3	1.8	3.0	0.8
Winston-Salem, NC	11.3	8.1	11.0	8.5	2.3	1.1	1.2	2.2	0.8
Worcester, MA	5.5	17.6	9.3	5.5	11.8	5.6	9.5	2.0	0.5
U.S.	12.8	9.6	8.1	5.7	5.0	2.7	2.2	1.6	1.1

Note: Figures are the percentage of the total population reporting a particular ancestry. The nine most commonly reported ancestries in the U.S. are shown. Figures include multiple ancestries (e.g. if a person reported being Irish and Italian, they were included in both columns); Figures cover the Metropolitan Statistical Area; (1) Excludes Basque
Source: U.S. Census Bureau, 2017-2021 American Community Survey 5-Year Estimates

Foreign-born Population: City

City	Any Foreign Country	Percent of Population Born in							
		Asia	Mexico	Europe	Caribbean	Central America[1]	South America	Africa	Canada
Albuquerque, NM	10.2	2.5	5.1	0.9	0.4	0.1	0.4	0.5	0.1
Allentown, PA	20.4	3.1	1.0	0.8	11.5	0.8	2.0	1.3	0.1
Anchorage, AK	11.0	6.1	0.7	1.0	0.6	0.2	0.5	0.6	0.4
Ann Arbor, MI	18.6	12.3	0.5	2.9	0.1	0.1	0.7	1.2	0.8
Athens, GA	9.5	2.9	2.4	0.9	0.3	1.0	1.0	1.0	0.2
Atlanta, GA	8.3	3.4	0.7	1.4	0.8	0.2	0.8	0.8	0.3
Austin, TX	18.5	6.3	6.3	1.5	0.6	1.7	0.8	0.9	0.3
Baltimore, MD	8.1	2.2	0.3	0.9	1.3	1.0	0.4	1.9	0.1
Boise City, ID	6.5	2.8	1.1	1.2	0.1	0.0	0.3	0.5	0.5
Boston, MA	28.1	7.6	0.4	3.1	8.6	2.5	2.3	3.0	0.4
Boulder, CO	10.6	4.4	0.9	3.0	0.2	0.5	0.7	0.3	0.5
Brownsville, TX	27.1	0.5	25.5	0.2	0.0	0.7	0.1	0.0	0.1
Cape Coral, FL	17.4	1.5	0.6	2.4	8.3	0.9	3.2	0.1	0.5
Cedar Rapids, IA	6.8	2.6	0.7	0.5	0.1	0.2	0.2	2.3	0.1
Charleston, SC	5.0	1.5	0.6	1.3	0.4	0.1	0.6	0.3	0.1
Charlotte, NC	17.3	5.3	2.5	1.3	1.2	3.1	1.5	2.1	0.2
Chicago, IL	20.2	5.1	8.1	3.4	0.3	0.9	1.1	1.0	0.2
Cincinnati, OH	6.6	1.9	0.4	0.9	0.2	0.8	0.3	2.0	0.1
Clarksville, TN	6.3	2.0	1.3	0.8	0.5	0.7	0.4	0.4	0.2
Cleveland, OH	6.0	2.4	0.4	1.1	0.6	0.4	0.3	0.7	0.1
College Station, TX	12.3	7.3	1.5	0.9	0.2	0.3	1.1	0.8	0.2
Colorado Springs, CO	7.5	2.2	2.0	1.5	0.3	0.4	0.4	0.4	0.4
Columbia, MO	8.4	5.1	0.6	0.9	0.1	0.2	0.3	1.0	0.1
Columbia, SC	4.8	2.1	0.3	0.6	0.6	0.2	0.4	0.5	0.1
Columbus, OH	13.3	5.0	1.1	0.9	0.5	0.8	0.4	4.7	0.1
Dallas, TX	23.8	2.8	13.9	0.8	0.4	2.9	0.7	2.1	0.2
Davenport, IA	4.5	1.6	1.8	0.4	0.2	0.1	0.0	0.2	0.1
Denver, CO	14.2	2.8	6.6	1.4	0.3	0.6	0.7	1.4	0.3
Des Moines, IA	13.8	5.2	3.6	0.8	0.1	1.1	0.1	2.8	0.1
Durham, NC	14.6	4.4	2.8	1.4	0.6	2.7	0.7	1.5	0.3
Edison, NJ	46.1	37.1	0.5	2.2	1.8	0.6	1.8	1.8	0.3
El Paso, TX	22.8	1.0	20.2	0.5	0.2	0.3	0.2	0.3	0.0
Fargo, ND	9.9	3.7	0.1	0.5	0.1	0.1	0.2	4.8	0.5
Fort Collins, CO	7.3	2.9	1.4	1.4	0.1	0.3	0.6	0.3	0.2
Fort Wayne, IN	8.6	4.3	2.0	0.6	0.1	0.6	0.2	0.6	0.1
Fort Worth, TX	16.7	3.7	9.2	0.6	0.3	0.8	0.6	1.3	0.2
Grand Rapids, MI	10.8	2.4	3.2	1.0	0.7	1.4	0.2	1.7	0.2
Greeley, CO	12.2	0.8	8.3	0.5	0.1	1.1	0.2	1.2	0.1
Green Bay, WI	9.2	2.0	5.2	0.4	0.2	0.4	0.3	0.6	0.1
Greensboro, NC	12.1	4.1	1.8	1.2	0.7	0.5	0.7	2.9	0.2
Honolulu, HI	27.5	22.9	0.2	0.9	0.2	0.1	0.2	0.2	0.2
Houston, TX	28.9	5.9	10.6	1.1	1.0	6.5	1.6	2.0	0.2
Huntsville, AL	6.4	1.9	1.5	0.8	0.3	0.5	0.3	0.7	0.1
Indianapolis, IN	10.0	3.0	2.8	0.5	0.5	0.9	0.4	1.9	0.1
Jacksonville, FL	12.0	4.2	0.6	1.9	2.2	0.8	1.4	0.6	0.2
Kansas City, MO	8.0	2.3	2.2	0.5	0.6	0.6	0.3	1.3	0.1
Lafayette, LA	5.5	2.3	0.4	0.7	0.2	1.1	0.6	0.1	0.1
Las Cruces, NM	11.0	2.3	7.0	0.8	0.1	0.1	0.2	0.4	0.1
Las Vegas, NV	20.8	5.3	8.8	1.6	1.1	2.4	0.8	0.4	0.4
Lexington, KY	10.1	3.8	2.0	1.1	0.3	0.7	0.5	1.5	0.2
Lincoln, NE	9.1	4.9	1.3	1.0	0.4	0.5	0.3	0.8	0.1
Little Rock, AR	7.1	2.6	1.7	0.5	0.1	1.1	0.4	0.4	0.1
Los Angeles, CA	36.2	10.9	12.0	2.4	0.3	8.4	1.1	0.7	0.4
Louisville, KY	8.6	2.6	0.8	0.9	2.0	0.5	0.3	1.4	0.2

Table continued on following page.

City	Percent of Population Born in								
	Any Foreign Country	Asia	Mexico	Europe	Caribbean	Central America[1]	South America	Africa	Canada
Madison, WI	12.0	6.2	1.4	1.6	0.2	0.3	1.0	1.0	0.3
Manchester, NH	14.6	4.3	0.5	2.7	1.7	1.4	1.0	2.1	1.0
Miami, FL	58.1	1.4	1.1	1.9	31.0	11.9	10.3	0.3	0.2
Midland, TX	15.1	2.1	9.0	0.2	1.0	0.5	0.5	1.3	0.5
Milwaukee, WI	10.1	2.8	4.9	0.7	0.4	0.3	0.2	0.8	0.1
Minneapolis, MN	14.8	3.7	1.8	1.2	0.3	0.4	1.5	5.8	0.3
Nashville, TN	13.7	4.0	2.8	0.9	0.3	2.0	0.3	3.0	0.3
New Haven, CT	17.4	4.2	2.7	2.4	2.6	1.3	2.3	1.5	0.3
New Orleans, LA	5.4	1.9	0.3	0.7	0.4	1.3	0.4	0.2	0.2
New York, NY	36.3	10.8	1.8	5.2	9.9	1.4	4.9	1.7	0.3
Oklahoma City, OK	11.6	3.2	5.3	0.5	0.2	1.2	0.4	0.6	0.2
Omaha, NE	10.8	3.3	3.4	0.7	0.1	1.2	0.4	1.5	0.2
Orlando, FL	22.8	2.8	0.6	2.0	6.7	1.1	8.8	0.5	0.3
Philadelphia, PA	14.3	5.5	0.5	2.1	2.9	0.7	0.9	1.6	0.1
Phoenix, AZ	19.2	3.2	11.7	1.4	0.4	0.9	0.4	0.8	0.4
Pittsburgh, PA	9.0	4.5	0.3	1.8	0.4	0.1	0.5	1.0	0.3
Portland, OR	13.1	6.0	1.9	2.5	0.2	0.4	0.3	0.9	0.5
Providence, RI	30.7	3.8	0.3	2.5	13.9	5.4	1.2	3.1	0.4
Provo, UT	11.3	1.9	4.3	0.4	0.4	0.9	2.4	0.4	0.4
Raleigh, NC	13.0	3.9	2.4	1.2	0.9	1.2	0.8	2.3	0.2
Reno, NV	15.6	5.4	5.1	1.4	0.2	1.7	0.4	0.6	0.4
Richmond, VA	7.5	1.6	0.6	0.8	0.6	2.7	0.4	0.7	0.1
Rochester, MN	13.6	5.4	1.0	1.7	0.1	0.2	0.5	4.5	0.2
Sacramento, CA	20.9	10.3	5.8	1.4	0.1	0.7	0.4	0.5	0.2
St. Louis, MO	6.8	2.8	0.7	1.2	0.2	0.3	0.2	1.3	0.1
Salem, OR	11.3	2.4	5.8	1.1	0.1	0.4	0.2	0.2	0.2
Salt Lake City, UT	15.3	4.1	4.9	1.9	0.2	0.7	1.3	1.0	0.4
San Antonio, TX	14.2	2.5	8.9	0.5	0.3	0.9	0.5	0.4	0.1
San Diego, CA	25.1	11.8	8.2	2.2	0.2	0.5	0.9	0.9	0.4
San Francisco, CA	34.1	22.0	2.4	4.5	0.2	2.4	1.1	0.5	0.6
San Jose, CA	40.7	26.4	8.6	2.3	0.1	1.2	0.7	0.8	0.3
Santa Rosa, CA	21.1	4.6	11.9	1.9	0.0	1.1	0.3	0.6	0.4
Savannah, GA	6.1	2.5	0.8	0.8	0.5	0.5	0.5	0.3	0.2
Seattle, WA	19.3	11.0	1.3	2.6	0.1	0.4	0.5	2.0	1.0
Sioux Falls, SD	8.7	2.1	0.5	1.1	0.1	1.1	0.1	3.4	0.1
Springfield, IL	4.4	2.3	0.5	0.5	0.1	0.1	0.2	0.6	0.0
Tampa, FL	18.1	3.8	1.1	1.8	7.1	1.2	2.3	0.5	0.3
Tucson, AZ	14.2	2.3	8.8	1.0	0.1	0.3	0.4	0.9	0.2
Tulsa, OK	11.0	2.6	5.2	0.6	0.2	1.0	0.5	0.6	0.1
Tuscaloosa, AL	4.5	2.3	1.0	0.4	0.1	0.3	0.1	0.2	0.1
Virginia Beach, VA	9.3	4.9	0.4	1.4	0.5	0.6	0.8	0.4	0.2
Washington, DC	13.5	3.0	0.6	2.4	1.2	2.4	1.5	2.1	0.3
Wichita, KS	9.9	3.7	4.2	0.5	0.1	0.5	0.3	0.5	0.1
Wilmington, NC	4.7	1.2	1.1	1.0	0.2	0.4	0.4	0.1	0.2
Winston-Salem, NC	10.2	2.2	4.1	0.6	0.5	1.5	0.7	0.7	0.1
Worcester, MA	21.9	6.1	0.3	3.6	3.0	1.3	2.5	4.9	0.1
U.S.	13.6	4.2	3.3	1.5	1.4	1.1	1.1	0.8	0.2

Note: (1) Excludes Mexico
Source: U.S. Census Bureau, 2017-2021 American Community Survey 5-Year Estimates

Foreign-born Population: Metro Area

Metro Area	Any Foreign Country	Asia	Mexico	Europe	Caribbean	Central America[1]	South America	Africa	Canada
Albuquerque, NM	8.9	1.9	4.9	0.8	0.3	0.2	0.3	0.4	0.1
Allentown, PA	9.7	2.7	0.4	1.4	2.8	0.5	1.1	0.6	0.1
Anchorage, AK	9.0	4.8	0.6	1.1	0.4	0.2	0.4	0.4	0.4
Ann Arbor, MI	12.5	7.3	0.6	2.3	0.1	0.2	0.5	0.9	0.6
Athens, GA	7.4	2.5	1.7	0.7	0.2	0.8	0.7	0.6	0.2
Atlanta, GA	14.1	4.7	2.3	1.1	1.6	1.2	1.2	1.7	0.2
Austin, TX	15.2	4.8	5.8	1.2	0.4	1.2	0.7	0.7	0.3
Baltimore, MD	10.5	4.3	0.4	1.3	0.8	1.1	0.5	1.9	0.1
Boise City, ID	6.5	1.5	2.7	1.0	0.0	0.2	0.4	0.3	0.3
Boston, MA	19.3	6.3	0.2	3.2	3.6	1.6	2.2	1.7	0.4
Boulder, CO	9.9	3.4	2.3	2.3	0.1	0.3	0.6	0.3	0.5
Brownsville, TX	22.8	0.6	20.8	0.2	0.1	0.7	0.1	0.0	0.1
Cape Coral, FL	17.1	1.3	2.3	2.0	6.3	1.9	2.2	0.1	0.9
Cedar Rapids, IA	4.3	1.8	0.4	0.3	0.1	0.1	0.1	1.2	0.1
Charleston, SC	5.8	1.5	1.0	1.1	0.3	0.6	0.7	0.2	0.2
Charlotte, NC	10.5	3.1	2.0	1.1	0.7	1.5	1.0	1.0	0.2
Chicago, IL	17.7	5.3	6.3	3.7	0.2	0.5	0.7	0.7	0.2
Cincinnati, OH	5.1	2.2	0.5	0.7	0.1	0.4	0.2	0.8	0.1
Clarksville, TN	4.9	1.5	0.9	0.6	0.3	0.4	0.3	0.6	0.2
Cleveland, OH	6.0	2.2	0.4	2.2	0.2	0.2	0.2	0.4	0.2
College Station, TX	11.5	3.8	5.0	0.7	0.2	0.5	0.7	0.5	0.1
Colorado Springs, CO	6.7	1.9	1.6	1.5	0.4	0.3	0.4	0.3	0.3
Columbia, MO	5.7	3.3	0.5	0.7	0.1	0.2	0.2	0.7	0.1
Columbia, SC	5.3	1.8	1.0	0.7	0.4	0.6	0.3	0.3	0.1
Columbus, OH	8.8	3.7	0.7	0.8	0.3	0.4	0.3	2.4	0.1
Dallas, TX	18.7	5.7	7.8	0.8	0.3	1.6	0.7	1.6	0.2
Davenport, IA	5.3	1.7	1.7	0.5	0.1	0.1	0.1	0.9	0.1
Denver, CO	12.0	3.3	4.6	1.4	0.2	0.5	0.6	1.1	0.3
Des Moines, IA	8.1	3.2	1.5	1.0	0.1	0.5	0.2	1.5	0.1
Durham, NC	11.8	3.6	2.7	1.4	0.4	1.8	0.6	1.0	0.3
Edison, NJ	29.4	8.7	1.4	4.3	6.9	1.9	4.5	1.4	0.2
El Paso, TX	23.7	0.9	21.3	0.4	0.2	0.3	0.2	0.2	0.0
Fargo, ND	7.0	2.8	0.1	0.5	0.1	0.0	0.1	3.0	0.4
Fort Collins, CO	5.8	1.8	1.4	1.2	0.1	0.2	0.5	0.3	0.2
Fort Wayne, IN	6.7	3.3	1.5	0.6	0.1	0.4	0.2	0.4	0.1
Fort Worth, TX	18.7	5.7	7.8	0.8	0.3	1.6	0.7	1.6	0.2
Grand Rapids, MI	6.6	2.1	1.6	0.9	0.4	0.5	0.2	0.7	0.2
Greeley, CO	8.9	0.8	6.0	0.5	0.1	0.7	0.2	0.5	0.1
Green Bay, WI	4.9	1.6	2.1	0.4	0.1	0.3	0.1	0.2	0.1
Greensboro, NC	9.1	3.0	2.4	0.8	0.4	0.5	0.5	1.4	0.1
Honolulu, HI	19.5	15.7	0.2	0.7	0.2	0.1	0.2	0.2	0.2
Houston, TX	23.5	6.0	8.4	1.1	0.8	3.8	1.6	1.5	0.3
Huntsville, AL	5.2	1.9	1.0	0.7	0.2	0.4	0.3	0.4	0.1
Indianapolis, IN	7.3	2.7	1.6	0.6	0.2	0.5	0.4	1.2	0.1
Jacksonville, FL	9.8	3.3	0.5	1.8	1.6	0.7	1.2	0.4	0.2
Kansas City, MO	6.8	2.3	2.0	0.5	0.2	0.6	0.2	0.8	0.1
Lafayette, LA	3.3	1.3	0.5	0.3	0.2	0.7	0.2	0.1	0.1
Las Cruces, NM	16.0	1.4	13.3	0.6	0.1	0.1	0.1	0.2	0.1
Las Vegas, NV	22.0	7.3	7.8	1.5	1.2	2.0	0.9	0.8	0.4
Lexington, KY	7.6	2.6	1.7	1.0	0.2	0.5	0.3	1.1	0.2
Lincoln, NE	8.0	4.2	1.1	0.9	0.3	0.4	0.2	0.7	0.1
Little Rock, AR	4.2	1.4	1.2	0.4	0.1	0.6	0.2	0.2	0.1
Los Angeles, CA	32.5	12.7	11.5	1.7	0.3	4.3	1.0	0.6	0.3
Louisville, KY	6.4	2.0	0.9	0.7	1.1	0.4	0.2	0.9	0.1

Table continued on following page.

Metro Area	Percent of Population Born in								
	Any Foreign Country	Asia	Mexico	Europe	Caribbean	Central America[1]	South America	Africa	Canada
Madison, WI	7.6	3.5	1.2	1.0	0.1	0.2	0.6	0.6	0.2
Manchester, NH	10.0	3.4	0.3	1.9	1.3	0.5	0.8	0.8	0.9
Miami, FL	41.2	2.2	1.2	2.3	20.9	4.2	9.5	0.4	0.6
Midland, TX	13.7	1.9	8.5	0.3	0.8	0.4	0.4	1.0	0.4
Milwaukee, WI	7.5	2.8	2.3	1.2	0.2	0.2	0.3	0.4	0.1
Minneapolis, MN	10.7	4.1	1.1	1.0	0.1	0.4	0.6	3.0	0.2
Nashville, TN	8.5	2.6	1.9	0.7	0.3	1.1	0.4	1.3	0.2
New Haven, CT	13.4	3.2	1.1	2.9	2.1	0.6	2.1	1.0	0.3
New Orleans, LA	7.6	2.1	0.5	0.5	0.9	2.7	0.4	0.3	0.1
New York, NY	29.4	8.7	1.4	4.3	6.9	1.9	4.5	1.4	0.2
Oklahoma City, OK	7.9	2.3	3.3	0.4	0.1	0.8	0.3	0.5	0.2
Omaha, NE	7.6	2.5	2.4	0.6	0.1	0.7	0.3	1.0	0.1
Orlando, FL	19.3	3.0	1.0	1.7	5.6	1.1	6.0	0.6	0.3
Philadelphia, PA	11.2	4.6	0.8	1.9	1.4	0.5	0.7	1.2	0.2
Phoenix, AZ	14.0	3.2	7.0	1.3	0.3	0.6	0.4	0.6	0.6
Pittsburgh, PA	4.1	2.0	0.1	0.9	0.2	0.1	0.2	0.3	0.1
Portland, OR	12.7	5.1	2.9	2.4	0.2	0.5	0.3	0.6	0.4
Providence, RI	13.9	2.3	0.3	4.1	2.6	1.6	1.2	1.6	0.2
Provo, UT	7.2	1.0	2.5	0.5	0.2	0.6	1.6	0.2	0.3
Raleigh, NC	12.2	4.7	2.4	1.3	0.6	0.9	0.6	1.2	0.3
Reno, NV	14.0	4.0	5.7	1.2	0.2	1.4	0.4	0.4	0.4
Richmond, VA	8.1	3.1	0.6	1.0	0.4	1.6	0.5	0.7	0.1
Rochester, MN	8.5	3.2	0.7	1.1	0.1	0.2	0.4	2.4	0.2
Sacramento, CA	18.6	9.1	4.3	2.7	0.1	0.7	0.4	0.4	0.3
St. Louis, MO	4.8	2.2	0.5	1.1	0.1	0.2	0.2	0.5	0.1
Salem, OR	11.5	1.5	7.2	1.1	0.1	0.5	0.3	0.1	0.2
Salt Lake City, UT	12.4	3.1	4.3	1.3	0.1	0.6	1.5	0.6	0.3
San Antonio, TX	11.7	2.1	7.1	0.6	0.3	0.7	0.4	0.3	0.1
San Diego, CA	22.7	8.8	9.6	1.8	0.2	0.6	0.7	0.6	0.4
San Francisco, CA	30.7	17.8	4.7	2.8	0.2	2.5	1.1	0.9	0.5
San Jose, CA	39.3	26.2	6.7	3.1	0.1	1.0	0.8	0.7	0.5
Santa Rosa, CA	16.3	3.1	8.9	1.9	0.1	0.9	0.4	0.3	0.4
Savannah, GA	6.0	1.9	1.2	1.0	0.6	0.3	0.4	0.3	0.2
Seattle, WA	19.5	10.4	2.3	2.8	0.2	0.6	0.6	1.6	0.7
Sioux Falls, SD	6.5	1.5	0.5	0.9	0.1	0.8	0.1	2.4	0.1
Springfield, IL	2.9	1.5	0.3	0.4	0.1	0.0	0.2	0.3	0.0
Tampa, FL	14.4	2.8	1.3	2.2	4.0	0.8	2.2	0.5	0.6
Tucson, AZ	12.2	2.2	7.0	1.2	0.2	0.3	0.3	0.6	0.3
Tulsa, OK	6.7	1.9	2.8	0.5	0.1	0.5	0.3	0.3	0.1
Tuscaloosa, AL	3.3	1.2	1.1	0.3	0.1	0.4	0.1	0.1	0.1
Virginia Beach, VA	6.6	2.8	0.4	1.1	0.6	0.7	0.4	0.4	0.1
Washington, DC	22.9	8.2	0.8	1.8	1.1	4.8	2.3	3.6	0.2
Wichita, KS	7.3	2.7	2.9	0.5	0.1	0.4	0.2	0.4	0.1
Wilmington, NC	4.6	1.0	1.0	0.9	0.1	0.6	0.4	0.2	0.2
Winston-Salem, NC	7.0	1.4	2.7	0.6	0.3	0.9	0.5	0.3	0.1
Worcester, MA	12.0	3.7	0.3	2.3	1.1	0.6	2.0	1.6	0.4
U.S.	13.6	4.2	3.3	1.5	1.4	1.1	1.1	0.8	0.2

Note: Figures cover the Metropolitan Statistical Area—see Appendix B for areas included; (1) Excludes Mexico
Source: U.S. Census Bureau, 2017-2021 American Community Survey 5-Year Estimates

Marital Status: City

City	Never Married	Now Married[1]	Separated	Widowed	Divorced
Albuquerque, NM	38.2	40.1	1.4	5.5	14.8
Allentown, PA	46.7	34.6	3.9	5.0	9.8
Anchorage, AK	33.6	48.9	1.9	3.6	12.0
Ann Arbor, MI	56.5	34.4	0.4	2.4	6.3
Athens, GA	53.8	31.8	1.7	3.7	9.0
Atlanta, GA	55.1	29.0	1.8	4.0	10.1
Austin, TX	43.0	41.9	1.4	3.0	10.6
Baltimore, MD	52.3	27.2	3.1	6.0	11.4
Boise City, ID	34.8	47.0	1.0	4.4	12.9
Boston, MA	55.7	30.9	2.5	3.6	7.3
Boulder, CO	56.1	31.2	0.7	2.5	9.5
Brownsville, TX	34.2	47.6	4.3	6.2	7.8
Cape Coral, FL	24.4	53.3	1.2	7.3	13.8
Cedar Rapids, IA	35.5	45.7	1.0	5.6	12.2
Charleston, SC	40.3	43.3	1.6	5.1	9.8
Charlotte, NC	41.4	42.0	2.4	3.9	10.3
Chicago, IL	48.9	35.5	2.3	5.0	8.3
Cincinnati, OH	52.6	29.1	2.2	4.5	11.7
Clarksville, TN	30.2	50.3	2.1	3.9	13.6
Cleveland, OH	53.1	24.0	2.9	5.9	14.1
College Station, TX	59.4	31.9	0.8	2.4	5.5
Colorado Springs, CO	30.9	50.2	1.6	4.5	12.9
Columbia, MO	47.8	39.2	1.3	3.1	8.7
Columbia, SC	55.7	29.6	2.3	4.0	8.4
Columbus, OH	45.4	36.7	2.1	4.2	11.6
Dallas, TX	42.3	40.2	2.9	4.3	10.3
Davenport, IA	36.9	43.5	1.3	5.6	12.7
Denver, CO	43.4	39.6	1.6	3.5	11.8
Des Moines, IA	39.5	39.8	2.1	5.5	13.0
Durham, NC	43.1	40.7	2.2	4.1	9.9
Edison, NJ	26.3	61.4	0.8	5.3	6.1
El Paso, TX	34.9	44.8	3.6	5.7	11.1
Fargo, ND	43.0	43.4	1.0	3.9	8.6
Fort Collins, CO	46.6	40.9	0.7	3.3	8.5
Fort Wayne, IN	36.1	44.2	1.5	5.9	12.3
Fort Worth, TX	35.5	46.7	2.2	4.4	11.1
Grand Rapids, MI	45.3	38.1	1.2	4.9	10.5
Greeley, CO	35.4	46.5	1.9	4.8	11.4
Green Bay, WI	37.4	42.2	1.2	5.2	14.0
Greensboro, NC	43.8	36.8	2.6	5.9	11.0
Honolulu, HI	37.5	44.7	1.1	6.7	10.0
Houston, TX	41.1	41.2	3.0	4.5	10.2
Huntsville, AL	36.1	43.6	2.1	5.9	12.4
Indianapolis, IN	41.8	39.4	1.7	4.8	12.3
Jacksonville, FL	36.0	42.4	2.1	5.5	14.0
Kansas City, MO	39.3	40.6	2.0	4.8	13.3
Lafayette, LA	40.6	41.4	2.1	6.0	9.9
Las Cruces, NM	41.9	39.4	1.7	4.7	12.4
Las Vegas, NV	35.6	43.7	2.0	5.2	13.5
Lexington, KY	38.6	43.4	1.5	4.6	11.8
Lincoln, NE	39.7	45.3	0.9	4.0	10.1
Little Rock, AR	38.2	40.4	1.8	5.6	14.1
Los Angeles, CA	46.1	38.9	2.5	4.4	8.1
Louisville, KY	36.9	42.0	2.1	6.3	12.7
Madison, WI	50.3	37.2	0.7	3.3	8.5
Manchester, NH	39.2	39.2	1.8	5.4	14.3

Table continued on following page.

City	Never Married	Now Married[1]	Separated	Widowed	Divorced
Miami, FL	39.7	37.3	3.5	6.0	13.6
Midland, TX	28.6	55.1	1.9	4.5	9.9
Milwaukee, WI	54.4	29.4	1.9	4.4	9.9
Minneapolis, MN	51.2	34.3	1.4	3.0	10.1
Nashville, TN	41.5	40.4	1.9	4.6	11.6
New Haven, CT	59.1	25.5	2.4	3.9	9.1
New Orleans, LA	49.7	29.4	2.6	5.5	12.8
New York, NY	43.8	39.9	2.9	5.3	8.1
Oklahoma City, OK	33.3	46.6	2.1	5.3	12.7
Omaha, NE	37.2	45.6	1.4	4.8	11.1
Orlando, FL	43.2	37.8	2.4	3.9	12.7
Philadelphia, PA	50.5	31.5	3.0	5.7	9.2
Phoenix, AZ	39.1	42.5	2.1	4.0	12.2
Pittsburgh, PA	53.1	30.4	1.9	5.4	9.2
Portland, OR	41.6	41.1	1.3	3.6	12.4
Providence, RI	53.6	31.9	2.0	4.2	8.4
Provo, UT	48.8	43.8	0.9	2.2	4.3
Raleigh, NC	43.2	40.0	2.1	3.8	11.0
Reno, NV	36.5	42.1	1.9	4.9	14.8
Richmond, VA	51.2	29.4	2.8	5.2	11.4
Rochester, MN	33.3	51.7	1.2	4.7	9.2
Sacramento, CA	40.5	41.1	2.6	4.8	11.2
St. Louis, MO	48.8	30.7	2.9	5.2	12.3
Salem, OR	34.6	45.1	1.6	5.2	13.4
Salt Lake City, UT	44.4	40.3	1.3	3.1	10.8
San Antonio, TX	38.3	41.7	2.8	5.1	12.0
San Diego, CA	40.1	44.8	1.6	4.0	9.5
San Francisco, CA	46.0	40.1	1.4	4.5	8.0
San Jose, CA	36.2	50.3	1.5	4.2	7.8
Santa Rosa, CA	33.8	46.4	2.0	5.4	12.3
Savannah, GA	47.5	32.1	2.6	5.6	12.2
Seattle, WA	45.5	40.3	1.2	3.0	10.0
Sioux Falls, SD	34.5	48.6	1.2	4.3	11.4
Springfield, IL	37.6	39.5	1.6	6.2	15.1
Tampa, FL	40.3	39.1	2.5	5.0	13.1
Tucson, AZ	42.0	36.7	2.2	5.2	13.9
Tulsa, OK	35.0	42.4	2.4	5.7	14.4
Tuscaloosa, AL	52.3	32.6	1.8	4.0	9.4
Virginia Beach, VA	30.9	50.8	2.1	5.1	11.2
Washington, DC	55.8	30.9	1.7	3.5	8.2
Wichita, KS	33.7	45.6	1.9	5.0	13.8
Wilmington, NC	41.6	39.1	2.2	5.3	11.7
Winston-Salem, NC	41.9	39.1	2.6	5.4	11.0
Worcester, MA	47.8	34.0	2.0	4.9	11.3
U.S.	33.8	48.0	1.8	5.6	10.8

Note: Figures are percentages and cover the population 15 years of age and older; (1) Excludes separated
Source: U.S. Census Bureau, 2017-2021 American Community Survey 5-Year Estimates

Marital Status: Metro Area

Metro Area	Never Married	Now Married[1]	Separated	Widowed	Divorced
Albuquerque, NM	35.6	43.5	1.4	5.5	14.1
Allentown, PA	32.7	49.3	1.9	6.2	9.9
Anchorage, AK	32.2	50.5	1.8	3.8	11.8
Ann Arbor, MI	43.1	44.4	0.7	3.6	8.1
Athens, GA	43.0	41.5	1.6	4.4	9.5
Atlanta, GA	35.7	47.6	1.8	4.4	10.6
Austin, TX	35.5	49.4	1.4	3.5	10.3
Baltimore, MD	36.0	46.3	1.9	5.7	10.0
Boise City, ID	29.1	53.3	1.1	4.3	12.2
Boston, MA	37.3	47.6	1.6	4.9	8.7
Boulder, CO	38.5	45.5	0.9	3.7	11.4
Brownsville, TX	33.6	48.2	3.5	6.3	8.4
Cape Coral, FL	25.9	51.9	1.5	7.9	12.8
Cedar Rapids, IA	30.6	51.3	1.1	5.5	11.5
Charleston, SC	33.8	48.5	2.1	5.3	10.3
Charlotte, NC	33.1	49.3	2.3	5.0	10.3
Chicago, IL	37.2	47.0	1.6	5.2	8.9
Cincinnati, OH	32.8	48.7	1.5	5.6	11.4
Clarksville, TN	29.6	51.1	1.9	4.9	12.5
Cleveland, OH	35.8	44.4	1.5	6.3	11.9
College Station, TX	45.5	40.1	1.8	4.1	8.5
Colorado Springs, CO	29.5	53.3	1.4	4.0	11.7
Columbia, MO	40.0	44.8	1.3	4.0	9.8
Columbia, SC	36.3	45.0	2.6	5.6	10.6
Columbus, OH	34.8	47.6	1.7	4.8	11.1
Dallas, TX	32.8	50.8	1.9	4.2	10.3
Davenport, IA	30.5	49.9	1.4	6.2	12.0
Denver, CO	33.6	49.8	1.4	3.8	11.5
Des Moines, IA	30.9	51.7	1.2	4.9	11.2
Durham, NC	37.3	46.1	2.0	4.8	9.8
Edison, NJ	38.1	46.1	2.2	5.5	8.1
El Paso, TX	34.9	45.8	3.5	5.4	10.4
Fargo, ND	37.5	49.1	0.9	4.0	8.5
Fort Collins, CO	34.5	51.3	0.8	4.0	9.4
Fort Wayne, IN	31.5	50.0	1.3	5.6	11.6
Fort Worth, TX	32.8	50.8	1.9	4.2	10.3
Grand Rapids, MI	32.2	52.1	0.9	4.5	10.3
Greeley, CO	28.7	55.2	1.4	4.0	10.7
Green Bay, WI	30.6	52.2	0.7	5.1	11.4
Greensboro, NC	34.1	45.5	2.8	6.2	11.4
Honolulu, HI	34.4	49.7	1.2	6.0	8.7
Houston, TX	33.8	50.2	2.3	4.3	9.4
Huntsville, AL	29.9	51.5	1.6	5.5	11.4
Indianapolis, IN	33.0	49.2	1.3	4.9	11.5
Jacksonville, FL	31.7	47.7	1.8	5.6	13.2
Kansas City, MO	30.8	50.5	1.5	5.0	12.1
Lafayette, LA	33.8	47.9	2.1	5.6	10.6
Las Cruces, NM	38.8	43.7	2.0	4.9	10.7
Las Vegas, NV	35.2	44.3	2.1	5.0	13.4
Lexington, KY	34.1	47.0	1.5	5.1	12.3
Lincoln, NE	37.3	48.1	0.8	4.1	9.7
Little Rock, AR	30.6	48.1	1.9	5.8	13.6
Los Angeles, CA	40.3	44.5	2.0	4.7	8.4
Louisville, KY	31.9	47.5	1.8	6.0	12.9
Madison, WI	37.1	48.2	0.8	4.1	9.9
Manchester, NH	31.3	50.2	1.2	5.1	12.1

Table continued on following page.

Metro Area	Never Married	Now Married[1]	Separated	Widowed	Divorced
Miami, FL	34.1	44.4	2.5	6.2	12.9
Midland, TX	27.9	55.4	1.7	4.5	10.5
Milwaukee, WI	37.4	46.2	1.1	5.1	10.1
Minneapolis, MN	33.7	51.0	1.0	4.1	10.1
Nashville, TN	32.6	50.0	1.5	4.9	11.0
New Haven, CT	38.2	43.7	1.6	5.7	10.8
New Orleans, LA	37.8	41.7	2.3	6.0	12.1
New York, NY	38.1	46.1	2.2	5.5	8.1
Oklahoma City, OK	31.4	49.2	1.8	5.4	12.3
Omaha, NE	32.2	51.3	1.2	4.7	10.7
Orlando, FL	35.2	46.2	2.0	5.0	11.6
Philadelphia, PA	37.3	45.8	2.0	5.7	9.2
Phoenix, AZ	33.7	48.2	1.6	4.8	11.7
Pittsburgh, PA	32.6	48.7	1.7	6.9	10.1
Portland, OR	32.8	49.6	1.3	4.3	12.0
Providence, RI	36.5	45.0	1.5	5.9	11.1
Provo, UT	33.0	58.1	0.8	2.5	5.5
Raleigh, NC	32.2	51.9	2.0	4.2	9.7
Reno, NV	32.4	47.4	1.7	4.9	13.7
Richmond, VA	34.7	46.7	2.3	5.6	10.7
Rochester, MN	29.0	56.0	0.9	4.7	9.3
Sacramento, CA	33.9	48.6	2.0	4.9	10.6
St. Louis, MO	32.2	48.7	1.7	5.9	11.4
Salem, OR	31.8	48.7	1.7	5.3	12.6
Salt Lake City, UT	32.7	52.3	1.4	3.6	10.1
San Antonio, TX	34.0	47.6	2.4	4.9	11.1
San Diego, CA	36.2	47.9	1.6	4.4	9.8
San Francisco, CA	36.6	48.6	1.4	4.6	8.7
San Jose, CA	34.4	52.7	1.4	4.1	7.4
Santa Rosa, CA	32.3	48.7	1.5	5.1	12.5
Savannah, GA	35.7	45.2	2.3	5.3	11.7
Seattle, WA	33.2	50.7	1.3	4.0	10.8
Sioux Falls, SD	30.6	53.2	1.0	4.4	10.8
Springfield, IL	32.4	46.6	1.3	6.1	13.6
Tampa, FL	31.3	46.5	1.9	6.8	13.5
Tucson, AZ	34.3	45.5	1.7	5.6	12.9
Tulsa, OK	29.1	49.8	1.9	6.1	13.0
Tuscaloosa, AL	39.5	43.1	1.7	5.4	10.3
Virginia Beach, VA	33.6	47.7	2.4	5.5	10.8
Washington, DC	36.2	49.2	1.7	4.2	8.7
Wichita, KS	30.3	50.2	1.4	5.4	12.7
Wilmington, NC	33.0	48.2	2.2	5.7	11.0
Winston-Salem, NC	31.0	48.9	2.4	6.4	11.3
Worcester, MA	34.4	47.7	1.5	5.4	11.0
U.S.	33.8	48.0	1.8	5.6	10.8

Note: Figures are percentages and cover the population 15 years of age and older; Figures cover the Metropolitan Statistical Area;
(1) Excludes separated
Source: U.S. Census Bureau, 2017-2021 American Community Survey 5-Year Estimates

Disability by Age: City

City	All Ages	Under 18 Years Old	18 to 64 Years Old	65 Years and Over
Albuquerque, NM	14.2	4.3	12.3	35.3
Allentown, PA	16.0	9.9	15.3	33.5
Anchorage, AK	11.1	3.8	10.0	33.3
Ann Arbor, MI	7.1	4.2	4.9	24.0
Athens, GA	11.8	6.1	9.6	35.6
Atlanta, GA	11.4	4.7	9.3	35.0
Austin, TX	8.7	4.1	7.4	28.5
Baltimore, MD	15.9	6.0	14.1	39.0
Boise City, ID	11.3	4.2	9.4	29.7
Boston, MA	11.8	6.3	8.7	38.3
Boulder, CO	6.6	2.9	4.7	23.1
Brownsville, TX	10.6	4.2	7.8	40.6
Cape Coral, FL	13.4	3.8	9.7	29.3
Cedar Rapids, IA	10.0	3.1	8.1	27.2
Charleston, SC	9.3	2.9	6.2	30.5
Charlotte, NC	7.8	2.6	6.5	27.9
Chicago, IL	10.9	3.3	8.8	34.8
Cincinnati, OH	12.8	5.2	11.8	32.0
Clarksville, TN	15.7	6.1	16.4	43.8
Cleveland, OH	19.5	8.4	18.5	41.9
College Station, TX	6.8	5.1	5.3	27.8
Colorado Springs, CO	13.1	5.2	12.1	30.9
Columbia, MO	11.4	4.6	9.8	33.9
Columbia, SC	12.8	5.1	10.7	38.5
Columbus, OH	11.6	5.2	10.3	34.5
Dallas, TX	10.5	4.5	9.0	34.3
Davenport, IA	13.1	5.2	11.3	31.6
Denver, CO	9.7	3.5	7.6	32.3
Des Moines, IA	13.7	5.3	12.8	35.6
Durham, NC	9.6	3.0	7.6	31.7
Edison, NJ	7.6	4.2	4.5	26.9
El Paso, TX	13.6	5.2	11.1	42.1
Fargo, ND	10.2	5.1	7.7	32.0
Fort Collins, CO	8.4	2.7	6.8	28.0
Fort Wayne, IN	13.9	5.5	12.8	34.2
Fort Worth, TX	9.7	3.4	8.6	34.4
Grand Rapids, MI	11.7	3.9	11.0	30.4
Greeley, CO	11.9	3.4	11.1	33.5
Green Bay, WI	13.8	6.7	12.2	34.9
Greensboro, NC	11.1	4.9	8.9	32.1
Honolulu, HI	11.5	3.1	6.9	32.4
Houston, TX	9.9	3.9	8.0	34.7
Huntsville, AL	13.5	4.4	11.3	33.7
Indianapolis, IN	13.5	5.3	12.4	35.5
Jacksonville, FL	13.1	4.8	11.3	35.3
Kansas City, MO	12.5	3.9	11.1	34.2
Lafayette, LA	12.1	2.8	9.7	34.5
Las Cruces, NM	15.9	7.9	13.6	38.0
Las Vegas, NV	12.5	4.0	10.4	34.8
Lexington, KY	12.5	4.9	10.8	33.2
Lincoln, NE	10.7	4.4	8.9	30.0
Little Rock, AR	13.2	4.7	11.6	34.5
Los Angeles, CA	10.3	3.1	7.5	36.6
Louisville, KY	14.3	4.5	12.8	35.6
Madison, WI	8.3	4.4	6.4	25.0

Table continued on following page.

City	All Ages	Under 18 Years Old	18 to 64 Years Old	65 Years and Over
Manchester, NH	13.9	6.6	11.8	34.7
Miami, FL	11.9	4.5	7.6	37.2
Midland, TX	9.8	2.7	8.1	41.1
Milwaukee, WI	12.5	5.0	11.6	36.6
Minneapolis, MN	11.0	4.9	9.8	32.2
Nashville, TN	11.2	4.6	9.1	34.5
New Haven, CT	10.3	4.2	8.8	33.4
New Orleans, LA	13.7	4.7	11.8	34.0
New York, NY	10.9	3.6	8.0	33.9
Oklahoma City, OK	13.1	4.3	11.9	36.6
Omaha, NE	10.9	3.6	9.6	30.9
Orlando, FL	9.6	4.9	7.7	32.0
Philadelphia, PA	16.9	7.0	15.0	42.0
Phoenix, AZ	10.8	4.2	9.7	32.9
Pittsburgh, PA	14.3	7.7	11.3	35.4
Portland, OR	12.1	4.8	9.9	33.4
Providence, RI	13.6	5.9	12.4	36.4
Provo, UT	9.6	4.9	8.1	41.8
Raleigh, NC	9.0	4.2	7.2	30.1
Reno, NV	11.2	3.2	9.0	31.1
Richmond, VA	14.2	6.5	12.1	35.7
Rochester, MN	10.3	4.2	7.9	30.7
Sacramento, CA	11.8	3.3	9.6	36.7
St. Louis, MO	15.4	6.2	13.3	38.5
Salem, OR	15.2	6.3	13.9	35.5
Salt Lake City, UT	11.0	4.0	9.4	32.6
San Antonio, TX	15.0	6.3	13.2	41.6
San Diego, CA	9.2	3.3	6.5	31.3
San Francisco, CA	10.1	2.6	6.3	33.5
San Jose, CA	8.9	3.1	6.0	33.1
Santa Rosa, CA	11.7	3.2	9.5	29.7
Savannah, GA	15.7	6.4	13.1	42.3
Seattle, WA	9.3	2.5	7.2	30.6
Sioux Falls, SD	10.1	3.4	9.0	28.9
Springfield, IL	14.7	6.2	13.0	31.2
Tampa, FL	12.1	3.7	9.6	38.9
Tucson, AZ	15.0	5.8	12.8	37.5
Tulsa, OK	14.2	4.7	13.1	34.6
Tuscaloosa, AL	9.9	2.9	8.3	28.0
Virginia Beach, VA	11.5	4.3	9.4	31.3
Washington, DC	11.2	4.4	9.2	33.7
Wichita, KS	14.8	5.7	13.7	35.4
Wilmington, NC	13.0	5.1	10.0	32.0
Winston-Salem, NC	11.3	3.5	9.9	30.6
Worcester, MA	14.3	4.7	12.9	37.3
U.S.	12.6	4.4	10.3	33.4

Note: Figures show percent of the civilian noninstitutionalized population that reported having a disability. Disability status is determined from from six types of difficulty: vision, hearing, cognitive, ambulatory, self-care, and independent living. For children under 5 years old, hearing and vision difficulty are used to determine disability status. For children between the ages of 5 and 14, disability status is determined from hearing, vision, cognitive, ambulatory, and self-care difficulties. For people aged 15 years and older, they are considered to have a disability if they have difficulty with any one of the six difficulty types.
Source: U.S. Census Bureau, 2017-2021 American Community Survey 5-Year Estimates

Disability by Age: Metro Area

Metro Area	All Ages	Under 18 Years Old	18 to 64 Years Old	65 Years and Over
Albuquerque, NM	15.1	4.2	13.2	36.3
Allentown, PA	12.7	5.5	10.2	30.3
Anchorage, AK	11.7	3.8	10.7	33.9
Ann Arbor, MI	9.7	3.8	7.7	27.2
Athens, GA	12.5	5.6	10.2	34.4
Atlanta, GA	10.3	4.0	8.6	31.5
Austin, TX	9.3	3.8	7.8	29.4
Baltimore, MD	11.8	4.6	9.7	30.8
Boise City, ID	12.1	4.4	10.6	31.6
Boston, MA	10.5	4.2	7.8	30.2
Boulder, CO	8.4	3.3	6.1	25.5
Brownsville, TX	12.2	5.6	9.5	39.0
Cape Coral, FL	13.6	3.9	9.8	26.9
Cedar Rapids, IA	10.3	4.1	8.1	27.2
Charleston, SC	11.6	3.9	9.2	32.1
Charlotte, NC	10.4	3.5	8.5	31.5
Chicago, IL	10.1	3.3	7.9	30.3
Cincinnati, OH	12.4	5.0	10.6	31.8
Clarksville, TN	16.7	7.1	16.3	42.9
Cleveland, OH	14.0	5.0	11.6	32.6
College Station, TX	9.9	5.5	7.6	33.3
Colorado Springs, CO	12.5	5.1	11.5	30.8
Columbia, MO	12.8	4.9	11.1	33.8
Columbia, SC	14.2	4.7	12.3	36.3
Columbus, OH	11.9	5.0	10.1	32.7
Dallas, TX	9.5	3.8	8.0	32.1
Davenport, IA	12.7	5.2	10.4	30.1
Denver, CO	9.7	3.5	7.8	29.8
Des Moines, IA	10.5	3.7	9.0	30.4
Durham, NC	11.0	3.4	8.6	30.7
Edison, NJ	10.1	3.3	7.3	30.5
El Paso, TX	13.3	5.4	10.9	43.0
Fargo, ND	9.8	4.0	7.8	31.7
Fort Collins, CO	10.0	2.7	7.7	28.8
Fort Wayne, IN	12.4	4.7	11.0	32.0
Fort Worth, TX	9.5	3.8	8.0	32.1
Grand Rapids, MI	10.9	3.8	9.4	29.8
Greeley, CO	10.7	3.6	9.1	34.7
Green Bay, WI	11.3	4.5	9.7	27.7
Greensboro, NC	13.1	4.9	10.9	32.7
Honolulu, HI	11.2	3.0	7.5	33.0
Houston, TX	9.6	3.8	7.9	32.6
Huntsville, AL	13.1	4.0	11.1	35.4
Indianapolis, IN	12.3	4.8	10.8	32.9
Jacksonville, FL	13.0	4.6	10.9	33.2
Kansas City, MO	11.7	4.0	9.9	32.2
Lafayette, LA	14.1	4.9	12.4	37.8
Las Cruces, NM	15.2	6.6	13.4	35.7
Las Vegas, NV	12.1	4.0	9.9	33.9
Lexington, KY	13.5	5.2	11.8	34.2
Lincoln, NE	10.7	4.1	8.8	30.4
Little Rock, AR	15.6	5.8	13.8	38.4
Los Angeles, CA	9.8	3.2	7.0	33.0
Louisville, KY	13.9	4.4	12.1	35.1
Madison, WI	8.9	4.2	6.9	24.6

Table continued on following page.

Metro Area	All Ages	Under 18 Years Old	18 to 64 Years Old	65 Years and Over
Manchester, NH	11.6	4.7	9.5	29.8
Miami, FL	10.8	3.7	7.2	31.1
Midland, TX	9.9	2.6	8.2	41.3
Milwaukee, WI	11.0	3.9	8.9	29.8
Minneapolis, MN	10.0	3.9	8.2	28.5
Nashville, TN	11.6	4.0	9.7	33.6
New Haven, CT	11.6	3.7	9.2	29.9
New Orleans, LA	14.9	5.4	12.7	36.4
New York, NY	10.1	3.3	7.3	30.5
Oklahoma City, OK	14.0	4.5	12.4	38.4
Omaha, NE	11.0	3.6	9.5	31.4
Orlando, FL	12.3	5.7	9.6	33.8
Philadelphia, PA	12.7	5.1	10.5	32.2
Phoenix, AZ	11.8	4.3	9.7	31.4
Pittsburgh, PA	14.4	5.7	11.3	32.5
Portland, OR	12.1	4.1	10.0	32.3
Providence, RI	13.7	5.4	11.5	31.9
Provo, UT	8.3	3.6	8.0	31.9
Raleigh, NC	9.7	3.9	7.9	30.4
Reno, NV	11.7	4.0	9.2	30.9
Richmond, VA	12.8	5.3	10.5	32.1
Rochester, MN	10.0	3.8	7.6	28.6
Sacramento, CA	11.5	3.4	9.0	33.7
St. Louis, MO	13.0	4.7	10.8	32.4
Salem, OR	14.9	5.3	13.0	36.5
Salt Lake City, UT	9.5	3.9	8.4	30.0
San Antonio, TX	14.1	5.9	12.3	38.7
San Diego, CA	10.0	3.3	7.4	31.7
San Francisco, CA	9.6	3.1	6.7	30.0
San Jose, CA	8.3	2.7	5.5	30.7
Santa Rosa, CA	11.6	3.4	8.8	28.4
Savannah, GA	14.2	4.9	12.5	36.6
Seattle, WA	10.8	3.9	8.7	32.8
Sioux Falls, SD	9.9	3.2	8.7	28.5
Springfield, IL	13.7	6.2	11.6	30.4
Tampa, FL	14.1	5.0	10.8	33.6
Tucson, AZ	14.9	5.3	12.1	33.4
Tulsa, OK	14.7	4.8	13.1	37.4
Tuscaloosa, AL	14.3	4.5	12.5	37.4
Virginia Beach, VA	13.3	5.3	11.3	33.7
Washington, DC	8.8	3.3	6.8	28.2
Wichita, KS	14.5	5.8	12.9	35.7
Wilmington, NC	12.9	4.5	10.6	30.3
Winston-Salem, NC	13.5	4.2	11.2	33.6
Worcester, MA	12.4	4.3	10.5	31.6
U.S.	12.6	4.4	10.3	33.4

Note: Figures show percent of the civilian noninstitutionalized population that reported having a disability. Disability status is determined from from six types of difficulty: vision, hearing, cognitive, ambulatory, self-care, and independent living. For children under 5 years old, hearing and vision difficulty are used to determine disability status. For children between the ages of 5 and 14, disability status is determined from hearing, vision, cognitive, ambulatory, and self-care difficulties. For people aged 15 years and older, they are considered to have a disability if they have difficulty with any one of the six difficulty types; Figures cover the Metropolitan Statistical Area
Source: U.S. Census Bureau, 2017-2021 American Community Survey 5-Year Estimates

Religious Groups by Family

Area[1]	Catholic	Baptist	Methodist	LDS[2]	Pentecostal	Lutheran	Islam	Adventist	Other
Albuquerque, NM	32.6	3.2	0.9	2.7	1.7	0.4	0.7	1.5	10.8
Allentown, PA	18.6	0.4	2.3	0.4	0.6	5.4	0.7	1.2	11.0
Anchorage, AK	4.9	3.4	1.0	5.1	1.7	1.5	0.1	1.7	16.3
Ann Arbor, MI	9.7	2.0	2.4	0.8	1.5	2.3	2.2	0.9	10.0
Athens, GA	6.4	12.8	5.7	1.0	2.4	0.3	0.2	1.3	7.9
Atlanta, GA	10.7	14.7	6.7	0.8	2.0	0.4	1.9	1.9	12.4
Austin, TX	18.8	6.5	2.2	1.3	0.7	1.1	1.0	1.0	9.9
Baltimore, MD	12.4	3.2	4.4	0.6	1.2	1.4	3.3	1.2	11.7
Boise City, ID	13.0	0.8	2.5	15.0	1.6	0.8	0.3	1.7	10.0
Boston, MA	37.0	1.0	0.7	0.5	0.7	0.2	2.2	0.9	7.1
Boulder, CO	16.0	0.3	0.7	0.7	0.5	1.7	0.4	0.9	15.2
Brownsville, TX	36.8	2.8	0.7	1.2	1.0	0.2	0.1	2.5	9.4
Cape Coral, FL	18.8	2.5	1.7	0.6	3.0	0.7	0.2	2.0	12.2
Cedar Rapids, IA	16.8	1.0	5.3	1.0	1.3	8.1	1.3	0.6	9.6
Charleston, SC	11.5	7.7	8.0	0.8	1.9	0.7	0.2	1.0	12.8
Charlotte, NC	12.1	13.9	7.0	0.7	2.2	1.1	1.7	1.4	15.9
Chicago, IL	28.6	3.4	1.4	0.3	1.5	2.1	4.7	1.1	9.2
Cincinnati, OH	17.0	5.7	2.3	0.6	1.5	0.8	1.1	0.7	21.8
Clarksville, TN	4.6	23.2	4.4	1.4	3.2	0.5	0.1	0.8	12.4
Cleveland, OH	26.1	4.3	2.3	0.4	1.5	1.8	1.1	1.3	16.8
College Station, TX	17.2	10.6	4.3	1.7	0.5	1.1	0.6	0.5	6.8
Colorado Springs, CO	16.4	2.6	1.3	3.0	1.0	1.2	0.1	1.0	16.2
Columbia, MO	7.1	9.0	3.5	1.7	1.1	1.6	1.4	1.2	12.4
Columbia, SC	6.6	15.1	8.5	1.2	3.8	2.3	0.3	1.3	15.4
Columbus, OH	11.7	3.4	3.0	0.8	1.9	1.7	2.1	0.9	17.5
Dallas, TX	14.2	14.3	4.7	1.4	2.2	0.5	1.8	1.3	13.8
Davenport, IA	13.2	3.2	3.6	0.8	1.5	6.6	0.7	0.8	6.7
Denver, CO	16.1	1.5	1.0	2.1	0.6	1.4	0.3	1.1	10.4
Des Moines, IA	12.1	1.8	4.0	0.9	2.5	6.6	1.6	0.8	8.7
Durham, NC	8.5	12.3	6.5	0.9	1.3	0.3	1.5	1.1	13.7
Edison, NJ	32.5	1.7	1.2	0.3	0.9	0.5	4.5	1.4	10.6
El Paso, TX	47.9	2.5	0.4	1.2	1.1	0.2	0.1	2.1	6.9
Fargo, ND	14.2	0.2	1.0	0.6	1.3	24.0	<0.1	0.6	8.1
Fort Collins, CO	9.9	1.2	1.3	4.0	2.7	2.5	<0.1	1.2	12.1
Fort Wayne, IN	13.1	8.1	3.9	0.4	1.1	7.1	1.0	0.9	17.6
Fort Worth, TX	14.2	14.3	4.7	1.4	2.2	0.5	1.8	1.3	13.8
Grand Rapids, MI	13.1	1.3	1.8	0.4	1.3	1.8	0.8	1.2	19.9
Greeley, CO	14.1	0.5	0.9	2.9	1.1	1.2	<0.1	1.1	6.1
Green Bay, WI	31.8	0.3	1.4	0.5	1.1	10.8	0.4	0.9	7.0
Greensboro, NC	7.9	10.0	8.0	0.7	2.8	0.4	1.5	1.4	17.8
Honolulu, HI	18.0	1.4	0.5	4.1	2.6	0.2	<0.1	1.9	9.8
Houston, TX	18.3	13.1	3.7	1.2	1.6	0.7	1.7	1.5	13.1
Huntsville, AL	7.5	23.6	6.6	1.4	1.2	0.4	0.8	2.7	17.5
Indianapolis, IN	11.5	6.2	3.3	0.7	1.3	1.1	1.1	1.0	17.4
Jacksonville, FL	13.0	14.5	3.0	1.0	1.4	0.4	0.6	1.3	20.5
Kansas City, MO	11.3	9.1	5.0	1.6	2.7	1.7	1.0	1.0	12.1
Lafayette, LA	44.3	9.3	2.0	0.4	1.8	0.1	0.1	0.8	7.0
Las Cruces, NM	19.3	4.1	1.6	2.5	2.5	0.4	0.6	2.2	4.2
Las Vegas, NV	26.2	1.9	0.3	5.8	1.5	0.6	0.3	1.3	5.5
Lexington, KY	5.8	14.9	5.5	1.2	1.6	0.3	0.5	1.2	16.6
Lincoln, NE	13.2	1.0	5.7	1.2	3.1	9.1	0.1	1.8	10.0
Little Rock, AR	4.9	23.5	6.2	0.8	3.7	0.4	0.4	1.0	13.6
Los Angeles, CA	31.1	2.6	0.8	1.5	2.4	0.4	1.4	1.5	9.1
Louisville, KY	11.9	14.5	3.2	0.8	0.9	0.5	1.0	1.0	12.4
Madison, WI	14.4	0.5	2.0	0.7	0.2	9.2	1.2	0.7	8.4
Manchester, NH	16.3	0.6	0.6	0.6	0.3	0.3	0.1	0.8	8.1

Table continued on following page.

Area[1]	Catholic	Baptist	Methodist	LDS[2]	Pentecostal	Lutheran	Islam	Adventist	Other
Miami, FL	23.8	5.1	0.9	0.5	1.3	0.3	0.8	2.4	11.1
Midland, TX	15.4	25.5	2.5	2.0	1.2	0.3	0.4	1.3	16.5
Milwaukee, WI	24.5	3.0	1.0	0.4	2.8	9.1	2.8	0.9	10.7
Minneapolis, MN	19.8	0.8	1.4	0.5	2.5	10.7	2.9	0.7	7.4
Nashville, TN	6.2	16.4	4.8	0.9	1.6	0.4	0.8	1.3	19.4
New Haven, CT	29.9	1.4	1.2	0.4	1.2	0.4	0.9	1.2	9.9
New Orleans, LA	42.1	9.3	2.5	0.5	2.1	0.5	1.4	1.0	8.0
New York, NY	32.5	1.7	1.2	0.3	0.9	0.5	4.5	1.4	10.6
Oklahoma City, OK	10.0	16.6	6.2	1.3	3.9	0.6	0.6	0.9	21.4
Omaha, NE	19.9	2.8	2.8	1.6	1.0	6.1	0.2	1.0	9.0
Orlando, FL	17.6	5.7	2.1	0.9	2.7	0.6	1.3	2.8	14.6
Philadelphia, PA	26.8	3.3	2.4	0.3	1.0	1.2	2.6	1.0	10.5
Phoenix, AZ	22.9	1.7	0.6	6.2	1.5	1.0	1.9	1.5	9.3
Pittsburgh, PA	30.6	1.9	4.3	0.4	1.3	2.5	0.6	0.6	12.5
Portland, OR	11.8	0.8	0.6	3.3	1.4	1.1	0.2	2.0	14.4
Providence, RI	37.9	0.9	0.6	0.3	0.6	0.3	0.5	0.9	6.1
Provo, UT	4.9	0.1	<0.1	82.6	0.1	<0.1	0.3	0.3	0.4
Raleigh, NC	12.4	9.8	5.4	1.2	1.9	0.7	3.2	1.5	12.8
Reno, NV	24.4	1.4	0.5	4.0	0.9	0.5	0.3	1.4	5.3
Richmond, VA	12.3	14.2	4.8	0.9	3.2	0.5	2.1	1.2	14.8
Rochester, MN	15.6	0.4	2.8	1.5	1.9	19.3	1.0	0.7	10.1
Sacramento, CA	17.1	1.9	1.1	3.1	2.2	0.6	1.9	1.9	8.2
St. Louis, MO	21.2	8.6	2.9	0.7	1.4	3.2	1.3	0.8	11.1
Salem, OR	19.5	0.5	0.6	3.8	2.9	1.2	n/a	2.5	10.7
Salt Lake City, UT	9.0	0.6	0.2	52.0	0.7	0.2	1.6	0.7	2.6
San Antonio, TX	27.3	6.4	2.1	1.4	1.6	1.1	0.5	1.5	11.0
San Diego, CA	22.9	1.5	0.6	2.1	1.0	0.6	1.5	1.9	9.4
San Francisco, CA	21.5	2.2	0.9	1.5	1.4	0.4	2.0	1.0	7.7
San Jose, CA	27.2	1.2	0.6	1.4	0.9	0.4	2.0	1.3	11.4
Santa Rosa, CA	23.5	1.1	0.5	1.4	0.5	0.5	0.2	1.8	6.9
Savannah, GA	5.5	11.9	4.8	0.8	1.5	1.1	0.2	1.4	12.3
Seattle, WA	11.0	1.0	0.7	2.6	2.8	1.2	0.6	1.4	19.8
Sioux Falls, SD	13.1	0.7	2.9	0.7	1.7	16.4	0.1	0.6	20.3
Springfield, IL	15.2	4.7	4.3	0.5	1.5	4.7	0.5	0.8	14.6
Tampa, FL	23.1	6.3	2.9	0.5	1.9	0.6	0.7	1.8	12.1
Tucson, AZ	18.9	1.9	0.6	2.8	1.3	1.1	1.0	1.4	9.7
Tulsa, OK	5.6	15.5	7.7	1.2	2.5	0.5	0.5	1.2	22.2
Tuscaloosa, AL	2.6	25.1	6.2	0.6	1.5	0.1	0.3	0.7	13.3
Virginia Beach, VA	8.3	9.5	4.8	0.7	2.0	0.5	1.0	0.9	16.1
Washington, DC	16.1	6.0	4.1	1.1	1.3	0.8	3.3	1.5	12.6
Wichita, KS	12.7	23.5	4.5	1.5	1.4	1.3	0.1	1.1	15.0
Wilmington, NC	13.2	9.9	8.1	1.0	1.0	0.7	0.7	1.4	12.6
Winston-Salem, NC	9.3	12.8	11.4	0.5	1.0	0.6	0.8	1.4	22.5
Worcester, MA	30.1	0.8	0.8	0.3	1.0	0.4	0.6	1.4	7.1
U.S.	18.7	7.3	3.0	2.0	1.8	1.7	1.3	1.3	11.6

Note: Figures are the number of adherents as a percentage of the total population; (1) Figures cover the Metropolitan Statistical Area; (2) Church of Jesus Christ of Latter-day Saints
Source: 2020 U.S. Religion Census, Association of Statisticians of American Religious Bodies; The Association of Religion Data Archives (ARDA)

Religious Groups by Tradition

Area	Catholic	Evangelical Protestant	Mainline Protestant	Black Protestant	Islam	Judaism	Hinduism	Orthodox	Buddhism
Albuquerque, NM	32.6	13.4	2.2	0.5	0.7	0.2	0.2	0.1	0.6
Allentown, PA	18.6	6.2	11.9	0.2	0.7	0.5	0.6	0.4	0.1
Anchorage, AK	4.9	19.2	2.4	0.9	0.1	0.1	0.1	0.5	1.3
Ann Arbor, MI	9.7	8.1	5.6	2.5	2.2	0.8	0.5	0.4	0.3
Athens, GA	6.4	19.1	7.2	2.6	0.2	0.2	0.2	0.1	<0.1
Atlanta, GA	10.7	22.3	7.4	5.3	1.9	0.5	0.7	0.3	0.2
Austin, TX	18.8	13.5	4.0	1.7	1.0	0.2	0.6	0.2	0.3
Baltimore, MD	12.4	10.6	5.9	3.3	3.3	1.7	0.1	0.5	0.1
Boise City, ID	13.0	11.9	3.9	<0.1	0.3	0.1	0.2	0.1	0.1
Boston, MA	37.0	3.4	3.2	0.3	2.2	1.1	0.3	0.9	0.4
Boulder, CO	16.0	12.7	3.4	n/a	0.4	0.7	0.5	0.2	1.0
Brownsville, TX	36.8	13.1	1.2	0.1	0.1	n/a	n/a	n/a	n/a
Cape Coral, FL	18.8	16.4	3.0	0.6	0.2	0.2	0.2	0.1	0.1
Cedar Rapids, IA	16.8	11.9	12.2	0.4	1.3	0.1	0.7	0.1	<0.1
Charleston, SC	11.5	17.1	6.8	6.6	0.2	0.4	<0.1	0.2	n/a
Charlotte, NC	12.1	26.4	9.5	3.4	1.7	0.2	0.2	0.4	0.1
Chicago, IL	28.6	8.2	3.7	3.6	4.7	0.7	0.4	0.7	0.4
Cincinnati, OH	17.0	24.9	4.1	2.0	1.1	0.4	0.3	0.3	0.1
Clarksville, TN	4.6	35.7	4.8	3.4	0.1	n/a	n/a	0.1	n/a
Cleveland, OH	26.1	15.1	5.6	3.5	1.1	1.3	0.3	0.8	0.2
College Station, TX	17.2	16.1	5.3	1.8	0.6	n/a	0.1	0.1	n/a
Colorado Springs, CO	16.4	18.3	2.9	0.9	0.1	<0.1	<0.1	0.1	0.3
Columbia, MO	7.1	19.4	6.3	1.9	1.4	0.2	0.1	0.1	<0.1
Columbia, SC	6.6	27.9	10.7	5.6	0.3	0.2	0.4	0.1	0.3
Columbus, OH	11.7	18.1	6.8	1.5	2.1	0.4	0.4	0.5	0.2
Dallas, TX	14.2	25.4	5.9	3.3	1.8	0.3	0.5	0.3	0.2
Davenport, IA	13.2	8.5	10.6	1.9	0.7	0.1	0.2	0.1	n/a
Denver, CO	16.1	9.6	2.8	0.6	0.3	0.4	0.5	0.4	0.5
Des Moines, IA	12.1	10.3	12.2	1.0	1.6	<0.1	0.2	0.1	0.1
Durham, NC	8.5	20.0	8.8	4.3	1.5	0.5	0.1	0.3	0.1
Edison, NJ	32.5	4.4	3.0	1.5	4.5	4.4	1.0	0.8	0.3
El Paso, TX	47.9	9.9	0.6	0.4	0.1	0.2	<0.1	<0.1	0.2
Fargo, ND	14.2	11.1	23.4	n/a	<0.1	<0.1	n/a	0.1	n/a
Fort Collins, CO	9.9	15.6	3.3	0.4	<0.1	n/a	0.1	0.1	0.1
Fort Wayne, IN	13.1	24.7	6.1	6.5	1.0	0.1	0.1	0.2	0.4
Fort Worth, TX	14.2	25.4	5.9	3.3	1.8	0.3	0.5	0.3	0.2
Grand Rapids, MI	13.1	17.6	7.4	1.0	0.8	0.1	0.2	0.2	<0.1
Greeley, CO	14.1	7.8	2.1	<0.1	<0.1	n/a	n/a	<0.1	0.2
Green Bay, WI	31.8	14.6	6.2	<0.1	0.4	n/a	n/a	<0.1	<0.1
Greensboro, NC	7.9	24.9	10.1	3.5	1.5	0.3	0.3	0.1	0.1
Honolulu, HI	18.0	8.1	2.3	0.2	<0.1	0.1	0.2	<0.1	4.0
Houston, TX	18.3	23.8	4.7	2.3	1.7	0.3	0.7	0.3	0.3
Huntsville, AL	7.5	34.8	8.2	7.2	0.8	0.1	0.9	0.1	0.1
Indianapolis, IN	11.5	16.8	7.6	4.2	1.1	0.4	0.2	0.3	0.1
Jacksonville, FL	13.0	29.8	3.5	5.6	0.6	0.3	0.3	0.3	0.2
Kansas City, MO	11.3	19.1	7.1	3.6	1.0	0.3	0.4	0.1	0.2
Lafayette, LA	44.3	12.6	2.4	5.0	0.1	n/a	<0.1	<0.1	0.1
Las Cruces, NM	19.3	9.8	2.4	0.2	0.6	0.1	0.2	<0.1	n/a
Las Vegas, NV	26.2	6.6	1.0	0.5	0.3	0.3	0.2	0.6	0.7
Lexington, KY	5.8	26.9	8.1	3.5	0.5	0.3	0.1	0.2	<0.1
Lincoln, NE	13.2	16.6	12.9	0.3	0.1	0.1	0.1	0.1	0.1
Little Rock, AR	4.9	32.1	6.6	8.5	0.4	0.1	<0.1	0.1	0.1
Los Angeles, CA	31.1	9.3	1.5	1.7	1.4	0.8	0.4	0.9	0.9
Louisville, KY	11.9	21.1	5.0	4.6	1.0	0.2	0.4	0.2	0.2
Madison, WI	14.4	8.0	10.6	0.2	1.2	0.4	0.1	0.1	0.9

Table continued on following page.

Area	Catholic	Evangelical Protestant	Mainline Protestant	Black Protestant	Islam	Judaism	Hinduism	Orthodox	Buddhism
Manchester, NH	16.3	5.8	2.7	n/a	0.1	0.3	<0.1	0.9	n/a
Miami, FL	23.8	13.7	1.6	2.2	0.8	1.2	0.3	0.2	0.3
Midland, TX	15.4	35.5	3.0	7.6	0.4	n/a	0.2	n/a	n/a
Milwaukee, WI	24.5	16.3	5.4	3.3	2.8	0.4	0.4	0.5	0.4
Minneapolis, MN	19.8	10.6	10.3	0.5	2.9	0.6	0.2	0.3	0.3
Nashville, TN	6.2	30.1	6.0	5.2	0.8	0.2	0.4	1.1	0.2
New Haven, CT	29.9	6.4	4.4	1.4	0.9	1.0	0.3	0.5	0.4
New Orleans, LA	42.1	13.5	3.0	4.9	1.4	0.4	0.3	0.1	0.3
New York, NY	32.5	4.4	3.0	1.5	4.5	4.4	1.0	0.8	0.3
Oklahoma City, OK	10.0	38.7	7.1	2.2	0.6	0.1	0.4	0.1	0.4
Omaha, NE	19.9	10.8	7.9	1.5	0.2	0.3	1.0	0.2	0.2
Orlando, FL	17.6	20.6	2.5	2.7	1.3	0.2	0.5	0.3	0.3
Philadelphia, PA	26.8	7.3	6.6	2.2	2.6	1.1	0.6	0.4	0.4
Phoenix, AZ	22.9	11.0	1.6	0.3	1.9	0.3	0.5	0.4	0.2
Pittsburgh, PA	30.6	8.8	10.1	1.3	0.6	0.6	1.2	0.6	0.1
Portland, OR	11.8	14.6	2.3	0.4	0.2	0.3	0.7	0.3	0.4
Providence, RI	37.9	4.0	3.2	0.1	0.5	0.6	0.1	0.5	0.2
Provo, UT	4.9	0.4	<0.1	n/a	0.3	n/a	0.1	n/a	n/a
Raleigh, NC	12.4	19.3	7.4	2.8	3.2	0.2	0.4	0.3	0.4
Reno, NV	24.4	6.8	1.3	0.2	0.3	0.1	0.1	0.1	0.2
Richmond, VA	12.3	23.1	9.3	3.1	2.1	0.3	1.3	0.4	0.2
Rochester, MN	15.6	15.0	19.1	n/a	1.0	0.1	0.1	0.2	0.2
Sacramento, CA	17.1	10.4	1.4	1.1	1.9	0.2	0.4	0.3	0.5
St. Louis, MO	21.2	16.1	5.7	3.9	1.3	0.6	0.2	0.2	0.3
Salem, OR	19.5	14.4	2.0	0.2	n/a	0.1	<0.1	<0.1	<0.1
Salt Lake City, UT	9.0	2.4	0.7	0.1	1.6	0.1	0.3	0.4	0.3
San Antonio, TX	27.3	17.7	3.1	0.8	0.5	0.2	0.1	0.1	0.3
San Diego, CA	22.9	9.5	1.5	0.6	1.5	0.4	0.3	0.4	0.7
San Francisco, CA	21.5	5.2	2.2	1.8	2.0	0.7	1.1	0.7	1.1
San Jose, CA	27.2	8.4	1.4	0.3	2.0	0.6	2.4	0.6	1.2
Santa Rosa, CA	23.5	5.3	1.5	<0.1	0.2	0.4	0.3	0.4	1.7
Savannah, GA	5.5	19.0	5.7	5.9	0.2	0.7	0.5	0.1	n/a
Seattle, WA	11.0	19.5	2.7	0.6	0.6	0.4	0.4	0.6	1.6
Sioux Falls, SD	13.1	21.0	20.2	0.1	0.1	n/a	n/a	0.8	<0.1
Springfield, IL	15.2	19.0	7.7	2.4	0.5	0.2	0.3	0.1	<0.1
Tampa, FL	23.1	16.9	3.8	1.7	0.7	0.4	0.3	0.8	0.4
Tucson, AZ	18.9	10.4	2.4	0.6	1.0	0.4	0.4	0.2	0.3
Tulsa, OK	5.6	37.8	8.6	1.7	0.5	0.2	0.1	0.1	<0.1
Tuscaloosa, AL	2.6	34.3	4.6	7.3	0.3	0.1	n/a	n/a	n/a
Virginia Beach, VA	8.3	21.3	6.9	3.7	1.0	0.3	0.2	0.3	0.3
Washington, DC	16.1	12.3	6.5	3.3	3.3	1.0	0.9	0.9	0.5
Wichita, KS	12.7	19.4	23.2	2.6	0.1	<0.1	0.1	0.2	0.5
Wilmington, NC	13.2	17.9	9.3	4.6	0.7	0.3	0.1	0.3	n/a
Winston-Salem, NC	9.3	31.4	13.6	3.4	0.8	n/a	<0.1	0.3	0.1
Worcester, MA	30.1	4.9	3.6	0.2	0.6	0.4	0.3	1.0	0.4
U.S.	18.7	16.5	5.2	2.3	1.3	0.6	0.4	0.4	0.3

Note: Figures are the number of adherents as a percentage of the total population; (1) Figures cover the Metropolitan Statistical Area
Source: 2020 U.S. Religion Census, Association of Statisticians of American Religious Bodies; The Association of Religion Data Archives (ARDA)

Gross Metropolitan Product

MSA[1]	2020	2021	2022	2023	Rank[2]
Albuquerque, NM	45.1	50.3	56.1	58.2	70
Allentown, PA	46.7	51.6	56.6	59.9	67
Anchorage, AK	25.8	28.3	31.3	32.6	112
Ann Arbor, MI	25.8	28.1	30.4	32.1	113
Athens, GA	10.5	11.5	12.8	13.4	213
Atlanta, GA	425.4	465.1	507.9	540.7	11
Austin, TX	168.4	192.3	215.9	231.0	22
Baltimore, MD	205.8	219.9	238.6	255.0	19
Boise City, ID	37.9	42.9	46.9	50.4	80
Boston, MA	480.3	526.5	569.8	601.7	8
Boulder, CO	29.7	32.7	35.9	38.1	101
Brownsville, TX	11.9	13.1	14.8	15.6	195
Cape Coral, FL	34.5	38.8	42.7	45.6	85
Cedar Rapids, IA	18.5	20.7	21.9	23.3	147
Charleston, SC	45.6	50.4	55.3	59.2	69
Charlotte, NC	184.0	204.1	222.9	238.2	21
Chicago, IL	693.0	757.2	819.9	861.2	3
Cincinnati, OH	152.1	165.2	178.8	190.5	27
Clarksville, TN	12.3	13.7	14.8	15.6	191
Cleveland, OH	133.6	144.9	157.7	167.2	35
College Station, TX	13.6	14.9	16.6	17.4	185
Colorado Springs, CO	39.5	43.7	47.3	49.9	78
Columbia, MO	10.4	11.6	12.5	13.3	211
Columbia, SC	44.4	48.2	51.8	55.2	74
Columbus, OH	137.3	151.0	164.2	175.3	33
Dallas, TX	538.4	608.8	686.1	722.1	5
Davenport, IA	22.1	24.6	26.3	27.6	126
Denver, CO	223.1	246.9	271.0	286.2	18
Des Moines, IA	55.0	63.3	67.6	71.4	57
Durham, NC	51.6	57.3	61.8	65.6	60
Edison, NJ	1,844.7	1,993.2	2,157.6	2,278.7	1
El Paso, TX	34.1	37.5	40.5	42.6	89
Fargo, ND	15.7	18.0	19.9	20.6	160
Fort Collins, CO	21.6	23.7	25.7	27.3	130
Fort Wayne, IN	24.3	27.3	29.8	31.6	114
Fort Worth, TX	538.4	608.8	686.1	722.1	5
Grand Rapids, MI	61.4	67.8	73.0	78.0	55
Greeley, CO	16.7	17.9	20.0	22.3	162
Green Bay, WI	20.5	22.2	24.3	26.0	139
Greensboro, NC	42.0	46.1	49.5	51.7	75
Honolulu, HI	62.1	66.8	74.3	80.2	56
Houston, TX	488.1	543.0	619.8	654.0	7
Huntsville, AL	30.9	33.5	36.5	39.2	98
Indianapolis, IN	146.9	163.9	178.6	190.0	28
Jacksonville, FL	91.0	100.3	109.1	115.5	42
Kansas City, MO	142.5	154.3	165.9	176.9	32
Lafayette, LA	20.6	22.6	24.8	26.2	135
Las Cruces, NM	7.6	8.5	9.6	10.0	258
Las Vegas, NV	119.4	134.8	151.1	164.0	36
Lexington, KY	29.8	32.5	35.1	36.8	103
Lincoln, NE	21.2	23.8	25.4	26.9	129
Little Rock, AR	38.6	42.3	45.8	48.0	81
Los Angeles, CA	1,007.0	1,129.4	1,226.9	1,295.5	2
Louisville, KY	75.6	83.6	90.5	94.4	47
Madison, WI	51.5	56.1	60.8	64.9	63
Manchester, NH	28.8	32.2	34.1	35.6	104

Table continued on following page.

MSA[1]	2020	2021	2022	2023	Rank[2]
Miami, FL	365.0	402.9	442.8	471.0	12
Midland, TX	21.8	25.3	30.1	33.9	121
Milwaukee, WI	102.4	110.1	119.2	126.3	38
Minneapolis, MN	270.7	298.9	324.7	344.9	15
Nashville, TN	136.6	157.4	173.7	184.5	31
New Haven, CT	53.0	57.1	61.7	64.7	61
New Orleans, LA	76.4	82.6	91.2	96.5	48
New York, NY	1,844.7	1,993.2	2,157.6	2,278.7	1
Oklahoma City, OK	74.4	81.6	92.9	98.2	49
Omaha, NE	69.1	77.9	83.2	88.2	50
Orlando, FL	144.1	160.5	180.2	194.2	30
Philadelphia, PA	439.1	478.2	521.7	553.7	9
Phoenix, AZ	281.0	310.1	336.3	358.7	14
Pittsburgh, PA	153.4	165.5	178.3	189.7	26
Portland, OR	168.4	184.1	201.8	214.4	25
Providence, RI	87.9	95.6	104.0	109.3	45
Provo, UT	31.9	36.5	40.2	43.1	91
Raleigh, NC	95.3	106.6	117.3	125.7	39
Reno, NV	31.8	35.9	39.3	41.9	92
Richmond, VA	91.2	97.3	104.5	110.5	44
Rochester, MN	14.2	15.8	17.1	18.1	178
Sacramento, CA	145.4	161.7	176.8	188.8	29
St. Louis, MO	171.5	187.7	201.8	212.8	23
Salem, OR	19.2	21.0	22.9	24.2	144
Salt Lake City, UT	103.9	114.9	124.5	132.3	37
San Antonio, TX	132.1	146.4	161.1	169.2	34
San Diego, CA	240.4	269.0	294.4	313.2	17
San Francisco, CA	588.3	652.7	713.1	748.9	4
San Jose, CA	360.5	400.1	431.2	450.9	13
Santa Rosa, CA	31.2	35.6	39.1	41.5	93
Savannah, GA	22.0	25.3	27.7	28.7	122
Seattle, WA	426.9	470.6	509.3	539.7	10
Sioux Falls, SD	23.4	26.6	28.7	30.6	118
Springfield, IL	11.7	13.1	13.8	14.6	196
Tampa, FL	169.3	187.4	205.4	217.8	24
Tucson, AZ	45.2	49.1	53.1	56.2	72
Tulsa, OK	53.7	58.3	65.1	68.5	59
Tuscaloosa, AL	11.4	12.2	13.2	13.9	205
Virginia Beach, VA	95.3	102.4	109.4	116.0	41
Washington, DC	560.7	600.8	647.6	688.6	6
Wichita, KS	36.7	40.2	44.0	47.1	83
Wilmington, NC	16.0	18.0	19.3	20.3	161
Winston-Salem, NC	34.0	37.6	40.9	43.7	88
Worcester, MA	50.9	55.1	59.3	62.5	64

Note: Figures are in billions of dollars; (1) Metropolitan Statistical Area; (2) Rank is based on 2021 data and ranges from 1 to 381.
Source: The U.S. Conference of Mayors, U.S. Metro Economies: U.S. Metros Compared to Global and State Economies,, June 2022

Economic Growth

MSA[1]	2018-20 (%)	2021 (%)	2022 (%)	2023	Rank[2]
Albuquerque, NM	-0.4	5.6	4.6	3.6	167
Allentown, PA	-0.3	5.9	3.6	2.6	159
Anchorage, AK	-2.4	0.4	2.3	2.9	323
Ann Arbor, MI	-0.4	5.0	2.9	2.6	164
Athens, GA	-2.1	5.6	6.1	1.6	288
Atlanta, GA	-0.1	5.9	3.3	3.1	151
Austin, TX	3.2	10.1	5.9	3.8	13
Baltimore, MD	-2.0	3.2	2.7	3.5	284
Boise City, ID	2.0	7.4	3.2	4.2	35
Boston, MA	-0.1	6.7	3.2	2.4	146
Boulder, CO	1.5	5.6	3.5	3.8	49
Brownsville, TX	1.3	6.2	4.4	2.9	56
Cape Coral, FL	-0.4	8.7	5.0	2.9	165
Cedar Rapids, IA	-2.3	4.9	-0.2	3.5	310
Charleston, SC	0.4	6.3	3.8	3.8	106
Charlotte, NC	0.5	6.6	3.2	3.6	103
Chicago, IL	-2.4	5.5	2.6	1.8	324
Cincinnati, OH	0.0	4.2	2.4	3.3	145
Clarksville, TN	0.7	7.1	3.0	1.6	91
Cleveland, OH	-1.3	4.3	3.1	2.7	238
College Station, TX	1.1	5.1	4.2	2.8	61
Colorado Springs, CO	1.6	6.0	2.1	3.0	47
Columbia, MO	2.1	5.6	2.9	3.3	29
Columbia, SC	0.1	4.4	1.7	3.2	137
Columbus, OH	0.1	5.8	3.1	3.5	136
Dallas, TX	0.8	8.3	5.3	3.2	84
Davenport, IA	-0.6	5.6	1.2	1.8	184
Denver, CO	0.8	6.2	3.5	3.1	82
Des Moines, IA	1.7	8.2	0.9	2.7	46
Durham, NC	2.7	6.7	2.5	2.9	19
Edison, NJ	-1.5	5.6	3.3	2.4	250
El Paso, TX	2.0	5.5	2.3	1.9	36
Fargo, ND	-0.4	6.0	-0.2	1.2	170
Fort Collins, CO	2.2	5.3	2.6	4.0	27
Fort Wayne, IN	-2.0	8.3	3.1	2.7	285
Fort Worth, TX	0.8	8.3	5.3	3.2	84
Grand Rapids, MI	-2.1	6.3	1.8	3.7	294
Greeley, CO	-4.3	3.2	5.5	9.1	366
Green Bay, WI	-2.5	3.7	3.7	3.9	326
Greensboro, NC	-2.2	5.4	1.5	1.4	302
Honolulu, HI	-5.4	3.6	5.2	4.6	376
Houston, TX	-1.6	4.9	4.4	4.7	254
Huntsville, AL	1.8	4.9	3.4	3.9	42
Indianapolis, IN	-0.2	7.3	3.2	3.1	155
Jacksonville, FL	2.1	6.1	3.1	2.6	30
Kansas City, MO	0.0	4.0	1.7	3.5	140
Lafayette, LA	-3.7	4.2	2.6	3.3	356
Las Cruces, NM	-1.8	6.3	7.3	3.2	273
Las Vegas, NV	-3.4	7.7	5.7	5.1	349
Lexington, KY	-1.6	4.1	1.8	1.6	261
Lincoln, NE	0.1	5.0	0.9	2.8	131
Little Rock, AR	-0.6	5.2	2.2	1.9	182
Los Angeles, CA	-1.6	8.8	3.3	2.6	256
Louisville, KY	-0.4	5.8	2.2	1.2	169
Madison, WI	0.1	4.4	2.7	3.7	132
Manchester, NH	0.9	8.3	1.2	1.0	78

Table continued on following page.

MSA[1]	2018-20 (%)	2021 (%)	2022 (%)	2023	Rank[2]
Miami, FL	-1.4	6.4	4.2	3.1	245
Midland, TX	3.5	15.8	10.1	12.3	12
Milwaukee, WI	-1.8	3.1	2.5	2.8	271
Minneapolis, MN	-1.9	5.9	2.8	3.0	276
Nashville, TN	-1.2	10.6	4.4	3.0	228
New Haven, CT	-0.9	4.6	2.8	1.7	206
New Orleans, LA	-2.2	2.6	1.8	3.3	304
New York, NY	-1.5	5.6	3.3	2.4	250
Oklahoma City, OK	-2.2	2.3	4.2	4.8	307
Omaha, NE	0.2	5.3	0.8	3.0	127
Orlando, FL	-1.2	7.5	6.4	4.4	229
Philadelphia, PA	-1.2	4.9	3.3	2.8	235
Phoenix, AZ	1.9	5.8	2.7	3.4	39
Pittsburgh, PA	-1.6	3.8	1.9	3.1	257
Portland, OR	-0.6	5.8	4.2	2.9	179
Providence, RI	-1.1	5.6	3.4	1.9	224
Provo, UT	5.1	10.9	6.1	4.3	3
Raleigh, NC	-0.1	7.7	4.4	4.0	148
Reno, NV	2.1	7.5	2.8	3.2	31
Richmond, VA	-0.3	3.0	1.7	2.3	160
Rochester, MN	-0.9	6.6	2.9	2.5	209
Sacramento, CA	0.0	7.4	3.6	3.6	142
St. Louis, MO	-1.2	5.3	1.6	2.0	232
Salem, OR	0.3	5.6	4.2	2.6	119
Salt Lake City, UT	1.9	6.1	2.7	3.1	38
San Antonio, TX	0.8	6.2	3.7	2.4	88
San Diego, CA	-0.5	8.2	3.9	3.3	174
San Francisco, CA	1.2	7.1	4.0	1.9	60
San Jose, CA	5.2	8.6	3.3	1.6	2
Santa Rosa, CA	-1.8	9.7	5.0	3.1	269
Savannah, GA	-1.6	10.3	4.8	0.1	262
Seattle, WA	2.2	7.2	3.3	2.6	26
Sioux Falls, SD	0.4	7.1	1.9	3.7	111
Springfield, IL	-3.3	9.4	0.6	2.6	346
Tampa, FL	1.0	7.2	4.1	2.8	72
Tucson, AZ	-1.3	4.0	2.1	2.5	240
Tulsa, OK	-1.7	1.1	3.1	3.5	266
Tuscaloosa, AL	0.9	3.1	3.9	2.4	80
Virginia Beach, VA	-1.4	3.5	1.1	2.5	247
Washington, DC	-0.7	4.0	2.5	3.0	192
Wichita, KS	-2.0	4.3	2.9	4.1	286
Wilmington, NC	1.5	8.5	1.8	1.3	52
Winston-Salem, NC	-4.0	6.0	2.8	3.6	358
Worcester, MA	-0.9	5.3	2.5	2.4	204
U.S.	-0.6	5.7	3.1	2.9	—

Note: Figures are real gross metropolitan product (GMP) growth rates and represent annual average percent change;
(1) Metropolitan Statistical Area; (2) Rank is based on 2020 2-year average annual percent change and ranges from 1 to 381
Source: The U.S. Conference of Mayors, U.S. Metro Economies: U.S. Metros Compared to Global and State Economies,, June 2022

Metropolitan Area Exports

MSA[1]	2016	2017	2018	2019	2020	2021	Rank[2]
Albuquerque, NM	999.7	624.2	771.5	1,629.7	1,265.3	2,215.0	101
Allentown, PA	3,657.2	3,639.4	3,423.2	3,796.3	3,207.4	4,088.7	68
Anchorage, AK	1,215.4	1,675.9	1,510.8	1,348.0	990.9	n/a	n/a
Ann Arbor, MI	1,207.9	1,447.4	1,538.7	1,432.7	1,183.1	1,230.7	141
Athens, GA	332.1	297.7	378.1	442.1	338.7	448.1	223
Atlanta, GA	20,480.1	21,748.0	24,091.6	25,800.8	25,791.0	28,116.4	16
Austin, TX	10,682.7	12,451.5	12,929.9	12,509.0	13,041.5	15,621.9	25
Baltimore, MD	5,288.6	4,674.3	6,039.2	7,081.8	6,084.6	8,200.6	43
Boise City, ID	3,021.7	2,483.3	2,771.7	2,062.8	1,632.9	1,937.1	110
Boston, MA	21,168.0	23,116.2	24,450.1	23,505.8	23,233.8	32,084.2	12
Boulder, CO	956.3	1,012.0	1,044.1	1,014.9	1,110.4	1,078.0	152
Brownsville, TX	5,016.7	n/a	6,293.0	4,741.8	n/a	6,953.0	47
Cape Coral, FL	540.3	592.3	668.0	694.9	654.8	797.5	183
Cedar Rapids, IA	945.0	1,071.6	1,025.0	1,028.4	832.0	980.0	160
Charleston, SC	9,508.1	8,845.2	10,943.2	16,337.9	6,110.5	3,381.6	77
Charlotte, NC	11,944.1	13,122.5	14,083.2	13,892.4	8,225.6	10,554.3	33
Chicago, IL	43,932.7	46,140.2	47,287.8	42,438.8	41,279.4	54,498.1	4
Cincinnati, OH	26,326.2	28,581.8	27,396.3	28,778.3	21,002.2	23,198.7	19
Clarksville, TN	376.1	360.2	435.5	341.8	246.8	288.7	268
Cleveland, OH	8,752.9	8,944.9	9,382.9	8,829.9	7,415.8	8,560.4	41
College Station, TX	113.2	145.4	153.0	160.5	114.9	110.3	346
Colorado Springs, CO	786.9	819.7	850.6	864.2	979.2	866.9	175
Columbia, MO	213.7	224.0	238.6	291.4	256.2	335.4	255
Columbia, SC	2,007.7	2,123.9	2,083.8	2,184.6	2,058.8	2,100.2	104
Columbus, OH	5,675.4	5,962.2	7,529.5	7,296.6	6,304.8	6,557.9	51
Dallas, TX	27,187.8	30,269.1	36,260.9	39,474.0	35,642.0	43,189.0	6
Davenport, IA	4,497.6	5,442.7	6,761.9	6,066.3	5,097.5	6,341.0	52
Denver, CO	3,649.3	3,954.7	4,544.3	4,555.6	4,604.4	4,670.8	62
Des Moines, IA	1,052.2	1,141.2	1,293.7	1,437.8	1,414.0	1,706.6	118
Durham, NC	2,937.4	3,128.4	3,945.8	4,452.9	3,359.3	3,326.4	78
Edison, NJ	89,649.5	93,693.7	97,692.4	87,365.7	75,745.4	103,930.9	2
El Paso, TX	26,452.8	25,814.1	30,052.0	32,749.6	27,154.4	32,397.9	11
Fargo, ND	474.5	519.5	553.5	515.0	438.3	539.4	210
Fort Collins, CO	993.8	1,034.1	1,021.8	1,060.0	1,092.5	1,132.5	146
Fort Wayne, IN	1,322.2	1,422.8	1,593.3	1,438.5	1,144.6	1,592.7	123
Fort Worth, TX	27,187.8	30,269.1	36,260.9	39,474.0	35,642.0	43,189.0	6
Grand Rapids, MI	5,168.5	5,385.8	5,420.9	5,214.1	4,488.3	5,171.7	57
Greeley, CO	1,539.6	1,492.8	1,366.5	1,439.2	1,480.4	2,022.6	109
Green Bay, WI	1,044.0	1,054.8	1,044.3	928.2	736.4	765.6	185
Greensboro, NC	3,730.4	3,537.9	3,053.5	2,561.8	2,007.3	2,356.2	97
Honolulu, HI	330.3	393.6	438.9	308.6	169.0	164.3	319
Houston, TX	84,105.5	95,760.3	120,714.3	129,656.0	104,538.2	140,750.4	1
Huntsville, AL	1,827.3	1,889.2	1,608.7	1,534.2	1,263.0	1,579.5	124
Indianapolis, IN	9,655.4	10,544.2	11,069.9	11,148.7	11,100.4	12,740.4	30
Jacksonville, FL	2,159.0	2,141.7	2,406.7	2,975.5	2,473.3	2,683.7	90
Kansas City, MO	6,709.8	7,015.0	7,316.9	7,652.6	7,862.7	9,177.6	38
Lafayette, LA	1,335.2	954.8	1,001.7	1,086.2	946.2	895.7	167
Las Cruces, NM	1,568.6	1,390.2	1,467.5	n/a	2,149.5	2,408.2	95
Las Vegas, NV	2,312.3	2,710.6	2,240.6	2,430.8	1,705.9	1,866.2	115
Lexington, KY	2,069.6	2,119.8	2,148.0	2,093.8	1,586.3	1,880.0	113
Lincoln, NE	796.9	860.9	885.6	807.0	726.3	872.6	171
Little Rock, AR	1,871.0	2,146.1	1,607.4	1,642.5	n/a	1,370.6	132
Los Angeles, CA	61,245.7	63,752.9	64,814.6	61,041.1	50,185.4	58,588.4	3
Louisville, KY	7,793.3	8,925.9	8,987.0	9,105.5	8,360.3	10,262.8	35
Madison, WI	2,204.8	2,187.7	2,460.2	2,337.6	2,450.5	2,756.3	89
Manchester, NH	1,465.2	1,714.7	1,651.4	1,587.1	1,704.9	2,077.6	106

Table continued on following page.

MSA[1]	2016	2017	2018	2019	2020	2021	Rank[2]
Miami, FL	32,734.5	34,780.5	35,650.2	35,498.9	29,112.1	36,011.3	7
Midland, TX	69.6	69.4	63.6	63.7	57.7	49.9	372
Milwaukee, WI	7,256.2	7,279.1	7,337.6	6,896.3	6,624.0	7,282.8	46
Minneapolis, MN	18,329.2	19,070.9	20,016.2	18,633.0	17,109.5	21,098.8	21
Nashville, TN	9,460.1	10,164.3	8,723.7	7,940.7	6,569.9	8,256.1	42
New Haven, CT	1,819.8	1,876.3	2,082.3	2,133.8	2,330.5	2,667.5	91
New Orleans, LA	29,518.8	31,648.5	36,570.4	34,109.6	31,088.4	35,773.5	8
New York, NY	89,649.5	93,693.7	97,692.4	87,365.7	75,745.4	103,930.9	2
Oklahoma City, OK	1,260.0	1,278.8	1,489.4	1,434.5	1,326.6	1,773.2	116
Omaha, NE	3,509.7	3,756.2	4,371.6	3,725.7	3,852.5	4,595.1	64
Orlando, FL	3,363.9	3,196.7	3,131.7	3,363.9	2,849.8	3,313.6	79
Philadelphia, PA	21,359.9	21,689.7	23,663.2	24,721.3	23,022.1	28,724.4	15
Phoenix, AZ	12,838.2	13,223.1	13,614.9	15,136.6	11,073.9	14,165.1	27
Pittsburgh, PA	7,971.0	9,322.7	9,824.2	9,672.9	7,545.1	9,469.6	36
Portland, OR	20,256.8	20,788.8	21,442.9	23,761.9	27,824.7	33,787.5	10
Providence, RI	6,595.7	7,125.4	6,236.6	7,424.8	6,685.2	6,708.2	49
Provo, UT	1,894.8	2,065.3	1,788.1	1,783.7	1,888.5	2,053.8	108
Raleigh, NC	2,620.4	2,865.8	3,193.2	3,546.8	3,372.0	3,962.7	71
Reno, NV	2,382.1	2,517.3	2,631.7	2,598.3	4,553.3	4,503.0	66
Richmond, VA	3,525.7	3,663.7	3,535.0	3,203.2	2,719.1	3,010.7	84
Rochester, MN	398.0	495.3	537.6	390.1	194.0	224.9	292
Sacramento, CA	7,032.1	6,552.6	6,222.8	5,449.2	4,980.9	5,682.3	54
St. Louis, MO	8,346.5	9,662.9	10,866.8	10,711.1	9,089.4	10,486.1	34
Salem, OR	358.2	339.0	410.2	405.7	350.5	372.0	244
Salt Lake City, UT	8,653.7	7,916.9	9,748.6	13,273.9	13,565.5	13,469.1	28
San Antonio, TX	5,621.2	9,184.1	11,678.1	11,668.0	10,987.9	13,086.4	29
San Diego, CA	18,086.6	18,637.1	20,156.8	19,774.1	18,999.7	23,687.8	18
San Francisco, CA	24,506.3	29,103.8	27,417.0	28,003.8	23,864.5	29,972.0	13
San Jose, CA	21,716.8	21,464.7	22,224.2	20,909.4	19,534.5	22,293.6	20
Santa Rosa, CA	1,194.3	1,168.2	1,231.7	1,234.5	1,131.4	1,301.8	137
Savannah, GA	4,263.4	4,472.0	5,407.8	4,925.5	4,557.0	5,520.5	55
Seattle, WA	61,881.0	59,007.0	59,742.9	41,249.0	23,851.0	28,866.7	14
Sioux Falls, SD	334.3	386.8	400.0	431.5	524.9	547.3	207
Springfield, IL	88.3	107.5	91.2	99.8	90.5	98.9	351
Tampa, FL	5,702.9	6,256.0	4,966.7	6,219.7	5,082.2	5,754.7	53
Tucson, AZ	2,563.9	2,683.9	2,824.8	2,943.7	2,640.7	2,846.1	87
Tulsa, OK	2,363.0	2,564.7	3,351.7	3,399.2	2,567.8	3,064.8	81
Tuscaloosa, AL	n/a	n/a	n/a	n/a	5,175.0	6,675.5	50
Virginia Beach, VA	3,291.1	3,307.2	3,950.6	3,642.4	4,284.3	4,566.3	65
Washington, DC	13,582.4	12,736.1	13,602.7	14,563.8	13,537.3	12,210.8	31
Wichita, KS	3,054.9	3,299.2	3,817.0	3,494.7	2,882.1	3,615.3	74
Wilmington, NC	598.7	759.8	634.4	526.4	553.6	497.8	218
Winston-Salem, NC	1,234.6	1,131.7	1,107.5	1,209.1	913.1	918.2	164
Worcester, MA	3,093.5	2,929.6	2,573.6	2,221.5	2,026.4	2,624.6	92

Note: Figures are in millions of dollars; (1) Metropolitan Statistical Area; (2) Rank is based on 2021 data and ranges from 1 to 388
Source: U.S. Department of Commerce, International Trade Administration, Office of Trade and Economic Analysis, Industry and Analysis, Exports by Metropolitan Area, extracted March 16, 2023

Building Permits: City

City	Single-Family			Multi-Family			Total		
	2021	2022	Pct. Chg.	2021	2022	Pct. Chg.	2021	2022	Pct. Chg.
Albuquerque, NM	773	707	-8.5	894	902	0.9	1,667	1,609	-3.5
Allentown, PA	0	27	–	0	0	0.0	0	27	–
Anchorage, AK	840	124	-85.2	293	31	-89.4	1,133	155	-86.3
Ann Arbor, MI	175	135	-22.9	52	4	-92.3	227	139	-38.8
Athens, GA	180	227	26.1	986	1,548	57.0	1,166	1,775	52.2
Atlanta, GA	855	1,775	107.6	1,558	10,078	546.9	2,413	11,853	391.2
Austin, TX	4,180	3,344	-20.0	14,542	15,102	3.9	18,722	18,446	-1.5
Baltimore, MD	191	118	-38.2	1,366	1,539	12.7	1,557	1,657	6.4
Boise City, ID	856	392	-54.2	1,165	1,210	3.9	2,021	1,602	-20.7
Boston, MA	53	53	0.0	3,459	3,882	12.2	3,512	3,935	12.0
Boulder, CO	41	35	-14.6	253	269	6.3	294	304	3.4
Brownsville, TX	883	817	-7.5	246	353	43.5	1,129	1,170	3.6
Cape Coral, FL	4,279	3,813	-10.9	1,133	922	-18.6	5,412	4,735	-12.5
Cedar Rapids, IA	158	129	-18.4	280	225	-19.6	438	354	-19.2
Charleston, SC	1,091	942	-13.7	378	459	21.4	1,469	1,401	-4.6
Charlotte, NC	n/a	n/a	n/a	n/a	n/a	n/a	n/a	n/a	n/a
Chicago, IL	414	412	-0.5	4,927	6,712	36.2	5,341	7,124	33.4
Cincinnati, OH	206	104	-49.5	932	689	-26.1	1,138	793	-30.3
Clarksville, TN	1,452	973	-33.0	1,813	2,160	19.1	3,265	3,133	-4.0
Cleveland, OH	104	158	51.9	27	363	1,244.4	131	521	297.7
College Station, TX	674	592	-12.2	318	97	-69.5	992	689	-30.5
Colorado Springs, CO	n/a	n/a	n/a	n/a	n/a	n/a	n/a	n/a	n/a
Columbia, MO	487	303	-37.8	189	135	-28.6	676	438	-35.2
Columbia, SC	804	772	-4.0	896	1,359	51.7	1,700	2,131	25.4
Columbus, OH	913	642	-29.7	3,555	5,535	55.7	4,468	6,177	38.2
Dallas, TX	2,245	2,349	4.6	7,769	7,880	1.4	10,014	10,229	2.1
Davenport, IA	84	160	90.5	0	0	0.0	84	160	90.5
Denver, CO	1,550	1,323	-14.6	8,450	6,973	-17.5	10,000	8,296	-17.0
Des Moines, IA	248	256	3.2	380	284	-25.3	628	540	-14.0
Durham, NC	1,960	1,595	-18.6	1,361	2,771	103.6	3,321	4,366	31.5
Edison, NJ	105	104	-1.0	250	17	-93.2	355	121	-65.9
El Paso, TX	1,961	1,649	-15.9	272	319	17.3	2,233	1,968	-11.9
Fargo, ND	410	413	0.7	736	820	11.4	1,146	1,233	7.6
Fort Collins, CO	381	287	-24.7	458	515	12.4	839	802	-4.4
Fort Wayne, IN	n/a	n/a	n/a	n/a	n/a	n/a	n/a	n/a	n/a
Fort Worth, TX	7,236	7,421	2.6	4,338	4,557	5.0	11,574	11,978	3.5
Grand Rapids, MI	43	23	-46.5	243	211	-13.2	286	234	-18.2
Greeley, CO	315	345	9.5	600	1,725	187.5	915	2,070	126.2
Green Bay, WI	58	37	-36.2	2	0	-100.0	60	37	-38.3
Greensboro, NC	529	467	-11.7	1,363	676	-50.4	1,892	1,143	-39.6
Honolulu, HI	n/a	n/a	n/a	n/a	n/a	n/a	n/a	n/a	n/a
Houston, TX	7,146	6,800	-4.8	8,103	8,945	10.4	15,249	15,745	3.3
Huntsville, AL	1,483	1,083	-27.0	1,328	47	-96.5	2,811	1,130	-59.8
Indianapolis, IN	1,221	1,099	-10.0	968	1,011	4.4	2,189	2,110	-3.6
Jacksonville, FL	6,191	5,484	-11.4	3,778	5,862	55.2	9,969	11,346	13.8
Kansas City, MO	890	746	-16.2	1,448	1,241	-14.3	2,338	1,987	-15.0
Lafayette, LA	n/a	n/a	n/a	n/a	n/a	n/a	n/a	n/a	n/a
Las Cruces, NM	763	685	-10.2	99	26	-73.7	862	711	-17.5
Las Vegas, NV	2,700	3,001	11.1	1,048	1,024	-2.3	3,748	4,025	7.4
Lexington, KY	792	686	-13.4	863	1,045	21.1	1,655	1,731	4.6
Lincoln, NE	1,093	943	-13.7	1,227	2,179	77.6	2,320	3,122	34.6
Little Rock, AR	666	377	-43.4	460	644	40.0	1,126	1,021	-9.3
Los Angeles, CA	2,475	3,182	28.6	11,613	13,525	16.5	14,088	16,707	18.6
Louisville, KY	1,382	1,151	-16.7	466	1,637	251.3	1,848	2,788	50.9

Table continued on following page.

City	Single-Family			Multi-Family			Total		
	2021	2022	Pct. Chg.	2021	2022	Pct. Chg.	2021	2022	Pct. Chg.
Madison, WI	327	314	-4.0	3,299	2,046	-38.0	3,626	2,360	-34.9
Manchester, NH	126	132	4.8	8	6	-25.0	134	138	3.0
Miami, FL	102	127	24.5	6,153	4,231	-31.2	6,255	4,358	-30.3
Midland, TX	858	593	-30.9	0	0	0.0	858	593	-30.9
Milwaukee, WI	28	42	50.0	176	134	-23.9	204	176	-13.7
Minneapolis, MN	63	55	-12.7	3,119	3,626	16.3	3,182	3,681	15.7
Nashville, TN	3,932	3,977	1.1	12,205	10,818	-11.4	16,137	14,795	-8.3
New Haven, CT	13	10	-23.1	286	491	71.7	299	501	67.6
New Orleans, LA	716	615	-14.1	860	1,007	17.1	1,576	1,622	2.9
New York, NY	151	61	-59.6	19,772	21,429	8.4	19,923	21,490	7.9
Oklahoma City, OK	4,127	3,298	-20.1	140	260	85.7	4,267	3,558	-16.6
Omaha, NE	1,620	1,217	-24.9	1,547	2,552	65.0	3,167	3,769	19.0
Orlando, FL	990	1,286	29.9	2,734	2,229	-18.5	3,724	3,515	-5.6
Philadelphia, PA	1,553	478	-69.2	23,704	2,745	-88.4	25,257	3,223	-87.2
Phoenix, AZ	4,922	3,982	-19.1	6,570	10,616	61.6	11,492	14,598	27.0
Pittsburgh, PA	198	115	-41.9	617	1,913	210.0	815	2,028	148.8
Portland, OR	474	489	3.2	2,554	1,708	-33.1	3,028	2,197	-27.4
Providence, RI	1	28	2,700.0	53	271	411.3	54	299	453.7
Provo, UT	98	134	36.7	617	327	-47.0	715	461	-35.5
Raleigh, NC	1,354	1,875	38.5	5,133	6,760	31.7	6,487	8,635	33.1
Reno, NV	1,414	1,158	-18.1	2,539	2,535	-0.2	3,953	3,693	-6.6
Richmond, VA	502	457	-9.0	565	2,192	288.0	1,067	2,649	148.3
Rochester, MN	251	234	-6.8	374	847	126.5	625	1,081	73.0
Sacramento, CA	1,004	905	-9.9	2,079	1,149	-44.7	3,083	2,054	-33.4
St. Louis, MO	146	122	-16.4	809	1,054	30.3	955	1,176	23.1
Salem, OR	447	318	-28.9	399	851	113.3	846	1,169	38.2
Salt Lake City, UT	172	144	-16.3	3,519	3,489	-0.9	3,691	3,633	-1.6
San Antonio, TX	6,567	4,686	-28.6	4,591	9,496	106.8	11,158	14,182	27.1
San Diego, CA	539	506	-6.1	4,249	3,916	-7.8	4,788	4,422	-7.6
San Francisco, CA	33	38	15.2	2,486	2,006	-19.3	2,519	2,044	-18.9
San Jose, CA	299	553	84.9	359	1,450	303.9	658	2,003	204.4
Santa Rosa, CA	420	286	-31.9	1,031	911	-11.6	1,451	1,197	-17.5
Savannah, GA	487	408	-16.2	5	24	380.0	492	432	-12.2
Seattle, WA	264	418	58.3	11,716	8,572	-26.8	11,980	8,990	-25.0
Sioux Falls, SD	1,313	1,036	-21.1	1,819	3,429	88.5	3,132	4,465	42.6
Springfield, IL	137	55	-59.9	87	10	-88.5	224	65	-71.0
Tampa, FL	1,312	1,058	-19.4	1,093	3,753	243.4	2,405	4,811	100.0
Tucson, AZ	1,134	918	-19.0	959	962	0.3	2,093	1,880	-10.2
Tulsa, OK	652	452	-30.7	165	369	123.6	817	821	0.5
Tuscaloosa, AL	401	299	-25.4	725	329	-54.6	1,126	628	-44.2
Virginia Beach, VA	335	231	-31.0	128	966	654.7	463	1,197	158.5
Washington, DC	376	409	8.8	4,364	7,296	67.2	4,740	7,705	62.6
Wichita, KS	760	787	3.6	368	276	-25.0	1,128	1,063	-5.8
Wilmington, NC	n/a	n/a	n/a	n/a	n/a	n/a	n/a	n/a	n/a
Winston-Salem, NC	1,087	1,291	18.8	0	0	0.0	1,087	1,291	18.8
Worcester, MA	66	94	42.4	112	718	541.1	178	812	356.2
U.S.	1,115,400	975,600	-12.5	621,600	689,500	10.9	1,737,000	1,665,100	-4.1

Note: Figures represent new, privately-owned housing units authorized (unadjusted data); All permit data are based on estimates with imputation

Source: U.S. Census Bureau, Manufacturing, Mining, and Construction Statistics, Building Permits, 2021, 2022

Building Permits: Metro Area

Metro Area	Single-Family			Multi-Family			Total		
	2021	2022	Pct. Chg.	2021	2022	Pct. Chg.	2021	2022	Pct. Chg.
Albuquerque, NM	2,535	2,002	-21.0	1,486	1,055	-29.0	4,021	3,057	-24.0
Allentown, PA	1,716	1,586	-7.6	890	723	-18.8	2,606	2,309	-11.4
Anchorage, AK	877	166	-81.1	306	47	-84.6	1,183	213	-82.0
Ann Arbor, MI	795	580	-27.0	121	49	-59.5	916	629	-31.3
Athens, GA	856	771	-9.9	992	1,574	58.7	1,848	2,345	26.9
Atlanta, GA	31,560	26,623	-15.6	7,906	21,484	171.7	39,466	48,107	21.9
Austin, TX	24,486	19,717	-19.5	26,421	22,647	-14.3	50,907	42,364	-16.8
Baltimore, MD	4,783	2,832	-40.8	3,051	3,756	23.1	7,834	6,588	-15.9
Boise City, ID	8,342	5,925	-29.0	3,854	4,550	18.1	12,196	10,475	-14.1
Boston, MA	4,820	3,985	-17.3	11,782	10,469	-11.1	16,602	14,454	-12.9
Boulder, CO	343	661	92.7	894	981	9.7	1,237	1,642	32.7
Brownsville, TX	1,573	1,940	23.3	479	569	18.8	2,052	2,509	22.3
Cape Coral, FL	11,020	9,145	-17.0	2,374	4,476	88.5	13,394	13,621	1.7
Cedar Rapids, IA	546	453	-17.0	352	494	40.3	898	947	5.5
Charleston, SC	5,913	6,329	7.0	2,369	2,994	26.4	8,282	9,323	12.6
Charlotte, NC	20,830	19,029	-8.6	9,296	8,183	-12.0	30,126	27,212	-9.7
Chicago, IL	10,071	8,563	-15.0	8,440	9,073	7.5	18,511	17,636	-4.7
Cincinnati, OH	5,358	4,126	-23.0	3,071	2,084	-32.1	8,429	6,210	-26.3
Clarksville, TN	2,217	1,501	-32.3	1,895	2,592	36.8	4,112	4,093	-0.5
Cleveland, OH	2,949	2,915	-1.2	391	820	109.7	3,340	3,735	11.8
College Station, TX	1,765	1,545	-12.5	535	230	-57.0	2,300	1,775	-22.8
Colorado Springs, CO	5,074	3,646	-28.1	4,261	5,198	22.0	9,335	8,844	-5.3
Columbia, MO	838	628	-25.1	191	151	-20.9	1,029	779	-24.3
Columbia, SC	5,853	4,101	-29.9	1,028	1,703	65.7	6,881	5,804	-15.7
Columbus, OH	6,844	5,623	-17.8	5,218	6,472	24.0	12,062	12,095	0.3
Dallas, TX	51,996	43,645	-16.1	26,709	34,249	28.2	78,705	77,894	-1.0
Davenport, IA	436	416	-4.6	193	181	-6.2	629	597	-5.1
Denver, CO	13,113	10,108	-22.9	16,893	13,368	-20.9	30,006	23,476	-21.8
Des Moines, IA	4,888	3,646	-25.4	2,081	2,476	19.0	6,969	6,122	-12.2
Durham, NC	3,735	3,170	-15.1	2,165	3,222	48.8	5,900	6,392	8.3
Edison, NJ	12,947	12,089	-6.6	43,714	46,323	6.0	56,661	58,412	3.1
El Paso, TX	2,655	2,147	-19.1	334	319	-4.5	2,989	2,466	-17.5
Fargo, ND	1,229	1,123	-8.6	1,060	1,191	12.4	2,289	2,314	1.1
Fort Collins, CO	2,149	1,385	-35.6	1,072	1,187	10.7	3,221	2,572	-20.1
Fort Wayne, IN	1,799	1,453	-19.2	179	882	392.7	1,978	2,335	18.0
Fort Worth, TX	51,996	43,645	-16.1	26,709	34,249	28.2	78,705	77,894	-1.0
Grand Rapids, MI	2,811	2,488	-11.5	894	1,710	91.3	3,705	4,198	13.3
Greeley, CO	3,814	3,203	-16.0	1,454	2,940	102.2	5,268	6,143	16.6
Green Bay, WI	830	627	-24.5	578	622	7.6	1,408	1,249	-11.3
Greensboro, NC	2,593	2,161	-16.7	1,371	832	-39.3	3,964	2,993	-24.5
Honolulu, HI	938	652	-30.5	500	1,901	280.2	1,438	2,553	77.5
Houston, TX	52,719	47,701	-9.5	16,544	28,027	69.4	69,263	75,728	9.3
Huntsville, AL	4,230	3,617	-14.5	1,942	418	-78.5	6,172	4,035	-34.6
Indianapolis, IN	10,159	8,578	-15.6	3,292	4,915	49.3	13,451	13,493	0.3
Jacksonville, FL	16,536	14,410	-12.9	6,202	8,759	41.2	22,738	23,169	1.9
Kansas City, MO	7,051	5,204	-26.2	4,203	6,015	43.1	11,254	11,219	-0.3
Lafayette, LA	3,040	2,051	-32.5	4	20	400.0	3,044	2,071	-32.0
Las Cruces, NM	1,239	1,079	-12.9	99	26	-73.7	1,338	1,105	-17.4
Las Vegas, NV	12,156	9,199	-24.3	4,151	3,867	-6.8	16,307	13,066	-19.9
Lexington, KY	1,760	1,460	-17.0	1,183	1,249	5.6	2,943	2,709	-8.0
Lincoln, NE	1,378	1,132	-17.9	1,229	2,217	80.4	2,607	3,349	28.5
Little Rock, AR	2,505	1,863	-25.6	1,130	1,475	30.5	3,635	3,338	-8.2
Los Angeles, CA	11,090	11,184	0.8	20,061	21,326	6.3	31,151	32,510	4.4
Louisville, KY	4,136	3,345	-19.1	1,372	2,111	53.9	5,508	5,456	-0.9

Table continued on following page.

Metro Area	Single-Family			Multi-Family			Total		
	2021	2022	Pct. Chg.	2021	2022	Pct. Chg.	2021	2022	Pct. Chg.
Madison, WI	1,737	1,530	-11.9	5,457	4,049	-25.8	7,194	5,579	-22.4
Manchester, NH	683	623	-8.8	659	224	-66.0	1,342	847	-36.9
Miami, FL	8,316	6,970	-16.2	16,997	13,051	-23.2	25,313	20,021	-20.9
Midland, TX	872	594	-31.9	0	0	0.0	872	594	-31.9
Milwaukee, WI	1,779	1,557	-12.5	1,150	1,609	39.9	2,929	3,166	8.1
Minneapolis, MN	11,734	9,114	-22.3	14,343	14,611	1.9	26,077	23,725	-9.0
Nashville, TN	17,422	15,388	-11.7	14,769	12,804	-13.3	32,191	28,192	-12.4
New Haven, CT	497	493	-0.8	486	770	58.4	983	1,263	28.5
New Orleans, LA	4,018	3,101	-22.8	1,264	1,065	-15.7	5,282	4,166	-21.1
New York, NY	12,947	12,089	-6.6	43,714	46,323	6.0	56,661	58,412	3.1
Oklahoma City, OK	7,637	5,971	-21.8	443	940	112.2	8,080	6,911	-14.5
Omaha, NE	3,677	2,651	-27.9	2,705	3,469	28.2	6,382	6,120	-4.1
Orlando, FL	17,795	16,213	-8.9	12,823	12,470	-2.8	30,618	28,683	-6.3
Philadelphia, PA	8,868	8,532	-3.8	27,439	5,881	-78.6	36,307	14,413	-60.3
Phoenix, AZ	34,347	26,857	-21.8	16,234	20,410	25.7	50,581	47,267	-6.6
Pittsburgh, PA	3,891	3,184	-18.2	1,332	2,481	86.3	5,223	5,665	8.5
Portland, OR	8,008	6,029	-24.7	7,015	6,949	-0.9	15,023	12,978	-13.6
Providence, RI	1,788	1,559	-12.8	470	563	19.8	2,258	2,122	-6.0
Provo, UT	7,562	5,153	-31.9	3,613	3,134	-13.3	11,175	8,287	-25.8
Raleigh, NC	14,227	12,488	-12.2	7,422	9,080	22.3	21,649	21,568	-0.4
Reno, NV	2,717	2,184	-19.6	2,620	3,628	38.5	5,337	5,812	8.9
Richmond, VA	5,946	4,503	-24.3	3,601	5,911	64.1	9,547	10,414	9.1
Rochester, MN	721	641	-11.1	414	1,080	160.9	1,135	1,721	51.6
Sacramento, CA	9,390	8,170	-13.0	3,044	2,630	-13.6	12,434	10,800	-13.1
St. Louis, MO	5,716	4,743	-17.0	2,610	4,388	68.1	8,326	9,131	9.7
Salem, OR	1,368	874	-36.1	786	1,943	147.2	2,154	2,817	30.8
Salt Lake City, UT	5,338	3,992	-25.2	6,304	6,110	-3.1	11,642	10,102	-13.2
San Antonio, TX	13,945	10,226	-26.7	8,319	14,113	69.6	22,264	24,339	9.3
San Diego, CA	3,227	3,517	9.0	6,821	5,829	-14.5	10,048	9,346	-7.0
San Francisco, CA	4,301	3,370	-21.6	9,305	7,834	-15.8	13,606	11,204	-17.7
San Jose, CA	2,400	3,899	62.5	2,129	4,308	102.3	4,529	8,207	81.2
Santa Rosa, CA	1,227	954	-22.2	1,391	1,310	-5.8	2,618	2,264	-13.5
Savannah, GA	2,752	2,228	-19.0	475	966	103.4	3,227	3,194	-1.0
Seattle, WA	8,828	7,029	-20.4	21,915	19,632	-10.4	30,743	26,661	-13.3
Sioux Falls, SD	1,893	1,626	-14.1	2,093	3,928	87.7	3,986	5,554	39.3
Springfield, IL	239	146	-38.9	93	64	-31.2	332	210	-36.7
Tampa, FL	19,305	15,678	-18.8	5,526	14,291	158.6	24,831	29,969	20.7
Tucson, AZ	5,116	3,735	-27.0	1,168	1,979	69.4	6,284	5,714	-9.1
Tulsa, OK	4,354	3,843	-11.7	566	1,280	126.1	4,920	5,123	4.1
Tuscaloosa, AL	771	714	-7.4	725	329	-54.6	1,496	1,043	-30.3
Virginia Beach, VA	4,712	3,680	-21.9	2,665	2,633	-1.2	7,377	6,313	-14.4
Washington, DC	13,729	11,657	-15.1	13,685	20,736	51.5	27,414	32,393	18.2
Wichita, KS	1,618	1,586	-2.0	766	1,264	65.0	2,384	2,850	19.5
Wilmington, NC	2,671	2,489	-6.8	1,747	1,932	10.6	4,418	4,421	0.1
Winston-Salem, NC	3,887	3,983	2.5	319	67	-79.0	4,206	4,050	-3.7
Worcester, MA	1,177	1,172	-0.4	876	1,080	23.3	2,053	2,252	9.7
U.S.	1,115,400	975,600	-12.5	621,600	689,500	10.9	1,737,000	1,665,100	-4.1

*Note: Figures cover the Metropolitan Statistical Area; Figures represent new, privately-owned
housing units authorized (unadjusted data); All permit data are based on estimates with imputation
Source: U.S. Census Bureau, Manufacturing, Mining, and Construction Statistics, Building Permits, 2021, 2022*

Housing Vacancy Rates

MSA[1]	Gross Vacancy Rate[2] (%)			Year-Round Vacancy Rate[3] (%)			Rental Vacancy Rate[4] (%)			Homeowner Vacancy Rate[5] (%)		
	2020	2021	2022	2020	2021	2022	2020	2021	2022	2020	2021	2022
Albuquerque, NM	5.1	5.3	5.3	4.9	5.1	5.1	5.4	6.4	5.5	1.4	0.5	1.0
Allentown, PA	4.9	5.2	8.7	4.8	4.3	8.0	3.9	4.0	6.1	0.7	0.1	1.2
Anchorage, AK	n/a	n/a	n/a	n/a	n/a	n/a	n/a	n/a	n/a	n/a	n/a	n/a
Ann Arbor, MI	n/a	n/a	n/a	n/a	n/a	n/a	n/a	n/a	n/a	n/a	n/a	n/a
Athens, GA	n/a	n/a	n/a	n/a	n/a	n/a	n/a	n/a	n/a	n/a	n/a	n/a
Atlanta, GA	5.8	6.1	5.9	5.4	5.7	5.7	6.4	5.2	6.7	0.8	1.0	0.8
Austin, TX	7.0	6.5	5.5	6.8	6.2	4.9	6.6	8.5	5.6	2.0	1.3	0.6
Baltimore, MD	7.2	6.8	5.9	7.0	6.6	5.7	7.0	6.1	5.3	1.0	1.0	0.5
Boise City, ID	n/a	n/a	n/a	n/a	n/a	n/a	n/a	n/a	n/a	n/a	n/a	n/a
Boston, MA	6.8	7.4	6.2	5.6	6.2	5.4	4.7	4.5	2.5	0.4	0.5	0.7
Boulder, CO	n/a	n/a	n/a	n/a	n/a	n/a	n/a	n/a	n/a	n/a	n/a	n/a
Brownsville, TX	n/a	n/a	n/a	n/a	n/a	n/a	n/a	n/a	n/a	n/a	n/a	n/a
Cape Coral, FL	35.1	36.4	38.2	15.8	13.0	16.9	15.5	10.7	11.6	1.9	2.4	3.9
Cedar Rapids, IA	n/a	n/a	n/a	n/a	n/a	n/a	n/a	n/a	n/a	n/a	n/a	n/a
Charleston, SC	18.1	12.9	10.6	16.5	10.5	7.5	27.7	15.4	8.8	2.3	1.3	0.4
Charlotte, NC	6.6	7.7	7.4	6.3	7.4	7.0	5.6	6.8	5.9	1.0	1.3	0.7
Chicago, IL	7.4	8.7	7.3	7.2	8.6	7.1	7.4	8.0	6.1	1.2	1.3	1.1
Cincinnati, OH	6.6	7.9	6.8	6.2	7.3	6.3	7.9	7.2	6.3	0.7	0.5	0.3
Clarksville, TN	n/a	n/a	n/a	n/a	n/a	n/a	n/a	n/a	n/a	n/a	n/a	n/a
Cleveland, OH	9.3	7.7	7.0	8.8	7.5	6.8	5.5	3.6	3.2	0.7	0.4	1.0
College Station, TX	n/a	n/a	n/a	n/a	n/a	n/a	n/a	n/a	n/a	n/a	n/a	n/a
Colorado Springs, CO	n/a	n/a	n/a	n/a	n/a	n/a	n/a	n/a	n/a	n/a	n/a	n/a
Columbia, MO	n/a	n/a	n/a	n/a	n/a	n/a	n/a	n/a	n/a	n/a	n/a	n/a
Columbia, SC	7.2	7.6	12.0	7.1	7.6	12.0	4.5	4.7	6.1	0.7	1.1	0.6
Columbus, OH	4.7	6.8	5.6	4.5	6.6	5.4	5.9	6.5	3.8	0.3	0.8	0.8
Dallas, TX	6.4	6.6	6.6	6.4	6.5	6.3	7.2	7.0	6.8	0.7	0.7	0.7
Davenport, IA	n/a	n/a	n/a	n/a	n/a	n/a	n/a	n/a	n/a	n/a	n/a	n/a
Denver, CO	5.8	6.5	5.8	5.1	5.3	5.2	4.8	4.6	5.1	0.5	1.0	0.3
Des Moines, IA	n/a	n/a	n/a	n/a	n/a	n/a	n/a	n/a	n/a	n/a	n/a	n/a
Durham, NC	n/a	n/a	n/a	n/a	n/a	n/a	n/a	n/a	n/a	n/a	n/a	n/a
Edison, NJ	9.1	9.8	8.2	7.8	8.7	7.0	4.5	5.2	3.5	1.3	1.2	1.0
El Paso, TX	n/a	n/a	n/a	n/a	n/a	n/a	n/a	n/a	n/a	n/a	n/a	n/a
Fargo, ND	n/a	n/a	n/a	n/a	n/a	n/a	n/a	n/a	n/a	n/a	n/a	n/a
Fort Collins, CO	n/a	n/a	n/a	n/a	n/a	n/a	n/a	n/a	n/a	n/a	n/a	n/a
Fort Wayne, IN	n/a	n/a	n/a	n/a	n/a	n/a	n/a	n/a	n/a	n/a	n/a	n/a
Fort Worth, TX	6.4	6.6	6.6	6.4	6.5	6.3	7.2	7.0	6.8	0.7	0.7	0.7
Grand Rapids, MI	7.1	7.0	4.9	4.7	4.2	3.0	4.6	3.4	2.4	1.1	0.7	0.1
Greeley, CO	n/a	n/a	n/a	n/a	n/a	n/a	n/a	n/a	n/a	n/a	n/a	n/a
Green Bay, WI	n/a	n/a	n/a	n/a	n/a	n/a	n/a	n/a	n/a	n/a	n/a	n/a
Greensboro, NC	8.3	5.9	8.7	8.2	5.9	8.7	7.2	2.7	10.2	0.7	0.5	0.7
Honolulu, HI	10.0	10.6	10.6	9.6	10.1	10.0	5.5	5.1	5.7	1.0	0.6	0.6
Houston, TX	6.8	7.2	6.9	6.3	6.6	6.3	9.7	8.8	8.9	1.1	0.8	0.6
Huntsville, AL	n/a	n/a	n/a	n/a	n/a	n/a	n/a	n/a	n/a	n/a	n/a	n/a
Indianapolis, IN	7.3	6.2	7.7	7.0	6.1	7.2	10.4	8.2	11.0	0.8	0.7	1.0
Jacksonville, FL	9.5	8.3	8.9	9.3	7.6	7.7	7.5	5.6	6.2	1.5	0.4	1.7
Kansas City, MO	9.1	8.3	7.1	9.1	8.2	7.1	9.4	8.9	7.8	0.7	1.2	0.6
Lafayette, LA	n/a	n/a	n/a	n/a	n/a	n/a	n/a	n/a	n/a	n/a	n/a	n/a
Las Cruces, NM	n/a	n/a	n/a	n/a	n/a	n/a	n/a	n/a	n/a	n/a	n/a	n/a
Las Vegas, NV	7.8	7.7	9.2	7.1	7.1	8.3	5.0	3.7	5.7	1.1	0.9	0.9
Lexington, KY	n/a	n/a	n/a	n/a	n/a	n/a	n/a	n/a	n/a	n/a	n/a	n/a
Lincoln, NE	n/a	n/a	n/a	n/a	n/a	n/a	n/a	n/a	n/a	n/a	n/a	n/a
Little Rock, AR	9.4	11.4	9.4	9.1	11.2	9.2	9.1	10.0	11.4	1.3	1.2	0.7
Los Angeles, CA	5.5	6.4	5.9	4.8	5.9	5.5	3.6	4.6	4.1	0.6	0.7	0.5
Louisville, KY	6.9	8.3	5.7	6.9	8.3	5.7	6.4	8.5	5.3	1.4	0.7	0.5

Table continued on following page.

MSA[1]	Gross Vacancy Rate[2] (%)			Year-Round Vacancy Rate[3] (%)			Rental Vacancy Rate[4] (%)			Homeowner Vacancy Rate[5] (%)		
	2020	2021	2022	2020	2021	2022	2020	2021	2022	2020	2021	2022
Madison, WI	n/a	n/a	n/a	n/a	n/a	n/a	n/a	n/a	n/a	n/a	n/a	n/a
Manchester, NH	n/a	n/a	n/a	n/a	n/a	n/a	n/a	n/a	n/a	n/a	n/a	n/a
Miami, FL	12.6	12.2	12.6	6.8	6.8	7.5	5.4	5.5	6.3	1.4	1.0	1.1
Midland, TX	n/a	n/a	n/a	n/a	n/a	n/a	n/a	n/a	n/a	n/a	n/a	n/a
Milwaukee, WI	6.6	5.2	5.2	6.3	5.1	5.1	4.6	2.2	5.9	0.6	0.5	0.1
Minneapolis, MN	4.7	5.3	4.8	3.7	4.6	4.5	4.0	4.9	6.7	0.5	0.6	0.8
Nashville, TN	6.5	7.1	7.6	6.1	6.8	7.1	7.3	7.9	6.4	0.7	1.0	0.9
New Haven, CT	9.4	7.9	6.8	8.4	7.2	6.4	7.8	5.4	2.6	0.2	0.5	1.1
New Orleans, LA	10.7	12.6	13.4	9.8	11.1	11.5	6.1	7.2	6.6	1.3	1.0	1.6
New York, NY	9.1	9.8	8.2	7.8	8.7	7.0	4.5	5.2	3.5	1.3	1.2	1.0
Oklahoma City, OK	7.5	6.1	8.6	7.3	6.0	8.5	6.4	5.7	10.6	0.9	0.8	0.9
Omaha, NE	5.6	6.0	5.4	5.3	5.7	5.0	6.5	5.1	4.2	0.5	0.7	0.8
Orlando, FL	12.9	9.5	9.6	9.8	7.5	7.4	8.6	7.5	6.5	1.2	0.5	1.4
Philadelphia, PA	6.0	6.1	5.5	5.8	5.9	5.4	5.4	4.8	4.2	0.7	0.5	1.0
Phoenix, AZ	8.9	9.0	10.9	5.3	5.6	6.7	4.9	4.9	6.4	0.7	0.6	0.9
Pittsburgh, PA	11.5	11.4	11.5	11.3	10.8	11.0	9.3	9.4	8.3	1.0	0.4	0.7
Portland, OR	5.5	6.0	5.4	4.9	5.6	5.1	4.3	5.2	4.0	0.8	0.9	1.2
Providence, RI	8.7	7.9	9.5	6.6	5.8	7.6	3.5	2.7	4.5	0.8	0.7	0.4
Provo, UT	n/a	n/a	n/a	n/a	n/a	n/a	n/a	n/a	n/a	n/a	n/a	n/a
Raleigh, NC	4.6	6.3	7.4	4.5	6.3	7.3	2.3	2.9	7.1	0.4	1.1	0.5
Reno, NV	n/a	n/a	n/a	n/a	n/a	n/a	n/a	n/a	n/a	n/a	n/a	n/a
Richmond, VA	6.0	5.8	6.1	6.0	5.8	6.1	2.7	1.8	3.0	0.9	1.0	0.7
Rochester, MN	n/a	n/a	n/a	n/a	n/a	n/a	n/a	n/a	n/a	n/a	n/a	n/a
Sacramento, CA	6.1	6.7	6.3	5.8	6.5	6.1	4.2	3.6	2.3	1.0	0.7	0.6
St. Louis, MO	6.4	7.0	7.2	6.3	7.0	7.1	5.3	6.5	6.8	0.7	0.5	1.4
Salem, OR	n/a	n/a	n/a	n/a	n/a	n/a	n/a	n/a	n/a	n/a	n/a	n/a
Salt Lake City, UT	5.7	4.1	5.1	5.6	3.9	4.5	6.2	4.1	4.6	0.3	0.8	0.6
San Antonio, TX	7.4	7.6	7.5	6.7	6.9	7.1	7.2	8.4	8.1	1.0	1.1	0.9
San Diego, CA	6.0	6.9	6.9	5.6	6.7	6.6	3.9	3.1	3.6	0.8	0.7	0.6
San Francisco, CA	6.4	7.6	7.9	6.2	7.3	7.7	5.3	6.5	5.4	0.5	1.1	1.3
San Jose, CA	4.7	5.9	5.8	4.7	5.6	5.8	4.4	6.6	4.7	n/a	0.4	0.4
Santa Rosa, CA	n/a	n/a	n/a	n/a	n/a	n/a	n/a	n/a	n/a	n/a	n/a	n/a
Savannah, GA	n/a	n/a	n/a	n/a	n/a	n/a	n/a	n/a	n/a	n/a	n/a	n/a
Seattle, WA	4.7	6.2	5.7	4.5	5.5	5.2	3.6	5.3	4.9	0.6	0.7	0.7
Sioux Falls, SD	n/a	n/a	n/a	n/a	n/a	n/a	n/a	n/a	n/a	n/a	n/a	n/a
Springfield, IL	n/a	n/a	n/a	n/a	n/a	n/a	n/a	n/a	n/a	n/a	n/a	n/a
Tampa, FL	13.0	14.2	13.3	10.1	10.5	9.9	8.9	7.3	8.1	1.5	1.0	1.2
Tucson, AZ	12.1	10.0	13.5	7.7	6.9	10.3	8.6	5.0	8.0	0.5	0.6	1.4
Tulsa, OK	9.4	11.0	8.9	8.8	10.0	8.5	8.6	5.3	5.6	0.8	1.5	0.7
Tuscaloosa, AL	n/a	n/a	n/a	n/a	n/a	n/a	n/a	n/a	n/a	n/a	n/a	n/a
Virginia Beach, VA	7.9	7.7	8.1	7.0	6.9	7.3	5.5	5.5	6.3	0.6	0.6	1.0
Washington, DC	6.5	5.5	5.2	6.2	5.3	5.0	5.5	5.9	5.3	0.7	0.5	0.6
Wichita, KS	n/a	n/a	n/a	n/a	n/a	n/a	n/a	n/a	n/a	n/a	n/a	n/a
Wilmington, NC	n/a	n/a	n/a	n/a	n/a	n/a	n/a	n/a	n/a	n/a	n/a	n/a
Winston-Salem, NC	n/a	n/a	n/a	n/a	n/a	n/a	n/a	n/a	n/a	n/a	n/a	n/a
Worcester, MA	4.8	5.5	4.5	4.6	4.9	4.0	1.3	2.2	1.6	0.4	0.7	0.4
U.S.	10.6	10.8	10.5	8.2	8.4	8.2	6.3	6.1	5.8	1.0	0.9	0.8

Note: (1) Metropolitan Statistical Area; (2) The percentage of the total housing inventory that is vacant; (3) The percentage of the housing inventory (excluding seasonal units) that is year-round vacant; (4) The percentage of rental inventory that is vacant for rent; (5) The percentage of homeowner inventory that is vacant for sale; n/a not available
Source: U.S. Census Bureau, Housing Vacancies and Homeownership Annual Statistics: 2020, 2021, 2022

Bankruptcy Filings

City	Area Covered	Business Filings			Nonbusiness Filings		
		2021	2022	% Chg.	2021	2022	% Chg.
Albuquerque, NM	Bernalillo County	21	15	-28.6	560	383	-31.6
Allentown, PA	Lehigh County	5	7	40.0	346	283	-18.2
Anchorage, AK	Anchorage Borough	12	4	-66.7	116	77	-33.6
Ann Arbor, MI	Washtenaw County	8	24	200.0	352	350	-0.6
Athens, GA	Clarke County	10	4	-60.0	162	212	30.9
Atlanta, GA	Fulton County	87	124	42.5	2,072	2,323	12.1
Austin, TX	Travis County	113	76	-32.7	443	372	-16.0
Baltimore, MD	Baltimore City	18	17	-5.6	1,323	1,167	-11.8
Boise City, ID	Ada County	13	16	23.1	393	326	-17.0
Boston, MA	Suffolk County	23	42	82.6	224	221	-1.3
Boulder, CO	Boulder County	13	27	107.7	216	160	-25.9
Brownsville, TX	Cameron County	0	4	n/a	171	195	14.0
Cape Coral, FL	Lee County	39	31	-20.5	928	711	-23.4
Cedar Rapids, IA	Linn County	6	10	66.7	193	166	-14.0
Charleston, SC	Charleston County	8	5	-37.5	176	228	29.5
Charlotte, NC	Mecklenburg County	56	21	-62.5	460	459	-0.2
Chicago, IL	Cook County	270	237	-12.2	10,430	10,849	4.0
Cincinnati, OH	Hamilton County	28	25	-10.7	1,500	1,164	-22.4
Clarksville, TN	Montgomery County	11	6	-45.5	333	352	5.7
Cleveland, OH	Cuyahoga County	48	53	10.4	3,240	2,994	-7.6
College Station, TX	Brazos County	8	4	-50.0	66	47	-28.8
Colorado Springs, CO	El Paso County	22	19	-13.6	728	609	-16.3
Columbia, MO	Boone County	1	5	400.0	193	171	-11.4
Columbia, SC	Richland County	8	13	62.5	348	424	21.8
Columbus, OH	Franklin County	128	38	-70.3	2,223	2,029	-8.7
Dallas, TX	Dallas County	186	237	27.4	1,797	1,984	10.4
Davenport, IA	Scott County	5	9	80.0	163	140	-14.1
Denver, CO	Denver County	72	37	-48.6	764	590	-22.8
Des Moines, IA	Polk County	22	17	-22.7	550	474	-13.8
Durham, NC	Durham County	10	5	-50.0	175	143	-18.3
Edison, NJ	Middlesex County	45	30	-33.3	843	746	-11.5
El Paso, TX	El Paso County	46	41	-10.9	961	1,092	13.6
Fargo, ND	Cass County	4	2	-50.0	131	100	-23.7
Fort Collins, CO	Larimer County	14	14	0.0	306	283	-7.5
Fort Wayne, IN	Allen County	6	13	116.7	872	767	-12.0
Fort Worth, TX	Tarrant County	151	200	32.5	2,277	2,447	7.5
Grand Rapids, MI	Kent County	8	10	25.0	469	439	-6.4
Greeley, CO	Weld County	9	16	77.8	447	400	-10.5
Green Bay, WI	Brown County	2	7	250.0	388	290	-25.3
Greensboro, NC	Guilford County	23	8	-65.2	369	336	-8.9
Honolulu, HI	Honolulu County	28	35	25.0	830	671	-19.2
Houston, TX	Harris County	269	213	-20.8	2,310	2,541	10.0
Huntsville, AL	Madison County	18	12	-33.3	894	806	-9.8
Indianapolis, IN	Marion County	45	37	-17.8	2,705	2,399	-11.3
Jacksonville, FL	Duval County	58	38	-34.5	1,336	1,226	-8.2
Kansas City, MO	Jackson County	22	16	-27.3	1,027	1,037	1.0
Lafayette, LA	Lafayette Parish	17	29	70.6	263	296	12.5
Las Cruces, NM	Dona Ana County	8	4	-50.0	187	178	-4.8
Las Vegas, NV	Clark County	181	163	-9.9	5,825	4,525	-22.3
Lexington, KY	Fayette County	8	7	-12.5	450	410	-8.9
Lincoln, NE	Lancaster County	6	14	133.3	430	304	-29.3
Little Rock, AR	Pulaski County	23	19	-17.4	1,157	1,352	16.9
Los Angeles, CA	Los Angeles County	672	626	-6.8	11,316	8,314	-26.5
Louisville, KY	Jefferson County	19	20	5.3	1,918	1,883	-1.8
Madison, WI	Dane County	26	10	-61.5	436	383	-12.2

Table continued on following page.

City	Area Covered	Business Filings			Nonbusiness Filings		
		2021	2022	% Chg.	2021	2022	% Chg.
Manchester, NH	Hillsborough County	19	11	-42.1	253	204	-19.4
Miami, FL	Miami-Dade County	201	224	11.4	6,432	5,081	-21.0
Midland, TX	Midland County	18	7	-61.1	64	73	14.1
Milwaukee, WI	Milwaukee County	20	20	0.0	3,237	2,957	-8.6
Minneapolis, MN	Hennepin County	52	55	5.8	1,240	1,200	-3.2
Nashville, TN	Davidson County	37	32	-13.5	959	989	3.1
New Haven, CT	New Haven County	14	12	-14.3	864	719	-16.8
New Orleans, LA	Orleans Parish	31	11	-64.5	263	287	9.1
New York, NY	Bronx County	23	27	17.4	1,219	862	-29.3
New York, NY	Kings County	108	212	96.3	1,238	1,062	-14.2
New York, NY	New York County	398	240	-39.7	721	595	-17.5
New York, NY	Queens County	82	126	53.7	1,447	1,478	2.1
New York, NY	Richmond County	24	25	4.2	310	352	13.5
Oklahoma City, OK	Oklahoma County	52	50	-3.8	1,424	1,199	-15.8
Omaha, NE	Douglas County	20	21	5.0	807	628	-22.2
Orlando, FL	Orange County	100	127	27.0	1,909	1,588	-16.8
Philadelphia, PA	Philadelphia County	31	28	-9.7	741	952	28.5
Phoenix, AZ	Maricopa County	223	172	-22.9	6,402	5,811	-9.2
Pittsburgh, PA	Allegheny County	79	72	-8.9	1,266	1,135	-10.3
Portland, OR	Multnomah County	33	17	-48.5	802	749	-6.6
Providence, RI	Providence County	16	21	31.3	638	507	-20.5
Provo, UT	Utah County	22	19	-13.6	814	790	-2.9
Raleigh, NC	Wake County	53	50	-5.7	614	536	-12.7
Reno, NV	Washoe County	25	26	4.0	592	467	-21.1
Richmond, VA	Richmond city	21	6	-71.4	590	511	-13.4
Rochester, MN	Olmsted County	0	1	n/a	90	119	32.2
Sacramento, CA	Sacramento County	80	61	-23.8	1,731	1,275	-26.3
St. Louis, MO	Saint Louis City	12	15	25.0	1,395	1,247	-10.6
Salem, OR	Marion County	7	4	-42.9	489	439	-10.2
Salt Lake City, UT	Salt Lake County	27	23	-14.8	2,389	2,147	-10.1
San Antonio, TX	Bexar County	143	84	-41.3	1,102	1,028	-6.7
San Diego, CA	San Diego County	194	158	-18.6	4,533	3,136	-30.8
San Francisco, CA	San Francisco County	65	55	-15.4	334	342	2.4
San Jose, CA	Santa Clara County	80	77	-3.8	868	655	-24.5
Santa Rosa, CA	Sonoma County	23	29	26.1	329	278	-15.5
Savannah, GA	Chatham County	9	7	-22.2	546	591	8.2
Seattle, WA	King County	56	55	-1.8	1,094	979	-10.5
Sioux Falls, SD	Minnehaha County	7	6	-14.3	221	201	-9.0
Springfield, IL	Sangamon County	6	5	-16.7	221	186	-15.8
Tampa, FL	Hillsborough County	87	94	8.0	2,061	1,686	-18.2
Tucson, AZ	Pima County	21	22	4.8	1,379	1,310	-5.0
Tulsa, OK	Tulsa County	30	51	70.0	874	758	-13.3
Tuscaloosa, AL	Tuscaloosa County	4	9	125.0	679	821	20.9
Virginia Beach, VA	Virginia Beach City	11	15	36.4	788	711	-9.8
Washington, DC	District of Columbia	36	36	0.0	264	200	-24.2
Wichita, KS	Sedgwick County	20	14	-30.0	760	658	-13.4
Wilmington, NC	New Hanover County	12	6	-50.0	144	138	-4.2
Winston-Salem, NC	Forsyth County	10	6	-40.0	240	240	0.0
Worcester, MA	Worcester County	24	26	8.3	569	550	-3.3
U.S.	U.S.	14,347	13,481	-6.0	399,269	374,240	-6.3

Note: Business filings include Chapter 7, Chapter 9, Chapter 11, Chapter 12, Chapter 13, Chapter 15, and Section 304; Nonbusiness filings include Chapter 7, Chapter 11, and Chapter 13

Source: Administrative Office of the U.S. Courts, Business and Nonbusiness Bankruptcy, County Cases Commenced by Chapter of the Bankruptcy Code, During the 12-Month Period Ending December 31, 2021 and Business and Nonbusiness Bankruptcy, County Cases Commenced by Chapter of the Bankruptcy Code, During the 12-Month Period Ending December 31, 2022

Income: City

City	Per Capita ($)	Median Household ($)	Average Household ($)
Albuquerque, NM	33,494	56,366	76,833
Allentown, PA	22,976	47,703	61,780
Anchorage, AK	43,125	88,871	113,873
Ann Arbor, MI	47,883	73,276	107,368
Athens, GA	27,194	43,466	65,960
Atlanta, GA	54,466	69,164	118,074
Austin, TX	48,550	78,965	111,233
Baltimore, MD	34,378	54,124	79,399
Boise City, ID	40,056	68,373	93,693
Boston, MA	50,344	81,744	120,939
Boulder, CO	52,057	74,902	123,606
Brownsville, TX	18,207	43,174	58,147
Cape Coral, FL	34,586	65,282	84,169
Cedar Rapids, IA	35,566	63,170	82,815
Charleston, SC	50,240	76,556	111,903
Charlotte, NC	43,080	68,367	104,228
Chicago, IL	41,821	65,781	100,347
Cincinnati, OH	34,060	45,235	73,412
Clarksville, TN	27,437	58,838	71,824
Cleveland, OH	23,415	33,678	49,942
College Station, TX	28,705	50,089	76,307
Colorado Springs, CO	37,979	71,957	93,740
Columbia, MO	32,784	57,463	80,898
Columbia, SC	32,954	48,791	79,637
Columbus, OH	32,481	58,575	75,482
Dallas, TX	37,719	58,231	92,785
Davenport, IA	32,431	56,315	76,281
Denver, CO	50,642	78,177	111,981
Des Moines, IA	31,276	58,444	74,131
Durham, NC	39,496	66,623	91,960
Edison, NJ	47,410	110,896	136,606
El Paso, TX	25,165	51,325	69,692
Fargo, ND	37,522	60,243	82,974
Fort Collins, CO	38,949	72,932	96,301
Fort Wayne, IN	29,268	53,978	70,654
Fort Worth, TX	32,569	67,927	90,141
Grand Rapids, MI	29,060	55,385	72,017
Greeley, CO	28,480	60,601	78,033
Green Bay, WI	29,822	55,221	70,879
Greensboro, NC	31,812	51,667	76,282
Honolulu, HI	41,571	76,495	105,724
Houston, TX	35,578	56,019	90,511
Huntsville, AL	38,838	60,959	87,475
Indianapolis, IN	31,538	54,321	75,792
Jacksonville, FL	32,654	58,263	79,817
Kansas City, MO	35,352	60,042	81,577
Lafayette, LA	35,348	55,329	82,752
Las Cruces, NM	26,290	47,722	64,425
Las Vegas, NV	33,363	61,356	86,008
Lexington, KY	37,475	61,526	88,901
Lincoln, NE	33,955	62,566	83,225
Little Rock, AR	39,141	56,928	89,748
Los Angeles, CA	39,378	69,778	106,931
Louisville, KY	34,195	58,357	81,393
Madison, WI	42,693	70,466	94,746
Manchester, NH	36,440	66,929	83,913

Table continued on following page.

City	Per Capita ($)	Median Household ($)	Average Household ($)
Miami, FL	34,295	47,860	79,886
Midland, TX	44,218	87,900	115,425
Milwaukee, WI	25,564	45,318	61,529
Minneapolis, MN	43,925	70,099	99,741
Nashville, TN	39,509	65,565	92,866
New Haven, CT	29,348	48,973	73,450
New Orleans, LA	34,036	45,594	76,715
New York, NY	43,952	70,663	113,315
Oklahoma City, OK	33,162	59,679	81,931
Omaha, NE	36,749	65,359	90,389
Orlando, FL	36,596	58,968	88,128
Philadelphia, PA	32,344	52,649	77,454
Phoenix, AZ	33,718	64,927	90,481
Pittsburgh, PA	37,655	54,306	80,248
Portland, OR	47,289	78,476	106,948
Providence, RI	31,757	55,787	83,046
Provo, UT	23,440	53,572	76,163
Raleigh, NC	42,632	72,996	102,100
Reno, NV	39,104	67,557	93,306
Richmond, VA	38,132	54,795	82,939
Rochester, MN	43,827	79,159	106,381
Sacramento, CA	35,793	71,074	93,320
St. Louis, MO	33,326	48,751	68,681
Salem, OR	31,610	62,185	82,450
Salt Lake City, UT	42,081	65,880	97,628
San Antonio, TX	28,579	55,084	74,154
San Diego, CA	46,460	89,457	121,230
San Francisco, CA	77,267	126,187	178,742
San Jose, CA	53,574	125,075	162,521
Santa Rosa, CA	41,880	84,823	108,164
Savannah, GA	27,952	49,832	69,653
Seattle, WA	68,836	105,391	144,955
Sioux Falls, SD	36,430	66,761	87,676
Springfield, IL	35,851	57,596	79,460
Tampa, FL	40,962	59,893	97,942
Tucson, AZ	26,373	48,058	63,665
Tulsa, OK	33,492	52,438	79,727
Tuscaloosa, AL	27,789	44,880	69,736
Virginia Beach, VA	41,803	81,810	105,521
Washington, DC	63,793	93,547	138,421
Wichita, KS	31,558	56,374	77,762
Wilmington, NC	38,890	54,066	83,853
Winston-Salem, NC	30,859	50,204	75,459
Worcester, MA	30,855	56,746	76,859
U.S.	37,638	69,021	97,196

Source: U.S. Census Bureau, 2017-2021 American Community Survey 5-Year Estimates

Income: Metro Area

Metro Area	Per Capita ($)	Median Household ($)	Average Household ($)
Albuquerque, NM	32,622	58,335	78,771
Allentown, PA	37,945	73,091	96,205
Anchorage, AK	41,201	86,252	109,817
Ann Arbor, MI	45,500	79,198	110,102
Athens, GA	31,392	52,958	80,272
Atlanta, GA	39,267	75,267	104,478
Austin, TX	44,830	85,398	114,103
Baltimore, MD	45,226	87,513	115,291
Boise City, ID	35,114	69,801	92,742
Boston, MA	53,033	99,039	135,411
Boulder, CO	52,401	92,466	128,190
Brownsville, TX	19,371	43,057	60,107
Cape Coral, FL	37,550	63,235	89,228
Cedar Rapids, IA	37,291	70,210	90,560
Charleston, SC	39,923	70,275	98,682
Charlotte, NC	38,783	69,559	98,559
Chicago, IL	42,097	78,790	109,339
Cincinnati, OH	37,846	70,308	94,687
Clarksville, TN	28,243	57,963	74,308
Cleveland, OH	36,907	61,320	85,864
College Station, TX	30,182	53,541	78,104
Colorado Springs, CO	37,650	75,641	97,647
Columbia, MO	33,131	61,901	82,741
Columbia, SC	32,508	58,992	79,903
Columbus, OH	38,167	71,020	95,315
Dallas, TX	38,609	76,916	105,647
Davenport, IA	34,859	63,282	83,352
Denver, CO	47,026	88,512	117,250
Des Moines, IA	39,333	75,134	97,364
Durham, NC	40,502	68,913	99,164
Edison, NJ	47,591	86,445	127,555
El Paso, TX	23,934	50,849	68,522
Fargo, ND	38,367	68,560	91,642
Fort Collins, CO	42,596	80,664	104,442
Fort Wayne, IN	32,207	62,031	80,675
Fort Worth, TX	38,609	76,916	105,647
Grand Rapids, MI	34,581	70,347	91,126
Greeley, CO	35,707	80,843	99,568
Green Bay, WI	35,678	68,952	87,144
Greensboro, NC	31,655	55,544	77,839
Honolulu, HI	40,339	92,600	118,470
Houston, TX	36,821	72,551	103,497
Huntsville, AL	38,800	71,057	94,763
Indianapolis, IN	36,867	67,330	92,858
Jacksonville, FL	36,316	66,664	91,361
Kansas City, MO	39,175	73,299	96,817
Lafayette, LA	30,758	55,539	77,448
Las Cruces, NM	24,645	47,151	65,405
Las Vegas, NV	33,461	64,210	87,879
Lexington, KY	36,123	63,360	88,439
Lincoln, NE	35,055	65,508	87,123
Little Rock, AR	33,523	58,441	81,542
Los Angeles, CA	39,895	81,652	115,584
Louisville, KY	35,613	64,533	87,361
Madison, WI	43,359	77,519	100,891
Manchester, NH	45,238	86,930	111,733

Table continued on following page.

Metro Area	Per Capita ($)	Median Household ($)	Average Household ($)
Miami, FL	36,174	62,870	94,059
Midland, TX	43,287	87,812	114,916
Milwaukee, WI	38,930	67,448	92,423
Minneapolis, MN	45,301	87,397	114,491
Nashville, TN	39,269	72,537	99,987
New Haven, CT	41,192	75,043	102,367
New Orleans, LA	33,792	57,656	83,052
New York, NY	47,591	86,445	127,555
Oklahoma City, OK	34,136	63,351	85,884
Omaha, NE	38,289	73,757	97,122
Orlando, FL	32,999	65,086	89,689
Philadelphia, PA	43,195	79,070	109,757
Phoenix, AZ	36,842	72,211	97,412
Pittsburgh, PA	39,416	65,894	90,001
Portland, OR	42,946	82,901	108,110
Providence, RI	39,267	74,422	97,540
Provo, UT	29,817	82,742	105,296
Raleigh, NC	42,554	83,581	110,195
Reno, NV	40,299	74,216	100,824
Richmond, VA	40,254	74,592	100,389
Rochester, MN	42,841	80,865	106,479
Sacramento, CA	39,510	81,264	107,069
St. Louis, MO	39,168	69,635	94,953
Salem, OR	31,447	65,881	85,642
Salt Lake City, UT	36,688	82,506	105,669
San Antonio, TX	32,580	65,355	88,127
San Diego, CA	42,696	88,240	118,474
San Francisco, CA	62,070	118,547	165,749
San Jose, CA	64,169	138,370	187,324
Santa Rosa, CA	47,580	91,607	121,206
Savannah, GA	34,908	64,703	89,172
Seattle, WA	51,872	97,675	130,964
Sioux Falls, SD	37,200	72,547	92,236
Springfield, IL	37,961	66,999	87,390
Tampa, FL	35,879	61,121	86,382
Tucson, AZ	33,016	59,215	80,772
Tulsa, OK	33,647	60,866	84,069
Tuscaloosa, AL	28,204	54,449	72,452
Virginia Beach, VA	37,548	71,612	93,415
Washington, DC	54,663	111,252	145,303
Wichita, KS	32,124	61,445	81,209
Wilmington, NC	38,607	63,036	89,355
Winston-Salem, NC	31,238	55,454	76,451
Worcester, MA	40,750	80,333	104,366
U.S.	37,638	69,021	97,196

Note: Figures cover the Metropolitan Statistical Area (MSA)
Source: U.S. Census Bureau, 2017-2021 American Community Survey 5-Year Estimates

Household Income Distribution: City

City	Under $15,000	$15,000 -$24,999	$25,000 -$34,999	$35,000 -$49,999	$50,000 -$74,999	$75,000 -$99,999	$100,000 -$149,999	$150,000 and up
Albuquerque, NM	13.1	8.9	9.8	12.9	18.0	11.6	14.8	10.9
Allentown, PA	13.0	12.4	10.9	16.1	19.7	11.2	10.9	5.7
Anchorage, AK	5.5	5.1	5.5	9.0	17.1	14.1	20.2	23.6
Ann Arbor, MI	14.5	6.2	6.2	8.9	15.2	11.2	15.7	22.2
Athens, GA	17.8	12.2	12.4	12.8	15.4	9.2	11.3	8.8
Atlanta, GA	14.2	8.1	7.3	9.4	14.5	11.0	13.5	22.0
Austin, TX	8.3	5.5	6.7	10.4	16.8	12.6	17.7	22.1
Baltimore, MD	16.6	9.1	8.9	12.2	17.1	10.8	12.7	12.8
Boise City, ID	7.6	7.6	8.6	12.4	18.5	13.9	15.7	15.7
Boston, MA	14.9	7.2	5.5	7.7	11.9	10.5	16.1	26.2
Boulder, CO	13.1	7.8	6.7	8.9	13.6	9.5	13.8	26.6
Brownsville, TX	18.6	13.1	10.0	13.0	18.2	10.7	10.6	5.9
Cape Coral, FL	7.6	6.2	8.7	13.7	20.5	15.4	17.2	10.6
Cedar Rapids, IA	7.1	8.5	9.5	13.6	19.9	14.8	14.9	11.7
Charleston, SC	9.1	6.5	6.2	11.3	15.8	12.3	18.6	20.3
Charlotte, NC	7.8	6.7	8.5	12.7	18.3	12.5	15.8	17.7
Chicago, IL	13.1	8.7	8.2	10.2	14.9	11.7	14.7	18.6
Cincinnati, OH	18.0	11.9	10.5	12.6	15.3	10.1	10.6	11.0
Clarksville, TN	9.6	6.8	9.9	15.2	20.6	15.3	15.5	7.2
Cleveland, OH	25.4	13.8	12.4	13.8	14.7	8.7	7.0	4.4
College Station, TX	19.7	10.2	8.8	11.2	15.3	10.0	12.3	12.4
Colorado Springs, CO	7.8	6.6	7.6	12.0	18.0	14.2	17.3	16.4
Columbia, MO	12.8	9.6	9.8	12.6	17.3	11.5	13.2	13.2
Columbia, SC	18.9	10.2	9.7	12.6	14.8	10.5	11.2	12.1
Columbus, OH	10.8	8.4	9.5	13.6	19.5	13.5	15.3	9.5
Dallas, TX	11.3	8.6	9.6	13.7	18.4	11.3	12.1	14.8
Davenport, IA	10.9	9.1	9.0	13.6	20.8	12.8	14.6	9.2
Denver, CO	8.6	6.1	6.4	10.3	16.9	12.4	17.0	22.2
Des Moines, IA	10.0	8.9	9.4	14.7	20.2	14.3	13.6	8.9
Durham, NC	8.9	6.8	9.7	12.2	17.2	13.1	15.7	16.4
Edison, NJ	4.6	3.4	3.5	7.2	13.3	12.4	21.8	34.0
El Paso, TX	13.8	11.4	10.6	13.3	18.8	10.7	12.7	8.8
Fargo, ND	9.8	9.1	9.7	12.9	18.4	13.0	15.5	11.7
Fort Collins, CO	9.6	6.7	7.5	11.0	16.5	13.0	17.2	18.5
Fort Wayne, IN	10.4	10.4	10.8	14.8	19.8	13.2	13.1	7.5
Fort Worth, TX	8.7	7.0	8.7	11.6	18.6	13.5	17.2	14.6
Grand Rapids, MI	12.5	9.8	8.1	14.1	19.0	14.1	14.3	8.0
Greeley, CO	10.3	8.2	9.7	13.9	16.1	13.7	17.9	10.3
Green Bay, WI	10.1	9.4	10.0	15.0	21.7	13.0	13.6	7.3
Greensboro, NC	12.2	9.7	10.9	15.7	17.5	11.3	12.7	9.9
Honolulu, HI	9.1	6.3	6.1	11.0	16.5	13.2	17.1	20.6
Houston, TX	11.9	9.5	10.6	13.1	17.1	10.7	12.1	14.9
Huntsville, AL	11.5	9.2	10.1	12.3	15.2	11.4	14.4	15.9
Indianapolis, IN	12.1	9.6	9.9	14.5	18.8	11.9	12.9	10.4
Jacksonville, FL	10.9	8.4	9.6	13.8	18.9	13.2	14.3	10.9
Kansas City, MO	11.4	8.8	9.6	12.7	17.2	12.7	15.2	12.3
Lafayette, LA	16.0	8.5	9.7	11.5	15.4	11.4	13.3	14.2
Las Cruces, NM	17.5	12.3	10.4	12.2	17.4	9.8	13.1	7.4
Las Vegas, NV	11.6	8.1	8.7	12.9	17.3	13.1	15.2	13.0
Lexington, KY	10.6	8.9	9.5	12.1	17.6	12.3	14.9	14.1
Lincoln, NE	8.4	7.9	9.8	13.0	20.2	12.4	16.1	12.0
Little Rock, AR	11.5	10.1	10.4	13.4	16.2	11.5	12.3	14.4
Los Angeles, CA	11.6	7.8	7.8	10.4	15.1	11.7	15.4	20.1
Louisville, KY	11.2	8.8	9.5	13.3	18.5	12.3	14.3	11.9

Table continued on following page.

City	Percent of Households Earning							
	Under $15,000	$15,000 -$24,999	$25,000 -$34,999	$35,000 -$49,999	$50,000 -$74,999	$75,000 -$99,999	$100,000 -$149,999	$150,000 and up
Madison, WI	10.0	6.8	7.5	11.0	17.5	14.1	16.9	16.0
Manchester, NH	8.0	7.7	7.3	13.7	19.8	14.0	17.0	12.5
Miami, FL	17.7	11.8	10.1	11.8	16.1	9.4	11.1	12.0
Midland, TX	8.0	5.8	6.5	8.5	14.7	12.5	19.6	24.4
Milwaukee, WI	16.5	11.5	11.7	14.6	17.8	11.6	10.5	5.8
Minneapolis, MN	11.3	7.1	7.5	11.0	16.1	12.6	15.9	18.5
Nashville, TN	9.1	7.1	8.2	12.9	19.1	13.2	15.6	14.8
New Haven, CT	18.5	11.0	9.8	11.2	17.2	10.3	11.4	10.6
New Orleans, LA	21.3	11.3	9.5	10.4	15.0	9.4	10.8	12.3
New York, NY	13.2	8.0	7.3	9.6	14.0	11.0	15.0	21.9
Oklahoma City, OK	10.7	7.7	9.6	13.9	18.7	12.8	14.6	12.1
Omaha, NE	9.5	7.3	8.4	12.5	18.9	13.7	15.5	14.1
Orlando, FL	11.2	9.3	8.7	13.6	17.9	11.7	13.0	14.5
Philadelphia, PA	17.1	9.8	9.2	12.0	16.4	11.3	12.4	11.7
Phoenix, AZ	8.4	7.6	8.8	13.5	18.2	13.5	15.3	14.8
Pittsburgh, PA	16.3	9.8	9.6	11.2	16.1	11.7	12.6	12.8
Portland, OR	9.8	6.3	6.7	9.7	15.7	12.6	17.5	21.8
Providence, RI	15.7	10.6	8.8	11.3	17.4	11.9	12.0	12.4
Provo, UT	11.4	10.2	11.3	14.1	19.1	12.7	10.7	10.5
Raleigh, NC	7.5	6.5	8.7	12.1	16.7	12.9	17.0	18.8
Reno, NV	8.6	7.7	8.6	11.5	18.1	13.4	16.7	15.3
Richmond, VA	14.1	9.6	9.4	13.7	17.4	11.3	11.7	12.7
Rochester, MN	6.9	6.3	5.8	10.4	18.0	13.9	18.8	19.9
Sacramento, CA	10.5	6.9	7.2	10.4	17.3	13.8	17.2	16.7
St. Louis, MO	17.0	10.3	10.7	12.9	17.5	10.5	12.1	8.9
Salem, OR	9.9	8.3	8.7	12.8	19.4	13.0	16.6	11.3
Salt Lake City, UT	11.2	6.9	8.6	10.9	18.1	13.1	15.0	16.2
San Antonio, TX	12.2	9.5	10.3	13.6	19.1	12.0	13.3	10.0
San Diego, CA	7.3	5.4	5.9	8.6	15.2	12.6	19.0	26.0
San Francisco, CA	9.2	4.9	4.5	6.0	9.1	8.3	14.9	43.2
San Jose, CA	5.2	4.2	4.2	6.3	10.9	9.9	17.7	41.6
Santa Rosa, CA	7.3	4.9	6.0	10.1	15.6	13.8	20.2	22.1
Savannah, GA	14.7	11.5	10.4	13.6	18.3	11.2	11.7	8.6
Seattle, WA	7.8	4.5	4.7	7.5	12.8	10.6	17.9	34.1
Sioux Falls, SD	7.3	7.4	9.7	12.4	19.1	15.0	17.1	11.9
Springfield, IL	13.8	9.1	9.7	11.9	16.0	13.3	15.0	11.2
Tampa, FL	12.9	8.5	9.4	12.0	15.8	10.8	13.3	17.3
Tucson, AZ	13.9	11.4	11.3	15.2	18.1	12.0	11.7	6.4
Tulsa, OK	12.7	9.8	11.0	14.2	17.7	11.5	11.7	11.5
Tuscaloosa, AL	19.5	10.8	10.9	11.9	15.4	8.7	12.8	10.0
Virginia Beach, VA	5.6	4.5	6.3	10.5	18.8	14.6	20.9	18.8
Washington, DC	11.9	5.1	5.5	6.8	12.2	11.3	15.9	31.3
Wichita, KS	10.8	9.3	10.3	14.0	18.9	12.8	13.6	10.3
Wilmington, NC	14.8	9.7	8.2	13.5	18.5	10.4	12.5	12.5
Winston-Salem, NC	13.8	10.6	11.2	14.2	16.4	12.3	11.7	9.8
Worcester, MA	15.5	9.8	8.5	12.0	15.8	11.7	14.8	11.8
U.S.	9.4	7.8	8.2	11.4	16.8	12.8	16.3	17.3

Source: U.S. Census Bureau, 2017-2021 American Community Survey 5-Year Estimates

Household Income Distribution: Metro Area

Metro Area	Percent of Households Earning							
	Under $15,000	$15,000 -$24,999	$25,000 -$34,999	$35,000 -$49,999	$50,000 -$74,999	$75,000 -$99,999	$100,000 -$149,999	$150,000 and up
Albuquerque, NM	12.0	8.9	9.3	13.0	18.0	12.3	15.0	11.5
Allentown, PA	7.3	7.6	7.6	11.8	17.0	13.7	17.9	17.2
Anchorage, AK	6.1	5.5	5.7	9.0	17.1	14.1	20.1	22.4
Ann Arbor, MI	9.7	6.0	6.9	9.7	15.5	12.5	17.4	22.3
Athens, GA	14.0	10.2	11.1	12.3	15.9	10.2	13.7	12.5
Atlanta, GA	7.6	6.5	7.5	11.1	17.2	13.3	17.3	19.5
Austin, TX	6.8	5.1	6.3	9.7	16.1	13.6	19.1	23.4
Baltimore, MD	8.0	5.5	5.9	9.3	14.8	12.5	18.8	25.1
Boise City, ID	7.0	7.1	7.6	12.0	20.4	14.6	17.3	14.2
Boston, MA	8.1	5.6	5.2	7.6	12.5	11.4	18.2	31.3
Boulder, CO	7.9	5.7	5.5	8.3	13.7	12.1	18.2	28.5
Brownsville, TX	16.8	13.4	11.5	12.9	17.9	10.7	10.6	6.3
Cape Coral, FL	9.1	7.9	9.2	13.2	19.0	13.8	14.9	12.8
Cedar Rapids, IA	6.6	7.4	8.5	12.1	19.2	14.9	17.0	14.4
Charleston, SC	8.4	7.7	7.8	11.6	17.3	13.4	17.1	16.7
Charlotte, NC	7.9	7.3	8.3	12.1	17.7	13.1	16.4	17.2
Chicago, IL	8.7	6.6	7.1	9.9	15.6	12.8	17.9	21.5
Cincinnati, OH	9.2	7.6	8.0	11.1	17.0	13.3	17.5	16.3
Clarksville, TN	10.8	7.6	10.3	14.0	19.6	14.5	14.8	8.5
Cleveland, OH	11.6	8.6	9.0	12.5	17.2	12.7	15.0	13.5
College Station, TX	16.0	9.6	8.9	12.5	17.0	11.2	13.1	11.7
Colorado Springs, CO	6.9	6.2	6.9	11.5	18.1	14.1	18.4	17.9
Columbia, MO	10.8	8.5	9.5	12.3	18.3	13.3	14.8	12.5
Columbia, SC	12.0	8.3	9.4	12.8	18.2	13.1	14.4	11.8
Columbus, OH	8.1	7.0	7.9	11.6	17.9	13.3	17.6	16.6
Dallas, TX	7.1	6.0	7.4	11.1	17.3	13.3	17.9	20.0
Davenport, IA	9.6	8.2	8.7	12.4	18.8	13.7	16.5	12.0
Denver, CO	6.2	4.8	5.7	9.5	16.3	13.2	19.9	24.5
Des Moines, IA	6.4	6.3	7.4	11.8	18.1	14.1	19.0	16.9
Durham, NC	9.2	7.1	9.1	11.5	16.4	12.4	15.6	18.8
Edison, NJ	9.7	6.6	6.3	8.6	13.3	11.2	16.7	27.5
El Paso, TX	13.8	11.2	10.7	13.5	19.0	10.9	12.5	8.3
Fargo, ND	8.7	7.9	7.9	11.8	17.3	13.8	17.9	14.7
Fort Collins, CO	7.9	6.2	6.6	10.0	16.0	14.2	18.8	20.3
Fort Wayne, IN	8.2	8.9	9.5	13.5	19.5	14.9	15.3	10.3
Fort Worth, TX	7.1	6.0	7.4	11.1	17.3	13.3	17.9	20.0
Grand Rapids, MI	7.1	7.4	7.5	12.3	19.2	14.8	17.9	13.9
Greeley, CO	6.6	5.7	7.3	10.2	16.7	14.3	22.2	16.9
Green Bay, WI	7.0	7.1	8.7	12.3	19.2	15.2	18.3	12.1
Greensboro, NC	11.3	9.5	10.3	14.5	17.9	12.1	13.8	10.5
Honolulu, HI	6.5	4.5	5.4	9.0	14.7	13.5	20.0	26.3
Houston, TX	8.4	7.1	8.2	11.0	16.6	12.3	16.5	19.8
Huntsville, AL	8.8	8.0	8.2	11.7	15.4	12.8	16.9	18.2
Indianapolis, IN	8.6	7.4	8.3	12.1	18.4	13.4	16.2	15.6
Jacksonville, FL	9.0	7.1	8.6	12.5	18.3	13.7	15.8	15.0
Kansas City, MO	7.5	6.9	8.1	11.4	17.1	13.9	18.1	17.0
Lafayette, LA	13.7	10.4	10.0	11.9	15.8	12.9	14.4	11.1
Las Cruces, NM	16.8	12.7	10.8	12.2	17.7	9.5	12.9	7.3
Las Vegas, NV	9.7	7.7	8.8	12.8	18.2	13.4	15.7	13.6
Lexington, KY	10.0	8.2	9.3	12.4	17.6	12.9	16.1	13.4
Lincoln, NE	7.8	7.5	9.4	12.6	19.7	12.8	17.1	13.1
Little Rock, AR	11.0	9.2	10.1	13.3	17.5	12.4	14.9	11.6
Los Angeles, CA	9.0	6.4	6.8	9.5	14.8	12.3	17.4	23.8
Louisville, KY	9.2	7.9	8.9	12.9	18.3	13.2	16.0	13.6

Table continued on following page.

Metro Area	Percent of Households Earning							
	Under $15,000	$15,000 -$24,999	$25,000 -$34,999	$35,000 -$49,999	$50,000 -$74,999	$75,000 -$99,999	$100,000 -$149,999	$150,000 and up
Madison, WI	6.9	6.0	6.7	11.1	17.7	14.3	18.9	18.3
Manchester, NH	5.4	5.5	6.2	10.2	15.7	13.2	20.1	23.7
Miami, FL	10.8	8.5	9.0	12.2	17.2	12.2	14.6	15.5
Midland, TX	7.6	5.8	7.1	8.8	14.1	12.8	19.2	24.6
Milwaukee, WI	9.4	7.8	8.5	11.8	17.1	13.2	16.7	15.5
Minneapolis, MN	6.1	5.2	6.1	9.7	16.0	13.7	20.2	23.2
Nashville, TN	7.4	6.5	7.4	12.1	18.2	13.9	17.5	16.9
New Haven, CT	9.4	7.6	6.9	10.1	15.8	12.5	17.1	20.4
New Orleans, LA	14.1	9.6	9.1	11.5	16.5	11.7	14.0	13.5
New York, NY	9.7	6.6	6.3	8.6	13.3	11.2	16.7	27.5
Oklahoma City, OK	9.4	7.9	9.1	13.0	18.6	13.4	15.6	12.8
Omaha, NE	7.6	6.5	7.7	11.3	17.7	14.2	18.5	16.4
Orlando, FL	8.3	7.9	9.0	12.9	18.5	13.6	15.8	14.0
Philadelphia, PA	9.3	6.7	7.1	9.7	15.1	12.5	17.3	22.5
Phoenix, AZ	7.4	6.6	7.7	12.0	18.1	13.9	17.7	16.7
Pittsburgh, PA	9.7	8.4	8.7	11.8	17.0	12.9	16.5	14.9
Portland, OR	7.2	5.7	6.3	10.0	16.3	13.6	19.5	21.5
Providence, RI	9.7	7.9	7.3	10.1	15.2	13.2	18.2	18.3
Provo, UT	5.1	5.0	6.4	10.4	17.9	15.7	20.8	18.6
Raleigh, NC	6.3	6.0	7.0	10.4	15.8	12.8	19.5	22.3
Reno, NV	7.2	6.7	7.8	10.8	18.0	14.0	18.3	17.2
Richmond, VA	7.9	6.7	7.2	11.2	17.2	13.1	18.3	18.3
Rochester, MN	6.2	6.0	6.4	10.1	17.8	14.0	20.1	19.5
Sacramento, CA	8.3	6.1	6.7	9.5	15.9	13.2	18.3	22.1
St. Louis, MO	8.6	7.4	8.1	11.8	17.5	13.5	16.9	16.3
Salem, OR	8.5	7.8	8.7	12.3	18.9	13.8	17.5	12.3
Salt Lake City, UT	6.0	4.8	6.3	10.2	17.9	14.8	20.6	19.3
San Antonio, TX	9.6	7.9	8.9	12.0	18.2	13.0	16.1	14.4
San Diego, CA	6.9	5.7	6.3	9.1	15.0	12.6	18.9	25.5
San Francisco, CA	6.7	4.3	4.5	6.4	10.8	10.0	17.1	40.0
San Jose, CA	4.9	3.6	3.7	5.5	9.9	9.2	16.8	46.6
Santa Rosa, CA	6.5	5.0	5.9	9.0	14.3	13.4	19.6	26.3
Savannah, GA	9.4	7.9	8.6	12.0	18.6	14.1	15.9	13.5
Seattle, WA	5.9	4.6	5.1	8.2	14.7	12.5	19.8	29.2
Sioux Falls, SD	6.2	6.7	8.7	11.8	18.7	15.7	18.9	13.3
Springfield, IL	10.4	7.9	8.4	11.5	16.2	14.1	18.0	13.7
Tampa, FL	9.9	8.6	9.5	13.2	18.0	12.7	14.6	13.7
Tucson, AZ	10.8	9.2	9.6	13.4	17.3	13.1	14.9	11.7
Tulsa, OK	9.6	8.5	9.9	13.1	18.6	12.8	15.3	12.2
Tuscaloosa, AL	14.3	9.9	10.2	12.1	17.3	12.0	14.5	9.6
Virginia Beach, VA	8.0	7.0	7.6	11.3	18.3	13.9	18.4	15.5
Washington, DC	5.7	3.7	4.4	6.8	12.6	12.0	19.6	35.4
Wichita, KS	9.2	8.6	9.1	13.4	19.6	13.4	15.5	11.0
Wilmington, NC	11.0	8.7	7.8	12.4	18.0	12.0	16.0	14.0
Winston-Salem, NC	11.0	10.0	10.7	13.7	18.1	13.1	13.3	10.1
Worcester, MA	8.6	6.8	7.0	9.6	15.3	12.5	18.5	21.8
U.S.	9.4	7.8	8.2	11.4	16.8	12.8	16.3	17.3

Note: Figures cover the Metropolitan Statistical Area (MSA)
Source: Source: U.S. Census Bureau, 2017-2021 American Community Survey 5-Year Estimates

Poverty Rate: City

City	All Ages	Under 18 Years Old	18 to 64 Years Old	65 Years and Over
Albuquerque, NM	16.2	21.0	15.7	11.7
Allentown, PA	23.3	34.9	19.6	16.6
Anchorage, AK	9.1	11.1	8.8	6.8
Ann Arbor, MI	22.5	10.8	27.7	6.3
Athens, GA	26.6	25.8	29.5	11.1
Atlanta, GA	18.5	27.1	16.5	16.9
Austin, TX	12.5	15.9	11.7	11.3
Baltimore, MD	20.3	27.9	18.2	18.6
Boise City, ID	11.6	13.8	11.6	8.6
Boston, MA	17.6	23.7	15.6	21.0
Boulder, CO	20.9	8.6	25.6	6.4
Brownsville, TX	26.5	36.4	21.2	28.2
Cape Coral, FL	9.9	15.4	8.7	8.8
Cedar Rapids, IA	11.2	15.5	10.9	6.4
Charleston, SC	12.0	14.6	12.6	6.4
Charlotte, NC	11.6	17.3	10.1	8.7
Chicago, IL	17.1	24.2	15.1	15.9
Cincinnati, OH	24.7	37.4	22.3	14.7
Clarksville, TN	13.2	16.9	12.4	7.2
Cleveland, OH	31.4	45.7	28.3	22.8
College Station, TX	28.2	13.2	34.3	5.9
Colorado Springs, CO	10.9	13.7	10.7	7.5
Columbia, MO	19.9	14.9	23.7	6.1
Columbia, SC	24.3	31.3	23.5	16.7
Columbus, OH	18.4	27.1	16.5	11.6
Dallas, TX	17.7	26.9	14.7	14.7
Davenport, IA	15.8	24.7	14.1	9.8
Denver, CO	11.6	16.0	10.4	11.3
Des Moines, IA	15.3	22.6	13.6	9.8
Durham, NC	13.5	19.6	12.5	8.9
Edison, NJ	5.8	7.1	5.1	6.6
El Paso, TX	18.3	25.3	15.1	19.1
Fargo, ND	12.9	14.1	14.1	4.8
Fort Collins, CO	15.7	8.9	18.7	7.3
Fort Wayne, IN	15.5	23.9	13.7	8.3
Fort Worth, TX	13.4	19.1	11.3	10.7
Grand Rapids, MI	18.6	25.6	17.1	13.9
Greeley, CO	15.3	20.5	14.5	9.1
Green Bay, WI	15.4	21.5	14.2	10.3
Greensboro, NC	17.4	24.3	15.9	13.0
Honolulu, HI	11.0	13.3	10.4	10.8
Houston, TX	19.5	29.7	16.3	15.1
Huntsville, AL	14.6	21.8	13.9	8.3
Indianapolis, IN	16.4	23.3	14.9	10.5
Jacksonville, FL	14.9	21.1	13.0	12.7
Kansas City, MO	15.0	22.2	13.4	10.1
Lafayette, LA	19.5	29.0	17.8	12.9
Las Cruces, NM	21.8	26.9	22.4	11.5
Las Vegas, NV	14.9	20.8	13.6	11.3
Lexington, KY	15.7	18.6	16.5	7.6
Lincoln, NE	13.0	13.5	14.4	6.1
Little Rock, AR	15.6	22.9	14.2	9.2
Los Angeles, CA	16.6	22.9	14.7	16.3
Louisville, KY	15.2	22.6	14.0	9.4
Madison, WI	16.6	13.0	19.2	7.1

Table continued on following page.

City	All Ages	Under 18 Years Old	18 to 64 Years Old	65 Years and Over
Manchester, NH	12.5	22.1	10.7	8.6
Miami, FL	20.9	27.8	16.6	30.9
Midland, TX	10.6	13.5	9.1	11.8
Milwaukee, WI	24.1	33.4	21.6	15.9
Minneapolis, MN	17.0	21.2	16.3	13.6
Nashville, TN	14.5	22.7	12.7	10.4
New Haven, CT	24.6	31.4	23.3	17.4
New Orleans, LA	23.8	33.8	21.5	20.6
New York, NY	17.0	23.2	14.7	17.8
Oklahoma City, OK	14.9	21.5	13.6	8.4
Omaha, NE	12.1	15.7	11.4	8.4
Orlando, FL	15.5	21.5	13.7	14.5
Philadelphia, PA	22.8	31.9	20.6	18.9
Phoenix, AZ	15.4	22.7	13.3	10.5
Pittsburgh, PA	19.7	28.8	19.0	14.0
Portland, OR	12.6	13.5	12.7	10.6
Providence, RI	21.5	30.3	18.8	19.5
Provo, UT	24.6	17.7	28.2	10.0
Raleigh, NC	12.1	15.8	11.8	7.2
Reno, NV	12.6	13.6	12.4	11.8
Richmond, VA	19.8	30.2	18.3	13.5
Rochester, MN	8.7	9.6	8.9	6.4
Sacramento, CA	14.8	18.5	14.1	12.1
St. Louis, MO	19.6	27.3	18.3	15.4
Salem, OR	14.7	18.0	14.5	10.2
Salt Lake City, UT	14.7	15.4	15.2	10.3
San Antonio, TX	17.6	25.8	15.3	13.6
San Diego, CA	11.6	13.9	11.3	9.4
San Francisco, CA	10.3	10.1	9.4	14.4
San Jose, CA	7.7	8.2	7.1	9.5
Santa Rosa, CA	9.8	12.9	9.0	9.0
Savannah, GA	19.8	29.7	18.1	12.1
Seattle, WA	10.0	9.5	9.9	11.2
Sioux Falls, SD	9.5	10.6	9.6	6.8
Springfield, IL	18.5	28.2	17.6	9.2
Tampa, FL	17.2	23.7	14.6	19.3
Tucson, AZ	19.8	25.3	19.7	12.5
Tulsa, OK	18.0	26.8	16.7	8.8
Tuscaloosa, AL	22.6	21.7	24.5	14.8
Virginia Beach, VA	7.8	10.5	7.6	4.8
Washington, DC	15.4	22.8	13.7	13.9
Wichita, KS	15.2	20.8	14.5	8.5
Wilmington, NC	18.8	25.3	19.8	8.7
Winston-Salem, NC	19.0	30.1	16.9	9.5
Worcester, MA	19.3	24.8	18.1	16.6
U.S.	12.6	17.0	11.8	9.6

Note: Figures are percentage of people whose income during the past 12 months was below the poverty level;
Source: U.S. Census Bureau, 2017-2021 American Community Survey 5-Year Estimates

Poverty Rate: Metro Area

Metro Area	All Ages	Under 18 Years Old	18 to 64 Years Old	65 Years and Over
Albuquerque, NM	15.3	19.5	14.9	11.3
Allentown, PA	10.4	15.9	9.4	7.3
Anchorage, AK	9.6	11.5	9.2	7.4
Ann Arbor, MI	13.4	11.1	15.8	5.8
Athens, GA	20.1	20.5	22.3	9.5
Atlanta, GA	11.1	15.5	9.9	8.5
Austin, TX	10.2	12.0	9.9	8.3
Baltimore, MD	9.8	12.7	9.0	8.8
Boise City, ID	9.9	11.2	9.9	7.6
Boston, MA	9.0	10.3	8.4	9.5
Boulder, CO	11.0	7.1	13.2	6.4
Brownsville, TX	26.3	37.9	21.2	21.8
Cape Coral, FL	12.0	18.7	11.5	9.0
Cedar Rapids, IA	9.5	12.0	9.4	6.5
Charleston, SC	12.1	18.2	10.9	8.1
Charlotte, NC	10.7	14.9	9.7	8.4
Chicago, IL	11.1	15.1	10.1	9.4
Cincinnati, OH	11.6	15.5	10.9	8.1
Clarksville, TN	13.5	17.0	12.6	9.2
Cleveland, OH	13.7	19.6	12.8	9.7
College Station, TX	22.3	20.5	25.3	8.6
Colorado Springs, CO	9.5	12.0	9.2	6.6
Columbia, MO	16.2	14.6	18.7	6.8
Columbia, SC	14.9	19.9	14.2	10.6
Columbus, OH	12.3	17.0	11.5	7.7
Dallas, TX	10.9	15.4	9.4	8.9
Davenport, IA	12.6	18.5	11.8	7.6
Denver, CO	8.1	10.2	7.6	7.1
Des Moines, IA	9.0	11.5	8.6	6.6
Durham, NC	13.2	17.8	12.9	8.2
Edison, NJ	12.3	16.6	10.8	12.1
El Paso, TX	19.3	26.5	15.9	20.0
Fargo, ND	11.3	12.1	12.2	5.5
Fort Collins, CO	11.1	8.8	13.0	6.6
Fort Wayne, IN	12.1	17.9	10.9	6.9
Fort Worth, TX	10.9	15.4	9.4	8.9
Grand Rapids, MI	9.8	11.7	9.5	7.8
Greeley, CO	9.7	12.1	9.0	7.7
Green Bay, WI	9.4	12.0	9.0	7.1
Greensboro, NC	15.1	21.5	14.0	10.3
Honolulu, HI	8.6	11.0	7.9	8.0
Houston, TX	13.3	18.9	11.5	10.5
Huntsville, AL	11.0	15.0	10.1	8.9
Indianapolis, IN	11.1	15.0	10.2	7.7
Jacksonville, FL	12.3	17.2	11.3	9.3
Kansas City, MO	9.8	13.5	9.0	7.0
Lafayette, LA	18.5	26.6	16.6	12.9
Las Cruces, NM	23.2	30.9	22.2	14.7
Las Vegas, NV	13.6	19.0	12.5	9.8
Lexington, KY	14.1	17.2	14.4	8.3
Lincoln, NE	11.8	11.9	13.1	5.9
Little Rock, AR	14.0	18.8	13.4	9.1
Los Angeles, CA	12.9	17.2	11.6	12.4
Louisville, KY	12.0	17.0	11.1	8.2
Madison, WI	10.1	9.0	11.5	5.8

Table continued on following page.

Metro Area	All Ages	Under 18 Years Old	18 to 64 Years Old	65 Years and Over
Manchester, NH	7.2	9.8	6.5	6.2
Miami, FL	13.6	18.0	11.6	15.6
Midland, TX	11.2	15.9	8.9	11.2
Milwaukee, WI	12.6	17.7	11.6	9.0
Minneapolis, MN	8.1	10.1	7.7	6.8
Nashville, TN	10.9	14.6	10.2	8.3
New Haven, CT	11.5	15.8	11.1	7.9
New Orleans, LA	17.3	24.6	15.7	13.3
New York, NY	12.3	16.6	10.8	12.1
Oklahoma City, OK	13.6	18.6	12.9	7.8
Omaha, NE	9.3	11.2	9.0	7.1
Orlando, FL	12.6	17.1	11.7	9.9
Philadelphia, PA	11.7	16.0	10.9	9.2
Phoenix, AZ	12.0	16.9	11.0	8.3
Pittsburgh, PA	10.7	14.2	10.3	8.3
Portland, OR	9.9	11.3	9.8	8.2
Providence, RI	11.2	15.2	10.3	9.6
Provo, UT	9.3	7.9	10.7	5.2
Raleigh, NC	9.3	12.1	8.7	6.9
Reno, NV	11.0	12.8	10.6	9.9
Richmond, VA	10.2	14.1	9.4	7.7
Rochester, MN	7.4	8.6	7.4	6.0
Sacramento, CA	12.2	14.9	12.0	8.8
St. Louis, MO	10.5	14.4	9.9	7.7
Salem, OR	13.1	16.8	12.8	8.8
Salt Lake City, UT	8.2	9.2	8.0	6.5
San Antonio, TX	13.8	19.4	12.1	10.7
San Diego, CA	10.7	13.2	10.3	8.9
San Francisco, CA	8.4	9.1	8.1	9.1
San Jose, CA	6.7	6.8	6.3	8.2
Santa Rosa, CA	8.7	10.3	8.6	7.4
Savannah, GA	12.5	17.5	11.5	8.6
Seattle, WA	8.3	9.7	7.9	7.8
Sioux Falls, SD	7.9	8.5	8.0	6.3
Springfield, IL	13.6	20.0	13.2	7.3
Tampa, FL	12.9	17.4	12.1	10.9
Tucson, AZ	15.1	20.2	15.5	8.6
Tulsa, OK	13.4	19.0	12.6	7.6
Tuscaloosa, AL	17.5	22.8	17.0	11.8
Virginia Beach, VA	10.9	16.1	9.8	7.6
Washington, DC	7.7	9.9	7.0	7.1
Wichita, KS	12.6	16.7	12.0	7.6
Wilmington, NC	13.4	16.6	14.2	7.0
Winston-Salem, NC	15.1	23.7	13.6	9.0
Worcester, MA	10.0	12.0	9.6	8.8
U.S.	12.6	17.0	11.8	9.6

Note: Figures are percentage of people whose income during the past 12 months was below the poverty level;
Figures cover the Metropolitan Statistical Area
Source: U.S. Census Bureau, 2017-2021 American Community Survey 5-Year Estimates

Employment by Industry

Metro Area[1]	(A)	(B)	(C)	(D)	(E)	(F)	(G)	(H)	(I)	(J)	(K)	(L)	(M)	(N)
Albuquerque, NM	6.2	n/a	16.6	5.0	19.4	1.4	10.6	4.2	n/a	2.9	16.6	10.5	3.7	2.8
Allentown, PA	3.4	n/a	20.9	3.3	10.0	1.3	8.6	10.5	n/a	3.7	13.2	10.4	11.0	3.7
Anchorage, AK	6.2	5.1	18.4	4.5	19.2	1.9	10.8	1.3	1.1	3.6	11.3	11.5	8.5	2.8
Ann Arbor, MI	2.0	n/a	13.1	3.1	38.2	2.6	7.0	5.5	n/a	2.6	13.6	7.2	2.2	3.0
Athens, GA	n/a	n/a	n/a	n/a	27.8	n/a	11.5	n/a	n/a	n/a	9.0	11.1	n/a	n/a
Atlanta, GA	4.7	4.6	13.1	6.7	11.3	3.8	9.8	5.9	0.1	3.5	19.4	10.1	6.5	5.3
Austin, TX	5.9	n/a	11.2	6.0	14.3	4.1	11.2	5.5	n/a	3.8	21.6	9.2	2.8	4.5
Baltimore, MD	6.0	n/a	19.1	5.5	16.0	1.1	8.6	4.2	n/a	3.4	17.7	9.0	5.8	3.7
Boise City, ID	8.4	n/a	14.8	5.8	13.2	1.2	10.1	7.6	n/a	3.4	15.4	10.6	4.4	5.0
Boston, MA[4]	3.9	n/a	22.9	8.3	10.3	3.6	9.0	4.0	n/a	3.4	21.9	7.2	2.5	3.0
Boulder, CO	2.9	n/a	12.7	3.5	19.4	4.0	9.5	10.8	n/a	4.0	20.6	8.0	1.1	3.6
Brownsville, TX	2.3	n/a	30.2	3.2	18.6	0.4	11.0	4.6	n/a	2.2	10.7	11.5	3.4	2.0
Cape Coral, FL	12.5	n/a	11.7	5.0	14.6	1.1	14.9	2.6	n/a	3.7	14.5	14.3	2.4	2.8
Cedar Rapids, IA	6.0	n/a	15.3	7.4	11.5	2.1	8.2	13.9	n/a	3.5	10.8	10.3	6.9	4.1
Charleston, SC	5.4	n/a	11.7	4.9	16.7	2.2	12.5	7.6	n/a	3.9	16.2	10.9	5.1	3.0
Charlotte, NC	5.6	n/a	10.4	9.1	12.2	2.0	10.6	8.3	n/a	3.7	16.9	10.5	6.0	4.8
Chicago, IL[2]	3.5	3.4	16.2	7.2	10.5	1.9	9.5	7.3	<0.1	4.1	19.2	8.9	6.6	5.0
Cincinnati, OH	4.5	n/a	14.7	6.8	11.2	1.2	10.4	10.4	n/a	3.5	16.2	9.4	6.4	5.1
Clarksville, TN	4.3	n/a	13.2	3.4	19.4	1.2	12.1	12.0	n/a	3.4	10.2	14.2	3.4	n/a
Cleveland, OH	3.7	n/a	19.4	7.0	12.3	1.5	9.0	11.4	n/a	3.6	14.4	9.1	3.6	5.0
College Station, TX	5.7	n/a	11.3	3.2	34.3	1.1	13.9	4.4	n/a	2.6	9.5	10.0	1.9	2.1
Colorado Springs, CO	5.9	n/a	13.8	5.8	17.7	1.6	12.1	3.7	n/a	6.8	17.0	10.3	3.3	2.0
Columbia, MO	n/a	n/a	n/a	n/a	28.2	n/a	n/a	n/a	n/a	n/a	n/a	10.5	n/a	n/a
Columbia, SC	4.0	n/a	12.8	8.6	19.9	1.2	9.2	7.6	n/a	4.1	13.7	10.8	4.2	3.8
Columbus, OH	4.2	n/a	14.1	7.3	16.0	1.6	9.1	6.4	n/a	3.8	16.5	9.0	8.5	3.6
Dallas, TX[2]	5.3	n/a	11.4	9.7	10.9	2.8	9.2	6.5	n/a	3.0	20.6	8.9	5.9	5.9
Davenport, IA	n/a	n/a	n/a	n/a	n/a	n/a	n/a	n/a	n/a	n/a	n/a	n/a	n/a	n/a
Denver, CO	6.9	n/a	12.2	7.3	12.7	3.3	10.6	4.5	n/a	4.1	19.6	8.9	5.0	4.9
Des Moines, IA	5.9	n/a	14.3	14.3	12.3	1.6	8.7	5.9	n/a	3.3	13.5	10.6	4.5	5.0
Durham, NC	2.9	n/a	21.9	4.8	18.9	1.8	7.7	8.5	n/a	3.4	17.5	7.1	2.5	2.8
Edison, NJ[2]	3.6	n/a	22.7	9.0	12.4	3.9	8.9	2.6	n/a	4.0	16.5	8.3	4.3	3.7
El Paso, TX	5.1	n/a	14.5	3.9	20.7	1.8	11.7	5.5	n/a	2.7	12.2	12.1	6.4	3.6
Fargo, ND	6.0	n/a	19.2	7.5	13.5	1.8	9.6	7.9	n/a	3.3	10.0	10.0	5.0	6.1
Fort Collins, CO	6.8	n/a	10.9	4.0	24.0	1.5	11.9	8.3	n/a	3.6	11.9	11.4	2.4	3.2
Fort Wayne, IN	5.2	n/a	18.4	5.5	9.4	0.8	9.0	16.4	n/a	5.0	9.7	10.7	5.1	4.8
Fort Worth, TX[2]	6.6	n/a	12.8	6.4	11.9	0.9	10.5	9.3	n/a	3.4	13.4	10.7	9.0	4.9
Grand Rapids, MI	4.7	n/a	16.5	4.8	8.6	1.2	8.2	20.0	n/a	3.9	13.8	8.7	3.5	6.0
Greeley, CO	15.1	n/a	9.9	4.1	16.5	0.5	9.3	12.3	n/a	3.2	10.5	10.6	4.2	4.0
Green Bay, WI	4.7	n/a	15.3	6.2	11.5	0.8	8.9	17.7	n/a	4.5	10.6	9.9	5.1	5.0
Greensboro, NC	4.8	n/a	14.6	4.6	11.9	1.1	9.9	13.8	n/a	3.4	12.6	11.2	6.3	5.8
Honolulu, HI	6.2	n/a	14.5	4.7	21.0	1.6	15.3	2.1	n/a	4.4	12.2	9.7	5.4	3.0
Houston, TX	8.8	6.7	13.2	5.5	13.4	1.0	10.3	6.9	2.0	3.5	16.6	9.8	5.9	5.2
Huntsville, AL	3.9	n/a	8.5	3.1	20.4	1.0	8.2	12.0	n/a	3.3	25.5	10.1	1.7	2.4
Indianapolis, IN	5.3	5.2	14.9	6.6	12.1	1.1	9.0	8.3	0.1	3.9	16.6	9.0	8.3	4.8
Jacksonville, FL	6.4	6.3	15.2	9.4	10.0	1.7	11.2	4.5	0.1	3.4	16.3	10.9	7.4	3.7
Kansas City, MO	5.1	n/a	14.5	7.0	12.9	1.5	9.7	7.6	n/a	4.0	17.1	9.8	6.3	4.6
Lafayette, LA	10.5	5.4	17.2	5.5	12.8	0.9	10.6	8.1	5.2	3.5	10.4	12.9	3.2	4.4
Las Cruces, NM	4.7	n/a	22.7	3.1	26.7	0.8	11.4	4.4	n/a	2.1	9.1	9.9	3.2	1.9
Las Vegas, NV	7.3	7.3	10.8	5.4	10.0	1.2	25.9	2.6	<0.1	2.9	14.8	10.4	6.4	2.4
Lexington, KY	4.8	n/a	13.0	4.0	19.0	1.0	11.1	10.8	n/a	4.4	13.2	10.2	4.5	3.8
Lincoln, NE	5.5	n/a	15.7	5.6	22.1	1.9	9.4	7.7	n/a	3.9	10.3	9.8	5.8	2.2
Little Rock, AR	4.9	n/a	16.2	6.4	17.9	1.5	8.6	5.1	n/a	6.6	12.3	10.2	5.8	4.6
Los Angeles, CA[2]	3.2	3.2	19.4	4.7	12.3	5.0	11.4	6.9	<0.1	3.4	14.9	9.2	5.1	4.4
Louisville, KY	4.3	n/a	14.7	6.8	10.5	1.3	9.3	12.4	n/a	3.7	12.9	9.4	10.2	4.6
Madison, WI	4.8	n/a	12.3	5.8	21.7	4.6	7.9	9.3	n/a	5.0	12.6	9.5	2.8	3.7
Manchester, NH[3]	5.0	n/a	22.7	6.5	10.3	2.2	8.4	6.9	n/a	4.1	16.2	10.8	3.0	3.9

Table continued on following page.

Metro Area[1]	(A)	(B)	(C)	(D)	(E)	(F)	(G)	(H)	(I)	(J)	(K)	(L)	(M)	(N)
Miami, FL[2]	4.0	4.0	16.4	7.1	10.9	1.9	11.1	3.4	<0.1	3.7	16.4	11.6	7.5	6.0
Midland, TX	33.3	n/a	6.6	4.5	8.4	1.0	9.8	4.2	n/a	3.5	9.8	8.3	4.9	5.7
Milwaukee, WI	4.0	3.9	20.3	6.0	9.6	1.4	8.4	13.5	0.1	5.2	13.9	8.9	4.2	4.6
Minneapolis, MN	4.1	n/a	18.0	7.6	12.5	1.5	8.9	10.5	n/a	3.6	15.4	9.3	4.3	4.3
Nashville, TN	5.2	n/a	14.6	6.7	10.9	2.8	11.0	7.5	n/a	4.1	17.3	9.2	6.6	4.2
New Haven, CT[3]	3.7	n/a	29.2	3.9	11.9	1.3	8.7	7.8	n/a	3.5	10.4	9.0	6.7	3.9
New Orleans, LA	5.6	5.1	19.0	5.1	12.1	1.6	14.0	5.3	0.6	4.0	13.5	10.6	5.3	3.9
New York, NY[2]	3.6	n/a	22.7	9.0	12.4	3.9	8.9	2.6	n/a	4.0	16.5	8.3	4.3	3.7
Oklahoma City, OK	6.6	4.9	15.4	5.4	18.8	0.9	11.2	5.2	1.6	4.2	13.3	10.4	5.2	3.4
Omaha, NE	6.3	n/a	16.3	8.3	13.3	2.0	9.7	6.9	n/a	3.8	14.2	10.5	5.3	3.3
Orlando, FL	6.0	6.0	12.6	6.3	8.9	1.9	19.4	3.7	<0.1	3.1	19.3	10.8	4.5	3.6
Philadelphia, PA[2]	2.5	n/a	31.6	6.5	12.7	2.0	9.1	3.3	n/a	4.0	14.5	7.4	4.2	2.4
Phoenix, AZ	6.6	6.4	15.9	9.3	10.2	1.8	10.1	6.4	0.1	3.1	17.0	10.5	5.1	4.0
Pittsburgh, PA	5.4	4.7	21.2	6.5	9.7	1.9	9.6	7.2	0.7	4.0	16.6	10.1	4.4	3.6
Portland, OR	6.7	6.6	15.0	6.2	12.2	2.3	9.4	10.2	0.1	3.4	16.2	9.7	4.3	4.6
Providence, RI[3]	4.8	4.8	20.8	6.4	12.8	1.2	10.6	8.6	<0.1	4.4	12.7	10.9	3.4	3.4
Provo, UT	10.0	n/a	19.8	4.2	11.7	4.7	8.6	7.7	n/a	2.3	15.0	11.7	1.8	2.5
Raleigh, NC	6.6	n/a	13.0	5.7	13.8	3.6	10.4	4.7	n/a	4.0	20.4	10.2	3.5	4.1
Reno, NV	8.4	8.3	11.1	4.4	12.1	1.4	14.4	10.8	0.1	2.4	12.7	9.3	9.4	3.9
Richmond, VA	5.8	n/a	14.1	8.0	16.2	0.9	9.2	4.6	n/a	4.5	17.7	9.6	5.4	4.0
Rochester, MN	4.0	n/a	43.3	2.4	10.5	0.9	8.5	7.9	n/a	3.0	5.4	9.9	2.1	2.1
Sacramento, CA	6.8	6.8	16.9	4.9	22.7	1.0	10.3	3.7	<0.1	3.5	14.0	9.6	4.0	2.6
Salem, OR	7.6	7.3	17.8	3.8	24.5	0.9	8.8	6.7	0.3	3.0	9.5	11.0	4.1	2.3
Salt Lake City, UT	7.0	n/a	11.5	7.6	13.6	3.2	8.3	7.8	n/a	2.8	17.8	9.9	5.8	4.5
San Antonio, TX	5.9	5.3	14.9	8.9	15.6	1.7	12.2	5.1	0.6	3.5	14.0	10.9	4.1	3.3
San Diego, CA	5.7	5.6	15.0	4.8	15.9	1.4	12.8	7.6	<0.1	3.6	18.6	9.1	2.7	2.8
San Francisco, CA[2]	3.4	3.4	13.1	7.4	10.9	10.6	10.2	3.3	<0.1	3.2	26.3	5.7	4.1	1.9
San Jose, CA	4.8	4.7	16.3	3.3	8.3	9.1	8.5	15.4	<0.1	2.1	21.7	6.4	1.8	2.4
Santa Rosa, CA	7.9	7.8	17.3	4.0	12.7	1.3	12.4	11.5	0.1	3.6	12.2	11.4	2.3	3.5
Savannah, GA	4.7	n/a	14.1	3.5	11.8	0.8	13.7	9.8	n/a	4.0	12.6	12.0	9.5	3.5
Seattle, WA[2]	6.1	6.0	12.9	5.0	11.7	7.9	8.7	8.1	<0.1	3.3	20.0	8.1	4.2	4.1
Sioux Falls, SD	5.8	n/a	21.6	9.1	9.1	1.5	9.5	8.7	n/a	3.9	9.8	11.8	3.8	5.5
Springfield, IL	3.4	n/a	19.2	5.6	24.1	2.0	9.6	3.3	n/a	5.5	11.4	10.9	2.3	2.9
St. Louis, MO	5.0	n/a	18.6	6.9	10.9	2.0	10.0	8.3	n/a	3.8	15.5	9.6	4.7	4.8
Tampa, FL	6.2	6.2	15.2	9.1	10.2	1.9	10.8	4.9	<0.1	3.3	19.3	11.3	3.6	4.1
Tucson, AZ	5.4	4.9	16.8	4.8	19.3	1.3	11.2	7.2	0.5	3.5	12.8	10.6	5.2	2.0
Tulsa, OK	6.1	5.3	16.0	5.2	12.7	1.2	10.1	10.7	0.8	4.5	13.8	11.0	5.2	3.7
Tuscaloosa, AL	5.7	n/a	8.5	3.5	25.7	0.7	10.3	16.8	n/a	4.1	9.3	10.4	3.1	1.9
Virginia Beach, VA	5.2	n/a	14.8	5.0	19.7	1.2	11.1	7.4	n/a	4.2	14.7	10.4	4.0	2.4
Washington, DC[2]	4.8	n/a	12.9	4.4	22.2	2.5	9.2	1.4	n/a	6.2	24.3	7.6	2.7	1.9
Wichita, KS	5.7	n/a	14.9	3.9	14.3	1.2	10.8	16.8	n/a	3.7	11.3	10.3	4.0	3.1
Wilmington, NC	7.4	n/a	17.0	5.1	12.6	2.0	14.8	4.2	n/a	4.2	13.1	12.7	3.3	3.5
Winston-Salem, NC	4.3	n/a	20.1	5.0	11.3	0.7	10.5	12.6	n/a	3.5	12.9	11.6	4.5	3.1
Worcester, MA[3]	4.1	n/a	23.5	4.8	15.7	0.9	8.3	9.2	n/a	3.6	11.1	10.2	5.3	3.2
U.S.	5.4	5.0	16.1	5.9	14.5	2.0	10.3	8.4	0.4	3.7	14.7	10.2	4.9	3.9

Note: All figures are percentages covering non-farm employment as of December 2022 and are not seasonally adjusted;
(1) Figures cover the Metropolitan Statistical Area (MSA) except where noted. See Appendix B for areas included; (2) Metropolitan Division; (3) New England City and Town Area; (4) New England City and Town Area Division; (A) Construction, Mining, and Logging (some areas report Construction separate from Mining and Logging); (B) Construction; (C) Private Education and Health Services; (D) Financial Activities; (E) Government; (F) Information; (G) Leisure and Hospitality; (H) Manufacturing; (I) Mining and Logging; (J) Other Services; (K) Professional and Business Services; (L) Retail Trade; (M) Transportation and Utilities; (N) Wholesale Trade; n/a not available
Source: Bureau of Labor Statistics, Current Employment Statistics, Employment, Hours, and Earnings, December 2022

Labor Force, Employment and Job Growth: City

City	Civilian Labor Force			Workers Employed		
	Dec. 2021	Dec. 2022	% Chg.	Dec. 2021	Dec. 2022	% Chg.
Albuquerque, NM	286,208	278,969	-2.5	272,867	270,719	-0.7
Allentown, PA	55,657	56,449	1.4	52,269	54,138	3.5
Anchorage, AK	154,601	155,471	0.5	148,017	150,605	1.7
Ann Arbor, MI	63,522	64,736	1.9	62,006	63,139	1.8
Athens, GA	60,379	61,240	1.4	58,643	59,627	1.6
Atlanta, GA	271,164	274,219	1.1	261,888	265,951	1.5
Austin, TX	626,475	642,058	2.4	609,403	625,541	2.6
Baltimore, MD	280,450	278,592	-0.6	262,676	266,256	1.3
Boise City, ID	135,152	140,433	3.9	132,075	137,857	4.3
Boston, MA	394,417	392,029	-0.6	379,015	380,790	0.4
Boulder, CO	66,246	67,538	1.9	64,727	66,197	2.2
Brownsville, TX	78,951	79,589	0.8	73,562	74,739	1.6
Cape Coral, FL	96,606	100,709	4.2	93,922	97,833	4.1
Cedar Rapids, IA	69,935	70,822	1.2	66,849	68,200	2.0
Charleston, SC	75,129	76,762	2.1	73,011	74,897	2.5
Charlotte, NC	498,644	513,354	2.9	481,757	496,911	3.1
Chicago, IL	1,370,152	1,365,082	-0.3	1,301,665	1,299,230	-0.1
Cincinnati, OH	147,147	145,962	-0.8	141,899	140,924	-0.6
Clarksville, TN	64,581	62,625	-3.0	62,259	60,449	-2.9
Cleveland, OH	154,230	153,656	-0.3	144,455	146,635	1.5
College Station, TX	63,443	64,403	1.5	61,598	62,625	1.6
Colorado Springs, CO	243,995	246,112	0.8	234,766	238,820	1.7
Columbia, MO	68,593	68,729	0.2	67,043	67,523	0.7
Columbia, SC	56,736	55,816	-1.6	54,797	54,043	-1.3
Columbus, OH	484,399	482,990	-0.2	469,341	467,547	-0.3
Dallas, TX	707,758	735,922	3.9	679,409	711,095	4.6
Davenport, IA	50,142	51,938	3.5	47,788	49,912	4.4
Denver, CO	428,646	439,359	2.5	411,447	426,400	3.6
Des Moines, IA	109,744	111,230	1.3	104,975	107,148	2.0
Durham, NC	155,641	159,589	2.5	151,405	155,264	2.5
Edison, NJ	55,370	56,778	2.5	53,727	55,594	3.4
El Paso, TX	302,469	303,815	0.4	288,907	292,314	1.1
Fargo, ND	72,514	72,188	-0.4	70,902	70,818	-0.1
Fort Collins, CO	100,891	102,741	1.8	98,235	100,394	2.2
Fort Wayne, IN	126,450	130,964	3.5	124,397	127,828	2.7
Fort Worth, TX	462,444	475,802	2.8	444,256	459,728	3.4
Grand Rapids, MI	101,134	105,118	3.9	96,771	100,836	4.2
Greeley, CO	51,681	51,829	0.2	49,366	50,105	1.5
Green Bay, WI	53,463	52,666	-1.4	52,235	51,500	-1.4
Greensboro, NC	143,008	144,251	0.8	137,220	138,826	1.1
Honolulu, HI	459,370	457,096	-0.5	440,467	441,407	0.2
Houston, TX	1,138,573	1,173,802	3.0	1,085,474	1,128,659	3.9
Huntsville, AL	102,295	104,297	1.9	100,086	102,254	2.1
Indianapolis, IN	450,127	464,032	3.0	441,617	452,513	2.4
Jacksonville, FL	470,543	493,413	4.8	456,509	481,988	5.5
Kansas City, MO	257,158	258,850	0.6	247,609	252,172	1.8
Lafayette, LA	59,534	60,606	1.8	57,818	58,830	1.7
Las Cruces, NM	48,477	48,211	-0.5	46,260	46,735	1.0
Las Vegas, NV	301,290	316,801	5.1	286,123	299,424	4.6
Lexington, KY	175,989	174,916	-0.6	170,668	170,430	-0.1
Lincoln, NE	161,763	164,641	1.7	159,144	161,093	1.2
Little Rock, AR	95,576	95,929	0.3	92,287	93,043	0.8
Los Angeles, CA	2,047,789	2,027,026	-1.0	1,931,445	1,935,875	0.2
Louisville, KY	400,329	398,800	-0.3	384,379	387,119	0.7
Madison, WI	162,642	161,298	-0.8	160,375	158,871	-0.9

Table continued on following page.

City	Civilian Labor Force			Workers Employed		
	Dec. 2021	Dec. 2022	% Chg.	Dec. 2021	Dec. 2022	% Chg.
Manchester, NH	63,249	66,044	4.4	61,619	64,357	4.4
Miami, FL	227,422	231,754	1.9	220,939	228,420	3.3
Midland, TX	83,370	84,916	1.8	80,102	82,715	3.2
Milwaukee, WI	272,797	266,036	-2.4	262,401	257,421	-1.9
Minneapolis, MN	241,913	246,063	1.7	235,948	240,094	1.7
Nashville, TN	413,734	407,521	-1.5	402,245	397,879	-1.0
New Haven, CT	65,615	66,515	1.3	62,503	64,310	2.8
New Orleans, LA	175,708	180,265	2.5	166,032	172,381	3.8
New York, NY	4,085,159	4,113,259	0.6	3,782,405	3,907,975	3.3
Oklahoma City, OK	327,538	333,291	1.7	320,689	324,655	1.2
Omaha, NE	250,414	253,695	1.3	244,895	246,725	0.7
Orlando, FL	168,524	173,274	2.8	162,788	169,122	3.8
Philadelphia, PA	712,569	723,233	1.5	667,785	690,464	3.4
Phoenix, AZ	865,943	889,029	2.6	842,267	864,868	2.6
Pittsburgh, PA	148,500	152,028	2.3	142,551	147,423	3.4
Portland, OR	387,410	393,179	1.4	373,537	376,724	0.8
Providence, RI	88,878	88,200	-0.7	85,136	85,603	0.5
Provo, UT	70,289	73,861	5.0	69,267	72,590	4.8
Raleigh, NC	255,398	264,381	3.5	247,896	256,967	3.6
Reno, NV	134,416	141,155	5.0	131,188	136,416	3.9
Richmond, VA	115,165	116,068	0.7	110,750	112,086	1.2
Rochester, MN	67,368	68,064	1.0	65,967	66,601	0.9
Sacramento, CA	237,842	239,915	0.8	226,017	231,146	2.2
Salem, OR	84,706	83,973	-0.8	81,711	80,171	-1.8
Salt Lake City, UT	121,702	125,773	3.3	119,545	123,299	3.1
San Antonio, TX	735,449	751,540	2.1	707,860	727,368	2.7
San Diego, CA	711,954	721,000	1.2	684,180	701,197	2.4
San Francisco, CA	560,450	578,421	3.2	543,659	566,695	4.2
San Jose, CA	546,462	558,687	2.2	529,424	546,728	3.2
Santa Rosa, CA	85,496	86,918	1.6	82,307	84,605	2.7
Savannah, GA	69,179	68,684	-0.7	66,698	66,661	0.0
Seattle, WA	483,713	490,565	1.4	471,546	477,991	1.3
Sioux Falls, SD	109,388	111,832	2.2	106,662	109,520	2.6
Springfield, IL	55,434	55,938	0.9	53,040	53,888	1.6
St. Louis, MO	150,418	149,690	-0.4	143,212	145,026	1.2
Tampa, FL	211,042	219,467	3.9	205,058	214,586	4.6
Tucson, AZ	257,903	262,655	1.8	249,443	254,180	1.9
Tulsa, OK	194,312	199,027	2.4	189,673	193,469	2.0
Tuscaloosa, AL	46,912	47,393	1.0	45,459	46,256	1.7
Virginia Beach, VA	222,270	227,788	2.4	216,500	221,941	2.5
Washington, DC	378,144	386,520	2.2	358,132	370,787	3.5
Wichita, KS	190,708	192,293	0.8	184,998	186,223	0.6
Wilmington, NC	65,317	66,641	2.0	63,471	64,589	1.7
Winston-Salem, NC	116,216	117,459	1.0	112,011	113,308	1.1
Worcester, MA	93,362	90,627	-2.9	88,807	87,239	-1.7
U.S.	161,696,000	164,224,000	1.6	155,732,000	158,872,000	2.0

Note: Data is not seasonally adjusted and covers workers 16 years of age and older
Source: Bureau of Labor Statistics, Local Area Unemployment Statistics

Labor Force, Employment and Job Growth: Metro Area

Metro Area[1]	Civilian Labor Force			Workers Employed		
	Dec. 2021	Dec. 2022	% Chg.	Dec. 2021	Dec. 2022	% Chg.
Albuquerque, NM	445,726	434,352	-2.5	424,396	421,074	-0.7
Allentown, PA	447,351	458,516	2.5	428,287	443,287	3.5
Anchorage, AK	205,827	206,845	0.4	196,305	199,569	1.6
Ann Arbor, MI	192,598	196,315	1.9	187,000	190,417	1.8
Athens, GA	102,226	103,727	1.4	99,578	101,194	1.6
Atlanta, GA	3,175,581	3,216,104	1.2	3,085,734	3,133,430	1.5
Austin, TX	1,339,834	1,372,624	2.4	1,301,083	1,335,791	2.6
Baltimore, MD	1,501,247	1,502,740	0.1	1,434,164	1,455,751	1.5
Boise City, ID	400,832	416,686	3.9	390,861	407,819	4.3
Boston, MA[4]	1,673,210	1,666,434	-0.4	1,614,446	1,622,005	0.4
Boulder, CO	198,590	201,887	1.6	193,073	197,458	2.2
Brownsville, TX	175,175	176,374	0.6	163,657	166,276	1.6
Cape Coral, FL	362,039	377,849	4.3	352,239	366,908	4.1
Cedar Rapids, IA	140,768	142,727	1.3	135,170	137,743	1.9
Charleston, SC	400,171	408,735	2.1	388,529	398,569	2.5
Charlotte, NC	1,377,149	1,414,791	2.7	1,332,923	1,371,461	2.8
Chicago, IL[2]	3,826,621	3,838,545	0.3	3,671,983	3,676,358	0.1
Cincinnati, OH	1,123,242	1,116,215	-0.6	1,088,875	1,082,108	-0.6
Clarksville, TN	120,311	117,511	-2.3	115,795	113,311	-2.1
Cleveland, OH	1,006,515	1,010,141	0.3	963,990	975,650	1.2
College Station, TX	138,941	140,832	1.3	134,636	136,870	1.6
Colorado Springs, CO	364,630	367,853	0.8	350,819	356,889	1.7
Columbia, MO	100,630	100,708	0.0	98,278	98,981	0.7
Columbia, SC	399,511	392,721	-1.7	387,182	381,702	-1.4
Columbus, OH	1,121,138	1,118,600	-0.2	1,088,089	1,084,246	-0.3
Dallas, TX[2]	2,825,024	2,943,498	4.1	2,723,620	2,851,201	4.6
Davenport, IA	185,485	190,708	2.8	177,815	183,615	3.2
Denver, CO	1,691,446	1,735,541	2.6	1,629,015	1,687,640	3.6
Des Moines, IA	362,322	367,598	1.4	350,192	357,259	2.0
Durham, NC	311,304	319,367	2.5	303,354	310,936	2.5
Edison, NJ[2]	6,978,612	7,057,593	1.1	6,599,840	6,759,099	2.4
El Paso, TX	365,233	366,661	0.3	347,953	352,057	1.1
Fargo, ND	143,613	142,810	-0.5	140,498	140,046	-0.3
Fort Collins, CO	208,863	212,087	1.5	202,604	207,057	2.2
Fort Wayne, IN	213,153	220,727	3.5	210,157	215,921	2.7
Fort Worth, TX[2]	1,345,295	1,384,350	2.9	1,295,323	1,340,078	3.4
Grand Rapids, MI	563,869	586,790	4.0	545,813	568,603	4.1
Greeley, CO	167,574	168,716	0.6	161,228	163,640	1.5
Green Bay, WI	173,797	170,959	-1.6	170,171	167,408	-1.6
Greensboro, NC	360,317	364,357	1.1	347,114	351,304	1.2
Honolulu, HI	459,370	457,096	-0.5	440,467	441,407	0.2
Houston, TX	3,460,832	3,565,905	3.0	3,294,015	3,425,418	3.9
Huntsville, AL	239,285	244,014	1.9	234,543	239,596	2.1
Indianapolis, IN	1,076,300	1,110,642	3.1	1,060,871	1,086,712	2.4
Jacksonville, FL	806,862	847,564	5.0	785,663	829,550	5.5
Kansas City, MO	1,138,286	1,149,586	0.9	1,105,453	1,121,442	1.4
Lafayette, LA	211,602	215,089	1.6	204,894	208,467	1.7
Las Cruces, NM	99,600	99,107	-0.5	94,429	95,399	1.0
Las Vegas, NV	1,093,227	1,149,504	5.1	1,039,029	1,087,331	4.6
Lexington, KY	275,622	274,006	-0.5	267,238	266,822	-0.1
Lincoln, NE	188,166	191,439	1.7	185,143	187,374	1.2
Little Rock, AR	350,674	353,640	0.8	341,122	343,843	0.8
Los Angeles, CA[2]	5,001,852	4,965,511	-0.7	4,701,620	4,747,043	0.9
Louisville, KY	672,926	678,057	0.7	650,589	659,926	1.4
Madison, WI	400,355	395,887	-1.1	393,718	389,430	-1.0

Table continued on following page.

Metro Area[1]	Civilian Labor Force			Workers Employed		
	Dec. 2021	Dec. 2022	% Chg.	Dec. 2021	Dec. 2022	% Chg.
Manchester, NH[3]	118,844	124,173	4.4	116,140	121,300	4.4
Miami, FL[2]	1,345,385	1,397,307	3.8	1,304,718	1,369,536	4.9
Midland, TX	103,649	105,497	1.7	99,519	102,761	3.2
Milwaukee, WI	817,582	799,375	-2.2	796,196	780,437	-1.9
Minneapolis, MN	1,991,752	2,028,489	1.8	1,943,478	1,975,295	1.6
Nashville, TN	1,124,910	1,111,047	-1.2	1,096,732	1,085,200	-1.0
New Haven, CT[3]	327,755	334,058	1.9	315,344	324,400	2.8
New Orleans, LA	582,640	600,820	3.1	558,375	579,744	3.8
New York, NY[2]	6,978,612	7,057,593	1.1	6,599,840	6,759,099	2.4
Oklahoma City, OK	699,178	711,592	1.7	685,472	694,168	1.2
Omaha, NE	502,000	508,654	1.3	490,956	495,693	0.9
Orlando, FL	1,366,646	1,407,116	2.9	1,323,163	1,374,399	3.8
Philadelphia, PA[2]	1,004,235	1,021,788	1.7	946,859	979,293	3.4
Phoenix, AZ	2,518,007	2,590,356	2.8	2,453,226	2,520,303	2.7
Pittsburgh, PA	1,147,805	1,177,164	2.5	1,096,709	1,134,155	3.4
Portland, OR	1,369,607	1,391,563	1.6	1,322,133	1,334,787	0.9
Providence, RI[3]	706,157	698,803	-1.0	679,845	680,282	0.0
Provo, UT	345,721	363,397	5.1	340,264	356,597	4.8
Raleigh, NC	737,649	764,883	3.6	718,092	744,560	3.6
Reno, NV	249,159	261,626	5.0	243,158	252,847	3.9
Richmond, VA	664,206	670,336	0.9	643,038	650,950	1.2
Rochester, MN	126,103	127,371	1.0	123,345	124,243	0.7
Sacramento, CA	1,102,380	1,115,511	1.1	1,055,002	1,078,900	2.2
Salem, OR	210,043	208,341	-0.8	202,733	198,916	-1.8
Salt Lake City, UT	699,196	722,471	3.3	686,309	707,898	3.1
San Antonio, TX	1,217,217	1,244,094	2.2	1,171,224	1,203,295	2.7
San Diego, CA	1,570,184	1,588,968	1.2	1,505,925	1,543,381	2.4
San Francisco, CA[2]	1,003,772	1,035,986	3.2	974,872	1,015,702	4.1
San Jose, CA	1,067,389	1,093,480	2.4	1,036,363	1,070,252	3.2
Santa Rosa, CA	243,938	248,408	1.8	235,525	242,101	2.7
Savannah, GA	199,752	198,853	-0.4	194,065	193,933	0.0
Seattle, WA[2]	1,724,262	1,779,111	3.1	1,675,402	1,725,495	2.9
Sioux Falls, SD	159,168	162,847	2.3	155,392	159,650	2.7
Springfield, IL	103,907	105,050	1.1	99,703	101,310	1.6
St. Louis, MO	1,460,514	1,459,027	-0.1	1,407,703	1,422,207	1.0
Tampa, FL	1,596,468	1,661,495	4.0	1,552,983	1,625,105	4.6
Tucson, AZ	482,383	492,280	2.0	468,330	477,224	1.9
Tulsa, OK	479,679	491,520	2.4	468,777	478,458	2.0
Tuscaloosa, AL	114,876	116,118	1.0	111,656	113,579	1.7
Virginia Beach, VA	821,309	840,432	2.3	795,009	815,342	2.5
Washington, DC[2]	2,676,340	2,681,074	0.1	2,582,644	2,604,564	0.8
Wichita, KS	317,498	320,744	1.0	309,104	311,289	0.7
Wilmington, NC	154,267	157,407	2.0	150,051	152,775	1.8
Winston-Salem, NC	322,524	326,477	1.2	312,552	316,261	1.1
Worcester, MA[3]	358,980	351,150	-2.1	344,046	339,514	-1.3
U.S.	161,696,000	164,224,000	1.6	155,732,000	158,872,000	2.0

Note: Data is not seasonally adjusted and covers workers 16 years of age and older; (1) Figures cover the Metropolitan Statistical Area (MSA) except where noted. See Appendix B for areas included; (2) Metropolitan Division; (3) New England City and Town Area; (4) New England City and Town Area Division
Source: Bureau of Labor Statistics, Local Area Unemployment Statistics

Unemployment Rate: City

City	2022											
	Jan.	Feb.	Mar.	Apr.	May	Jun.	Jul.	Aug.	Sep.	Oct.	Nov.	Dec.
Albuquerque, NM	4.9	4.3	4.0	3.9	3.7	4.4	4.1	4.0	4.0	3.6	3.2	3.0
Allentown, PA	7.3	6.5	6.1	6.0	5.8	6.2	6.2	6.5	5.0	4.6	4.6	4.1
Anchorage, AK	4.8	4.4	4.0	3.9	3.7	3.8	3.6	2.9	2.9	3.1	3.3	3.1
Ann Arbor, MI	2.7	3.1	2.5	2.5	3.0	3.4	3.3	2.9	2.7	2.7	2.5	2.5
Athens, GA	3.2	3.2	3.2	2.3	2.7	3.5	2.9	3.2	2.5	3.1	2.7	2.6
Atlanta, GA	4.0	3.8	3.9	2.9	3.1	3.7	3.4	3.5	3.1	3.4	3.2	3.0
Austin, TX	3.2	3.2	2.6	2.4	2.6	2.9	2.9	2.9	2.7	2.7	2.6	2.6
Baltimore, MD	6.3	6.1	5.8	4.9	5.1	6.1	5.6	5.9	5.1	5.6	5.0	4.4
Boise City, ID	2.8	2.7	2.5	2.0	2.0	2.4	2.2	2.3	2.3	2.4	2.3	1.8
Boston, MA	4.4	3.5	3.2	3.0	3.2	3.5	3.6	3.5	3.0	2.9	2.7	2.9
Boulder, CO	2.6	2.7	2.3	2.1	2.2	2.8	3.0	2.4	2.3	2.6	2.7	2.0
Brownsville, TX	7.9	7.4	6.1	6.0	6.1	7.1	6.9	6.4	5.9	5.5	5.7	6.1
Cape Coral, FL	3.4	2.9	2.6	2.3	2.4	2.8	2.7	2.6	2.5	4.2	3.6	2.9
Cedar Rapids, IA	4.9	3.9	3.6	2.7	2.9	3.4	3.7	3.8	3.3	3.4	3.7	3.7
Charleston, SC	3.1	3.5	2.9	2.1	2.5	2.8	2.6	2.6	2.4	2.8	2.2	2.4
Charlotte, NC	4.0	3.8	3.7	3.5	3.5	3.9	3.6	3.9	3.3	3.8	3.7	3.2
Chicago, IL	5.8	5.5	5.0	4.7	4.9	5.7	5.8	5.9	5.6	5.2	5.3	4.8
Cincinnati, OH	4.6	4.2	3.8	3.5	3.5	4.6	4.8	4.8	3.9	4.2	3.3	3.5
Clarksville, TN	4.0	3.6	3.4	3.5	3.9	4.8	4.6	4.1	3.6	4.1	3.9	3.5
Cleveland, OH	7.7	8.0	8.2	7.5	7.2	7.7	6.5	6.0	5.9	6.4	5.8	4.6
College Station, TX	3.5	3.4	2.7	2.6	2.8	3.6	3.3	3.3	3.0	3.0	3.2	2.8
Colorado Springs, CO	4.1	4.2	3.6	3.2	3.1	3.4	3.8	3.6	3.5	3.7	3.5	3.0
Columbia, MO	3.0	2.2	2.4	1.7	2.4	1.9	2.4	2.5	1.5	1.9	1.9	1.8
Columbia, SC	3.7	4.3	3.5	2.9	3.9	4.0	3.9	3.7	3.4	4.2	3.3	3.2
Columbus, OH	3.9	3.8	3.4	3.1	3.1	3.9	3.8	4.0	3.4	3.7	2.9	3.2
Dallas, TX	4.5	4.4	3.6	3.4	3.5	4.0	4.0	3.9	3.6	3.6	3.5	3.4
Davenport, IA	5.5	4.4	4.1	3.1	3.2	4.0	4.0	3.9	3.3	3.4	3.8	3.9
Denver, CO	4.3	4.3	3.9	3.4	3.3	3.4	3.6	3.6	3.5	3.7	3.4	2.9
Des Moines, IA	5.7	4.7	4.3	3.0	2.8	3.0	3.2	3.3	2.8	2.9	3.2	3.7
Durham, NC	3.2	3.0	3.0	2.9	3.1	3.5	3.1	3.3	2.7	3.4	3.2	2.7
Edison, NJ	3.3	3.0	2.9	2.5	2.5	2.8	2.7	2.6	2.0	2.1	2.1	2.1
El Paso, TX	5.1	5.0	4.1	4.0	4.2	4.7	4.5	4.4	4.1	4.1	4.1	3.8
Fargo, ND	2.7	2.5	2.7	2.1	1.8	2.2	1.7	1.8	1.4	1.5	1.6	1.9
Fort Collins, CO	3.0	3.2	2.7	2.4	2.4	2.8	2.9	2.7	2.6	2.8	2.8	2.3
Fort Wayne, IN	2.5	2.7	2.8	2.5	2.6	3.3	3.6	3.1	2.3	2.9	2.9	2.4
Fort Worth, TX	4.5	4.4	3.6	3.4	3.6	4.2	4.2	4.0	3.7	3.6	3.5	3.4
Grand Rapids, MI	5.0	5.0	4.3	4.2	4.6	5.2	5.0	4.6	4.3	4.2	4.0	4.1
Greeley, CO	4.9	5.0	4.4	3.7	3.5	3.9	4.5	3.9	3.8	3.9	3.7	3.3
Green Bay, WI	3.1	3.1	3.1	2.9	2.8	3.4	3.2	3.4	3.3	2.9	2.5	2.2
Greensboro, NC	4.6	4.5	4.4	4.3	4.3	4.8	4.6	4.8	4.0	4.5	4.4	3.8
Honolulu, HI	3.7	3.5	3.2	3.3	3.4	3.9	3.5	3.4	3.3	3.4	3.8	3.4
Houston, TX	5.3	5.2	4.3	4.1	4.2	4.7	4.8	4.6	4.2	4.1	4.0	3.8
Huntsville, AL	2.8	2.6	2.1	1.7	2.1	3.0	2.8	2.6	2.3	2.3	2.1	2.0
Indianapolis, IN	2.7	3.0	3.0	2.5	2.8	3.5	3.8	3.4	2.4	2.9	3.0	2.5
Jacksonville, FL	3.6	3.2	2.7	2.5	2.6	3.3	3.2	3.1	2.7	2.8	2.7	2.3
Kansas City, MO	4.3	4.3	4.1	3.1	3.2	2.6	3.4	3.4	2.2	2.7	2.7	2.6
Lafayette, LA	3.6	3.1	3.1	2.9	3.1	3.9	3.8	3.2	3.0	2.7	2.6	2.9
Las Cruces, NM	4.8	3.9	3.6	3.5	3.4	4.9	4.7	4.6	4.5	3.8	3.4	3.1
Las Vegas, NV	5.9	5.4	5.2	5.2	5.4	5.8	5.7	5.8	5.4	5.8	5.7	5.5
Lexington, KY	3.3	3.0	3.1	2.8	2.9	3.5	3.3	3.0	2.8	3.3	3.1	2.6
Lincoln, NE	2.3	2.1	2.2	1.8	1.9	2.4	2.3	2.1	1.9	2.1	2.1	2.2
Little Rock, AR	4.3	4.2	3.7	3.8	3.6	4.1	4.6	3.9	3.9	3.3	3.2	3.0
Los Angeles, CA	6.3	5.5	5.0	4.9	4.6	5.3	5.2	5.1	4.6	4.6	4.6	4.5
Louisville, KY	4.7	3.9	4.7	3.1	4.1	3.8	4.1	3.4	3.0	3.5	3.3	2.9
Madison, WI	1.9	2.0	2.0	1.9	2.2	2.8	2.5	2.4	2.6	2.2	2.0	1.5

Table continued on following page.

City	2022											
	Jan.	Feb.	Mar.	Apr.	May	Jun.	Jul.	Aug.	Sep.	Oct.	Nov.	Dec.
Manchester, NH	3.6	2.6	2.5	2.3	1.9	2.0	2.0	2.4	2.4	2.7	2.7	2.6
Miami, FL	3.0	2.6	2.8	2.4	2.2	2.0	2.2	2.2	1.9	1.7	1.5	1.4
Midland, TX	4.3	4.3	3.4	3.2	3.2	3.6	3.5	3.3	3.0	3.0	2.8	2.6
Milwaukee, WI	4.8	5.1	5.0	5.0	4.9	5.4	5.5	5.5	4.8	4.6	4.1	3.2
Minneapolis, MN	3.0	2.2	2.4	1.5	1.7	2.4	2.2	2.3	2.0	1.9	2.0	2.4
Nashville, TN	3.3	2.9	2.7	2.7	2.9	3.5	3.2	2.9	2.5	2.8	2.7	2.4
New Haven, CT	5.5	5.4	4.4	4.1	4.8	5.0	5.6	5.4	4.7	4.7	4.0	3.3
New Orleans, LA	6.5	6.0	5.9	5.5	5.5	6.5	6.6	5.5	4.8	4.1	4.0	4.4
New York, NY	7.8	7.2	6.3	5.7	5.4	5.5	5.4	5.2	4.5	5.0	5.0	5.0
Oklahoma City, OK	2.9	3.0	2.9	2.7	2.8	3.4	3.0	3.3	3.2	3.4	2.9	2.6
Omaha, NE	2.9	2.8	2.7	2.3	2.3	2.9	3.1	2.7	2.4	2.6	2.5	2.7
Orlando, FL	3.9	3.6	3.1	2.9	2.9	3.3	3.1	3.1	2.7	2.8	2.7	2.4
Philadelphia, PA	7.7	6.8	6.3	6.0	5.7	6.2	6.2	6.4	4.9	4.7	4.8	4.5
Phoenix, AZ	3.4	3.3	2.5	2.8	3.0	3.4	3.4	3.5	3.6	3.5	3.0	2.7
Pittsburgh, PA	4.9	4.1	4.0	3.8	3.9	4.3	4.4	4.4	3.2	3.1	3.0	3.0
Portland, OR	4.5	3.9	3.9	3.4	3.0	3.5	3.7	4.1	3.8	3.8	4.1	4.2
Providence, RI	5.5	5.3	3.7	3.3	3.5	3.5	4.0	5.0	4.3	4.1	4.3	2.9
Provo, UT	1.8	1.5	1.6	1.7	2.0	2.4	1.8	1.8	1.6	1.8	1.8	1.7
Raleigh, NC	3.3	3.3	3.2	3.1	3.3	3.6	3.4	3.5	3.0	3.5	3.4	2.8
Reno, NV	3.1	2.8	2.5	2.7	2.9	3.3	3.2	3.5	3.1	3.6	3.5	3.4
Richmond, VA	4.6	4.1	3.7	3.5	3.9	3.8	3.7	4.1	3.4	3.5	3.9	3.4
Rochester, MN	2.6	2.0	2.1	1.2	1.3	1.9	1.7	1.8	1.6	1.5	1.6	2.1
Sacramento, CA	5.7	4.9	4.3	3.7	3.3	3.8	3.8	4.1	3.8	3.9	4.2	3.7
Salem, OR	4.4	4.0	4.0	3.7	3.1	3.8	4.2	4.5	4.1	4.2	4.3	4.5
Salt Lake City, UT	2.4	2.1	2.0	2.1	2.1	2.3	2.1	2.1	1.9	2.1	2.0	2.0
San Antonio, TX	4.3	4.2	3.5	3.3	3.5	4.0	3.9	3.8	3.5	3.5	3.4	3.2
San Diego, CA	4.5	3.9	3.3	2.9	2.6	3.0	2.9	3.2	2.9	3.0	3.2	2.7
San Francisco, CA	3.5	3.0	2.5	2.2	1.9	2.2	2.1	2.3	2.1	2.2	2.3	2.0
San Jose, CA	3.5	3.1	2.6	2.3	2.0	2.4	2.3	2.5	2.2	2.3	2.5	2.1
Santa Rosa, CA	4.3	3.8	3.3	2.7	2.4	2.8	2.7	2.9	2.7	2.8	3.1	2.7
Savannah, GA	4.2	4.0	4.1	3.1	3.2	3.8	3.3	3.5	3.0	3.4	3.1	2.9
Seattle, WA	3.0	2.5	2.1	1.6	1.9	2.4	2.6	2.8	2.6	2.6	2.7	2.6
Sioux Falls, SD	2.6	2.8	2.4	2.0	1.9	2.1	1.7	2.0	1.6	1.9	1.8	2.1
Springfield, IL	5.3	5.0	4.6	4.9	5.2	4.6	4.8	4.9	4.3	4.5	4.3	3.7
St. Louis, MO	5.4	5.0	4.9	3.6	3.8	3.3	4.1	4.1	2.5	3.0	3.2	3.1
Tampa, FL	3.5	3.0	2.6	2.3	2.4	2.9	2.8	2.8	2.6	2.7	2.6	2.2
Tucson, AZ	4.0	3.9	3.1	3.4	3.6	4.2	4.2	4.3	4.3	4.2	3.6	3.2
Tulsa, OK	3.2	3.3	3.2	3.0	3.1	3.7	3.4	3.7	3.6	3.7	3.2	2.8
Tuscaloosa, AL	3.6	3.4	2.6	2.4	2.9	4.1	4.0	3.4	2.9	3.1	2.7	2.4
Virginia Beach, VA	3.2	2.7	2.6	2.4	2.9	2.9	2.8	3.0	2.5	2.7	2.9	2.6
Washington, DC	6.3	5.6	5.1	4.2	4.3	4.9	4.7	4.6	4.1	4.3	4.1	4.1
Wichita, KS	3.7	3.6	3.6	2.8	3.2	3.5	4.1	3.8	3.1	3.2	3.1	3.2
Wilmington, NC	3.4	3.4	3.2	3.3	3.5	3.9	3.5	3.7	3.1	3.6	3.6	3.1
Winston-Salem, NC	4.1	4.0	3.9	3.8	4.0	4.5	4.3	4.4	3.8	4.3	4.1	3.5
Worcester, MA	5.5	4.6	4.1	3.9	4.2	4.6	4.6	4.6	4.0	3.7	3.5	3.7
U.S.	4.4	4.1	3.8	3.3	3.4	3.8	3.8	3.8	3.3	3.4	3.4	3.3

Note: Data is not seasonally adjusted and covers workers 16 years of age and older; All figures are percentages
Source: Bureau of Labor Statistics, Local Area Unemployment Statistics

Unemployment Rate: Metro Area

Metro Area[1]	2022											
	Jan.	Feb.	Mar.	Apr.	May	Jun.	Jul.	Aug.	Sep.	Oct.	Nov.	Dec.
Albuquerque, NM	5.1	4.4	4.1	4.0	3.8	4.6	4.3	4.1	4.2	3.7	3.3	3.1
Allentown, PA	5.5	4.8	4.5	4.1	3.9	4.4	4.5	4.5	3.3	3.2	3.3	3.3
Anchorage, AK	5.3	4.9	4.5	4.3	4.0	4.2	3.9	3.2	3.2	3.3	3.6	3.5
Ann Arbor, MI	3.3	3.7	3.1	3.0	3.6	4.1	4.0	3.5	3.3	3.3	3.1	3.0
Athens, GA	2.9	2.9	2.9	2.1	2.5	3.1	2.6	2.9	2.3	2.9	2.5	2.4
Atlanta, GA	3.3	3.2	3.2	2.4	2.6	3.2	2.8	3.0	2.5	2.9	2.7	2.6
Austin, TX	3.3	3.3	2.7	2.5	2.7	3.1	3.1	3.0	2.8	2.8	2.8	2.7
Baltimore, MD	4.2	4.3	4.2	3.3	3.6	4.6	4.1	4.3	3.7	4.0	3.5	3.1
Boise City, ID	3.1	3.0	2.8	2.4	2.2	2.7	2.6	2.7	2.5	2.6	2.5	2.1
Boston, MA[4]	4.2	3.4	3.1	2.8	2.9	3.1	3.0	3.0	2.7	2.7	2.5	2.7
Boulder, CO	3.1	3.2	2.8	2.4	2.4	2.8	2.9	2.6	2.5	2.8	2.6	2.2
Brownsville, TX	7.6	7.3	6.1	5.9	6.0	6.9	6.8	6.4	5.8	5.6	5.7	5.7
Cape Coral, FL	3.4	2.9	2.5	2.2	2.4	2.9	2.8	2.7	2.6	4.0	3.6	2.9
Cedar Rapids, IA	4.9	4.0	3.7	2.6	2.6	3.0	3.2	3.4	2.9	3.0	3.3	3.5
Charleston, SC	3.2	3.6	2.9	2.3	2.8	3.0	2.7	2.8	2.7	3.1	2.2	2.5
Charlotte, NC	3.7	3.7	3.5	3.2	3.4	3.8	3.4	3.6	3.1	3.7	3.5	3.1
Chicago, IL[2]	5.2	5.0	4.4	4.3	4.5	5.3	5.1	5.2	4.6	4.5	4.4	4.2
Cincinnati, OH	3.9	3.8	3.5	3.0	3.0	3.9	3.9	3.8	3.3	3.6	3.0	3.1
Clarksville, TN	4.1	3.7	3.6	3.6	4.0	4.7	4.5	4.1	3.6	4.0	3.9	3.6
Cleveland, OH	5.6	6.0	5.6	4.8	4.9	5.3	4.9	4.5	4.1	3.9	3.6	3.4
College Station, TX	3.7	3.5	2.9	2.7	2.9	3.6	3.5	3.5	3.1	3.1	3.1	2.8
Colorado Springs, CO	4.1	4.2	3.8	3.3	3.3	3.5	3.9	3.6	3.5	3.8	3.6	3.0
Columbia, MO	3.0	2.3	2.6	1.7	2.3	1.8	2.3	2.4	1.4	1.9	1.8	1.7
Columbia, SC	3.5	3.8	3.1	2.5	3.0	3.3	3.1	3.1	2.9	3.4	2.6	2.8
Columbus, OH	3.8	3.7	3.3	2.9	2.9	3.8	3.7	3.8	3.3	3.5	2.7	3.1
Dallas, TX[2]	4.1	4.0	3.3	3.1	3.3	3.8	3.7	3.6	3.4	3.3	3.2	3.1
Davenport, IA	5.3	4.6	4.4	3.7	3.8	3.7	3.8	3.8	3.4	3.5	3.7	3.7
Denver, CO	4.0	4.0	3.6	3.2	3.1	3.3	3.5	3.3	3.2	3.5	3.3	2.8
Des Moines, IA	4.2	3.4	3.2	2.1	2.2	2.5	2.6	2.7	2.3	2.5	2.8	2.8
Durham, NC	3.0	2.9	2.8	2.8	3.0	3.4	3.1	3.2	2.7	3.3	3.2	2.6
Edison, NJ[2]	6.1	5.6	5.1	4.7	4.6	4.9	5.3	5.4	4.1	4.1	4.2	4.2
El Paso, TX	5.4	5.3	4.3	4.2	4.3	4.9	4.8	4.6	4.4	4.3	4.2	4.0
Fargo, ND	2.8	2.4	2.7	1.9	1.6	2.1	1.7	1.7	1.4	1.4	1.5	1.9
Fort Collins, CO	3.4	3.5	3.1	2.7	2.6	2.9	3.0	2.8	2.7	2.9	2.8	2.4
Fort Wayne, IN	2.2	2.4	2.6	2.2	2.3	3.0	3.2	2.8	2.0	2.7	2.6	2.2
Fort Worth, TX[2]	4.2	4.2	3.4	3.2	3.4	3.9	3.9	3.8	3.5	3.4	3.4	3.2
Grand Rapids, MI	3.7	3.8	3.3	3.1	3.4	3.9	3.8	3.4	3.2	3.1	3.0	3.1
Greeley, CO	4.2	4.3	3.9	3.4	3.3	3.6	3.8	3.6	3.4	3.7	3.5	3.0
Green Bay, WI	2.8	3.0	3.0	2.7	2.6	3.2	3.0	3.0	2.9	2.6	2.4	2.1
Greensboro, NC	4.2	4.1	4.0	3.8	4.0	4.5	4.2	4.4	3.7	4.3	4.1	3.6
Honolulu, HI	3.7	3.5	3.2	3.3	3.4	3.9	3.5	3.4	3.3	3.4	3.8	3.4
Houston, TX	5.5	5.3	4.4	4.1	4.3	4.8	4.8	4.6	4.2	4.1	4.0	3.9
Huntsville, AL	2.6	2.4	1.9	1.6	1.9	2.7	2.6	2.3	2.1	2.2	2.0	1.8
Indianapolis, IN	2.2	2.5	2.5	2.0	2.4	3.0	3.3	2.8	2.1	2.6	2.6	2.2
Jacksonville, FL	3.2	2.9	2.5	2.2	2.3	2.9	2.8	2.8	2.5	2.5	2.5	2.1
Kansas City, MO	3.4	3.7	3.3	2.4	2.7	2.6	3.2	3.1	2.2	2.6	2.5	2.4
Lafayette, LA	3.8	3.4	3.4	3.1	3.2	4.1	4.0	3.3	3.2	2.8	2.7	3.1
Las Cruces, NM	5.7	5.1	4.8	4.8	4.4	5.3	5.0	4.6	4.8	4.2	4.0	3.7
Las Vegas, NV	5.8	5.3	5.0	5.0	5.2	5.7	5.6	5.7	5.3	5.6	5.6	5.4
Lexington, KY	3.4	3.1	3.1	2.8	2.9	3.5	3.3	3.0	2.8	3.3	3.1	2.6
Lincoln, NE	2.3	2.1	2.1	1.8	1.9	2.4	2.3	2.1	1.9	2.0	2.1	2.1
Little Rock, AR	3.8	3.8	3.3	3.2	3.2	3.7	4.0	3.5	3.5	2.8	2.9	2.8
Los Angeles, CA[2]	6.5	5.8	5.2	4.8	4.5	4.9	4.9	4.7	4.3	4.5	4.5	4.4
Louisville, KY	4.1	3.5	4.3	2.8	3.7	3.5	3.8	3.1	2.7	3.3	3.1	2.7
Madison, WI	2.3	2.5	2.4	2.1	2.2	2.8	2.5	2.5	2.6	2.2	2.0	1.6

Table continued on following page.

Metro Area[1]	2022											
	Jan.	Feb.	Mar.	Apr.	May	Jun.	Jul.	Aug.	Sep.	Oct.	Nov.	Dec.
Manchester, NH[3]	3.3	2.3	2.3	2.1	1.8	1.9	1.9	2.2	2.3	2.5	2.4	2.3
Miami, FL[2]	3.2	2.9	3.0	2.6	2.5	2.6	2.8	2.9	2.6	2.4	2.1	2.0
Midland, TX	4.4	4.3	3.5	3.2	3.3	3.6	3.5	3.3	3.0	2.9	2.8	2.6
Milwaukee, WI	3.4	3.7	3.6	3.5	3.4	4.0	4.0	3.9	3.6	3.3	3.0	2.4
Minneapolis, MN	3.0	2.4	2.6	1.5	1.6	2.2	2.0	2.2	1.9	1.7	1.9	2.6
Nashville, TN	2.9	2.7	2.4	2.5	2.8	3.4	3.1	2.7	2.4	2.7	2.6	2.3
New Haven, CT[3]	4.6	4.6	3.9	3.5	3.8	3.9	4.2	4.1	3.7	3.7	3.3	2.9
New Orleans, LA	4.9	4.5	4.4	4.1	4.1	5.1	5.0	4.1	3.8	3.3	3.1	3.5
New York, NY[2]	6.1	5.6	5.1	4.7	4.6	4.9	5.3	5.4	4.1	4.1	4.2	4.2
Oklahoma City, OK	2.8	2.9	2.7	2.6	2.7	3.2	2.9	3.1	3.1	3.3	2.8	2.4
Omaha, NE	2.9	2.7	2.6	2.1	2.1	2.7	2.7	2.5	2.2	2.4	2.4	2.5
Orlando, FL	3.8	3.4	2.9	2.6	2.7	3.2	3.0	2.9	2.7	2.8	2.7	2.3
Philadelphia, PA[2]	7.0	6.2	5.7	5.5	5.2	5.7	5.7	5.9	4.5	4.3	4.4	4.2
Phoenix, AZ	3.2	3.1	2.4	2.7	2.9	3.4	3.3	3.4	3.5	3.5	3.0	2.7
Pittsburgh, PA	5.8	5.1	4.6	4.2	4.0	4.6	4.7	4.8	3.4	3.3	3.5	3.7
Portland, OR	4.4	3.9	3.9	3.4	3.1	3.5	3.6	4.0	3.7	3.7	3.9	4.1
Providence, RI[3]	4.9	4.7	3.4	3.0	2.9	3.0	3.3	4.0	3.4	3.3	3.4	2.7
Provo, UT	2.0	1.8	1.8	1.8	2.0	2.3	1.8	1.9	1.7	1.9	1.9	1.9
Raleigh, NC	3.1	3.0	2.9	2.9	3.1	3.4	3.1	3.3	2.8	3.3	3.2	2.7
Reno, NV	3.2	2.8	2.6	2.7	2.9	3.3	3.2	3.5	3.1	3.5	3.5	3.4
Richmond, VA	3.7	3.2	2.9	2.8	3.2	3.2	3.1	3.4	2.8	3.0	3.2	2.9
Rochester, MN	3.0	2.3	2.4	1.3	1.3	1.9	1.7	1.8	1.5	1.4	1.6	2.5
Sacramento, CA	5.0	4.4	3.7	3.3	2.9	3.4	3.3	3.6	3.3	3.4	3.7	3.3
Salem, OR	4.5	3.9	3.9	3.6	3.1	3.7	4.0	4.4	4.0	4.2	4.3	4.5
Salt Lake City, UT	2.4	2.2	2.1	2.1	2.2	2.4	2.1	2.1	1.9	2.1	2.0	2.0
San Antonio, TX	4.3	4.2	3.5	3.3	3.5	4.0	4.0	3.8	3.5	3.5	3.4	3.3
San Diego, CA	4.7	4.0	3.4	3.0	2.7	3.2	3.1	3.4	3.1	3.2	3.3	2.9
San Francisco, CA[2]	3.3	2.9	2.4	2.1	1.8	2.1	2.1	2.3	2.1	2.1	2.3	2.0
San Jose, CA	3.4	3.0	2.5	2.2	1.9	2.3	2.2	2.4	2.2	2.2	2.4	2.1
Santa Rosa, CA	4.0	3.5	3.0	2.6	2.3	2.7	2.6	2.8	2.6	2.6	2.9	2.5
Savannah, GA	3.3	3.2	3.2	2.4	2.6	3.1	2.7	2.9	2.5	2.9	2.6	2.5
Seattle, WA[2]	3.3	2.8	2.6	2.3	2.6	3.0	3.3	3.3	3.3	3.4	2.9	3.0
Sioux Falls, SD	2.5	2.7	2.3	1.9	1.9	2.1	1.7	2.0	1.5	1.8	1.7	2.0
Springfield, IL	5.1	4.8	4.5	4.6	4.7	4.2	4.3	4.3	3.8	3.9	3.9	3.6
St. Louis, MO	4.3	3.7	3.7	2.9	3.2	2.8	3.2	3.3	2.3	2.7	2.7	2.5
Tampa, FL	3.3	2.9	2.5	2.3	2.4	2.9	2.7	2.7	2.5	2.6	2.6	2.2
Tucson, AZ	3.6	3.6	2.8	3.1	3.3	3.9	3.9	4.0	4.1	4.0	3.4	3.1
Tulsa, OK	3.1	3.3	3.1	2.9	3.0	3.6	3.3	3.4	3.4	3.5	3.0	2.7
Tuscaloosa, AL	3.5	3.2	2.5	2.1	2.5	3.6	3.4	3.0	2.6	2.7	2.4	2.2
Virginia Beach, VA	3.9	3.4	3.1	3.0	3.4	3.4	3.3	3.6	3.0	3.2	3.4	3.0
Washington, DC[2]	4.0	3.6	3.5	3.0	3.3	3.6	3.4	3.6	3.0	3.2	3.1	2.9
Wichita, KS	3.4	3.3	3.3	2.6	3.0	3.2	3.8	3.5	2.9	3.0	2.9	2.9
Wilmington, NC	3.3	3.2	3.1	3.0	3.3	3.7	3.3	3.5	3.0	3.6	3.4	2.9
Winston-Salem, NC	3.6	3.5	3.4	3.3	3.6	4.0	3.6	3.8	3.3	3.8	3.7	3.1
Worcester, MA[3]	5.0	4.4	3.9	3.4	3.5	3.7	3.7	3.8	3.3	3.2	3.0	3.3
U.S.	4.4	4.1	3.8	3.3	3.4	3.8	3.8	3.8	3.3	3.4	3.4	3.3

Note: Data is not seasonally adjusted and covers workers 16 years of age and older; All figures are percentages; (1) Figures cover the Metropolitan Statistical Area (MSA) except where noted. See Appendix B for areas included; (2) Metropolitan Division; (3) New England City and Town Area; (4) New England City and Town Area Division
Source: Bureau of Labor Statistics, Local Area Unemployment Statistics

Average Hourly Wages: Occupations A – C

Metro Area[1]	Accountants/ Auditors	Automotive Mechanics	Book-keepers	Carpenters	Cashiers	Computer Program-mers	Computer Systems Analysts
Albuquerque, NM	35.62	21.48	20.91	23.25	13.53	39.45	44.30
Allentown, PA	38.74	23.90	21.73	26.50	12.78	48.46	45.52
Anchorage, AK	38.08	28.88	25.34	35.06	16.27	47.28	47.93
Ann Arbor, MI	41.17	24.91	22.53	27.04	13.30	46.31	50.46
Athens, GA	35.00	22.03	20.51	23.47	11.77	29.81	35.56
Atlanta, GA	42.89	23.34	23.13	24.77	12.29	47.05	50.28
Austin, TX	41.33	25.45	22.37	24.23	13.85	46.80	48.67
Baltimore, MD	42.20	24.80	24.11	26.91	14.41	50.01	51.61
Boise City, ID	34.92	22.86	21.24	21.41	13.64	37.89	44.85
Boston, MA[2]	46.85	25.85	27.28	34.31	16.21	55.26	57.55
Boulder, CO	46.88	27.50	24.94	27.55	16.30	71.67	61.71
Brownsville, TX	31.30	20.87	17.66	18.88	11.54	n/a	40.71
Cape Coral, FL	37.19	23.44	21.35	21.78	12.98	43.01	46.18
Cedar Rapids, IA	36.04	23.48	22.67	24.39	13.19	42.82	43.29
Charleston, SC	38.80	22.64	20.63	23.50	12.44	n/a	51.58
Charlotte, NC	45.21	24.42	22.12	22.36	12.80	54.86	52.23
Chicago, IL	42.15	25.15	25.13	35.45	14.91	43.54	49.11
Cincinnati, OH	38.18	21.73	22.50	26.23	12.78	44.15	50.79
Clarksville, TN	32.20	21.35	19.54	21.38	11.96	n/a	39.23
Cleveland, OH	39.26	22.70	22.17	27.47	12.94	40.92	48.16
College Station, TX	36.77	21.75	19.34	20.12	12.47	36.69	39.40
Colorado Springs, CO	36.34	25.04	21.56	25.51	14.94	56.28	53.00
Columbia, MO	32.30	21.77	20.39	25.95	12.91	37.12	38.74
Columbia, SC	31.51	22.42	19.63	22.23	11.56	46.56	41.41
Columbus, OH	38.54	23.63	22.84	26.80	12.98	44.12	48.82
Dallas, TX	43.06	24.09	22.81	23.70	13.14	46.27	54.07
Davenport, IA	34.44	23.03	21.58	25.54	13.39	41.58	42.03
Denver, CO	43.21	26.75	24.91	26.47	16.03	59.06	58.10
Des Moines, IA	36.71	23.68	23.50	25.01	13.40	44.45	45.98
Durham, NC	42.03	24.33	23.51	22.09	12.86	51.67	48.44
Edison, NJ	54.94	26.81	26.44	37.06	16.55	57.97	60.54
El Paso, TX	33.19	19.58	18.00	18.84	11.04	32.89	38.82
Fargo, ND	33.62	23.74	21.80	24.78	14.30	43.53	46.07
Fort Collins, CO	40.07	25.91	23.02	25.81	15.48	47.61	50.60
Fort Wayne, IN	35.91	21.07	20.51	24.46	12.43	41.88	40.51
Fort Worth, TX	43.06	24.09	22.81	23.70	13.14	46.27	54.07
Grand Rapids, MI	36.05	23.88	21.43	25.03	13.24	43.23	45.05
Greeley, CO	40.39	26.16	22.81	25.71	14.89	42.19	47.48
Green Bay, WI	35.84	24.15	21.27	27.33	13.29	48.63	44.13
Greensboro, NC	39.53	23.26	20.74	21.12	11.95	47.79	44.56
Honolulu, HI	35.01	25.53	23.01	40.03	15.19	40.35	44.09
Houston, TX	45.35	24.26	22.16	23.53	12.84	44.09	53.59
Huntsville, AL	38.65	23.32	19.18	21.60	12.06	48.90	59.97
Indianapolis, IN	38.48	24.17	21.02	26.70	12.72	55.30	46.41
Jacksonville, FL	37.78	21.66	22.39	21.96	12.81	45.61	47.46
Kansas City, MO	37.26	22.90	22.32	28.49	13.42	32.32	43.98
Lafayette, LA	33.20	21.50	19.60	21.95	10.71	46.32	40.06
Las Cruces, NM	31.08	19.52	19.12	19.82	12.79	32.88	40.51
Las Vegas, NV	32.32	23.93	22.52	31.29	12.95	46.77	45.39
Lexington, KY	34.78	19.88	21.74	24.79	12.65	41.29	41.63
Lincoln, NE	33.19	25.66	21.09	22.21	12.89	42.91	38.01
Little Rock, AR	34.54	21.76	20.43	20.73	12.61	39.86	36.35
Los Angeles, CA	44.41	27.03	25.38	32.48	16.40	52.39	56.78
Louisville, KY	37.30	20.62	21.86	24.50	12.91	39.53	43.77
Madison, WI	37.27	24.24	22.60	27.63	14.13	56.02	44.74

Table continued on following page.

Metro Area[1]	Accountants/ Auditors	Automotive Mechanics	Book-keepers	Carpenters	Cashiers	Computer Program-mers	Computer Systems Analysts
Manchester, NH[2]	38.41	25.34	23.03	25.30	13.47	37.37	55.74
Miami, FL	40.21	23.98	22.09	23.23	13.04	57.52	49.49
Midland, TX	45.27	22.73	23.16	24.74	13.53	46.24	60.82
Milwaukee, WI	38.84	25.28	22.52	27.42	13.47	48.26	47.82
Minneapolis, MN	41.61	26.35	24.93	31.05	14.83	56.92	51.73
Nashville, TN	37.26	23.62	22.19	23.17	13.16	55.27	45.76
New Haven, CT[2]	40.18	25.11	25.93	29.63	14.82	46.28	50.48
New Orleans, LA	35.71	22.89	21.05	23.83	11.45	n/a	42.24
New York, NY	54.94	26.81	26.44	37.06	16.55	57.97	60.54
Oklahoma City, OK	37.21	22.78	20.87	21.48	12.66	43.42	43.52
Omaha, NE	36.79	24.01	22.22	22.88	13.40	45.89	44.58
Orlando, FL	39.04	22.82	21.76	22.25	13.41	44.68	49.23
Philadelphia, PA	41.83	25.23	23.94	30.34	13.39	48.86	51.32
Phoenix, AZ	40.79	24.61	23.11	24.95	14.93	42.27	50.03
Pittsburgh, PA	36.77	22.54	21.77	27.30	12.18	44.53	44.54
Portland, OR	40.08	26.62	24.24	30.98	16.34	54.65	56.22
Providence, RI[2]	44.90	22.35	24.22	29.76	14.61	43.32	51.67
Provo, UT	36.53	24.47	21.59	22.45	13.70	50.42	42.69
Raleigh, NC	40.68	23.79	21.92	22.09	12.55	51.36	48.99
Reno, NV	36.36	26.22	23.68	30.24	13.43	47.35	51.99
Richmond, VA	39.80	24.06	22.01	22.95	13.04	46.05	49.01
Rochester, MN	39.00	23.13	22.86	28.86	14.39	43.06	50.23
Sacramento, CA	41.27	28.35	25.70	32.41	16.67	54.48	52.53
Salem, OR	37.81	26.17	23.29	27.37	15.07	43.99	48.05
Salt Lake City, UT	38.26	24.06	23.32	24.89	13.79	48.36	47.68
San Antonio, TX	40.79	22.70	21.14	21.56	13.19	42.04	48.72
San Diego, CA	43.86	27.06	25.51	32.52	16.54	61.76	55.08
San Francisco, CA	54.83	31.95	30.30	38.33	18.96	64.89	70.44
San Jose, CA	55.92	37.42	29.94	37.76	19.15	70.63	79.75
Santa Rosa, CA	44.48	28.50	27.43	37.66	17.71	51.79	53.46
Savannah, GA	37.20	21.80	21.94	22.17	12.01	40.03	51.98
Seattle, WA	45.25	28.69	26.09	35.16	17.95	64.30	62.53
Sioux Falls, SD	36.65	24.92	19.54	20.96	13.46	31.23	41.70
Springfield, IL	37.41	23.85	22.33	28.27	13.91	43.32	48.50
St. Louis, MO	37.46	23.04	23.29	29.99	13.92	39.08	49.69
Tampa, FL	39.60	22.77	21.91	22.26	12.70	42.78	47.41
Tucson, AZ	34.99	23.11	21.61	21.37	14.27	39.03	51.23
Tulsa, OK	39.68	22.38	20.66	21.83	12.73	44.62	44.82
Tuscaloosa, AL	35.59	21.58	19.16	21.27	11.34	40.66	45.86
Virginia Beach, VA	36.48	23.14	20.67	23.04	12.50	45.16	49.26
Washington, DC	48.98	27.98	26.17	28.25	15.21	59.90	58.64
Wichita, KS	36.01	21.40	19.47	23.61	12.22	33.61	40.07
Wilmington, NC	37.58	21.31	19.94	21.32	11.98	51.25	42.16
Winston-Salem, NC	38.18	21.78	20.62	20.32	11.93	48.29	46.37
Worcester, MA[2]	42.78	26.08	24.24	29.55	15.32	49.03	50.87

Notes: (1) Figures cover the Metropolitan Statistical Area (MSA) except where noted. See Appendix B for areas included; (2) New England City and Town Area; n/a not available
Source: Bureau of Labor Statistics, May 2022 Metro Area Occupational Employment and Wage Estimates

Average Hourly Wages: Occupations C – E

Metro Area	Comp. User Support Specialists	Construction Laborers	Cooks, Restaurant	Customer Service Reps.	Dentists	Electricians	Engineers, Electrical
Albuquerque, NM	25.04	17.98	15.25	17.46	92.90	27.76	63.45
Allentown, PA	29.17	23.73	15.53	19.08	76.30	35.65	52.01
Anchorage, AK	31.03	26.21	18.32	20.61	86.58	38.38	51.77
Ann Arbor, MI	26.14	23.76	16.10	19.39	76.15	34.45	48.28
Athens, GA	23.39	17.59	14.12	16.00	83.95	25.40	51.99
Atlanta, GA	30.05	19.06	14.12	19.35	n/a	27.76	56.29
Austin, TX	28.69	19.04	15.59	19.39	85.63	27.12	62.22
Baltimore, MD	28.42	20.10	16.72	20.48	78.23	31.44	56.06
Boise City, ID	26.11	19.73	15.37	18.74	71.88	26.06	55.65
Boston, MA[2]	35.38	31.95	19.78	24.00	89.08	39.81	61.23
Boulder, CO	37.04	20.81	18.99	21.92	77.69	28.91	61.37
Brownsville, TX	21.36	14.98	12.36	16.29	n/a	21.42	44.90
Cape Coral, FL	27.26	18.06	16.07	18.46	77.81	23.54	48.44
Cedar Rapids, IA	27.05	22.70	14.19	20.25	95.40	28.53	47.69
Charleston, SC	26.98	18.51	15.93	18.41	87.52	25.86	46.55
Charlotte, NC	30.39	18.19	15.26	19.72	98.68	25.03	49.35
Chicago, IL	29.52	32.85	17.06	21.26	67.54	42.79	50.03
Cincinnati, OH	25.81	24.39	15.01	19.74	86.77	28.47	48.44
Clarksville, TN	22.21	17.54	13.67	17.08	n/a	25.15	45.92
Cleveland, OH	26.60	26.17	15.16	20.42	78.04	29.88	46.94
College Station, TX	22.57	17.19	13.51	16.40	n/a	25.15	44.21
Colorado Springs, CO	31.65	20.22	17.67	19.52	88.61	27.65	54.86
Columbia, MO	26.05	25.63	14.43	17.49	80.29	27.19	40.87
Columbia, SC	26.44	18.07	14.25	17.29	76.98	25.73	41.58
Columbus, OH	26.03	26.04	15.34	20.25	69.07	29.48	53.22
Dallas, TX	28.45	18.68	15.57	19.64	76.46	26.46	50.66
Davenport, IA	27.11	23.89	14.54	19.17	75.24	30.25	46.40
Denver, CO	33.31	20.88	18.61	21.35	73.17	29.06	53.05
Des Moines, IA	27.24	22.43	14.73	21.45	80.98	30.12	48.91
Durham, NC	31.57	18.55	15.87	19.93	106.19	27.22	56.69
Edison, NJ	35.55	30.93	19.55	23.75	89.01	41.22	53.37
El Paso, TX	20.96	15.44	12.46	15.69	78.62	21.95	40.61
Fargo, ND	27.94	22.00	15.80	19.82	80.70	29.07	47.71
Fort Collins, CO	30.99	20.70	17.57	19.06	n/a	28.15	54.42
Fort Wayne, IN	25.05	22.43	14.31	19.63	81.34	29.66	48.26
Fort Worth, TX	28.45	18.68	15.57	19.64	76.46	26.46	50.66
Grand Rapids, MI	27.43	21.17	15.94	19.17	88.95	27.51	43.36
Greeley, CO	33.01	20.70	17.40	18.44	65.47	27.92	50.58
Green Bay, WI	29.31	22.68	15.04	20.32	81.73	30.20	43.80
Greensboro, NC	25.86	17.39	14.20	18.33	85.11	24.46	46.74
Honolulu, HI	29.83	32.93	19.44	20.16	n/a	43.15	50.24
Houston, TX	27.70	18.56	14.67	18.59	74.27	27.69	55.91
Huntsville, AL	24.38	16.49	14.48	17.51	87.97	25.26	53.71
Indianapolis, IN	25.93	23.51	14.76	20.25	98.07	31.79	46.72
Jacksonville, FL	27.33	18.20	15.75	19.12	82.64	24.62	48.04
Kansas City, MO	28.08	22.55	15.09	19.33	85.61	32.19	49.54
Lafayette, LA	26.07	17.53	12.87	16.84	63.45	25.23	43.20
Las Cruces, NM	22.91	17.03	14.13	15.26	76.28	25.44	44.62
Las Vegas, NV	25.53	21.97	17.17	18.68	n/a	33.87	42.86
Lexington, KY	25.84	20.07	14.54	17.87	n/a	25.25	44.15
Lincoln, NE	25.23	19.61	15.58	17.91	73.53	25.71	47.33
Little Rock, AR	22.91	17.13	14.00	18.06	85.98	21.91	46.55
Los Angeles, CA	33.66	25.96	18.92	22.21	n/a	37.09	65.13
Louisville, KY	26.08	21.24	14.55	19.09	87.22	28.92	45.08
Madison, WI	29.94	23.76	16.05	20.72	83.83	34.25	46.88

Table continued on following page.

Metro Area	Comp. User Support Specialists	Construction Laborers	Cooks, Restaurant	Customer Service Reps.	Dentists	Electricians	Engineers, Electrical
Manchester, NH[2]	30.81	20.40	17.24	20.95	139.57	28.40	53.87
Miami, FL	27.62	18.58	16.91	19.16	80.27	25.35	47.59
Midland, TX	29.09	19.01	15.29	19.91	n/a	29.47	42.56
Milwaukee, WI	27.77	24.14	15.78	21.30	86.72	36.15	46.03
Minneapolis, MN	30.92	27.61	17.93	22.61	93.89	37.09	50.35
Nashville, TN	25.45	19.33	15.20	18.93	89.30	28.19	47.79
New Haven, CT[2]	31.79	25.19	17.29	21.99	95.87	33.24	50.00
New Orleans, LA	25.14	18.62	13.82	17.57	88.12	27.99	51.29
New York, NY	35.55	30.93	19.55	23.75	89.01	41.22	53.37
Oklahoma City, OK	26.61	19.08	14.94	18.11	84.37	27.58	47.89
Omaha, NE	26.48	20.49	15.05	18.92	78.54	27.41	47.76
Orlando, FL	26.77	17.79	17.07	18.69	91.27	24.05	50.65
Philadelphia, PA	31.04	26.48	16.51	21.24	93.37	38.35	53.63
Phoenix, AZ	29.29	21.22	18.08	19.49	87.37	25.61	49.97
Pittsburgh, PA	29.16	24.33	14.67	19.68	68.86	34.15	49.62
Portland, OR	30.08	25.00	18.56	21.22	91.21	41.15	51.53
Providence, RI[2]	29.79	26.46	17.00	21.03	97.31	30.94	54.51
Provo, UT	28.02	21.54	15.72	18.34	65.12	26.76	56.26
Raleigh, NC	31.64	18.40	15.45	19.52	107.63	24.71	52.39
Reno, NV	26.75	25.44	17.06	19.43	56.35	32.25	48.35
Richmond, VA	28.49	17.43	15.43	18.72	79.72	27.27	50.41
Rochester, MN	31.25	25.20	16.86	20.61	83.58	33.41	51.22
Sacramento, CA	44.86	26.69	18.68	22.15	81.12	35.93	59.48
Salem, OR	29.88	23.00	17.44	19.55	94.78	37.27	52.49
Salt Lake City, UT	30.53	20.17	16.82	20.02	64.38	28.08	58.74
San Antonio, TX	26.07	18.15	14.44	18.47	90.08	25.79	50.10
San Diego, CA	31.80	26.98	18.75	22.23	70.37	33.63	61.94
San Francisco, CA	40.10	31.48	20.39	25.95	98.09	46.31	77.67
San Jose, CA	39.13	30.35	21.53	26.29	103.12	47.71	n/a
Santa Rosa, CA	34.14	28.67	19.90	23.15	79.52	36.36	60.81
Savannah, GA	26.01	17.96	15.06	16.30	n/a	25.68	56.50
Seattle, WA	36.00	28.67	21.69	24.71	84.44	44.45	60.98
Sioux Falls, SD	21.59	18.01	15.46	18.54	69.39	26.54	46.30
Springfield, IL	26.48	30.22	16.03	19.00	72.48	35.32	47.34
St. Louis, MO	30.84	27.50	15.55	20.00	n/a	33.40	50.08
Tampa, FL	29.20	18.14	15.73	18.73	77.98	24.40	49.32
Tucson, AZ	27.18	19.78	16.51	17.76	87.60	24.71	56.86
Tulsa, OK	26.87	19.26	14.72	18.17	83.90	27.67	48.62
Tuscaloosa, AL	29.58	15.23	14.27	17.16	93.58	25.75	55.16
Virginia Beach, VA	26.21	17.52	14.70	17.30	78.65	27.29	47.22
Washington, DC	33.96	21.29	18.00	22.02	85.40	34.04	59.45
Wichita, KS	27.25	18.13	13.72	17.53	76.11	28.57	43.15
Wilmington, NC	25.96	18.29	14.56	18.04	76.66	23.28	48.09
Winston-Salem, NC	26.98	17.33	14.50	18.08	91.37	23.79	49.50
Worcester, MA[2]	31.83	28.53	18.32	21.98	n/a	37.55	57.13

Notes: (1) Figures cover the Metropolitan Statistical Area (MSA) except where noted. See Appendix B for areas included;
(2) New England City and Town Area; n/a not available
Source: Bureau of Labor Statistics, May 2022 Metro Area Occupational Employment and Wage Estimates

Average Hourly Wages: Occupations F – J

Metro Area	Fast Food and Counter Workers	Financial Managers	First-Line Supervisors/ of Office Workers	General and Operations Managers	Hair-dressers/ Cosme-tologists	Home Health and Personal Care Aides	Janitors/ Cleaners
Albuquerque, NM	12.75	59.44	27.81	58.98	13.60	13.30	14.36
Allentown, PA	12.66	74.84	31.48	58.15	16.54	13.96	16.71
Anchorage, AK	14.73	72.72	32.44	54.98	15.13	17.28	16.95
Ann Arbor, MI	13.66	71.39	31.10	62.22	19.87	14.08	17.50
Athens, GA	11.00	67.23	27.18	47.82	17.24	12.56	14.99
Atlanta, GA	11.65	83.96	31.25	59.75	18.59	12.95	15.06
Austin, TX	12.48	81.29	32.79	56.28	16.04	12.07	14.63
Baltimore, MD	14.31	76.62	32.11	55.22	19.90	15.32	16.24
Boise City, ID	11.97	56.23	27.15	38.95	15.45	13.80	14.80
Boston, MA[2]	16.22	88.25	36.88	74.45	23.51	17.13	19.76
Boulder, CO	16.24	90.26	34.38	77.36	23.64	17.40	18.80
Brownsville, TX	10.12	59.69	25.20	41.63	12.81	10.33	12.36
Cape Coral, FL	12.56	69.72	30.29	51.54	18.15	15.99	14.30
Cedar Rapids, IA	12.59	60.69	29.72	45.54	15.24	16.20	15.98
Charleston, SC	11.69	65.85	29.33	52.71	16.62	13.41	13.93
Charlotte, NC	12.43	84.45	30.59	64.62	18.90	12.92	14.10
Chicago, IL	14.28	78.05	33.78	63.64	21.49	15.66	17.40
Cincinnati, OH	12.33	74.98	31.83	54.62	19.64	13.84	15.79
Clarksville, TN	11.02	59.25	27.42	46.82	16.59	12.82	13.88
Cleveland, OH	12.12	74.24	31.50	57.05	17.94	13.45	16.17
College Station, TX	10.89	65.41	26.24	47.87	13.68	11.46	13.57
Colorado Springs, CO	14.73	83.92	31.26	65.50	23.17	16.66	16.75
Columbia, MO	12.77	n/a	27.71	47.42	18.61	13.29	15.66
Columbia, SC	10.98	59.98	30.75	48.46	15.32	12.35	13.42
Columbus, OH	12.65	71.54	32.35	57.91	20.68	13.75	16.00
Dallas, TX	12.14	79.36	31.46	56.66	16.24	11.66	14.42
Davenport, IA	12.80	60.84	29.38	47.04	16.42	14.44	16.52
Denver, CO	15.81	94.94	34.80	75.18	21.59	16.85	17.70
Des Moines, IA	13.07	72.01	31.64	49.19	16.70	15.41	15.75
Durham, NC	13.08	84.49	31.92	70.01	22.31	13.24	16.43
Edison, NJ	16.08	110.67	38.32	83.82	20.85	17.10	20.14
El Paso, TX	10.10	62.87	24.90	40.58	13.11	9.83	12.05
Fargo, ND	13.47	68.39	30.87	48.98	16.61	16.62	16.77
Fort Collins, CO	14.91	86.90	31.88	63.72	26.75	16.84	17.15
Fort Wayne, IN	11.84	56.74	29.78	57.29	15.67	13.51	15.11
Fort Worth, TX	12.14	79.36	31.46	56.66	16.24	11.66	14.42
Grand Rapids, MI	13.09	65.10	29.78	55.04	18.45	14.38	15.34
Greeley, CO	14.57	83.73	32.68	64.82	19.24	16.62	17.37
Green Bay, WI	11.72	67.97	32.04	64.87	16.41	14.33	15.45
Greensboro, NC	11.81	73.43	28.58	57.79	18.33	12.20	13.36
Honolulu, HI	13.92	65.00	29.47	57.59	15.94	15.75	16.29
Houston, TX	11.74	84.66	31.01	56.99	13.81	11.18	13.63
Huntsville, AL	11.05	69.15	28.19	67.02	18.45	12.03	13.17
Indianapolis, IN	12.43	70.85	32.23	62.85	15.39	14.07	15.71
Jacksonville, FL	12.07	73.04	31.15	55.91	16.72	13.54	14.39
Kansas City, MO	13.01	74.13	31.26	52.71	19.13	13.99	16.10
Lafayette, LA	10.23	58.26	26.05	58.46	12.89	9.92	12.05
Las Cruces, NM	12.21	46.68	25.64	50.87	13.04	12.29	13.56
Las Vegas, NV	12.19	58.11	29.10	60.12	13.20	15.34	15.69
Lexington, KY	11.82	65.06	29.85	45.50	13.22	14.88	14.75
Lincoln, NE	12.48	61.87	26.83	47.07	17.83	14.17	14.69
Little Rock, AR	12.41	56.25	26.41	41.68	13.73	12.92	13.43
Los Angeles, CA	16.43	87.66	34.56	67.77	22.18	15.68	18.46
Louisville, KY	11.98	70.09	32.22	48.89	14.19	15.29	14.97

Table continued on following page.

Metro Area	Fast Food and Counter Workers	Financial Managers	First-Line Supervisors/ of Office Workers	General and Operations Managers	Hair-dressers/ Cosme-tologists	Home Health and Personal Care Aides	Janitors/ Cleaners
Madison, WI	12.42	72.88	33.73	65.92	17.32	14.89	16.04
Manchester, NH[2]	13.09	72.83	33.58	67.22	16.38	15.63	17.06
Miami, FL	12.93	81.34	31.90	56.01	15.37	13.24	14.03
Midland, TX	12.27	94.45	32.60	59.45	14.46	12.12	14.35
Milwaukee, WI	12.08	74.52	33.87	68.48	18.97	13.83	15.71
Minneapolis, MN	14.79	76.74	34.96	56.37	20.87	15.64	17.94
Nashville, TN	12.17	72.46	32.48	67.20	19.75	13.96	15.14
New Haven, CT[2]	14.76	71.48	34.08	70.00	18.17	16.48	18.12
New Orleans, LA	12.70	67.00	26.71	61.48	14.26	11.09	12.91
New York, NY	16.08	110.67	38.32	83.82	20.85	17.10	20.14
Oklahoma City, OK	11.19	64.38	30.11	48.66	17.09	12.14	13.56
Omaha, NE	12.76	65.55	28.58	47.42	21.04	14.54	15.19
Orlando, FL	12.49	77.76	30.12	55.62	17.02	13.54	13.87
Philadelphia, PA	13.26	78.78	33.31	68.82	17.70	14.31	17.24
Phoenix, AZ	15.53	76.99	30.64	54.46	20.15	15.17	15.82
Pittsburgh, PA	11.65	73.72	29.71	55.74	16.69	13.88	16.22
Portland, OR	15.88	75.43	32.27	56.83	18.86	17.48	18.11
Providence, RI[2]	14.82	81.58	34.07	65.29	15.61	17.07	17.99
Provo, UT	12.33	68.82	29.37	47.51	18.44	15.63	13.80
Raleigh, NC	12.10	74.45	29.75	64.48	21.68	13.39	14.13
Reno, NV	12.62	59.63	29.96	61.79	16.20	17.81	15.57
Richmond, VA	12.47	80.46	31.31	59.05	18.60	13.05	14.79
Rochester, MN	14.09	65.15	31.71	51.56	19.51	15.54	18.28
Sacramento, CA	16.46	79.36	35.50	67.53	21.69	15.29	18.34
Salem, OR	14.60	64.50	30.14	46.82	18.25	17.28	17.05
Salt Lake City, UT	13.19	69.34	30.21	53.16	19.62	16.45	14.30
San Antonio, TX	11.50	73.39	30.02	50.98	14.16	10.89	14.02
San Diego, CA	16.37	83.73	33.77	n/a	21.87	16.23	18.06
San Francisco, CA	18.38	107.34	40.24	80.86	23.34	16.61	21.39
San Jose, CA	18.80	103.92	41.82	90.32	20.99	17.24	20.64
Santa Rosa, CA	17.13	81.95	34.88	64.13	21.59	16.52	22.75
Savannah, GA	11.64	71.42	27.26	51.37	16.53	12.70	14.18
Seattle, WA	17.49	87.94	37.50	72.41	23.93	18.81	20.41
Sioux Falls, SD	13.18	76.40	28.08	71.87	19.15	15.27	15.35
Springfield, IL	13.61	64.09	30.02	52.04	18.76	14.39	16.63
St. Louis, MO	13.40	72.89	31.51	54.93	18.85	13.32	16.09
Tampa, FL	12.44	76.40	30.65	53.47	17.46	13.80	13.88
Tucson, AZ	14.40	62.10	27.35	44.86	19.75	14.57	15.53
Tulsa, OK	11.21	72.14	29.35	51.65	16.50	12.65	14.02
Tuscaloosa, AL	11.34	62.63	28.60	55.95	17.32	11.32	14.40
Virginia Beach, VA	12.47	72.27	28.99	54.70	17.34	12.57	14.20
Washington, DC	15.12	87.75	35.74	72.97	22.54	15.70	17.34
Wichita, KS	11.16	70.00	28.52	46.78	16.45	12.10	14.45
Wilmington, NC	11.32	74.45	26.02	53.42	19.04	12.45	13.87
Winston-Salem, NC	12.15	74.71	27.78	58.23	18.87	12.67	13.23
Worcester, MA[2]	15.52	71.84	32.65	61.97	21.83	16.77	18.83

Notes: (1) Figures cover the Metropolitan Statistical Area (MSA) except where noted. See Appendix B for areas included;
(2) New England City and Town Area; n/a not available
Source: Bureau of Labor Statistics, May 2022 Metro Area Occupational Employment and Wage Estimates

Average Hourly Wages: Occupations L – N

Metro Area	Landscapers	Lawyers	Maids/House-keepers	Main-tenance/ Repairers	Marketing Managers	Network Admin.	Nurses, Licensed Practical
Albuquerque, NM	16.24	54.41	13.69	20.91	61.49	44.73	28.50
Allentown, PA	17.57	64.68	14.89	24.13	66.34	41.40	26.64
Anchorage, AK	21.00	58.26	15.86	24.49	52.64	42.70	31.62
Ann Arbor, MI	17.82	60.75	15.15	22.11	66.72	43.40	28.93
Athens, GA	15.97	n/a	12.50	19.81	54.36	36.48	24.20
Atlanta, GA	17.07	84.73	13.58	21.53	73.79	50.54	26.03
Austin, TX	16.91	72.31	13.88	20.40	70.73	46.20	27.17
Baltimore, MD	18.68	77.46	14.74	23.34	69.41	52.41	28.83
Boise City, ID	17.90	48.56	15.14	20.73	51.10	39.68	27.38
Boston, MA[2]	21.78	97.55	19.01	27.11	80.96	52.37	33.67
Boulder, CO	21.69	n/a	17.31	27.19	85.56	48.32	29.85
Brownsville, TX	12.90	56.07	10.80	15.45	56.84	36.42	22.93
Cape Coral, FL	16.34	58.21	14.40	20.21	65.93	42.44	25.89
Cedar Rapids, IA	16.78	57.59	13.71	22.16	61.42	41.95	25.54
Charleston, SC	16.99	53.48	13.47	21.41	52.80	46.31	25.74
Charlotte, NC	17.24	78.03	13.43	22.36	71.03	44.85	26.52
Chicago, IL	18.93	78.47	17.07	26.11	70.74	44.98	30.01
Cincinnati, OH	16.69	64.18	13.58	23.48	69.92	46.45	25.99
Clarksville, TN	16.66	51.48	11.75	22.30	50.21	34.09	22.40
Cleveland, OH	17.23	64.28	14.02	23.06	69.27	45.69	26.09
College Station, TX	15.78	75.98	12.68	18.38	57.23	37.16	23.08
Colorado Springs, CO	n/a	53.62	16.06	22.51	79.04	47.29	27.54
Columbia, MO	15.24	58.60	13.42	20.64	52.19	38.68	23.50
Columbia, SC	15.84	53.72	12.62	20.68	59.00	43.75	25.20
Columbus, OH	17.46	65.26	13.91	23.16	69.18	47.97	26.41
Dallas, TX	16.86	87.42	13.78	21.23	67.66	45.36	26.59
Davenport, IA	16.43	56.57	13.68	22.09	60.27	40.41	25.09
Denver, CO	20.25	84.07	16.80	25.27	86.32	50.59	30.30
Des Moines, IA	17.60	59.08	14.22	22.01	64.50	44.01	25.09
Durham, NC	17.41	73.85	14.21	23.68	75.77	48.52	26.52
Edison, NJ	20.81	92.92	21.40	26.67	93.41	55.75	30.31
El Paso, TX	13.79	65.20	11.07	16.87	49.29	37.25	22.95
Fargo, ND	19.28	61.05	14.33	22.10	61.40	39.32	25.14
Fort Collins, CO	19.43	88.05	16.17	22.69	87.40	43.41	28.74
Fort Wayne, IN	16.18	62.54	13.34	23.13	56.84	37.68	25.80
Fort Worth, TX	16.86	87.42	13.78	21.23	67.66	45.36	26.59
Grand Rapids, MI	17.18	64.19	14.27	21.10	64.10	41.89	27.34
Greeley, CO	20.33	67.70	16.09	25.25	80.70	41.55	29.06
Green Bay, WI	17.41	72.57	14.43	22.47	75.00	42.60	23.59
Greensboro, NC	15.69	66.92	13.04	21.27	64.13	41.11	25.19
Honolulu, HI	19.21	50.95	23.06	25.25	59.72	44.72	27.07
Houston, TX	16.29	84.79	14.27	20.87	71.45	47.28	26.65
Huntsville, AL	15.92	69.72	11.97	20.71	68.35	45.60	22.75
Indianapolis, IN	17.19	74.02	14.20	23.30	65.78	42.49	27.80
Jacksonville, FL	16.00	62.74	13.79	20.57	72.46	43.58	24.97
Kansas City, MO	17.47	70.16	14.27	22.59	68.75	42.01	26.30
Lafayette, LA	14.42	53.24	10.93	18.12	47.53	41.24	21.48
Las Cruces, NM	15.38	53.03	12.60	18.02	n/a	41.48	27.19
Las Vegas, NV	17.85	82.94	17.87	23.05	51.14	49.43	30.50
Lexington, KY	15.64	51.22	12.88	22.07	55.36	38.28	24.21
Lincoln, NE	16.86	56.01	13.97	21.04	49.76	40.83	24.46
Little Rock, AR	15.21	50.96	12.84	18.37	51.80	38.74	23.12
Los Angeles, CA	19.81	93.69	18.69	24.86	81.73	49.56	32.95
Louisville, KY	16.00	52.07	13.67	23.69	68.37	40.49	25.32
Madison, WI	18.73	66.28	14.97	22.80	70.25	43.19	25.83

Table continued on following page.

Metro Area	Landscapers	Lawyers	Maids/ House- keepers	Main- tenance/ Repairers	Marketing Managers	Network Admin.	Nurses, Licensed Practical
Manchester, NH[2]	19.05	69.50	15.17	23.02	70.51	42.70	31.39
Miami, FL	16.61	69.69	14.17	20.30	73.31	45.42	26.47
Midland, TX	16.75	87.92	13.55	20.19	76.35	46.75	26.25
Milwaukee, WI	17.75	80.34	14.73	22.70	68.47	46.07	26.39
Minneapolis, MN	19.96	83.25	17.58	25.64	78.99	46.85	27.70
Nashville, TN	17.05	73.05	13.44	21.40	76.32	44.89	23.71
New Haven, CT[2]	20.86	73.87	15.86	24.69	71.85	45.08	30.20
New Orleans, LA	14.72	68.27	12.41	20.69	61.89	39.84	24.25
New York, NY	20.81	92.92	21.40	26.67	93.41	55.75	30.31
Oklahoma City, OK	16.15	53.26	12.31	18.75	64.04	41.84	23.45
Omaha, NE	17.69	59.74	14.69	22.11	58.09	44.11	25.44
Orlando, FL	16.23	70.07	14.29	20.33	76.95	43.75	26.40
Philadelphia, PA	18.71	76.88	15.47	23.49	71.68	47.15	28.52
Phoenix, AZ	17.31	72.30	16.08	22.41	68.83	45.37	30.07
Pittsburgh, PA	16.84	66.28	14.29	22.49	60.70	45.38	25.74
Portland, OR	20.88	73.57	17.60	24.55	66.94	48.17	33.26
Providence, RI[2]	20.58	74.38	16.14	24.78	79.73	51.47	31.28
Provo, UT	18.30	72.07	14.71	21.46	62.12	43.16	25.28
Raleigh, NC	17.40	67.47	14.15	22.67	71.21	45.26	26.69
Reno, NV	18.37	72.00	16.74	23.76	64.64	55.57	32.19
Richmond, VA	16.43	80.05	13.35	22.55	72.33	48.67	25.75
Rochester, MN	18.74	57.71	15.90	23.54	62.16	48.04	25.78
Sacramento, CA	20.30	79.67	20.36	24.95	77.80	43.18	34.27
Salem, OR	19.59	67.46	16.44	22.28	52.32	46.22	30.83
Salt Lake City, UT	18.82	65.12	16.12	23.79	65.16	45.48	29.02
San Antonio, TX	15.69	68.81	13.15	19.50	60.00	41.81	25.93
San Diego, CA	19.61	89.63	18.37	24.59	84.68	49.31	32.57
San Francisco, CA	23.72	115.06	22.92	29.95	100.73	61.21	38.69
San Jose, CA	24.14	128.77	22.48	30.88	113.98	72.84	38.75
Santa Rosa, CA	21.42	88.92	20.35	26.12	75.37	46.00	36.88
Savannah, GA	15.94	n/a	11.85	20.32	68.95	44.17	24.10
Seattle, WA	23.52	83.85	18.50	27.19	82.15	53.30	35.34
Sioux Falls, SD	16.41	60.68	13.76	20.54	66.13	35.57	22.26
Springfield, IL	18.70	61.68	16.39	23.40	62.68	36.92	25.11
St. Louis, MO	17.58	68.34	14.77	24.01	64.07	45.06	26.06
Tampa, FL	15.63	66.40	13.55	19.72	72.41	44.44	25.31
Tucson, AZ	16.04	61.60	14.58	20.08	58.86	41.53	29.01
Tulsa, OK	15.90	60.61	12.45	19.66	69.45	41.63	24.26
Tuscaloosa, AL	15.89	55.63	11.48	18.71	54.09	37.32	21.53
Virginia Beach, VA	16.35	61.10	13.16	21.28	70.40	44.66	24.37
Washington, DC	19.67	101.85	17.03	25.65	84.53	55.96	29.10
Wichita, KS	15.78	54.07	12.87	19.99	63.35	40.60	23.92
Wilmington, NC	16.23	61.99	12.83	19.80	67.91	39.92	25.28
Winston-Salem, NC	16.17	81.73	13.42	21.32	72.60	42.13	25.36
Worcester, MA[2]	20.03	69.75	17.11	24.75	73.90	47.65	30.85

Notes: (1) Figures cover the Metropolitan Statistical Area (MSA) except where noted. See Appendix B for areas included;
(2) New England City and Town Area; n/a not available
Source: Bureau of Labor Statistics, May 2022 Metro Area Occupational Employment and Wage Estimates

Average Hourly Wages: Occupations N – P

Metro Area	Nurses, Registered	Nursing Assistants	Office Clerks	Physical Therapists	Physicians	Plumbers	Police Officers
Albuquerque, NM	41.94	16.74	16.26	44.66	129.51	25.36	27.99
Allentown, PA	39.14	17.79	20.19	48.05	n/a	32.16	36.38
Anchorage, AK	49.59	20.50	22.26	49.64	112.03	43.11	47.16
Ann Arbor, MI	41.54	18.36	19.11	46.21	120.10	33.25	34.05
Athens, GA	38.59	14.53	19.23	49.24	106.67	26.88	24.49
Atlanta, GA	43.40	17.12	19.42	46.86	123.80	28.56	26.02
Austin, TX	41.69	16.17	19.06	47.33	136.94	28.42	35.58
Baltimore, MD	43.03	17.71	19.28	45.91	120.21	28.83	34.65
Boise City, ID	39.06	17.88	17.66	43.44	148.73	28.88	30.67
Boston, MA[2]	51.44	20.42	23.38	46.36	106.88	39.70	36.32
Boulder, CO	44.57	19.72	25.81	48.20	142.09	32.34	40.88
Brownsville, TX	35.07	13.19	14.88	45.71	116.21	20.29	26.68
Cape Coral, FL	38.04	16.24	19.43	43.77	177.87	24.29	31.19
Cedar Rapids, IA	33.68	17.02	19.34	40.86	125.70	32.41	31.90
Charleston, SC	36.96	17.18	17.46	41.79	141.24	24.76	25.12
Charlotte, NC	38.24	15.93	18.96	46.12	133.48	25.11	28.24
Chicago, IL	40.99	18.37	21.22	48.81	100.40	43.17	41.59
Cincinnati, OH	38.82	16.53	19.80	45.46	108.34	31.67	33.83
Clarksville, TN	34.52	14.53	16.20	42.52	143.21	24.18	23.65
Cleveland, OH	38.95	17.21	20.05	47.43	79.22	31.97	34.02
College Station, TX	37.59	14.34	15.70	46.21	n/a	24.11	31.36
Colorado Springs, CO	39.78	18.31	23.24	45.18	n/a	28.01	37.67
Columbia, MO	34.00	15.71	18.99	41.76	132.62	28.50	24.89
Columbia, SC	35.37	15.81	16.30	41.97	142.61	22.81	24.96
Columbus, OH	38.80	16.67	20.13	48.56	102.84	31.99	37.43
Dallas, TX	42.24	16.34	18.59	50.76	118.86	26.94	35.82
Davenport, IA	32.77	16.26	18.58	41.53	n/a	32.66	32.09
Denver, CO	42.21	19.35	24.74	47.13	156.83	31.18	41.85
Des Moines, IA	34.16	17.50	19.96	41.72	105.11	31.79	34.32
Durham, NC	n/a	16.82	19.49	40.71	n/a	26.00	25.40
Edison, NJ	50.41	21.50	21.90	53.25	128.42	42.38	42.43
El Paso, TX	36.36	13.69	15.17	45.54	105.87	22.73	30.10
Fargo, ND	36.60	17.94	22.07	40.35	105.75	29.18	34.03
Fort Collins, CO	40.85	18.30	23.55	42.61	n/a	29.30	43.64
Fort Wayne, IN	35.21	15.77	18.98	44.25	n/a	33.18	31.73
Fort Worth, TX	42.24	16.34	18.59	50.76	118.86	26.94	35.82
Grand Rapids, MI	36.98	17.03	20.33	42.66	126.06	30.06	31.96
Greeley, CO	41.14	17.60	23.36	47.67	n/a	26.96	36.95
Green Bay, WI	37.41	17.41	19.40	44.40	177.48	33.56	34.37
Greensboro, NC	38.59	14.93	17.77	45.22	n/a	23.39	24.52
Honolulu, HI	55.38	19.29	20.72	49.00	132.28	37.07	43.41
Houston, TX	42.73	16.18	18.74	52.20	138.31	28.24	32.31
Huntsville, AL	31.99	14.59	13.92	46.53	139.48	24.93	25.54
Indianapolis, IN	38.68	16.97	20.15	45.55	161.40	33.28	32.70
Jacksonville, FL	37.74	15.99	19.42	44.49	132.91	23.81	27.88
Kansas City, MO	36.82	17.33	20.48	44.96	104.46	31.93	29.20
Lafayette, LA	35.91	12.92	13.92	44.44	140.81	25.47	22.67
Las Cruces, NM	37.30	14.84	15.58	40.75	135.79	22.92	27.37
Las Vegas, NV	46.96	19.90	19.84	51.20	126.98	31.07	36.94
Lexington, KY	37.36	16.43	17.56	40.93	146.74	29.90	24.95
Lincoln, NE	35.52	16.53	16.75	44.49	131.40	25.79	33.34
Little Rock, AR	34.48	15.09	17.64	44.50	90.44	22.44	23.08
Los Angeles, CA	60.26	20.49	21.66	52.02	113.43	34.45	50.13
Louisville, KY	39.08	16.62	18.11	43.91	144.45	29.23	25.96
Madison, WI	41.46	18.71	20.66	43.49	152.61	35.91	35.34

Table continued on following page.

Metro Area	Nurses, Registered	Nursing Assistants	Office Clerks	Physical Therapists	Physicians	Plumbers	Police Officers
Manchester, NH[2]	39.38	18.40	22.10	43.45	n/a	28.32	30.78
Miami, FL	39.33	16.17	19.87	42.11	102.65	24.64	43.87
Midland, TX	39.34	16.60	20.43	50.09	124.58	26.81	34.27
Milwaukee, WI	39.44	17.93	19.83	45.40	104.93	35.62	35.72
Minneapolis, MN	44.32	22.36	22.34	43.60	145.35	39.07	39.69
Nashville, TN	37.13	16.08	17.70	44.33	131.73	26.77	26.07
New Haven, CT[2]	46.18	18.43	21.09	48.79	130.80	34.63	36.86
New Orleans, LA	38.18	14.49	14.52	46.62	151.73	27.73	23.68
New York, NY	50.41	21.50	21.90	53.25	128.42	42.38	42.43
Oklahoma City, OK	37.19	14.90	16.78	44.06	126.14	24.68	33.22
Omaha, NE	36.18	17.53	18.19	43.62	142.86	32.29	34.43
Orlando, FL	38.04	16.41	18.94	45.58	133.16	23.14	29.83
Philadelphia, PA	42.23	18.17	21.08	48.69	n/a	34.76	37.93
Phoenix, AZ	42.03	18.44	21.73	48.80	98.99	28.48	35.65
Pittsburgh, PA	36.65	17.51	19.95	45.42	59.50	34.72	36.66
Portland, OR	53.66	21.15	21.40	46.36	111.11	40.51	40.50
Providence, RI[2]	42.39	18.87	21.07	45.70	100.09	32.22	34.35
Provo, UT	34.96	15.59	18.82	43.16	82.30	25.73	28.90
Raleigh, NC	37.82	16.03	19.56	42.43	140.14	24.57	26.56
Reno, NV	44.85	19.69	21.19	49.42	142.69	32.67	35.21
Richmond, VA	39.75	15.79	18.79	46.28	79.68	25.66	29.03
Rochester, MN	43.30	19.09	21.24	41.61	143.61	37.05	34.21
Sacramento, CA	69.82	21.17	21.97	58.89	145.43	33.87	48.52
Salem, OR	46.17	21.59	20.38	45.54	158.13	34.34	37.37
Salt Lake City, UT	38.16	16.66	19.23	45.74	120.76	30.62	32.06
San Antonio, TX	39.92	15.47	18.02	45.42	145.35	24.88	31.55
San Diego, CA	56.65	20.39	21.38	52.92	125.61	34.09	47.51
San Francisco, CA	79.21	25.13	26.29	60.61	114.31	44.23	57.43
San Jose, CA	76.94	24.81	25.56	64.33	124.09	46.57	62.36
Santa Rosa, CA	72.67	20.99	22.86	60.31	112.97	36.74	49.57
Savannah, GA	40.41	14.89	18.02	45.44	100.61	28.19	25.28
Seattle, WA	50.74	21.40	24.29	50.43	120.27	41.46	48.78
Sioux Falls, SD	30.18	15.47	15.70	41.62	n/a	25.38	31.52
Springfield, IL	37.80	17.22	20.11	46.06	146.21	38.31	34.84
St. Louis, MO	36.14	16.41	20.76	44.14	142.81	35.55	29.89
Tampa, FL	38.42	16.72	19.64	46.29	132.49	23.00	33.26
Tucson, AZ	40.19	17.25	20.55	44.89	n/a	25.56	30.75
Tulsa, OK	38.32	15.05	17.16	43.95	78.82	26.43	26.48
Tuscaloosa, AL	30.81	14.13	13.87	48.68	105.13	23.92	27.48
Virginia Beach, VA	38.20	15.13	18.11	45.34	n/a	26.56	27.70
Washington, DC	44.61	18.33	22.52	49.52	101.91	30.71	37.25
Wichita, KS	33.08	15.61	14.16	43.47	100.53	27.23	25.83
Wilmington, NC	36.27	14.86	17.25	41.09	112.33	22.57	23.49
Winston-Salem, NC	38.57	15.34	17.36	47.28	n/a	22.79	24.14
Worcester, MA[2]	47.38	18.71	21.03	44.80	108.84	40.47	30.41

Notes: (1) Figures cover the Metropolitan Statistical Area (MSA) except where noted. See Appendix B for areas included;
(2) New England City and Town Area; n/a not available
Source: Bureau of Labor Statistics, May 2022 Metro Area Occupational Employment and Wage Estimates

Average Hourly Wages: Occupations P – S

Metro Area	Postal Mail Carriers	R.E. Sales Agents	Retail Sales-persons	Sales Reps., Technical/ Scientific	Secretaries, Exc. Leg./ Med./Exec.	Security Guards	Surgeons
Albuquerque, NM	26.30	22.73	15.08	37.39	20.16	15.37	n/a
Allentown, PA	27.45	27.37	16.75	51.14	20.39	17.28	n/a
Anchorage, AK	25.73	34.80	18.27	36.27	20.62	20.74	n/a
Ann Arbor, MI	27.10	33.57	16.77	128.93	22.52	18.34	n/a
Athens, GA	25.97	21.38	14.84	41.34	17.79	19.33	n/a
Atlanta, GA	26.65	28.00	15.55	52.79	19.44	16.02	212.04
Austin, TX	27.22	39.51	16.52	44.57	21.45	17.41	n/a
Baltimore, MD	27.22	32.50	15.99	50.13	21.48	20.09	162.71
Boise City, ID	27.00	21.80	16.72	41.57	18.67	16.67	n/a
Boston, MA[2]	28.27	38.33	18.39	54.97	25.44	19.80	148.22
Boulder, CO	28.10	49.41	18.86	n/a	22.19	21.46	n/a
Brownsville, TX	26.80	24.87	14.27	n/a	16.45	15.55	n/a
Cape Coral, FL	26.49	24.97	15.73	53.67	18.53	14.53	n/a
Cedar Rapids, IA	27.18	30.06	15.63	51.91	20.40	17.15	n/a
Charleston, SC	26.88	29.27	15.26	37.04	19.15	14.67	n/a
Charlotte, NC	27.50	27.29	15.72	54.96	20.17	14.89	276.15
Chicago, IL	27.84	21.56	17.49	56.01	23.34	17.98	136.81
Cincinnati, OH	28.15	27.69	16.23	51.86	20.51	17.09	184.17
Clarksville, TN	25.40	28.07	15.47	32.81	18.04	18.30	n/a
Cleveland, OH	27.79	20.71	16.56	52.20	20.38	17.47	n/a
College Station, TX	26.30	31.28	14.39	39.76	18.70	14.38	n/a
Colorado Springs, CO	26.35	34.84	17.44	46.25	19.90	17.50	n/a
Columbia, MO	26.18	20.94	14.99	n/a	18.33	16.33	n/a
Columbia, SC	25.68	28.52	14.63	40.39	18.64	13.48	n/a
Columbus, OH	27.37	21.29	16.00	58.13	20.96	17.83	n/a
Dallas, TX	27.30	38.08	16.19	43.31	20.33	16.99	142.82
Davenport, IA	26.31	33.24	15.72	50.09	19.78	18.10	n/a
Denver, CO	28.16	40.40	19.03	54.91	22.11	19.02	146.05
Des Moines, IA	27.78	34.49	15.88	54.80	21.22	17.63	n/a
Durham, NC	27.82	26.02	15.72	58.46	21.42	18.04	n/a
Edison, NJ	27.72	47.01	19.51	63.64	23.24	19.89	149.60
El Paso, TX	26.59	27.97	14.09	n/a	16.30	15.14	n/a
Fargo, ND	27.52	29.08	17.14	54.63	20.53	16.86	n/a
Fort Collins, CO	27.22	33.68	17.51	46.18	21.02	16.93	n/a
Fort Wayne, IN	26.91	27.25	14.91	51.06	18.31	17.67	n/a
Fort Worth, TX	27.30	38.08	16.19	43.31	20.33	16.99	142.82
Grand Rapids, MI	27.01	27.56	16.20	52.99	20.23	14.75	121.07
Greeley, CO	26.49	52.77	18.12	47.78	20.32	16.95	n/a
Green Bay, WI	27.20	29.62	16.28	34.34	20.34	16.22	n/a
Greensboro, NC	27.21	26.84	15.24	42.34	19.33	14.54	n/a
Honolulu, HI	26.72	26.75	17.85	54.70	23.30	17.09	205.79
Houston, TX	26.87	38.86	16.04	46.77	20.43	15.78	162.09
Huntsville, AL	26.36	41.38	14.54	38.34	20.21	15.35	n/a
Indianapolis, IN	27.71	32.61	15.60	52.85	20.15	16.75	185.56
Jacksonville, FL	27.22	29.37	15.49	46.55	19.30	15.13	n/a
Kansas City, MO	27.63	26.48	16.44	53.53	19.21	18.98	119.29
Lafayette, LA	26.29	17.52	13.84	40.17	17.91	13.48	n/a
Las Cruces, NM	25.66	22.91	13.98	n/a	18.37	15.27	n/a
Las Vegas, NV	26.97	38.35	16.82	41.45	21.22	15.06	n/a
Lexington, KY	27.17	27.67	15.76	45.14	20.09	14.57	n/a
Lincoln, NE	27.48	19.09	15.39	43.72	19.78	14.91	n/a
Little Rock, AR	26.80	n/a	14.90	44.97	18.48	15.34	n/a
Los Angeles, CA	28.35	35.65	18.93	52.61	24.22	18.19	n/a
Louisville, KY	27.28	22.31	15.89	49.19	19.91	16.60	194.02
Madison, WI	27.00	33.85	16.03	36.52	21.15	17.01	n/a

Table continued on following page.

Metro Area	Postal Mail Carriers	R.E. Sales Agents	Retail Sales-persons	Sales Reps., Technical/ Scientific	Secretaries, Exc. Leg./ Med./Exec.	Security Guards	Surgeons
Manchester, NH[2]	27.77	30.34	16.93	41.73	20.73	18.41	n/a
Miami, FL	27.09	26.19	16.30	50.86	20.66	16.16	92.08
Midland, TX	25.08	48.44	16.59	48.08	20.58	17.08	n/a
Milwaukee, WI	27.42	24.00	16.36	39.18	20.72	16.44	n/a
Minneapolis, MN	27.77	n/a	17.68	47.57	23.29	18.79	176.40
Nashville, TN	27.31	19.02	16.18	40.84	20.51	15.94	135.32
New Haven, CT[2]	26.76	29.22	18.46	45.89	26.88	18.52	n/a
New Orleans, LA	26.86	24.99	14.66	40.90	18.95	15.17	n/a
New York, NY	27.72	47.01	19.51	63.64	23.24	19.89	149.60
Oklahoma City, OK	27.22	n/a	15.14	39.45	18.26	15.95	n/a
Omaha, NE	27.42	29.75	16.07	41.32	19.89	17.42	158.30
Orlando, FL	26.72	26.11	15.51	46.62	18.93	15.30	n/a
Philadelphia, PA	27.23	27.12	16.66	57.64	21.81	18.05	196.21
Phoenix, AZ	27.93	29.19	17.07	46.98	21.31	17.03	n/a
Pittsburgh, PA	26.80	30.60	15.60	50.53	19.68	16.59	n/a
Portland, OR	27.17	28.64	19.03	56.64	24.16	18.14	n/a
Providence, RI[2]	27.29	35.48	17.17	39.71	22.88	17.75	n/a
Provo, UT	27.30	27.88	16.90	43.62	19.25	15.75	n/a
Raleigh, NC	27.38	27.61	16.28	55.59	20.25	15.48	n/a
Reno, NV	27.69	24.89	17.26	42.94	22.47	16.07	n/a
Richmond, VA	26.92	35.50	15.56	47.20	19.90	17.63	n/a
Rochester, MN	27.15	n/a	16.90	35.30	21.71	17.79	156.35
Sacramento, CA	28.15	32.19	19.11	58.98	23.74	18.43	n/a
Salem, OR	26.44	29.11	17.64	53.51	22.97	18.21	n/a
Salt Lake City, UT	28.08	26.96	18.75	57.43	20.26	17.09	219.11
San Antonio, TX	26.74	32.87	15.92	41.27	19.44	15.80	n/a
San Diego, CA	27.48	41.65	18.69	57.24	23.50	18.37	n/a
San Francisco, CA	29.20	39.87	21.47	60.73	28.82	21.09	75.20
San Jose, CA	29.08	36.25	21.34	78.03	28.34	21.24	n/a
Santa Rosa, CA	27.31	39.25	19.94	53.84	25.29	19.11	n/a
Savannah, GA	26.97	23.15	14.40	40.36	18.89	15.54	n/a
Seattle, WA	28.57	34.93	19.75	74.86	26.09	20.72	97.57
Sioux Falls, SD	27.07	n/a	18.12	57.97	17.76	16.09	n/a
Springfield, IL	26.37	26.10	16.08	39.68	20.55	17.77	n/a
St. Louis, MO	27.22	23.21	17.00	48.57	19.80	17.68	n/a
Tampa, FL	26.91	27.94	16.01	45.68	18.84	15.00	191.11
Tucson, AZ	27.62	27.03	16.59	48.00	19.49	15.65	n/a
Tulsa, OK	27.22	40.04	15.59	38.20	18.07	15.18	n/a
Tuscaloosa, AL	27.01	29.05	14.09	n/a	19.12	15.31	n/a
Virginia Beach, VA	26.24	33.80	15.11	45.63	20.00	16.42	n/a
Washington, DC	27.72	36.03	17.61	62.98	24.44	23.65	186.07
Wichita, KS	26.65	27.02	15.34	51.87	17.74	15.50	n/a
Wilmington, NC	26.03	28.16	15.41	60.83	19.24	15.17	n/a
Winston-Salem, NC	27.50	33.61	14.59	44.22	19.35	16.60	n/a
Worcester, MA[2]	27.11	n/a	17.84	55.25	23.77	18.53	n/a

Notes: (1) Figures cover the Metropolitan Statistical Area (MSA) except where noted. See Appendix B for areas included;
(2) New England City and Town Area; n/a not available
Source: Bureau of Labor Statistics, May 2022 Metro Area Occupational Employment and Wage Estimates

Average Hourly Wages: Occupations T – W

Metro Area	Teacher Assistants[3]	Teachers, Secondary School[3]	Telemarketers	Truck Drivers, Heavy	Truck Drivers, Light	Waiters/ Waitresses
Albuquerque, NM	14.88	28.99	20.16	22.67	20.43	16.14
Allentown, PA	16.36	35.24	14.10	27.04	22.74	15.35
Anchorage, AK	17.44	36.14	n/a	27.93	26.04	13.47
Ann Arbor, MI	15.21	35.99	n/a	24.45	23.48	17.37
Athens, GA	11.12	31.25	n/a	26.85	22.03	13.09
Atlanta, GA	14.07	34.25	15.50	26.24	21.28	14.52
Austin, TX	15.16	30.16	16.31	23.73	22.03	13.42
Baltimore, MD	19.37	34.31	18.80	26.63	22.04	17.63
Boise City, ID	14.04	27.88	17.64	25.05	24.37	14.76
Boston, MA[2]	20.14	40.58	19.82	27.78	23.55	19.76
Boulder, CO	18.12	35.67	17.68	26.67	24.66	20.98
Brownsville, TX	13.50	26.50	n/a	22.21	18.91	10.94
Cape Coral, FL	14.90	33.25	16.95	22.84	20.22	15.70
Cedar Rapids, IA	14.26	28.59	n/a	25.17	19.97	13.27
Charleston, SC	12.32	27.85	n/a	25.58	19.54	11.64
Charlotte, NC	13.20	26.35	16.09	25.66	19.89	13.70
Chicago, IL	16.89	37.13	15.52	27.99	24.27	15.53
Cincinnati, OH	16.00	33.81	14.72	26.16	21.77	14.51
Clarksville, TN	14.59	26.06	n/a	22.96	19.13	11.97
Cleveland, OH	16.13	35.16	14.85	25.57	20.45	14.38
College Station, TX	13.43	25.97	n/a	22.43	22.97	12.47
Colorado Springs, CO	15.06	26.75	19.45	24.71	22.21	19.75
Columbia, MO	14.65	n/a	n/a	24.11	22.20	15.51
Columbia, SC	12.00	26.34	10.78	23.99	19.35	10.82
Columbus, OH	16.49	34.42	15.65	26.61	22.93	15.07
Dallas, TX	14.09	30.46	18.24	24.73	22.27	13.17
Davenport, IA	15.10	31.35	14.97	26.12	20.97	13.22
Denver, CO	17.40	32.50	20.16	27.32	23.68	18.48
Des Moines, IA	14.28	32.05	15.86	26.85	21.17	13.46
Durham, NC	13.63	26.62	15.07	24.94	19.89	14.16
Edison, NJ	18.07	45.24	20.35	29.43	23.63	23.01
El Paso, TX	12.23	27.72	14.74	20.95	18.70	11.05
Fargo, ND	16.83	28.97	n/a	27.94	23.00	14.71
Fort Collins, CO	16.36	28.98	18.28	25.19	22.91	19.93
Fort Wayne, IN	13.32	27.57	15.78	25.45	20.20	13.17
Fort Worth, TX	14.09	30.46	18.24	24.73	22.27	13.17
Grand Rapids, MI	15.09	31.35	15.93	24.69	20.89	17.53
Greeley, CO	16.03	27.26	n/a	26.14	23.11	18.76
Green Bay, WI	15.77	29.64	n/a	25.81	21.30	15.02
Greensboro, NC	12.50	24.32	18.68	24.84	18.97	12.88
Honolulu, HI	16.06	29.35	16.92	26.64	21.01	16.89
Houston, TX	13.73	30.64	17.46	24.72	22.19	13.02
Huntsville, AL	10.75	28.00	n/a	23.90	20.20	11.55
Indianapolis, IN	14.25	30.46	17.62	26.92	23.09	13.35
Jacksonville, FL	14.72	31.72	15.08	24.87	21.39	15.33
Kansas City, MO	15.24	28.68	20.21	26.24	22.59	15.86
Lafayette, LA	11.25	24.62	n/a	21.71	17.50	11.88
Las Cruces, NM	14.06	33.00	n/a	21.52	17.37	15.04
Las Vegas, NV	16.36	30.96	15.02	24.98	20.79	13.18
Lexington, KY	16.94	29.65	n/a	26.48	21.58	14.02
Lincoln, NE	12.27	28.33	13.08	35.10	21.50	14.17
Little Rock, AR	14.46	25.70	n/a	26.45	22.85	13.89
Los Angeles, CA	20.58	43.33	18.39	26.10	22.77	18.08
Louisville, KY	15.01	30.29	15.36	27.04	23.90	13.48
Madison, WI	16.63	29.79	n/a	25.52	20.60	15.98

Table continued on following page.

Metro Area	Teacher Assistants[3]	Teachers, Secondary School[3]	Telemarketers	Truck Drivers, Heavy	Truck Drivers, Light	Waiters/ Waitresses
Manchester, NH[2]	16.19	33.56	15.33	25.70	20.52	16.61
Miami, FL	14.59	31.87	16.79	24.62	21.37	16.13
Midland, TX	13.37	30.50	n/a	25.69	20.91	12.89
Milwaukee, WI	16.86	33.03	16.38	26.40	21.54	15.68
Minneapolis, MN	18.50	31.91	22.98	28.77	23.50	13.34
Nashville, TN	13.61	26.44	n/a	26.23	21.56	11.99
New Haven, CT[2]	18.30	36.32	23.10	26.23	21.59	19.08
New Orleans, LA	14.50	27.00	n/a	24.66	19.53	12.15
New York, NY	18.07	45.24	20.35	29.43	23.63	23.01
Oklahoma City, OK	11.92	27.00	18.98	24.66	20.54	12.33
Omaha, NE	13.94	28.50	13.51	32.23	21.83	15.36
Orlando, FL	13.42	26.07	14.29	24.63	21.37	16.41
Philadelphia, PA	16.04	35.76	16.16	27.40	22.39	15.81
Phoenix, AZ	15.19	30.07	17.98	25.42	22.85	22.24
Pittsburgh, PA	15.05	39.73	16.91	25.67	20.10	14.85
Portland, OR	19.64	41.94	19.08	28.25	22.77	18.37
Providence, RI[2]	17.68	36.31	16.60	27.14	22.45	16.64
Provo, UT	13.34	31.61	17.82	25.28	20.06	17.18
Raleigh, NC	12.44	25.67	15.51	24.80	19.06	14.41
Reno, NV	18.08	36.23	n/a	26.51	21.26	13.12
Richmond, VA	14.32	37.47	n/a	24.27	20.61	16.35
Rochester, MN	17.00	31.98	n/a	26.90	21.79	12.51
Sacramento, CA	19.35	41.56	18.78	26.24	23.03	17.51
Salem, OR	19.13	39.59	16.13	26.69	21.33	16.15
Salt Lake City, UT	14.52	33.46	15.85	26.89	21.89	17.80
San Antonio, TX	14.17	29.61	17.04	22.61	20.69	13.14
San Diego, CA	19.50	47.51	17.68	25.83	22.99	17.49
San Francisco, CA	22.38	44.23	22.03	30.83	25.29	18.52
San Jose, CA	22.29	46.64	20.56	29.99	24.72	19.37
Santa Rosa, CA	20.52	43.10	n/a	27.66	24.22	18.13
Savannah, GA	15.18	29.79	n/a	24.85	20.20	13.87
Seattle, WA	22.89	44.03	20.78	30.34	24.18	23.47
Sioux Falls, SD	12.99	24.57	n/a	26.46	21.01	13.23
Springfield, IL	15.04	30.36	n/a	24.23	23.13	14.77
St. Louis, MO	15.52	29.12	18.25	26.27	22.92	16.19
Tampa, FL	14.33	32.73	14.35	23.41	20.06	15.84
Tucson, AZ	14.47	23.84	n/a	23.82	21.31	20.77
Tulsa, OK	12.67	28.15	18.01	24.99	19.91	11.71
Tuscaloosa, AL	10.07	26.64	n/a	24.19	20.50	10.78
Virginia Beach, VA	16.04	31.98	17.71	23.13	19.47	15.39
Washington, DC	19.39	40.33	20.08	27.54	23.67	19.91
Wichita, KS	14.41	28.44	n/a	23.66	20.17	14.48
Wilmington, NC	12.82	25.18	15.79	22.70	20.42	13.33
Winston-Salem, NC	11.63	25.01	n/a	24.69	18.96	12.01
Worcester, MA[2]	19.32	38.25	19.51	26.93	22.55	18.31

Notes: (1) Figures cover the Metropolitan Statistical Area (MSA) except where noted. See Appendix B for areas included; (2) New England City and Town Area; (3) Hourly wages were calculated from annual wage data assuming a 40 hour work week; n/a not available
Source: Bureau of Labor Statistics, May 2022 Metro Area Occupational Employment and Wage Estimates

Means of Transportation to Work: City

City	Car/Truck/Van		Public Transportation			Bicycle	Walked	Other Means	Worked at Home
	Drove Alone	Car-pooled	Bus	Subway	Railroad				
Albuquerque, NM	76.6	8.9	1.3	0.0	0.1	0.8	1.9	1.1	9.4
Allentown, PA	67.4	15.5	3.7	0.0	0.0	0.1	4.4	1.9	6.9
Anchorage, AK	73.7	12.1	1.4	0.0	0.0	0.9	2.6	2.1	7.1
Ann Arbor, MI	48.5	4.9	7.9	0.2	0.0	3.1	15.5	0.6	19.1
Athens, GA	72.0	8.0	2.7	0.0	0.0	1.4	4.8	1.0	10.2
Atlanta, GA	59.8	4.8	4.8	3.6	0.2	1.0	4.4	2.8	18.6
Austin, TX	66.2	7.7	2.5	0.1	0.1	1.0	2.6	1.4	18.4
Baltimore, MD	58.2	7.8	11.8	1.2	1.1	0.8	5.9	2.7	10.8
Boise City, ID	73.8	6.9	0.5	0.0	0.0	2.5	2.9	1.6	11.7
Boston, MA	36.1	5.5	10.6	15.5	1.1	2.0	14.4	2.6	12.3
Boulder, CO	45.8	4.3	6.5	0.0	0.0	8.8	9.1	1.3	24.3
Brownsville, TX	80.7	10.2	0.7	0.0	0.0	0.1	1.3	1.2	5.7
Cape Coral, FL	79.3	7.8	0.1	0.0	0.0	0.2	0.9	1.9	9.8
Cedar Rapids, IA	80.2	7.6	0.4	0.0	0.0	0.5	2.0	1.0	8.5
Charleston, SC	74.5	6.2	0.8	0.0	0.0	1.8	3.8	1.3	11.6
Charlotte, NC	68.8	8.6	1.9	0.3	0.1	0.1	1.8	1.8	16.7
Chicago, IL	47.4	7.5	11.1	10.7	1.4	1.5	5.8	2.2	12.3
Cincinnati, OH	69.0	8.5	6.1	0.0	0.0	0.3	5.5	1.4	9.2
Clarksville, TN	84.5	7.7	0.7	0.0	0.0	0.0	1.2	1.4	4.5
Cleveland, OH	68.6	9.9	7.3	0.4	0.1	0.5	4.7	1.7	6.9
College Station, TX	74.7	8.8	2.1	0.0	0.0	1.8	2.6	0.9	9.0
Colorado Springs, CO	74.7	9.8	0.7	0.0	0.0	0.5	1.7	1.1	11.4
Columbia, MO	75.0	9.0	0.9	0.0	0.0	1.2	6.4	0.7	6.8
Columbia, SC	63.8	5.7	1.5	0.0	0.0	0.4	20.3	1.6	6.7
Columbus, OH	75.0	7.2	2.5	0.0	0.0	0.4	2.7	1.1	11.0
Dallas, TX	72.3	11.2	2.3	0.3	0.2	0.2	2.2	1.6	9.7
Davenport, IA	83.4	6.5	0.6	0.0	0.0	0.2	2.3	0.7	6.3
Denver, CO	62.7	6.8	3.5	0.6	0.4	2.0	4.4	2.3	17.2
Des Moines, IA	75.4	10.6	1.4	0.1	0.0	0.5	2.4	1.4	8.2
Durham, NC	70.7	8.0	2.6	0.0	0.0	0.5	2.2	1.3	14.6
Edison, NJ	64.0	8.1	0.7	0.5	9.9	0.1	1.1	1.3	14.1
El Paso, TX	79.1	10.2	1.4	0.0	0.0	0.1	1.1	2.4	5.7
Fargo, ND	79.5	7.8	1.2	0.0	0.0	0.5	3.5	1.9	5.5
Fort Collins, CO	66.7	6.3	1.8	0.0	0.0	4.4	4.3	1.1	15.5
Fort Wayne, IN	80.9	9.6	1.0	0.0	0.0	0.5	1.5	0.8	5.8
Fort Worth, TX	77.3	11.0	0.5	0.0	0.1	0.2	1.3	1.0	8.6
Grand Rapids, MI	71.5	10.0	3.3	0.0	0.0	0.9	4.4	1.0	8.8
Greeley, CO	76.0	12.4	0.5	0.0	0.0	0.5	3.1	0.7	6.8
Green Bay, WI	77.7	10.7	1.1	0.0	0.0	0.2	2.3	1.1	6.9
Greensboro, NC	78.2	7.7	2.3	0.0	0.0	0.2	2.3	1.0	8.3
Honolulu, HI	57.7	13.1	9.4	0.0	0.0	1.6	8.2	3.6	6.4
Houston, TX	73.7	9.8	3.4	0.1	0.0	0.4	1.9	2.4	8.3
Huntsville, AL	81.8	6.2	0.4	0.0	0.0	0.2	1.2	0.8	9.4
Indianapolis, IN	77.6	9.3	1.6	0.0	0.0	0.4	1.9	0.9	8.4
Jacksonville, FL	77.3	8.7	1.4	0.0	0.0	0.3	1.4	2.0	8.8
Kansas City, MO	77.2	7.4	2.2	0.0	0.0	0.2	1.7	1.5	9.8
Lafayette, LA	83.4	4.8	0.8	0.0	0.0	0.5	2.4	1.0	7.0
Las Cruces, NM	74.3	13.2	0.5	0.0	0.0	1.6	1.7	1.4	7.4
Las Vegas, NV	75.5	9.8	2.8	0.0	0.0	0.2	1.3	2.9	7.4
Lexington, KY	77.0	8.1	1.7	0.0	0.0	0.6	3.5	1.1	8.2
Lincoln, NE	78.2	9.1	1.0	0.0	0.0	0.8	3.3	0.7	7.0
Little Rock, AR	78.5	9.7	0.7	0.0	0.0	0.2	1.8	1.5	7.7
Los Angeles, CA	65.2	8.9	6.6	0.8	0.1	0.7	3.2	2.1	12.4
Louisville, KY	76.6	8.4	2.6	0.0	0.0	0.3	1.9	1.6	8.5

Table continued on following page.

City	Car/Truck/Van		Public Transportation			Bicycle	Walked	Other Means	Worked at Home
	Drove Alone	Car-pooled	Bus	Subway	Railroad				
Madison, WI	60.5	6.6	7.0	0.0	0.1	3.6	8.9	1.3	12.1
Manchester, NH	77.8	8.9	0.5	0.0	0.0	0.2	2.6	1.2	8.8
Miami, FL	65.9	7.7	6.1	1.1	0.1	0.8	4.8	3.5	10.1
Midland, TX	82.4	10.4	0.2	0.0	0.0	0.3	0.6	0.7	5.5
Milwaukee, WI	71.2	9.5	5.8	0.0	0.0	0.6	4.1	1.0	7.7
Minneapolis, MN	56.4	6.3	8.6	0.6	0.2	2.9	6.6	2.6	15.8
Nashville, TN	72.8	9.1	1.6	0.0	0.1	0.2	2.2	1.3	12.7
New Haven, CT	58.6	8.0	7.5	0.1	1.1	2.1	11.6	1.9	9.1
New Orleans, LA	65.6	8.9	4.6	0.1	0.0	2.6	5.4	2.9	9.9
New York, NY	22.4	4.4	9.7	38.4	1.2	1.4	9.5	2.5	10.7
Oklahoma City, OK	80.0	9.7	0.4	0.0	0.0	0.2	1.6	1.4	6.8
Omaha, NE	77.2	8.9	1.3	0.0	0.0	0.2	2.1	1.0	9.3
Orlando, FL	75.2	8.1	2.3	0.0	0.0	0.6	1.4	2.7	9.7
Philadelphia, PA	48.3	7.8	13.5	5.2	2.2	2.0	7.6	2.7	10.8
Phoenix, AZ	70.8	11.5	2.1	0.0	0.0	0.5	1.5	1.9	11.5
Pittsburgh, PA	52.1	6.6	14.5	0.3	0.0	1.2	9.7	1.8	13.9
Portland, OR	53.8	7.4	7.2	0.5	0.2	4.7	5.1	3.2	18.0
Providence, RI	64.0	11.3	3.3	0.1	1.0	0.9	7.3	1.7	10.4
Provo, UT	59.2	11.2	3.2	0.1	0.9	2.0	11.8	1.0	10.5
Raleigh, NC	70.9	7.1	1.7	0.0	0.0	0.2	1.4	1.4	17.2
Reno, NV	71.1	12.0	2.7	0.0	0.0	0.7	2.8	2.5	8.3
Richmond, VA	67.8	8.5	4.2	0.1	0.0	1.8	4.5	1.6	11.5
Rochester, MN	67.8	11.9	5.4	0.0	0.0	0.8	4.2	1.2	8.8
Sacramento, CA	68.9	9.6	1.7	0.2	0.3	1.6	2.9	2.2	12.6
St. Louis, MO	69.9	6.6	5.8	0.4	0.1	0.9	4.4	1.4	10.5
Salem, OR	71.7	9.5	2.2	0.0	0.0	1.4	3.4	1.2	10.5
Salt Lake City, UT	63.1	8.8	3.8	0.3	0.6	2.1	4.8	3.2	13.2
San Antonio, TX	74.6	11.8	2.1	0.0	0.0	0.2	1.8	1.6	8.0
San Diego, CA	68.9	8.2	2.8	0.1	0.1	0.7	3.2	2.0	14.0
San Francisco, CA	29.4	6.5	17.8	7.0	1.3	3.3	11.0	5.6	18.0
San Jose, CA	69.2	10.5	2.0	0.3	0.9	0.6	1.9	1.8	13.0
Santa Rosa, CA	76.1	10.3	1.4	0.1	0.1	0.8	1.8	1.4	7.9
Savannah, GA	71.7	10.7	3.1	0.0	0.0	1.2	4.2	1.8	7.3
Seattle, WA	40.5	6.1	15.4	1.0	0.1	2.8	9.7	2.9	21.4
Sioux Falls, SD	81.7	7.8	0.6	0.0	0.0	0.3	2.1	0.7	6.8
Springfield, IL	79.6	6.4	1.6	0.1	0.0	0.5	1.6	1.7	8.7
Tampa, FL	71.9	8.2	1.9	0.0	0.0	0.8	2.1	1.9	13.2
Tucson, AZ	71.3	10.4	2.6	0.0	0.0	1.9	2.9	1.7	9.2
Tulsa, OK	78.4	9.9	0.6	0.0	0.0	0.2	1.8	1.9	7.2
Tuscaloosa, AL	80.0	9.7	1.4	0.0	0.0	0.5	1.8	1.0	5.6
Virginia Beach, VA	79.1	7.6	0.7	0.0	0.0	0.4	2.1	1.6	8.4
Washington, DC	30.7	4.7	10.0	16.7	0.2	3.7	11.3	2.7	19.8
Wichita, KS	81.4	9.8	0.6	0.0	0.0	0.4	1.2	1.4	5.1
Wilmington, NC	75.4	7.5	0.7	0.0	0.0	0.6	2.5	0.8	12.6
Winston-Salem, NC	77.7	8.9	1.3	0.0	0.0	0.3	2.1	1.2	8.5
Worcester, MA	68.3	11.4	1.9	0.2	0.6	0.2	6.2	2.9	8.3
U.S.	73.2	8.6	2.0	1.6	0.5	0.5	2.5	1.5	9.7

Note: Figures are percentages and cover workers 16 years of age and older
Source: U.S. Census Bureau, 2017-2021 American Community Survey 5-Year Estimates

Means of Transportation to Work: Metro Area

Metro Area	Car/Truck/Van		Public Transportation			Bicycle	Walked	Other Means	Worked at Home
	Drove Alone	Car-pooled	Bus	Subway	Railroad				
Albuquerque, NM	76.8	9.4	1.0	0.0	0.1	0.6	1.7	1.1	9.4
Allentown, PA	78.4	7.9	1.2	0.1	0.1	0.1	2.3	1.2	8.7
Anchorage, AK	73.7	11.5	1.2	0.0	0.0	0.8	2.4	3.0	7.4
Ann Arbor, MI	66.1	6.5	4.1	0.1	0.0	1.3	6.9	0.8	14.2
Athens, GA	75.1	8.0	1.6	0.0	0.0	0.8	3.4	1.2	9.9
Atlanta, GA	72.7	8.7	1.5	0.7	0.1	0.2	1.2	1.7	13.2
Austin, TX	69.7	8.4	1.3	0.0	0.1	0.6	1.8	1.3	16.8
Baltimore, MD	72.5	7.4	3.4	0.7	0.7	0.2	2.3	1.5	11.2
Boise City, ID	76.4	7.9	0.2	0.0	0.0	1.1	1.9	1.3	11.0
Boston, MA	62.2	6.6	3.2	5.5	1.8	0.9	5.0	1.7	13.0
Boulder, CO	60.1	6.6	3.9	0.0	0.0	3.6	4.0	1.1	20.8
Brownsville, TX	81.3	9.1	0.4	0.0	0.0	0.1	1.6	1.2	6.3
Cape Coral, FL	76.3	9.6	0.5	0.0	0.0	0.7	1.0	2.3	9.6
Cedar Rapids, IA	80.3	7.0	0.3	0.0	0.0	0.3	1.8	0.8	9.4
Charleston, SC	79.1	7.6	0.6	0.0	0.0	0.6	1.8	1.2	9.1
Charlotte, NC	74.7	8.4	0.9	0.1	0.0	0.1	1.3	1.3	13.1
Chicago, IL	66.7	7.6	3.7	3.6	2.6	0.6	2.8	1.5	10.9
Cincinnati, OH	78.8	7.7	1.4	0.0	0.0	0.2	1.9	0.9	9.1
Clarksville, TN	82.2	8.6	0.5	0.0	0.0	0.2	2.9	1.3	4.3
Cleveland, OH	77.9	7.4	2.1	0.1	0.0	0.3	2.1	1.2	8.8
College Station, TX	78.2	9.5	1.1	0.0	0.0	1.1	1.7	1.2	7.2
Colorado Springs, CO	73.8	9.6	0.5	0.0	0.0	0.3	3.2	1.0	11.4
Columbia, MO	77.1	9.6	0.6	0.0	0.0	0.8	4.4	0.8	6.7
Columbia, SC	78.7	8.1	0.6	0.0	0.0	0.1	4.2	1.6	6.7
Columbus, OH	77.1	6.7	1.3	0.0	0.0	0.3	2.0	1.0	11.6
Dallas, TX	75.8	9.5	0.6	0.1	0.2	0.1	1.2	1.3	11.1
Davenport, IA	83.9	6.8	0.7	0.0	0.0	0.2	2.2	0.7	5.6
Denver, CO	69.8	7.5	2.2	0.3	0.2	0.8	2.1	1.7	15.4
Des Moines, IA	78.3	7.6	0.6	0.0	0.0	0.2	1.7	1.1	10.5
Durham, NC	70.8	7.7	2.6	0.0	0.0	0.6	2.3	1.3	14.5
Edison, NJ	47.4	6.1	6.7	17.4	3.1	0.7	5.5	2.3	10.6
El Paso, TX	78.6	10.6	1.1	0.0	0.0	0.1	1.4	2.3	5.8
Fargo, ND	79.8	8.0	0.9	0.0	0.0	0.4	2.6	1.4	6.9
Fort Collins, CO	70.7	6.4	1.1	0.1	0.0	2.4	2.8	1.1	15.4
Fort Wayne, IN	82.1	8.7	0.7	0.0	0.0	0.4	1.3	0.7	6.2
Fort Worth, TX	75.8	9.5	0.6	0.1	0.2	0.1	1.2	1.3	11.1
Grand Rapids, MI	79.0	8.5	1.2	0.0	0.0	0.4	2.2	0.7	7.9
Greeley, CO	76.7	10.4	0.4	0.0	0.0	0.2	1.9	0.8	9.5
Green Bay, WI	81.4	7.6	0.5	0.0	0.0	0.1	1.8	0.8	7.8
Greensboro, NC	79.8	8.8	1.1	0.0	0.0	0.2	1.5	1.1	7.5
Honolulu, HI	65.4	13.2	6.3	0.0	0.0	0.9	5.2	2.5	6.4
Houston, TX	77.1	9.3	1.7	0.0	0.0	0.3	1.2	1.6	8.7
Huntsville, AL	83.6	5.8	0.2	0.0	0.0	0.1	0.7	1.0	8.6
Indianapolis, IN	78.7	8.2	0.7	0.0	0.0	0.2	1.4	0.9	9.8
Jacksonville, FL	76.8	8.2	0.9	0.0	0.0	0.4	1.3	1.9	10.5
Kansas City, MO	79.0	7.3	0.7	0.0	0.0	0.1	1.1	1.0	10.6
Lafayette, LA	83.9	6.7	0.3	0.0	0.0	0.2	1.9	1.2	5.8
Las Cruces, NM	76.4	12.3	0.4	0.0	0.0	0.9	1.7	1.3	7.1
Las Vegas, NV	75.8	10.1	2.6	0.0	0.0	0.2	1.3	2.5	7.4
Lexington, KY	78.2	8.4	1.1	0.0	0.0	0.4	2.9	1.0	8.0
Lincoln, NE	78.5	8.9	0.8	0.0	0.0	0.8	3.2	0.7	7.2
Little Rock, AR	81.6	9.4	0.4	0.0	0.0	0.1	1.1	1.1	6.3
Los Angeles, CA	70.9	9.3	3.4	0.4	0.2	0.6	2.3	1.8	11.2
Louisville, KY	78.9	8.2	1.5	0.0	0.0	0.2	1.4	1.1	8.7

Table continued on following page.

Metro Area	Car/Truck/Van		Public Transportation			Bicycle	Walked	Other Means	Worked at Home
	Drove Alone	Car-pooled	Bus	Subway	Railroad				
Madison, WI	71.0	6.5	3.3	0.0	0.0	1.8	4.9	1.0	11.5
Manchester, NH	77.6	7.2	0.6	0.1	0.1	0.2	1.8	0.9	11.5
Miami, FL	75.1	9.1	2.1	0.3	0.1	0.5	1.5	2.1	9.2
Midland, TX	82.7	9.9	0.1	0.0	0.0	0.2	1.2	0.7	5.1
Milwaukee, WI	77.4	7.1	2.4	0.0	0.0	0.4	2.3	0.8	9.5
Minneapolis, MN	72.1	7.4	3.2	0.1	0.1	0.6	2.1	1.3	13.1
Nashville, TN	76.7	8.6	0.7	0.0	0.1	0.1	1.2	1.1	11.6
New Haven, CT	74.9	8.1	2.3	0.1	0.7	0.4	3.4	1.3	8.7
New Orleans, LA	76.2	9.6	1.7	0.0	0.0	0.9	2.4	1.7	7.4
New York, NY	47.4	6.1	6.7	17.4	3.1	0.7	5.5	2.3	10.6
Oklahoma City, OK	80.6	9.1	0.3	0.0	0.0	0.3	1.6	1.2	7.0
Omaha, NE	79.5	8.0	0.7	0.0	0.0	0.1	1.7	1.0	9.0
Orlando, FL	75.8	9.4	1.1	0.0	0.1	0.4	1.1	1.9	10.2
Philadelphia, PA	68.2	7.1	4.2	1.7	1.7	0.6	3.2	1.5	11.7
Phoenix, AZ	71.6	10.3	1.3	0.0	0.0	0.6	1.4	1.8	13.0
Pittsburgh, PA	73.0	7.4	4.2	0.2	0.0	0.2	3.0	1.3	10.8
Portland, OR	66.2	8.4	3.6	0.4	0.2	1.7	3.1	2.0	14.4
Providence, RI	77.8	8.3	1.2	0.1	0.7	0.2	2.7	1.0	7.8
Provo, UT	70.1	10.3	1.0	0.1	0.7	0.7	3.3	1.0	12.8
Raleigh, NC	72.9	7.4	0.7	0.0	0.0	0.1	1.1	1.0	16.8
Reno, NV	73.1	12.0	2.0	0.0	0.0	0.5	2.0	2.0	8.3
Richmond, VA	76.2	7.7	1.2	0.0	0.1	0.4	1.4	1.1	11.9
Rochester, MN	71.2	11.0	3.4	0.0	0.0	0.5	3.5	1.0	9.4
Sacramento, CA	72.1	8.8	1.3	0.1	0.2	1.1	1.6	1.7	13.1
St. Louis, MO	79.2	6.7	1.4	0.2	0.1	0.2	1.6	1.0	9.8
Salem, OR	74.3	10.1	1.3	0.0	0.0	0.8	2.6	1.1	9.8
Salt Lake City, UT	71.0	10.3	1.5	0.2	0.4	0.6	1.9	1.7	12.5
San Antonio, TX	75.6	10.7	1.3	0.0	0.0	0.2	1.6	1.4	9.1
San Diego, CA	71.6	8.4	2.0	0.1	0.1	0.5	2.9	2.0	12.5
San Francisco, CA	53.4	8.6	6.1	5.7	1.2	1.6	4.3	2.8	16.3
San Jose, CA	67.1	9.4	1.8	0.3	1.0	1.4	2.1	1.6	15.3
Santa Rosa, CA	72.8	10.0	1.2	0.1	0.2	0.6	2.3	1.5	11.3
Savannah, GA	79.8	8.6	1.3	0.0	0.0	0.6	1.9	1.7	6.2
Seattle, WA	62.4	9.1	6.7	0.3	0.4	0.9	3.6	1.6	14.9
Sioux Falls, SD	81.7	7.6	0.5	0.0	0.0	0.3	1.9	0.6	7.4
Springfield, IL	81.6	6.4	0.9	0.1	0.0	0.4	1.4	1.3	8.0
Tampa, FL	74.8	8.2	1.0	0.0	0.0	0.5	1.3	1.6	12.4
Tucson, AZ	73.4	9.7	1.7	0.0	0.0	1.2	2.1	1.7	10.3
Tulsa, OK	80.7	9.1	0.3	0.0	0.0	0.1	1.3	1.3	7.1
Tuscaloosa, AL	82.3	10.3	0.8	0.0	0.0	0.2	0.9	0.6	5.0
Virginia Beach, VA	78.3	7.9	1.3	0.0	0.0	0.3	3.1	1.6	7.5
Washington, DC	60.7	8.5	3.6	5.8	0.6	0.7	2.9	1.7	15.4
Wichita, KS	82.2	8.7	0.4	0.0	0.0	0.3	1.5	1.3	5.6
Wilmington, NC	77.5	8.0	0.3	0.0	0.0	0.4	1.4	0.6	11.8
Winston-Salem, NC	80.7	8.8	0.6	0.0	0.0	0.1	1.3	0.9	7.6
Worcester, MA	76.2	7.6	0.7	0.2	0.7	0.2	2.6	1.7	10.2
U.S.	73.2	8.6	2.0	1.6	0.5	0.5	2.5	1.5	9.7

Note: Figures are percentages and cover workers 16 years of age and older; (1) Figures cover the Metropolitan Statistical Area
Source: U.S. Census Bureau, 2017-2021 American Community Survey 5-Year Estimates

Travel Time to Work: City

City	Less Than 10 Minutes	10 to 19 Minutes	20 to 29 Minutes	30 to 44 Minutes	45 to 59 Minutes	60 to 89 Minutes	90 Minutes or More
Albuquerque, NM	11.0	35.9	27.8	18.1	3.1	2.5	1.6
Allentown, PA	10.6	33.2	30.0	15.2	4.3	4.6	2.1
Anchorage, AK	16.1	44.4	23.4	11.2	2.1	1.2	1.6
Ann Arbor, MI	13.9	45.7	18.6	14.0	5.0	2.4	0.5
Athens, GA	18.0	45.8	16.6	9.8	3.5	3.5	2.8
Atlanta, GA	6.9	29.5	25.6	21.8	7.3	5.4	3.5
Austin, TX	9.7	32.0	24.5	21.7	6.9	3.7	1.5
Baltimore, MD	6.7	23.6	23.3	25.6	8.7	7.4	4.7
Boise City, ID	13.6	44.5	26.2	11.4	1.6	1.5	1.2
Boston, MA	6.9	20.4	19.6	29.8	12.1	9.1	2.1
Boulder, CO	19.7	44.5	16.1	9.5	5.8	3.2	1.2
Brownsville, TX	8.7	42.9	28.9	14.3	2.5	1.7	1.0
Cape Coral, FL	8.0	25.3	22.2	27.4	9.4	5.4	2.3
Cedar Rapids, IA	20.0	48.9	17.0	9.2	1.9	1.5	1.5
Charleston, SC	11.4	30.7	26.6	20.6	7.6	1.6	1.4
Charlotte, NC	8.6	29.6	26.7	23.2	6.5	3.3	2.1
Chicago, IL	4.7	16.4	18.4	30.5	15.1	11.9	3.1
Cincinnati, OH	11.4	33.0	26.8	19.1	4.3	3.2	2.1
Clarksville, TN	10.3	33.0	25.3	14.1	6.8	8.5	2.2
Cleveland, OH	10.2	34.0	27.0	20.0	3.9	3.0	2.1
College Station, TX	17.6	55.5	17.1	6.2	0.5	2.0	1.1
Colorado Springs, CO	11.5	35.9	28.0	15.9	3.3	2.9	2.5
Columbia, MO	20.0	54.4	13.7	7.3	2.5	1.0	1.1
Columbia, SC	29.8	36.0	19.0	10.0	2.1	1.8	1.4
Columbus, OH	10.3	34.2	30.4	18.7	3.2	1.9	1.3
Dallas, TX	8.2	26.9	23.3	25.8	8.0	5.9	1.9
Davenport, IA	16.5	47.5	22.0	8.2	3.1	1.8	1.0
Denver, CO	7.9	29.0	24.7	26.0	7.2	3.7	1.4
Des Moines, IA	13.5	43.1	26.6	12.3	2.2	1.3	1.1
Durham, NC	9.2	38.4	25.5	17.9	4.8	2.7	1.4
Edison, NJ	7.6	22.0	18.1	17.8	12.2	12.6	9.6
El Paso, TX	9.5	33.5	28.5	19.7	4.7	2.2	1.8
Fargo, ND	20.6	56.3	15.2	3.6	1.4	1.9	0.9
Fort Collins, CO	15.4	43.8	20.6	10.0	5.4	3.3	1.5
Fort Wayne, IN	12.8	38.2	28.0	13.5	3.0	2.6	1.8
Fort Worth, TX	7.7	29.0	22.9	23.9	8.7	5.8	2.0
Grand Rapids, MI	14.5	44.0	23.5	11.6	3.7	2.0	0.8
Greeley, CO	15.9	37.3	15.3	14.4	5.9	9.2	1.9
Green Bay, WI	18.2	48.6	19.5	8.5	2.8	1.3	1.1
Greensboro, NC	12.5	40.0	23.6	15.9	3.2	3.0	2.0
Honolulu, HI	8.7	38.2	22.6	20.6	5.0	3.6	1.2
Houston, TX	7.2	25.5	23.0	27.7	8.9	5.9	1.8
Huntsville, AL	13.1	41.0	26.2	15.5	2.5	1.0	0.8
Indianapolis, IN	9.5	30.4	28.8	22.7	4.3	2.4	1.8
Jacksonville, FL	8.7	28.5	27.2	25.4	6.0	2.8	1.4
Kansas City, MO	11.6	33.4	27.9	20.3	4.0	1.7	1.2
Lafayette, LA	15.8	44.0	19.3	11.9	2.8	3.6	2.6
Las Cruces, NM	16.2	49.2	16.2	9.5	3.5	4.8	0.7
Las Vegas, NV	7.3	24.0	30.6	27.4	6.2	2.7	1.9
Lexington, KY	13.2	39.5	26.2	13.9	2.9	2.4	1.8
Lincoln, NE	16.7	44.7	22.8	9.9	2.6	2.1	1.2
Little Rock, AR	15.4	45.3	23.6	11.0	2.3	1.5	0.9
Los Angeles, CA	5.9	22.2	19.3	28.5	10.5	10.1	3.6
Louisville, KY	9.6	32.6	31.4	19.1	3.9	2.0	1.4
Madison, WI	14.9	39.6	24.8	15.1	3.0	1.8	0.8

Table continued on following page.

City	Less Than 10 Minutes	10 to 19 Minutes	20 to 29 Minutes	30 to 44 Minutes	45 to 59 Minutes	60 to 89 Minutes	90 Minutes or More
Manchester, NH	12.6	35.5	23.4	14.6	6.4	5.1	2.4
Miami, FL	6.0	21.8	24.7	30.5	9.1	6.6	1.4
Midland, TX	14.2	47.3	18.9	12.0	2.9	2.4	2.4
Milwaukee, WI	10.4	36.6	26.1	19.1	3.5	2.7	1.7
Minneapolis, MN	7.9	32.6	30.2	20.9	4.5	2.7	1.1
Nashville, TN	9.1	29.0	26.6	23.2	7.0	3.6	1.5
New Haven, CT	13.2	40.4	21.6	13.6	4.5	4.2	2.5
New Orleans, LA	11.0	34.8	24.2	19.5	5.0	3.5	2.0
New York, NY	4.0	12.3	13.5	27.1	16.3	19.2	7.6
Oklahoma City, OK	10.5	36.0	29.0	18.2	3.5	1.4	1.4
Omaha, NE	14.5	41.2	26.7	12.4	2.5	1.9	0.9
Orlando, FL	7.2	25.4	27.6	26.6	7.2	3.9	2.2
Philadelphia, PA	6.1	19.2	20.2	28.1	12.9	9.5	4.0
Phoenix, AZ	8.6	26.6	26.6	24.5	7.4	4.5	1.8
Pittsburgh, PA	9.4	32.3	26.6	21.8	4.6	3.6	1.7
Portland, OR	8.3	28.2	26.8	24.0	7.1	4.1	1.5
Providence, RI	10.3	40.4	19.4	15.3	6.2	5.5	2.8
Provo, UT	21.4	44.2	16.8	9.8	3.5	3.1	1.2
Raleigh, NC	9.3	32.4	27.0	20.8	5.7	3.0	1.8
Reno, NV	15.6	40.3	22.8	12.5	4.7	2.7	1.4
Richmond, VA	11.4	37.4	27.3	16.8	2.9	2.7	1.5
Rochester, MN	17.7	55.5	14.1	6.5	2.8	2.2	1.2
Sacramento, CA	8.4	31.3	24.9	22.4	5.6	4.2	3.1
St. Louis, MO	9.2	35.2	26.5	19.7	4.3	2.9	2.1
Salem, OR	13.0	41.0	19.7	12.7	6.0	6.0	1.6
Salt Lake City, UT	14.1	45.1	21.4	12.6	3.5	2.2	1.2
San Antonio, TX	9.4	31.4	26.3	21.8	6.0	3.4	1.7
San Diego, CA	7.7	32.9	27.5	20.9	5.7	3.6	1.7
San Francisco, CA	4.5	19.3	21.4	29.5	11.6	10.1	3.7
San Jose, CA	5.6	24.6	23.2	26.1	10.1	7.5	3.0
Santa Rosa, CA	12.6	40.1	21.3	14.4	4.3	4.0	3.3
Savannah, GA	15.7	39.1	22.8	13.3	4.8	2.8	1.5
Seattle, WA	7.3	24.0	24.1	27.6	10.6	5.0	1.5
Sioux Falls, SD	16.7	51.6	22.0	5.8	1.7	1.2	1.0
Springfield, IL	17.4	53.1	17.9	6.3	1.8	2.3	1.3
Tampa, FL	11.1	30.2	22.5	23.4	6.8	4.3	1.8
Tucson, AZ	11.8	34.9	25.4	19.6	4.7	2.0	1.6
Tulsa, OK	14.2	44.9	26.3	10.1	1.9	1.4	1.2
Tuscaloosa, AL	16.8	46.6	21.7	7.6	3.1	3.1	1.1
Virginia Beach, VA	10.1	30.9	27.9	22.0	5.3	2.5	1.4
Washington, DC	5.3	19.0	22.3	33.1	11.6	6.6	2.1
Wichita, KS	14.3	44.9	26.7	9.9	1.6	1.4	1.2
Wilmington, NC	16.1	47.0	21.7	9.5	2.5	1.7	1.5
Winston-Salem, NC	14.0	40.3	22.6	14.3	4.6	2.6	1.7
Worcester, MA	13.4	34.6	19.5	17.8	5.9	6.3	2.5
U.S.	12.4	28.5	21.0	20.9	8.2	6.2	2.9

Note: Figures are percentages and include workers 16 years old and over
Source: U.S. Census Bureau, 2017-2021 American Community Survey 5-Year Estimates

Travel Time to Work: Metro Area

Metro Area	Less Than 10 Minutes	10 to 19 Minutes	20 to 29 Minutes	30 to 44 Minutes	45 to 59 Minutes	60 to 89 Minutes	90 Minutes or More
Albuquerque, NM	10.7	31.5	26.0	20.7	5.7	3.5	1.8
Allentown, PA	12.6	27.7	23.5	18.5	7.3	6.6	3.8
Anchorage, AK	15.0	40.4	21.8	11.4	4.5	4.1	2.7
Ann Arbor, MI	11.5	32.6	24.5	19.1	7.3	3.8	1.1
Athens, GA	14.2	38.2	21.9	13.5	5.2	4.0	3.0
Atlanta, GA	6.9	22.5	19.9	25.2	12.2	9.6	3.5
Austin, TX	9.3	26.6	22.1	23.8	10.1	6.3	1.9
Baltimore, MD	8.0	23.3	21.0	24.7	11.0	8.3	3.7
Boise City, ID	12.8	33.4	25.0	19.7	5.5	2.2	1.4
Boston, MA	9.1	22.7	18.6	24.4	11.7	10.1	3.3
Boulder, CO	14.5	33.4	20.5	17.6	7.6	4.8	1.6
Brownsville, TX	12.8	40.5	25.7	15.0	3.4	1.6	1.0
Cape Coral, FL	8.6	25.3	22.8	26.0	9.8	5.2	2.3
Cedar Rapids, IA	18.8	40.1	20.6	12.8	4.3	2.0	1.5
Charleston, SC	8.8	26.0	24.1	25.1	9.5	4.8	1.7
Charlotte, NC	9.8	27.8	22.6	23.3	9.3	5.1	2.1
Chicago, IL	8.5	21.9	19.0	25.3	12.2	10.0	3.1
Cincinnati, OH	10.9	28.2	25.2	23.1	7.5	3.5	1.6
Clarksville, TN	14.8	31.0	22.4	16.1	6.5	6.5	2.7
Cleveland, OH	11.6	28.2	25.9	23.2	6.7	2.9	1.6
College Station, TX	16.1	49.4	18.4	10.4	2.3	2.1	1.4
Colorado Springs, CO	11.5	32.8	26.9	18.0	4.7	3.6	2.5
Columbia, MO	17.3	44.2	19.4	11.9	3.8	1.7	1.7
Columbia, SC	12.6	28.8	24.1	22.2	6.9	3.3	2.2
Columbus, OH	11.4	29.5	26.7	21.7	6.1	3.1	1.5
Dallas, TX	8.6	25.2	21.7	25.6	10.3	6.7	2.0
Davenport, IA	18.3	36.1	24.9	13.1	3.9	2.4	1.3
Denver, CO	8.4	25.1	23.0	26.5	9.6	5.5	1.9
Des Moines, IA	15.0	35.0	27.5	16.1	3.7	1.5	1.1
Durham, NC	9.8	31.4	24.8	21.0	7.3	4.2	1.5
Edison, NJ	7.0	18.5	16.3	24.0	12.7	14.7	6.8
El Paso, TX	10.3	31.9	27.4	21.0	5.2	2.3	1.9
Fargo, ND	17.8	52.1	18.3	6.0	2.4	1.9	1.4
Fort Collins, CO	13.5	35.4	21.8	15.9	6.3	4.9	2.2
Fort Wayne, IN	13.0	35.3	28.4	15.7	3.4	2.4	1.8
Fort Worth, TX	8.6	25.2	21.7	25.6	10.3	6.7	2.0
Grand Rapids, MI	14.8	35.3	24.7	16.1	5.0	2.6	1.5
Greeley, CO	11.6	26.7	18.8	22.8	9.8	8.1	2.3
Green Bay, WI	17.9	40.4	21.9	13.0	3.6	1.7	1.4
Greensboro, NC	12.8	34.6	24.4	18.6	4.8	3.0	1.9
Honolulu, HI	9.8	26.1	19.9	24.9	9.4	7.3	2.6
Houston, TX	7.6	23.2	20.4	26.7	11.6	8.2	2.3
Huntsville, AL	10.1	31.7	27.7	22.1	5.2	1.9	1.2
Indianapolis, IN	11.4	27.7	23.9	24.5	7.4	3.4	1.7
Jacksonville, FL	9.1	26.1	24.3	26.1	8.6	4.2	1.6
Kansas City, MO	12.3	30.6	25.5	21.6	6.3	2.5	1.3
Lafayette, LA	13.3	33.5	20.9	18.5	5.9	3.8	4.0
Las Cruces, NM	13.9	40.3	20.0	14.2	5.2	4.8	1.7
Las Vegas, NV	7.8	27.5	29.4	25.4	5.4	2.6	1.9
Lexington, KY	14.5	35.6	24.5	16.8	4.3	2.6	1.7
Lincoln, NE	16.9	41.6	23.5	11.6	3.0	2.2	1.3
Little Rock, AR	13.0	32.7	22.6	20.4	7.0	2.9	1.4
Los Angeles, CA	7.1	24.8	19.9	25.4	9.9	9.3	3.5
Louisville, KY	9.7	30.1	28.8	22.0	5.7	2.4	1.5
Madison, WI	15.9	32.2	24.8	18.2	5.3	2.5	1.1

Table continued on following page.

Metro Area	Less Than 10 Minutes	10 to 19 Minutes	20 to 29 Minutes	30 to 44 Minutes	45 to 59 Minutes	60 to 89 Minutes	90 Minutes or More
Manchester, NH	10.9	29.7	21.2	19.5	8.7	6.7	3.4
Miami, FL	6.6	22.6	22.7	27.7	10.2	7.6	2.6
Midland, TX	14.7	42.7	21.0	13.5	3.3	2.5	2.2
Milwaukee, WI	12.1	32.1	25.7	21.2	5.0	2.5	1.4
Minneapolis, MN	10.6	28.0	25.2	23.2	7.7	4.0	1.4
Nashville, TN	9.4	26.2	21.5	23.5	10.9	6.5	2.0
New Haven, CT	11.7	31.6	23.1	19.7	6.3	4.6	3.0
New Orleans, LA	10.9	30.8	21.8	20.7	8.0	5.5	2.4
New York, NY	7.0	18.5	16.3	24.0	12.7	14.7	6.8
Oklahoma City, OK	11.9	32.3	25.4	20.6	5.7	2.5	1.6
Omaha, NE	14.1	36.1	27.3	16.0	3.6	1.9	1.1
Orlando, FL	7.2	22.9	22.3	28.1	11.2	6.0	2.4
Philadelphia, PA	9.6	23.9	20.6	24.0	11.1	7.8	3.1
Phoenix, AZ	9.9	26.1	24.0	23.6	8.9	5.6	1.9
Pittsburgh, PA	11.8	27.0	21.3	22.9	9.1	5.8	2.1
Portland, OR	10.8	27.5	23.0	22.7	8.9	5.1	2.0
Providence, RI	11.7	30.4	21.3	19.8	7.8	6.2	2.8
Provo, UT	17.1	34.7	20.2	16.5	6.2	3.9	1.5
Raleigh, NC	8.6	26.7	24.4	24.4	9.1	4.9	1.9
Reno, NV	13.0	35.6	24.5	17.2	5.2	2.9	1.6
Richmond, VA	9.3	28.8	26.7	23.5	6.6	3.1	2.1
Rochester, MN	18.1	41.7	18.6	12.6	4.3	2.9	1.9
Sacramento, CA	9.9	28.3	22.4	23.1	7.9	4.7	3.7
St. Louis, MO	11.0	27.3	24.4	24.0	7.9	3.8	1.7
Salem, OR	13.7	32.6	20.9	16.9	7.6	6.3	2.0
Salt Lake City, UT	10.8	33.5	26.9	19.2	5.5	3.0	1.2
San Antonio, TX	9.2	27.8	24.1	23.2	8.7	4.8	2.2
San Diego, CA	8.1	29.4	24.5	23.5	7.5	5.0	2.1
San Francisco, CA	7.0	22.9	17.8	23.6	11.9	12.0	4.9
San Jose, CA	7.0	26.5	23.0	24.3	9.1	7.0	3.1
Santa Rosa, CA	14.0	32.4	20.4	17.1	6.4	6.0	3.8
Savannah, GA	11.0	29.3	24.8	21.8	8.2	3.6	1.5
Seattle, WA	8.2	22.3	21.1	25.2	11.2	8.6	3.4
Sioux Falls, SD	16.8	43.8	24.1	10.0	2.6	1.4	1.2
Springfield, IL	15.0	43.3	23.5	11.8	2.5	2.1	1.8
Tampa, FL	9.6	26.9	21.0	23.7	10.2	6.3	2.3
Tucson, AZ	10.6	29.4	24.7	24.1	7.0	2.4	1.7
Tulsa, OK	13.3	33.7	26.9	18.0	4.6	2.1	1.4
Tuscaloosa, AL	11.1	33.8	23.3	17.4	6.7	5.7	2.0
Virginia Beach, VA	11.1	31.1	23.5	21.4	7.1	4.0	1.7
Washington, DC	6.1	19.3	18.2	26.2	13.7	12.1	4.3
Wichita, KS	16.1	37.2	26.2	15.1	2.7	1.5	1.3
Wilmington, NC	12.7	38.0	22.6	16.0	5.7	2.8	2.1
Winston-Salem, NC	12.5	32.5	24.3	19.3	6.1	3.2	2.2
Worcester, MA	12.3	26.0	18.5	20.6	10.4	8.5	3.8
U.S.	12.4	28.5	21.0	20.9	8.2	6.2	2.9

Note: Figures are percentages and include workers 16 years old and over; Figures cover the Metropolitan Statistical Area
Source: U.S. Census Bureau, 2017-2021 American Community Survey 5-Year Estimates

2020 Presidential Election Results

City	Area Covered	Biden	Trump	Jorgensen	Hawkins	Other
Albuquerque, NM	Bernalillo County	61.0	36.6	1.5	0.5	0.4
Allentown, PA	Lehigh County	53.1	45.5	1.2	0.1	0.2
Anchorage, AK	State of Alaska	42.8	52.8	2.5	0.0	1.9
Ann Arbor, MI	Washtenaw County	72.4	25.9	0.9	0.3	0.4
Athens, GA	Clarke County	70.1	28.1	1.6	0.1	0.1
Atlanta, GA	Fulton County	72.6	26.2	1.2	0.0	0.0
Austin, TX	Travis County	71.4	26.4	1.5	0.3	0.4
Baltimore, MD	Baltimore City	87.3	10.7	0.7	0.6	0.7
Boise City, ID	Ada County	46.1	50.0	2.0	0.1	1.8
Boston, MA	Suffolk County	80.6	17.5	0.9	0.5	0.5
Boulder, CO	Boulder County	77.2	20.6	1.2	0.3	0.6
Brownsville, TX	Cameron County	56.0	42.9	0.6	0.3	0.1
Cape Coral, FL	Lee County	39.9	59.1	0.5	0.1	0.3
Cedar Rapids, IA	Linn County	55.6	41.9	1.6	0.3	0.7
Charleston, SC	Charleston County	55.5	42.6	1.5	0.3	0.1
Charlotte, NC	Mecklenburg County	66.7	31.6	1.0	0.3	0.5
Chicago, IL	Cook County	74.2	24.0	0.8	0.5	0.5
Cincinnati, OH	Hamilton County	57.1	41.3	1.2	0.3	0.0
Clarksville, TN	Montgomery County	42.3	55.0	1.9	0.2	0.7
Cleveland, OH	Cuyahoga County	66.4	32.3	0.7	0.3	0.3
College Station, TX	Brazos County	41.4	55.7	2.1	0.3	0.4
Colorado Springs, CO	El Paso County	42.7	53.5	2.4	0.3	1.0
Columbia, MO	Boone County	54.8	42.3	2.2	0.3	0.4
Columbia, SC	Richland County	68.4	30.1	1.0	0.4	0.1
Columbus, OH	Franklin County	64.7	33.4	1.2	0.3	0.4
Dallas, TX	Dallas County	64.9	33.3	1.0	0.4	0.4
Davenport, IA	Scott County	50.7	47.2	1.2	0.2	0.7
Denver, CO	Denver County	79.6	18.2	1.2	0.3	0.7
Des Moines, IA	Polk County	56.5	41.3	1.3	0.2	0.7
Durham, NC	Durham County	80.4	18.0	0.8	0.3	0.4
Edison, NJ	Middlesex County	60.2	38.2	0.7	0.3	0.6
El Paso, TX	El Paso County	66.7	31.6	1.0	0.5	0.2
Fargo, ND	Cass County	46.8	49.5	2.9	0.0	0.7
Fort Collins, CO	Larimer County	56.2	40.8	1.8	0.3	0.9
Fort Wayne, IN	Allen County	43.2	54.3	2.2	0.0	0.3
Fort Worth, TX	Tarrant County	49.3	49.1	1.2	0.3	0.0
Grand Rapids, MI	Kent County	51.9	45.8	1.5	0.3	0.5
Greeley, CO	Weld County	39.6	57.6	1.7	0.2	0.9
Green Bay, WI	Brown County	45.5	52.7	1.3	0.0	0.5
Greensboro, NC	Guilford County	60.8	37.7	0.8	0.2	0.4
Honolulu, HI	Honolulu County	62.5	35.7	0.9	0.6	0.4
Houston, TX	Harris County	55.9	42.7	1.0	0.3	0.0
Huntsville, AL	Madison County	44.8	52.8	1.9	0.0	0.5
Indianapolis, IN	Marion County	63.3	34.3	1.8	0.1	0.4
Jacksonville, FL	Duval County	51.1	47.3	1.0	0.2	0.5
Kansas City, MO	Jackson County	59.8	37.9	1.4	0.4	0.5
Lafayette, LA	Lafayette Parish	34.7	63.3	1.3	0.0	0.7
Las Cruces, NM	Dona Ana County	58.0	39.7	1.4	0.5	0.4
Las Vegas, NV	Clark County	53.7	44.3	0.9	0.0	1.1
Lexington, KY	Fayette County	59.2	38.5	1.6	0.1	0.6
Lincoln, NE	Lancaster County	52.3	44.6	2.4	0.0	0.7
Little Rock, AR	Pulaski County	60.0	37.5	1.0	0.3	1.3
Los Angeles, CA	Los Angeles County	71.0	26.9	0.8	0.5	0.8
Louisville, KY	Jefferson County	58.9	38.8	1.2	0.1	1.0
Madison, WI	Dane County	75.5	22.9	1.1	0.1	0.6
Manchester, NH	Hillsborough County	52.8	45.2	1.7	0.0	0.3

Table continued on following page.

City	Area Covered	Biden	Trump	Jorgensen	Hawkins	Other
Miami, FL	Miami-Dade County	53.3	46.0	0.3	0.1	0.3
Midland, TX	Midland County	20.9	77.3	1.3	0.2	0.2
Milwaukee, WI	Milwaukee County	69.1	29.3	0.9	0.0	0.7
Minneapolis, MN	Hennepin County	70.5	27.2	1.0	0.3	1.0
Nashville, TN	Davidson County	64.5	32.4	1.1	0.2	1.8
New Haven, CT	New Haven County	58.0	40.6	0.9	0.4	0.0
New Orleans, LA	Orleans Parish	83.1	15.0	0.9	0.0	1.0
New York, NY	Bronx County	83.3	15.9	0.2	0.3	0.3
New York, NY	Kings County	76.8	22.1	0.3	0.4	0.4
New York, NY	New York County	86.4	12.2	0.5	0.4	0.5
New York, NY	Queens County	72.0	26.9	0.3	0.4	0.4
New York, NY	Richmond County	42.0	56.9	0.4	0.3	0.4
Oklahoma City, OK	Oklahoma County	48.1	49.2	1.8	0.0	0.9
Omaha, NE	Douglas County	54.4	43.1	2.0	0.0	0.6
Orlando, FL	Orange County	60.9	37.8	0.7	0.2	0.4
Philadelphia, PA	Philadelphia County	81.2	17.9	0.7	0.1	0.2
Phoenix, AZ	Maricopa County	50.1	48.0	1.5	0.0	0.3
Pittsburgh, PA	Allegheny County	59.4	39.0	1.2	0.0	0.4
Portland, OR	Multnomah County	79.2	17.9	1.2	0.6	1.0
Providence, RI	Providence County	60.5	37.6	0.8	0.0	1.0
Provo, UT	Utah County	26.3	66.7	3.6	0.3	3.1
Raleigh, NC	Wake County	62.3	35.8	1.2	0.3	0.5
Reno, NV	Washoe County	50.8	46.3	1.4	0.0	1.5
Richmond, VA	Richmond City	82.9	14.9	1.5	0.0	0.6
Rochester, MN	Olmsted County	54.2	43.4	1.2	0.3	0.9
Sacramento, CA	Sacramento County	61.4	36.1	1.4	0.5	0.7
St. Louis, MO	St. Louis City	81.9	16.0	1.1	0.4	0.5
Salem, OR	Marion County	48.9	47.7	2.0	0.5	0.9
Salt Lake City, UT	Salt Lake County	53.0	42.1	2.2	0.4	2.2
San Antonio, TX	Bexar County	58.2	40.1	1.1	0.4	0.2
San Diego, CA	San Diego County	60.2	37.5	1.3	0.5	0.5
San Francisco, CA	San Francisco County	85.3	12.7	0.7	0.6	0.7
San Jose, CA	Santa Clara County	72.6	25.2	1.1	0.5	0.6
Santa Rosa, CA	Sonoma County	74.5	23.0	1.3	0.6	0.6
Savannah, GA	Chatham County	58.6	39.9	1.4	0.0	0.0
Seattle, WA	King County	75.0	22.2	1.5	0.5	0.8
Sioux Falls, SD	Minnehaha County	43.8	53.3	2.8	0.0	0.0
Springfield, IL	Sangamon County	46.5	50.9	1.4	0.6	0.6
Tampa, FL	Hillsborough County	52.7	45.8	0.8	0.2	0.5
Tucson, AZ	Pima County	58.4	39.8	1.5	0.0	0.3
Tulsa, OK	Tulsa County	40.9	56.5	1.8	0.0	0.8
Tuscaloosa, AL	Tuscaloosa County	41.9	56.7	1.0	0.0	0.4
Virginia Beach, VA	Virginia Beach City	51.6	46.2	1.8	0.0	0.4
Washington, DC	District of Columbia	92.1	5.4	0.6	0.5	1.4
Wichita, KS	Sedgwick County	42.6	54.4	2.4	0.0	0.5
Wilmington, NC	New Hanover County	50.2	48.0	1.2	0.3	0.4
Winston-Salem, NC	Forsyth County	56.2	42.3	0.9	0.2	0.4
Worcester, MA	Worcester County	57.6	39.7	1.7	0.6	0.4
U.S.	U.S.	51.3	46.8	1.2	0.3	0.5

Note: Results are percentages and may not add to 100% due to rounding
Source: Dave Leip's Atlas of U.S. Presidential Elections

House Price Index (HPI)

Metro Area[1]	National Ranking[3]	Quarterly Change (%)	One-Year Change (%)	Five-Year Change (%)	Since 1991Q1 (%)
Albuquerque, NM	67	0.95	14.03	58.76	256.02
Allentown, PA	104	-0.97	12.09	52.30	165.53
Anchorage, AK	215	-0.36	8.00	27.30	235.38
Ann Arbor, MI	210	-4.46	8.26	40.08	220.18
Athens, GA	33	0.64	16.98	76.16	301.70
Atlanta, GA	40	-0.35	16.14	73.42	274.52
Austin, TX	222	-5.35	7.56	75.92	618.91
Baltimore, MD	199	0.91	8.63	34.77	214.03
Boise City, ID	256	-6.44	1.06	96.45	501.63
Boston, MA[2]	195	-1.14	8.90	44.63	310.81
Boulder, CO	150	-1.96	10.66	47.80	588.29
Brownsville, TX	n/a	n/a	n/a	n/a	n/a
Cape Coral, FL	6	-0.47	20.91	83.64	358.39
Cedar Rapids, IA	243	-4.60	5.29	30.92	170.24
Charleston, SC	29	-0.34	17.51	66.55	441.52
Charlotte, NC	19	0.48	18.66	78.79	310.41
Chicago, IL[2]	205	-1.86	8.51	31.58	168.46
Cincinnati, OH	96	-0.52	12.38	55.37	199.65
Clarksville, TN	n/a	n/a	n/a	n/a	n/a
Cleveland, OH	189	-1.76	9.23	49.32	153.83
College Station, TX	n/a	n/a	n/a	n/a	n/a
Colorado Springs, CO	231	-3.83	6.63	67.59	425.90
Columbia, MO	148	1.10	10.69	48.19	225.68
Columbia, SC	23	1.44	18.32	59.58	209.37
Columbus, OH	94	-1.27	12.41	59.08	243.03
Dallas, TX[2]	43	-1.44	15.77	61.60	325.13
Davenport, IA	220	0.26	7.72	30.21	202.26
Denver, CO	216	-2.41	7.96	52.15	548.72
Des Moines, IA	108	0.29	12.00	40.34	223.17
Durham, NC	45	-3.85	15.68	66.89	294.13
Edison, NJ[2]	212	-0.09	8.22	34.61	258.57
El Paso, TX	21	2.05	18.42	54.29	201.64
Fargo, ND	133	0.78	11.14	32.39	270.20
Fort Collins, CO	141	-2.34	10.88	51.04	508.13
Fort Wayne, IN	68	1.56	14.01	67.52	186.04
Fort Worth, TX[2]	53	-1.47	15.09	66.00	306.95
Grand Rapids, MI	116	n/a	11.72	62.74	262.62
Greeley, CO	207	-3.14	8.35	53.74	462.73
Green Bay, WI	25	3.83	17.89	59.68	250.27
Greensboro, NC	26	0.70	17.71	64.64	188.62
Honolulu, HI	122	-5.39	11.51	33.52	222.93
Houston, TX	81	0.53	13.01	46.44	300.24
Huntsville, AL	109	-1.12	11.99	73.58	211.74
Indianapolis, IN	99	-1.53	12.29	62.22	209.62
Jacksonville, FL	35	-1.80	16.79	76.35	371.41
Kansas City, MO	102	-0.14	12.17	58.36	257.00
Lafayette, LA	179	-0.60	9.73	25.29	232.27
Las Cruces, NM	n/a	n/a	n/a	n/a	n/a
Las Vegas, NV	157	-3.37	10.38	70.87	260.78
Lexington, KY	72	0.70	13.70	53.19	235.38
Lincoln, NE	107	0.03	12.01	49.08	257.46
Little Rock, AR	119	0.21	11.59	41.21	196.34
Los Angeles, CA[2]	200	-1.90	8.62	46.01	298.97
Louisville, KY	147	1.02	10.70	47.57	251.74
Madison, WI	121	-1.67	11.52	45.50	303.94

Table continued on following page.

Metro Area[1]	National Ranking[3]	Quarterly Change (%)	One-Year Change (%)	Five-Year Change (%)	Since 1991Q1 (%)
Manchester, NH	126	-0.32	11.34	59.79	253.04
Miami, FL[2]	4	2.23	21.62	75.85	539.14
Midland, TX	n/a	n/a	n/a	n/a	n/a
Milwaukee, WI	134	-1.54	11.11	45.94	239.44
Minneapolis, MN	239	-1.83	6.08	41.05	273.41
Nashville, TN	34	-1.19	16.94	75.36	429.41
New Haven, CT	113	0.91	11.80	48.13	135.81
New Orleans, LA	202	0.06	8.58	36.52	291.68
New York, NY[2]	212	-0.09	8.22	34.61	258.57
Oklahoma City, OK	97	0.36	12.37	49.27	260.86
Omaha, NE	161	-0.79	10.26	51.61	252.12
Orlando, FL	13	0.53	19.76	74.99	330.12
Philadelphia, PA[2]	187	1.72	9.32	47.35	257.72
Phoenix, AZ	144	-4.25	10.82	83.46	453.06
Pittsburgh, PA	224	-1.54	7.43	42.48	223.87
Portland, OR	247	-2.87	4.63	43.13	493.76
Providence, RI	153	-0.93	10.48	54.47	232.15
Provo, UT	206	-3.27	8.39	75.92	514.28
Raleigh, NC	57	-2.71	14.97	69.49	298.33
Reno, NV	244	-1.71	5.01	60.21	333.43
Richmond, VA	79	-0.25	13.11	53.64	254.70
Rochester, MN	234	-3.55	6.25	42.75	234.69
Sacramento, CA	253	-3.63	3.17	45.83	234.41
St. Louis, MO	190	-0.80	9.10	40.60	193.95
Salem, OR	204	-1.19	8.51	62.82	461.52
Salt Lake City, UT	197	-2.92	8.70	74.37	596.70
San Antonio, TX	50	0.79	15.27	62.24	345.76
San Diego, CA	181	-2.11	9.62	51.34	344.82
San Francisco, CA[2]	177	3.28	9.77	19.08	360.06
San Jose, CA	101	1.47	12.23	31.21	389.33
Santa Rosa, CA	250	-4.80	3.50	26.56	276.48
Savannah, GA	12	1.20	19.86	70.81	361.13
Seattle, WA[2]	236	-3.59	6.21	48.84	436.06
Sioux Falls, SD	92	-1.20	12.49	55.67	315.04
Springfield, IL	158	-0.16	10.38	29.11	125.30
Tampa, FL	10	-0.71	19.98	91.22	438.13
Tucson, AZ	73	-1.74	13.68	74.77	329.80
Tulsa, OK	58	0.72	14.67	52.24	236.95
Tuscaloosa, AL	n/a	n/a	n/a	n/a	n/a
Virginia Beach, VA	131	0.74	11.17	43.79	243.78
Washington, DC[2]	238	-1.35	6.16	35.79	253.98
Wichita, KS	151	-1.84	10.63	47.99	197.78
Wilmington, NC	18	-1.23	18.70	72.00	356.80
Winston-Salem, NC	37	0.94	16.66	66.13	201.85
Worcester, MA	184	-1.36	9.48	52.36	218.67
U.S.[4]	—	0.34	8.41	58.44	289.08

Note: The HPI is a weighted repeat sales index. It measures average price changes in repeat sales or refinancings on the same properties. This information is obtained by reviewing repeat mortgage transactions on single-family properties whose mortgages have been purchased or securitized by Fannie Mae or Freddie Mac since January 1975; all figures are for the period ended December 31, 2022; (1) figures cover the Metropolitan Statistical Area (MSA) unless noted otherwise; (2) Metropolitan Division; (3) Rankings are based on annual percentage change, for all MSAs containing at least 15,000 transactions over the last 10 years and ranges from 1 to 257; (4) figures based on a weighted division average; (a) Not ranked because of increased index variability due to smaller sample size; n/a not available
Source: Federal Housing Finance Agency, Change in FHFA Metropolitan Area House Price Indexes, 2022Q4

Home Value: City

City	Under $100,000	$100,000 -$199,999	$200,000 -$299,999	$300,000 -$399,999	$400,000 -$499,999	$500,000 -$999,999	$1,000,000 or more	Median ($)
Albuquerque, NM	8.2	36.2	31.9	13.0	5.9	4.2	0.6	214,600
Allentown, PA	19.9	58.7	14.0	3.6	1.8	1.4	0.5	145,700
Anchorage, AK	6.7	10.2	25.3	28.2	13.9	14.3	1.4	327,500
Ann Arbor, MI	2.4	10.8	20.5	24.6	18.8	19.9	3.0	366,600
Athens, GA	16.0	34.3	25.3	10.4	5.8	6.9	1.2	199,300
Atlanta, GA	8.9	17.3	17.4	13.6	10.3	23.2	9.3	346,600
Austin, TX	3.6	8.4	20.6	21.5	15.3	24.7	6.0	381,400
Baltimore, MD	21.5	35.5	21.4	10.3	4.3	5.9	1.0	175,300
Boise City, ID	5.2	12.8	27.2	22.0	13.5	17.2	2.3	322,300
Boston, MA	2.6	1.0	5.5	11.1	15.0	48.4	16.5	610,400
Boulder, CO	5.2	3.5	3.6	5.3	6.9	44.1	31.4	790,100
Brownsville, TX	53.5	34.4	9.1	1.4	0.6	0.8	0.1	95,700
Cape Coral, FL	3.4	25.6	35.3	19.8	6.7	8.1	1.2	255,700
Cedar Rapids, IA	18.6	53.5	19.0	5.4	1.7	1.5	0.3	149,000
Charleston, SC	3.1	7.6	23.0	23.5	11.5	23.2	8.1	369,500
Charlotte, NC	7.8	27.5	23.8	14.8	8.8	13.3	4.0	258,000
Chicago, IL	8.5	22.4	24.5	16.5	9.6	14.2	4.3	277,600
Cincinnati, OH	24.5	35.2	17.3	9.2	4.7	7.2	1.8	162,300
Clarksville, TN	13.0	51.0	25.3	6.3	1.6	2.6	0.3	172,700
Cleveland, OH	67.7	23.2	4.6	2.2	0.7	1.3	0.2	74,700
College Station, TX	2.2	18.2	39.2	25.7	7.6	6.3	0.7	269,100
Colorado Springs, CO	4.6	11.0	28.1	26.0	14.7	14.1	1.4	324,100
Columbia, MO	8.9	35.8	29.2	14.1	6.5	5.1	0.5	215,300
Columbia, SC	17.9	34.1	18.9	9.7	5.5	11.7	2.2	193,100
Columbus, OH	19.2	40.1	25.2	9.3	2.9	2.8	0.5	174,400
Dallas, TX	17.6	27.3	15.3	11.0	8.6	14.8	5.5	230,000
Davenport, IA	28.0	44.6	17.1	7.5	1.1	1.4	0.3	138,000
Denver, CO	2.3	4.6	12.8	20.0	17.5	34.9	7.9	459,100
Des Moines, IA	20.9	53.8	17.0	4.6	1.5	1.9	0.3	149,700
Durham, NC	5.0	24.8	31.4	20.4	8.2	9.0	1.1	264,100
Edison, NJ	3.9	3.9	14.5	26.0	20.3	29.1	2.3	408,100
El Paso, TX	25.7	52.3	14.1	4.5	1.7	1.4	0.3	137,600
Fargo, ND	7.4	30.1	36.2	16.5	4.6	4.4	0.7	232,900
Fort Collins, CO	4.0	2.8	10.0	24.0	29.5	27.3	2.4	431,300
Fort Wayne, IN	32.7	46.5	14.2	4.0	1.2	1.1	0.2	130,700
Fort Worth, TX	15.9	29.7	31.6	12.1	4.7	4.8	1.2	212,300
Grand Rapids, MI	16.4	49.8	24.0	6.0	2.0	1.4	0.3	168,700
Greeley, CO	9.3	8.9	33.0	31.0	10.6	6.8	0.3	296,300
Green Bay, WI	17.2	57.2	16.1	5.1	2.4	1.8	0.2	151,000
Greensboro, NC	19.7	40.5	20.3	9.3	4.4	4.8	1.0	169,100
Honolulu, HI	1.6	1.6	5.5	11.7	10.7	41.2	27.6	726,000
Houston, TX	19.1	30.8	17.1	11.0	6.7	11.3	4.0	200,700
Huntsville, AL	21.0	30.5	21.8	12.5	6.6	6.4	1.1	194,500
Indianapolis, IN	23.7	43.7	17.7	7.2	3.1	3.9	0.7	156,300
Jacksonville, FL	17.0	32.0	28.0	12.0	4.8	4.9	1.4	203,400
Kansas City, MO	23.0	34.6	21.2	11.4	4.1	4.8	0.8	175,400
Lafayette, LA	13.7	33.6	25.7	11.7	7.0	6.7	1.6	209,100
Las Cruces, NM	17.4	49.1	21.5	7.7	1.5	2.5	0.3	167,800
Las Vegas, NV	4.3	14.0	31.2	23.5	11.7	13.1	2.2	302,100
Lexington, KY	9.0	36.1	25.2	14.5	6.4	7.6	1.2	216,800
Lincoln, NE	9.6	42.9	27.9	11.1	4.5	3.2	0.7	193,800
Little Rock, AR	22.0	33.4	17.9	11.1	5.5	8.4	1.6	179,500
Los Angeles, CA	2.2	1.3	2.4	6.2	11.3	50.1	26.6	705,900
Louisville, KY	17.5	40.5	20.3	10.8	5.0	5.1	0.9	174,400
Madison, WI	3.4	18.6	35.0	22.5	10.9	8.3	1.3	277,800

Table continued on following page.

City	Under $100,000	$100,000 -$199,999	$200,000 -$299,999	$300,000 -$399,999	$400,000 -$499,999	$500,000 -$999,999	$1,000,000 or more	Median ($)
Manchester, NH	4.7	21.9	39.9	23.6	6.6	3.1	0.1	258,100
Miami, FL	4.5	9.8	20.4	22.1	14.7	20.0	8.4	369,100
Midland, TX	11.2	22.4	32.5	17.2	6.3	8.8	1.5	250,300
Milwaukee, WI	30.6	48.6	14.1	3.3	1.2	1.8	0.5	135,600
Minneapolis, MN	4.2	19.5	31.1	20.3	9.7	12.6	2.5	284,400
Nashville, TN	4.4	18.9	29.1	21.3	9.6	13.3	3.3	291,400
New Haven, CT	11.0	36.4	29.4	10.5	5.4	5.7	1.6	207,600
New Orleans, LA	9.7	28.7	20.4	13.4	8.3	15.2	4.2	255,500
New York, NY	4.3	3.6	5.5	8.2	10.8	44.7	22.9	660,700
Oklahoma City, OK	23.1	38.5	21.4	8.2	3.8	3.8	1.2	168,900
Omaha, NE	15.7	42.7	23.3	9.7	4.0	3.9	0.7	177,700
Orlando, FL	7.5	23.3	22.9	20.6	10.8	12.3	2.6	283,700
Philadelphia, PA	21.6	33.0	22.8	10.0	4.6	6.6	1.4	184,100
Phoenix, AZ	7.3	19.8	28.5	18.6	9.6	13.8	2.4	277,700
Pittsburgh, PA	33.7	31.4	13.9	7.9	4.8	7.2	1.1	147,600
Portland, OR	2.6	2.8	9.9	21.8	20.5	38.3	4.1	462,800
Providence, RI	4.9	27.5	34.7	14.0	4.1	11.6	3.2	248,900
Provo, UT	5.3	9.2	27.9	26.4	12.3	16.1	2.7	328,500
Raleigh, NC	4.0	21.6	28.3	18.3	11.0	14.2	2.7	285,400
Reno, NV	5.9	5.9	14.6	25.8	20.2	24.1	3.5	391,500
Richmond, VA	9.5	26.4	21.0	16.5	8.6	14.2	3.8	263,000
Rochester, MN	5.8	30.7	30.8	16.9	8.6	6.8	0.5	236,400
Sacramento, CA	4.0	5.0	19.4	25.1	19.3	24.0	3.0	385,500
St. Louis, MO	29.9	36.3	17.8	8.4	3.4	3.4	0.9	153,200
Salem, OR	7.5	13.6	32.7	26.7	11.1	7.9	0.5	289,500
Salt Lake City, UT	3.8	10.8	19.8	19.3	14.6	26.2	5.3	380,200
San Antonio, TX	24.0	38.4	21.9	8.7	3.3	3.1	0.6	167,700
San Diego, CA	2.6	1.4	3.1	8.1	13.7	51.4	19.8	664,000
San Francisco, CA	1.5	0.8	1.0	1.9	1.6	26.1	67.1	1,194,500
San Jose, CA	2.3	2.5	2.0	1.6	2.6	40.3	48.6	986,700
Santa Rosa, CA	4.1	2.6	4.0	7.3	13.6	60.0	8.4	598,700
Savannah, GA	19.1	41.2	21.4	6.7	4.4	5.9	1.3	170,500
Seattle, WA	1.1	0.6	2.7	6.3	8.6	55.3	25.4	767,500
Sioux Falls, SD	10.1	32.4	31.9	12.6	6.1	5.6	1.3	218,600
Springfield, IL	34.4	38.8	15.9	6.3	2.4	1.9	0.4	132,900
Tampa, FL	9.0	22.7	22.8	14.6	9.9	14.9	6.1	277,700
Tucson, AZ	17.8	41.3	26.3	8.4	3.0	2.4	0.7	177,800
Tulsa, OK	28.0	36.9	15.4	8.2	4.4	5.5	1.5	151,500
Tuscaloosa, AL	14.2	37.7	19.5	11.1	6.0	10.0	1.6	194,500
Virginia Beach, VA	3.8	15.6	32.0	21.6	11.7	12.8	2.6	295,900
Washington, DC	1.8	2.2	7.5	12.3	12.7	42.1	21.4	635,900
Wichita, KS	31.2	39.6	17.3	6.7	2.2	2.7	0.3	145,300
Wilmington, NC	5.9	23.6	25.8	19.2	8.2	13.7	3.7	279,900
Winston-Salem, NC	22.4	44.2	16.7	7.0	3.5	5.6	0.6	158,600
Worcester, MA	4.7	20.1	40.8	22.2	6.8	4.6	0.9	259,800
U.S.	16.2	24.2	20.1	13.6	8.3	13.6	4.1	244,900

Note: Figures are percentages except for median and cover owner-occupied housing units.
Source: U.S. Census Bureau, 2017-2021 American Community Survey 5-Year Estimates

Home Value: Metro Area

MSA[1]	Under $100,000	$100,000 -$199,999	$200,000 -$299,999	$300,000 -$399,999	$400,000 -$499,999	$500,000 -$999,999	$1,000,000 or more	Median ($)
Albuquerque, NM	11.7	34.6	28.4	12.3	5.9	5.9	1.1	210,700
Allentown, PA	9.9	31.5	28.8	17.1	7.2	5.1	0.6	227,900
Anchorage, AK	6.7	12.7	28.8	26.2	12.5	12.0	1.1	306,700
Ann Arbor, MI	9.2	18.2	24.0	19.4	12.7	14.5	1.9	293,800
Athens, GA	16.8	30.0	23.5	12.5	7.6	8.0	1.7	211,500
Atlanta, GA	8.9	26.9	25.0	16.1	9.3	11.7	2.0	252,100
Austin, TX	6.2	12.5	25.9	20.6	12.6	18.1	4.1	326,400
Baltimore, MD	6.7	15.8	23.5	20.6	12.8	18.2	2.4	319,500
Boise City, ID	6.9	15.9	25.8	21.3	13.1	14.9	2.1	306,300
Boston, MA	2.5	3.6	10.6	18.0	17.3	38.5	9.4	487,600
Boulder, CO	4.1	2.1	5.7	13.1	16.3	44.3	14.5	575,700
Brownsville, TX	53.6	31.8	8.9	2.9	1.1	1.4	0.2	94,200
Cape Coral, FL	12.0	23.6	27.5	16.4	7.3	10.5	2.8	248,300
Cedar Rapids, IA	17.2	44.7	22.6	8.4	3.7	3.0	0.5	165,500
Charleston, SC	10.8	21.0	24.9	16.5	8.1	14.0	4.6	270,700
Charlotte, NC	13.0	27.8	23.7	15.3	8.0	10.0	2.3	237,300
Chicago, IL	8.6	25.3	26.7	17.5	8.5	10.9	2.5	258,500
Cincinnati, OH	16.4	37.7	23.2	11.6	4.9	5.4	0.9	187,000
Clarksville, TN	19.0	41.2	23.4	9.2	2.9	3.7	0.7	174,300
Cleveland, OH	23.8	37.8	20.5	9.2	4.1	3.9	0.6	164,400
College Station, TX	20.3	25.9	24.8	14.8	5.2	7.7	1.3	213,600
Colorado Springs, CO	4.6	10.9	26.6	25.1	14.8	16.3	1.6	331,300
Columbia, MO	14.6	36.8	24.4	12.8	5.2	5.2	1.0	195,600
Columbia, SC	22.5	38.6	19.7	9.2	4.2	4.9	1.0	167,800
Columbus, OH	14.2	32.0	25.3	14.2	6.8	6.6	0.9	213,600
Dallas, TX	10.9	24.1	26.2	17.0	9.3	10.2	2.4	255,600
Davenport, IA	27.9	41.0	17.1	8.3	2.8	2.6	0.4	145,200
Denver, CO	3.2	3.4	11.5	22.5	21.7	32.8	4.9	443,400
Des Moines, IA	12.8	35.7	26.8	13.6	5.6	5.0	0.6	205,200
Durham, NC	10.6	23.8	24.0	17.7	9.2	12.7	1.9	264,400
Edison, NJ	3.5	5.2	11.1	16.7	16.1	36.2	11.2	483,500
El Paso, TX	29.8	49.6	13.5	4.1	1.4	1.2	0.3	131,200
Fargo, ND	8.0	29.3	32.7	16.9	6.0	6.3	0.8	235,600
Fort Collins, CO	4.9	3.0	11.4	25.9	23.2	28.1	3.4	420,200
Fort Wayne, IN	26.2	42.9	18.0	6.8	2.7	2.8	0.5	150,600
Fort Worth, TX	10.9	24.1	26.2	17.0	9.3	10.2	2.4	255,600
Grand Rapids, MI	14.0	34.9	27.4	12.2	5.7	4.7	1.1	203,500
Greeley, CO	7.1	7.0	21.1	28.5	17.5	17.3	1.5	352,000
Green Bay, WI	12.8	41.4	26.0	10.9	4.6	3.6	0.7	188,800
Greensboro, NC	22.8	39.9	19.0	9.0	4.4	4.2	0.7	162,700
Honolulu, HI	1.6	1.6	3.6	8.3	9.7	53.8	21.5	726,800
Houston, TX	13.5	30.4	25.4	13.7	6.5	8.0	2.5	221,400
Huntsville, AL	17.1	33.2	24.5	12.5	6.2	5.8	0.7	199,000
Indianapolis, IN	17.1	37.2	22.1	11.7	5.5	5.6	0.9	186,700
Jacksonville, FL	13.2	26.5	26.7	15.0	7.8	8.5	2.2	235,300
Kansas City, MO	15.2	31.5	24.6	14.0	6.8	6.8	1.1	211,900
Lafayette, LA	28.0	34.1	21.1	9.0	3.7	3.3	0.7	167,400
Las Cruces, NM	26.6	38.7	19.7	7.3	3.9	3.4	0.4	162,200
Las Vegas, NV	5.6	12.8	29.4	25.2	12.4	12.3	2.3	308,800
Lexington, KY	10.9	37.5	24.2	13.2	6.0	7.1	1.2	206,000
Lincoln, NE	9.4	39.9	27.0	12.5	5.5	4.7	0.9	202,300
Little Rock, AR	23.2	39.9	20.4	8.5	3.2	4.0	0.8	164,200
Los Angeles, CA	3.2	1.7	3.2	7.0	11.9	52.3	20.7	671,700
Louisville, KY	15.4	37.8	23.3	12.0	5.0	5.4	0.9	189,900
Madison, WI	5.1	20.5	30.8	21.7	10.9	9.4	1.6	277,400

Table continued on following page.

MSA[1]	Under $100,000	$100,000 -$199,999	$200,000 -$299,999	$300,000 -$399,999	$400,000 -$499,999	$500,000 -$999,999	$1,000,000 or more	Median ($)
Manchester, NH	4.2	13.5	30.7	27.5	12.9	10.7	0.5	306,000
Miami, FL	8.7	15.9	21.8	20.7	12.8	15.2	4.9	317,800
Midland, TX	16.5	20.8	29.5	16.1	6.9	8.7	1.4	243,400
Milwaukee, WI	10.6	29.0	27.8	16.4	7.5	7.4	1.2	235,100
Minneapolis, MN	4.6	17.1	32.2	21.8	11.2	11.4	1.7	287,600
Nashville, TN	6.6	19.5	27.4	19.2	9.9	14.1	3.2	286,800
New Haven, CT	6.4	25.9	29.4	18.7	10.0	8.3	1.2	259,400
New Orleans, LA	11.5	34.6	25.7	13.3	5.8	7.5	1.7	214,300
New York, NY	3.5	5.2	11.1	16.7	16.1	36.2	11.2	483,500
Oklahoma City, OK	21.7	39.2	20.6	9.0	4.1	4.1	1.2	169,300
Omaha, NE	13.4	38.4	24.8	12.5	5.4	4.7	0.8	195,000
Orlando, FL	10.4	20.5	30.9	19.9	8.1	8.3	1.9	260,800
Philadelphia, PA	9.6	21.9	25.7	18.4	10.4	12.1	1.8	270,400
Phoenix, AZ	8.3	15.9	27.3	20.3	11.4	13.9	2.9	294,700
Pittsburgh, PA	25.5	34.6	19.9	9.9	4.5	4.9	0.7	167,500
Portland, OR	4.2	3.7	12.4	25.2	21.3	29.7	3.5	421,300
Providence, RI	3.5	12.7	31.4	24.1	12.7	13.5	2.1	309,600
Provo, UT	3.1	6.2	22.3	28.1	17.5	20.2	2.6	365,500
Raleigh, NC	7.0	20.0	25.5	20.2	12.4	13.2	1.7	289,700
Reno, NV	5.5	6.4	16.4	25.0	18.1	22.9	5.9	387,400
Richmond, VA	6.4	24.3	29.8	18.4	9.3	10.4	1.5	262,900
Rochester, MN	9.2	29.8	26.8	16.1	8.6	8.3	1.2	234,700
Sacramento, CA	4.1	3.6	11.7	22.0	20.6	33.7	4.4	441,800
St. Louis, MO	20.0	33.1	22.7	12.1	5.2	5.7	1.2	189,600
Salem, OR	8.1	12.8	29.6	24.3	12.1	12.1	1.0	298,400
Salt Lake City, UT	3.8	8.2	22.9	24.5	16.6	21.1	2.9	361,600
San Antonio, TX	18.7	31.5	24.5	12.0	5.8	6.2	1.3	199,200
San Diego, CA	4.2	2.2	3.5	7.9	14.3	52.3	15.7	627,200
San Francisco, CA	2.0	1.4	1.7	3.8	5.9	40.7	44.4	933,300
San Jose, CA	2.1	2.0	1.7	1.6	2.3	32.2	58.0	1,113,700
Santa Rosa, CA	3.9	2.9	2.9	5.1	9.9	58.1	17.2	665,800
Savannah, GA	14.2	32.9	25.4	11.2	5.1	9.1	2.1	210,400
Seattle, WA	3.3	3.2	9.5	16.3	15.8	39.3	12.5	518,000
Sioux Falls, SD	11.0	31.1	29.9	14.0	6.4	6.5	1.2	221,500
Springfield, IL	29.8	38.6	19.5	7.3	2.4	2.0	0.4	148,000
Tampa, FL	16.4	25.3	26.4	14.8	6.9	8.1	2.0	229,400
Tucson, AZ	15.0	29.7	26.3	13.5	6.8	7.4	1.3	217,700
Tulsa, OK	24.2	39.1	19.5	8.6	3.5	4.1	0.9	163,100
Tuscaloosa, AL	24.9	35.9	20.8	9.4	3.6	4.6	0.8	171,100
Virginia Beach, VA	6.5	23.8	31.1	18.5	9.8	9.0	1.3	261,800
Washington, DC	2.4	4.9	14.2	19.7	16.6	34.4	7.8	453,100
Wichita, KS	28.6	40.0	18.4	7.4	2.6	2.6	0.4	151,900
Wilmington, NC	9.2	24.0	25.8	18.0	8.9	11.6	2.4	262,500
Winston-Salem, NC	20.7	42.5	19.5	8.7	3.7	4.4	0.5	165,000
Worcester, MA	3.6	16.4	30.3	22.9	12.3	13.1	1.3	298,900
U.S.	16.2	24.2	20.1	13.6	8.3	13.6	4.1	244,900

Note: (1) Figures cover the Metropolitan Statistical Area (MSA); Figures are percentages except for median and cover owner-occupied housing units.
Source: U.S. Census Bureau, 2017-2021 American Community Survey 5-Year Estimates

Homeownership Rate

Metro Area	2015	2016	2017	2018	2019	2020	2021	2022
Albuquerque, NM	64.3	66.9	67.0	67.9	70.0	69.5	66.5	67.3
Allentown, PA	69.2	68.9	73.1	72.1	67.8	68.8	70.4	73.1
Anchorage, AK	n/a	n/a	n/a	n/a	n/a	n/a	n/a	n/a
Ann Arbor, MI	n/a	n/a	n/a	n/a	n/a	n/a	n/a	n/a
Athens, GA	n/a	n/a	n/a	n/a	n/a	n/a	n/a	n/a
Atlanta, GA	61.7	61.5	62.4	64.0	64.2	66.4	64.2	64.4
Austin, TX	57.5	56.5	55.6	56.1	59.0	65.4	62.2	62.4
Baltimore, MD	65.3	68.5	67.5	63.5	66.5	70.7	67.5	70.4
Boise City, ID	n/a	n/a	n/a	n/a	n/a	n/a	n/a	n/a
Boston, MA	59.3	58.9	58.8	61.0	60.9	61.2	60.7	59.4
Boulder, CO	n/a	n/a	n/a	n/a	n/a	n/a	n/a	n/a
Brownsville, TX	n/a	n/a	n/a	n/a	n/a	n/a	n/a	n/a
Cape Coral, FL	62.9	66.5	65.5	75.1	72.0	77.4	76.1	70.8
Cedar Rapids, IA	n/a	n/a	n/a	n/a	n/a	n/a	n/a	n/a
Charleston, SC	65.8	62.1	67.7	68.8	70.7	75.5	73.2	71.9
Charlotte, NC	62.3	66.2	64.6	67.9	72.3	73.3	70.0	68.7
Chicago, IL	64.3	64.5	64.1	64.6	63.4	66.0	67.5	66.8
Cincinnati, OH	65.9	64.9	65.7	67.3	67.4	71.1	72.1	67.1
Clarksville, TN	n/a	n/a	n/a	n/a	n/a	n/a	n/a	n/a
Cleveland, OH	68.4	64.8	66.6	66.7	64.4	66.3	64.7	63.0
College Station, TX	n/a	n/a	n/a	n/a	n/a	n/a	n/a	n/a
Colorado Springs, CO	n/a	n/a	n/a	n/a	n/a	n/a	n/a	n/a
Columbia, MO	n/a	n/a	n/a	n/a	n/a	n/a	n/a	n/a
Columbia, SC	66.1	63.9	70.7	69.3	65.9	69.7	69.4	70.9
Columbus, OH	59.0	57.5	57.9	64.8	65.7	65.6	64.6	61.5
Dallas, TX	57.8	59.7	61.8	62.0	60.6	64.7	61.8	60.4
Davenport, IA	n/a	n/a	n/a	n/a	n/a	n/a	n/a	n/a
Denver, CO	61.6	61.6	59.3	60.1	63.5	62.9	62.8	64.6
Des Moines, IA	n/a	n/a	n/a	n/a	n/a	n/a	n/a	n/a
Durham, NC	n/a	n/a	n/a	n/a	n/a	n/a	n/a	n/a
Edison, NJ	49.9	50.4	49.9	49.7	50.4	50.9	50.7	50.5
El Paso, TX	n/a	n/a	n/a	n/a	n/a	n/a	n/a	n/a
Fargo, ND	n/a	n/a	n/a	n/a	n/a	n/a	n/a	n/a
Fort Collins, CO	n/a	n/a	n/a	n/a	n/a	n/a	n/a	n/a
Fort Wayne, IN	n/a	n/a	n/a	n/a	n/a	n/a	n/a	n/a
Fort Worth, TX	57.8	59.7	61.8	62.0	60.6	64.7	61.8	60.4
Grand Rapids, MI	75.8	76.2	71.7	73.0	75.2	71.8	65.0	68.1
Greeley, CO	n/a	n/a	n/a	n/a	n/a	n/a	n/a	n/a
Green Bay, WI	n/a	n/a	n/a	n/a	n/a	n/a	n/a	n/a
Greensboro, NC	65.4	62.9	61.9	63.2	61.7	65.8	61.9	70.0
Honolulu, HI	59.6	57.9	53.8	57.7	59.0	56.9	55.9	57.7
Houston, TX	60.3	59.0	58.9	60.1	61.3	65.3	64.1	63.7
Huntsville, AL	n/a	n/a	n/a	n/a	n/a	n/a	n/a	n/a
Indianapolis, IN	64.6	63.9	63.9	64.3	66.2	70.0	70.1	68.8
Jacksonville, FL	62.5	61.8	65.2	61.4	63.1	64.8	68.1	70.6
Kansas City, MO	65.0	62.4	62.4	64.3	65.0	66.7	63.8	63.8
Lafayette, LA	n/a	n/a	n/a	n/a	n/a	n/a	n/a	n/a
Las Cruces, NM	n/a	n/a	n/a	n/a	n/a	n/a	n/a	n/a
Las Vegas, NV	52.1	51.3	54.4	58.1	56.0	57.3	57.7	58.7
Lexington, KY	n/a	n/a	n/a	n/a	n/a	n/a	n/a	n/a
Lincoln, NE	n/a	n/a	n/a	n/a	n/a	n/a	n/a	n/a
Little Rock, AR	65.8	64.9	61.0	62.2	65.0	67.7	64.6	64.4
Los Angeles, CA	49.1	47.1	49.1	49.5	48.2	48.5	47.9	48.3
Louisville, KY	67.7	67.6	71.7	67.9	64.9	69.3	71.4	71.7
Madison, WI	n/a	n/a	n/a	n/a	n/a	n/a	n/a	n/a
Manchester, NH	n/a	n/a	n/a	n/a	n/a	n/a	n/a	n/a

Table continued on following page.

Metro Area	2015	2016	2017	2018	2019	2020	2021	2022
Miami, FL	58.6	58.4	57.9	59.9	60.4	60.6	59.4	58.3
Midland, TX	n/a	n/a	n/a	n/a	n/a	n/a	n/a	n/a
Milwaukee, WI	57.0	60.4	63.9	62.3	56.9	58.5	56.8	57.3
Minneapolis, MN	67.9	69.1	70.1	67.8	70.2	73.0	75.0	73.0
Nashville, TN	67.4	65.0	69.4	68.3	69.8	69.8	65.7	70.4
New Haven, CT	64.6	59.4	58.7	65.0	65.1	63.4	61.0	63.3
New Orleans, LA	62.8	59.3	61.7	62.6	61.1	66.3	66.2	66.3
New York, NY	49.9	50.4	49.9	49.7	50.4	50.9	50.7	50.5
Oklahoma City, OK	61.4	63.1	64.7	64.6	64.3	68.3	61.9	64.8
Omaha, NE	69.6	69.2	65.5	67.8	66.9	68.6	68.6	67.9
Orlando, FL	58.4	58.5	59.5	58.5	56.1	64.2	63.0	62.1
Philadelphia, PA	67.0	64.7	65.6	67.4	67.4	69.2	69.8	68.2
Phoenix, AZ	61.0	62.6	64.0	65.3	65.9	67.9	65.2	68.0
Pittsburgh, PA	71.0	72.2	72.7	71.7	71.5	69.8	69.1	72.7
Portland, OR	58.9	61.8	61.1	59.2	60.0	62.5	64.1	65.2
Providence, RI	60.0	57.5	58.6	61.3	63.5	64.8	64.1	66.3
Provo, UT	n/a	n/a	n/a	n/a	n/a	n/a	n/a	n/a
Raleigh, NC	67.4	65.9	68.2	64.9	63.0	68.2	62.7	65.1
Reno, NV	n/a	n/a	n/a	n/a	n/a	n/a	n/a	n/a
Richmond, VA	67.4	61.7	63.1	62.9	66.4	66.5	64.9	66.3
Rochester, MN	n/a	n/a	n/a	n/a	n/a	n/a	n/a	n/a
Sacramento, CA	60.8	60.5	60.1	64.1	61.6	63.4	63.2	63.5
St. Louis, MO	68.7	66.4	65.6	65.8	68.1	71.1	73.8	69.9
Salem, OR	n/a	n/a	n/a	n/a	n/a	n/a	n/a	n/a
Salt Lake City, UT	69.1	69.2	68.1	69.5	69.2	68.0	64.1	66.6
San Antonio, TX	66.0	61.6	62.5	64.4	62.6	64.2	62.7	62.9
San Diego, CA	51.8	53.3	56.0	56.1	56.7	57.8	52.6	51.6
San Francisco, CA	56.3	55.8	55.7	55.6	52.8	53.0	54.7	56.4
San Jose, CA	50.7	49.9	50.4	50.4	52.4	52.6	48.4	53.1
Santa Rosa, CA	n/a	n/a	n/a	n/a	n/a	n/a	n/a	n/a
Savannah, GA	n/a	n/a	n/a	n/a	n/a	n/a	n/a	n/a
Seattle, WA	59.5	57.7	59.5	62.5	61.5	59.4	58.0	62.7
Sioux Falls, SD	n/a	n/a	n/a	n/a	n/a	n/a	n/a	n/a
Springfield, IL	n/a	n/a	n/a	n/a	n/a	n/a	n/a	n/a
Tampa, FL	64.9	62.9	60.4	64.9	68.0	72.2	68.3	68.4
Tucson, AZ	61.4	56.0	60.1	63.8	60.1	67.1	63.5	71.6
Tulsa, OK	65.2	65.4	66.8	68.3	70.5	70.1	63.8	63.7
Tuscaloosa, AL	n/a	n/a	n/a	n/a	n/a	n/a	n/a	n/a
Virginia Beach, VA	59.4	59.6	65.3	62.8	63.0	65.8	64.4	61.4
Washington, DC	64.6	63.1	63.3	62.9	64.7	67.9	65.8	66.2
Wichita, KS	n/a	n/a	n/a	n/a	n/a	n/a	n/a	n/a
Wilmington, NC	n/a	n/a	n/a	n/a	n/a	n/a	n/a	n/a
Winston-Salem, NC	n/a	n/a	n/a	n/a	n/a	n/a	n/a	n/a
Worcester, MA	64.2	65.5	64.9	63.4	62.7	65.9	68.7	64.8
U.S.	63.7	63.4	63.9	64.4	64.6	66.6	65.5	65.8

Note: Figures are percentages and cover the Metropolitan Statistical Area; n/a not available
Source: U.S. Census Bureau, Housing Vacancies and Homeownership Annual Statistics: 2015-2022

Year Housing Structure Built: City

City	2020 or Later	2010 -2019	2000 -2009	1990 -1999	1980 -1989	1970 -1979	1960 -1969	1950 -1959	1940 -1949	Before 1940	Median Year
Albuquerque, NM	0.2	5.7	16.1	14.9	15.1	19.1	9.8	11.8	4.3	3.1	1981
Allentown, PA	0.1	2.3	4.6	3.4	5.3	10.8	11.5	15.0	7.2	39.7	1952
Anchorage, AK	<0.1	4.7	11.9	11.9	25.8	28.0	10.2	5.8	1.2	0.5	1982
Ann Arbor, MI	0.2	5.0	5.8	11.7	11.3	16.9	18.0	11.1	5.0	15.0	1971
Athens, GA	0.1	5.7	17.6	18.6	15.8	15.8	12.5	6.6	2.2	5.1	1985
Atlanta, GA	0.4	12.7	22.0	10.2	7.6	7.7	11.0	10.6	5.7	12.1	1984
Austin, TX	0.2	17.5	17.1	14.7	18.6	15.0	7.7	4.5	2.1	2.6	1990
Baltimore, MD	<0.1	3.4	3.6	3.9	4.3	5.7	8.6	15.8	11.9	42.8	1946
Boise City, ID	0.1	9.0	11.0	22.5	15.8	17.1	7.8	6.8	3.9	6.2	1985
Boston, MA	0.2	7.2	6.6	4.4	5.6	7.5	7.6	7.3	5.4	48.2	1943
Boulder, CO	0.1	7.9	7.7	12.0	16.7	19.6	17.7	9.0	1.7	7.7	1977
Brownsville, TX	0.2	12.9	22.9	18.0	14.8	15.5	6.2	4.4	2.8	2.3	1992
Cape Coral, FL	0.1	8.4	34.8	17.6	21.6	11.7	4.6	0.8	0.2	0.1	1996
Cedar Rapids, IA	0.1	7.7	11.5	10.5	7.1	14.6	14.8	12.8	4.1	16.8	1971
Charleston, SC	0.3	18.9	20.0	10.6	12.0	8.8	8.5	5.5	3.4	11.9	1990
Charlotte, NC	0.2	13.2	21.5	19.3	14.4	11.2	8.7	6.3	2.5	2.7	1992
Chicago, IL	<0.1	3.8	8.0	5.1	4.8	7.7	9.6	11.8	8.8	40.3	1951
Cincinnati, OH	0.1	3.3	3.7	4.2	6.0	9.4	12.2	11.5	8.4	41.4	1950
Clarksville, TN	0.2	15.6	22.2	20.2	12.9	12.0	7.2	4.8	2.8	2.1	1994
Cleveland, OH	0.1	2.9	3.5	3.4	2.8	5.5	7.8	12.7	11.2	50.0	<1940
College Station, TX	0.6	20.8	20.7	20.0	16.6	14.8	3.5	2.0	0.4	0.6	1996
Colorado Springs, CO	0.3	9.5	14.7	15.4	18.9	17.2	9.4	7.0	2.0	5.5	1985
Columbia, MO	0.1	15.5	20.0	18.1	11.8	12.1	10.5	4.4	2.3	5.3	1992
Columbia, SC	0.2	9.3	15.2	11.3	10.2	10.2	10.2	13.9	10.1	9.5	1976
Columbus, OH	0.1	8.0	11.7	15.1	12.9	14.3	11.5	10.4	4.3	11.8	1978
Dallas, TX	0.2	9.8	10.5	10.8	16.4	16.5	12.5	13.2	4.9	5.2	1979
Davenport, IA	<0.1	3.9	8.5	8.7	6.8	15.2	12.5	10.9	5.6	27.8	1965
Denver, CO	0.3	12.8	11.1	6.7	7.6	12.7	10.6	14.2	5.8	18.2	1971
Des Moines, IA	0.1	5.5	6.7	7.0	6.4	13.6	10.0	14.9	7.8	28.0	1960
Durham, NC	0.4	17.0	17.9	16.6	14.6	10.4	8.1	5.7	3.3	5.9	1991
Edison, NJ	0.1	2.5	5.7	9.8	24.2	11.6	18.6	17.8	4.0	5.5	1973
El Paso, TX	0.1	12.1	14.1	12.9	14.4	16.3	10.5	11.1	3.7	4.8	1982
Fargo, ND	0.3	18.3	14.2	15.1	13.1	14.2	6.1	8.0	2.3	8.3	1988
Fort Collins, CO	0.3	13.1	18.0	21.0	15.0	16.8	6.7	3.0	1.5	4.6	1991
Fort Wayne, IN	0.1	2.2	6.7	13.6	11.5	17.5	14.9	12.8	6.5	14.2	1971
Fort Worth, TX	0.3	14.8	21.3	12.3	13.5	9.4	7.7	10.2	4.9	5.7	1989
Grand Rapids, MI	<0.1	3.8	4.9	6.3	6.6	8.5	9.0	14.9	8.9	37.1	1953
Greeley, CO	0.1	9.4	17.2	16.7	10.2	21.2	9.4	6.4	2.2	7.2	1984
Green Bay, WI	0.1	2.3	7.0	10.4	12.0	18.6	12.9	15.6	6.5	14.7	1970
Greensboro, NC	0.1	8.0	15.0	16.8	16.5	13.3	11.3	10.2	3.7	5.1	1984
Honolulu, HI	0.1	6.0	6.8	8.2	9.8	26.1	21.0	11.9	5.2	5.0	1973
Houston, TX	0.2	11.8	12.7	9.8	14.6	19.6	13.0	10.0	4.2	4.2	1980
Huntsville, AL	0.2	13.6	12.4	11.0	15.8	12.8	20.6	8.6	2.4	2.6	1982
Indianapolis, IN	0.1	5.0	9.2	12.5	11.5	12.9	13.6	12.8	6.2	16.3	1971
Jacksonville, FL	0.6	8.4	18.1	14.7	15.6	12.4	9.9	10.8	4.5	5.0	1985
Kansas City, MO	0.2	6.9	9.8	9.2	8.9	11.8	12.5	13.4	5.9	21.3	1968
Lafayette, LA	<0.1	10.1	10.7	10.1	19.5	22.0	12.8	9.0	3.2	2.5	1980
Las Cruces, NM	0.3	10.7	19.9	15.0	16.9	15.5	8.1	8.9	2.1	2.6	1988
Las Vegas, NV	0.2	7.1	21.8	31.0	16.3	10.1	7.6	4.2	1.1	0.5	1993
Lexington, KY	0.2	8.4	14.2	16.5	13.2	15.2	13.5	8.9	2.9	7.1	1982
Lincoln, NE	0.1	10.3	13.1	14.2	10.4	15.4	9.4	10.7	3.4	13.0	1979
Little Rock, AR	0.0	8.0	11.4	12.3	13.7	18.5	13.8	9.4	5.1	7.8	1978
Los Angeles, CA	0.1	4.8	5.5	6.0	10.6	13.4	13.6	16.8	9.3	19.7	1963
Louisville, KY	0.2	6.6	11.0	11.1	6.9	12.4	13.6	14.6	7.2	16.5	1969
Madison, WI	0.1	10.1	13.5	12.8	9.8	13.7	11.8	9.4	4.5	14.2	1977

Table continued on following page.

City	2020 or Later	2010 -2019	2000 -2009	1990 -1999	1980 -1989	1970 -1979	1960 -1969	1950 -1959	1940 -1949	Before 1940	Median Year
Manchester, NH	0.3	2.5	6.2	8.3	16.3	11.9	8.1	10.1	7.2	29.1	1965
Miami, FL	0.2	11.5	18.0	6.6	7.5	12.8	10.0	14.4	9.9	9.1	1975
Midland, TX	0.2	18.2	8.1	13.4	18.0	11.7	8.9	17.8	2.6	1.2	1984
Milwaukee, WI	0.1	2.6	3.5	3.3	4.1	8.7	11.4	19.5	10.4	36.5	1952
Minneapolis, MN	<0.1	7.3	6.3	4.0	6.8	8.2	7.5	9.0	6.9	43.9	1949
Nashville, TN	0.8	13.4	13.8	12.3	14.5	13.5	11.6	9.7	4.0	6.4	1983
New Haven, CT	0.0	3.8	4.6	3.1	6.8	9.5	11.2	10.3	7.4	43.2	1949
New Orleans, LA	0.1	4.4	6.9	3.3	7.6	13.9	10.9	12.1	7.3	33.4	1958
New York, NY	<0.1	4.1	5.4	3.8	4.9	7.0	12.5	12.9	9.5	39.9	1950
Oklahoma City, OK	0.3	12.0	13.4	9.9	14.2	15.9	11.5	10.0	5.0	7.9	1980
Omaha, NE	0.1	5.1	8.3	12.4	10.9	15.1	14.4	10.9	4.6	18.3	1971
Orlando, FL	0.2	13.7	20.3	14.7	15.6	14.5	7.2	8.3	2.8	2.8	1989
Philadelphia, PA	0.1	3.6	3.0	3.2	4.0	7.4	11.1	15.7	11.2	40.7	1948
Phoenix, AZ	0.2	6.4	16.3	15.4	17.5	19.4	11.0	9.6	2.4	1.9	1983
Pittsburgh, PA	0.1	3.9	3.0	3.6	4.4	6.6	8.3	13.2	8.3	48.8	1941
Portland, OR	0.2	8.9	9.9	7.9	6.8	10.8	8.6	11.4	7.8	27.7	1964
Providence, RI	0.1	1.2	4.6	4.6	5.7	7.9	5.4	7.1	5.7	57.7	<1940
Provo, UT	0.4	6.9	10.7	18.8	14.4	18.5	9.9	7.8	5.0	7.6	1981
Raleigh, NC	0.3	14.6	23.4	18.5	16.8	9.9	7.6	4.2	1.6	3.1	1994
Reno, NV	1.0	9.8	19.0	17.3	13.8	18.0	8.8	6.1	3.1	3.1	1988
Richmond, VA	0.1	6.5	5.3	5.8	7.1	9.9	11.8	14.7	9.1	29.6	1958
Rochester, MN	0.4	12.3	18.0	14.4	12.0	12.5	10.0	8.8	3.4	8.1	1986
Sacramento, CA	0.1	4.6	14.5	8.7	15.6	14.2	11.4	12.3	7.3	11.3	1975
St. Louis, MO	<0.1	2.4	4.0	3.0	3.2	4.4	6.5	10.2	8.1	58.2	<1940
Salem, OR	0.2	6.9	12.5	16.8	9.7	19.9	9.5	10.6	4.9	9.0	1978
Salt Lake City, UT	0.2	8.1	6.8	6.4	7.6	11.3	9.8	12.8	9.2	27.8	1960
San Antonio, TX	0.2	10.2	14.9	12.9	16.2	14.4	10.3	9.9	5.5	5.4	1983
San Diego, CA	0.2	5.7	10.2	11.0	17.5	20.7	12.5	11.5	4.1	6.7	1977
San Francisco, CA	0.1	5.4	6.3	4.2	5.4	7.2	7.9	8.6	8.8	46.2	1944
San Jose, CA	0.2	6.4	9.2	10.1	12.5	24.3	18.0	11.1	2.8	5.3	1975
Santa Rosa, CA	0.5	4.6	12.5	13.2	17.9	21.1	12.0	8.1	4.7	5.5	1979
Savannah, GA	0.1	9.6	9.7	6.5	10.9	11.5	12.2	14.5	8.0	17.0	1969
Seattle, WA	0.1	14.7	11.9	8.3	7.6	7.7	8.3	9.1	8.0	24.2	1971
Sioux Falls, SD	0.3	17.8	17.9	14.7	9.7	12.1	7.0	8.3	3.1	9.1	1990
Springfield, IL	<0.1	3.0	8.6	13.0	8.8	17.4	12.6	10.8	6.0	19.7	1971
Tampa, FL	0.3	10.8	17.3	12.5	11.9	11.3	9.3	13.0	5.1	8.6	1982
Tucson, AZ	0.1	3.4	12.6	13.3	17.2	20.5	11.0	13.9	4.6	3.4	1978
Tulsa, OK	0.1	4.6	6.2	9.2	13.4	20.6	14.4	16.5	6.4	8.7	1972
Tuscaloosa, AL	0.1	16.7	16.7	14.4	11.6	14.9	9.8	8.3	3.9	3.6	1988
Virginia Beach, VA	0.1	6.4	11.1	14.1	27.1	20.4	12.4	6.1	1.2	1.1	1983
Washington, DC	0.2	10.3	7.9	3.1	4.7	6.8	11.1	12.1	10.8	32.9	1955
Wichita, KS	0.1	5.9	9.9	12.2	12.3	13.1	9.8	18.6	8.0	10.2	1973
Wilmington, NC	0.1	10.8	15.0	17.3	15.3	12.9	6.7	6.8	5.5	9.6	1986
Winston-Salem, NC	0.1	6.4	13.2	13.0	14.3	16.4	11.8	12.2	4.9	7.7	1978
Worcester, MA	0.0	2.1	4.6	5.2	10.1	7.9	7.8	11.6	7.5	43.3	1949
U.S.	0.2	7.3	13.6	13.6	13.2	14.8	10.3	10.0	4.7	12.2	1979

Note: Figures are percentages except for median year
Source: U.S. Census Bureau, 2017-2021 American Community Survey 5-Year Estimates

Year Housing Structure Built: Metro Area

Metro Area	2020 or Later	2010 -2019	2000 -2009	1990 -1999	1980 -1989	1970 -1979	1960 -1969	1950 -1959	1940 -1949	Before 1940	Median Year
Albuquerque, NM	0.2	5.9	17.2	17.3	16.8	17.8	8.7	9.3	3.6	3.2	1984
Allentown, PA	0.1	4.0	11.4	10.3	11.0	12.0	9.5	10.9	5.2	25.7	1969
Anchorage, AK	0.1	6.4	17.2	13.3	25.0	23.5	8.3	4.7	1.0	0.5	1985
Ann Arbor, MI	0.2	4.8	12.8	17.0	11.2	16.0	12.4	9.7	4.5	11.5	1977
Athens, GA	0.2	7.5	17.8	20.4	16.4	15.2	10.0	5.3	1.9	5.2	1988
Atlanta, GA	0.3	9.4	23.6	20.8	17.1	12.4	7.3	4.5	1.7	2.8	1992
Austin, TX	0.6	22.4	22.8	16.7	15.5	10.6	4.9	3.0	1.5	2.1	1997
Baltimore, MD	0.1	6.0	9.4	13.4	13.4	12.9	10.4	12.8	6.2	15.4	1974
Boise City, ID	0.5	14.3	23.2	20.7	9.8	14.1	5.2	4.3	2.8	5.2	1994
Boston, MA	0.1	5.8	7.5	7.4	10.4	10.8	10.1	10.7	5.0	32.2	1962
Boulder, CO	0.2	9.4	11.7	19.4	16.4	19.7	10.6	4.8	1.3	6.3	1984
Brownsville, TX	0.2	11.0	22.2	17.0	17.9	16.0	5.7	5.3	2.6	2.1	1990
Cape Coral, FL	0.2	8.9	29.7	17.4	21.0	14.4	5.2	2.2	0.4	0.6	1994
Cedar Rapids, IA	0.1	8.3	13.7	12.7	7.2	13.8	12.3	10.4	3.5	18.0	1974
Charleston, SC	0.3	16.4	20.8	15.5	15.4	13.0	7.7	4.8	2.4	3.7	1992
Charlotte, NC	0.2	13.6	22.6	18.9	12.9	10.8	7.7	6.3	2.9	4.1	1993
Chicago, IL	0.1	3.6	11.4	11.2	9.1	14.1	11.5	12.7	5.9	20.5	1969
Cincinnati, OH	0.1	5.3	12.0	13.8	10.7	13.8	10.5	11.6	4.8	17.3	1974
Clarksville, TN	0.4	13.8	19.7	20.2	12.2	13.9	7.9	6.0	2.9	3.0	1992
Cleveland, OH	0.1	3.4	6.8	8.9	6.9	12.4	13.6	17.7	7.6	22.5	1962
College Station, TX	0.6	17.0	18.8	18.0	16.6	14.4	6.0	4.3	2.1	2.3	1992
Colorado Springs, CO	0.3	10.7	17.8	16.4	17.6	16.2	8.1	6.2	1.6	5.1	1987
Columbia, MO	<0.1	12.1	18.1	17.6	13.2	14.8	9.6	4.7	2.6	7.2	1988
Columbia, SC	0.3	11.3	18.6	18.3	13.7	14.9	9.2	6.7	3.2	3.7	1989
Columbus, OH	0.2	8.0	14.2	15.9	11.6	13.8	10.7	9.8	3.7	12.2	1980
Dallas, TX	0.4	14.0	19.1	15.6	17.3	13.3	8.3	7.1	2.4	2.6	1989
Davenport, IA	0.1	4.6	7.9	8.5	6.8	15.9	12.8	12.1	7.2	24.2	1965
Denver, CO	0.3	10.7	16.0	14.8	13.8	17.2	9.0	9.0	2.6	6.5	1984
Des Moines, IA	0.3	14.1	15.7	12.5	8.0	13.3	7.9	8.8	3.9	15.4	1981
Durham, NC	0.5	13.4	17.9	18.2	15.3	12.0	8.4	6.1	2.9	5.3	1990
Edison, NJ	0.1	4.1	6.5	6.2	7.8	9.7	13.5	15.6	8.5	28.1	1959
El Paso, TX	0.2	14.0	15.8	14.1	14.5	15.2	9.2	9.4	3.3	4.3	1986
Fargo, ND	0.4	17.5	17.3	13.6	10.2	15.0	6.8	7.8	2.5	8.9	1989
Fort Collins, CO	0.4	14.9	18.1	19.1	12.4	17.9	6.6	3.3	1.8	5.6	1991
Fort Wayne, IN	0.2	5.9	11.5	14.3	10.4	15.3	12.4	11.0	5.4	13.7	1975
Fort Worth, TX	0.4	14.0	19.1	15.6	17.3	13.3	8.3	7.1	2.4	2.6	1989
Grand Rapids, MI	0.2	6.9	12.6	15.8	11.3	13.6	9.3	10.0	5.1	15.2	1978
Greeley, CO	0.7	16.2	26.7	15.4	7.2	14.6	5.6	3.9	1.9	7.7	1996
Green Bay, WI	<0.1	7.5	13.4	16.3	11.6	15.4	9.8	9.5	4.3	12.3	1979
Greensboro, NC	0.1	7.3	15.8	17.9	14.5	14.4	10.4	9.5	4.1	6.0	1984
Honolulu, HI	0.1	6.7	9.7	11.8	12.4	24.3	17.9	10.1	3.8	3.1	1976
Houston, TX	0.4	15.6	20.3	13.9	15.3	15.8	8.1	5.9	2.4	2.4	1990
Huntsville, AL	0.2	14.6	18.9	16.7	16.1	10.6	13.0	5.9	1.9	2.1	1990
Indianapolis, IN	0.2	8.8	14.9	16.3	10.3	12.1	10.6	10.1	4.5	12.3	1980
Jacksonville, FL	0.7	11.2	21.2	15.9	16.4	12.0	7.7	7.7	3.2	4.0	1989
Kansas City, MO	0.2	7.1	13.3	14.1	12.0	14.7	11.7	11.0	4.3	11.7	1978
Lafayette, LA	0.2	12.8	14.8	12.9	15.8	15.9	10.3	9.0	3.7	4.5	1984
Las Cruces, NM	0.2	11.0	17.9	19.3	18.3	15.3	7.0	6.3	1.9	2.7	1989
Las Vegas, NV	0.3	10.0	29.1	27.6	14.2	10.6	4.9	2.1	0.7	0.4	1996
Lexington, KY	0.2	8.7	16.1	17.4	13.4	14.8	11.1	7.7	3.0	7.6	1984
Lincoln, NE	0.1	10.1	13.5	14.2	10.1	15.6	9.6	9.8	3.3	13.7	1979
Little Rock, AR	0.3	12.0	17.4	16.6	14.0	15.9	10.0	6.8	3.2	3.8	1987
Los Angeles, CA	0.1	4.2	6.1	7.7	12.4	16.1	15.5	18.2	8.0	11.7	1968
Louisville, KY	0.2	6.7	12.8	13.8	9.2	14.8	12.1	12.2	5.9	12.3	1975
Madison, WI	0.2	9.4	15.4	15.5	10.7	14.3	9.5	7.6	3.5	13.9	1981

Table continued on following page.

Metro Area	2020 or Later	2010 -2019	2000 -2009	1990 -1999	1980 -1989	1970 -1979	1960 -1969	1950 -1959	1940 -1949	Before 1940	Median Year
Manchester, NH	0.1	4.2	9.7	10.9	20.4	15.6	9.5	7.0	3.8	18.8	1977
Miami, FL	0.2	6.0	12.7	14.6	19.2	21.0	11.9	9.8	2.7	2.1	1981
Midland, TX	0.2	19.5	11.0	14.2	17.8	10.9	7.8	14.6	2.6	1.4	1987
Milwaukee, WI	0.1	4.2	8.2	10.9	7.8	12.9	11.5	15.7	6.9	21.8	1965
Minneapolis, MN	0.2	7.0	13.5	13.9	14.2	14.3	9.8	9.5	3.7	13.8	1979
Nashville, TN	0.6	15.4	18.5	16.8	13.5	12.5	8.8	6.4	2.8	4.5	1991
New Haven, CT	<0.1	2.5	5.8	7.4	12.6	13.6	12.2	14.8	7.1	23.9	1963
New Orleans, LA	0.2	5.1	12.1	10.0	13.3	19.0	12.9	9.7	4.6	13.0	1975
New York, NY	0.1	4.1	6.5	6.2	7.8	9.7	13.5	15.6	8.5	28.1	1959
Oklahoma City, OK	0.3	11.8	14.7	11.0	14.3	16.8	11.4	9.2	4.6	5.9	1981
Omaha, NE	0.3	9.0	14.4	12.5	9.8	14.1	11.7	8.4	3.5	16.3	1977
Orlando, FL	0.3	12.7	22.2	19.4	19.4	12.6	5.8	5.1	1.2	1.5	1992
Philadelphia, PA	0.1	4.3	7.9	9.4	9.8	12.0	12.0	15.3	7.2	22.0	1965
Phoenix, AZ	0.3	9.8	24.5	19.4	16.8	15.4	6.9	4.8	1.2	0.9	1992
Pittsburgh, PA	0.1	4.0	6.2	7.6	7.7	12.0	11.4	16.5	8.6	25.9	1959
Portland, OR	0.3	9.2	14.0	17.3	11.3	16.7	8.2	6.9	4.5	11.7	1982
Providence, RI	0.1	2.7	6.1	8.1	11.2	12.1	10.7	11.5	6.0	31.4	1961
Provo, UT	0.4	19.6	24.2	17.6	8.9	12.7	4.7	5.0	2.7	4.2	1997
Raleigh, NC	0.5	17.9	23.9	21.6	14.6	8.6	5.4	3.4	1.4	2.7	1996
Reno, NV	0.7	8.8	20.1	18.8	14.8	18.9	8.6	4.7	2.3	2.3	1989
Richmond, VA	0.2	8.7	14.2	15.0	15.6	14.5	9.6	8.8	4.3	9.0	1982
Rochester, MN	0.3	9.6	17.9	14.4	10.8	13.2	9.0	7.6	3.4	13.8	1983
Sacramento, CA	0.2	5.3	16.9	14.9	16.7	18.0	10.6	9.7	3.4	4.2	1982
St. Louis, MO	0.2	5.3	11.4	12.1	11.1	13.0	12.6	12.6	5.5	16.2	1972
Salem, OR	0.2	6.5	13.4	17.3	9.7	22.3	10.3	8.0	4.0	8.4	1979
Salt Lake City, UT	0.2	12.6	14.8	15.1	11.9	17.4	8.6	8.3	3.5	7.5	1984
San Antonio, TX	0.5	16.2	19.2	13.9	14.5	12.4	8.0	7.2	3.8	4.3	1990
San Diego, CA	0.2	5.1	11.8	12.2	18.6	22.2	11.9	10.5	3.4	4.2	1979
San Francisco, CA	0.1	4.6	7.6	8.1	10.9	14.7	13.1	13.6	7.7	19.7	1967
San Jose, CA	0.2	7.5	8.9	10.0	12.1	21.3	17.6	13.9	3.5	5.0	1975
Santa Rosa, CA	0.3	4.0	10.3	13.7	18.2	20.6	11.6	8.9	4.4	8.0	1978
Savannah, GA	0.3	13.3	19.8	14.7	13.2	11.2	7.6	7.8	4.2	8.0	1989
Seattle, WA	0.2	10.6	14.7	15.2	14.1	13.4	10.8	7.1	4.2	9.7	1983
Sioux Falls, SD	0.2	16.0	18.0	14.9	8.7	12.7	6.7	7.4	3.2	12.2	1989
Springfield, IL	<0.1	4.3	10.0	13.2	8.7	17.3	11.7	11.0	6.0	17.8	1972
Tampa, FL	0.3	8.2	15.8	14.0	19.9	19.9	9.1	8.3	2.0	2.6	1984
Tucson, AZ	0.2	6.2	18.1	17.3	17.7	19.1	8.4	8.2	2.8	2.0	1985
Tulsa, OK	0.3	9.1	13.7	12.1	14.1	18.8	10.5	10.5	4.3	6.7	1980
Tuscaloosa, AL	0.1	12.4	18.5	18.3	13.5	14.7	9.0	6.6	3.2	3.6	1989
Virginia Beach, VA	0.2	8.0	12.6	14.8	18.4	15.2	11.6	9.3	4.2	5.7	1982
Washington, DC	0.2	9.0	14.0	14.0	15.4	13.5	11.8	8.9	4.9	8.3	1982
Wichita, KS	0.1	6.7	11.8	13.5	12.4	13.1	8.8	16.4	6.5	10.7	1976
Wilmington, NC	0.3	12.4	20.4	20.9	15.1	12.0	5.6	4.6	3.4	5.3	1992
Winston-Salem, NC	0.1	6.8	15.2	16.6	14.8	16.6	10.2	9.2	4.1	6.2	1982
Worcester, MA	0.1	3.8	8.7	9.5	12.4	11.3	8.9	11.0	5.6	28.9	1965
U.S.	0.2	7.3	13.6	13.6	13.2	14.8	10.3	10.0	4.7	12.2	1979

Note: Figures are percentages except for median year; Figures cover the Metropolitan Statistical Area
Source: U.S. Census Bureau, 2017-2021 American Community Survey 5-Year Estimates

Gross Monthly Rent: City

City	Under $500	$500 -$999	$1,000 -$1,499	$1,500 -$1,999	$2,000 -$2,499	$2,500 -$2,999	$3,000 and up	Median ($)
Albuquerque, NM	7.3	49.4	31.5	9.8	1.1	0.5	0.5	932
Allentown, PA	7.6	31.1	44.6	14.9	1.3	0.3	0.3	1,100
Anchorage, AK	4.8	20.1	34.7	23.1	11.6	4.0	1.8	1,350
Ann Arbor, MI	3.9	17.0	37.0	24.4	9.7	3.5	4.4	1,382
Athens, GA	5.4	52.2	29.1	9.4	2.2	0.8	0.8	939
Atlanta, GA	11.0	18.0	31.3	25.2	9.2	2.9	2.4	1,342
Austin, TX	2.8	10.6	43.9	26.9	10.3	3.0	2.6	1,415
Baltimore, MD	14.9	22.2	37.2	17.6	5.5	1.5	1.1	1,146
Boise City, ID	4.2	34.8	42.3	15.3	1.9	0.7	0.8	1,103
Boston, MA	14.1	10.7	13.3	20.9	17.7	9.6	13.6	1,783
Boulder, CO	3.1	6.2	29.1	27.4	16.5	6.4	11.3	1,711
Brownsville, TX	20.5	54.9	19.9	3.9	0.7	0.2	0.0	794
Cape Coral, FL	1.2	11.9	40.8	37.8	5.8	0.9	1.5	1,456
Cedar Rapids, IA	12.8	56.9	24.8	3.1	0.6	0.2	1.7	836
Charleston, SC	5.1	13.9	39.7	27.1	8.4	2.8	3.0	1,400
Charlotte, NC	3.4	19.6	48.2	21.7	4.5	1.5	1.2	1,260
Chicago, IL	8.6	25.4	32.7	17.7	8.6	3.9	3.2	1,209
Cincinnati, OH	15.9	52.7	21.5	6.4	2.1	0.7	0.7	814
Clarksville, TN	4.2	44.4	38.0	10.4	2.6	0.3	0.1	1,016
Cleveland, OH	20.3	53.7	19.1	4.7	1.3	0.6	0.4	774
College Station, TX	2.2	44.2	33.0	14.9	3.9	1.4	0.5	1,042
Colorado Springs, CO	3.3	21.7	39.4	25.1	6.5	2.8	1.2	1,300
Columbia, MO	5.7	52.3	30.3	6.6	4.2	0.8	0.1	935
Columbia, SC	10.3	38.9	37.0	11.2	2.0	0.3	0.3	1,007
Columbus, OH	5.2	37.8	43.6	10.1	2.3	0.4	0.6	1,061
Dallas, TX	3.5	28.7	42.6	16.5	5.2	1.7	1.8	1,178
Davenport, IA	9.4	61.7	21.9	4.3	0.7	0.5	1.5	815
Denver, CO	7.1	10.5	32.7	27.6	14.0	5.1	3.0	1,495
Des Moines, IA	7.8	52.1	31.7	6.4	1.7	0.2	0.2	916
Durham, NC	6.7	26.5	44.8	17.4	3.1	0.4	1.1	1,157
Edison, NJ	3.2	3.3	26.6	39.0	22.8	4.0	1.1	1,716
El Paso, TX	12.3	48.4	31.0	6.7	1.2	0.3	0.2	910
Fargo, ND	5.7	65.4	21.2	5.3	1.9	0.3	0.2	841
Fort Collins, CO	2.0	17.4	34.7	28.6	13.4	2.2	1.7	1,443
Fort Wayne, IN	9.5	63.9	22.8	3.0	0.4	0.2	0.2	823
Fort Worth, TX	3.7	28.4	40.5	19.2	5.9	1.4	0.9	1,187
Grand Rapids, MI	10.7	38.1	37.4	9.2	3.4	0.8	0.4	1,013
Greeley, CO	9.1	29.7	37.4	16.2	6.0	1.1	0.5	1,134
Green Bay, WI	9.1	66.5	22.1	1.8	0.2	0.0	0.2	805
Greensboro, NC	5.7	53.2	33.2	5.9	1.2	0.3	0.6	944
Honolulu, HI	6.7	10.1	27.5	24.0	13.2	7.9	10.7	1,620
Houston, TX	3.4	34.1	38.9	15.8	4.4	1.5	1.8	1,136
Huntsville, AL	7.5	52.1	31.9	6.8	0.7	0.5	0.5	912
Indianapolis, IN	6.0	49.3	34.3	7.9	1.7	0.4	0.4	962
Jacksonville, FL	5.4	29.0	43.7	17.5	3.6	0.5	0.4	1,146
Kansas City, MO	7.2	39.0	38.6	11.6	2.4	0.7	0.5	1,040
Lafayette, LA	6.9	50.5	32.1	8.7	1.0	0.2	0.6	948
Las Cruces, NM	13.0	56.6	25.0	4.0	1.0	0.1	0.4	824
Las Vegas, NV	4.0	25.7	42.9	20.6	4.9	1.0	0.9	1,219
Lexington, KY	6.4	47.7	34.5	8.1	2.3	0.5	0.4	967
Lincoln, NE	6.2	53.4	30.1	7.6	1.4	0.3	1.1	920
Little Rock, AR	7.8	49.3	33.3	6.7	1.4	0.7	0.8	940
Los Angeles, CA	4.9	11.1	27.1	24.6	15.1	8.1	9.2	1,641
Louisville, KY	11.4	47.2	32.6	6.8	1.2	0.2	0.6	931
Madison, WI	4.2	25.0	44.1	17.9	5.5	1.6	1.7	1,212

Table continued on following page.

City	Under $500	$500 -$999	$1,000 -$1,499	$1,500 -$1,999	$2,000 -$2,499	$2,500 -$2,999	$3,000 and up	Median ($)
Manchester, NH	7.0	21.3	43.4	20.8	5.4	1.4	0.8	1,220
Miami, FL	9.1	17.6	31.5	20.1	11.7	5.0	4.9	1,361
Midland, TX	2.8	19.5	44.3	19.5	9.2	3.6	1.1	1,273
Milwaukee, WI	7.7	55.0	28.4	6.3	1.6	0.6	0.4	910
Minneapolis, MN	10.9	27.0	33.1	17.8	7.4	2.0	1.9	1,159
Nashville, TN	7.4	20.6	41.1	20.6	6.9	1.9	1.5	1,250
New Haven, CT	13.5	14.2	40.8	20.6	7.4	2.4	1.1	1,267
New Orleans, LA	10.9	31.7	36.8	13.8	4.6	1.2	0.8	1,079
New York, NY	9.5	12.4	24.4	23.3	13.3	6.6	10.5	1,579
Oklahoma City, OK	6.5	51.2	32.1	7.8	1.6	0.4	0.4	933
Omaha, NE	5.4	44.7	36.8	10.2	1.6	0.4	0.9	999
Orlando, FL	3.4	15.1	45.7	26.9	6.3	1.6	1.1	1,346
Philadelphia, PA	9.3	27.7	38.4	15.3	5.5	2.0	1.8	1,149
Phoenix, AZ	3.8	28.5	43.3	18.5	4.2	0.9	0.8	1,175
Pittsburgh, PA	13.0	33.7	31.0	13.9	5.5	2.0	0.9	1,043
Portland, OR	5.6	14.2	37.6	25.6	10.8	3.9	2.3	1,406
Providence, RI	19.3	21.5	38.2	14.8	3.7	1.3	1.2	1,098
Provo, UT	9.1	44.7	29.6	11.4	4.1	0.5	0.6	973
Raleigh, NC	3.2	19.5	52.4	19.0	4.3	0.9	0.9	1,237
Reno, NV	5.7	27.4	37.5	21.1	6.4	1.0	1.0	1,213
Richmond, VA	11.2	26.1	41.7	16.2	3.6	0.6	0.7	1,132
Rochester, MN	7.8	34.8	32.6	17.7	3.4	1.3	2.4	1,120
Sacramento, CA	5.5	16.1	33.0	30.1	11.3	2.5	1.6	1,434
St. Louis, MO	10.6	54.3	26.8	6.1	1.7	0.3	0.2	873
Salem, OR	6.3	30.7	43.7	15.2	2.8	0.6	0.7	1,125
Salt Lake City, UT	8.0	30.3	36.6	17.7	5.4	1.2	0.8	1,141
San Antonio, TX	6.2	34.8	41.6	13.5	2.6	0.7	0.6	1,090
San Diego, CA	2.7	6.1	19.8	27.8	21.3	11.6	10.7	1,885
San Francisco, CA	8.6	10.0	13.7	14.1	13.3	11.6	28.5	2,130
San Jose, CA	3.7	5.6	9.3	17.0	19.6	18.0	26.7	2,366
Santa Rosa, CA	4.9	5.3	21.2	27.5	21.2	11.7	8.1	1,837
Savannah, GA	8.6	29.0	45.1	13.3	2.8	0.5	0.7	1,116
Seattle, WA	5.4	6.3	21.6	27.9	19.6	9.7	9.6	1,801
Sioux Falls, SD	6.2	58.7	27.7	5.7	0.6	0.4	0.8	892
Springfield, IL	10.6	58.7	23.8	4.8	0.9	0.8	0.4	852
Tampa, FL	7.4	21.2	39.2	19.4	8.2	2.4	2.1	1,249
Tucson, AZ	6.0	53.6	30.2	8.0	1.2	0.5	0.6	907
Tulsa, OK	8.9	54.8	28.8	4.8	1.3	0.5	0.9	882
Tuscaloosa, AL	11.0	51.3	28.3	5.9	2.0	0.6	0.9	907
Virginia Beach, VA	2.3	9.1	45.2	30.5	8.6	2.5	1.8	1,433
Washington, DC	9.2	10.4	22.3	22.4	15.2	9.2	11.3	1,681
Wichita, KS	8.1	60.2	26.3	3.9	0.8	0.2	0.5	856
Wilmington, NC	10.1	31.3	40.1	15.0	2.5	0.5	0.6	1,093
Winston-Salem, NC	8.8	57.2	26.5	5.3	1.3	0.3	0.6	871
Worcester, MA	13.8	21.1	41.4	18.7	3.6	0.7	0.7	1,179
U.S.	8.1	30.5	30.8	16.8	7.3	3.1	3.5	1,163

Note: Figures are percentages except for Median; Gross rent is the contract rent plus the estimated average monthly cost of utilities (electricity, gas, and water and sewer) and fuels (oil, coal, kerosene, wood, etc.) if these are paid by the renter (or paid for the renter by someone else).

Source: U.S. Census Bureau, 2017-2021 American Community Survey 5-Year Estimates

Gross Monthly Rent: Metro Area

MSA[1]	Under $500	$500 -$999	$1,000 -$1,499	$1,500 -$1,999	$2,000 -$2,499	$2,500 -2,999	$3,000 and up	Median ($)
Albuquerque, NM	7.2	47.4	32.9	10.2	1.3	0.4	0.5	952
Allentown, PA	8.9	28.4	39.4	17.7	3.9	0.9	0.9	1,141
Anchorage, AK	5.1	21.7	34.9	22.4	10.8	3.5	1.5	1,314
Ann Arbor, MI	5.1	24.0	40.6	18.9	6.1	2.2	3.1	1,218
Athens, GA	5.6	51.9	28.9	9.1	2.7	0.9	0.8	939
Atlanta, GA	4.3	19.1	43.9	23.8	6.2	1.5	1.2	1,294
Austin, TX	2.6	12.4	43.5	26.5	9.9	2.7	2.4	1,398
Baltimore, MD	8.2	14.4	35.1	26.4	11.0	3.0	2.0	1,387
Boise City, ID	6.5	32.7	40.5	16.2	2.6	0.8	0.7	1,107
Boston, MA	10.9	10.8	20.5	24.5	16.4	8.4	8.6	1,659
Boulder, CO	3.5	7.0	27.3	31.3	15.9	6.9	8.0	1,694
Brownsville, TX	18.4	59.0	18.3	3.2	0.7	0.2	0.2	785
Cape Coral, FL	3.6	19.1	45.6	21.7	5.9	1.8	2.4	1,307
Cedar Rapids, IA	13.4	57.1	23.0	4.2	0.8	0.1	1.4	806
Charleston, SC	4.6	20.9	43.3	20.1	6.9	2.0	2.1	1,274
Charlotte, NC	4.8	31.3	41.3	16.7	3.6	1.2	1.0	1,147
Chicago, IL	6.9	25.3	36.0	18.6	7.6	2.9	2.5	1,209
Cincinnati, OH	10.6	49.6	28.4	7.8	2.1	0.7	0.8	906
Clarksville, TN	7.7	45.9	35.8	8.3	1.9	0.2	0.1	967
Cleveland, OH	11.5	52.2	27.1	6.5	1.4	0.5	0.8	880
College Station, TX	5.0	44.7	32.9	12.3	3.1	1.2	0.7	1,003
Colorado Springs, CO	3.3	20.8	36.2	28.6	7.6	2.6	1.1	1,349
Columbia, MO	7.4	52.9	29.9	5.6	3.5	0.6	0.2	917
Columbia, SC	7.1	43.7	35.6	9.8	2.7	0.5	0.5	993
Columbus, OH	6.0	38.6	41.3	10.3	2.4	0.7	0.6	1,049
Dallas, TX	2.6	22.1	43.0	21.2	7.7	1.9	1.5	1,264
Davenport, IA	12.9	58.7	21.1	4.7	1.2	0.4	1.1	808
Denver, CO	4.5	9.6	32.5	31.5	14.2	5.0	2.7	1,554
Des Moines, IA	6.8	46.8	34.7	8.9	2.0	0.3	0.6	972
Durham, NC	6.6	30.7	41.7	15.5	3.6	0.7	1.3	1,127
Edison, NJ	8.4	11.4	26.5	24.9	13.4	6.3	9.1	1,573
El Paso, TX	12.0	48.6	30.8	7.0	1.2	0.2	0.2	908
Fargo, ND	6.6	60.9	22.5	7.6	1.6	0.4	0.3	855
Fort Collins, CO	2.8	17.7	34.1	28.7	12.2	2.9	1.7	1,433
Fort Wayne, IN	8.9	62.4	23.7	4.1	0.6	0.2	0.2	839
Fort Worth, TX	2.6	22.1	43.0	21.2	7.7	1.9	1.5	1,264
Grand Rapids, MI	8.4	45.1	34.9	7.7	2.5	0.9	0.6	973
Greeley, CO	7.1	26.4	33.6	21.2	7.5	2.6	1.6	1,234
Green Bay, WI	6.8	64.8	24.4	2.9	0.3	0.3	0.4	851
Greensboro, NC	9.0	55.6	28.9	4.6	1.1	0.3	0.6	900
Honolulu, HI	5.4	8.4	20.9	20.8	15.0	12.0	17.6	1,870
Houston, TX	3.3	29.1	39.7	19.2	5.7	1.5	1.6	1,189
Huntsville, AL	8.0	51.8	30.9	7.1	1.1	0.6	0.5	912
Indianapolis, IN	5.7	46.0	35.5	9.7	2.0	0.5	0.6	987
Jacksonville, FL	4.9	27.9	41.7	18.9	4.6	1.0	1.0	1,175
Kansas City, MO	6.5	38.5	38.5	11.8	3.0	0.8	0.9	1,052
Lafayette, LA	13.8	54.5	25.3	4.8	1.1	0.1	0.4	853
Las Cruces, NM	16.4	55.8	22.5	3.8	1.2	0.1	0.3	785
Las Vegas, NV	2.3	24.0	42.7	23.4	5.6	1.2	0.8	1,257
Lexington, KY	7.5	50.4	32.5	7.0	1.8	0.4	0.3	934
Lincoln, NE	6.5	53.2	30.0	7.4	1.5	0.3	1.1	918
Little Rock, AR	8.1	55.9	29.1	5.3	0.9	0.4	0.4	893
Los Angeles, CA	3.8	8.7	24.8	26.8	17.5	8.9	9.5	1,737
Louisville, KY	11.0	47.2	33.5	6.2	1.3	0.2	0.6	934
Madison, WI	4.5	31.5	41.8	15.7	4.3	1.1	1.2	1,143

Table continued on following page.

MSA[1]	Under $500	$500 -$999	$1,000 -$1,499	$1,500 -$1,999	$2,000 -$2,499	$2,500 -2,999	$3,000 and up	Median ($)
Manchester, NH	6.7	18.6	40.2	24.7	6.8	1.9	1.1	1,305
Miami, FL	4.5	11.5	34.6	28.5	12.9	4.5	3.6	1,492
Midland, TX	4.2	19.9	43.6	19.0	9.0	3.3	1.0	1,271
Milwaukee, WI	6.9	48.0	32.3	9.1	2.4	0.7	0.5	963
Minneapolis, MN	8.1	24.0	37.9	20.4	6.3	1.7	1.6	1,207
Nashville, TN	6.7	25.1	39.7	20.0	5.7	1.6	1.2	1,211
New Haven, CT	10.6	19.5	41.4	19.9	5.6	1.6	1.4	1,223
New Orleans, LA	8.0	35.7	39.3	12.2	3.5	0.7	0.6	1,064
New York, NY	8.4	11.4	26.5	24.9	13.4	6.3	9.1	1,573
Oklahoma City, OK	6.8	50.2	32.3	8.0	1.6	0.5	0.6	937
Omaha, NE	6.4	43.7	36.5	10.2	1.7	0.5	1.2	1,000
Orlando, FL	2.7	16.2	43.2	27.2	7.5	1.9	1.2	1,363
Philadelphia, PA	7.2	22.3	40.2	19.2	6.7	2.3	2.0	1,230
Phoenix, AZ	3.0	23.1	41.3	22.9	6.3	1.7	1.7	1,268
Pittsburgh, PA	14.0	47.0	26.4	7.9	2.9	0.9	0.9	892
Portland, OR	4.1	12.6	38.8	28.4	10.8	3.2	2.0	1,434
Providence, RI	14.9	29.3	35.5	14.2	4.1	1.0	0.9	1,066
Provo, UT	4.6	31.0	36.2	20.0	6.2	1.0	1.1	1,193
Raleigh, NC	4.4	22.5	46.4	19.1	5.2	1.2	1.2	1,230
Reno, NV	4.8	26.6	36.7	22.2	6.7	1.5	1.5	1,250
Richmond, VA	6.6	23.4	45.3	18.7	3.9	0.9	1.2	1,202
Rochester, MN	10.2	39.0	30.7	14.7	2.8	1.0	1.8	1,013
Sacramento, CA	4.3	14.1	34.2	27.8	13.3	3.9	2.5	1,465
St. Louis, MO	7.9	47.8	33.0	7.6	2.1	0.6	1.1	952
Salem, OR	5.9	30.4	45.3	14.0	2.9	1.0	0.5	1,128
Salt Lake City, UT	4.6	21.7	43.4	22.2	6.0	1.1	0.9	1,253
San Antonio, TX	5.6	32.5	41.5	15.3	3.5	0.9	0.7	1,122
San Diego, CA	2.9	5.9	21.1	29.4	19.7	10.6	10.4	1,842
San Francisco, CA	5.6	7.0	13.2	18.3	19.2	14.0	22.8	2,155
San Jose, CA	3.0	4.7	7.8	14.7	19.4	18.5	31.9	2,511
Santa Rosa, CA	4.8	7.8	19.2	25.6	21.0	11.3	10.3	1,856
Savannah, GA	5.5	26.3	47.1	16.1	3.7	0.6	0.6	1,161
Seattle, WA	4.3	8.4	25.0	30.5	17.7	7.5	6.6	1,701
Sioux Falls, SD	7.0	57.8	27.5	5.8	0.8	0.3	0.7	889
Springfield, IL	10.4	57.4	25.5	4.8	0.8	0.6	0.5	857
Tampa, FL	4.1	24.2	42.4	19.8	6.2	1.8	1.5	1,230
Tucson, AZ	5.5	46.8	33.6	10.3	1.9	0.8	1.1	976
Tulsa, OK	8.7	51.9	30.3	6.3	1.6	0.4	0.8	909
Tuscaloosa, AL	14.9	50.5	27.1	4.8	1.5	0.6	0.5	879
Virginia Beach, VA	6.1	22.2	42.3	21.1	5.5	1.5	1.3	1,227
Washington, DC	4.3	6.4	20.9	32.5	19.2	8.6	8.1	1,783
Wichita, KS	8.8	57.8	26.3	5.4	0.9	0.4	0.5	868
Wilmington, NC	8.0	29.7	41.7	15.1	3.2	1.5	0.8	1,118
Winston-Salem, NC	11.0	59.4	23.7	4.3	1.0	0.2	0.4	834
Worcester, MA	13.2	26.4	37.7	15.9	4.7	1.2	1.0	1,126
U.S.	8.1	30.5	30.8	16.8	7.3	3.1	3.5	1,163

Note: (1) Figures cover the Metropolitan Statistical Area (MSA); Figures are percentages except for Median; Gross rent is the contract rent plus the estimated average monthly cost of utilities (electricity, gas, and water and sewer) and fuels (oil, coal, kerosene, wood, etc.) if these are paid by the renter (or paid for the renter by someone else).
Source: U.S. Census Bureau, 2017-2021 American Community Survey 5-Year Estimates

Highest Level of Education: City

City	Less than H.S.	H.S. Diploma	Some College, No Deg.	Associate Degree	Bachelors Degree	Masters Degree	Profess. School Degree	Doctorate Degree
Albuquerque, NM	9.1	21.8	22.7	9.1	20.4	11.5	2.9	2.6
Allentown, PA	19.4	36.5	19.3	7.5	11.5	3.8	1.1	0.8
Anchorage, AK	5.8	23.7	25.0	8.6	22.8	9.8	2.8	1.3
Ann Arbor, MI	2.2	7.6	8.9	4.0	30.5	26.8	8.3	11.6
Athens, GA	10.3	19.2	17.0	6.4	23.4	14.8	2.7	6.1
Atlanta, GA	7.9	17.5	13.6	5.4	31.6	15.8	5.6	2.7
Austin, TX	9.4	14.4	15.7	5.4	34.2	14.9	3.5	2.6
Baltimore, MD	13.7	28.1	18.8	5.2	17.2	11.3	3.2	2.5
Boise City, ID	4.8	20.4	22.8	8.3	28.0	10.8	2.8	2.0
Boston, MA	11.8	18.5	12.9	4.7	27.8	15.7	5.1	3.6
Boulder, CO	3.1	5.9	10.6	3.6	37.1	25.0	5.7	9.0
Brownsville, TX	32.0	24.2	16.0	7.3	14.6	4.7	0.9	0.3
Cape Coral, FL	7.1	37.1	23.0	9.2	15.6	5.3	1.5	1.3
Cedar Rapids, IA	6.2	25.7	22.8	12.5	22.7	7.2	2.0	0.8
Charleston, SC	4.2	16.8	16.1	7.3	34.5	13.6	4.8	2.9
Charlotte, NC	10.3	16.9	19.2	7.9	29.5	12.2	2.9	1.2
Chicago, IL	13.7	21.9	17.0	5.7	24.1	12.2	3.6	1.8
Cincinnati, OH	11.4	24.0	17.6	7.4	23.0	11.0	3.4	2.2
Clarksville, TN	6.4	26.9	26.3	11.6	18.7	8.2	0.8	1.1
Cleveland, OH	17.4	33.3	22.8	7.4	11.4	5.2	1.7	0.8
College Station, TX	5.2	13.1	17.0	6.7	30.3	15.4	2.1	10.3
Colorado Springs, CO	6.1	19.1	24.0	10.7	24.3	12.0	2.3	1.7
Columbia, MO	4.5	17.5	17.6	6.6	28.4	15.5	4.6	5.3
Columbia, SC	9.5	19.3	18.8	7.7	25.1	11.7	4.5	3.3
Columbus, OH	9.7	24.8	20.3	7.4	24.3	10.0	2.1	1.6
Dallas, TX	20.4	21.8	17.4	4.8	22.1	9.0	3.2	1.3
Davenport, IA	7.9	31.4	22.0	11.7	17.9	6.6	1.6	0.9
Denver, CO	10.0	16.0	16.0	5.6	32.0	13.9	4.5	2.1
Des Moines, IA	12.9	29.6	20.2	9.2	19.3	6.2	1.8	0.8
Durham, NC	9.4	16.2	14.7	6.9	27.7	15.8	4.3	5.0
Edison, NJ	7.9	18.1	11.9	5.8	30.1	21.4	2.6	2.3
El Paso, TX	18.6	23.1	22.7	8.8	17.7	6.6	1.4	1.0
Fargo, ND	5.2	19.3	20.3	13.6	28.1	9.9	1.8	2.0
Fort Collins, CO	3.0	14.4	17.3	8.6	32.8	17.5	2.5	3.8
Fort Wayne, IN	11.1	28.9	21.9	10.1	19.0	7.1	1.1	0.8
Fort Worth, TX	16.5	24.5	20.8	7.2	20.6	7.8	1.6	1.1
Grand Rapids, MI	11.3	22.2	20.1	7.6	25.6	9.7	2.2	1.4
Greeley, CO	16.4	26.0	22.8	8.8	15.9	7.7	1.4	1.2
Green Bay, WI	12.2	31.3	19.7	11.7	18.3	5.0	0.9	0.8
Greensboro, NC	9.8	21.3	20.4	9.0	24.5	10.7	2.4	1.9
Honolulu, HI	9.6	23.1	18.1	10.8	24.0	9.1	3.1	2.1
Houston, TX	20.5	21.6	17.2	6.0	20.9	9.1	3.0	1.8
Huntsville, AL	8.9	17.6	20.9	7.9	26.7	13.7	1.9	2.5
Indianapolis, IN	13.3	27.3	18.8	7.6	21.1	8.2	2.3	1.2
Jacksonville, FL	9.7	28.7	21.5	9.9	20.3	7.2	1.6	1.0
Kansas City, MO	9.0	24.9	22.2	7.4	23.0	9.8	2.6	1.2
Lafayette, LA	9.7	26.2	19.5	5.2	24.9	8.7	3.9	1.9
Las Cruces, NM	12.5	19.8	22.0	9.3	20.5	11.7	2.2	2.0
Las Vegas, NV	14.6	27.4	24.0	8.0	16.7	6.4	1.9	0.9
Lexington, KY	7.6	18.9	20.0	7.9	25.9	12.2	4.2	3.4
Lincoln, NE	7.1	20.7	20.9	11.2	25.3	9.8	2.2	2.8
Little Rock, AR	8.1	21.7	19.8	6.4	25.3	11.8	4.3	2.8
Los Angeles, CA	21.6	18.8	17.2	6.3	23.7	8.1	3.0	1.5
Louisville, KY	9.8	28.2	22.1	8.3	18.9	9.0	2.1	1.5
Madison, WI	4.4	14.2	15.4	7.5	32.5	15.9	4.2	5.9

Table continued on following page.

City	Less than H.S.	H.S. Diploma	Some College, No Deg.	Associate Degree	Bachelors Degree	Masters Degree	Profess. School Degree	Doctorate Degree
Manchester, NH	11.4	28.8	18.8	9.1	21.5	8.0	1.5	1.0
Miami, FL	20.8	25.8	12.6	7.8	19.8	8.2	3.9	1.1
Midland, TX	15.5	23.4	22.1	8.1	22.5	6.4	1.4	0.6
Milwaukee, WI	15.1	30.9	21.1	7.4	16.3	6.7	1.4	1.0
Minneapolis, MN	9.3	14.2	16.4	7.4	31.7	14.5	3.9	2.5
Nashville, TN	10.0	21.5	18.4	6.2	27.5	10.7	3.2	2.6
New Haven, CT	14.6	30.2	14.2	4.6	16.3	11.9	4.0	4.3
New Orleans, LA	11.8	22.4	21.6	5.0	21.9	10.4	4.5	2.2
New York, NY	16.8	23.6	13.5	6.5	22.9	11.8	3.3	1.6
Oklahoma City, OK	12.5	24.6	22.5	8.1	20.5	8.0	2.6	1.2
Omaha, NE	9.7	21.7	22.0	7.8	24.9	9.1	3.1	1.6
Orlando, FL	8.4	23.2	16.8	11.5	25.0	10.3	3.1	1.7
Philadelphia, PA	13.4	31.4	16.7	6.0	18.4	9.3	3.0	1.8
Phoenix, AZ	16.5	22.9	22.1	8.0	19.1	8.2	2.1	1.2
Pittsburgh, PA	6.5	24.7	14.9	8.2	23.5	13.7	4.6	3.9
Portland, OR	6.7	15.1	19.4	6.9	31.2	13.9	4.3	2.4
Providence, RI	16.5	30.6	14.6	5.1	17.4	9.5	3.5	2.9
Provo, UT	7.3	14.4	25.3	8.6	31.6	8.7	1.6	2.4
Raleigh, NC	7.7	15.7	16.9	7.3	32.7	13.7	3.5	2.5
Reno, NV	10.2	22.7	23.3	8.3	21.6	9.2	2.5	2.3
Richmond, VA	12.3	20.4	19.2	5.0	25.1	12.1	3.7	2.2
Rochester, MN	5.6	18.6	15.8	11.3	26.6	13.1	5.2	3.6
Sacramento, CA	13.6	20.3	22.6	8.4	22.2	8.4	3.2	1.4
St. Louis, MO	10.8	24.4	20.3	6.5	21.3	11.3	3.2	2.2
Salem, OR	11.6	23.2	25.8	9.4	18.4	8.4	1.8	1.4
Salt Lake City, UT	8.9	16.6	17.9	6.7	28.3	13.4	4.6	3.5
San Antonio, TX	16.7	25.5	22.5	8.0	16.9	7.2	2.0	1.2
San Diego, CA	10.7	15.4	18.6	7.7	27.9	12.8	3.6	3.4
San Francisco, CA	11.2	11.4	12.7	5.2	35.4	16.0	5.1	3.0
San Jose, CA	14.5	16.3	16.2	7.6	26.0	14.5	2.2	2.8
Santa Rosa, CA	14.5	18.0	23.2	10.0	21.3	8.7	3.0	1.3
Savannah, GA	11.2	26.9	24.6	6.8	19.3	7.9	2.1	1.2
Seattle, WA	4.5	9.7	13.9	6.0	37.3	19.4	5.3	3.9
Sioux Falls, SD	6.7	24.6	20.5	12.2	24.3	8.3	2.4	1.0
Springfield, IL	8.7	26.6	22.1	8.2	20.2	9.6	3.5	1.2
Tampa, FL	11.6	23.4	15.3	7.9	24.8	10.6	4.4	2.0
Tucson, AZ	13.7	22.8	25.7	8.9	17.5	8.2	1.4	1.8
Tulsa, OK	12.1	25.3	22.1	8.0	20.7	7.7	2.7	1.3
Tuscaloosa, AL	9.9	27.1	18.6	6.8	20.5	11.0	2.1	4.0
Virginia Beach, VA	5.5	20.8	24.1	11.0	24.3	10.7	2.3	1.4
Washington, DC	7.8	15.5	12.4	3.0	25.5	21.9	9.7	4.3
Wichita, KS	11.8	26.2	23.4	8.1	19.3	8.4	1.7	1.1
Wilmington, NC	6.5	19.7	20.0	10.3	28.3	10.2	3.2	1.8
Winston-Salem, NC	12.0	24.9	20.7	7.7	20.3	9.2	2.8	2.2
Worcester, MA	14.2	28.3	17.1	8.2	19.2	8.8	2.0	2.3
U.S.	11.1	26.5	20.0	8.7	20.6	9.3	2.2	1.5

Note: Figures cover persons age 25 and over
Source: U.S. Census Bureau, 2017-2021 American Community Survey 5-Year Estimates

Highest Level of Education: Metro Area

Metro Area	Less than H.S.	H.S. Diploma	Some College, No Deg.	Associate Degree	Bachelors Degree	Masters Degree	Profess. School Degree	Doctorate Degree
Albuquerque, NM	10.0	23.8	23.2	9.2	18.6	10.5	2.4	2.2
Allentown, PA	9.1	33.6	16.6	9.4	19.5	8.7	1.6	1.4
Anchorage, AK	6.0	26.2	25.5	9.1	20.9	8.8	2.4	1.2
Ann Arbor, MI	4.3	14.6	17.0	6.9	26.9	19.0	5.0	6.2
Athens, GA	10.6	22.7	17.6	7.4	20.8	13.0	3.2	4.7
Atlanta, GA	9.5	23.3	18.9	7.8	24.9	11.1	2.6	1.6
Austin, TX	9.0	18.2	18.9	6.5	30.1	12.7	2.6	2.0
Baltimore, MD	8.4	24.1	18.9	6.9	22.7	13.7	3.0	2.3
Boise City, ID	7.9	24.1	24.9	9.2	22.6	8.1	1.9	1.3
Boston, MA	7.9	21.2	14.1	7.1	26.9	15.8	3.6	3.5
Boulder, CO	4.5	11.1	15.0	6.6	34.5	19.1	3.9	5.3
Brownsville, TX	30.5	26.1	17.1	7.4	13.2	4.4	0.9	0.5
Cape Coral, FL	10.2	30.8	20.5	9.4	17.8	7.5	2.3	1.4
Cedar Rapids, IA	5.2	28.0	21.3	13.4	22.1	7.4	1.7	0.9
Charleston, SC	8.5	24.3	19.7	9.5	24.0	10.0	2.6	1.4
Charlotte, NC	10.1	22.9	20.5	9.4	24.5	9.7	2.0	0.9
Chicago, IL	10.5	23.4	19.0	7.3	23.8	11.6	2.8	1.5
Cincinnati, OH	8.2	29.3	18.7	8.4	21.9	9.8	2.1	1.5
Clarksville, TN	8.6	28.9	25.1	11.0	17.0	7.4	1.2	0.9
Cleveland, OH	8.6	28.5	21.3	8.8	19.8	9.2	2.5	1.3
College Station, TX	12.1	23.4	19.3	6.7	21.6	9.8	2.0	5.1
Colorado Springs, CO	5.4	19.8	24.4	10.9	23.9	12.0	1.9	1.6
Columbia, MO	5.9	23.1	18.3	7.5	25.4	12.6	3.3	3.8
Columbia, SC	9.4	26.0	21.5	9.5	20.5	9.2	2.1	1.8
Columbus, OH	7.9	26.7	19.4	7.6	24.0	10.4	2.5	1.5
Dallas, TX	13.4	22.0	20.6	7.3	23.8	9.8	1.9	1.2
Davenport, IA	8.2	29.9	22.9	11.1	17.8	7.7	1.5	0.9
Denver, CO	8.1	19.2	18.9	7.6	29.1	12.5	2.8	1.8
Des Moines, IA	6.6	25.6	19.5	10.7	25.8	8.4	2.1	1.3
Durham, NC	9.9	19.0	15.8	7.9	24.4	14.1	4.1	4.8
Edison, NJ	12.7	24.0	14.4	6.8	24.2	12.7	3.4	1.7
El Paso, TX	20.4	23.8	22.3	9.0	16.5	6.0	1.3	0.8
Fargo, ND	4.8	19.7	21.1	14.1	27.8	8.9	1.8	1.7
Fort Collins, CO	3.7	17.4	20.4	9.1	29.5	14.4	2.4	3.1
Fort Wayne, IN	9.8	29.0	21.0	11.0	19.8	7.1	1.5	1.0
Fort Worth, TX	13.4	22.0	20.6	7.3	23.8	9.8	1.9	1.2
Grand Rapids, MI	7.7	26.7	21.6	9.5	22.5	9.1	1.8	1.2
Greeley, CO	11.9	25.4	23.8	9.5	19.3	7.8	1.3	1.1
Green Bay, WI	7.5	31.5	19.1	12.8	20.5	6.3	1.4	0.8
Greensboro, NC	11.8	26.7	21.4	9.7	19.8	7.9	1.5	1.3
Honolulu, HI	7.3	25.6	19.8	11.1	23.2	8.9	2.5	1.6
Houston, TX	15.6	22.7	20.2	7.4	21.6	8.8	2.2	1.5
Huntsville, AL	9.2	20.9	21.0	8.0	25.2	12.4	1.5	1.8
Indianapolis, IN	9.4	27.3	18.9	8.0	23.2	9.4	2.3	1.3
Jacksonville, FL	8.6	27.5	21.0	9.9	21.6	8.4	2.0	1.1
Kansas City, MO	7.3	25.1	21.6	8.0	23.8	10.6	2.4	1.3
Lafayette, LA	14.0	36.5	18.4	6.5	17.0	5.1	1.7	0.8
Las Cruces, NM	19.3	21.5	20.9	8.3	17.5	9.2	1.7	1.7
Las Vegas, NV	13.6	28.0	24.3	8.3	17.1	6.2	1.7	0.9
Lexington, KY	8.3	23.8	20.5	8.3	22.4	10.8	3.4	2.5
Lincoln, NE	6.6	21.4	20.7	11.7	25.1	9.8	2.1	2.6
Little Rock, AR	8.4	29.1	22.2	8.3	19.9	8.6	2.2	1.4
Los Angeles, CA	18.4	19.6	18.8	7.2	23.2	8.6	2.7	1.5
Louisville, KY	9.1	29.3	21.7	8.7	18.9	8.8	2.1	1.4
Madison, WI	4.3	20.6	17.5	9.8	28.8	12.3	3.1	3.5

Table continued on following page.

Metro Area	Less than H.S.	H.S. Diploma	Some College, No Deg.	Associate Degree	Bachelors Degree	Masters Degree	Profess. School Degree	Doctorate Degree
Manchester, NH	7.1	25.6	17.7	9.9	25.0	11.4	1.7	1.6
Miami, FL	13.5	25.8	16.9	9.6	21.1	8.6	3.2	1.3
Midland, TX	15.6	24.5	23.1	8.2	20.0	6.8	1.2	0.5
Milwaukee, WI	7.9	26.1	19.7	8.9	24.3	9.4	2.3	1.5
Minneapolis, MN	6.0	20.5	19.4	10.6	28.3	10.9	2.6	1.7
Nashville, TN	9.0	25.7	19.6	7.3	24.9	9.4	2.3	1.8
New Haven, CT	9.7	29.6	16.7	7.3	19.4	11.9	3.2	2.2
New Orleans, LA	11.9	26.9	22.4	6.5	20.0	8.0	2.9	1.3
New York, NY	12.7	24.0	14.4	6.8	24.2	12.7	3.4	1.7
Oklahoma City, OK	10.2	26.4	22.9	8.1	20.7	8.1	2.2	1.4
Omaha, NE	7.7	23.1	22.0	9.4	24.3	9.6	2.4	1.4
Orlando, FL	9.9	25.4	19.4	11.6	21.9	8.6	2.0	1.1
Philadelphia, PA	8.4	27.9	16.5	7.3	23.3	11.5	2.9	2.0
Phoenix, AZ	11.3	22.8	23.8	9.0	20.9	9.0	2.0	1.3
Pittsburgh, PA	5.5	31.4	16.0	10.5	22.2	10.3	2.3	1.7
Portland, OR	7.2	20.1	22.9	8.9	25.5	10.8	2.7	2.0
Providence, RI	12.0	28.7	17.5	8.6	20.2	9.4	2.0	1.6
Provo, UT	4.9	17.2	25.6	10.4	29.0	9.4	1.7	1.7
Raleigh, NC	7.4	17.3	17.7	9.0	30.1	13.6	2.6	2.3
Reno, NV	11.4	23.8	23.9	8.6	19.8	8.5	2.2	1.8
Richmond, VA	8.9	24.6	19.9	7.6	23.7	11.0	2.5	1.7
Rochester, MN	5.3	23.2	17.8	12.6	23.9	10.6	4.1	2.4
Sacramento, CA	10.2	20.8	24.1	9.9	22.3	8.3	2.8	1.5
St. Louis, MO	7.2	25.7	21.7	9.2	21.5	10.9	2.2	1.6
Salem, OR	13.2	25.1	26.3	9.7	16.7	6.8	1.3	1.0
Salt Lake City, UT	8.2	22.8	23.5	9.2	23.4	9.3	2.2	1.5
San Antonio, TX	13.6	25.2	22.7	8.2	19.0	8.2	1.9	1.2
San Diego, CA	11.7	18.2	21.5	8.4	24.5	10.5	2.9	2.3
San Francisco, CA	10.3	15.1	16.5	6.7	29.9	14.5	3.9	3.1
San Jose, CA	11.0	14.1	14.7	6.9	27.5	18.7	2.8	4.4
Santa Rosa, CA	10.8	18.3	24.2	9.5	23.2	9.2	3.3	1.5
Savannah, GA	9.3	26.5	22.9	7.8	20.7	9.0	2.4	1.5
Seattle, WA	6.8	19.1	20.3	9.4	27.1	12.5	2.7	2.0
Sioux Falls, SD	6.3	25.7	20.2	13.0	24.1	7.8	2.0	1.0
Springfield, IL	7.1	28.0	22.7	8.8	20.3	9.4	2.6	1.1
Tampa, FL	9.6	28.1	20.0	9.8	20.8	8.2	2.2	1.2
Tucson, AZ	10.6	21.4	24.6	9.0	19.7	10.2	2.2	2.2
Tulsa, OK	10.0	28.8	23.3	9.2	19.2	6.7	1.8	1.0
Tuscaloosa, AL	11.5	31.7	20.2	8.8	16.6	7.6	1.2	2.4
Virginia Beach, VA	7.6	24.7	23.8	10.1	20.6	9.8	1.9	1.4
Washington, DC	8.5	17.7	15.5	6.0	26.4	18.2	4.6	3.3
Wichita, KS	9.8	26.5	23.8	8.8	20.1	8.5	1.5	1.0
Wilmington, NC	7.2	20.8	21.3	10.9	26.2	9.4	2.8	1.5
Winston-Salem, NC	12.0	29.1	21.8	9.6	17.7	6.7	1.7	1.3
Worcester, MA	8.7	27.8	17.9	9.2	21.5	11.4	1.8	1.8
U.S.	11.1	26.5	20.0	8.7	20.6	9.3	2.2	1.5

Note: Figures cover persons age 25 and over; Figures cover the Metropolitan Statistical Area
Source: U.S. Census Bureau, 2017-2021 American Community Survey 5-Year Estimates

School Enrollment by Grade and Control: City

City	Preschool (%)		Kindergarten (%)		Grades 1 - 4 (%)		Grades 5 - 8 (%)		Grades 9 - 12 (%)	
	Public	Private	Public	Private	Public	Private	Public	Private	Public	Private
Albuquerque, NM	57.2	42.8	86.7	13.3	86.7	13.3	90.7	9.3	91.7	8.3
Allentown, PA	80.2	19.8	86.2	13.8	87.7	12.3	90.5	9.5	89.0	11.0
Anchorage, AK	50.1	49.9	91.5	8.5	87.5	12.5	89.0	11.0	92.0	8.0
Ann Arbor, MI	34.0	66.0	86.6	13.4	88.7	11.3	87.6	12.4	94.0	6.0
Athens, GA	61.1	38.9	96.2	3.8	91.8	8.2	88.7	11.3	91.8	8.2
Atlanta, GA	50.7	49.3	75.7	24.3	85.9	14.1	78.5	21.5	79.9	20.1
Austin, TX	52.0	48.0	87.1	12.9	88.8	11.2	87.9	12.1	90.9	9.1
Baltimore, MD	69.2	30.8	83.5	16.5	84.0	16.0	85.0	15.0	85.3	14.7
Boise City, ID	32.0	68.0	77.1	22.9	89.8	10.2	91.7	8.3	88.4	11.6
Boston, MA	51.0	49.0	87.0	13.0	84.7	15.3	86.1	13.9	88.8	11.2
Boulder, CO	50.4	49.6	88.4	11.6	88.7	11.3	90.1	9.9	89.7	10.3
Brownsville, TX	95.8	4.2	92.3	7.7	95.6	4.4	94.7	5.3	97.5	2.5
Cape Coral, FL	73.5	26.5	96.9	3.1	88.6	11.4	94.2	5.8	90.2	9.8
Cedar Rapids, IA	69.1	30.9	85.6	14.4	88.0	12.0	91.4	8.6	87.2	12.8
Charleston, SC	42.4	57.6	81.0	19.0	83.5	16.5	83.8	16.2	76.6	23.4
Charlotte, NC	48.9	51.1	86.9	13.1	89.2	10.8	85.8	14.2	89.3	10.7
Chicago, IL	54.2	45.8	80.2	19.8	82.7	17.3	84.1	15.9	86.0	14.0
Cincinnati, OH	64.4	35.6	70.7	29.3	76.8	23.2	78.9	21.1	80.3	19.7
Clarksville, TN	61.1	38.9	85.7	14.3	93.4	6.6	92.1	7.9	87.1	12.9
Cleveland, OH	71.3	28.7	80.0	20.0	81.4	18.6	78.8	21.2	78.0	22.0
College Station, TX	51.4	48.6	86.9	13.1	91.0	9.0	93.9	6.1	88.3	11.7
Colorado Springs, CO	56.0	44.0	89.3	10.7	88.6	11.4	89.0	11.0	91.0	9.0
Columbia, MO	42.1	57.9	84.4	15.6	86.5	13.5	85.4	14.6	91.4	8.6
Columbia, SC	50.6	49.4	75.0	25.0	88.4	11.6	86.6	13.4	91.7	8.3
Columbus, OH	63.4	36.6	78.5	21.5	84.4	15.6	84.8	15.2	86.2	13.8
Dallas, TX	71.3	28.7	91.0	9.0	91.3	8.7	91.4	8.6	90.6	9.4
Davenport, IA	59.7	40.3	83.7	16.3	85.5	14.5	86.6	13.4	94.0	6.0
Denver, CO	57.4	42.6	85.2	14.8	90.6	9.4	89.6	10.4	91.8	8.2
Des Moines, IA	73.4	26.6	90.8	9.2	89.8	10.2	89.4	10.6	92.0	8.0
Durham, NC	53.6	46.4	84.7	15.3	89.3	10.7	84.4	15.6	88.5	11.5
Edison, NJ	18.4	81.6	71.4	28.6	88.2	11.8	89.7	10.3	91.9	8.1
El Paso, TX	88.6	11.4	92.5	7.5	94.3	5.7	94.0	6.0	95.8	4.2
Fargo, ND	43.0	57.0	92.4	7.6	92.6	7.4	90.6	9.4	94.5	5.5
Fort Collins, CO	44.8	55.2	89.3	10.7	93.6	6.4	93.0	7.0	93.8	6.2
Fort Wayne, IN	50.8	49.2	76.9	23.1	79.4	20.6	82.2	17.8	79.9	20.1
Fort Worth, TX	62.1	37.9	83.6	16.4	90.6	9.4	90.1	9.9	92.2	7.8
Grand Rapids, MI	66.8	33.2	74.2	25.8	78.3	21.7	82.3	17.7	82.3	17.7
Greeley, CO	72.4	27.6	92.8	7.2	94.1	5.9	92.8	7.2	94.4	5.6
Green Bay, WI	70.8	29.2	87.5	12.5	87.8	12.2	84.9	15.1	91.3	8.7
Greensboro, NC	55.5	44.5	90.0	10.0	93.3	6.7	91.0	9.0	89.1	10.9
Honolulu, HI	40.2	59.8	73.5	26.5	79.4	20.6	75.4	24.6	71.9	28.1
Houston, TX	64.5	35.5	89.1	10.9	93.1	6.9	92.0	8.0	92.5	7.5
Huntsville, AL	58.2	41.8	85.2	14.8	81.8	18.2	78.4	21.6	82.1	17.9
Indianapolis, IN	58.5	41.5	86.4	13.6	83.9	16.1	84.2	15.8	87.5	12.5
Jacksonville, FL	54.4	45.6	85.0	15.0	83.7	16.3	80.4	19.6	84.8	15.2
Kansas City, MO	55.9	44.1	86.9	13.1	87.6	12.4	88.5	11.5	83.8	16.2
Lafayette, LA	63.6	36.4	67.4	32.6	70.2	29.8	72.4	27.6	79.5	20.5
Las Cruces, NM	84.8	15.2	91.5	8.5	92.9	7.1	96.6	3.4	96.2	3.8
Las Vegas, NV	63.4	36.6	88.2	11.8	90.3	9.7	91.1	8.9	92.5	7.5
Lexington, KY	37.3	62.7	84.6	15.4	83.2	16.8	83.9	16.1	85.4	14.6
Lincoln, NE	50.3	49.7	73.0	27.0	83.5	16.5	83.1	16.9	87.0	13.0
Little Rock, AR	67.9	32.1	88.9	11.1	78.3	21.7	79.1	20.9	76.2	23.8
Los Angeles, CA	57.1	42.9	85.7	14.3	88.0	12.0	87.6	12.4	89.1	10.9
Louisville, KY	51.6	48.4	80.2	19.8	82.9	17.1	82.3	17.7	78.3	21.7
Madison, WI	51.2	48.8	87.9	12.1	88.7	11.3	88.1	11.9	90.6	9.4

Table continued on following page.

City	Preschool (%)		Kindergarten (%)		Grades 1 - 4 (%)		Grades 5 - 8 (%)		Grades 9 - 12 (%)	
	Public	Private	Public	Private	Public	Private	Public	Private	Public	Private
Manchester, NH	58.7	41.3	86.5	13.5	89.0	11.0	93.0	7.0	92.0	8.0
Miami, FL	58.9	41.1	85.5	14.5	85.8	14.2	84.2	15.8	90.8	9.2
Midland, TX	70.6	29.4	83.7	16.3	83.1	16.9	77.6	22.4	83.9	16.1
Milwaukee, WI	74.3	25.7	77.9	22.1	75.8	24.2	74.5	25.5	81.4	18.6
Minneapolis, MN	55.0	45.0	85.0	15.0	87.3	12.7	88.9	11.1	90.7	9.3
Nashville, TN	48.4	51.6	84.0	16.0	84.6	15.4	80.0	20.0	81.9	18.1
New Haven, CT	80.4	19.6	89.7	10.3	95.2	4.8	93.4	6.6	92.5	7.5
New Orleans, LA	49.2	50.8	78.4	21.6	81.5	18.5	81.9	18.1	80.2	19.8
New York, NY	63.8	36.2	79.0	21.0	81.8	18.2	80.9	19.1	80.3	19.7
Oklahoma City, OK	70.9	29.1	87.6	12.4	89.5	10.5	88.2	11.8	88.1	11.9
Omaha, NE	52.7	47.3	81.2	18.8	82.9	17.1	83.3	16.7	83.2	16.8
Orlando, FL	62.9	37.1	84.3	15.7	88.0	12.0	87.0	13.0	86.7	13.3
Philadelphia, PA	54.6	45.4	78.1	21.9	79.2	20.8	80.8	19.2	79.4	20.6
Phoenix, AZ	61.2	38.8	86.5	13.5	90.6	9.4	91.6	8.4	93.1	6.9
Pittsburgh, PA	50.4	49.6	76.4	23.6	76.9	23.1	76.5	23.5	79.5	20.5
Portland, OR	37.9	62.1	84.9	15.1	87.2	12.8	88.2	11.8	87.1	12.9
Providence, RI	56.9	43.1	80.9	19.1	88.4	11.6	84.5	15.5	89.6	10.4
Provo, UT	63.9	36.1	91.4	8.6	92.1	7.9	95.5	4.5	90.2	9.8
Raleigh, NC	37.3	62.7	87.2	12.8	85.6	14.4	87.7	12.3	87.7	12.3
Reno, NV	59.8	40.2	92.4	7.6	94.3	5.7	92.0	8.0	93.1	6.9
Richmond, VA	50.9	49.1	89.3	10.7	85.0	15.0	84.6	15.4	83.6	16.4
Rochester, MN	52.1	47.9	90.2	9.8	90.8	9.2	88.0	12.0	89.3	10.7
Sacramento, CA	65.0	35.0	91.0	9.0	93.1	6.9	91.5	8.5	90.9	9.1
St. Louis, MO	56.8	43.2	73.9	26.1	82.9	17.1	78.8	21.2	80.6	19.4
Salem, OR	61.3	38.7	87.8	12.2	90.0	10.0	93.3	6.7	96.5	3.5
Salt Lake City, UT	42.5	57.5	86.4	13.6	88.6	11.4	91.0	9.0	94.8	5.2
San Antonio, TX	74.0	26.0	89.7	10.3	92.1	7.9	92.3	7.7	91.5	8.5
San Diego, CA	46.8	53.2	89.4	10.6	90.4	9.6	91.7	8.3	91.2	8.8
San Francisco, CA	34.0	66.0	67.4	32.6	71.0	29.0	66.6	33.4	75.5	24.5
San Jose, CA	43.4	56.6	81.8	18.2	87.0	13.0	87.6	12.4	85.9	14.1
Santa Rosa, CA	53.7	46.3	86.2	13.8	92.9	7.1	89.1	10.9	93.8	6.2
Savannah, GA	77.0	23.0	89.0	11.0	91.9	8.1	91.5	8.5	88.5	11.5
Seattle, WA	36.3	63.7	79.0	21.0	79.2	20.8	73.5	26.5	77.3	22.7
Sioux Falls, SD	53.8	46.2	92.3	7.7	86.4	13.6	88.8	11.2	84.6	15.4
Springfield, IL	53.6	46.4	80.8	19.2	80.5	19.5	86.1	13.9	86.8	13.2
Tampa, FL	51.4	48.6	81.9	18.1	87.9	12.1	83.5	16.5	82.2	17.8
Tucson, AZ	70.3	29.7	84.3	15.7	86.8	13.2	88.9	11.1	93.6	6.4
Tulsa, OK	63.6	36.4	82.4	17.6	85.0	15.0	83.0	17.0	81.8	18.2
Tuscaloosa, AL	78.7	21.3	94.7	5.3	84.3	15.7	96.4	3.6	94.9	5.1
Virginia Beach, VA	35.4	64.6	75.9	24.1	90.1	9.9	90.1	9.9	92.2	7.8
Washington, DC	74.2	25.8	90.9	9.1	88.6	11.4	82.4	17.6	80.7	19.3
Wichita, KS	62.8	37.2	84.4	15.6	86.4	13.6	83.7	16.3	84.5	15.5
Wilmington, NC	62.4	37.6	84.8	15.2	75.5	24.5	74.3	25.7	88.8	11.2
Winston-Salem, NC	56.5	43.5	90.6	9.4	91.7	8.3	91.4	8.6	91.9	8.1
Worcester, MA	54.7	45.3	96.0	4.0	93.5	6.5	92.0	8.0	88.1	11.9
U.S.	58.8	41.2	86.3	13.7	88.3	11.7	88.6	11.4	89.4	10.6

Note: Figures shown cover persons 3 years old and over
Source: U.S. Census Bureau, 2017-2021 American Community Survey 5-Year Estimates

School Enrollment by Grade and Control: Metro Area

Metro Area	Preschool (%)		Kindergarten (%)		Grades 1 - 4 (%)		Grades 5 - 8 (%)		Grades 9 - 12 (%)	
	Public	Private	Public	Private	Public	Private	Public	Private	Public	Private
Albuquerque, NM	57.8	42.2	84.8	15.2	86.4	13.6	89.8	10.2	90.8	9.2
Allentown, PA	52.6	47.4	86.9	13.1	89.7	10.3	91.2	8.8	91.3	8.7
Anchorage, AK	51.6	48.4	90.9	9.1	87.2	12.8	88.1	11.9	90.9	9.1
Ann Arbor, MI	49.9	50.1	89.4	10.6	87.1	12.9	88.1	11.9	93.0	7.0
Athens, GA	64.9	35.1	93.2	6.8	89.6	10.4	87.0	13.0	88.4	11.6
Atlanta, GA	54.8	45.2	85.7	14.3	89.8	10.2	88.2	11.8	89.0	11.0
Austin, TX	49.5	50.5	89.5	10.5	90.6	9.4	89.8	10.2	91.7	8.3
Baltimore, MD	47.8	52.2	82.9	17.1	85.3	14.7	84.6	15.4	83.2	16.8
Boise City, ID	35.5	64.5	84.5	15.5	87.8	12.2	90.3	9.7	89.0	11.0
Boston, MA	45.1	54.9	88.5	11.5	91.0	9.0	89.6	10.4	86.5	13.5
Boulder, CO	50.1	49.9	84.8	15.2	90.1	9.9	90.4	9.6	94.6	5.4
Brownsville, TX	95.5	4.5	95.8	4.2	97.0	3.0	96.5	3.5	96.7	3.3
Cape Coral, FL	60.7	39.3	89.9	10.1	90.4	9.6	90.7	9.3	90.5	9.5
Cedar Rapids, IA	69.0	31.0	86.7	13.3	89.3	10.7	90.5	9.5	91.0	9.0
Charleston, SC	46.6	53.4	83.0	17.0	86.2	13.8	88.5	11.5	88.5	11.5
Charlotte, NC	50.3	49.7	87.4	12.6	89.5	10.5	87.5	12.5	89.9	10.1
Chicago, IL	56.6	43.4	84.4	15.6	88.3	11.7	88.6	11.4	90.3	9.7
Cincinnati, OH	53.2	46.8	79.7	20.3	82.8	17.2	83.5	16.5	82.3	17.7
Clarksville, TN	62.6	37.4	88.2	11.8	86.8	13.2	88.6	11.4	87.0	13.0
Cleveland, OH	52.8	47.2	79.0	21.0	81.1	18.9	82.0	18.0	82.4	17.6
College Station, TX	59.9	40.1	86.3	13.7	91.4	8.6	92.1	7.9	92.3	7.7
Colorado Springs, CO	58.9	41.1	87.2	12.8	88.7	11.3	90.1	9.9	90.8	9.2
Columbia, MO	52.3	47.7	87.6	12.4	85.9	14.1	87.6	12.4	91.3	8.7
Columbia, SC	58.5	41.5	90.7	9.3	92.0	8.0	92.7	7.3	92.9	7.1
Columbus, OH	57.3	42.7	82.1	17.9	87.4	12.6	87.9	12.1	88.7	11.3
Dallas, TX	59.0	41.0	88.8	11.2	91.3	8.7	91.6	8.4	91.9	8.1
Davenport, IA	68.6	31.4	88.3	11.7	91.0	9.0	92.0	8.0	92.1	7.9
Denver, CO	58.0	42.0	88.1	11.9	90.8	9.2	90.9	9.1	91.5	8.5
Des Moines, IA	67.2	32.8	90.4	9.6	91.9	8.1	90.5	9.5	92.2	7.8
Durham, NC	47.9	52.1	81.8	18.2	88.9	11.1	86.0	14.0	90.4	9.6
Edison, NJ	56.6	43.4	81.6	18.4	84.6	15.4	84.8	15.2	84.1	15.9
El Paso, TX	88.3	11.7	93.1	6.9	94.3	5.7	94.7	5.3	96.3	3.7
Fargo, ND	59.7	40.3	91.9	8.1	91.0	9.0	91.1	8.9	91.6	8.4
Fort Collins, CO	45.2	54.8	88.9	11.1	88.9	11.1	86.8	13.2	88.3	11.7
Fort Wayne, IN	46.6	53.4	75.5	24.5	76.6	23.4	77.4	22.6	80.7	19.3
Fort Worth, TX	59.0	41.0	88.8	11.2	91.3	8.7	91.6	8.4	91.9	8.1
Grand Rapids, MI	61.5	38.5	81.4	18.6	82.3	17.7	85.8	14.2	85.3	14.7
Greeley, CO	71.5	28.5	91.2	8.8	92.1	7.9	91.7	8.3	94.2	5.8
Green Bay, WI	67.1	32.9	86.7	13.3	88.4	11.6	86.7	13.3	91.8	8.2
Greensboro, NC	55.7	44.3	86.7	13.3	88.5	11.5	88.1	11.9	88.2	11.8
Honolulu, HI	38.4	61.6	78.3	21.7	82.6	17.4	79.3	20.7	75.9	24.1
Houston, TX	56.6	43.4	88.9	11.1	92.0	8.0	92.4	7.6	92.5	7.5
Huntsville, AL	57.2	42.8	80.7	19.3	82.7	17.3	81.5	18.5	81.8	18.2
Indianapolis, IN	52.2	47.8	87.2	12.8	86.8	13.2	87.0	13.0	88.4	11.6
Jacksonville, FL	54.8	45.2	86.3	13.7	84.9	15.1	83.2	16.8	87.2	12.8
Kansas City, MO	59.2	40.8	88.2	11.8	88.3	11.7	89.5	10.5	88.8	11.2
Lafayette, LA	66.3	33.7	78.7	21.3	80.8	19.2	78.8	21.2	78.7	21.3
Las Cruces, NM	83.3	16.7	92.7	7.3	90.3	9.7	96.5	3.5	94.7	5.3
Las Vegas, NV	60.9	39.1	88.6	11.4	91.5	8.5	92.4	7.6	92.7	7.3
Lexington, KY	44.3	55.7	82.5	17.5	85.0	15.0	84.0	16.0	86.6	13.4
Lincoln, NE	49.5	50.5	74.6	25.4	81.6	18.4	83.9	16.1	87.2	12.8
Little Rock, AR	70.5	29.5	90.1	9.9	87.0	13.0	86.6	13.4	86.4	13.6
Los Angeles, CA	55.8	44.2	86.9	13.1	90.0	10.0	90.1	9.9	91.1	8.9
Louisville, KY	52.4	47.6	81.8	18.2	82.3	17.7	82.4	17.6	80.7	19.3
Madison, WI	67.4	32.6	88.0	12.0	89.6	10.4	90.2	9.8	94.3	5.7

Table continued on following page.

Metro Area	Preschool (%)		Kindergarten (%)		Grades 1 - 4 (%)		Grades 5 - 8 (%)		Grades 9 - 12 (%)	
	Public	Private	Public	Private	Public	Private	Public	Private	Public	Private
Manchester, NH	49.7	50.3	81.7	18.3	87.4	12.6	87.8	12.2	88.9	11.1
Miami, FL	51.1	48.9	82.4	17.6	85.2	14.8	85.6	14.4	86.1	13.9
Midland, TX	75.7	24.3	79.8	20.2	83.8	16.2	82.0	18.0	85.2	14.8
Milwaukee, WI	58.0	42.0	78.8	21.2	79.9	20.1	79.6	20.4	85.4	14.6
Minneapolis, MN	61.4	38.6	87.3	12.7	89.0	11.0	89.6	10.4	91.6	8.4
Nashville, TN	50.2	49.8	85.0	15.0	85.7	14.3	84.7	15.3	83.3	16.7
New Haven, CT	65.6	34.4	93.4	6.6	92.1	7.9	90.4	9.6	88.9	11.1
New Orleans, LA	54.1	45.9	76.7	23.3	77.8	22.2	77.5	22.5	74.9	25.1
New York, NY	56.6	43.4	81.6	18.4	84.6	15.4	84.8	15.2	84.1	15.9
Oklahoma City, OK	71.5	28.5	87.9	12.1	89.2	10.8	88.8	11.2	89.1	10.9
Omaha, NE	57.9	42.1	83.0	17.0	85.1	14.9	85.4	14.6	85.4	14.6
Orlando, FL	50.4	49.6	81.5	18.5	84.1	15.9	85.5	14.5	87.5	12.5
Philadelphia, PA	46.2	53.8	81.2	18.8	84.8	15.2	84.6	15.4	83.3	16.7
Phoenix, AZ	61.7	38.3	86.0	14.0	89.6	10.4	91.1	8.9	92.7	7.3
Pittsburgh, PA	50.8	49.2	82.7	17.3	88.7	11.3	89.0	11.0	89.6	10.4
Portland, OR	41.3	58.7	85.1	14.9	87.5	12.5	89.1	10.9	90.2	9.8
Providence, RI	56.5	43.5	88.3	11.7	90.4	9.6	89.4	10.6	88.4	11.6
Provo, UT	54.2	45.8	89.1	10.9	91.5	8.5	93.7	6.3	94.4	5.6
Raleigh, NC	33.6	66.4	84.1	15.9	86.7	13.3	86.5	13.5	88.1	11.9
Reno, NV	54.1	45.9	89.2	10.8	93.0	7.0	92.3	7.7	92.1	7.9
Richmond, VA	44.8	55.2	87.7	12.3	88.8	11.2	89.4	10.6	90.2	9.8
Rochester, MN	63.8	36.2	91.4	8.6	90.6	9.4	89.8	10.2	91.2	8.8
Sacramento, CA	59.9	40.1	90.0	10.0	91.7	8.3	91.9	8.1	91.7	8.3
St. Louis, MO	53.6	46.4	80.8	19.2	83.8	16.2	82.7	17.3	85.1	14.9
Salem, OR	59.7	40.3	86.9	13.1	89.6	10.4	91.7	8.3	93.9	6.1
Salt Lake City, UT	55.1	44.9	86.9	13.1	90.6	9.4	93.7	6.3	93.7	6.3
San Antonio, TX	67.2	32.8	89.3	10.7	91.6	8.4	91.2	8.8	91.1	8.9
San Diego, CA	49.0	51.0	89.7	10.3	90.8	9.2	91.8	8.2	92.3	7.7
San Francisco, CA	40.5	59.5	83.1	16.9	85.1	14.9	84.7	15.3	86.2	13.8
San Jose, CA	36.0	64.0	78.9	21.1	85.4	14.6	86.0	14.0	85.9	14.1
Santa Rosa, CA	48.2	51.8	87.3	12.7	92.4	7.6	89.8	10.2	92.0	8.0
Savannah, GA	53.9	46.1	81.7	18.3	85.0	15.0	88.0	12.0	85.4	14.6
Seattle, WA	42.0	58.0	82.0	18.0	86.4	13.6	86.9	13.1	90.2	9.8
Sioux Falls, SD	56.2	43.8	91.6	8.4	87.3	12.7	90.0	10.0	87.1	12.9
Springfield, IL	58.6	41.4	85.1	14.9	85.1	14.9	89.7	10.3	90.4	9.6
Tampa, FL	54.7	45.3	82.3	17.7	84.8	15.2	85.9	14.1	87.4	12.6
Tucson, AZ	67.5	32.5	85.8	14.2	87.9	12.1	88.9	11.1	91.0	9.0
Tulsa, OK	66.3	33.7	85.2	14.8	86.1	13.9	86.5	13.5	85.9	14.1
Tuscaloosa, AL	71.4	28.6	87.3	12.7	86.8	13.2	89.9	10.1	88.1	11.9
Virginia Beach, VA	50.5	49.5	79.9	20.1	88.8	11.2	90.0	10.0	90.1	9.9
Washington, DC	45.8	54.2	84.0	16.0	87.7	12.3	87.4	12.6	88.2	11.8
Wichita, KS	64.9	35.1	83.7	16.3	86.6	13.4	86.2	13.8	87.4	12.6
Wilmington, NC	48.0	52.0	81.2	18.8	83.4	16.6	82.0	18.0	88.8	11.2
Winston-Salem, NC	52.2	47.8	88.5	11.5	90.0	10.0	89.8	10.2	88.4	11.6
Worcester, MA	59.0	41.0	91.1	8.9	92.2	7.8	90.6	9.4	90.5	9.5
U.S.	58.8	41.2	86.3	13.7	88.3	11.7	88.6	11.4	89.4	10.6

Note: Figures shown cover persons 3 years old and over; Figures cover the Metropolitan Statistical Area
Source: U.S. Census Bureau, 2017-2021 American Community Survey 5-Year Estimates

Educational Attainment by Race: City

City	High School Graduate or Higher (%)					Bachelor's Degree or Higher (%)				
	Total	White	Black	Asian	Hisp.[1]	Total	White	Black	Asian	Hisp.[1]
Albuquerque, NM	90.9	93.0	94.3	87.7	84.8	37.4	41.1	36.2	54.1	24.3
Allentown, PA	80.6	84.7	83.6	80.4	70.5	17.3	21.5	11.2	42.3	7.7
Anchorage, AK	94.2	96.4	93.2	88.4	85.6	36.8	44.0	21.6	26.4	24.5
Ann Arbor, MI	97.8	98.5	93.2	98.0	92.7	77.2	79.5	36.4	85.6	69.9
Athens, GA	89.7	94.3	83.2	92.5	67.4	47.1	59.0	23.3	72.4	27.0
Atlanta, GA	92.1	98.3	86.3	96.7	84.0	55.6	79.9	29.9	86.1	48.0
Austin, TX	90.6	93.2	89.5	92.7	76.2	55.1	59.5	31.6	76.5	30.9
Baltimore, MD	86.3	91.5	84.1	90.2	72.2	34.2	59.7	18.7	71.6	32.9
Boise City, ID	95.2	96.2	78.5	90.0	82.7	43.7	43.9	31.0	57.7	26.7
Boston, MA	88.2	94.7	85.2	80.6	72.7	52.1	68.7	25.0	57.1	25.7
Boulder, CO	96.9	98.2	89.2	95.5	81.4	76.8	78.0	34.2	84.3	51.2
Brownsville, TX	68.0	67.8	78.7	92.7	66.5	20.5	20.4	37.3	61.2	19.3
Cape Coral, FL	92.9	94.0	84.8	87.3	88.5	23.6	23.9	22.7	44.4	16.4
Cedar Rapids, IA	93.8	95.3	83.0	86.2	82.8	32.8	33.6	17.8	51.5	22.4
Charleston, SC	95.8	97.8	89.2	98.6	86.5	55.7	63.7	24.3	66.2	41.3
Charlotte, NC	89.7	94.7	91.2	84.3	60.8	45.7	59.2	30.8	61.5	19.1
Chicago, IL	86.3	90.8	86.4	87.6	70.9	41.7	55.5	23.5	64.1	18.5
Cincinnati, OH	88.6	92.9	83.1	94.7	76.9	39.6	54.9	16.8	80.3	33.3
Clarksville, TN	93.6	94.2	94.0	87.4	87.1	28.7	30.6	25.3	37.3	17.2
Cleveland, OH	82.6	85.7	81.1	75.3	71.4	19.2	27.6	11.2	46.9	9.2
College Station, TX	94.8	95.9	91.0	94.2	87.1	58.0	58.7	31.9	78.7	41.2
Colorado Springs, CO	93.9	95.5	93.8	85.8	82.6	40.2	43.4	28.1	42.7	20.4
Columbia, MO	95.5	96.6	92.6	94.7	89.1	53.8	56.5	29.4	68.9	47.1
Columbia, SC	90.5	96.2	83.5	95.7	87.6	44.7	63.4	21.6	76.0	35.4
Columbus, OH	90.3	93.0	87.0	86.5	73.5	37.9	44.5	20.1	60.7	24.1
Dallas, TX	79.6	80.5	88.4	87.4	55.4	35.6	44.3	22.3	66.0	13.5
Davenport, IA	92.1	93.9	87.7	71.8	78.3	27.1	29.1	13.6	35.3	15.4
Denver, CO	90.0	93.6	89.8	85.6	69.6	52.5	60.7	27.7	56.5	19.4
Des Moines, IA	87.1	91.9	82.1	58.6	60.2	28.1	31.1	16.4	21.8	10.1
Durham, NC	90.6	93.8	90.0	93.0	54.7	52.8	65.7	35.4	77.8	19.8
Edison, NJ	92.1	94.0	95.0	92.0	86.3	56.4	38.6	43.0	76.2	25.0
El Paso, TX	81.4	84.1	96.1	88.5	77.8	26.7	28.7	32.3	56.8	22.7
Fargo, ND	94.8	96.7	79.3	82.7	91.6	41.8	43.5	19.0	57.2	16.4
Fort Collins, CO	97.0	97.6	91.7	93.4	87.4	56.6	58.0	36.7	73.4	33.1
Fort Wayne, IN	88.9	93.5	85.4	47.6	63.7	28.0	31.6	15.3	21.6	11.6
Fort Worth, TX	83.5	88.1	89.1	80.9	63.5	31.0	37.5	22.7	44.5	14.4
Grand Rapids, MI	88.7	92.6	86.4	80.6	57.7	38.8	46.0	20.4	44.7	13.3
Greeley, CO	83.6	86.1	69.8	81.6	64.7	26.1	28.3	21.9	50.3	9.1
Green Bay, WI	87.8	90.7	76.5	75.1	57.7	25.1	27.0	16.9	26.0	9.3
Greensboro, NC	90.2	93.9	89.3	77.0	68.0	39.5	50.5	26.7	47.0	19.3
Honolulu, HI	90.4	97.9	94.5	87.4	93.9	38.4	54.2	31.3	37.9	31.6
Houston, TX	79.5	82.2	89.1	87.1	59.6	34.7	42.7	25.0	62.3	15.5
Huntsville, AL	91.1	93.8	86.8	88.8	72.3	44.8	51.8	29.4	56.2	29.2
Indianapolis, IN	86.7	89.7	85.3	70.5	60.6	32.9	38.4	20.9	44.3	15.8
Jacksonville, FL	90.3	92.0	88.2	87.8	83.9	30.2	33.0	21.3	49.4	27.0
Kansas City, MO	91.0	93.9	88.6	86.1	71.3	36.5	45.2	16.9	48.4	19.0
Lafayette, LA	90.3	95.1	80.3	92.2	72.5	39.4	49.1	15.2	63.9	33.0
Las Cruces, NM	87.5	90.4	83.9	85.3	83.2	36.4	38.7	47.4	63.0	24.8
Las Vegas, NV	85.4	89.5	88.3	91.9	66.0	25.9	29.4	18.8	43.3	11.6
Lexington, KY	92.4	94.8	88.9	89.4	64.1	45.6	49.7	23.7	69.0	25.3
Lincoln, NE	92.9	95.0	87.1	79.8	69.0	40.1	41.7	26.6	43.7	19.9
Little Rock, AR	91.9	94.1	90.0	87.5	67.6	44.1	57.8	25.7	61.9	13.0
Los Angeles, CA	78.4	84.6	89.3	90.9	58.3	36.2	44.9	29.3	56.8	14.0
Louisville, KY	90.2	91.8	88.2	80.0	77.1	31.6	35.2	18.8	50.7	24.4
Madison, WI	95.6	97.2	88.8	92.4	79.2	58.5	60.9	24.7	70.9	40.0

Table continued on following page.

City	High School Graduate or Higher (%)					Bachelor's Degree or Higher (%)				
	Total	White	Black	Asian	Hisp.[1]	Total	White	Black	Asian	Hisp.[1]
Manchester, NH	88.6	90.4	78.2	81.0	67.1	31.9	32.9	17.6	40.8	13.0
Miami, FL	79.2	80.7	75.7	96.5	76.5	33.1	37.3	15.6	68.9	29.6
Midland, TX	84.5	88.0	88.2	72.1	71.2	30.9	35.0	16.2	45.8	15.5
Milwaukee, WI	84.9	90.5	84.9	74.8	64.4	25.5	37.6	13.5	32.7	10.8
Minneapolis, MN	90.7	96.7	74.7	84.7	66.1	52.6	63.7	17.2	57.3	25.6
Nashville, TN	90.0	92.2	89.3	80.3	59.3	43.9	50.7	28.8	52.3	17.2
New Haven, CT	85.4	87.2	87.3	94.8	71.6	36.5	49.2	22.5	78.5	14.5
New Orleans, LA	88.2	96.4	83.7	76.7	80.9	39.1	65.3	21.0	47.9	40.4
New York, NY	83.2	90.5	84.7	76.8	70.8	39.6	54.6	25.3	44.0	20.1
Oklahoma City, OK	87.5	89.5	91.2	80.6	57.6	32.3	35.4	24.3	42.3	10.4
Omaha, NE	90.3	93.1	87.9	72.2	60.3	38.7	42.8	17.7	49.8	13.8
Orlando, FL	91.6	94.7	84.5	92.5	90.2	40.1	48.5	20.6	54.5	32.2
Philadelphia, PA	86.6	91.8	86.9	73.2	71.9	32.5	46.4	19.3	41.4	18.1
Phoenix, AZ	83.5	87.0	89.8	86.8	65.5	30.6	33.8	25.9	60.2	12.0
Pittsburgh, PA	93.5	95.0	89.1	92.5	87.3	45.7	51.2	19.8	77.7	49.3
Portland, OR	93.3	95.7	89.2	79.9	79.1	51.9	56.1	26.6	43.6	34.5
Providence, RI	83.5	88.8	85.7	84.1	73.3	33.3	41.9	27.0	50.4	12.3
Provo, UT	92.7	94.5	95.3	84.4	73.5	44.3	46.4	17.0	47.4	19.3
Raleigh, NC	92.3	96.3	91.6	89.4	62.6	52.4	64.4	32.6	61.7	23.0
Reno, NV	89.8	93.9	90.8	92.4	66.3	35.5	38.3	31.1	49.5	13.5
Richmond, VA	87.7	94.7	81.5	88.6	58.3	43.1	68.0	14.8	70.7	22.5
Rochester, MN	94.4	96.8	70.6	88.5	76.7	48.7	49.9	19.9	61.8	33.6
Sacramento, CA	86.4	91.5	91.3	81.6	75.4	35.1	42.6	24.8	39.3	21.6
St. Louis, MO	89.2	94.4	83.1	87.1	79.1	38.0	53.9	16.6	57.9	36.7
Salem, OR	88.4	92.3	95.0	84.5	61.8	30.0	32.6	27.1	44.4	11.1
Salt Lake City, UT	91.1	95.3	84.5	83.1	69.3	49.8	54.8	32.1	57.8	21.2
San Antonio, TX	83.3	84.8	91.5	86.1	76.7	27.3	28.9	25.7	55.7	18.0
San Diego, CA	89.3	91.8	91.2	89.2	73.4	47.6	52.0	28.3	55.1	22.6
San Francisco, CA	88.8	97.3	87.3	80.4	79.2	59.5	75.4	31.5	48.9	38.1
San Jose, CA	85.5	90.9	91.4	87.6	69.6	45.4	48.2	38.3	57.5	16.6
Santa Rosa, CA	85.5	92.6	83.5	86.8	62.4	34.3	40.0	27.4	48.4	14.4
Savannah, GA	88.8	94.8	84.1	78.6	84.0	30.5	45.4	16.3	50.7	31.9
Seattle, WA	95.5	98.2	89.8	90.1	85.7	65.9	70.7	32.9	66.9	46.5
Sioux Falls, SD	93.3	95.3	83.9	74.3	73.5	36.0	37.9	20.0	44.2	17.9
Springfield, IL	91.3	93.6	80.0	94.0	86.8	34.4	37.2	14.3	69.9	43.3
Tampa, FL	88.4	91.9	84.1	87.7	78.2	41.8	49.8	18.7	65.4	26.7
Tucson, AZ	86.3	89.9	84.2	87.3	75.0	28.9	32.7	20.8	51.6	15.5
Tulsa, OK	87.9	90.8	89.6	74.0	59.8	32.4	37.6	17.8	37.0	11.5
Tuscaloosa, AL	90.1	95.5	85.9	91.4	66.5	37.6	57.4	15.7	67.5	20.2
Virginia Beach, VA	94.5	96.0	92.5	89.5	87.4	38.6	41.7	29.3	40.9	30.1
Washington, DC	92.2	98.6	88.0	94.4	78.6	61.4	90.8	31.1	82.4	52.8
Wichita, KS	88.2	91.6	87.8	73.7	63.9	30.5	33.6	17.7	35.1	13.3
Wilmington, NC	93.5	95.6	87.4	84.0	78.0	43.6	49.0	20.9	60.7	32.3
Winston-Salem, NC	88.0	90.7	88.1	89.9	58.9	34.6	43.0	20.9	70.4	15.1
Worcester, MA	85.8	88.9	89.5	74.9	69.5	32.2	33.9	31.7	41.7	13.9
U.S.	88.9	91.4	87.2	87.6	71.2	33.7	35.5	23.3	55.6	18.4

Note: Figures shown cover persons 25 years old and over; (1) People of Hispanic origin can be of any race
Source: U.S. Census Bureau, 2017-2021 American Community Survey 5-Year Estimates

Educational Attainment by Race: Metro Area

Metro Area	High School Graduate or Higher (%)					Bachelor's Degree or Higher (%)				
	Total	White	Black	Asian	Hisp.[1]	Total	White	Black	Asian	Hisp.[1]
Albuquerque, NM	90.0	92.1	92.0	89.6	83.8	33.7	37.5	34.4	54.4	21.7
Allentown, PA	90.9	92.5	87.6	89.0	77.5	31.2	32.2	21.7	61.7	15.7
Anchorage, AK	94.0	95.8	92.9	88.2	86.4	33.3	38.1	21.8	26.1	24.3
Ann Arbor, MI	95.7	96.8	90.8	95.7	87.2	57.2	58.9	29.1	82.1	46.1
Athens, GA	89.4	92.3	82.2	89.7	69.1	41.7	46.6	21.7	67.5	30.6
Atlanta, GA	90.5	92.5	91.5	87.7	67.2	40.4	44.6	32.6	59.7	22.9
Austin, TX	91.0	93.4	92.3	92.8	77.1	47.4	50.3	33.1	73.7	26.1
Baltimore, MD	91.6	93.9	89.0	89.1	76.2	41.8	46.4	28.4	63.1	32.4
Boise City, ID	92.1	94.1	80.8	88.2	70.7	33.9	35.1	25.3	52.0	16.6
Boston, MA	92.1	95.1	86.2	86.6	73.7	49.7	52.5	29.6	64.1	24.9
Boulder, CO	95.5	97.0	86.9	92.5	75.8	62.9	64.6	30.4	70.8	31.3
Brownsville, TX	69.5	70.7	82.1	89.3	66.1	19.0	18.7	26.6	59.8	16.2
Cape Coral, FL	89.8	92.0	81.0	91.5	74.4	29.0	30.9	16.7	50.0	14.7
Cedar Rapids, IA	94.8	95.7	83.9	87.6	79.9	32.1	32.5	18.5	49.3	23.6
Charleston, SC	91.5	94.6	85.7	89.7	70.2	38.0	45.2	18.5	50.8	23.0
Charlotte, NC	89.9	92.2	89.9	86.7	65.7	37.1	40.0	28.1	60.8	20.5
Chicago, IL	89.5	92.9	88.7	91.1	70.5	39.7	44.4	24.5	66.5	16.8
Cincinnati, OH	91.8	92.7	87.3	89.4	77.4	35.4	36.4	21.6	65.9	29.4
Clarksville, TN	91.4	91.9	90.6	87.5	85.7	26.5	27.3	23.3	42.7	18.7
Cleveland, OH	91.4	93.3	86.1	86.8	77.9	32.7	36.2	16.8	63.5	17.6
College Station, TX	87.9	89.3	87.7	94.5	67.8	38.6	40.7	18.3	76.8	17.3
Colorado Springs, CO	94.6	95.8	95.1	87.2	84.7	39.4	41.9	29.6	42.2	21.4
Columbia, MO	94.1	94.7	91.6	94.2	88.0	45.1	46.2	25.5	67.1	38.5
Columbia, SC	90.6	92.8	88.1	92.3	70.0	33.6	37.9	24.7	62.2	23.1
Columbus, OH	92.1	93.6	87.6	88.4	76.8	38.4	40.3	22.7	64.1	27.4
Dallas, TX	86.6	88.9	91.8	88.8	63.9	36.8	38.9	30.0	62.8	16.2
Davenport, IA	91.8	93.9	80.3	78.7	75.3	27.9	29.0	11.8	51.7	16.9
Denver, CO	91.9	94.5	90.4	84.9	74.1	46.2	50.1	29.2	53.1	19.6
Des Moines, IA	93.4	95.6	84.8	71.0	68.2	37.6	39.0	20.7	37.1	15.8
Durham, NC	90.1	93.0	87.9	92.8	56.5	47.4	54.2	30.3	77.1	21.3
Edison, NJ	87.3	92.2	86.3	84.1	73.1	42.0	49.1	26.8	56.0	21.3
El Paso, TX	79.6	82.4	96.1	89.2	76.0	24.6	26.5	32.2	54.0	20.8
Fargo, ND	95.2	96.5	78.9	85.9	86.7	40.3	41.5	20.4	55.6	21.7
Fort Collins, CO	96.3	96.9	94.2	93.2	84.3	49.4	50.0	33.0	66.7	28.5
Fort Wayne, IN	90.2	93.3	86.0	55.8	66.3	29.3	31.4	16.4	30.4	12.5
Fort Worth, TX	86.6	88.9	91.8	88.8	63.9	36.8	38.9	30.0	62.8	16.2
Grand Rapids, MI	92.3	94.3	87.7	75.5	69.4	34.5	36.4	20.6	40.5	16.2
Greeley, CO	88.1	90.1	79.6	89.1	67.8	29.5	31.3	31.0	41.1	10.1
Green Bay, WI	92.5	94.3	76.4	83.4	61.7	29.1	29.8	19.0	47.3	13.4
Greensboro, NC	88.2	90.3	87.8	78.5	61.1	30.5	32.9	24.1	47.0	14.3
Honolulu, HI	92.7	97.6	97.1	90.3	95.1	36.2	50.0	33.8	37.4	28.7
Houston, TX	84.4	86.6	91.8	87.3	66.4	34.2	36.5	30.0	56.9	16.7
Huntsville, AL	90.8	92.5	87.5	89.5	74.7	40.9	43.4	32.1	60.6	27.7
Indianapolis, IN	90.6	92.5	86.5	81.0	67.3	36.3	38.5	22.9	55.5	21.3
Jacksonville, FL	91.4	92.8	88.4	89.4	85.5	33.1	35.6	22.0	49.9	27.9
Kansas City, MO	92.7	94.3	89.8	88.2	72.4	38.0	40.9	20.4	56.2	19.1
Lafayette, LA	86.0	88.8	79.2	76.0	70.7	24.6	27.7	13.2	38.0	19.1
Las Cruces, NM	80.7	83.8	84.8	88.6	73.5	30.0	32.5	44.9	60.3	19.8
Las Vegas, NV	86.4	90.0	89.9	90.6	68.4	25.8	28.3	19.8	41.0	11.9
Lexington, KY	91.7	93.3	89.0	89.2	63.6	39.0	40.9	22.8	65.5	22.1
Lincoln, NE	93.4	95.2	87.1	79.5	69.3	39.6	40.9	26.6	43.4	20.1
Little Rock, AR	91.6	92.8	90.2	87.1	70.1	32.1	34.4	24.8	51.1	15.5
Los Angeles, CA	81.6	86.5	90.5	88.8	64.5	36.0	40.8	29.5	54.5	15.1
Louisville, KY	90.9	91.9	88.1	85.5	73.8	31.1	32.7	19.7	57.5	21.6
Madison, WI	95.7	96.8	90.1	90.5	77.2	47.7	48.1	25.2	68.5	30.6

Table continued on following page.

Metro Area	High School Graduate or Higher (%)					Bachelor's Degree or Higher (%)				
	Total	White	Black	Asian	Hisp.[1]	Total	White	Black	Asian	Hisp.[1]
Manchester, NH	92.9	93.8	82.8	89.8	73.6	39.6	39.8	20.5	62.1	19.0
Miami, FL	86.5	88.7	83.6	87.9	81.2	34.1	38.5	21.2	54.3	29.8
Midland, TX	84.4	87.4	89.1	75.0	71.5	28.5	31.3	16.7	51.6	14.1
Milwaukee, WI	92.1	95.2	85.9	86.1	71.0	37.4	42.3	15.1	53.3	16.6
Minneapolis, MN	94.0	96.6	82.8	82.7	73.9	43.5	46.1	23.6	46.0	24.1
Nashville, TN	91.0	92.2	90.0	86.0	64.9	38.4	39.9	30.0	55.3	19.4
New Haven, CT	90.3	92.7	88.2	89.7	74.5	36.6	39.8	23.0	64.1	15.6
New Orleans, LA	88.1	91.7	84.1	80.3	74.7	32.2	39.2	19.9	43.4	22.4
New York, NY	87.3	92.2	86.3	84.1	73.1	42.0	49.1	26.8	56.0	21.3
Oklahoma City, OK	89.8	91.3	91.6	83.3	62.2	32.4	34.4	24.0	47.2	13.2
Omaha, NE	92.3	94.2	88.8	75.9	66.1	37.7	39.7	20.5	49.0	17.3
Orlando, FL	90.1	92.1	85.6	89.2	85.5	33.7	36.3	23.3	52.0	25.7
Philadelphia, PA	91.6	94.4	89.0	84.5	73.0	39.8	44.5	23.0	58.3	20.7
Phoenix, AZ	88.7	91.3	91.7	89.3	71.8	33.1	35.2	28.2	59.7	14.9
Pittsburgh, PA	94.5	95.1	90.8	87.5	88.5	36.6	37.0	21.6	69.2	37.5
Portland, OR	92.8	94.6	90.8	87.6	73.2	41.0	41.6	31.3	54.0	22.1
Providence, RI	88.0	89.8	84.7	86.4	73.3	33.2	34.9	25.8	53.2	15.5
Provo, UT	95.1	95.8	95.1	93.1	79.7	41.9	42.6	34.1	54.0	24.9
Raleigh, NC	92.6	95.1	91.1	92.7	65.6	48.6	52.8	32.3	75.7	21.1
Reno, NV	88.6	92.8	90.7	92.0	64.2	32.3	34.9	28.0	47.1	13.2
Richmond, VA	91.1	94.0	87.4	89.9	68.9	38.9	45.5	22.8	65.6	22.8
Rochester, MN	94.7	96.1	71.8	88.1	77.4	41.0	41.1	19.5	59.6	31.3
Sacramento, CA	89.8	93.2	91.2	84.7	76.7	35.0	36.8	25.5	44.8	20.1
St. Louis, MO	92.8	94.2	87.5	90.8	82.3	36.2	38.6	20.4	68.0	31.3
Salem, OR	86.8	90.9	92.8	81.5	60.7	25.7	28.0	25.2	37.3	10.0
Salt Lake City, UT	91.8	94.9	84.6	86.6	73.5	36.4	38.9	25.4	49.1	17.1
San Antonio, TX	86.4	88.1	92.7	87.8	78.4	30.3	32.0	31.4	53.9	19.4
San Diego, CA	88.3	90.8	91.6	90.0	73.1	40.3	43.2	27.4	53.0	19.6
San Francisco, CA	89.7	95.0	91.3	88.1	73.1	51.4	58.7	31.6	57.6	23.9
San Jose, CA	89.0	92.7	92.4	91.4	71.9	53.4	53.4	41.7	67.5	19.0
Santa Rosa, CA	89.2	94.2	87.2	88.3	66.1	37.1	41.5	32.1	48.5	15.9
Savannah, GA	90.7	93.4	87.0	83.3	84.4	33.6	39.7	21.0	51.4	25.1
Seattle, WA	93.2	95.5	90.8	90.0	75.9	44.3	44.9	27.5	58.3	25.0
Sioux Falls, SD	93.7	95.1	84.5	75.7	73.0	34.8	36.1	19.6	44.4	18.6
Springfield, IL	92.9	94.4	80.8	90.9	89.3	33.4	34.8	15.5	68.2	42.6
Tampa, FL	90.4	91.9	88.7	85.1	81.4	32.4	33.1	25.0	51.8	24.6
Tucson, AZ	89.4	92.5	87.6	87.7	77.9	34.4	38.1	27.6	55.7	18.5
Tulsa, OK	90.0	91.7	90.1	76.7	65.8	28.7	31.1	19.6	34.9	14.0
Tuscaloosa, AL	88.5	91.2	84.9	86.9	64.6	27.8	34.2	15.3	61.0	17.4
Virginia Beach, VA	92.4	94.9	88.7	88.4	84.8	33.8	38.2	23.8	44.2	28.3
Washington, DC	91.5	95.1	92.4	91.3	70.4	52.4	61.3	37.2	66.0	28.0
Wichita, KS	90.2	92.8	87.6	74.2	66.9	31.1	33.0	19.0	35.5	16.4
Wilmington, NC	92.8	94.4	87.9	82.0	78.9	39.9	43.0	22.5	63.9	27.1
Winston-Salem, NC	88.0	89.3	87.7	88.3	60.1	27.4	28.9	21.0	54.6	13.5
Worcester, MA	91.3	92.9	89.3	85.0	73.7	36.4	36.4	34.4	59.8	16.6
U.S.	88.9	91.4	87.2	87.6	71.2	33.7	35.5	23.3	55.6	18.4

Note: Figures shown cover persons 25 years old and over; Figures cover the Metropolitan Statistical Area; (1) People of Hispanic origin can be of any race
Source: U.S. Census Bureau, 2017-2021 American Community Survey 5-Year Estimates

Cost of Living Index

Urban Area	Composite	Groceries	Housing	Utilities	Transp.	Health	Misc.
Albuquerque, NM	93.8	104.8	84.5	87.7	97.2	99.8	96.6
Allentown, PA	104.4	98.4	114.0	103.4	104.8	94.6	100.6
Anchorage, AK	124.5	132.6	140.0	124.0	114.8	144.2	109.7
Ann Arbor, MI	n/a	n/a	n/a	n/a	n/a	n/a	n/a
Athens, GA	n/a	n/a	n/a	n/a	n/a	n/a	n/a
Atlanta, GA	102.8	103.4	103.5	85.1	103.6	107.1	106.0
Austin, TX	99.7	91.2	105.5	95.2	90.7	105.8	101.4
Baltimore, MD	n/a	n/a	n/a	n/a	n/a	n/a	n/a
Boise City, ID	98.7	94.5	97.5	81.9	108.5	103.0	102.8
Boston, MA	151.0	109.3	228.6	120.5	112.0	118.3	129.3
Boulder, CO	n/a	n/a	n/a	n/a	n/a	n/a	n/a
Brownsville, TX	76.6	80.2	58.0	108.2	88.1	80.3	79.6
Cape Coral, FL	100.6	107.8	89.6	98.8	98.7	108.5	106.3
Cedar Rapids, IA	96.2	94.8	83.0	102.1	96.6	107.0	103.9
Charleston, SC	97.2	99.7	93.2	120.4	86.6	97.5	95.9
Charlotte, NC	98.2	101.7	88.8	95.6	90.7	105.1	106.0
Chicago, IL	120.6	101.9	155.7	92.4	125.9	100.0	109.4
Cincinnati, OH	99.7	91.2	105.5	95.2	90.7	105.8	101.4
Clarksville, TN	n/a	n/a	n/a	n/a	n/a	n/a	n/a
Cleveland, OH	96.9	106.0	83.3	96.1	99.4	104.4	102.6
College Station, TX	n/a	n/a	n/a	n/a	n/a	n/a	n/a
Colorado Springs, CO	101.1	95.9	101.3	97.2	97.7	108.6	104.1
Columbia, MO	91.8	95.5	75.0	100.0	92.0	102.6	99.8
Columbia, SC	93.5	103.1	72.7	126.2	87.1	79.9	100.5
Columbus, OH	92.6	98.6	81.2	89.1	95.5	88.5	99.7
Dallas, TX	108.2	100.2	118.8	106.8	96.7	105.4	106.7
Davenport, IA	92.0	99.7	76.9	98.9	105.8	105.3	93.7
Denver, CO	111.3	98.3	139.3	80.5	100.9	103.6	106.6
Des Moines, IA	89.9	95.2	80.2	90.1	99.1	95.4	92.3
Durham, NC[1]	n/a	n/a	n/a	n/a	n/a	n/a	n/a
Edison, NJ[2]	120.6	108.7	149.3	105.8	107.8	102.5	112.4
El Paso, TX	87.7	102.3	73.7	85.7	99.0	99.3	89.0
Fargo, ND	98.6	111.5	77.6	90.5	100.4	120.1	108.9
Fort Collins, CO	n/a	n/a	n/a	n/a	n/a	n/a	n/a
Fort Wayne, IN	86.9	86.7	62.3	95.7	99.5	101.5	98.6
Fort Worth, TX	94.9	92.4	88.4	107.2	96.9	101.5	96.2
Grand Rapids, MI	94.1	92.8	87.4	98.5	104.1	92.3	96.3
Greeley, CO	n/a	n/a	n/a	n/a	n/a	n/a	n/a
Green Bay, WI	91.1	91.0	77.9	97.4	97.7	101.8	96.6
Greensboro, NC	n/a	n/a	n/a	n/a	n/a	n/a	n/a
Honolulu, HI	192.9	165.0	332.6	172.3	138.2	118.8	124.2
Houston, TX	95.8	88.4	91.2	105.8	95.2	92.0	100.3
Huntsville, AL	91.3	95.1	66.6	99.0	97.3	96.4	104.7
Indianapolis, IN	92.4	94.1	78.4	105.4	97.9	90.6	98.0
Jacksonville, FL	91.7	98.4	88.0	97.7	86.0	83.7	92.7
Kansas City, MO	95.8	102.4	82.6	100.6	92.6	105.9	101.7
Lafayette, LA	88.9	101.8	72.0	88.0	104.7	88.0	93.3
Las Cruces, NM	n/a	n/a	n/a	n/a	n/a	n/a	n/a
Las Vegas, NV	103.6	95.8	118.3	98.6	114.0	100.2	94.2
Lexington, KY	92.7	89.9	83.7	95.6	96.7	78.9	100.7
Lincoln, NE	93.0	95.6	78.7	90.2	93.4	105.8	102.2
Little Rock, AR	96.0	95.1	88.1	97.4	94.7	89.6	103.2
Los Angeles, CA	146.7	116.3	230.6	106.2	134.8	110.8	112.0
Louisville, KY	94.1	91.8	79.8	94.6	98.1	105.2	103.7
Madison, WI	107.0	107.6	108.6	99.8	104.4	124.0	106.0
Manchester, NH	108.9	102.2	109.6	117.9	104.1	116.0	108.9

Table continued on following page.

Urban Area	Composite	Groceries	Housing	Utilities	Transp.	Health	Misc.
Miami, FL	115.0	110.5	144.3	102.0	101.5	100.6	102.7
Midland, TX	102.1	93.6	91.5	106.6	104.1	96.5	112.6
Milwaukee, WI	96.7	93.4	100.5	94.8	99.8	115.9	92.4
Minneapolis, MN	106.6	103.6	102.9	97.5	104.4	105.6	113.9
Nashville, TN	98.9	99.5	98.5	97.0	97.9	92.4	100.4
New Haven, CT	122.3	111.0	128.5	136.7	110.6	115.8	121.9
New Orleans, LA	105.0	102.6	125.5	81.5	101.3	115.1	96.1
New York, NY[3]	181.6	128.4	339.0	121.4	113.7	107.1	123.1
Oklahoma City, OK	86.0	93.3	69.6	95.3	86.2	95.0	92.1
Omaha, NE	92.3	96.8	83.6	99.4	98.3	96.4	93.3
Orlando, FL	92.1	100.7	85.1	97.2	89.3	88.3	94.1
Philadelphia, PA	110.9	118.7	116.5	105.6	116.1	101.8	104.8
Phoenix, AZ	99.3	99.7	103.8	109.5	107.2	90.1	91.9
Pittsburgh, PA	103.1	111.9	105.7	116.1	114.0	93.1	92.6
Portland, OR	134.7	112.4	186.4	87.1	131.0	115.6	119.4
Providence, RI	119.2	106.7	132.8	126.4	112.1	109.3	114.6
Provo, UT	98.2	93.0	96.1	84.7	100.7	94.5	105.4
Raleigh, NC	95.4	92.7	89.0	98.3	90.9	103.8	100.9
Reno, NV	114.1	118.7	125.8	85.9	126.3	113.9	107.6
Richmond, VA	94.2	89.0	86.0	97.6	86.9	106.7	102.1
Rochester, MN	n/a	n/a	n/a	n/a	n/a	n/a	n/a
Sacramento, CA	118.4	120.2	134.2	102.9	139.0	113.6	104.8
Saint Louis, MO	n/a	n/a	n/a	n/a	n/a	n/a	n/a
Salem, OR	n/a	n/a	n/a	n/a	n/a	n/a	n/a
Salt Lake City, UT	103.6	108.0	106.7	87.8	103.6	105.7	103.6
San Antonio, TX	89.5	88.0	82.2	87.6	89.1	87.2	96.5
San Diego, CA	142.1	116.1	216.3	123.2	129.2	107.3	107.3
San Francisco, CA	197.9	131.3	368.9	123.0	145.3	129.6	133.4
San Jose, CA	n/a	n/a	n/a	n/a	n/a	n/a	n/a
Santa Rosa, CA	n/a	n/a	n/a	n/a	n/a	n/a	n/a
Savannah, GA	89.5	95.7	66.2	96.0	94.9	106.1	100.0
Seattle, WA	157.5	129.1	227.6	108.0	137.8	128.6	136.2
Sioux Falls, SD	92.5	96.3	86.3	84.7	91.9	107.7	96.3
Springfield, IL	n/a	n/a	n/a	n/a	n/a	n/a	n/a
Tampa, FL	91.2	104.8	79.2	85.9	99.4	98.3	93.7
Tucson, AZ	97.5	100.5	87.9	99.9	101.1	98.7	102.0
Tulsa, OK	86.0	96.2	62.7	99.5	84.4	91.6	96.1
Tuscaloosa, AL	n/a	n/a	n/a	n/a	n/a	n/a	n/a
Virginia Beach, VA[4]	94.1	92.7	89.1	97.4	92.2	90.4	98.7
Washington, DC	159.9	116.0	277.1	117.9	110.6	95.8	118.1
Wichita, KS	91.1	94.3	69.6	99.3	95.3	96.1	102.5
Wilmington, NC	n/a	n/a	n/a	n/a	n/a	n/a	n/a
Winston-Salem, NC	90.8	101.4	66.7	94.6	92.0	119.5	100.5
Worcester, MA	n/a	n/a	n/a	n/a	n/a	n/a	n/a
U.S.	100.0	100.0	100.0	100.0	100.0	100.0	100.0

Note: The Cost of Living Index measures regional differences in the cost of consumer goods and services, excluding taxes and non-consumer expenditures, for professional and managerial households in the top income quintile. It is based on more than 50,000 prices covering almost 60 different items for which prices are collected three times a year by chambers of commerce, economic development organizations or university applied economic centers in each participating urban area. The numbers shown should be read as a percentage above or below the national average of 100. For example, a value of 115.4 in the groceries column indicates that grocery prices are 15.4% higher than the national average. Small differences in the index numbers should not be interpreted as significant. In cases where data is not available for the city, data for the metro area or for a neighboring city has been provided and noted as follows: (1) Chapel Hill NC; (2) Middlesex-Monmouth NJ; (3) Brooklyn, NY; (4) Hampton Roads-SE Virginia
Source: The Council for Community and Economic Research, Cost of Living Index, 2022

Grocery Prices

Urban Area	T-Bone Steak ($/pound)	Frying Chicken ($/pound)	Whole Milk ($/half gal.)	Eggs ($/dozen)	Orange Juice ($/64 oz.)	Coffee ($/11.5 oz.)
Albuquerque, NM	11.88	1.01	2.29	2.30	3.89	5.52
Allentown, PA	15.80	1.61	2.56	2.11	3.74	3.90
Anchorage, AK	16.43	2.25	2.85	2.16	4.61	6.29
Ann Arbor, MI	n/a	n/a	n/a	n/a	n/a	n/a
Athens, GA	n/a	n/a	n/a	n/a	n/a	n/a
Atlanta, GA	12.23	1.21	1.94	1.87	3.63	4.51
Austin, TX	11.44	1.08	2.14	2.18	3.36	4.26
Baltimore, MD	15.04	1.96	2.45	2.54	4.38	5.31
Boise City, ID	13.59	1.60	2.21	1.69	3.58	5.27
Boston, MA	n/a	n/a	n/a	n/a	n/a	n/a
Boulder, CO	n/a	n/a	n/a	n/a	n/a	n/a
Brownsville, TX	10.74	1.02	2.10	2.06	3.34	3.77
Cape Coral, FL	14.43	2.34	2.55	1.83	4.28	4.04
Cedar Rapids, IA	14.03	1.66	2.19	2.32	3.68	5.08
Charleston, SC	12.23	1.63	2.11	2.00	4.07	4.90
Charlotte, NC	13.63	1.23	2.11	2.12	3.68	5.31
Chicago, IL	n/a	n/a	n/a	n/a	n/a	n/a
Cincinnati, OH	13.66	2.66	2.15	1.68	3.92	6.05
Clarksville, TN	n/a	n/a	n/a	n/a	n/a	n/a
Cleveland, OH	16.00	2.16	1.86	2.08	3.91	4.91
College Station, TX	n/a	n/a	n/a	n/a	n/a	n/a
Colorado Springs, CO	14.09	1.35	2.17	2.04	3.53	5.14
Columbia, MO	12.00	1.39	3.08	2.51	3.99	5.68
Columbia, SC	12.03	1.56	2.36	2.02	3.66	4.95
Columbus, OH	14.20	1.44	1.93	1.99	4.00	5.76
Dallas, TX	12.76	1.26	2.34	2.12	3.60	4.62
Davenport, IA	13.66	2.17	2.57	2.18	3.81	5.91
Denver, CO	13.30	1.65	2.07	2.07	3.66	4.97
Des Moines, IA	11.66	2.33	2.79	2.40	3.41	5.05
Durham, NC[1]	13.15	1.77	1.97	2.14	4.23	5.04
Edison, NJ[2]	n/a	n/a	n/a	n/a	n/a	n/a
El Paso, TX	14.35	2.08	2.19	2.14	3.96	5.58
Fargo, ND	n/a	n/a	n/a	n/a	n/a	n/a
Fort Collins, CO	n/a	n/a	n/a	n/a	n/a	n/a
Fort Wayne, IN	12.91	1.22	2.46	1.84	3.53	4.98
Fort Worth, TX	13.46	1.51	2.16	2.25	3.40	4.73
Grand Rapids, MI	15.24	1.48	1.92	2.07	3.33	3.68
Greeley, CO	n/a	n/a	n/a	n/a	n/a	n/a
Green Bay, WI	15.09	1.55	2.25	1.74	3.86	4.01
Greensboro, NC	n/a	n/a	n/a	n/a	n/a	n/a
Honolulu, HI	18.12	2.74	4.32	4.32	5.31	8.59
Houston, TX	11.65	1.42	2.10	2.00	3.76	4.58
Huntsville, AL	14.42	1.54	2.22	2.04	3.86	5.03
Indianapolis, IN	14.69	1.70	2.12	1.99	3.50	4.75
Jacksonville, FL	13.82	1.79	2.26	2.53	3.59	4.86
Kansas City, MO	13.21	1.90	2.42	2.03	3.44	4.53
Lafayette, LA	12.53	1.49	2.57	3.19	3.66	5.04
Las Cruces, NM	13.28	1.47	2.51	2.47	3.97	5.37
Las Vegas, NV	14.35	1.87	2.51	2.43	4.05	5.47
Lexington, KY	13.65	1.26	2.02	1.80	3.65	4.54
Lincoln, NE	13.05	1.58	2.23	1.79	3.20	4.97
Little Rock, AR	12.30	1.41	2.12	2.08	3.74	3.90
Los Angeles, CA	14.79	1.77	2.76	3.66	4.20	6.21
Louisville, KY	14.49	1.35	1.51	1.48	3.61	4.28
Madison, WI	16.50	1.80	2.27	1.88	3.60	5.26

Table continued on following page.

Urban Area	T-Bone Steak ($/pound)	Frying Chicken ($/pound)	Whole Milk ($/half gal.)	Eggs ($/dozen)	Orange Juice ($/64 oz.)	Coffee ($/11.5 oz.)
Manchester, NH	16.69	1.85	2.66	2.57	4.36	5.25
Miami, FL	11.37	1.69	3.62	2.72	4.62	5.14
Midland, TX	12.66	1.09	2.11	2.23	3.77	4.78
Milwaukee, WI	15.29	1.57	2.52	2.18	3.77	4.12
Minneapolis, MN	14.32	1.95	2.28	1.83	3.78	4.69
Nashville, TN	14.63	1.68	2.33	1.83	3.95	4.92
New Haven, CT	13.03	1.44	2.84	2.53	3.81	4.79
New Orleans, LA	15.23	1.37	2.57	2.32	3.68	4.26
New York, NY[3]	16.18	1.70	2.88	2.77	4.42	4.89
Oklahoma City, OK	12.72	1.51	2.34	2.04	3.32	4.72
Omaha, NE	15.11	1.71	2.00	1.72	3.59	5.20
Orlando, FL	13.49	1.37	2.67	2.44	3.89	3.89
Philadelphia, PA	16.43	1.91	2.57	2.47	4.19	5.67
Phoenix, AZ	14.66	1.65	2.06	2.51	4.00	5.82
Pittsburgh, PA	16.67	2.16	2.50	1.93	3.90	5.33
Portland, OR	12.15	1.28	2.88	2.75	4.10	6.48
Providence, RI	15.73	1.68	2.42	2.52	3.90	3.94
Provo, UT	14.23	1.44	2.04	2.18	4.02	5.39
Raleigh, NC	11.98	1.14	1.99	1.71	4.00	3.54
Reno, NV	13.35	1.68	2.82	2.46	3.75	5.69
Richmond, VA	12.49	1.38	2.09	1.44	3.87	4.49
Rochester, MN	n/a	n/a	n/a	n/a	n/a	n/a
Sacramento, CA	12.12	1.51	3.08	3.34	4.02	5.25
Saint Louis, MO	17.61	1.85	1.97	2.17	3.66	4.65
Salem, OR	n/a	n/a	n/a	n/a	n/a	n/a
Salt Lake City, UT	13.19	1.85	2.28	2.25	4.46	5.46
San Antonio, TX	11.06	1.05	2.20	1.86	3.41	4.07
San Diego, CA	14.80	1.85	2.70	3.71	4.32	5.91
San Francisco, CA	18.36	1.95	3.38	3.83	4.48	7.00
San Jose, CA	n/a	n/a	n/a	n/a	n/a	n/a
Santa Rosa, CA	n/a	n/a	n/a	n/a	n/a	n/a
Savannah, GA	13.73	1.29	2.24	1.99	3.42	4.55
Seattle, WA	17.83	2.43	2.97	2.23	4.41	6.55
Sioux Falls, SD	12.85	1.47	2.61	2.26	3.63	5.53
Springfield, IL	14.11	2.05	1.85	1.54	3.88	4.88
Tampa, FL	12.92	1.93	2.78	2.83	4.18	4.31
Tucson, AZ	12.19	1.47	2.37	2.22	4.03	5.97
Tulsa, OK	13.52	1.46	2.57	1.97	3.57	4.66
Tuscaloosa, AL	n/a	n/a	n/a	n/a	n/a	n/a
Virginia Beach, VA[4]	12.02	1.45	2.24	1.64	3.95	3.93
Washington, DC	13.41	1.21	2.91	2.62	4.08	5.36
Wichita, KS	13.71	1.63	2.05	1.95	4.15	4.95
Wilmington, NC	n/a	n/a	n/a	n/a	n/a	n/a
Winston-Salem, NC	13.05	1.11	2.31	2.28	3.98	4.30
Worcester, MA	n/a	n/a	n/a	n/a	n/a	n/a
Average*	13.81	1.59	2.43	2.25	3.85	4.95
Minimum*	10.17	0.90	1.51	1.30	2.90	3.46
Maximum*	19.35	3.30	4.32	4.32	5.31	8.59

*Note: **T-Bone Steak** (price per pound); **Frying Chicken** (price per pound, whole fryer); **Whole Milk** (half gallon carton); **Eggs** (price per dozen, Grade A, large); **Orange Juice** (64 oz. Tropicana or Florida Natural); **Coffee** (11.5 oz. can, vacuum-packed, Maxwell House, Hills Bros, or Folgers); (*) Average, minimum, and maximum values for all 286 areas in the Cost of Living Index report; n/a not available; In cases where data is not available for the city, data for the metro area or for a neighboring city has been provided and noted as follows: (1) Chapel Hill NC; (2) Middlesex-Monmouth NJ; (3) Brooklyn, NY; (4) Hampton Roads-SE Virginia*
Source: The Council for Community and Economic Research, Cost of Living Index, 2022

Housing and Utility Costs

Urban Area	New Home Price ($)	Apartment Rent ($/month)	All Electric ($/month)	Part Electric ($/month)	Other Energy ($/month)	Telephone ($/month)
Albuquerque, NM	383,227	1,215	-	107.21	43.71	191.37
Allentown, PA	485,339	1,679	-	99.25	82.35	193.11
Anchorage, AK	656,122	1,516	-	102.07	130.31	188.62
Ann Arbor, MI	n/a	n/a	n/a	n/a	n/a	n/a
Athens, GA	n/a	n/a	n/a	n/a	n/a	n/a
Atlanta, GA	489,573	1,551	-	90.61	44.15	188.95
Austin, TX	484,044	1,807	-	101.22	51.85	196.79
Baltimore, MD	440,295	1,868	-	92.51	93.60	196.85
Boise City, ID	576,971	1,640	-	63.81	63.35	174.27
Boston, MA	n/a	n/a	n/a	n/a	n/a	n/a
Boulder, CO	n/a	n/a	n/a	n/a	n/a	n/a
Brownsville, TX	274,631	757	-	139.72	54.99	196.56
Cape Coral, FL	495,794	1,824	182.94	-	-	195.37
Cedar Rapids, IA	339,825	846	-	106.96	45.22	189.46
Charleston, SC	423,780	1,572	224.48	-	-	195.28
Charlotte, NC	377,295	1,498	155.34	-	-	184.19
Chicago, IL	n/a	n/a	n/a	n/a	n/a	n/a
Cincinnati, OH	368,833	1,083	-	76.34	81.75	184.60
Clarksville, TN	n/a	n/a	n/a	n/a	n/a	n/a
Cleveland, OH	347,809	1,302	-	89.55	82.10	188.12
College Station, TX	n/a	n/a	n/a	n/a	n/a	n/a
Colorado Springs, CO	497,622	1,512	-	104.56	85.71	186.39
Columbia, MO	442,644	861	-	96.49	65.29	194.74
Columbia, SC	322,903	1,107	-	112.85	167.25	190.68
Columbus, OH	366,506	1,200	-	88.37	72.63	184.15
Dallas, TX	439,403	1,563	-	136.69	79.10	196.79
Davenport, IA	285,682	1,014	-	88.01	57.06	198.79
Denver, CO	639,886	1,841	-	58.60	78.48	190.08
Des Moines, IA	337,128	741	-	79.63	53.25	188.32
Durham, NC[1]	582,565	1,411	-	85.31	62.68	176.30
Edison, NJ[2]	n/a	n/a	n/a	n/a	n/a	n/a
El Paso, TX	292,519	1,130	-	93.81	47.74	200.02
Fargo, ND	n/a	n/a	n/a	n/a	n/a	n/a
Fort Collins, CO	n/a	n/a	n/a	n/a	n/a	n/a
Fort Wayne, IN	296,241	1,083	-	105.04	65.35	191.60
Fort Worth, TX	372,205	1,327	-	137.89	75.49	199.27
Grand Rapids, MI	384,672	1,273	-	105.38	79.74	190.37
Greeley, CO	n/a	n/a	n/a	n/a	n/a	n/a
Green Bay, WI	382,340	881	-	83.06	80.95	186.93
Greensboro, NC	n/a	n/a	n/a	n/a	n/a	n/a
Honolulu, HI	1,605,915	3,589	309.47	-	-	182.54
Houston, TX	378,106	1,292	-	123.18	45.33	195.79
Huntsville, AL	350,811	1,023	173.74	-	-	186.08
Indianapolis, IN	340,588	1,325	-	111.24	89.87	188.71
Jacksonville, FL	385,800	1,507	187.84	-	-	196.12
Kansas City, MO	439,207	1,471	-	98.92	78.39	198.58
Lafayette, LA	284,856	1,063	-	89.62	58.12	186.23
Las Cruces, NM	364,513	926	-	95.18	40.12	192.31
Las Vegas, NV	491,447	1,600	-	121.78	57.89	196.21
Lexington, KY	351,975	982	-	90.87	109.72	189.80
Lincoln, NE	359,724	1,066	-	63.75	64.03	199.14
Little Rock, AR	395,450	946	-	81.77	91.69	204.44
Los Angeles, CA	1,098,874	3,182	-	123.99	84.34	192.21
Louisville, KY	338,400	1,315	-	90.92	105.78	184.63
Madison, WI	475,954	1,205	-	114.02	94.46	183.66

Table continued on following page.

Urban Area	New Home Price ($)	Apartment Rent ($/month)	All Electric ($/month)	Part Electric ($/month)	Other Energy ($/month)	Telephone ($/month)
Manchester, NH	441,922	2,064	-	107.51	118.35	184.25
Miami, FL	584,754	2,690	192.68	-	-	195.67
Midland, TX	366,614	927	-	121.06	40.30	195.66
Milwaukee, WI	432,791	1,481	-	104.40	98.25	186.18
Minneapolis, MN	404,076	1,318	-	102.55	74.40	188.30
Nashville, TN	483,320	1,465	-	90.92	51.95	190.02
New Haven, CT	434,014	2,127	-	166.18	115.11	186.44
New Orleans, LA	654,349	1,851	-	71.40	46.62	187.68
New York, NY[3]	1,349,755	3,727	-	106.15	87.34	195.04
Oklahoma City, OK	333,325	860	-	90.04	66.60	195.02
Omaha, NE	350,853	1,290	-	92.74	60.25	198.80
Orlando, FL	448,493	1,766	154.33	-	-	192.14
Philadelphia, PA	430,067	1,542	-	105.62	103.27	196.34
Phoenix, AZ	497,561	2,083	187.70	-	-	185.99
Pittsburgh, PA	418,872	1,281	-	118.68	149.99	194.84
Portland, OR	661,664	2,636	-	80.74	76.64	181.33
Providence, RI	462,061	2,085	-	132.22	119.10	193.25
Provo, UT	532,268	1,449	-	67.96	72.66	194.35
Raleigh, NC	400,445	1,614	-	112.40	74.47	184.19
Reno, NV	576,610	1,515	-	97.93	44.46	185.65
Richmond, VA	383,637	1,334	-	95.49	99.23	182.67
Rochester, MN	n/a	n/a	n/a	n/a	n/a	n/a
Sacramento, CA	582,334	2,402	-	152.89	43.30	189.21
Saint Louis, MO	339,758	981	-	80.89	68.47	201.40
Salem, OR	n/a	n/a	n/a	n/a	n/a	n/a
Salt Lake City, UT	575,689	1,609	-	77.74	74.42	194.94
San Antonio, TX	327,632	1,388	-	99.94	37.03	198.89
San Diego, CA	1,001,748	3,057	-	145.75	74.47	183.97
San Francisco, CA	1,502,557	3,585	-	172.31	95.33	201.38
San Jose, CA	n/a	n/a	n/a	n/a	n/a	n/a
Santa Rosa, CA	n/a	n/a	n/a	n/a	n/a	n/a
Savannah, GA	297,041	1,176	158.44	-	-	186.50
Seattle, WA	940,665	3,031	188.83	-	-	198.78
Sioux Falls, SD	450,933	1,111	-	84.19	47.87	182.72
Springfield, IL	408,667	1,152	-	91.51	94.77	185.67
Tampa, FL	414,223	1,528	167.09	-	-	192.89
Tucson, AZ	481,931	1,410	-	103.78	69.05	186.26
Tulsa, OK	313,413	852	-	90.90	68.43	190.79
Tuscaloosa, AL	n/a	n/a	n/a	n/a	n/a	n/a
Virginia Beach, VA[4]	395,804	1,258	-	98.78	95.60	184.73
Washington, DC	1,156,418	3,220	-	117.06	100.23	188.98
Wichita, KS	314,516	978	-	93.16	71.97	198.70
Wilmington, NC	n/a	n/a	n/a	n/a	n/a	n/a
Winston-Salem, NC	319,961	1,290	157.68	-	-	180.76
Worcester, MA	n/a	n/a	n/a	n/a	n/a	n/a
Average*	450,913	1,371	176.41	99.93	76.96	190.22
Minimum*	229,283	546	100.84	31.56	27.15	174.27
Maximum*	2,434,977	4,569	356.86	249.59	272.24	208.31

Note: **New Home Price** (2,400 sf living area, 8,000 sf lot, in urban area with full utilities); **Apartment Rent** (950 sf 2 bedroom/1.5 or 2 bath, unfurnished, excluding all utilities except water); **All Electric** (average monthly cost for an all-electric home); **Part Electric** (average monthly cost for a part-electric home); **Other Energy** (average monthly cost for natural gas, fuel oil, coal, wood, and any other forms of energy except electricity); **Telephone** (price includes the base monthly rate plus taxes and fees for three lines of mobile phone service); (*) Average, minimum, and maximum values for all 286 areas in the Cost of Living Index report; n/a not available; In cases where data is not available for the city, data for the metro area or for a neighboring city has been provided and noted as follows: (1) Chapel Hill NC; (2) Middlesex-Monmouth NJ; (3) Brooklyn, NY; (4) Hampton Roads-SE Virginia
Source: The Council for Community and Economic Research, Cost of Living Index, 2022

Health Care, Transportation, and Other Costs

Urban Area	Doctor ($/visit)	Dentist ($/visit)	Optometrist ($/visit)	Gasoline ($/gallon)	Beauty Salon ($/visit)	Men's Shirt ($)
Albuquerque, NM	114.36	105.38	123.65	3.81	45.00	29.72
Allentown, PA	107.20	115.92	108.43	4.12	53.07	35.54
Anchorage, AK	228.37	152.08	252.89	4.49	55.00	34.08
Ann Arbor, MI	n/a	n/a	n/a	n/a	n/a	n/a
Athens, GA	n/a	n/a	n/a	n/a	n/a	n/a
Atlanta, GA	115.86	132.58	128.60	3.87	51.09	40.24
Austin, TX	122.17	119.14	118.78	3.47	52.91	34.72
Baltimore, MD	80.00	115.58	87.78	3.67	56.91	27.22
Boise City, ID	140.88	86.46	138.00	4.43	39.00	43.44
Boston, MA	n/a	n/a	n/a	n/a	n/a	n/a
Boulder, CO	n/a	n/a	n/a	n/a	n/a	n/a
Brownsville, TX	90.00	91.61	73.32	3.46	23.67	13.19
Cape Coral, FL	127.67	112.88	96.64	3.86	50.60	29.74
Cedar Rapids, IA	139.68	101.88	94.68	3.84	34.39	26.11
Charleston, SC	146.94	92.17	71.32	3.61	59.17	37.27
Charlotte, NC	140.33	135.13	125.78	3.68	31.70	49.35
Chicago, IL	n/a	n/a	n/a	n/a	n/a	n/a
Cincinnati, OH	142.44	100.47	107.60	4.01	43.10	45.33
Clarksville, TN	n/a	n/a	n/a	n/a	n/a	n/a
Cleveland, OH	113.00	109.47	94.21	3.86	35.71	41.99
College Station, TX	n/a	n/a	n/a	n/a	n/a	n/a
Colorado Springs, CO	134.96	108.29	123.36	3.96	47.60	44.38
Columbia, MO	125.84	92.11	110.19	3.84	43.33	29.87
Columbia, SC	124.17	82.50	53.00	3.26	42.36	37.12
Columbus, OH	118.38	87.19	61.70	3.77	42.53	38.24
Dallas, TX	141.13	129.77	139.62	3.39	64.32	38.33
Davenport, IA	136.67	84.83	102.07	3.46	34.89	37.75
Denver, CO	106.00	118.21	115.00	3.72	47.09	35.52
Des Moines, IA	131.59	90.21	119.28	3.34	39.44	39.61
Durham, NC[1]	143.27	113.91	132.86	3.70	53.11	22.22
Edison, NJ[2]	n/a	n/a	n/a	n/a	n/a	n/a
El Paso, TX	146.74	84.59	98.23	3.61	28.33	30.52
Fargo, ND	n/a	n/a	n/a	n/a	n/a	n/a
Fort Collins, CO	n/a	n/a	n/a	n/a	n/a	n/a
Fort Wayne, IN	140.00	105.42	88.55	3.70	34.67	39.66
Fort Worth, TX	92.61	96.41	111.17	3.58	55.08	32.87
Grand Rapids, MI	104.35	109.29	109.72	4.13	36.00	26.03
Greeley, CO	n/a	n/a	n/a	n/a	n/a	n/a
Green Bay, WI	152.75	98.67	75.78	3.45	27.46	26.90
Greensboro, NC	n/a	n/a	n/a	n/a	n/a	n/a
Honolulu, HI	168.32	97.93	209.95	5.03	75.67	53.63
Houston, TX	99.00	115.42	103.21	3.53	64.48	26.78
Huntsville, AL	124.50	99.17	88.78	3.55	49.33	33.22
Indianapolis, IN	97.22	99.33	68.63	3.65	39.23	42.46
Jacksonville, FL	90.43	93.90	72.66	3.68	63.00	25.84
Kansas City, MO	90.64	101.00	89.60	3.40	33.07	36.41
Lafayette, LA	109.56	100.77	100.99	3.43	43.28	30.76
Las Cruces, NM	114.46	118.68	146.98	3.89	41.11	36.87
Las Vegas, NV	108.58	98.81	101.71	4.55	46.52	20.35
Lexington, KY	97.28	98.17	80.03	3.78	58.71	52.93
Lincoln, NE	157.42	104.71	103.26	3.64	38.48	50.37
Little Rock, AR	116.78	58.25	94.06	3.52	52.55	37.55
Los Angeles, CA	130.00	128.20	132.27	5.54	82.67	36.49
Louisville, KY	82.50	87.22	61.89	4.13	84.44	45.50
Madison, WI	207.78	115.45	65.67	3.59	54.45	43.08

Table continued on following page.

Urban Area	Doctor ($/visit)	Dentist ($/visit)	Optometrist ($/visit)	Gasoline ($/gallon)	Beauty Salon ($/visit)	Men's Shirt ($)
Manchester, NH	175.70	152.18	115.00	4.03	59.17	41.12
Miami, FL	109.83	94.65	100.82	3.81	80.15	24.94
Midland, TX	118.20	107.50	108.50	3.51	45.00	25.17
Milwaukee, WI	181.86	123.58	75.00	3.66	37.70	33.64
Minneapolis, MN	161.06	88.15	100.90	3.94	37.88	35.74
Nashville, TN	106.23	100.08	86.77	3.57	41.35	27.39
New Haven, CT	146.79	125.96	131.33	4.04	46.14	28.74
New Orleans, LA	168.89	125.56	105.55	3.92	42.78	39.00
New York, NY[3]	124.61	125.08	113.20	4.34	68.52	42.89
Oklahoma City, OK	111.16	120.92	115.53	3.36	43.00	21.10
Omaha, NE	140.67	89.91	120.78	3.75	30.74	28.27
Orlando, FL	98.00	108.72	79.50	3.83	60.44	45.42
Philadelphia, PA	136.17	96.17	118.67	4.19	63.11	34.67
Phoenix, AZ	99.00	99.00	117.08	4.30	50.83	19.04
Pittsburgh, PA	98.25	112.80	96.58	3.99	37.03	20.62
Portland, OR	142.04	113.83	122.48	4.72	56.61	32.88
Providence, RI	143.54	117.33	120.06	3.98	51.00	34.08
Provo, UT	105.44	95.74	116.76	4.24	40.94	46.89
Raleigh, NC	121.09	115.41	113.39	3.86	50.42	26.62
Reno, NV	124.83	110.67	109.50	4.63	36.67	21.59
Richmond, VA	145.32	104.74	115.73	3.61	49.08	29.41
Rochester, MN	n/a	n/a	n/a	n/a	n/a	n/a
Sacramento, CA	176.26	109.67	149.00	5.48	57.08	33.30
Saint Louis, MO	86.89	101.96	85.05	3.81	39.83	21.57
Salem, OR	n/a	n/a	n/a	n/a	n/a	n/a
Salt Lake City, UT	114.47	93.33	109.59	4.14	39.28	46.00
San Antonio, TX	123.35	111.47	125.52	3.43	58.84	35.83
San Diego, CA	116.25	118.33	126.18	5.50	66.33	36.49
San Francisco, CA	174.07	148.07	154.96	5.42	85.61	50.77
San Jose, CA	n/a	n/a	n/a	n/a	n/a	n/a
Santa Rosa, CA	n/a	n/a	n/a	n/a	n/a	n/a
Savannah, GA	119.64	141.34	89.22	3.40	37.92	35.96
Seattle, WA	176.92	144.83	170.85	4.95	65.43	43.45
Sioux Falls, SD	164.33	103.08	126.50	3.57	33.33	24.13
Springfield, IL	120.00	103.33	123.00	3.95	28.33	17.09
Tampa, FL	100.17	104.90	106.73	3.80	31.35	28.97
Tucson, AZ	140.00	101.33	108.10	4.09	39.50	37.99
Tulsa, OK	126.65	101.50	105.72	3.23	43.68	29.27
Tuscaloosa, AL	n/a	n/a	n/a	n/a	n/a	n/a
Virginia Beach, VA[4]	88.07	115.80	111.36	3.72	40.74	32.74
Washington, DC	129.71	105.20	75.00	3.98	81.00	37.83
Wichita, KS	106.36	92.39	162.06	3.75	41.30	51.01
Wilmington, NC	n/a	n/a	n/a	n/a	n/a	n/a
Winston-Salem, NC	142.38	133.67	132.58	3.71	45.00	35.83
Worcester, MA	n/a	n/a	n/a	n/a	n/a	n/a
Average*	124.91	107.77	117.66	3.86	43.31	34.21
Minimum*	36.61	58.25	51.79	2.90	22.18	13.05
Maximum*	250.21	162.58	371.96	5.54	85.61	63.54

Note: **Doctor** (general practitioners routine exam of an established patient); **Dentist** (adult teeth cleaning and periodic oral examination); **Optometrist** (full vision eye exam for established adult patient); **Gasoline** (one gallon regular unleaded, national brand, including all taxes, cash price at self-service pump if available); **Beauty Salon** (woman's shampoo, trim, and blow-dry); **Men's Shirt** (cotton/polyester dress shirt, pinpoint weave, long sleeves); (*) Average, minimum, and maximum values for all 286 areas in the Cost of Living Index report; n/a not available; In cases where data is not available for the city, data for the metro area or for a neighboring city has been provided and noted as follows: (1) Chapel Hill NC; (2) Middlesex-Monmouth NJ; (3) Brooklyn, NY; (4) Hampton Roads-SE Virginia
Source: The Council for Community and Economic Research, Cost of Living Index, 2022

Number of Medical Professionals

City	Area Covered	MDs[1]	DOs[1,2]	Dentists	Podiatrists	Chiropractors	Optometrists
Albuquerque, NM	Bernalillo County	472.2	22.0	87.6	8.9	25.1	16.3
Allentown, PA	Lehigh County	359.4	84.6	88.1	12.5	28.8	20.8
Anchorage, AK	Anchorage Borough	383.0	45.1	130.5	5.6	64.2	31.2
Ann Arbor, MI	Washtenaw County	1,319.8	42.2	198.4	7.9	26.8	18.4
Athens, GA	Clarke County	326.1	16.3	52.1	4.7	22.5	15.5
Atlanta, GA	Fulton County	536.7	14.7	74.5	5.3	58.4	19.8
Austin, TX	Travis County	327.2	18.8	74.5	4.5	35.0	17.9
Baltimore, MD	Baltimore City	1,113.1	23.8	82.9	8.3	14.9	16.0
Boise City, ID	Ada County	283.7	33.7	81.1	3.9	53.3	20.7
Boston, MA	Suffolk County	1,576.4	17.2	235.9	9.9	15.7	36.8
Boulder, CO	Boulder County	361.2	31.7	107.7	6.1	82.8	27.9
Brownsville, TX	Cameron County	140.1	7.1	31.4	3.1	7.8	6.6
Cape Coral, FL	Lee County	203.1	31.1	53.7	8.1	27.9	13.2
Cedar Rapids, IA	Linn County	182.0	23.5	74.3	7.9	58.5	17.5
Charleston, SC	Charleston County	831.9	31.3	113.3	5.8	52.1	24.5
Charlotte, NC	Mecklenburg County	343.0	16.9	72.0	3.7	35.2	14.5
Chicago, IL	Cook County	434.1	22.5	95.4	12.6	29.2	21.1
Cincinnati, OH	Hamilton County	614.9	25.9	76.1	10.2	20.5	22.8
Clarksville, TN	Montgomery County	97.7	16.3	43.0	2.2	12.3	11.8
Cleveland, OH	Cuyahoga County	715.5	51.1	110.1	18.9	19.1	17.3
College Station, TX	Brazos County	270.8	16.2	55.3	3.4	17.7	16.5
Colorado Springs, CO	El Paso County	207.1	31.6	104.2	5.3	45.4	25.1
Columbia, MO	Boone County	808.6	57.6	71.6	5.4	38.2	28.5
Columbia, SC	Richland County	357.2	15.4	93.7	7.2	22.5	19.8
Columbus, OH	Franklin County	442.5	62.5	93.6	7.6	25.4	28.6
Dallas, TX	Dallas County	357.1	21.3	93.4	4.3	37.6	14.7
Davenport, IA	Scott County	240.7	53.3	81.0	4.6	184.3	17.2
Denver, CO	Denver County	611.2	31.8	81.0	6.5	39.4	16.9
Des Moines, IA	Polk County	215.9	99.2	77.3	11.3	59.4	21.7
Durham, NC	Durham County	1,130.5	16.3	75.4	4.3	19.9	14.1
Edison, NJ	Middlesex County	377.3	20.2	88.4	9.9	24.9	20.0
El Paso, TX	El Paso County	204.1	13.3	47.4	3.9	9.1	10.4
Fargo, ND	Cass County	404.1	21.1	82.5	4.3	75.6	32.7
Fort Collins, CO	Larimer County	251.3	31.4	83.6	6.1	56.8	21.2
Fort Wayne, IN	Allen County	263.0	29.3	66.9	5.9	23.4	26.0
Fort Worth, TX	Tarrant County	190.1	33.9	62.9	4.5	29.2	16.6
Grand Rapids, MI	Kent County	358.3	69.8	76.9	5.0	39.2	25.4
Greeley, CO	Weld County	126.4	18.1	46.2	2.1	23.2	12.9
Green Bay, WI	Brown County	253.8	27.9	80.9	3.0	49.7	18.5
Greensboro, NC	Guilford County	257.0	14.8	60.5	4.8	14.4	10.3
Honolulu, HI	Honolulu County	351.4	16.2	97.1	3.6	20.4	24.8
Houston, TX	Harris County	348.8	12.3	73.7	4.9	23.1	21.2
Huntsville, AL	Madison County	274.6	13.3	51.6	3.3	23.5	19.0
Indianapolis, IN	Marion County	451.2	21.7	92.0	6.4	16.8	20.9
Jacksonville, FL	Duval County	341.1	22.8	79.5	7.1	25.9	15.9
Kansas City, MO	Jackson County	314.4	59.1	91.9	6.4	47.6	20.2
Lafayette, LA	Lafayette Parish	377.7	11.6	71.7	3.7	32.8	14.3
Las Cruces, NM	Dona Ana County	166.0	13.6	59.1	6.3	18.5	8.6
Las Vegas, NV	Clark County	182.9	36.0	65.4	4.5	20.5	14.1
Lexington, KY	Fayette County	764.3	38.2	146.7	7.8	24.5	26.4
Lincoln, NE	Lancaster County	223.6	13.0	102.6	5.5	47.1	21.3
Little Rock, AR	Pulaski County	743.0	15.3	77.7	4.8	22.1	21.9
Los Angeles, CA	Los Angeles County	315.0	14.6	94.2	6.5	30.7	19.7
Louisville, KY	Jefferson County	480.0	18.7	104.9	8.1	27.8	16.6
Madison, WI	Dane County	615.0	20.6	73.4	4.8	45.0	20.9
Manchester, NH	Hillsborough County	240.8	24.4	82.8	5.7	26.2	21.9

Table continued on following page.

City	Area Covered	MDs[1]	DOs[1,2]	Dentists	Podiatrists	Chiropractors	Optometrists
Miami, FL	Miami-Dade County	375.0	18.6	75.2	10.2	19.4	15.6
Midland, TX	Midland County	157.4	7.6	63.7	2.4	13.1	12.5
Milwaukee, WI	Milwaukee County	388.3	22.2	88.0	7.1	21.1	11.5
Minneapolis, MN	Hennepin County	532.0	24.0	103.5	5.2	77.1	21.6
Nashville, TN	Davidson County	647.1	14.1	81.0	5.3	26.8	17.5
New Haven, CT	New Haven County	577.3	10.3	77.7	9.6	27.2	16.6
New Orleans, LA	Orleans Parish	887.3	24.0	81.2	4.2	10.1	8.2
New York, NY	New York City	471.8	16.8	87.4	13.4	16.3	18.2
Oklahoma City, OK	Oklahoma County	423.1	43.0	109.1	5.3	28.9	20.5
Omaha, NE	Douglas County	547.3	26.0	101.4	5.0	42.2	21.7
Orlando, FL	Orange County	323.9	23.6	51.7	3.8	28.7	13.2
Philadelphia, PA	Philadelphia County	587.8	43.6	81.6	16.8	15.4	19.0
Phoenix, AZ	Maricopa County	255.3	33.2	71.1	7.0	33.9	16.7
Pittsburgh, PA	Allegheny County	640.1	44.3	97.1	9.2	44.0	20.7
Portland, OR	Multnomah County	646.7	32.2	101.6	5.1	76.3	24.8
Providence, RI	Providence County	489.8	17.1	58.3	9.7	21.1	21.6
Provo, UT	Utah County	119.4	20.8	59.3	4.7	26.4	11.7
Raleigh, NC	Wake County	289.4	12.4	72.7	3.7	28.3	16.8
Reno, NV	Washoe County	298.1	20.5	69.5	3.9	29.0	23.9
Richmond, VA	Richmond City	777.8	27.8	150.5	11.9	7.5	16.8
Rochester, MN	Olmsted County	2,470.7	46.0	125.4	6.7	44.1	22.6
Sacramento, CA	Sacramento County	329.3	16.6	80.7	4.6	21.8	18.4
St. Louis, MO	St. Louis City	1,222.5	35.3	63.1	4.8	21.1	19.4
Salem, OR	Marion County	182.0	15.0	84.4	5.8	34.0	16.4
Salt Lake City, UT	Salt Lake County	387.4	18.7	79.5	6.4	28.2	14.1
San Antonio, TX	Bexar County	329.0	18.9	94.2	5.4	17.2	18.9
San Diego, CA	San Diego County	346.3	19.7	96.3	4.7	35.5	20.4
San Francisco, CA	San Francisco County	834.7	13.1	171.0	11.8	43.1	31.8
San Jose, CA	Santa Clara County	445.9	12.0	124.2	6.9	45.0	28.8
Santa Rosa, CA	Sonoma County	284.4	19.0	96.7	7.4	43.0	18.3
Savannah, GA	Chatham County	352.3	19.0	68.5	6.7	20.2	13.8
Seattle, WA	King County	502.8	16.6	113.5	6.3	47.7	22.8
Sioux Falls, SD	Minnehaha County	369.1	23.8	56.1	5.5	58.1	19.0
Springfield, IL	Sangamon County	644.3	24.0	86.3	5.6	39.0	21.6
Tampa, FL	Hillsborough County	366.3	31.8	61.6	6.0	27.7	15.0
Tucson, AZ	Pima County	372.3	24.5	67.2	5.9	19.2	17.0
Tulsa, OK	Tulsa County	264.3	111.5	70.3	4.3	38.8	23.6
Tuscaloosa, AL	Tuscaloosa County	223.2	9.2	44.9	4.0	18.9	15.9
Virginia Beach, VA	Virginia Beach City	259.3	14.6	80.6	6.6	26.2	17.3
Washington, DC	District of Columbia	817.4	19.0	128.8	9.6	10.4	14.0
Wichita, KS	Sedgwick County	252.9	34.0	69.1	1.9	43.3	29.0
Wilmington, NC	New Hanover County	359.2	30.5	82.1	8.7	36.7	24.9
Winston-Salem, NC	Forsyth County	680.1	29.8	65.6	6.0	17.6	18.4
Worcester, MA	Worcester County	360.6	19.0	75.4	6.6	19.8	18.9
U.S.	U.S.	289.3	23.5	72.5	6.2	28.7	17.4

Note: All figures are rates per 100,000 population; Data as of 2021 unless noted; (1) Data as of 2020 and includes all active, non-federal physicians; (2) Doctor of Osteopathic Medicine
Source: U.S. Department of Health and Human Services, Health Resources and Services Administration, Bureau of Health Professions, Area Resource File (ARF) 2021-2022

Health Insurance Coverage: City

City	With Health Insurance	With Private Health Insurance	With Public Health Insurance	Without Health Insurance	Population Under Age 19 Without Health Insurance
Albuquerque, NM	92.1	60.6	44.2	7.9	4.3
Allentown, PA	88.6	46.4	50.2	11.4	4.7
Anchorage, AK	89.5	69.7	32.7	10.5	7.6
Ann Arbor, MI	97.4	87.5	20.3	2.6	1.3
Athens, GA	87.5	70.8	25.1	12.5	9.1
Atlanta, GA	89.4	70.1	27.0	10.6	6.2
Austin, TX	87.2	74.3	20.3	12.8	7.9
Baltimore, MD	94.1	59.3	45.9	5.9	3.4
Boise City, ID	92.1	75.5	28.2	7.9	4.2
Boston, MA	96.6	68.6	35.9	3.4	1.7
Boulder, CO	96.0	83.6	21.0	4.0	1.1
Brownsville, TX	69.2	37.3	35.7	30.8	18.5
Cape Coral, FL	87.2	64.4	38.6	12.8	10.1
Cedar Rapids, IA	95.2	73.2	34.4	4.8	2.2
Charleston, SC	93.2	79.8	25.0	6.8	2.4
Charlotte, NC	87.2	68.2	26.4	12.8	7.7
Chicago, IL	90.2	61.6	35.5	9.8	3.6
Cincinnati, OH	92.7	60.4	40.5	7.3	5.2
Clarksville, TN	91.5	71.6	34.9	8.5	3.5
Cleveland, OH	92.5	44.5	56.6	7.5	3.3
College Station, TX	91.3	84.1	14.3	8.7	5.6
Colorado Springs, CO	92.1	69.2	36.4	7.9	4.6
Columbia, MO	92.5	80.0	22.1	7.5	3.8
Columbia, SC	91.4	70.7	30.7	8.6	3.4
Columbus, OH	90.7	63.4	34.7	9.3	5.6
Dallas, TX	76.5	53.3	29.3	23.5	16.0
Davenport, IA	93.3	66.2	39.9	6.7	4.9
Denver, CO	90.4	66.9	31.3	9.6	5.5
Des Moines, IA	93.7	63.7	42.0	6.3	2.2
Durham, NC	88.1	69.6	27.9	11.9	7.7
Edison, NJ	95.2	80.5	23.8	4.8	1.9
El Paso, TX	80.0	54.6	33.9	20.0	10.2
Fargo, ND	93.8	79.9	25.1	6.2	3.8
Fort Collins, CO	93.9	78.5	23.9	6.1	5.1
Fort Wayne, IN	90.8	64.6	37.0	9.2	6.2
Fort Worth, TX	81.2	61.1	26.9	18.8	12.5
Grand Rapids, MI	91.6	63.6	37.7	8.4	4.9
Greeley, CO	90.2	60.8	40.2	9.8	5.1
Green Bay, WI	91.7	64.2	36.7	8.3	5.5
Greensboro, NC	90.3	66.3	34.1	9.7	4.1
Honolulu, HI	96.0	76.9	36.2	4.0	1.9
Houston, TX	76.2	51.7	30.5	23.8	14.5
Huntsville, AL	90.1	72.6	33.3	9.9	3.9
Indianapolis, IN	90.2	62.4	37.4	9.8	6.3
Jacksonville, FL	87.9	64.4	34.2	12.1	6.9
Kansas City, MO	88.2	68.9	28.9	11.8	6.9
Lafayette, LA	91.5	64.4	38.6	8.5	4.0
Las Cruces, NM	92.0	54.9	50.8	8.0	2.2
Las Vegas, NV	87.1	60.7	36.0	12.9	8.6
Lexington, KY	93.2	70.9	33.1	6.8	3.1
Lincoln, NE	92.6	77.1	26.4	7.4	4.9
Little Rock, AR	91.3	63.9	38.7	8.7	4.4
Los Angeles, CA	89.3	55.1	40.8	10.7	3.8
Louisville, KY	94.4	66.2	41.2	5.6	3.4
Madison, WI	96.0	82.9	23.3	4.0	2.4

Table continued on following page.

City	With Health Insurance	With Private Health Insurance	With Public Health Insurance	Without Health Insurance	Population Under Age 19 Without Health Insurance
Manchester, NH	90.9	65.9	35.1	9.1	3.8
Miami, FL	81.0	49.9	34.5	19.0	8.1
Midland, TX	83.5	69.9	20.7	16.5	14.2
Milwaukee, WI	90.6	54.1	44.8	9.4	3.5
Minneapolis, MN	93.9	68.8	33.0	6.1	3.1
Nashville, TN	87.6	68.7	29.3	12.4	8.2
New Haven, CT	92.2	51.9	46.3	7.8	3.1
New Orleans, LA	91.2	54.1	45.3	8.8	5.0
New York, NY	93.1	58.8	43.6	6.9	2.4
Oklahoma City, OK	85.6	64.7	32.3	14.4	7.5
Omaha, NE	89.7	70.8	28.7	10.3	7.0
Orlando, FL	84.9	64.3	27.5	15.1	8.9
Philadelphia, PA	92.6	57.7	45.8	7.4	4.1
Phoenix, AZ	85.5	57.9	35.0	14.5	10.0
Pittsburgh, PA	94.5	73.0	33.7	5.5	3.9
Portland, OR	93.9	72.1	31.8	6.1	2.3
Providence, RI	93.2	55.8	45.4	6.8	3.9
Provo, UT	89.3	78.1	17.5	10.7	10.8
Raleigh, NC	89.6	74.3	24.5	10.4	6.1
Reno, NV	90.0	69.1	30.5	10.0	8.4
Richmond, VA	89.3	63.7	35.5	10.7	6.9
Rochester, MN	96.2	79.1	30.9	3.8	2.0
Sacramento, CA	94.3	64.2	40.8	5.7	2.4
St. Louis, MO	89.5	62.6	35.2	10.5	4.3
Salem, OR	92.9	64.7	41.5	7.1	2.1
Salt Lake City, UT	88.9	74.0	22.7	11.1	9.9
San Antonio, TX	82.8	58.9	33.4	17.2	9.2
San Diego, CA	92.8	71.1	31.1	7.2	3.7
San Francisco, CA	96.4	76.2	29.5	3.6	1.9
San Jose, CA	94.9	72.9	29.9	5.1	2.1
Santa Rosa, CA	92.4	68.5	36.9	7.6	5.5
Savannah, GA	84.3	58.4	35.4	15.7	7.7
Seattle, WA	95.6	80.7	23.5	4.4	1.5
Sioux Falls, SD	92.0	77.5	26.1	8.0	5.2
Springfield, IL	95.7	69.7	41.8	4.3	1.4
Tampa, FL	88.9	63.5	33.0	11.1	5.1
Tucson, AZ	88.7	57.2	42.3	11.3	7.6
Tulsa, OK	83.3	58.7	35.8	16.7	8.7
Tuscaloosa, AL	92.1	70.9	32.9	7.9	2.3
Virginia Beach, VA	92.9	79.8	27.6	7.1	4.3
Washington, DC	96.6	71.9	34.7	3.4	2.2
Wichita, KS	87.8	65.8	33.6	12.2	5.8
Wilmington, NC	88.9	70.3	32.6	11.1	6.5
Winston-Salem, NC	87.7	62.3	36.6	12.3	4.5
Worcester, MA	97.0	61.1	46.4	3.0	1.5
U.S.	91.2	67.8	35.4	8.8	5.3

Note: Figures are percentages that cover the civilian noninstitutionalized population
Source: U.S. Census Bureau, 2017-2021 American Community Survey 5-Year Estimates

Health Insurance Coverage: Metro Area

Metro Area	With Health Insurance	With Private Health Insurance	With Public Health Insurance	Without Health Insurance	Population Under Age 19 Without Health Insurance
Albuquerque, NM	92.0	60.1	45.5	8.0	4.7
Allentown, PA	94.6	72.8	35.7	5.4	2.9
Anchorage, AK	88.6	68.1	33.5	11.4	9.0
Ann Arbor, MI	96.6	82.5	27.2	3.4	1.8
Athens, GA	88.1	70.2	27.8	11.9	7.0
Atlanta, GA	87.4	69.4	27.2	12.6	7.9
Austin, TX	87.7	75.1	21.7	12.3	8.1
Baltimore, MD	95.2	75.1	33.7	4.8	3.2
Boise City, ID	90.5	72.3	30.7	9.5	5.4
Boston, MA	97.0	76.8	32.6	3.0	1.6
Boulder, CO	95.4	79.9	26.0	4.6	2.3
Brownsville, TX	71.5	38.4	38.3	28.5	17.1
Cape Coral, FL	86.9	61.9	43.5	13.1	9.8
Cedar Rapids, IA	96.2	75.9	33.5	3.8	1.8
Charleston, SC	89.7	71.5	31.4	10.3	6.7
Charlotte, NC	89.7	70.1	29.6	10.3	5.5
Chicago, IL	92.4	70.5	31.6	7.6	3.3
Cincinnati, OH	94.6	72.7	33.0	5.4	3.5
Clarksville, TN	91.6	69.8	36.8	8.4	5.6
Cleveland, OH	94.6	68.7	38.7	5.4	3.4
College Station, TX	87.5	73.3	23.8	12.5	8.4
Colorado Springs, CO	92.7	71.3	35.4	7.3	4.7
Columbia, MO	92.4	78.6	25.0	7.6	4.7
Columbia, SC	90.4	69.8	34.4	9.6	4.5
Columbus, OH	93.0	71.1	31.8	7.0	4.5
Dallas, TX	83.4	66.4	24.5	16.6	11.7
Davenport, IA	94.5	71.5	37.8	5.5	3.5
Denver, CO	92.2	72.6	29.1	7.8	4.7
Des Moines, IA	95.7	76.3	31.8	4.3	2.2
Durham, NC	90.0	71.8	30.0	10.0	5.7
Edison, NJ	93.2	67.3	36.5	6.8	3.0
El Paso, TX	78.7	52.8	33.7	21.3	10.9
Fargo, ND	94.5	80.8	25.2	5.5	4.4
Fort Collins, CO	94.0	76.6	28.9	6.0	4.4
Fort Wayne, IN	91.9	69.8	33.3	8.1	6.1
Fort Worth, TX	83.4	66.4	24.5	16.6	11.7
Grand Rapids, MI	95.0	76.1	31.3	5.0	3.0
Greeley, CO	91.2	68.7	32.3	8.8	4.7
Green Bay, WI	94.9	74.8	31.6	5.1	3.7
Greensboro, NC	89.9	64.9	36.0	10.1	4.5
Honolulu, HI	96.5	79.2	34.3	3.5	2.3
Houston, TX	81.3	61.6	26.6	18.7	12.3
Huntsville, AL	91.9	77.2	29.5	8.1	3.1
Indianapolis, IN	92.4	71.4	31.8	7.6	5.2
Jacksonville, FL	89.3	68.7	33.1	10.7	6.7
Kansas City, MO	90.9	74.8	27.2	9.1	5.6
Lafayette, LA	91.9	61.3	41.3	8.1	3.5
Las Cruces, NM	89.4	48.3	52.6	10.6	4.8
Las Vegas, NV	88.1	63.3	34.7	11.9	8.0
Lexington, KY	93.9	71.2	34.6	6.1	3.4
Lincoln, NE	93.1	78.1	26.2	6.9	4.7
Little Rock, AR	92.3	66.2	39.1	7.7	4.3
Los Angeles, CA	91.4	61.2	37.6	8.6	3.6
Louisville, KY	94.6	70.7	37.3	5.4	3.5
Madison, WI	96.1	83.0	25.6	3.9	2.4

Table continued on following page.

Metro Area	With Health Insurance	With Private Health Insurance	With Public Health Insurance	Without Health Insurance	Population Under Age 19 Without Health Insurance
Manchester, NH	93.8	77.2	28.7	6.2	3.4
Miami, FL	85.3	59.9	33.0	14.7	8.3
Midland, TX	84.0	69.8	21.3	16.0	13.0
Milwaukee, WI	94.3	71.8	34.1	5.7	2.8
Minneapolis, MN	95.7	77.9	29.9	4.3	2.8
Nashville, TN	90.5	72.7	28.4	9.5	5.7
New Haven, CT	94.9	66.9	39.6	5.1	2.5
New Orleans, LA	91.2	58.8	42.8	8.8	4.5
New York, NY	93.2	67.3	36.5	6.8	3.0
Oklahoma City, OK	87.4	68.4	31.5	12.6	6.9
Omaha, NE	92.3	75.4	27.6	7.7	5.0
Orlando, FL	87.8	65.8	31.3	12.2	6.8
Philadelphia, PA	94.7	73.0	34.8	5.3	3.2
Phoenix, AZ	89.2	65.8	34.2	10.8	8.6
Pittsburgh, PA	96.3	76.2	36.5	3.7	1.9
Portland, OR	93.9	73.0	32.9	6.1	3.1
Providence, RI	96.0	70.2	39.4	4.0	2.2
Provo, UT	92.2	82.4	17.0	7.8	6.2
Raleigh, NC	90.9	75.9	25.2	9.1	5.2
Reno, NV	90.2	69.8	31.2	9.8	7.8
Richmond, VA	92.5	74.5	31.1	7.5	4.7
Rochester, MN	95.7	79.6	30.8	4.3	3.3
Sacramento, CA	95.1	70.1	38.0	4.9	2.6
St. Louis, MO	93.7	74.5	30.5	6.3	3.4
Salem, OR	92.2	63.8	41.9	7.8	3.1
Salt Lake City, UT	90.2	77.7	20.2	9.8	8.2
San Antonio, TX	85.0	64.7	31.2	15.0	8.9
San Diego, CA	92.5	69.4	33.6	7.5	3.9
San Francisco, CA	95.9	76.0	30.5	4.1	2.3
San Jose, CA	95.8	77.5	26.7	4.2	1.9
Santa Rosa, CA	94.1	72.5	36.2	5.9	3.5
Savannah, GA	87.2	68.1	30.9	12.8	6.3
Seattle, WA	94.3	75.8	29.2	5.7	2.6
Sioux Falls, SD	92.8	79.1	25.2	7.2	4.7
Springfield, IL	96.2	74.4	37.3	3.8	1.4
Tampa, FL	88.3	63.7	36.4	11.7	6.2
Tucson, AZ	91.1	62.9	42.4	8.9	6.9
Tulsa, OK	86.3	65.3	33.3	13.7	7.7
Tuscaloosa, AL	92.6	70.5	34.5	7.4	2.6
Virginia Beach, VA	92.3	74.5	32.6	7.7	4.4
Washington, DC	92.7	77.8	26.4	7.3	4.5
Wichita, KS	89.8	70.6	31.6	10.2	5.2
Wilmington, NC	89.7	72.8	32.3	10.3	7.2
Winston-Salem, NC	89.0	65.0	36.4	11.0	4.8
Worcester, MA	97.4	73.0	37.5	2.6	1.3
U.S.	91.2	67.8	35.4	8.8	5.3

Note: Figures are percentages that cover the civilian noninstitutionalized population; Figures cover the Metropolitan Statistical Area (MSA)—see Appendix B for areas included
Source: U.S. Census Bureau, 2017-2021 American Community Survey 5-Year Estimates

Crime Rate: City

City	Total Crime	Violent Crime Rate				Property Crime Rate		
		Murder	Rape	Robbery	Aggrav. Assault	Burglary	Larceny -Theft	Motor Vehicle Theft
Albuquerque, NM	6,355.7	14.2	78.5	256.0	994.9	902.9	3,225.8	883.3
Allentown, PA[1]	2,669.6	5.7	52.5	139.5	188.7	427.6	1,656.1	199.4
Anchorage, AK	4,659.4	6.3	194.8	194.8	816.4	504.2	2,541.7	401.2
Ann Arbor, MI	1,563.2	0.8	40.6	31.5	170.7	126.8	1,125.6	67.1
Athens, GA	3,463.9	3.1	81.9	79.6	345.7	465.9	2,213.8	273.9
Atlanta, GA[2]	5,423.2	17.7	49.4	221.5	480.1	621.2	3,366.4	666.8
Austin, TX	4,098.2	4.4	47.8	110.1	304.7	477.3	2,747.3	406.6
Baltimore, MD[1]	6,169.9	58.3	54.2	813.1	933.1	906.5	2,745.1	659.5
Boise City, ID	1,933.2	1.7	73.5	23.8	193.8	207.2	1,312.6	120.7
Boston, MA	2,490.8	8.3	26.4	131.8	457.9	243.5	1,439.4	183.6
Boulder, CO	4,092.0	1.9	29.1	67.5	223.3	613.5	2,808.7	348.0
Brownsville, TX	2,250.2	3.8	45.2	83.3	269.6	219.5	1,563.0	65.9
Cape Coral, FL	1,195.5	0.5	9.0	10.0	108.3	152.9	848.1	66.7
Cedar Rapids, IA	3,488.4	8.2	11.9	75.9	225.6	619.4	2,132.8	414.7
Charleston, SC	2,771.1	12.2	38.7	71.6	343.2	233.6	1,747.4	324.5
Charlotte, NC	4,076.6	12.4	25.6	184.0	614.4	449.9	2,478.9	311.4
Chicago, IL	n/a	28.6	50.0	292.1	616.2	320.9	n/a	373.2
Cincinnati, OH	4,576.3	30.2	70.6	246.1	546.1	762.0	2,427.1	494.2
Clarksville, TN	2,852.9	9.3	52.1	48.4	500.1	273.6	1,715.6	253.8
Cleveland, OH	5,727.5	42.2	103.7	420.2	1,090.7	973.8	2,321.2	775.7
College Station, TX	2,082.2	1.7	45.5	22.3	110.1	265.7	1,463.2	173.8
Colorado Springs, CO	3,976.6	7.4	82.5	77.5	429.6	533.5	2,344.8	501.4
Columbia, MO	3,106.6	10.4	71.3	46.5	314.0	323.6	1,985.1	355.7
Columbia, SC	5,227.8	14.4	65.3	156.3	516.0	552.4	3,442.2	481.1
Columbus, OH	3,686.0	19.1	89.5	197.1	249.9	609.1	2,180.6	340.7
Dallas, TX	4,291.0	17.3	41.7	241.5	544.2	727.6	1,955.6	763.1
Davenport, IA	4,661.8	9.8	65.8	133.6	527.5	895.8	2,568.6	460.7
Denver, CO	5,506.6	13.1	90.8	165.1	588.9	708.0	2,800.8	1,139.9
Des Moines, IA	4,606.3	15.3	55.3	114.3	519.8	894.1	2,347.1	660.5
Durham, NC	4,596.6	12.6	43.9	219.7	582.6	668.9	2,730.2	338.7
Edison, NJ	1,242.2	1.0	9.0	31.1	62.3	131.5	889.7	117.5
El Paso, TX	1,557.6	4.1	38.1	42.2	231.9	123.6	1,057.2	60.6
Fargo, ND	3,929.0	5.5	84.3	48.1	322.2	800.5	2,302.1	366.4
Fort Collins, CO[1]	2,389.9	0.6	24.0	21.1	171.5	204.8	1,834.5	133.4
Fort Wayne, IN	2,659.5	14.3	35.6	90.0	272.9	240.6	1,818.8	187.3
Fort Worth, TX	3,274.2	11.8	48.0	93.3	387.9	366.9	1,988.9	377.4
Grand Rapids, MI	2,666.0	13.8	59.7	94.8	544.2	228.6	1,437.9	286.9
Greeley, CO	2,888.6	8.1	48.0	70.6	298.6	333.9	1,774.6	354.7
Green Bay, WI	2,056.4	5.7	67.8	43.0	410.9	196.8	1,222.2	109.9
Greensboro, NC	4,513.0	19.7	31.7	193.7	656.6	737.6	2,501.9	371.8
Honolulu, HI	n/a	n/a	n/a	n/a	n/a	n/a	n/a	n/a
Houston, TX	5,435.1	17.0	48.5	373.2	817.5	672.9	2,875.9	630.0
Huntsville, AL	n/a	n/a	n/a	n/a	n/a	n/a	n/a	n/a
Indianapolis, IN	4,440.6	24.3	64.3	243.2	538.9	580.6	2,376.9	612.5
Jacksonville, FL	3,569.3	15.2	49.5	100.8	532.3	419.3	2,129.5	322.6
Kansas City, MO	5,705.4	35.2	76.5	257.3	1,216.8	615.2	2,595.1	909.2
Lafayette, LA	5,081.3	11.1	13.4	116.0	421.5	843.9	3,352.6	322.9
Las Cruces, NM[1]	4,077.5	9.7	61.8	55.1	370.0	631.8	2,652.6	296.6
Las Vegas, NV	2,738.2	5.7	63.1	100.8	358.1	416.8	1,390.7	403.0
Lexington, KY	3,191.6	8.6	54.6	102.8	154.1	445.0	2,108.3	318.2
Lincoln, NE[1]	3,133.7	1.7	110.9	57.0	213.3	339.4	2,255.4	155.9
Little Rock, AR	6,707.0	24.8	99.1	190.2	1,535.8	772.4	3,572.3	512.4
Los Angeles, CA	2,869.9	8.8	49.6	200.3	463.3	344.3	1,274.6	529.1
Louisville, KY[1]	4,578.4	13.9	29.8	149.2	494.0	638.9	2,670.2	582.4

Table continued on following page.

City	Total Crime	Violent Crime Rate				Property Crime Rate		
		Murder	Rape	Robbery	Aggrav. Assault	Burglary	Larceny -Theft	Motor Vehicle Theft
Madison, WI	3,099.3	3.8	28.2	62.8	225.7	497.5	2,034.7	246.6
Manchester, NH	2,858.0	4.4	64.6	97.3	426.5	253.9	1,854.6	156.6
Miami, FL	3,305.4	12.8	19.7	128.1	394.9	305.2	2,104.0	340.7
Midland, TX	2,436.7	6.6	53.8	33.2	271.0	268.4	1,494.1	309.6
Milwaukee, WI	4,325.4	32.4	73.2	326.8	1,164.5	578.5	1,388.2	761.8
Minneapolis, MN	5,713.0	18.2	83.0	409.5	644.2	899.8	2,747.1	911.3
Nashville, TN	5,228.7	16.4	56.0	253.2	830.1	544.3	3,086.9	441.9
New Haven, CT	4,218.8	16.1	22.3	257.9	411.4	419.8	2,507.3	584.0
New Orleans, LA	5,863.9	51.0	180.8	280.9	811.6	506.4	3,138.3	894.9
New York, NY	2,136.3	5.6	27.1	158.8	386.2	167.5	1,279.4	111.5
Oklahoma City, OK	4,621.5	9.5	84.2	123.1	509.1	881.3	2,444.3	569.9
Omaha, NE	3,805.8	7.7	73.1	96.6	453.9	316.7	2,227.2	630.7
Orlando, FL	4,663.8	10.6	57.6	172.8	619.4	408.4	3,003.8	391.3
Philadelphia, PA[2]	4,005.6	22.1	69.0	331.6	486.0	409.4	2,329.5	357.9
Phoenix, AZ	3,788.0	10.9	62.5	191.8	533.2	433.4	2,121.4	434.7
Pittsburgh, PA[2]	3,594.8	18.8	40.0	230.0	289.9	443.2	2,331.9	241.0
Portland, OR	5,261.6	8.0	39.5	121.7	353.4	567.0	3,211.0	960.9
Providence, RI	2,900.8	9.5	36.7	101.9	338.0	335.2	1,776.7	302.9
Provo, UT[1]	1,623.0	0.9	37.5	11.1	65.7	139.1	1,259.5	109.2
Raleigh, NC	2,412.8	4.4	34.2	97.0	256.5	270.0	1,468.3	282.4
Reno, NV	2,710.2	6.6	108.4	110.4	338.0	426.4	1,345.1	375.4
Richmond, VA	3,269.8	28.3	8.6	117.4	194.6	330.4	2,328.7	261.8
Rochester, MN	2,172.3	4.2	61.5	36.6	147.1	275.9	1,519.1	128.0
Sacramento, CA	3,428.4	8.1	24.1	169.3	481.8	546.0	1,715.2	483.8
Saint Louis, MO	7,846.6	88.1	78.4	416.2	1,433.5	855.2	3,895.8	1,079.3
Salem, OR	4,187.2	1.1	15.9	83.8	294.4	383.8	2,780.4	627.9
Salt Lake City, UT	8,274.5	8.4	137.0	240.9	536.1	764.1	5,503.8	1,084.1
San Antonio, TX	4,362.2	8.3	75.5	137.5	514.2	503.4	2,679.8	443.7
San Diego, CA	2,060.6	3.9	33.7	84.0	247.3	231.2	1,116.0	344.5
San Francisco, CA	4,938.4	5.4	22.5	270.9	245.3	845.4	2,872.2	676.8
San Jose, CA	2,741.2	3.9	55.0	115.1	251.0	392.9	1,237.2	686.2
Santa Rosa, CA	2,120.0	2.3	62.2	76.3	375.3	306.3	1,059.7	237.9
Savannah, GA[2]	2,865.5	11.6	35.1	110.2	248.5	364.9	1,824.4	270.8
Seattle, WA	5,498.9	6.7	39.0	190.7	389.9	1,351.5	2,884.6	636.5
Sioux Falls, SD	3,729.0	6.9	51.8	54.4	484.6	365.1	2,273.0	493.1
Springfield, IL	n/a	9.7	88.7	171.2	676.8	822.6	n/a	223.0
Tampa, FL	1,885.4	10.1	24.8	79.8	405.5	227.1	980.2	157.8
Tucson, AZ	4,319.0	11.1	84.1	177.7	425.3	381.0	2,898.7	341.2
Tulsa, OK	6,244.2	17.9	94.0	184.3	836.5	1,095.8	3,045.0	970.7
Tuscaloosa, AL[2]	4,843.6	4.9	46.2	137.6	316.4	739.9	3,289.0	309.5
Virginia Beach, VA	1,610.5	3.8	13.3	27.5	54.1	110.7	1,262.7	138.4
Washington, DC	4,389.2	27.8	43.1	309.8	577.3	275.4	2,683.2	472.8
Wichita, KS[1]	6,462.8	9.0	94.1	118.2	919.8	686.3	4,044.6	590.9
Wilmington, NC	3,175.8	17.5	52.5	113.7	445.2	473.0	1,915.8	158.2
Winston-Salem, NC	n/a	n/a	n/a	n/a	n/a	n/a	n/a	n/a
Worcester, MA	2,631.3	5.4	21.6	113.6	491.8	360.8	1,396.3	241.8
U.S.	2,356.7	6.5	38.4	73.9	279.7	314.2	1,398.0	246.0

Note: Figures are crimes per 100,000 population in 2020 except where noted; n/a not available; (1) 2019 data; (2) 2018 data; Due to the transition to the National Incident-Based Reporting System (NIBRS), limited city and metro area data was released for 2021
Source: FBI Uniform Crime Reports, 2018, 2019, 2020

Crime Rate: Suburbs

Suburbs[1]	Total Crime	Violent Crime Rate				Property Crime Rate		
		Murder	Rape	Robbery	Aggrav. Assault	Burglary	Larceny -Theft	Motor Vehicle Theft
Albuquerque, NM	2,025.9	1.9	34.6	40.4	405.3	354.2	870.1	319.4
Allentown, PA	n/a	n/a	n/a	n/a	n/a	n/a	n/a	n/a
Anchorage, AK	3,312.3	0.0	63.6	42.4	445.2	233.2	2,247.1	280.9
Ann Arbor, MI	1,734.3	3.2	74.1	38.7	378.3	167.6	942.7	129.7
Athens, GA	1,270.6	2.3	20.5	11.4	171.1	219.0	735.7	110.6
Atlanta, GA[3]	2,666.3	4.6	24.0	82.5	168.8	373.2	1,770.4	242.7
Austin, TX	1,578.6	2.3	40.3	25.2	129.8	227.0	1,028.7	125.3
Baltimore, MD[2]	2,213.3	3.9	31.8	88.1	260.3	217.8	1,485.2	126.1
Boise City, ID	1,206.5	1.9	52.0	6.9	189.1	178.4	674.0	104.3
Boston, MA	1,043.0	1.2	21.0	22.6	147.3	96.5	677.6	76.8
Boulder, CO	2,552.6	0.9	66.0	30.7	181.8	304.8	1,686.2	282.2
Brownsville, TX	2,358.5	2.5	38.8	39.2	248.9	317.7	1,598.9	112.6
Cape Coral, FL	1,333.2	5.3	37.6	48.3	222.8	148.9	761.7	108.6
Cedar Rapids, IA	1,291.6	0.7	39.3	10.0	135.0	318.6	660.1	127.9
Charleston, SC	2,958.7	11.2	35.6	81.5	313.9	324.5	1,914.7	277.3
Charlotte, NC	n/a	n/a	n/a	n/a	n/a	n/a	n/a	n/a
Chicago, IL	n/a	n/a	n/a	n/a	n/a	n/a	n/a	n/a
Cincinnati, OH	1,469.5	1.9	27.0	24.3	78.3	177.6	1,049.2	111.1
Clarksville, TN	1,659.2	4.0	32.5	25.9	161.9	300.0	988.2	146.7
Cleveland, OH	1,328.9	3.0	20.9	35.0	104.7	154.4	907.3	103.7
College Station, TX	2,209.2	5.4	86.2	41.4	262.1	349.1	1,310.7	154.2
Colorado Springs, CO	1,620.4	4.1	66.6	24.3	191.2	193.8	966.8	173.6
Columbia, MO	1,789.7	2.3	52.8	19.9	179.4	218.1	1,128.2	188.8
Columbia, SC	3,572.6	8.2	37.6	61.2	415.2	504.0	2,183.1	363.3
Columbus, OH	1,664.0	1.5	28.2	27.2	77.2	205.1	1,223.7	101.1
Dallas, TX	n/a	n/a	n/a	n/a	n/a	n/a	n/a	n/a
Davenport, IA	n/a	5.8	57.2	48.2	268.5	345.6	n/a	174.3
Denver, CO	3,233.8	3.8	57.7	70.7	238.2	357.6	1,904.0	601.8
Des Moines, IA	1,384.2	2.2	25.9	9.9	141.1	218.8	859.4	126.9
Durham, NC	1,768.6	4.6	17.6	32.3	169.1	319.6	1,113.7	111.7
Edison, NJ	n/a	n/a	n/a	n/a	n/a	n/a	n/a	n/a
El Paso, TX	1,026.7	3.1	36.2	20.0	217.8	121.7	554.9	73.0
Fargo, ND	2,397.0	5.8	53.5	17.3	159.7	489.9	1,455.9	214.9
Fort Collins, CO[2]	1,855.9	1.1	44.9	14.6	189.3	184.4	1,296.7	124.9
Fort Wayne, IN	988.4	1.4	22.3	16.7	146.5	136.7	579.0	85.8
Fort Worth, TX	n/a	n/a	n/a	n/a	n/a	n/a	n/a	n/a
Grand Rapids, MI	1,390.3	2.5	70.8	21.3	172.1	149.8	837.9	135.8
Greeley, CO	2,286.0	3.2	56.2	25.4	188.9	212.4	1,410.9	389.1
Green Bay, WI	816.1	0.9	22.7	3.2	54.1	122.4	580.0	32.8
Greensboro, NC	2,458.1	7.5	28.3	53.6	282.3	415.1	1,477.5	193.7
Honolulu, HI	n/a	n/a	n/a	n/a	n/a	n/a	n/a	n/a
Houston, TX	2,188.3	5.4	42.8	68.3	212.3	270.6	1,338.7	250.2
Huntsville, AL	n/a	n/a	n/a	n/a	n/a	n/a	n/a	n/a
Indianapolis, IN	n/a	n/a	n/a	n/a	n/a	n/a	n/a	n/a
Jacksonville, FL	1,375.4	2.4	28.0	23.8	169.5	172.0	880.2	99.5
Kansas City, MO	n/a	n/a	n/a	n/a	n/a	n/a	n/a	n/a
Lafayette, LA	2,189.8	7.4	23.9	35.5	344.1	400.2	1,210.2	168.4
Las Cruces, NM[2]	1,781.8	1.7	52.3	10.5	546.8	362.8	699.5	108.1
Las Vegas, NV	1,944.4	5.0	31.6	99.0	209.5	261.9	1,057.0	280.4
Lexington, KY	2,178.6	1.5	29.6	28.6	75.6	317.7	1,508.9	216.6
Lincoln, NE[2]	1,017.1	0.0	77.9	0.0	41.1	119.0	705.4	73.6
Little Rock, AR	3,185.5	8.9	56.1	52.4	493.6	457.2	1,830.0	287.2
Los Angeles, CA	2,435.2	4.2	28.0	102.7	228.4	355.9	1,303.4	412.7
Louisville, KY[2]	1,847.8	1.9	21.7	30.8	98.0	230.7	1,263.0	201.7

Table continued on following page.

Suburbs[1]	Total Crime	Violent Crime Rate				Property Crime Rate		
		Murder	Rape	Robbery	Aggrav. Assault	Burglary	Larceny -Theft	Motor Vehicle Theft
Madison, WI	1,304.6	1.7	21.3	17.4	85.0	157.7	930.9	90.6
Manchester, NH	801.4	0.0	34.0	8.8	36.6	64.3	609.1	48.6
Miami, FL	2,551.6	7.0	31.8	85.7	280.9	220.2	1,689.2	236.7
Midland, TX	2,973.5	8.2	30.0	13.6	360.1	349.2	1,606.8	605.6
Milwaukee, WI	1,624.3	1.5	20.3	29.8	78.2	114.7	1,274.1	105.6
Minneapolis, MN	n/a	n/a	n/a	n/a	n/a	n/a	n/a	n/a
Nashville, TN	1,755.3	3.0	29.0	27.7	266.9	199.9	1,090.1	138.6
New Haven, CT	2,076.3	4.2	20.2	61.1	82.9	193.7	1,413.6	300.7
New Orleans, LA	2,268.4	8.6	24.1	45.2	233.6	244.1	1,581.0	131.9
New York, NY	n/a	n/a	n/a	n/a	n/a	n/a	n/a	n/a
Oklahoma City, OK	2,313.8	6.3	37.1	28.2	177.5	392.7	1,432.3	239.8
Omaha, NE	1,602.2	1.5	37.1	23.2	163.9	191.7	977.7	207.1
Orlando, FL	1,994.4	5.4	40.1	59.7	267.8	251.1	1,217.2	153.1
Philadelphia, PA[3]	1,935.5	7.6	16.3	96.8	235.8	202.8	1,235.3	140.9
Phoenix, AZ	2,118.2	3.8	35.2	43.8	211.2	276.5	1,380.4	167.3
Pittsburgh, PA[3]	1,402.7	3.5	23.7	33.2	168.7	159.1	958.5	55.9
Portland, OR	n/a	n/a	41.7	37.9	150.0	262.3	1,381.0	296.2
Providence, RI	1,264.5	1.7	40.2	29.7	189.1	149.7	749.5	104.7
Provo, UT[2]	1,312.0	1.1	30.2	7.2	46.1	131.5	1,018.1	77.8
Raleigh, NC	1,376.5	2.8	12.2	21.8	100.3	201.3	956.0	82.2
Reno, NV	1,808.3	4.5	59.7	39.2	243.4	304.1	959.0	198.4
Richmond, VA	1,784.2	5.9	23.2	30.9	126.7	136.3	1,342.0	119.3
Rochester, MN	824.5	1.0	36.1	2.9	75.1	191.3	456.7	61.5
Sacramento, CA	2,102.6	3.8	27.9	64.5	196.3	323.1	1,274.4	212.6
Saint Louis, MO	n/a	5.6	29.6	39.0	241.8	262.7	n/a	283.8
Salem, OR	2,400.4	1.9	29.2	29.6	123.4	258.0	1,578.0	380.3
Salt Lake City, UT	3,411.8	4.1	53.4	45.4	176.7	364.6	2,327.6	439.9
San Antonio, TX	1,759.0	3.9	36.2	22.5	151.5	297.8	1,074.4	172.6
San Diego, CA	1,655.8	3.1	25.4	69.7	229.9	210.0	887.9	229.9
San Francisco, CA	3,106.9	5.3	33.9	157.3	219.7	345.9	1,757.2	587.6
San Jose, CA	2,331.9	1.7	27.1	56.1	116.6	343.6	1,474.4	312.3
Santa Rosa, CA	1,554.3	1.9	41.1	41.8	329.5	232.8	807.9	99.2
Savannah, GA[3]	3,497.3	5.3	37.2	67.1	245.2	497.1	2,366.1	279.1
Seattle, WA	3,022.6	4.0	29.2	70.5	168.3	442.6	1,893.4	414.8
Sioux Falls, SD	1,410.7	2.3	31.5	8.2	172.8	462.4	597.9	135.5
Springfield, IL	n/a	1.1	36.1	21.9	259.1	349.8	n/a	122.4
Tampa, FL	1,648.1	3.1	34.5	42.4	204.3	176.5	1,068.6	118.6
Tucson, AZ	2,196.1	4.9	16.1	37.5	172.4	257.0	1,582.6	125.6
Tulsa, OK	2,005.9	3.6	31.0	21.9	174.2	380.7	1,150.1	244.3
Tuscaloosa, AL[3]	2,503.0	3.3	28.5	41.7	249.6	518.3	1,449.1	212.5
Virginia Beach, VA	2,536.3	12.5	30.6	67.3	327.6	197.9	1,701.5	198.8
Washington, DC	n/a	n/a	n/a	n/a	n/a	n/a	n/a	n/a
Wichita, KS[2]	n/a	1.6	42.3	14.5	156.8	271.8	n/a	129.8
Wilmington, NC	1,803.5	2.3	27.7	24.3	135.2	300.9	1,220.4	92.7
Winston-Salem, NC	n/a	n/a	n/a	n/a	n/a	n/a	n/a	n/a
Worcester, MA	922.7	0.4	32.3	16.3	166.2	115.4	522.3	69.7
U.S.	2,356.7	6.5	38.4	73.9	279.7	314.2	1,398.0	246.0

Note: Figures are crimes per 100,000 population in 2020 except where noted; n/a not available; (1) All areas within the metro area that are located outside the city limits; (2) 2019 data; (3) 2018 data; Due to the transition to the National Incident-Based Reporting System (NIBRS), limited city and metro area data was released for 2021
Source: FBI Uniform Crime Reports, 2018, 2019, 2020

Crime Rate: Metro Area

Metro Area[1]	Total Crime	Violent Crime Rate				Property Crime Rate		
		Murder	Rape	Robbery	Aggrav. Assault	Burglary	Larceny -Theft	Motor Vehicle Theft
Albuquerque, NM	4,660.5	9.4	61.3	171.6	764.1	688.1	2,303.5	662.5
Allentown, PA[3]	n/a	n/a	n/a	n/a	n/a	n/a	n/a	n/a
Anchorage, AK	4,576.1	5.9	186.7	185.4	793.4	487.5	2,523.4	393.8
Ann Arbor, MI	1,678.4	2.4	63.2	36.3	310.4	154.3	1,002.5	109.3
Athens, GA	2,572.9	2.8	57.0	51.9	274.8	365.6	1,613.3	207.6
Atlanta, GA[4]	2,895.7	5.7	26.1	94.1	194.7	393.9	1,903.2	278.0
Austin, TX	2,682.2	3.2	43.6	62.4	206.4	336.6	1,781.5	248.5
Baltimore, MD[3]	3,057.2	15.5	36.6	242.7	403.8	364.7	1,753.9	239.9
Boise City, ID	1,424.4	1.8	58.5	11.9	190.5	187.0	865.5	109.2
Boston, MA[2]	1,249.7	2.2	21.8	38.2	191.6	117.5	786.3	92.1
Boulder, CO	3,053.3	1.2	54.0	42.7	195.3	405.2	2,051.3	303.6
Brownsville, TX	2,311.6	3.1	41.6	58.3	257.9	275.1	1,583.3	92.3
Cape Coral, FL	1,298.3	4.1	30.4	38.6	193.8	149.9	783.6	98.0
Cedar Rapids, IA	2,367.4	4.4	25.9	42.3	179.4	465.9	1,381.3	268.3
Charleston, SC	2,926.8	11.3	36.1	79.8	318.9	309.0	1,886.2	285.4
Charlotte, NC	n/a	n/a	n/a	n/a	n/a	n/a	n/a	n/a
Chicago, IL[2]	n/a	n/a	n/a	n/a	n/a	n/a	n/a	n/a
Cincinnati, OH	1,894.4	5.7	33.0	54.6	142.3	257.5	1,237.7	163.5
Clarksville, TN	2,276.1	6.7	42.6	37.5	336.7	286.4	1,364.1	202.0
Cleveland, OH	2,145.2	10.3	36.2	106.5	287.7	306.5	1,169.7	228.4
College Station, TX	2,152.0	3.7	67.9	32.8	193.6	311.5	1,379.4	163.0
Colorado Springs, CO	3,139.6	6.2	76.8	58.6	344.9	412.8	1,855.2	384.9
Columbia, MO	2,572.2	7.1	63.8	35.7	259.4	280.8	1,637.3	288.0
Columbia, SC	3,830.0	9.2	41.9	76.0	430.9	511.5	2,378.9	381.6
Columbus, OH	2,523.0	9.0	54.3	99.3	150.6	376.7	1,630.2	202.9
Dallas, TX[2]	n/a	n/a	n/a	n/a	n/a	n/a	n/a	n/a
Davenport, IA	n/a	6.9	59.6	71.2	338.3	493.9	n/a	251.4
Denver, CO	3,793.1	6.1	65.8	93.9	324.5	443.9	2,124.7	734.2
Des Moines, IA	2,362.1	6.2	34.8	41.6	256.0	423.8	1,310.9	288.8
Durham, NC	3,000.9	8.1	29.1	113.9	349.3	471.8	1,818.1	210.6
Edison, NJ[2]	n/a	n/a	n/a	n/a	n/a	n/a	n/a	n/a
El Paso, TX	1,457.0	3.9	37.7	38.0	229.2	123.2	962.0	62.9
Fargo, ND	3,180.0	5.6	69.3	33.0	242.8	648.6	1,888.3	292.3
Fort Collins, CO[3]	2,112.3	0.8	34.8	17.7	180.7	194.2	1,555.0	129.0
Fort Wayne, IN	2,083.1	9.9	31.0	64.7	229.3	204.7	1,391.1	152.3
Fort Worth, TX[2]	n/a	n/a	n/a	n/a	n/a	n/a	n/a	n/a
Grand Rapids, MI	1,628.8	4.6	68.8	35.1	241.6	164.6	950.1	164.0
Greeley, CO	2,487.0	4.8	53.4	40.4	225.5	253.0	1,532.2	377.6
Green Bay, WI	1,216.1	2.5	37.3	16.0	169.2	146.4	787.1	57.6
Greensboro, NC	3,250.8	12.2	29.6	107.7	426.7	539.5	1,872.7	262.4
Honolulu, HI[3]	n/a	n/a	n/a	n/a	n/a	n/a	n/a	n/a
Houston, TX	3,249.2	9.2	44.7	167.9	410.0	402.1	1,841.0	374.3
Huntsville, AL	n/a	n/a	n/a	n/a	n/a	n/a	n/a	n/a
Indianapolis, IN	n/a	n/a	n/a	n/a	n/a	n/a	n/a	n/a
Jacksonville, FL	2,653.0	9.9	40.5	68.6	380.8	316.0	1,607.7	229.4
Kansas City, MO	n/a	n/a	n/a	n/a	n/a	n/a	n/a	n/a
Lafayette, LA	2,937.4	8.4	21.2	56.3	364.1	514.9	1,764.1	208.4
Las Cruces, NM[3]	2,871.0	5.5	56.8	31.6	462.9	490.4	1,626.2	197.5
Las Vegas, NV	2,525.2	5.5	54.6	100.3	318.2	375.2	1,301.2	370.1
Lexington, KY	2,811.4	5.9	45.2	75.0	124.6	397.2	1,883.4	280.1
Lincoln, NE[3]	2,843.7	1.5	106.4	49.2	189.7	309.2	2,043.0	144.7
Little Rock, AR	4,117.3	13.1	67.5	88.9	769.4	540.6	2,291.0	346.8
Los Angeles, CA[2]	2,567.7	5.6	34.6	132.5	300.0	352.3	1,294.6	448.2
Louisville, KY[3]	3,300.8	8.3	26.0	93.8	308.7	447.9	2,011.8	404.3

Table continued on following page.

Metro Area[1]	Total Crime	Violent Crime Rate				Property Crime Rate		
		Murder	Rape	Robbery	Aggrav. Assault	Burglary	Larceny -Theft	Motor Vehicle Theft
Madison, WI	2,007.2	2.5	24.0	35.2	140.1	290.7	1,363.0	151.7
Manchester, NH	1,355.7	1.2	42.2	32.7	141.6	115.4	944.8	77.7
Miami, FL[2]	2,609.4	7.5	30.9	88.9	289.6	226.7	1,721.0	244.7
Midland, TX	2,541.9	6.9	49.1	29.4	288.5	284.2	1,516.1	367.5
Milwaukee, WI	2,634.0	13.1	40.0	140.8	484.3	288.1	1,316.8	350.9
Minneapolis, MN	n/a	n/a	n/a	n/a	n/a	n/a	n/a	n/a
Nashville, TN	2,968.8	7.7	38.4	106.5	463.7	320.3	1,787.7	244.5
New Haven, CT	2,425.5	6.1	20.5	93.2	136.5	230.5	1,591.8	346.9
New Orleans, LA	3,378.9	21.7	72.5	118.0	412.2	325.1	2,061.9	367.5
New York, NY[2]	n/a	n/a	n/a	n/a	n/a	n/a	n/a	n/a
Oklahoma City, OK	3,387.0	7.8	59.0	72.3	331.7	619.9	1,902.9	393.3
Omaha, NE	2,710.6	4.6	55.2	60.1	309.8	254.6	1,606.2	420.2
Orlando, FL	2,288.9	5.9	42.0	72.2	306.6	268.4	1,414.3	179.4
Philadelphia, PA[2,4]	3,462.1	18.3	55.2	270.0	420.3	355.2	2,042.3	300.9
Phoenix, AZ	2,681.7	6.2	44.4	93.8	319.9	329.5	1,630.4	257.5
Pittsburgh, PA[4]	1,687.7	5.5	25.8	58.8	184.5	196.1	1,137.0	80.0
Portland, OR	n/a	n/a	41.1	60.0	203.7	342.7	1,864.0	471.6
Providence, RI	1,445.8	2.5	39.8	37.7	205.6	170.2	863.3	126.6
Provo, UT[3]	1,368.4	1.1	31.6	7.9	49.6	132.9	1,061.8	83.5
Raleigh, NC	1,727.9	3.3	19.7	47.3	153.3	224.6	1,129.7	150.1
Reno, NV	2,291.8	5.6	85.8	77.4	294.1	369.6	1,165.9	293.3
Richmond, VA	2,050.3	9.9	20.6	46.4	138.8	171.1	1,518.7	144.8
Rochester, MN	1,552.4	2.7	49.8	21.1	114.0	237.0	1,030.4	97.4
Sacramento, CA	2,393.6	4.8	27.0	87.5	259.0	372.0	1,371.2	272.1
Saint Louis, MO	n/a	14.3	34.8	79.2	368.7	325.8	n/a	368.6
Salem, OR	3,123.1	1.6	23.8	51.5	192.6	308.9	2,064.3	480.4
Salt Lake City, UT	4,200.7	4.8	67.0	77.1	235.0	429.5	2,842.9	544.4
San Antonio, TX	3,339.5	6.6	60.1	92.3	371.7	422.6	2,049.1	337.2
San Diego, CA	1,830.5	3.4	29.0	75.8	237.4	219.1	986.3	279.3
San Francisco, CA[2]	3,448.3	5.3	31.8	178.5	224.5	439.0	1,965.0	604.2
San Jose, CA	2,543.9	2.8	41.6	86.7	186.2	369.1	1,351.5	506.0
Santa Rosa, CA	1,758.4	2.0	48.7	54.2	346.0	259.4	898.8	149.2
Savannah, GA[4]	3,107.5	9.2	35.9	93.7	247.2	415.6	2,032.0	274.0
Seattle, WA[2]	3,496.7	4.5	31.1	93.5	210.7	616.6	2,083.1	457.2
Sioux Falls, SD	3,001.8	5.5	45.4	39.9	386.8	395.6	1,747.6	381.0
Springfield, IL	n/a	5.8	65.2	104.7	490.8	612.0	n/a	178.2
Tampa, FL	1,678.0	4.0	33.3	47.1	229.7	182.8	1,057.5	123.6
Tucson, AZ	3,298.3	8.1	51.4	110.3	303.7	321.4	2,265.9	237.5
Tulsa, OK	3,701.1	9.3	56.2	86.8	439.1	666.7	1,908.0	534.9
Tuscaloosa, AL[4]	3,445.1	4.0	35.6	80.3	276.5	607.5	2,189.7	251.6
Virginia Beach, VA	2,301.0	10.3	26.2	57.2	258.1	175.7	1,590.0	183.5
Washington, DC[2]	n/a	n/a	n/a	n/a	n/a	n/a	n/a	n/a
Wichita, KS[3]	n/a	6.1	74.0	77.9	623.3	525.2	n/a	411.7
Wilmington, NC	2,373.9	8.6	38.0	61.5	264.0	372.4	1,509.5	120.0
Winston-Salem, NC	n/a	n/a	n/a	n/a	n/a	n/a	n/a	n/a
Worcester, MA	1,285.0	1.5	30.1	36.9	235.2	167.5	707.6	106.2
U.S.	2,356.7	6.5	38.4	73.9	279.7	314.2	1,398.0	246.0

Note: Figures are crimes per 100,000 population in 2020 except where noted; n/a not available; (1) Figures cover the Metropolitan Statistical Area except where noted; (2) Metropolitan Division (MD); (3) 2019 data; (4) 2018 data; Due to the transition to the National Incident-Based Reporting System (NIBRS), limited city and metro area data was released for 2021
Source: FBI Uniform Crime Reports, 2018, 2019, 2020

Temperature & Precipitation: Yearly Averages and Extremes

City	Extreme Low (°F)	Average Low (°F)	Average Temp. (°F)	Average High (°F)	Extreme High (°F)	Average Precip. (in.)	Average Snow (in.)
Albuquerque, NM	-17	43	57	70	105	8.5	11
Allentown, PA	-12	42	52	61	105	44.2	32
Anchorage, AK	-34	29	36	43	85	15.7	71
Ann Arbor, MI	-21	39	49	58	104	32.4	41
Athens, GA	-8	52	62	72	105	49.8	2
Atlanta, GA	-8	52	62	72	105	49.8	2
Austin, TX	-2	58	69	79	109	31.1	1
Baltimore, MD	-7	45	56	65	105	41.2	21
Boise City, ID	-25	39	51	63	111	11.8	22
Boston, MA	-12	44	52	59	102	42.9	41
Boulder, CO	-25	37	51	64	103	15.5	63
Brownsville, TX	16	65	74	83	106	25.8	Trace
Cape Coral, FL	26	65	75	84	103	53.9	0
Cedar Rapids, IA	-34	36	47	57	105	34.4	33
Charleston, SC	6	55	66	76	104	52.1	1
Charlotte, NC	-5	50	61	71	104	42.8	6
Chicago, IL	-27	40	49	59	104	35.4	39
Cincinnati, OH	-25	44	54	64	103	40.9	23
Clarksville, TN	-17	49	60	70	107	47.4	11
Cleveland, OH	-19	41	50	59	104	37.1	55
College Station, TX	-2	58	69	79	109	31.1	1
Colorado Springs, CO	-24	36	49	62	99	17.0	48
Columbia, MO	-20	44	54	64	111	40.6	25
Columbia, SC	-1	51	64	75	107	48.3	2
Columbus, OH	-19	42	52	62	104	37.9	28
Dallas, TX	-2	56	67	77	112	33.9	3
Davenport, IA	-24	40	50	60	108	31.8	33
Denver, CO	-25	37	51	64	103	15.5	63
Des Moines, IA	-24	40	50	60	108	31.8	33
Durham, NC	-9	48	60	71	105	42.0	8
Edison, NJ	-8	46	55	63	105	43.5	27
El Paso, TX	-8	50	64	78	114	8.6	6
Fargo, ND	-36	31	41	52	106	19.6	40
Fort Collins, CO	-25	37	51	64	103	15.5	63
Fort Wayne, IN	-22	40	50	60	106	35.9	33
Fort Worth, TX	-1	55	66	76	113	32.3	3
Grand Rapids, MI	-22	38	48	57	102	34.7	73
Greeley, CO	-25	37	51	64	103	15.5	63
Green Bay, WI	-31	34	44	54	99	28.3	46
Greensboro, NC	-8	47	58	69	103	42.5	10
Honolulu, HI	52	70	77	84	94	22.4	0
Houston, TX	7	58	69	79	107	46.9	Trace
Huntsville, AL	-11	50	61	71	104	56.8	4
Indianapolis, IN	-23	42	53	62	104	40.2	25
Jacksonville, FL	7	58	69	79	103	52.0	0
Kansas City, MO	-23	44	54	64	109	38.1	21
Lafayette, LA	8	57	68	78	103	58.5	Trace
Las Cruces, NM	-8	50	64	78	114	8.6	6
Las Vegas, NV	8	53	67	80	116	4.0	1
Lexington, KY	-21	45	55	65	103	45.1	17
Lincoln, NE	-33	39	51	62	108	29.1	27
Little Rock, AR	-5	51	62	73	112	50.7	5
Los Angeles, CA	27	55	63	70	110	11.3	Trace
Louisville, KY	-20	46	57	67	105	43.9	17
Madison, WI	-37	35	46	57	104	31.1	42

Table continued on following page.

City	Extreme Low (°F)	Average Low (°F)	Average Temp. (°F)	Average High (°F)	Extreme High (°F)	Average Precip. (in.)	Average Snow (in.)
Manchester, NH	-33	34	46	57	102	36.9	63
Miami, FL	30	69	76	83	98	57.1	0
Midland, TX	-11	50	64	77	116	14.6	4
Milwaukee, WI	-26	38	47	55	103	32.0	49
Minneapolis, MN	-34	35	45	54	105	27.1	52
Nashville, TN	-17	49	60	70	107	47.4	11
New Haven, CT	-7	44	52	60	103	41.4	25
New Orleans, LA	11	59	69	78	102	60.6	Trace
New York, NY	-2	47	55	62	104	47.0	23
Oklahoma City, OK	-8	49	60	71	110	32.8	10
Omaha, NE	-23	40	51	62	110	30.1	29
Orlando, FL	19	62	72	82	100	47.7	Trace
Philadelphia, PA	-7	45	55	64	104	41.4	22
Phoenix, AZ	17	59	72	86	122	7.3	Trace
Pittsburgh, PA	-18	41	51	60	103	37.1	43
Portland, OR	-3	45	54	62	107	37.5	7
Providence, RI	-13	42	51	60	104	45.3	35
Provo, UT	-22	40	52	64	107	15.6	63
Raleigh, NC	-9	48	60	71	105	42.0	8
Reno, NV	-16	33	50	67	105	7.2	24
Richmond, VA	-8	48	58	69	105	43.0	13
Rochester, MN	-40	34	44	54	102	29.4	47
Sacramento, CA	18	48	61	73	115	17.3	Trace
Saint Louis, MO	-18	46	56	66	115	36.8	20
Salem, OR	-12	41	52	63	108	40.2	7
Salt Lake City, UT	-22	40	52	64	107	15.6	63
San Antonio, TX	0	58	69	80	108	29.6	1
San Diego, CA	29	57	64	71	111	9.5	Trace
San Francisco, CA	24	49	57	65	106	19.3	Trace
San Jose, CA	21	50	59	68	105	13.5	Trace
Santa Rosa, CA	23	42	57	71	109	29.0	n/a
Savannah, GA	3	56	67	77	105	50.3	Trace
Seattle, WA	0	44	52	59	99	38.4	13
Sioux Falls, SD	-36	35	46	57	110	24.6	38
Springfield, IL	-24	44	54	63	112	34.9	21
Tampa, FL	18	63	73	82	99	46.7	Trace
Tucson, AZ	16	55	69	82	117	11.6	2
Tulsa, OK	-8	50	61	71	112	38.9	10
Tuscaloosa, AL	-6	51	63	74	106	53.5	2
Virginia Beach, VA	-3	51	60	69	104	44.8	8
Washington, DC	-5	49	58	67	104	39.5	18
Wichita, KS	-21	45	57	68	113	29.3	17
Wilmington, NC	0	53	64	74	104	55.0	2
Winston-Salem, NC	-8	47	58	69	103	42.5	10
Worcester, MA	-13	38	47	56	99	47.6	62

Source: National Climatic Data Center, International Station Meteorological Climate Summary, 9/96; NOAA

Weather Conditions

City	Temperature			Daytime Sky			Precipitation		
	10°F & below	32°F & below	90°F & above	Clear	Partly cloudy	Cloudy	0.01 inch or more precip.	1.0 inch or more snow/ice	Thunder-storms
Albuquerque, NM	4	114	65	140	161	64	60	9	38
Allentown, PA	n/a	123	15	77	148	140	123	20	31
Anchorage, AK	n/a	194	n/a	50	115	200	113	49	2
Ann Arbor, MI	n/a	136	12	74	134	157	135	38	32
Athens, GA	1	49	38	98	147	120	116	3	48
Atlanta, GA	1	49	38	98	147	120	116	3	48
Austin, TX	< 1	20	111	105	148	112	83	1	41
Baltimore, MD	6	97	31	91	143	131	113	13	27
Boise City, ID	n/a	124	45	106	133	126	91	22	14
Boston, MA	n/a	97	12	88	127	150	253	48	18
Boulder, CO	24	155	33	99	177	89	90	38	39
Brownsville, TX	n/a	n/a	116	86	180	99	72	0	27
Cape Coral, FL	n/a	n/a	115	93	220	52	110	0	92
Cedar Rapids, IA	n/a	156	16	89	132	144	109	28	42
Charleston, SC	< 1	33	53	89	162	114	114	1	59
Charlotte, NC	1	65	44	98	142	125	113	3	41
Chicago, IL	n/a	132	17	83	136	146	125	31	38
Cincinnati, OH	14	107	23	80	126	159	127	25	39
Clarksville, TN	5	76	51	98	135	132	119	8	54
Cleveland, OH	n/a	123	12	63	127	175	157	48	34
College Station, TX	< 1	20	111	105	148	112	83	1	41
Colorado Springs, CO	21	161	18	108	157	100	98	33	49
Columbia, MO	17	108	36	99	127	139	110	17	52
Columbia, SC	< 1	58	77	97	149	119	110	1	53
Columbus, OH	n/a	118	19	72	137	156	136	29	40
Dallas, TX	1	34	102	108	160	97	78	2	49
Davenport, IA	n/a	137	26	99	129	137	106	25	46
Denver, CO	24	155	33	99	177	89	90	38	39
Des Moines, IA	n/a	137	26	99	129	137	106	25	46
Durham, NC	n/a	n/a	39	98	143	124	110	3	42
Edison, NJ	n/a	90	24	80	146	139	122	16	46
El Paso, TX	1	59	106	147	164	54	49	3	35
Fargo, ND	n/a	180	15	81	145	139	100	38	31
Fort Collins, CO	24	155	33	99	177	89	90	38	39
Fort Wayne, IN	n/a	131	16	75	140	150	131	31	39
Fort Worth, TX	1	40	100	123	136	106	79	3	47
Grand Rapids, MI	n/a	146	11	67	119	179	142	57	34
Greeley, CO	24	155	33	99	177	89	90	38	39
Green Bay, WI	n/a	163	7	86	125	154	120	40	33
Greensboro, NC	3	85	32	94	143	128	113	5	43
Honolulu, HI	n/a	n/a	23	25	286	54	98	0	7
Houston, TX	n/a	n/a	96	83	168	114	101	1	62
Huntsville, AL	2	66	49	70	118	177	116	2	54
Indianapolis, IN	19	119	19	83	128	154	127	24	43
Jacksonville, FL	< 1	16	83	86	181	98	114	1	65
Kansas City, MO	22	110	39	112	134	119	103	17	51
Lafayette, LA	< 1	21	86	99	150	116	113	< 1	73
Las Cruces, NM	1	59	106	147	164	54	49	3	35
Las Vegas, NV	< 1	37	134	185	132	48	27	2	13
Lexington, KY	11	96	22	86	136	143	129	17	44
Lincoln, NE	n/a	145	40	108	135	122	94	19	46
Little Rock, AR	1	57	73	110	142	113	104	4	57
Los Angeles, CA	0	< 1	5	131	125	109	34	0	1
Louisville, KY	8	90	35	82	143	140	125	15	45

Table continued on following page.

City	Temperature			Daytime Sky			Precipitation		
	10°F & below	32°F & below	90°F & above	Clear	Partly cloudy	Cloudy	0.01 inch or more precip.	1.0 inch or more snow/ice	Thunder-storms
Madison, WI	n/a	161	14	88	119	158	118	38	40
Manchester, NH	n/a	171	12	87	131	147	125	32	19
Miami, FL	n/a	n/a	55	48	263	54	128	0	74
Midland, TX	1	62	102	144	138	83	52	3	38
Milwaukee, WI	n/a	141	10	90	118	157	126	38	35
Minneapolis, MN	n/a	156	16	93	125	147	113	41	37
Nashville, TN	5	76	51	98	135	132	119	8	54
New Haven, CT	n/a	n/a	7	80	146	139	118	17	22
New Orleans, LA	0	13	70	90	169	106	114	1	69
New York, NY	n/a	n/a	18	85	166	114	120	11	20
Oklahoma City, OK	5	79	70	124	131	110	80	8	50
Omaha, NE	n/a	139	35	100	142	123	97	20	46
Orlando, FL	n/a	n/a	90	76	208	81	115	0	80
Philadelphia, PA	5	94	23	81	146	138	117	14	27
Phoenix, AZ	0	10	167	186	125	54	37	< 1	23
Pittsburgh, PA	n/a	121	8	62	137	166	154	42	35
Portland, OR	n/a	37	11	67	116	182	152	4	7
Providence, RI	n/a	117	9	85	134	146	123	21	21
Provo, UT	n/a	128	56	94	152	119	92	38	38
Raleigh, NC	n/a	n/a	39	98	143	124	110	3	42
Reno, NV	14	178	50	143	139	83	50	17	14
Richmond, VA	3	79	41	90	147	128	115	7	43
Rochester, MN	n/a	165	9	87	126	152	114	40	41
Sacramento, CA	0	21	73	175	111	79	58	< 1	2
Saint Louis, MO	13	100	43	97	138	130	109	14	46
Salem, OR	n/a	66	16	78	118	169	146	6	5
Salt Lake City, UT	n/a	128	56	94	152	119	92	38	38
San Antonio, TX	n/a	n/a	112	97	153	115	81	1	36
San Diego, CA	0	< 1	4	115	126	124	40	0	5
San Francisco, CA	0	6	4	136	130	99	63	< 1	5
San Jose, CA	0	5	5	106	180	79	57	< 1	6
Santa Rosa, CA	n/a	43	30	n/a	365	n/a	n/a	n/a	2
Savannah, GA	< 1	29	70	97	155	113	111	< 1	63
Seattle, WA	n/a	38	3	57	121	187	157	8	8
Sioux Falls, SD	n/a	n/a	n/a	95	136	134	n/a	n/a	n/a
Springfield, IL	19	111	34	96	126	143	111	18	49
Tampa, FL	n/a	n/a	85	81	204	80	107	< 1	87
Tucson, AZ	0	18	140	177	119	69	54	2	42
Tulsa, OK	6	78	74	117	141	107	88	8	50
Tuscaloosa, AL	1	57	59	91	161	113	119	1	57
Virginia Beach, VA	< 1	53	33	89	149	127	115	5	38
Washington, DC	2	71	34	84	144	137	112	9	30
Wichita, KS	13	110	63	117	132	116	87	13	54
Wilmington, NC	< 1	42	46	96	150	119	115	1	47
Winston-Salem, NC	3	85	32	94	143	128	113	5	43
Worcester, MA	n/a	141	4	81	144	140	131	32	23

Note: Figures are average number of days per year
Source: National Climatic Data Center, International Station Meteorological Climate Summary, 9/96; NOAA

Air Quality Index

MSA[1] (Days[2])	Percent of Days when Air Quality was...					AQI Statistics	
	Good	Moderate	Unhealthy for Sensitive Groups	Unhealthy	Very Unhealthy	Maximum	Median
Albuquerque, NM (365)	23.6	70.7	5.2	0.5	0.0	166	62
Allentown, PA (365)	69.9	29.0	0.8	0.3	0.0	153	43
Anchorage, AK (365)	80.3	18.6	0.8	0.3	0.0	160	25
Ann Arbor, MI (365)	76.2	23.8	0.0	0.0	0.0	100	40
Athens, GA (365)	71.8	27.9	0.3	0.0	0.0	107	41
Atlanta, GA (365)	57.3	40.5	2.2	0.0	0.0	150	47
Austin, TX (365)	68.2	31.5	0.3	0.0	0.0	101	43
Baltimore, MD (365)	68.8	27.1	4.1	0.0	0.0	140	45
Boise City, ID (365)	55.1	39.5	4.4	1.1	0.0	168	49
Boston, MA (365)	77.0	21.6	1.1	0.3	0.0	153	40
Boulder, CO (365)	55.9	34.5	8.8	0.8	0.0	159	48
Brownsville, TX (365)	64.4	35.6	0.0	0.0	0.0	99	43
Cape Coral, FL (365)	91.0	9.0	0.0	0.0	0.0	97	36
Cedar Rapids, IA (365)	64.4	34.5	1.1	0.0	0.0	123	44
Charleston, SC (365)	79.5	20.5	0.0	0.0	0.0	93	40
Charlotte, NC (365)	64.4	34.8	0.8	0.0	0.0	128	46
Chicago, IL (365)	34.2	58.1	7.1	0.5	0.0	169	58
Cincinnati, OH (365)	45.8	52.1	2.2	0.0	0.0	140	52
Clarksville, TN (365)	70.4	29.3	0.3	0.0	0.0	138	43
Cleveland, OH (365)	47.4	50.4	2.2	0.0	0.0	122	52
College Station, TX (356)	87.6	12.4	0.0	0.0	0.0	84	30
Colorado Springs, CO (365)	64.7	27.7	7.7	0.0	0.0	140	47
Columbia, MO (245)	95.1	4.9	0.0	0.0	0.0	77	37
Columbia, SC (365)	74.0	25.5	0.5	0.0	0.0	102	41
Columbus, OH (365)	71.2	28.8	0.0	0.0	0.0	100	43
Dallas, TX (365)	54.0	37.5	7.4	0.8	0.3	209	49
Davenport, IA (365)	56.2	43.0	0.8	0.0	0.0	112	49
Denver, CO (365)	30.1	51.5	13.7	4.7	0.0	177	61
Des Moines, IA (365)	77.8	21.9	0.3	0.0	0.0	110	40
Durham, NC (365)	81.6	18.4	0.0	0.0	0.0	90	40
Edison, NJ (365)	54.8	39.5	4.9	0.8	0.0	154	49
El Paso, TX (365)	38.6	56.2	5.2	0.0	0.0	150	54
Fargo, ND (363)	76.6	18.7	2.2	2.5	0.0	192	37
Fort Collins, CO (365)	54.0	36.4	8.8	0.8	0.0	156	50
Fort Wayne, IN (365)	70.7	29.3	0.0	0.0	0.0	100	41
Fort Worth, TX (365)	54.0	37.5	7.4	0.8	0.3	209	49
Grand Rapids, MI (365)	62.2	36.4	1.4	0.0	0.0	143	44
Greeley, CO (365)	54.5	36.2	9.0	0.3	0.0	154	49
Green Bay, WI (365)	73.4	25.2	1.4	0.0	0.0	125	40
Greensboro, NC (365)	75.9	24.1	0.0	0.0	0.0	100	42
Honolulu, HI (365)	99.7	0.3	0.0	0.0	0.0	52	26
Houston, TX (365)	38.6	53.2	5.8	2.5	0.0	179	54
Huntsville, AL (357)	75.4	24.1	0.6	0.0	0.0	105	41
Indianapolis, IN (365)	42.2	55.9	1.9	0.0	0.0	114	53
Jacksonville, FL (365)	73.4	26.6	0.0	0.0	0.0	93	43
Kansas City, MO (365)	52.9	43.6	3.6	0.0	0.0	147	50
Lafayette, LA (365)	81.6	18.4	0.0	0.0	0.0	87	38
Las Cruces, NM (365)	38.4	53.2	5.5	2.2	0.3	665	55
Las Vegas, NV (365)	32.6	58.1	8.5	0.8	0.0	174	59
Lexington, KY (363)	77.4	22.0	0.6	0.0	0.0	108	40
Lincoln, NE (276)	93.1	6.9	0.0	0.0	0.0	84	35
Little Rock, AR (365)	58.4	41.1	0.5	0.0	0.0	112	47
Los Angeles, CA (365)	10.7	62.5	19.5	7.1	0.3	281	77
Louisville, KY (365)	60.8	37.3	1.9	0.0	0.0	143	46

Table continued on following page.

MSA[1] (Days[2])	Percent of Days when Air Quality was...					AQI Statistics	
	Good	Moderate	Unhealthy for Sensitive Groups	Unhealthy	Very Unhealthy	Maximum	Median
Madison, WI (365)	67.1	32.6	0.3	0.0	0.0	101	42
Manchester, NH (365)	91.8	7.7	0.5	0.0	0.0	144	36
Miami, FL (365)	70.4	28.8	0.8	0.0	0.0	135	44
Midland, TX (n/a)	n/a	n/a	n/a	n/a	n/a	n/a	n/a
Milwaukee, WI (365)	57.3	39.5	3.3	0.0	0.0	129	47
Minneapolis, MN (365)	63.0	34.8	1.4	0.8	0.0	182	44
Nashville, TN (365)	60.5	38.1	1.4	0.0	0.0	133	46
New Haven, CT (365)	77.0	19.2	3.3	0.5	0.0	159	40
New Orleans, LA (365)	76.4	22.7	0.8	0.0	0.0	108	42
New York, NY (365)	54.8	39.5	4.9	0.8	0.0	154	49
Oklahoma City, OK (365)	48.2	49.0	2.7	0.0	0.0	140	51
Omaha, NE (365)	72.9	25.8	1.4	0.0	0.0	150	42
Orlando, FL (365)	82.7	17.3	0.0	0.0	0.0	97	39
Philadelphia, PA (365)	49.9	46.0	3.6	0.5	0.0	152	51
Phoenix, AZ (365)	3.0	32.1	28.2	16.7	20.0	272	123
Pittsburgh, PA (365)	44.9	52.6	2.2	0.3	0.0	153	53
Portland, OR (365)	79.7	20.0	0.0	0.3	0.0	161	37
Providence, RI (365)	76.2	22.7	1.1	0.0	0.0	147	41
Provo, UT (365)	60.0	35.3	4.7	0.0	0.0	144	46
Raleigh, NC (365)	71.0	29.0	0.0	0.0	0.0	97	43
Reno, NV (365)	54.2	36.2	4.4	4.4	0.8	291	49
Richmond, VA (365)	76.4	22.7	0.8	0.0	0.0	112	42
Rochester, MN (361)	83.4	16.1	0.6	0.0	0.0	125	36
Sacramento, CA (365)	37.8	46.3	10.4	3.3	1.4	448	62
St. Louis, MO (365)	38.1	57.8	3.6	0.5	0.0	187	55
Salem, OR (363)	87.1	12.9	0.0	0.0	0.0	93	33
Salt Lake City, UT (365)	47.4	39.5	10.7	2.5	0.0	177	52
San Antonio, TX (365)	54.5	42.2	3.3	0.0	0.0	147	48
San Diego, CA (365)	26.8	68.8	4.4	0.0	0.0	133	64
San Francisco, CA (365)	58.1	39.2	2.5	0.3	0.0	151	46
San Jose, CA (365)	60.5	37.5	1.9	0.0	0.0	147	46
Santa Rosa, CA (365)	87.9	12.1	0.0	0.0	0.0	88	33
Savannah, GA (363)	75.8	24.0	0.3	0.0	0.0	103	41
Seattle, WA (365)	72.1	26.0	1.4	0.5	0.0	177	43
Sioux Falls, SD (349)	81.7	16.9	0.9	0.6	0.0	182	36
Springfield, IL (362)	80.7	19.3	0.0	0.0	0.0	97	38
Tampa, FL (365)	72.9	26.8	0.3	0.0	0.0	129	44
Tucson, AZ (365)	39.2	57.0	3.6	0.0	0.0	315	53
Tulsa, OK (365)	60.3	37.0	2.2	0.5	0.0	163	47
Tuscaloosa, AL (281)	94.3	5.7	0.0	0.0	0.0	90	31
Virginia Beach, VA (365)	85.8	14.2	0.0	0.0	0.0	94	38
Washington, DC (365)	61.6	35.6	2.5	0.3	0.0	153	46
Wichita, KS (365)	59.7	38.9	1.4	0.0	0.0	147	47
Wilmington, NC (360)	89.4	10.6	0.0	0.0	0.0	93	34
Winston-Salem, NC (365)	67.4	31.8	0.8	0.0	0.0	124	44
Worcester, MA (365)	81.6	17.5	0.8	0.0	0.0	140	39

Note: The Air Quality Index (AQI) is an index for reporting daily air quality. EPA calculates the AQI for five major air pollutants regulated by the Clean Air Act: ground-level ozone, particle pollution (also known as particulate matter), carbon monoxide, sulfur dioxide, and nitrogen dioxide. The AQI runs from 0 to 500. The higher the AQI value, the greater the level of air pollution and the greater the health concern. There are six AQI categories: "Good" The AQI is between 0 and 50. Air quality is considered satisfactory; "Moderate" The AQI is between 51 and 100. Air quality is acceptable; "Unhealthy for Sensitive Groups" When AQI values are between 101 and 150, members of sensitive groups may experience health effects; "Unhealthy" When AQI values are between 151 and 200 everyone may begin to experience health effects; "Very Unhealthy" AQI values between 201 and 300 trigger a health alert; "Hazardous" AQI values over 300 trigger health warnings of emergency conditions; (1) Data covers the Metropolitan Statistical Area; (2) Number of days with AQI data in 2021
Source: U.S. Environmental Protection Agency, Air Quality Index Report, 2021

Air Quality Index Pollutants

MSA[1] (Days[2])	Percent of Days when AQI Pollutant was...					
	Carbon Monoxide	Nitrogen Dioxide	Ozone	Sulfur Dioxide	Particulate Matter 2.5	Particulate Matter 10
Albuquerque, NM (365)	0.0	0.0	49.6	(3)	16.7	33.7
Allentown, PA (365)	0.0	1.6	48.8	(3)	49.6	0.0
Anchorage, AK (365)	0.0	0.0	0.0	(3)	68.5	31.5
Ann Arbor, MI (365)	0.0	0.0	62.5	(3)	37.5	0.0
Athens, GA (365)	0.0	0.0	32.9	(3)	67.1	0.0
Atlanta, GA (365)	0.0	3.6	40.8	(3)	55.6	0.0
Austin, TX (365)	0.0	1.6	50.7	(3)	46.6	1.1
Baltimore, MD (365)	0.0	7.4	60.5	(3)	32.1	0.0
Boise City, ID (365)	0.0	0.8	44.9	(3)	51.2	3.0
Boston, MA (365)	0.0	3.3	53.4	(3)	43.0	0.3
Boulder, CO (365)	0.0	0.0	74.8	(3)	24.7	0.5
Brownsville, TX (365)	0.0	0.0	31.2	(3)	68.8	0.0
Cape Coral, FL (365)	0.0	0.0	66.0	(3)	32.9	1.1
Cedar Rapids, IA (365)	0.0	0.0	35.1	(3)	64.7	0.3
Charleston, SC (365)	0.0	0.0	41.4	(3)	58.6	0.0
Charlotte, NC (365)	0.0	0.3	59.2	(3)	40.5	0.0
Chicago, IL (365)	0.0	4.9	34.2	(3)	51.0	9.9
Cincinnati, OH (365)	0.0	3.0	28.8	(3)	64.1	4.1
Clarksville, TN (365)	0.0	0.0	47.4	(3)	52.6	0.0
Cleveland, OH (365)	0.0	1.4	35.9	(3)	60.8	1.9
College Station, TX (356)	0.0	0.0	0.0	(3)	100.0	0.0
Colorado Springs, CO (365)	0.0	0.0	95.1	(3)	4.9	0.0
Columbia, MO (245)	0.0	0.0	100.0	(3)	0.0	0.0
Columbia, SC (365)	0.0	0.0	51.8	(3)	48.2	0.0
Columbus, OH (365)	0.0	2.7	44.7	(3)	52.6	0.0
Dallas, TX (365)	0.0	3.3	61.4	(3)	35.3	0.0
Davenport, IA (365)	0.0	0.0	33.4	(3)	46.8	19.7
Denver, CO (365)	0.0	18.6	63.6	(3)	11.2	6.6
Des Moines, IA (365)	0.0	3.6	43.3	(3)	51.8	1.4
Durham, NC (365)	0.0	0.0	51.8	(3)	48.2	0.0
Edison, NJ (365)	0.0	12.3	41.4	(3)	46.3	0.0
El Paso, TX (365)	0.0	5.8	53.2	(3)	35.9	5.2
Fargo, ND (363)	0.0	1.4	54.5	(3)	44.1	0.0
Fort Collins, CO (365)	0.0	0.0	91.0	(3)	9.0	0.0
Fort Wayne, IN (365)	0.0	0.0	51.0	(3)	49.0	0.0
Fort Worth, TX (365)	0.0	3.3	61.4	(3)	35.3	0.0
Grand Rapids, MI (365)	0.0	1.9	50.1	(3)	47.9	0.0
Greeley, CO (365)	0.0	0.3	78.6	(3)	21.1	0.0
Green Bay, WI (365)	0.0	0.0	48.8	(3)	51.2	0.0
Greensboro, NC (365)	0.0	0.0	52.9	(3)	46.3	0.8
Honolulu, HI (365)	0.3	0.8	83.8	(3)	11.5	3.6
Houston, TX (365)	0.0	0.8	38.9	(3)	55.3	4.9
Huntsville, AL (357)	0.0	0.0	33.3	(3)	63.0	3.6
Indianapolis, IN (365)	0.0	2.2	25.5	(3)	72.3	0.0
Jacksonville, FL (365)	0.0	0.0	36.4	(3)	63.6	0.0
Kansas City, MO (365)	0.0	0.3	38.6	(3)	50.1	11.0
Lafayette, LA (365)	0.0	0.0	61.9	(3)	38.1	0.0
Las Cruces, NM (365)	0.0	2.5	58.1	(3)	6.3	33.2
Las Vegas, NV (365)	0.0	1.6	66.6	(3)	24.9	6.8
Lexington, KY (363)	0.0	5.5	38.3	(3)	55.9	0.3
Lincoln, NE (276)	0.0	0.0	78.6	(3)	21.4	0.0
Little Rock, AR (365)	0.0	1.6	27.9	(3)	70.4	0.0
Los Angeles, CA (365)	0.0	6.6	46.0	(3)	45.2	2.2
Louisville, KY (365)	0.0	2.2	39.5	(3)	58.4	0.0

Table continued on following page.

MSA[1] (Days[2])	Percent of Days when AQI Pollutant was...					
	Carbon Monoxide	Nitrogen Dioxide	Ozone	Sulfur Dioxide	Particulate Matter 2.5	Particulate Matter 10
Madison, WI (365)	0.0	0.0	39.2	(3)	60.8	0.0
Manchester, NH (365)	0.0	0.0	92.1	(3)	7.9	0.0
Miami, FL (365)	0.0	6.8	33.7	(3)	59.5	0.0
Midland, TX (n/a)	n/a	n/a	n/a	(3)	n/a	n/a
Milwaukee, WI (365)	0.0	1.4	52.3	(3)	43.6	2.7
Minneapolis, MN (365)	0.0	3.3	47.7	(3)	41.1	7.9
Nashville, TN (365)	0.0	5.2	33.4	(3)	61.4	0.0
New Haven, CT (365)	0.0	5.2	55.9	(3)	37.5	1.4
New Orleans, LA (365)	0.0	0.0	48.2	(3)	51.5	0.3
New York, NY (365)	0.0	12.3	41.4	(3)	46.3	0.0
Oklahoma City, OK (365)	0.0	3.0	41.6	(3)	54.8	0.5
Omaha, NE (365)	0.0	0.0	53.4	(3)	38.4	8.2
Orlando, FL (365)	0.0	0.0	66.0	(3)	33.2	0.8
Philadelphia, PA (365)	0.0	6.0	39.7	(3)	54.0	0.3
Phoenix, AZ (365)	0.0	0.0	75.3	(3)	6.3	18.4
Pittsburgh, PA (365)	0.0	0.3	32.6	(3)	67.1	0.0
Portland, OR (365)	0.0	0.5	61.1	(3)	38.4	0.0
Providence, RI (365)	0.0	2.2	63.0	(3)	34.8	0.0
Provo, UT (365)	0.0	3.3	78.9	(3)	16.4	1.4
Raleigh, NC (365)	0.0	0.5	53.7	(3)	45.8	0.0
Reno, NV (365)	0.0	1.4	72.6	(3)	24.9	1.1
Richmond, VA (365)	0.0	6.3	51.8	(3)	41.9	0.0
Rochester, MN (361)	0.0	0.0	61.5	(3)	38.5	0.0
Sacramento, CA (365)	0.0	0.0	66.0	(3)	33.4	0.5
St. Louis, MO (365)	0.0	0.5	25.8	(3)	70.1	3.6
Salem, OR (363)	0.0	0.0	39.7	(3)	60.3	0.0
Salt Lake City, UT (365)	0.0	7.9	64.4	(3)	24.1	3.6
San Antonio, TX (365)	0.0	0.3	44.9	(3)	54.2	0.5
San Diego, CA (365)	0.0	1.1	59.5	(3)	38.6	0.8
San Francisco, CA (365)	0.0	1.1	47.9	(3)	51.0	0.0
San Jose, CA (365)	0.0	0.0	54.8	(3)	44.1	1.1
Santa Rosa, CA (365)	0.0	0.0	59.5	(3)	37.5	3.0
Savannah, GA (363)	0.0	0.0	24.5	(3)	75.5	0.0
Seattle, WA (365)	0.0	2.2	62.2	(3)	35.6	0.0
Sioux Falls, SD (349)	0.0	4.6	65.9	(3)	22.3	7.2
Springfield, IL (362)	0.0	0.0	43.1	(3)	56.9	0.0
Tampa, FL (365)	0.0	0.0	51.2	(3)	48.2	0.5
Tucson, AZ (365)	0.0	0.0	54.8	(3)	15.9	29.3
Tulsa, OK (365)	0.0	0.0	52.9	(3)	46.3	0.8
Tuscaloosa, AL (281)	0.0	0.0	72.6	(3)	27.4	0.0
Virginia Beach, VA (365)	0.0	6.8	49.6	(3)	43.6	0.0
Washington, DC (365)	0.0	8.5	52.1	(3)	39.5	0.0
Wichita, KS (365)	0.0	0.5	42.7	(3)	48.8	7.9
Wilmington, NC (360)	0.0	0.0	46.7	(3)	53.3	0.0
Winston-Salem, NC (365)	0.0	1.6	46.6	(3)	51.8	0.0
Worcester, MA (365)	0.0	2.5	58.1	(3)	39.2	0.3

Note: The Air Quality Index (AQI) is an index for reporting daily air quality. EPA calculates the AQI for five major air pollutants regulated by the Clean Air Act: ground-level ozone, particle pollution (also known as particulate matter), carbon monoxide, sulfur dioxide, and nitrogen dioxide. The AQI runs from 0 to 500. The higher the AQI value, the greater the level of air pollution and the greater the health concern; (1) Data covers the Metropolitan Statistical Area—see Appendix B for areas included; (2) Number of days with AQI data in 2021; (3) Sulfur dioxide is no longer included in this table (as of December 8, 2021) because SO$_2$ concentrations tend to be very localized and not necessarily representative of broad geographical areas like counties and CBSAs.
Source: U.S. Environmental Protection Agency, Air Quality Index Report, 2021

Air Quality Trends: Ozone

MSA[1]	1990	1995	2000	2005	2010	2015	2018	2019	2020	2021
Albuquerque, NM	0.072	0.070	0.072	0.073	0.066	0.066	0.074	0.067	0.071	0.071
Allentown, PA	0.093	0.091	0.091	0.086	0.080	0.070	0.067	0.064	0.063	0.063
Anchorage, AK	n/a	n/a	n/a	n/a	n/a	n/a	n/a	n/a	n/a	n/a
Ann Arbor, MI	0.025	0.034	0.035	0.023	0.034	0.064	0.072	0.058	0.067	0.063
Athens, GA	n/a	n/a	n/a	n/a	n/a	n/a	n/a	n/a	n/a	n/a
Atlanta, GA	0.088	0.089	0.089	0.077	0.067	0.069	0.068	0.070	0.059	0.064
Austin, TX	0.088	0.089	0.088	0.082	0.074	0.073	0.072	0.065	0.066	0.066
Baltimore, MD	0.100	0.103	0.088	0.089	0.084	0.073	0.071	0.070	0.064	0.071
Boise City, ID	n/a	n/a	n/a	n/a	n/a	n/a	n/a	n/a	n/a	n/a
Boston, MA	0.078	0.085	0.067	0.075	0.066	0.065	0.061	0.052	0.053	0.059
Boulder, CO	n/a	n/a	n/a	n/a	n/a	n/a	n/a	n/a	n/a	n/a
Brownsville, TX	n/a	n/a	n/a	n/a	n/a	n/a	n/a	n/a	n/a	n/a
Cape Coral, FL	0.069	0.066	0.073	0.071	0.065	0.058	0.065	0.062	0.061	0.055
Cedar Rapids, IA	n/a	n/a	n/a	n/a	n/a	n/a	n/a	n/a	n/a	n/a
Charleston, SC	0.068	0.071	0.078	0.073	0.067	0.054	0.058	0.064	0.059	0.062
Charlotte, NC	0.094	0.091	0.099	0.089	0.082	0.071	0.070	0.073	0.060	0.067
Chicago, IL	0.074	0.094	0.073	0.084	0.070	0.066	0.073	0.069	0.076	0.071
Cincinnati, OH	0.083	0.082	0.074	0.075	0.069	0.069	0.073	0.067	0.067	0.065
Clarksville, TN	n/a	n/a	n/a	n/a	n/a	n/a	n/a	n/a	n/a	n/a
Cleveland, OH	0.084	0.090	0.079	0.084	0.074	0.069	0.072	0.067	0.069	0.066
College Station, TX	n/a	n/a	n/a	n/a	n/a	n/a	n/a	n/a	n/a	n/a
Colorado Springs, CO	n/a	n/a	n/a	n/a	n/a	n/a	n/a	n/a	n/a	n/a
Columbia, MO	n/a	n/a	n/a	n/a	n/a	n/a	n/a	n/a	n/a	n/a
Columbia, SC	0.091	0.079	0.089	0.082	0.069	0.058	0.059	0.063	0.053	0.061
Columbus, OH	0.090	0.091	0.085	0.084	0.073	0.066	0.062	0.060	0.062	0.061
Dallas, TX	0.094	0.103	0.096	0.096	0.079	0.078	0.079	0.070	0.070	0.076
Davenport, IA	0.065	0.072	0.064	0.065	0.057	0.060	0.067	0.066	0.063	0.066
Denver, CO	0.077	0.070	0.069	0.072	0.070	0.073	0.071	0.068	0.079	0.080
Des Moines, IA	n/a	n/a	n/a	n/a	n/a	n/a	n/a	n/a	n/a	n/a
Durham, NC	0.078	0.080	0.082	0.079	0.074	0.061	0.063	0.063	0.051	0.063
Edison, NJ	0.101	0.105	0.089	0.090	0.080	0.074	0.073	0.067	0.064	0.069
El Paso, TX	0.080	0.078	0.082	0.074	0.072	0.071	0.077	0.074	0.076	0.071
Fargo, ND	n/a	n/a	n/a	n/a	n/a	n/a	n/a	n/a	n/a	n/a
Fort Collins, CO	0.066	0.072	0.074	0.075	0.072	0.070	0.073	0.065	0.070	0.077
Fort Wayne, IN	0.086	0.094	0.086	0.081	0.067	0.061	0.071	0.063	0.064	0.062
Fort Worth, TX	0.094	0.103	0.096	0.096	0.079	0.078	0.079	0.070	0.070	0.076
Grand Rapids, MI	0.098	0.092	0.073	0.084	0.069	0.066	0.070	0.063	0.074	0.067
Greeley, CO	0.076	0.072	0.069	0.078	0.073	0.073	0.073	0.065	0.072	0.076
Green Bay, WI	n/a	n/a	n/a	n/a	n/a	n/a	n/a	n/a	n/a	n/a
Greensboro, NC	0.097	0.089	0.089	0.082	0.076	0.064	0.067	0.064	0.057	0.066
Honolulu, HI	0.034	0.049	0.044	0.042	0.046	0.048	0.046	0.053	0.044	0.045
Houston, TX	0.119	0.114	0.102	0.087	0.079	0.083	0.073	0.074	0.067	0.072
Huntsville, AL	0.079	0.080	0.088	0.075	0.071	0.063	0.065	0.063	0.057	0.061
Indianapolis, IN	0.085	0.095	0.081	0.081	0.070	0.065	0.076	0.066	0.065	0.067
Jacksonville, FL	0.080	0.068	0.072	0.076	0.068	0.060	0.060	0.062	0.057	0.061
Kansas City, MO	0.075	0.095	0.087	0.082	0.067	0.063	0.072	0.061	0.064	0.067
Lafayette, LA	n/a	n/a	n/a	n/a	n/a	n/a	n/a	n/a	n/a	n/a
Las Cruces, NM	0.073	0.075	0.075	0.070	0.060	0.070	0.072	0.068	0.071	0.079
Las Vegas, NV	n/a	n/a	n/a	n/a	n/a	n/a	n/a	n/a	n/a	n/a
Lexington, KY	0.078	0.088	0.077	0.078	0.070	0.069	0.063	0.059	0.060	0.064
Lincoln, NE	0.057	0.060	0.057	0.056	0.050	0.061	0.062	0.056	0.054	0.059
Little Rock, AR	0.080	0.086	0.090	0.083	0.072	0.063	0.066	0.059	0.062	0.066
Los Angeles, CA	0.128	0.109	0.090	0.086	0.074	0.082	0.082	0.080	0.096	0.076
Louisville, KY	0.082	0.091	0.087	0.083	0.076	0.071	0.069	0.064	0.063	0.064
Madison, WI	0.077	0.084	0.072	0.079	0.062	0.064	0.066	0.059	0.070	0.066
Manchester, NH	0.085	0.088	0.070	0.082	0.067	0.061	0.066	0.054	0.055	0.061

Table continued on following page.

MSA[1]	1990	1995	2000	2005	2010	2015	2018	2019	2020	2021
Miami, FL	0.068	0.072	0.075	0.065	0.064	0.061	0.064	0.058	0.058	0.057
Midland, TX	n/a	n/a	n/a	n/a	n/a	n/a	n/a	n/a	n/a	n/a
Milwaukee, WI	0.095	0.106	0.082	0.092	0.079	0.069	0.073	0.066	0.074	0.072
Minneapolis, MN	0.068	0.084	0.065	0.074	0.066	0.061	0.065	0.059	0.060	0.067
Nashville, TN	0.089	0.092	0.084	0.078	0.073	0.065	0.068	0.064	0.061	0.064
New Haven, CT	0.121	0.117	0.087	0.092	0.079	0.081	0.077	0.084	0.080	0.083
New Orleans, LA	0.082	0.088	0.091	0.079	0.074	0.067	0.065	0.062	0.061	0.060
New York, NY	0.101	0.105	0.089	0.090	0.080	0.074	0.073	0.067	0.064	0.069
Oklahoma City, OK	0.080	0.087	0.083	0.077	0.071	0.067	0.072	0.065	0.066	0.068
Omaha, NE	0.054	0.075	0.063	0.069	0.058	0.055	0.063	0.050	0.055	0.055
Orlando, FL	0.081	0.075	0.080	0.083	0.069	0.060	0.062	0.062	0.059	0.061
Philadelphia, PA	0.102	0.109	0.099	0.091	0.083	0.074	0.075	0.067	0.065	0.068
Phoenix, AZ	0.080	0.086	0.082	0.077	0.075	0.072	0.073	0.071	0.079	0.079
Pittsburgh, PA	0.080	0.100	0.084	0.083	0.077	0.070	0.070	0.062	0.066	0.066
Portland, OR	0.081	0.065	0.059	0.059	0.056	0.064	0.062	0.058	0.058	0.058
Providence, RI	0.106	0.107	0.087	0.090	0.072	0.070	0.074	0.064	0.065	0.067
Provo, UT	n/a	n/a	n/a	n/a	n/a	n/a	n/a	n/a	n/a	n/a
Raleigh, NC	0.093	0.081	0.087	0.082	0.071	0.065	0.063	0.064	0.054	0.062
Reno, NV	0.074	0.069	0.067	0.069	0.068	0.071	0.077	0.063	0.073	0.078
Richmond, VA	0.083	0.089	0.080	0.082	0.079	0.062	0.062	0.061	0.054	0.061
Rochester, MN	n/a	n/a	n/a	n/a	n/a	n/a	n/a	n/a	n/a	n/a
Sacramento, CA	0.087	0.092	0.085	0.084	0.072	0.073	0.074	0.067	0.072	0.073
St. Louis, MO	0.077	0.084	0.074	0.078	0.069	0.067	0.072	0.066	0.066	0.067
Salem, OR	n/a	n/a	n/a	n/a	n/a	n/a	n/a	n/a	n/a	n/a
Salt Lake City, UT	n/a	n/a	n/a	n/a	n/a	n/a	n/a	n/a	n/a	n/a
San Antonio, TX	0.090	0.095	0.078	0.084	0.072	0.079	0.072	0.075	0.069	0.070
San Diego, CA	0.110	0.085	0.079	0.074	0.073	0.068	0.069	0.069	0.078	0.068
San Francisco, CA	0.062	0.077	0.060	0.060	0.063	0.064	0.056	0.062	0.062	0.064
San Jose, CA	0.078	0.084	0.065	0.063	0.072	0.067	0.059	0.061	0.066	0.067
Santa Rosa, CA	0.063	0.071	0.061	0.050	0.053	0.059	0.055	0.052	0.052	0.052
Savannah, GA	n/a	n/a	n/a	n/a	n/a	n/a	n/a	n/a	n/a	n/a
Seattle, WA	0.082	0.062	0.056	0.053	0.053	0.059	0.067	0.052	0.052	0.052
Sioux Falls, SD	n/a	n/a	n/a	n/a	n/a	n/a	n/a	n/a	n/a	n/a
Springfield, IL	n/a	n/a	n/a	n/a	n/a	n/a	n/a	n/a	n/a	n/a
Tampa, FL	0.080	0.075	0.081	0.075	0.067	0.062	0.065	0.065	0.063	0.060
Tucson, AZ	0.073	0.078	0.074	0.075	0.068	0.065	0.069	0.065	0.070	0.068
Tulsa, OK	0.086	0.091	0.081	0.072	0.069	0.061	0.067	0.062	0.061	0.063
Tuscaloosa, AL	n/a	n/a	n/a	n/a	n/a	n/a	n/a	n/a	n/a	n/a
Virginia Beach, VA	0.085	0.084	0.083	0.078	0.074	0.061	0.061	0.059	0.053	0.057
Washington, DC	0.075	0.083	0.073	0.069	0.069	0.067	0.068	0.064	0.057	0.066
Wichita, KS	0.077	0.069	0.080	0.074	0.075	0.064	0.064	0.062	0.059	0.061
Wilmington, NC	0.082	0.079	0.080	0.075	0.062	0.057	0.062	0.059	0.054	0.062
Winston-Salem, NC	0.084	0.086	0.089	0.080	0.078	0.065	0.064	0.062	0.058	0.062
Worcester, MA	0.097	0.096	0.076	0.085	0.070	0.063	0.065	0.060	0.063	0.063
U.S.	0.087	0.089	0.081	0.080	0.072	0.067	0.069	0.065	0.065	0.067

Note: (1) Data covers the Metropolitan Statistical Area; n/a not available. The values shown are the composite ozone concentration averages among trend sites based on the highest fourth daily maximum 8-hour concentration in parts per million. These trends are based on sites having an adequate record of monitoring data during the trend period. Data from exceptional events are included.
Source: U.S. Environmental Protection Agency, Air Quality Monitoring Information, "Air Quality Trends by City, 1990-2021"

Maximum Air Pollutant Concentrations: Particulate Matter, Ozone, CO and Lead

Metro Aea	PM 10 (ug/m³)	PM 2.5 Wtd AM (ug/m³)	PM 2.5 24-Hr (ug/m³)	Ozone (ppm)	Carbon Monoxide (ppm)	Lead (ug/m³)
Albuquerque, NM	221	11.3	28	0.076	1	n/a
Allentown, PA	44	9.9	27	0.069	n/a	0.06
Anchorage, AK	97	6	21	n/a	2	n/a
Ann Arbor, MI	n/a	8.8	18	0.066	n/a	n/a
Athens, GA	n/a	10.1	25	0.06	n/a	n/a
Atlanta, GA	44	9.7	22	0.07	2	n/a
Austin, TX	91	9.4	21	0.066	1	n/a
Baltimore, MD	27	8.9	21	0.075	1	n/a
Boise City, ID	113	9.2	37	0.075	1	n/a
Boston, MA	50	8.3	18	0.067	1	n/a
Boulder, CO	51	10	54	0.082	n/a	n/a
Brownsville, TX	n/a	9.2	24	0.056	n/a	n/a
Cape Coral, FL	54	7.3	17	0.055	n/a	n/a
Cedar Rapids, IA	57	8.8	24	0.064	n/a	n/a
Charleston, SC	40	9.5	20	0.059	n/a	n/a
Charlotte, NC	39	9.3	21	0.067	1	n/a
Chicago, IL	166	10.8	27	0.079	1	0.03
Cincinnati, OH	178	12.1	27	0.07	2	n/a
Clarksville, TN	n/a	10.4	27	0.06	n/a	n/a
Cleveland, OH	89	12.6	29	0.072	2	0.01
College Station, TX	n/a	8	21	n/a	n/a	n/a
Colorado Springs, CO	39	6	21	0.078	1	n/a
Columbia, MO	n/a	n/a	n/a	0.058	n/a	n/a
Columbia, SC	42	9	22	0.064	1	n/a
Columbus, OH	32	9.9	24	0.064	1	n/a
Dallas, TX	56	9.6	23	0.085	1	0.02
Davenport, IA	137	9.4	26	0.066	1	n/a
Denver, CO	96	10.3	41	0.089	2	n/a
Des Moines, IA	54	8.3	23	0.061	n/a	n/a
Durham, NC	40	8	18	0.063	n/a	n/a
Edison, NJ	40	9.8	26	0.079	2	n/a
El Paso, TX	153	9.2	37	0.073	3	n/a
Fargo, ND	n/a	11	60	0.063	n/a	n/a
Fort Collins, CO	n/a	8.5	29	0.085	1	n/a
Fort Wayne, IN	n/a	9	21	0.065	n/a	n/a
Fort Worth, TX	56	9.6	23	0.085	1	0.02
Grand Rapids, MI	42	10.1	26	0.069	1	n/a
Greeley, CO	n/a	9.8	31	0.083	1	n/a
Green Bay, WI	n/a	8.7	26	0.068	n/a	n/a
Greensboro, NC	35	7.7	18	0.066	n/a	n/a
Honolulu, HI	34	3.3	6	0.047	2	n/a
Houston, TX	103	11.4	24	0.083	2	n/a
Huntsville, AL	36	7.5	17	0.061	n/a	n/a
Indianapolis, IN	55	12.6	32	0.067	2	n/a
Jacksonville, FL	54	8.8	18	0.061	1	n/a
Kansas City, MO	103	11.2	31	0.071	1	n/a
Lafayette, LA	56	7.6	16	0.063	n/a	n/a
Las Cruces, NM	439	9.3	26	0.086	n/a	n/a
Las Vegas, NV	176	9.9	33	0.076	2	n/a
Lexington, KY	27	9.6	23	0.064	n/a	n/a
Lincoln, NE	n/a	7.1	21	0.059	n/a	n/a
Little Rock, AR	32	9.7	25	0.067	1	n/a
Los Angeles, CA	113	13.4	48	0.097	3	0.06
Louisville, KY	46	11.2	28	0.073	1	n/a
Madison, WI	49	9.5	27	0.066	n/a	n/a

Table continued on following page.

Metro Aea	PM 10 (ug/m³)	PM 2.5 Wtd AM (ug/m³)	PM 2.5 24-Hr (ug/m³)	Ozone (ppm)	Carbon Monoxide (ppm)	Lead (ug/m³)
Manchester, NH	n/a	4.5	13	0.062	1	n/a
Miami, FL	73	9.5	26	0.058	1	n/a
Midland, TX	n/a	n/a	n/a	n/a	n/a	n/a
Milwaukee, WI	70	10.2	27	0.073	1	n/a
Minneapolis, MN	115	8.8	30	0.07	2	0.08
Nashville, TN	50	9.4	24	0.066	2	n/a
New Haven, CT	68	8.8	22	0.083	1	n/a
New Orleans, LA	45	7.6	17	0.063	1	0.05
New York, NY	40	9.8	26	0.079	2	n/a
Oklahoma City, OK	64	11.2	28	0.07	1	n/a
Omaha, NE	70	8.9	26	0.066	1	0.09
Orlando, FL	51	7.6	15	0.062	1	n/a
Philadelphia, PA	60	10.1	25	0.077	1	0
Phoenix, AZ	225	12.7	36	0.083	3	n/a
Pittsburgh, PA	81	11.8	30	0.068	4	0
Portland, OR	29	6.4	16	0.062	1	n/a
Providence, RI	29	9.3	21	0.069	1	n/a
Provo, UT	100	7.7	31	0.077	1	n/a
Raleigh, NC	56	9.2	22	0.066	1	n/a
Reno, NV	284	12.4	105	0.08	2	n/a
Richmond, VA	40	8.3	19	0.066	1	n/a
Rochester, MN	n/a	n/a	n/a	0.067	n/a	n/a
Sacramento, CA	406	11.3	57	0.085	1	n/a
St. Louis, MO	161	10	23	0.073	1	0.06
Salem, OR	n/a	n/a	n/a	0.063	n/a	n/a
Salt Lake City, UT	103	10.3	43	0.087	1	n/a
San Antonio, TX	87	8.9	22	0.078	1	n/a
San Diego, CA	119	11.2	24	0.078	1	0.02
San Francisco, CA	35	9.1	23	0.074	2	n/a
San Jose, CA	76	10.9	25	0.074	1	n/a
Santa Rosa, CA	53	n/a	n/a	0.055	1	n/a
Savannah, GA	n/a	10.1	22	0.058	n/a	n/a
Seattle, WA	22	7.1	22	0.078	1	n/a
Sioux Falls, SD	110	n/a	n/a	0.065	1	n/a
Springfield, IL	n/a	8.7	22	0.057	n/a	n/a
Tampa, FL	61	8.5	18	0.063	1	0.08
Tucson, AZ	249	6.6	14	0.068	1	n/a
Tulsa, OK	99	10.1	29	0.068	1	n/a
Tuscaloosa, AL	n/a	7.8	20	0.053	n/a	n/a
Virginia Beach, VA	44	7.2	16	0.061	1	n/a
Washington, DC	47	9.6	21	0.072	2	n/a
Wichita, KS	89	11.3	31	0.067	n/a	n/a
Wilmington, NC	41	4.8	13	0.062	n/a	n/a
Winston-Salem, NC	41	9.2	41	0.066	n/a	n/a
Worcester, MA	31	9.1	19	0.068	1	n/a
NAAQS[1]	150	15.0	35	0.075	9	0.15

Note: Data from exceptional events are included; Data covers the Metropolitan Statistical Area; (1) National Ambient Air Quality Standards; ppm = parts per million; ug/m³ = micrograms per cubic meter; n/a not available
Concentrations: Particulate Matter 10 (coarse particulate)—highest second maximum 24-hour concentration; Particulate Matter 2.5 Wtd AM (fine particulate)—highest weighted annual mean concentration; Particulate Matter 2.5 24-Hour (fine particulate)—highest 98th percentile 24-hour concentration; Ozone—highest fourth daily maximum 8-hour concentration; Carbon Monoxide—highest second maximum non-overlapping 8-hour concentration; Lead—maximum running 3-month average
Source: U.S. Environmental Protection Agency, Air Quality Monitoring Information, "Air Quality Statistics by City, 2021"

Maximum Air Pollutant Concentrations: Nitrogen Dioxide and Sulfur Dioxide

Metro Area	Nitrogen Dioxide AM (ppb)	Nitrogen Dioxide 1-Hr (ppb)	Sulfur Dioxide AM (ppb)	Sulfur Dioxide 1-Hr (ppb)	Sulfur Dioxide 24-Hr (ppb)
Albuquerque, NM	8	44	n/a	3	n/a
Allentown, PA	10	42	n/a	6	n/a
Anchorage, AK	n/a	n/a	n/a	n/a	n/a
Ann Arbor, MI	n/a	n/a	n/a	n/a	n/a
Athens, GA	n/a	n/a	n/a	n/a	n/a
Atlanta, GA	17	50	n/a	4	n/a
Austin, TX	13	44	n/a	3	n/a
Baltimore, MD	16	51	n/a	16	n/a
Boise City, ID	10	45	n/a	2	n/a
Boston, MA	12	45	n/a	9	n/a
Boulder, CO	n/a	n/a	n/a	n/a	n/a
Brownsville, TX	n/a	n/a	n/a	n/a	n/a
Cape Coral, FL	n/a	n/a	n/a	n/a	n/a
Cedar Rapids, IA	n/a	n/a	n/a	40	n/a
Charleston, SC	n/a	n/a	n/a	9	n/a
Charlotte, NC	7	37	n/a	2	n/a
Chicago, IL	17	54	n/a	73	n/a
Cincinnati, OH	16	49	n/a	28	n/a
Clarksville, TN	n/a	n/a	n/a	n/a	n/a
Cleveland, OH	9	38	n/a	39	n/a
College Station, TX	n/a	n/a	n/a	11	n/a
Colorado Springs, CO	n/a	n/a	n/a	10	n/a
Columbia, MO	n/a	n/a	n/a	n/a	n/a
Columbia, SC	n/a	n/a	n/a	1	n/a
Columbus, OH	10	47	n/a	2	n/a
Dallas, TX	13	48	n/a	8	n/a
Davenport, IA	n/a	n/a	n/a	4	n/a
Denver, CO	26	71	n/a	7	n/a
Des Moines, IA	6	34	n/a	n/a	n/a
Durham, NC	n/a	n/a	n/a	1	n/a
Edison, NJ	19	65	n/a	17	n/a
El Paso, TX	14	57	n/a	n/a	n/a
Fargo, ND	4	31	n/a	n/a	n/a
Fort Collins, CO	n/a	n/a	n/a	n/a	n/a
Fort Wayne, IN	n/a	n/a	n/a	n/a	n/a
Fort Worth, TX	13	48	n/a	8	n/a
Grand Rapids, MI	8	39	n/a	4	n/a
Greeley, CO	6	42	n/a	n/a	n/a
Green Bay, WI	n/a	n/a	n/a	5	n/a
Greensboro, NC	n/a	n/a	n/a	n/a	n/a
Honolulu, HI	3	22	n/a	44	n/a
Houston, TX	12	49	n/a	16	n/a
Huntsville, AL	n/a	n/a	n/a	n/a	n/a
Indianapolis, IN	12	40	n/a	3	n/a
Jacksonville, FL	11	41	n/a	39	n/a
Kansas City, MO	10	44	n/a	9	n/a
Lafayette, LA	n/a	n/a	n/a	n/a	n/a
Las Cruces, NM	8	48	n/a	n/a	n/a
Las Vegas, NV	22	53	n/a	3	n/a
Lexington, KY	6	n/a	n/a	5	n/a
Lincoln, NE	n/a	n/a	n/a	n/a	n/a
Little Rock, AR	7	38	n/a	6	n/a
Los Angeles, CA	25	76	n/a	4	n/a
Louisville, KY	15	50	n/a	13	n/a
Madison, WI	n/a	n/a	n/a	2	n/a

Table continued on following page.

Metro Area	Nitrogen Dioxide AM (ppb)	Nitrogen Dioxide 1-Hr (ppb)	Sulfur Dioxide AM (ppb)	Sulfur Dioxide 1-Hr (ppb)	Sulfur Dioxide 24-Hr (ppb)
Manchester, NH	n/a	n/a	n/a	1	n/a
Miami, FL	13	49	n/a	2	n/a
Midland, TX	n/a	n/a	n/a	n/a	n/a
Milwaukee, WI	13	42	n/a	n/a	n/a
Minneapolis, MN	8	38	n/a	14	n/a
Nashville, TN	13	52	n/a	4	n/a
New Haven, CT	12	48	n/a	3	n/a
New Orleans, LA	9	37	n/a	56	n/a
New York, NY	19	65	n/a	17	n/a
Oklahoma City, OK	13	47	n/a	1	n/a
Omaha, NE	n/a	n/a	n/a	48	n/a
Orlando, FL	n/a	n/a	n/a	n/a	n/a
Philadelphia, PA	14	54	n/a	6	n/a
Phoenix, AZ	26	59	n/a	7	n/a
Pittsburgh, PA	10	36	n/a	54	n/a
Portland, OR	9	31	n/a	3	n/a
Providence, RI	16	36	n/a	3	n/a
Provo, UT	9	42	n/a	n/a	n/a
Raleigh, NC	8	31	n/a	2	n/a
Reno, NV	12	47	n/a	3	n/a
Richmond, VA	13	48	n/a	3	n/a
Rochester, MN	n/a	n/a	n/a	n/a	n/a
Sacramento, CA	7	41	n/a	n/a	n/a
St. Louis, MO	10	46	n/a	34	n/a
Salem, OR	n/a	n/a	n/a	n/a	n/a
Salt Lake City, UT	16	51	n/a	7	n/a
San Antonio, TX	7	32	n/a	3	n/a
San Diego, CA	13	54	n/a	1	n/a
San Francisco, CA	12	40	n/a	11	n/a
San Jose, CA	12	39	n/a	2	n/a
Santa Rosa, CA	3	20	n/a	n/a	n/a
Savannah, GA	n/a	n/a	n/a	50	n/a
Seattle, WA	16	49	n/a	3	n/a
Sioux Falls, SD	n/a	n/a	n/a	n/a	n/a
Springfield, IL	n/a	n/a	n/a	n/a	n/a
Tampa, FL	9	37	n/a	29	n/a
Tucson, AZ	8	38	n/a	1	n/a
Tulsa, OK	7	38	n/a	5	n/a
Tuscaloosa, AL	n/a	n/a	n/a	n/a	n/a
Virginia Beach, VA	7	40	n/a	3	n/a
Washington, DC	15	50	n/a	3	n/a
Wichita, KS	7	39	n/a	4	n/a
Wilmington, NC	n/a	n/a	n/a	n/a	n/a
Winston-Salem, NC	6	32	n/a	4	n/a
Worcester, MA	9	44	n/a	2	n/a
NAAQS[1]	53	100	30	75	140

Note: Data from exceptional events are included; Data covers the Metropolitan Statistical Area; (1) National Ambient Air Quality Standards; ppb = parts per billion; n/a not available
Concentrations: Nitrogen Dioxide AM—highest arithmetic mean concentration; Nitrogen Dioxide 1-Hr—highest 98th percentile 1-hour daily maximum concentration; Sulfur Dioxide AM—highest annual mean concentration; Sulfur Dioxide 1-Hr—highest 99th percentile 1-hour daily maximum concentration; Sulfur Dioxide 24-Hr—highest second maximum 24-hour concentration
Source: U.S. Environmental Protection Agency, Air Quality Monitoring Information, "Air Quality Statistics by City, 2021"

Appendix B: Metropolitan Area Definitions

Metropolitan Statistical Areas (MSA), Metropolitan Divisions (MD), New England City and Town Areas (NECTA), and New England City and Town Area Divisions (NECTAD)

Note: In March 2020, the Office of Management and Budget (OMB) announced changes to metropolitan and micropolitan statistical area definitions. Both current and historical definitions (December 2009) are shown below. If the change only affected the name of the metro area, the counties included were not repeated.

Albuquerque, NM MSA
Bernalillo, Sandoval, Torrance, and Valencia Counties

Allentown-Bethlehem-Easton, PA-NJ MSA
Carbon, Lehigh, and Northampton Counties, PA; Warren County, NJ

Anchorage, AK MSA
Anchorage Municipality and Matanuska-Susitna Borough

Ann Arbor, MI MSA
Washtenaw County

Athens-Clarke County, GA MSA
Clarke, Madison, Oconee, and Oglethorpe Counties

Atlanta-Sandy Springs-Roswell, GA MSA
Barrow, Bartow, Butts, Carroll, Cherokee, Clayton, Cobb, Coweta, Dawson, DeKalb, Douglas, Fayette, Forsyth, Fulton, Gwinnett, Haralson, Heard, Henry, Jasper, Lamar, Meriwether, Morgan, Newton, Paulding, Pickens, Pike, Rockdale, Spalding, and Walton Counties
Previously Atlanta-Sandy Springs-Marietta, GA MSA
Barrow, Bartow, Butts, Carroll, Cherokee, Clayton, Cobb, Coweta, Dawson, DeKalb, Douglas, Fayette, Forsyth, Fulton, Gwinnett, Haralson, Heard, Henry, Jasper, Lamar, Meriwether, Newton, Paulding, Pickens, Pike, Rockdale, Spalding, and Walton Counties

Austin-Round Rock, TX MSA
Previously Austin-Round Rock-San Marcos, TX MSA
Bastrop, Caldwell, Hays, Travis, and Williamson Counties

Baltimore-Columbia-Towson, MD MSA
Previously Baltimore-Towson, MD MSA
Baltimore city; Anne Arundel, Baltimore, Carroll, Harford, Howard, and Queen Anne's Counties

Boise City, ID MSA
Previously Boise City-Nampa, ID MSA
Ada, Boise, Canyon, Gem, and Owyhee Counties

Boston, MA

Boston-Cambridge-Newton, MA-NH MSA
Previously Boston-Cambridge-Quincy, MA-NH MSA
Essex, Middlesex, Norfolk, Plymouth, and Suffolk Counties, MA; Rockingham and Strafford Counties, NH

Boston, MA MD
Previously Boston-Quincy, MA MD
Norfolk, Plymouth, and Suffolk Counties

Boston-Cambridge-Nashua, MA-NH NECTA
Includes 157 cities and towns in Massachusetts and 34 cities and towns in New Hampshire
Previously Boston-Cambridge-Quincy, MA-NH NECTA
Includes 155 cities and towns in Massachusetts and 38 cities and towns in New Hampshire

Boston-Cambridge-Newton, MA NECTA Division
Includes 92 cities and towns in Massachusetts
Previously Boston-Cambridge-Quincy, MA NECTA Division
Includes 97 cities and towns in Massachusetts

Boulder, CO MSA
Boulder County

Brownsville-Harlingen, TX MSA
Cameron County

Cape Coral-Fort Myers, FL MSA
Lee County

Cedar Rapids, IA, MSA
Benton, Jones, and Linn Counties

Charleston-North Charleston, SC MSA
Previously Charleston-North Charleston-Summerville, SC MSA
Berkeley, Charleston, and Dorchester Counties

Charlotte-Concord-Gastonia, NC-SC MSA
Cabarrus, Gaston, Iredell, Lincoln, Mecklenburg, Rowan, and Union Counties, NC; Chester, Lancaster, and York Counties, SC
Previously Charlotte-Gastonia-Rock Hill, NC-SC MSA
Anson, Cabarrus, Gaston, Mecklenburg, and Union Counties, NC; York County, SC

Chicago, IL

Chicago-Naperville-Elgin, IL-IN-WI MSA
Previous name: Chicago-Joliet-Naperville, IL-IN-WI MSA
Cook, DeKalb, DuPage, Kane, Kendall, Lake, McHenry, and Will Counties, IL; Jasper, Lake, Newton, and Porter Counties, IN; Kenosha County, WI

Chicago-Naperville-Arlington Heights, IL MD
Cook, DuPage, Grundy, Kendall, McHenry, and Will Counties
Previous name: Chicago-Joliet-Naperville, IL MD
Cook, DeKalb, DuPage, Grundy, Kane, Kendall, McHenry, and Will Counties

Elgin, IL MD
DeKalb and Kane Counties
Previously part of the Chicago-Joliet-Naperville, IL MD

Gary, IN MD
Jasper, Lake, Newton, and Porter Counties

Lake County-Kenosha County, IL-WI MD
Lake County, IL; Kenosha County, WI

Cincinnati, OH-KY-IN MSA
Brown, Butler, Clermont, Hamilton, and Warren Counties, OH; Boone, Bracken, Campbell, Gallatin, Grant, Kenton, and Pendleton County, KY; Dearborn, Franklin, Ohio, and Union Counties, IN
Previously Cincinnati-Middletown, OH-KY-IN MSA
Brown, Butler, Clermont, Hamilton, and Warren Counties, OH; Boone, Bracken, Campbell, Gallatin, Grant, Kenton, and Pendleton County, KY; Dearborn, Franklin, and Ohio Counties, IN

Clarksville, TN-KY MSA
Montgomery and Stewart Counties, TN; Christian and Trigg Counties, KY

Cleveland-Elyria-Mentor, OH MSA
Cuyahoga, Geauga, Lake, Lorain, and Medina Counties

College Station-Bryan, TX MSA
Brazos, Burleson and Robertson Counties

Colorado Springs, CO MSA
El Paso and Teller Counties

Columbia, MO MSA
Boone and Howard Counties

Columbia, SC MSA
Calhoun, Fairfield, Kershaw, Lexington, Richland and Saluda Counties

Columbus, OH MSA
Delaware, Fairfield, Franklin, Licking, Madison, Morrow, Pickaway, and Union Counties

Dallas, TX

Dallas-Fort Worth-Arlington, TX MSA
Collin, Dallas, Denton, Ellis, Hunt, Johnson, Kaufman, Parker, Rockwall, Tarrant, and Wise Counties

Dallas-Plano-Irving, TX MD
Collin, Dallas, Denton, Ellis, Hunt, Kaufman, and Rockwall Counties

Davenport-Moline-Rock Island, IA-IL MSA
Henry, Mercer, and Rock Island Counties, IA; Scott County

Denver-Aurora-Lakewood, CO MSA
Previously Denver-Aurora-Broomfield, CO MSA
Adams, Arapahoe, Broomfield, Clear Creek, Denver, Douglas, Elbert, Gilpin, Jefferson, and Park Counties

Des Moines-West Des Moines, IA MSA
Dallas, Guthrie, Madison, Polk, and Warren Counties

Durham-Chapel Hill, NC MSA
Chatham, Durham, Orange, and Person Counties

Edison, NJ
See New York, NY (New York-Jersey City-White Plains, NY-NJ MD)

El Paso, TX MSA
El Paso County

Fargo, ND-MN MSA
Cass County, ND; Clay County, MN

Fort Collins, CO MSA
Previously Fort Collins-Loveland, CO MSA
Larimer County

Fort Wayne, IN MSA
Allen, Wells, and Whitley Counties

Fort Worth, TX

Dallas-Fort Worth-Arlington, TX MSA
Collin, Dallas, Denton, Ellis, Hunt, Johnson, Kaufman, Parker, Rockwall, Tarrant, and Wise Counties

Fort Worth-Arlington, TX MD
Hood, Johnson, Parker, Somervell, Tarrant, and Wise Counties

Grand Rapids-Wyoming, MI MSA
Barry, Kent, Montcalm, and Ottawa Counties
Previously Grand Rapids-Wyoming, MI MSA
Barry, Ionia, Kent, and Newaygo Counties

Greeley, CO MSA
Weld County

Green Bay, WI MSA
Brown, Kewaunee, and Oconto Counties

Greensboro-High Point, NC MSA
Guilford, Randolph, and Rockingham Counties

Honolulu, HI MSA
Honolulu County

Houston-The Woodlands-Sugar Land-Baytown, TX MSA
Austin, Brazoria, Chambers, Fort Bend, Galveston, Harris, Liberty, Montgomery, and Waller Counties
Previously Houston-Sugar Land-Baytown, TX MSA
Austin, Brazoria, Chambers, Fort Bend, Galveston, Harris, Liberty, Montgomery, San Jacinto, and Waller Counties

Huntsville, AL MSA
Limestone and Madison Counties

Indianapolis-Carmel, IN MSA
Boone, Brown, Hamilton, Hancock, Hendricks, Johnson, Marion, Morgan, Putnam, and Shelby Counties

Jacksonville, FL MSA
Baker, Clay, Duval, Nassau, and St. Johns Counties

Kansas City, MO-KS MSA
Franklin, Johnson, Leavenworth, Linn, Miami, and Wyandotte Counties, KS; Bates, Caldwell, Cass, Clay, Clinton, Jackson, Lafayette, Platte, and Ray Counties, MO

Lafayette, LA MSA
Acadia, Iberia, Lafayette, St. Martin, and Vermilion Parishes

Las Cruces, NM MSA
Doña Ana County
Previously Las Cruces, NM MSA
Doña Ana and San Miguel Counties

Las Vegas-Henderson-Paradise, NV MSA
Previously Las Vegas-Paradise, NV MSA
Clark County

Lexington-Fayette, KY MSA
Bourbon, Clark, Fayette, Jessamine, Scott, and Woodford Counties

Lincoln, NE MSA
Lancaster and Seward Counties

Little Rock-North Little Rock-Conway, AR MSA
Faulkner, Grant, Lonoke, Perry, Pulaski, and Saline Counties

Los Angeles, CA

Los Angeles-Long Beach-Anaheim, CA MSA
Previously Los Angeles-Long Beach-Santa Ana, CA MSA
Los Angeles and Orange Counties

Los Angeles-Long Beach-Glendale, CA MD
Los Angeles County

Anaheim-Santa Ana-Irvine, CA MD
Previously Santa Ana-Anaheim-Irvine, CA MD
Orange County

Louisville/Jefferson, KY-IN MSA
Clark, Floyd, Harrison, Scott, and Washington Counties, IN; Bullitt, Henry, Jefferson, Oldham, Shelby, Spencer, and Trimble Counties, KY

Madison, WI MSA
Columbia, Dane, and Iowa Counties

Manchester, NH

Manchester-Nashua, NH MSA
Hillsborough County

Manchester, NH NECTA
Includes 11 cities and towns in New Hampshire
Previously Manchester, NH NECTA
Includes 9 cities and towns in New Hampshire

Miami, FL

Miami-Fort Lauderdale-West Palm Beach, FL MSA
Previously Miami-Fort Lauderdale-Pompano Beach, FL MSA
Broward, Miami-Dade, and Palm Beach Counties

Miami-Miami Beach-Kendall, FL MD
Miami-Dade County

Midland, TX MSA
Martin, and Midland Counties

Milwaukee-Waukesha-West Allis, WI MSA
Milwaukee, Ozaukee, Washington, and Waukesha Counties

Minneapolis-St. Paul-Bloomington, MN-WI MSA
Anoka, Carver, Chisago, Dakota, Hennepin, Isanti, Le Sueur, Mille
Lacs, Ramsey, Scott, Sherburne, Sibley, Washington, and Wright
Counties, MN; Pierce and St. Croix Counties, WI

Nashville-Davidson-Murfreesboro-Franklin, TN MSA
Cannon, Cheatham, Davidson, Dickson, Hickman, Macon, Robertson,
Rutherford, Smith, Sumner, Trousdale, Williamson, and Wilson Counties

New Haven-Milford, CT MSA
New Haven County

New Orleans-Metarie-Kenner, LA MSA
Jefferson, Orleans, Plaquemines, St. Bernard, St. Charles, St. James,
St. John the Baptist, and St. Tammany Parish
Previously New Orleans-Metarie-Kenner, LA MSA
Jefferson, Orleans, Plaquemines, St. Bernard, St. Charles, St. John the
Baptist, and St. Tammany Parish

New York, NY

New York-Newark-Jersey City, NY-NJ-PA MSA
Bergen, Essex, Hudson, Hunterdon, Middlesex, Monmouth, Morris,
Ocean, Passaic, Somerset, Sussex, and Union Counties, NJ; Bronx,
Dutchess, Kings, Nassau, New York, Orange, Putnam, Queens,
Richmond, Rockland, Suffolk, and Westchester Counties, NY; Pike
County, PA
Previous name: New York-Northern New Jersey-Long Island,
NY-NJ-PA MSA
Bergen, Essex, Hudson, Hunterdon, Middlesex, Monmouth, Morris,
Ocean, Passaic, Somerset, Sussex, and Union Counties, NJ; Bronx,
Kings, Nassau, New York, Putnam, Queens, Richmond, Rockland,
Suffolk, and Westchester Counties, NY; Pike County, PA

Dutchess County-Putnam County, NY MD
Dutchess and Putnam Counties
Dutchess County was previously part of the
Poughkeepsie-Newburgh-Middletown, NY MSA. Putnam County was
previously part of the New York-Wayne-White Plains, NY-NJ MD

Nassau-Suffolk, NY MD
Nassau and Suffolk Counties

New York-Jersey City-White Plains, NY-NJ MD
Bergen, Hudson, Middlesex, Monmouth, Ocean, and Passaic
Counties, NJ; Bronx, Kings, New York, Orange, Queens, Richmond,
Rockland, and Westchester Counties, NY
Previous name: New York-Wayne-White Plains, NY-NJ MD
Bergen, Hudson, and Passaic Counties, NJ; Bronx, Kings, New York,
Putnam, Queens, Richmond, Rockland, and Westchester Counties, NY

Newark, NJ-PA MD
Essex, Hunterdon, Morris, Somerset, Sussex, and Union Counties, NJ;
Pike County, PA
Previous name: Newark-Union, NJ-PA MD
Essex, Hunterdon, Morris, Sussex, and Union Counties, NJ; Pike
County, PA

Oklahoma City, OK MSA
Canadian, Cleveland, Grady, Lincoln, Logan, McClain, and Oklahoma
Counties

Omaha-Council Bluffs, NE-IA MSA
Harrison, Mills, and Pottawattamie Counties, IA; Cass, Douglas,
Sarpy, Saunders, and Washington Counties, NE

Orlando-Kissimmee-Sanford, FL MSA
Lake, Orange, Osceola, and Seminole Counties

Philadelphia, PA

Philadelphia-Camden-Wilmington, PA-NJ-DE-MD MSA
New Castle County, DE; Cecil County, MD; Burlington, Camden,
Gloucester, and Salem Counties, NJ; Bucks, Chester, Delaware,
Montgomery, and Philadelphia Counties, PA

Camden, NJ MD
Burlington, Camden, and Gloucester Counties

Montgomery County-Bucks County-Chester County, PA MD
Bucks, Chester, and Montgomery Counties
Previously part of the Philadelphia, PA MD

Philadelphia, PA MD
Delaware and Philadelphia Counties
Previous name: Philadelphia, PA MD
Bucks, Chester, Delaware, Montgomery, and Philadelphia Counties

Wilmington, DE-MD-NJ MD
New Castle County, DE; Cecil County, MD; Salem County, NJ

Phoenix-Mesa-Scottsdale, AZ MSA
Previously Phoenix-Mesa-Glendale, AZ MSA
Maricopa and Pinal Counties

Pittsburgh, PA MSA
Allegheny, Armstrong, Beaver, Butler, Fayette, Washington, and
Westmoreland Counties

Portland-Vancouver-Hillsboro, OR-WA MSA
Clackamas, Columbia, Multnomah, Washington, and Yamhill
Counties, OR; Clark and Skamania Counties, WA

Providence, RI

Providence-New Bedford-Fall River, RI-MA MSA
Previously Providence-New Bedford-Fall River, RI-MA MSA
Bristol County, MA; Bristol, Kent, Newport, Providence, and
Washington Counties, RI

Providence-Warwick, RI-MA NECTA
Includes 12 cities and towns in Massachusetts and 36 cities and towns
in Rhode Island
Previously Providence-Fall River-Warwick, RI-MA NECTA
Includes 12 cities and towns in Massachusetts and 37 cities and towns
in Rhode Island

Provo-Orem, UT MSA
Juab and Utah Counties

Raleigh, NC MSA
Previously Raleigh-Cary, NC MSA
Franklin, Johnston, and Wake Counties

Reno, NV MSA
Previously Reno-Sparks, NV MSA
Storey and Washoe Counties

Richmond, VA MSA
Amelia, Caroline, Charles City, Chesterfield, Dinwiddie, Goochland, Hanover, Henrico, King William, New Kent, Powhatan, Prince George, and Sussex Counties; Colonial Heights, Hopewell, Petersburg, and Richmond Cities

Rochester, MN MSA
Dodge, Fillmore, Olmsted, and Wabasha Counties

Sacramento—Roseville—Arden-Arcade, CA MSA
El Dorado, Placer, Sacramento, and Yolo Counties

Saint Louis, MO-IL MSA
Bond, Calhoun, Clinton, Jersey, Macoupin, Madison, Monroe, and St. Clair Counties, IL; St. Louis city; Franklin, Jefferson, Lincoln, St. Charles, St. Louis, and Warren Counties, MO
Previously Saint Louis, MO-IL MSA
Bond, Calhoun, Clinton, Jersey, Macoupin, Madison, Monroe, and St. Clair Counties, IL; St. Louis city; Crawford (part), Franklin, Jefferson, Lincoln, St. Charles, St. Louis, Warren, and Washington Counties, MO

Salem, OR MSA
Marion and Polk Counties

Salt Lake City, UT MSA
Salt Lake and Tooele Counties

San Antonio-New Braunfels, TX MSA
Atascosa, Bandera, Bexar, Comal, Guadalupe, Kendall, Medina, and Wilson Counties

San Diego-Carlsbad, CA MSA
Previously San Diego-Carlsbad-San Marcos, CA MSA
San Diego County

San Francisco, CA

San Francisco-Oakland-Hayward, CA MSA
Previously San Francisco-Oakland- Fremont, CA MSA
Alameda, Contra Costa, Marin, San Francisco, and San Mateo Counties

San Francisco-Redwood City-South San Francisco, CA MD
San Francisco and San Mateo Counties

Previously San Francisco-San Mateo-Redwood City, CA MD
Marin, San Francisco, and San Mateo Counties

San Jose-Sunnyvale-Santa Clara, CA MSA
San Benito and Santa Clara Counties

Santa Rosa, CA MSA
Previously Santa Rosa-Petaluma, CA MSA
Sonoma County

Savannah, GA MSA
Bryan, Chatham, and Effingham Counties

Seattle, WA

Seattle-Tacoma-Bellevue, WA MSA
King, Pierce, and Snohomish Counties

Seattle-Bellevue-Everett, WA MD
King and Snohomish Counties

Sioux Falls, SD MSA
Lincoln, McCook, Minnehaha, and Turner Counties

Springfield, IL MSA
Menard and Sangamon Counties

Tampa-St. Petersburg-Clearwater, FL MSA
Hernando, Hillsborough, Pasco, and Pinellas Counties

Tucson, AZ MSA
Pima County

Tulsa, OK MSA
Creek, Okmulgee, Osage, Pawnee, Rogers, Tulsa, and Wagoner Counties

Tuscaloosa, AL MSA
Hale, Pickens, and Tuscaloosa Counties

Virginia Beach-Norfolk-Newport News, VA-NC MSA
Currituck County, NC; Chesapeake, Hampton, Newport News, Norfolk, Poquoson, Portsmouth, Suffolk, Virginia Beach and Williamsburg cities, VA; Gloucester, Isle of Wight, James City, Mathews, Surry, and York Counties, VA

Washington, DC

Washington-Arlington-Alexandria, DC-VA-MD-WV MSA
District of Columbia; Calvert, Charles, Frederick, Montgomery, and Prince George's Counties, MD; Alexandria, Fairfax, Falls Church, Fredericksburg, Manassas Park, and Manassas cities, VA; Arlington, Clarke, Culpepper, Fairfax, Fauquier, Loudoun, Prince William, Rappahannock, Spotsylvania, Stafford, and Warren Counties, VA; Jefferson County, WV
Previously Washington-Arlington-Alexandria, DC-VA-MD-WV MSA
District of Columbia; Calvert, Charles, Frederick, Montgomery, and Prince George's Counties, MD; Alexandria, Fairfax, Falls Church, Fredericksburg, Manassas Park, and Manassas cities, VA; Arlington, Clarke, Fairfax, Fauquier, Loudoun, Prince William, Spotsylvania, Stafford, and Warren Counties, VA; Jefferson County, WV

Washington-Arlington-Alexandria, DC-VA-MD-WV MD
District of Columbia; Calvert, Charles, and Prince George's Counties, MD; Alexandria, Fairfax, Falls Church, Fredericksburg, Manassas Park, and Manassas cities, VA; Arlington, Clarke, Culpepper, Fairfax, Fauquier, Loudoun, Prince William, Rappahannock, Spotsylvania, Stafford, and Warren Counties, VA; Jefferson County, WV
Previously Washington-Arlington-Alexandria, DC-VA-MD-WV MD
District of Columbia; Calvert, Charles, and Prince George's Counties, MD; Alexandria, Fairfax, Falls Church, Fredericksburg, Manassas Park, and Manassas cities, VA; Arlington, Clarke, Fairfax, Fauquier, Loudoun, Prince William, Spotsylvania, Stafford, and Warren Counties, VA; Jefferson County, WV

Wichita, KS MSA
Butler, Harvey, Kingman, Sedgwick, and Sumner Counties

Wilmington, NC MSA
New Hanover and Pender Counties
Previously Wilmington, NC MSA
Brunswick, New Hanover and Pender Counties

Winston-Salem, NC MSA
Davidson, Davie, Forsyth, Stokes, and Yadkin Counties

Worcester, MA

Worcester, MA-CT MSA
Windham County, CT; Worcester County, MA
Previously Worcester, MA MSA
Worcester County

Worcester, MA-CT NECTA
Includes 40 cities and towns in Massachusetts and 8 cities and towns in Connecticut
Previously Worcester, MA-CT NECTA
Includes 37 cities and towns in Massachusetts and 3 cities and towns in Connecticut

Appendix C: Government Type and Primary County

This appendix includes the government structure of each place included in this book. It also includes the county or county equivalent in which each place is located. If a place spans more than one county, the county in which the majority of the population resides is shown.

Albuquerque, NM
Government Type: City
County: Bernalillo

Allentown, PA
Government Type: City
County: Lehigh

Anchorage, AK
Government Type: Municipality
Borough: Anchorage

Ann Arbor, MI
Government Type: City
County: Washtenaw

Athens, GA
Government Type: Consolidated
   city-county
County: Clarke

Atlanta, GA
Government Type: City
County: Fulton

Austin, TX
Government Type: City
County: Travis

Baltimore, MD
Government Type: Independent city

Baton Rouge, LA
Government Type: Consolidated city-parish
Parish: East Baton Rouge

Boise City, ID
Government Type: City
County: Ada

Boston, MA
Government Type: City
County: Suffolk

Boulder, CO
Government Type: City
County: Boulder

Brownsville, TX
Government Type: City
County: Cameron

Cape Coral, FL
Government Type: City
County: Lee

Cedar Rapids, IA
Government Type: City
County: Linn

Charleston, SC
Government Type: City
County: Charleston

Charlotte, NC
Government Type: City
County: Mecklenburg

Chicago, IL
Government Type: City
County: Cook

Cincinnati, OH
Government Type: City
County: Hamilton

Clarksville, TN
Government Type: City
County: Montgomery

Cleveland, OH
Government Type: City
County: Cuyahoga

College Station, TX
Government Type: City
County: Brazos

Colorado Springs, CO
Government Type: City
County: El Paso

Columbia, MO
Government Type: City
County: Boone

Columbia, SC
Government Type: City
County: Richland

Columbus, OH
Government Type: City
County: Franklin

Dallas, TX
Government Type: City
County: Dallas

Davenport, IA
Government Type: City
County: Scott

Denver, CO
Government Type: City
County: Denver

Des Moines, IA
Government Type: City
County: Polk

Durham, NC
Government Type: City
County: Durham

Edison, NJ
Government Type: Township
County: Middlesex

El Paso, TX
Government Type: City
County: El Paso

Fargo, ND
Government Type: City
County: Cass

Fort Collins, CO
Government Type: City
County: Larimer

Fort Wayne, IN
Government Type: City
County: Allen

Fort Worth, TX
Government Type: City
County: Tarrant

Grand Rapids, MI
Government Type: City
County: Kent

Greeley, CO
Government Type: City
County: Weld

Green Bay, WI
Government Type: City
County: Brown

Greensboro, NC
Government Type: City
County: Guilford

Honolulu, HI
Government Type: Census Designated Place (CDP)
County: Honolulu

Houston, TX
Government Type: City
County: Harris

Huntsville, AL
Government Type: City
County: Madison

Indianapolis, IN
Government Type: City
County: Marion

Jacksonville, FL
Government Type: City
County: Duval

Kansas City, MO
Government Type: City
County: Jackson

Lafayette, LA
Government Type: City
Parish: Lafayette

Las Cruces, NM
Government Type: City
County: Doña Ana

Las Vegas, NV
Government Type: City
County: Clark

Lexington, KY
Government Type: Consolidated city-county
County: Fayette

Lincoln, NE
Government Type: City
County: Lancaster

Little Rock, AR
Government Type: City
County: Pulaski

Los Angeles, CA
Government Type: City
County: Los Angeles

Louisville, KY
Government Type: Consolidated city-county
County: Jefferson

Madison, WI
Government Type: City
County: Dane

Manchester, NH
Government Type: City
County: Hillsborough

Memphis, TN
Government Type: City
County: Shelby

Miami, FL
Government Type: City
County: Miami-Dade

Midland, TX
Government Type: City
County: Midland

Milwaukee, WI
Government Type: City
County: Milwaukee

Minneapolis, MN
Government Type: City
County: Hennepin

Nashville, TN
Government Type: Consolidated city-county
County: Davidson

New Haven, CT
Government Type: City
County: New Haven

New Orleans, LA
Government Type: City
Parish: Orleans

New York, NY
Government Type: City
Counties: Bronx; Kings; New York; Queens;
   Staten Island

Oklahoma City, OK
Government Type: City
County: Oklahoma

Omaha, NE
Government Type: City
County: Douglas

Orlando, FL
Government Type: City
County: Orange

Philadelphia, PA
Government Type: City
County: Philadelphia

Phoenix, AZ
Government Type: City
County: Maricopa

Pittsburgh, PA
Government Type: City
County: Allegheny

Portland, OR
Government Type: City
County: Multnomah

Providence, RI
Government Type: City
County: Providence

Provo, UT
Government Type: City
County: Utah

Raleigh, NC
Government Type: City
County: Wake

Reno, NV
Government Type: City
County: Washoe

Richmond, VA
Government Type: Independent city

Riverside, CA
Government Type: City
County: Riverside

Rochester, MN
Government Type: City
County: Olmsted

Rochester, NY
Government Type: City
County: Monroe

Sacramento, CA
Government Type: City
County: Sacramento

Saint Louis, MO
Government Type: Independent city

Salem, OR
Government Type: City
County: Marion

Salt Lake City, UT
Government Type: City
County: Salt Lake

San Antonio, TX
Government Type: City
County: Bexar

San Diego, CA
Government Type: City
County: San Diego

San Francisco, CA
Government Type: City
County: San Francisco

San Jose, CA
Government Type: City
County: Santa Clara

Santa Rosa, CA
Government Type: City
County: Sonoma

Savannah, GA
Government Type: City
County: Chatham

Seattle, WA
Government Type: City
County: King

Sioux Falls, SD
Government Type: City
County: Minnehaha

Springfield, IL
Government Type: City
County: Sangamon

Tampa, FL
Government Type: City
County: Hillsborough

Tucson, AZ
Government Type: City
County: Pima

Tulsa, OK
Government Type: City
County: Tulsa

Tuscaloosa, AL
Government Type: City
County: Tuscaloosa

Virginia Beach, VA
Government Type: Independent city

Washington, DC
Government Type: City
County: District of Columbia

Wichita, KS
Government Type: City
County: Sedgwick

Wilmington, NC
Government Type: City
County: New Hanover

Winston-Salem, NC
Government Type: City
County: Forsyth

Worcester, MA
Government Type: City
County: Worcester

Appendix D: Chambers of Commerce

Albuquerque, NM
Albuquerque Chamber of Commerce
P.O. Box 25100
Albuquerque, NM 87125
Phone: (505) 764-3700
Fax: (505) 764-3714
www.abqchamber.com

Albuquerque Economic Development Dept
851 University Blvd SE, Suite 203
Albuquerque, NM 87106
Phone: (505) 246-6200
Fax: (505) 246-6219
www.cabq.gov/econdev

Allentown, PA
Greater Lehigh Valley Chamber of
Commerce
Allentown Office
840 Hamilton Street, Suite 205
Allentown, PA 18101
Phone: (610) 751-4929
Fax: (610) 437-4907
www.lehighvalleychamber.org

Anchorage, AK
Anchorage Chamber of Commerce
1016 W Sixth Avenue
Suite 303
Anchorage, AK 99501
Phone: (907) 272-2401
Fax: (907) 272-4117
www.anchoragechamber.org

Anchorage Economic Development
Department
900 W 5th Avenue
Suite 300
Anchorage, AK 99501
Phone: (907) 258-3700
Fax: (907) 258-6646
aedcweb.com

Ann Arbor, MI
Ann Arbor Area Chamber of Commerce
115 West Huron
3rd Floor
Ann Arbor, MI 48104
Phone: (734) 665-4433
Fax: (734) 665-4191
www.annarborchamber.org

Ann Arbor Economic Development
Department
201 S Division
Suite 430
Ann Arbor, MI 48104
Phone: (734) 761-9317
www.annarborspark.org

Athens, GA
Athens Area Chamber of Commerce
246 W Hancock Avenue
Athens, GA 30601
Phone: (706) 549-6800
Fax: (706) 549-5636
www.aacoc.org

Athens-Clarke County Economic
Development Department
246 W. Hancock Avenue
Athens, GA 30601
Phone: (706) 613-3233
Fax: (706) 613-3812
www.athensbusiness.org

Atlanta, GA
Metro Atlanta Chamber of Commerce
235 Andrew Young International Blvd NW
Atlanta, GA 30303
Phone: (404) 880-9000
Fax: (404) 586-8464
www.metroatlantachamber.com

Austin, TX
Greater Austin Chamber of Commerce
210 Barton Springs Road
Suite 400
Austin, TX 78704
Phone: (512) 478-9383
Fax: (512) 478-6389
www.austin-chamber.org

Baltimore, MD
Baltimore City Chamber of Commerce
P.O. Box 43121
Baltimore, MD 21236
443-860-2020
baltimorecitychamber.org

Baltimore County Chamber of Commerce
102 W. Pennsylvania Avenue
Suite 305
Towson, MD, 21204
Phone: (410) 825-6200
Fax: (410) 821-9901
www.baltcountychamber.com

Boise City, ID
Boise Metro Chamber of Commerce
250 S 5th Street
Suite 800
Boise City, ID 83701
Phone: (208) 472-5200
Fax: (208) 472-5201
www.boisechamber.org

Boston, MA
Greater Boston Chamber of Commerce
265 Franklin Street
12th Floor
Boston, MA 02110
Phone: (617) 227-4500
Fax: (617) 227-7505
www.bostonchamber.com

Boulder, CO
Boulder Chamber of Commerce
2440 Pearl Street
Boulder, CO 80302
Phone: (303) 442-1044
Fax: (303) 938-8837
www.boulderchamber.com

City of Boulder Economic Vitality Program
P.O. Box 791
Boulder, CO 80306
Phone: (303) 441-3090
www.bouldercolorado.gov

Brownsville, TX
Brownsville Chamber of Commerce
1600 University Blvd.
Brownsville, TX 78520
Phone: (956) 542-4341
brownsvillechamber.com

Cape Coral, FL
Chamber of Commerce of Cape Coral
2051 Cape Coral Parkway East
Cape Coral, FL 33904
Phone: (239) 549-6900
Fax: (239) 549-9609
www.capecoralchamber.com

Cedar Rapids, IA
Cedar Rapids Chamber of Commerce
424 First Avenue NE
Cedar Rapids, IA 52401
Phone: (319) 398-5317
Fax: (319) 398-5228
www.cedarrapids.org

Cedar Rapids Economic Development
50 Second Avenue Bridge, Sixth Floor
Cedar Rapids, IA 52401-1256
Phone: (319) 286-5041
Fax: (319) 286-5141
www.cedar-rapids.org

Charleston, SC
Charleston Metro Chamber of Commerce
P.O. Box 975
Charleston, SC 29402
Phone: (843) 577-2510
www.charlestonchamber.net

Charlotte, NC
Charlotte Chamber of Commerce
330 S Tryon Street
P.O. Box 32785
Charlotte, NC 28232
Phone: (704) 378-1300
Fax: (704) 374-1903
www.charlottechamber.com

Charlotte Regional Partnership
1001 Morehead Square Drive, Suite 200
Charlotte, NC 28203
Phone: (704) 347-8942
Fax: (704) 347-8981
www.charlotteusa.com

Chicago, IL
Chicagoland Chamber of Commerce
200 E Randolph Street
Suite 2200
Chicago, IL 60601-6436
Phone: (312) 494-6700
Fax: (312) 861-0660
www.chicagolandchamber.org

City of Chicago Department of Planning
and Development
City Hall, Room 1000
121 North La Salle Street
Chicago, IL 60602
Phone: (312) 744-4190
Fax: (312) 744-2271
www.cityofchicago.org/city/en/depts/dcd.html

Cincinnati, OH
Cincinnati USA Regional Chamber
3 East 4th Street, Suite 200
Cincinnati, Ohio 45202
Phone: (513) 579-3111
www.cincinnatichamber.com

Clarksville, TN
Clarksville Area Chamber of Commerce
25 Jefferson Street, Suite 300
Clarksville, TN 37040
Phone: (931) 647-2331
www.clarksvillechamber.com

Cleveland, OH
Greater Cleveland Partnership
1240 Huron Rd. E, Suite 300
Cleveland, OH 44115
Phone: (216) 621-3300
www.gcpartnership.com

College Station, TX
Bryan-College Station Chamber of
Commerce
4001 East 29th St, Suite 175
Bryan, TX 77802
Phone: (979) 260-5200
www.bcschamber.org

Colorado Springs, CO
Colorado Springs Chamber and EDC
102 South Tejon Street
Suite 430
Colorado Springs, CO 80903
Phone: (719) 471-8183
coloradospringschamberedc.com

Columbia, MO
Columbia Chamber of Commerce
300 South Providence Rd.
P.O. Box 1016
Columbia, MO 65205-1016
Phone: (573) 874-1132
Fax: (573) 443-3986
www.columbiamochamber.com

Columbia, SC
The Columbia Chamber
930 Richland Street
Columbia, SC 29201
Phone: (803) 733-1110
Fax: (803) 733-1113
www.columbiachamber.com

Columbus, OH
Greater Columbus Chamber
37 North High Street
Columbus, OH 43215
Phone: (614) 221-1321
Fax: (614) 221-1408
www.columbus.org

Dallas, TX
City of Dallas Economic Development
Department
1500 Marilla Street
5C South
Dallas, TX 75201
Phone: (214) 670-1685
Fax: (214) 670-0158
www.dallas-edd.org

Greater Dallas Chamber of Commerce
700 North Pearl Street
Suite1200
Dallas, TX 75201
Phone: (214) 746-6600
Fax: (214) 746-6799
www.dallaschamber.org

Davenport, IA
Quad Cities Chamber
331 W. 3rd Street
Suite 100
Davenport, IA 52801
Phone: (563) 322-1706
quadcitieschamber.com

Denver, CO
Denver Metro Chamber of Commerce
1445 Market Street
Denver, CO 80202
Phone: (303) 534-8500
Fax: (303) 534-3200
www.denverchamber.org

Downtown Denver Partnership
511 16th Street
Suite 200
Denver, CO 80202
Phone: (303) 534-6161
Fax: (303) 534-2803
www.downtowndenver.com

Des Moines, IA
Des Moines Downtown Chamber
301 Grand Ave
Des Moines, IA 50309
Phone: (515) 309-3229
desmoinesdowntownchamber.com

Greater Des Moines Partnership
700 Locust Street
Suite 100
Des Moines, IA 50309
Phone: (515) 286-4950
Fax: (515) 286-4974
www.desmoinesmetro.com

Durham, NC
Durham Chamber of Commerce
P.O. Box 3829
Durham, NC 27702
Phone: (919) 682-2133
Fax: (919) 688-8351
www.durhamchamber.org

North Carolina Institute of Minority
Economic Development
114 W Parish Street
Durham, NC 27701
Phone: (919) 956-8889
Fax: (919) 688-7668
www.ncimed.com

Edison, NJ
Edison Chamber of Commerce
939 Amboy Avenue
Edison, NJ 08837
Phone: (732) 738-9482
www.edisonchamber.com

El Paso, TX
City of El Paso Department of Economic
Development
2 Civic Center Plaza
El Paso, TX 79901
Phone: (915) 541-4000
Fax: (915) 541-1316
www.elpasotexas.gov

Greater El Paso Chamber of Commerce
10 Civic Center Plaza
El Paso, TX 79901
Phone: (915) 534-0500
Fax: (915) 534-0510
www.elpaso.org

Fargo, ND
Chamber of Commerce of Fargo Moorhead
202 First Avenue North
Fargo, ND 56560
Phone: (218) 233-1100
Fax: (218) 233-1200
www.fmchamber.com

Greater Fargo-Moorhead Economic
Development Corporation
51 Broadway, Suite 500
Fargo, ND 58102
Phone: (701) 364-1900
Fax: (701) 293-7819
www.gfmedc.com

Fort Collins, CO
Fort Collins Chamber of Commerce
225 South Meldrum
Fort Collins, CO 80521
Phone: (970) 482-3746
Fax: (970) 482-3774
fortcollinschamber.com

Fort Wayne, IN
City of Fort Wayne Economic Development
1 Main St
1 Main Street
Fort Wayne, IN 46802
Phone: (260) 427-1111
Fax: (260) 427-1375
www.cityoffortwayne.org

Greater Fort Wayne Chamber of Commerce
826 Ewing Street
Fort Wayne, IN 46802
Phone: (260) 424-1435
Fax: (260) 426-7232
www.fwchamber.org

Fort Worth, TX
City of Fort Worth Economic Development
City Hall
900 Monroe Street
Suite 301
Fort Worth, TX 76102
Phone: (817) 392-6103
Fax: (817) 392-2431
www.fortworthgov.org

Fort Worth Chamber of Commerce
777 Taylor Street, Suite 900
Fort Worth, TX 76102-4997
Phone: (817) 336-2491
Fax: (817) 877-4034
www.fortworthchamber.com

Grand Rapids, MI
Grands Rapids Area Chamber of Commerce
111 Pearl Street N.W.
Grand Rapids, MI 49503
Phone: (616) 771-0300
Fax: (616) 771-0318
www.grandrapids.org

Greeley, CO
Greeley Area Chamber of Commerce
902 7th Avenue
Greeley, CO 80631
Phone: (970) 352-3566
www.greeleychamber.com

Green Bay, WI
Economic Development
100 N Jefferson Street
Room 202
Green Bay, WI 54301
Phone: (920) 448-3397
Fax: (920) 448-3063
www.ci.green-bay.wi.us

Green Bay Area Chamber of Commerce
300 N. Broadway
Suite 3A
Green Bay, WI 54305-1660
Phone: (920) 437-8704
Fax: (920) 593-3468
www.titletown.org

Greensboro, NC
Greensboro Chamber of Commerce
111 W. February One Place
Greensboro, NC 27401
Phone: (336) 387-8301
greensboro.org

Honolulu, HI
The Chamber of Commerce of Hawaii
1132 Bishop Street
Suite 402
Honolulu, HI 96813
Phone: (808) 545-4300
Fax: (808) 545-4369
www.cochawaii.com

Houston, TX
Greater Houston Partnership
1200 Smith Street, Suite 700
Houston, TX 77002-4400
Phone: (713) 844-3600
Fax: (713) 844-0200
www.houston.org

Huntsville, AL
Chamber of Commerce of
Huntsville/Madison County
225 Church Street
Huntsville, AL 35801
Phone: (256) 535-2000
Fax: (256) 535-2015
www.huntsvillealabamausa.com

Indianapolis, IN
Greater Indianapolis Chamber of Commerce
111 Monument Circle, Suite 1950
Indianapolis, IN 46204
Phone: (317) 464-2222
Fax: (317) 464-2217
www.indychamber.com

The Indy Partnership
111 Monument Circle, Suite 1800
Indianapolis, IN 46204
Phone: (317) 236-6262
Fax: (317) 236-6275
indypartnership.com

Jacksonville, FL
Jacksonville Chamber of Commerce
3 Independent Drive
Jacksonville, FL 32202
Phone: (904) 366-6600
Fax: (904) 632-0617
www.myjaxchamber.com

Kansas City, MO
Greater Kansas City Chamber of Commerce
2600 Commerce Tower
911 Main Street
Kansas City, MO 64105
Phone: (816) 221-2424
Fax: (816) 221-7440
www.kcchamber.com

Kansas City Area Development Council
2600 Commerce Tower
911 Main Street
Kansas City, MO 64105
Phone: (816) 221-2121
Fax: (816) 842-2865
www.thinkkc.com

Lafayette, LA
Greater Lafayette Chamber of Commerce
804 East Saint Mary Blvd.
Lafayette, LA 70503
Phone: (337) 233-2705
Fax: (337) 234-8671
www.lafchamber.org

Las Cruces, NM
Greater Las Cruces Chamber of Commerce
505 S Main Street, Suite 134
Las Cruces, NM 88001
Phone: (575) 524-1968
Fax: (575) 527-5546
www.lascruces.org

Las Vegas, NV
Las Vegas Chamber of Commerce
6671 Las Vegas Blvd South
Suite 300
Las Vegas, NV 89119
Phone: (702) 735-1616
Fax: (702) 735-0406
www.lvchamber.org

Las Vegas Office of Business Development
400 Stewart Avenue
City Hall
Las Vegas, NV 89101
Phone: (702) 229-6011
Fax: (702) 385-3128
www.lasvegasnevada.gov

Lexington, KY
Greater Lexington Chamber of Commerce
330 East Main Street
Suite 100
Lexington, KY 40507
Phone: (859) 254-4447
Fax: (859) 233-3304
www.commercelexington.com

Lexington Downtown Development
Authority
101 East Vine Street
Suite 500
Lexington, KY 40507
Phone: (859) 425-2296
Fax: (859) 425-2292
www.lexingtondda.com

Lincoln, NE
Lincoln Chamber of Commerce
1135 M Street
Suite 200
Lincoln, NE 68508
Phone: (402) 436-2350
Fax: (402) 436-2360
www.lcoc.com

Little Rock, AR
Little Rock Regional Chamber
One Chamber Plaza
Little Rock, AR 72201
Phone: (501) 374-2001
Fax: (501) 374-6018
www.littlerockchamber.com

Los Angeles, CA
Los Angeles Area Chamber of Commerce
350 South Bixel Street
Los Angeles, CA 90017
Phone: (213) 580-7500
Fax: (213) 580-7511
www.lachamber.org

Los Angeles County Economic
Development Corporation
444 South Flower Street
34th Floor
Los Angeles, CA 90071
Phone: (213) 622-4300
Fax: (213) 622-7100
www.laedc.org

Louisville, KY
The Greater Louisville Chamber of
Commerce
614 West Main Street
Suite 6000
Louisville, KY 40202
Phone: (502) 625-0000
Fax: (502) 625-0010
www.greaterlouisville.com

Madison, WI
Greater Madison Chamber of Commerce
615 East Washington Avenue
P.O. Box 71
Madison, WI 53701-0071
Phone: (608) 256-8348
Fax: (608) 256-0333
www.greatermadisonchamber.com

Manchester, NH
Greater Manchester Chamber of Commerce
889 Elm Street
Manchester, NH 03101
Phone: (603) 666-6600
Fax: (603) 626-0910
www.manchester-chamber.org

Manchester Economic Development Office
One City Hall Plaza
Manchester, NH 03101
Phone: (603) 624-6505
Fax: (603) 624-6308
www.yourmanchesternh.com

Miami, FL
Greater Miami Chamber of Commerce
1601 Biscayne Boulevard
Miami, FL 33132-1260
Phone: (305) 350-7700
Fax: (305) 374-6902
www.miamichamber.com

The Beacon Council
80 Southwest 8th Street, Suite 2400
Miami, FL 33130
Phone: (305) 579-1300
Fax: (305) 375-0271
www.beaconcouncil.com

Midland, TX
Midland Chamber of Commerce
109 N. Main
Midland, TX 79701
Phone: (432) 683-3381
Fax: (432) 686-3556
www.midlandtxchamber.com

Milwaukee, WI
Greater Milwaukee Chamber of Commerce
6815 W. Capitol Drive
Suite 300
Milwaukee, WI 53216
Phone: (414) 465-2422
www.gmcofc.org

Metropolitan Milwaukee Association of
Commerce
756 N. Milwaukee Street
Suite 400
Milwaukee, WI 53202
Phone: (414) 287-4100
Fax: (414) 271-7753
www.mmac.org

Minneapolis, MN
Minneapolis Regional Chamber
81 South Ninth Street, Suite 200
Minneapolis, MN 55402
Phone: (612) 370-9100
Fax: (612) 370-9195
www.minneapolischamber.org

Minneapolis Community Development
Agency
Crown Roller Mill
105 5th Avenue South
Suite 200
Minneapolis, MN 55401
Phone: (612) 673-5095
Fax: (612) 673-5100
www.ci.minneapolis.mn.us

Nashville, TN
Nashville Area Chamber of Commerce
211 Commerce Street, Suite 100
Nashville, TN 37201
Phone: (615) 743-3000
Fax: (615) 256-3074
www.nashvillechamber.com

Tennessee Valley Authority Economic
Development
400 West Summit Hill Drive
Knoxville TN 37902
Phone: (865) 632-2101
www.tvaed.com

New Haven, CT
Greater New Haven Chamber of Commerce
900 Chapel Street, 10th Floor
New Haven, CT 06510
Phone: (203) 787-6735
www.gnhcc.com

New Orleans, LA
New Orleans Chamber of Commerce
1515 Poydras Street
Suite 1010
New Orleans, LA 70112
Phone: (504) 799-4260
Fax: (504) 799-4259
www.neworleanschamber.org

New York, NY
New York City Economic Development
Corporation
110 William Street
New York, NY 10038
Phone: (212) 619-5000
www.nycedc.com

The Partnership for New York City
One Battery Park Plaza
5th Floor
New York, NY 10004
Phone: (212) 493-7400
Fax: (212) 344-3344
www.pfnyc.org

Oklahoma City, OK
Greater Oklahoma City Chamber of
Commerce
123 Park Avenue
Oklahoma City, OK 73102
Phone: (405) 297-8900
Fax: (405) 297-8916
www.okcchamber.com

Omaha, NE
Omaha Chamber of Commerce
1301 Harney Street
Omaha, NE 68102
Phone: (402) 346-5000
Fax: (402) 346-7050
www.omahachamber.org

Orlando, FL
Metro Orlando Economic Development
Commission of Mid-Florida
301 East Pine Street, Suite 900
Orlando, FL 32801
Phone: (407) 422-7159
Fax: (407) 425.6428
www.orlandoedc.com

Orlando Regional Chamber of Commerce
75 South Ivanhoe Boulevard
P.O. Box 1234
Orlando, FL 32802
Phone: (407) 425-1234
Fax: (407) 839-5020
www.orlando.org

Philadelphia, PA
Greater Philadelphia Chamber of
Commerce
200 South Broad Street
Suite 700
Philadelphia, PA 19102
Phone: (215) 545-1234
Fax: (215) 790-3600
www.greaterphilachamber.com

Phoenix, AZ
Greater Phoenix Chamber of Commerce
201 North Central Avenue
27th Floor
Phoenix, AZ 85073
Phone: (602) 495-2195
Fax: (602) 495-8913
www.phoenixchamber.com

Greater Phoenix Economic Council
2 North Central Avenue
Suite 2500
Phoenix, AZ 85004
Phone: (602) 256-7700
Fax: (602) 256-7744
www.gpec.org

Pittsburgh, PA
Allegheny County Industrial Development
Authority
425 6th Avenue
Suite 800
Pittsburgh, PA 15219
Phone: (412) 350-1067
Fax: (412) 642-2217
www.alleghenycounty.us

Greater Pittsburgh Chamber of Commerce
425 6th Avenue
12th Floor
Pittsburgh, PA 15219
Phone: (412) 392-4500
Fax: (412) 392-4520
www.alleghenyconference.org

Portland, OR
Portland Business Alliance
200 SW Market Street
Suite 1770
Portland, OR 97201
Phone: (503) 224-8684
Fax: (503) 323-9186
www.portlandalliance.com

Providence, RI
Greater Providence Chamber of Commerce
30 Exchange Terrace
Fourth Floor
Providence, RI 02903
Phone: (401) 521-5000
Fax: (401) 351-2090
www.provchamber.com

Rhode Island Economic Development
Corporation
Providence City Hall
25 Dorrance Street
Providence, RI 02903
Phone: (401) 421-7740
Fax: (401) 751-0203
www.providenceri.com

Provo, UT
Provo-Orem Chamber of Commerce
51 South University Avenue, Suite 215
Provo, UT 84601
Phone: (801) 851-2555
Fax: (801) 851-2557
www.thechamber.org

Raleigh, NC
Greater Raleigh Chamber of Commerce
800 South Salisbury Street
Raleigh, NC 27601-2978
Phone: (919) 664-7000
Fax: (919) 664-7099
www.raleighchamber.org

Reno, NV
Greater Reno-Sparks Chamber of Commerce
1 East First Street, 16th Floor
Reno, NV 89505
Phone: (775) 337-3030
Fax: (775) 337-3038
www.reno-sparkschamber.org

The Chamber Reno-Sparks-Northern Nevada
449 S. Virginia Street, 2nd Floor
Reno, NV 89501
Phone: (775) 636-9550
www.thechambernv.org

Richmond, VA
Greater Richmond Chamber
600 East Main Street
Suite 700
Richmond, VA 23219
Phone: (804) 648-1234
www.grcc.com

Greater Richmond Partnership
901 East Byrd Street
Suite 801
Richmond, VA 23219-4070
Phone: (804) 643-3227
Fax: (804) 343-7167
www.grpva.com

Rochester, MN
Rochester Area Chamber of Commerce
220 South Broadway
Suite 100
Rochester, MN 55904
Phone: (507) 288-1122
Fax: (507) 282-8960
www.rochestermnchamber.com

Sacramento, CA
Sacramento Metro Chamber
One Capitol Mall
Suite 700
Sacramento, CA 95814
Phone: (916) 552-6800
metrochamber.org

Saint Louis, MO
St. Louis Regional Chamber
One Metropolitan Square, Suite 1300
St. Louis, MO 63102
Phone: (314) 231-5555
www.stlregionalchamber.com

Salem, OR
Salem Chamber
1110 Commercial Street NE
Salem, OR 97301
Phone: (503) 581-1466
salemchamber.org

Salt Lake City, UT
Salt Lake Chamber
175 E. University Blvd. (400 S), Suite 600
Salt Lake City, UT 84111
Phone: (801) 364-3631
www.slchamber.com

San Antonio, TX
The Greater San Antonio Chamber of
Commerce
602 E. Commerce Street
San Antonio, TX 78205
Phone: (210) 229-2100
Fax: (210) 229-1600
www.sachamber.org

San Antonio Economic Development
Department
P.O. Box 839966
San Antonio, TX 78283-3966
Phone: (210) 207-8080
Fax: (210) 207-8151
www.sanantonio.gov/edd

San Diego, CA
San Diego Economic Development Corp.
401 B Street
Suite 1100
San Diego, CA 92101
Phone: (619) 234-8484
Fax: (619) 234-1935
www.sandiegobusiness.org

San Diego Regional Chamber of Commerce
402 West Broadway
Suite 1000
San Diego, CA 92101-3585
Phone: (619) 544-1300
Fax: (619) 744-7481
www.sdchamber.org

San Francisco, CA
San Francisco Chamber of Commerce
235 Montgomery Street
12th Floor
San Francisco, CA 94104
Phone: (415) 392-4520
Fax: (415) 392-0485
www.sfchamber.com

San Jose, CA
Office of Economic Development
60 South Market Street
Suite 470
San Jose, CA 95113
Phone: (408) 277-5880
Fax: (408) 277-3615
www.sba.gov

The Silicon Valley Organization
101 W Santa Clara Street
San Jose, CA 95113
Phone: (408) 291-5250
www.thesvo.com

Santa Rosa, CA
Santa Rosa Chamber of Commerce
1260 North Dutton Avenue
Suite 272
Santa Rosa, CA 95401
Phone: (707) 545-1414
www.santarosachamber.com

Savannah, GA
Economic Development Authority
131 Hutchinson Island Road
4th Floor
Savannah, GA 31421
Phone: (912) 447-8450
Fax: (912) 447-8455
www.seda.org

Savannah Chamber of Commerce
101 E. Bay Street
Savannah, GA 31402
Phone: (912) 644-6400
Fax: (912) 644-6499
www.savannahchamber.com

Seattle, WA
Greater Seattle Chamber of Commerce
1301 Fifth Avenue
Suite 2500
Seattle, WA 98101
Phone: (206) 389-7200
Fax: (206) 389-7288
www.seattlechamber.com

Sioux Falls, SD
Sioux Falls Area Chamber of Commerce
200 N. Phillips Avenue
Suite 102
Sioux Falls, SD 57104
Phone: (605) 336-1620
Fax: (605) 336-6499
www.siouxfallschamber.com

Springfield, IL
The Greater Springfield Chamber of
Commerce
1011 S. Second Street
Springfield, IL 62704
Phone: (217) 525-1173
Fax: (217) 525-8768
www.gscc.org

Tampa, FL
Greater Tampa Chamber of Commerce
P.O. Box 420
Tampa, FL 33601-0420
Phone: (813) 276-9401
Fax: (813) 229-7855
www.tampachamber.com

Tucson, AZ
Tucson Metro Chamber
212 E. Broadway Blvd
Tucson, AZ 85701
Phone: (520) 792-1212
tucsonchamber.org

Tulsa, OK
Tulsa Regional Chamber
One West Third Street
Suite 100
Tulsa, OK 74103
Phone: (918) 585-1201
www.tulsachamber.com

Tuscaloosa, AL
The Chamber of Commerce of West
Alabama
2201 Jack Warner Parkway
Building C
Tuscaloosa, AL 35401
Phone: (205) 758-7588
tuscaloosachamber.com

Virginia Beach, VA
Hampton Roads Chamber of Commerce
500 East Main Street, Suite 700
Virginia Beach, VA 23510
Phone: (757) 664-2531
www.hamptonroadschamber.com

Washington, DC
District of Columbia Chamber of Commerce
1213 K Street NW
Washington, DC 20005
Phone: (202) 347-7201
Fax: (202) 638-6762
www.dcchamber.org

District of Columbia Office of Planning and
Economic Development
J.A. Wilson Building
1350 Pennsylvania Ave NW, Suite 317
Washington, DC 20004
Phone: (202) 727-6365
Fax: (202) 727-6703
www.dcbiz.dc.gov

Wichita, KS
Wichita Regional Chamber of Commerce
350 W Douglas Avennue
Wichita, KS 67202
Phone: (316) 265-7771
www.wichitachamber.org

Wilmington, NC
Wilmington Chamber of Commerce
One Estell Lee Place
Wilmington, NC 28401
Phone: (910) 762-2611
www.wilmingtonchamber.org

Winston-Salem, NC
Winston-Salem Chamber of Commerce
411 West Fourth Street
Suite 211
Winston-Salem, NC 27101
Phone: (336) 728-9200
www.winstonsalem.com

Worcester, MA
Worcester Regional Chamber of Commerce
311 Main Street, Suite 200
Worcester, MA 01608
Phone: (508) 753-2924
worcesterchamber.org

Appendix E: State Departments of Labor

Alabama
Alabama Department of Labor
P.O. Box 303500
Montgomery, AL 36130-3500
Phone: (334) 242-3072
www.labor.alabama.gov

Alaska
Dept of Labor and Workforce Devel.
P.O. Box 11149
Juneau, AK 99822-2249
Phone: (907) 465-2700
www.labor.state.ak.us

Arizona
Industrial Commission or Arizona
800 West Washington Street
Phoenix, AZ 85007
Phone: (602) 542-4411
www.azica.gov

Arkansas
Department of Labor
10421 West Markham
Little Rock, AR 72205
Phone: (501) 682-4500
www.labor.ar.gov

California
Labor and Workforce Development
445 Golden Gate Ave., 10th Floor
San Francisco, CA 94102
Phone: (916) 263-1811
www.labor.ca.gov

Colorado
Dept of Labor and Employment
633 17th St., 2nd Floor
Denver, CO 80202-3660
Phone: (888) 390-7936
cdle.colorado.gov

Connecticut
Department of Labor
200 Folly Brook Blvd.
Wethersfield, CT 06109-1114
Phone: (860) 263-6000
www.ctdol.state.ct.us

Delaware
Department of Labor
4425 N. Market St., 4th Floor
Wilmington, DE 19802
Phone: (302) 451-3423
dol.delaware.gov

District of Columbia
Department of Employment Services
614 New York Ave., NE, Suite 300
Washington, DC 20002
Phone: (202) 671-1900
does.dc.gov

Florida
Florida Department of Economic Opportunity
The Caldwell Building
107 East Madison St. Suite 100
Tallahassee, FL 32399-4120
Phone: (800) 342-3450
www.floridajobs.org

Georgia
Department of Labor
Sussex Place, Room 600
148 Andrew Young Intl Blvd., NE
Atlanta, GA 30303
Phone: (404) 656-3011
dol.georgia.gov

Hawaii
Dept of Labor & Industrial Relations
830 Punchbowl Street
Honolulu, HI 96813
Phone: (808) 586-8842
labor.hawaii.gov

Idaho
Department of Labor
317 W. Main St.
Boise, ID 83735-0001
Phone: (208) 332-3579
www.labor.idaho.gov

Illinois
Department of Labor
160 N. LaSalle Street, 13th Floor
Suite C-1300
Chicago, IL 60601
Phone: (312) 793-2800
www.illinois.gov/idol

Indiana
Indiana Department of Labor
402 West Washington Street, Room W195
Indianapolis, IN 46204
Phone: (317) 232-2655
www.in.gov/dol

Iowa
Iowa Workforce Development
1000 East Grand Avenue
Des Moines, IA 50319-0209
Phone: (515) 242-5870
www.iowadivisionoflabor.gov

Kansas
Department of Labor
401 S.W. Topeka Blvd.
Topeka, KS 66603-3182
Phone: (785) 296-5000
www.dol.ks.gov

Kentucky
Department of Labor
1047 U.S. Hwy 127 South, Suite 4
Frankfort, KY 40601-4381
Phone: (502) 564-3070
www.labor.ky.gov

Louisiana
Louisiana Workforce Commission
1001 N. 23rd Street
Baton Rouge, LA 70804-9094
Phone: (225) 342-3111
www.laworks.net

Maine
Department of Labor
45 Commerce Street
Augusta, ME 04330
Phone: (207) 623-7900
www.state.me.us/labor

Maryland
Department of Labor, Licensing & Regulation
500 N. Calvert Street
Suite 401
Baltimore, MD 21202
Phone: (410) 767-2357
www.dllr.state.md.us

Massachusetts
Dept of Labor & Workforce Development
One Ashburton Place
Room 2112
Boston, MA 02108
Phone: (617) 626-7100
www.mass.gov/lwd

Michigan
Department of Licensing and Regulatory
Affairs
611 W. Ottawa
P.O. Box 30004
Lansing, MI 48909
Phone: (517) 373-1820
www.michigan.gov/lara

Minnesota
Dept of Labor and Industry
443 Lafayette Road North
Saint Paul, MN 55155
Phone: (651) 284-5070
www.doli.state.mn.us

Mississippi
Dept of Employment Security
P.O. Box 1699
Jackson, MS 39215-1699
Phone: (601) 321-6000
www.mdes.ms.gov

Missouri
Labor and Industrial Relations
P.O. Box 599
3315 W. Truman Boulevard
Jefferson City, MO 65102-0599
Phone: (573) 751-7500
labor.mo.gov

Montana
Dept of Labor and Industry
P.O. Box 1728
Helena, MT 59624-1728
Phone: (406) 444-9091
www.dli.mt.gov

Nebraska
Department of Labor
550 S 16th Street
Lincoln, NE 68508
Phone: (402) 471-9000
dol.nebraska.gov

Nevada
Dept of Business and Industry
3300 W. Sahara Ave, Suite 425
Las Vegas, NV 89102
Phone: (702) 486-2750
business.nv.gov

New Hampshire
Department of Labor
State Office Park South
95 Pleasant Street
Concord, NH 03301
Phone: (603) 271-3176
www.nh.gov/labor

New Jersey
Department of Labor & Workforce Devel.
John Fitch Plaza, 13th Floor, Suite D
Trenton, NJ 08625-0110
Phone: (609) 777-3200
lwd.dol.state.nj.us/labor

New Mexico
Department of Workforce Solutions
401 Broadway, NE
Albuquerque, NM 87103-1928
Phone: (505) 841-8450
www.dws.state.nm.us

New York
Department of Labor
State Office Bldg. # 12
W.A. Harriman Campus
Albany, NY 12240
Phone: (518) 457-9000
www.labor.ny.gov

North Carolina
Department of Labor
4 West Edenton Street
Raleigh, NC 27601-1092
Phone: (919) 733-7166
www.labor.nc.gov

North Dakota
North Dakota Department of Labor and
Human Rights
State Capitol Building
600 East Boulevard, Dept 406
Bismark, ND 58505-0340
Phone: (701) 328-2660
www.nd.gov/labor

Ohio
Department of Commerce
77 South High Street, 22nd Floor
Columbus, OH 43215
Phone: (614) 644-2239
www.com.state.oh.us

Oklahoma
Department of Labor
4001 N. Lincoln Blvd.
Oklahoma City, OK 73105-5212
Phone: (405) 528-1500
www.ok.gov/odol

Oregon
Bureau of Labor and Industries
800 NE Oregon St., #32
Portland, OR 97232
Phone: (971) 673-0761
www.oregon.gov/boli

Pennsylvania
Dept of Labor and Industry
1700 Labor and Industry Bldg
7th and Forster Streets
Harrisburg, PA 17120
Phone: (717) 787-5279
www.dli.pa.gov

Rhode Island
Department of Labor and Training
1511 Pontiac Avenue
Cranston, RI 02920
Phone: (401) 462-8000
www.dlt.state.ri.us

South Carolina
Dept of Labor, Licensing & Regulations
P.O. Box 11329
Columbia, SC 29211-1329
Phone: (803) 896-4300
www.llr.state.sc.us

South Dakota
Department of Labor & Regulation
700 Governors Drive
Pierre, SD 57501-2291
Phone: (605) 773-3682
dlr.sd.gov

Tennessee
Dept of Labor & Workforce Development
Andrew Johnson Tower
710 James Robertson Pkwy
Nashville, TN 37243-0655
Phone: (615) 741-6642
www.tn.gov/workforce

Texas
Texas Workforce Commission
101 East 15th St.
Austin, TX 78778
Phone: (512) 475-2670
www.twc.state.tx.us

Utah
Utah Labor Commission
160 East 300 South, 3rd Floor
Salt Lake City, UT 84114-6600
Phone: (801) 530-6800
laborcommission.utah.gov

Vermont
Department of Labor
5 Green Mountain Drive
P.O. Box 488
Montpelier, VT 05601-0488
Phone: (802) 828-4000
labor.vermont.gov

Virginia
Dept of Labor and Industry
Powers-Taylor Building
13 S. 13th Street
Richmond, VA 23219
Phone: (804) 371-2327
www.doli.virginia.gov

Washington
Dept of Labor and Industries
P.O. Box 44001
Olympia, WA 98504-4001
Phone: (360) 902-4200
www.lni.wa.gov

West Virginia
Division of Labor
749 B Building 6
Capitol Complex
Charleston, WV 25305
Phone: (304) 558-7890
labor.wv.gov

Wisconsin
Dept of Workforce Development
201 E. Washington Ave., #A400
P.O. Box 7946
Madison, WI 53707-7946
Phone: (608) 266-6861
dwd.wisconsin.gov

Wyoming
Department of Workforce Services
1510 East Pershing Blvd.
Cheyenne, WY 82002
Phone: (307) 777-7261
www.wyomingworkforce.org

Titles from Grey House

Visit www.GreyHouse.com for Product Information, Table of Contents, and Sample Pages.

Opinions Throughout History

Opinions Throughout History: Church & State
Opinions Throughout History: Conspiracy Theories
Opinions Throughout History: The Death Penalty
Opinions Throughout History: Diseases & Epidemics
Opinions Throughout History: Drug Use & Abuse
Opinions Throughout History: The Environment
Opinions Throughout History: Free Speech & Censorship
Opinions Throughout History: Gender: Roles & Rights
Opinions Throughout History: Globalization
Opinions Throughout History: Guns in America
Opinions Throughout History: Immigration
Opinions Throughout History: Law Enforcement in America
Opinions Throughout History: Mental Health
Opinions Throughout History: Nat'l Security vs. Civil & Privacy Rights
Opinions Throughout History: Presidential Authority
Opinions Throughout History: Robotics & Artificial Intelligence
Opinions Throughout History: Social Media Issues
Opinions Throughout History: The Supreme Court
Opinions Throughout History: Voters' Rights
Opinions Throughout History: War & the Military
Opinions Throughout History: Workers Rights & Wages

This is Who We Were

This is Who We Were: Colonial America (1492-1775)
This is Who We Were: 1880-1899
This is Who We Were: In the 1900s
This is Who We Were: In the 1910s
This is Who We Were: In the 1920s
This is Who We Were: A Companion to the 1940 Census
This is Who We Were: In the 1940s (1940-1949)
This is Who We Were: In the 1950s
This is Who We Were: In the 1960s
This is Who We Were: In the 1970s
This is Who We Were: In the 1980s
This is Who We Were: In the 1990s
This is Who We Were: In the 2000s
This is Who We Were: In the 2010s

Working Americans

Working Americans—Vol. 1: The Working Class
Working Americans—Vol. 2: The Middle Class
Working Americans—Vol. 3: The Upper Class
Working Americans—Vol. 4: Children
Working Americans—Vol. 5: At War
Working Americans—Vol. 6: Working Women
Working Americans—Vol. 7: Social Movements
Working Americans—Vol. 8: Immigrants
Working Americans—Vol. 9: Revolutionary War to the Civil War
Working Americans—Vol. 10: Sports & Recreation
Working Americans—Vol. 11: Inventors & Entrepreneurs
Working Americans—Vol. 12: Our History through Music
Working Americans—Vol. 13: Education & Educators
Working Americans—Vol. 14: African Americans
Working Americans—Vol. 15: Politics & Politicians
Working Americans—Vol. 16: Farming & Ranching
Working Americans—Vol. 17: Teens in America
Working Americans—Vol. 18: Health Care Workers
Working Americans—Vol. 19: The Performing Arts

Grey House Health & Wellness Guides

Addiction Handbook & Resource Guide
The Autism Spectrum Handbook & Resource Guide
Autoimmune Disorders Handbook & Resource Guide
Cardiovascular Disease Handbook & Resource Guide
Dementia Handbook & Resource Guide
Depression Handbook & Resource Guide
Diabetes Handbook & Resource Guide
Nutrition, Obesity & Eating Disorders Handbook & Resource Guide

Consumer Health

Complete Mental Health Resource Guide
Complete Resource Guide for Pediatric Disorders
Complete Resource Guide for People with Chronic Illness
Complete Resource Guide for People with Disabilities
Older Americans Information Resource
Parenting: Styles & Strategies
Teens: Growing Up, Skills & Strategies

General Reference

American Environmental Leaders
Constitutional Amendments
Encyclopedia of African-American Writing
Encyclopedia of Invasions & Conquests
Encyclopedia of Prisoners of War & Internment
Encyclopedia of the Continental Congresses
Encyclopedia of the United States Cabinet
Encyclopedia of War Journalism
The Environmental Debate
Financial Literacy Starter Kit
From Suffrage to the Senate
The Gun Debate: Gun Rights & Gun Control in the U.S.
Historical Warrior Peoples & Modern Fighting Groups
Human Rights and the United States
Political Corruption in America
Privacy Rights in the Digital Age
The Religious Right and American Politics
Speakers of the House of Representatives, 1789-2021
US Land & Natural Resources Policy
The Value of a Dollar 1600-1865 Colonial to Civil War
The Value of a Dollar 1860-2019

Business Information

Business Information Resources
Complete Broadcasting Industry Guide: TV, Radio, Cable & Streaming
Directory of Mail Order Catalogs
Environmental Resource Handbook
Food & Beverage Market Place
The Grey House Guide to Homeland Security Resources
The Grey House Performing Arts Industry Guide
Guide to Healthcare Group Purchasing Organizations
Guide to U.S. HMOs and PPOs
Guide to Venture Capital & Private Equity Firms
Hudson's Washington News Media Contacts Guide
New York State Directory
Sports Market Place

Grey House Publishing | Salem Press | H.W. Wilson | 4919 Route 22, PO Box 56, Amenia, NY 12501-0056

Grey House Imprints

Visit www.GreyHouse.com for Product Information, Table of Contents, and Sample Pages.

Grey House Titles, continued

Education

Complete Learning Disabilities Resource Guide
Digital Literacy: Skills & Strategies
Educators Resource Guide
The Comparative Guide to Elem. & Secondary Schools
Special Education: Policy & Curriculum Development

Statistics & Demographics

America's Top-Rated Cities
America's Top-Rated Smaller Cities
The Comparative Guide to American Suburbs
Profiles of America
Profiles of California
Profiles of Florida
Profiles of Illinois
Profiles of Indiana
Profiles of Massachusetts
Profiles of Michigan
Profiles of New Jersey
Profiles of New York
Profiles of North Carolina & South Carolina
Profiles of Ohio
Profiles of Pennsylvania
Profiles of Texas
Profiles of Virginia
Profiles of Wisconsin

Weiss Financial Ratings

Financial Literacy Basics
Financial Literacy: How to Become an Investor
Financial Literacy: Planning for the Future
Weiss Ratings Consumer Guides
Weiss Ratings Guide to Banks
Weiss Ratings Guide to Credit Unions
Weiss Ratings Guide to Health Insurers
Weiss Ratings Guide to Life & Annuity Insurers
Weiss Ratings Guide to Property & Casualty Insurers
Weiss Ratings Investment Research Guide to Bond & Money Market
    Mutual Funds
Weiss Ratings Investment Research Guide to Exchange-Traded Funds
Weiss Ratings Investment Research Guide to Stock Mutual Funds
Weiss Ratings Investment Research Guide to Stocks

Canadian Resources

Associations Canada
Canadian Almanac & Directory
Canadian Environmental Resource Guide
Canadian Parliamentary Guide
Canadian Venture Capital & Private Equity Firms
Canadian Who's Who
Cannabis Canada
Careers & Employment Canada
Financial Post: Directory of Directors
Financial Services Canada
FP Bonds: Corporate
FP Bonds: Government
FP Equities: Preferreds & Derivatives
FP Survey: Industrials
FP Survey: Mines & Energy
FP Survey: Predecessor & Defunct
Health Guide Canada
Libraries Canada

Books in Print Series

American Book Publishing Record® Annual
American Book Publishing Record® Monthly
Books In Print®
Books In Print® Supplement
Books Out Loud™
Bowker's Complete Video Directory™
Children's Books In Print®
El-Hi Textbooks & Serials In Print®
Forthcoming Books®
Law Books & Serials In Print™
Medical & Health Care Books In Print™
Publishers, Distributors & Wholesalers of the US™
Subject Guide to Books In Print®
Subject Guide to Children's Books In Print®

Titles from Salem Press

Visit www.SalemPress.com for Product Information, Table of Contents, and Sample Pages.

LITERATURE

Critical Insights: Authors

Louisa May Alcott
Sherman Alexie
Isabel Allende
Maya Angelou
Isaac Asimov
Margaret Atwood
Jane Austen
James Baldwin
Saul Bellow
Roberto Bolano
Ray Bradbury
The Brontë Sisters
Gwendolyn Brooks
Albert Camus
Raymond Carver
Willa Cather
Geoffrey Chaucer
John Cheever
Joseph Conrad
Charles Dickens
Emily Dickinson
Frederick Douglass
T. S. Eliot
George Eliot
Harlan Ellison
Ralph Waldo Emerson
Louise Erdrich
William Faulkner
F. Scott Fitzgerald
Gustave Flaubert
Horton Foote
Benjamin Franklin
Robert Frost
Neil Gaiman
Gabriel Garcia Marquez
Thomas Hardy
Nathaniel Hawthorne
Robert A. Heinlein
Lillian Hellman
Ernest Hemingway
Langston Hughes
Zora Neale Hurston
Henry James
Thomas Jefferson
James Joyce
Jamaica Kincaid
Stephen King
Martin Luther King, Jr.
Barbara Kingsolver
Abraham Lincoln
C.S. Lewis
Mario Vargas Llosa
Jack London
James McBride
Cormac McCarthy
Herman Melville
Arthur Miller
Toni Morrison
Alice Munro
Tim O'Brien
Flannery O'Connor
Eugene O'Neill
George Orwell

Sylvia Plath
Edgar Allan Poe
Philip Roth
Salman Rushdie
J.D. Salinger
Mary Shelley
John Steinbeck
Amy Tan
Leo Tolstoy
Mark Twain
John Updike
Kurt Vonnegut
Alice Walker
David Foster Wallace
Edith Wharton
Walt Whitman
Oscar Wilde
Tennessee Williams
Virginia Woolf
Richard Wright
Malcolm X

Critical Insights: Works

Absalom, Absalom!
Adventures of Huckleberry Finn
The Adventures of Tom Sawyer
Aeneid
All Quiet on the Western Front
All the Pretty Horses
Animal Farm
Anna Karenina
The Awakening
The Bell Jar
Beloved
Billy Budd, Sailor
The Book Thief
Brave New World
The Canterbury Tales
Catch-22
The Catcher in the Rye
The Color Purple
The Crucible
Death of a Salesman
The Diary of a Young Girl
Dracula
Fahrenheit 451
The Grapes of Wrath
Great Expectations
The Great Gatsby
Hamlet
The Handmaid's Tale
Harry Potter Series
Heart of Darkness
The Hobbit
The House on Mango Street
How the Garcia Girls Lost Their Accents
The Hunger Games Trilogy
I Know Why the Caged Bird Sings
In Cold Blood
The Inferno
Invisible Man
Jane Eyre
The Joy Luck Club
Julius Caesar
King Lear

The Kite Runner
Life of Pi
Little Women
Lolita
Lord of the Flies
The Lord of the Rings
Macbeth
The Merchant of Venice
The Metamorphosis
Midnight's Children
A Midsummer Night's Dream
Moby-Dick
Mrs. Dalloway
Nineteen Eighty-Four
The Odyssey
Of Mice and Men
The Old Man and the Sea
On the Road
One Flew Over the Cuckoo's Nest
One Hundred Years of Solitude
Othello
The Outsiders
Paradise Lost
The Pearl
The Plague
The Poetry of Baudelaire
The Poetry of Edgar Allan Poe
A Portrait of the Artist as a Young Man
Pride and Prejudice
A Raisin in the Sun
The Red Badge of Courage
Romeo and Juliet
The Scarlet Letter
Sense and Sensibility
Short Fiction of Flannery O'Connor
Slaughterhouse-Five
The Sound and the Fury
A Streetcar Named Desire
The Sun Also Rises
A Tale of Two Cities
The Tales of Edgar Allan Poe
Their Eyes Were Watching God
Things Fall Apart
To Kill a Mockingbird
War and Peace
The Woman Warrior

Critical Insights: Themes

The American Comic Book
American Creative Non-Fiction
The American Dream
American Multicultural Identity
American Road Literature
American Short Story
American Sports Fiction
The American Thriller
American Writers in Exile
Censored & Banned Literature
Civil Rights Literature, Past & Present
Coming of Age
Conspiracies
Contemporary Canadian Fiction
Contemporary Immigrant Short Fiction
Contemporary Latin American Fiction
Contemporary Speculative Fiction

Titles from Salem Press

Visit www.SalemPress.com for Product Information, Table of Contents, and Sample Pages.

Crime and Detective Fiction
Crisis of Faith
Cultural Encounters
Dystopia
Family
The Fantastic
Feminism Flash Fiction
Gender, Sex and Sexuality
Good & Evil
The Graphic Novel
Greed
Harlem Renaissance
The Hero's Quest
Historical Fiction
Holocaust Literature
The Immigrant Experience
Inequality
LGBTQ Literature
Literature in Times of Crisis
Literature of Protest
Love
Magical Realism
Midwestern Literature
Modern Japanese Literature
Nature & the Environment
Paranoia, Fear & Alienation
Patriotism
Political Fiction
Postcolonial Literature
Power & Corruption
Pulp Fiction of the '20s and '30s
Rebellion
Russia's Golden Age
Satire
The Slave Narrative
Social Justice and American Literature
Southern Gothic Literature
Southwestern Literature
Survival
Technology & Humanity
Truth & Lies
Violence in Literature
Virginia Woolf & 20th Century Women Writers
War

Critical Insights: Film

Bonnie & Clyde
Casablanca
Alfred Hitchcock
Stanley Kubrick

Critical Approaches to Literature

Critical Approaches to Literature: Feminist
Critical Approaches to Literature: Moral
Critical Approaches to Literature: Multicultural
Critical Approaches to Literature: Psychological

Literary Classics

Recommended Reading: 600 Classics Reviewed

Novels into Film

Novels into Film: Adaptations & Interpretation
Novels into Film: Adaptations & Interpretation, Volume 2

Critical Surveys of Literature

Critical Survey of American Literature
Critical Survey of Drama
Critical Survey of Long Fiction
Critical Survey of Mystery and Detective Fiction
Critical Survey of Poetry
Critical Survey of Poetry: Contemporary Poets
Critical Survey of Science Fiction & Fantasy Literature
Critical Survey of Shakespeare's Plays
Critical Survey of Shakespeare's Sonnets
Critical Survey of Short Fiction
Critical Survey of World Literature
Critical Survey of Young Adult Literature

Critical Surveys of Graphic Novels

Heroes & Superheroes
History, Theme, and Technique
Independents & Underground Classics
Manga

Critical Surveys of Mythology & Folklore

Creation Myths
Deadly Battles & Warring Enemies
Gods & Goddesses
Heroes and Heroines
Love, Sexuality, and Desire
World Mythology

Cyclopedia of Literary Characters & Places

Cyclopedia of Literary Characters
Cyclopedia of Literary Places

Introduction to Literary Context

American Poetry of the 20th Century
American Post-Modernist Novels
American Short Fiction
English Literature
Plays
World Literature

Magill's Literary Annual

Magill's Literary Annual, 2023
Magill's Literary Annual, 2022
Magill's Literary Annual, 2021
Magill's Literary Annual (Backlist Issues 2020-1977)

Masterplots

Masterplots, Fourth Edition
Masterplots, 2010-2018 Supplement

Notable Writers

Notable African American Writers
Notable American Women Writers
Notable Mystery & Detective Fiction Writers
Notable Writers of the American West & the Native American
    Experience
Notable Writers of LGBTQ+ Literature

Grey House Publishing | Salem Press | H.W. Wilson | 4919 Route, 22 PO Box 56, Amenia NY 12501-0056

Titles from Salem Press
Visit www.SalemPress.com for Product Information, Table of Contents, and Sample Pages.

HISTORY
The Decades
The 1910s in America
The Twenties in America
The Thirties in America
The Forties in America
The Fifties in America
The Sixties in America
The Seventies in America
The Eighties in America
The Nineties in America
The 2000s in America
The 2010s in America

Defining Documents in American History
Defining Documents: The 1900s
Defining Documents: The 1910s
Defining Documents: The 1920s
Defining Documents: The 1930s
Defining Documents: The 1950s
Defining Documents: The 1960s
Defining Documents: The 1970s
Defining Documents: The 1980s
Defining Documents: American Citizenship
Defining Documents: The American Economy
Defining Documents: The American Revolution
Defining Documents: The American West
Defining Documents: Business Ethics
Defining Documents: Capital Punishment
Defining Documents: Civil Rights
Defining Documents: Civil War
Defining Documents: The Constitution
Defining Documents: The Cold War
Defining Documents: Dissent & Protest
Defining Documents: Domestic Terrorism & Extremism
Defining Documents: Drug Policy
Defining Documents: The Emergence of Modern America
Defining Documents: Environment & Conservation
Defining Documents: Espionage & Intrigue
Defining Documents: Exploration and Colonial America
Defining Documents: The First Amendment
Defining Documents: The Free Press
Defining Documents: The Great Depression
Defining Documents: The Great Migration
Defining Documents: The Gun Debate
Defining Documents: Immigration & Immigrant Communities
Defining Documents: The Legacy of 9/11
Defining Documents: LGBTQ+
Defining Documents: Manifest Destiny and the New Nation
Defining Documents: Native Americans
Defining Documents: Political Campaigns, Candidates & Discourse
Defining Documents: Postwar 1940s
Defining Documents: Prison Reform
Defining Documents: Secrets, Leaks & Scandals
Defining Documents: Slavery
Defining Documents: Supreme Court Decisions
Defining Documents: Reconstruction Era
Defining Documents: The Vietnam War
Defining Documents: U.S. Involvement in the Middle East
Defining Documents: Workers' Rights
Defining Documents: World War I
Defining Documents: World War II

Defining Documents in World History
Defining Documents: The 17th Century
Defining Documents: The 18th Century
Defining Documents: The 19th Century
Defining Documents: The 20th Century (1900-1950)
Defining Documents: The Ancient World
Defining Documents: Asia
Defining Documents: Genocide & the Holocaust
Defining Documents: Human Rights
Defining Documents: The Middle Ages
Defining Documents: The Middle East
Defining Documents: Nationalism & Populism
Defining Documents: The Nuclear Age
Defining Documents: Pandemics, Plagues & Public Health
Defining Documents: Renaissance & Early Modern Era
Defining Documents: Revolutions
Defining Documents: Women's Rights

Great Events from History
Great Events from History: American History, Exploration to the
    Colonial Era, 1492-1775
Great Events from History: The Ancient World
Great Events from History: The Middle Ages
Great Events from History: The Renaissance & Early Modern Era
Great Events from History: The 17th Century
Great Events from History: The 18th Century
Great Events from History: The 19th Century
Great Events from History: The 20th Century, 1901-1940
Great Events from History: The 20th Century, 1941-1970
Great Events from History: The 20th Century, 1971-2000
Great Events from History: Modern Scandals
Great Events from History: African American History
Great Events from History: The 21st Century, 2000-2016
Great Events from History: LGBTQ Events
Great Events from History: Human Rights
Great Events from History: Women's History

Great Lives from History
Great Athletes
Great Athletes of the Twenty-First Century
Great Lives from History: The 17th Century
Great Lives from History: The 18th Century
Great Lives from History: The 19th Century
Great Lives from History: The 20th Century
Great Lives from History: The 21st Century, 2000-2017
Great Lives from History: African Americans
Great Lives from History: The Ancient World
Great Lives from History: American Heroes
Great Lives from History: American Women
Great Lives from History: Asian and Pacific Islander Americans
Great Lives from History: Autocrats & Dictators
Great Lives from History: The Incredibly Wealthy
Great Lives from History: Inventors & Inventions
Great Lives from History: Jewish Americans
Great Lives from History: Latinos
Great Lives from History: The Middle Ages
Great Lives from History: The Renaissance & Early Modern Era
Great Lives from History: Scientists and Science

SALEM
PRESS

Titles from Salem Press

SALEM
PRESS

Visit www.SalemPress.com for Product Information, Table of Contents, and Sample Pages.

History & Government

American First Ladies
American Presidents
The 50 States
The Ancient World: Extraordinary People in Extraordinary Societies
The Bill of Rights
The Criminal Justice System
The U.S. Supreme Court

Innovators

Computer Technology Innovators
Fashion Innovators
Human Rights Innovators
Internet Innovators
Music Innovators
Musicians and Composers of the 20th Century
World Political Innovators

SOCIAL SCIENCES

Civil Rights Movements: Past & Present
Countries, Peoples and Cultures
Countries: Their Wars & Conflicts: A World Survey
Education Today: Issues, Policies & Practices
Encyclopedia of American Immigration
Ethics: Questions & Morality of Human Actions
Issues in U.S. Immigration
Principles of Sociology: Group Relationships & Behavior
Principles of Sociology: Personal Relationships & Behavior
Principles of Sociology: Societal Issues & Behavior
Racial & Ethnic Relations in America
Weapons, Warfare & Military Technology
World Geography

HEALTH

Addictions, Substance Abuse & Alcoholism
Adolescent Health & Wellness
Aging
Cancer
Community & Family Health Issues
Integrative, Alternative & Complementary Medicine
Genetics and Inherited Conditions
Infectious Diseases and Conditions
Magill's Medical Guide
Nutrition
Parenting: Styles & Strategies
Psychology & Behavioral Health
Teens: Growing Up, Skills & Strategies
Women's Health

Principles of Health

Principles of Health: Allergies & Immune Disorders
Principles of Health: Anxiety & Stress
Principles of Health: Depression
Principles of Health: Diabetes
Principles of Health: Nursing
Principles of Health: Obesity
Principles of Health: Occupational Therapy & Physical Therapy
Principles of Health: Pain Management
Principles of Health: Prescription Drug Abuse

SCIENCE

Ancient Creatures
Applied Science
Applied Science: Engineering & Mathematics
Applied Science: Science & Medicine
Applied Science: Technology
Biomes and Ecosystems
Digital Literacy: Skills & Strategies
Earth Science: Earth Materials and Resources
Earth Science: Earth's Surface and History
Earth Science: Earth's Weather, Water and Atmosphere
Earth Science: Physics and Chemistry of the Earth
Encyclopedia of Climate Change
Encyclopedia of Energy
Encyclopedia of Environmental Issues
Encyclopedia of Global Resources
Encyclopedia of Mathematics and Society
Forensic Science
Notable Natural Disasters
The Solar System
USA in Space

Principles of Science

Principles of Aeronautics
Principles of Anatomy
Principles of Astronomy
Principles of Behavioral Science
Principles of Biology
Principles of Biotechnology
Principles of Botany
Principles of Chemistry
Principles of Climatology
Principles of Computer-aided Design
Principles of Computer Science
Principles of Digital Arts & Multimedia
Principles of Ecology
Principles of Energy
Principles of Fire Science
Principles of Forestry & Conservation
Principles of Geology
Principles of Information Technology
Principles of Marine Science
Principles of Mathematics
Principles of Mechanics
Principles of Microbiology
Principles of Modern Agriculture
Principles of Pharmacology
Principles of Physical Science
Principles of Physics
Principles of Programming & Coding
Principles of Robotics & Artificial Intelligence
Principles of Scientific Research
Principles of Sports Medicine & Exercise Science
Principles of Sustainability
Principles of Zoology

Grey House Publishing | Salem Press | H.W. Wilson | 4919 Route, 22 PO Box 56, Amenia NY 12501-0056

Titles from Salem Press

Visit www.SalemPress.com for Product Information, Table of Contents, and Sample Pages.

CAREERS

Careers: Paths to Entrepreneurship
Careers in Archaeology & Museum Services
Careers in Artificial Intelligence
Careers in the Arts: Fine, Performing & Visual
Careers in the Automotive Industry
Careers in Biology
Careers in Biotechnology
Careers in Building Construction
Careers in Business
Careers in Chemistry
Careers in Communications & Media
Careers in Cybersecurity
Careers in Education & Training
Careers in Engineering
Careers in Environment & Conservation
Careers in Financial Services
Careers in Fish & Wildlife
Careers in Forensic Science
Careers in Gaming
Careers in Green Energy
Careers in Healthcare
Careers in Hospitality & Tourism
Careers in Human Services
Careers in Information Technology
Careers in Law, Criminal Justice & Emergency Services
Careers in the Music Industry
Careers in Manufacturing & Production
Careers in Nursing
Careers in Physics
Careers in Protective Services
Careers in Psychology & Behavioral Health
Careers in Public Administration
Careers in Sales, Insurance & Real Estate
Careers in Science & Engineering
Careers in Social Media
Careers in Sports & Fitness
Careers in Sports Medicine & Training
Careers in Technical Services & Equipment Repair
Careers in Transportation
Careers in Writing & Editing
Careers Outdoors
Careers Overseas
Careers Working with Infants & Children
Careers Working with Animals

BUSINESS

Principles of Business: Accounting
Principles of Business: Economics
Principles of Business: Entrepreneurship
Principles of Business: Finance
Principles of Business: Globalization
Principles of Business: Leadership
Principles of Business: Management
Principles of Business: Marketing

Grey House Publishing | Salem Press | H.W. Wilson | 4919 Route, 22 PO Box 56, Amenia NY 12501-0056

Titles from H.W. Wilson

Visit www.HWWilsonInPrint.com for Product Information, Table of Contents, and Sample Pages.

The Reference Shelf

Affordable Housing
Aging in America
Alternative Facts, Post-Truth and the Information War
The American Dream
Artificial Intelligence
The Business of Food
Campaign Trends & Election Law
College Sports
Democracy Evolving
The Digital Age
Embracing New Paradigms in Education
Food Insecurity & Hunger in the United States
Future of U.S. Economic Relations: Mexico, Cuba, & Venezuela
Gene Editing & Genetic Engineering
Global Climate Change
Guns in America
Hacktivism
Hate Crimes
Immigration
Income Inequality
Internet Abuses & Privacy Rights
Internet Law
LGBTQ in the 21st Century
Marijuana Reform
Mental Health Awareness
Money in Politics
National Debate Topic 2014/2015: The Ocean
National Debate Topic 2015/2016: Surveillance
National Debate Topic 2016/2017: US/China Relations
National Debate Topic 2017/2018: Education Reform
National Debate Topic 2018/2019: Immigration
National Debate Topic 2019/2021: Arms Sales
National Debate Topic 2020/2021: Criminal Justice Reform
National Debate Topic 2021/2022: Water Resources
National Debate Topic 2022/2023: Emerging Technologies & International Security
National Debate Topic 2023/2024: Economic Inequality
New Frontiers in Space
Policing in 2020
Pollution
Prescription Drug Abuse
Propaganda and Misinformation
Racial Tension in a Postracial Age
Reality Television
Renewable Energy
Representative American Speeches, Annual Editions
Rethinking Work
Revisiting Gender
The South China Sea Conflict
Sports in America
The Supreme Court
The Transformation of American Cities
The Two Koreas
UFOs
Vaccinations
Voting Rights
Whistleblowers

Core Collections

Children's Core Collection
Fiction Core Collection
Graphic Novels Core Collection
Middle & Junior High School Core
Public Library Core Collection: Nonfiction
Senior High Core Collection
Young Adult Fiction Core Collection

Current Biography

Current Biography Cumulative Index 1946-2021
Current Biography Monthly Magazine
Current Biography Yearbook

Readers' Guide to Periodical Literature

Abridged Readers' Guide to Periodical Literature
Readers' Guide to Periodical Literature

Indexes

Index to Legal Periodicals & Books
Short Story Index
Book Review Digest

Sears List

Sears List of Subject Headings
Sears List of Subject Headings, Online Database
Sears: Lista de Encabezamientos de Materia

History

American Game Changers: Invention, Innovation & Transformation
American Reformers
Speeches of the American Presidents

Facts About Series

Facts About the 20th Century
Facts About American Immigration
Facts About China
Facts About the Presidents
Facts About the World's Languages

Nobel Prize Winners

Nobel Prize Winners: 1901-1986
Nobel Prize Winners: 1987-1991
Nobel Prize Winners: 1992-1996
Nobel Prize Winners: 1997-2001
Nobel Prize Winners: 2002-2018

Famous First Facts

Famous First Facts
Famous First Facts About American Politics
Famous First Facts About Sports
Famous First Facts About the Environment
Famous First Facts: International Edition

American Book of Days

The American Book of Days
The International Book of Days

Grey House Publishing | Salem Press | H.W. Wilson | 4919 Route, 22 PO Box 56, Amenia NY 12501-0056